September 19–23
Minneapolis, Minnesota, USA

Association for
Computing Machinery

Advancing Computing as a Science & Profession

PACT'12

Proceedings of the 21st International Conference on
Parallel Architectures and Compilation Techniques

Sponsored by:
ACM SIGARCH

Sponsored by:
IFIP WG 10.3, IEEE CS TCAA and CS TCPP

Supported by:
IEEE Computer Society, IFIP, NSF, Intel, UNISYS, CRAY, NVIDIA, IBM Research, and AMD

Association for
Computing Machinery

Advancing Computing as a Science & Profession

The Association for Computing Machinery
2 Penn Plaza, Suite 701
New York, New York 10121-0701

Notice to Past Authors of ACM-Published Articles
ACM intends to create a complete electronic archive of all articles and/or other material previously published by ACM. If you have written a work that has been previously published by ACM in any journal or conference proceedings prior to 1978, or any SIG Newsletter at any time, and you do NOT want this work to appear in the ACM Digital Library, please inform permissions@acm.org, stating the title of the work, the author(s), and where and when published.

ISBN: 978-1-4503-1762-7 (Digital)

ISBN: 978-1-4503-1884-6 (Print)

Additional copies may be ordered prepaid from:

ACM Order Department
PO Box 30777
New York, NY 10087-0777, USA

Phone: 1-800-342-6626 (USA and Canada)
+1-212-626-0500 (Global)
Fax: +1-212-944-1318
E-mail: acmhelp@acm.org
Hours of Operation: 8:30 am – 4:30 pm ET

Printed in the USA

Welcome from the Chairs

It is our pleasure to welcome you to the 21st International Conference on Parallel Architectures and Compilation Techniques (PACT 2012) in Minneapolis, Minnesota, the Land of Ten Thousand Lakes.

This year the conference received 207 complete paper submissions, which is almost exactly the same number received last year. These papers were rigorously reviewed by a combination of a 42-member technical program committee and more than 300 additional external reviewers. More than 800 total reviews were submitted with a typical program committee member personally reviewing 11-12 papers each. After almost all of the reviews had been received, the authors were given several days to read and respond to the reviewers' comments. The program committee members evaluated these responses during an online discussion period before the formal program committee meeting.

On June 9, 2012, the program committee met in Minneapolis for a full day's discussion of the submitted papers. Committee members who had conflicts-of-interest with papers as they were brought up for discussion were asked to leave the room. After thorough discussions of the reviews and author responses, 39 papers were selected for the main conference program. The final acceptance rate of 19% was similar to previous years. The authors of an additional 41 papers were invited to submit posters of their papers during a special poster session at the conference, and to prepare an extended abstract for publication in the conference proceedings. A total of 25 authors accepted this poster invitation.

We are pleased to have three distinguished keynote speakers for the conference, two of them are from academia. They are Dr. Bill Cramer from the National Center for Supercomputing Applications (NCSA) at the University of Illinois at Urbana-Champaign and Dr. Kathy Yelick (University of California, Berkeley, also with Lawrence Berkeley National Laboratory). One keynote speaker is from industry, Peter J. Ungaro from Cray. They provide their insights into the future directions of parallel computing.

We particularly thank ACM, IEEE, and IFIP for their continued sponsorship of PACT as well as several companies providing financial support for this year's conference. Those companies include Cray, Intel, Unisys, AMD, IBM and NVidia. Their strong support has made our technical and social programs possible. A number of organizations, including NSF, ACM SIGARCH and IEEE Computer Society (TCCA and TCPP), offered generous student travel grants. In addition, we thank the organizing committee for all their tireless hard work. The number of e-mails exchanged between the committee members reached 1,700 and is still counting as of this writing. The organizing committee includes Rajeev Balasubramonian (ACM Student Research Competition Chair), John Cavazos (Tutorials Chair), Yoonseo Choi (Publications Chair), Nikos Hardavellas (Web Chair), Byeong Kil Lee (Submissions Chair), Xiaorui Wang (Finance Chair), Jon Weissman (Local Arrangements Chair), Thomas Wenisch (Workshops Chair) and Antonia Zhai (Registration Chair), as well as four Publicity Chairs: Barry Rountree (Americas), Mainak Chaudhuri (India), Marcelo Cintra (Europe), Xiaobing Feng (China) and Kei Hiraki (Pacific). They have performed their jobs with dedication and efficiency, and it has been a great pleasure and a privilege to work with them all. Finally, we thank the workshop and tutorial organizers and program committee members for their efforts and contributions to the conference.

We hope you enjoy this year's conference in Minneapolis.

Sangyeun Cho, Luiz DeRose, David Lilja and Pen-Chung Yew
(General and Program Co-Chairs)

Table of Contents

Session 4: Best Papers

Session 5: Keynote Address

Session 6a: Transactional Memory

Session 6b: Debugging and Error Detection

Session 7: Keynote Address

Session 8a: Multicore and Multithread

Session 8b: Optimization

Session 9a: Memory System (I)

Session 9b: Hybrid Systems

Session 10a: Memory System (II)

Session 10b: Accelerators

PACT Poster Papers

ACM SRC Abstracts

PACT 2012 Organization

General Co-Chairs: Pen-Chung Yew (*University of Minnesota*)
Sangyeun Cho *(University of Pittsburgh)*

Program Co-Chairs: Luiz DeRose *(Cray, Inc.)*
David J. Lilja *(University of Minnesota)*

ACM Student Research Competition Chair: Rajeev Balasubramonian *(University of Utah)*

Finance Chair: Xiaorui Wang *(Ohio State University)*

Local Arrangements Chair: Jon Weissman *(University of Minnesota)*

Publicity Chair - America: Barry Rountree *(Lawrence Livermore National Lab.)*

Publicity Chair - China: Xiaobing Feng *(ICT)*

Publicity Chair - Europe: Marcelo Cintra *(University of Edinburgh)*

Publicity Chair - India: Mainak Chaudhuri *(IIT Kanpur)*

Publicity Chair - Pacific: Kei Hiraki *(University of Tokyo)*

Publication Chair: Yoonseo Choi *(Samsung Adv. Institute of Tech.)*

Registration Chair: Antonia Zhai *(University of Minnesota)*

Tutorials Chair: John Cavazos *(University of Delaware)*

Workshops Chair: Thomas Wenisch *(University of Michigan)*

Web Chair: Nikos Hardavellas *(Northwestern University)*

Submissions Chair: Byeong Kil Lee *(University of Texas, San Antonio)*

Student Travel Grant Chair: Xin Fu *(University of Kansas)*

Program Committee: Luiz DeRose *(Co-Chair, Cray, Inc.)*
David J. Lilja *(Co-Chair, University of Minnesota)*
Tarek Abdelrahman *(University of Toronto)*
Dennis Abts *(Google)*
Nancy Amato *(Texas A&M University)*
Dorian Arnold *(University of New Mexico)*
Brad Beckmann *(AMD)*
John Carter *(IBM Research)*
Daniel Chavarria *(Pacific Northwest National Lab.)*
Derek Chiou *(University of Texas - Austin)*
Marcelo Cintra *(University of Edinburgh)*
Tom Conte *(Georgia Tech.)*
Bronis R. de Supinski *(Lawrence Livermore National Lab.)*
Evelyn Duesterwald *(IBM Research)*
Rudi Eigenmann *(Purdue University)*
Dan Ernst *(Cray, Inc.)*
Guang Gao *(University of Delaware)*
Michael Garland *(NVIDIA)*
Michael Gerndt *(Technical Univ. Munich, Germany)*
Kei Hiraki *(University of Tokyo)*
Amir Hormati *(Microsoft Research)*
Vijay Janapa Reddi *(University of Texas - Austin)*
Alex Jones *(University of Pittsburgh)*
Karen Karavanic *(Portland State University)*
Jaejin Lee *(Seoul National University, Korea)*
Sally A. McKee *(Chalmers University of Technology, Sweden)*
Jose Moreira *(IBM Research)*
Satish Narayanasamy *(University of Michigan)*
Kunle Olukotun *(Stanford University)*
Vijay Pai *(Purdue University)*
Shaz Qadeer *(Microsoft Research)*
Lawrence Rauchwerger *(Texas A&M University)*
Martin Schulz *(Lawrence Livermore National Lab)*
Resit Sendag *(University of Rhode Island)*
James M. Stichnoth *(Intel)*
Mary Lou Soffa *(University of Virginia)*
Michael Taylor *(University of California, San Diego)*
Cheng Wang *(Intel)*
Felix Wolf *(RWTH Aachen University, Germany)*
Antonia Zhai *(University of Minnesota)*
Xiaodong Zhang *(Ohio State University)*

PACT 2012 Sponsor & Supporters

Sponsor: SIGARCH

Technical Supporters: IEEE Computer Society, ifip

Gold Supporter: NSF

Silver Supporters: intel, UNISYS, CRAY THE SUPERCOMPUTER COMPANY

Bronze Supporters: NVIDIA, IBM Research, AMD

The Changing Role of Supercomputing

Peter J. Ungaro
Cray Inc.
Seattle, Washington
ungaro@cray.com

Categories and Subject Descriptors

C.5.1 [Computer System Implementation]: Large and Medium ("Mainframe") Computers - *Super (very large) computers*

Keywords:

architecture

BIOGRAPHY

Peter Ungaro serves as President and Chief Executive Officer of Cray Inc., a leader in the supercomputing marketplace. Prior to his appointment as President and CEO in 2005, Ungaro was the Senior Vice President responsible for sales, marketing and service. Ungaro was recently named CEO of the Year for 2006 by Seattle Business Monthly magazine for his leadership in turning around the company and one of the "40 under 40" by Corporate Leader Magazine in 2008. He has also been appointed to the Department of Commerce's Manufacturing Council. The Council advises the Secretary of Commerce on matters relating to the competitiveness of the manufacturing sector and government policies and programs that affect U.S. manufacturers.

Before joining Cray in 2003, Ungaro served as Vice President of Sales for Worldwide Deep Computing, at IBM. In that role, he led global sales of all IBM server and storage products for high performance computing, life sciences, digital media and business intelligence markets. He held a variety of other sales leadership positions since joining IBM in 1991. Ungaro received a B.A. in business administration from Washington State University.

PACT'12, September 19–23, 2012, Minneapolis, Minnesota, USA.
ACM 978-1-4503-1182-3/12/09.

Power-Aware Multi-Core Simulation for Early Design Stage Hardware/Software Co-Optimization

Wim Heirman*† Souradip Sarkar*† Trevor E. Carlson*†
Ibrahim Hur‡† Lieven Eeckhout*

*ELIS Department, Ghent University, Belgium
†ExaScience Lab, Leuven, Belgium
‡Intel, Leuven, Belgium

ABSTRACT

Stringent performance targets and power constraints push designers towards building specialized workload-optimized systems across a broad spectrum of the computing arena, including supercomputing applications as exemplified by the IBM BlueGene and Intel MIC architectures. In this paper, we make the case for hardware/software co-design during early design stages of processors for scientific computing applications. Considering an important scientific kernel, namely stencil computation, we demonstrate that performance and energy-efficiency can be improved by a factor of 1.66× and 1.25×, respectively, by co-optimizing hardware and software.

To enable hardware/software co-design in early stages of the design cycle, we propose a novel simulation infrastructure by combining high-abstraction performance simulation using Sniper with power modeling using McPAT and custom DRAM power models. Sniper/McPAT is fast — simulation speed is around 2 MIPS on an 8-core host machine — because it uses analytical modeling to abstract away core performance during multi-core simulation. We demonstrate Sniper/McPAT's accuracy through validation against real hardware; we report average performance and power prediction errors of 22.1% and 8.3%, respectively, for a set of SPEComp benchmarks.

Categories and Subject Descriptors

C.4 [**Computer Systems Organization** – **Performance of Systems**]: Modeling techniques

General Terms

Performance, Experimentation, Design

Keywords

Performance modeling, power modeling, hardware/software co-design, design space exploration, multi-core processor

PACT'12, September 19–23, 2012, Minneapolis, Minnesota, USA.

1. INTRODUCTION

With limited increases in clock frequency because of power constraints, improving next-generation processor performance has become a real challenge. One increasingly attractive way to improve performance within a given power and energy budget is to optimize the system for a specific workload — a paradigm that is broadly adopted for the design of smartphones, tablets, game machines, data centers and supercomputers. Because computer systems are increasingly power and energy-constrained, it is to be expected that workload-optimized system design will become even more prevalent in the future. Notable examples of processors optimized for supercomputing applications are IBM's BlueGene processors and Intel's Many Integrated Core (MIC) architecture. However, optimizing the hardware alone might not be sufficient moving forward. Instead, co-optimizing the workload along with the hardware — hardware/software co-design — can be even more promising, as we experimentally demonstrate in this paper. Hardware/software co-design is already the design paradigm of choice for embedded system design, however, it is not generally employed for high-performance processor design.

A fundamental challenge regarding co-designing hardware and software is how to evaluate design decisions and make trade-offs early in the design cycle. A common approach in architecture design is to employ detailed cycle-accurate simulation. Unfortunately, cycle-accurate simulators are extremely slow, are difficult to scale to large multi-core systems, and take a long time to develop, hence they are inappropriate for early design stages. To make things even worse, making a detailed cycle-accurate simulator power and energy-aware further increases development and evaluation time. Clearly, driving hardware/software co-design through cycle-accurate simulation is particularly problematic.

In this paper, we make the case for architectural simulation at a higher level of abstraction for driving early design stage hardware/software trade-off explorations, while considering both performance and power. Our simulation methodology leverages a mechanistic analytical performance model to abstract away core performance, i.e., core performance is estimated through an analytical model while simulating the uncore (memory hierarchy, interconnection network, etc.) at some level of detail in order to capture inter-core performance interactions. Coupling this high-abstraction performance simulation approach, called interval simulation as implemented in Sniper [6], with high-level power modeling using McPAT [18] and custom DRAM power models, we achieve both good accuracy and speed.

We demonstrate the power of Sniper/McPAT which is a hardware-validated, accurate (for both performance and power), parallel simulator that can run multi-threaded and multi-programmed workloads on multi-core hardware.

Having established the accuracy and speed of our simulation methodology, we perform a number of architecture explorations and we make the case for hardware/software co-design towards higher levels of performance and energy efficiency. To this end, we consider a widely used numerical kernel, namely stencil computation. This case study illustrates the huge potential of hardware/software co-design, which we believe is going to be a crucial design principle towards future processor systems.

More specifically, we make the following contributions in this paper.

- We propose Sniper/McPAT, a high-abstraction simulation methodology for simulating performance and power of large multi-core systems. Sniper is a parallel simulator that benefits from running on multi-core hosts. Further, it employs analytical core modeling to raise the level of abstraction. Both features make up for a fast simulation approach, which enables running more and longer running simulations within a given time budget. With our simulation methodology, we achieve simulation speeds around 2 MIPS when simulating a 16-core target system on an 8-core host system.

- We validate Sniper/McPAT against real hardware and we report good accuracy for both performance and power. We find the average accuracy to be within 22.1% and 8.3% compared to real hardware (Intel Nehalem processor system with 8 cores) for performance and power, respectively, when running benchmarks from SPEComp [2]. These results show that even basic statistics can yield accurate power predictions. Detailed inputs such as activity factors and bit toggles, as done in other power modeling frameworks such as Wattch [5], are not needed in Sniper/McPAT: basic event counts such as the number of cache misses and duty cycles yield good accuracy. Power modeling is part of the public Sniper release, which can be downloaded from `http://snipersim.org`.

- We use Sniper/McPAT to drive architecture explorations using multi-threaded benchmarks from the SPLASH-2, PARSEC, Rodinia, and SPEComp suites in which we explore the performance and power impact of 3D stacking, multi-core processing, core width, and power settings. We show that 3D stacking, in which the increase in memory bandwidth allows cache size to be traded in for more cores, is an advantageous design point for a broad range of multi-threaded applications.

- We make the case for hardware/software co-design of processor chips for scientific applications. Using stencil computation as a driver numerical kernel, we demonstrate that co-designing the architecture along with the software leads to improvements of a factor 1.66× in terms of performance and 1.25× in terms of energy efficiency.

2. BACKGROUND

Before introducing Sniper/McPAT, we first briefly describe its building blocks, namely interval simulation using Sniper, and power modeling using McPAT.

2.1 Interval simulation

Interval simulation is a recently proposed simulation paradigm for simulating multi/many-core and multi-processor systems at a higher level of abstraction than current practice of detailed cycle-accurate simulation [10]. Interval simulation leverages a mechanistic analytical model to abstract core performance by driving the timing simulation of an individual core without the detailed tracking of individual instructions through the core's pipeline stages. The mechanistic analytical model is constructed from the underlying mechanisms of a superscalar processor core. The foundation of the model is that miss events (e.g., branch mispredictions, cache misses, serializing instructions) divide the smooth streaming of instructions through the pipeline into so-called *intervals*, and that progress between miss events is determined by the amount of processor-exposed instruction-level parallelism (number of inter-instruction dependencies and instruction execution latencies). The branch predictor, memory hierarchy, cache coherence and interconnection network simulators determine the miss events while the analytical model derives the timing of each interval. The co-operation between the mechanistic analytical model and the miss event simulators enables modeling of the tight performance entanglement between co-executing threads on multi-core processors at a higher level of abstraction than detailed cycle-accurate simulators. The implementation of interval simulation in Sniper, a parallel multi-core x86 simulator, results in an accurate, high-abstraction level performance simulator [6].

2.2 McPAT

McPAT [18] is a recently proposed and fully-integrated power, area and timing modeling framework. It models all types of power dissipation and provides an integrated solution for multithreaded and multi-core processors. The timing and area models in this tool are derived from CACTI [27]. The dynamic power model is similar to Wattch [5], while adding short circuit and leakage models.

3. SNIPER/MCPAT SIMULATION

Sniper/McPAT combines Sniper for performance modeling with McPAT and custom DRAM models for power modeling. Sniper, in addition to generating an overall performance estimate, also generates a number of statistics that serve as input for estimating power consumption using McPAT (see Figure 1). Hence, we keep Sniper and McPAT as separate executables. We first run Sniper to obtain performance data and various other statistics. Once the performance simulation is finished, a separate script parses the results and generates an XML input file for McPAT. Finally, the output from McPAT is parsed, and final representations such as total power and/or per-component energy stacks are generated.

3.1 Generating input for McPAT

McPAT's input file consists of two main types of information: architectural parameters and statistics about the

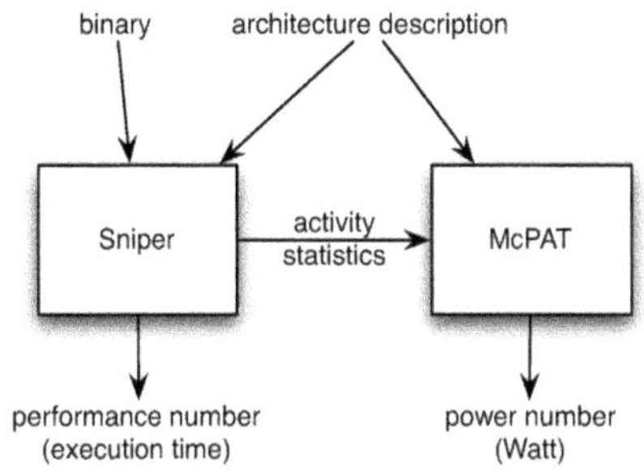

Figure 1: High-level overview of Sniper/McPAT.

activity of various architecture components during application runtime. The architecture parameters, such as the processor's reorder buffer size and issue width, and the size, associativity and latency of each cache level, are used to calculate power and energy costs for each component, for a specific technology node. We picked these parameters using public information [15] when modeling an Intel Nehalem-like system in our setup.

The activity statistics take the form of duty cycles which indicate what fraction of time a component is in use, as well as counts for events that have a per-event energy cost such as a memory access. For high-level components such as hits and misses at the various levels of the memory hierarchy, these values are trivially obtained from Sniper's output statistics. Activities for other components, especially those related to structures inside the core — which interval simulation does not model deliberately in order to raise the level of abstraction and improve simulation speed — need to be estimated. For instance, reads and writes to the reorder buffer (ROB) or register allocation table (RAT) are not explicitly modeled by interval simulation. Instead, we assume a constant usage pattern by each instruction and estimate these statistics as a fixed ratio of the number of instructions, e.g., one ROB read and write per instruction, etc.

For other components such as ALUs and the load-store units, McPAT expects an activity factor. We calculate these using the following assumption. We assume these components to achieve a throughput of one instruction per cycle. This means that each instruction that uses a given component, occupies this component for exactly one cycle. The fact that the component is internally pipelined does not matter from a modeling perspective, as each pipeline stage is kept busy by this instruction for just one cycle; even though the activity caused by the instruction might be spread out over multiple clock cycles, it still causes the complete component to be active for one cycle, assuming aggressive clock gating when parts of a component are not used. Thus, the activity factor of the unit can be estimated by taking the number of instructions that use it, implicitly multiplying this number by one active cycle per instruction, and dividing it by the total number of clock cycles the simulation took. We also extended Sniper to output the dynamic instruction mix, which allows us to compute the usage of the respective execution units.

3.2 DRAM power

McPAT does not model DRAM power, although this can represent a significant fraction of total system power [17]. We therefore added a basic first-order DRAM power model. Using Micron's DDR3 System-Power calculator [21], we calculate idle (static plus refresh) power and per-operation energy for reads and writes. Power consumption of the DRAM interface, both for the regular DDR3 case as for 3D stacked memory, is calculated according to the models from [9]. We thus calculate static and dynamic DRAM chip and interface power, and add these to McPAT's power numbers.

3.3 Sniper/McPAT limitations

By using a high-abstraction user-level simulation infrastructure such as Sniper/McPAT, we opt for simulation speed and short simulator development time at the expense of sacrificing some accuracy. Hence, Sniper/McPAT has its limitations and should not be used for detailed microarchitecture studies inside the core of a multi-core processor; however, we believe Sniper/McPAT is an ideal simulation platform for studying system-level design trade-offs at early stages in the design cycle.

We now briefly summarize Sniper/McPAT's limitations. Sniper is a user-level simulator, hence, it does not model system-level code. As we focus on HPC benchmarks, which spend most of their time in user-level code [20], this is a valid trade-off. Second, Sniper is built on top of Pin [19], which is a dynamic binary instrumentation tool. This implies that Pin enables instrumenting correct-path instructions only, i.e., wrong-path execution is not modeled. Again, HPC workloads typically have a high branch prediction accuracy [20], hence, this is a viable assumption. Third, Sniper does not model the internals of a superscalar out-of-order processor core, hence, it is unable to track the occupancy and activity factors inside the core. (Recall the key motivation behind interval simulation is to abstract away these details in order to achieve higher simulation speed.) We therefore need to approximate some of these core internal statistics, as described in the previous section. Yet, in spite of these limitations and simplifying modeling assumptions, Sniper/McPAT is accurate compared against real hardware, as we show in Section 5.

3.4 Simulation speed

Sniper's simulation speed is up to around 2 MIPS when simulating 16-core architectures on an 8-core host machine [6]. To enable power modeling, we extended Sniper to export some additional statistics as described in Section 3.1. All of these changes to the performance simulator do not slow down simulation. Parsing the various statistics files and generating McPAT's input file is straightforward and takes less than a second, as does parsing McPAT's output and generating the final results. The runtime for McPAT itself can be up to a few minutes, mainly taken up by CACTI which searches for the optimum register file and cache organization. Still, compared to performance simulation using Sniper, which takes several hours when running realistic benchmarks, the total increase in simulation time because of power modeling is insignificant.

We can therefore state that, from a simulation time perspective, power modeling is essentially free in Sniper/McPAT. This is in contrast to a more detailed approach such as Wattch, which incurs a slowdown of the SimpleScalar performance simulator in which it is integrated, by about 30% [5]. The reason for this slowdown in Wattch/Simplescalar is that detailed activity factors and the

Component	Parameters
Processor	2 sockets, 4 cores per socket
Core	2.66 GHz, 4-way issue, 128-entry ROB
Branch predictor	Pentium M [28], 17 cycles penalty
L1-I	32 KB, 4 way, 4 cycle access time
L1-D	32 KB, 8 way, 4 cycle access time
L2 cache	256 KB per core, 8 way, 8 cycle
L3 cache	8 MB per 4 cores, 16 way, 30 cycle
Main memory	65 ns access time, 8 GB/s per socket

Table 1: Simulated system characteristics for the dual-socket quad-core Intel Nehalem baseline architecture.

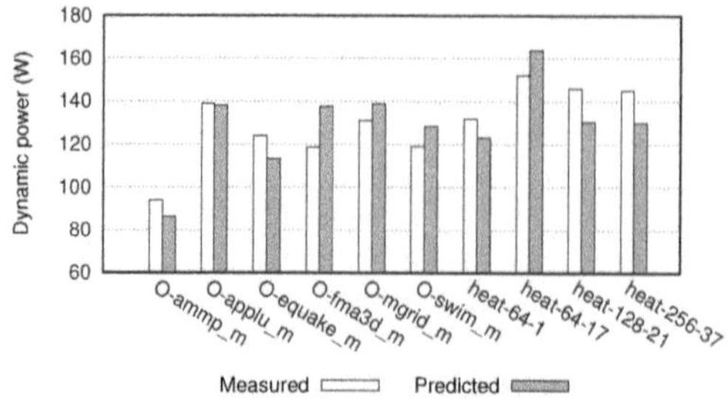

Figure 2: Measured versus predicted dynamic power consumption using Sniper/McPAT.

number of bit toggles need to be computed during performance simulation.

3.5 Sniper/McPAT output

McPAT computes chip area and both static and dynamic power, broken down into several architectural components such as the reorder buffer and other core structures, caches, etc. By multiplying total power consumption with the benchmark's execution time as obtained from Sniper's performance simulation, derived metrics such as static and dynamic energy, or energy-delay products can be computed — both for the complete system or broken down per component. In addition, power traces can be computed as well, by running McPAT on a time series of runtime statistics produced by Sniper. Examples will be given in the results section.

4. EXPERIMENTAL SETUP

4.1 Baseline processor configuration

Our baseline processor configuration is configured after a dual-socket, quad-core Intel Nehalem machine. The Nehalem chips consist of four 4-wide out-of-order cores running at 2.66 GHz with private L1 and L2 caches and a shared L3 last-level cache. More details can be found in Table 1.

4.2 Benchmarks

Results in this paper combine applications from four benchmark suites: SPLASH-2 [31], PARSEC [3], Rodinia [7] and SPEComp [2], compiled with GCC 4.3.2. The input sizes used are `simsmall` and `simlarge` for PARSEC and `train` from SPEComp (medium). For SPLASH-2 and Rodinia, we used the inputs defined in [12]. We only enable performance modeling during the parallel section of the benchmark (the region of interest, ROI); the sequential parts at the beginning and end of a benchmark execution are not included in any timing or energy results given in this paper.

In addition to these standardized benchmark suites, we also include a scientific kernel, namely stencil computation, for driving a hardware/software co-design case study. Stencil computation is part of the Berkeley dwarfs [1] (Structured Grid), and is a widely used kernel in many applications, such as physical dynamics simulations. This particular application models heat transfer across a 2-D grid; we will refer to this application as the `heat` benchmark. A more detailed description can be found in Section 7.1.

5. HARDWARE VALIDATION

In this section, we evaluate the accuracy of Sniper/McPAT against real hardware. We specifically focus on power consumption here; Sniper has been hardware-validated for performance previously, by Carlson et al. [6].

5.1 Setup

Our validation experiments compare McPAT's *Peak Dynamic Power* prediction against that of a dual-socket, 45 nm Intel Nehalem processor based server machine (an IBM x3650 M2). Total system power was measured using a Racktivity RC0816 [24] Power Distribution Unit (PDU) with integrated power metering. This PDU performs real-time true RMS measurements of the server's 230V AC power supply and allows us to read out the server's power consumption once every second; the reported number is the average power consumed over the second. We run our benchmarks on real hardware and measure total system power. Since we only have one power measurement per second, we selected only benchmarks for which the ROI was longer than two seconds to make sure we always have at least one valid power measurement from the ROI. Out of the extensive set of benchmarks that we considered in this work (see Section 4.2), only six of the benchmarks from the SPEComp suite and the `heat` benchmark run longer than two seconds; the other benchmarks from SPLASH-2, PARSEC, Rodinia and SPEComp did not run long enough to obtain meaningful power numbers. Each benchmark is run for two minutes. During the first minute we allow the system to reach a thermal equilibrium. We then report the average power consumption during the second minute for those samples that completely overlap with the benchmark's ROI. Finally, for validation purposes of Sniper/McPAT's dynamic power estimates, we subtract the system's idle power so our numbers do not include power consumed by disks, motherboard, network interfaces, etc., but account for processor and DRAM dynamic energy only.

5.2 Results

Figure 2 compares measured against predicted dynamic power consumption using Sniper/McPAT, for the selected SPEComp benchmarks and several configurations of the `heat` benchmark. The numbering scheme for the configurations of `heat` consists of the tile size and number of steps (s) computed per tile. These parameters can be used to tweak the memory access behavior of this application, as we will explain in more detail in Section 7.1. As expected, power consumption is benchmark-dependent. Sniper/McPAT captures the trend fairly accurately with an average absolute error of 8.3% and a maximum error of 16% for SPEComp's `fma3d`. We also re-evaluated Sniper's performance accuracy and found the average absolute error for this set of benchmarks to be 22.1%, which is in line with the results reported by Carlson et al. [6].

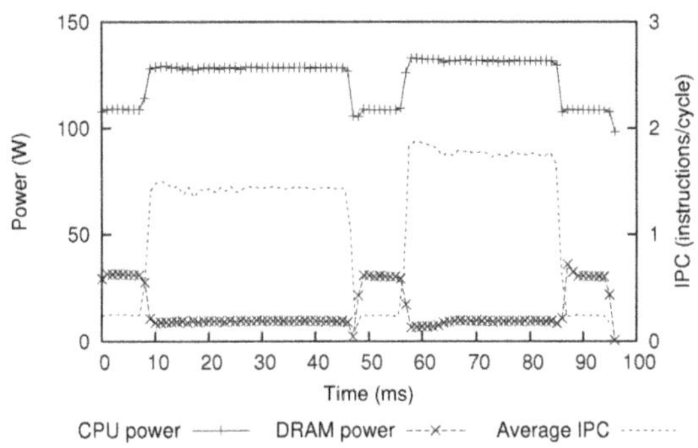

Figure 3: Simulated execution behavior for `fft`.

Figure 3 plots a trace of CPU and DRAM dynamic power consumption over time for the **fft** benchmark, along with an IPC trace (averaged across all eight cores). Execution phases with low IPC are memory-intensive. Hence, CPU power consumption is relatively low while DRAM power consumption is high. During compute-intensive, high-IPC phases, CPU power is high while DRAM power is relatively low. This illustrates that Sniper/McPAT's power predictions track resource usage as expected.

Finally, we wanted to verify whether computing power consumption at the end of the performance simulation using aggregate performance and activity statistics yields any differences compared to computing power consumption at smaller time granularities. We therefore ran McPAT once per one millisecond time interval to obtain a power trace over time. Computing the total energy consumption from this power trace yielded the same total energy within two percent as obtained from aggregate performance and activity statistics. This is because the power models in McPAT are mostly linear; moreover, the thermal response of the chip is slow enough such that short bursts in activity do not significantly affect overall temperature.

6. ARCHITECTURAL EXPLORATION

Using our validated simulation framework, we now perform a design space exploration in which we compare four architecture design points. We consider the processor configuration inspired by the dual-socket Nehalem system as described in Table 1 as a starting point, and asked ourselves the following question:

> *Given a technological advancement by two technology nodes, from 45 nm to 22 nm, how can we best use the available improvements in transistor density and energy efficiency?*

The first architecture considered is a conservative integration, in which we integrate the eight cores of the dual-socket quad-core Nehalem machine onto a single chip. Along with an increase in clock frequency from 2.66 GHz to 3.059 GHz, and cache size (from 256 KB to 512 KB for L2, and from 8 MB to 32 MB for L3), this forms our *8-core* design point.

In addition to this conservative scaling option, we also explore several more drastic modifications. The three alternate architecture design points that we consider in this trade-off study all have 16 cores (twice the number of cores), with each core having half the L2 cache size (256 KB instead of 512 KB). Other modifications are as follows:

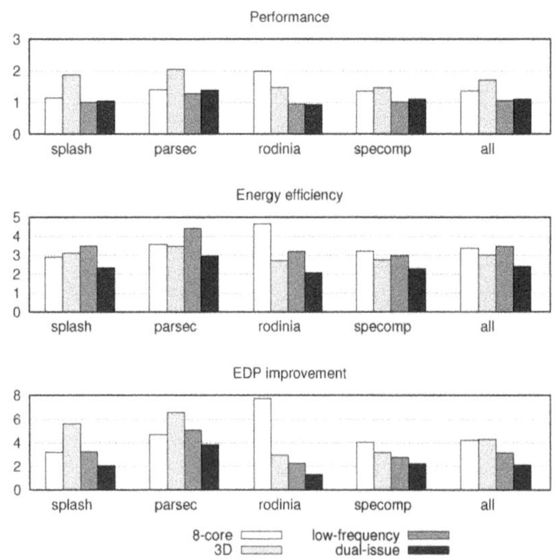

Figure 4: Average improvements per benchmark suite for the four 22 nm architecture design points over the 45 nm Nehalem baseline machine in terms of performance, energy efficiency and energy-delay product (EDP).

- The *3D* design point does not integrate an L3 cache but uses 3D stacked memory instead, which has a higher memory bandwidth and slightly shorter memory access time compared to regular DDR3 memory. This architecture results in a slightly bigger chip and nearly twice the power budget.
- The *low-frequency* design point reduces clock frequency and operating voltage which enables integrating 16 cores in a smaller power envelope. We assume a 16 MB L3 cache (2 times 8 MB per 8 cores) in order to reduce off-chip memory bandwidth pressure.
- The *dual-issue* design point replaces the 4-wide out-of-order cores with 16 less aggressive dual-issue cores. Reducing cache sizes compared to the 8-core architecture allows for integrating twice the number of cores at a slight increase in chip area.

The simulation parameters for these architectures are described in Table 2, along with chip area estimates and maximum observed power consumption for any of the benchmarks, as reported by Sniper/McPAT.

Note that the relatively high power consumption of the *3D* design point is caused by the fact that, for most of the benchmarks, the processor cores are much more active: compared to the other architectures, the time spent waiting for DRAM is lower here. Power consumption in 3D-stacked DRAM itself is slightly lower than that of the other architectures, mainly because long-distance off-chip communication on the DRAM bus is replaced by much more efficient short-range communication using through-silicon vias (TSVs).

6.1 Results

Figure 4 summarizes the average improvements per benchmark suite for the four 22 nm architecture design points over the 45 nm baseline architecture in terms of performance, energy efficiency and energy-delay product (EDP). (Energy

Parameter	Nehalem	8-core	3D	low-frequency	dual-issue
Sockets per system	2	1	1	1	1
Cores per socket	4	8	16	16	16
Core frequency	2.66 GHz	3.059 GHz	3.059 GHz	1.8 GHz	3.059 GHz
Core voltage	1.2 V	1.2 V	1.2 V	1.025 V	1.2 V
Issue width	4	4	4	4	2
ROB size	128	128	128	128	32
L2 cache size (per core)	256 KB	512 KB	256 KB	256 KB	256 KB
L3 cache size	8 MB per chip	32 MB	—	8 MB per 8 cores	8 MB per 8 cores
Memory bandwidth	8 GB/s	8 GB/s	128 GB/s	8 GB/s	8 GB/s
Memory latency	65 ns	65 ns	50 ns	65 ns	65 ns
Technology node	45 nm	22 nm	22 nm	22 nm	22 nm
Chip area	2× 243 mm^2	151 mm^2	181 mm^2	208 mm^2	187 mm^2
Maximum observed power	2× 99 W	80 W	130 W	58 W	102 W

Table 2: Simulated system characteristics used in the architectural exploration study.

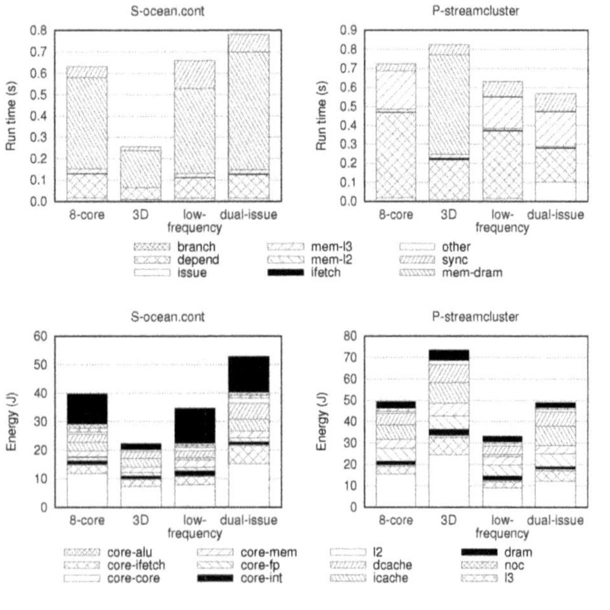

Figure 5: Time and energy stacks for `ocean.cont` from SPLASH-2 and `streamcluster` from PARSEC.

consumption in these results includes both dynamic and static energy consumption as reported by Sniper/McPAT.) Whereas the *3D* design point yields the highest absolute improvement in performance, its power consumption is rather high so it does not lead to the best architecture when energy consumption is taken into account. Instead, when optimizing for energy, the *low-frequency* design point is the optimum configuration for this set of benchmarks.

The high performance of the *3D* design point is especially apparent for benchmarks that are DRAM bandwidth bound. One such example is **`S-ocean.cont`**, see Figure 5 (left column) for cycle and energy stacks. For other applications with moderate working set sizes, the *3D* architecture suffers from the absence of an L3 cache. **`P-streamcluster`** for instance (Figure 5, right column) has a working set that does fit in the L3 cache for the *8-core*, *low-frequency* and *dual-issue* design points; on the *3D* architecture on the other hand, this benchmark needs to go out to the stacked DRAM, which — even though it is faster and more energy-efficient than regular DRAM — is still more expensive than using data that can be found in on-chip caches.

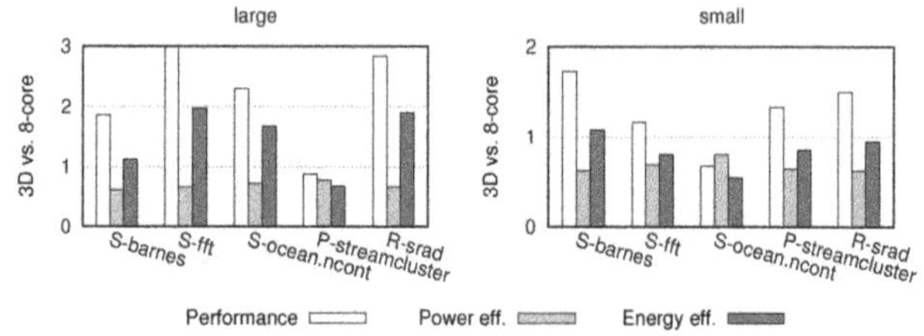

Figure 6: Improvement of the 3D design point over the 8-core design point in terms of performance, power and energy efficiency, using large (left) versus small (right) inputs: Different input sizes lead to different conclusions.

Out of the four benchmark suites, Rodinia is the one that stands out by having poor performance on all of the 16-core architectures. Even though Rodinia is written with GPUs in mind, which have many small cores, the Rodinia benchmarks do not seem to parallelize very well on a multi-core CPU environment. One problem is that the data sets are not very large, which makes them fit in the caches — removing the benefit the *3D* design point had. Also, its fine-grained parallelism using short inner loops does not work well in a context where threads are heavy-weight and inter-core synchronization is relatively expensive, as is the case in the GNU OpenMP runtime that was used.

6.2 Dependence on input size

It is well understood that a benchmark's input size may have a major impact on performance, and simulations using a small input may therefore not be a reliable proxy for larger inputs. This is because working set size often scales with input size, which may lead to very different cache behavior. Therefore, simulations need to be done using larger and more realistic input sizes, which further emphasizes the need for a fast simulator because of increased runtimes.

This not only applies to performance, but also to power and energy consumption. As an example, Figure 6 plots performance, power and energy efficiency of the *3D* design point relative to the *8-core* design point for a selection of benchmarks, using both large and small inputs. For some benchmarks, such as **`S-barnes`**, the conclusion as to which architecture is more power or energy-efficient is the same irrespective of the input size; however, for other benchmarks, the conclusion is reversed. For instance, using the small input, one would conclude that *3D*'s energy efficiency is worse compared to *8-core* for all of the selected benchmarks. However, when using the large input, *3D* is considerably more energy-efficient for three out of five of the applications considered. This shows that architecture studies should take caution when using reduced input sizes.

7. HARDWARE/SOFTWARE CO-DESIGN

We now go one step further and we use Sniper/McPAT to drive a case study in which we optimize both hardware and software. We do this for an important scientific kernel, namely stencil computation. Our kernel implementation allows for trading off data locality with redundant computation, which enables finding an optimum software configuration for a given hardware setting, and vice versa.

7.1 Heat transfer application

Our stencil computation benchmark models heat transfer across a regular 2D grid over a number of time steps. The heat transfer equation involves stencil computation in which temperature at a given point in time at each grid location is a linear combination of the temperatures of that location and its neighbors at the previous time step.

A naive implementation of the heat transfer equation computes a single time step at a time, and iterates over the complete grid to apply the stencil operation at each grid location (data element). This implementation has very poor data reuse because each data element is used only once per time step. By the time a data element is used again — at the next time step — the processor will have touched all other data elements, and hence, when simulating a large grid, likelihood for seeing a hit in the cache is small.

To improve memory locality, the algorithm has been reorganized to compute multiple time steps (s) on a small tile of the complete grid. This allows the tile's data elements to be reused multiple times, before moving on to the next tile. Additionally, when the application is parallelized by distributing tiles across cores, synchronization can be postponed by allowing each core to do more independent work before shared data at the tile boundaries needs to be communicated. A disadvantage is that at the edges of a tile, data from a neighboring tile about future time steps is needed — which is yet to be computed. This can be solved at the expense of doing some redundant work, by overlapping the edges of the tiles and letting the overlap decrease (by the width of the stencil) at each iteration. This way, the computation evolves — when time is represented as a dimension perpendicular to the grid plane — in a pyramid-shaped fashion, see Figure 7.

The heat benchmark was implemented using Intel Thread Building Blocks (TBB). Tasks are spawned which each simulate s time steps for a single tile, which TBB's work-stealing scheduler distributes over the available cores. There are many more tiles than cores so even in the presence of non-homogeneous memory access latencies the load balance of this application is typically very good.

7.2 Roofline model

The roofline model [30] provides a useful framework for high-level reasoning about algorithm efficiency and performance on a particular hardware platform. Figure 8 illustrates the roofline model for this particular application on our baseline architecture. The horizontal axis denotes the *arithmetic intensity* which is defined as the number of

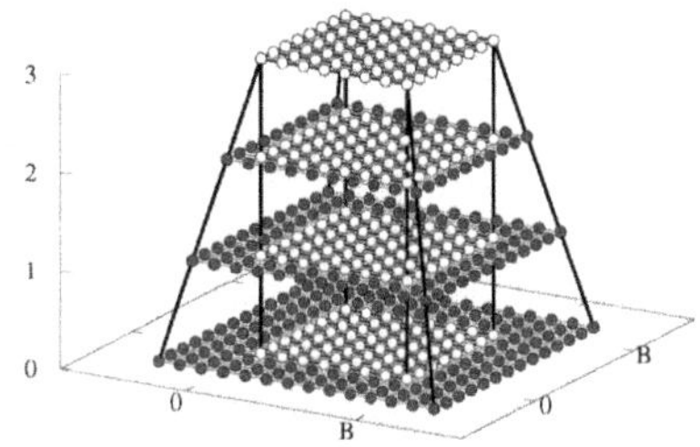

Figure 7: Illustration of three iterations of the heat transfer simulation, applied to an 8×8 tile. To satisfy the data dependencies up to the third step of the stencil, redundant computations (on the darker dots) are performed at the boundaries of the tile. From [11].

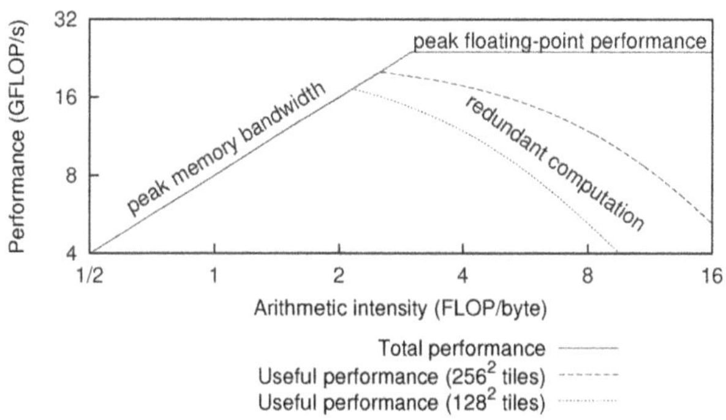

Figure 8: Expected performance profile of the heat benchmark using the roofline model [30], for the 8-core configuration with 128^2 and 256^2-sized tiles.

floating-point operations performed per byte loaded from memory. Initially, at low arithmetic intensities the problem is essentially memory bandwidth bound. Improving data reuse increases arithmetic intensity and increases performance, up to the peak floating-point performance of the machine.

In this kernel, arithmetic intensity can be raised by increasing the number of time steps computed per tile. Unfortunately, this optimization also increases redundant work, which causes useful performance to fall back once the amount of redundant computation becomes too high (dotted lines in Figure 8). The crossover point at which redundant work offsets the additional benefit of increased locality, moves towards higher values of s (higher levels of arithmetic intensity, to the right in Figure 8) for larger tile sizes. In addition, introducing too much redundant work will also flatten the useful performance curve, in the sense that an increasing fraction of the available machine's peak performance will be used for doing redundant work.

Trading off the amount of redundant computation against the increase in data locality is the main challenge in optimizing the heat transfer algorithm in particular, and stencil computations in general. This problem is difficult to solve analytically or through intuition because of the complex interplay between redundant work versus improving locality and how this affects energy consumption and performance. This reinforces the need for a fast simulation methodology

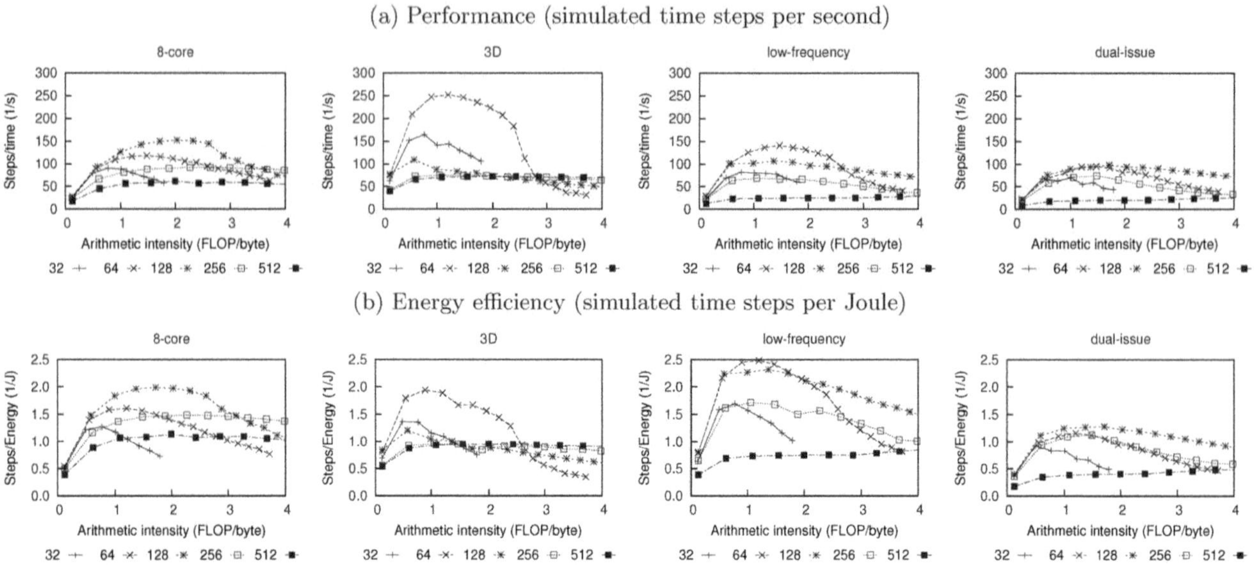

Figure 9: Hardware/software co-design for the heat benchmark when optimizing for performance and energy efficiency: four architecture design points are considered while varying software parameters such as tile size (see legend) and arithmetic intensity (horizontal axes).

for performance and power to explore these trade-offs and hardware/software interactions.

7.3 Co-design analysis

Figure 9 plots the simulation results for hardware/software co-design for the heat benchmark application. The grid domain is 4096×4096 elements. This domain is split up into square tiles measuring between 32 and 512 data points on each side. The complete domain is 128 MB in total and does not fit in the last-level cache for any of the architectures considered, so tiles always have to be loaded from main memory. The number of time steps performed on each tile before moving on to the next one varies between 1 and 65 steps. The graphs plot the achieved number of time steps per second, or per Joule of consumed energy, as a function of arithmetic intensity. The performance graphs in Figure 9(a) follow the basic roofline model from Figure 8: initially, increasing the number of time steps improves performance, which later falls back once the amount of redundant computation becomes too high. Additionally, each architecture has an optimal tile size which maximizes data reuse while still fitting in the cache. For example, the *8-core* design point reach a performance level of around 150 simulated time steps per second, using a tile size of 128×128. The working set of this application is two tiles worth of data, corresponding to the previous and current time steps. At one double-precision floating-point number or 8 bytes per element, the working set of 256 KB for the 128^2-sized tile fits in a core's private 512 KB L2 cache, whereas for the larger 256^2 tiles it does not — which makes performance significantly lower than that predicted by the roofline model. The three other architectures, which have an L2 cache of only 256 KB, reach their optimal performance using the smaller 64^2 tiles.

If we consider the effect of arithmetic intensity on energy rather than performance, we see that generally the optimum has shifted towards the left, meaning that less redundant work — and a slightly increased access rate to main memory — is preferred. This is because the ratio between access times of caches and DRAM is very high, making the performance aspect of more redundant work cheap when compared to extra DRAM accesses. On the other hand, when comparing the energy cost of DRAM accesses versus that of extra computation, the ratio is lower which makes the relative cost of the redundant work higher. Note that this extra cost consists of not just extra floating-point operations, which are in themselves very cheap (in the order of 0.5 nJ per double-precision operation, vs. 100 nJ per DRAM access[1]) but also the cost of extra instructions flowing through all stages of the out-of-order pipeline, extra cache accesses, etc. (In Figure 5, floating-point ALU energy represents only a small fraction of total core energy.)

When considering performance alone, the *3D* architecture clearly wins for this benchmark. The additional bandwidth of the 3D stacked memory allows for a steeper performance slope in the leftmost part of the performance graph, while the availability of 16 full-sized cores results in the highest peak performance across all architecture design points considered. Yet, tiles have to be kept small enough such that they fit in L2 cache; this architecture does not have an L3 cache so the cost of L2 misses, which become significant with tile sizes larger than 64^2, is much higher here than in the other architectures.

On the other hand, the *low-frequency* architecture, while being less high-performance than both the *8-core* and *3D* design points, reaches the highest energy efficiency. Because this application scales fairly good with core count, and the power envelope of the *low-frequency* chip is still modest, one could even consider another doubling of the number of cores which should almost double performance at very little additional cost in energy.

[1]According to the relevant component in the dynamic energy stacks computed by Sniper/McPAT, scaled by the number of FP operations or DRAM accesses throughout the benchmark, respectively.

Finally, the *dual-issue* architecture performs poorly for all software configurations. It was designed to be a middle-of-the-road out-of-order core, with a ROB size of 32 entries. This usually makes sense, as the complexity of a ROB (and hence area and energy cost) doubles superlinearly with its size, and it is not useful to discover more parallelism than the dual-issue execution stage is able to exploit. Yet, for this particular benchmark, performance is limited by dependencies, not the core's issue width. Significant amounts of instruction-level and memory-level parallelism do exist in the code; but since they are hidden behind long chains of dependencies, this parallelism would only be uncovered by a larger ROB.

The benefit from co-design. This case study clearly illustrates the necessity and huge potential of hardware/software co-design in order to achieve optimum performance and energy efficiency. If the algorithm would have been tuned for a specific architecture only, say the *8-core* design point, this would have yielded a maximum performance of 152 time steps per second or 1.99 time steps per Joule. However, by co-optimizing the hardware and the software, substantially better performance and energy efficiency can be achieved, up to 252 time steps per second if optimized for performance through the *3D* design point — an improvement by a factor 1.66× — or up to 2.48 time steps per Joule if optimized for energy through the *low-frequency* design point — an improvement by a factor 1.25×.

8. RELATED WORK

We now briefly describe related work in modeling and simulation, and architecture exploration.

8.1 Modeling and simulation

Architects in industry and academia heavily rely on detailed cycle-accurate simulation. The key benefit of cycle-accurate simulation obviously is accuracy, however, its slow speed is a significant limitation. Industry simulators typically run at a speed of 1 to 10 kHz. Academic simulators, such as gem5 [4] and PTLsim [34], are not truly cycle-accurate compared to real hardware, and therefore they are typically faster, with simulation speeds in the tens to hundreds of KIPS (kilo simulated instructions per second) range. Whereas cycle-accurate simulation is indispensable for detailed microarchitecture design studies inside a processor core, it does not scale to large multi-core systems.

Speeding up architectural simulation is an active field of research. Sampled simulation is likely the most widely used simulation speedup technique. The idea of sampled simulation is to simulate a limited, but representative number of simulation points [8, 25, 32]. Another approach that has gained interest recently is to accelerate simulation by mapping timing models on FPGAs [22, 29]. The timing models in FPGA-accelerated simulators are typically cycle-accurate, with the speedup coming from the fine-grained parallelism in the FPGA. Higher abstraction simulation, as employed in Sniper/McPAT, uses a different, and orthogonal, method for speeding up simulation: it models the processor at a higher level of abstraction. By doing so, higher abstraction models not only speed up simulation, they also reduce simulator complexity and development time compared to sampled and FPGA-accelerated simulation.

Existing power simulation methodologies typically rely on detailed activity factors. Wattch [5] uses SimpleScalar to obtained these activity factors at the cost of a 30% hit in simulation speed. PrEsto [26] incorporates power modeling in an FPGA-based simulation platform. Other work focuses on increasing the abstraction level of power modeling by using few high-level parameters and analytical scaling models [14, 18, 23]. Sniper/McPAT combines the high-abstraction levels for both performance (interval simulation) and power modeling (McPAT) into a fast yet accurate, hardware-validated simulation framework, that is still of low implementation complexity. All these characteristics are essential in allowing simulation to be used at early stages of design, and in achieving a short turn-around time for hardware/software co-design.

8.2 Design space exploration

The goal of architectural simulation is to drive design space exploration. A typical approach is to vary one architecture parameter at a time while holding the other architecture parameters constant in order to understand the sensitivity to that parameter. The number of simulation experiments that need to be performed quickly explodes with a large number of architecture parameters. Yi et al. [33] propose a method for identifying the most important architecture parameters to explore through a limited number of experiments. Empirical modeling is another popular approach to more quickly explore large design spaces, see for example [13, 16]. All of this prior work focuses on architecture exploration only, and is unlikely to be effective for hardware/software co-design, because these techniques rely on detailed cycle-accurate simulation to build the models. Employing these approaches for hardware/software co-design would require numerous detailed simulations for each version of the software; this would be prohibitively time-consuming.

9. CONCLUSIONS

There are significant performance and energy benefits to be achieved by co-designing hardware and software for high-performance processors and scientific applications. We argued that making design decisions that involve both hardware and software changes should be done early in the design cycle, so that correct high-level design decisions are made and both hardware and software evolve in the right direction. In order to do so, we developed Sniper/McPAT, a fast simulation platform that predicts both performance and power. Sniper, which is a parallel, high-abstraction multi-core performance simulator, predicts activity statistics that serve as input to McPAT which then predicts power consumption. We validated Sniper/McPAT against real hardware and we report average performance and power errors of 22.1% and 8.3%, respectively. Collecting activity statistics for McPAT does not slow down performance simulation in Sniper, which achieves a simulation speed around 2 MIPS on an 8-core simulation host machine.

Sniper/McPAT is a useful tool for driving architecture explorations as well as hardware/software co-design studies. Through a case study in which we considered an important scientific kernel, namely stencil computation, we demonstrated that co-designing hardware and software can lead to substantial performance and energy-efficiency improvements that cannot be achieved by exploring the architecture space only. More specifically, for our case study, we reported 1.66×

and 1.25× improvements in performance and energy efficiency, respectively. Overall, this paper makes the case for hardware/software co-design as an important and promising design paradigm for future processor system design.

10. ACKNOWLEDGEMENTS

We thank the anonymous reviewers for their valuable feedback. This work is supported by Intel and the Institute for the Promotion of Innovation through Science and Technology in Flanders (IWT). Experiments were run on computing infrastructure at the ExaScience Lab, Leuven, Belgium; the Intel HPC Lab, Swindon, UK; and the VSC Flemish Supercomputer Center. Additional support is provided by the European Research Council under the European Community's Seventh Framework Programme (FP7/2007-2013) / ERC Grant agreement no. 259295.

11. REFERENCES

[1] K. Asanovic, R. Bodik, B. C. Catanzaro, J. J. Gebis, P. Husbands, K. Keutzer, D. A. Patterson, W. Lester, Plishker, J. Shalf, S. W. Williams, and K. A. Yelick. The landscape of parallel computing research: A view from Berkeley. Technical Report UCB/EECS-2006-183, EECS Department, University of California at Berkeley, 2006.

[2] V. Aslot, M. Domeika, R. Eigenmann, G. Gaertner, W. Jones, and B. Parady. SPEComp: A new benchmark suite for measuring parallel computer performance. In *OpenMP Shared Memory Parallel Programming, LNCS*, 2104:1–10, 2001.

[3] C. Bienia, S. Kumar, J. P. Singh, and K. Li. The PARSEC benchmark suite: Characterization and architectural implications. In *PACT*, pages 72–81, 2008.

[4] N. Binkert, B. Beckmann, G. Black, S. K. Reinhardt, A. Saidi, A. Basu, J. Hestness, D. R. Hower, T. Krishna, S. Sardashti, R. Sen, K. Sewell, M. Shoaib, N. Vaish, M. D. Hill, and D. A. Wood. The gem5 simulator. *SIGARCH Comput. Archit. News*, 39(2):1–7, 2011.

[5] D. Brooks, V. Tiwari, and M. Martonosi. Wattch: A framework for architectural-level power analysis and optimizations. In *ISCA*, pages 83–94, 2000.

[6] T. E. Carlson, W. Heirman, and L. Eeckhout. Sniper: Exploring the level of abstraction for scalable and accurate parallel multi-core simulations. In *SuperComputing*, 2011.

[7] S. Che, M. Boyer, J. Meng, D. Tarjan, J. W. Sheaffer, S.-H. Lee, and K. Skadron. Rodinia: A benchmark suite for heterogeneous computing. In *IISWC*, pages 44–54, 2009.

[8] T. M. Conte, M. A. Hirsch, and K. N. Menezes. Reducing state loss for effective trace sampling of superscalar processors. In *ICCD*, pages 468–477, 1996.

[9] M. Facchini, T. E. Carlson, A. Vignon, M. Palkovic, F. Catthoor, W. Dehaene, L. Benini, and P. Marchal. System-level power/performance evaluation of 3D stacked DRAMs for mobile applications. In *DATE*, pages 923–928, 2009.

[10] D. Genbrugge, S. Eyerman, and L. Eeckhout. Interval simulation: Raising the level of abstraction in architectural simulation. In *HPCA*, pages 307–318, 2010.

[11] P. Ghysels, P. Klosiewicz, and W. Vanroose. Improving the arithmetic intensity of multigrid with the help of polynomial smoothers. In *Copper Mountain Conference on Multigrid Methods*, 2011.

[12] W. Heirman, T. E. Carlson, S. Che, K. Skadron, and L. Eeckhout. Using cycle stacks to understand scaling bottlenecks in multi-threaded workloads. In *IISWC*, 2011.

[13] E. İpek, S. A. McKee, R. Caruana, B. R. de Supinski, and M. Schulz. Efficiently exploring architectural design spaces via predictive modeling. In *ASPLOS*, 2006.

[14] H. Jacobson, A. Buyuktosunoglu, P. Bose, E. Acar, and R. Eickemeyer. Abstraction and microarchitecture scaling in early-stage power modeling. In *HPCA*, pages 394–405, 2011.

[15] D. Kanter. Inside Nehalem: Intel's future processor and system. `http://www.realworldtech.com`, 2008.

[16] B. Lee, J. Collins, H. Wang, and D. Brooks. CPR: Composable performance regression for scalable multiprocessor models. In *MICRO*, pages 270–281, 2008.

[17] C. Lefurgy, K. Rajamani, F. Rawson, W. Felter, M. Kistler, and T. W. Keller. Energy management for commercial servers. *IEEE Computer*, 36:39–48, 2003.

[18] S. Li, J. H. Ahn, R. D. Strong, J. B. Brockman, D. M. Tullsen, and N. P. Jouppi. McPAT: An integrated power, area, and timing modeling framework for multicore and manycore architectures. In *MICRO*, MICRO 42, pages 469–480. 2009.

[19] C.-K. Luk, R. Cohn, R. Muth, H. Patil, A. Klauser, G. Lowney, S. Wallace, V. J. Reddi, and K. Hazelwood. Pin: Building customized program analysis tools with dynamic instrumentation. In *PLDI*, pages 190–200. 2005.

[20] A. M. G. Maynard, C. M. Donnelly, and B. R. Olszewski. Contrasting characteristics and cache performance of technical and multi-user commercial workloads. In *ASPLOS*, pages 145–156, 1994.

[21] Micron. TN-41-01: Calculating memory system power for DDR3, 2007.

[22] M. Pellauer, M. Adler, M. Kinsy, A. Parashar, and J. Emer. HAsim: FPGA-based high-detail multicore simulation using time-division multiplexing. In *HPCA*, pages 406–417, 2011.

[23] M. Powell, A. Biswas, J. Emer, S. Mukherjee, B. Sheikh, and S. Yardi. CAMP: A technique to estimate per-structure power at run-time using a few simple parameters. In *HPCA*, pages 289–300, 2009.

[24] Racktivity RC0816 datasheet. Available from `http://www.racktivity.com`.

[25] T. Sherwood, E. Perelman, G. Hamerly, and B. Calder. Automatically characterizing large scale program behavior. In *ASPLOS*, pages 45–57, 2002.

[26] D. Sunwoo, G. Y. Wu, N. A. Patil, and D. Chiou. PrEsto: An FPGA-accelerated power estimation methodology for complex systems. In *FPL*, pages 310–317, 2010.

[27] S. Thoziyoor, J. Ahn, M. Monchiero, J. Brockman, and N. Jouppi. A comprehensive memory modeling tool and its application to the design and analysis of future memory hierarchies. In *ISCA*, pages 51–62, 2008.

[28] V. Uzelac and A. Milenkovic. Experiment flows and microbenchmarks for reverse engineering of branch predictor structures. In *ISPASS*, pages 207–217, 2009.

[29] J. Wawrzynek, D. Patterson, M. Oskin, S.-L. Lu, C. Kozyrakis, J. C. Hoe, D. Chiou, and K. Asanovic. RAMP: Research accelerator for multiple processors. *IEEE Micro*, 27(2):46–57, 2007.

[30] S. Williams, A. Waterman, and D. A. Patterson. Roofline: An insightful visual performance model for multicore architectures. *Communications of the ACM*, 52(4):65–76, Apr. 2009.

[31] S. C. Woo, M. Ohara, E. Torrie, J. P. Singh, and A. Gupta. The SPLASH-2 programs: Characterization and methodological considerations. In *ISCA*, pages 24–36, 1995.

[32] R. E. Wunderlich, T. F. Wenisch, B. Falsafi, and J. C. Hoe. SMARTS: Accelerating microarchitecture simulation via rigorous statistical sampling. In *ISCA*, pages 84–95, 2003.

[33] J. Yi, D. Lilja, and D. Hawkins. A statistically rigorous approach for improving simulation methodology. In *HPCA*, pages 281–291, 2003.

[34] M. Yourst. PTLsim: A cycle accurate full system x86-64 microarchitectural simulator. In *ISPASS*, pages 23–34. 2007.

PGCapping: Exploiting Power Gating for Power Capping and Core Lifetime Balancing in CMPs

Kai Ma and Xiaorui Wang
Department of Electrical and Computer Engineering
The Ohio State University
Columbus, OH 43210
{mak, xwang}@ece.osu.edu

ABSTRACT

Optimizing the performance of a chip multiprocessor (CMP) within a power cap has recently received a lot of attention. However, most existing solutions rely solely on DVFS, which is anticipated to have only limited actuation ranges in the future. Power gating shuts down idling cores in a CMP, such that more power can be shifted to the cores that run applications for better CMP performance. However, current preliminary studies on integrating the two knobs focus on deciding the power gating and DVFS levels in a tightly coupled fashion, with much less attention given to the direction of decoupled designs. By decoupling the two knobs that may interfere with each other, individual knob management algorithms can be less complex and more efficient to take advantage of the characteristics of different knobs. This paper proposes *PGCapping*, a decoupled design to integrate power gating with DVFS for CMP power capping. To fully utilize the power headroom that is reserved through power gating, *PGCapping* enables per-core overclocking on turned-on cores that run sequential applications. However, per-core overclocking may make some cores age much faster than others and thus become the reliability bottleneck in the whole system. Therefore, *PGCapping* also uses power gating to balance the core lifetimes. Our empirical results on a hardware testbed show that the proposed scheme achieves up to 42.0% better average application performance than five state-of-the-art power capping baselines for realistic multi-core applications, i.e., a mixed group of PARSEC and SPEC CPU2006 benchmarks. Furthermore, our extensive simulation results with real-world traces demonstrate that a lightweight lifetime balancing algorithm (based on power gating) can increase the CMP lifetime by 9.2% on average.

Categories and Subject Descriptors

C.4 [**Performance of Systems**]: Design studies; C.1.4 [**Processor Architectures**]: Parallel architectures

PACT'12, September 19–23, 2012, Minneapolis, Minnesota, USA.

General Terms

Design, Management, Performance, Experimentation

Keywords

Chip multiprocessor, power capping, power control, power gating, lifetime balancing, control theory

1. INTRODUCTION

Power has become a first-class constraint in current microprocessor design due to packaging, cooling, and power delivery circuit limits. An important research challenge is to optimize the performance of a Chip Multiprocessor (CMP) within a given power constraint (i.e., power capping). Recently, many research studies have been conducted to utilize Dynamic Voltage and Frequency Scaling (DVFS) as a knob for power capping. Unfortunately, in recent generations of technology scaling, to keep leakage current under control, the decrease in the threshold voltage (V_{th}) of transistors has stopped [13]. This, in turn, has prevented the supply voltage (V_{dd}) from further decreasing. As a result, DVFS alone may no longer be able to fully address the power capping issue. Power gating is a technique that cuts off the power supply of a logic block by inserting a gate (or sleep transistor) in a series with the power supply [27]. Gating the power supply results in almost no power consumption in the gated block [15]. Power gating complements DVFS by providing an effective mechanism to reduce leakage power. Therefore, it is preferable to integrate power gating and DVFS in power capping for further improved CMP performance.

In this paper, we consider the case of per-core power gating (PCPG) because it has been implemented in mainstream processors (e.g., Intel Core i7 [15]). PCPG and DVFS have different characteristics in terms of their transition overheads and interactions with OS, which requires a decoupled design to address their differences. PCPG has a larger transition time and energy overhead [27, 23]. Furthermore, since PCPG changes the number of turned-on cores, the OS scheduler may reallocate the thread-core mapping in each power gating interval. Therefore, the algorithm designed for PCPG should track long-term trends and avoid actuation oscillations. In contrast, DVFS has a smaller transition overhead (e.g., $10\mu s$ in Nehalem processors [15]). Moreover, it does not change the on/off states of the cores. Therefore, DVFS is preferable to explore short-term workload variations (e.g., multiple DVFS adjustment intervals within one scheduling interval) [37, 28]. However, existing efforts [21, 3] on integrating power gating and DVFS for power capping simply treat the power gating state as an extra-low power state below the existing DVFS levels and consider power gating and DVFS state in a coupled fashion at a coarse time scale. These coupled designs cannot either take advantage of fine-grain DVFS or avoid unnecessary actuations for power gating. Furthermore, these coupled designs usually require manually disabling the OS scheduler to have a fixed thread-core mapping, because if OS changes the thread-core mapping, the current statistics of one core cannot be used to decide the power state for the next interval. Therefore, a decoupled design that can meet the different requirements of power gating and DVFS, as well as can be deployed with native OS, needs to be developed.

Through PCPG, the wasted leakage power of certain under-utilized cores (in DVFS alone systems) can be proactively transformed into the dynamic power headroom for accelerating useful applications. Hardware overclocking provides CMPs with the capability of fully utilizing the dynamic power headroom for optimized performance. However, many existing CMPs have only homogeneous cores with *chip-level* overclocking capability (e.g., Intel TurboBoost [15]), which cannot fully explore the variations of different applications among cores during runtime. Since the benefit of per-core DVFS has been discussed in detail [20], we consider the case that with the per-core overclocking enabled, CMPs with homogeneous cores can mimic the functionality of heterogeneous cores to dynamically provide more powerful cores to meet the runtime requirement of applications. Even in the systems without physically implemented per-core DVFS (e.g., multi-power-island chips), Rangan et al. [34] have shown that thread migration on systems with only two power states can be used to approximate the functionality of per-core DVFS. Compared with TurboBoost, which only adjusts the *chip-level* DVFS levels, this paper addresses a different issue of coordinating the DVFS (overclocking) states for multiple on-chip cores to improve the CMP performance within a chip-level power cap.

While per-core DVFS and overclocking offer new opportunities to explore the power-performance trade-off, they also pose serious challenges to CMP reliability. Overclocking directly leads to a higher wear-out rate on the overclocked cores [19]. The practice of employing per-core DVFS/overclocking aggravates the case that some cores may age much faster than others and become the reliability bottleneck for the whole system, which thus significantly reduces the system service life [14]. Previous studies [9] have developed effective algorithms to use per-core DVFS to balance the service lifetime of on-chip cores. However, the solution of lifetime-balancing algorithms may conflict with the solution of power-capping algorithms. For example, lifetime-balancing per-core DVFS algorithms may throttle the cores running high-activity applications (e.g., high IPC) to reduce wear-out. However, those cores are probably the same cores that performance-power optimization algorithms usually seek to boost performance. It is unlikely to be able to coordinate those conflicting goals by using just one knob. Fortunately, power gating offers new opportunities to manage the core lifetime balancing issue, because the power-gated cores do not experience measurable wear-out [19]. Therefore, it is possible to achieve lifetime balancing through modulating the power gating state of each core.

Base on the above observations, this paper proposes *PG-Capping* (Power Gating for Capping), a decoupled design to integrate power gating with per-core DVFS/overclocking for CMP power capping and also discuss how to use power gating to balance the core lifetimes. Specifically, *PGCapping* consists of a Proportional-Integral (PI) controller based on feedback control theory to manage power gating and a *Quicksearch* algorithm for DVFS/overclocking management. Both the PI controller and *Quicksearch* algorithm are invoked periodically. We select different intervals for the PI controller and *Quicksearch* to decouple them. The PI controller adjusts the number of turned-on cores to control the chip power at a coarse time scale with theoretically provable stability guarantee. At a finer time scale, *Quicksearch* employs per-core DVFS to fully handle the short-term workload variations. Core-level lifetime balancing is achieved by selecting which core(s) to be turned on/off after the power controller decides the number of turned-on cores.

Specifically, this paper makes the following major contributions:

- We propose a novel algorithm *PGCapping*, which integrates power gating, DVFS, and core overclocking to optimize the CMP performance within a power cap. *PGCapping* explores a novel decoupled design direction, which has not been addressed sufficiently by previous studies. PGCapping conducts power gating at a coarser time scale for reduced runtime overhead and DVFS at a finer time scale to handle short-term workload variations.
- Since overclocking may have negative impacts on the core aging rates and lead to unnecessarily shortened CMP lifetime, *PGCapping* integrates core lifetime balancing as an integral part of the proposed power capping framework and uses a power-gating-based balancing algorithm to maximize the CMP lifetime.
- While most existing work has only simulation results, we implement the proposed *PGCapping* solution on a 12-core AMD Opteron processor and present empirical results. Our results show that our decoupled design achieves up to 42.0% better average application performance than five state-of-the-art baselines for mixed PARSEC and SPEC CPU 2006 benchmarks.

The rest of this paper is organized as follows. Section 2 highlights the differences between this paper and related work. Section 3 describes the decoupled design. Section 4 introduces our hardware testbed, simulation setups, and the implementation details of our solutions. Section 5 presents our baselines and evaluation results. Section 6 concludes this paper.

2. RELATED WORK

A well-known industry practice to integrate DVFS, overclocking and power gating is the Intel TurboBoost technology [15]. However, TurboBoost, as well as the studies in Li et al. [25] and Lee et al. [21], discusses chip-wide DVFS rather than per-core DVFS, which limits the optimization space. Because chip-wide DVFS *cannot* fully explore the inter-core variations. Since per-core frequency scaling has been available in commercial processors (e.g., AMD [1]) and on-chip regulators has been proposed [20] for per-core DVFS, this paper focuses on integrating power gating and per-core DVFS. Compared with power gating and chip-level DVFS, this paper addresses a different but more challenging problem because we need to coordinate the power state (i.e.,

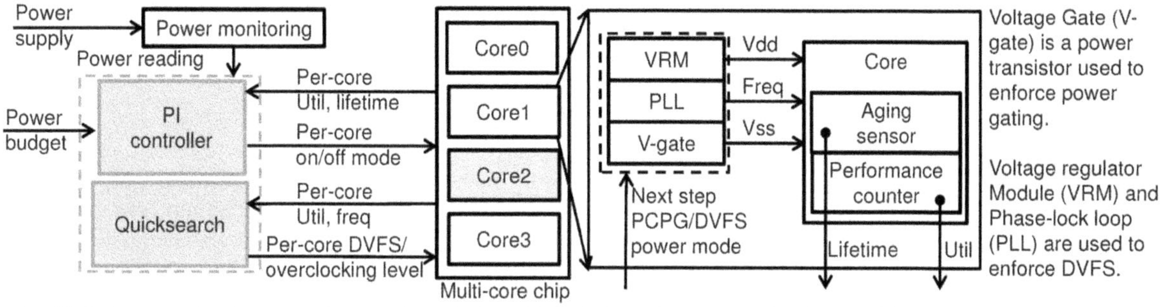

Figure 1: *PGCapping* features a decoupled design that takes the power budget, chip power measurement, per-core utilization, temperature, lifetime as inputs. *PGCapping* computes next-step power mode (e.g., on/off, DVFS levels, overclocking state) of each core to cap the entire chip power, boost performance, and balance core lifetimes.

power gating state and DVFS level) of each core for optimized performance. Many power-capping solutions [37, 28] based on the per-core DVFS have been proposed. However, they do not discuss the coordination with the power gating technology. Bircher et al. [3] use both the per-core DVFS and power gating. However, they focus on proposing and validating a workload phase predictor for the power management. The impact of the real-world OS scheduling, which is crucial to the workload-based power management, has not been sufficiently addressed in their work.

Karpuzcu et al. [19] have proposed to use per-core overclocking to boost sequential application execution. However, they only overclock one core each time until it runs out and then they cut that core off from the on-chip logic and power network. In contrast, our scheme allows multiple cores to simultaneously stay at the overclocking state within a desired power budget and we balance the service lifetime of each core.

Power capping has been previously addressed at different levels, such as CMP [40, 16, 3], server [22, 8], server cluster [38, 33], and data center [39]. However, all the prior studies rely only on DVFS without core lifetime balancing.

The core-level lifetime balancing issue of multi-core processors has been extensively studied. However, previous explorations mainly focus on the per-core DVFS and scheduling [14, 9]. Using per-core power gating as a reliability management knob and the impact of overclocking are rarely touched. Compared with previous art, this paper discusses using power gating as a reliability management knob and specifically considers the overclocking scenarios.

3. SYSTEM DESIGN

In this section, we introduce *PGCapping*, which integrates power gating, DVFS, and overclocking to optimize the CMP performance within a power cap. *PGCapping* is a novel decoupled design that conducts power gating at a coarse time scale for reduced runtime overhead and DVFS at a fine time scale to handle short-term workload variations.

As shown in Figure 1, we design one power gating management module (i.e., *PI controller*) and one DVFS/overclocking management module (i.e., *Quicksearch* algorithm) to conduct power capping at different time scales. *PI controller* adjusts the number of turned-on cores to control the chip power based on the power measurement and budget at a coarse time interval. Core-level lifetime balancing is achieved through assigning the on/off state of each core based on its utilization. At a fine-gained time interval, the power control and performance optimization are realized by adjusting the DVFS level of each core. We treat the overclocking states as extra DVFS levels higher than the labeled peak DVFS levels. Therefore, the assignment of overclocking state is also conducted in *Quicksearch*.

Both *PI controller* and *Quicksearch* are invoked periodically. We select different intervals for *PI controller* and *Quicksearch* to decouple them. The interval of *PI controller* is set to be much longer than the OS scheduling interval to give OS enough time for spreading and balancing workload among turned-on cores. The interval of *Quicksearch* is selected to be much shorter than that of OS scheduling. Therefore, before the next *PI controller* interval starts, *Quicksearch* has already settled at the optimal point with the current power gating setting. As a result, the *PI controller* does not introduce oscillations to the DVFS management. On the other side, since *Quicksearch* converges quickly, the impacts of DVFS on PCPG are observed to be negligible. Therefore, the two loops will not interfere with each other and can be designed independently. Moreover, both loops are decoupled from OS scheduling, so native OS scheduling without modification can be used in this decoupled design.

3.1 Design of PCPG Management Module

In this section, we introduce the design of *PI controller* that controls the power consumption of the entire chip to a desired power budget by adjusting the number of turned-on cores at a coarse time interval.

The power of the chip generally has a monotonic relationship with the number of turned-on cores. However, the runtime variations (e.g., different applications or DVFS) make it unlikely to develop an accurate model for all possible cases. Therefore, we adopt feedback control theory to design a PI controller to decide the number of turned-on cores. A key advantage of the control theory design approach is that it can tolerate a certain degree of modeling errors and adapt to online model variations based on dynamic feedback [10]. Therefore, our solution does not rely on power models that are perfectly accurate, which is in sharp contrast to open-loop solutions that would fail without an accurate model.

Controller Design. Following standard PI control theory design procedures [10], our controller is designed as:

$$N(k) = N(k-1) + \frac{(P_t - cp(k))}{a}. \qquad (1)$$

$N(k)$ is the number of turned-on cores on the chip in the kth control period. P_t is the power budget of the entire chip, which can be determined by the thermal and power supply constraints of the processor or specified by the user during runtime. $cp(k)$ is the power consumption of the entire

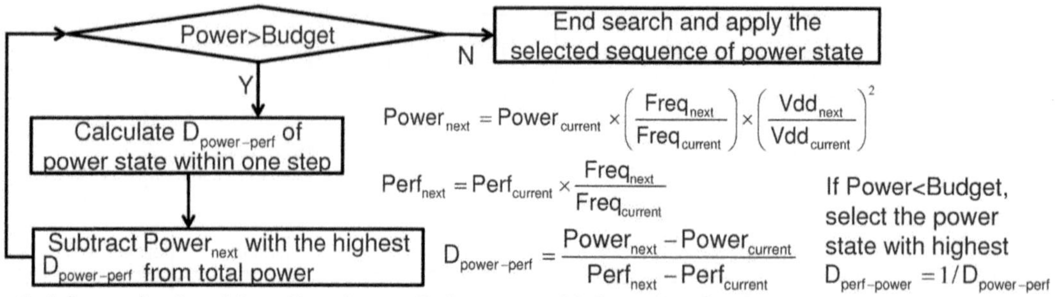

Figure 2: *Quicksearch* algorithm flowchart. Only power-higher-than-budget case is presented for concision.

chip in the kth control period. Parameter a characterizes the power consumption of one core, which may vary for different chips and applications. In our design, we derive a by using the datasheet full power range (from the idle power to the maximum power of the chip [2]) divided by the dynamic range of $N(k)$ (e.g., a=5.9).

Controller Analysis. A fundamental benefit of the control-theoretic approach is that it offers a mathematical framework to analyze the system stability and performance, even when the system power model may change at runtime due to variations. By applying pole analysis [10] on our controller, we prove that the closed-loop system is stable as long as $0 \leq a \leq 11.8$. In our experiments, the variation never exceeds the range. Please note in our PI controller design, we only use three datasheet numbers (idle power, TDP, the number of cores) without the need to profiling the power efficiency of each core. This design methodology is in sharp contrast with previous studies, which typically requires extensive profiling tests.

Actuation refinement. Through the controller calculation, we have derived the number of cores N_a that should be at the turned-on state in order to optimize the CMP performance within the desired power cap. Next, we get the number of unfinished tasks N_b from OS. We then enforce $min(N_a, N_b)$ cores at turned-on state for the next interval to transform saved leakage power to the dynamic power headroom that can be used to improve the CMP performance.

3.2 Design of DVFS Management Module

Since the power gating state of each core has been decided by the PI controller, we now introduce *Quicksearch* algorithm to explore short-term workload variations with per-core DVFS/overclocking.

Quicksearch uses the performance/power ratio to decide the power state (i.e., the DVFS/overclocking level) of each core. Specifically, we define $Perf = Util * Freq$ as our performance metric. As discussed in [19], the aggregated frequency $Freq$ is a high-level computational capacity metric. We extend their metric by weighting frequency with utilization $Util$ to deduct the idling cycles. As shown in Figure 2, *Quicksearch* starts with the current power states of all the cores. If the current power is higher than the chip-wide budget, the algorithm selects the application/core pair that would provide the highest $D_{power-perf}$ (i.e., power reduction to performance loss ratio). The chip-level power consumption with this new configuration is estimated by adding $Power_{next}$-$Power_{current}$ to the current chip power. If the new estimated chip power is still higher than the budget, *Quicksearch* is again invoked from the new configuration. This process is repeated until the power budget is met. If the current power is lower than the chip-wide budget, the algorithm selects the application/core pair that provides the highest ratio of performance gain to power increase $D_{perf-power}$. The chip power consumption of this new configuration is estimated by adding $Power_{next}$-$Power_{current}$ to the current chip power. If the new estimated chip power is still lower than the budget, *Quicksearch* is again invoked from the new configuration. This process is repeated until the power budget is met. *Quicksearch* extends the *SteepestDrop* algorithm [41] to consider overclocking states. In an overclocking-enabled system, the final peak DVFS level might not be fixed [1]. Starting from the peak configuration (as in original *SteepestDrop*) is not always possible. Therefore, *Quicksearch* uses the current configuration as the search starting point. Moreover, there are relatively fewer power mode transitions in the stable execution phases. Therefore, *Quicksearch* reduces the search time. As a greedy algorithm, *Quicksearch* cannot completely avoid ending at a local optimum. Fortunately, DVFS impacts the performance approximately in a linear way unless the application is extremely memory-bounded, which is not a common case.

Overclocking and parallel applications. In *Quicksearch*, we do not explicitly discuss the core acceleration because we consider the overclocking states as extra DVFS levels above the labeled peak DVFS level. For parallel applications, hardware or software spin loop detectors [26] can be used to identify the active waiting loops within applications to deduct spinning cycles from working cycles. In that case, the utilization-weighted frequency represents the amount of real work that a core is doing. Selecting the steps to maximize the performance/power ratio in *Quicksearch* is still valid. We can even further improve the parallel application performance by on-line detecting the critical thread and overclocking the critical thread [28]. Please note we address the core-to-core power efficiency variations by using per-core DVFS (or per-core frequency scaling) in *Quicksearch*. *Quicksearch* first dynamically estimates the perf/power ratio of each core; then it raises the frequency of a high perf/power ratio core if the current power is lower than the budget; if the current power is higher than the budget, it lowers the frequency of a low perf/power ratio core.

3.3 Lifetime Balancing

In this section, we introduce the core lifetime balancing algorithm in *PGCapping*.

We propose to organize all the cores to two lists. One list contains all the turned-on cores. The other list contains all the turned-off cores. When we need to turn on one core, we find the core with the longest estimated lifetime in the turned-off core list to turn on. When we turn off one core, we find the core with the shortest estimated lifetime in the turned-on core list to turn off. Wear-out information can be estimated by using aging sensors that dynamically measure the increase in critical path delays due to aging [5]. Please note lifetime balancing only takes place when some cores are turned on/off. Therefore, this balancing algorithm does not interfere with the power-capping algorithm introduced earlier. Our experiments have shown that this balancing strategy can achieve decent core-level lifetime balance results (in Section 5.4). Compared with previous sophisticated designs (e.g., [9]), which usually require on-line workload characteristic evaluation and then use scheduling or per-core DVFS to balance the lifetime of each core, the algorithm we present does not require any modification about OS scheduling or DVFS management. There are mainly two reasons why such a lightweight algorithm can work well: 1) in real production environment, there are always variations (e.g., processor utilization and power budget variations) for us to turn on/off cores; 2) the normal wear-out process takes place gradually since we eliminate catastrophic overheating through power capping.

4. IMPLEMENTATION

In this section, we introduce the physical testbed for power capping evaluation and simulation environment for lifetime balancing evaluation.

4.1 Power Capping Evaluation Testbed

Our testbed is a 12-core AMD Opteron 6168 processor running OpenSUSE 11.3. 6168 does not support per-core DVFS and PCPG [2]. We use per-core p-state assignment to emulate per-core DVFS. 6168 has 5 p-states (0.8GHz/-0.975V, 1.0GHz/1.0V, 1.3GHz/1.025V, 1.5GHz/1.0625V, and 1.9GHz /1.1125V). When we assign a p-state to one core, the frequency of that core is enforced independently as the defined value. However, the core voltage is decided by the highest frequency among the cores because all the cores share the same voltage plane [2]. We use CPU Hotplug [31] to emulate PCPG as in [23]. CPU Hotplug was originally intended for systems with hardware support to install and remove CPU modules without interruption, which mimics precisely the behavior necessary to model per-core power gating. The per-core p-state assignment and CPU Hotplug can emulate the performance impact of per-core DVFS and PCPG.

A challenge we face is to estimate the power consumption because the direct measured CPU power does not factor in the power impact of core-grained voltage scaling and PCPG. Our hybrid power estimation (based on real-time measurement), which considers the power impact of per-core DVFS and PCPG, works as follows. First we measure the power consumption of 6168 as in [17]. An Agilent 34410A digital multimeter is used together with a Fluke i410 current probe to measure the current running through the 12V power lines that power the processor. The accuracy of this measurement is ±3.5% of reading. We first set all the cores to the same p-state and measure the idling power P_{idle}. Our measure is: 44.0W(0.8GHz), 46.4W(1.0GHz), 51.3W(1.3GHz), 55.1W(1.5GHz), 61.3W-(1.9GHz). Then we calculate the activity factor β in model (2) [18, 28].

$$mPow = \sum_{j=0}^{N-1} \beta * \frac{Freq(j)}{1.9} * (\frac{V_{DD}}{1.1125})^2 * Util(j) + P_{idle} \quad (2)$$

where $mPow$ is the *measured* power of the entire chip. Parameter $Freq(j)$ is the frequency of the jth core. V_{DD} is the Vdd corresponding to the highest frequency among all the cores because all the cores share one voltage plane. $Util(j)$ is the utilization of the jth core. $mPow$ is measured. P_{idle} at different chip-level p-states (decided by the peak frequency among the cores) has been measured. $Freq(j)$ and $Util(j)$ can be derived from OS. By using those inputs, we can compute the chip-level activity factor β. Using chip-level activity factor is a trade-off between estimation accuracy and estimation complexity [18, 28]. In our extensive validation experiments, the average error is 1.1W (the worst case is 3.6W) between the estimated and measured power for this estimation methodology. Once we derive β, we estimate the power of each core as:

$$Pow(j) = \beta * \frac{Freq(j)}{1.9} * (\frac{V_{DD}(j)}{1.1125})^2 * Util(j) + \frac{P_{idle}}{12} \quad (3)$$

where $Pow(j)$ is the estimated power of the jth core. Please note $V_{DD}(j)$ is the voltage of the jth core at current DVFS level. The chip power is estimated as $Pow = \sum_{j=0}^{N-1} Pow(j)$. We assume $Pow(j)=0$ if it is power-gated. We report Pow in our experiment part because it accounts for the power impact of per-core DVFS and PCPG. We do not explicitly consider the dynamic power of the uncore part because the uncore power is actually driven by the core part. We attribute uncore part power to the corresponding core part, which is has been shown to be sufficiently accurate for the power management purpose [18, 28].

Table 1: Workload mixes used on physical testbed.

Mixes	PARSEC 2.1, SPEC2006 [1]	Aggregate Effect
mix1	12-mcf	memory intensive
mix2	12-perlbench	CPU intensive
mix3	8-swaptions, 4-omnetpp	no-barrier parallel
mix4	4-(blackscholes, bodytrack) 2-(xalancbmk, povray)	low-barrier and high-barrier parallel
mix5	4-x264, 8-fluidanimate	high-lock parallel
mix6	4-(vips,facesim) 1-(libq,astar,soplex,dealII)	random mix

We evaluate the proposed solution with the PARSEC and SPEC workload mixes (Table 1), which cover a variety of different aggregate effects [28].

On our prototype testbed, we implement the control algorithm as an OS daemon process to control the target processor. The intervals of our designs are decided as follows. First, our physical testbed measurement shows that the overhead of DVFS is $35\mu s$ (close to $10\mu s$ in Nehalem [15]) and the average overhead of PCPG is 127ms and the worst case is 220ms (close to the 100ms measurement result in [23]). Second, we study the key intervals in the OS. Although the minimum Linux time quantum can reach 10ms, the default time slice is 100ms [6]. The default load balancing interval is 200ms. Third, we decide our design intervals. In the decoupled design, we select 2s as PCPG interval to give the kernel sufficient time to balance the workloads in the decoupled design. We select DVFS interval to be 50ms, which is smaller than the default time slice to test fine-grain DVFS.

4.2 Lifetime Balancing Evaluation Simulator

6168 does not have aging sensors. Therefore, we evaluate the lifetime balancing part in a simulator [29]. We model the core of Opteron 6168 (e.g., voltage, DVFS levels, frequency). In each time interval (e.g., DVFS interval), per-core power is modeled as in [21] with two parts: the dynamic power is based on utilization and DVFS level, the leakage power is based on temperature. The temperature is modeled

[1] The number-appname notation is the number of threads of the application with the name of appname for PARSEC; for SPEC2006 workload, it is the number of copies of the application with the name of appname.

as in [19] based on the total power. Since the total power impacts temperature and the temperature impacts leakage power. These two parts are entangled together. We run multiple iterations of calculation until both power and temperature readings converge (e.g., no more than 5% change between two consecutive iterations). We use RAMP2.0 to model the service lifetime. The different failure models and key parameters are the same as those used in [35].

4.3 Discussion on Per-core DVFS

We assume per-core DVFS as one possible power adjustment knob (which is also assumed in [20, 21, 24, 41]) and emulate per-core DVFS with per-core frequency scaling in our testbed. However, *PGCapping* does not rely on per-core DVFS. In fact, *PGCapping* already works with pre-core frequency scaling on our testbed. To physically enable fast voltage adjustment required by per-core DVFS, on-chip voltage regulators are needed [20]. Recently, IBM Watson Lab demonstrated a 2.5D on-chip integrated regulator [36], showing the new manufacturing break-through in enabling fine-grain DVFS. Moreover, even in the systems without physically implemented per-core DVFS, Rangan et al. [34] have shown that thread migration on systems with only two power states can be used to approximate the functionality of per-core DVFS. Therefore, this paper emulates per-core DVFS in our evaluation and explores the integration of per-core DVFS and power gating.

5. EVALUATION

In this section, we compare the power control accuracy, application performance, core-level lifetime balancing results of *PGCapping* and baselines in both physical testbed and simulator.

5.1 Baselines

In this section, we introduce the five studied policies.

Our first baseline is *per-core-DVFS-only*. It adopts the original *SteepestDrop* algorithm [41], without PCPG or overclocking states. We select *SteepestDrop* as an example of state-of-the-art per-core DVFS based solutions. However, the dynamic range of *per-core-DVFS-only* is limited due to the lack of overclocking states and PCPG.

Our second baseline is *PCPG-only*. We disable DVFS and use PCPG as the only knob to control power. When the current power $cp(k)$ is lower than the budget P_t, we need to turn on cores. In order to achieve a fast convergence, we turn on multiple cores each time. We randomly pick a core in the turned-off core list, then we use the power when it was turned off as an estimation and add that power to $cp(k)$. If $cp(k)$ is still lower than P_t, we pick another core and so on, until $cp(k)$ is higher than P_t. When the current power $cp(k)$ is higher than the budget P_t, we do just the opposite. We allow turn on/off multiple cores each time to achieve fast convergence because PCPG takes place at a coarse time interval. We design *PCPG-only* as an example of using PCPG as the only knob to control the chip-level power consumption in a heuristic way. However, this simple heuristic cannot avoid the oscillation.

Our third baseline *ETurboBoost* is an extended version of Intel TurboBoost [15]. It uses chip-level DVFS and PCPG. Original TurboBoost does not turn off cores when all the cores are running applications and adjusts the DVFS level of the entire chip to fit the power budget by one level at each DVFS interval. *ETurboBoost* extends original TurboBoost by using the PI controller to control the number of cores when the assigned power budget is lower than the power consumption that all the cores are running at the lowest frequency levels. We implement *ETurboBoost* as an example of state-of-the-art power capping solution through power gating and chip-level DVFS.

Our fourth baseline *Per-core-DVFS+PCPG* is using PI controller for PCPG and per-core DVFS with *Quicksearch* but without overclocking states. We select this baseline to show the necessity to include overclocking states to fully explore the power headroom.

We design our fifth baseline *EQuicksearch* (i.e., Enhanced Quicksearch) to be a very competitive coupled solution to integrate per-core DVFS/overclocking with power gating. *EQuicksearch* extends power gating state to *Quicksearch*. We take the power gating state as the extra-low power state under the labeled lowest DVFS level as in previous coupled design [21]. We assume the power and performance of a turned-off core to be zero. We estimate $Power_{next}$ and $Perf_{next}$ of a currently turned-off core as the average power and performance of all the turned-on cores at the last interval. We also add the transition power to $Power_{next}$ and deduct the transition time from $Perf_{next}$ to minimize the undesirable oscillation. We take *EQuicksearch* as an example of coupled solutions because it demonstrates two key features of a coupled solution: 1) the coupled solution has the opportunity to select from the entire available adjustment space; 2) due to the huge search space, pruning strategies (e.g., greedy algorithm like *SteepestDrop*) usually need to be employed. We consider *EQuicksearch* as a state-of-the-art coupled design because its predecessor *SteepestDrop* has been shown to outperform many other recently published solutions [30, 37] and intuitive baselines [41]. Since *EQuicksearch* may change the power gating states of multiple cores, we set the interval to be sufficiently long to conduct the required actuations. In our experiment, we invoke *EQuicksearch* every 1s to get the trade-off between actuation overhead and system responsiveness. Please note coupled solutions (either *EQuicksearch* or previous studies like [21]) may change the on/off states of cores at each control interval. As a result, OS might reschedule the thread-core mapping, which makes the last interval statistic based decision-making invalid. Therefore, we have to manually assign thread-core affinity when we use coupled solutions. In contrast, our proposed decoupled design can work with native OS without any manual intervention because the PCPG and DVFS parts have been decoupled with OS through interval selection.

5.2 Power Control

In this section, we present the physical testbed results. We set 1.3GHz as the normal peak working state. We have three DVFS states (0.8GHz, 1.0GHz, 1.3GHz) and two overclocking states (1.5GHz, 1.9GHz). The overclocking setting agrees with the overclocking potential analysis in [12] (e.g., normally 10-40%).

In Figure 3, we run 7 copies of a randomly selected benchmark *gobmk* from SPEC CPU2006 on Opteron 6168. We reduce the power budget at 40s from 55W to 35W to emulate a power budget cut scenario due to various reasons (e.g., thermal emergency). The power budget is then raised back to 55W at 80s after the emergency is resolved. Initially, we turn on all cores at the lowest DVFS level as in Linux default case.

Figure 3a shows the results of *per-core-DVFS-only*. Be-

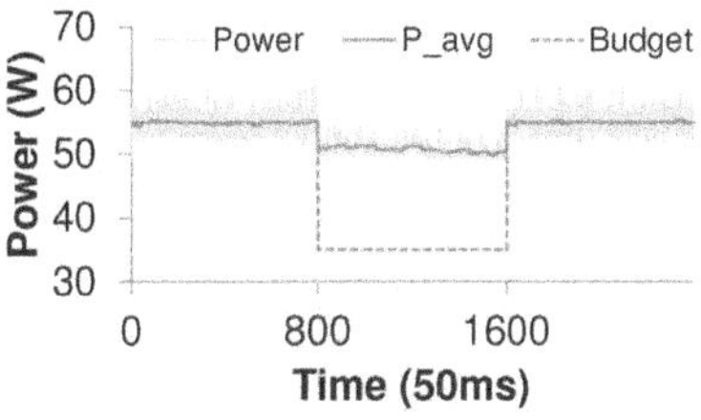

(a) *Per-core-DVFS-only.*

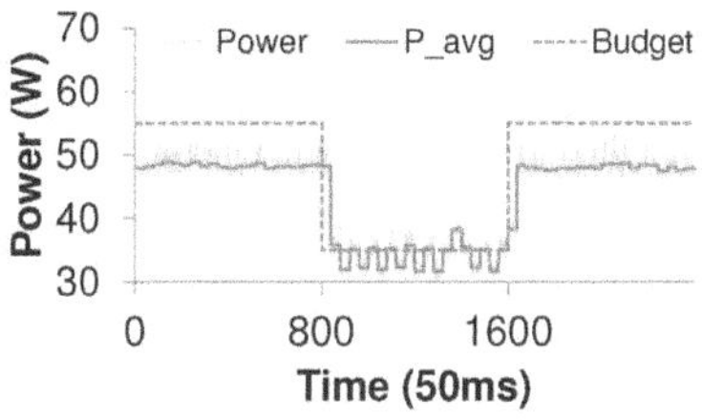

(b) *PCPG-only.*

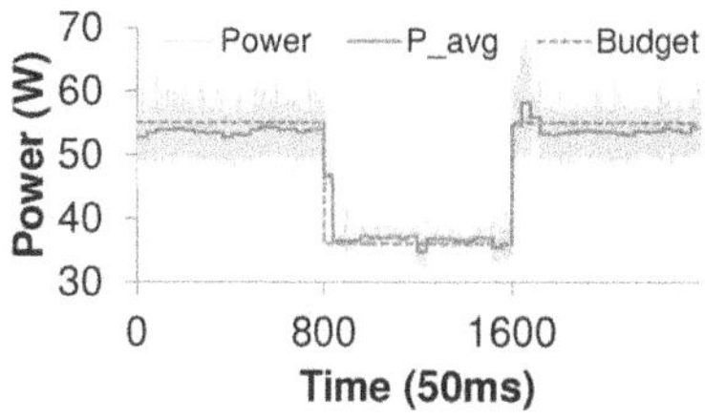

(c) *ETurboBoost.*

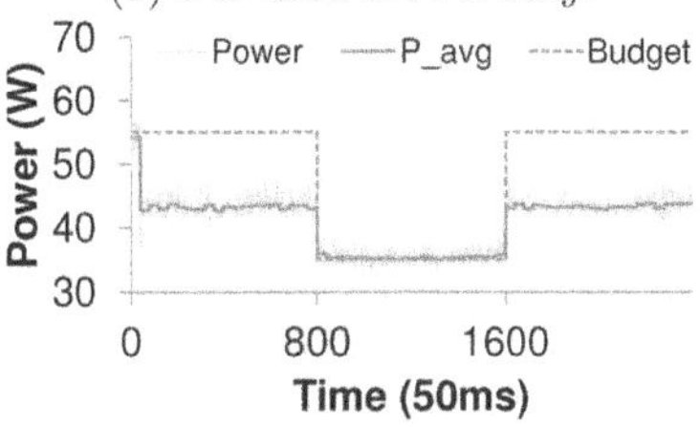

(d) *Per-core-DVFS+PCPG.*

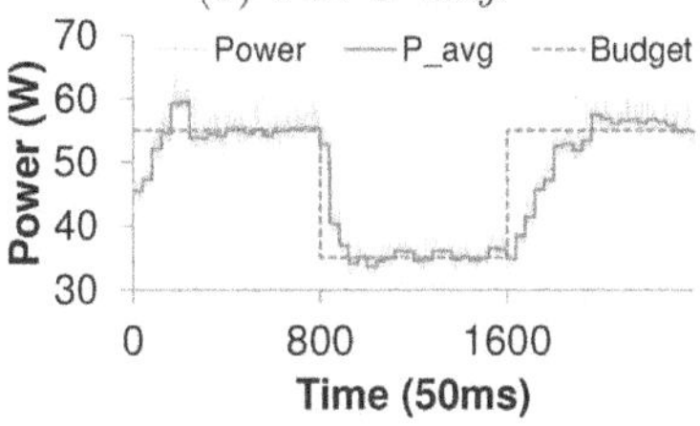

(e) *EQuicksearch.*

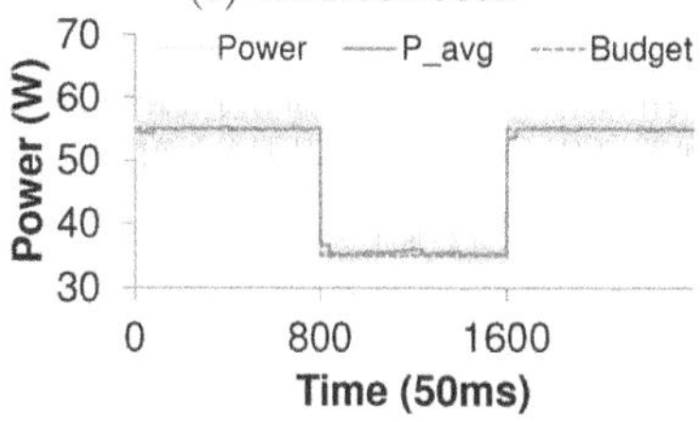

(f) *PGCapping.*

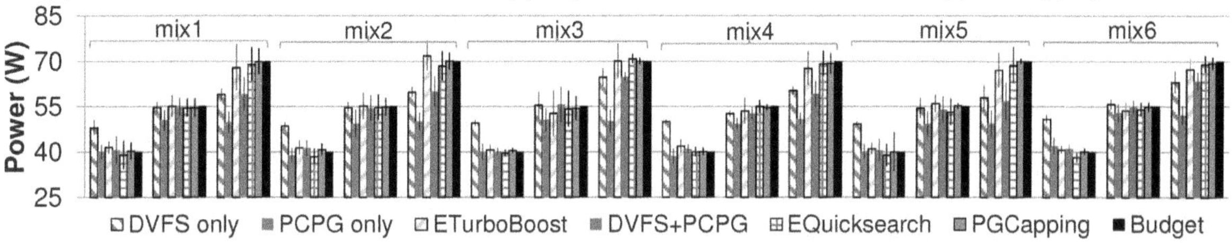

(g) Power comparison with different budgets and different benchmarks.

Figure 3: Hardware testbed results to show that *PGCapping* can precisely enforce the power budget by using PCPG, DVFS and overclocking in both the high and low power budget cases. We calculate the average power with a 2s window as P_avg to clearly present the general trend.

cause the frequencies of all the cores have been set to the lowest level, *per-core-DVFS-only* cannot further reduce power to enforce power budget cut at 40-80s. This might introduce system crash or other undesirable failures. In Figure 3b, with PCPG, the system can successfully reach the low power budget. However, the frequently turning on/off cores introduces large power oscillations and potential large thermal cycling. Figure 3c shows the results of *ETurboBoost*. *ETurboBoost* can enforce the desired power budget. However, *ETurboBoost* uses chip-level DVFS and introduces large power oscillations. More importantly, *ETurboBoost* always oscillates between two adjacent DVFS levels of the entire chip, even in the steady state. As a result, even on average, it never settles to the set point. Please note there is averagely an 2.5W power gap between the 2s-window average power and the budget curve during 0-40s and 40-80s. Potential performance benefits could be gained by fully utilizing the power budget. Moreover, the processor is running on average 0.7W higher than the budget during 40-80s, which may possibly introduce undesirable failures. In Figure 3d, we show the case of per-core DVFS with PCPG but no overclocking. Our PI controller with refinement (Section 3.1) can identify that there are only 7 cores are used in our experiment and turn off the rest 5 cores. However, without overclocking, even with all the cores set to the peak DVFS level, the power budget still cannot be fully utilized. Figure 3e shows that *EQuicksearch* can enforce the power budget. However, *EQuicksearch* has larger oscillations due to coarser time interval. Figure 3f shows that *PGCapping* can precisely enforce the power budget. In steady state, *PGCapping* oscillates between two adjacent DVFS levels of one core, which is much smaller than oscillating between two adjacent DVFS levels of the entire chip in *ETurboBoost*. As more and more cores are expected to be integrated on-chip with future process technology scaling, the benefit of one core adaptation instead of whole chip adaptation will become more significant. We also notice although *PGCapping* tracks the power budget closely in Figure 3f, it exceeds the budget sometimes for very short time periods. We believe those small and short noise will not introduce serious issues because modern computer systems are extensively equipped with capacitors in the system to address potential voltage or power variations. Moreover, the power overdraw protection is usually implemented by circuit breakers, which are usually designed to tolerate short period of time of overdraw (typically seconds [11]). Therefore, an extremely short period power overdraw can be masked by those factors. In our physical testbed results, the power overdraw is at the order of milliseconds and the average power is strictly controlled to the set point.

Figure 3g shows that *per-core-DVFS-only*, *PCPG-only*, *ETurboBoost*, and *Per-core-DVFS+PCPG* cannot adjust the processor to the desired power budget in certain cases for the reasons analyzed above. In contrast, *PGCapping* and *EQuicksearch* can always control the power to the assigned setting point for different benchmark mixes with different power budgets.

5.3 Application Performance

In Figure 4, we present the corresponding frequency, number of turned-on cores traces of Figure 3 to show the performance impact of different policies. The frequencies of the turned-off cores are counted as 0. In Figure 4a, *per-core-DVFS-only* policy has no PCPG. Therefore, during 40-80s, the frequencies of all the cores have been set to the low-

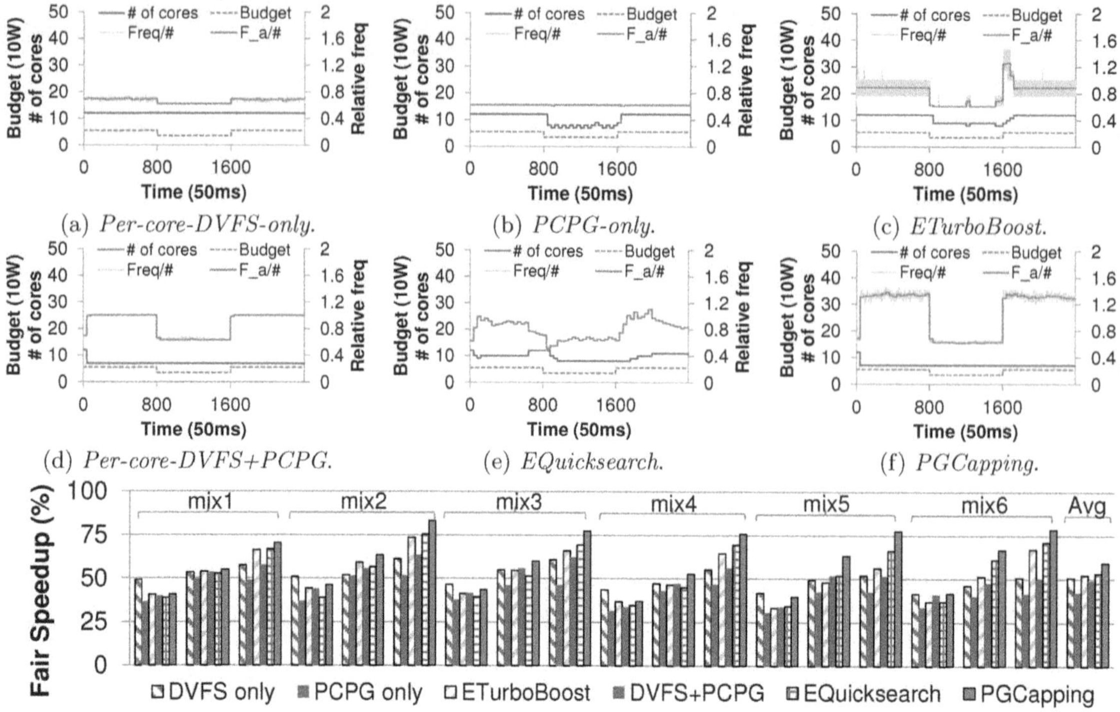

(a) *Per-core-DVFS-only.* (b) *PCPG-only.* (c) *ETurboBoost.*

(d) *Per-core-DVFS+PCPG.* (e) *EQuicksearch.* (f) *PGCapping.*

(g) Performance comparison with different budgets and different benchmarks.

Figure 4: Hardware testbed results to show that *PGCapping* can reserve power headroom by using PCPG and accelerate cores running useful workload by using overclocking. The frequencies are normalized to the peak frequency of one core (i.e., Relative freq). The Freq/# is calculated by dividing the total aggregated relative frequency of the entire chip by the number of turned-on cores, which can be interpreted as a high-level computing capability that each turned-on core can offer (the higher is preferable). We also calculate average Freq/# with a 2s window as F_a/#.

est level continuously and could not go lower to enforce desired power budget. Figure 4b shows the results of *PCPG-only*. Because *PCPG-only* does not change the DVFS levels of the cores, it only adjusts the number of turned-on cores to fit the power budget. We can observe that the cores are always turned on/off frequently. This is not desirable because PCPG has a high overhead compared with DVFS. Frequently turning on/off cores negatively impacts performance. In Figure 4c, *ETurboBoost* adjusts the DVFS level of the entire chip up/down around the power budget, which could not explore the inter-core variations. Moreover, due to the large granularity of chip-level DVFS, DVFS and PCPG have large interference at transition time, leading to the large overshoot at 80s. Figure 4d shows the results of per-core DVFS with PCPG but no overclocking. We can see from 0-40s and 40-80s, when the power budget is high, due to the lack of overclocking state, the DVFS levels of the cores could not be raised further, which fails to achieve optimal performance. In Figure 4e, *EQuicksearch* purely relies on a heuristic algorithm to decide the power state of each core in a coupled fashion (e.g., using DVFS or on/off state to adjust power consumption). Therefore, the adaptation is limited to a coarse level. Furthermore, *EQuicksearch* cannot avoid unnecessary oscillation of power state due to the system noises and workload variations. Please note we already minimize the power gating oscillation by considering the transition power and time overhead in *EQuicksearch* algorithm. In Figure 4f, *PGCapping* can identify the idling cores and turn them off to reserve the power budget headroom. It then uses overclocking to fully utilize the headroom. Please note that a core is running at a higher DVFS level on average when managed by *PGCapping* than *ETurboBoost* and *EQuicksearch* because *PGCapping* can fully utilize the power budget. In addition, *PGCapping* can fully explore the runtime variations among different cores by using per-core DVFS and per-core overclocking. Figure 4g shows the performance comparison for different policies on different benchmark mixes. In this paper, we use Fair Speedup (FS) as our performance indicator. The FS of a partitioning scheme is defined as the harmonic mean of per-application speedup with respect to the equal resource share case (i.e., peak frequency for all applications) [4]. The FS achieved by a scheme can be expressed as

$$FS(scheme) = N_{app} / \sum_{i=1}^{N_{app}} \frac{ET_{app_i(scheme)}}{ET_{app_i(base)}} \quad (4)$$

$ET_{app_i(scheme)}$ is the execution time of the ith application under a certain power management scheme. $ET_{app_i(base)}$ is the execution time of running the ith application of the peak frequency level all the time. N_{app} is the number of applications in the system, i.e., the set of applications that execute together. FS is an indicator of the overall improvement in execution efficiency gained across the applications. Figure 4g shows that *PGCapping* outperforms *per-core-DVFS-only*, *PCPG-only*, *ETurboBoost*, and *Per-core-DVFS+PCPG* by 16.9%, 42.0%, 13.9%, 21.4% on average, respectively. In general, the reason that *PGCapping* can outperform baselines is that it fully utilizes the power budget. Therefore, the cores are generally running at a higher frequency level. Specifically, *PGCapping* reserves power headroom for cores running useful workload by turning off unused cores. There-

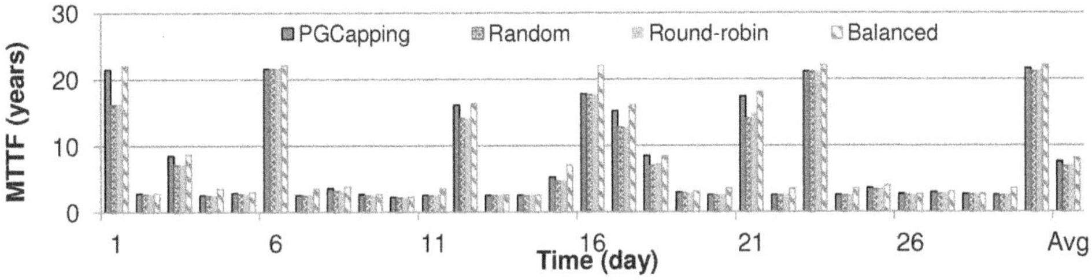

(a) Lifetime-balancing results with real-world data center utilization traces.

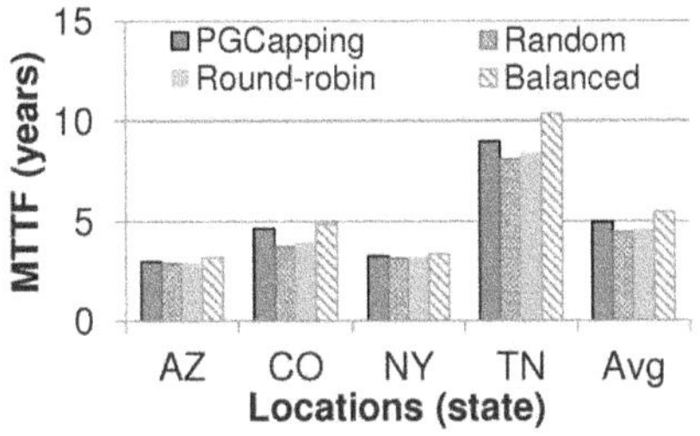

(b) Lifetime-balancing with solar power budget.

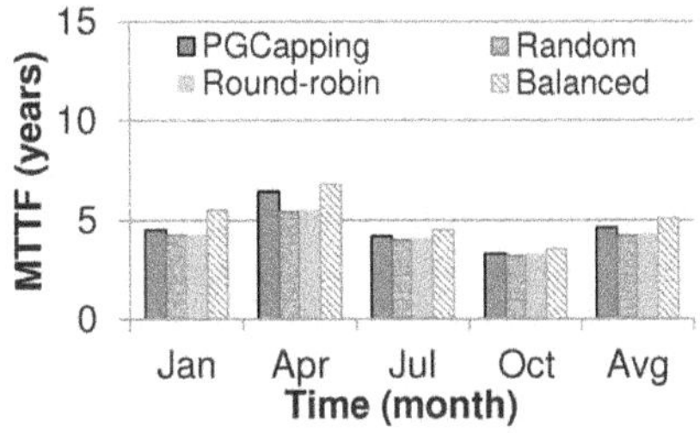

(c) Combined test.

Figure 5: *PGCapping* achieves very close core lifetime balancing performance with *Balanced* (a state-of-the-art core lifetime balancing scheme [9]). *PGCapping* outperforms *Random* and *Round-robin* baselines.

fore, it outperforms *per-core-DVFS-only*. Then, *PGCapping* uses per-core DVFS/overclocking to fully utilize the power headroom and explore the runtime inter-core variations for optimized performance. Therefore, *PGCapping* can outperform *ETurboBoost*, and *Per-core-DVFS+PCPG*. Althought *EQuicksearch* has a full set of the possible configuratioin combination to explore for optimized performance at a coarse time interval, it cannot eliminate unnecessary oscillation of power gating due to system noises. In contrast, *PGCapping* benefits from fine-time-grain DVFS and robust PI controller in the power gating part. Therefore, *PGCapping* achieves 11.5% better performance than *EQuicksearch* on average.

5.4 Lifetime Balancing

In this section, we first introduce three baselines for our lifetime balancing part. Next, we present our simulation results.

We use three baselines to compare with our power-gating-based lifetime balancing algorithm in *PGCapping* (Section 3.3). The first baseline is *Random*: when we need to turn on cores, we randomly select the turned-off cores to turn on; when we turn off cores, we randomly select the turned-on cores to turn off. The second baseline is *Round-robin* [19]: when we turn off cores, we start from the first core, then the second, and so on. When we turn on cores, we also start with the first. If it is already turned on, we turn to the next. The third baseline *Balanced* is an extension of the lifetime balancing algorithm discussed in [9]. *Balanced* sorts the cores in lifetime descended order and the next step available precore DVFS levels or on/off states in descended order. Next, it maps the two lists. *Balanced* strictly enforces lifetime balancing among cores at each DVFS and PCPG interval without considering the actuation overhead. *Balanced* negatively impacts performance. Therefore, it is not suitable for real-world implementation. However, it has been suggested as a reasonable approximation for the best-effort per-core DVFS based lifetime balancing [9].

In Figure 5, we conduct three test cases to evaluate the lifetime balancing with real-world workload and power budget variations.

In Figure 5a, we evaluate our proposed life-balancing solution in *PGCapping* with real-world workload variations. We assign a fixed power cap (e.g., 62W) to the processor while using a continuous 30-day real-world server utilization trace [42]. We derive the 62W budget by calculating the overall 30-day average utilization and test run the simulator with the average utilization at peak frequency. *PGCapping* outperforms *Random* and *Round-robin* by 9.2% and 8.1%. *PGCapping* achieves 92.3% of *Balanced* in the mean time to failure (MTTF). In Figure 5b, we evaluate our proposed life-balancing solution with real-world power budget variations. We assume the processor is powered by a solar panel (e.g. BP3180N [7]) and hosting HPC applications, which is a newly proposed green-energy solution [24]. Therefore, the power budget changes with the solar radiation but the utilization is fixed to 100%. We use meteorological data from the Measurement and Instrumentation Data Center (MIDC) [32] at the locations that have different solar energy resource potentials (e.g., AZ, CO, NY, TN) across different seasons (e.g. the middle of Jan., Apr., Jul. of 2011 and Oct. of 2010) to calculate the maximum available solar power envelopes. Then, we run our simulator with the power budget envelopes. On average, *PGCapping* outperforms *Random* and *Round-robin* by 11.0% and 7.1%. *PGCapping* achieves 90.7% of *Balanced* in MTTF. In Figure 5c, we assume the processor is powered by a solar panel with real-world server utilization trace. We exhaustively test the 30-day trace with 4 different seasons and 4 different locations and present the result in Figure 5c (e.g., totally 4x4 30-day tests). *PGCapping* outperforms *Random* and *Round-robin* by 9.2% and 7.2%. It achieves 90.4% of *Balanced* in terms of MTTF in this test case. Interestingly, we observe that certain location (e.g., TN) has longer MTTF and greater differences among different policies. From the analysis of the solar radiation traces [32], the available solar power is relatively low (longer MTTF) and irregular (greater difference among different policies) in Tennessee (TN), possibly due to the valley location and related weather.

When *PGCapping* uses PCPG to enforce the power budget, it always turns on the longer-lifetime cores and turns off the shorter-lifetime cores. Therefore, none of the on-chip cores becomes significantly worn out. That is the reason why *PGCapping* can outperform *Random* and *Round-robin*. Due to real-world power budget and utilization variations, there are always certain chances to turn on/off some cores. Therefore, although *PGCapping* does not strictly balance lifetime among cores at each DVFS and PCPG interval, it still achieves a CMP lifetime that is 90.4% of that of *Balanced*.

6. CONCLUSION

Both DVFS and power gating are anticipated to be important power adaptation knobs. However, current studies on integrating power gating and DVFS focus on deciding the power gating and DVFS levels in a tightly coupled fashion, with much less attention given to the direction of decoupled designs. In this paper, we have explored *PGCapping*, a decoupled design to integrate per-core power gating with DVFS/overclocking for CMP power capping. However, both per-core DVFS and overclocking may make some cores age much faster than others and thus become the reliability bottleneck in the whole system. Therefore, *PGCapping* also balances the lifetimes of the CMP cores using power gating. Our empirical results show that *PGCapping* achieves up to 42.0% better average application performance than five state-of-the-art baselines. Furthermore, our extensive simulation results with real-world traces demonstrate that *PGCapping* can increase the CMP lifetime by 9.2% on average.

7. ACKNOWLEDGMENT

This work was supported, in part, by NSF under grants CCF-1143605, CNS-0915959, and CNS-1143607 (NSF CAREER Award), and by ONR under grant N00014-09-1-0750.

8. REFERENCES

[1] AMD. AMD dragon platform technology performance tuning guide, 2009.
[2] AMD. AMD family 10h server and workstation processor power and thermal data sheet, 2010.
[3] W. L. Bircher et al. Predictive power management for multi-core processors. In *WEED*, 2010.
[4] R. Bitirgen et al. Coordinated management of multiple interacting resources in chip multiprocessors: A machine learning approach. In *MICRO*, 2008.
[5] J. Blome et al. Self-calibrating online wearout detection. In *MICRO*, 2007.
[6] D. P. Bovet and M. Cesati. *Understanding the Linux Kernel, Third Edition*. O'Reilly, 1997.
[7] BP. BP3180N datasheet. http://www.solardepot.com/pdf/BP3180N.pdf, 2009.
[8] M. Chen et al. Coordinating processor and main memory for efficient server power control. In *ICS*, 2011.
[9] A. K. Coskun et al. Evaluating the impact of job scheduling and power management on processor lifetime for chip multiprocessors. In *MMCS*, SIGMETRICS, 2009.
[10] G. F. Franklin et al. *Digital Control of Dynamic Systems, 3rd edition*. Addition-Wesley, 1997.
[11] X. Fu, X. Wang, and C. Lefurgy. How much power oversubscription is safe and allowed in data centers? In *ICAC*, 2011.
[12] B. Greskamp and J. Torrellas. Paceline: Improving single-thread performance in nanoscale cmps through core overclocking. In *PACT*, 2007.
[13] M. Horowitz. Scaling, power, and the future of CMOS. In *VLSID*, 2007.
[14] L. Huang et al. Lifetime reliability-aware task allocation and scheduling for MPSoC platforms. In *DATE*, 2009.
[15] Intel. Intel Core i7 processor extreme edition and Intel Core i7 processor datasheet. Technical report, Intel Corporation, November 2008.
[16] C. Isci et al. An analysis of efficient multi-core global power management policies: Maximizing performance for a given power budget. In *MICRO*, 2006.
[17] C. Isci and M. Martonosi. Runtime power monitoring in high-end processors: Methodology and empirical data. In *MICRO*, 2003.
[18] A. Kansal et al. Virtual machine power metering and provisioning. In *SoCC*, 2010.
[19] U. R. Karpuzcu et al. The bubblewrap many-core: popping cores for sequential acceleration. In *MICRO*, 2009.
[20] W. Kim et al. System level analysis of fast, per-core DVFS using on-chip switching regulators. In *HPCA*, 2008.
[21] J. Lee and N. S. Kim. Optimizing throughput of power- and thermal-constrained multicore processors using dvfs and per-core power-gating. In *DAC*, 2009.
[22] C. Lefurgy et al. Server-level power control. In *ICAC*, 2007.
[23] J. Leverich et al. Power management of datacenter workloads using per-core power gating. *IEEE Comput. Archit. Lett.*, 8, 2009.
[24] C. Li et al. Solarcore: Solar energy driven multi-core architecture power management. In *HPCA*, 2011.
[25] J. Li et al. Dynamic power-performance adaptation of parallel computation on chip multiprocessors. In *HPCA*, 2006.
[26] T. Li et al. Spin detection hardware for improved management of multithreaded systems. *IEEE Trans. Parallel Distrib. Syst.*, 17(6), 2006.
[27] A. Lungu et al. Dynamic power gating with quality guarantees. In *ISLPED*, 2009.
[28] K. Ma, X. Li, M. Chen, and X. Wang. Scalable power control for many-core architectures running multi-threaded applications. In *ISCA*, 2011.
[29] N. Madan et al. A case for guarded power gating in multi-core processors. In *HPCA*, 2011.
[30] K. Meng et al. Multi-optimization power management for chip multiprocessors. In *PACT*, 2008.
[31] Z. Mwaikambo and A. Raj. Linux kernel hotplug CPU support. *Linux Symposium*, 2, 2004.
[32] NREL. Measurement and instrumentation data center. http://www.nrel.gov/midc, 2011.
[33] R. Raghavendra et al. No power struggles: Coordinated multi-level power management for the data center. In *ASPLOS*, 2008.
[34] K. Rangan et al. Thread motion: Fine-grained power management for multi-core systems. In *ISCA*, 2009.
[35] J. Srinivasan et al. Lifetime reliability: toward an architectural solution. *Micro, IEEE*, 2005.
[36] N. Sturcken et al. A 2.5d integrated voltage regulator using coupled-magnetic-core inductors on silicon interposer delivering 10.8a/mm2. In *ISSCC*, 2012.
[37] R. Teodorescu and J. Torrellas. Variation-aware application scheduling and power management for chip multiprocessors. In *ISCA*, 2008.
[38] X. Wang and M. Chen. Cluster-level feedback power control for performance optimization. In *HPCA*, 2008.
[39] X. Wang et al. SHIP: Scalable hierarchical power control for large-scale data centers. In *PACT*, 2009.
[40] Y. Wang, K. Ma, and X. Wang. Temperature-constrained power control for chip multiprocessors with online model estimation. In *ISCA*, 2009.
[41] J. A. Winter et al. Scalable thread scheduling and global power management for heterogeneous many-core architectures. In *PACT*, 2010.
[42] C. Zhuo et al. Process variation and temperature-aware reliability management. In *DATE*, 2010.

Power-Efficient Time-Sensitive Mapping in Heterogeneous Systems*

Cong Liu
University of North Carolina at Chapel Hill
Dept. of Computer Science
cong@cs.unc.edu

Jian Li
IBM Austin Research Laboratory
jianli@us.ibm.com

Wei Huang
IBM Austin Research Laboratory
huangwe@us.ibm.com

Juan Rubio
IBM Austin Research Laboratory
rubioj@us.ibm.com

Evan Speight
IBM Austin Research Laboratory
speight@us.ibm.com

Felix Xiaozhu Lin
Rice University
Dept. of Computer Science
xzl@rice.edu

ABSTRACT

Heterogeneous systems that contain multiple types of resources, such as CPUs and GPUs, are becoming increasingly popular thanks to the potential of achieving high performance and energy efficiency. In such systems, the problem of data mapping and communication for time-sensitive applications while reducing power and energy consumption is more challenging, since applications may have varied data management and computing patterns on different types of resources. In this paper, we propose power-aware mapping techniques for CPU/GPU heterogeneous system that are able to meet applications' timing requirements while reducing power and energy consumption by applying DVFS on both CPUs and GPUs. We have implemented the proposed techniques in a real CPU/GPU heterogeneous system. Experimental results with several data analytics workloads show that compared to performance-driven mapping, our power-efficient mapping techniques can often achieve a reduction of more than 20% in power and energy consumption.

Categories and Subject Descriptors

C.1.4 [**Processor Architectures**]: Parallel Architectures; C.4 [**Performance of Systems**]: *design studies, modeling techniques*; F.2.2 [**Analysis of Algorithms and Problem Complexity**]: Nonnumerical Algorithms and Problems—*scheduling*

*This work was performed while Cong Liu and Felix Xiaozhu Lin were interns at IBM Austin Research Laboratory.

General Terms

Algorithms, Management, Measurement, Performance, Design, Theory, Experimentation

Keywords

Multi-Core Architectures, Heterogeneous CPU/GPU Multiprocessors, Power-Efficient Scheduling

1. INTRODUCTION

Given the need to achieve higher performance without driving up power consumption, energy usage and heat dissipation, most chip manufacturers have shifted to multicore architectures. An important subcategory of such architectures are those that are heterogeneous in design. By integrating specific-purpose processing elements with general-purpose computing elements, such architectures can provide high performance and power efficiency [17, 21]. Heterogeneous architectures have been widely adopted in various computing domains, ranging from embedded systems to high performance computing systems.

One of the most prominent early examples of a heterogeneous multicore architecture is the IBM/Sony Cell® architecture, which consists of a Power processor and eight synergistic processors on the same chip. More recently, Graphic Processing Units (GPUs) have seen wide-spread use in heterogeneous systems. GPUs are able to execute data-parallel applications efficiently, due to their highly multithreaded architecture and high-bandwidth memory. Major chip vendors have already released products that integrate CPUs and GPUs on the same chip, such as AMD's Fusion® APU chip.

By providing heterogeneous processing elements with different performance and energy characteristics in the same system, heterogeneous architectures are expected to provide more flexibility for better energy efficiency[21, 17]. Indeed, prior work [17] has shown that heterogeneous systems are able to reduce power and energy consumption compared to homogeneous systems. However, without power-aware application and data mapping methods that explicitly consider heterogeneity, such advantages cannot be fully exploited. Such methods are of interest for other reasons as well. For example, excessive power consumption may cause system unreliability (due to power constraints and local hot spots).

In work on homogeneous systems, much work has been directed at techniques that reduce power and energy consumption by applying dynamic voltage/frequency scaling (DVFS) techniques to lower CPUs' voltages/frequencies. With the growing prevalence of such heterogeneous architectures, there is a need to evolve such techniques so they can be applied in systems with different computing resources. One important category of applications that could benefit from such techniques is those that are time-sensitive; examples include data analytics, stock trading, avionics, real-time scoring of bank transactions, live video processing, etc. Such applications range from desktop-level systems to systems that require significant computational capacity. As an example of the latter, systems processing time-sensitive business transactions have been implemented by Azul Systems on top of the highly-parallel Vega3 platform, which consists of CPUs and GPUs with up to 864 cores [22]. In this paper, such time-sensitive applications are our focus.

The driving problem that motivates our research is that of determining how to run analytics workloads[1]efficiently in terms of timing guarantees and power/energy efficiency on heterogeneous architectures. This can be very beneficial to systems design in the era of "Big Data" analytics [14]. "Big Data" analytics thrives to monetize insights in both structured and unstructured data generated from all sorts of sources [2], and make businesses more agile. Ongoing research [24] has shown that running such analytics workloads on GPUs often provides much better performance with respect to response times and power/energy efficiency. Analytics workloads often have strict response time requirements in order to make business decisions in realtime. As an example, IBM recently released a new multicore-based stream computing platform called IBM InfoSphere Streams System®, which enables massive amounts of data from "living entities" to be analyzed in real time, delivering fast, accurate insights to enable smarter business decision-making. Yet another example is IBM InfoSphere BigInsights®that brings the power of Hadoop to the enterprise for peta-scale Big Data analytics.

Motivated by the above observations, in this paper, we address the problem of devising power-efficient mappings of time-sensitive applications onto CPU/GPU heterogeneous systems. This problem can be divided into two subproblems. First, since applications may have different performance characteristics when executed on CPUs than GPUs, efficient mapping techniques are needed to provide performance guarantees[3]while considering heterogeneity. It has been shown that the general problem of mapping applications with deadlines onto heterogeneous systems consisting of at least two types of resources (e.g., CPUs and GPUs) is NP-hard in the strong sense [5]. Thus, it is important to design efficient mapping heuristics that can provide a measurable guarantee (such as a speed-up factor, as shown in Sec. 4) to meet applications' deadlines. Secondly, in order to reduce power and energy consumption, power-efficient techniques such as DVFS are needed that can be applied on both CPUs and GPUs. Our proposed strategy is to first map applications onto CPUs and GPUs, and to then apply DVFS on each CPU and GPU.

More specifically, our mapping techniques consider the characteristics of both resources and applications to make mapping decisions. An application is always mapped to a resource that can execute it with the fastest speed while meeting its deadline. We propose mapping techniques that can be applied both initially and when applications dynamically arrive at run-time. Additionally, by leveraging the fact that at run-time some applications typically exhibit actual execution times that are lower than their worst-case execution time, we propose and apply techniques to dynamically and aggressively reduce voltages/frequencies on CPUs and GPUs. Note that our strategy should generally apply to other heterogeneous systems containing two different types of computing resources, such as systems with CPUs and FPGAs, CPU with on-chip accelerators, etc. Our overall strategy is based on several components:

1. An offline scheme for mapping the initial set of applications and computing the appropriate voltage/frequency to minimize power and energy consumption while meeting all deadlines (Sec. 4).

2. An online scheme for dynamically mapping applications arriving at run-time and re-evaluating the voltage/frequency settings (Sec. 5).

3. A speculative voltage/frequency scaling scheme that aggressively reduces voltage/frequency by exploiting average-case execution time information (Sec. 6).

We evaluated the above strategy by implementing it on a real CPU/GPU heterogeneous system and running several analytics workloads, such as Non-Negative Matrix Factorization (NMF)[4][18] implemented using OpenCL [8]. Experimental results using real power measurements demonstrate that our proposed algorithms can achieve much better power and energy efficiency than performance-driven mapping algorithms that always map applications to resources with the fastest response time. Our experiments show that power and energy consumption can be further reduced by exploiting earlier-than-worst-case completions and by aggressively reducing voltages/frequencies by exploiting average-case execution time information.

The rest of this paper is organized as follows. Section 2 describes related work. Section 3 presents our system model. Sections 4-6 describe the proposed power-efficient mapping techniques in detail. Section 7 discusses our implementation methodology and experimental results. Section 8 concludes.

2. RELATED WORK

Kumar et al. [17] were among the first work to demonstrate that heterogeneous architectures have advantages over

[1]The term "application" used in this paper refers to such analytics workloads. In the evaluation section (Sec. 7), we implement several such analytics workloads to evaluate the performance.

[2]Everyday, 2.5 quintillion bytes of data are created [14], coming from many sources: from sensors used to gather climate information, posts to social media sites, digital pictures and videos posted online, transaction records of online purchases, and cell phone GPS signals to name a few.

[3]In this paper, the required performance guarantee is meeting applications' deadlines.

[4]NMF has been used in many data analyzing problems such as text mining, spectral data analysis, and scalable Internet distance prediction [18].

homogeneous ones in terms of throughput and power efficiency. In work on throughput-oriented systems, Luk et al. [21] proposed an adaptive mapping technique to map applications onto a heterogeneous system consisting of CPUs and GPUs. This mapping algorithm has been implemented in an experimental system called Qilin for programming CPUs and GPUs. Evaluation results show that compared to manual mapping (e.g., manually done by the programmer), their adaptive mapping performs close in both execution time and energy consumption, but can better adapt to changes in input sizes, and hardware and software configurations. In [4], Augonnet et al. proposed an efficient mapping technique that overlaps communication with computation to support application graphs in heterogeneous systems consisting of CPUs and GPUs. Moreover, several [13, 15] propose scheduling techniques in heterogeneous systems in order to improve performance and/or energy efficiency, at either user-level and operating system kernel-level. Also much work (see [20] for a survey) has been done on DVFS-based power-aware scheduling techniques for homogeneous systems.

In real-time and embedded systems, much work has been done on power- and energy-efficient scheduling on DVFS-enabled platforms, including uniprocessor and multiprocessor systems. An overview of such work can be found in [6]. However, none of this prior work targets heterogeneous systems consisting of CPUs and GPUs. In contrast to our work, where power/energy measurements were obtained in a real heterogeneous system by running real workloads, in most prior work, a simulation-based evaluation approach was used.

3. SYSTEM MODEL

We consider the problem of mapping n independent applications $J = \{J_1, J_2, J_3, ..., J_n\}$ arriving at time 0, and a number of dynamically arriving applications, onto m processors $\{P_1, P_2, ..., P_m\}$. Each processor is either a CPU or a GPU. Each application J_i has an arrival time r_i, a deadline d_i, and a worst-case execution time of e_i^c (resp., e_i^g) if executed on a CPU (resp., GPU) under the maximum voltage/frequency. The execution time and deadline can range from milliseconds to hours, depending on the specific application. We can obtain the worst-case execution time of an application by either using a worst-case execution time analysis tool [12] or by sampling runs.[5] Any application J_i must complete its execution by time d_i. We require that for any application J_i, $e_i^c + r_i \leq d_i$ and $e_i^g + r_i \leq d_i$ hold; otherwise, deadlines cannot be met. Our techniques can also be extended to be applied to more generalized real-time execution models. A summary of important notations is given in Table 1.

Table 1: Notation Summary.

n	number of applications arriving at time 0
m	number of processors
J_i	i^{th} application
P_i	i^{th} processor (either a CPU or a GPU)
r_i	arrival time of J_i
d_i	deadline of J_i
e_i^c	worst-case execution time of J_i executed on a CPU under its maximum voltage
e_i^g	worst-case execution time of J_i executed on a GPU under its maximum voltage
v_k	k^{th} voltage level on a processor
v_{maxi}	maximum voltage level on P_i

Power model. Prior work has shown that the power/energy consumption of a processor is a monotonically increasing superlinear function of the supply voltage [23]. The dominant components of power consumption in widely adopted CMOS technology are active and idle power dissipation. Similar to previous work [7, 11, 16], we can approximate the power consumption p_{total} of an on-chip system by the following:

$$p_{total} = p_{idle} + \sum_{i=1}^{m} \lambda_i \cdot f_i^3.$$

In this expression, p_{idle} denotes the idle power dissipation, which is assumed to include the base power consumption of the CPU and the power consumption of all other components. Additionally, each processor P_i also consumes power $\lambda_i \cdot f_i^3$ that depends on the processor's operating frequency f_i. (Note that frequency is proportional to voltage [23] with a small offset.) Thus, the active energy consumed by processor P_i during a time interval with length t is given by $\lambda_i \cdot f_i^3 \cdot t$, where λ_i is a coefficient term that includes power loss due to power supply inefficiency. Furthermore, the execution time of an application is inversely proportional to voltage and frequency [11, 23]. As seen from this model, DVFS is able to reduce power/energy consumption by reducing the voltage/frequency.

We assume that both CPUs and GPUs have a fixed number of voltage steps, which is often the case in practice. Moreover, most modern processors specify voltage/frequency pairs (referred to as a *P-state*) instead of separate voltage and frequency values. Thus, for conciseness, we use voltage in this paper to represent the voltage/frequency pair. Let $\{v_1, v_2, ..., 1.0\}$ $(v_j \leq v_{j+1} \leq 1.0)$ denote the normalized voltage levels of processor P_i (the maximum normalized voltage level on any processor is 1.0). Each workload J_i has a worst-case execution time e_i^c on a CPU under the maximum voltage level, or e_i^g on a GPU under the maximum voltage level. Since the execution time of an application is inversely proportional to voltage, the execution time of J_i executed on any CPU (respectively, GPU) P_i under a specific voltage level v_k is thus given by $\frac{e_i^c}{v_k}$ (respectively, $\frac{e_i^g}{v_k}$).

Preemptive vs. non-preemptive execution. Preemptive execution is allowed on CPUs. However, on GPUs, executions are often non-preemptive [10]. That is, once an application starts execution on a GPU, it cannot be preempted by other applications until its completion. We thus assume that executions are preemptive on CPUs but non-preemptive on GPUs.

[5] Sampling techniques have been commonly used to obtain worst-case execution times in prior related work (see [12] for a survey).

Earliest-deadline-first. As shown in Sec. 4, we use earliest-deadline-first (EDF) to order applications on each processor. Under EDF, applications are prioritized by their deadlines, and any ties are broken by application ID.

4. STATIC MAPPING

In this section, we present the offline mapping algorithm for the initial set of applications arriving at time 0, assuming that each application's worst-case execution time is known. In later sections, we show how to adapt to the dynamic case where workloads arrive at run-time.

The algorithm contains an assignment phase, a load-balancing phase, and a voltage scaling phase. The assignment phase assigns applications to processors (i.e., CPUs and GPUs), the load-balancing phase balances loads among processors, and the voltage scaling phase adjusts the voltage/frequency on each processor. The goal is to reduce power and energy consumption (i.e., adjust each processor's voltage/frequency to the lowest possible level) while meeting all deadlines. A *feasible* mapping is one that meets all deadlines.

Assignment. The problem of assigning applications to heterogeneous systems containing at least two types of processors while meeting all deadlines has been shown to be NP-hard in the strong sense [5]. An assignment algorithm for such systems named FF-3C , recently proposed by Andersson et. al [3], provides provable quantitive performance guarantee on meeting deadlines. FF-3C was designed for assigning real-time *periodic* [6]applications onto two different types of processors. As shown in [3], FF-3C has a speed-competitive ratio of 2, which implies that if any feasible mapping algorithm exists for a set of applications over A, then FF-3C can provide a feasible mapping for the same set of applications over a computing platform A' each of whose processors has at least twice the speed of the corresponding processor in A. A low speed-competitive ratio of 2 indicates high performance of the FF-3C algorithm.

Our proposed assignment phase is designed based upon FF-3C. Compared to the original FF-3C algorithm, the only modification is to order applications in a certain way before making the assignment decisions (as shown later). The intuition behind the ordering process is to increase the likelihood that applications that run faster on a specific type of processor are mapped onto processors of that type. The pseudo-code of the assignment algorithm is shown in Fig. 1. Before describing the algorithm, we give several necessary definitions.

Definition 1. *The load of an application J_i executed on CPU (resp., GPU) under the maximum voltage is given by $load_i^c = \frac{e_i^c}{d_i - r_i}$ (resp., $load_i^g = \frac{e_i^g}{d_i - r_i}$). An application J_i is termed to be heavy on a CPU (resp., a GPU) if $load_i^c > 1/2$ (resp., $load_i^g > 1/2$).*

Definition 2. *The heterogeneity ratio of an application J_i is defined to be $H_i = max(\frac{e_i^c}{e_i^g}, \frac{e_i^g}{e_i^c})$. For any application*

[6]A periodic application generates a potentially infinite sequence of jobs with deadlines. Jobs arrive exactly p time units apart where p is often called period. Note that the periodic task model generalizes the application model used in this paper. This is because each application under our model can be deemed as a periodic task that only releases one job.

ASSIGNMENT

1 Sort applications in J^h and J^{nh} by largest-heterogeneity-ratio-first
2 **for** each application J_k in J^h **do**
3   Assign J_k to its favorite processors by first-fit
4 **for** each application J_k in J^{nh} **do**
5   Assign J_k to its favorite processors by first-fit
6 **for** each remaining application J_k in J^{nh} **do**
7   Assign J_k to its non-favorite processors by first-fit
8 **for** each processor P_i **do**
9   Sort applications assigned to P_i by EDF

Figure 1: The psuedo-code of Algorithm *Assignment.*

J_i, $\frac{e_i^c}{e_i^g} > 1$ implies that J_i is more suitable to be executed on a GPU than on a CPU. The favorite processor type of an application J_i is a GPU if $\frac{e_i^c}{e_i^g} > 1$ and a CPU otherwise.

Definition 3. *Let $J_1, J_2, ..., J_{q_i}$ denote applications that are assigned to processor P_i, ordered by EDF (i.e., $d_k \leq d_{k+1}$) that are not completed at time t. Then, the processor load on CPU (respectively, GPU) P_i at time t is given by $load(P_i, t) = max_{k=1}^{q_i}\left(\frac{\sum_{o=1}^{k} \overline{e}_o^c}{d_k - t}\right)$ (resp., $load(P_i) = max_{k=1}^{q_i}\left(\frac{\sum_{o=1}^{k} \overline{e}_o^g}{d_k - t}\right)$), where $\overline{e}_o^c$ ($\overline{e}_o^g$) denotes the remaining execution time of J_o at time t on CPU (resp., GPU). At time 0, $load(P_i, 0) = max_{k=1}^{q_i}\left(\frac{\sum_{o=1}^{k} e_o^c}{d_k}\right)$ (resp., $load(P_i) = max_{k=1}^{q_i}\left(\frac{\sum_{o=1}^{k} e_o^g}{d_k}\right)$) if P_i is a CPU (resp., GPU).*

Example Consider assigning two applications J_1 and J_2 onto a CPU P_1, where $(e_1^c, d_1 = 1, 4)$ and $(e_2^c, d_2 = 3, 12)$. Thus, we have $load(P_1, 0) = max(1/4, (1+3)/12) = 1/3$.

Now we describe the pseudo-code of the assignment algorithm. Note that the *first-fit* policy used in this algorithm represents the classical first-fit bin-packing policy, which assigns an application to the first processor that can accommodate it. In our problem context, a processor can accommodate an application if and only if the application's deadline can be met (which can be checked by Theorem 1 shown later).

Algorithm description. Algorithm *Assignment* assigns applications to processors. First, applications are divided into two sets: a set J^h in which applications are heavy on their non-favorite processors and a set J^{nh} in which applications are non-heavy on both CPUs and GPUs. Then, within each set, applications are sorted by largest-heterogeneity-ratio-first (Line 1). This is to give applications with a larger heterogeneity ratio a greater chance to be assigned to their favorite processors. Then applications in J^h and J^{nh} in order are assigned to their favorite type of processor by first-fit (Lines 2-5). Any remaining applications in J^{nh} are assigned to their non-favorite type of processor by first fit (Lines 6-7). Finally applications on each processor are ordered by EDF (Lines 8-9). Note that if an application cannot be assigned to a processor (while meeting its deadline) in Lines 3, 5, and 7, then the algorithm fails to produce a feasible assignment.

So far we have not yet discussed the criteria for successfully mapping an application to a processor to meet its deadline. To provide such a criteria, we apply a well-known result on scheduling independent applications with deadlines on a uniprocessor under EDF, as stated in the following theorem.

Theorem 1. *[19] For executing applications arriving at time 0 on CPU (or GPU) P_i in EDF order, all deadlines are guaranteed to be met if load$(P_i, 0) \leq 1$, where load$(P_i, 0)$ is the processor load at time 0 as defined in Def. 3.*

Time complexity. It can be shown that Algorithm *Assignment* has a time complexity of $O(n^2 \cdot m)$, where n is the number of applications and m is the number of processors.[7]

Performance guarantee provided by the assignment algorithm. It has been shown in [3] that FF-3C has a speed competitive ratio of 2. There are only two differences between our assignment algorithm and FF-3C. First, we sort applications within sets J^h and J^{nh} by largest-heterogeneity-first where FF-3C does not assume any specific ordering among tasks. Second, we target independent applications with deadlines where FF-3C targets periodic applications with deadlines. Due to the facts that the order of applications used in our algorithm can be viewed as a specific case of all possible orders supported by FF-3C and the periodic application model generalizes the independent application model, our mapping algorithm also yields a speed competitive ratio of 2. (Note that the load-balancing and the voltage/frequency scaling schemes as presented next do not invalidate this speed competitive ratio result since they are executed after the assignment process.)

Example Consider assigning a set of six applications onto a heterogeneous system with a CPU P_1 and a GPU P_2. The parameters of these applications are: $J_1(6, 2, 10)$, $J_2(2, 1, 5)$, $J_3(4, 3, 15)$, $J_4(6, 1, 8)$, $J_5(3, 4, 12)$, $J_6(1, 3, 4)$, where $J_i(a, b, c)$ denotes that $e_i^c = a$, $e_i^g = b$, and $d_i = c$. The heterogeneity ratios of these applications can be calculated by Def. 2 as follows: $H_1 = 3$, $H_2 = 2$, $H_3 = 4/3$, $H_4 = 6$, $H_5 = 4/3$, and $H_6 = 3$. By the definitions of J_h and J_{nh}, in this example, $J_h = \{J_1, J_4, J_6\}$ and $J_{nh} = \{J_2, J_3, J_5\}$. By Algorithm *Assignment* shown in Fig. 1, applications J_5 and J_6 are assigned to CPU P_1, and the other four applications are assigned to GPU P_2. All deadlines are guaranteed to be met since under this assignment, by Def. 3, load$(P_1) = 1/3 < 1$ and load$(P_2) = 7/15 < 1$. (This example system will be used throughput this paper.)

Load-balancing. After mapping applications onto processors, it may be the case that some processors have much heavier loads than others. This is undesirable from the perspective of reducing the overall system power and energy consumption because the whole system may need to run longer due to the imbalanced load. This may cause other system components such as disks and memory to consume more energy. Thus, we propose to balance loads among processors after the initial mapping to avoid such problems. We set up a threshold denoted thr $(0 \leq thr \leq 1)$ to trigger the load-balancing process. That is, if the difference between the maximum demand (as defined below) and the average demand among processors becomes larger than thr, then load-balancing is performed. The pseudo-code of the algorithm is shown in Fig. 2.

LOAD-BALANCING

1 **while** $demand_{max} > (1 + thr) \cdot demand_{avg}$ **do**
2   Order applications on P_{max}
      by shortest-exeuction-time-first
3   **for** each application J_k on P_{max} in order **do**
4   **if** $e_k < dem_{max} - demand_{min}$ and
        J_k can be assigned to P_{min} **then**
5   Remove J_k from P_{max} and assign it to P_{min}
6   Update $demand_{avg}$, $demand_{max}$, P_{max}
7   **if** $demand_{avg}$, $demand_{max}$, and P_{max}
      remain unchanged **then**
8   Terminate

Figure 2: The psuedo-code of Algorithm *Load-Balancing.*

Definition 4. *The demand of CPU (resp., GPU) P_i is defined to be demand$(P_i) = \sum_{k=1}^{q_i} e_k^c$ (resp., $\sum_{k=1}^{q_i} e_i^g$). Let $demand_{max}$, $demand_{min}$, and $demand_{avg}$ denote the maximum, the minimum, and the average demand among processors respectively. Let P_{max} (resp. P_{min}) denote the processor that has the maximum (resp. minimum) demand.*

Algorithm description. If the condition shown on Line 1 of the pseudo-code of the algorithm in Fig. 2 holds, then the loads on some processors exceed the average load by more than *thr*. Lines 2-4 balance loads between P_{max} and P_{min}. Specifically, Lines 2-4 try to re-assign some application that is originally assigned to P_{max} to P_{min} while still meeting all deadlines (Line 4). Lines 5-7 provide a termination condition if $demand_{max}$, $demand_{avg}$, and P_{max} remain unchanged, which implies that the algorithm cannot further balance the load. Note that a small value of *thr* can lead to more balanced loads but at the expense of higher complexity.[8]

Example Consider the example assignment shown in Example 2. For this example, demand$(P_1) = 4$, $demand_{max}$ = demand$(P_2) = 7$, $demand_{avg} = 5.5$. Let $thr = 20\%$ for this example. By Algorithm *Load-Balancing*, since J_2 has the smallest execution cost and can be assigned to P_1, J_2 is removed from P_2 and assigned to P_1. This leads to more balanced loads between P_1 and P_2, where demand(P_1) = demand$(P_2) = demand_{max} = demand_{avg} = 6$.

Voltage/frequency scaling. After the assignment and the load-balancing phase, we adjust the voltage level on each processor in order to reduce power and energy consumption. The following theorem computes the voltage level that should be set at time 0 in order to achieve the best energy-efficiency.

Theorem 2. *At time 0, the optimal voltage level on processor P_i (either a CPU or a GPU) to minimize power and energy consumption while meeting all the deadlines is constant and equal to $max(v_1, v(load(P_i, 0)))$, where load$(P_i, 0)$*

[7]Note that in order to apply the mapping algorithm in a large-scale systems with many nodes and achieve minimal mapping overheads, the algorithm can be loop unrolled and parallelized, and hence introduces negligible overhead.

[8]Since both the assignment and the load-balancing can be executed offline, in practice it might be desirable to have a small value of *thr* in order to obtain a more balanced mapping.

is the processor load of P_i and $v(load(P_i,0))$ denotes the lowest voltage level of P_i that is no less than $load(P_i,0)$.

PROOF. Since the power-voltage relationship is a monotonic function (as discussed in Sec. 3), we can reduce the power and energy consumption by maintaining a fixed voltage level while fully utilizing the processor to the maximum extent. Thus, power and energy consumption can be reduced to the maximum extent under the lowest voltage level under which deadlines can be guaranteed. Thus, to prove the theorem, it is sufficient to prove that $max(v_1, v(load(P_i,0)))$ is the lowest voltage level under which all deadlines can be guaranteed. Depending on the relationship between v_1 and $v(load(P_i,0))$, we have two cases.

Case 1: $v(load(P_i,0)) \leq v_1$**.** In this case, $max(v_1, v(load(P_i,0))) = v_1$, which is the lowest possible voltage level on P_i. For conciseness, assume that P_i is a CPU (the argument holds for the case where P_i is a GPU as well). As discussed in Sec. 3, under v_1, for any application J_o, its execution time is given by $\frac{e_o^c}{v_1}$. By Def. 3 and the definition of $v(load(P_i,0))$, we have

$$v_1 \geq v(load(P_i,0)) \geq load(P_i,0). \quad (1)$$

Thus, for P_i operated under voltage level v_1, its processor load can be re-calculated by $max_{k=1}^{q_i}\left(\frac{\sum_{o=1}^{k} e_o^c/v_1}{d_k}\right) = load(P_i,0)/v_1 \overset{\{by\ (1)\}}{\leq} 1$. Therefore, by Theorem 1, v_1 is the lowest voltage level under which all deadlines are met.

Case 2: $v(load(P_i,0)) > v_1$**.** In this case, $max(v_1, v(load(P_i,0))) = v(load(P_i,0))$, which from the statement of the theorem is the lowest voltage level of P_i that is no less than $load(P_i,0)$. That is,

$$v(load(P_i,0)) \geq load(P_i,0) \quad (2)$$

holds. Under $v(load(P_i,0))$, for any application J_o, its execution time is given by $\frac{e_o^c}{v(load(P_i,0))}$. Thus, for P_i operated under voltage level $v(load(P_i,0))$, its processor load can be re-calculated by $max_{k=1}^{q_i}\left(\frac{\sum_{o=1}^{k} e_o^c/v(load(P_i,0))}{d_k}\right) = load(P_i,0)/v(load(P_i,0)) \overset{\{by\ (2)\}}{\leq} 1$. Thus, under voltage level $v(load(P_i,0))$, all deadlines are met. Now we prove that $v(load(P_i,0))$ is the lowest voltage level that guarantees to meet all deadlines. For P_i operated under any voltage level $v' < load(P_i,0)$, the execution time of any application J_o is given by $\frac{e_o^c}{v'}$. Therefore, the processor load on P_i under v' becomes $v(load(P_i,0)) = max_{k=1}^{q_i}\left(\frac{\sum_{o=1}^{k} e_o^c/v'}{d_k}\right) = load(P_i,0)/v' > 1$, which by Theorem 1 implies that deadlines may be missed under v'. □

Example Again, reconsider the system given in Example 4. Assume that both CPUs and GPUs have three voltage/frequency steps: $v_1 = 0.5$, $v_2 = 0.8$, and $v_{max} = 1$. By Theorem 2, since $load(P_1,0) = 3/5$ and $load(P_2,0) = 6/15$, we have $v(load(P_1,0)) = v_2 = 0.8$ and $v(load(P_2,0)) = v_1 = 0.5$. Thus, P_1 can be operated under a voltage of v_2 and P_2 can be operated under a voltage of v_1. All applications can still meet their deadlines after reducing voltages.

DYNAMIC-MAPPING

1 Assign J_k to its favorite processors by first-fit
2 **if** J_k cannot be assigned **then**
3   **for** each processor P_i of J_k's favorite type **do**
4   Order applications on P_i by lowest-heterogeneity-ratio-first
5   **for** each application J_h on P_i in order **do**
6   **for** each processor P_a other than P_i **do**
7   **if** J_h can be assigned to P_a and J_k can be assigned to P_i after removing J_h from P_i **then**
8   Assign J_h to P_a and assign J_k to P_i
9   Order applications on P_a and P_i by EDF
10   **if** J_k still cannot be assigned to any processor **then**
11   **for** each processor P_i of J_k's non-favorite type **do**
12   Assign J_k to P_i
13   Order applications on P_i by EDF
14 **for** each processor P_i whose application queue is changed **do**
15   Re-adjust P_i's voltage to be $max(v_1, v(load(P_i,t)))$
16 **if** an early completion is detected on processor P_i at time t **then**
17   Re-adjust P_i's voltage to be $max(v_1, v(load(P_i,t)))$

Figure 3: The pseudo-code of Algorithm *Dynamic-Mapping*.

5. DYNAMIC MAPPING WITH BUDGET RECLAMATION

In practice, it is often the case that applications arrive at run-time. Thus, in this section, we propose an algorithm based upon the static mapping algorithm to handle the dynamic arrival case. In practice, applications may often complete earlier than under the worst case. Thus, if an application completes earlier, then our algorithm takes advantage of processing capacity made available and adjusts the voltage on that application's processor on-the-fly to enable more power and energy savings. Finally, if an incoming application with a large heterogeneity ratio cannot be assigned to its favorite processor, then our algorithm swaps this application with some application with a small heterogeneity ratio that has been assigned to one of the incoming application's favorite processors.

Under the dynamic mapping algorithm, the voltage level will be re-adjusted in two circumstances: (*i*) when a new application arrives, and (*ii*) an early completion is detected. The pseudo-code of the algorithm is shown in Fig. 3. Assume that an application J_k arrives at time t.

Algorithm description. Algorithm *Dynamic-Mapping* assigns an application arriving at run-time to a processor and re-adjusts the processor's voltage accordingly. When an application J_k arrives at run-time, J_k is assigned to some processor of its favorite type (Line 1). If none of J_k's favorite processors can accommodate it, then the algorithm checks whether there exists an application J_h queued[9]on one of J_k's favorite processors P_i such that J_k can be assigned to P_i after removing J_h from P_i, and J_h can be assigned to some other processor P_a (Lines 2-7). If J_k still cannot be assigned to one of its favorite type of processors, then J_k is assigned to one of its non-favorite type of processors (Lines 8-10). Finally, if any processor's queue has been changed or an early completion is detected, then the voltage/frequency of this

[9]Note that J_h must be queued and is not executing

processor is re-adjusted (Lines 11-14). Note that the algorithm fails if the application cannot be assigned in Lines 1, 8, and 12. Also note that since compilation at run-time, which is needed in order to dynamically map application, may cost significant power and energy consumption, one optimization step is to pre-compile all types of applications that arrive at run-time.

As discussed in Sec. 3, executions on GPUs are non-preemptive. Thus, we are not able to apply Theorem 1 as a criteria for successful assignment since it assumes preemptive EDF and targets applications that arrive at time 0. The following theorem provides such a criteria for the dynamic arrival case. Consider the case where an application J_k comes at time t at run-time and is mapped to processor P_i by Algorithm *Dynamic-Mapping*. Let J_x denote the application that is executing or just completes at t. Let e_x' denote the remaining execution time of J_x after t.

Theorem 3. *An application J_k arriving at time t at run-time can be successfully assigned to processor P_i if $load(P_i, t) \leq 1$ and $load(P_i, t + e_x') \leq 1$.*

PROOF. If J_x completes at t or J_k has a later deadline than J_x, then by Theorem 1, $load(P_i, t) \leq 1$ is a sufficient condition for J_k to be successfully assigned to P_i because in these cases no preemption may occur after t. The other case is that J_x is executing at t but has a deadline later than J_k. Under this case, J_k has an earlier deadline than J_x but cannot preempt J_x. Thus, we need to check the processor load again when J_x completes. When J_x completes at time $t+e_x'$, applications queued on P_i including J_k can be executed in the EDF order and no preemption may occur after $t + e_x'$. That is, $load(P_i, t + e_x') \leq 1$ provides a sufficient condition for J_k to be successfully assigned to P_i. □

Time complexity. The time complexity of Algorithm *Dynamic-Mapping* is dominated by the three loops in Lines 3-7, which have a complexity of $O(m^2 \cdot n^2)$.

Example Consider the same system as presented in Examples 4-4. Now assume that an application J_7 arrives at time 4 at run-time, whose $e_7^c = 4$, $e_7^g = 6$, and $d_7 = 11$. By Def. 2, CPU is the favorite type of processor of J_7. By Theorem 1, it cannot be assigned to P_1. By Algorithm *Dynamic-Mapping*, J_5 is removed from P_1 and assigned to P_2, and J_7 can be assigned to P_1. After the assignment, $load(P_1, 4) = 4/7$ and $load(P_2, 4) = 0.79$. Thus, by Theorem 2, both P_1 and P_2 can be operated with a voltage of v_2.

6. AGGRESSIVE VOLTAGE REDUCTION

Although the static and dynamic mapping algorithms provide sound assignment and voltage scaling schemes, they all assume the worst-case workloads. This assumption is conservative and pessimistic since the run-time execution time is often shorter than the worst-case. In this section, we propose an aggressive voltage reduction scheme by speculating that workloads will most likely present an average-case computational demand that is lower than the worst-case demand.

The mapping scheme is the same as the algorithm presented in previous sections, except that voltages are set assuming average-case execution times instead of the worst-case.[10] Since we assume average-case execution times, we may need to adjust the voltage/frequency when an early or late completion is detected. We apply similar schemes as used in Algorithm *Dynamic-Mapping* for the adjustment. Specifically, when an early or late completion is detected on processor P_i at time t, $load(P_i, t)$ is re-computed and P_i's voltage is adjusted to be $max(v_1, v(load(P_i, t)))$. Note that some applications may miss their deadlines if late completions occur. Thus, the aggressive voltage reduction algorithm may reduce power and energy consumption at the cost of missing deadlines.

Example For the example application system as presented in Example 4, assume that the average execution time for all six applications is 0.5 time unit less than the corresponding worst-case execution time. Then, by the above aggressive voltage reduction algorithm, both P_1 and P_2 can be operated under a voltage of v_3 since by using the average-case execution times, $load(P_1, 0) = 0.3$ and $load(P_2, 0) = 0.4$. This further reduces the voltage compared to the case where the static or the dynamic mapping algorithm is used.

In order to balance the tradeoff between performance and energy efficiency, we introduce a parameter K for each processor to determine the aggressiveness level. On any processor, K can be set to be $\frac{v_{avg}}{v_{worst}} \leq K \leq 1$, where v_{avg} is the voltage level calculated by assuming average-case execution times and v_{worst} is the voltage level calculated by assuming worst-case execution times.[11] For applications whose run-time execution times are often consistent, it is preferable to set $K = \frac{v_{avg}}{v_{worst}}$ in order to achieve maximal power and energy efficiency. On the other hand, for applications whose run-time execution times often vary, it is preferable to set K to be a larger value than $\frac{v_{avg}}{v_{worst}}$ in order to avoid late completions that may cause deadline misses.

7. EVALUATION

In this section, we present the implementation methodology and experimental results used to evaluate the effectiveness of our proposed algorithms.

7.1 Methodology

We implemented the proposed algorithms in a real heterogeneous desktop computer consisting of a CPU and a GPU. The hardware specification is given in Table 2. The benchmarks used in the experiments are listed in Table 3. Each benchmark set consists of the same corresponding application but with multiple input sizes. For the GPU implementations of the benchmarks, we used the ones provided by IBM or in the AMD OpenCL Software Development Kit (SDK) [9] if available.

Regarding the software architecture of the implemented experimental system, we provide an API to programmers for writing GPU-parallelizable operations at the application level. The API is built on top of C/C++ so that it can be easily adopted. Beneath the API layer is the system layer,

[10]The average-case information may not need to be accurate, as we shall discuss later.

[11]Note that since K can be considered as a run-time optimization parameter, we do not require accurate information on a workload's average-case execution time. If the actual run-time execution time is more or less than the assumed average-case execution time, then we can adjust K and the voltage/frequency accordingly.

Table 2: Experimental Hardware Specification.

	CPU	GPU
Architecture	Intel Xeon 5160	AMD Radeon HD 5770
Voltage/Frequency levels	3GHz (1.5v) / 2GHz (1.2v)	850MHz(1.25v) / 500MHz(1v) / 148MHz(0.95v)
TDP	80W	108W
OS	64-bit Linux Ubuntu lucid	

Table 3: Benchmarks.

Benchmarks	Description	Source
Non-negative Matrix Factorization (NMF)	OpenCL implementation of NMF	IBM
MatrixMultiplication (MM)	Dense matrix multiplication	AMD OpenCL SDK
MatrixTranspose (MT)	Dense matrix Transpose	AMD OpenCL SDK
MatrixOperation (MO)	Mixed operations on dense matrix	AMD OpenCL SDK

which consists of a compiler and a scheduler. The compiler intercepts OpenCL function calls at compile, replacing them with functionally equivalent calls into its heterogeneous scheduling runtime. It transforms an input OpenCL program to use all OpenCL devices available. Our proposed scheduling algorithms are implemented in the scheduler that schedules applications to run on the CPU or GPU.

We compared the static mapping scheme, the dynamic mapping scheme with budget reclamation, and the aggressive voltage reduction scheme with each other. Moreover, we compared these three proposed schemes with a performance-driven mapping algorithm, which is called earliest-response-time-first (ERF). ERF maps an application onto the resource that provides the shortest response time. In all experimental results presented below, we denote our static mapping, dynamic mapping with budget reclamation, aggressive voltage reduction schemes, and the ERF scheme as "Static," "Dynamic," "Aggressive," and "ERF" respectively.

Our evaluation metrics are the power and energy consumption. We measured the entire system power (including the CPU, GPU, memory, and disks) using the WT210 digital power meter [25]. Also we measured the wall-clock execution time for each experiment. Then the total energy consumption can be obtained by computing the product of power and execution time.

Generate application parameters. In our experiments, the benchmark sets were generated as follows. For each experiment, we randomly generated a number of benchmarks with different input matrix files. To obtain the execution time of a benchmark, we ran the benchmark repeatedly for thirty minutes and recorded the maximum execution time among these runs as the measured execution time. The worst-case execution time (WCET) of each benchmark was then calculated based upon the corresponding measured execution time (MET): $WCET = 120\% \cdot MET$. Per-benchmark loads were uniformly distributed in [0.001, 0.1]. Benchmark deadlines were then calculated from worst-case execution times and benchmark loads. For each experiment, the cap on the sum of all benchmarks' loads was varied by three values: 1 (light system load), 1.4 (medium system load), and 1.8 (heavy system load). Each benchmark set was generated by creating benchmarks until the sum of all benchmarks' loads exceeded the corresponding system load cap, and by then reducing the last benchmark's load so that the sum of all benchmarks' loads equalled the system load cap.

Applying DVFS on CPUs and GPUs. To enable voltage/frequency scaling on the CPU, we applied the CPUFreq kernel infrastructure [2] that implements CPU voltage/frequency scaling. It enables the operating system to scale the CPU voltage/frequency up or down in order to save power/energy. Most modern operating systems including Linux Ubuntu Lucid support CPUFreq.

Unfortunately, voltage/frequency scaling on GPUs is not easy. The major difficulty is that there is no OpenCL-supported ATI GPU driver that supports voltage/frequency scaling. The official ATI GPU driver supports OpenCL, but does not support voltage/frequency scaling. On the other hand, the open-source ATI GPU driver called RadeonDriver [1] that comes with Ubuntu supports voltage/frequency scaling via the Kernel Mode Setting (KMS). However, RadeonDriver does not support OpenCL. Therefore, we applied a modeling approach to obtain the GPU power values under different voltage levels, as explained below.

By using the RadeonDriver, we are able to obtain the GPU power when running non-OpenCL applications under different voltage/frequency levels. Let $P(1, A)$ (respectively, $P(v_i, A)$) denote the GPU power when running non-OpenCL application A under the maximum voltage level (respectively, the ith voltage level v_i). Moreover, by using the official ATI GPU driver, we are able to obtain GPU power when running OpenCL applications under the maximum voltage/frequency. Let $P(v_{max}, A_{CL})$ denote the GPU power when running OpenCL application A_{CL} under the maximum voltage/frequency. Then, we can calculate the GPU power when running A_{CL} under the ith voltage/frequency level, denoted $P(v_i, A_{CL})$, as follows.

$$P(v_i, A_{CL}) = \frac{P(v_{max}, A_{CL})}{P(v_{max}, A)} \cdot P(v_i, A).$$

7.2 Results

In this section, we present results on power and energy consumption that compare different algorithms.

Power consumption. Figs. 4 (a)-(c) show the power consumption results under light, medium, and heavy system loads. Each box in each figure plots the normalized power consumption under ERF, Static, Dynamic, and Aggressive for running the four benchmarks. As seen, our proposed algorithms can achieve a much better power efficiency compared to ERF in all scenarios. For example, under the light load, our algorithms can reduce the power consumption for around 20%. Another observation is that under the light system load, Static, Dynamic, and Aggressive achieve the same power consumption. This is due to the fact that when the system load is light, Static (as well as Dynamic and Aggressive) can reduce the voltage on CPUs and GPUs to the lowest level. While under medium and heavy system loads, it is seen that Aggressive and Dynamic can reduce more power consumption compared to static. This is because Aggressive and Dynamic can utilize the budget due to the difference between the actual execution time and the worst-case execution time to further reduce the voltage/frequency.

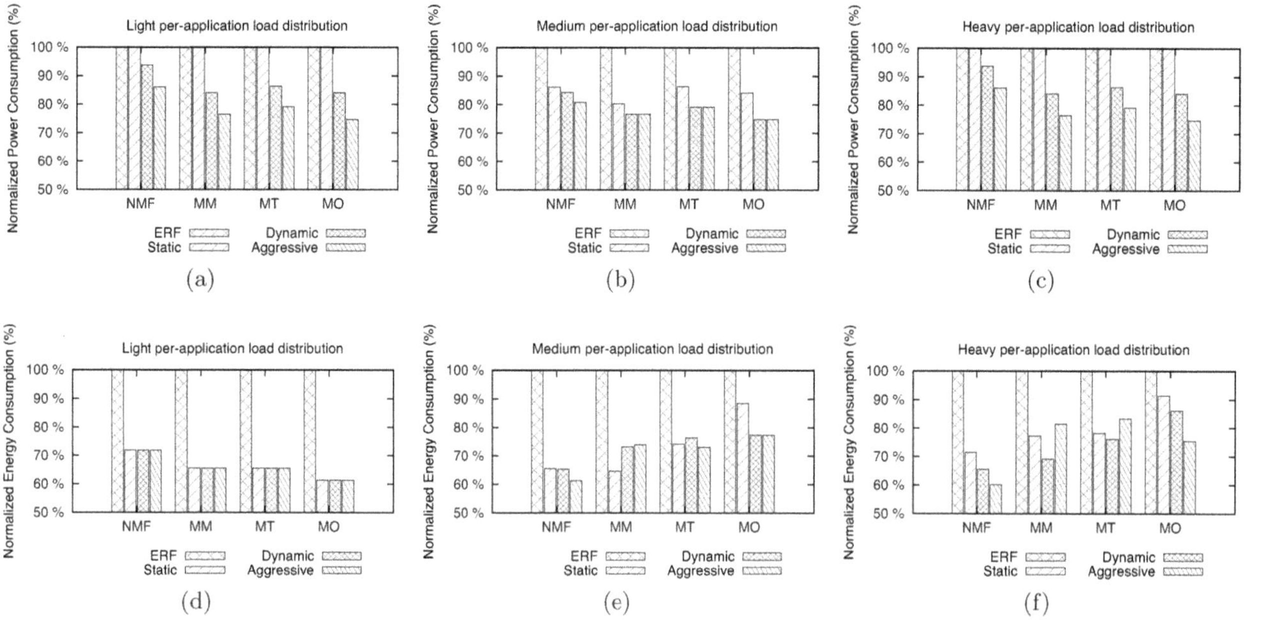

Figure 4: Power and energy consumption results. In the first (resp., second and third) column of graphs, light (resp., medium and heavy) loads are assumed. The first (resp., second) row shows the power (resp., energy) consumption results.

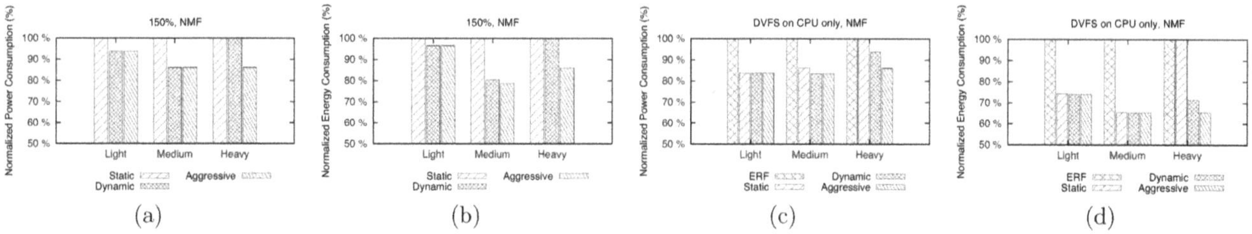

Figure 5: (a)-(b). Results when the worst-case execution times equal 150% of the measured execution times. (a) and (b) show the power and energy consumption results. (c)-(d). Results with CPU DVFS only. (c) and (d) show the power and energy consumption results.

Energy consumption. Figs. 4 (d)-(f) show the energy consumption results under light, medium, and heavy system loads. Each box in each figure plots the normalized energy consumption under ERF, Static, Dynamic, and Aggressive for running the four benchmarks. It can be observed that Static, Dynamic, and Aggressive can achieve a much better energy efficiency compared to ERF in all scenarios. For example, under the light system load, Static, Dynamic, and Aggressive can reduce the energy consumption for more than 27%. In certain scenarios, such improvement can reach up to 40% (e.g., when running NMF under the heavy per-application load distribution using Aggressive). An interesting observation is that under medium and heavy system loads, Aggressive consumes more energy than Static and Dynamic for certain benchmarks such as MatrixMultiply. This is because when the voltage is reduced, the execution time increases, which causes an increase on the energy consumed by the whole system (including memory and disks).

More conservative worst-case execution times. As seen in Fig. 4, in most cases, Aggressive achieves power and energy consumption results that are close to those of Static and Dynamic. In this experiment set, we want to evaluate the effectiveness of Aggressive when the ratio of the worst-case execution time over the measured execution time increases. Intuitively, Aggressive is expected to reduce more power/energy consumption when this ratio increases, since in this case Aggressive is able to reduce the voltage to the lowest possible level by assuming the average-case execution time. Thus, in this experiment set, we set the worst-case execution times to equal 150% of the measured execution times. Fig. 5 (a) and (b) show the power and energy consumption under Static, Dynamic, and Aggressive for running the NMF benchmark.[12] As seen, compared to the case shown in Fig. 4, Aggressive is able to reduce power and energy consumption more. For example, under the heavy system load, Aggressive can reduce 13% more power and energy consumption compared to Static and Dynamic. From these results, we claim that for benchmarks whose worst-case execution times are often longer than the average-case, Aggressive can achieve better energy efficiency.

DVFS on CPUs only. Since we can only apply a modeling approach to obtain the GPU power under different voltage levels, it is important to know whether the proposed

[12]Note that ERF is not included in this experiment set since our focus is to evaluate whether Aggressive can achieve better performance by exploiting average-case execution time information.

algorithm can still save power/energy by applying DVFS on CPUs only. Thus, we conducted an additional set of experiments, in which voltages on CPUs are still scaled according to the proposed algorithm, but GPUs are always set to run under the maximum voltage level (i.e., the DVFS step of the algorithms is not executed on GPUs). Fig. 5 (c) and (d) show the power and energy under ERF, Static, Dynamic, and Aggressive for running the NMF benchmark. As seen, our proposed algorithms reduce the power and energy consumption by a considerable amount compared to ERF in all scenarios. For example, under the light load, our algorithms can reduce 16% more power consumption and 25% more energy consumption.

8. CONCLUSION

In this paper, we proposed power-efficient time-sensitive mapping techniques for heterogeneous systems consisting of CPUs and GPUs. These techniques were implemented in a real CPU/GPU heterogeneous system. Experimental results demonstrate the effectiveness of the proposed techniques in reducing both power and energy consumption.

Several interesting avenues for further work exist. It would be interesting to consider heterogeneous systems consisting of more than two types of processors (e.g., a system containing CPUs, GPUs, and FPGAs). Moreover, contrary to our current strategy where each GPU and CPU has its own scheduler and application queue, designing a centralized scheduler that captures the information on both CPUs and GPUs at run-time may be able to make better mapping decisions in terms of reducing power and energy consumption.

9. REFERENCES

[1] AMD GPU Open-Source Drivers. www.help.ubuntu.com/community/RadeonDriver, 2011.

[2] CPUFreq technology. www.wiki.archlinux.org/index.php, 2011.

[3] B. Andersson, G. Raravi, and K. Bletsas. Assigning real-time tasks on heterogeneous multiprocessors with two unrelated types of processors. In *Proc. of the 31st Real-Time Sys. Symp.*, pp. 239-248, 2010.

[4] C. Augonnet, J. Clet-Ortega, S. Thibault, and R. Namyst. Data-aware task scheduling on multi-accelerator based platforms. In *Proc. of the 16th international conference on parallel and distributed systems*, 2010.

[5] S. Baruah. Partitioning real-time tasks among heterogeneous multiprocessors. In *Proc. of the 33rd International Conference on Parallel Processing*, pp. 467-474, 2004.

[6] J.J. Chen and C. F. Kuo. Energy-efficient scheduling for real-time systems on dynamic voltage scaling (dvs) platforms. In *Proc. of the 13th International Conference on Embedded and Real-Time Computing Systems and Applications*, pp. 28-38, 2007.

[7] Y. Chen, A. Das, W. Qin, A. Sivasubramaniam, Q. Wang, and N. Gautam. Managing server energy and operational costs in hosting centers. In *Proc. of the 2005 ACM SIGMETRICS International conference on Measurement and modeling of computer systems*, pp. 303-314, 2005.

[8] Khronos Corporation. The OpenCL Language. www.khronos.org/opencl, 2011.

[9] Advanced Micro Devices. AMD APP SDK. www.developer.amd.com/sdks/AMDAPPSDK/, 2011.

[10] G. Elliott and J. Anderson. Real-World Constraints of GPUs in Real-Time Systems. In *Proceedings of the First International Workshop on Cyber-Physical Systems, Networks, and Applications*, pp. 48-54, 2011.

[11] M. Elnozahy, M. Kistler, and R. Rajamony. Energy-efficient server clusters. In *Proc. of the 2nd Workshop on Power Aware Computing Sys.*, 2002.

[12] R. Wilhelm et al. The worst-case execution-time problem-overview of methods and survey of tools. In *ACM Transactions on Embedded Computing Systems*, Vol. 7, Issue 3, 2008.

[13] S. Ghiasi, T. Keller, and F. Rawson. Scheduling for heterogeneous processors in server systems. In *Proc. of the 2nd Conference on Computing Frontiers*, pp. 199-210, 2005.

[14] IBM. Big data analytics. http://www.ibm.com/software/data/infosphere/bigdata-analytics.html, 2011.

[15] V. Jimenez, L. Vilanova, I. Gelado, M. Gil, G. Fursin, and N. Navarro. Predictive runtime code scheduling for heterogeneous architectures. In *Proc. of the 4th International Conference on High Performance Embedded Architectures and Compilers*, pp. 19-33, 2009.

[16] Nam Sung Kim, Todd Austin, David Blaauw, Trevor Mudge, Krisztián Flautner, Jie S. Hu, Mary Jane Irwin, Mahmut Kandemir, and Vijaykrishnan Narayanan. Leakage current: Moore's law meets static power. *Computer*, 36(12):68–75, December 2003.

[17] R. Kumar, D. Tullsen, N. Jouppi, and P. Ranganathan. Heterogeneous Chip Multiprocessors. In *IEEE Computer*, pp. 32-38, 2005.

[18] D. Lee and H. S. Seung. Algorithms for non-negative matrix factorization. In *Proc. of the Intl. Conf. on Neural Info. Processing Sys.*, pp. 556-562, 2000.

[19] J. Liu. Real-time systems. In *Prentice Hall*, 2000.

[20] Y. Liu and H. Zhu. A survey of the reserach on power management techniques for high-performance systems. In *Journal of Software - Practice and Experience*, Vol. 40, Issue 11, 2010.

[21] C. Luk, S. Hong, and H. Kim. Qilin: Exploiting parallelism on heterogeneous multiprocessors with adaptive mapping. In *Proc. of the 42nd International Symp. on Microarchitecture*, pp. 45-55, 2009.

[22] S. Pak. Azul Systems extends leadership in business critical Java applications performance with the new Vega series. www.azulsystems.com/press/052008vega3.htm, May 2008.

[23] J. Rabaey. Digital integrated circuits. In *Prentice Hall*, 1996.

[24] R. Wu, B. Zhang, and M. Hsu. GPU-Accelerated Large Scale Analytics. In *HP Labotories Technical Report*, HPL-2009-38, 2009.

[25] Yokogawa. Wt210 digital power meter. www.yokogawa.com/tm/Bu/WT210, 2011.

Fast and Efficient Automatic Memory Management for GPUs using Compiler-Assisted Runtime Coherence Scheme

Sreepathi Pai R. Govindarajan Matthew J. Thazhuthaveetil
Supercomputer Education and Research Centre,
Indian Institute of Science, Bangalore, India.
{sree@hpc.serc, govind@serc, mjt@serc}.iisc.ernet.in

Abstract

Exploiting the performance potential of GPUs requires managing the data transfers to and from them efficiently which is an error-prone and tedious task. In this paper, we develop a software coherence mechanism to fully automate all data transfers between the CPU and GPU without any assistance from the programmer. Our mechanism uses compiler analysis to identify potential stale accesses and uses a runtime to initiate transfers as necessary. This allows us to avoid redundant transfers that are exhibited by all other existing automatic memory management proposals.

We integrate our automatic memory manager into the X10 compiler and runtime, and find that it not only results in smaller and simpler programs, but also eliminates redundant memory transfers. Tested on eight programs ported from the Rodinia benchmark suite it achieves (i) a 1.06x speedup over hand-tuned manual memory management, and (ii) a 1.29x speedup over another recently proposed compiler–runtime automatic memory management system. Compared to other existing runtime-only and compiler-only proposals, it also transfers 2.2x to 13.3x less data on average.

Categories and Subject Descriptors D.3.4 [*Programming Languages*]: Processors—Compilers, Run-time environments, Optimization

Keywords GPU, Memory Management, Data Transfers, Automatic, Software Coherence

1. Introduction

GPUs are now widely used in high performance computing. Three of the current top 5 supercomputers in the world [20] are accelerated by GPUs. Performance obtained on GPUs is often an order of magnitude greater than that obtainable on modern multicore CPUs [13]. A key aspect of GPU performance is the use of local, high-bandwidth *GPU memory* that is distinct from CPU memory. Programs that run on the GPU, called *kernels*, can only access this memory. All data consumed or produced by them must therefore reside in GPU memory. Programs on the CPU which share data with GPU kernels must use explicit transfers between CPU and GPU memories in order to communicate. Current programming models for the GPU, such as CUDA [14] and OpenCL [10], require the programmer to manually perform allocations of GPU memory and transfers of shared data between the CPU and GPU. This manual memory management is tedious, error-prone and a source of performance and portability issues. CUDA 4.0 [15] unifies CPU and GPU memory into a single 64-bit address space ("unified virtual address"), but the GPU and CPU still cannot directly access each other's memory and programmers must continue to perform explicit memory transfers.

CUDA and OpenCL are based on C and C++ and are fairly low-level. Some higher-level languages support programming GPUs directly without the use of CUDA or OpenCL. In particular, the partitioned global address space (PGAS) languages X10 [3] and Chapel [2] already support programming the GPU directly. These languages have built-in support for expressing parallelism, asynchronous communication and execution, and notions of remote and local data. Therefore GPUs can be integrated into these programming languages in a more natural fashion than is possible with CUDA or OpenCL. However, neither X10 nor Chapel fully abstracts CUDA. In X10CUDA [21] (the X10 compiler and runtime for CUDA) the programmer is still required to manually perform GPU memory allocations and transfers. GPU memory management therefore continues to be a source of programming difficulty and potential performance problems even in these languages.

Although there are several proposals that can automate CPU–GPU memory management [6, 8, 9, 11], our analysis (Section 3) shows that all of them introduce redundant transfers. These transfers increase the execution time of programs when compared to the use of hand-tuned manual transfers. Thus, the problem is not only to automate data transfers, but do so in an *efficient* manner. Our proposal differs from past work in the following ways:

- We present the design of the first *full* software coherence mechanism for automating transfers between the CPU and GPU.
- Designed as a compiler–runtime hybrid scheme, it requires no OS or hardware support (unlike [6, 9, 17]), and is therefore widely applicable to accelerators beyond GPUs.
- Importantly, our design treats the GPU and CPU as peers, by keeping full coherence state for both, allowing it to avoid redundant transfers. Hence it outperforms all existing proposals and is also highly competitive with manual memory management.

We integrate our automatic memory management system into X10CUDA, making the following specific contributions:

- We describe compiler analyses, code transformations and runtime support for AMM, a fast and efficient software coher-

```
var J:Rail[Float]! = Rail.make[Float](...);

val J_cuda = Rail.makeRemote[Float](gpu, ...);
val E_c = Rail.makeRemote[Float](gpu, ...)
...
for (iter=0; iter< niter; iter++){
    for (...) {
      for(...) {
        // read J
      }
    }

    finish J.copyTo(..., J_cuda, ...);

    //Run GPU kernels
    srad_cuda_1(gpu, E_c, ..., J_cuda, ...);
    srad_cuda_2(gpu, E_c, ..., J_cuda, ...);

    finish J.copyFrom(..., J_cuda, ...);
}
```

Listing 1. Code excerpt from Rodinia's srad ported to X10CUDA with manual memory management

ence scheme that performs automatic memory management for GPUs. We implement the scheme as *X10CUDA with Automatic Memory Management* (X10CUDA+AMM).

- On programs from the Rodinia Benchmark suite, X10CUDA+AMM obtains a geometric mean speedup of 1.06x over the original programs that use hand-tuned programmer-specified memory management.
- X10CUDA+AMM is 1.29x faster than CGCM [8], a recent automatic memory management proposal.
- Comparison with ADSM [6] and OpenMPC [11] reveals that they are slower by 1.32x and 3.72x than the original programs. On average (geomeans), they also transfer 2.2x and 13.3x more data than AMM.

The rest of the paper is organized as follows. We compare manual memory management in X10CUDA to automatic memory management in X10CUDA+AMM in Section 2. We then investigate a naive compiler-based automatic memory management system in Section 3 and demonstrate that it performs poorly because of large number of redundant transfers. Section 4 presents an overview of our scheme, while the compiler analyses, code transformations and runtime support are described in Section 5. We describe our port of CGCM to X10CUDA, resulting in X10CUDA+CGCM in Section 6. The results of our evaluation of X10CUDA+CGCM and X10CUDA+AMM are presented in Section 7. Other relevant related work is discussed in Section 8.

2. Background

Programs for NVIDIA GPUs are written in a C++ dialect called CUDA. CUDA code is structured as *kernels* which execute atomically on the GPU. A kernel's data must reside in GPU memory, which is a distinct address space from that of the CPU. The CUDA API provides functions which a programmer can use to create copies of shared data on the GPU and keep them updated.

X10CUDA [21] provides an X10 dialect of CUDA. Kernels are written as X10 Closures and are translated by the X10CUDA compiler to CUDA code. A GPU is exposed to the programmer as an X10 *Place* which is an X10 construct used to distribute data and schedule computations. Data is transferred using the X10 *Rail* type which is a C array-like type whose contents must reside entirely in a single Place. The Rail type provides methods to create Rails in GPU Places and to transfer data between a CPU-side Rail and a GPU-side Rail.

Listing 1 shows an excerpt from the Rodinia [4] srad benchmark program that we have ported to X10CUDA with the original hand-tuned memory management statements suitably translated, but intact. First, `Rail.makeRemote` is used to create GPU-side copies of CPU-side arrays (akin to CUDA's `cudaMalloc()`). In srad, J_cuda is the GPU copy of J and must therefore be kept in sync with it. There is no CPU-side equivalent for E_c because it is private to the GPU and communicates intermediate data between the two kernels (`srad_cuda_1` and `srad_cuda_2`). It appears in CPU code because GPU memory must be allocated by the CPU as kernels lack the ability to allocate memory.

```
var J:Rail[Float]! = Rail.make[Float](...);
val E_c = Rail.make[Float](...)
...
for (iter=0; iter< niter; iter++){
    for (...) {
      for(...) {
        // read J
      }
    }

    //Run GPU kernels
    srad_cuda_1(E_c, ..., J, ...);
    srad_cuda_2(E_c, ..., J, ...);
}
```

Listing 2. Rodinia's srad in X10CUDA with implicit memory management

Next, the programmer inserts the necessary memory transfers. The $J.copyTo$ and $J.copyFrom$ statements copy to and from the GPU respectively (akin to CUDA's `cudaMemcpy()`). The `srad_cuda_1` kernel reads J_cuda and writes E_c. Therefore, the programmer updates J_cuda on the GPU using the `copyTo` call on J. The `srad_cuda_2` kernel reads from E_c and writes to J_cuda, so the `copyFrom` call is used to update the CPU-side version J. No calls are made to transfer the E_c array since it is never read or written to on the CPU.

Listing 2 shows the same srad program without explicit memory management. In this *implicit* version, no copies of Rails on the GPU are created by the programmer. Nor are memory transfers explicitly specified. The compiler and runtime automatically create copies on the GPU and keep them updated by performing memory transfers when required. This version of srad is therefore much easier to write and involves considerably less book-keeping by the programmer. By removing explicit GPU-specific memory transfers from the source code, we have also increased the portability of the code.

This increase in convenience, productivity and portability cannot come at the expense of performance. In well-written hand-tuned programs, memory transfers are usually not the primary determinants of performance and occupy only a small fraction of execution time. Inefficient automatic memory management can unfortunately change this, as we shall see in the next section.

3. The Need for Efficient Memory Management

Figure 1 shows the total data transferred between the CPU and GPU by a naive automatic scheme for eight applications from the Rodinia [4] benchmark suite written in implicit X10CUDA. The results are normalized to the total data transferred by the original X10CUDA program where transfers are specified manually by the programmer.

This naive automatic scheme transfers the read set into the GPU when a kernel is invoked, and copies the write set to the CPU immediately after the kernel ends[1]. It is easy to implement in a compiler and has been used in an initial version of Chapel [19]

[1] In both the manual and naive versions, the granularity of transfer is an entire Rail (array).

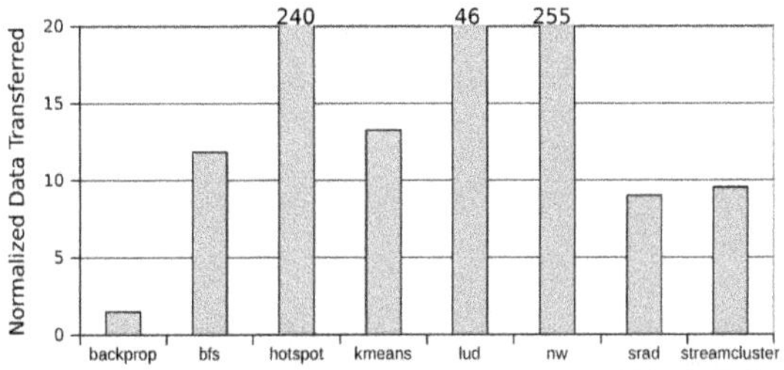

Figure 1. Total data transferred by a naive automatic memory transfer scheme normalized to that transferred by explicitly-specified transfers

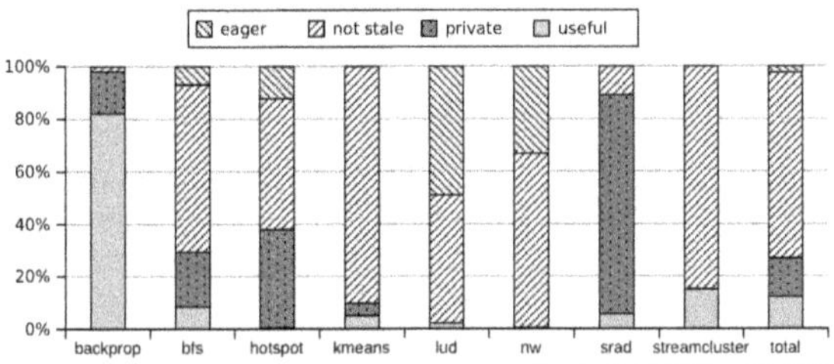

Figure 2. Breakup of data transferred by the naive automatic memory manager

for the GPU and with minor variations in the OpenMP to GPU compiler [12]. The scheme keeps the data always coherent in CPU memory, but it performs a large number of redundant transfers that cause it to transfer 1.5x to 255x more data than manually-specified transfers. We classify these redundant data transfers into three main categories described below and plot this information in Figure 2.

Transfers of non-stale data On kernel invocation, the naive scheme often transfers data which is not stale on the GPU. This happens, for example, when the CPU acts as a read-only consumer of data produced by the GPU kernel. The original copy of such data is in GPU memory and does not need to be transferred back. The naive scheme does not track the state of shared data making these transfers hard to avoid. Consider also the case of the streamcluster benchmark which uses a randomized CPU algorithm that only occasionally writes to shared data between kernel invocations. Thus, for some invocations, the GPU will have a non-stale copy of the data since the CPU has not written to it, but for others, it will have to update its copy of the data from the CPU. A pure compiler-only scheme would end up transferring data redundantly every time. The redundant transfers in this case are referred to as "not stale" in Figure 2. A scheme can prevent non-stale redundant transfers by only transferring data that has changed.

Eager transfers of data The naive scheme transfers data eagerly back to the CPU immediately after the kernel finishes. This can lead to redundant transfers, especially in loops that invoke kernels. Consider the following extract from the main loop of the lud benchmark, where all the functions invoked are GPU kernels:

```
for (...) {
  lud_diagonal_gpu(m, ...)
  lud_perimeter_gpu(m, ...);
  lud_internal_gpu(m, ...);
}
lud_diagonal_gpu(m, ...);
```

As there is no CPU-side code that reads or writes shared data inside the loop, it is sufficient to transfer the matrix `m` once at the beginning and once at the end of the loop. In this case, even the transfer at the end of the loop can be postponed to after the `lud_diagonal_gpu` outside the loop has executed. The naive scheme fails to utilize the opportunity presented by such loops to reduce the number of transfers since it always transfers data before kernel invocation and immediately after the kernel ends. Such loops are not the only source of such redundant transfers. Calls to GPU kernels with no intervening CPU-side reads or writes, like the calls to `srad_cuda_1` and `srad_cuda_2` in Listing 2, also cause redundant transfers in schemes that transfer data eagerly[2]. A scheme can avoid eager transfers by only initiating transfers when it knows the data will be read.

Scheme	Only Non-stale to Stale		Prevents Eager	
	C2G	G2C	C2G	G2C
Naive	N	Y	Y	N
ADSM [6] (Lazy)	Y	N	Y	Y
ADSM [6] (Rolling)	Y	N	N	Y
OpenMPC [11]	N	Y	Y	N
CGCM [8]	N	Y	Y	N
DyManD [9]	N	N	N	P
AMM	Y	Y	Y	Y

Table 1. A comparison of the ability of automatic memory management systems to eliminate redundant transfers. *Legend: P = Partial, C2G = CPU-to-GPU, G2C = GPU-to-CPU*

Transfers of private GPU-only data The naive scheme also transfers private GPU-only data between the CPU and GPU. This is data that is resident on the GPU and never read or written by the CPU. It is used by GPU kernels to communicate intermediate data between themselves (e.g., E_c in Listing 2) or across multiple invocations of the same kernel. Since a GPU kernel cannot allocate GPU memory on its own, the CPU must perform the allocation on its behalf and pass the kernel the pointer to the allocated memory. In an automatic scheme, a private GPU array would end up being represented by a CPU array that is never read or written by CPU code, but it would still feature in the read and write sets of GPU kernels. Not knowing that the CPU never reads or writes this array, the naive memory manager would keep this array coherent in CPU memory with transfers that are redundant. In srad, of the six same-sized arrays allocated on the GPU, *five* are private to the GPU and are only used for communication between the two kernels. Avoiding redundant transfers of GPU-only private data requires identification of GPU-only private data, but a scheme can also take advantage of the fact that the CPU does not read or write GPU-only private data.

So, of the total data transferred by the naive memory manager, only 12% is useful in that the transfer updates a stale copy of the data. Private data constitutes 14%, eager transfers about 2.5%, while over 70% of data transferred simply overwrites a non-stale copy (Figure 2).

We conclude that an automatic memory management scheme can eliminate redundant data transfers by: (i) not doing eager data transfers, (ii) ensuring that data is only transferred from a non-stale copy to a stale copy, (iii) transferring data only if it will change the destination copy. In practice, the third requirement can be costly to implement, so we assume data that was written to has its value changed as well.

Table 1 evaluates existing automatic memory management schemes against the first two requirements. These schemes span from pure compiler-only schemes (OpenMPC) to compiler–runtime schemes (CGCM, DyManD) and fully runtime schemes (ADSM). We see that *all* current systems fail to eliminate redundant transfers. For example, ADSM does not track changes on the GPU, so it always copies back data from the GPU leading to non-stale transfers. Similarly, compiler-based OpenMPC and CGCM are conservative and transfer modified data eagerly from the GPU back to the CPU

[2] In srad's case, these eager transfers are actually of private GPU-only data, and therefore accounted as "private" in Figure 2.

even when there is no CPU reader. Some of DyManD's transfers, too, are redundant non-stale transfers, because it tracks ownership of data but not whether data has changed or not. It also exhibits eager transfers, because although, like ADSM, it only transfers data back to the CPU on a read or a write, on occasion it brings back all GPU data to the CPU leading to eager transfers. We describe and evaluate these schemes quantitatively in Section 7.

To address these inefficiencies, we propose AMM, a compiler-assisted runtime coherence scheme for automatic GPU memory management. Our scheme reduces redundant data transfers by (i) tracking data staleness, (ii) identifying and preventing transfers of private GPU-only data, and (iii) transferring data in a lazy fashion.

4. Overview of Automatic Memory Management using Software Coherence

Since the CPU and GPU have distinct address spaces, programmers are forced to maintain copies of shared data in each address space. Without a hardware coherence mechanism, these copies must be kept coherent by software, usually by programmers manually performing data transfers. An automatic software coherence mechanism is therefore a natural alternative to manual GPU memory management. Such a mechanism would detect accesses to shared data and automatically schedule data transfers whenever accesses to stale data are detected. Thus, instead of statically inserting memory transfers to keep data coherent, we insert *coherence checks* to ensure that data accessed is not stale. These checks cause the runtime to trigger data transfers dynamically as required.

In this section, we present an overview of how GPU memory is automatically managed using our software coherence scheme in our implementation of X10CUDA+AMM. We discuss what our scheme keeps coherent, how it checks the coherence status of data on the CPU and GPU, and how it initiates data transfers. We then apply our scheme to the `srad` benchmark and demonstrate how it eliminates redundant transfers. The details of compiler analyses, transformations and runtime support required to implement our software coherence scheme outlined here are discussed in Section 5. For simplicity of presentation, we assume a system with one GPU in the text, however, our scheme is trivially extensible to multiple GPUs.

4.1 Implementing Coherence for Rails

The primary data type that must be kept coherent in an X10CUDA program is the Rail. X10CUDA+AMM kernels also accept primitive types, but these are passed by value. In general, CUDA kernels can accept arbitrary pointer parameters, e.g., to structures in GPU memory. However, X10CUDA does not yet support passing structures to its kernels. Nevertheless, our description of implementing coherence for Rails can be generalized easily to other non-primitive types.

We choose to implement software coherence at the granularity of an entire Rail. This granularity is also used by the manual versions of almost all of the benchmarks we tested. In these benchmarks, GPU kernels are written expecting Rails to be transferred in their entirety before and after kernel execution. We speculate that this is the result of the large parallelism available on the GPU, the atomic nature of kernel executions and the inability to transfer data mid-kernel to the GPU.

We associate with each Rail state information indicating its coherence status ("stale", "not stale") on each device (CPU, GPU) as well as addresses of the buffers on each device if allocated. This state is maintained by the runtime as described in Section 5.3. All Rails start out as not stale on all devices until the first write. Then the device that performed the write owns the copy of the Rail, and the other copies are marked as stale.

4.2 Maintaining Coherence on the GPU

A GPU kernel cannot transfer data while executing, so inserting coherence checks into kernels would be futile – we cannot update stale GPU copies mid-kernel execution. Therefore, X10CUDA+AMM must check and update all the Rails in a kernel's read set before it begins execution.

When a kernel is invoked, checks inserted by our compiler cause our coherence mechanism to update all the stale Rails in the kernel's read set from their CPU copies. If this is the first time a particular Rail is being transferred to the GPU, our coherence mechanism also allocates memory on the GPU for it before the transfer.

The coherence status of all the Rails written to by the kernel must also be updated on the CPU. Compiler-inserted calls to our coherence mechanism mark the CPU copy of each Rail in the kernel's write set as stale.

To prevent eager transfers, our approach *does not* transfer the non-stale GPU copy of a Rail back to the CPU immediately after the kernel finishes. Transfer to the CPU of a Rail updated on the GPU is initiated only when a compiler-inserted check on the CPU detects a stale access to that Rail.

4.3 Maintaining Coherence on the CPU

Unlike GPU code, where a kernel's entry and exit points are convenient points to insert coherence checks, there are no clearly defined boundaries in CPU code where checks to maintain coherence can be inserted.

Our coherence mechanism therefore tracks all CPU reads and writes to every Rail in the program. Each read or write of a Rail in CPU code is preceded by a coherence check inserted by our X10CUDA+AMM compiler. If the check detects a stale Rail, it updates the Rail from its GPU copy and sets its coherence status to not stale, so redundant transfers are avoided.

Since checking every read or write would be inefficient, we develop a compiler analysis that conservatively identifies a set of reads and writes that need to have checks inserted before them (Section 5.2.1). Only these reads or writes trigger coherence checks. To prevent overhead from redundant execution of checks at runtime, we also optimize the placement of these checks (Section 5.2.2).

4.4 Putting it all together

We demonstrate how our software coherence scheme triggers data transfers and avoids redundant transfers in the `srad` benchmark, whose high-level description was given in Section 2.

Figure 3 shows the flow of control during `srad`'s execution. We annotate the edges with changes in coherence status for the two Rails J and E_c. The initial part of `srad` reads an image and initializes J. It then executes a loop (Listing 2) that consists of a CPU-side reduction of J and consecutive calls to the two CUDA kernels `srad_cuda_1` and `srad_cuda_2`.

Inside the loop, J and E_c experience changes in their coherence status on CPU and GPU due to the code execution on these devices. Data transfers are only triggered based on the coherence status of the Rails. These transfers occur at kernel boundaries (for CPU to GPU transfers) and before the actual read/write (for GPU to CPU transfers). The elimination of redundant transfers happens as follows.

Elimination of non-stale data transfers The Rail J is initialized by the CPU causing its GPU copy to be marked as stale. The first GPU kernel, `srad_cuda_1` reads J, so in the first iteration of the loop our coherence mechanism transfers it to the GPU. The second GPU kernel, `srad_cuda_2`, writes to J causing the CPU copy to be marked as stale. When the reduce node inside the loop attempts to read J, the compiler-inserted check before the read of J operation

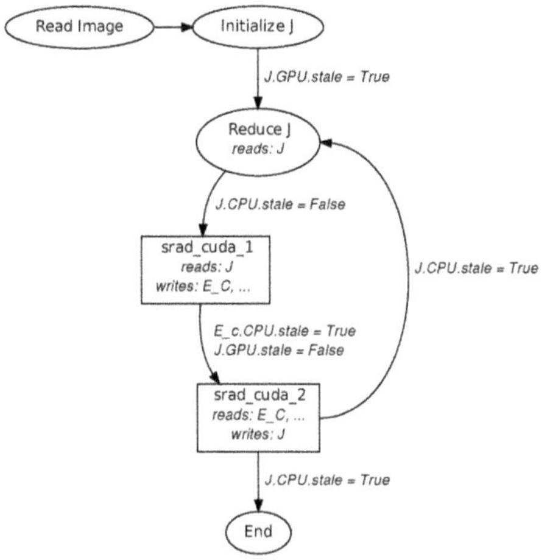

Figure 3. srad runtime control flow. The labels on the edges denote changes in coherence status for the Rails J and E_c on a per-device (CPU/GPU) basis. J is never stale on the GPU after the first iteration of the loop, a fact used by the runtime to eliminate redundant transfers of J to the GPU.

detects the stale access, and a transfer is initiated to update the CPU copy of J. There is no CPU code in the loop that writes to J, so the copy on the GPU is never stale. Hence, in subsequent iterations, transfers guarded by the coherence checks avoid the transfer and no transfers of J to the GPU occur in later iterations of the loop.

Although the redundant transfer in this example can be eliminated by purely compiler-based approaches (e.g., using loop peeling transformation), there are situations (e.g. in streamcluster as explained in Section 3) where runtime techniques are indeed needed to avoid some redundant data transfers.

Elimination of private GPU-only data transfers In srad, E_c is private GPU-only data. It starts out as not stale on the GPU and CPU, and since it is never written by the CPU, the first invocation of `srad_cuda_1` causes a GPU memory allocation for it but no transfer takes place since it is not stale on the GPU. This GPU kernel writes to E_c so the CPU-held copy of E_c is marked as stale. However, no CPU code ever reads E_c hence there are no stale accesses to it and hence no transfers back to the CPU are triggered by the coherence mechanism. Thus, transfers of private GPU-only data are completely avoided.

Elimination of eager transfers Since the software coherence mechanism only transfers data when there are stale accesses, there are no eager transfers. If the srad loop consisted only of kernel calls and the reduction code was eliminated, no reads or writes from the CPU would occur, and data would not be transferred back to the CPU during execution of the loop.

As shown above, our software coherence scheme automatically manages shared data between the GPU and CPU and avoids redundant transfers.

4.5 Coherence Checks versus Data Transfers

Earlier compiler-based approaches [2, 8, 11, 12] insert data transfers statically and use increasingly sophisticated analyses and transformations to avoid redundant transfers. However, the conservativeness inherent in a compiler-only approach cannot avoid all redundant transfers. Our approach of using the compiler to only insert coherence checks while utilizing runtime coherence state to eliminate redundant transfers allows us to avoid this fundamental limitation that plagues earlier work. Compiler conservativeness can only result in redundant coherence checks in our approach, not redundant transfers.

X10CUDA	E.g.	Usage description	X10CUDA+AMM
`makeRemote`	J_c	GPU copy of shared data	*not needed*
	E_c	GPU private data	`Rail.make`
`copyFrom`, `copyTo`		Manual transfers between CPU and GPU	*not needed*
Remote GPU Rail references	J_c	Arguments to kernel functions	Original (J)

Table 2. Differences between X10CUDA and X10CUDA+AMM language features for GPU programs. Examples are from Listing 1.

5. X10CUDA+AMM

Our X10CUDA+AMM compiler is based on the publicly available X10CUDA compiler [21]. Through it, we extend the X10CUDA compiler to insert coherence checks in CPU code and optimize their placement. These coherence checks then invoke our runtime coherence mechanism which maintains coherence status for all Rails and performs dynamic data transfers as required. The X10CUDA runtime uses the asynchronous CUDA API to overlap computation with communication, we plan to use this to perform ahead-of-time transfers to the GPU in the future.

5.1 X10CUDA+AMM Programs

Programs written for X10CUDA+AMM differ from those written for X10CUDA in several ways by not requiring explicit memory management. Table 2 compares X10CUDA and X10CUDA+AMM languages features used for GPU programming.

To summarize, X10CUDA+AMM programs do not to allocate GPU Rails and transfer them between the CPU and GPU manually. If a GPU kernel requires the use of private data, the programmer simply allocates the private data as a standard CPU-side Rail. Even the arguments passed to GPU kernels refer to the original CPU Rails treating GPU kernels as if they were standard CPU functions. This results in programs that look like Listing 2, i.e., smaller, simpler and more portable than their X10CUDA versions.

5.2 Compiler Analyses and Transformations

To determine which Rails must be kept coherent across devices, the compiler conservatively identifies the read and write sets of each GPU kernel using a standard def–use analysis. It then inserts before each call to a kernel, coherence checks for each Rails in the kernel's read and write set. At runtime, before the kernel is invoked, these checks make the GPU copies coherent by transferring them as necessary.

The procedure to insert coherence checks in CPU code relies on compiler analysis to determine which reads or writes in the source code are likely to access stale data. The checks are then placed just before these reads or writes. Since this placement might result in redundant checks executed at runtime, our compiler optimizes their placement. The analysis to insert these checks and the optimization of their placement are discussed in detail in the following sections.

5.2.1 Inserting Coherence Checks in CPU code

As previously discussed in Section 4.3, CPU code lacks the clearly defined boundaries of a GPU kernel where coherence checks can be inserted. The coherence mechanism must therefore check every read or write on the CPU to ensure that no stale data is read or written. We implement this check in the form of two methods, `check_read()` (Section 5.3.2) and `check_write()` (Section 5.3.3), that are invoked on a Rail object before a read and a write respectively. If the data in the Rail is stale, these methods trigger memory transfers and ensure that data available to subsequent

$$
\begin{aligned}
OUT_{WRITE}(ENTRY) &= \emptyset \\
IN_{WRITE}(s) &= \cap_{p,p \in pred(s)} OUT_{WRITE}(p) \\
OUT_{WRITE}(s) &= (IN_{WRITE}(s) \cup write_s) - kill_s \\
FIRST\_WRITTEN(s) &= OUT_{WRITE}(s) - IN_{WRITE}(s)
\end{aligned}
$$

$$
\begin{aligned}
OUT_{READ}(ENTRY) &= \emptyset \\
IN_{READ}(s) &= \cap_{p,p \in pred(s)} OUT_{READ}(p) \\
OUT_{READ}(s) &= (IN_{READ}(s) \cup read_s) - kill_s \\
FIRST\_READ(s) &= (OUT_{READ}(s) - IN_{READ}(s)) \\
&\quad - IN_{WRITE}(s)
\end{aligned}
$$

Figure 4. Data flow equations to determine placement of coherence checks

reads or writes is updated. They also update the Rail's coherence status to not stale, so that redundant transfers are prevented.

Our compiler could insert calls to these functions before every statement that read or wrote to a Rail, but that would be inefficient because of the overheads involved. Not all of these calls are necessary, though. A Rail's coherence status on the CPU can only change when a GPU kernel that reads or writes it is invoked. If it can be determined that a static reference (read or write) would always access coherent data the check can be eliminated. For example, if a static reference to a Rail is preceded by another reference to the same Rail and no GPU kernel invocations occur in between these two references, the second reference is guaranteed to always access coherent data, since the Rail would have been made coherent by the first reference[3].

Our analysis identifies such references so that the compiler can eliminate coherence checks whenever possible. Specifically, for every statement, our approach ultimately calculate two sets: $FIRST\_READ$ and $FIRST\_WRITTEN$ that contain Rails for which that statement is the first reader or writer respectively along some path from entry or the previous GPU kernel call. Our compiler then inserts `check_read()` and `check_write()` calls for these Rails before the statement. Note that there may be one first read or first write for a Rail after each GPU kernel call.

The data flow analysis to calculate $FIRST\_READ$ and $FIRST\_WRITTEN$ (Figure 4) begins by initializing three sets for each statement: the $read_s$ set which contains all Rails read in that statement, the $write_s$ set which contains all Rails written to in that statement, and the $kill_s$ set which contains Rails which may have gone stale during execution of that statement. The $kill_s$ set for a kernel invocation, for example, contains all the Rails read or written to by that kernel.

The dataflow equations in Figure 4 are iterated over the control-flow graph. This produces the set of Rails already read ($IN_{read}(s)$) and written ($IN_{write}(s)$) along all paths from ENTRY to statement s. Intuitively, these sets contain Rails that have reads or writes respectively along all paths from ENTRY to s. If R is a Rail in one of these sets, and if s reads or writes R, we do not need to invoke `check_read()` or `check_write()` on R because a prior read or write would have already done so – a coherent copy of R is available on all paths to s. It is, therefore, the difference of the OUT and IN sets for reads and writes that gives us the Rails first read or written to in this statement.

Once the dataflow analysis has converged, calls to `check_read()` and `check_write()` are inserted for each statement for Rails in that statement's $FIRST\_READ(s)$ and $FIRST\_WRITTEN(s)$ sets respectively.

[3] Note that the coherence is maintained at the granularity of the whole Rail.

```
var J:Rail[Float]! = Rail.make[Float](...);
val E_c = Rail.make[Float](...)
...
for (iter=0; iter< niter; iter++){
  J.CPU.check_read()
  for (...) {
    for(...) {
      // read J
    }
  }

  //Run GPU kernels
  E_c.GPU.check_write()
  J.GPU.check_read()
  srad_cuda_1(E_c, ..., J, ...);

  E_c.GPU.check_read()
  J.GPU.check_write()
  srad_cuda_2(E_c, ..., J, ...);
}
```

Listing 3. Listing 2 after insertion and of placement optimization of checks

5.2.2 Optimizing Placement of Coherence Checks

The analysis of the previous section inserts `check_read()` and `check_write()` as close to a read or write as possible. However, this can result in sub-optimal placements. Consider this example:

```
for(i = ...) {
  R.CPU.check_read();
  ... = R(i)
}
```

In this code, `R.CPU.check_read()` will check if R is coherent in every iteration of the loop. However, the loop in this example contains no calls to GPU kernels, and hence R cannot go stale during execution of this loop. If R was stale on entry to the loop, the first dynamic instance of `R.CPU.check_read` will result in a transfer, but the subsequent dynamic instances from the loop will be redundant.

We can hoist this call out of the loop, resulting in:

```
R.CPU.check_read();
for(i = ...) {
  ... = R(i)
}
```

We implement a pass in our compiler that moves calls to `check_write()` or `check_read()` for a Rail R out of a loop if the following conditions hold: (i) The reference to R is loop invariant, (ii) No statement in that loop causes R to possibly go stale on the CPU (directly or indirectly calls a GPU kernel).

This pass is repeated until no calls are moved. Listing 3 is the result of compiling Listing 2 by our compiler. Checks have been inserted at the appropriate points, and the check for J has been hoisted out of the doubly-nested reduction loop.

5.3 Runtime Support

The X10CUDA+AMM runtime is responsible for tracking the coherence state of a Rail during program execution. It also initiates data transfers dynamically across the CPU and GPU as required.

5.3.1 Modifications to the Rail type

In X10CUDA+AMM, the Rail type is extended to maintain state that is used by the coherence mechanism. Each Rail object contains a coherence status for each device (CPU, GPU) which marks it as "stale" or "not stale" on that device.

This new state also includes the locations of buffers allocated for this Rail on each device. Buffers on the GPU are only allocated the first time data is transferred to it.

We also add the `check_read()` and `check_write()` methods to the Rail type. These methods maintain the coherence status for the Rail, and also initiate transfers as necessary. The Rail is always coherent after these methods are invoked.

5.3.2 The check_read() method

The `check_read()` method (Algorithm 1) signals the coherence mechanism that the CPU or GPU will read the Rail's data in the code to follow.

This method updates the coherence status of the Rail on the device (CPU or GPU) by marking it not stale on that device, after updating the stale Rail by transferring from another non-stale copy if necessary.

In our implementation, we use a highly optimized version of this method to implement checks in CPU code to lower overheads.

Algorithm 1 Pseudocode for the Rail's `check_read()` method

```
if device == GPU then
    if GPU.data_ptr == NULL then
        GPU.data_ptr = cuMemAlloc(Rail.length)
    if GPU.stale then
        copy(destination = GPU.data_ptr, source = CPU.data_ptr)
        GPU.stale ← False
else
    if CPU.stale then
        copy(destination = CPU.data_ptr, source = GPU.data_ptr)
        CPU.stale ← False
```

5.3.3 The check_write() method

The `check_write()` method (Algorithm 2) signals the coherence mechanism that the CPU or GPU will write to the Rail.

The `check_write()` method first performs the equivalent of a `check_read()`, updating a stale Rail from a non-stale copy. The coherence status of the Rail on the device is then set to not stale while all other copies of the Rail are marked as stale.

Again, like `check_read()`, our implementation uses an optimized check to lower overheads. Also, in the case of some X10 library functions that completely overwrite a Rail, our implementation skips the call to `check_read()`, saving on the transfer of data that would be overwritten anyway.

Algorithm 2 Pseudocode for the Rail's `check_write()` method

```
if device == GPU then
    if GPU.data_ptr == NULL then
        GPU.data_ptr = cuMemAlloc(Rail.length)
    if GPU.stale then
        copy(destination = GPU.data_ptr, source = CPU.data_ptr)
        GPU.stale ← False
    CPU.stale ← True
else
    if CPU.stale then
        copy(destination = CPU.data_ptr, source = GPU.data_ptr)
        CPU.stale ← False
    GPU.stale ← True
```

6. CPU–GPU Communications Manager (CGCM) for X10CUDA

The CPU–GPU Communications Manager (CGCM) [8] is a system that automates memory allocations and transfers of data between the CPU and GPU. In that work, CGCM is coupled to an auto-parallelization system that produces GPU code from the programs written in C/C++. In order to compare this state-of-the-art system with X10CUDA+AMM, we port CGCM to X10CUDA, resulting in X10CUDA+CGCM.

Transfers in CGCM are handled by `map`, `unmap` and `release` calls placed into the code by the compiler. The compiler brackets each kernel invocation site with these calls for every Rail in the kernel's read and write set. Simplistically, a `map` and its corresponding `unmap` transfer data to and from the GPU, whereas `map` and `release` manipulate a runtime reference count to prevent some redundant transfers.

To decrease redundant transfers, the CGCM compiler performs *map promotion*, which hoists the above function calls out of loops and function bodies. Map promotion does not succeed if there are CPU references or modifications to the Rails inside the loop/function.

To improve the applicability of map promotion, CGCM performs *glue kernel identification* whereby CPU code that interferes with map promotion is converted to a single-threaded GPU function where possible. We perform map promotions and glue kernel identifications faithfully for all our benchmarks as well.

7. Evaluation

Our objective is to evaluate the AMM scheme and its impact on program execution time. We compare the performance of our AMM implementation against (i) X10CUDA implementation which uses programmer inserted (manual) memory management, and (ii) X10CUDA+CGCM in Sections 7.2–7.4. In Section 7.5, we contrast AMM against the compiler-only OpenMPC and the runtime-only ADSM schemes. In Section 7.6, we quantify the overheads of our implementation.

7.1 Methodology

The benchmarks used in the evaluation are taken from the Rodinia Benchmark suite (v1) [4]. The original benchmarks are available as C++ and CUDA programs and contain manually parallelized kernels and explicit hand-tuned memory allocations and transfers. We port these benchmarks to X10CUDA as faithfully as possible, maintaining the same memory allocations and transfers as in the C++ version. These programs are referred to as the X10CUDA (manual) versions.

X10CUDA does not support passing arrays of structures to the GPU, so we convert programs that use arrays of structures extensively (backprop, bfs, streamcluster) to use structures of arrays instead. The version of X10CUDA used in our work also does not support GPU textures or constant memory, so we modify the kmeans benchmark which uses these features to work without them.

The heartwall, leucocyte, cfd and mummergpu benchmarks are not included because they make extensive use of C/C++ native libraries, GPU SIMD types and structures as kernel arguments, none of which are supported by the base X10CUDA compiler.

We run hotspot for 360 iterations and srad for 100 iterations as described in the Rodinia paper [4].

We rewrite each X10CUDA version of the benchmark for X10CUDA+AMM using Table 2 as a guide. In this rewritten version, all data transfers are implicit. We convert GPU-only private Rails to CPU-side Rails.

To obtain the X10CUDA+CGCM versions, we take the implicit version of the benchmark produced for X10CUDA+AMM and perform Map Insertion, Map Promotion and Glue Kernel Identification manually. Map promotion hoists the map calls for Rails out of all loops in all programs except kmeans and streamcluster. In hotspot, the main loop limits map promotion because the Rodinia source code refers to Rails used by the GPU kernels in a loop-dependent fashion. In srad, a glue kernel for the CPU-side reduction improves the applicability of map promotion. No such opportunities are found in kmeans or streamcluster.

Lastly, the naive version of each benchmark uses the same source code as the X10CUDA+AMM but has transfers inserted

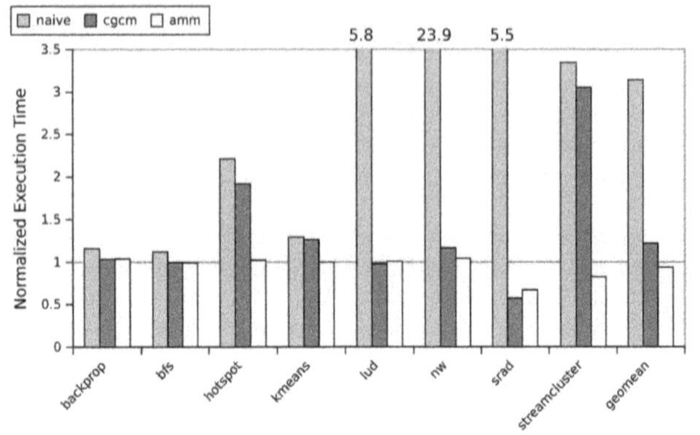

Figure 5. Normalized execution time of benchmarks using automatic memory management relative to the manual version. Lower is better.

statically by the compiler. Note that the manual version of each benchmark acts as the baseline for all our experiments.

All of the resulting versions are compiled using the same base X10 compiler, which invokes gcc 4.4.5 and CUDA 2.3 compilers with -O3 optimizations. The benchmarks are run on a system equipped with an NVIDIA Tesla C1060 with 4GB RAM. The CPUs are two quad-core Intel Xeon E5405 2GHz with 16GB RAM. In all our experiments the CPU code and the GPU code are executed in a single X10 Place, which uses two CPU cores (the default) and a single GPU. Each program was run 10 times, and the runtime averaged across those ten runs.

We report normalized execution time of X10CUDA+AMM, X10CUDA+CGCM and X10CUDA+Naive relative to the runtime of the manual version of the program which has hand-tuned memory transfers as in the original Rodinia source code. Normalized execution times are aggregated using geometric means.

7.2 Performance of Individual Schemes

Figure 5 shows the normalized execution times of the implicit X10CUDA+Naive, X10CUDA+CGCM and X10CUDA+AMM versions over their manual version.

First, for reasons discussed in Section 3, the X10CUDA+Naive implementation of memory management performs very poorly for all programs, slowing down execution time by 3.14x (geomean).

Second, X10CUDA+AMM is able to perform as well as the manual version except for nw and backprop where it is within 4%. In two benchmarks, srad and streamcluster, AMM outperforms the manual version of the benchmarks by 34% and 18% respectively. This is due to the reduction in redundant transfers as explained later in Section 7.3.

While X10CUDA+CGCM achieves a higher performance in srad (improvement of 44% primarily due to the glue kernel optimization which reduces the overall data transferred) and comparable performance in bfs, lud and nw, it suffers significant slowdowns in hotspot, kmeans and streamcluster – 91%, 26% and 205% respectively – compared to the manual versions.

Overall, X10CUDA+CGCM is slower than manual by 22%. X10CUDA+AMM, on the other hand, is 6% faster than manual. X10CUDA+AMM is 1.29x faster than X10CUDA+CGCM and 3.33x faster than X10CUDA+Naive.

Next, we compare the amount of data transferred by these schemes to understand their speedups.

7.3 Data Transferred by X10CUDA+AMM

From Figure 6, other than in streamcluster, X10CUDA+AMM does not transfer more data than the equivalent manual version. Further,

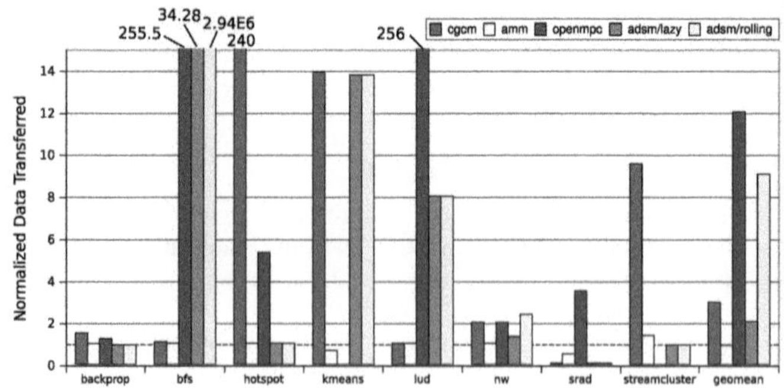

Figure 6. Size of data transferred by X10CUDA+AMM, X10CUDA+CGCM, Cetus+OpenMPC, ADSM versions normalized to data transferred by the manual version. Lower is better.

for three of the benchmarks – backprop, srad, kmeans, it actually transfers *less* data than the manual version.

Examination of the source code for backprop, srad, kmeans reveals they have redundant transfers in the original Rodinia source code that transfer non-stale data to the GPU. X10CUDA+AMM detects and eliminates these transfers. In srad's case, for example, as we noted in Section 4.4, the $J.copyTo$ inside the loop (Listing 1) is redundant after the first iteration.

The case of streamcluster is more complicated. The excess data transferred is not due to X10CUDA+AMM transferring non-stale or private data or even through eager data transfers. It turns out that streamcluster is the only benchmark that performs partial transfers of a Rail in the manual version. Since X10CUDA+AMM always transfers back an entire Rail, the automatic version of streamcluster transfers back more data (3.91x) for one Rail (`work_mem_h`), than the manual version.

However, there are other Rails in streamcluster that are transferred from the CPU to the GPU. These Rails (`p_assign`, `p_weight` and `p_cost`) are only modified occasionally by the CPU inside a randomized algorithm. The manual version of streamcluster transfers these Rails on every kernel invocation, but as X10CUDA+AMM tracks the coherence state of each Rail, they are only transferred if they have been modified by the CPU. In this case, X10CUDA+AMM transfers only 9.5GB instead of 11.5GB transferred by the manual version. Overall, X10CUDA+AMM transfers 1.37x more data than manual in streamcluster. However, the automatic version of streamcluster is 20% faster than the manual version. Overall X10CUDA+AMM transfers on average 0.9x the data transferred by manual.

7.4 Data Transferred by X10CUDA+CGCM

Figure 6 shows that for six of the eight programs, X10CUDA+CGCM transfers more data than the equivalent programmer-tuned manual version. The amount of data transferred is as high as 240x for hotspot, 9.5x for streamcluster and 13.9x for kmeans. In lud, the amount of data transferred under X10CUDA+CGCM is equal to that transferred under manual because the map promotion successfully hoists the map outside the main loop, and then outside the function. In srad, the glue kernel leads to all code being run on the GPU therefore transferring only 0.06x of the data transferred by manual.

To examine why X10CUDA+CGCM transfers more data for the remaining six programs we use the analysis of Section 3 to plot in Figure 7, a breakup of the data transferred by X10CUDA+CGCM. As described in Section 6, X10CUDA+CGCM does not track CPU reads or writes at all. This causes it to transfer non-stale data redundantly, prevents it from identifying private GPU-only data and also causes eager transfers. Note that GPU-only private data has no CPU

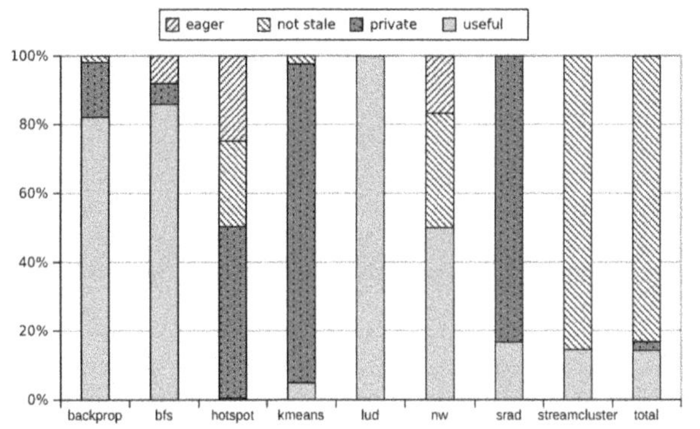

Figure 7. Breakup of data transfers performed by X10CUDA+CGCM

reads or writes, so map promotion does succeed in reducing the amount of private data transferred. However, X10CUDA+CGCM still ends up transferring GPU-only private data at least once.

Loops in which map promotion failed end up contributing to both non-stale redundant transfers and eager transfers. In kmeans and streamcluster, where opportunities to perform map promotion were not found, X10CUDA+CGCM performs equivalent to the naive scheme.

To summarize, X10CUDA+CGCM ends up transferring 2.9x more data (geomean) than manual and only 14% of the total data transferred by X10CUDA+CGCM turns out to be useful. Compared to this, all the data transferred by our X10CUDA+AMM is useful.

7.5 Comparison with Cetus+OpenMPC, ADSM and DyManD

To contrast CGCM and AMM with a compiler-only approach, we present data transfer information for benchmarks compiled by the OpenMPC compiler [11] which translates OpenMP programs to CUDA. It inserts data transfers statically by performing interprocedural analysis to identify GPU-resident and CPU-live variables. We were only able to compile six Rodinia benchmarks with Cetus 1.3. Figure 6 shows that the OpenMPC compiler transfers from 1.22x to 256x the data transferred by the manual versions for these six benchmarks, even when the benchmarks were compiled with the highest level of memory transfer optimizations as supported by OpenMPC. Overall, OpenMPC transfers 12x (geomean) more data.

We also evaluate ADSM [6] which is a fully runtime scheme, but requires the programmer to annotate shared data. It uses OS-level memory protection mechanisms to intercept reads and writes to this shared data. We use the libgmac 0.0.20 [7] implementation and evaluate both Lazy and Rolling schemes. We find that Lazy is faster and transfers less data as compared to the Rolling scheme. ADSM handles partial data transfers and tracks coherence information on the CPU so it is able to eliminate redundant transfers in srad and streamcluster. However, since it does not track GPU coherence information, it transfers non-stale data from the GPU, for example in kmeans. We observe that data structure initialization can confuse ADSM's Rolling scheme leading to repeated redundant transfers. In the extreme case exhibited by bfs, this transfers 2.94×10^6 times more data. Compared to manual, on average ADSM transfers 2x more data for Lazy, and 9x (1.4x without bfs) more data for Rolling.

These excess data transfers lead to loss of performance, as seen in Figure 8 which shows the performance of the ADSM schemes normalized to Rodinia CUDA code. ADSM is faster than manual only for srad, and is upto 2.2x slower for kmeans. Overall, ADSM Lazy is 32% (geomean) slower than the manual Rodinia code and Rolling is 4x slower (39% without bfs). Similarly, OpenMPC's excess data transfers cause it to never be faster than manual for any program. Overall it is 3.72x (geomean) slower than manual.

DyManD [9] extends CGCM with a memory optimization framework similar to ADSM. However its state machine is considerably less detailed than that of ADSM – tracking only ownership but not coherence state. We therefore believe that its performance will be similar to that of ADSM.

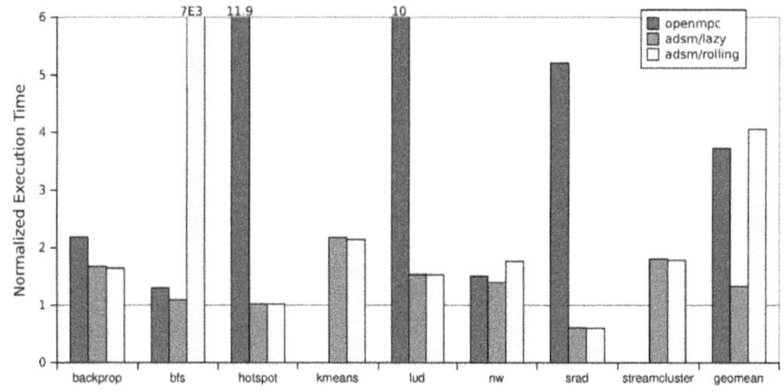

Figure 8. Normalized execution time for OpenMPC and ADSM relative to the Rodinia CUDA manual benchmarks

Benchmark	check_read()	check_write()	OoL
backprop	24	15	29
bfs	3	11	12
lud	9	2	9
nw	6	8	10
srad	4	3	6
hotspot	4	2	6
kmeans	13	11	19
streamcluster	53	37	44

Table 3. Number of coherence checks inserted and hoisted per benchmark. OoL refers to checks that have been placed outside-of-loops.

Benchmark	reads + writes	check_write	check_read
backprop	18,088,926	2,228,377	2,228,345
bfs	859,964	65	12
hotspot	1,835,384	5	3
kmeans	1,975,962,573	6487	6516
lud	65,537	1	1
nw	16,822,812	264	2
srad	14,221,329	2	103
streamcluster	4,733,235,158	21,228,272	26,905,978

Table 4. Number of dynamic `check_write()` and `check_read()` executions compared to number of dynamic reads and writes per benchmark

7.6 Overheads of redundant check_read() and check_write()

Table 3 shows the number of `check_read()` and `check_write()` calls that are inserted by our compiler into each benchmark. The *OoL* entry in the table corresponds to the sum of `check_read()` and `check_write()` calls that end up outside loops after the optimization procedure described in Section 5.2.2. The calls that are not hoisted are in loops that contain GPU kernel calls and/or that have loop-dependent references to Rails. In addition, in our current implementation, we do not hoist checks that are inside conditional blocks of code, so as to prevent redundant transfers, even if those conditional blocks lie inside a loop.

Table 4 shows the number of actual dynamic calls that are executed during a run of each benchmark. The absolute number of dynamic `check_read()` and `check_write()` calls are low when compared to the actual number of reads and writes. Only in backprop do they form a significant fraction (12.3%) of the number of reads and writes. This is because of a loop that iterates over the outermost index of a 2D Rail in the innermost loop, thus creating a loop dependence that prevents the hoisting of the `check_read()` and `check_write()` calls. For all other benchmarks, the fraction of checks to reads and writes is less than 0.01% with the exception of streamcluster for which the checks fraction is 1%.

From this we estimate the runtime overhead for execution of these checks. We measure the cycles taken by `check_read()` and `check_write()` using the `RDTSC` instruction [16]. On average, these methods take 8–9 cycles per call[4] when no data is transferred. The overhead in execution time is very low (the maximum of 2.46% is experienced by backprop) with the average overhead being around 0.35% of runtime.

8. Related Work

Software caching schemes have been used on the Cell accelerator [5] to communicate data between the CPU and the Cell's SPUs. However, unlike SPUs, GPUs cannot initiate memory transfers, so it is not possible to realize software caches on current GPUs.

The OpenMPC compiler translates OpenMP code to GPU kernels [11] and inserts transfers by using an interprocedural analysis to identify GPU-resident and CPU-live variables at compile-time. Our scheme identifies possibly stale reads or writes instead and inserts coherence checks, not transfers. OpenMPC is evaluated in Section 7.5.

Baskaran et al. develop an automatic polyhedral model-based framework [1] to insert data transfers statically. Their method is closely tied to their parallelization framework and does not involve any runtime coherence mechanism to avoid transfers of non-stale data. Our work can automate transfers for both manually-written kernels as well as automatically parallelized GPU code.

Saha et al. describe a programming model for C on heterogeneous x86 platforms [17] which provides a logical shared address space between the CPU and an accelerator modeled on the Larrabee [18]. Coherence is maintained by the CPU and the accelerator by intercepting reads and writes using the operating system's memory protection mechanisms. However, this requires the accelerator to support virtual memory and protection to support its coherence mechanisms, something current GPUs lack.

The ADSM/GMAC [6] system also provides shared pointers, but does so via an asymmetric distributed memory system that does not require the GPU to participate in coherence management. It is implemented as a layer over CUDA. Reads and writes on the CPU are intercepted using the operating system memory protection mechanisms. Shared objects are annotated by a programmer. Our work does not require operating system support or annotations.

Our work is closely related to the CGCM [8] system which provides a compiler and runtime to automatically manage memory for CUDA programs written in C++. DyManD [9] extends CGCM by adding a runtime ADSM-like memory optimization framework.

We have compared and evaluated our work against CGCM, ADSM and OpenMPC in this paper.

9. Conclusions

In this paper, we have presented the AMM system which is a hybrid compiler-assisted runtime coherence scheme to automatically manage all aspects of CPU–GPU communication including allocations and memory transfers. Our design was motivated by the observation that not all redundant transfers can be completely eliminated at compile time. Our system can be used both by a programmer writing GPU kernels manually and as part of a parallelizing compiler. It significantly eases the task of programming the GPU by eliminating a potential source of errors and performance problems.

We have incorporated AMM into the X10CUDA compiler and runtime, and evaluated it on a set of benchmark programs from the Rodinia suite. The AMM system achieves comparable performance to programmer-inserted manual memory management. In fact it achieves a speedup of 1.06x over manual by eliminating some redundant data transfers. Compared to a state-of-the-art memory management system, CGCM [8], our AMM system is faster by 1.29x. Moreover, compared to other existing runtime-only and compiler-only proposals, it also transfers 2.2x to 13.3x less data on average.

Acknowledgments

The authors acknowledge partial funding from Microsoft Corporation towards this work.

References

[1] M. M. Baskaran, U. Bondhugula, et al. Automatic data movement and computation mapping for multi-level parallel architectures with explicitly managed memories. In *PPoPP*, 2008.

[2] B. L. Chamberlain, D. Callahan, and H. P. Zima. Parallel programmability and the Chapel language. *International Journal of High Performance Computing Applications*, 21:291–312, 2007.

[3] P. Charles, C. Grothoff, V. Saraswat, et al. X10: An object-oriented approach to non-uniform cluster computing. In *OOPSLA*, 2005.

[4] S. Che, M. Boyer, J. Meng, et al. Rodinia: A benchmark suite for heterogeneous computing. In *IISWC*, 2009.

[5] A. E. Eichenberger, K. O'Brien, et al. Optimizing compiler for the CELL processor. In *PACT*, 2005.

[6] I. Gelado, J. E. Stone, et al. An asymmetric distributed shared memory model for heterogeneous parallel systems. In *ASPLOS*, 2010.

[7] I. Gelado et al. GMAC: Global Memory for Accelerators (version 0.0.20). URL `http://code.google.com/p/adsm/`.

[8] T. B. Jablin, P. Prabhu, et al. Automatic CPU-GPU communication management and optimization. In *PLDI*, 2011.

[9] T. B. Jablin, J. A. Jablin, et al. Dynamically Managed Data for CPU-GPU architectures. In *CGO*, March 2012.

[10] Khronos. OpenCL: The open standard for parallel programming of heterogeneous systems. URL `http://www.khronos.org/opencl`.

[11] S. Lee and R. Eigenmann. OpenMPC: Extended OpenMP programming and tuning for GPUs. In *SC*, 2010.

[12] S. Lee, S.-J. Min, and R. Eigenmann. OpenMP to GPGPU: a compiler framework for automatic translation and optimization. In *PPoPP*, 2009.

[13] V. W. Lee, C. Kim, et al. Debunking the 100X GPU vs. CPU myth: an evaluation of throughput computing on CPU and GPU. In *ISCA*, 2010.

[14] NVIDIA. CUDA: Compute Unified Device Architecture. URL `http://developer.nvidia.com/cuda`.

[15] NVIDIA. NVIDIA CUDA C Programming Guide version 4.0. 2011.

[16] G. Paoloni. How to benchmark code execution times on Intel IA-32 and IA-64 instruction set architectures. 2010.

[17] B. Saha, X. Zhou, et al. Programming model for a heterogeneous x86 platform. In *PLDI*, 2009.

[18] L. Seiler, D. Carmean, et al. Larrabee: A many-core x86 architecture for visual computing. *ACM Trans. Graph.*, 27(3), 2008.

[19] A. Sidelnik, B. L. Chamberlain, M. J. Garzaran, and D. Padua. Using the High Productivity Language Chapel to target GPGPU architectures. Technical report, UIUC Dept. of Computer Science, 2011.

[20] TOP500.org. The Top 500. URL `http://www.top500.org/`.

[21] x10 lang.org. X10 2.1 cuda. URL `http://docs.codehaus.org/display/XTENLANG/X10+2.1+CUDA`.

[4] Our implementation is very efficient. In an experiment where *all* reads and writes were subject to coherence checks, we observed noticeable slowdowns only in kmeans (19%) and streamcluster (8%).

Riposte: A Trace-Driven Compiler and Parallel VM for Vector Code in R

Justin Talbot
Stanford University
jtalbot@stanford.edu

Zachary DeVito
Stanford University
zdevito@stanford.edu

Pat Hanrahan
Stanford University
hanrahan@cs.stanford.edu

ABSTRACT

There is a growing utilization gap between modern hardware and modern programming languages for data analysis. Due to power and other constraints, recent processor design has sought improved performance through increased SIMD and multi-core parallelism. At the same time, high-level, dynamically typed languages for data analysis have become popular. These languages emphasize ease of use and high productivity, but have, in general, low performance and limited support for exploiting hardware parallelism.

In this paper, we describe Riposte, a new runtime for the R language, which bridges this gap. Riposte uses *tracing*, a technique commonly used to accelerate scalar code, to dynamically discover and extract sequences of vector operations from arbitrary R code. Once extracted, we can fuse traces to eliminate unnecessary memory traffic, compile them to use hardware SIMD units, and schedule them to run across multiple cores, allowing us to fully utilize the available parallelism on modern shared-memory machines. Our evaluation shows that Riposte can run vector R code near the speed of hand-optimized C, 5–50x faster than the open source implementation of R, and can also linearly scale to 32 cores for some tasks. Across 12 different workloads we achieve an overall average speed-up of over 150x without explicit programmer parallelization.

Categories and Subject Descriptors

D.3.4 [**Processors**]: incremental compilers, code generation, interpreters

Keywords

R language, just-in-time compilation, tracing, data parallel

1. INTRODUCTION

Recent trends in hardware have increased available parallelism by widening SIMD units, increasing core counts, and adding specialized hardware accelerators, such as GPUs. These trends challenge traditional programming models, which focus on scalar code, leading to interest in developing more effective parallel programming models.

We approach this challenge from the domain of data analysis where there is increasing interest in programmer-friendly, high productivity languages, such as R, Matlab, and Python. These languages are now widely used in statistics, data mining, and machine learning, as well as in application areas such as social sciences, biology, and finance. Analytic languages commonly include arbitrary-length homogeneous arrays ("vectors") as basic types in addition to standard scalar types. Vector types and their associated operations are a good fit to data analysis workloads which often contain linear algebra-style arithmetic and substantial processing of tabular data sets. More importantly, these vector types and operations provide regions of implicit data parallelism that should allow users to transparently exploit emerging parallel hardware.

However, the dynamically typed semantics of these languages make it difficult to extract this data parallelism. Necessary type checks and other dynamic control flow lead to virtual machine implementations that execute a single vector operation at a time, resulting in large intermediate values that consume memory and bandwidth. In such implementations, vector operations are memory-bound and fail to take advantage of data parallel hardware.

Work on addressing this problem has focused on two approaches: (1) supplementing or replacing dynamically typed languages with statically-typed ones that are easier to analyze and compile [9, 23, 25], or (2) exposing parallelism by adding coarse-grained *explicit* task parallel constructs to the language [37, 29]. Both of these approaches give up productivity and familiarity. The second approach additionally sacrifices fine-grained parallelism, including the use of SIMD units and GPUs.

A more promising direction is suggested by the recent work on accelerating languages such as Javascript [1, 13] and Lua [2]. This work maintains the original semantics of the dynamic language, but achieves good performance through runtime type specialization and just-in-time compilation. However, this work has focused primarily on scalar code, making little use of parallel hardware.

In this paper, we tackle the challenge of efficiently executing a dynamically-typed data analytic language with vector types. Our solution uses a *trace-based* approach to dynamically separate the complex scalar code, including dynamic type checks and other difficult semantics, from the simpler vector operations. Once separated, we can aggressively optimize the vector operations for modern parallel hardware—performing vector fusion to eliminate memory traffic, JIT compiling to SIMD machine code, and scheduling across multiple cores on a shared memory machine.

We have implemented our tracing approach in Riposte, a prototype virtual machine for the R programming language. For code using R's vector operations, Riposte achieves a 5–50x speed up over the open source R interpreter [27] on a single core and demonstrates near linear scalability for some workloads out to 32 cores.

This paper makes the following contributions:

- We demonstrate that a *vector-based, dynamically typed* language can be an effective and efficient parallel programming model for data analysis tasks.
- We present a tracing approach inspired by deferred evaluation that can extract simple, compilable vector sequences from dynamic R code. This is augmented with a dynamic liveness analysis pass that can eliminate unnecessary intermediate outputs recorded in the trace, decreasing our memory and bandwidth usage.
- We describe a simple vector virtual machine designed to support the straight-line vector code produced by tracing and show that the semantics of the virtual machine make vector fusion easy. We also describe our VM's simple just-in-time compiler and its parallel runtime for shared-memory machines.
- We validate our approach by comparing Riposte to the existing open-source R interpreter, showing large speed-ups, and to hand-written, vectorized, C code, showing performance within a small factor of optimal. We also show that Riposte can scale well to 32 cores.

In Section 2, we give a high-level overview of our design through a worked example. Then in Section 3, we describe our tracing approach in more detail. Section 4 explains how we perform vector fusion on the traces. In Section 5 we explain how we optimize, JIT, and execute the fused code. We evaluate Riposte in Section 6 and then end with related work and discussion.

2. DESIGN OVERVIEW

We provide an overview of our system by describing how our trace-based approach will execute the simple program in Figure 1 that computes the average income of males over 40 from a dataset. This example code, while simple, uses some high-level dynamic features of R. The `incomes_of` function takes an arbitrary first-class filtering function as a parameter; the function `males_over_40` is generic and can operate on entire vectors; and the semantics of R dictate that function arguments be lazily evaluated. As Riposte executes, it separates this dynamic language functionality from the vector operations, so that the latter can be executed efficiently.

Riposte interprets the example normally until it reaches line 6. At this point the interpreter must evaluate the subexpression `a >= 40`. Since `a` is the vector `age`, R's semantics require that this operation actually perform 20 million greater-than or equal comparisons. We could execute this immediately (this is what the open source R interpreter does), but that commits us to materializing the 20 million result values, consuming substantial memory and bandwidth. Instead, the Riposte interpreter checks the length of the operands dynamically; if `a` is a long vector, we delay the `>=` instruction by inserting it into a *vector trace* (lines 1–3 of Figure 2) and inserting a *future* into the interpreter's result slot. Continuing execution, the operators `==` and `&` (line 6) are similarly recorded and delayed. The interpreter then returns a future from the function `males_over_40` instead of an actual value. In addition to simple operations, like `>=`, which operate element-wise over the array, we also delay and record instruction, like filters (`[]`, line 11) and reductions (`mean`, line 14), which change the shape of the vector.

Tracing ends when the interpreter encounters `print`. The final vector trace, shown in Figure 2, is handed to the JIT to be compiled. Note that unlike the interpreter's bytecodes, the instructions in the

```
1   age <- read.table("ages") #20 million elements
2   gender <- read.table("genders")
3   income <- read.table("incomes")
4
5   males_over_40 <- function(a,g) {
6       a >= 40 & g == 1
7   }
8
9   incomes_of <- function(filter_function) {
10      mask <- filter_function(age,gender)
11      income[mask]
12  }
13
14  print(mean(incomes_of(males_over_40)))
```

Figure 1: R code that computes the mean income for a subset of a sample, a simple data analysis task. Dynamic types and control flow (such as the dynamic function call used in `incomes_of`) make static analysis of this R code difficult. Tracing permits us to recover blocks of vector code as a first step to compilation.

```
n0 : double[1]          = constant 40
n1 : double[20M]        = load age
n2 : logical[20M]       = ge    n1 n0
n3 : double[1]          = constant 1
n4 : double[20M]        = load gender
n5 : logical[20M]       = eq    n4 n3
n6 : logical[20M]       = and   n2 n5
n7 : double[20M]        = load income
n8 : logical[20M[n6]]= filter n7 n6
n9 : double[1]          = mean n8
```

Figure 2: Vector trace generated from the example code in Figure 1. Dynamic types and control flow have been eliminated. Each instruction has both a concrete type (e.g. `double`) and shape (e.g. `20M` elements).

vector trace contain both the type (e.g. double), and shape of arrays (e.g. 20 million elements), making it possible to generate efficient code.

At this point, multiple futures exist in the interpreter's state, but some of these futures have become unreachable. The results associated with them do not have to be written out, saving memory and bandwidth. For instance, the variable `mask` holds a future referencing the output of value `n6` in the trace. But `mask` is no longer reachable because the `income_of` function has returned, so the output of `n6` does not have to be materialized.

After eliminating dead futures, we fuse together the vector trace and JIT it to hardware vector instructions (e.g. SSE), shown as pseudocode in Figure 3. The compiled code is inserted into a task queue where it is collaboratively completed by worker threads through task stealing.

Finally, the result replaces the future in the argument to `print` and the interpreter resumes computation, printing out the average income of males over 40.

We can compare Riposte's trace-based execution of this program to the standard behavior of R's interpreter. R's interpreter will execute each vector operation completely before continuing, materializing intermediates that are as large as the original arrays. In this case, intermediates are created to hold the temporaries for the results of the `>=`, `==`, and `&` operators. Further, R implements the filter

```
double2 sum = {0,0};
for(int i = 0; i < 20000000; i += 2) {
    bool2 a = age[i] >= 40;
    bool2 b = gender[i] == 1;
    bool2 c = a & b;
    double2 new_sum = sum + income[i];
    sum = blend(c,new_sum,sum);
}
double mean = (sum[0] + sum[1]) / 20000000;
```

Figure 3: Pseudocode of the generated machine code from the trace in Figure 2. It is vectorized and can be executed in parallel by multiple threads. (`blend` **is the vectorized ternary operator:** `?:`)

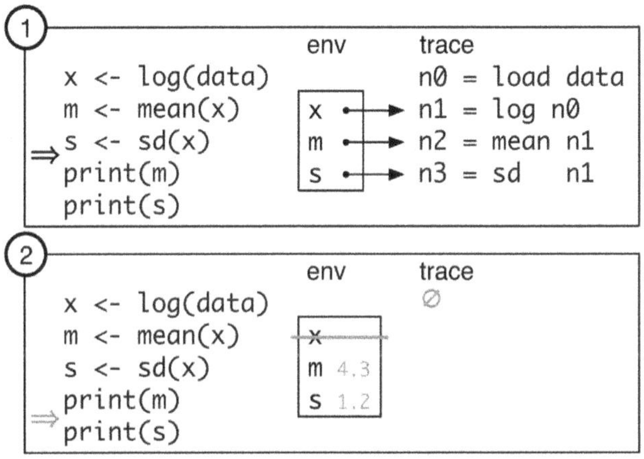

Figure 4: The state of the interpreter (1) before and (2) after executing a trace. The statement `print(m)` **requires the value for** `m`**. The value for** `s` **will be used later, so it should also be materialized to avoid recomputation. The value** `x` **is dead, so it should not be materialized.**

operator (`[]`) by first creating an array of indexes where the filter is true, and then using it to gather the list of valid incomes, creating two additional temporaries. Assuming the worst case (where the filter removes no values), the R version will need to read 9 arrays of 20 million elements, and allocate/write 5 arrays. In contrast, Riposte will only need to read the 3 input arrays. The result is that the Riposte trace-based JIT runs this example 6.5 times faster than standard R.

3. EXTRACTING VECTOR TRACES FROM DYNAMIC CODE

The following sections describe our vector tracing approach in more detail. First, we explain the deferred evaluation tracing strategy. Then we describe our liveness analysis which determines the set of trace outputs that should be materialized.

3.1 Vector Tracing via Deferred Evaluation

Tracing is typically done on scalar code [14]. In this case, one observes the execution of an early iteration of a loop, and then generates type-specialized machine code to run the remainder of the iterations. Scalar operators execute relatively quickly, so interpreting the first few iterations of the loop is feasible. In contrast, the cost of vector operations is dependent on the size of the vector. For large vectors, each individual vector operation is itself an expensive loop. If we waited until the second time we saw such vector operations before optimizing their execution, we would miss a large number of critical loops.

This leads us to use a tracing approach based on deferred evaluation. Rather than executing vector instructions immediately, we delay their execution through the creation of futures that reference entries in the vector trace. This allows us to record and compile vector operators the first time they are seen. Figure 4 (1) illustrates this process. After executing the first three instructions, the values of `x`, `m`, and `s` are futures pointing into the trace rather than concrete values. Since recording and compilation have a cost, we only delay evaluation if the lengths of the operands are long enough to amortize the overhead introduced. As we discuss in Section 5.2, this currently occurs at 512 elements.

After creating futures, the interpreter can propagate them through later instructions. Vector operations that have futures as operands can be recorded and new futures are created for their output (as with `mean` and `sd` in Figure 4). Futures used in many other operations can be propagated through unchanged. For example, futures can be assigned to variables in environments and passed to and returned from functions. Since the trace entry referenced by the future is typed, futures can also be used in dynamic dispatch without being evaluated. Vector operations in loops will be recorded multiple times as interpreter execution unrolls the loop.

Modifying the interpreter to support tracing may add overhead. A naïve approach would introduce a future check and a length check into each vector operation in the interpreter. We found that this approach can add 20% or more to the runtime of tight scalar loops. We eliminate the overhead of the future check by including futures as a built-in interpreter type and folding the check for futures into the already existing type check in each operation. We avoid the cost of the length check by placing it after special-case dispatch logic for scalar operands. Since we treat the futures as a type in the interpreter, futures can also be adapted to work with more sophisticated approaches based on inline caching [8].

The infrastructure to store and execute traced instructions requires additional memory allocations and bookkeeping. To minimize this cost, we limit the total number of traced instructions. If a trace grows too large, we simply execute it even if a future has not been requested. This allows us to use fixed-size buffers to store the trace and all compilation intermediates.

3.2 Selective Materialization through Dynamic Liveness Analysis

Our vector tracing approach produces blocks of vector code that we can easily fuse and compile, but it adds an additional complexity. Each trace can contain multiple outputs in the form of unevaluated futures in the interpreter. These outputs may be (1) required by the interpreter to continue execution, (2) required at a later point, or (3) dead (i.e. the future represents an intermediate value that is never used again). Consider Figure 4 (1). The value `m` is required by the interpreter in order to execute the next `print` statement, `s` will be needed in the next line, and `x` is never used again. There are two problems that arise in handling these outputs.

First, for outputs in group (2) there is a classic time vs. space trade off. Since they are not yet needed by the interpreter, we could delay materializing them at the cost of potentially executing the trace multiple times. Or we could materialize them the first time the trace runs at the cost of increased storage. We use the latter approach since it will never materialize more outputs than the standard R execution strategy. Thus, in Figure 4 (2), after evaluating the first `print` statement, the futures for both `m` and `s` have been materialized. In contrast, recomputing values can perform considerably worse than the current R interpreter in certain cases. In Figure 4, had we not evaluated `s` at the same time as `m`, we would have had to evaluate `x` twice, duplicating the expensive `log` operation.

Second, if we were to materialize dead outputs, we would generate unnecessary memory traffic. For example, in Figure 4, the value of `x` is never used again after the `print` statement, therefore there is no need to materialize it at all. If we fail to detect this, we will allocate and write to an unnecessary result vector.

Since static analysis of R code is difficult, we use a dynamic liveness analysis pass that determines the set of futures that are reachable from the interpreter's state. Unreachable futures are dead and their outputs can be safely eliminated. This pass is conceptually very similar to garbage collection. The most straightforward approach is to give each future a reference count, but we found that this introduces an unacceptable cost on non-vector code since each stack-stack or stack-environment move must check whether the moved value is a future before updating its reference count.

Instead, we use a strategy similar to a tracing garbage collector. While recording instructions we maintain a conservative root set containing environments and stack frames that may contain futures. This can be done entirely off the fast path since this set only changes when recording an instruction in the vector trace, along function call boundaries, and in some infrequently-used environment manipulation operations. Then, before executing the trace, we traverse the root set looking for futures. Any futures not found are known to be dead and their outputs from the trace are not materialized.

4. FUSING VECTOR TRACES

Vector fusion—combining the individual vector operations into a single loop—is important in getting high performance. In fused code, intermediate values can be stored in registers. In contrast, unfused operators store intermediates in memory. For long vectors, where the intermediates exceed the cache size, fusion will replace expensive cache misses with reads from a register.

Similar to the Stream Fusion approach [11], Riposte considers only the subset of potential fusion opportunities that will result in a single fused loop; we never generate nested loops. We have designed our vector virtual machine to make this fusion easy to derive from the vector's shape.

We first describe the design of the vector virtual machine and then show how we can use the vector shapes to group operations into fused loops.

4.1 Vector Virtual Machine

Our vector virtual machine supports immutable 1D vectors of uniform type (currently `double`, 64-bit `integer`, and `logical`, each of which also include R's special missing value `NA`). Each vector has a shape consisting of an integer length, and optionally, a *filter* defined by a logical vector and/or a *group by* defined by an integer vector.

It supports three classes of vector operations:

1. generators, e.g. `gather` (read from an already materialized vector) or `seq` (generate an arithmetic sequence),
2. unary, binary, and ternary operations mapped over vector(s), e.g. `sqrt`, `add`, or `blend`, and
3. reductions, e.g. `sum`, `min`, or `scatter` (write a new vector out to memory).

Two special operators, `filter` and `groupby` semantically change the shape of their input, but do no actual computation.

Map operators are defined to apply element-wise to all vectors regardless of shape. Thus, on grouped vectors, map operators apply to each element of each group, not to the groups themselves. In contrast, the behavior of reductions depends upon their input shape. If the shape has a *filter*, filtered elements are not included in the reduction. If the shape has a *group by*, a grouped reduction is computed. (A grouped `scatter` produces a list of vectors.)

4.2 Shape-based Fusion

The semantics of the vector virtual machine make it easy to determine that operators on vectors of the same length can always be fused. Generators, maps, and reductions on simple vectors of the same length are trivially fuseable since they have the same implicit loop iteration count and the loops are implicitly aligned. Operations on filtered vectors can be fused with operations on the unfiltered length since this translates to a simple conditional on the filter inside the fused loop. Similarly, operations on grouped vectors can also be fused with operations on the ungrouped length. This is true since maps apply element-wise regardless of the grouping and reductions can handle the grouping by generating additional code inside the loop to scatter the output to the correct location for the group.

Binary and ternary map operations can have operands with different lengths in R. R semantically handles this case by repeating the shorter operand(s) to the length of the longest one. While it might be profitable in some cases to fuse such operations, in general, repeating the shorter vector in a fused fashion can cause unnecessary repeated computation. Instead, we handle this case by always materializing the shorter operand(s) and then fusing with the longest operand. Note that handling scalar-vector operations is a special case of this heuristic—the scalar operand is materialized by the interpreter and fusion continues on the vector.

Given this heuristic, we can implement fusion by grouping vector operations by the length of their largest input. Since vector length is known as we record instructions, we implement this grouping by recording multiple length-specific traces. If we encounter an instruction with operands of different lengths, we immediately execute the trace associated with the shorter operand and then delay and record the instruction into the longer operand's trace.

5. COMPILING AND PARALLELIZING VECTOR TRACES

Riposte's just-in-time compiler transforms vector traces into executable code. Creating a compiler is typically very involved. However, an advantage of a trace-based approach is that vector traces have no control flow, simplifying the compilation process. In the following two sections, we describe our simple vector JIT. Then in the final section, we discuss scheduling the compiled traces on multiple cores.

5.1 Optimization

Since vector traces contain no control flow, standard optimizations such as constant propagation, algebraic simplification, common subexpression elimination, and dead code elimination can be implemented as single passes over the vector trace.

In addition to improving user-written expressions, these passes also improve less-than-optimal code generated by our tracing approach. For example, R vectors use 1-based indexing, but our vector language uses 0-based indexing for easier compilation. This results in traces littered with code to add and subtract 1. The algebraic simplification pass eliminates most of these. Similarly, our tracing based approach unrolls loops, which can generate many replicates of the body of the loop. Common subexpression elimination removes copies of loop invariant code.

5.2 JIT

Code generation for straight-line vector traces is simple enough that we emit x86-64 machine code directly. Our fusion approach guarantees that each trace will only contain operands of a single length, and we only have to generate code for a single loop over the vector length. We can generate the body of this loop by replacing the each variable-length vector operation in the trace with a fixed-length hardware equivalent. For the map operations this is often a single SSE instruction. But for operations not supported by the hardware instruction set, we either inline short instruction sequences or emit calls to vectorized functions. Generators are also relatively straightforward, though they must update loop-carried dependencies.

The code generation for reductions is more complicated due to `filters` and `groupbys`. A standard way to handle filters in vector code is to use predicated instructions that are disabled when the filter is false. However, x86-64 has poor support for predicated instructions. Instead, we execute all map operations regardless of the filter state, and only predicate the reductions, via an SSE blend operation or a branch. When the cardinality of a reduction's `groupby` is low, or there is no `groupby`, we maintain multiple aggregates, one per vector lane per group, allowing the reductions to be vectorized. For large cardinality reductions, this increase in the working set size can negatively impact performance; so, in these cases, we serialize the reductions and only store a single aggregate per group.

Register allocation is accomplished using the linear scan algorithm [26]. For operations whose output needs to be stored into a live future, we generate store instructions as needed. Additionally, we JIT a loop header that initializes loop-carried state, such as reduction variables or sequence iterators, in the thread-local stack space.

As a further simplification, we do not attempt to reuse vector traces. This means that the JIT does not have to generate code to guard dynamic control flow decisions or to restore the interpreter to the correct state when a guard fails. For sufficiently long vectors, the overhead of compilation is still low because it is amortized over the vector length. For the current implementation, the break-even point occurs at 512 elements. We see only incremental benefits in optimizing for vectors shorter than this. Such vectors will fit in the L1 cache, so they benefit less from fusion; they may be better addressed using standard scalar compilation techniques.

As an alternative to JIT compiling vector traces, we considered strip-mining [7, 12, 35]. However, in a preliminary experiment, we found that strip-mining performed 33% worse than JIT compilation on our BLACK-SCHOLES benchmark. Similarly, other work has reported that strip-mining performs 2 times slower than hand-written compiled code [7].

5.3 Scheduling to Multicore

The compiled code consists of a single fully fused loop which is nearly data-parallel. To partition the iterations of this loop across multiple threads there are two cases we have to handle specially: generators and reductions. Vector generation functions (e.g. `seq`) may have loop-carried dependencies. When we partition the loop iterations we have to initialize the loop-carried dependencies to their proper state. This is straightforward for the set of generators we support. We only support reductions that are commutative and associative, making them easy to parallelize. Each thread allocates separate space in different cache lines to store partial reductions so that the threads operate independently and avoid false sharing. After the computation has finished, the separate partial reductions are then aggregated together.

Table 1: Workloads

BLACK-SCHOLES	Compute 10M options
DATA CLEANING	On 20M element vector: filter invalid values, compute z-scores, and count outliers
FILTER 1-D	7-element 1-D convolution applied to a 10M element vector
HISTOGRAM	100M element vector with 100 distinct values
K-MEANS	1M 2D data points, 5 means
LOGISTIC REGRESSION	Compute via gradient descent on 30 continuous predictors with 1M data points
MANDELBROT	2048×1538 resolution in the domain $(-2,-1) \times (1,1)$
COVARIANCE MATRIX	50 variables with 1M data points
RAY-SPHERE INTERSECTION	Distance to the closest intersection of a ray with 10M spheres
SAMPLING MIXTURE OF NORMALS	Draw 10M samples from mixture of 3 normals using CDF inversion
SPARSE MATRIX-VECTOR MULTIPLICATION	$500K \times 500K$ matrix with 20M non-zero entries
TPC-H QUERY 1	Database query with filter and aggregations (Scale Factor 10 = $\sim$60M rows)

We don't yet support the output of filtered or grouped vectors without an aggregate when executing in multiple threads. Doing so correctly requires a parallel prefix scan which is not yet included in our vector language.

The fused loop is scheduled on multiple cores using Lazy Binary Splitting [33], a recent work stealing-based scheduling strategy that attempts to dynamically discover an appropriate task block size. In our experience, this has been quite robust.

6. EVALUATION

In this section we evaluate our tracing-based approach. First, we demonstrate that our trace-based vector fusion and liveness analysis can eliminate a substantial fraction of memory accesses by comparing Riposte with the open source implementation of R, which does no fusion. We show that eliminating these memory accesses achieves a substantial speed-up. Next, we compare Riposte to vectorized C code executing the same benchmarks to show that we can effectively utilize vector hardware and that vector traces can achieve very high absolute performance. Finally, we examine the scalability of our trace scheduling and show that leveraging the implicit parallelism in R vector code results in a substantial performance improvement.

We use a set of twelve workloads, shown in Table 1, covering a range of problem domains. Riposte and the open source R implementation execute nearly the same high-level R code for each workload. (In a couple cases, we had to write non-idiomatic R in order to work around severe performance limitations of its blend operation (`ifelse`). And in one case, we worked around the fact that

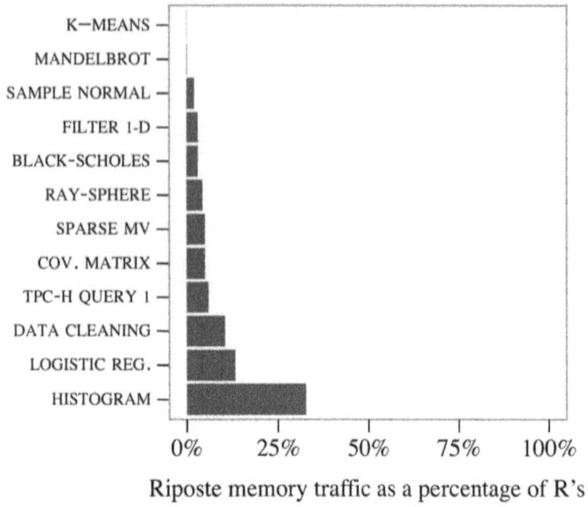

Figure 5: Vector fusion substantially reduces Riposte's main memory traffic (total number of requests to main memory, measured using hardware counters) compared to R.

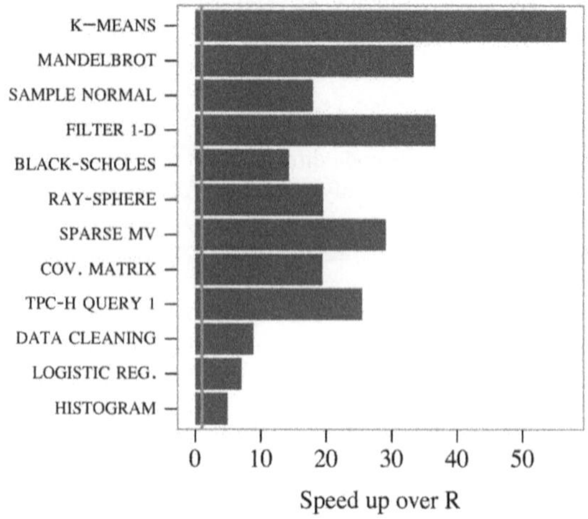

Figure 6: Performance of Riposte (including all interpreter and JIT overhead) normalized to R. The red line is at 1x (no speed-up). Riposte outperforms R on all benchmarks.

Riposte does not yet store futures in objects.) Since we are evaluating the use of vector primitives, we restricted the set of workloads to ones that can be written in vectorized R code. Thus, none of these benchmarks are bottlenecked on interpreter performance. Additionally, to clearly evaluate the benefits of runtime fusion of vector code, we also avoided calling R standard library functions which implement hand-fused sequences in C code.

To make the comparisons as fair as possible, we compiled R 2.14.2, Riposte, and our C implementations of the workloads using ICC 12.0.0. We used the flags `-O3` and `-fp-model fast` to enable ICC's floating-point optimizations and loop autovectorization. ICC failed to autovectorize half of our C implementations. We hand vectorized these cases using SSE intrinsics or the Intel SPMD Program Compiler (ISPC) [24]. We also spot-checked the generated assembly of R's vector math operations to ensure that they were correctly autovectorized. The system we used for evaluation is a shared memory machine with 4 8-core Nehalem-EX X7560 processors running at 2.2Ghz and 128GB of RAM. All measurements of speed-up are reported using the minimum execution time of 3 runs of the reference code and the maximum execution time of 3 runs of Riposte.

6.1 Effectiveness of Fusion

The goal of vector fusion is to reduce memory traffic by eliminating intermediates and by rearranging data access patterns to be more cache friendly. Figure 5 shows the main memory traffic of Riposte as a fraction of the main memory traffic of R for all our benchmarks, measured using the *offcore_response_0* counter on Intel Nehalem chips. Fusion succeeds in eliminating a substantial portion of the memory traffic. Both K-MEANS and MANDELBROT are iterative workloads and R has very high memory traffic as it repeatedly cycles the working set in and out of cache. In Riposte, fusion succeeds in reducing the working set below the L3 cache size. Thus, Riposte only touches main memory once, on the first iteration, for a substantially memory traffic reduction. In contrast, the HISTOGRAM workload is a single pass. Riposte is able to eliminate one intermediate (1 store + 1 read), but still must do the initial read, resulting in a comparatively high 33% traffic rate.

Figure 6 shows the speed of Riposte normalized to R. Speed-ups range from 5x to more than 50x. The harmonic mean speed up across all 12 workloads is 14.4x. The speed-up is roughly a function of the percent of memory accesses eliminated by fusion (note the inverse relationship between Figures 5 and 6. However, other factors such as the memory access pattern resulting from fusion and the task-specific instruction mix also affect the speed up.

For example, for workloads such as FILTER 1-D, K-MEANS, and MANDELBROT, which have a large number of simple math operators and a small set of input vectors, Riposte achieves a 35–50x speed-up. When R runs these workloads, it is extremely memory bound and there is lots of room for improvement. For other workloads that have a much larger input set, like COVARIANCE MATRIX and LOGISTIC REGRESSION, the improvements are smaller (5–20x) since the fraction of memory traffic that fusion can eliminate is lower.

6.2 Absolute Performance

We next compare Riposte to vectorized C implementations of the same tasks to evaluate absolute performance. Figure 7 shows the performance of Riposte normalized to vectorized C. The harmonic mean speed-up across all workloads is 0.74x. Despite the simplicity of our JIT compiler, Riposte performs almost as well as well-written vectorized C code, which indicates that Riposte is getting most of the speed-up possible over R.

The two slowest workloads, MANDELBROT and SAMPLE NORMAL, suffer from our lack of support for true conditional operations. We currently always generate branches as blend operations which require evaluating both sides of the branch. This is costly in these workloads because the amount of work performed in the conditional is not trivial. The lower performance of the TPC-H workload is caused by missed opportunities for common subexpression elimination because we don't decompose grouped reduction instructions.

To better understand the pay off of vectorization, we also compared Riposte to unvectorized C implementations (Figure 8). Since Riposte primarily operates on doubles and 64-bit integers, on SSE the maximum speed up possible is 2x. We achieve a more moderate 10%–50% improvement on some workloads compared to C. As vector lengths increase, we expect the payoff of vectorization to grow.

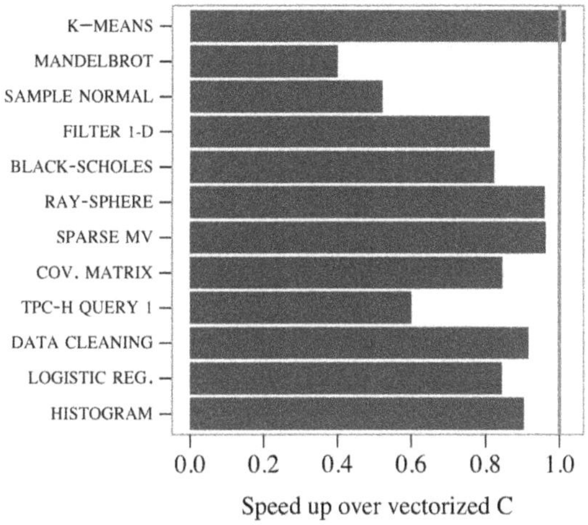

Figure 7: Performance of Riposte (including all interpreter and JIT overhead) normalized to vectorized C implementations. On average, Riposte performs within a small factor of C.

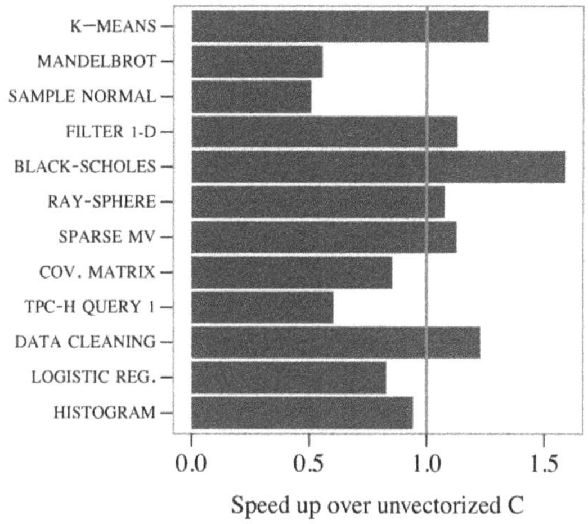

Figure 8: Performance of Riposte normalized to unvectorized C. Riposte's support for 2-wide SSE operations provides moderate performance gains on some, but not all, workloads.

6.3 Scalability

Finally, we examine the scalability of Riposte, shown in Figure 9. Most workloads demonstrate reasonable scalability out to 16 or 32 cores; some even benefit from hyper-threading.

The operating system limits scaling in DATA CLEANING and FILTER 1-D. Both read in a large vector and output a vector of similar size. Creating the new vector requires allocating fresh pages—both examples spend 30–50% of their time allocating pages. Scaling is limited by the performance of the page allocator in Linux, which has been shown to only scale to 8 cores [34].

SPARSE MATRIX-VECTOR MULTIPLICATION scales very poorly due to our simple parallel reduction strategy. We allocate separate output vectors for each thread which are merged at the end. As the number of threads grows, the amount of memory allocated for the reduction exceeds the L3 cache and performance degrades. High-cardinality reductions are a well-known challenge in parallel runtime design [36].

Riposte does not always find the maximum amount of fusion possible. For instance, the loops in COVARIANCE MATRIX are too long to unroll completely meaning that Riposte must execute the loops in multiple traces. While this introduces only minor overhead into single-threaded code, it creates a synchronization point between each trace, which limits scaling. In the standard R implementation, parallelizing individual operations yields only limited improvements because of this problem [31].

Excluding the outlying SPARSE MATRIX-VECTOR MULTIPLICATION benchmark, Riposte's overall speed up on 32 threads compared to R's scalar performance ranges from 55–670x with a harmonic mean of 155x.

7. RELATED WORK

Previous work has applied trace-based just-in-time compilation to optimize scalar code. The Dynamo optimization system traced native machine code to perform runtime optimizations [6]. Gal et al. used tracing to optimize Java bytecodes [14]. Tracing has also been used to accelerate dynamic languages such as Javascript [1, 13] or Lua [2]. Riposte adapts these techniques to vector code.

Delaying array operations in a dynamic language in order to expose opportunities for later optimization was a feature of the APL Machine [4, 19, 16], a proposed (but never built) physical machine with an APL-like instruction set. Riposte demonstrates that a similar approach, designed for modern hardware, can be effectively implemented in software.

Other work has applied vector optimizations in the context of statically compiled languages. Intel's Array Building Blocks [21] and the PeakStream platform [22] add support for array-based programming to C++ through a JIT compiler. Data-parallel Haskell, a compiled functional language, implements nested array operations using a vector machine that supports segmented operations [23]. Coutts et al. use Haskell's algebraic data-types and user-defined rewrite rules to implement static fusion of a number of "streamable" operations [11]. Keller et al. apply loop fusion on a functional representation of delayed arrays written in Haskell, and transparently parallelize the code [17].

Morandat et al. have studied the semantics and performance of the current open source R implementation [20]. Schmidberger et al. provide a good analysis of existing parallel libraries for R [29]. There are a number of other projects that have tried to improve the implementation of the R language. Tierney has developed a new bytecode interpreter for R that is progressively replacing the existing AST-walking interpreter in the standard distribution [32]. It improves the performance of scalar code. Tierney has also explored hand-fusion and parallelization of R code [31]. Milborrow has developed an experimental just-in-time compiler for R that can accelerate scalar arithmetic loops [3]. Garvin has developed an R-to-C cross compiler that also focuses on scalar performance. The CXXR project is refactoring the open source R implementation to ease future development, but it has not yet focused on performance improvements [28]. While this paper was in submission, NVIDIA released an experimental R-to-PTX compiler based on an LLVM backend [15]. Like Riposte, it does aggressive vector fusion, but is currently limited to compiling simple sequences of map operations.

The growth of big data analysis problems has created interest in making other higher-level data analytic languages more scalable. McVM [10] is a function-based JIT for Matlab. It has been used to explore static [18] and profile-based [5] optimization techniques to Matlab. Copperhead [9] compiles a statically analyzable subset of Python to GPUs.

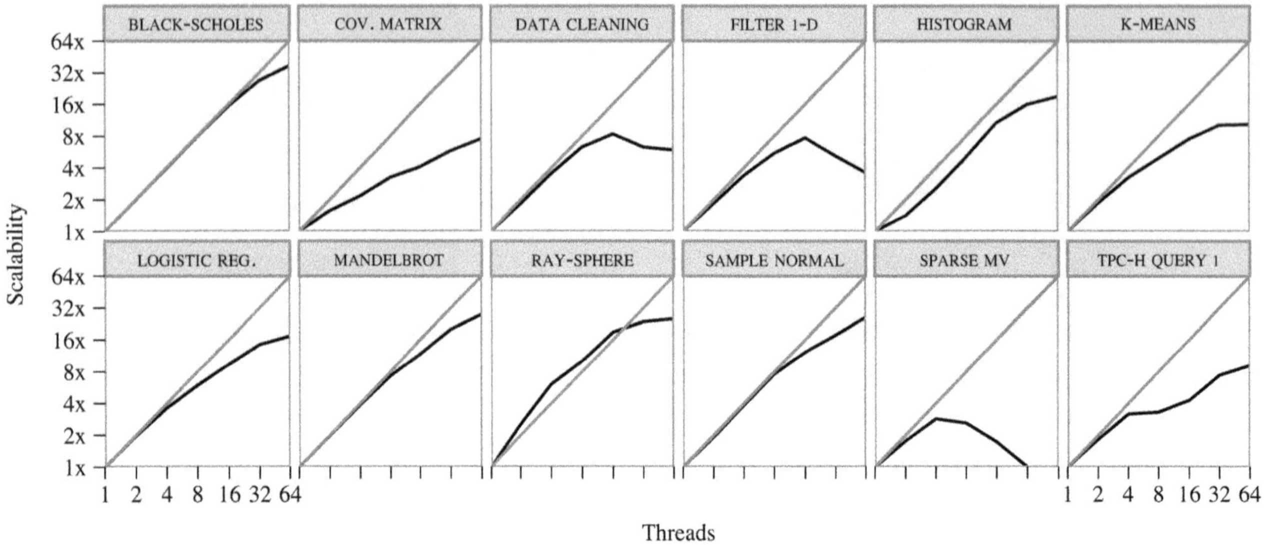

Figure 9: Scalability of Riposte on a 32-core Nehalem machine with hyperthreading. The red line is linear scalability. Riposte scales well on most workloads. The poor scalability in the SPARSE MATRIX-VECTOR MULTIPLICATION **workload is due to poor support for high-cardinality multi-threaded reductions in our current implementation.**

8. CONCLUSION

We have presented a trace-based approach for efficiently executing dynamically typed data analytic languages on modern hardware. The resulting virtual machine performs 5–50x faster than standard R—nearly as well as vectorized C code—and can scale well on multicore, shared memory machines. Thus, without changing to a statically-typed programming language or having to explicitly parallelize, R programmers using Riposte can see an overall speed-up of two orders of magnitude on interesting data analytic workloads.

Substantial work remains to be done to improve our Riposte implementation. We want to address the limitations of Riposte's current parallel runtime highlighted in our evaluation by adding support for prefix scans and a better high-cardinality reduction implementation [36]. We also want to increase the set of operators that can be delayed. This should increase the average length of traces and thus the benefits from fusion, as well as increase the likelihood that we will be able to identify futures as dead, decreasing unnecessary memory usage.

Even though Riposte currently uses an interpreter to run scalar code, we want to integrate our vector virtual machine with modern techniques for executing dynamic scalar code such as function- or trace-based JITs. We will also continue to improve the performance of our JIT compiler (currently 90% of its time is spent in the optimization passes), allowing us to compile shorter vectors profitably. These two directions will permit us to experiment with efficiently supporting short vector code and mixed scalar/vector code.

Finally, we plan to expand the design of our vector virtual machine to support compilation to newer vector architectures such as GPUs and Intel's AVX or MIC [30] architectures, and to consider the issues of scheduling vector code on distributed memory clusters.

In summary, Riposte allows data analysts to leverage emerging hardware trends to improve the performance and scale of their analyses while continuing to code easily and productively.

9. ACKNOWLEDGMENTS

This work was supported by NSF grant CCF-1111943.

10. REFERENCES

[1] Google V8 Javascript engine. `http://code.google.com/p/v8/`.

[2] The LuaJIT project. `http://http://luajit.org/`.

[3] The Ra extension to R. `http://www.milbo.users.sonic.net/ra/`.

[4] P. S. Abrams. *An APL Machine*. PhD thesis, Stanford Linear Accelerator Center, Stanford University, Stanford, CA, USA, 1970.

[5] A. Aslam and L. Hendren. McFLAT: a profile-based framework for Matlab loop analysis and transformations. In *Proceedings of the 23rd international conference on Languages and compilers for parallel computing*, LCPC'10, pages 1–15, Berlin, Heidelberg, 2011. Springer-Verlag.

[6] V. Bala, E. Duesterwald, and S. Banerjia. Dynamo: a transparent dynamic optimization system. In *Proceedings of the ACM SIGPLAN 2000 conference on Programming language design and implementation*, PLDI '00, pages 1–12, New York, NY, USA, 2000. ACM.

[7] P. A. Boncz, M. Zukowski, and N. Nes. MonetDB/X100: Hyper-Pipelining Query Execution. In *CIDR*, pages 225–237, 2005.

[8] S. Brunthaler. Inline caching meets quickening. In *Proceedings of the 24th European conference on Object-oriented programming*, ECOOP'10, pages 429–451, Berlin, Heidelberg, 2010. Springer-Verlag.

[9] B. Catanzaro, M. Garland, and K. Keutzer. Copperhead: Compiling an embedded data parallel language. In *Proceedings of the 16th ACM symposium on Principles and practice of parallel programming*, PPoPP '11, pages 47–56, New York, NY, USA, 2011. ACM.

[10] M. Chevalier-Boisvert, L. Hendren, and C. Verbrugge. Optimizing Matlab through just-in-time specialization. In R. Gupta, editor, *Compiler Construction*, volume 6011 of *Lecture Notes in Computer Science*, pages 46–65. Springer Berlin / Heidelberg, 2010. 10.1007/978-3-642-11970-5_4.

[11] D. Coutts, R. Leshchinskiy, and D. Stewart. Stream fusion: From lists to streams to nothing at all. In *Proceedings of the 12th ACM SIGPLAN international conference on Functional programming*, ICFP '07, pages 315–326, New York, NY, USA, 2007. ACM.

[12] A. Das, W. J. Dally, and P. Mattson. Compiling for stream processing. In *Proceedings of the 15th international conference on Parallel architectures and compilation techniques*, PACT '06, pages 33–42, New York, NY, USA, 2006. ACM.

[13] A. Gal, B. Eich, M. Shaver, D. Anderson, D. Mandelin, M. R. Haghighat, B. Kaplan, G. Hoare, B. Zbarsky, J. Orendorff, J. Ruderman, E. W. Smith, R. Reitmaier, M. Bebenita, M. Chang, and M. Franz. Trace-based just-in-time type specialization for dynamic languages. In *Proceedings of the 2009 ACM SIGPLAN conference on Programming language design and implementation*, PLDI '09, pages 465–478, New York, NY, USA, 2009. ACM.

[14] A. Gal, C. W. Probst, and M. Franz. HotpathVM: An effective JIT compiler for resource-constrained devices. In *Proceedings of the 2nd international conference on Virtual execution environments*, VEE '06, pages 144–153, New York, NY, USA, 2006. ACM.

[15] V. Grover and Y. Lin. Compiling CUDA and other languages for GPUs. In *GPU Technology Conference (GTC)*, 2012.

[16] L. J. Guibas and D. K. Wyatt. Compilation and delayed evaluation in APL. In *Proceedings of the 5th ACM SIGACT-SIGPLAN symposium on Principles of programming languages*, POPL '78, pages 1–8, New York, NY, USA, 1978. ACM.

[17] G. Keller, M. M. Chakravarty, R. Leshchinskiy, S. Peyton Jones, and B. Lippmeier. Regular, shape-polymorphic, parallel arrays in Haskell. In *Proceedings of the 15th ACM SIGPLAN international conference on Functional programming*, ICFP '10, pages 261–272, New York, NY, USA, 2010. ACM.

[18] N. Lameed and L. Hendren. Staged static techniques to efficiently implement array copy semantics in a Matlab JIT compiler. In *Proceedings of the 20th international conference on Compiler construction: part of the joint European conferences on theory and practice of software*, CC'11/ETAPS'11, pages 22–41, Berlin, Heidelberg, 2011. Springer-Verlag.

[19] T. C. Miller. Tentative compilation: A design for an APL compiler. *SIGAPL APL Quote Quad*, 9:88–95, May 1979.

[20] F. Morandat, B. Hill, L. Osvald, and J. Vitek. Evaluating the design of the R language. In *ECOOP 2012 Object-Oriented Programming*, Lecture Notes in Computer Science, 2012.

[21] C. Newburn, B. So, Z. Liu, M. McCool, A. Ghuloum, S. Toit, Z. G. Wang, Z. H. Du, Y. Chen, G. Wu, P. Guo, Z. Liu, and D. Zhang. Intel's Array Building Blocks: A retargetable, dynamic compiler and embedded language. In *Code Generation and Optimization (CGO) 2011*, pages 224–235, April 2011.

[22] M. Papakipos. The PeakStream platform: High productivity software development for multi-core processors. Technical report, 2006.

[23] S. Peyton Jones. Harnessing the multicores: Nested data parallelism in Haskell. In *Proceedings of the 6th Asian Symposium on Programming Languages and Systems*, APLAS '08, pages 138–138, Berlin, Heidelberg, 2008. Springer-Verlag.

[24] M. Pharr and W. R. Mark. ispc: A SPMD compiler for high-performance CPU programming. In *Proceedings of the 2012 Innovative Parallel Computing: Foundations & Applications of GPU, Manycore, and Heterogeneous Systems*, InPar '12, 2012.

[25] R. Pike, S. Dorward, R. Griesemer, and S. Quinlan. Interpreting the data: Parallel analysis with Sawzall. *Sci. Program.*, 13(4):277–298, Oct. 2005.

[26] M. Poletto and V. Sarkar. Linear scan register allocation. *ACM Trans. Program. Lang. Syst.*, 21(5):895–913, Sept. 1999.

[27] R Development Core Team. *R: A Language and Environment for Statistical Computing*. R Foundation for Statistical Computing, Vienna, Austria, 2011. ISBN 3-900051-07-0.

[28] A. R. Runnalls and C. A. Silles. CXXR: An ideas hatchery for future R development. In *Proceedings of the 2011 Joint Statistical Meetings (JSM)*, 2011.

[29] M. Schmidberger, M. Morgan, D. Eddelbuettel, H. Yu, L. Tierney, and U. Mansmann. State of the art in parallel computing with R. *Journal of Statistical Software*, 31(1):1–27, 8 2009.

[30] L. Seiler, D. Carmean, E. Sprangle, T. Forsyth, M. Abrash, P. Dubey, S. Junkins, A. Lake, J. Sugerman, R. Cavin, R. Espasa, E. Grochowski, T. Juan, and P. Hanrahan. Larrabee: A many-core x86 architecture for visual computing. In *ACM SIGGRAPH 2008 papers*, SIGGRAPH '08, pages 18:1–18:15, New York, NY, USA, 2008. ACM.

[31] L. Tierney. Code analysis and parallelizing vector operations in R. *Computational Statistics*, 24:217–223, 2009. 10.1007/s00180-008-0117-9.

[32] L. Tierney. A byte code compiler for R. Technical report, 2012.

[33] A. Tzannes, G. C. Caragea, R. Barua, and U. Vishkin. Lazy binary-splitting: A run-time adaptive work-stealing scheduler. In *Proceedings of the 15th ACM SIGPLAN Symposium on Principles and Practice of Parallel Programming*, PPoPP '10, pages 179–190, New York, NY, USA, 2010. ACM.

[34] D. Wentzlaff and A. Agarwal. Factored operating systems (FOS): The case for a scalable operating system for multicores. *SIGOPS Oper. Syst. Rev.*, 43(2):76–85, Apr. 2009.

[35] M. Wolfe. More iteration space tiling. In *Proceedings of the 1989 ACM/IEEE conference on Supercomputing*, Supercomputing '89, pages 655–664, New York, NY, USA, 1989. ACM.

[36] Y. Ye, K. A. Ross, and N. Vesdapunt. Scalable aggregation on multicore processors. In *Proceedings of the Seventh International Workshop on Data Management on New Hardware*, DaMoN '11, pages 1–9, New York, NY, USA, 2011. ACM.

[37] Y. Zhao, M. Hategan, B. Clifford, I. Foster, G. von Laszewski, V. Nefedova, I. Raicu, T. Stef-Praun, and M. Wilde. Swift: Fast, reliable, loosely coupled parallel computation. In *Services, 2007 IEEE Congress on*, pages 199 –206, July 2007.

Auto-Parallelizing Stateful Distributed Streaming Applications

Scott Schneider†, Martin Hirzel†, Buğra Gedik◇ and Kun-Lung Wu†
† IBM Thomas J. Watson Research Center, IBM Research, Hawthorne, New York, 10532, USA
◇ Department of Computer Engineering, Bilkent University, Bilkent, Ankara, 06800, Turkey
{scott.a.s,hirzel,klwu}@us.ibm.com, bgedik@cs.bilkent.edu.tr

ABSTRACT

Streaming applications transform possibly infinite streams of data and often have both high throughput and low latency requirements. They are comprised of operator graphs that produce and consume data tuples. The streaming programming model naturally exposes task and pipeline parallelism, enabling it to exploit parallel systems of all kinds, including large clusters. However, it does not naturally expose data parallelism, which must instead be extracted from streaming applications. This paper presents a compiler and runtime system that automatically extract data parallelism for distributed stream processing. Our approach guarantees safety, even in the presence of stateful, selective, and user-defined operators. When constructing parallel regions, the compiler ensures safety by considering an operator's selectivity, state, partitioning, and dependencies on other operators in the graph. The distributed runtime system ensures that tuples always exit parallel regions in the same order they would without data parallelism, using the most efficient strategy as identified by the compiler. Our experiments using 100 cores across 14 machines show linear scalability for standard parallel regions, and near linear scalability when tuples are shuffled across parallel regions.

Categories and Subject Descriptors

D.1.3 [**Programming Techniques**]: Concurrent Programming–Parallel programming; D.3.4 [**Programming Languages**]: Language Classifications–Concurrent, distributed, and parallel languages

Keywords

distributed stream processing; automatic parallelization

1. INTRODUCTION

Stream processing is a programming paradigm that naturally exposes task and pipeline parallelism. Streaming applications are directed graphs where vertices are operators and edges are data streams. Because the operators are independent of each other, and they are fed continuous streams of tuples, they can naturally execute in parallel. The only communication between operators is through the streams that connect them. When operators are connected in chains, they expose inherent pipeline parallelism. When the same streams are fed to multiple operators that perform distinct tasks, they expose inherent task parallelism.

Being able to easily exploit both task and pipeline parallelism makes the streaming paradigm popular in domains such as telecommunications, financial trading, web-scale data analysis, and social media analytics. These domains require high throughput, low latency applications that can scale with both the number of cores in a machine, and with the number of machines in a cluster. Such applications contain user-defined operators (for domain-specific algorithms), operator-local state (e.g., for aggregation or enrichment), and dynamic selectivity[1] (e.g., for data-dependent filtering, compression, or time-based windows).

While pipeline and task parallelism occur naturally in stream graphs, data parallelism requires intervention. In the streaming context, data parallelism involves splitting data streams and replicating operators. The parallelism obtained through replication can be more well-balanced than the inherent parallelism in a particular stream graph, and is easier to scale to the resources at hand. Such data parallelism allows operators to take advantage of additional cores and hosts that the task and pipeline parallelism are unable to exploit.

Extracting data parallelism by hand is possible, but is usually cumbersome. Developers must identify where potential data parallelism exists, while at the same time considering if applying data parallelism is safe. The difficulty of developers doing this optimization by hand grows quickly with the size of the application and the interaction of the subgraphs that comprise it. After identifying where parallelism is both possible and legal, developers may have to enforce ordering on their own. All of these tasks are tedious and error-prone—exactly the kind of tasks that compiler optimizations should handle for developers. As hardware grows increasingly parallel, automatic exploitation of parallelism will become an expected compiler optimization.

Prior work on auto-parallelizing streaming applications is either unsafe [17, 22], or safe but restricted to stateless operators and static selectivity [10, 21]. Our work is the first to automatically exploit data parallelism in streaming ap-

[1]Selectivity is the number of tuples produced per tuples consumed; e.g., selectivity 0.1 means produce 1 tuple for every 10 consumed.

PACT'12, September 19–23, 2012, Minneapolis, Minnesota, USA.

plications with stateful and dynamic operators. Our compiler analyzes the code to determine which subgraphs can be parallelized with which technique. The runtime system implements the various techniques (round-robin or hashing, with sequence numbers as needed) to back the compiler's decisions. We implemented our automatic data parallelization in SPL [13], the stream processing language for System S [1]. System S is a high-performance streaming platform running on a cluster of commodity machines. The compiler is oblivious to the actual size and configuration of the cluster, and only decides which operators belong to which parallel region, but not the degree of parallelism. The actual degree of parallelism in each region is decided at job submission time, which can adapt to system conditions at that moment. This decoupling increases performance portability of streaming applications.

This paper makes the following contributions:

- Language and compiler support for automatically discovering safe parallelization opportunities in the presence of stateful and user-defined operators.
- Runtime support for enforcing safety while exploiting the concrete number of cores and hosts of a given distributed, shared-nothing cluster.
- A side-by-side comparison of the fundamental techniques used to maintain safety in the design space of streaming optimizations.

2. DATA PARALLELISM IN STREAMING

This paper is concerned with extracting data parallelism by replicating operators. In a streaming context, replication of operators is data parallelism because each replica of an operator performs the same task on a different portion of the data. Data parallelism has the advantage that it is not limited by the number of operators in the original stream graph. Our auto-parallelizer is *automatic*, *safe*, and *system independent*. It is automatic, since the source code of the application does not indicate parallel regions. It is safe, since the observable behavior of the application is unchanged. And it is system independent, since the compiler forms parallel regions without hard-coding their degree of parallelism.

Our programming model is asynchronous, which is in direct contrast to synchronous data flow languages [16] such as StreamIt [10]. In synchronous data flow, the selectivity of each operator is known statically, at compile time. Compilers can create a static schedule for the entire stream graph, which specifies exactly how many tuples each operator will consume and produce every time it fires. Such static schedules enable aggressive compile-time optimizations, making synchronous data flow languages well suited for digital signal processors and embedded devices.

As our programming model is asynchronous, operators can have dynamic selectivity. We can still use static analysis to classify an operator's selectivity, but unlike synchronous languages, the classification may be a range of values rather than a constant. Such dynamic selectivity means that the number of tuples produced per tuples consumed can depend on runtime information. As a result, we cannot always produce static schedules for our stream graphs. Our operators consume one tuple at a time, and determine at runtime how many (if any) tuples to produce. This dynamic behavior is often required for big-data stream processing.

```
composite Main {
 type
  Entry = tuple<uint32 uid, rstring server, rstring msg>;
  Summary = tuple<uint32 uid, int32 total>;
 graph
  stream<Entry> Messages = ParSrc() {
   param  servers:     "logs.*.com";
          partitionBy: server;
  }
  stream<Summary> Summaries = Aggregate(Messages) {
   window Messages:    tumbling, time(5), partitioned;
   param  partitionBy: uid;
   output Summaries: uid = Any(uid), total = Count();
  }
  stream<Summary> Suspects = Filter(Summaries) {
   param  filter:      total > 100;
  }
  () as Sink = FileSink(Suspects) {
   param  file:        "suspects.csv";
          format:      csv;
  }
}
```

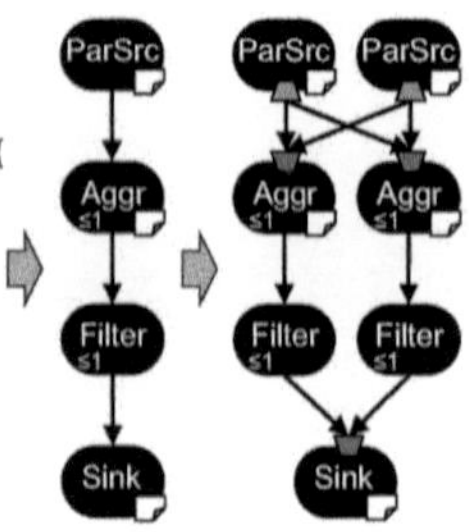

Figure 1: Example SPL program (left), its stream graph (middle), and the parallel transformation of that graph (right). The paper icons in the lower right of an operator indicate that that operator has state, and the numbers in the lower left indicate that operator's selectivity.

Another way of thinking about selectivity is the consumption to production ratio. In synchronous data flow, the ratio is $m : n$, where m and n can be any integers, but they must be known statically. In our model, the general ratio is $1 : *$. When an operator fires, it always consumes a single tuple, but it can produce any number of output tuples, including none. This number can be different at each firing, hence we call this dynamic selectivity.

Figure 1 presents a sample SPL program [13] on the left. The program is a simplified version of a common streaming application: network monitoring. The application continually reads server logs, aggregates the logs based on user IDs, looks for unusual behavior, and writes the results to a file.

The types Entry and Summary describe the structure of the *tuples* in this application. A tuple is a data item consisting of attributes, where each attribute has a type (such as uint32) and a name (such as uid). The stream graph consists of operator invocations, where operators transform streams of a particular tuple type.

The first operator invocation, ParSrc, is a source, so it does not consume any streams. It produces an output stream called Messages, and all tuples on that stream are of type Entry. The ParSrc operator takes two parameters. The partitionBy parameter indicates that the data is *partitioned* on the server attribute that is a part of tuple type Entry. We consider {server} to be the partitioning *key* for this operator.

The Aggregate operator invocation consumes the Messages stream, indicated by being "passed in" to the Aggregate operator. The window clause specifies the tuples to operate on, and the output clause describes how to aggregate input tuples (of type Entry) into output tuples (of type Summary). This operator is also partitioned, but this time the key is the uid attribute of the Entry tuples. Because the Aggregate operator is stateful, we consider this operator invocation to have *partitioned state*. The Aggregate operator maintains separate aggregations for each instance of the partitioning key ({uid} in this case). In general, programmers can provide multiple attributes to partitionBy, and each attribute is used in combination to create the partitioning key. The operator maintains separate state for each partitioning key.[2]

[2]In our runtime, operators maintain a map of keys to their associated

The Filter operator invocation drops all tuples from the aggregation that have no more than 100 entries. Finally, the FileSink operator invocation writes all of the tuples that represent anomalous behavior to a file.

The middle of Figure 1 shows the stream graph that programmers reason about. In general, SPL programs can specify arbitrary graphs, but the example consists of just a simple pipeline of operators. We consider the stream graph from the SPL source code the *sequential semantics*, and our work seeks to preserve such semantics. The right of Figure 1 shows the stream graph that our runtime will actually execute. First, the compiler determines that the first three operators have data parallelism, and it allows the runtime to replicate those operators. The operator instances ParSrc and Aggregate are partitioned on different keys. Because the keys are incompatible, the compiler instructs the runtime to perform a *shuffle* between them, so the correct tuples are routed to the correct operator replica. The Filter operator instances are stateless and can accept any tuple. Hence, tuples can flow directly from the Aggregate replicas to the Filter replicas, without another shuffle. Finally, the FileSink operator instance is not parallelizable, which implies that there must be a merge before it to ensure it sees tuples in the same order as in the sequential semantics.

Note that there are no programmer annotations in the SPL code to enable the extraction of data parallelism. Our compiler inspects the SPL code, performs the allowable transformations to the graph, and informs the runtime how to safely execute the application. The operators themselves are written in C++ or Java and have operator models describing their behavior. Our compiler uses these operator models in conjunction with SPL code inspection to extract data parallelism. While this program is entirely declarative, SPL allows programmers to embed custom, imperative logic in operator invocations. Our static analysis includes such custom logic that is expressed in SPL. Many applications do *not* implement their own operators, and instead only use existing operators. In our example, operators Aggregate, Filter and FileSink come from the SPL Standard Toolkit, and operator ParSrc is user-defined.

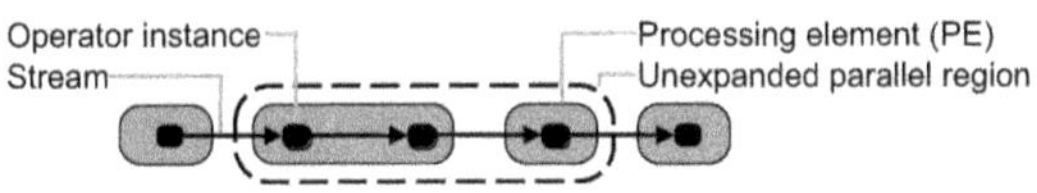

Figure 2: Stream graph, from the compiler's perspective.

Parts of the stream graph that the compiler determines are safe to parallelize are called *parallel regions*. To be system independent, the compiler produces *unexpanded parallel regions* as shown in Figure 2. Besides auto-parallelization, another important streaming optimization is fusion [10, 15]. Fusion combines multiple operators into a single operating-system process to reduce communication overhead. We refer to fused operators as *PE*s (processing elements). Our compiler ensures that PEs never span parallel region boundaries.

The runtime expands parallel regions by replicating their PEs as shown in Figure 3. A *port* is the point where a PE and a stream connect. The runtime implements *split* as a special form of output port, and *merge* as a special form

state. Operators obtain keys by hashing the values of the attributes from the partitioning set. So, given a state map, a current tuple and the set of partitioning attributes {a1–an}, each operator firing accesses state[partition(tuple.a1, tuple.a2, ..., tuple.an)].

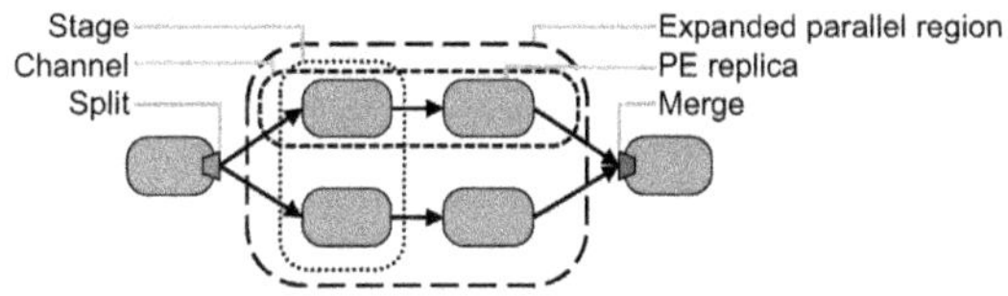

Figure 3: Stream graph, from the runtime's perspective.

of input port. We refer to each path through an expanded parallel region as a *channel*. The set of replicas of the same PE is called a *stage*.

Finally, our runtime is distributed. Each PE can run on a separate host machine, which means that we must carefully consider what information to communicate across PEs.

3. COMPILER

The compiler's task is to decide which operator instances belong to which parallel regions. Furthermore, the compiler picks implementation strategies for each parallel region, but not the degree of parallelism. One can think of the compiler as being in charge of safety while avoiding platform-dependent profitability decisions.

3.1 Safety Conditions

This section lists sufficient pre-conditions for auto-parallelization. As usual in compiler optimization, our approach is conservative: the conditions may not always be necessary, but they imply safety. The conditions for parallelizing an individual operator instance are:

- ***No state or partitioned state:*** The operator instance must be either stateless, or its state must be a map where the *key* is a set of attributes from the input tuple. Each time the operator instance fires, it only updates its state for the given key. This makes it safe to parallelize by giving each operator replica a disjoint partition of the key domain.
- ***Selectivity of at most one:*** As mentioned before, selectivity is the number of output tuples per input tuple. Requiring selectivity ≤ 1 enables the runtime to implement ordering with a simple sequence number scheme. Note that unlike synchronous data flow [16], SPL supports dynamic selectivity. For example, a filtering operator can have data-dependent predicates where it drops some tuples, but forwards others. Such an operator has a selectivity of ≤ 1, as the consumption to production ratio is $1 : [0, 1]$.
- ***At most one predecessor and successor:*** The operator instance must have fan-in and fan-out ≤ 1. This means parallel regions have a single entry and exit where the runtime can implement ordering.

The conditions for forming larger parallel regions with multiple operator instances are:

- ***Compatible keys:*** If there are multiple stateful operator instances in the region, their keys must be compatible. A key is a set of attributes, and keys are compatible if their intersection is non-empty. Parallel regions are not required to have the exact same partitioning as the operators they contain so long as the region's partitioning key is formed from attributes that all operators in the region are also partitioned on. In other words, the partitioning cannot degenerate to the empty key, where there is only a single partition. It is safe to use a coarser partitioning at the parallel region level because it acts as first-level routing. The operators themselves can still be partitioned on a finer grained key, and that finer grained routing will happen inside the operator itself.

- ***Forwarded keys:*** Care must be taken that the region key as seen by a stateful operator instance o indeed has the same value as at the start of the parallel region. This is because the split at the start of the region uses the key to route tuples, whereas o uses the key to access its partitioned state map. All operator instances along the way from the split to o must forward the key unchanged. In other words, they must copy the attributes of the region key unmodified from input tuples to output tuples.
- ***Region-local fusion dependencies:*** SPL programmers can influence fusion decisions with pragmas. If the pragmas require two operator instances to be fused into the same PE, and one of them is in a parallel region, the other one must be in the same parallel region. This ensures that the PE replicas after expansion can be placed on different hosts of the cluster.

3.2 Compiler Analysis

This section describes how the compiler establishes the safety conditions from the previous section. We must first distinguish an operator definition from an operator invocation. The *operator definition* is a template, such as an Aggregate operator. It provides different configuration options, such as what window to aggregate over or which function (Count, Avg, etc.) to use. Since users have domain-specific code written in C++ or Java, we support user-defined operators that encapsulate such code. Each operator definition comes with an *operator model* describing its configuration options to the compiler. The *operator invocation* is written in SPL and configures a specific instance of the operator, as shown in Figure 1. The operator instance is a vertex in the stream graph.

We take a two-pronged approach to establishing safety conditions: *program analysis* for operator invocations in SPL, and *properties* in the operator model for operator definitions. This is a pragmatic approach, and requires some trust: if the author of the operator deceives the compiler by using the wrong properties in the operator model, then our optimization may be unsafe. This situation is analogous to what happens in other multi-lingual systems. For instance, the Java keyword **final** is a property that makes a field of an object immutable. However, the author of the Java code may be lying, and actually modify the field through C++ code. The Java compiler cannot detect this. By correctly modeling standard library operators, and choosing safe defaults for new operators that can then be overridden by their authors, we discharge our part of the responsibility for safety.

The following flags in the operator model support auto-parallelization. The default for each is Unknown.

- state $\in$ {Stateless, ParameterPartitionBy, Unknown}.
  In the ParameterPartitionBy case, the partitionBy parameter in the operator invocation specifies the key.
- selectivity $\in$ {ExactlyOne, NoParamFilter, AtMostOne, Unknown}.
  In the NoParamFilter case, the selectivity is $= 1$ if the operator invocation specifies no filter parameter, and ≤ 1 otherwise. (In SPL, filter parameters are optional predicates which determine if the operator will drop a tuple, or send it downstream.) Using consumption to production ratios, a selectivity of $= 1$ is $1:1$, ≤ 1 is $1:[0,1]$ and Unknown is $1:[0,\infty)$.
- forwarding $\in$ {Always, FunctionAny, Unknown}.
  In the Always case, all attributes are forwarded unless the operator invocation explicitly changes or drops them. The FunctionAny case is used for aggregate operators, which forward only attributes that use an Any function in the operator invocation.

In most cases, analyzing an SPL operator invocation is straightforward given its operator model. However, operator invocations can also contain imperative code, which may affect safety conditions. State can be affected by mutating expressions such as n++ or foo(n), if function foo modifies its parameter or is otherwise stateful. SPL's type system supports the analysis by making parameter mutability and statefulness of functions explicit [13]. Selectivity can be affected if the operator invocation calls submit to send tuples to output streams. Our compiler uses data-flow analysis to count submit-calls. If submit-calls appear inside of if-statements, the analysis computes the minimum and maximum selectivity along each path. If submit-calls appear in loops, the analysis assumes that selectivity is Unknown.

3.3 Parallel Region Formation

After the compiler analyzes all operator instances to determine the properties that affect safety, it forms parallel regions. In general, there is an exponential number of possible choices, so we employ a simple heuristic to pick one. This leads to a faster algorithm and more predictable results for users.

Our heuristic is to always form regions left-to-right. In other words, the compiler starts parallel regions as close to sources as possible, and keeps adding operator instances as long as all safety conditions are satisfied. This is motivated by the observation that in practice, more operators are selective than prolific, since streaming applications tend to reduce the data volume early to reduce overall cost [26]. Furthermore, our policy of only parallelizing operator instances with selectivity ≤ 1 ensures that the number of tuples in a region shrinks from left to right. Therefore, our left-to-right heuristic minimizes the number of tuples traveling across region boundaries, where they incur split or merge costs.

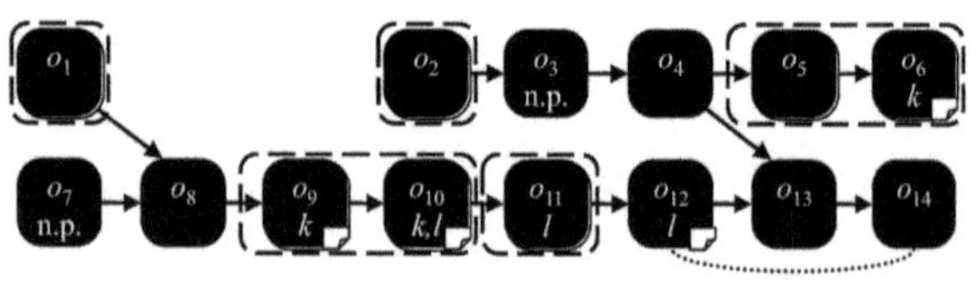

Figure 5: Parallel region formation example. Operator instances labeled "n.p." are not parallelizable, for example, due to unknown state or selectivity > 1. The letters k and l indicate key attributes. The dotted line from o_{12} to o_{14} indicates a fusion dependency. Dashed ovals indicate unexpanded parallel regions as in Figure 2. The paper icons in the lower right of an operator indicate the operator is stateful.

The example stream graph in Figure 5 illustrates our algorithm. The first parallel region contains just o_1, since its successor o_8 violates the fan-in $= 1$ condition. Similarly, the

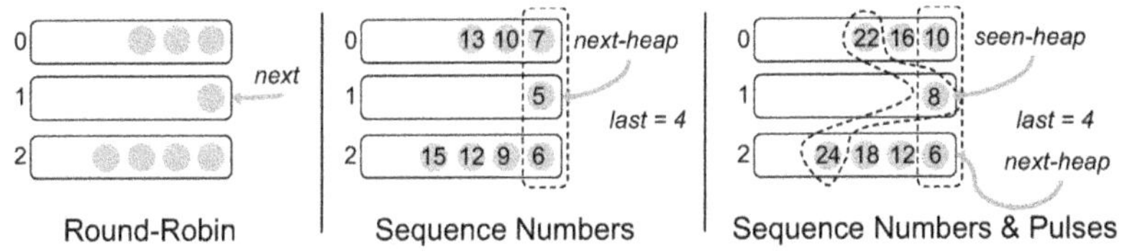

Figure 4: Merge ordering mechanisms after receiving a new tuple.

next region contains just o_2, since its successor o_3 is "n.p." (not parallelizable). Operator instances o_5 and o_6 are combined in a single region, since o_5 is stateless and o_6 has state partitioned by key $\{k\}$. The region with o_9 and o_{10} ends before o_{11}, because adding o_{11} would lead to an empty region key. This illustrates our left-to-right heuristic: another safe alternative would have been to combine o_{10} with o_{11} instead of o_9. Finally, o_{12} is not in a parallel region, because it has a fusion dependency with o_{14}. (Recall that programmers can request that multiple operators be fused together into one PE.) That means they would have to be in the same parallel region, but o_{13} is in the way and violates the fan-in = 1 condition.

3.4 Implementation Strategy Selection

Besides deciding which operator instances belong to which parallel region, the compiler also decides the implementation strategy for each parallel region. We refer to the single entry and single exit of a region as the *first joint* and *last joint*, respectively. The first joint can be a parallel source, split, or shuffle. Likewise, the last joint can be a parallel sink, merge, or shuffle. The compiler decides the joint types, as well as their implementation strategies. Later, the runtime picks up these decisions and enforces them.

Our region formation algorithm keeps track of the region key and overall selectivity as it incrementally adds operator instances to the region. When it is done forming a region, the compiler uses the key to pick a tuple-routing strategy (for example, hashing), and it uses the selectivity to pick an ordering strategy (for example, round-robin). After region formation, the compiler inserts shuffles between each pair of adjacent parallel regions, and adjusts their joint types and ordering strategies accordingly.

4. RUNTIME

The runtime has two primary tasks: route tuples to parallel channels, and enforce tuple ordering. Parallel regions should be semantically equivalent to their sequential counterparts. In a streaming context, that equivalence is maintained by ensuring that the same tuples leave parallel regions in the same order regardless of the number of parallel channels.

The distributed nature of our runtime—PEs can run on separate hosts—has influenced every design decision. We favored a design which does not add out-of-band communication between PEs. Instead, we either attach the extra information the runtime needs for parallelization to the tuples themselves, or add it to the stream.

4.1 Splitters and Mergers

Routing and ordering are achieved through the same mechanisms: *splitters* and *mergers* in the PEs at the edges of parallel regions (as shown in Figure 3). Splitters exist on the output ports of the last PE before the parallel region. Their job is to route tuples to the appropriate parallel channel, and add any information needed to maintain proper tuple ordering. Mergers exist on the input ports of the first PE after the parallel region. Their job is to take all of the different streams from each parallel channel and merge those tuples into one, well-ordered output stream. The splitter and merger must perform their jobs invisibly to the operators both inside and outside the parallel region.

	= 1	≤ 1	unknown
no state	round-robin	seqno & pulses	*n/a*
partitioned state	seqno	seqno & pulses	*n/a*
unknown state	*n/a*	*n/a*	*n/a*

Table 1: Ordering strategies determined by state and selectivity. Entries marked *n/a* are not parallelized.

4.2 Routing

When parallel regions only have stateless operators, the splitters route tuples in round-robin fashion, regardless of the ordering strategy. When parallel regions have partitioned state, the splitter uses all of the attributes that define the partition key to compute a hash value. That hash value is then used to route the tuple, ensuring that the same attribute values are always routed to the same operators.

4.3 Ordering

There are three different ordering strategies: round-robin, sequence numbers, and sequence numbers and pulses. The situations in which the three strategies must be employed depend on the presence of state and the region's selectivity, as shown in Table 1.

Internally, all kinds of mergers maintain queues for each channel. PEs work on a push, not a pull basis. So a PE will likely receive many tuples from a channel, even though the merger is probably not yet ready to send those tuples downstream. The queues exist so that the merger can accept tuples from the transport layer, and then later pop them off of the queues as dictated by their ordering strategy.

In fact, all of the merging strategies follow the same algorithm when they receive a tuple. Upon receiving a tuple from the transport layer, the merge places that tuple into the appropriate queue. It then attempts to drain the queues as much as possible based on the status of the queues and its ordering strategy. All of the tuples in each queue *are* ordered. If a tuple appears ahead of another tuple in the same channel queue, then we know that it must be submitted downstream first. Mergers, then, are actually performing a merge across ordered sources. Several of the ordering strategies take advantage of this fact.

4.3.1 Round-Robin

The simplest ordering strategy is *round-robin*, and it can only be employed with parallel regions that have stateless operators with a selectivity of 1. Because there is no state, the splitter has the freedom to route any tuple to any parallel channel. On the other end, the merger can exploit the fact that there will always be an output tuple for every input tuple. Tuple ordering can be preserved by enforcing that the merger pops tuples from the channel queues in the same order that the splitter sends them.

The left side of Figure 4 shows an example of a round-robin merge. The merger has just received a tuple on channel 1. Channel 1 is *next* in the round-robin order, so the merger will submit the tuple on channel 1. It will also submit the front tuples on 2 and 0, and will once again wait on 1.

4.3.2 Sequence Numbers

The second ordering strategy is *sequence numbers*, where the splitter adds a sequence number to each outgoing tuple. The PE runtime inside of each parallel channel is responsible for ensuring that sequence numbers are preserved; if a tuple with sequence number x is the cause of an operator sending a tuple, the resulting tuple must also carry x as its sequence number. When tuples have sequence numbers, the merger's job is to submit tuples downstream in sequential order.

The merger maintains order by keeping track of the sequence number of the last tuple it submitted. If that sequence number is y, then it knows that the next tuple to be submitted must be $y + 1$; this condition holds because sequence numbers without pulses are used only when the selectivity is 1. The merger also maintains a minimum-heap of the head of each channel queue. The top of the heap is the tuple with the lowest sequence number across all of the channel queues; it is the best candidate to be submitted. We call this heap the *next-heap*. Using a heap ensures that obtaining the next tuple to submit (as required during a drain) is a $\log N$ operation where N is the number of incoming channels.

The middle of Figure 4 shows an example of a sequence number merge which has just received a tuple on channel 1. The merger uses the *next-heap* to keep track of the lowest sequence number across all channel queues. In this instance, it knows that $last = 4$, so the next tuple to be submitted must be 5. The top of the next-heap is 5, so it is submitted. Tuples 6 and 7 are also drained from their queues, and the merger is then waiting for 8.

4.3.3 Sequence Numbers and Pulses

The most general strategy is *sequence numbers and pulses*, which permits operators with selectivity less than 1, meaning they may drop tuples. In that case, if the last tuple to be submitted was y, the merger cannot wait until $y + 1$ shows up—it may *never* come. But the merger cannot simply use a timeout either, because the channel that $y+1$ would come in on may simply be slow. The merger must handle a classic problem in distributed systems: discriminating between something that is gone, and something that is merely slow.

Pulses solve this problem. The splitter periodically sends a pulse on all channels, and the length of this period is an *epoch*. Each pulse receives the same sequence number, and pulses are merged along with tuples. Operators in parallel channels forward pulses regardless of their selectivity; even an operator that drops all tuples will still forward pulses.

The presence of pulses guarantees that the merger will receive information on all incoming channels at least once per epoch. The merger uses pulses and the fact that all tuples and pulses come in sequential order on a channel to infer when a tuple has been dropped. In addition to the *next-heap*, the merger maintains an additional minimum-heap of the tuples last seen on each channel, which are the backs of the channel queues. This heap keeps track of the minimum of the maximums; the back of each channel queue is the highest sequence number seen on that channel, and the top of this heap is the minimum of those. We call this heap the *seen-heap*. Using a heap ensures that finding the min-of-the-maxes is a $\log N$ operation.

Consider the arrival of the tuple with sequence number z. As in the sequence number case, if $z - 1 = last$ where $last$ is the sequence number of the tuple submitted last, then z is ready to be submitted. If that is not the case, we may still submit z if we have enough information to infer that tuple $z - 1$ has been dropped. The top of the seen-heap can provide that information: if $z - 1$ is less than the top of the seen-heap, then we know for certain that $z - 1$ is never coming. Recall that the top of the seen-heap is the lowest sequence number among the backs of the channel queues (the min-of-the-maxes), and that the channel queues are in sequential order. So we use the seen-heap to check the status of *all* of the channels. And if $z - 1$ (the tuple that z must wait on) is less than the backs of all of the channel queues, then it is impossible for $z - 1$ to arrive on *any* channel.

The right of Figure 4 shows an example of a sequence number and pulses merger that has just received a tuple on channel 1. In addition to the next-heap, the merger uses the seen-heap to track the lowest sequence number among the backs of the queues. In this instance, $last = 4$, so the merger needs to either see 5 or be able to conclude it is never coming. After 8 arrives on channel 1 and becomes the top of the seen-heap, the merger is able to conclude that 5 is never coming—the top of the seen-heap is the lowest sequence number of the backs of the queues, and $5 < 8$. The merger then submits 6, and it also has enough information to submit 8. It cannot submit 10 because it does not have enough information to determine if 9 has been dropped.

4.4 Shuffles

When the compiler forms parallel regions (Section 3.3), it aggressively tries to merge adjacent regions. Adjacent parallel regions that are not merged are sequential bottlenecks. When possible, the compiler merges parallel regions by simply removing adjacent mergers and splitters. Section 3.1 lists the safety conditions for when merging parallel regions is possible. However, when adjacent parallel regions have incompatible keys, they cannot be merged. Instead, the compiler inserts a shuffle: all channels of the left parallel region end with a split, and all channels of the right parallel region begin with a merge. Shuffles preserve safety while avoiding a sequential bottleneck.

In principle, shuffles are just splits and merges at the edges of adjacent parallel regions. However, splits and merges in a shuffle modify their default behavior, as shown in Figure 7.

Ordinary splitters have both routing and ordering responsibilities. The ordering responsibility for an ordinary splitter is to create and attach sequence numbers (if needed) to each outgoing tuple. When tuples arrive at a splitter in a shuffle, those tuples already have sequence numbers. The PE itself preserves sequence numbers, so a splitter in a shuffle only has routing responsibilities. Splitters inside of a shuffle also

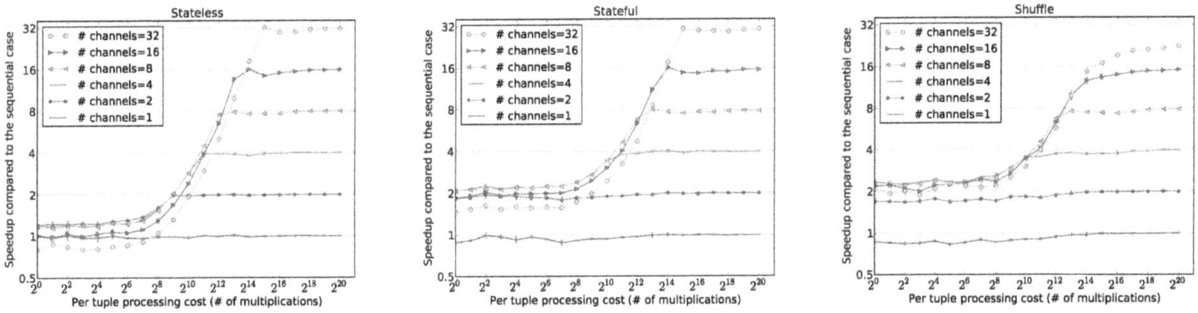

Figure 6: Scalability benchmarks.

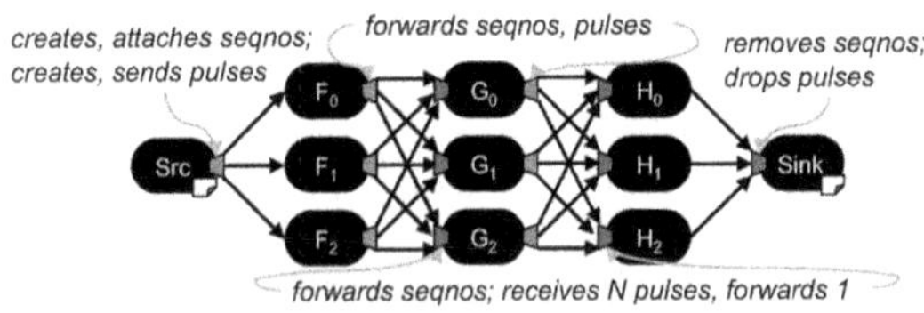

Figure 7: Splitter and merger responsibilities in a shuffle.

do not generate pulses; they were already generated by the splitter at the beginning of the parallel region.

When mergers exist at the edge of parallel regions, they are responsible for stripping off the sequence numbers from tuples and dropping pulses. Mergers that are a part of a shuffle must preserve sequence numbers and pulses. But they cannot do so naively, since mergers inside of a shuffle will actually receive N copies of every pulse, where N is the number of parallel channels. The split before them has to forward each pulse it receives to all of the mergers in the shuffle, meaning that each merger will receive a copy of each pulse. The merger prevents this problem from exploding by ensuring that only one copy of each pulse is fowarded on through the channel. If the merger did not drop duplicated pulses, then the number of pulses that arrived at the final merger would be on the order of N^s where s is the number of stages connected by shuffles.

5. RESULTS

We use three classes of benchmarks. The scalability benchmarks are designed to show that simple graphs with data parallelism will scale using our techniques. Our microbenchmarks are designed to measure the overhead of runtime mechanisms that are necessary to ensure correct ordering. Finally, we use five application kernels to show that our techniques can improve the performance of stream graphs inspired by real applications.

All of our experiments were performed on machines with 2 Intel Xeon processors where each processor has 4 cores. In total, each machine has 8 cores and 64 GB of memory.

Our *Large-scale* experiment uses 112 cores across 14 machines. The large-scale experiments demonstrate the inherent scalability of our runtime, and indicate that the linear trends seen in the other experiments are likely to continue. The remainder of our experiments use 4 machines connected with Infiniband.

We vary the amount of work per tuple on the x-axis, where work is the number of integer multiplications performed per tuple. We scale this exponentially so that we can explore how our system behaves with both very cheap and very expensive tuples. When there is little work per tuple, scalability will be more difficult to achieve because the parallelization overhead will be significant compared to the actual work. Hence, the low end of the spectrum—the left side of the x-axis—is more sensitive to the runtime parallelization overheads. The high end of the spectrum—the right side of the x-axis—shows the scalability that is possible when there is sufficient work.

All data points in our experiments represent the average of at least three runs, with error bars showing the standard deviation.

5.1 Scalability Benchmarks

The scalability benchmarks, Figure 6, demonstrate our runtime's scalability across a wider range of parallel channels. These experiments use 4 machines (32 cores). When there is a small amount of work per tuple (left side of the x-axis), these experiments also show how sensitive the runtime is to having more active parallel channels than exploitable parallelism.

The *Stateless* scalability experiment has a stream graph with a single stateless operator inside of a parallel region. Because the operator in the parallel region is stateless, the compiler recognizes that the runtime can use the least expensive ordering strategy, round-robin. Hence, we observe linear scalability, up to 32 times the sequential case when 32 parallel channels are used with 32 cores available. Just as importantly, when there is very little work—when the amount of work to be done is closer to the parallelization cost—additional parallel channels do not harm performance.

The stream graph is the same for the *Stateful* scalability experiment, but the operator is an aggregator that has local state. The compiler instructs the runtime to use sequence numbers and pulses to ensure proper ordering. The scalability is linear for 2–16 parallel channels, and achieves 31.3 times the sequential case for 32 parallel channels when using 32 cores. However, all cases see some performance improvement with very inexpensive work, with all but the 32-channel cases never dropping below 2 times improvement. The 32-channel case never has less than 1.4 time improvement for very inexpensive work. This result indicates that our runtime has little overhead. Note that in the *Stateful* experiment, inexpensive work exhibits more than 2 times improvement for 1–8 channels, which is not the case with the *Stateless* experiment. Even though the per-tuple cost is the same for both experiments, the aggregation itself adds a fixed cost. Hence, operators in the *Stateful* experiment do more work than operators in the *Stateless* experiment.

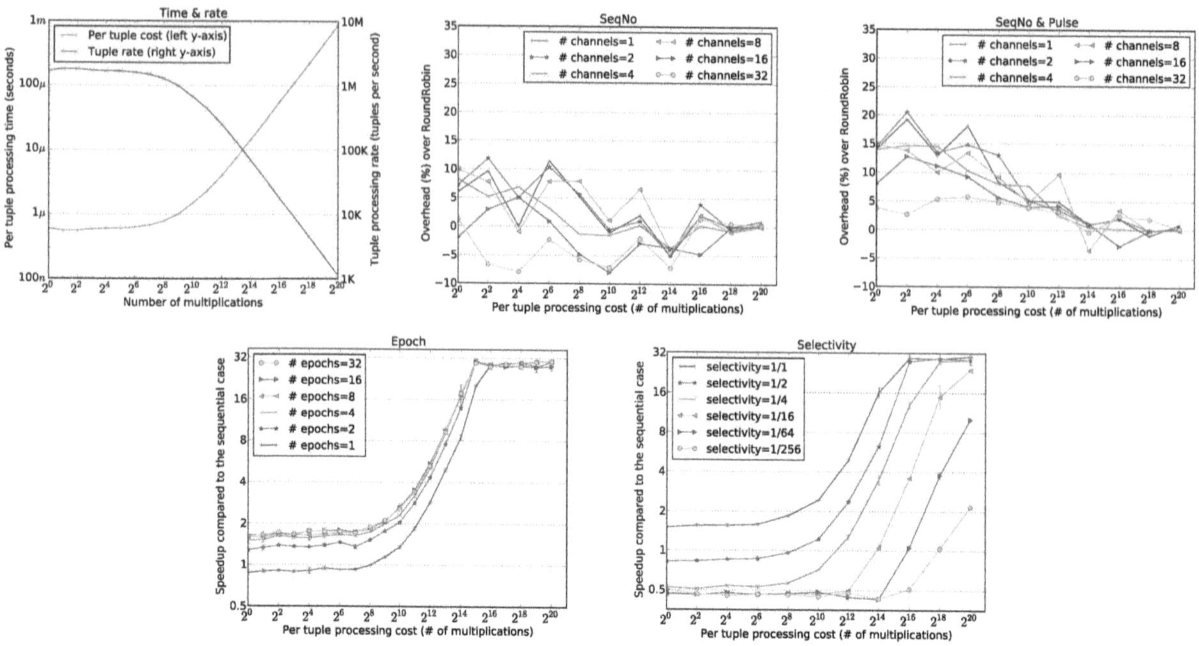

Figure 8: Microbenchmarks.

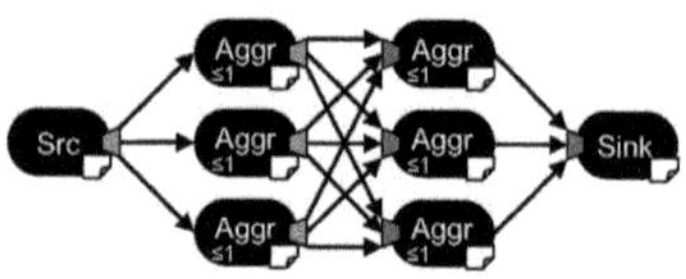

Figure 9: Expanded stream graph for a two-way shuffle.

Very inexpensive work in the *Stateful* experiment is benefiting from both pipeline and data parallelism.

Figure 9 shows the stream graph for the *Shuffle* experiment, which has two aggregations partitioned on different keys, requiring a shuffle between them. When there are 32 channels in the *Shuffle* experiment, there are actually 64 processes running on 32 cores. Hence, the 32-channel case is an over-subscribed system by a factor of 2, and it only scales to 22.6 times. The 16-channel case has 32 PEs, which is a fully subscribed system, and it scales to 15.3 times. As with the *Stateful* experiment, the inexpensive end of the work spectrum benefits from pipeline as well as data parallelism, achieving over 2 times improvement for 4–32 channels.

Note that the effect of pipeline parallelism for low tuple costs is least pronounced in the *Stateless* experiment, and most pronounced in *Shuffle*. In the sequential case with low-tuple costs, the one PE worker is the bottleneck; it must receive, process, and send tuples. The splitter only sends tuples. As the number of parallel channels increases, the work on each worker PE decreases, making the splitter the bottleneck. The more costly the work is, the stronger the effect becomes, which is why it is weakest in the *Stateless* experiment and strongest in the *Shuffle* experiment.

The *Large-scale* experiment in Figure 10 demonstrates the scalability the runtime system is able to achieve with a large number of cores across many machines. This experiment uses a total of 14 machines. One machine (8 cores) is dedicated to the source and sink, which includes the split and merge at the edges of the parallel region. The other 13 machines (104 cores) are dedicated to the PEs in the parallel region. The stream graph for the *stateful* experiment is a single, stateful aggregation in a parallel region with 100 parallel channels. The *stateful* experiment shows near linear scalability, maxing out at 93 times improvement.

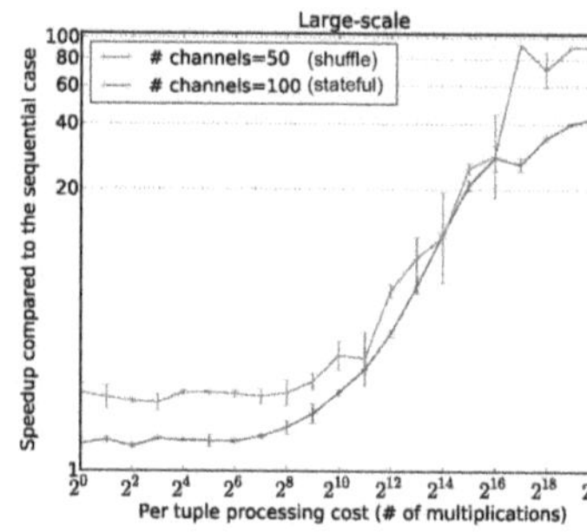

Figure 10: Large-scale scalability.

The *shuffle* experiment in Figure 10 has the same stream graph as shown in Figure 9. As explained with the *Shuffle* experiment, there are twice as many processes as parallel channels. When there are 50 parallel channels in each of its two parallel regions, it maxes out at 42 times improvement. The *shuffle* experiment cannot scale as high as the *stateful* experiment because with 50 parallel channels, there are 100 PEs.

5.2 Microbenchmarks

All of the microbenchmarks are shown in Figure 8. The stream graph for all of the microbenchmarks is a parallel region with a single stateless operator.

The *Time & Rate* benchmark shows the relationship between the amount of work done and the time it takes to do that work. For all our of results, we characterize the work done in the number of multiplications performed per tuple. This experiment maps those multiplications to both an elapsed time (left y-axis) and a processing rate (right

y-axis). The elapsed time range is from 600 nanoseconds to 1 millisecond, and the processing rate is from 1.6 million tuples a second to one thousand tuples a second. This cost experiment is a "calibration" experiment that shows the relationship between the amount of work done, the time it takes to do that work, and the throughput on all of our other experiments.

As described in Section 4.3, adding sequence numbers to tuples and inserting pulses on all channels will incur some overhead. We measured this overhead in Figure 8, using pure round-robin ordering as the baseline. As expected, as the work-per-tuple increases, the cost of adding a sequence number to each tuple becomes negligible compared to the actual work done. However, even when relatively little work is done, the highest average overhead is only 12%. Pulses add more overhead, but never more than 21%. As with sequence numbers alone, the overhead goes towards zero as the cost of the work increases.

Epochs, as explained in Section 4.3, are the number of tuples on each channel between generating pulses on all channels. The *Epoch* experiment in Figure 8 measures how sensitive performance is to the epoch length. An epoch of e means that the splitter will send eN tuples, where N is the total number of channels, before generating a pulse on each channel. We scale the epoch with the number of channels to ensure that each channel receives e tuples before it receives a single pulse. The default epoch is $e = 10$. Our results show that beyond an epoch length of 8, speedup does not vary more than 8% in the range 8–32.

In the *Selectivity* experiment, we fixed the number of parallel channels at 32. Each line in the graph represents a progressively more selective aggregator. So, when selectivity is 1:1, the operator performs an aggregation for every tuple it receives. When selectivity is 1:256, it performs 1 aggregation for every 256 tuples it receives. When per-tuple cost is low, and the selectivity increases, the worker PEs do very little actual work; they mostly receive tuples. However, the cost for the splitter remains constant, as it always has 32 channels. When selectivity is high, the splitter is paying the cost to split to 32 channels, but there is no benefit to doing so, since real work is actually a rare event. As a result, as selectivity increases, there is actually slowdown until the cost of processing one of the selected tuples become large.

5.3 Application Kernels

This section further explores performance using five real-world application kernels shown in Figure 11. All of these application kernels have selective or stateful parallel regions, which require the techniques presented in this paper to be parallelized. They are representative of big data use cases.

The *Network monitoring* kernel monitors multiple servers, looking for suspicious user behavior. The filters remove values below a "suspicious" threshold. The left parallel region is partitioned by the server, while the right parallel region is partitioned by users, with a shuffle in the middle. Note, however, that because there are parallel sources on the left and parallel sinks on the right, tuples are *not* ordered in this application. The compiler recognizes this and informs the runtime that it has only routing responsibilities.

The *PageRank* kernel uses a feedback loop to iteratively rank pages in a web graph [18]. This application is typically associated with MapReduce, but is also easy to express in a streaming language. Each iteration multiplies the rank vector with the web graph adjacency matrix. In the first iteration, MulAdd reads the graph from disk. Each iteration uses the parallel channels of MulAdd to multiply the previous rank vector with some rows of the matrix, and uses Add to assemble the next rank vector. The input consists of a synthetic graph of 2 million vertices with a sparsity of 0.001, in other words, 4 billion uniformly distributed edges.

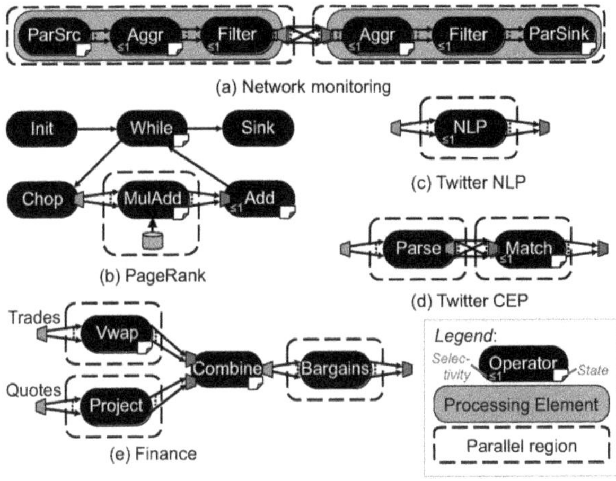

Figure 11: Stream graphs for the application kernels.

	operators					
Network	Left	33 μs	Right	23 μs		
PageRank	MulAdd	11 s				
Twitter NLP	NLP	103 μs				
Twitter CEP	Parse	140 μs	Match	3.5 ms		
Finance	Vwap	81 μs	Project	26 μs	Bargains	2.5 μs

Table 2: Average processing time per tuple.

The *Twitter NLP* kernel uses a natural language processing engine [5] to analyze tweets. The input is a stream of tweet contents as strings, and the output is a tuple containing a list of the words used in the message, a list with the lengths of the words, and the average length of the words. The stream graph has a parallel region with a single, stateless, operator. The NLP engine is implemented in Java, so tuples that enter the NLP operator must be serialized, copied into the JVM, processed, then deserialized and copied out from the JVM.

The *Twitter CEP* kernel uses complex event processing to detect patterns across sequences of tweets [12]. The Parse operator turns an XML tweet into a tuple with author, contents, and timestamp. The Match operator detects sequences of five consecutive tweets by the same author with identical hash-tags. This pattern is a pathological case for this input stream, which causes the finite state machine that implements the pattern matching to generate and check many partial matches for most tuples. Both Parse and Match are parallelized, with a shuffle to partition by author before Match. The topology is similar to that of the *Network monitoring* kernel, but since there is no parallel source or sink, ordering matters.

The *Finance* kernel detects bargains when a quote exceeds the VWAP (volume-weighted average price) of its stock symbol. The graph has three parallelizable operators. Only the Combine operator, which merges its two input streams in timestamp order, is not parallel.

Figure 12 shows the parallel speedups of the five applica-

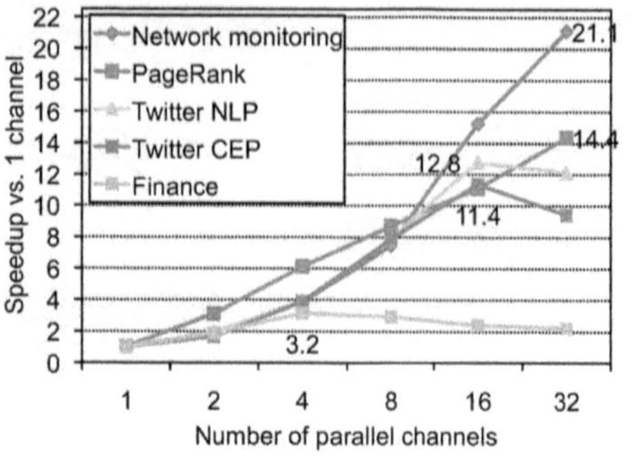

Figure 12: Performance results for the application kernels.

tion kernels on a cluster of 4 machines with 8 cores each, for a total of 32 cores. In these experiments, all parallel regions are replicated to the same number of parallel channels. For example, when the number of channels is 32, *Twitter CEP* has a total of 64 operator instances, thus over-subscribing the cores. Most of the kernels have near-perfect scaling up to 8 channels. The exception is *Finance*, which tops out at a speedup of 3.2× with 4 channels, at which point the Combine operator becomes the bottleneck. The other application kernels scale well, topping out at either 16 or 32 channels, with speedups between 11.4× and 21.1× over sequential.

Table 2 shows the average time it takes for all operators in parallel regions to process tuples. Combining this data with the *Time & Rate* experiment in Figure 8 allows us to calibrate the application kernels to the scalability benchmarks in Figure 6. Note, however, that this is a rough calibration, as the integer multiplications in the microbenchmarks occur in a tight loop, operating on a register. The average timings in Table 2 will include a mix of integer and floating point operations that could potentially include cache misses and branch mispredictions.

6. RELATED WORK

Table 3 compares this paper to prior work on data-parallel streaming. Stateful indicates whether the parallelizer can handle stateful operators, which are necessary for aggregation, enrichment, and detecting composite events across sequences of tuples. Dynamic indicates whether the parallelizer can handle operators with dynamic selectivity, which are necessary for data-dependent filtering, compression, and time-based windows. Safety indicates whether the parallelizer guarantees that the order of tuples in the output stream is the same as without parallelization, which is necessary for deterministic applications and simplifies testing and accountability. Finally, Scaling indicates the maximum number of cores for which results were reported. Our work is the first that is both general (with respect to state and dynamism) and safe. Furthermore, our paper includes results for scaling further than prior stream-processing papers.

The compiler for the StreamIt language auto-parallelizes operators using round-robin to guarantee ordering [10]. The StreamIt language supports stateful and dynamic operators, but the StreamIt auto-parallelization technique only works for operators that are stateless and have static selectivity. We treat it as a special case of our more general framework, which also supports stateful operators and dynamic selectivity. Furthermore, unlike StreamIt, we support more general topologies that eliminate bottle-necks, including parallel sources, shuffles, and parallel sinks.

Auto-parallel streaming system	**Generality Stateful**	**Generality Dynamic**	**Safety Order**	**Scaling #Cores**
StreamIt [10]	no	no	yes	64
PS-DSWP [21]	no	no	yes	6
Brito et al. [3]	yes	no	yes	8
Elastic operators [22]	no	yes	no	16
S4 [17]	yes	yes	no	64
This paper	yes	yes	yes	100

Table 3: Comparison to prior work on parallel streaming.

To achieve our scaling results for stateful operators, we adapt an idea from distributed databases [9, 11]: we partition the state by keys. This same technique is also the main factor in the success of the MapReduce [8] and Dryad [14] batch processing systems. However, unlike parallel databases, MapReduce, and Dryad, our approach works in a streaming context. This required us to invent novel techniques for enforcing output ordering. For instance, MapReduce uses a batch sorting stage for output ordering, but that is not an option in a streaming system. Furthermore, whereas parallel databases rely on relational algebra to guarantee that data parallelism is safe, MapReduce and Dryad leave this up to the programmer. Our system, on the other hand, uses static analysis to infer sufficient safety preconditions.

There are several efforts, including Hive [25], Pig [20] and FlumeJava [4], that provide higher-level abstractions for MapReduce. These projects provide a programming model that abstracts away the details of using a high performance, distributed system. Since these languages and libraries are abstractions for MapReduce, they do not work in a streaming context, and do not have the ordering guarantees that our system does.

There has been prior work on making batch data processing systems more incremental. MapReduce Online reports approximate results early, and increases accuracy later [7]. The Percolator allows observers to trigger when intermediate results are ready [19]. Unlike these hybrid systems, which still experience high latencies, our system is fully streaming.

Storm is an open-source project for distributed stream computing [24]. The programming model is similar to ours—programmers implement asynchronous *bolts* which can have dynamic selectivity. Developers can achieve data parallelism on any bolt by requesting multiple copies of it. However, such data parallelism does not enforce sequential semantics; safety is left entirely to the developers. S4 is another open-source streaming system [17], which was inspired by both MapReduce and the foundational work behind System S [1]. In S4, the runtime creates replica PEs at runtime for each new instance of a key value. Creating replica PEs enables data parallelism, but S4 has no mechanisms to enforce tuple ordering. Again, safety is left to developers.

There are extensions to the prior work on data-flow parallelization that are complementary to our work. River performs load-balancing for parallel flows [2], and Flux supports fault-tolerance for parallel flows [23]. Both River and Flux focus on batch systems, and both leave safety to the user. Elastic operators [22] and flexible filters [6] adapt the degree of parallelism dynamically, but do not address stateful operators in a distributed system or safey analysis. Finally, Brito et al. describes how to parallelize stateful operators with STM (software transactional memory) [3], but only if memory is shared and operator selectivity is exactly one.

7. CONCLUSIONS

We have presented a compiler and runtime system that are capable of automatically extracting data parallelism from streaming applications. Our work differs from prior work by being able to extract such parallelism with safety guarantees in the presence of operators that can be stateful, selective, and user-defined. We have demonstrated that these techniques can scale with available resources and exploitable parallelism. The result is a programming model in which developers can naturally express task and pipeline parallelism, and let the compiler and runtime automatically exploit data parallelism.

Acknowledgements

We would like to thank Rohit Khandekar for modifying the fusion algorithm implementation to accommodate the changes in the stream graph caused by auto-parallelization. We would also like to thank the anonymous reviewers whose detailed feedback substantially improved our paper.

8. REFERENCES

[1] L. Amini, H. Andrade, R. Bhagwan, F. Eskesen, R. King, P. Selo, Y. Park, and C. Venkatramani. SPC: A distributed, scalable platform for data mining. In *International Workshop on Data Mining Standards, Services, and Platforms*, 2006.

[2] R. H. Arpaci-Dusseau, E. Anderson, N. Treuhaft, D. E. Culler, J. M. Hellerstein, D. Patterson, and K. Yelick. Cluster I/O with River: Making the fast case common. In *Workshop on I/O in Parallel and Distributed Systems (IOPADS)*, 1999.

[3] A. Brito, C. Fetzer, H. Sturzrehm, and P. Felber. Speculative out-of-order event processing with software transaction memory. In *Conference on Distributed Event-Based Systems (DEBS)*, 2008.

[4] C. Chambers, A. Raniwala, F. Perry, S. Adams, R. R. Henry, R. Bradshaw, and N. Weizenbaum. FlumeJava: easy, efficient data-parallel pipelines. In *Proceedings of the 2010 ACM SIGPLAN conference on Programming Language Design and Implementation (PLDI)*, 2010.

[5] L. Chiticariu, R. Krishnamurthy, Y. Li, S. Raghavan, F. R. Reiss, and S. Vaithyanathan. SystemT: an algebraic approach to declarative information extraction. In *Proceedings of the 48th Annual Meeting of the Association for Computational Linguistics (ACL)*, 2010.

[6] R. L. Collins and L. P. Carloni. Flexible filters: Load balancing through backpressure for stream programs. In *International Conference on Embedded Software (EMSOFT)*, 2009.

[7] T. Condie, N. Conway, P. Alvaro, J. M. Hellerstein, K. Elmeleegy, and R. Sears. MapReduce online. In *Networked Systems Design and Implementation*, 2010.

[8] J. Dean and S. Ghemawat. MapReduce: Simplified Data Processing on Large Clusters. In *Operating Systems Design and Implementation (OSDI)*, 2004.

[9] D. J. Dewitt, S. Ghandeharizadeh, D. A. Schneider, A. Bricker, H. I. Hsiao, and R. Rasmussen. The Gamma database machine project. *Transactions on Knowledge and Data Engineering*, 2(1), 1990.

[10] M. I. Gordon, W. Thies, and S. Amarasinghe. Exploiting coarse-grained task, data, and pipeline parallelism in stream programs. In *Architectural Support for Programming Languages and Operating Systems (ASPLOS)*, 2006.

[11] G. Graefe. Encapsulation of parallelism in the Volcano query processing system. In *International Conference on Management of Data (SIGMOD)*, 1990.

[12] M. Hirzel. Partition and compose: Parallel complex event processing. In *Conference on Distributed Event-Based Systems (DEBS)*, 2012.

[13] M. Hirzel, H. Andrade, B. Gedik, V. Kumar, G. Losa, M. Mendell, H. Nasgaard, R. Soulé, and K.-L. Wu. Streams processing language specification. Research Report RC24897, IBM, 2009.

[14] M. Isard, M. B. Y. Yu, A. Birrell, and D. Fetterly. Dryad: Distributed data-parallel program from sequential building blocks. In *European Conference on Computer Systems (EuroSys)*, 2007.

[15] R. Khandekar, I. Hildrum, S. Parekh, D. Rajan, J. Wolf, K.-L. Wu, H. Andrade, and B. Gedik. COLA: Optimizing stream processing applications via graph partitioning. In *International Conference on Middleware*, 2009.

[16] E. A. Lee and D. G. Messerschmitt. Synchronous data flow. *Proceedings of the IEEE*, 75(9), 1987.

[17] L. Neumeyer, B. Robbins, A. Nair, and A. Kesari. S4: Distributed stream processing platform. In *KDCloud*, 2010.

[18] L. Page, S. Brin, R. Motwani, and T. Winograd. The pagerank citation ranking: Bringing order to the web. Technical Report 1999-66, Stanford InfoLab, November 1999.

[19] D. Peng and F. Dabek. Large-scale incremental processing using distributed transactions and notifications. In *Operating Systems Design and Implementation (OSDI)*, 2010.

[20] Pig. `http://pig.apache.org/`. Retrieved July, 2012.

[21] E. Raman, G. Ottoni, A. Raman, M. J. Bridges, and D. I. August. Parallel-stage decoupled software pipelining. In *Code Generation and Optimization (CGO)*, 2008.

[22] S. Schneider, H. Andrade, B. Gedik, A. Biem, and K.-L. Wu. Elastic scaling of data parallel operators in stream processing. In *International Parallel & Distributed Processing Symposium (IPDPS)*, 2009.

[23] M. A. Shah, J. M. Hellerstein, and E. Brewer. Highly Available, Fault-Tolerant, Parallel Dataflows. In *International Conference on Management of Data (SIGMOD)*, 2004.

[24] Storm. `http://storm-project.net/`. Retrieved July, 2012.

[25] A. Thusoo, J. S. Sarma, N. Jain, Z. Shao, P. Chakka, S. Anthony, H. Liu, P. Wyckoff, and R. Murthy. Hive: a warehousing solution over a map-reduce framework. *Proc. VLDB Endow.*, 2(2):1626–1629, Aug. 2009.

[26] D. Turaga, H. Andrade, B. Gedik, C. Venkatramani, O. Verscheure, J. D. Harris, J. Cox, W. Szewczyk, and P. Jones. Design principles for developing stream processing applications. *Software—Practice and Experience (SP&E)*, 40(12), Nov. 2010.

PEPON: Performance-Aware Hierarchical Power Budgeting for NoC Based Multicores*

Akbar Sharifi, Asit K. Mishra, Shekhar Srikantaiah, Mahmut Kandemir and Chita R. Das
Department of CSE
The Pennsylvania State University
University Park, PA 16802, USA
{akbar, amishra, srikanta, kandemir, das}@cse.psu.edu

ABSTRACT

Targeting NoC based multicores, we propose a two-level power budget distribution mechanism, called PEPON, where the first level distributes the overall power budget of the multicore system among various types of on-chip resources like the cores, caches, and NoC, and the second level determines the allocation of power to individual instances of each type of resource. Both these distributions are oriented towards maximizing workload performance without exceeding the specified power budget. Extensive experimental evaluations of the proposed power distribution scheme using a full system simulation and detailed power models emphasize the importance of power budget partitioning at both levels. Specifically, our results show that the proposed scheme can provide up to 29% performance improvement as compared to no power budgeting, and performs 13% better than a competing scheme, under the same chip-wide power cap.

Categories and Subject Descriptors

C.1.2 [**Computer Systems Organization**]: Multiprocessors; Interconnection architectures; C.4 [**Performance of Systems**]: Design studies

General Terms

Design, Experimentation, Management, Performance

Keywords

Power Budgeting, NoC-based Multicores, Performance

1. INTRODUCTION

Power budgeting and performance optimization under a given power budget in multicore systems have received considerable attention recently [19, 20, 24, 32]. A majority of these solutions focus on power budgeting at the processor level and the only *knob* they use to control the power of a multicore processor is the voltage/frequency level of the cores. While modulating the voltage/frequency level of the cores in a multicore processor has the potential to control power consumption of the processor, it provides no direct control on the efficiency (performance per Watt) of the processor. This is because the performance of an application is not controlled by the core frequency alone (although it has a vital influence), but is also influenced by other on-chip components; specifically, the last-level-cache and the network-on-chip (NoC). In fact, the significance of the power consumption of the non-core components is increasing and projected to be quickly on par with the power consumption of cores themselves, if not greater [11, 12, 23]. Our experimental studies also reinforce these observations made in the literature. For example, our experiments on a 16-core machine with 8MB last-level cache and a 4 × 4 mesh-based NoC show that about 33% of the power is consumed by the non-core components on average (15% and 18% by the last-level cache banks and the NoC, respectively).

A recent network based multicore from Intel [12] reports 31% and 79% non-core power contribution in full power and low power operating modes, respectively. Despite the fact that the power consumptions of caches and NoC are on par with that of the cores, to the best of our knowledge, there has been *no* prior work on distributing the power budget among all these resources to maximize performance, while maintaining the same overall power budget of the system as a whole. We believe significant performance improvements can be achieved by distributing the overall power intelligently among the resources based on the workload's sensitivity to core/NoC frequency and cache allocation.

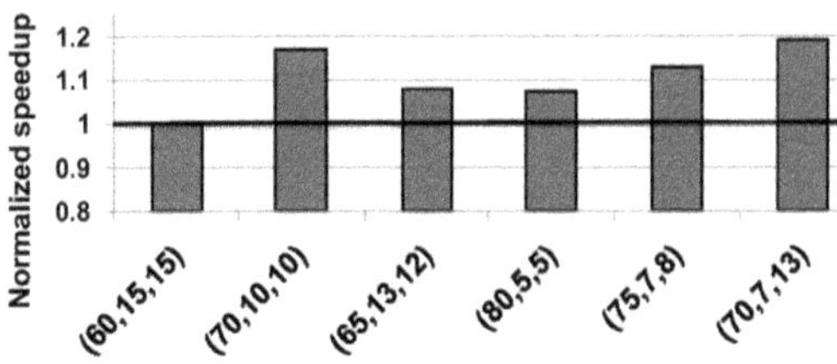

Figure 1: Performance (normalized weighted speedup) of a mix of 16 applications on a 16-core machine under different distributions of the same power budget (90W). All bars are normalized to the first bar. (x,y,z) on the x-axes indicates the specified core, cache and NoC power budgets (in watts), respectively.

To illustrate the key insight leveraged by this paper, that different distributions of the overall system power can lead to different system performances (despite keeping the overall power budget the same), we performed a simple experiment. We allocated different percentages of a fixed chip-wide power cap (90W) to different resources in the system. The core frequency is tuned so that the overall power allocation to the cores is respected. Similarly, the number

*This research is supported in part by NSF grants #1213052, #1152479, #1147388, #1139023, #1017882, #0963839, #0811687 and a grant from Microsoft Corporation.

of active cache ways in a set-associative last-level cache (LLC) are tuned such that the overall cache power remains within the allocated budget, and the NoC frequency is set such that the NoC power budget is also respected. The performance of a multiprogrammed workload mix of 16 applications on a 16-core 4×4 system as measured by the normalized weighted speedup under various distributions of the (same) overall power budget is shown in Figure 1. From this figure, we can see that different power budget distributions (x-axis) result in significantly different system performance, under the same power budget. Note that, the results presented in Figure 1 are only with a *static distribution* of the overall power among different resources, which does not react to changes in the workload behavior. Further, any changes in the power allocation to a specific resource requires tracking the actual (now-limited) resource allocation to applications over time. Therefore, a *dynamic distribution* of the power budget can potentially achieve much higher overall performance and a mechanism to track the allocated power among applications can also ensure that the power budget is always respected despite changing workload behavior.[1]

To this end, in this paper, we propose a power budget distribution mechanism (called *PEPON*) that distributes the chip-wide power budget among various types of critical resources like the cores, caches, and NoC to maximize performance, while respecting the allocated budget in the corresponding resources, thereby respecting the overall power budget. Specifically, the main contributions of the paper can be summarized as follows:

• We propose a novel *two-level* power distribution scheme that distributes a specified power budget among different resources by carefully managing the allocated power to attain best possible performance for a given workload. This scheme employs different models at different power distribution levels and uses feedback controllers to enforce the core and NoC power allocations.

• Extensive evaluation of the proposed technique using a full system simulation and detailed power/performance models shows that carefully distributing the power budget among all the on-chip resources not only ensures that the power cap on the processor is respected, but also optimizes the system performance. Our experimental analysis indicates that overall workload performance can be improved by as much as 29%, as compared to the case where no power distribution is implemented. Further, with respect to a recently-proposed power budgeting scheme that considers redistribution of only core power [20], our scheme achieves, on average, about 13% performance improvement –under the same chip-wide power budget.

2. TARGET MULTICORE SYSTEM

Figure 2 shows an NoC-based multicore architecture. It is a shared-memory based two-dimensional mesh structure, where each node contains a processor core, private L1 data or instruction caches, a shared L2 cache bank, and a router through which it gets connected to the neighboring nodes. Although all nodes share the same logical on-chip L2 cache space, data access latencies depend on the distance between the requesting core and the cache bank that holds the requested data. The set of links used during an access to a data element in some other node's L2 is determined by the routing policy, which is XY-routing [17] in this work.

[1]Note that, while (for a given workload/configuration), one may find a static partitioning that comes close to the dynamic one, one would need an exhaustive search to achieve this (which is not possible in practice). Further, in other cases, one may not even find a comparable static partitioning (since static partitionings do not consider dynamic modulations in workload behavior).

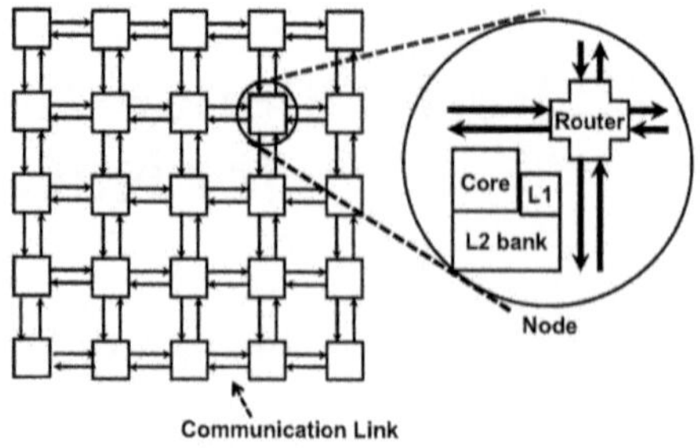

Figure 2: An NoC-based multicore architecture.

One of the critical issues in designing such multicore architectures is *power consumption*, which mainly comes from three sources: cores, on-chip cache components (shared L2 banks), and the NoC. To reduce the power consumption of cores, prior *dynamic voltage/frequency scaling* (DVFS) based methods [4, 12, 14] proposed in the literature can be employed. The idea of DVFS is to exploit the variance in processor utilization by lowering the voltage/frequency when the processor is lightly loaded and increasing the voltage-/frequency when the processor is highly utilized. Like processor cores, there is also a wide variance in cache line utilization in on-chip memories as well as link utilization in NoC-based multicore architectures, depending on applications' communication/data sharing patterns. In fact, one can obtain up to $10\times$ power savings, by accurately shutting down unused cache ways or lowering frequency and voltage of links when link usage is decreased [16]. We exploit DVFS for varying the power allocations of cores and the NoC.

3. OUR PROPOSED APPROACH

3.1 High-Level View of PEPON

Targeting the multicore architecture shown in Figure 2, our goal in this work is to maximize workload performance under a chip-wide power budget constraint. More specifically, given a multicore-wide power budget, we want to distribute/redistribute it across different hardware components such that (i) the given power budget is not exceeded and (ii) performance is maximized. Consequently, we are not interested in solutions that maximize workload performance but violate the specified power budget. Further, among all solutions that satisfy the power budget constraint, we are interested in finding the one that maximizes performance.

Figure 3(a) illustrates the high level operation of our proposed two-level power budget distribution strategy (PEPON). In the first level of this strategy, the overall power budget is partitioned among cores, NoC and L2 caches. In the second level, the power budget assigned to cores is further partitioned among individual cores and, similarly, the power budget assigned to L2 caches is further partitioned across individual L2 caches. While it is also possible to divide the NoC into voltage islands [26] and distribute the power allocated to the NoC across these islands, we did not pursue that direction in this work because such a partitioning can have a non-deterministic impact on different applications. Instead, in this work, we treated the NoC as a single monolithic entity, all components of which have the same voltage/frequency level at a given time (i.e., when voltage/frequency scaling is applied, it is applied to the entire NoC).

At each level of this power distribution strategy, a different approach is employed. Specifically, for the first-level distribution, we adopt a *regression-based* performance model that guides us to decide the most performance-efficient distribution of power. For the second-level distribution, on the other hand, we use different strate-

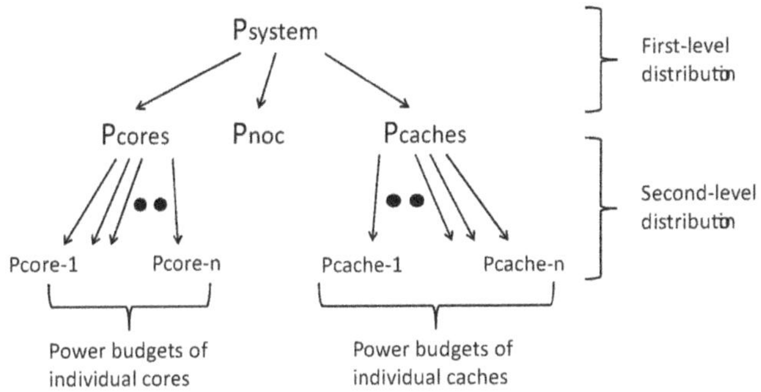

(a) Power budget distribution.

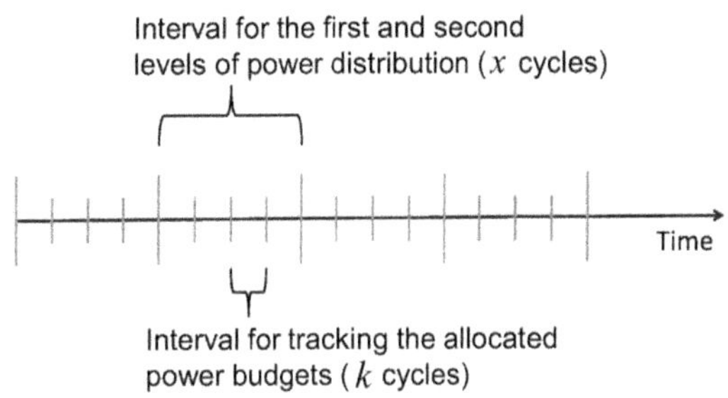

(b) Control intervals.

Figure 3: High level view of PEPON.

gies for caches and cores. The power budget assigned to cores is distributed using a control theoretic approach. On the other hand, for power budget distribution across different L2 banks, we employ a *utility-based* model. The technical details of these models as well as the details of our two-level power distribution strategy and our power control knobs are described next.

3.2 Design Details of PEPON

For the first level power distribution, the system power budget (P_{system}) is partitioned among different types of components, namely, cores (P_{cores}), cache banks (P_{caches}), and NoC (P_{noc}). That is, we have: $P_{system} = P_{cores} + P_{caches} + P_{noc}$. At the second level, P_{cores} is distributed among the cores and P_{caches} is distributed among the cache banks. Both the first and the second-level distributions are performed at every x million cycles. Further, each component of interest (each core, cache bank and NoC) has a *controller* associated with it, which tracks the allocated budget. As illustrated in Figure 3(b), the longer epochs (x million cycles) are divided into several sub-epochs, and the controller associated with each component is invoked every k million cycles (sub-epochs) to track its power budget, which is determined at every x million cycles. While we performed experiments with different values of x and k parameters, the default values used in most of our experiments are 100 and 20, respectively.

3.2.1 *First-Level Power Distribution*

At this level, we employ a *regression-based* estimator:

$$Perf = \epsilon + a_1 \times P_{cores} + a_2 \times P_{caches} + a_3 \times P_{noc}. \quad (1)$$

In this expression, $Perf$ is the overall workload performance, a_i ($1 \leq i \leq 3$) represent model coefficients, and ϵ captures the model error value. This model gives the overall performance ($Perf$) expected to be achieved over an epoch when the total power budget is partitioned into P_{cores}, P_{caches} and P_{noc} values in that epoch. In our model, we define the overall workload performance ($Perf$) over each time interval as $\sum_i \frac{IPS_i^k}{Avg\_IPS_i}$, where IPS_i^k is the *instruction per second* (IPS) of the ith application over the kth time interval and Avg_IPS_i is the average measured IPS of that application when it is executed without any power constraint. Avg_IPS_i can be obtained for each application by running that application on a core with the highest possible frequency and without imposing any power budget constraint.

At each time interval, first, the coefficients are updated based on the measured performance and allocated power budgets in the previous epoch and then our scheme increases the power budget of the component with the largest coefficient and reduces the power budget of the component with the smallest coefficient. As an example, if $a_1 > a_2 > a_3$, then P_{cores} and P_{noc} are increased by δ and reduced by $\delta - \epsilon_1$, respectively (δ is an increment/decrement unit and ϵ_1 is a small number and helps the regression to be computable). To update the model, we keep a *window* (*table*) with *four* entries that store the power budget allocations and corresponding measured performance numbers for the four recent epochs. Each entry in this table is in the form of ($Perf$, P_{cores}, P_{caches}, P_{noc}); an example table is given in Table 1. At each budget distribution epoch (the longer of the intervals shown in Figure 3(b)), first, the oldest entry in the table is replaced with the new entry ($Perf^k$, P^k_{cores}, P^k_{caches}, P^k_{noc}), where $Perf^k$ is the measured overall system performance over the last epoch and P^k_{cores}, P^k_{caches} and P^k_{noc} are the recent power budgets assigned to the cores, caches and NoC, respectively. The data stored in Table 1 and the model coefficients can be stacked together and written as follows:

$Perf^k$	P^k_{cores}	P^k_{caches}	P^k_{noc}
$Perf^{k-1}$	P^{k-1}_{cores}	P^{k-1}_{caches}	P^{k-1}_{noc}
$Perf^{k-2}$	P^{k-2}_{cores}	P^{k-2}_{caches}	P^{k-2}_{noc}
$Perf^{k-3}$	P^{k-3}_{cores}	P^{k-3}_{caches}	P^{k-3}_{noc}

Table 1: A sample window (table) of the power budget allocations and corresponding performance numbers (first column).

$$PF = P \times A + \epsilon, \quad \text{where}$$

$$PF = \begin{pmatrix} Perf^k \\ Perf^{k-1} \\ Perf^{k-2} \\ Perf^{k-3} \end{pmatrix}, \quad P = \begin{pmatrix} P^k_{cores} & P^k_{caches} & P^k_{noc} \\ P^{k-1}_{cores} & P^{k-1}_{caches} & P^{k-1}_{noc} \\ P^{k-2}_{cores} & P^{k-2}_{caches} & P^{k-2}_{noc} \\ P^{k-3}_{cores} & P^{k-3}_{caches} & P^{k-3}_{noc} \end{pmatrix},$$

$$A = \begin{pmatrix} a_1 \\ a_2 \\ a_3 \end{pmatrix}, \quad \epsilon = \begin{pmatrix} \epsilon_1 \\ \epsilon_2 \\ \epsilon_3 \end{pmatrix}.$$

After updating the regression history, we use the *least square method* to estimate a_1, a_2 and a_3 values. In the least square method, regression coefficients are computed as: $A = (P^T \times P)^{-1} P^T \times PF$. PEPON then increases the power budget with the largest coefficient and reduces the power budget with the smallest coefficient, since these values reflect the impact of varying the power budget of the corresponding components on the overall performance improvement.

3.2.2 *Second-Level Power Distribution*

At the second level, we employ different power distribution strategies for cores and caches. To distribute P_{cores} across the different cores in the multicore system, we use the approach proposed in [20]. Specifically, we allocate a power budget of P_i to core i

based on its $\frac{IPS}{watt}$ (performance per watt) over the last epoch ($\frac{IPS}{watt}$ = $\frac{Instruction\ per\ second}{power\ consumption}$). The allocated budgets are proportional to this parameter. In mathematical terms, if IPS_i and Pow_i are the measured IPS and the estimated power consumption of the application running on core i over the last epoch, and Avg_IPS_i is the average IPS of that application when it is running without any power constraint, then the power budget allocated to core i would be computed as:

$$Power\_Budget_{core}(i) = \frac{\frac{IPS_i}{Avg\_IPS_i}/Pow_i}{\sum_{core\ j}(\frac{IPS_j}{Avg\_IPS_j}/Pow_j)} \times P_{cores}.$$

Note that, in this equation, $\frac{IPS_i}{Avg\_IPS_i}$ is used instead of IPS_i since some applications intrinsically has low IPS numbers even when they are executed without any power budget constraint. We can obtain Avg_IPS for each application by running that application on a core with the frequency set to the highest possible value and without imposing any power budget constraint. Note that, this profiling is performed once for each application (not for workloads). Previous work such as [31], also uses the average IPS value as a baseline. In Section 4.2, we present experimental results to show that partitioning power only at the core level (as in the case of [20]) may not be sufficient to maximize performance. Once the power budget of each core is determined, the controller associated with each core attempts to track the budget by adjusting frequency/voltage of the core. As stated before, we use DVFS as our knob to control power consumption of the cores. More details are given later in this section.

To distribute P_{caches} among different cache banks, we employ a *utility-based* strategy. More specifically, the power share of each bank is proportional to its utility over the last epoch. Our goal is to allocate more power budget to the cache banks which are likely to bring more benefits towards the overall system performance. Different strategies can be used to compute utility of cache banks. As an example, the utility of a bank can be computed as the total number of accesses to that bank over the last epoch. However, this would not be a good metric for power budget partitioning since those accesses may have a small cache footprint and it is not probably beneficial to allocate more power budget to the bank with higher utility (note that, more budget means larger size for the banks). The approach adopted in this work is based on *cache footprints*. In this approach, we consider the number of unique cache lines that are hits in a cache bank over the last epoch as the *utility* of that cache bank. To implement this scheme, a small bit vector is associated with each cache bank. This bit vector is used as a hash table. Once a miss occurs in a cache bank, a bit in its bit vector is set to '1'. This bit is indexed using the tag of the new data as the key (the key is hashed using an efficient hardware function). At the same time, the corresponding bit of the evicted data is set to '0'. Consequently, within a period of time, the '1's in the bit vector of a cache bank indicate the number of unique active cache lines that have been accessed. Since a cache line may not be accessed over a long time after the first access, we reset the bit vectors at the beginning of each time interval. In PEPON, the power budget share of each cache bank is proportional to its utility (i.e., the number of '1's in the bit vector) over the last epoch.

Note that, in our system, each core runs a single-application, whereas NoC and cache-banks are shared. Therefore, a pure application-centric budget-partitioning is not possible for an NoC or caches. This is why we take a component-centric partitioning strategy instead.

3.2.3 Design of the Power Controllers

In this subsection, we explain how the power budgets assigned by PEPON are tracked by the controllers associated with different hardware components.

{0.25 , 7}	{0.41 , 0.8}	{0.60 , 0.9}	{0.65 , 0.94}	{0.76 , 1}
{0.84 , 1.05}	{0.93 , 1.1}	{1.0 , 1.14}	{1.23 , 1.28}	{1.33 , 1.34}

Table 2: {frequency (GHz) , voltage (V)} levels considered for the cores.

{0.06 , 0.55}	{0.55 , 0.7}	{0.88 , 0.8}	{1.24 , 0.91}	{1.34 , 0.94}
{1.54 , 1}	{1.7 , 1.05}	{2.0 , 1.14}	{2.23 , 1.21}	{2.46 , 1.28}

Table 3: {frequency (GHz) , voltage (V)} levels considered for the NoC.

Core and NoC Controllers. As stated before, we use the frequency/voltage of the cores and the NoC as our knob to control power consumption of these modules (we employ DVFS). Tables 2 and 3 give the frequency/voltage pairs we consider in our DVFS scheme. A simple *P (proportional) feedback controller* is configured and associated with each core as well as the NoC to modulate the frequency levels, with the goal of tracking the allocated power budgets. Figure 4 illustrates the high level view of how our controllers operate.[2] We employ *P* controllers in PEPON due to two main reasons: (i) they are relatively easy to design and implement with low overhead since the control output is the control error multiplied by a constant value, and (ii) they are fast to take the system output to the desired value (we need this property in PEPON, since the controllers have only limited number of time intervals to reach the desired power budgets). In this section, based on our system model, we show that employing only the *P* component of a *PID* controller provides a fast and stable controller with zero *steady error*[3].

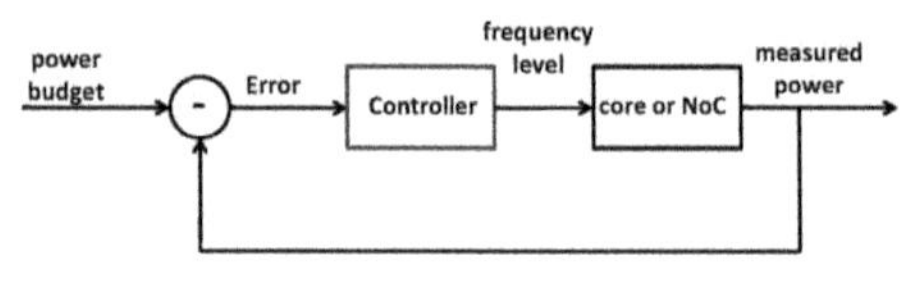

Figure 4: Feedback control loop for regulating the core/NoC power.

At each epoch, the controller compares the current power budget and the measured power over the last epoch and, based on the result of that comparison, adjusts (increases or decreases) the frequency level to *minimize* the measured error value (which is the difference between the power budget and the actual power). Each controller in PEPON implements the following rule to modulate the frequency level:

$$f(T+1) = f(T) + K \times (P_{budget} - P_{current}), \quad (2)$$

where $f(T)$ is the frequency at T^{th} time interval, K is a constant value, and P_{budget} and $P_{current}$ are the specified power budget and the current power, respectively. The controller first computes $f(T+1)$ and then sets the current frequency level to the level which is the closest one to $f(T+1)$. The controller ensures that its output be one of the available frequency levels in Tables 2 and 3. As can be observed from this control rule, if the measured power is greater than the reference power, the controller reduces the frequency level to reduce power consumption over the next epoch.

The next step to configure the controller is to determine the value of K. This value is computed based on the system power behavior

[2]The *P* controller [10] is a type of controller in which the output of the controller is *proportional* to the error value, which is the difference between the target value and the current system output.

[3]Although most our experiments are performed using a *P* controller, we later report results with a *PID* controller as well.

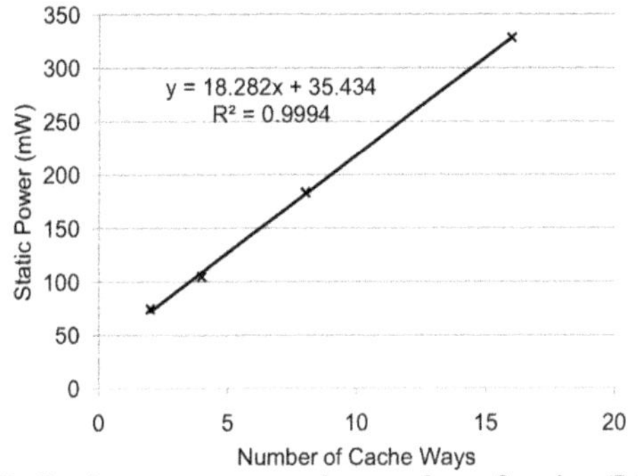

Figure 5: Static power versus the number of active (L2) cache ways.

(core/NoC) when the frequency level is varied. As shown in [24], the impact of varying the frequency on power consumption can be estimated linearly as follows:

$$P_2 = P_1 + a \times \Delta F, \tag{3}$$

where P_1 is the power being consumed at the old frequency and P_2 is the power consumption after the frequency is increased by ΔF. The value of a can be estimated offline by performing experiments with different applications and frequencies and averaging over the obtained values for a. By combining Equations (2) and (3), we observe that, if we set the K value to $\frac{1}{a}$ in the controller, the frequency is changed towards reaching the reference (target) power budget (the value of K is 60M in our scheme).

Control System Analysis. One of the main methods to characterize a control system is to analyze it in the frequency-domain [10]. In this method, the system is represented by a *transfer function* that shows the correlation between its input and output in frequency-domain (*z-transform* is used for discrete time systems). Our system, which is modeled by Equation(3), can be represented as $\frac{Y(z)}{X(z)} = \frac{a}{z-1}$, where $Y(z)$ is the power consumption of the system and $X(z)$ is the variation in the operating frequency in *z-domain*. Since we employ a *P* controller, our closed loop transfer function can be obtained as $H(z) = \frac{Y(z)}{R(z)} = \frac{K \times a}{z-1+K \times a}$, where $R(z)$ is the power budget target.

In formal control theory, a control system is stable and tracks the target over the steady state if the *poles* of the closed loop transfer function is placed inside the unit circle in *z-plane*. The poles of the transfer function are obtained by solving the characteristic equation (setting the nominator of the transfer function to zero). Therefore, as can be observed, our frequency control system has a pole at $z = 1 - K \times a$. Further, as mentioned before, the value of the K parameter is set to $\frac{1}{a}$, which ensures the stability of the system.

Steady state error is another important metric for a control system. This error is defined as the difference between the input reference and the actual system output when the controller reaches its steady state. It can be shown that the steady state error equals $\lim_{z \to 0} \frac{1}{1+H(z)}$ for step reference inputs, where $H(z)$ is the closed loop transfer function. In our control system, the reference inputs are step signals since they vary between two different frequency levels instantly. If we replace $H(z)$ with our system transfer function, one can observe that the steady error would be zero based on the mathematical analysis. Note that, although our analysis shows an accurate control system, there may still be some inaccuracies in tracking the reference targets as will be discussed in our experimental evaluations. These imprecisions can occur because we employ a linear estimation for modeling the system (see Equation(3)) and it does not ideally capture the dynamic behavior of co-runner applications.

Cache Bank Controller. As technology scales down, static (leakage) power of caches becomes an important part of the overall power consumption. The static power highly depends on the size of the caches. As an example, Figure 5 plots the leakage power of a 512KB, 16-way set associative cache manufactured with the 45nm technology, when the number of "active" cache ways varies. This figure clearly indicates that there is a *linear correlation* between the number of active cache ways and the static power consumption. Motivated by this observation, in PEPON, power is controlled in cache banks by turning 'ON' or 'OFF' the cache ways. Specifically, at each epoch, the controller associated with each cache bank compares the current power and the reference power budget and, using the data in Figure 5, decides to turn on or off a number of cache ways, to minimize the difference between the actual and reference power.

3.2.4 Implementation Overheads

PEPON is implemented in software at the OS level with support from hardware. One of the overheads imposed by PEPON is the process of computing the individual power budgets. This includes simple mathematical and matrix operations to partition power at the first and second levels. These overheads are minimal, since the scheme is implemented in software and executed only in every 100-million cycles. In comparison, the controllers are invoked with a higher frequency to track the power budgets. It should be noted, however, that our controllers perform a simple operation (subtraction and multiplication) since they are implemented as *P* controllers. Therefore, the additional overheads caused by our controllers are also not very high. *The power and performance numbers presented in the next section include all the overheads incurred by PEPON.* In addition to these software-level overheads, PEPON assumes that the underlying system has support for DVFS, which is a standard in almost all processors today. We make the same assumption for the DVFS overheads as in [20] (20us DVFS actuation overhead). If the voltage/frequency values are enforced every 20-million cycles (our default value) and if the system operates at 500MHz, the resulting DVFS overhead (20us) would be about 0.05%. In addition, PEPON also assumes that the processor has support for software level control for reconfiguring (turning on/off) cache ways in the L2 cache and tuning the operating frequency of the NoC.

4. EXPERIMENTAL EVALUATION

In this section, we experimentally evaluate PEPON, and compare it against alternate power budgeting strategies quantitatively. We use SIMICS [21], which is a full-system simulator for multicores, as our simulation framework. For our experiments, SIMICS is enhanced with detailed latency models as well as power models from CACTI [29], Orion [30] and Wattch [3], to estimate the power consumption of different components in our target multicore architecture.

4.1 Power Estimation Models

Power model for cores. We use the same model as in [24] to estimate power consumption of the cores. The power consumed by a core depends almost linearly on the utility of the core. In other words, once an application starts its execution, the average power consumption of the core can be estimated based on this equation: $P_i = k_0 \times U_i + k_1$, where P_i is the power consumption of core i, U_i is its utilization, and k_0 and k_1 are constant values. Note that the values of k_0 and k_1 may be different for different applications. In this work, we estimated values of these constants by running each application independently and using Wattch [3] for monitoring power consumption over execution.

Power model for caches. We use numbers obtained from CACTI [29] to estimate power consumption of the caches. Power of each cache bank can be estimated as:

$$Power = Leakage\ Power + (read\ power \times \#\ of\ reads) + (write\ power \times \#\ of\ writes),$$

where the leakage power linearly depends on the cache size. Since, in our scheme, we use the number of active cache ways as the knob to control the power consumption of a cache bank, the leakage power can be estimated considering the active cache size at each time interval over the execution.

Power model for the NoC. The average power consumption of the NoC, over a time interval T, is estimated as follows: $P_{noc} = P_{dynamic} + P_{static} = \frac{NH_{noc} \times E_{noc}}{T} + P_{static}$, where NH_{noc} is the total number of hops that all the packets in the network traverse over T and E_{noc} is the energy per hop. In this expression, "energy per hop" is the amount of energy consumed when a packet passes through a router. We used the energy values obtained from Orion [30] to estimate the total power consumption of the NoC.

Processors	16 cores with private L1 data and instruction caches
NoC Architecture	4 × 4
Processor Model	4-way issue superscalar
Private L1 Data and Instr Caches	Direct mapped, 32KB, 64 bytes block size, 3 cycle access latency
Number of L2 Cache Banks	16 (distributed over the network)
L2 Cache	64 bytes block size, 10 cycle access latency
L2 Cache Bank Size	512KB per core
Memory	4GB, 200 cycle off–chip access latency
Power Budget Control Enforcement Interval	100 Million cycles
Tracking Control Enforcement Interval	20 Million cycles
δ	1

Table 4: Baseline configuration.

Table 4 gives the baseline configuration we use in our experimental evaluation. In our baseline configuration, the power budget allocated to each component by PEPON is computed and enforced every 100-million cycles. Further, the controller assigned to each component has the opportunity to track its power target over five intervals with 20-million cycles duration. We form six application mixes (workloads) using the SPEC CPU 2006 benchmark suite [1] for our experimental evaluation. Each of our application mixes consists of 16 applications. We consider one-to-one mapping, that is, in each experiment, 16 applications of a mix are mapped and executed on 16 different cores in our system (one application per core). These six workloads are given in Table 5. In forming these workloads, we tried to have diversity in terms of memory access behavior. For each application, we skip the first 1-billion cycles for warm-up, and then the simulation continues with the next 10-billion cycles (100 power budget enforcement intervals).

4.1.1 *Schemes for Performance Evaluation*

Table 6 lists the five different schemes we consider in our experimental evaluation to compare with PEPON. In this table, "*dynamic*" indicates that the corresponding power budget is varied over the execution. As can be observed from Table 6, all the entries are shown as "*dynamic*" for PEPON, indicating that the power budgets are varied over the execution in *both* the first and second levels of the budget partitioning. However, in other schemes (Schemes 1 through 4), the power budgets are fixed at the first level of partitioning during runtime (i.e., P_{cores}, P_{caches} and P_{noc} are fixed as given in Table 6). This table also gives the actual power budget values (for the high and low power modes) assigned when using the different partitioning schemes. However, in Scheme 1, the total power budget of the cores and the cache banks are still partitioned among the individual components dynamically. All the power budgets of different components are fixed in Scheme 2, and the total power budget of the cores and the caches are evenly distributed among them. In Schemes 3 and 4, on the other hand, only one of the power budget distribution mechanisms is enabled at the second level (for cores in Scheme 3 and for caches in Scheme 4). Note that, Scheme 3 mimics a recently-proposed approach to power budget partitioning in multicores [20]. In addition to these schemes, we also implemented another scheme in which at the first level, the total power budget is distributed dynamically and at the second one, the power budgets of the cores and cache banks – from the first level – are partitioned statistically (evenly) among the individual components (cores and caches). We observed that PEPON improves the performance over this last scheme by about 8% on average. The detailed results for this scheme is omitted due to space concerns.

4.2 Results

4.2.1 *Performance Results*

We performed our experiments under two power modes: (i) *Low power mode.* In this case, the total power budget of the chip is set to be 40 watts, and (ii) *High power mode.* The total power budget is set to be 90 watts in this case. These power budgets are partitioned in two levels by PEPON over the course of execution. For the other schemes (Schemes 1-4) in Table 6, the total power budgets at the first level of the power budget partitioning which are fixed during the runtime, to be about 80% and 40% of the maximum power value in each case as given in Table 6. Figure 6(a-b) plots the normalized weighted speedup values achieved for different mixes when employing the schemes listed in Table 6. The weighted speedup for n applications is computed as follows:

$$Weighted\ Speedup = \sum_{i=0}^{i=n-1} \frac{IPS^{i}_{scheme}}{IPS^{i}_{alone}},$$

where IPS^{i}_{scheme} is the achieved instruction per second (IPS) by the employed scheme for application i and IPS^{i}_{alone} is the measured IPS achieved when the application is executed alone without any power constraints. The weighted speedup values in Figure 6 are normalized to *Scheme 2* (assumed to be the *base scheme*) in Table 6, where power budgets are not modulated over the execution (i.e., all power distributions are fixed throughout the execution). Note that, we consider IPS instead of instruction per cycle (IPC) to compute the speedup values since we use the operating frequency as a knob to control the power consumption of the cores and the IPC value does not change by varying the core frequency.

Figures 6(a) and (b) show that PEPON achieves significant performance (workload speedup) improvements in both the low and high power modes (more than 25% in the low power case and more than 20% in the high power case). Further, the total power consumptions track the power budgets quite closely as shown in Figures 6(c) and 6(d). These plots reveal that partitioning the total power budget at the first level by PEPON plays a significant role in achieving better performance under a certain power budget. As an example, as can be seen from Figure 6(a), although performance is improved by partitioning the power budget at the second level among the cores and cache banks in Mix-2 (Schemes 1 , 3, and 4),

Workload	Applications
Mix-1	*mcf, soplex, libquantum, GemsFDTD, lbm, leslie3d, milc, sphinx3, xalancbmk, cactusADM, mcf, soplex, libquantum, GemsFDTD, lbm, leslie3d*
Mix-2	*gobmk, sjeng, gcc, wrf, dealII, namd, perlbench, calculix, tonto, povray, povray, tonto, calculix, perlbench, namd, dealII*
Mix-3	*mcf, soplex, libquantum, GemsFDTD, lbm, leslie3d, milc, sphinx3, xalancbmk, cactusADM, omnetpp, astar, hmmer, bzip2, h264ref, gromacs*
Mix-4	*gobmk, sjeng, gcc, wrf, dealII, namd, perlbench, calculix, tonto, povray, omnetpp, astar, hmmer, bzip2, h264ref, gromacs,*
Mix-5	*mcf, soplex, libquantum, GemsFDTD, lbm, leslie3d, milc, sphinx3, xalancbmk, cactusADM, gobmk, sjeng, gcc, wrf, dealII, namd,*
Mix-6	*gobmk, sjeng, gcc, wrf, dealII, namd, perlbench, calculix, tonto, povray, cactusADM, xalancbmk, sphinx3, milc, leslie3d, mcf,*

Table 5: Various mixes of applications considered for our multiprogrammed workloads.

Scheme	$\sum CorePowerBudget(i)$	$CorePowerBudget(i)$	$\sum BankPowerBudget(i)$	$BankPowerBudget(i)$	$NoCPowerBudget$
PEPON	dynamic	dynamic	dynamic	dynamic	dynamic
Scheme1	static (29 watt – 68 watt)	dynamic	static (5 watt – 10 watt)	dynamic	static (6 watt – 12 watt)
Scheme2	static (29 watt – 68 watt)	static (29/16 watt – 68/16 watt)	static (5 watt – 10 watt)	static (5/16 watt – 10/16 watt)	static(6 watt – 12 watt)
Scheme3	static (29 watt – 68 watt)	dynamic	static (5 watt – 10 watt)	static (5/16 watt – 10/16 watt)	static (6 watt – 12 watt)
Scheme4	static (29 watt – 68 watt)	static (29/16 watt – 68/16 watt)	static (5 watt – 10 watt)	dynamic	static (6 watt – 12 watt)

Table 6: Various experimental schemes with the fixed power budget values.

it is less than the improvement achieved by PEPON since the budgets are fixed at the first level in all those schemes. We also note that there is a significant difference between PEPON and Scheme 3 (which mimics a recently proposed scheme [20]), further emphasizing power budgeting at *both* the levels.

Figures 6(a) and (b) also show the average speedup values achieved by different schemes across all the workloads. One can observe that, PEPON improves the overall workload performance significantly as compared to the other schemes tested in both high and low power modes (about 21% in the low power mode and 17% in the high power mode). Also, as can be seen, the performance improvement achieved by Scheme 1 is higher than the other schemes (Schemes 2, 3 and 4). This is because this scheme takes advantage of partitioning the power budgets among both the cores and cache banks at the second level, whereas in all other schemes tested (except ours), power budgets (among the cores or caches or both) are fixed at the second level.

4.2.2 Dynamics of PEPON

We next focus on how the total power budget is dynamically partitioned by PEPON over the course of execution to achieve the performance enhancements shown in Figure 6. Here, we present the results for one of our workloads (Mix1); the remaining workloads exhibit similar behavior.

Figures 7(a)-(c) plot the power budgets assigned to cores, caches and NoC by PEPON during runtime for Mix-1, when the total power budget is set to 40 watts. These figures also plot the measured power consumption for different components. As can be observed, PEPON first distributes the total budget at the first level and then, the budget targets are successfully tracked at each group. The accumulated power consumptions of the cores, caches and NoC are plotted in Figure 7(d) (this chart shows the total power consumption and *not* the total power budget). It is important to note that the power budget violation experienced when using PEPON is very low (less than 2%); the power budget violations will be further discussed later. There are two other important points in Figures 7(a)-(c) that should be noted: (i) the power consumption of the cores and NoC (Figures 7(a) and (c)) oscillate around the target power budgets and the budgets are slightly violated over the execution, whereas the power consumption of the caches is always below the budget, and (ii) the power budget of the caches is tracked faster. As an example, at time '0', as shown in Figures 7(a) and (c), the power budgets of the cores and NoC are not the same as their power consumptions, and the power budgets are tracked after some intervals. The main reason for these two differences is that the type of the controllers employed for the caches are different from the ones associated with the cores and NoC. As stated before, in the caches, power consumption is dominated by the static power and the static power exact model is known (the correlation between the number of active ways and power consumption). Therefore, the controllers associated with the caches are able to select the correct number of active cache ways based on the model in a short time, such that the power budget is not violated. On the other hand, we employ *P* controllers for the cores and NoC in which the exact model is not known and the frequencies are determined based on the *error* values, leading to small oscillations.

Figure 8 plots the power budget distribution at the first level for Mix-1 (similar to Figure 7) but when our total budget is 90 watts (high power mode). As one can observe, the power budget is successfully partitioned and tracked when we are operating at high power mode, too. We observed the same dynamic behavior at the first level of power budget partitioning from our other mixes as well. Note that, the NoC power in these experiments is controlled directly by modulating the NoC frequeny/voltage level. However, the power budgets of the cores and caches are not directly controlled and are distributed further among the individual components. Therefore, tracking the total power budgets of the cores and caches at the first level (as shown in this set of figures) implies that each individual component (cores and caches) has been successful in tracking its own budget.

Figures 9 illustrates how the power budgets determined at the first level are partitioned among the individual components (cores and caches) at the second level over the execution for Mix-1. As can be observed from each of these plots, the total power budget is partitioned into 16 pieces, and the size of each piece indicates the amount of power budget allocated to each component. Different components receive different shares from the power budget since the total budgets are distributed based on the utility of the caches or the performance power ratio of the cores over the recent time interval (the schemes that we employ at the second level). The controller configured for each hardware component tracks the target power budget by adjusting the voltage-frequency and the number of active cache ways of the cores and caches, respectively. To better understand these power distribution curves, we plot in Figure 10 the selected frequencies for the cores and the number of cache ways for Mix-1. We see that the values of these knobs are also different for different components at a specific time. As an example, at time 10, the frequencies assigned to some of the cores are low as compared to the others. This is because, the power budgets are not the same for different cores. Note also that even if the budgets were the same, the different cores would consume different amounts of energy when they operate at the same frequency since they execute different applications.

Controller Selection. As discussed before, we employ simple and fast *P* controllers to modulate the frequency of the cores and the

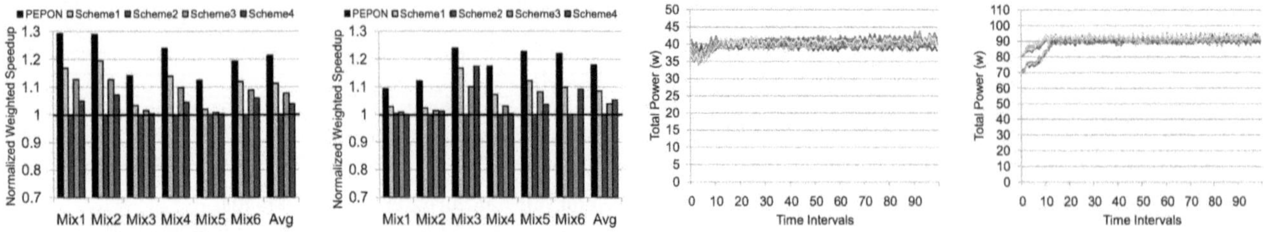

(a) Low power mode (b) High power mode (c) Low power mode (d) High power mode

Figure 6: (a-b) Normalized weighted speedup values achieved by different schemes under certain power budget, and (c-d) Dynamic tracking of the total power budget. Note that both (c) and (d) plot all the mixes together. The point here is that, in the low power case, chip-wide power consumptions of our mixes approach 40W, and similarly, in the high power case, chip-wide power consumptions of our mixes approach 90W.

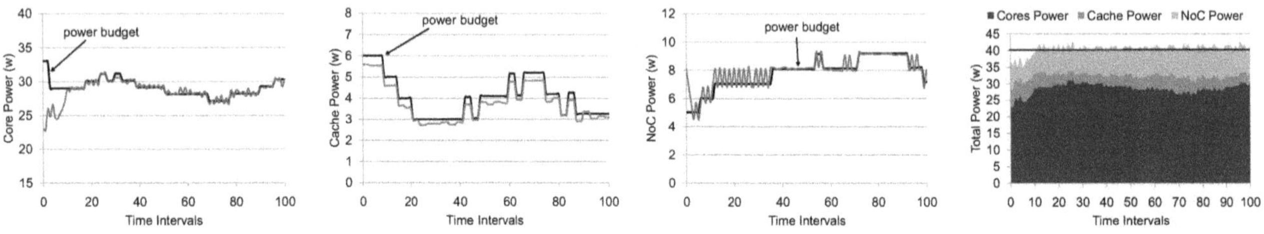

(a) Core power. (b) Cache power. (c) NoC power. (d) Total power consumption (not power budget).

Figure 7: Power budget partitioning and tracking at the first level of PEPON for Mix-1 (low power mode).

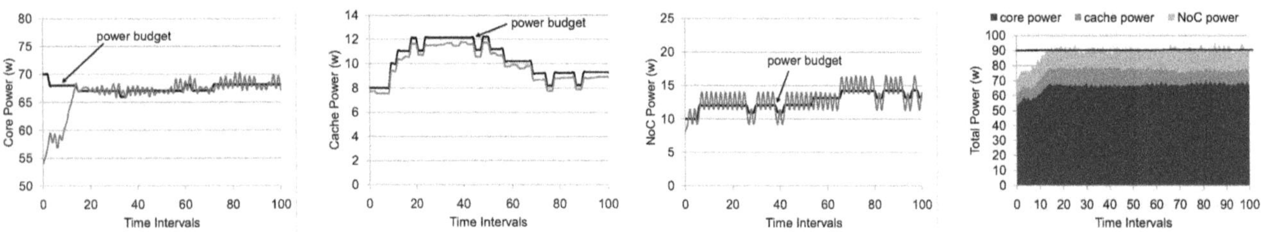

(a) Core power. (b) Cache power. (c) NoC power. (d) Total power consumption (not power budget).

Figure 8: Power budget partitioning and tracking at the first level of PEPON for Mix-1 (high power mode).

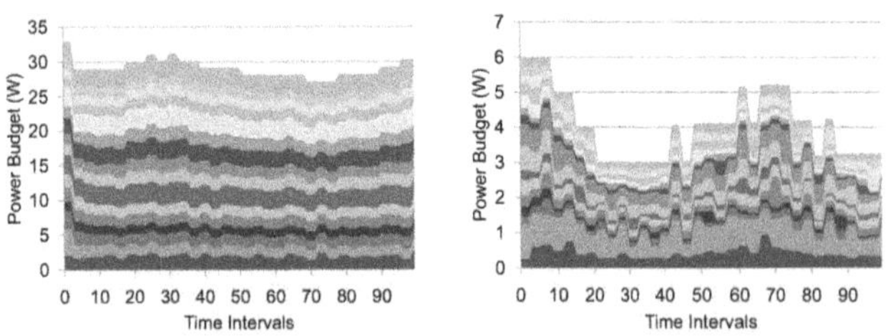

(a) Cores' power budgets (low power mode). (b) Caches' power budgets (low power mode).

Figure 9: Power budget partitioning at the second level (Mix-1). Note that each graph plots all 16 core (or cache) components.

NoC to track the specified power budgets. Instead of a *P* controller, one may suggest to employ a more complicated *PID* controller for frequency modulation. One of the main advantages of employing *PID* controllers is that they can drive steady-state errors to zero. As discussed before, in our system, this error is already zero when employing *P* controllers. Figure 11 plots how the power budgets (which is assigned to one of the cores in Mix-1 experiment) are tracked by *P* and *PID* controllers over the course of execution. As can be observed from this figure, the *P* controller is able to track the targets as well as the *PID* controller. However, the *PID* controller slightly reduces the number of oscillations at some time intervals (e.g., at 30th time interval). On the flip side, the *P* controller has the capability to respond more quickly to the target variation (e.g., at 70th time interval). In addition, as compared to the *PID* controller, the *P* controller incurs less overhead.

4.2.3 Sensitivity Experiments

We also measured sensitivity of Mix-1 (under the low power mode) to different parameters. As stated before, at each epoch, the power budgets are increased and decreased by δ and $\delta - \epsilon_1$, respectively at the first level of power budget partitioning tree. Recall from Table 4 that the default value for δ is 1 in our experimental evaluations. Figure 12 plots the speedups achieved for Mix-1, when the δ value is set to 2 (the results with a value of 1 are reproduced for ease of comparison). We see that increasing the δ value has a negative impact on the achieved speedup by PEPON. This is because, the power budgets may oscillate around the optimal values and not reach the optimal ones by having a larger δ.

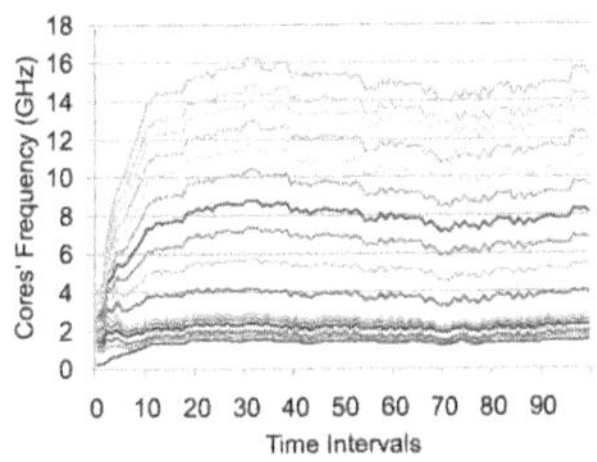

(a) Cores' frequencies (low power mode).

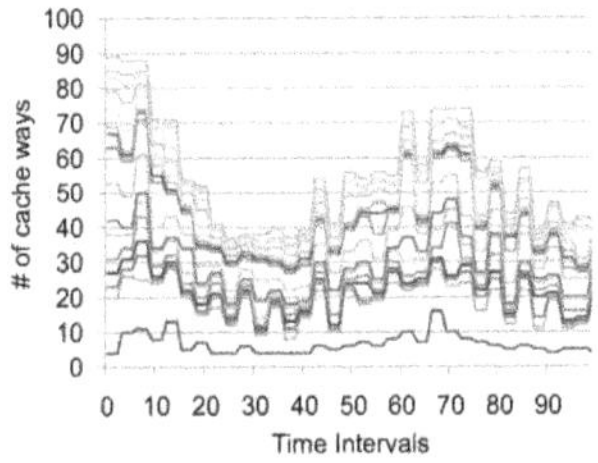

(b) Number of caches' ways (low power mode).

Figure 10: Modulation of core frequencies and the number of active cache ways over execution (Mix-1). Note that, the curves are stacked on top of each other for better visibility. Note also that, time intervals where the cumulative number of (cache) ways activated is low correspond to periods where caches are not allocated much power.

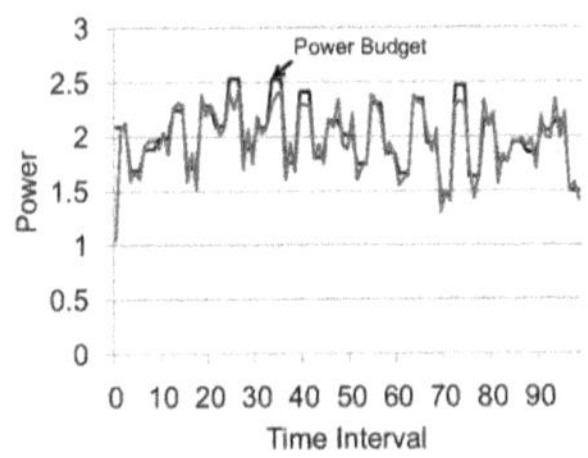

(a) P controller

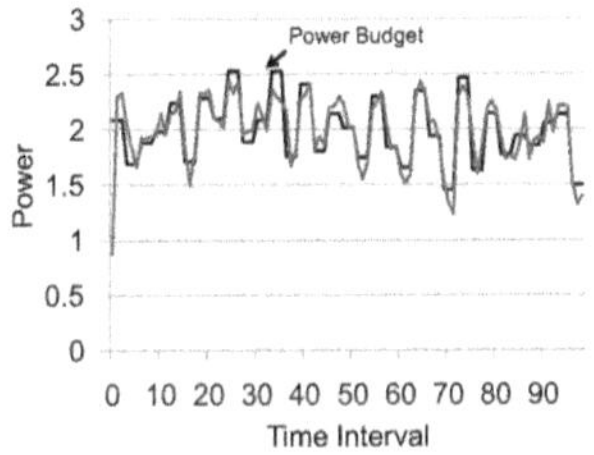

(b) PID controller

Figure 11: Employing P and PID controllers.

Our experiments with different cache sizes show that our speedups are not very sensitive to the cache bank sizes, since in this case, due to the low budget allocated to the cache banks, even when more cache space is available, only a portion of them is used during runtime. One of the parameters that affects the performance improvements achieved by PEPON is the frequency at which the control decisions are made and enforced (our epoch sizes). Our experiments show that the speedup achieved for small epoch sizes is generally higher. This is because, in this case PEPON is invoked more frequently, and the behaviors of the running applications are monitored with a higher frequency; as a result, we may end up achieving better performance improvements. However, this also means more overhead.

4.3 Power Budget Violations

As can be observed from Figures 7(d), 8(d), the overall power budget could not always be tracked with 100% accuracy and is violated over the course of execution (although this violation is in general very low). Also, in some cases, the budget is not fully utilized. This is because the power consumption of the individual components at the bottom of the partitioning tree (see Figure 3(a)), is not always exactly the same as their power budgets. There are two main reasons for this: (i) the knobs used by the controllers can only take values from a set of discrete levels and cannot be varied continuously. As an example, the frequency/voltage of a core can only be set to the one of the discrete values selected from Table 2. Consequently, the frequency chosen by the controller may not be the exact one required to reach the power budget; and (ii) when the target power budget of a controller is modulated, it takes time for the controller to track the new target and, during that time, the output power may fluctuate. Even if the budget is fixed, the controller needs to compensate for the potential change in the behavior of the running application. One of the methods using which these over- and under-utilizations of the available power budget can be handled is through dynamically changing the reference budgets. For example, if we under-utilize the available budget in the previous interval by $x\%$, we could increase the reference budget value by $x\%$. Investigating this and similar compensation schemes is in our future research agenda.

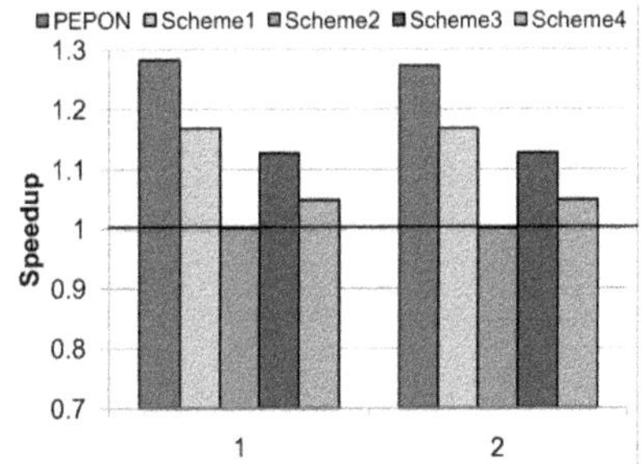

Figure 12: Performance improvements achieved for Mix-1 by varying the default values of configuration parameters.

5. RELATED WORK

Control theory as a tool for power management has recently gained popularity but most prior control centric works do not account for chip-wide power management that takes into account cores, on-chip caches, and the underlying NoC. We have already quantitatively compared our work with [20] and show that our proposal fares better since it is a more holistic approach that considers the on-chip cores, caches and the NoC. In this section, we discuss the most relevant prior works to our proposal.

5.1 Feedback Control Based Power Management

[24] proposes a control theoretic framework for power management in multi-clock domain architectures, where each domain is controlled by a separate clock. In this work, a two-tier power management architecture is proposed, where the first tier allocates a target budget to each local island and the second tier controls the power. The solution becomes simpler in this case since it is implicitly assumed that all cores (and their caches) in a domain would be running *similar* applications, i.e., all cores in a particular domain would either host CPU intensive or memory intensive applications. This allows for DVFS of an entire domain using the per domain clock. Compared to this architecture, our solution targets a realistic CMP with cores, shared caches and an NoC, where domain level clock management is prohibitive. To tackle this, our proposal has a two level power control: The first level allocates power budget among the cores, shared caches and the NoC, and the second level redistributes the core power among different cores, and the cache power among different caches. Other related works advocating control theory for power and thermal management include [6, 15, 31, 32, 33]. In [6], a PI-based core thermal controller is proposed and an outer control loop is used to decide process migrations on thermal emergencies. The proposal in [15] extended [33] and proposes a distributed version of the scheme, applying the basic mechanics of the formal approach to CMPs. In [31], a hierarchical control architecture is proposed that controls the total power consumption of a large-scale data center to stay within a constraint imposed by its power distribution capacity. This work, however, only models cores in a processor when it comes to power management. In [32], Wang et al. propose a multi-input multi-output solution to CMP temperature management. One major difference between our proposal and the work in [32] is that, while our approach is simple

and flexible (in fact flexibility policy was one of the prime design time consideration behind our proposed approach), [32] use sophisticated controllers whose complexity is proportional to the number of cores in the chip. Consequently, it is hard to apply the same to really large CMPs. Further, when compared to the work in [20], our proposal targets all major components in a CMP (cores, caches and NoC), whereas [20] only targets power control in cores.

5.2 Ad-hoc Power and Thermal Management

There are many prior proposals focussing on the design of power and thermal management schemes [5, 9, 13, 18, 22, 25, 28]. These works highlight the importance of adapting to workload behavior under power and thermal constraints. However, most of these works adopt a combination of independent local schemes in the architecture or scheduling decisions in the operating system. Meng et al. [22] proposed an adaptive, multi-optimization strategy for multicore power management and addressed the problem of meeting a global chip-wide power budget through run-time adaptation of configurable processor cores. Isci et al. [13] also used a global power manager, similar to ours, that provides a mechanism to sense the per-core power and performance state of the chip at periodic intervals; it then sets the operating power level or mode of each core to enforce adherence to known chip-level power budgets. However, the local monitoring used to enforce these power budgets were based on open loop control and does not provide the same robustness as the formal feedback control in our work. Furthermore, the constraints on the achievable performance were less stringent as they perform per-core DVFS as opposed to core, cache and NoC as we do in our work. Prior proposals like [2, 8, 27] have looked at energy saving mechanisms for cache alone by dynamically reconfiguring the cache hierarchy or partitioning a shared cache among multiple applications. Works such as [7] have investigated memory cell sizing for cache energy efficiency. Our work also uses cache reconfiguration for energy management, but we do so as part of managing the energy consumption of an entire CMP rather than the on-chip caches alone.

6. CONCLUDING REMARKS

The main contribution of this paper is a two-level power distribution strategy oriented towards maximizing system performance under a specified power budget. The results collected from our experiments with 6 workloads formed using 16 applications selected from a set of 30 applications clearly demonstrate the importance of power distribution at both the levels. Specifically, our experimental results indicate that, when using PEPON, overall performance can be improved by as much as 29% over the case when no power distribution is adopted. Further, our results also show that distributing power only at a core level (as done in a recent study [20]) may not be sufficient for maximizing performance.

7. REFERENCES

[1] `http://www.spec.org/cpu2006/`.

[2] R. Balasubramonian, et al. Memory hierarchy reconfiguration for energy and performance in general-purpose processor architectures. In *MICRO'00*.

[3] D. Brooks, et al. Wattch: a framework for architectural-level power analysis and optimizations. In *ISCA'00*.

[4] T. Burd and R. Brodersen. Design issues for dynamic voltage scaling. In *ISLPED'00*.

[5] J. D. Davis, J. Laudon, and K. Olukotun. Maximizing CMP throughput with mediocre cores. In *PACT'05*.

[6] J. Donald and M. Martonosi. Techniques for multicore thermal management: classification and new exploration. In *ISCA'06*.

[7] R. G. Dreslinski, et al. Reconfigurable energy efficient near threshold cache architectures. In *MICRO'08*.

[8] S. Dropsho, et al. Integrating adaptive on-chip storage structures for reduced dynamic power. In *PACT'02*.

[9] M. Gomaa, et al. Heat-and-run: leveraging smt and CMP to manage power density through the operating system. In *ASPLOS'04*.

[10] J. L. Hellerstein, et al. *Feedback Control of Computing Systems*. 2004.

[11] Y. Hoskote, et al. A 5-GHz mesh interconnect for a teraflops processor. *IEEE Micro*, 27:51–61, September 2007.

[12] J. Howard, et al. A 48-Core IA-32 Message-passing processor with DVFS in 45nm CMOS. In *ISSCC'10*.

[13] C. Isci, et al. An analysis of efficient multi-core global power management policies: Maximizing performance for a given power budget. In *MICRO'06*.

[14] N. K. Jha. Low power system scheduling and synthesis. In *ICCAD'01*.

[15] P. Juang, Q. Wu, L.-S. Peh, M. Martonosi, and D. W. Clark. Coordinated, distributed, formal energy management of chip multiprocessors. In *ISLPED '05*.

[16] J. Kim and M. Horowitz. Adaptive supply serial links with sub-1v operation and per-pin clock recovery. In *ISSCC'02*.

[17] J. F. Kurose and K. W. Ross. *Computer Networking: A Top-Down Approach Featuring the Internet*. Addison Wesley, 2003.

[18] J. Li and J. F. Martínez. Dynamic power-performance adaptation of parallel computation on chip multiprocessors. In *HPCA'06*.

[19] S.-H. Lim, et al. Migration, assignment, and scheduling of jobs in virtualized environment. In *ATC'11*.

[20] K. Ma, et al. Scalable power control for many-core architectures running multi-threaded applications. In *ISCA'11*.

[21] P. S. Magnusson, et al. Simics: A full system simulation platform. *Computer*, 2002.

[22] K. Meng, et al. Multi-optimization power management for chip multiprocessors. In *PACT'08*.

[23] Y. Meng, et al. On the limits of leakage power reduction in caches. In *HPCA'05*.

[24] A. K. Mishra, et al. CPM in CMPs: Coordinated power management in chip-multiprocessors. In *SC'10*.

[25] M. Monchiero, et al. Power/performance/thermal design-space exploration for multicore architectures. *IEEE Trans. Parallel Distrib. Syst.*, 19:666–681, May 2008.

[26] U. Y. Ogras, et al. Voltage-frequency island partitioning for GALS-based networks-on-chip. In *DAC'07*.

[27] M. K. Qureshi and Y. N. Patt. Utility-based cache partitioning: A low-overhead, high-performance, runtime mechanism to partition shared caches. In *MICRO'06*.

[28] J. Sharkey, et al. Evaluating design tradeoffs in on-chip power management for cmps. In *ISLPED '07*.

[29] S. Thoziyoor, et al. CACTI 5.1. *Technical Report, Hewlett-Packard Company*, 2009.

[30] H. Wang, et al. Orion: A power-performance simulator for interconnection networks. In *MICRO'02*.

[31] X. Wang, et al. SHIP: Scalable hierarchical power control for large-scale data centers. In *PACT'09*.

[32] Y. Wang, et al. Temperature-constrained power control for chip multiprocessors with online model estimation. In *ISCA'09*.

[33] Q. Wu, et al. Formal online methods for voltage/frequency control in multiple clock domain microprocessors. *SIGARCH Comput. Archit. News*, 32:248–259, October 2004.

XPoint Cache: Scaling Existing Bus-Based Coherence Protocols for 2D and 3D Many-Core Systems

Ronald G. Dreslinski, Thomas Manville, Korey Sewell, Reetuparna Das, Nathaniel Pinckney, Sudhir Satpathy, David Blaauw, Dennis Sylvester, Trevor Mudge

Department of Electrical Engineering and Computer Science
The University of Michigan, Ann Arbor – Ann Arbor, MI, 48109

ABSTRACT

With multi-core processors now mainstream, the shift to many-core processors poses a new set of design challenges. In particular, the scalability of coherence protocols remains a significant challenge. While complex Network-on-Chip interconnect fabrics have been proposed and in some cases implemented, most of industry has slowly evolved existing coherence solutions to meet the needs of a growing number of cores. Industries' slow adoption of Network-on-Chip designs is in large part due to the significant effort needed to design and verify the system. However, simply scaling bus-based coherence is not straightforward either because of increased contention and latency on the bus for large core counts.

This paper proposes a new architecture, *XPoint*, which does not need to modify existing bus-based snooping coherence protocols to scale to 64 core systems. *XPoint* employs interleaved cache structures with detailed floorplaning and system analysis to reduce contention at high core counts. Results show that the *XPoint* system achieves, on average, a 28× and 35× speedup over a single core design on the Splash2 benchmarks for a 32 and 64 core system respectively (a 1.6× improvement over a 64 core conventional bus). *XPoint* is also evaluated as a 3D stacked system to reduce further bus latency. Results show a 29× and 45× speedup for 32 and 64 core systems respectively (a 2.1× improvement over a 64 core conventional bus and within 8% of the speedup of a 64 core system with an ideal interconnect). Measurements also show that the *XPoint* system decreases bus contention of a 64 core system to only 13% higher than that of an 8-core design (a 29× improvement over a 64 core conventional bus).

Categories and Subject Descriptors

B.0 [**Hardware**]: General; C.0 [**Computer Systems Organization**]: General

Keywords

3D Integration, Bus Design, Cache Coherence, Interconnect

PACT'12, September 19–23, 2012, Minneapolis, Minnesota, USA.

1. INTRODUCTION

Shared memory multi-core processors have become mainstream. As core counts in these systems continue to rise, it becomes important to support scalable cache coherence protocols. While complex systems have been proposed for directory based Network-on-Chip (NoC) interconnects, they have only been adopted in a limited number of commercial systems [3]. Meanwhile, many manufacturers continue to run on evolved versions of older snooping based designs, such as the rings in the IBM Power 4/5 series [41] and the Intel Sandybridge [36]. Other systems have taken small steps away from snooping protocols by adopting crossbars to interconnect the chip such as Sun's Niagara 2 [26] and IBM's BlueGene/Q [24].

The reluctance of industry to move to NoC designs is in part driven by the difficulty of system verification. There is a significant infrastructure [31] around existing coherence solutions, which makes validating evolutionary coherence solutions much less costly in both engineering effort and time to market. Thus, an interconnect that scales to many-core systems without modifying the underlying coherence protocol is desirable.

In this paper, we propose a new interconnect architecture, *XPoint*, which employs address-interleaved cache architectures to scale unmodified snooping coherence protocol designs to many-core systems as large as 64 cores. Address interleaving of the memory system, coupled with the aid of point-to-point interconnects and optimized layout designs, helps to reduce the contention for shared resources in the system while leaving the coherence protocol *unmodified*. Detailed floorplaning and analysis is done in a 32nm technology which shows that the design can easily scale to 64 cores in a conventional 2D layout—*XPoint 2D*. A 32 core *XPoint 2D* system only increases the bus contention by 9% on average when compared to an 8 core design, and has 10× less bus contention than a 32 core system with a conventional design. A 32 and 64 core *XPoint 2D* system achieves, on average, a 28× and 35× speedup over a single core, which is a 1.6× improvement over a 64 core conventional design.

While the *XPoint 2D* system itself scales to 64 cores, at the higher core counts (32-64) there is still room for improvement. The bus delay of the system at this point is much larger than the 8 core system, and leads to increased bus contention and longer L1 miss latencies. We show that the *XPoint* design extends naturally to 3-dimensions (3D). While 3D integration is itself a speculative technology, recent designs [17, 29] have supported the feasibility of such systems with fabricated test chips. The work by Fick *et al.* [17] demonstrates a 7-layer, 3D-stacked system with 128 ARM cores on 4 layers of CMOS logic and 256*MB* of DRAM on the remaining 3 layers. With optimized floorplans the *XPoint 3D* system can reduce the bus delay of a 64 core *XPoint 2D* system to that of a 16 core system. This reduction in bus delay shows that an *XPoint 3D* system with 64 cores only increases bus contention by 13% on average over an 8 core system and has 29× less contention than a 64 core conventional design. The *XPoint 3D* also improves the average speedup of the system to 29× and 45× for a 32 and 64 core system, which is a 2.1× improvement over a 64 core conventional design and is within 8% of the speedup of an ideal interconnect.

An important concern for 3D stacked systems is cooling. Thermal analysis shows it is possible to stack 4 layers of *XPoint 2D* systems in a single chip that can be cooled by conventional means.

The main contributions of this paper are:

- An architecture that uses snooping buses with *unmodified* coherence protocols coupled with address-interleaved caches and point-to-point links to reduce shared bus contention in on-die many-core chips
- Detailed floorplaning and spice analysis of the buses and other key components in 32nm
- An extension of the design in a proven 3D technology, including thermal analysis, that reduces the latency of shared buses
- Detailed analysis of the performance of this design from 8 to 64 cores, showing the system readily scales to 64 cores in both 2D and 3D implementations

The rest of the paper is organized as follows: In Section 2 we will motivate the advantage of simply extending existing snooping protocols and illustrates the key barriers. Section 3 will present the *XPoint Cache* architecture. Experimental methodology is presented in Section 4 and the results in Section 5. A brief summary of related work is presented in Section 6. Finally we provide concluding remarks in Section 7.

2. MOTIVATION

Broadcast-based snooping protocols are a common approach to building multicore processors [8]. In the past, there has been considerable effort to retain and scale snooping protocols by adapting them for split transaction buses [18], hierarchical buses [40], and address broadcast trees [11] that provide a "logical bus" ordering. Existing products, like the IBM Power4/5 and the Intel Sandybridge, retain and scale snooping coherence protocols for ring interconnects [36,41].

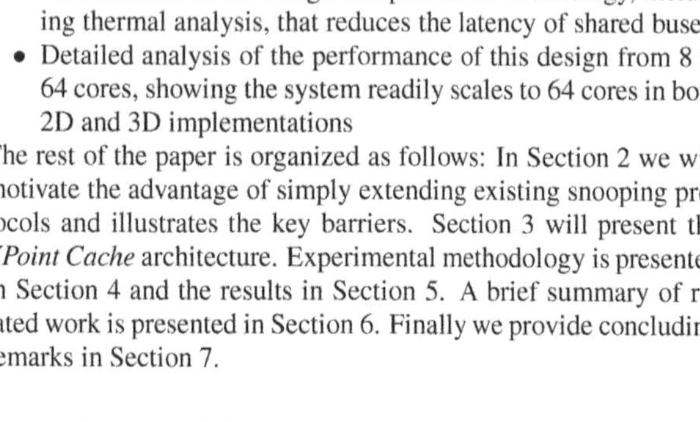

Figure 1: State transition diagram for the MESTI coherence protocol [32] including spit-transactions and race conditions (Containing 47-states). Industry protocols similar to this have an extensive infrastructure to verify state interaction.

While more advanced approaches have been discussed in literature, industry designers have been more comfortable evolving their existing snooping-based system over the years. One of the reasons such effort has been devoted towards continuously scaling and supporting snooping protocols is the prohibitive design and verification complexity of any coherence protocol [31]. While it is possible to formally verify relatively simple state machines at the abstract level [14,16,19,38,39], verifying the concrete system with detailed interactions is difficult and requires a mixture of pre-silicon [49] and post silicon validation [9,13,35,43]. Although significant efforts have been devoted to the verification of protocols, coherence bugs in commercial processors often go undetected [25]. In fact, the need for simpler verification has even led architects to propose coherence protocols designed explicitly for verification [50].

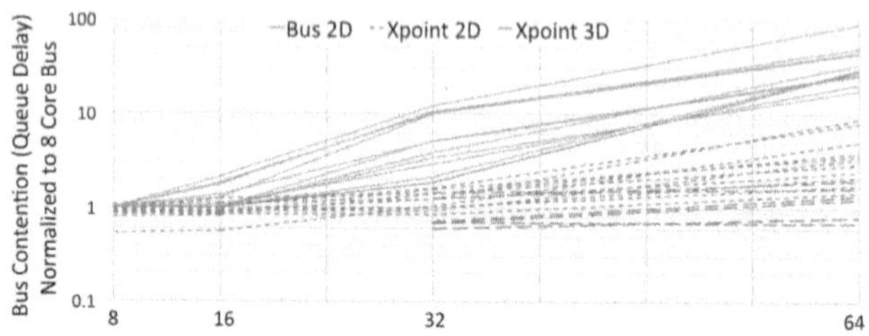

Figure 2: Bus Utilization for 8-64 Cores on the SPLASH2 Benchmarks. Each line represents one benchmark. The conventional bus based system sees a 50-100× increase in contention, while the *XPoint* designs limit this to much lower amounts.

Some designs, such as the AMD Opteron [27] and IBM Blue-Gene/Q [24], have migrated to a directory based approach for modest core counts. These designs are built on top of either point-to-point interconnects or crossbar based designs. Directory protocols are more complex than snooping, but because the interconnects in these systems are predictable and contain no intermediate buffering within the interconnect itself, the increased verification effort is bounded. Meanwhile, in the research community even more complex directory systems have been proposed. These systems typically employ a Network-on-Chip (NoC) approach to address the scalability of many-core systems, however very few commercial chips have adopted this approach [3].

Although NoC systems scale towards large core counts, transitioning to such a design represents a more radical change than just evolving an existing snooping system with well defined design flow and verification infrastructure. The MESTI [32] protocol for snooping shown in Figure 1 contains 47 states, while the directory protocol used in the *gem5* simulator [6] for an NoC system requires 65 states for the L2, 15 states for the L1, 19 states for the directory, and 3 states for the DMA engine. The product of all the potential states that need to be verified in such systems becomes daunting, particularly when many of these controllers are instantiated multiple times in the system. Compounding this problem is the internal buffering and routing algorithms employed in the NoC which create unpredictable, non-uniform latencies. This, in turn, increases the number of transient states and makes post-silicon verification more difficult as routing algorithms and buffering solutions also need to be verified.

The goal of this work is to extend the snooping bus based coherence protocol to many core systems without modifying the underlying implementation of snooping protocols. However, the increasing bandwidth pressure and latency on the bus as the core count increases provide two significant hurdles to scalability. The proposed *XPoint* design challenges the conventional wisdom that bus-based approaches cannot scale to many-core systems [12]. While

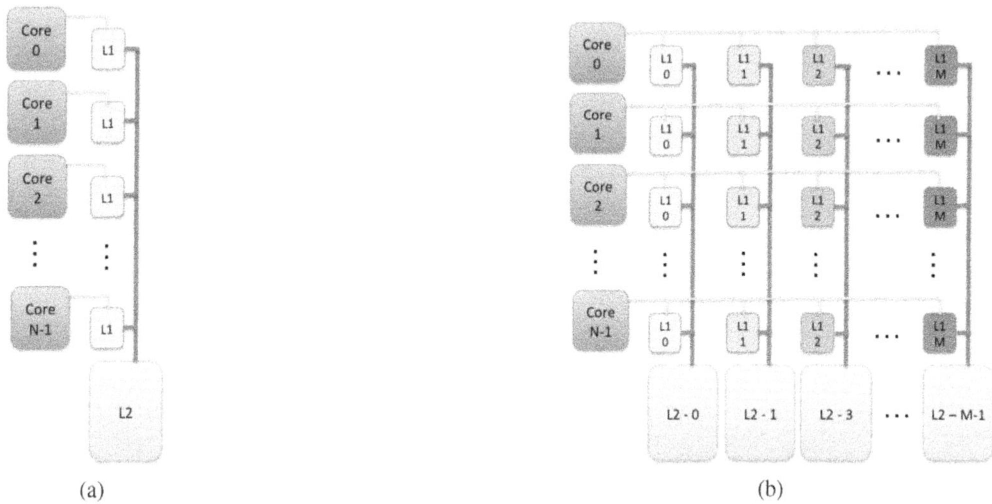

Figure 3: High level view of (a) a conventional bus based architecture, and (b) The *XPoint* architecture. Caches in a vertical column are all assigned to the same address range. No snooping is required between vertical columns. The vertical buses represent independent unmodified snooping busses. The horizontal connections are made with fast point-to-point links.

the *XPoint* design does not scale indefinitely, detailed results show that in a 32nm technology it can easily scale to at least 32 cores in a conventional 2D layout and to at leaset 64 cores when 3D integration techniques are employed.

To better understand the barriers associated with scaling snooping coherence on a bus based interconnect Figure 2 shows the bus contention rate for the SPLASH2 benchmarks at various core counts. The methodology and configuration parameters are presented later in Section 4. The bus contention rate, approximated by the average L1 queueing delay, is normalized to an 8 core system. Each line in the diagram represents one SPLASH2 benchmark. As the core count is increased, the bus contention of traditional designs (solid lines) grows dramatically. At a core count of 64, an 8× increase in the number of cores, the benchmarks experience 20-100× increases in bus contention. To extend unmodified snooping coherence a two pronged approach will be necessary that attacks the contention on the bus as well as the bus latency. The *XPoint 2D* system (short dashed lines) employs techniques to reduce contention, as a result 32 cores only increase the contention on the bus by 1.6× in the worst case. As the *XPoint 2D* system is scaled further to 64 cores, the increased delay on the bus pushes contention higher to 8.9× that of the baseline 8 core system. The *XPoint 3D* system (long dashed lines) tackles the delay scalability of the bus using 3D integration. At 64 cores the bus contention for *XPoint 3D* is, on average, only 13% higher than that of an 8-core system, even though it supports 8× the number of cores.

3. CROSSPOINT CACHE ARCHITECTURE

In the following subsections we will present architectures which overcome the two major hurdles of scaling bus based snooping protocols. First we tackle the bus contention with an architecture called *XPoint 2D*. *XPoint 2D* uses multiple cache line interleaved buses supporting unmodified coherence protocols. Results in Section 5 will show this system scales readily to 64 cores. The *XPoint* architecture naturally extends to 3D allowing further scaling by overcoming the increasing bus latency—*XPoint 3D*. The section concludes with thermal analysis of *XPoint 3D* and the applicability of the *XPoint* to other bus-based systems.

3.1 XPoint 2D - Overcoming Bus Contention

To understand the *XPoint 2D* architecture a brief review of a traditional bus based system follows. Figure 3(a) shows a high level view of a traditional bus based system. Each core is connected to a private L1, each of the L1's are connected to a shared snooping bus, which in turn is connected to the L2. As the number of cores grows, the contention on the shared bus becomes a bottleneck in the system. The *XPoint 2D* architecture addresses this bottleneck while leaving the coherence protocol unmodified.

Our baseline builds on memory interleaving techniques developed in the 1980's to address interconnect congestion in board level multi-processors [46]. However, integration levels and pin constraints limited their practicality. We show that with new architectural techniques these designs are now practical for single chip implementations, where point-to-point connections, higher cache associativites, and a greater number of wires are available. In addition we explore the implications of such designs on coherence mechanisms.

The *XPoint 2D* system exploits address-interleaving to reduce bandwidth pressure on the shared bus fabric. Figure 3(b) shows the logical layout of our proposed architecture. To scale the coherence protocol to n cores, each core's last level of private cache (L1 in this diagram) is split into m equal slices. The core can access all the m slices via direct point-to-point channels. By using point-to-point connections, the speed of the interconnect can be much faster than a traditional bus which requires bi-directional repeaters and arbitration units. The shared L2 cache is also split into m equal slices. A bus connects a vertical column of private cache slices (n L1 slices) to a shared L2 cache slice, all of which map to the same addresses. This isolates the coherence traffic separately on each vertical bus from the other vertical buses in the system. The result is a multi-bus system with simple, unmodified coherence that reduces contention and increases bandwidth.

3.1.1 *Architectural Impacts*

The floorplan of the *XPoint 2D* system is shown in Figure 4. The introduction of point-to-point links from the core to the L1 increases the access latency. By keeping the connections point-to-

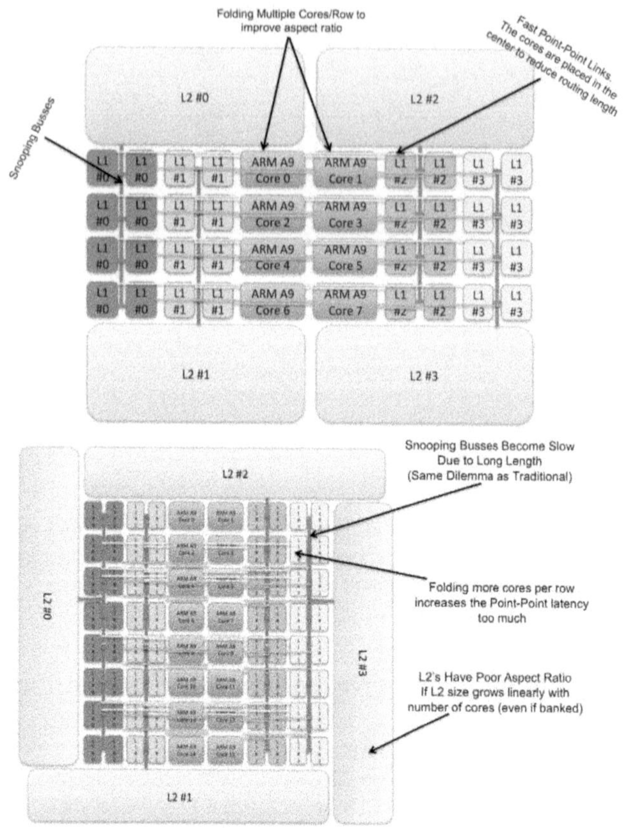

Figure 4: Floorplan view of a *XPoint 2D* system for 8 and 16 cores.

point, rather than bus based, the system can communicate to/from the L1 slices in one additional cycle. To help hide this new latency a 4 cache line, fully-associative L0 buffer is inserted in the core. The L0 and L1 are accessed in parallel, so hits in the L0 take a single cycle, and hits in the L1 take two cycles. Coherence of the L0 is maintained by keeping a copy of the tags in the L1 slices. When snoops occur on addresses contained in the L0 that must be invalidated, the L1 can signal the L0 via a point-to-point invalidation wire. We will show with results, that the increase in L1 access time is offset by the increased bandwidth and reduced contention of the *XPoint 2D* system in Section 5.

Splitting the cache into slices has the potential to produce different cache miss/hit behavior. For the *XPoint* architecture we propose smaller associativities for slices. The lowest bits of the set index are used to determine address mappings to the slices. In addition, because the accesses are split across the buses, prefetch mechanisms should be located at the core/L0 to observe the entire pattern.

3.1.2 Coherence and Consistency

In Figure 3(b) each vertical bus is an *unmodified* snooping based interconnect, and because each vertical bus is independent of the other vertical buses (different address ranges), no snooping is needed for caches in the horizontal direction. By splitting the bus into m slices, the total bandwidth to memory is m-times larger, and the contention on the bus is $1/m^{th}$ that of a traditional design.

Although the coherence mechanism remains unmodified, there may still be consistency issues. Coherence is an ordering of requests to the same block, so splitting the bus into slices means there is no ordering constraints between vertical buses. Consistency on the other hand is an ordering of requests to different addresses, and therefore requires some guarantees across vertical slices. However, for x86 systems which support a form of processor consistency, the consistency can be maintained by the store buffer in the core itself, insuring that all stores are drained from the processor in program order. More constrained consistency models will require the processor to properly order requests to each of the slices.

3.1.3 Interleaving Mechanism

As mentioned earlier, by splitting the bus resource there is the potential for uneven utilization of the vertical slices. For uniform-random traffic the bus utilization is even. However, if the system is split into four slices, a program with an access pattern where the stride is a harmonic of 4 will access only a subset of slices creating an uneven utilization.

To address these concerns a more complex mapping scheme can be used to determine the slice index of the system. In the results section we present a system with simple address interleaving on low order bits and show that for all but 3 benchmarks utilization is not significantly impacted. For the 3 benchmarks impacted by the interleaving, they still outperform the baseline bus system, however the optimal solution is a system with only 2 or 4 slices, instead of 8. We leave more detailed analysis of other interleaving hash functions as future work.

3.1.4 Remaining Scaling Limitations

While the *XPoint 2D* system addresses the increased contention on the shared bus, it does not address the increased latency of the bus in the system. Figure 4(b) shows the *XPoint 2D* architecture scaled to 32 cores. This system still has several limits on ultimate scalability. First, the bus length grows linearly with the number of cores, the same obstacle faced by a traditional system. Second the aspect ratios of the L2 cache become large, meaning that the cache banks are spread out which increases latency and power consumption.

3.2 XPoint 3D - Overcoming Bus Latency

The *XPoint* architecture naturally extends to 3D allowing further scaling by overcoming the increasing bus latency of the *XPoint 2D* system. The following subsections will discuss the 3D technology used for our study and present the *XPoint 3D* architecture.

3.2.1 3D Integration Technology

There are many techniques for 3D integration. Simple techniques such as face-to-face bonding allow simple stacks of 2 chips while more complicated techniques that use wafer thinning allow for larger stack systems. For our analysis we use figures from a 3D integration technology by Tezzaron [23]. Their technique is a via-first, back-end-of-line integration technology and has been demonstrated in several test chips [17,29]. In the system by Fick *et al.* [17] the Tezzaron technology is used to stack four layers of CMOS logic on top of three layers of DRAM. Figure 5 (left) shows a diagram of the system implemented by Fick *et al.* Figure 5 (right) shows a cross section [29] of the through-silicon-via (TSV) technology from Tezzaron. The layers are thinned to less than 12 microns, and the TSV's themselves are less than 6 microns thick. The size of the TSV's are 1.4 square microns, and can be placed with a density of 62,000 TSV's per square mm.

The resistance ($<.35\Omega$) and capacitance ($2fF$) of these TSV's are extremely small compared to other 3D integration technologies. They allow for extremely fast and short connections between lay-

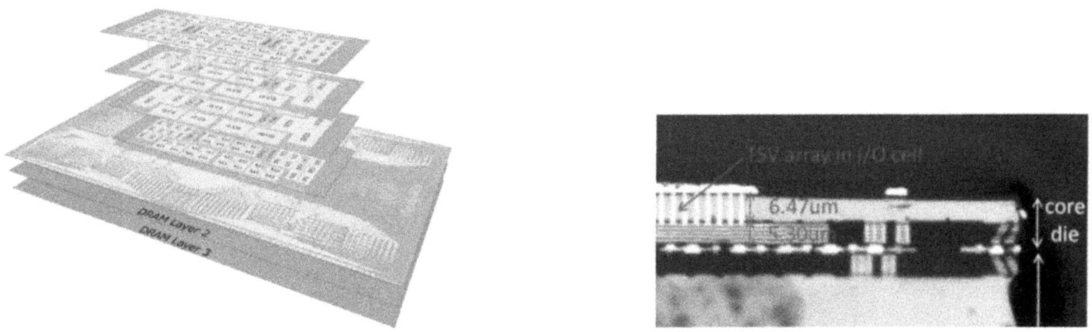

Figure 5: Top level view of the Centip3De 7-layer 3D system [17] built on Tezzaron 3D stacking technology and a cross section of the same process on the 3D-MAPS system [29]. Note the TSV's are only 6.47 microns deep and the wafer is thinned to less than 12 microns which is important for reducing thermal resistance and RC delays.

ers. In fact, in a 4 layer stack the length of a TSV running the whole distance of the stack is <50 microns. This allows the *XPoint 3D* system to create buses that run in the 3rd dimension that add minimal latency to the 2D bus.

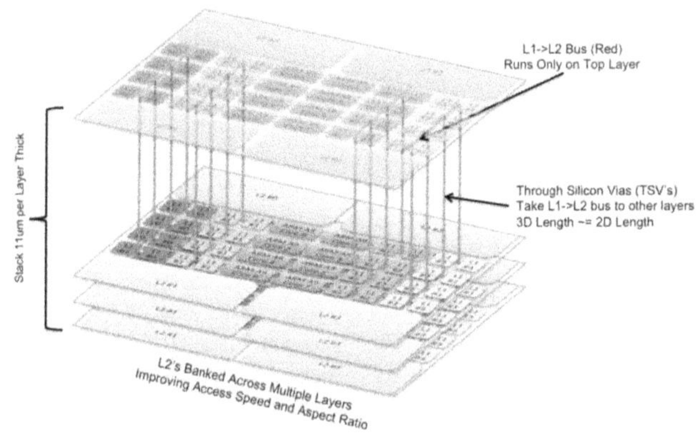

Figure 6: Diagram of the *XPoint 3D* design.

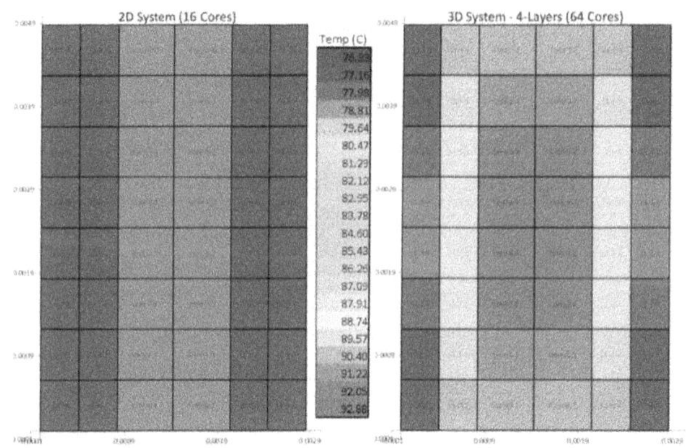

Figure 7: HotSpot simulation of the *XPoint* system on 1 layer,16 core system and across a 4 layer, 64 core system. The peak temperature of the chip is 92 degrees Celsius on 4-layers.

3.2.2 XPoint 3D Architecture

Figure 6 shows the proposed *XPoint 3D* system. The coherent buses are run only along the top layer, and connections to L2's at lower levels are made with TSV's which are 11 microns long per layer. This pitchfork layout creates a 3D bus that is approximately the same length as the bus on the top layer. This means that the effective length of the bus is halved when the system contains 2-layers, and quartered when spread across 4-layers. To a first order the latency of the bus grows linearly with $cores/layers$ instead of linearly with $cores$ as it does in a 2D system. In addition the L2 cache is banked across multiple layers to improve the aspect ratio of the cache itself, thereby improving access times and power consumption of the L2.

3.2.3 Thermal Constraints

As with any 3D chip design, thermal constraints can be a matter of concern. To verify the system operates in a thermal region that can be cooled by conventional solutions, we perform analysis of the system with the HotSpot 5.1 [42] simulator. The thermal characteristics of the Tezzaron process were modeled in HotSpot and peak power draw numbers were used for the core. Power numbers for the Cortex-A9 were based on published data [2] and scaled to 32nm. Figure 7 shows the simulated system for a single layer and a 4-layer stack. The low power design of the Cortex-A9 processor helps to make stacking feasible. The peak temperature of the 4-layer system reaches 92 degrees centigrade, well within conventional cooling solutions. Had the thermal profile been more of an issue, designs where cores are placed on the left side of the L1's on even numbered layers and the right side of the L1's on odd numbered layers could be used to reduce the thermal profile at the expense of more power to drive the longer point-to-point links. The HotSpot analysis did not consider the thermal dissipating characteristics of the TSV's, which would have further reduced the peak temperature. More details on the component models and methodology can be found in Section 4.

3.3 Other Opportunities

This architectural design was done with a system containing private L1 caches and shared L2 caches. Many commercial systems implement private L2 caches and shared L3 caches. The coherence protocol for these systems is different, however the techniques of interleaving the system will also work in such designs without modification of the coherence protocol. In such systems the L2 caches would be interleaved the interleaving would be done on the

L2 caches and the L1 could remain coupled with the processor in either interleaved slices, or as a single L1.

4. EXPERIMENTAL METHODOLOGY

4.1 Component Models

The following sections will describe the models used for simulation. A summary of the components area and speed can be found in Table 1, details on how each value was arrived at are found in the corresponding sub-section.

Table 1: Component Areas and Speeds in 32nm

	Area/Length	Speed/Latency
ARM Cortex-A9	$0.38mm^2$	$1.25GHz$
L1 (64kB I&D) per core	$0.61mm^2$	1 cycle
L2 (256 kB) per core	$1.33mm^2$	8 cycles
Coherent Bus	$0.31mm/core$	160 ps/mm

Table 2: 2D Floorplan Sizes and Bus Speeds

Num. of Cores	Die Size	Bus Length	Bus Speed	Total L2 Size
8	$19mm^2$	$2.48mm$	$>$1.25 GHz	$2MB$
16	$38mm^2$	$4.96mm$	1.25 GHz	$4MB$
32	$78mm^2$	$10.1mm$	~630 MHz	$8MB$
64	$156mm^2$	$20.1mm$	~315 MHz	$16MB$

Cores: The system is based on ARM Cortex-A9 cores. Area and power estimates are drawn from ARM data sheets [2] and scaled to 32nm. The core area in 32nm is $0.38mm^2$, the speed is $1.25GHz$, and the power is $0.5W$.

Caches: Cache sizes and speeds are obtained from a comercial memory compiler. The total L1 cache size per core is $64kB$ for both I- and D-Cache. The cache area is $0.6mm^2$. The L1 access time is 1 cycle for the bus based system and 2 cycles in the *XPoint* cache system due to the point-to-point link latency. To hide this latency in the *XPoint* cache system a 4 cache line, fully-associative buffer is added as a L0 next to the core. The L0 and L1 are accessed in parallel. The associativity of the entire L1 is 4-way. When the system is interleaved, the associativity of each slice is divided. When the system is split into 8-banks, the associativity is 1-way per 8 bank caches. The L2 cache size is $256kB$ per core, 16-way associative. The die area of the L2 is $1.33mm^2$ per core, and the access latency is 8 cycles. The L2 size and associativity are divided among interleaved slices in the same manner as the L1.

Busses: Bus delays and power estimations were obtained using a 13-layer metallization stack from an industrial 32nm process. In this metallization stack there are five *1X*, three *2X*, two *4X*, two *8X*, and one *16X* metal layers. The *1X* metal layers and one of the *2X* metal layers are reserved for local routing (within the core/-cache). The *8X* and *16X* metal layers are reserved for power and clock routing. That leaves two *2X* and two *4X* layers for global routing. Bus delays were calculated using wire models from the design kit and calculated using SPICE including wire parasitics, repeaters, and worst case cross-coupling capacitance of neighboring wires and metal layers. Repeater placement is done using optimally interleaved spacing as described by Ghoneima and Ismail [20].

The L1 uni-directional point-to-point links can achieve a speed of $54ps/mm$ in double spaced *4X* metal, permitting a delay of less than one clock cycle to/from the L1 banks. The L2 snooping bus requires more complicated bi-directional repeaters and achieves a maximum speed of $160ps/mm$ in double spaced *4X* metal. Assuming the L1 caches in the traditional bus based system are mirrored across the snooping bus to reduce wire length, the bus length is $0.31mm$ per core (about half the length of a core due to mirroring). Table 2 shows the achieved speeds of the bus for each core count. For the 8 and 16 core system, the bus can operate at the speed of the cores ($1.25GHz$), for larger systems the bus is slower.

Table 3: *gem5* Simulation Parameters

Component	Bus Based System	*XPoint System*
Processor	ARM Cortex-A9, 1.25 GHz, 2-Wide, 56 Physical Registers	
Cache Block Size	64 Bytes	
L0 Cache	None	4-entry, fully associative, 1-cycle
L1 Cache	64kB Split I and D Caches	
	4-way Associative, 1-Cycle	Div. by number of Slices Associativity 4-way/#Slices, 2 -cycle
L2 Cache	256 kB per Core, 16-way, 8-cycle	
Coherent Bus	312-1250 MHz, 64Bytes	
Main Memory	2GB, 50 Cycle Latency	

4.2 Simulator & Benchmarks

We evaluate the *Bus 2D* (conventional bus), *XPoint 2D*, and *XPoint 3D* architectures using the *gem5* full-system simulator [6]. The *gem5* simulator was extended to accommodate the *XPoint* interleaved architecture. No modifications to the coherence protocol were necessary. The *gem5* simulator accurately tracks data throughout the memory system. Because the data is accurately passed through the system, any bugs in the coherence protocol would manifest themselves as errors while simulating. Table 3 details the simulation parameters for the studies. To account for non-determinism in threaded workloads, we randomly perturb memory access latencies and run multiple simulations to arrive at stable runtimes following the approach described by Alameldeen *et al.* [1]. A comparison to an ideal interconnect is presented in Table 4, which simulates an interconnect with infinite bandwidth and zero-contention. Results show the *XPoint* system achieves speedups within 8% of ideal, obviating the need for a comparison to an NoC based system.

We use benchmarks from the SPLASH2 [48] suite to test the systems. The SPLASH2 benchmarks are of particular interest for the study of on-chip interconnects as they have many sharing and data migration patterns. This is illustrated in the work of Barrow-Williams *et al.* [4].

5. RESULTS

In the following sub-sections we will present the results. First the *XPoint 2D* system will be analyzed against a traditional bus based system, showing the decreased bus contention and improved scalability of the system across various numbers of *XPoint* slices. Next results will be presented showing how the improvement of the bus latency impacts the *XPoint 3D* system to take scalability even further. Then an analysis of the speedups of the best configurations for all 2D and 3D systems will be presented.

5.1 Reducing Bus Contention - XPoint 2D

Analysis of the *XPoint 2D* system is made based on three key metrics: Runtime/Speedup, Bus Utilization, and Bus Contention. The bus contention is plotted in Figure 2, and a description of the results is presented at the end of Section 2. Figure 8 presents the other key metrics. The plots in Figure 8 show, on a log-log plot, the normalized runtime (solid lines) and bus utilization (dotted lines).

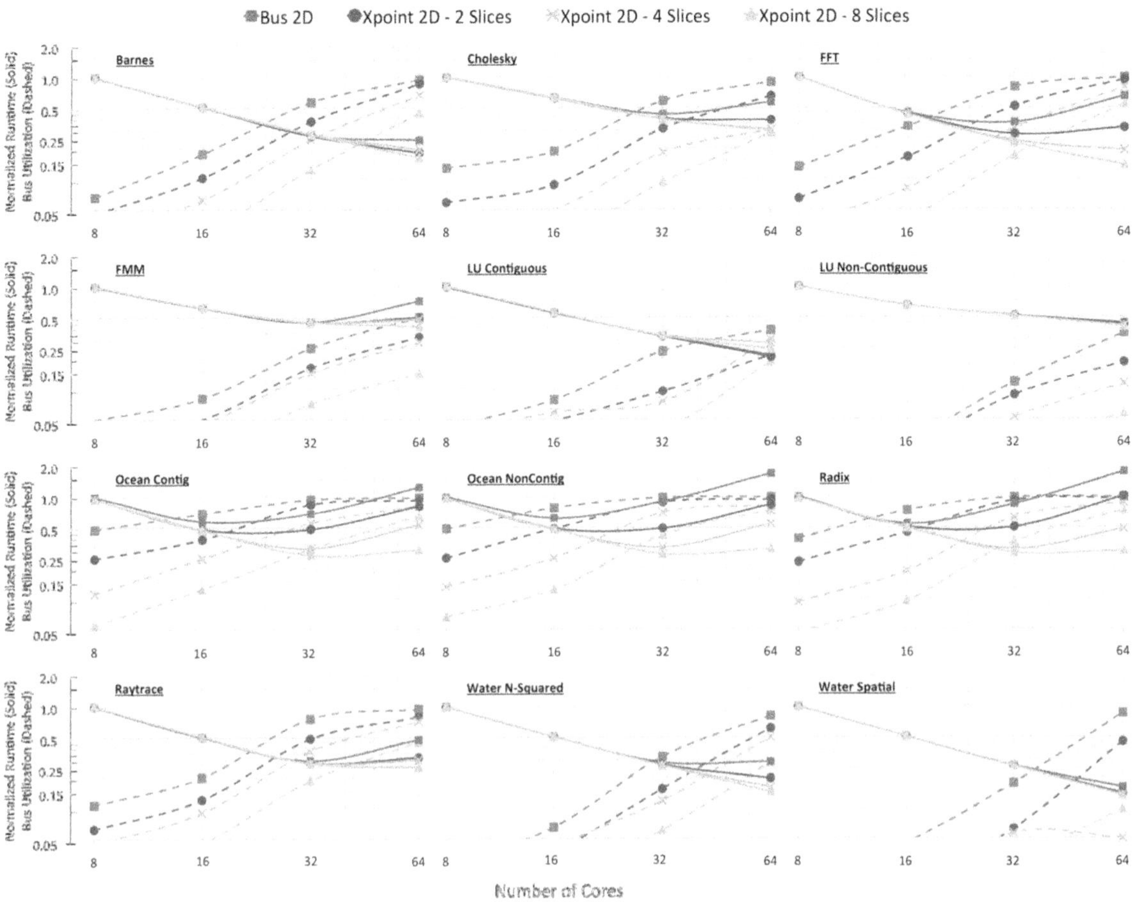

Figure 8: Runtime (solid lines) and Bus Utilization (dotted lines) plotted across core counts. A straight line for runtime represents ideal scaling of the benchmark. As the core count is increased the contention/utilization of the bus is increased, this leads to non-ideal speedup. For the *Bus 2D* system many benchmarks do not scale well beyond 16 cores. The *XPoint 2D* system improves the scalability to higher core counts.

The ideal scaling of these benchmarks would be a straight line (for runtime) where the slope is determined by the efficiency of the parallel scaling in the application itself (workload imbalance and/or ratios of serial to parallel code). Bus utilization is a metric from 0 to 1, describing how often the bus is utilized. The bus utilization numbers saturate for the *Bus 2D* systems for most benchmarks around 32 cores. This saturation correlates with the dramatic increase in bus contention plotted in Figure 2. As the bus utilization and contention increase, the overall runtimes of the benchmarks increase. Eventually the increase in contention outweighs the performance gains of more cores, yielding an optimal number of cores for the system. For the *Ocean Contig*, *Ocean NonContig*, and *Radix* benchmarks the optimal point for a *Bus 2D* system is 16 cores. Beyond this point the runtime increases, even with the addition of more cores. Some benchmarks scale slightly better to 32 cores. There are only two benchmarks that scale to 64 cores on a conventional system. The first is *Water Spatial* where the working set fits in the L1 cache. For the second, *LU Non-Contig*, the runtime line is straight but with a small slope due to workload imbalance. Giving this workload 8× the number of cores only results in a 2× speedup.

The *XPoint 2D* architecture targets benchmarks with scalability limitations due to contention. The plot shows the effects of different degrees of slicing. For the benchmarks whose *Bus 2D* line is not straight, the *XPoint* cache reduces bus contention and lowers the runtime at high core counts—making the line straighter. For many benchmarks, like *Water N-Squared* the *XPoint 2D* system brings the line back to linear at 64 cores. However, for some benchmarks, like *Ocean Non-Contig*, the *XPoint 2D* system is only effective up to 32 cores. This limit occurs because the bus latency is increasing as the core count is increased, reducing the total bandwidth of the system effectively creating more contention.

5.1.1 Cache Slice Fairness

As mentioned in Section 3.1.3, by splitting the cache, unfairness can occur in the allocation of cache lines to slices. This will result in higher L1 miss rates, as less of the cache is being utilized. This effect is particularly evident in strided accesses. To quantify the impact of the cache slicing mechanism we plot a fairness metric in Figure 10. The metric is derived by dividing the number of accesses to the most accessed bank by the number of accesses to the least accessed bank. A fairness of 1 indicates that the cache lines are divided evenly amongst the slices. For all but 3 benchmarks the fairness is good, around 1.2. However, for *Barnes*, *FMM*, and *LU* there is less balance. This corresponds to designs that favor less slicing for optimal runtime (Figure 8). Overall, there are some benchmarks that show sensitivity to the slicing allocation, however

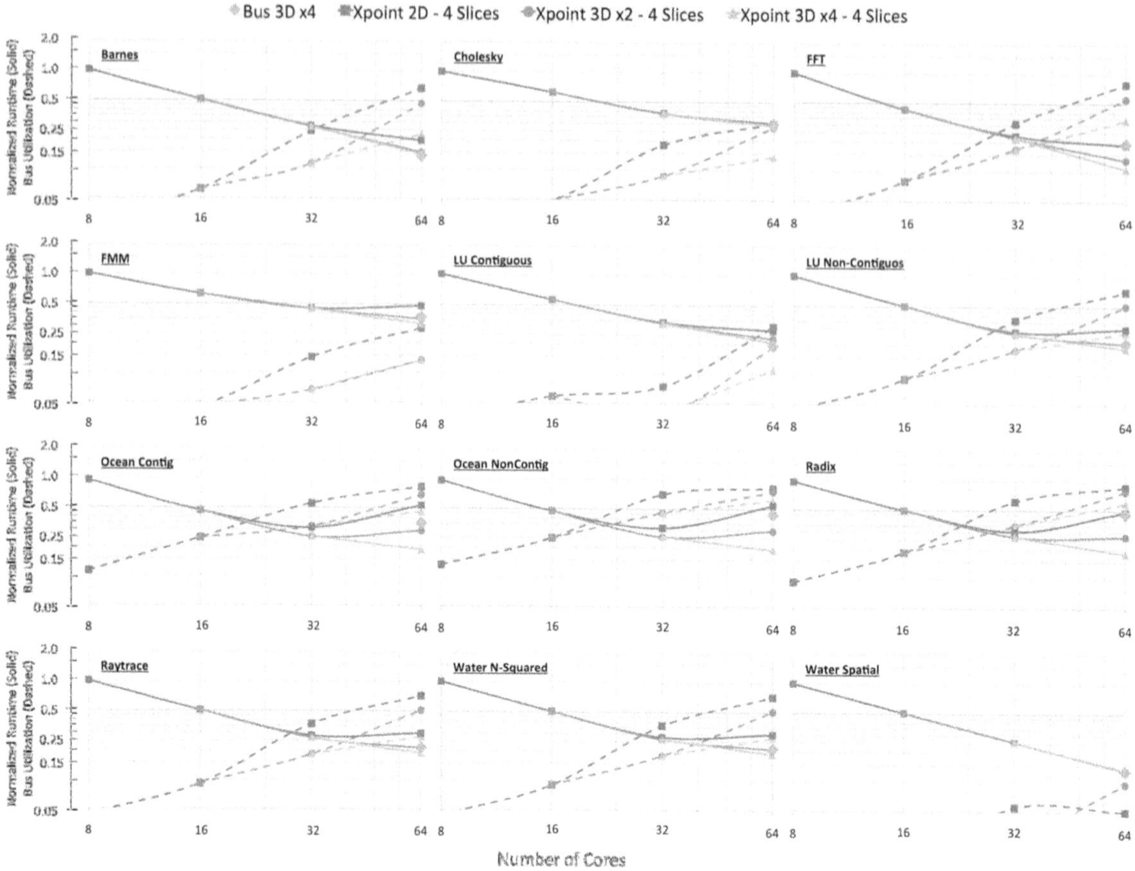

Figure 9: Runtime (solid lines) and Bus Utilization (dotted lines) plotted across core counts. A straight line for runtime represents ideal scaling of the benchmark. All configurations use a cache slicing of 4. *XPoint 3D* improves the scaling compared to the *XPoint 2D*.

the system still shows improvement. We leave exploring more complex hashing functions to balance interleaving for future work.

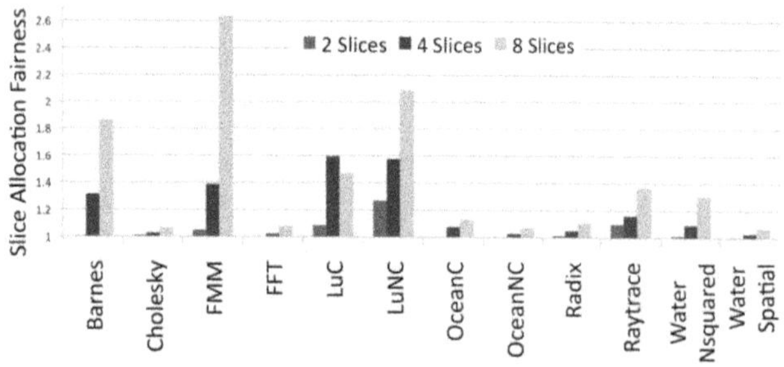

Figure 10: Fairness of slice allocation. Calculated as the total number of accesses to the most accessed cache slice divided by the total number of accesses to the least accessed cache slice. A completely even distribution has a fairness of 1.

5.2 Improving Bus Latency - XPoint 3D

While the results show that the *XPoint2D* system scaled well to 32 cores, there were several benchmarks that still had scaling limitations resulting from increased bus delay. By extending the system in 3D, the bus latencies are decreased and further scaling is possible for these benchmarks. Figure 9 shows runtime and bus utilization on the same axes as before, but for *XPoint 2D* and *XPoint 3D* designs with 4-slices. For the *XPoint 2D* benchmarks that did not scale well—*FMM*, *Ocean Contig*, *Ocean Non-Contig*, *Radix*, and *Water Spatial*—the use of *XPoint 3D* helps reduce the runtime at 64 cores, making the trend closer to linear. On average, the *XPoint 3D* improves performance by 28% over the *XPoint 2D* system at 64 cores.

5.3 Best Configurations

The best performing configurations for each benchmark on each type of system is listed in Table 4. For systems with uneven slice utilization the optimal number of slices is less than 8, which correspond to the same benchmarks shown in Section 5.1.1. The average speedup achieved by the *XPoint 2D* system is 35× , the *XPoint 3D* system further improves that number to 45×. On average the *XPoint 2D* system performs 1.6× better than the bus, it also outperforms the conventional bus in 3D for all but 3 benchmarks. Overall the *XPoint 3D* system improves performance by 2.1× compared to the 2D conventional bus. The *XPoint 3D* system achieves speedups within 8% of an ideal interconnect, showing that both the *XPoint 2D* and *XPoint 3D* take the scalability of bus based systems farther than commonly thought, making them ideal architectures for many-core systems of 32-64 cores.

Table 4: A Breakdown of the best performing parameters on each system for each benchmark. Speedup is presented over a uniprocessor system with 2MB L2. Ideal Interconnect allows infinite requests on the bus simultaneously, with a single cycle latency. Super linear speedups occur for FFT due to the increased L2 size available in the 64 core system. The *XPoint 3D* design is within 8% of the speedup of an ideal interconnect.

	Bus 2D		*XPoint 2D*			Bus 3D			*XPoint 3D*				Ideal Interconnect	
	Cores	Speedup	Cores	Slices	Speedup	Cores	Layers	Speedup	Cores	Slices	Layers	Speedup	Cores	Speedup
Barnes	64	33×	64	8	49×	64	4	58×	64	2	4	**60×**	64	64×
Cholesky	64	18×	64	8	28×	64	4	27×	64	2	4	**29×**	64	30×
FFT	32	22×	64	8	59×	64	4	41×	64	8	4	**83×**	64	86×
FMM	32	17×	64	8	19×	64	4	21×	64	8	4	**25×**	64	39×
Lu Contig	64	38×	64	2	39×	64	4	41×	64	2	4	**41×**	64	42×
Lu NonContig	64	18×	64	8	19×	64	4	20×	64	4	4	**21×**	64	22×
Ocean Contig	16	13×	32	8	30×	64	4	23×	64	8	4	**54×**	64	60×
Ocean NonContig	16	13×	32	8	29×	64	4	18×	64	8	4	**53×**	64	63×
Radix	16	15×	32	8	28×	64	4	17×	64	8	4	**48×**	64	50×
Raytrace	32	27×	64	8	32×	64	4	38×	64	8	4	**43×**	64	52×
Water NSquared	32	28×	64	8	55×	64	4	51×	64	8	4	**59×**	64	59×
Water Spatial	64	50×	64	4	60×	64	4	61×	64	8	4	**62×**	64	62×
Geometric Mean		22×			35×			31×				**45×**		49×

Overall, the results have shown that the *XPoint* architecture scales to 64 core systems with an unmodified bus based snooping protocol. Given the infrastructure already in place for verifying these types of systems, *XPoint 2D* presents a desirable approach to interconnect at 32-64 cores in 32nm. As 3D technology becomes part of the commercial mainstream the *XPoint 3D* systems will further scale bus based designs to higher core counts.

6. RELATED WORK

Our baseline builds on memory interleaving techniques developed in the 1980's to address interconnect congestion in board level multi-processors [46]. However, integration levels and pin constraints limited their practicality. We show that with new architectural techniques these designs are now practical for single chip implementations, where higher cache associativites and a greater number of wires are available. We further differentiate our design from theirs with the use of on-die point-to-point connections from the core to the L1's to improve latency, the addition of L0 buffers to hide increased L1 access time, and 3D integration to reduce bus latency. Many other researchers have looked at multiple bus systems in both interleaved and non-interleaved architectures [5, 10, 15, 44]. However, none of their work explicitly shows how interleaved busses can be used to scale *unmodified* coherence protocols. Recent work by Udipi *et al.* [45] also seeks to scale conventional snooping coherence to many-core systems with the design of a segmented bus and an associated filtering mechanism. Only in passing do they mention interleaved buses and they leave the evaluation of such designs as future work. In addition the *XPoint* system shows how 3D integration can be used to improve the scalability of the bus, an approach not considered in any of these previous works.

There have also been many papers on the topic of 3D integration [7, 28, 34, 47]. While these papers target increased system performance, scaling coherence protocols were not their primary purpose. Other papers on 3D interconnects [30, 33, 37] have extended the research of NoC designs to 3D chips. These papers seek to reduce hop counts in NoC systems by leveraging the 3rd dimension to implement higher radix NoC topologies, such as hyper-cubes and flattened butterflies. The *XPoint 3D* architecture shows that both 2D and 3D stacked systems with conventional snooping coherence can be extended to systems of 64 cores, without the need for complex designs that require extensive verification effort.

Finally there has also been some related work on interleaving main memory [21] and caches [22] for VLIW systems, however none of these designs addresses the scalability of cache coherence protocols or 3D integration.

7. CONCLUSION

Design, verification, and validation of coherence protocols in comercial chips is difficult and expensive. Within industry there is a large amount of infrastructure built around validating current interconnect solutions. While distributed directory architectures represent one approach to scalability, their design is more complex and less familiar compared to current bus-based snooping mechanisms and therefore present a significant hurdle to current validation techniques. On the other hand, simply scaling traditional bus solutions leads to increased contention and latency on the bus.

To address the scalability of existing solutions while leaving the coherence protocol unmodified, this paper proposed the *XPoint* architecture. The *XPoint* system showed that bus-based snooping coherence can scale to 64 core systems by leveraging architectural and layout enhancements designed to combat the degraded speed of long busses and increased contention at large core counts. Overall the *XPoint* system showed a 29× and 45× speedup for 32 and 64 core systems respectively(a 2.1× improvement over a 64 core conventional bus and within 8% of a 64 core system with an ideal interconnect). Measurements also showed that the *XPoint* system decreased the bus contention of a 64 core system to only 13% higher than that of an 8-core design.

8. REFERENCES

[1] A. Alameldeen and D. Wood. Variability in architectural simulations of multi-threaded workloads. In *The Ninth International Symposium on High-Performance Computer Architecture*, Feb 2003.

[2] ARM Ltd. http://www.arm.com/products/processors/cortex-a/cortex-a9.php, 2011.

[3] M. Baron. Tilera's Cores Communicate Better: Mesh Networks and Distributed Memory Reduce Contention Among Cores. *Microprocessor Report*, 2007.

[4] N. Barrow-Williams, C. Fensch, and S. Moore. A communication characterisation of SPLASH-2 and parsec. In *IISWC*, 2009.

[5] J. Bertoni, J.-L. Baer, and W.-H. Wang. Scaling shared-bus multi-processors with multiple buses and shared caches: a

performance study. *Microprocess. Microsyst.*, 16:339–350, September 1992.

[6] N. L. Binkert, R. G. Dreslinski, L. R. Hsu, K. T. Lim, A. G. Saidi, and S. K. Reinhardt. The M5 simulator: Modeling networked systems. *IEEE Micro*, 26(4):52–60, 2006.

[7] B. Black, M. Annavaram, N. Brekelbaum, J. Devale, L. Jiang, G. H. Loh, D. Mccauley, P. Morrow, D. W. Nelson, D. Pantuso, P. Reed, J. Rupley, S. Shankar, J. Shen, and C. Webb. Die stacking (3D) microarchitecture. In *In Proceedings of MICRO-39*, 2006.

[8] G. Blake, R. Dreslinski, and T. Mudge. A survey of multicore processors. In *Signal Processing Magazine*. IEEE, 2009.

[9] J. F. Cantin, M. H. Lipasti, and J. E. Smith. Dynamic verification of cache coherence protocols, 2001.

[10] M. J. Carlton. Multiple-bus, scalable, shared-memory multiprocessors, 1995.

[11] A. Charlesworth. Starfire: Extending the SMP envelope. In *IEEE Micro*, 1998.

[12] D. Culler, J. Singh, and A. Gupta. *Parallel Computer Architecture: A Hardware/Software Approach*. Morgan Kaufmann, 1998. The Morgan Kaufmann Series in Computer Architecture and Design.

[13] A. DeOrio, A. Bauserman, and V. Bertacco. Post-silicon verification for cache coherence. In *Computer Design, 2008. ICCD 2008. IEEE International Conference on*, pages 348 –355, oct. 2008.

[14] D. Dill, A. Drexler, A. Hu, and C. Yang. Protocol verification as a hardware design aid. In *Computer Design: VLSI in Computers and Processors, 1992. ICCD '92. Proceedings., IEEE 1992 International Conference on*, pages 522 –525, oct 1992.

[15] M. Dubois. Throughput analysis of cache-based multiprocessors with multiple buses. *Computers, IEEE Transactions on*, 37(1):58 –70, jan 1988.

[16] E. A. Emerson and V. Kahlon. Exact and efficient verification of parameterized cache coherence protocols. In *Correct Hardware Design and Verification Methods (CHARME'03), LNCS 2860*, pages 247–262. Springer, 2003.

[17] D. Fick, R. Dreslinski, B. Giridhar, G. Kim, S. Seo, M. Fojtik, S. Satpathy, Y. Lee, D. Kim, N. Liu, M. Wieckowski, G. Chen, T. Mudge, D. Sylvester, and D. Blaauw. Centip3De: A 3930 dmips/w configurable near-threshold 3D stacked system with 64 ARM Cortex-M3 cores. *To appear in IEEE International Solid-State Circuits Conference, San Francisco, CA, 2012*, 2012.

[18] M. Galles and E. Williams. Performance optimizations, implementation, and verification of the sgi challenge multiprocessor. In *System Sciences, 1994. Proceedings of the Twenty-Seventh Hawaii International Conference on*, 1994.

[19] S. M. German. Formal design of cache memory protocols in ibm. *Form. Methods Syst. Des.*, 22:133–141, March 2003.

[20] M. Ghoneima and Y. Ismail. Optimum positioning of interleaved repeaters in bidirectional buses. *Computer-Aided Design of Integrated Circuits and Systems, IEEE Transactions on*, 24(3):461 – 469, march 2005.

[21] S. Ghosh, J. Ghosh, and S. Ray. Architecture of configurable k-way c-access interleaved memory. In *Process Automation, Control and Computing (PACC)*, pages 1 –5, july 2011.

[22] E. Gibert, J. Sanchez, and A. Gonzalez. An interleaved cache clustered VLIW processor. *Architecture*, pages 210–219, 2002.

[23] S. Gupta, M. Hibert, S. Hong, and R. Patti. Techniques for producing 3D ICs with high-density interconnect. *White Paper*, 2004.

[24] R. Haring. The IBM Blue Gene/Q Compute chip+SIMD floating-point unit. In *HotChips 23: A Symposium on High-Performance Chips*, 2011.

[25] Intel. Intel core2 extreme processor x6800 and intel core2 duo desktop processor e6000 and e4000 sequence, 2008.

[26] T. Johnson and U. Nawathe. An 8-core, 64-thread, 64-bit power efficient sparc soc (niagara2). In *International symposium on Physical design*, ISPD '07, pages 2–2, New York, NY, USA, 2007. ACM.

[27] C. N. Keltcher, K. J. McGrath, A. Ahmed, and P. Conway. The amd opteron processor for multiprocessor servers. *IEEE Micro*, 23:66–76, March 2003.

[28] T. Kgil, S. D'Souza, A. G. Saidi, N. L. Binkert, R. G. Dreslinski, T. N. Mudge, S. K. Reinhardt, and K. Flautner. PicoServer: using 3D stacking technology to enable a compact energy efficient chip multiprocessor. In *ASPLOS*, pages 117–128, 2006.

[29] D. H. Kim, K. Athikulwongse, M. B. Healy, M. M. Hossain, M. Jung, I. Khorosh, G. Kumar, Y.-J. Lee, D. L. Lewis, T.-W. Lin, C. Liu, S. Panth, M. Pathak, M. Ren, G. Shen, T. Song, D. H. Woo, X. Zhao, J. Kim, H. Choi, G. H. Loh, H.-H. S. Lee, and S. K. Lim. 3D-MAPS: 3D massively parallel processor with stacked memory. *To appear in IEEE International Solid-State Circuits Conference, San Francisco, CA, 2012*, 2012.

[30] J. Kim, C. Nicopoulos, D. Park, R. Das, Y. Xie, V. Narayanan, M. S. Yousif, and C. R. Das. A novel dimensionally-decomposed router for on-chip communication in 3D architectures. *SIGARCH Comput. Archit. News*, 35:138–149, June 2007.

[31] J. Leary, M. Talupur, and M. R. Tuttle. Protocol verification using flows: An industrial experience. In *IEEE Formal Methods in Computer-Aided Design*, 2009.

[32] K. M. Lepak and M. H. Lipasti. Temporally silent stores. In *In Proceedings of PACT-2000*, pages 30–41, 2002.

[33] F. Li, C. Nicopoulos, T. Richardson, Y. Xie, V. Narayanan, and M. Kandemir. Design and management of 3D chip multiprocessors using network-in-memory. In *Computer Architecture, 2006. ISCA '06. 33rd International Symposium on*, pages 130 –141, 0-0 2006.

[34] G. H. Loh, Y. Xie, and B. Black. Processor design in 3D die-stacking technologies. *Micro, IEEE*, 27(3):31 –48, may-june 2007.

[35] A. Meixner. Error detection via online checking of cache coherence with token coherence signatures. In *In Proceedings of HPCA-13*, pages 145–156, 2007.

[36] R. Merritt. Inside Intel's Sandy Bridge architecture.

[37] V. Pavlidis and E. Friedman. 3-D topologies for networks-on-chip. *Very Large Scale Integration (VLSI) Systems, IEEE Transactions on*, 15(10):1081 –1090, oct. 2007.

[38] A. Pnueli, S. Ruah, and L. Zuck. Automatic deductive verification with invisible invariants, 2001.

[39] F. Pong and M. Dubois. Verification techniques for cache coherence protocols. *ACM Comput. Surv.*, 29:82–126, March 1997.

[40] J. Schanin. The design and development of a very high speed

system bus - the encore multimax nanobus. In *ACM Fall Joint Computer Conference*, 1986.

[41] B. Sinharoy, R. Kalla, J. Tendler, R. Eickemeyer, and J. Joyner. Power5 system microarchitecture. In *IBM Journal of Research and Development*, 2005.

[42] K. Skadron, M. Stan, W. Huang, S. Velusamy, K. Sankaranarayanan, and D. Tarjan. Temperature-aware microarchitecture. In *Computer Architecture, 2003. Proceedings. 30th Annual International Symposium on*, pages 2 – 13, june 2003.

[43] D. Sorin, M. Hill, and D. Wood. Dynamic verification of end-to-end multiprocessor invariants. In *Dependable Systems and Networks*, pages 281 – 290, june 2003.

[44] S. Thakkar, M. Dubois, A. Laundrie, and G. Sohi. Scalable shared-memory multiprocessor architectures. *Computer*, 23(6):71 –74, jun 1990.

[45] A. Udipi, N. Muralimanohar, and R. Balasubramonian. Towards scalable, energy-efficient, bus-based on-chip networks. In *High Performance Computer Architecture (HPCA), 2010 IEEE 16th International Symposium on*, pages 1 –12, jan. 2010.

[46] D. Winsor and T. N. Mudge. Crosspoint cache architectures. In *In International Symposium on Computer Architecture*, pages 266–269, 1987.

[47] D. H. Woo, N. H. Seong, D. Lewis, and H.-H. Lee. An optimized 3D-stacked memory architecture by exploiting excessive, high-density TSV bandwidth. In *High Performance Computer Architecture (HPCA), 2010 IEEE 16th International Symposium on*, pages 1 –12, jan. 2010.

[48] S. C. Woo, M. Ohara, E. Torrie, J. P. Singh, and A. Gupta. The splash-2 programs: characterization and methodological considerations. In *ISCA '95: Proceedings of the 22nd annual international symposium on Computer architecture*, pages 24–36, New York, NY, USA, 1995. ACM.

[49] D. Wood, G. Gibson, and R. Katz. Verifying a multiprocessor cache controller using random test generation. *Design Test of Computers, IEEE*, 7(4):13 –25, aug 1990.

[50] M. Zhang, A. R. Lebeck, and D. J. Sorin. Fractal coherence: Scalably verifiable cache coherence. In *Proceedings of the 2010 43rd Annual IEEE/ACM International Symposium on Microarchitecture*, MICRO '43, pages 471–482, Washington, DC, USA, 2010. IEEE Computer Society.

APCR: An Adaptive Physical Channel Regulator for On-Chip Interconnects

Lei Wang, Poornachandran Kumar, Ki Hwan Yum, and Eun Jung Kim
Department of Computer Science and Engineering, Texas A&M University
College Station, TX, US
{wanglei, chandran, yum, ejkim}@cse.tamu.edu

ABSTRACT

Chip Multi-Processor (CMP) architectures have become mainstream for designing processors. With a large number of cores, Network-On-Chip (NOC) provides a scalable communication method for CMP architectures, where wires become abundant resources available inside the chip. NOC must be carefully designed to meet constraints of power and area, and provide ultra low latencies. In this paper, we propose an Adaptive Physical Channel Regulator (APCR) for NOC routers to exploit huge wiring resources. The flit size in an APCR router is less than the physical channel width (phit size) to provide finer granularity flow control. An APCR router allows flits from different packets or flows to share the same physical channel in a single cycle. The three regulation schemes (Monopolizing, Fair-sharing and Channel-stealing) intelligently allocate the output channel resources considering not only the availability of physical channels but the occupancy of input buffers. In an APCR router, each Virtual Channel can forward a dynamic number of flits every cycle depending on the run-time network status. Our simulation results using a detailed cycle-accurate simulator show that an APCR router improves the network throughput by over 100% in synthetic workloads, compared with a traditional design with the same buffer size. An APCR router can outperform a traditional router even if the buffer size is halved.

Categories and Subject Descriptors

C.1.2 [**Computer Systems Organization**]: Multiprocessors—*Interconnection architectures*

Keywords

Channel Regulator, CMP, On-Chip Interconnects

1. INTRODUCTION

Moore's law has steadily increased on-chip transistor density and integrated dozens of components on a single die. Providing efficient communication in a single die is becoming a critical factor for high performance Chip Multi-Processors (CMPs) [23]. Traditional shared buses and dedicated wires do not meet the communication demands for future multi-core architectures. Moreover, the shrinking technology exacerbates the imbalance between transistors and wires in terms of delay, and power has embarked on a fervent search for efficient communication designs [12]. In this regime, Network-On-Chip (NOC) with packet-switching is a promising architecture that orchestrates chip-wide communications towards future many-core processors.

As feature size is shrinking, wires are becoming abundant resources available in NOC [3, 22].Since NOC can benefit from high wire density due to no limits on the number of pins and faster signaling rates, it is very critical in the NOC router design to find a way that fully utilizes the wire resources to provide high performance. There have been a handful studies exploiting abundant wire resources to explore different topologies with high degree channels such as Flattened Butterfly [15] and Express Cube [10]. Meanwhile, this wiring capability has led to networks with very wide transmission channels between routers, which facilitate low latency due to small serialization delay [3, 6]. However, as shown in Figure 1, if we simply increase the channel width and define the flit size to be the same as the channel width or phit size, we cannot achieve significant performance improvement for the same router buffer budget. It is interesting to observe that the performance with 512-bit channels is worse than the one with 256-bit channels. Due to the limited buffer area budget, increasing flit size proportionately decreases the virtual channel (VC) depth, which incurs more contention and, in turn, more performance degradation. To reduce the network contention, it is obvious to define a smaller flit size for finer granularity flow control. Therefore, to balance the trade-off between serialization latency and contention delay, the flit size should be carefully re-examined to exploit wide channels for the NOC router design.

Furthermore, diverse packet sizes found in the CMP communications also limit the usage of wide channels. The majority of on-chip communication emanates from cache traffic, such as cache coherence messages or L1/L2 cache blocks. A cache coherence message, like a request or an invalidation, consists of a small header and a memory address only, which are around 64 bits, while a packet that carries a L1/L2 cache block is as large as 512 bits (64 Bytes). Recently, Das et al. [8] suggest to define two kinds of flits (short and long) to maximize the usage of the physical channel. However, it is not trivial to provide two different flit sizes in a network due to the complicated credit management. Therefore, we attempt to solve this challenging problem to utilize wide channel resources in NOC without defining multiple flit sizes for different packet lengths.

In this paper, we propose an Adaptive Physical Channel Regulator (APCR) for NOC routers. Even though there may exist different packet lengths (short or long) in the same network, an APCR router only defines one constant flit size, which is typically smaller

PACT'12, September 19–23, 2012, Minneapolis, Minnesota, USA.

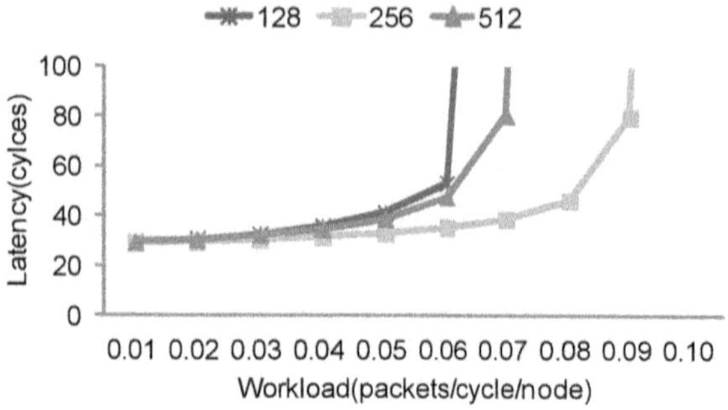

Figure 1: Average Packet Latencies with Three (128, 256 and 512 bits) Different Channel Widths and a Fixed Router Buffer Size in an (8×8) Mesh Network (Detailed simulation configuration can be found in Section 5.).

than the channel width. An APCR router allows VCs to transmit multiple small flits in one cycle. The number of flits being transmitted every cycle dynamically changes according to the network status. We present three regulation schemes for APCR: Monopolizing, Fair-sharing and Channel-stealing. Monopolizing allows only one packet to use the physical channel every cycle, while in Fair-sharing multiple packets can traverse at the same time. Channel-stealing is most flexible, where idle physical channels can be utilized by any ready packet. Routers become run-time configurable to different packet lengths with these three regulation schemes. It is similar to providing routers with diverse flit sizes to meet the requirements of different packet lengths. Long packets with multiple flits can transmit more than one flit in a cycle when no other packets want to use the same physical channel (This occurs in a low-workload network.). Short packets, normally containing one flit, use only a portion of the physical channel and leave other portions utilized by other packets, or the unused portions are fully shut down thus consuming only static power. Furthermore, an APCR allocates the channel resources using the occupancy of input buffers, thoroughly utilizing the wide channel and providing high network throughput. Our simulation results show that an APCR router outperforms a traditional router with double the buffer size. When buffer sizes are identical, an APCR router achieves more than 100% throughput improvement in synthetic workloads without negative effect on zero-load latency. Moreover, it is observed that an APCR router improves the network performance regardless of the underlying topologies. Monopolizing achieves 30% improvement in both Flattened Butterfly and Express Cube while Channel-stealing gets 40%, which demonstrates the synergy effect of the two approaches (wide transmission channels and high degree channels) exploiting abundant wire resources.

The rest of this paper is organized as follows. We briefly summarize the related work in Section 2. We present the three channel regulation schemes in Section 3. Section 4 gives details on the microarchitecture of an APCR router. In Section 5, we describe the evaluation methodology and summarize the simulation results. Finally, we draw conclusions in Section 6.

2. RELATED WORK

Several NOC topologies have been proposed to explore abundant channel resources. MeshX2 [3] increases the wire and area utilization by introducing a second parallel network. Each subnetwork of the MeshX2 transports a disjoint subset of packets, one subnetwork for long packets and the other for short packets. However, partitioning the networks based on the packet lengths performs poorly when such a partitioning fails to maximize the available wire resources usage. Flattened butterfly [15] shows the benefit of having multiple parallel channels, and each parallel channel connects to a different switch in the same row or column. Hence, the number of ports in a switch will be increased. Since some of the parallel channels are multi-hop channels, the wires have to cross the chip, increasing the complexity of the floorplan. Express Cube topologies [10] get rid of the multiple parallel channels among routers. Instead, Multidrop Express Channels (MECS), a one-to-many communication fabric, are introduced to connect each router. It is our understanding that this design relies heavily on the intelligent repeaters in the MECS, and the design complexity of the intelligent repeaters can be high, because the intelligent repeaters should control the point-to-multipoint unidirectional links at run-time.

There are also some designs that share the channel among different flits in a single cycle. Das et al. [8] look into multiple flits sharing a channel. In their network, there are two kinds of flits, short and long. The sharing condition is simple: if two short flits are routed to the same output port, they can simultaneously traverse the crossbar and output channel. For long flits, no sharing is applied. The flow control can be challenging to support two flit sizes in a network, since it makes the credit management complicated. Leroy et al. [17] introduce Spatial Division Multiplexing (SDM) into the NOC design by providing a fully free reconfigurable wire level data path. The results show that SDM is a more interesting approach than Time Division Multiplexing (TDM), due to the high complexity and power needed by buffers to store the TDM configuration for each clock cycle. In [25, 26], abundant wire resources are explored, where the main goal is to provide more path diversity.

3. ADAPTIVE PHYSICAL CHANNEL REGULATION SCHEMES

In this section, we primarily elucidate three regulation schemes (Monopolizing, Fair-sharing and Channel-stealing) used in an APCR Router, while Section 4 delves into its detailed microarchitecture.

3.1 Monopolizing

Monopolizing allows only one VC to use the total bandwidth of the physical channel every cycle. In a generic router design, the flit size is usually the same as the phit size, thus a VC can fully use the whole bandwidth of the physical channel. However, in the APCR router the flit size is smaller than the phit size, so potentially multiple flits can be delivered in the same channel concurrently. Monopolizing allows a VC to transmit a different number of flits in one cycle. There is one restriction on this situation: a VC is only allowed to transmit the flits that belong to the same packet to prevent different packets in the same VC from interleaving. The maximum number of transmitted flits depends on how many flits stored in a VC belong to the same packet, not on how many flits the physical channel can process. In Figure 2 the phit size is four times the flit size, which implies the physical channel can transmit at most four flits in one cycle. Meanwhile, the VC depth is also four, and each packet consists of four filts (one head flit, two middle flits and one tail flit). Assume that VC_0 wins the arbitration of the output channel, and it contains four flits as follows: one middle flit at the head of VC_0 followed by a tail flit belonging to the same packet, then a head flit and a middle flit belonging to a different packet. In this case, although the physical channel can transmit four flits at a time, only the first two flits are allowed to be transmitted. The head and middle flits of the next packet should wait until the next cycle because they belong to a different packet that may have a different routing direction.

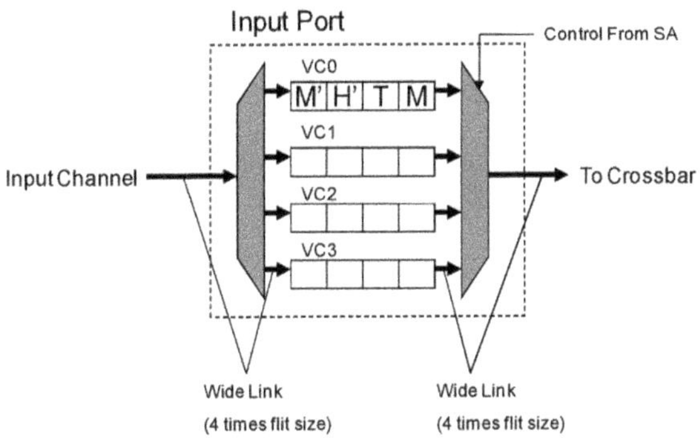

Figure 2: Monopolizing: Flits M and T belong to a packet, and flits H' and M' are from another packet. VC_0 wins the arbitration of the output channel. However, only M and T can be transmitted in the same cycle.

Compared with the generic router design, a smaller flit size can provide finer granularity of traffic control. The best case occurs when VC_0 always buffers four flits from the same packet, since VC_0 can transmit four flits every cycle that will occupy the whole bandwidth of the physical channel. This situation is similar to defining the flit size equal to the phit size. If we treat the term "flit" as the unit that a VC sends every cycle, an APCR router makes the "flit" size run-time configurable according to the status of the network, and routers use different "flit" sizes at the same time. However, Monopolizing can potentially waste the channel bandwidth, as shown in Figure 3. We assume that each VC has at least one flit and within each VC the flits to be sent are going to the same direction. If VC_2 wins the output channel, according to Monopolizing, only one quarter of the physical channel is utilized even though other VCs have flits waiting to be sent through the same physical channel.

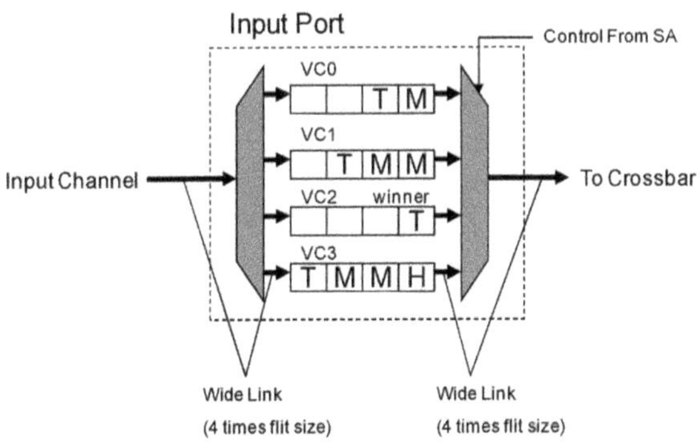

Figure 3: Monopolizing Wasting the Channel Bandwidth: VC_2 wins the arbitration of the physical channel. However, VC_2 has only one flit to be sent, thus wastes three quarters of the channel bandwidth.

3.2 Fair-sharing

Considering the inefficient channel utilization described above, we propose Fair-sharing, where VCs fairly share the physical channel resources. In Fair-sharing, a wide physical channel needs to be divided into several small parts, called sub-channels. We reserve a separate sub-channel for each VC in an input port. If a physical channel is divided into four sub-channels and each input port has four VCs, each VC of the same input port can have one sub-channel of its own (VC_0 uses sub-channel$_0$, VC_1 uses sub-channel$_1$, and so forth.). In addition, VCs from different input ports can share a sub-channel. For example, all VC_0s of different input ports share sub-channel$_0$. To simplify the hardware design, the ID of a VC is bound with the ID of a sub-channel. Since the width of a sub-channel is a flit, multiple VCs can send flits concurrently even though they belong to the same input port. If the number of sub-channels is bigger than the number of VCs in an input port, each VC can be assigned more than one sub-channel.

Compared with Monopolizing, Fair-sharing utilizes the wide channel more efficiently, because the chance of sending multiple flits from multiple VCs is normally higher than sending multiple flits from a single VC, especially at high workload. Fair-sharing still has its own limitations, as illustrated in Figure 4, where VC_0 has two flits, VC_1 has three, but VC_2 and VC_3 are empty. According to Fair-sharing, VC_0 and VC_1 will use sub-channel$_0$ and sub-channel$_1$ to send one flit each. Since VC_2 and VC_3 have no flits, sub-channel$_2$ and sub-channel$_3$ are empty. Even though VC_0 and VC_1 have more flits to be sent, they cannot use sub-channel$_2$ and sub-channel$_3$ because they are not bound to sub-channel$_2$ and sub-channel$_3$.

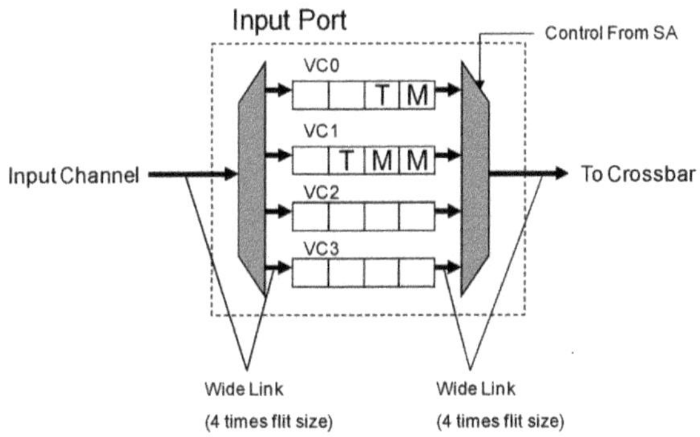

Figure 4: Fair-sharing: VC_0 and VC_1 can only send one flit each using their own sub-channels. VC_2 and VC_3 waste their sub-channels because they do not have any flits. These wasted sub-channels cannot be used by VC_0 and VC_1.

3.3 Channel-stealing

To improve the utilization of wide channels further, we propose Channel-stealing, which is built upon Fair-sharing. If a VC finally has no flit to be sent, its sub-channel can be stolen by other VCs. Here the stealing can occur in two different ways. One is stealing from VCs belonging to the same input port, and the other is stealing from VCs of different input ports that have no flits to be sent in the same output direction. Channel-stealing can explore the channel resources thoroughly. It optimizes the arbitration of output channels by using the buffer occupancy information from each VC and finally increases the network throughput. In Figure 4, since

VC_2 and VC_3 have no flits to be sent, VC_0 and VC_1 can steal the sub-channels assigned to VC_2 and VC_3, and send more than one flit. There are two options: Both VC_0 and VC_1 send two flits each or VC_0 sends one flit while VC_1 sends three flits. Choosing from the two options depends on the scheduling policy. In this study, we adopt Round-Robin as our scheduling policy, which fairly allocates the extra free sub-channels to other VCs with more flits.

4. APCR ROUTER MICROARCHITECTURE DESIGN

To support three channel regulation schemes in Section 3, a generic NOC router microarchitecture has to be enhanced. In this section, we first briefly explain a generic NOC router microarchitecture and the functionality of each pipeline stage. Then we propose the APCR router microarchitecture design and analyze each main component.

4.1 A Generic NOC Router

Figure 5 (a) shows a generic NOC router architecture [7] for a 2D mesh network. In most implementations, there are 5 ports in the router: four from/to the four cardinal directions (NORTH, EAST, SOUTH and WEST) and one from/to local Processing Element (PE). The main building blocks for a generic NOC router are input buffer, route computation logic, VC allocator, switch allocator, and crossbar. To achieve high performance, routers process packets with four pipeline stages, which are routing computation (RC), VC allocation (VA), switch allocation (SA), and switch traversal (ST). First, the RC stage directs a packet to a proper output port by looking up its destination address. Next, the VA stage allocates one available VC of the downstream router determined by RC. The SA stage arbitrates input and output ports of the crossbar, and successfully granted flits traverse the crossbar during the ST stage. Due to the stringent area budget of a chip, routers use flit level buffering in a wormhole-switching network as opposed to packet level buffering. Additionally, the buffer is managed with credit-based flow control, where downstream routers provide back-pressure to upstream routers to prevent buffer overflow. Considering that only the head flit needs routing computation and middle flits always have to stall at the RC stage, low-latency router designs parallelize RC, VA and SA using lookahead routing [9] and speculative switch allocation [24]. The functionality of lookahead routing is the same as the normal RC stage, calculating the output ports. However, instead of calculating routing information for the current router, lookahead routing does the same for the downstream router and stores the routing information in the head flit. In this way the RC and VA stages can be overlapped because the VC allocator does not need to wait for the output of the RC logic. Speculative switch allocation [24] predicts the winner of the VA stage and performs SA based on the prediction. If the packet fails to allocate a VC, the pipeline stalls and both the VA and SA stages will be repeated in the next cycle. These two modifications lead to two-stage and even single-stage [21] routers, which parallelize the various stages in the router. In this paper, we use a two-stage router as the baseline router.

4.2 APCR Router Microarchitecture

Figure 5 (b) shows the microarchitecture of an APCR router, where the differences from a generic router are shaded. In an APCR router, the VC allocator is the same as a generic router for the three regulation schemes. Also no modification will be needed to the crossbar. Even with wide channels, the number of input and output ports will be the same (5×5 crossbar for a 2D mesh topology). The APCR component works together with switch allocator and input buffers. First, based on the characteristics of the regulation schemes selected, APCR decides the number of flits each VC can send. For example, Monopolizing allows a VC to send multiple flits but selects only one VC from each input port, while in Fair-sharing a VC can only send one flit but no competition exists among VCs of the same input port. Second, APCR controls the input buffer operations according to the allocation results. In the following we describe the design of each main component in an APCR router.

4.2.1 *Buffer Management*

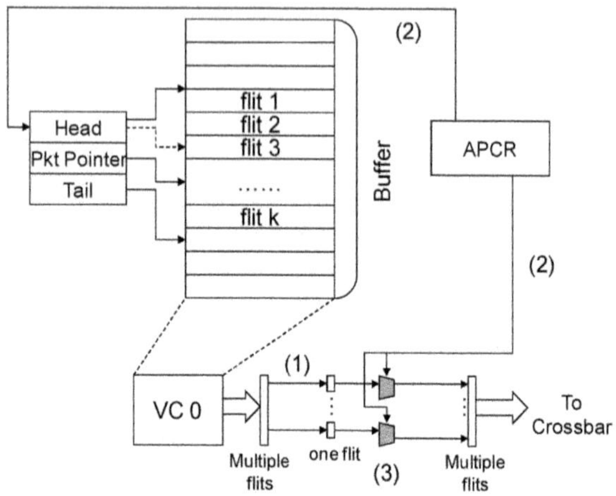

Figure 7: Three Steps of Buffer Management: (1) VC_0 reads multiple flits out (the number of flits depends on the relationship between the flit size and phit size.). (2) APCR sets up the head of each input buffer and the output. (3) The guaranteed flits are sent through the crossbar. The remaining flits will be dropped and read out again in the next cycle.

Due to the limitations of power and area, NOC routers rely on simple buffer structures. As shown in Figure 6 (a), each input port has v VCs, each of which has dedicated k-flit FIFO buffer. Recent NOC routers have small input buffers to minimize their overhead. The necessity for low latency buffer operation mandates the use of a parallel FIFO as illustrated in Figure 6 (b). As opposed to a serial FIFO implementation [30], the parallel FIFO eliminates the need for a flit to traverse all slots in a pipelined manner before exiting the buffer. This fine-grained control uses read and write pointers to maintain the FIFO order. Figure 6 (c) shows a data structure to represent parallel FIFO buffers. When a read operation is performed, the flit pointed by the head is sent out and the head pointer is automatically moved to the next position. Similarly, when a write operation comes, the flit is written to the position pointed by the tail and the tail pointer is increased by one. When the head is equal to the tail after a read, the buffer is empty. When the tail is equal to the head after a write, the buffer becomes full. We use this parallel FIFO implementation for our study.

The three regulation schemes (Monopolizing, Fair-sharing and Channel-stealing) require different buffer structures. While the input buffer for Fair-sharing is the same as that of a generic router since every cycle only one flit can be sent from a VC, Monopolizing and Channel-stealing need a different buffer structure. Since Monopolizing and Channel-stealing allow a VC to send multiple

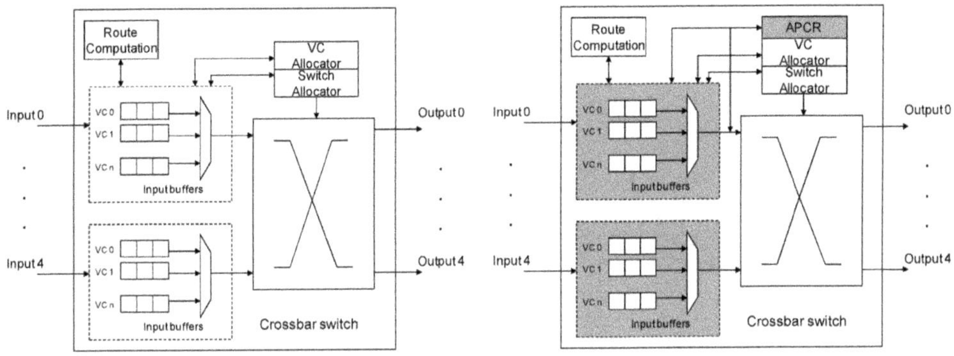

(a) A Generic NOC Router Architecture (b) An APCR Router Architecture

Figure 5: Generic Router and APCR Router Architectures.

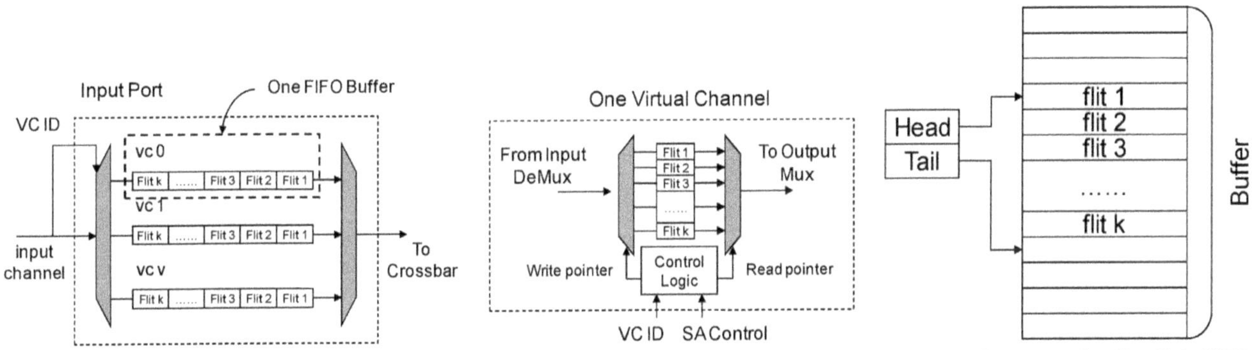

(a) Input Buffer Organization (b) VC Design with Parallel FIFO Implementation (c) Data Structure for Parallel FIFO Buffers

Figure 6: Generic NOC Router Input Buffer Architecture.

flits to the output channel per cycle, the input buffer should support multiple-flit read or write operations. Instead of the multiple read or write ports buffer design [27] that incurs significant overhead, the proposed buffer design reads data from each VC as wide as the output channel bandwidth. Note that all the data (e.g. 4 flits) read from a VC may not be sent to the output channel in a cycle. Then those flits that were read out but not sent should be dropped. To support the functionality of reading and dropping flits, the data structure shown in Figure 6 (c) should be modified, since it is necessary to add a packet pointer which points to the end position of a packet. Also the input buffer should be notified how many flits are effectively sent out. After each read operation, the head can be moved to the correct position. This information is gathered from the APCR component after the SA stage. Meanwhile, the channel allocation information should be transmitted to the downstream router through control links, since flits in different parts of the channel may enter different VCs. It does not incur any extra router delays, because the transmission can overlap with the ST and Link Traverse (LT) stages.

Figure 7 describes the whole procedure of the buffer management in an APCR router that supports Monopolizing and Channel-stealing. VC_0 buffers multiple flits that belong to the same packet. At step (1) multiple flits will be read out since the buffer output width is equal to the router output channel width, a multiple of the flit size. After the SA stage, the APCR component has the information of how many flits each VC can eventually send. At step (2) the allocation information will be used to set up the head pointer in each input buffer and the control signals of each output. At step (3) the guaranteed flits will be sent to downstream routers through the crossbar and the remaining read-out flits are dropped. These dropped flits will be read out from the input buffers again in the next cycle. The buffer write adopts the same method as the buffer read. Obviously, these redundant operations will incur more energy consumption. Compared with Fair-sharing, Monopolizing and Channel-stealing consume average 13% more energy for delivering one packet[1].

4.2.2 VC and Switch Allocation

The VC allocation in an APCR router is the same as that in a generic router. However, the switch allocation is different, which brings the main overhead. Figure 8 (a) shows the two-stage arbitration used in a generic router[2]. The first stage is to select one VC from each input port. It needs p $(v : 1)$ arbiters. The second stage is for output ports, selecting one valid request from p input ports which have the same output direction. Hence, each output port needs a $(p : 1)$ arbiter and the total number of the second stage arbiters adds up to p. Monopolizing has the same SA structure as a generic router, which does not incur any SA overhead.

[1]We use Orion 2.0 [13] for energy and area estimation in 45nm technology.

[2]We assume the router has p input ports and each input port has v virtual channels.

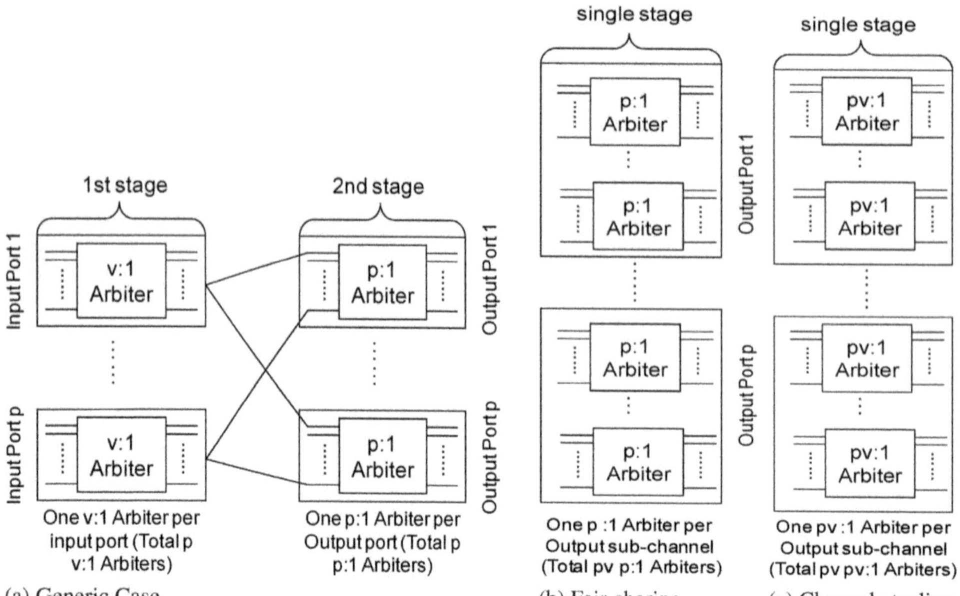

(a) Generic Case (b) Fair-sharing (c) Channel-stealing

Figure 8: Switch Allocation.

Switch allocation for Fair-sharing is different as shown in Figure 8 (b). In Fair-sharing, each VC of the same input port has its own reserved sub-channel, which guarantees one flit bandwidth. There is no competition among the VCs of the same input port. They share the wide channel between the input buffer and the crossbar, each occupying one flit bandwidth. This removes the first stage arbitration of a generic router. However, each output sub-channel needs an arbiter to decide the current winner because it receives requests from VCs of different input ports. Considering VCs are bound with output sub-channels in Fair-sharing[3], the number of inputs of an output sub-channel arbiter is the same as the number of input ports, p. Assuming that the number of sub-channels of an output port is equivalent to the number of VCs of an input port (v), pv ($p : 1$) arbiters should be provided. Channel-stealing needs even more complex SA structure because it provides the most flexible channel usage. Similar to Fair-sharing, only a single stage arbitration is required, as shown in Figure 8 (c). However, Channel-stealing does not bind VCs with sub-channels, which means a VC can request any sub-channel in the same output direction. Hence, each output sub-channel needs a ($pv : 1$) arbiter and the whole SA requires pv ($pv : 1$) arbiters.

Figure 9 shows the normalized area for the three schemes. We can see that an APCR router incurs less than 1% area overhead. The difference mainly comes from the SA arbiters. Monopolizing and Channel-stealing require extra control logic in buffer management, which does not incur much area overhead. Compared with other components, the area used by the arbiters and control logic is negligible. This explains why we cannot see much area difference when we consider the total router area.

4.2.3 *Credit-Based Flow Control*

With credit-based flow control, the upstream router keeps a record of the number of free buffers in each VC of downstream routers. Every cycle, when the upstream router forwards a flit, it will consume one credit until the credit counter becomes zero, which means the VC of the corresponding downstream router is full. In the opposite way, when the downstream forwards a flit and frees the associated buffer, it sends a credit to the upstream, causing the credit counter to increase by one. In the generic NOC design, the flit size is the same as the phit size, which means every cycle the current router can forward at most one flit to its downstream router in each direction. This triggers a credit to be sent to the corresponding upstream router. However, in an APCR router the flit size is no more equivalent to the phit size (normally smaller), which causes

[3] VC_0 from any input port can only use sub-channel$_0$ of all the output ports.

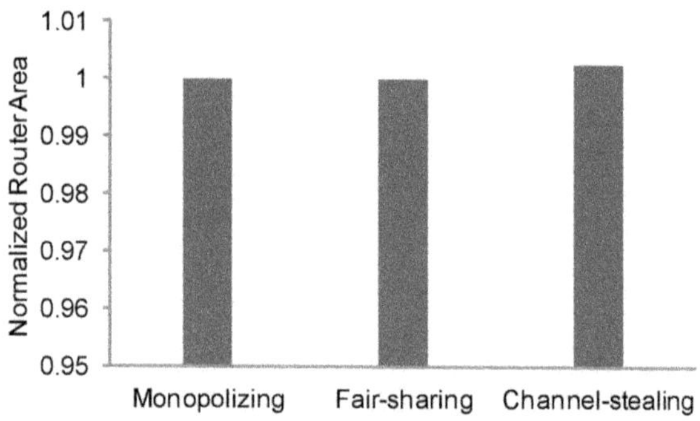

Figure 9: Total Router Area Normalized to a Generic Router.

Table 1: Time Analysis of the SA Stage Delay from HSPICE Simulations Using 45nm Technology.

Generic	Monopolizing	Fair-sharing	Channel-stealing
247 ps	247 ps	122 ps	333 ps

Table 2: Basic Network Configuration and Variations.

Characteristic	Basic	Variations
Topology	8×8 2D Mesh	MeshX2, MeshX4, FBFLY, MECS
Routing	XY	–
Router Arch	Two-stage Speculative	APCR Router
Per-hop Latency	3 cycles: 2 cycle in a router, 1 cycle to cross a link	–
Virtual Channels/Port	4	–
Phit Size (Channel Width)	512 bits	–
Flit Size	512 bits	128 bits
Packet Length (flits)	one (control packet), five (data packet)	–
Traffic Pattern	Uniform Random, Bit Complement, Transpose	SPEComp, SPECjbb, SPLASH-2 and PARSEC
Simulation Warm-up Cycles	10,000	–
Total Simulation Cycles	200,000	10,000,000 (Benchmarks)

Table 3: CMP System Parameters.

Clock Frequency	4 GHz
Core Count	32
L1 I and D cache	1-way and 4-way, 32KB, 1 cycle
L2 cache	16-way, 16MB, 512KB per bank, 32 banks, 20 cycles
L1/L2 cache block	64B
Memory Latency	300 cycles

the number of credits sent in each direction to be greater than one. To solve this problem, more wires are needed between two neighboring routers to transmit the credit information. Considering the depth of a VC is not big, the overhead of credit wires can be trivial.

4.2.4 *APCR's Effect on the Router Pipeline*

NOC router pipeline stage delays are quite imbalanced unlike the processor pipeline [24].Normally, the VA stage is the bottleneck [20]. The VA stage in an APCR router is the same as in a generic NOC router, but the SA stage is different. In the following time analysis, we mainly focus on the SA stage. Table 1 shows the SA stage delays for a generic router and three different regulation schemes. These results are obtained from HSPICE simulations using 45nm technology. Since Monopolizing has the same SA as a generic router, they have the same SA delay. Fair-sharing has the lowest delay, because of two main reasons: first, Fair-sharing only needs a single stage arbitration; second, binding VCs with output sub-channels makes the number of inputs of an output port arbiter small. Channel-stealing has the highest SA stage delay because of its complicated arbitration. However, when we compare these delays with the VA stage delay (328ps), the SA stage delays of all the schemes are still affordable. Additionally, according to the time stealing technology proposed by Das et al. [20], a slower stage in the router gains evaluation time by stealing it from successive or previous router pipeline stages. Considering the relative lower delay of the ST stage, the SA stage can steal time from the ST stage by delaying the triggering edge of the clock to all the subsequent latches. By adopting the time stealing technology, the APCR component is expected to have marginal effects on the router clock cycle time.

5. EXPERIMENTAL EVALUATION

In this section, we present a detailed evaluation of the proposed design.

5.1 Methodology

We evaluate the performance of our proposed schemes with a cycle-accurate network simulator that models all router pipeline delays and wire latencies. To achieve a fair comparison, we assume the same hardware budgets for the baseline router and the APCR router, including buffer and wire resources. We model a link as 512 parallel wires, which takes advantage of abundant metal resources provided by future multi-layer interconnects. In the baseline router, the flit size is the same as the link width (512 bits), while an APCR router uses a 128-bit flit. We simulate two kinds of packets in the network: control packets (short packets) and data packets (long packets). Note that each packet, whether it is short or long, has the same number of bits in both the baseline and the APCR router designs. With different filt sizes, the packet size of the baseline router is different from that of the APCR router. For example, a one-flit short packet and a five-flit long packet in the APCR design correspond to a one-flit short packet and a two-flit long packet in the baseline design. We choose an 8×8 2DMesh topology and XY routing algorithm, and configure four VCs for each port. Table 2 summarizes the network simulator configuration.

The workloads for our evaluation consist of synthetic workloads and real applications. Three different synthetic traffic patterns, Uniform Random (UR), Bit Complement (BC) and Transpose (TP), are used in our evaluation. In synthetic workloads, the percentage of short packets is 60%[4]. The packet generation rate for each node is

[4]The percentage is taken from SIMICS with GEMS [19] extension [5].

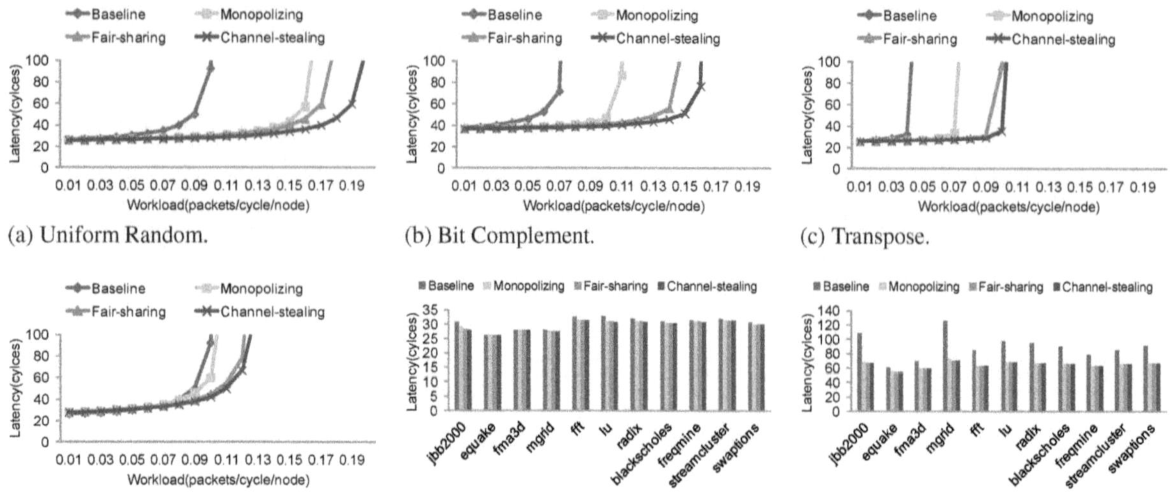

(a) Uniform Random. (b) Bit Complement. (c) Transpose.

(d) Uniform Random with the buffer size of the APCR Router halved. (e) Real Applications. (f) Average Latencies in the Congestion Period.

Figure 10: Packet Latencies with Three Synthetic Traffic Patterns and Real Applications.

constant. The real application workloads considered in this paper are three programs (fft, lu, radix) from SPLASH-2 [29], four benchmarks (blackscholes, streamcluster, swaptions and freqmine) from the PARSEC suite [4], three programs (equake,fma3d and mgrid) from SPEComp2001 [2], and SPECjbb2000 [1].

To extract traces from real applications, we use Simics [18], a full-system simulator, configured for UltraSPARCIII+ multiprocessors running Solaris 9 operating system. We develop a customized timing-model interface modeling out-of-order cores with 4 MSHRs per each processing core to implement a self-throttling CMP network [16]. Our CMP configuration has 32 out-of-order processors and 32 L2 cache banks in a single chip, modeling static non-uniform cache architecture (S-NUCA) [14]. Processing cores and L2 cache banks are connected through the on-chip interconnection network with 2D Mesh topology. All the cache related delays and area parameters are determined by CACTI [28]. Table 3 shows the main parameters of our CMP system.

5.2 Performance Results

We first evaluate the average packet latencies for the three schemes and the baseline router design. Since the flit sizes in the APCR design and the baseline design are different, we use *packet per node per cycle* as the metric of workloads to ensure a fair comparison.

Standard Synthetic Workloads: Figure 10 (a), (b) and (c) show the simulation results using three synthetic workloads. The results are consistent with our expectations. The trends observed in all the three traffic patterns are the same. When the packet injection rate is low, the performance of the four schemes only has minor differences. However, with high injection rates, an APCR router outperforms the baseline router. For example, when the injection rate is 0.1, Monopolizing improves the performance by 67% for the Uniform Random traffic. Among the three regulation schemes, Channel-stealing is the best, since it utilizes the output channels most efficiently. If there are flits ready in any VC and the downstream routers have enough credits, the output channel can always be utilized, since no channel usage restrictions exist in Channel-stealing. In the baseline design, if a flit is transmitted through the channel, the wide channel is also fully used, since the flit size is the same as the channel width. However, a big flit size can affect the VC depth if we keep the router buffer size constant. When the packet injection rate is high, with shallow VC depth, contention occurs and the network can easily get saturated. An APCR router makes more packets share the same channel resources, which potentially relieves the network congestion. The three schemes perform much better than the baseline when the packet injection rate is more than 0.1. Also when the network congestion is relieved, the network throughput is improved. It is observed that Channel-stealing increases the throughput by more than 100% for all three traffic patterns compared with the baseline design. Figure 10 (d) shows the performance result with the buffer size of the APCR router halved. We can see that the APCR router can still outperform the baseline router.

Real Applications: Figure 10 (e) shows the average packet latency with real applications. Channel-stealing delivers the best performance while the baseline is the worst. Since the packet injection rate of each node in these real applications is very low (below 0.01), the latency improvement of the three schemes over the baseline is not obvious (jbb2000 gets 9.3% improvement while fft gets 4.3% and lu gets 6.6%.). However, when we analyze the communication latency in the congestion period[5] for these real programs, as shown in Figure 10 (f), an APCR router can improve the communication latency by 25% in most of the benchmarks.

5.3 Topology Studies

In this section, we evaluate the performance of an APCR router in different topologies. Note that MeshX, such as MeshX2 and MeshX4, explores the channel resources by introducing multiple parallel networks. First, we compare the performance of an APCR router with that of MeshX using UR, as shown in Figure 11 (a). We assume that each design has the same buffer budget and bisection bandwidth, and that the flit size is always equal to the phit size in MeshX. It is observed that MeshX1, MeshX2 and MeshX4 have higher latency than the three APCR schemes before the network saturation point. Although MeshX divides the workload into mul-

[5] We define the congestion period as the time period when the average ratio of buffer occupancy in injection ports is above a threshold, which is set to 75% in our study.

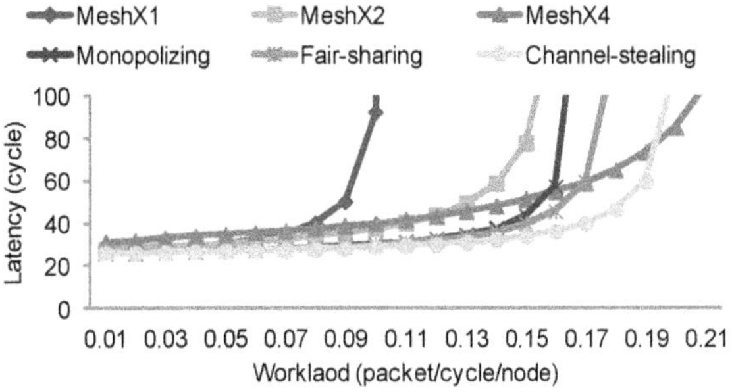

(a) Performance of MeshX and an APCR Router.

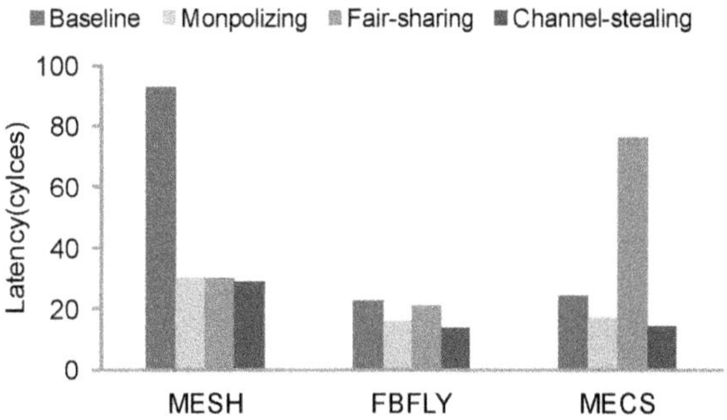

(b) Performance of an APCR Router in Various Network Topologies.

Figure 11: Topology Studies.

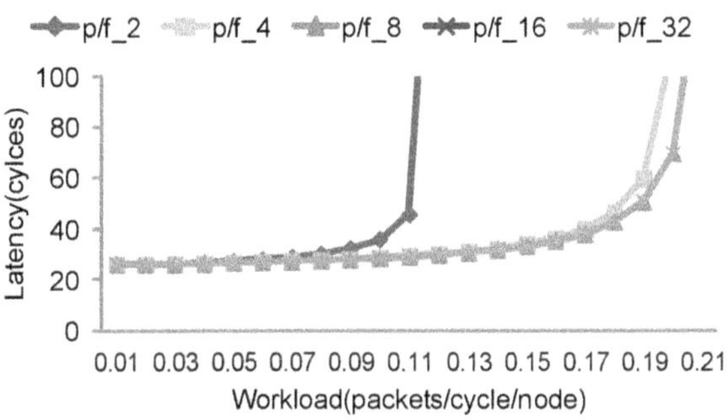

(a) Impact of the Number of Sub-channels on Packet Latency.

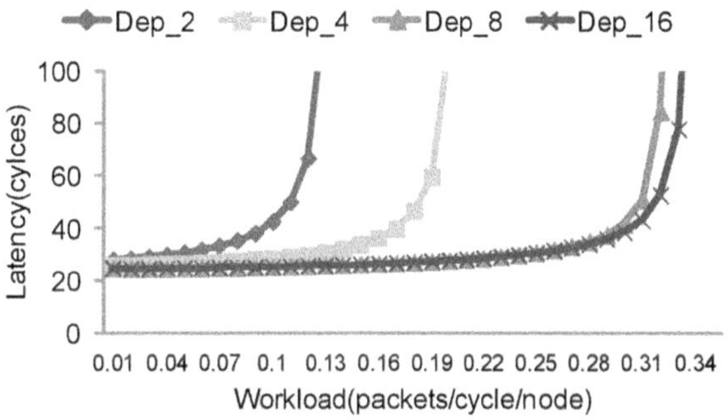

(b) Impact of the VC Depth on Packet Latency.

Figure 12: Sensitivity Studies with Different Network Design Points.

tiple parallel networks, these networks share the same amount of buffer space, which limits the VC depth of each port, making the network congested easier. MeshX4 produces the highest network throughput, benefiting from its multi-network design. However, MeshX4 increases the complexity of the crossbar, which incurs a big area overhead [11].

Next, we investigate the performance of an APCR router in recently proposed topologies, as shown in Figure 11 (b). We use a 2D Mesh, Flattened Butterfly (**FBFLY**) [15] and Multitask Express Channels (**MECS**) [10] with Uniform Random traffic[6], assuming each physical channel has the same bandwidth. We can see that an APCR router improves the network performance regardless of the underlying topologies. Monopolizing achieves 30% improvement in both FBFLY and MECS while Channel-stealing gets 40%. An exception comes from the MECS topology with the Fair-sharing scheme. Unlike FBFLY, MECS does not have any replicated channel, which implies all the multi-hop channels share a physical channel. If a physical channel is used as a two-hop channel, it cannot be used as a one-hop or three-hop channel in the same cycle. This reduces the probability of sharing physical channels from different packets, which hurts the performance of Fair-sharing.

5.4 Sensitivity to Network Design Points

In this section, we present variations that provide insight into the performance of an APCR router in different environments. Observing that Channel-stealing delivers the best performance, we use Channel-stealing for our experiments in the sensitivity study. The key idea of an APCR router is that the flit size is smaller than the phit size. The effect of the ratio between the phit size and flit size on the performance is shown in Figure 12 (a) where "p/f_2" means the phit size is two times the flit size. In this situation, the output channel is divided into two sub-channels. We can see that from "p/f_2" to "p/f_4" the network throughput is almost doubled. However, as the value of "p/f" keeps on increasing, there is no significant improvement. The main reason is that the VC depth is fixed as four. Even though the router has many free sub-channels, such as 16 or 32, the maximum flits stored in a VC is four. Hence, VCs cannot provide enough flits to completely utilize the sub-channels.

To further study how the VC depth in the number of flits affects the performance of an APCR router, we simulate with different VC depths. Each output channel is divided into four sub-channels, which also means that the flit size is one quarter of the phit size. The number of VCs is also fixed as four. Figure 12 (b) summarizes our experiments. Firstly, we observe that increasing the VC depth improves the network throughput. For example, changing the VC depth from 2 to 4 causes the network throughput to be improved by more than 53%. From 4 to 8, we get around 60% improvement. However, if we further increase the VC depth from 8 to 16, the improvement is marginal. One reason for this can be deduced from the packet size. In our experiment, the maximum packet size is five flits. VCs, whose depth is 8 or 16, can always hold one whole packet. The number of credits provided by the downstream

[6] We observe that other traffic patterns have the same trend.

router can also be greater than five. However, due to the regulation schemes, flits belonging to different packets cannot be transmitted in the same cycle. Therefore the maximum number of flits a VC can send is no more than five. Another reason is from the number of sub-channels. Since there are only four sub-channels, the output channel can only process four flits in a cycle. Thus, even with a long VC depth, the network throughput cannot be improved further.

6. CONCLUSIONS

Abundant wires inside a chip infer that it is important to organize this huge wiring capability efficiently. In this paper, we propose an Adaptive Physical Channel Regulator (APCR) for NOC routers to efficiently allocate the huge wiring resources. By defining the small flit, an APCR router allows flits from different packets or flows to share the same output channel in a single cycle. The three regulation schemes (Monopolizing, Fair-sharing and Channel-stealing) intelligently allocate the output channel resources considering not only the availability of physical channels but the occupancy of input buffers. Among the three schemes, Channel-stealing provides the most flexible usage of wide channels and, thus, achieves the best performance. An APCR router allows VCs to transmit multiple flits every cycle. The number of flits being transmitted every cycle dynamically changes according to the network status. Our simulation results using a detailed cycle-accurate simulator show that an APCR router improves the network throughput by over 100% in synthetic workloads. An APCR router can still outperform the baseline router when the buffer size is halved. It is also observed that an APCR router improves the network performance regardless of the underlying topologies.

7. REFERENCES

[1] Specjbb 2000 Benchmark. http://www.spec.org/jbb2000/.
[2] Specomp 2001 Benchmark Suite. http://www.spec.org/omp/.
[3] J. D. Balfour and W. J. Dally. Design Tradeoffs for Tiled CMP On-Chip Networks. In *ICS*, pages 187–198, 2006.
[4] C. Bienia, S. Kumar, J. P. Singh, and K. Li. The PARSEC Benchmark Suite: Characterization and Architectural Implications. In *PACT*, pages 72–81, 2008.
[5] B. Cuesta, A. Robles, and J. Duato. An Effective Starvation Avoidance Mechanism to Enhance the Token Coherence Protocol. In *PDP*, pages 47–54, 2007.
[6] W. J. Dally and B. Towles. Route Packets, Not Wires: On-Chip Interconnection Networks. In *Proceedings of DAC*, pages 684–689, 2001.
[7] W. J. Dally and B. Towles. *Principles and Practices of Interconnection Networks*. Morgan Kaufmann, 2003.
[8] R. Das, S. Eachempati, A. K. Mishra, N. Vijaykrishnan, and C. R. Das. Design and Evaluation of a Hierarchical On-Chip Interconnect for Next-Generation CMPs. In *HPCA*, pages 175–186, 2009.
[9] M. Galles. Scalable Pipelined Interconnect for Distributed Endpoint Routing: The SGI SPIDER chip. In *Proceedings of Hot Interconnect 4*, pages 141–146, 1996.
[10] B. Grot, J. Hestness, S. W. Keckler, and O. Mutlu. Express Cube Topologies for On-Chip Interconnects. In *HPCA*, pages 163–174, 2009.
[11] B. Grot, S. W. Keckler, and O. Mutlu. Topology-aware Quality-of-Service Support in Highly Integrated Chip Multiprocessors. In *WIOSCA*, 2010.
[12] R. Ho, K. Mai, and M. Horowitz. The Future of Wires. In *Proceedings of the IEEE*, pages 490–504, 2001.
[13] A. B. Kahng, B. Li, L.-S. Peh, and K. Samadi. ORION 2.0: A Fast and Accurate NoC Power and Area Model for Early-Stage Design Space Exploration. In *DATE*, pages 423–428, 2009.
[14] C. Kim, D. Burger, and S. W. Keckler. An Adaptive, Non-Uniform Cache Structure for Wire-Delay Dominated On-Chip Caches. In *ASPLOS*, pages 211–222, 2002.
[15] J. Kim, J. Balfour, and W. J. Dally. Flattened Butterfly Topology for On-Chip Networks. In *Proceedings of MICRO*, pages 172–182, 2007.
[16] D. Kroft. Lockup-Free Instruction Fetch/Prefetch Cache Organization. In *ISCA*, pages 81–88, 1981.
[17] A. Leroy, P. Marchal, A. Shickova, F. Catthoor, F. Robert, and D. Verkest. Spatial Division Multiplexing: A Novel Approach for Guaranteed Throughput on NoCs. In *CODES+ISSS*, pages 81–86, 2005.
[18] P. S. Magnusson, M. Christensson, J. Eskilson, D. Forsgren, G. Hållberg, J. Högberg, F. Larsson, A. Moestedt, and B. Werner. Simics: A Full System Simulation Platform. *IEEE Computer*, 35(2):50–58, 2002.
[19] M. M. K. Martin, D. J. Sorin, B. M. Beckmann, M. R. Marty, M. Xu, A. R. Alameldeen, K. E. Moore, M. D. Hill, and D. A. Wood. Multifacet's General Execution-driven Multiprocessor Simulator (GEMS) Toolset. *SIGARCH Computer Architecture News*, 33(4):92–99, 2005.
[20] A. K. Mishra, R. Das, S. Eachempati, R. Iyer, N. Vijaykrishnan, and C. R. Das. A Case for Dynamic Frequency Tuning in On-Chip Networks. In *MICRO*, pages 292–303, 2009.
[21] R. D. Mullins, A. West, and S. W. Moore. Low-Latency Virtual-Channel Routers for On-Chip Networks. In *Proceedings of ISCA*, pages 188–197, 2004.
[22] R. D. Mullins, A. West, and S. W. Moore. The Design and Implementation of a Low-Latency On-Chip Network. In *ASP-DAC*, pages 164–169, 2006.
[23] J. D. Owens, W. J. Dally, R. Ho, D. N. Jayasimha, S. W. Keckler, and L.-S. Peh. Research Challenges for On-Chip Interconnection Networks. *IEEE Micro*, 27(5):96–108, 2007.
[24] L.-S. Peh and W. J. Dally. A Delay Model and Speculative Architecture for Pipelined Routers. In *Proceedings of HPCA*, pages 255–266, 2001.
[25] C. G. Requena, M. E. Gómez, P. López, and J. Duato. Exploiting Wiring Resources on Interconnection Network: Increasing Path Diversity. In *PDP*, pages 20–29, 2008.
[26] C. G. Requena, M. E. Gómez, P. J. L. Rodríguez, and J. Duato. An Efficient Switching Technique for NoCs with Reduced Buffer Requirements. In *ICPADS*, pages 713–720, 2008.
[27] Y. Tamir and G. L. Frazier. High-Performance Multi-Queue Buffers for VLSI Communication Switches. In *Proceedings of ISCA*, pages 343–354, 1988.
[28] S. Thoziyoor, N. Muralimanohar, J. H. Ahn, and N. P. Jouppi. CACTI 5.1. Technical report, HP Laboratories, 2008.
[29] S. C. Woo, M. Ohara, E. Torrie, J. P. Singh, and A. Gupta. The SPLASH-2 Programs: Characterization and Methodological Considerations. In *ISCA*, pages 24–36, 1995.
[30] A. Yakovlev, A. Koelmans, and L. Lavagno. High-Level Modeling and Design of Asynchronous Interface Logic. *IEEE Design & Test of Computers*, 12(1):32–40, 1995.

Pointy: A Hybrid Pointer Prefetcher for Managed Runtime Systems

Ioana Burcea*
IBM Research T.J. Watson
ioana@us.ibm.com

Livio Soares*
IBM Research T.J. Watson
lsoares@us.ibm.com

Andreas Moshovos
University of Toronto
moshovos@eecg.toronto.edu

ABSTRACT

This work proposes *Pointy*, a software assisted hardware pointer prefetcher for Java applications. *Pointy* exploits the strengths of both software and hardware. Its runtime software component communicates points-to relationships between objects to the underlying hardware. This points-to information is maintained and tracked in any managed runtime that implements automatic garbage collection. *Pointy* stores the object connectivity information in a separate hardware structure and uses it to generate timely pointer prefetches. To achieve a low-cost hardware implementation, *Pointy* spills the object metadata to the conventional memory hierarchy and retrieves it only when needed. Taking advantage of its hybrid design, *Pointy* can selectively communicate points-to metadata to the hardware based on class profiling that is readily available at the runtime level, while impractical to extract at the hardware level.

Experimental results show that *Pointy* improves performance for pointer intensive benchmarks even in the presence of conventional prefetchers. When used in conjunction with traditional prefetchers, such as striding and next line, *Pointy* improves application performance by 53% for SpecJBB 2005 and by 72% on average[1], which represents a speedup of 19% and 18%, respectively, compared to traditional prefetchers.

Categories and Subject Descriptors

C4 [**Performance of Systems**]: Design studies; D3.4 [**Processors**]: Memory management

Keywords

computer architecture, runtime systems, pointer prefetching, hybrid software-hardware prefetching

*Research done while at the University of Toronto.

[1]Average performance is computed using the geometric mean across the speedup obtained for individual benchmarks.

PACT'12, September 19–23, 2012, Minneapolis, Minnesota, USA.

1. INTRODUCTION

The last decade has witnessed the widespread adoption of managed programming languages [19]. The popularity of these languages stems, in part, from their ease of programming, rich libraries and managed runtimes. However, the high level abstraction of these languages comes at the cost of lower performance compared to non-dynamic languages [9, 15].

Many managed applications have large memory footprints and would benefit from effective data prefetching. Predicting memory accesses of managed applications is difficult due to the heavy use of *pointers* and the inherently dynamic memory layout. Previous prefetching proposals for managed runtimes fall into two broad categories: hardware-only and software-only.

The effectiveness of hardware data prefetchers has been shown to be limited for managed applications [1, 17, 21]. The main challenge in designing a hardware-based prefetcher for managed runtimes is inferring application memory layout at the hardware-level. Reconstructing memory layout information in hardware has been reported to be only partially successful, even for non-managed applications [4, 5]. The automatic memory management present in modern runtimes (i.e., garbage collection) makes this task more difficult and error-prone. In addition, reconstructing memory layout information in hardware is fundamentally more expensive than leveraging the information that is readily available in the software runtime.

A different approach is to delegate the responsibility of prefetching completely to software. In this case, prefetch instructions are directly inserted into application code [1, 10]. Since it is instruction-based, the main challenge of software prefetching is that *what* to prefetch and *when* to prefetch must be explicitly inserted into application code. The dynamic nature of both the memory layout and the access pattern of managed applications make it difficult to design an instruction-based prefetcher that can cope with run-time changes. For example, extending a modern Java just-in-time compiler to dynamically prefetch objects has been demonstrated to be a complex task, with limited success [1]. In general, we believe that, as systems and applications become more complex, a stronger collaboration among computing stack layers can help achieve more efficient systems with higher application performance.

Fundamentally, implementing data prefetchers for managed runtimes solely in software or solely in hardware implies using complex heuristics, which potentially leads to limited accuracy. This paper demonstrates that, by delegating responsibilities to the *appropriate layer* in the compute stack, it is possible to design a simple, yet effective data prefetcher for managed runtimes.

This work presents *Pointy*, a software-guided hardware object pointer prefetcher for Java applications. In *Pointy*, the runtime is responsible for exposing points-to relationships between objects to the hardware, while the hardware uses this information to generate data prefetches. Points-to relationships are readily available in the runtime system as these relationships are tracked to implement efficient garbage collection. Thus, the runtime code modifications necessary to communicate this information to the hardware are easy to implement. At the hardware-level, application memory accesses can be cheaply monitored allowing for timely triggering of prefetch requests using the points-to information supplied by the software runtime.

Complex applications exhibit large pointer footprints. Storing all object pointer metadata in dedicated on-chip storage is impractical. Thus, to allow for a cost-effective implementation, instead of dedicating on-chip resources to store pointer metadata, we *virtualize* the pointer table [2]. In the virtualized design, the metadata table is stored in physical memory and its entries are retrieved as needed. The metadata retrieval is performed using regular memory requests injected starting at the L2 cache level, which naturally leads to metadata being stored in the L2 cache. This technique does not require changes to the existing memory system, except for the ability to insert metadata requests alongside application data and instruction requests.

As expected, not all pointers are created equal. The performance potential for prefetching varies across pointers. We implement a runtime feedback mechanism that focuses prefetching on delinquent class fields. By selectively exposing only delinquent fields to the hardware, the runtime can dynamically reduce the aggressiveness of the prefetcher while maintaining, or improving, its effectiveness. This type of filtering highlights an advantage of *Pointy*'s hybrid architecture: the class-level information is readily available at the runtime level, however, the same information would be hard and expensive to infer at the hardware level.

Pointy was implemented in the widely deployed Java Virtual Machine OpenJDK 7. Our experimental results show that *Pointy* improves overall application performance for a series of pointer-intensive applications using less than 1KB of dedicated hardware storage. When used in conjunction with traditional prefetchers, such as striding and next line, *Pointy* improves application performance by 53% for SpecJBB 2005 and by 72% on average, which represents a speedup of 19% and 18%, respectively, compared to the traditional prefetchers alone. Our evaluation also shows that *Pointy* complements a state-of-the-art pattern-based data prefetcher [11], improving overall the cost-performance trade-off. While our implementation uses the Java runtime system, we do not employ any Java specific features. We expect similar optimizations to be possible in any managed runtime system that implements some form of automatic memory management (i.e., garbage collection).

The novelty of *Pointy* is two-fold. First, the runtime system is responsible for collecting and communicating application metadata to the underlying hardware, eliminating the need for complicated heuristics at either hardware or software level. Second, the hardware component employs virtualization to implement a cost-effective prefetcher.

2. SOFTWARE RUNTIME ASSISTED OBJECT POINTER PREFETCHING

This work proposes a new hybrid (software/hardware) data prefetcher, *Pointy*, that targets inter-object references in managed applications. The design of *Pointy* follows the principle of delegating responsibilities to the appropriate layer in the computing stack. In the case of an object pointer prefetcher, the prefetcher must (1) collect and update the information about program memory layout and access pattern, (2) efficiently store this metadata for subsequent prefetch predictions, and (3) trigger prefetch requests. In the following paragraphs, we describe challenges of each of these requirements, as well as summarize how *Pointy* addresses them.

Managed applications delegate the management of memory, typically in the form of data structures or objects, to the language and runtime layers. For these applications, which make use of numerous logically linked objects, extracting stable access patterns at the processor-level is difficult and error-prone. Conversely, managed runtimes track the memory layout of application objects, and their relationships (points-to information), in order to support efficient automatic memory management (i.e., garbage collection). For this reason, we advocate that the runtime should *expose* object-level relationships to the hardware to enable effective prefetching. Not only is this information readily available, making it easy to implement and collect, but the runtime also has the most up-to-date information. This is more important for managed applications than non-managed ones, since objects are generally moved by the runtime during garbage collection.

Storing the points-to information in a hardware structure impacts the amount of on-chip resources dedicated to the prefetcher. As we show in Section 4, the size of pointer footprints can grow to tens of megabytes. Reserving this much storage for pointer information alone is unlikely to yield performance benefits over using the storage to augment the capacity of the general purpose processor caches, specially when considering a wide spectrum of applications. For this reason, we *virtualize Pointy*'s object pointer table, storing it in main memory, while taking advantage of the processor cache hierarchy for partially storing pointer metadata and timely accessing table entries [2]. The virtualized design of the prefetcher requires only 1K of dedicated storage.

The main challenge in virtualizing *Pointy*'s object pointer table is that virtualization delays prefetch predictions when table entries are not found in the dedicated storage and need to be fetched from the on-chip caches. To amortize the misses to the dedicated table with several prefetches generated from the same information, we apply simple techniques to both compress the pointer metadata, as well as collocate various entries in the same cache line. Our results show that these techniques allow the virtualized prefetcher to remain effective at improving overall performance, even when accounting for additional delays in retrieving prefetching metadata.

Finally, prefetch request generation is best suited to be implemented at the hardware level. A close collaboration with the processor pipeline allows the prefetcher to observe application memory requests at runtime. This information is fundamental in guiding both *what* to prefetch, and *when* to prefetch. By observing memory addresses, the prefetcher can easily infer which objects are being accessed by the application and can predict which objects are likely to be accessed in the near future based on previously provided object pointer information.

Figure 1 depicts a simple example of how *Pointy* works. The first diagram (a) shows the software runtime view of the application objects and their connectivity. The second diagram (b) shows the corresponding *Pointy* table (Object Metadata Table) that stores a compressed view of the points-to relationships, and (c) shows a sample execution where the *Pointy* hardware prefetcher monitors memory accesses to trigger prefetch requests, according to the contents of the object metadata table.

The implementation of *Pointy* comprises the following components:

- Simple JVM extensions to communicate pointer information to the prefetcher, including pointer creations and mutations due to object relocation during garbage collection.

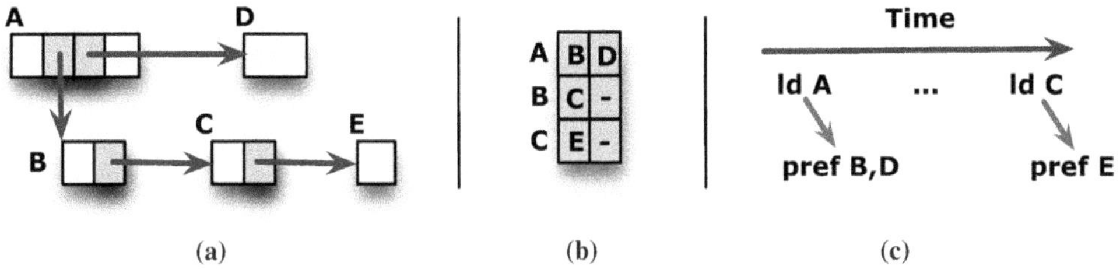

Figure 1: Overview of the *Pointy* prefetcher. (a) The software-level view of five objects and their points-to relationships, which are maintained within the Java virtual machine, (b) The *Pointy* hardware table stores a compressed view of the points-to relationships, (c) A sample execution where the *Pointy* hardware prefetcher monitors memory accesses and triggers prefetch requests, according to the contents of the hardware table.

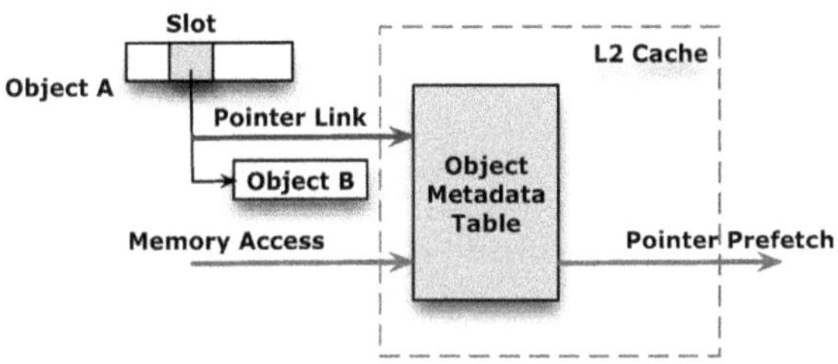

Figure 2: Overview of the software runtime assisted object pointer prefetching.

Figure 3: Pointer link.

- A hardware *Object Metadata Table* that stores the object metadata supplied by the software runtime. To minimize the amount of dedicated storage, we apply virtualization to the table, spilling its content to the on-chip and off-chip memory hierarchy.
- An L2 cache hardware prefetcher that monitors application memory accesses and generates prefetch requests using the pointer information in the Object Metadata Table.

Next, we describe the design and implementation of *Pointy*, detailing each of the three components.

2.1 Extending the Java Runtime System

To be able to perform automatic garbage collection, runtime systems keep track of all relationships between objects. To expose these relationships to the hardware, we annotate both the just-in-time compiler, as well as the garbage collector, in all contexts where links between objects are created or updated. There are two main points where links between objects are modified: 1) in the compiled code of the application, whenever an object is attributed to another object field and 2) at garbage collection time, when objects are moved in memory. Pointers create links between objects, as shown in Figure 3. We refer to these links as *pointer links*. Upon the creation or modification of a pointer link, the two addresses *(Slot, Pointer)* are communicated to the hardware. *Slot* is the address in memory that contains the value of the *Pointer*; in other words, *Slot* is the address of the object field that gets modified.

Once pointer links are monitored inside the JVM, they can be communicated to the hardware by several means, such as using either a new instruction or piggy-backing on regular stores with a memory-mapped interface. The latter can be a less intrusive change to the ISA.

For ease of development, in our implementation of *Pointy*, we added a new instruction, *pointer-link*, to the ISA. This instruction requires two memory addresses as operands, the first corresponding to the *Slot* address of the pointer link, and the second the *Pointer* address of the pointer link. During its execution, once the *pointer-link* instruction gets decoded, the two addresses are sent to the prefetcher. Since no other processing is required, the overhead of the *pointer-link* instructions is limited. These *pointer-link* instructions are advisory and can be ignored or discarded at will, making it easy to maintain compatibility in future implementations. For the applications we studied, the percentage of the dynamic *pointer-link* instructions is less than 1% of the total application instructions.

We modified the *OpenJDK 7* source code to provide the object metadata through the addition of *pointer-link* instructions. The modifications are straightforward, as all information needed is readily available in the just-in-time compiler and garbage collector. The modifications consist of 290 lines of code across 12 files.

2.2 Object Metadata Table

Pointy stores the information provided by the runtime in a hardware *Object Metadata Table*, as shown in Figure 2. The goal of this metadata table is to record the memory addresses of application objects, as well as their connectivity.

An entry in this table can be seen as a compressed description of an object, containing all the addresses of the objects it has access to through its object fields. A row in the table may contain multiple such entries. In practice, to optimize for space and to simplify table lookups, we store information at cache-line granularity. In other words, we assume that all pointers in a cache line belong to the same object. Thus, each entry in the table corresponds to a memory block equal in size to the L2 cache line. When the *pointer-link* instruction is executed, a pair of two addresses (*Slot*, *Pointer*) are provided to the table. The cache-line address of the *Slot* is used to index and retrieve the corresponding entry from the table. The content of the retrieved entry is updated with the new *Pointer* value to reflect that the object located at the *Pointer* address is reachable from this entry. If all locations within the retrieved entry are already pointing to existing objects, the oldest pointer value is overwritten with the new value, effectively implementing a FIFO replacement policy.

2.2.1 *Virtualizing the Object Metadata Table*

To achieve the full benefits of *Pointy*, given that complex applications have large pointer footprints, the hardware storage for the object pointer metadata needs to be large. Dedicating on-chip storage for such a large structure is impractical for several reasons. First, dedicating a large portion of the processor chip to one optimization reduces the resources available to implement other optimizations or functionality. Second, applications vary in their requirement for the size of the object metadata table. Third, some applications may not be using this optimization at all, in which case, the dedicated on-chip storage is completely wasted. Predictor virtualization mitigates the limitations of one-size-fits-all optimization storage by emulating large tables using the conventional memory hierarchy to store application metadata [2].

For a cost-effective hardware implementation, we apply virtualization to the object metadata table. In the virtualized design, the table is conceptually moved to main memory, as shown in Figure 4. A small dedicated on-chip metadata cache holds the active entries of the table. The contents from the large, in-memory table are retrieved as needed by the prefetcher, using regular memory requests injected starting at the L2 cache level. As a consequence, the content of the table is partially stored in the L2 cache, competing with application data and instructions for cache capacity.

In the virtualized approach, several entries from the object metadata table are packed together and stored in one cache block in the L2 cache. Whenever metadata is required for prefetching, the dedicated cache is checked first. If the metadata is found in the dedicated cache, it is immediately used for prefetching. Otherwise, on a miss to the dedicated cache, a request is sent to the memory hierarchy to retrieve the necessary metadata. Upon the retrieval of the metadata from the memory hierarchy, the entries received are unpacked and installed in the dedicated cache. Several entries are retrieved with one memory request and all metadata entries are installed in the dedicated cache.

To track the outstanding metadata requests, a series of request status registers (MSHRs) are used. These type of registers are already employed in current processors to track the outstanding memory request at each level in the memory hierarchy. Similarly, these registers hold information about the pending metadata requests. Upon a miss to the dedicated cache, the status registers are checked for a match before forwarding the request to the memory hierarchy. This avoids sending multiple L2 requests for the same metadata.

Upon the modification of a pointer link, the contents of the rest of the corresponding L2 cache line needs to be retrieved to be able to propagate the modification to the memory hierarchy. Pending modifications are tracked by a series of write buffers. The number of MSHRs and write buffers used impacts the number of requests that can be serviced without losing any information. Whenever these registers are not sufficient to store in-progress requests, some information is lost, i.e., either some prefetch information is not retrieved or some pointer links are not updated. Experimental analysis shows that, for the benchmarks studied, 16 MSHRs and four write buffers are sufficient to monitor all pending requests such that no information is dropped.

A direct consequence of virtualization is the higher latency of accessing the object metadata. This affects the timeliness of the prefetches and, for this reason, a virtualized prefetcher generally shows lower performance than the equivalent scheme where all the table is in dedicated hardware. Section 4 shows that virtualization is by far beneficial when considering the trade-off between the performance and the hardware overhead.

2.3 Pointer Prefetcher

Prefetches are injected in the second level of the on-chip processor cache. We chose the second level cache for two reasons. First, since first level caches are generally small, they are highly sensitive to the pollution introduced by prefetching. Second, application performance suffers mostly due to accesses that experience the full latency to main memory.

Pointy consults the information in the object metadata table to predict subsequent application memory accesses. Due to the object-oriented nature of Java applications, memory is traversed according to the paths described by pointer links among objects. As such, it is possible to anticipate the objects to be accessed in the near future based on the pointer links of currently accessed objects.

Upon a demand access to the L2 cache, the object metadata table is searched for any corresponding slots within the accessed cache block. If such a slot exists, it means that the cache block being accessed contains pointers to other memory locations. These pointers are prefetched proactively such that, if accessed, the latency to retrieve the data from memory is partially or fully hidden. *Pointy* installs prefetches directly in the L2 cache, without any intermediate buffering.

In general, L2 caches are accessed with physical memory addresses. Since the object metadata table contains virtual addresses, a virtual-to-physical translation is needed for the prefetcher. Accessing the same TLB used for translating demand requests would increase the contention on this structure. Thus, we assume that prefetching uses a lazily-updated shadow TLB. Since prefetches are advisory in nature and are not required for the correctness of the application, lazy updates to the shadow TLB are sufficient. We do not include the hardware storage of the TLB in the storage overhead of the prefetcher. Such a shadow TLB can be shared among several optimizations. To further reduce the dedicated space, the TLB can also be virtualized.

3. CLASS ORIENTED OBJECT METADATA FILTERING

Not all object pointers are created equal. Some type of pointer links are traversed more often, and, as a consequence, they generate more L2 cache misses and exhibit higher potential for prefetching. One way to increase the benefit of prefetching is to focus on such pointer links with higher prefetch potential. In this section, we describe one programmer transparent mechanism we experimented with, implemented completely in software, to filter out pointer links that are less likely to yield beneficial prefetching opportunities.

With this goal in mind, we implemented a profile analysis in the runtime system that tracks which pointer links generate the most L2 cache misses. In this analysis, we focused on understanding the behavior of object pointers with respect to the *class* each object instantiates. There are several advantages to filtering at the class level. First, class level information is easily accessible within the Java runtime, and can be used to decide which pointer links to communicate to the hardware. Second, as Section 4.5 shows, the distribution of *delinquent pointers* is biased to a small set of class fields, making it a good criteria for discarding a large portion of pointer links without sacrificing prefetching opportunities. Third, the runtime overhead resulting from filtering at class-field granularity is expected to be low, since a simple general check can decide to include, or not, the new *pointer-link* instruction. This would not be the case for filtering specific objects or specific pointer links.

For all the classes loaded by an application, we attempt to identify the specific class fields that contribute to the largest portion of *delinquent pointers*. To do so, we extend the software runtime in the following way. Each pointer link of an object corresponds to a particular field of the class that the object instantiates. Whenever an L2 cache miss occurs, we map the miss address to a pointer link,

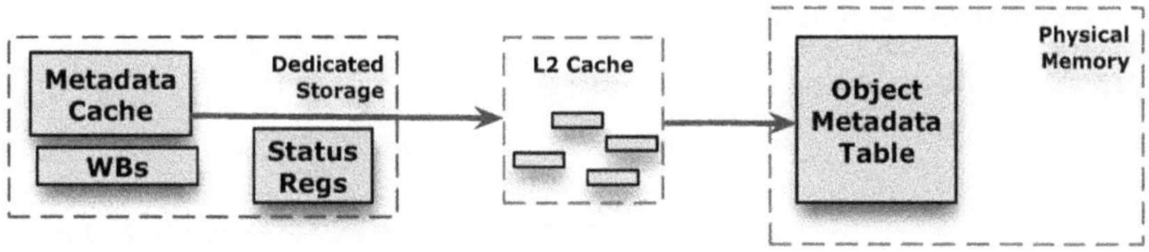

Figure 4: Virtualization is applied to the object pointer metadata.

and subsequently map the delinquent link to its corresponding class field. We increment a counter for the corresponding class field on each delinquent pointer miss. After a profiling phase, we can rank the class fields according to counter values.

When communicating the pointer links to the underlying hardware, the software runtime can choose to filter out the object metadata and communicate only the pointer links resulting from the topmost class fields in the ranking. These pointer links are predicted to be delinquent, and, in consequence, we expect that their prefetching potential is higher.

Filtering the object metadata has several consequences. First, there is less contention for storage capacity in the object metadata table. By filtering the most important pointers, we eliminate the potential overwriting of useful pointers by non-useful ones that can occur due to aliasing. Thus, filtering out non-useful pointers can lead to higher application performance. Second, less updates to the table translates into less accesses to the L2 cache. Third, a smaller object metadata footprint leads to lower pollution in the L2 cache due to the virtualization of the metadata table. In Section 4 we show how filtering improves performance for certain benchmarks and reduces the pressure on the L2 cache.

4. EXPERIMENTAL EVALUATION

In this section we evaluate the performance of *Pointy*. First, we present the methodology used in our study, our benchmarks and the simulation infrastructure. Second, we analyze the potential performance improvement for software assisted pointer prefetchers. Third, we present the evaluation of both dedicated and virtualized pointer prefetchers. Motivated by our analysis on distribution of delinquent pointer links, we propose a class-level profiling technique that focuses the prefetching to a limited number of class pointer fields. We compare this approach with an idealized filtering and study the performance improvement and the impact on the memory hierarchy.

4.1 Experimental Methodology

In our experiments, we used a simulation infrastructure based on PIN, a dynamic binary instrumentation framework [14]. We use PIN to simulate each workload on an in-order processor core, in which each instruction, except for memory instructions, takes one cycle to execute. The latency of memory instructions is determined by simulating a memory hierarchy with a 32KB first level data cache (2-way set-associative) and a 4MB second level cache (16-way set-associative). The latency of the L1 cache is one cycle, the latency of the L2 cache is 12 cycles and the latency of the main memory is 400 cycles. The cache block size used in all caches is 64 bytes.

In our study, we focused on pointer-intensive benchmarks with high L2 cache MPKI. We used two workloads from the Java implementation of the Olden benchmark suite: *em3d* and *mst*. For *em3d*, we present results for two different sets of inputs, since they exhibit different behavior. In addition, we include results for a benchmark that was recently used to analyze the performance and the features of different programming languages [9].[2] The benchmark is an implementation of an algorithm that analyzes code to recognize reducible and irreducible loops, described by Havlak [8]. The benchmark builds a large control flow graph containing 4-deep loop nests with a total of 76,000 loops. The benchmark performs loop recognition on this graph 50 times. The benchmark comes with several versions. In our experiments, we used the optimized Java implementation for this benchmark. In the text and in the graphs, we refer to this benchmark as *loop*. The last benchmark used in our study is SpecJBB 2005 modified to execute a fixed number of transactions, as it is used in several Java studies under the name of *pseudo-SpecJBB*. The input parameters used to run the benchmarks are specified in Table 1. All results were collected using our modified OpenJDK 7 JVM for the x86 32-bit backend.

Benchmark	Input Parameters
em3d-A	10,000 nodes, degree 4
em3d-B	20,000 nodes, degree 5
mst	1,024 nodes
Havlak-loop	default
specjbb	warehouse_population = 2,000 jbb_transactions=100,000

Table 1: Input parameters used for running the benchmarks

To avoid the interference of the just-in-time compiler on our measurements, we forced OpenJDK to JIT-compile all code with the optimizing compiler. We verified by running the benchmarks on a real machine that the Java runtime produces efficient code when run with this option. For all experiments, several iterations of the benchmark are run before any timing measurement is performed. This ensures that all methods involved in the benchmark execution are compiled to native code. For all benchmarks, we collect time measurements for the fifth iteration of the benchmark. Based on our experiments on a real machine, the performance stabilizes by the fifth iteration. For all benchmarks except SpecJBB, we report performance numbers for a complete run of one benchmark iteration. For SpecJBB, we report performance numbers for running the first four billion instructions in the fifth benchmark iteration. The benchmarks runs are sufficiently long that garbage collection is triggered during the execution. Thus, our measurements include the effects of garbage collection.

In all experiments, we enable two additional orthogonal, simple hardware prefetchers that have been widely deployed: stride and next-line prefetchers. For the stride prefetcher we use a table with 128 entries to identify instruction-based striding patterns in the memory access stream [3]. Next-line prefetching is triggered

[2]The full benchmark sources are available as open-source, hosted by at *http://code.google.com/p/multi-language-bench/*.

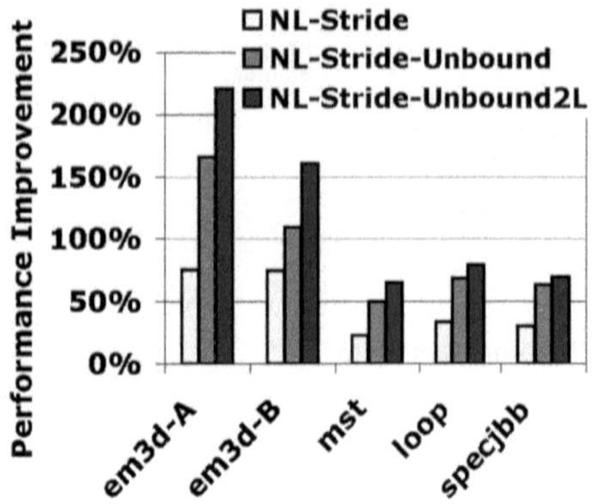

Figure 5: The performance improvement potential for *Pointy*, with unbounded storage capacity.

on misses at the second level cache. All prefetches are directly inserted in the L2 cache, without intermediate buffering.

4.2 The Potential of Software Runtime Assisted Pointer Prefetching

In this section, we quantify the potential of *Pointy* to improve application performance. For this set of experiments, the Java runtime communicates all object pointer links upon their creation or modification. We assume that the *Object Metadata Table* is unbounded in size, and, thus, it stores all pointer links. While this is an impractical assumption, our goal is to quantify the potential of the proposed prefetching scheme. We discuss a realistic implementation in the next section.

Whenever an L2 cache block is accessed, the unbounded table is searched for all possible *Slot* addresses corresponding to the access (i.e., in our 32-bit system, for a 64-byte cache line, there are 16 possible addresses). If such a *Slot* address exists in the table, the corresponding *Pointer* is retrieved, and a prefetch for the address *Pointer* is generated, provided the corresponding memory block is not already present in the L2 cache. Since objects can span multiple cache line or nearby objects may be accessed close in time, we vary the number of cache lines prefetched. Thus, we experiment with generating prefetches for up to two cache lines: the one containing the address *Pointer* and the subsequent cache block in memory.

Figure 5 shows the percentage performance improvement relative to a baseline with no prefetching for three different prefetching techniques: 1) *NL-Stride*: next-line and stride prefetching running together, 2) *NL-Stride-Unbound*: the unbounded pointer prefetching technique when run in conjunction with the next-line and stride prefetching, and 3) *NL-Stride-Unbound2L*: the same as the previous scheme, but with up to two cache lines prefetched as explained above.

As expected, traditional prefetching schemes improve the performance of memory intensive applications. These schemes work for regular access patterns and also for object pointers that happen to be aligned in memory at constant strides. However, a runtime assisted pointer prefetcher adds considerably to the performance improvement. As the graph shows, the potential performance for such a scheme is significant across all applications, with a 70% performance improvement for SpecJBB. Across all applications, prefetching the subsequent line for an object pointer is beneficial, therefore, for the rest of the experiments presented in the paper, prefetching is always performed for two consecutive cache lines. Further experiments (not shown in here) with prefetching more than two consecutive lines at a time resulted in smaller performance improvements due to increased cache pollution.

While these results are promising, they are obtained with an unrealistic hardware implementation that assumes unbounded resources to store the object metadata. In the next section, we study the prefetching performance under realistic conditions, limiting the resources available for storing metadata.

4.3 The Performance of a Practical Pointer Prefetcher

In this section, we show that even a considerably large dedicated table is not sufficient to capture the full potential of the prefetcher. To address this issue, we virtualize the object metadata table as explained in Section 2.2.1 and compare its performance with the dedicated approach.

For the first set of experiments, the object metadata table is limited to a fixed size. Each entry in the table corresponds to a 64-byte memory block and can store up to four pointer addresses (i.e., up to four pointer addresses that exist in the 64-byte memory block; the table loses information for memory blocks with higher pointer density). The pointer information is stored using a FIFO replacement policy. The table is two-way set associative, which performs slightly better than a direct mapped table.

To break the limitations of the on-chip resources, we virtualize the object metadata table. Virtualization allows for increased storage capacity without the cost of dedicated on-chip resources. The drawback of virtualization is the increased pressure on the memory hierarchy and an increase in prefetch latency.

In Figure 6 we present the performance improvement over a baseline with no prefetching for the following schemes: 1) *NL-Stride*: next-line and stride prefetching, 2) *NL-Stride-Small-Dedicated*: next-line and stride prefetching run in conjunction with a pointer prefetcher with a dedicated table with 256K sets, 3) *NL-Stride-NoFiltering-Dedicated*: same as the previous scheme, but, in this case, the table has 2M sets (i.e., $2*2^{20}$ sets), 4) *NL-Stride-NoFiltering-Virtual*: the table in the previous scheme is virtualized, and 5) *NL-Stride-Unbound2L*: the unbound version of the pointer prefetcher. The *NL-Stride* and *NL-Stride-Unbound2L* are the same as in Figure 5 and are included for reference.

For the benchmarks with smaller pointer footprints, the small table provides considerable performance improvement on top of the traditional prefetchers. However, for the benchmarks with larger pointer footprints, the smaller table is insufficient to achieve the true performance potential. Even the small dedicated table occupies considerable on-chip resources, which may not be available in a real-world processor design. Virtualization represents a viable solution for such hardware optimizations that require large tables to achieve their potential. We apply virtualization for the large pointer metadata table.

Figure 6 presents the results for a large dedicated table and the corresponding virtualized design (*NL-Stride-NoFiltering-Dedicated* and *NL-Stride-NoFiltering-Virtual*). The large dedicated table, while not fully achieving all the performance potential, makes the pointer prefetching come close to the performance of the unbound table. However, the size of the table is prohibitively high to be implemented on-chip. Applying virtualization loses some of the performance obtained by the large dedicated table, since some of the cache space is allocated to store object metadata and the timeliness of the prefetches is affected by storing metadata in the cache. When considering the trade-off between performance and dedicated space, the virtualized prefetcher is a viable option: most of the performance potential is achieved with limited dedicated resources.

For *em3d-B*, virtualization shows visibly less performance than the dedicated table. In this case, the object metadata causes consid-

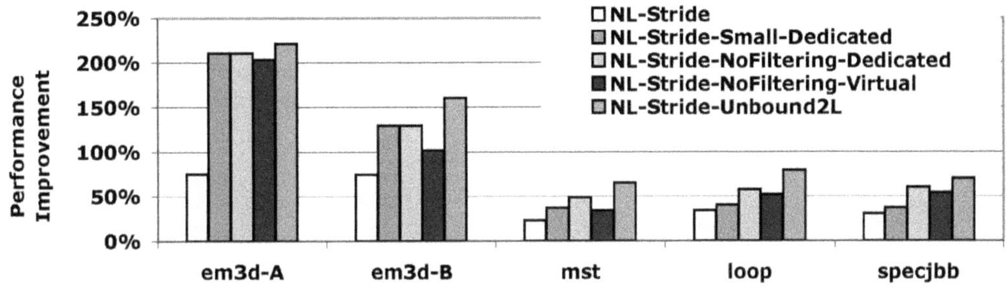

Figure 6: Performance comparison of *Pointy* when changing the design of Object Metadata Table. *NL-Stride-Unbound2L* and *NL-Stride-NoFiltering-Dedicated* have unrealistic storage requirements, while *NL-Stride-Small-Dedicated* and *NL-Stride-NoFiltering-Virtual* capture most the performance improvements, with significantly lower storage requirements (6.75MB and under 1KB, respectively).

Scheme	Dedicated storage
NL-Stride-Small-Dedicated	6.75 MB
NL-Stride-NoFiltering-Dedicated	52MB
NL-Stride-NoFiltering-Virtual	879.5 bytes

Table 2: Dedicated on-chip storage requirements for the Object Metadata Table under different *Pointy* designs.

erable pollution on the L2 cache. In fact, for *em3d-B*, virtualizing a smaller table can achieve higher performance. Tuning the size of the virtual table depending on the application is possible and deferred for future work.

To better understand the benefits of virtualization, we present the storage required for each of the schemes presented. For all schemes, the tables are tagged with the remaining bits after indexing is performed. Each entry in the table has sufficient space to store metadata for up to four pointers. Each pointer metadata represents a memory address aligned to a memory block of 128 bytes (i.e., the two 64-byte cache lines to be prefetched). Table 2 shows the amount of storage required for each of the prefetching schemes. The storage for the virtualized approach includes the resources needed for the status registers and write buffers. The trade-off between dedicated space and performance makes the virtualized pointer prefetcher a promising candidate.

As discussed in Section 3, not all pointer links contribute equally to the performance improvement. The results presented so far did not attempt at filtering the object metadata stored for prefetching. In the next section, we experiment with filtering of object metadata to achieve higher performance.

4.4 The Potential of Object Metadata Filtering

For the prefetchers discussed so far, the runtime communicates *all* object pointers to the processor. However, not all prefetches issued by the prefetcher are useful. In fact, since the capacity of the table is smaller than the pointer footprint of the applications, it is possible that useful pointer metadata is overwritten, due to aliasing, by metadata that does not contribute to any increase in performance. In this section, we aim to quantify how much additional performance object metadata filtering could provide, using hindsight information.

To identify which pointer links to filter out, we ran the unbounded scheme and mark which pointers are both prefetched and used by the application before being replaced from the L2 cache. We call these pointers *useful pointers*. To understand the potential of metadata filtering, we run the virtualized prefetcher described in the previous section, this time with only useful pointers being communicated to the hardware. Note that the useful pointer footprint is still larger than the capacity of the virtual table, and, in consequence, some entries may be overwritten.

Figure 7 shows the performance improvement of filtering useful pointers (i.e., the bar labeled *NL-Stride-Useful-Virtual*) compared to schemes presented previously. For the *em3d* runs, the capacity of the virtual table is sufficient to store most of the application pointers and, as a consequence, filtering ends up reducing the potential in performance. However, for the rest of the benchmarks, that have higher pointer footprints, filtering object metadata visibly increases the performance potential. For example, for the *loop* benchmark, the performance improvement increases from 51% to 68%. For *specjbb*, the filtering brings the performance within 6% of the idealized unbound prefetching scheme.

While the useful-pointer filtering presented in this section shows performance improvement, the filtering is performed with information not available at runtime. In the next section we analyze the distribution of useful pointers that inspired the practical filtering scheme, based on class fields, presented in Section 3.

4.5 Distribution of Useful Pointer Fields

Due to application access patterns, certain object pointer types are more frequently traversed than others. For example, in the *mst* benchmark, the pointer fields that link the buckets within a hash-table are traversed more often than the object pointers that refer to the data stored in each entry in the hash-table. For this reason, prefetching bucket links is more beneficial than prefetching data links. In this section, we experiment with filtering object metadata based on class object pointer types. To better understand the potential of such a filtering technique, we analyze the distribution of useful pointer fields. We are interested in studying the percentage of unique class fields that contribute to most of the useful prefetches. To collect these statistics, we mark the pointers that are useful using the unbounded scheme. Once all pointer links are collected, we identify the unique class fields that generate at least 100 useful pointer prefetches.

Figure 8 shows the cumulative distribution of unique class fields that contribute to useful prefetches. These results show that a small fraction of the pointer fields contribute to most of the useful prefetches. The most notable example is *mst* for which only two pointers contribute to more than 90% of the useful pointers. Even for the more complex benchmarks, such as *loop* and *specjbb*, less than a quarter of class fields contribute to more than 80% of the useful prefetches. For *em3d*, both runs look similar, with most of the pointers contributing to the useful prefetches, and we therefore

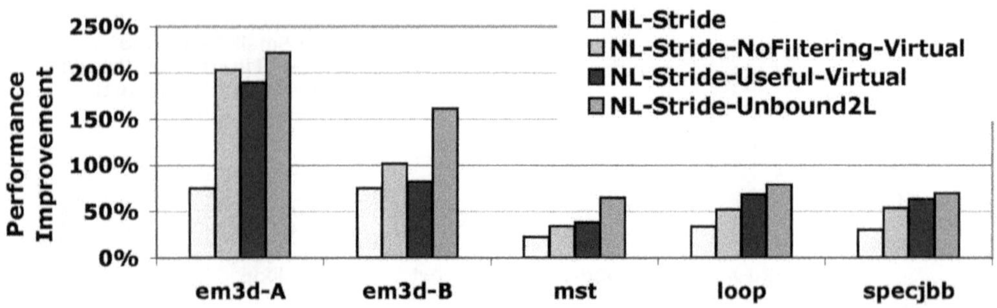

Figure 7: Potential performance improvement of *Pointy* by filtering information using hindsight useful pointer links.

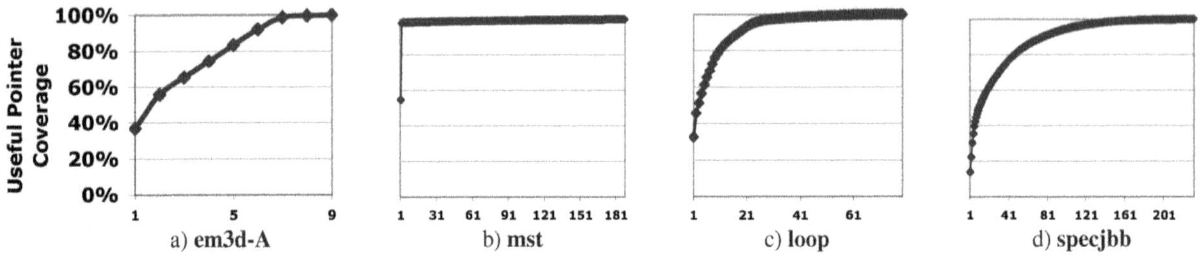

Figure 8: The distribution of pointer fields for useful prefetches.

omit the graph for *em3d-B*. Since the pointer footprints are small for these benchmarks, the virtual table can accommodate all object metadata. For the rest of the paper, we exclude *em3d* from our analysis, to focus on the benchmarks that can benefit from pointer link filtering.

These results indicate that filtering the object metadata to focus prefetching on a subset of the pointer fields can potentially achieve higher performance. Reducing the amount of metadata to be stored in the table diminishes aliasing, increasing the efficiency of the table. In addition, the pressure of the virtual table on the cache capacity may decrease, since it may store less information. In the next section we experiment with one type of object metadata filtering and study its benefits.

4.6 Class Oriented Object Metadata Filtering

In this section we study filtering pointer links based on class field types. Using the statistics collected in the previous section, we restrict prefetching to the most beneficial class pointer fields by communicating to the hardware only pointer links that correspond to the class fields with higher contributions to the useful prefetches. While this type of filtering is not practical, we include it as a reference point for our practical runtime filtering scheme.

One way to filter object metadata is to focus on delinquent pointer links. In this filtering, we account which pointer field traversals lead to misses in the L2 cache. As misses are observed, they are attributed to the corresponding class fields that generated the memory access. This type of runtime profiling is similar in spirit to the one presented by Adl-Tabatabai et al. [1]. Based on this profiling, we rank the class pointer fields and restrict prefetching to the pointer links corresponding to the top-most delinquent class fields.

Figure 9 shows the performance results for three virtual prefetching schemes: no filtering, filtering based on runtime delinquent pointer fields and filtering based on useful prefetches using hindsight information (see Section 4.4). Filtering shows the most performance benefits for *loop*, with an increase in performance of 6% and 8% for the two filtering techniques over no filtering.

Filtering object metadata leads less pressure on the virtual table. This has implications on the amount of metadata stored and retrieved from the memory hierarchy. To understand the impact of filtering on the memory hierarchy, we next analyze the memory traffic caused by the virtual prefetching scheme with and without filtering.

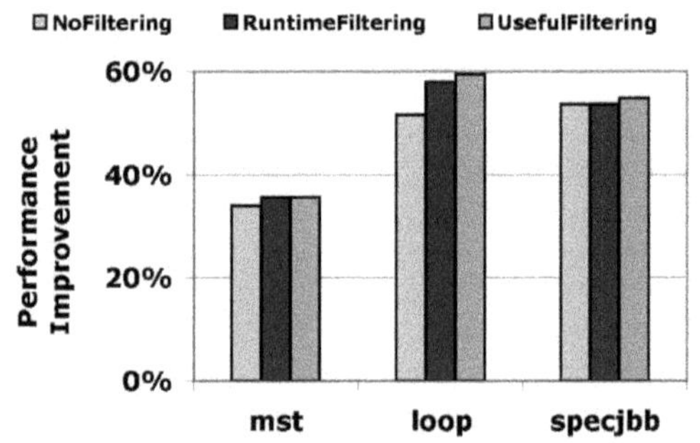

Figure 9: Performance improvement of *Pointy* with pointer link filtering performed by the runtime.

Table 3 shows several statistics that characterizes the traffic to the L2 cache as a percentage difference between filtering and no filtering. For all metrics presented, there is a slight decrease for the scheme that employs filtering. The decrease is more pronounced for writebacks, both application data and object metadata writebacks. With filtering, the footprint of the metadata in the cache is smaller, which leads to less cache replacements, and, as a consequence, less application writebacks. In addition, filtering implies less updates to the virtual table, which means less object metadata writebacks.

The last line in the table captures the maximum cache capacity used to store metadata. The table entry shows the maximum number of cache lines that store metadata in the L2 cache throughout the execution of the application. For the more complex benchmarks, the metadata reaches almost a third of the cache capacity. Metadata steals capacity from the application and translates it in increased performance. This result is a reinforcement of the fact that locality is poor for pointer-intensive applications and the cache

Statistic	mst	loop	specjbb	Statistic	mst	loop	specjbb
Demand Misses	-0.03%	-6.91%	-0.28%	Attempted Prefetches	-2.56%	-9.11%	-4.70%
Writebacks	-0.89%	-28.65%	-5.76%	Metadata Misses	-0.09%	0.18%	0.09%
Prefetches	-0.97%	-0.60%	1.71%	Metadata Writebacks	-0.89%	-28.66%	-5.78%
Useful Prefetches	-0.08%	4.26%	0.16%	Metadata Max Lines	14.23K	20.7K	22.84K

Table 3: L2 cache statistics differences for the filtering scheme when compared to no filtering.

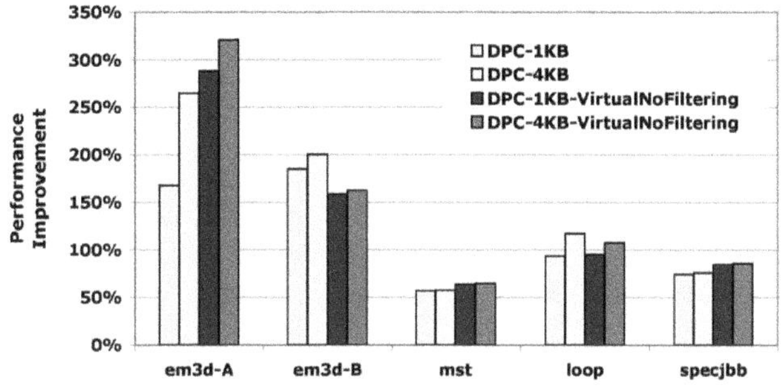

Figure 10: Prefetching champion run without and with *Pointy* prefetching.

storage is better utilized to store object metadata to help prefetching rather than using the same capacity for traditional application data caching.

An important benefit of delegating metadata collection to the software runtime layer, as opposed to implementing it fully in hardware, is the higher flexibility at a lower cost. The profiling scheme presented in this section exemplifies this benefit. With no changes to our proposed hardware, or the interface, the software runtime is able to leverage various sources of information about its memory layout and specific application access patterns, to provide more relevant information to the hardware pointer prefetcher.

4.7 Object Pointer Prefetching and State-of-the-Art Prefetching

So far, we have used and compared *Pointy* with next-line and striding prefetchers. This is motivated by the wide availability of these two prefetchers in current processors. In this section, we strive to understand how the *Pointy* performs when run in conjunction with a state-of-the-art pattern-based prefetcher.

Due to the performance penalties of long memory latencies, data prefetching is a well-researched topic with a plethora of proposals. For the purpose of this section, we chose to use the winner from the first data prefetching championship [11]. We implemented this prefetcher in our simulation infrastructure and we refer to it as the DPC (data prefetching champion). For the experiments included in this section, we used two different configurations for the DPC: the original proposal (i.e., 4KB of dedicated space) and a reduced-storage design with only 1KB of dedicated storage.

Figure 10 shows the results for the DPC when run without and with *Pointy* prefetching. The results vary across the benchmarks used in this study. For *em3d-B* and *loop*, there is a negative interference between the DPC and the object pointer prefetcher, leading to a slight slowdown when the two prefetchers are run together. However, for *em3d-A*, *mst* and *specjbb*, the object pointer prefetcher always adds to the application performance obtained with the DPC in both configurations used. In particular, a DPC-1KB with *Pointy* performs better than the DPC-4KB with a larger dedicated storage. This shows that using precise object pointer information in prefetching exposes a performance potential that is difficult to be covered by pattern-based prefetchers alone.

5. RELATED WORK

As the disparity between the speed of processors and main memory continues to impact the performance of modern computers, a large body of prefetching techniques have been proposed and studied. In particular, prefetching linked data structures is a well-researched topic with various proposals [1, 4, 5, 7, 12, 13, 16, 20, 21, 22, 23]. In this section, we outline the schemes that are most similar to *Pointy*.

Content-directed prefetching [5] inspects the data fetched into the on-chip caches and uses a simple heuristic to determine which slots within a cache line could potentially contain virtual addresses. All these potential virtual addresses are used to generate prefetches. One major drawback with this approach is the timeliness of the prefetches. To be able to identify which slots contain pointers, the data needs to be brought from the main memory before it is inspected. Consequently, the distance in time between the prefetch and the actual demand request is reduced to the point that most prefetches are ineffective. To address this issue, the pointer cache technique stores the identified pointers in a dedicated on-chip structure [4]. This technique requires large dedicated resources to be effective. Both the content-directed data prefetching and the pointer cache rely on heuristics to determine pointer links. In contrast, in our approach, the pointer links are communicated by the runtime system and no heuristic is needed. Ebrahimi et al. improve on the content-directed data prefetching by using compiler hints to indicate which words within a cache line should be considered for prefetching [7]. The compiler hints rely on a static object layout, which is generally not the case for managed languages. Ebrahimi et al. also propose heuristics to ensure a better collaboration between the traditional prefetchers and the pointer prefetcher. These heuristics are orthogonal to the prefetching scheme in use and can be deployed in conjunction with our approach for a better utilization of the memory bandwidth and cache capacity.

Among the existing hardware proposals, address-correlating prefetchers indirectly address pointer accesses [6, 18]. However, in the presence of garbage collection, that restructures the object memory layout, address correlation becomes more difficult.

Several prefetching techniques for linked data structures rely on compiler and/or programmer support [10, 16, 20, 23]. In contrast to existing proposals, our scheme is transparent to the programmer and uses information readily available to the runtime system.

The research most similar, in spirit, to our proposal is the work of Adl-Tabatabai et al., which identifies delinquent pointer links in Java applications and generates prefetches for these links [1]. The main difference between the two proposals is how the prefetches are generated. Adl-Tabatabai et al. rely on the ability of the runtime system to reposition the objects in memory and try to preserve the distances between objects. The prefetches are generated in software using constant distances between objects. In our approach, the relationship between objects is communicated to the hardware, which stores this metadata and uses it to generate the pointer prefetches in hardware. Our scheme does not depend on a fixed memory object layout and does not require repositioning of objects in memory. In general, applications exhibit complex object layouts, which makes it hard to preserve distances between certain objects. For example, in the case of SPEC JBB2000, only 20% of memory references can be correctly predicted using constant deltas [1].

The fundamental difference between our work and other proposals is that we do not require heuristics to determine points-to relationships. Even if performance improvements of our proposal and previous ones are similar for specific applications, our proposal yields fundamentally more accurate information and is simpler to implement, since it delegates the roles of detecting and prefetching memory accesses to the appropriate layers (i.e., software and hardware layer, respectively).

6. CONCLUDING REMARKS

The computing industry is experiencing an inflection point: no significant increase in application performance is possible by simply upgrading the underlying hardware or by applying optimizations solely at the software level. We believe that coordinated innovations across multiple layers of the computing stack are needed to deliver the expected application performance.

In this paper we presented *Pointy*, a software-hardware collaborative scheme for software runtime assisted object pointer prefetching. Managed runtimes record rich metadata on object memory layout that is not available to the underlying hardware. Through a thin interface, we communicate the links between objects to the hardware. Using this information, the hardware generates pointer prefetches based on the memory access stream of the application. To achieve a cost-effective hardware implementation, the object metadata is spilled to the memory hierarchy and retrieved only when needed. This alleviates the need for large, dedicated, on-chip structures and makes the prefetching scheme practical.

We experimented with object metadata filtering based on delinquent pointer links. We analyzed the pointer links that lead to most misses observed by the L2 cache and focus the prefetching only on the class pointer fields that generate the most misses. This filtering reduces the amount of object metadata stored in the hardware and results in slightly higher application performance with less traffic to the L2 cache and main memory. The analysis of the delinquent pointer links is performed at the runtime level, with information that is readily available. Such an analysis is impractical at the hardware level since the underlying hardware is oblivious to the object memory layout or relationships between objects.

Experimental results show that *Pointy* improves performance for pointer intensive benchmarks even in the presence of conventional prefetchers. When used in conjunction with traditional prefetchers, such as striding and next line, *Pointy* improves application performance by 53% for SpecJBB 2005 and by 72% on average, which represents a speedup of 19% and 18%, respectively, compared to traditional prefetchers alone. Our evaluation also shows that the new proposal complements a state-of-the-art pattern-based data prefetcher, improving overall application performance.

7. ACKNOWLEDGMENTS

The authors would like to thank the anonymous reviewers for their comments and suggestions. Ioana Burcea was partially funded by an IBM PhD Fellowship and a Google Anita Borg Memorial Scholarship.

References

[1] A.-R. Adl-Tabatabai, R. L. Hudson, M. J. Serrano, and S. Subramoney. Prefetch injection based on hardware monitoring and object metadata. In *PLDI*, 2004.

[2] I. Burcea, S. Somogyi, A. Moshovos, and B. Falsafi. Predictor virtualization. In *ASPLOS*, 2008.

[3] T. Chen and J. Baer. Effective hardware based data prefetching for high-performance processors. *IEEE Transactions on Computers*, 1995.

[4] J. Collins, S. Sair, B. Calder, and D. M. Tullsen. Pointer cache assisted prefetching. In *MICRO*, 2002.

[5] R. Cooksey, S. Jourdan, and D. Grunwald. A stateless, content-directed data prefetching mechanism. In *ASPLOS*, 2002.

[6] D. G. Doug Joseph. Prefetching using Markov Predictors. In *ISCA*, 1997.

[7] E. Ebrahimi, O. Mutlu, and Y. N. Patt. Techniques for bandwidth-efficient prefetching of linked data structures in hybrid prefetching systems. In *HPCA*, 2009.

[8] P. Havlak. Nesting of reducible and irreducible loops. *ACM Trans. Program. Lang. Syst.*, 1997.

[9] R. Hundt. Loop Recognition in C++/Java/Go/Scala. In *Scala Days*, 2011.

[10] T. Inagaki, T. Onodera, H. Komatsu, and T. Nakatani. Stride prefetching by dynamically inspecting objects. In *PLDI*, 2003.

[11] Y. Ishii, M. Inaba, and K. Hiraki. Access map pattern matching for high performance data cache prefetch. *Journal of Instruction-Level Parallelism*, 2011.

[12] M. Karlsson, F. Dahlgren, and P. Stenstrom. A prefetching technique for irregular accesses to linked data structures. In *HPCA*, 2000.

[13] M. H. Lipasti, W. J. Schmidt, S. R. Kunkel, and R. R. Roediger. SPAID: software prefetching in pointer- and call-intensive environments. In *MICRO*, 1995.

[14] C.-K. Luk, R. Cohn, R. Muth, H. Patil, A. Klauser, G. Lowney, S. Wallace, V. J. Reddi, and K. Hazelwood. Pin: building customized program analysis tools with dynamic instrumentation. In *PLDI*, 2005.

[15] L. Prechelt. An Empirical Comparison of Seven Programming Languages. *IEEE Computer*, 2000.

[16] A. Roth and G. S. Sohi. Effective jump-pointer prefetching for linked data structures. In *ISCA*, 1999.

[17] Y. Shuf, M. Gupta, H. Franke, A. Appel, and J. P. Singh. Creating and preserving locality of Java applications at allocation and garbage collection times. In *OOPSLA*, 2002.

[18] S. Somogyi, T. Wenisch, A. Ailamaki, B. Falsafi, and A. Moshovos. Spatial Memory Streaming. In *ISCA*, 2006.

[19] TIOBE. Tiobe Index, retrieved Sep. 2011. http://www.tiobe.com/index.php/content/paperinfo/tpci/.

[20] Z. Wang, D. Burger, K. S. McKinley, S. K. Reinhardt, and C. C. Weems. Guided region prefetching: a cooperative hardware/software approach. In *ISCA*, 2003.

[21] Q. Wu, A. Pyatakov, A. Spiridonov, E. Raman, D. W. Clark, and D. I. August. Exposing memory access regularities using object-relative memory profiling. In *CGO*, 2004.

[22] Y. Wu. Efficient discovery of regular stride patterns in irregular programs and its use in compiler prefetching. In *PLDI*, 2002.

[23] X. Zhuang and H.-H. Lee. A hardware-based cache pollution filtering mechanism for aggressive prefetches. In *ICPP*, 2003.

Scalability-Based Manycore Partitioning

Hiroshi Sasaki
Kyushu University
744 Motooka Nishi-ku
Fukuoka, Japan
sasaki@soc.ait.kyushu-u.ac.jp

Teruo Tanimoto*
The University of Tokyo
7-3-1 Bunkyo-ku, Hongo
Tokyo, Japan
tanimoto@hal.ipc.i.u-tokyo.ac.jp

Koji Inoue
Kyushu University
744 Motooka Nishi-ku
Fukuoka, Japan
inoue@ait.kyushu-u.ac.jp

Hiroshi Nakamura
The University of Tokyo
7-3-1 Bunkyo-ku, Hongo
Tokyo, Japan
nakamura@hal.ipc.i.u-tokyo.ac.jp

ABSTRACT

Multicore processors have been popular for years, and the industry is gradually shifting towards the era of manycore processors. Single-thread performance of microprocessors is not growing at a historical rate, but the existence of a number of active processes in the computer system and the continuing development of multi-threaded applications benefit from the growing core counts to sustain system throughput. This trend brings us a situation where a number of parallel applications simultaneously being executed on a single system. Since multi-threaded applications try to maximize its throughput by utilizing the whole system, each of them usually create equal or larger number of threads compared to underlying logical core counts. This introduces much greater number of threads to be co-scheduled in the entire system. However, each program has different characteristics (or scalability) and contends for shared resources, which are the CPU cores and memory hierarchies, with each other. Therefore, it is clear that OS thread scheduling will play a major role in achieving high system performance under such conditions. We develop a sophisticated scheduler that (1) dynamically predicts the scalability of programs via the use of hardware performance monitoring units, (2) decides the optimal number of cores to be allocated for each program, and (3) allocates the cores to programs while maximizing the system utilization to achieve fair and maximum performance. The evaluation results on a 48-core AMD Opteron system show improvements over the Linux scheduler for a variety of multiprogramming workloads.

*The author is currently with FUJITSU LABORATORIES LTD.

Categories and Subject Descriptors

D.4.1 [**Operating Systems**]: Process Management—*scheduling, multiprocessing/multiprogramming/multitasking*

General Terms

Experimentation, Measurement, Performance

Keywords

Multicore/manycore processors, process scheduling, multi-threaded applications, scalability, performance prediction, dynamic optimization

1. INTRODUCTION

The end of clock frequency scaling has led the processor architecture design towards multiple processors on a chip (known as *multicore processors* or *CMPs*) which exploits thread level parallelism to improve performance [14]. The trend of increasing the core count tends to continue and push the industry and researchers to face *manycore processors* in the near future [24, 27]. The shift from single-core to multicore has broaden the range of applications, and the focus of research has shifted from executing one single-threaded application on a system to either (1) concurrently executing multiple single-threaded applications or (2) running one multi-threaded application on a system. However, considering that not all programs can best utilize the potential of manycore architectures, further shift towards manycore processors will force us to manage dozens of simultaneously executed programs which are heavily multi-threaded.

In such a scenario, shared resource contention is one of the most fundamental and important problems which have to be solved. Prior work have showed that contention should be minimized by (1) isolating (or partitioning) shared resource accesses as much as possible, and at the same time, (2) allocating appropriate amount of shared resources to each program [23]. For single-threaded multiprogramming workloads, trying to reduce contention at the last level cache (LLC), memory controller or the prefetcher which lie down in the memory hierarchy is the main objective [2, 5, 6, 12, 15, 19,

30]. However, memory hierarchy is not the only shared resource when scheduling multi-threaded applications. Parallel programs tend to be executed by creating equal or larger number of threads than the underlying logical core counts to fully make use of the system. Therefore, the computing resources (i.e., CPU cores) which directly contribute to performance is the most important shared resource that we have to carefully allocate to each program in order to achieve high performance.

Allocation should be done dynamically according to program's characteristics at the point of creation or termination of programs, and therefore the runtime layer such as the OS scheduler or the programming language runtime system [16, 21] will play a major role in it. Traditional OS scheduler tries to assign equal CPU time to each thread to ensure the *fairness* property. Therefore, we can consider that CPU cores are evenly shared among each program, controlled by the OS scheduler. This approach is simple and fair from an OS point of view, however, there is still room for improvement and we can still perform better in terms of performance by taking the *scalability* of each program into account.

In this paper, we propose a sophisticated OS scheduler for multi-threaded multiprogramming workloads on manycore processors. The proposed scheduler is able to optimize against various performance metrics which can be determined by either the user or the system software. Several performance metrics are used to evaluate the multiprogramming workloads in the literature: total throughput, weighted speedup [28], harmonic mean of the per program speedup [18], or average normalized turnaround time (i.e., execution time) or ANTT [11]. We insist that the manycore OS scheduler should be flexible enough to optimize against different needs (or metrics) and the key to achieve this is to take the scalability of each program into account. The principle behind our technique is that the speedup obtained from multi-threading on manycore processors heavily depends on several details of the program, and are quite different between them. For example, some program might double its performance by doubling the number of cores, while other might achieve no performance improvement or even degrade its performance. Therefore, we can achieve better performance than the evenly (or fairly) partitioned allocation which is achieved in the Linux scheduler by allocating optimal number of cores to each program according to their scalability.

The main contributions of this paper include the following:

- We find that state-of-the-art Linux default scheduler performs poorly in a multi-threaded multiprogramming environment because of lacking the consideration of scalability of its scheduled programs.
- We propose a scheduling algorithm which predicts the scalability of multi-threaded applications to dynamically allocate the appropriate number of cores to each program in order to optimize system performance. We also introduce a couple of sophisticated enhancements to the scheduler which attempt to get the most out of manycore environments.
- We implement a practical user level scheduler called SBMP (pronounced *S-Bump*) scheduler which (1) requires no changes to the OS kernel, (2) works on existing Linux systems and uses existing hardware performance monitoring units (PMUs), and (3) works with any unmodified application binaries.
- We evaluate the proposed SBMP scheduler with an AMD 48-core system, which shows our design well outperforms the Linux default scheduler for a series of multiprogramming workloads comprised of emerging PARSEC benchmark suite [4].

The remainder of the paper is structured as follows. Next section motivates our work on developing *scalability-based manycore partitioning scheduler (SBMP scheduler)* by showing the poor performance of Linux default scheduler when multiple multi-threaded workloads are simultaneously executed on a manycore environment. Section 3 describes our scheduler algorithm and implementation in detail along with some novel improvements added to enhance our scheduler design. Section 4 explains our evaluation framework and Section 5 shows the performance of the proposed scheduler with wide variety of evaluations. Section 6 introduces related work, and finally the conclusions and future work are stated in Section 7.

2. MOTIVATION

Figure 1 shows how Linux default scheduler performs poorly in a multi-threaded multiprogramming environment. The figure shows performance result of four multi-threaded applications (`canneal`, `ferret`, `raytrace` and `streamcluster` chosen from PARSEC benchmark suite) when they are simultaneously executed on a 48-core symmetric multi-processor system*. Bars in Figure 1 indicate the normalized turnaround time (NTT) [11]. NTT is a lower-is-better metric which has a value larger than or equal to one†, and quantifies the turnaround time slowdown due to multiprogrammed execution. Right most group of bars shows the average NTT (ANTT). ANTT is a reciprocal of the commonly used harmonic mean metric of the relative throughputs under multiprogramming environment compared to their solo-runs [18]. ANTT has a system-level meaning rather than the harmonic mean metric, and we believe it is a good indicator to represent system performance in multiprogramming environments. Therefore, we use this metric throughout this work. The results of Linux default scheduler and the *best static partitioning* are shown in the figure.

For these applications, the best partitioning (or core allocation) is: 12 cores for `canneal` and `raytrace` each, 18 cores for `ferret`, and six cores for `streamcluster`. Note that all programs create 48 threads (or more, according to the program) in order to fully utilize the processor, and threads of each program are packed onto the specified number of cores [7] when partitioned. The best partitioning was obtained by trying all the possible allocations. There are several ways to assign the cores to programs even the number of cores to be assigned are the same. Figure 3 shows two possible assignments which are (a) distributing or (b) centralizing the threads on the system. We have compared the ANTT for these two types of assignments for all the workloads and found that centralizing the threads gives higher or

*Figure 2 shows the base node architecture of the evaluation system we use throughout this paper. It consists of four CMPs with each CMP having 12 core multi-chip module processor consisting of two six core dies. Further details of the experimental environment is described in Section 4.

†Note that the origin of all the graphs which show the NTT begins with one.

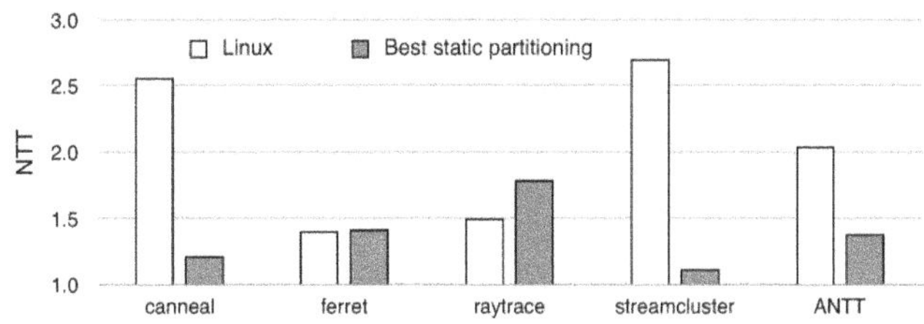

Figure 1: Normalized turnaround time (NTT) of Linux scheduler and static space sharing.

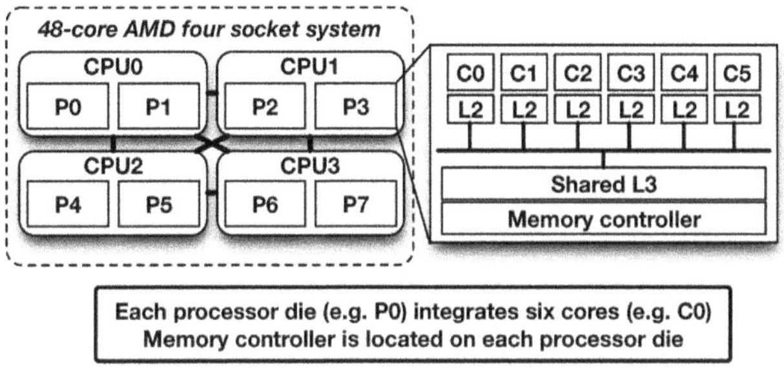

Figure 2: Node architecture of the evaluation platform.

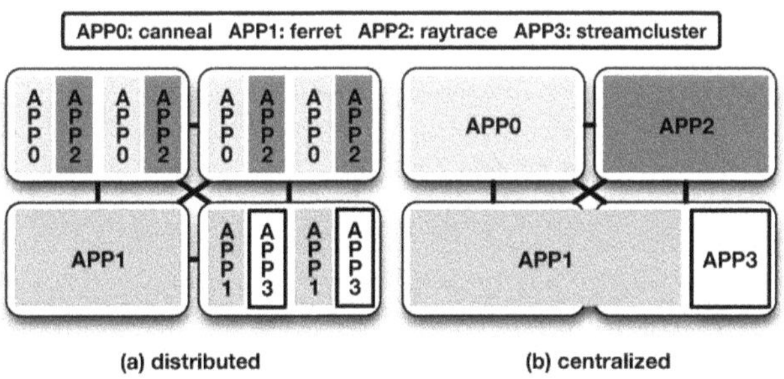

Figure 3: Two possible program-to-core assignments of best partitioning.

at least the same performance in most cases. This is quite intuitive because of the low latency of accessing the shared data (including coherency messages) and minimized interference or contention between programs. Therefore, we use the centralized assignment of cores throughout this work.

Also, we decided to use the processor die in Figure 2 as a minimum unit of allocation to programs. That is, each program is provided a number of cores which is a multiple of six in the experimental platform. This restriction still leaves us plenty of room for optimization, while eliminating the unexpected contention by potentially giving exclusive use of the portion of LLC which is on the same die. We can say that the memory subsystem is partitioned as well as the cores, which means that the program with a greater number of cores also gets larger amount of LLC. More sophisticated memory managements such as applying page coloring technique [17] in order to give larger amount of LLC to a program with fewer number of cores can be considered, but those optimizations are left for future work, and we focus on the scheduling of CPU cores in this study. Note that we dedicate each core to only a single program at a time, which means that no two programs share the same core[‡]. These partitioning methods are also used in the proposed scheduler.

We can see the poor ANTT of the Linux default scheduler from Figure 1 which is 2.04, where the ANTT of best static core allocation is 1.38, and significantly improves over the Linux scheduler. To understand the reason of the result shown in Figure 1, we display the scalability of the PARSEC applications in Figure 4. The x-axis indicates the number of cores allocated and y-axis shows relative performance to the maximum. The benchmarks are classified into three groups named with colors according to their scalability characteristics, namely *Green*, *Yellow* and *Red*, which are used in the later section for discussions. The numbers on top of each graph show the maximum speedup obtained compared to the case when a single core is assigned.

The key factor of this improvement is to appropriately controlling the number of cores to be assigned to each application by considering their scalability. This can be seen from the scalability curve of the evaluated four programs, especially `ferret` and `streamcluster`. The best partitioning allocates 18 cores to `ferret` and six cores to `streamcluster`. `Streamcluster` achieves its maximum performance at six cores so there is no reason to allocate greater number of cores from a performance point of view. Other three programs show similar shapes of scalability curve, however, the number on top of the graph showing the maximum speedup against a single core assignment is the largest for `ferret` which is 17.22x. Therefore, it is beneficial to give the resource to `ferret` to maximize the multiprogramming performance. This result motivates us that the scalability of programs should be taken into account by the OS scheduler to achieve good performance.

We have seen the potential performance improvement of static partitioning approach thus far, however, it is not practical to apply the static scheduling in a general purpose OS scheduler because: (1) the best core assignment cannot be easily obtained in advance without the knowledge of the scalability of programs *a priori*, (2) the best core allocation might change during runtime because applications can be composed of several phases which shows different scalability characteristics, and (3) applications are dynamically executed on a general purpose OS so that we do not know which applications will be co-scheduled at what time. We address the above issues by dynamically detecting the program's *scalability* along with several enhancements which are stated in Section 3.

3. SCHEDULER DESIGN

We designed and implemented **SBMP** scheduler, a *scalability-based manycore partitioning* scheduler which achieves high system performance under multi-threaded multiprogramming execution. SBMP scheduler dynamically predicts the scalability of each multi-threaded application by using a simple performance model and select the appropriate amount of cores to be assigned. The model is obtained by slightly modifying the Amdahl's law equation. The key idea behind this allocation is that, we do not give fair amount of CPU time and resources as in the traditional OS scheduler, instead we provide the resources considering their scalability,

[‡]Later in Section 3, we propose an enhancement to the scheduler which relaxes this constraint to allow up to two programs sharing each core to improve performance.

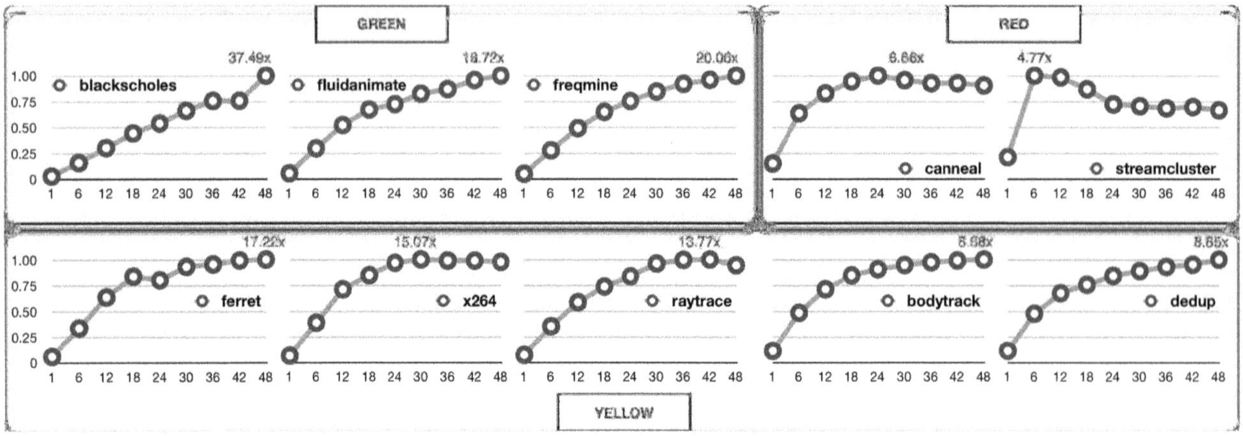

Figure 4: Scalability of the evaluated PARSEC benchmarks.

giving more resources to programs that make more use of them. That is, SBMP scheduler attempts to balance the utilization of resources, not the physical amount of resources. This section provides the scheduling overview, as well as the description of the prediction model and its usage, and the scheduling algorithm and implementation of SBMP scheduler in detail.

3.1 Scheduler Overview

The basic overview of the scheduling algorithm is shown in Figure 5. The top view of the algorithm is fairly simple constructing a loop which consists of the following: (1) SBMP scheduler decides to change the core partitioning when it detects that the optimal partitioning has changed, (2) predicts the scalability of the target program, and (3) calculates the optimal core allocation based on the optimization metric and re-schedules the programs according to it. The detail of (1) through (3) is discussed in Subsections 3.3, 3.2, and in the following paragraphs of this subsection, respectively. Subsection 3.4 describes a key improvement technique to the SBMP scheduler which is called *Core Donation* which aims to maximize the CPU utilization ratio by relaxing the constraint that each core is exclusively used by a single program.

As stated in Section 2, we target in optimizing (minimizing) the average normalized turnaround time or ANTT metric because we believe it is a good metric to represent system performance of multiprogramming workloads. However, the key idea of the proposed scheduler which predicts and utilizes the scalability is not only restricted for optimizing the system against ANTT, but can be used to target different performance metrics such as the weighted speedup metric, if required. This can easily be accomplished by changing the function which seeks for the optimal allocation inside the scheduler.

ANTT is computed as

$$ANTT = \frac{1}{n}\sum_{i=1}^{n} NTT_i = \frac{1}{n}\sum_{i=1}^{n} \frac{C_i^{MP}}{C_i^{SP}} \quad (1)$$

where C_i^{SP} and C_i^{MP} denote the number of clock cycles to execute a program i under solo and multiprogrammed runs, respectively. Minimizing ANTT means that all the programs are fairly achieving high performance compared to its peak performance (achievable only when occupying

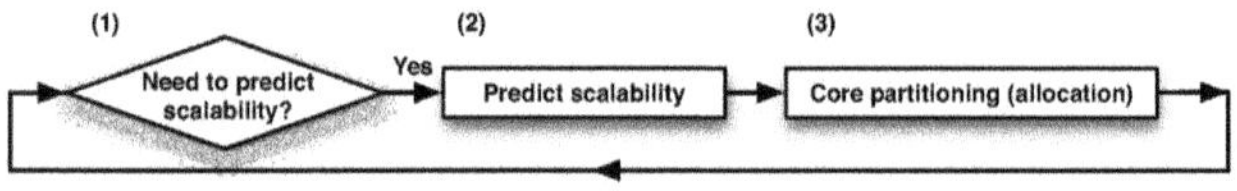

Figure 5: Algorithm overview of SBMP.

the whole system by itself). Therefore, programs that scale almost linearly (such as the applications labeled Green in Figure 4) are removed from the co-scheduling candidate and run in isolation, or gang-scheduling [3].

SBMP scheduler maintains a table called *scalability-table* for each multi-threaded program which consists of pairs of values: each pair consists of a *key* and a *value* where key stores the number of cores to be allocated, and the value stores the relative performance against its peak when executed at the *key* number of cores. Note that having this table is identical with being able to draw the scalability curve shown in Figure 4. The value in the table represents C_i^{MP}/C_i^{SP} in Equation (1), so the scheduler is able to compute ANTT for different core allocations during runtime. The number of possible core assignments is computed as $(N_{core}-1)!/(N_{core}-N_{app})!(N_{app}-1)!$ where $N_{core} > N_{app}$ holds, N_{core} and N_{app} being the number of cores in the system and number of programs that are being scheduled, respectively. It becomes unpractical to calculate and search through all the possible ANTT values to find the optimal allocation when N_{core} and/or N_{app} grow. Therefore, we use a simple hill climbing algorithm similar to the technique used in [8] to find the near optimal assignment.

3.2 Predicting the Scalability

SBMP scheduler needs to know the relative performance against its best solo run for all the co-scheduled programs during runtime to perform its scheduling. We propose to use the number of *cumulative retired instructions* of the program to indicate the performance. That is, we store the cumulative retired instructions per second (IPS) to the *value* of the scalability-table associated with each program. The key notion behind this is the fact that changing the core assignments does not affect the total number of instructions. Figure 6 supports our idea. It shows the number of cores allocated on the x-axis and the number of total instructions on the y-axis for PARSEC benchmarks. All the bars are ob-

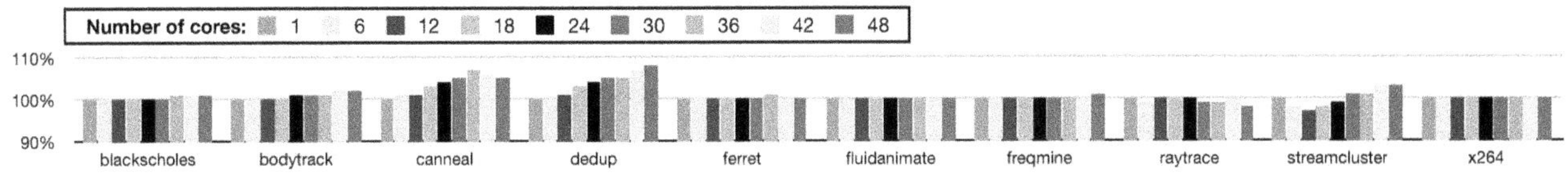

Figure 6: Total number of dynamic instructions of PARSEC benchmarks for different core assignments.

tained by spawning 48 threads, assuming SBMP scheduling. We can see that the applications whose number of instructions varies the most are `canneal` and `dedup` which shows slight variation of up to 8% in the worst case, which is still acceptable for our purpose considering measurement errors. Instruction counts of all the other programs are stable with respect to the number of cores. Therefore, IPS is a perfect indicator to measure the scalability of a program.

As IPS values can be easily obtained by performance monitoring units (PMUs) which come with most of today's microprocessors, it is possible for the scheduler to directly measure the values to fill the scalability-table. For example, the scheduler can dynamically change the allocations during runtime, and run the program for a fixed amount of time to obtain the values. However, we found out that the overhead of measuring the IPS in this manner is not negligible: earning a stable IPS value for a new assignment requires the OS to actually migrate the threads to the new allocation and run for a while to warm up the caches and branch predictors. This requires up to few hundred milliseconds per assignment in the evaluated environment. Recall that we use the processor die in Figure 2 as a minimum unit of allocation, so there are eight (48 divided by six) possible allocations to a single program. Even after careful tuning of the software, it took over three seconds to fill the table, and this overhead will become larger according to the increasing number of cores in the future. Therefore, we introduce a simple model to predict the IPS values. By using the model, we can compute the IPS to fill the scalability-table by sampling the IPS for only a few allocations.

The prediction model we use in this work is the following.

$$\frac{IPS_{N_1}}{IPS_{N_{core}}} = \alpha + \frac{\beta}{N_{core}} + \gamma N_{core} \quad (\alpha + \beta + \gamma = 1) \qquad (2)$$

IPS_{N_1} and $IPS_{N_{core}}$ indicate the IPS when allocated a single core and N cores, respectively. The left side of the equation represents the relative turnaround time against single core execution, and the left two terms of the right side is the same as that of Amdahl's law equation [1]. Recall that Amdahl's law is a simple yet powerful model that models the scalability of a parallel program. The formula is quite intuitive and the scalability curve is known to fit well with real world programs. However, as can be seen from Figure 4, the scalability of some applications tend to not only saturate at some point but also degrade its performance by adding more number of cores. This cannot be represented by the original Amdahl's law. Therefore, we added the last term γN_{core} which we expect to represent some overhead associated with adding more number of cores. The condition equation in the parentheses follows the original condition of the Amdahl's law that the sum of the coefficients equals one, and this is because we assume that the parallel portion of the program represented as β in the original equation, can be divided into two sections where one can be parallelized ($\frac{\beta}{N_{core}}$) and the other adds an overhead (γN_{core}). Therefore, we set the condition as the sum of α, β and γ equals one.

To obtain the values of the coefficients, we use the least squares approach. Therefore, we need to at least collect the IPS with three configurations (two different configurations in addition to single core execution) in order to obtain the three coefficients because Equation (2) has two individual parameters.

3.3 Re-partitioning Algorithm

As seen from Figure 5, SBMP scheduler tries to change the core partitioning when it considers that the optimal allocation has changed during the multiprogramming execution. There are mainly two events that invokes the SBMP scheduler to re-partition during execution. Those events are (1) creation or termination of a program and (2) phase transition detected in any of the programs.

The first is natural, because it means that the multiprogramming workload has changed, and thus there is a chance to find a better partitioning. When any of the program finishes its execution, SBMP simply calculates the optimal allocation using the existing scalability-table and allocates the cores according to it. When a new program is created, then SBMP scheduler predicts the scalability of it as described in Subsection 3.2, and performs the partitioning.

The second is more aggressive which utilizes the information obtained online to dynamically find a better core assignment. Programs are typically composed of different execution phases which show different characteristics, and SBMP scheduler attempts to keep up with the optimal core partitioning. Researchers have tried to detect phases to perform dynamic optimization, and there exists different definition of phases according to the optimization techniques. In this paper, we consider phase as a region of program having different scalability.

Figure 7 shows an example execution trace of `x264` showing the execution phases having different scalability. x-axis and y-axis of Figure 7 (a) represents time in milliseconds and the cumulative execution cycles, respectively. The thick dotted line on top of the figure shows the maximum available cumulative cycles which is equivalent to the cumulative execution cycles when the CPU is 100% utilized. The cumulative cycles is sampled every 50 ms. CPU utilization ratio is obtained by dividing the cumulative execution cycles by the maximum available cumulative cycles. We can see from the figure that the trace can be divided into three regions or phases by focusing on the cumulative execution cycles (identical to CPU utilization), which we named phase A, B and C. Three figures of Figure 7 (b) on the right side show the scalability for those three phases. X-axis indicates the number of cores allocated and the y-axis shows the relative performance against a single-core execution. We can see similar trends for phases A and C which show a gentle curve giving the maximum performance at the maximum number of cores, and a much steeper scalability curve for phase B showing the

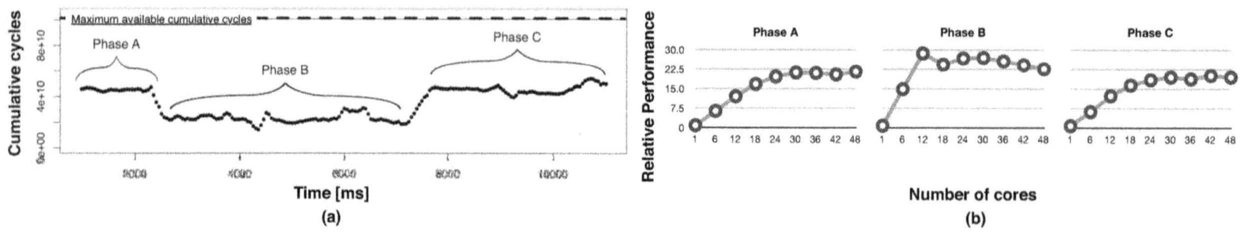

Figure 7: Execution trace of x264 showing the relationships between CPU utilization ratio and scalability. (a) Time series plots of cumulative cycles and (b) scalability of different points are shown.

Table 1: CPU utilization ratio (%) of PARSEC benchmarks

# of cores	bl	fl	fr	fe	x2	ra	bo	de	ca	st
6	98.6	96.7	96.4	99.9	99.5	89.0	73.7	73.9	82.1	92.6
12	93.6	90.4	86.8	92.7	97.2	78.4	55.5	59.0	71.1	80.7
18	89.8	83.4	65.4	95.4	83.9	71.9	46.4	51.1	68.5	67.3
24	85.3	74.8	68.6	87.9	72.2	62.9	39.0	44.8	69.8	56.7
30	84.4	68.0	61.3	74.7	59.3	60.2	32.5	38.8	67.3	50.6
36	80.5	62.0	43.1	82.2	46.1	50.5	29.9	34.9	66.2	45.7
42	69.6	58.8	34.9	72.6	38.7	43.8	26.8	31.4	70.4	42.3
48	85.7	54.5	44.5	72.1	33.3	37.6	24.1	28.7	65.9	37.7

highest performance at 12 cores. These graphs motivate us to detect the phase changes online and dynamically perform a re-partitioning. Also, we can see that the CPU utilization ratio which can be obtained from cumulative execution cycles is a good indicator to detect phase transition. Therefore, SBMP scheduler detects the phase change by monitoring its cumulative execution cycles. SBMP scheduler monitors the PMUs every *epoch* (or time window), and whenever a change of the counter values greater than a certain *threshold* compared to the previous epoch has been observed, SBMP scheduler enters the scalability prediction process to perform re-scheduling.

3.4 Core Donation

The design of SBMP scheduler is described in the above subsections, and here we introduce *Core Donation*, a sophisticated technique to improve the system performance in SBMP scheduler. As we have shown in Figure 7, different programs have different CPU utilization ratios. Table 1 shows the average CPU utilization ratio of PARSEC benchmarks (benchmark names are represented with their first two letters) for different number of cores being allocated. We can see a trend across benchmarks that by allocating more number of cores, the CPU utilization tends to decrease. This is a fundamental problem in multi-threaded applications which does not have linear scalability, so we have to overcome this tendency to achieve high performance. In addition, there are variability in the utilization ratio that some programs have high utilization (`blackscholes`, `ferret`, and `fluidanimate`) while others have poor utilization (`bodytrack` and `canneal`). One of the most important aspects of the OS scheduler is to keep the CPU as busy as possible by continuously assigning threads that are ready to execute. However, SBMP scheduler partitions the processor, and only a single program is allowed to run on each core which tends to waste the precious CPU time.

We provide a solution to this problem by letting a program which has a utilization ratio lower than a certain threshold to be a "donor" of CPU cores (or CPU time). After allocating the cores to each program, SBMP scheduler checks if any of the program meets the requirement of a donor. If it finds a correspondent program, SBMP scheduler picks another program which benefits the most by getting additional cores (which has a high utilization ratio and good scalability) from the scalability-table, and sets the program as a "donee". SBMP scheduler allows the donee program to be executed on the donor's cores by allocating the program to its original partition and also the donor's partition. Therefore, there are two multi-threaded applications which can run on donor's cores. Donee is kept from interfering with the donor's threads by executing its threads only when the donor cannot utilize the CPU. We use the thread priority mechanism to achieve this requirement by making the priority of donee program much lower than that of the donor. This makes the situation where donor can preempt donee's execution while the opposite is not possible. Core Donation is applied after core partitioning (see (3) of Figure 5).

The interesting point of Core Donation is that it works in synergy with the SBMP scheduler by optimizing against different granularities. SBMP scheduler assigns the cores to programs by using the processor die as a minimal unit, which is six cores in the evaluation platform. This is rather a coarse grain spatial optimization while Core Donation tries to fill in the gap and apply finer granularity optimization after a rough optimization done by SBMP scheduler. Also, Core Donation works in a much finer time granularity than the original SBMP, and is possible to increase the CPU utilization to improve system performance. Therefore, by applying the partitioning of SBMP scheduler and the optimization of Core Donation, the proposed set of techniques make the most out of manycore architectures to achieve high performance.

We have to be careful that the utilization ratio to detect a phase change for donee programs should be only measured at its original partition (there might be some disturbance by the donor program at the donor's cores). Note that each program is allowed to either be a donor or donee but not both, and a donor is only allowed to have one donee.

4. EXPERIMENTAL SETUP

4.1 Hardware Platform

We perform experiments on a quad socket IBM System x3755 M3 server which consists of four 12-core AMD Opteron 6172 microprocessors running at 2.1 GHz forming a 48-core system. Each socket integrates two six-core dies with each core having its own private L1 and L2 caches along with a shared 12 MB L3 cache. Table 2 shows relevant hardware parameters of the evaluation platform.

Table 2: Parameters of the evaluation platform

Processor:	4 × AMD Opteron 6172
# of dies per processor	2
# of cores per die:	6
Total # of cores:	48
L3 cache size:	12 MB per socket
Main memory:	96 GB DDR3 PC3-10600

Table 3: Parameters of the SBMP scheduler

Threshold of phase change detection:	Utilization ratio more than doubles or gets smaller than half of the previous epoch
Length of epoch:	2.5 seconds
Length of the first epoch after re-scheduling:	10 seconds
# of samples for prediction: (# of cores)	four points (1, 12, 24 and 48)
Overhead of prediction:	≈ 550 milliseconds
Threshold of becoming a "donor" in Core Donation:	70%

4.2 SBMP Scheduler Implementation

We have implemented a prototype of SBMP scheduler as a user level software. The evaluation system runs Linux kernel 2.6.37.6, and the modified version of `perf-tools` toolset is used to allow periodical access to the PMUs. CPU clock frequency scaling is disabled to avoid measurement variance. We use standard Linux API (`sched_setaffinity(2)` and `setpriority(2)`) to control the CPU affinity of processes to bind the programs to specific cores and to manage the priority (niceness) of each program in order to apply Core Donation technique.

Detailed values of parameters used inside the SBMP scheduler are shown in Table 3. Threshold to detect phase change and its length of sampling epoch is experimentally obtained by taking the overhead of prediction into account. Also, we set the first epoch after re-scheduling to 10 seconds to prevent oscillation of re-scheduling. For the sampling points, increasing the number of samples tends to increase the fitting accuracy but the associated overhead of sampling also becomes larger (≈150ms for each sample). Therefore, we constructed a model of all the possible combinations for each benchmark in advance and compared the fitting accuracy to the plot shown in Figure 4. As a result, four sample points with 1, 12, 24 and 48 cores gave us a good balance between fitting accuracy (coefficient of determination over 0.99) and the overhead on average and we chose them as shown in the table. We apply Core Donation if the utilization of any of the programs being executed is below 70%.

4.3 Workloads

We use PARSEC benchmark suite 2.1 [4] to evaluate SBMP scheduler against the Linux default scheduler. PARSEC benchmark suite is designed to evaluate shared-memory computers, and is composed of a set of emerging workloads for future manycore processors. We compile PARSEC with GCC-4.1 with "`-O3 -funroll-loops -fprefetch-loop-arrays`" options. We use *native* input sets for all benchmarks except `dedup`. Because the execution time of `dedup` was too short compared to other programs, we use a larger input (the Fedora 16 x86_64 DVD ISO).

We have shown 10 out of 13 PARSEC benchmarks in figures 4 and 6 where `facesim`, `swaptions` and `vips` are excluded because we could not correctly compile them on the evaluation platform. Additionally, we exclude `blackscholes` and `fluidanimate` which are categorized as Green in Figure 4. Highly scalable applications prefer being executed in a gang-scheduling manner as shown in other work [3], where SBMP scheduler can detect these applications as having good scalability by checking the scalability-table, and remove from co-scheduling in order to perform gang-scheduling. Although categorized as Green, we left `freqmine` in the evaluation workloads because it has a reduction operation which shows multiple phase changes during its execution and is used to show the effectiveness of our phase detection capability.

We evaluate SBMP scheduler with variety of workloads where each workload is composed of four benchmark programs. SBMP scheduler is designed to optimize the scheduling under multiprogramming environment with a number of parallel programs with wide varieties of scalability, however, increasing the number of applications within each workload reduces the possible allocations resulting in no space to optimize. For example, as we give each program at least six cores, having more than four programs within a workload results in giving at least one program to only stick on the minimum allocation of six cores. Therefore, we chose four as a number to create each workload because it gives us a good balance between the optimization flexibility as well as enough load on the target system.

Because the main target of SBMP scheduler is efficient co-scheduling of parallel regions of multi-threaded multiprogramming workloads, we use Berkeley Lab Checkpoint/Restart (BLCR) tools [13] to set up an environment which enables *checkpoint and restart* of programs to evaluate only the parallel region called the *region of interest (ROI)* of PARSEC, which is marked in the original source code. Our evaluation is conducted using this system running from the beginning till the end of ROI for all benchmarks.

The evaluation methodology is similar to the one originally proposed for SMT job scheduling [26], and a number of following work have been evaluated in a similar manner [2, 12, 15, 29]. To account for the varieties of execution times (from tens to hundreds of seconds), we restart an application instantaneously when it finishes execution until all the programs are executed at least three times to completion. We measure the execution time of each application using the `time` command in Linux.

5. EVALUATION RESULTS

5.1 Programs with a Single Phase

First, we show the results with the workloads which does not include applications that have multiple phases within programs. For this purpose, we have set up six workloads which include two applications classified as Red (`canneal` and `streamcluster`), and the other two from Yellow benchmarks (`bodytrack`, `dedup`, `ferret` and `raytrace`). The Red applications have low scalability and thus assigning a large number of cores will hurt system performance. Therefore, we can see if SBMP scheduler can accurately predict the scalability of the program. Evaluated workloads are shown in Table 4.

Figure 8 shows the ANTT for each workload of *SBMP-base*, which is the simplest implementation of SBMP scheduler which does not have the ability of phase prediction nor

Table 4: Multiprogrammed workloads to evaluate SBMP-base

ID	Benchmarks	Type
1	bo-ca-de-st	YYRR
2	bo-ca-fe-st	YYRR
3	bo-ca-ra-st	YYRR
4	ca-de-fe-st	YYRR
5	ca-de-ra-st	YYRR
6	ca-fe-ra-st	YYRR

Table 5: Multiprogrammed workloads to evaluate SBMP-PP

ID	Benchmarks	Type	ID	Benchmarks	Type
7	bo-ca-fe-fr	GYYR	16	de-fr-st-x2	GYYR
8	bo-ca-fr-x2	GYYR	17	fe-fr-ra-st	GYYR
9	bo-fe-fr-st	GYYR	18	fr-ra-st-x2	GYYR
10	bo-fr-st-x2	GYYR	19	bo-ca-fe-x2	YYYR
11	ca-de-fe-fr	GYYR	20	bo-fe-st-x2	YYYR
12	ca-de-fr-x2	GYYR	21	ca-de-fe-x2	YYYR
13	ca-fe-fr-ra	GYYR	22	ca-fe-ra-x2	YYYR
14	ca-fr-ra-x2	GYYR	23	de-fe-st-x2	YYYR
15	de-fe-fr-st	GYYR	24	fe-ra-st-x2	YYYR

Table 6: Multiprogrammed workloads to evaluate SBMP-CD

ID	Benchmarks	Type	ID	Benchmarks	Type
25	bo-de-fe-fr	GYYY	32	bo-de-ra-x2	YYYY
26	bo-de-fe-x2	GYYY	33	bo-ca-de-fe	YYYR
27	bo-de-fr-ra	GYYY	34	bo-ca-de-ra	YYYR
28	bo-de-fr-x2	GYYY	35	bo-ca-de-x2	YYYR
29	bo-ca-de-fr	GYYR	36	bo-de-fe-st	YYYR
30	bo-de-fr-st	GYYR	37	bo-de-ra-st	YYYR
31	bo-de-fe-ra	YYYY	38	bo-de-st-x2	YYYR

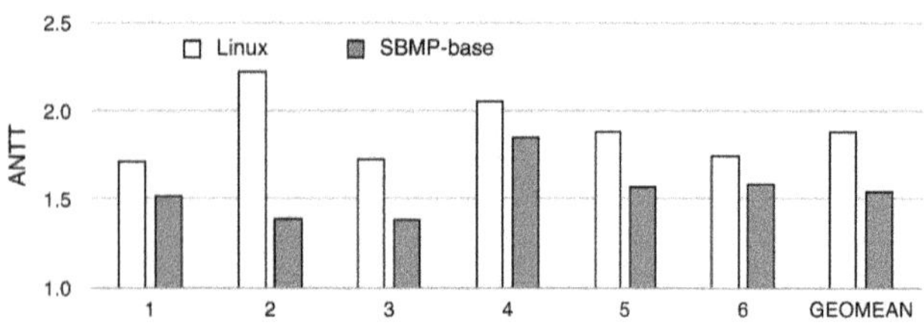

Figure 8: ANTT of Linux and SBMP-base schedulers for applications with a single phase.

Core Donation, is compared against Linux scheduler. Average ANTT of Linux scheduler is 1.88, and SBMP-base whose average ANTT is 1.54 well outperforms Linux scheduler for all the workloads evaluated. The results show that effectively choosing the core allocation based on the scalability of each program gives performance benefit over Linux scheduler. From these results, we can conclude that the proposed scalability prediction algorithm described in Subsection 3.2 succeeds in predicting the scalability of programs.

5.2 Programs with Multiple Phases

Next, we present the results by evaluating the workloads which contain applications that have multiple phases within the program such as `x264` shown in Figure 7. The evaluated workloads are shown in Table 5. All the workloads include two out of three applications which have multiple phases (`freqmine`, `ferret` and `x264`), one from Yellow applications, and another from Red applications.

Figure 9 shows the result of the Linux scheduler, SBMP-base and *SBMP-PP* which is SBMP-base with phase prediction enabled. Average ANTT of the Linux scheduler, SBMP-base and SBMP-PP are 1.89, 2.09 and 1.77, respectively. We can see that while SBMP-base shows lower performance than the Linux scheduler, SBMP-PP significantly outperforms both, showing the superiority of SBMP-PP. The representative contribution of SBMP-PP can be seen in many workloads such as 10, 11, 12, 13 and so on, where SBMP-base has the worst case ANTT. Because SBMP-base only predicts the scalability of each program at the point of creation/termination, it tremendously suffers from making a wrong decision at the point of re-scheduling. However, because SBMP-PP has the ability to dynamically detect phase transition, it can recover from making a bad decision. This reveals us that the aggressive re-scheduling based on phase detection is beneficial for programs which are composed of multiple phases. We have presented that detecting and optimizing against the scalability, which is the key insight of SBMP scheduling, is effective in scheduling multi-threaded multiprogramming workloads.

5.3 Programs with Various CPU Utilizations

Now, we show whether Core Donation can improve performance against the Linux scheduler and SBMP-PP. The 14 workloads which are evaluated are presented in Table 6. These workloads are comprised of two applications which have low CPU utilization (`bodytrack` and `dedup` as can be seen from Table 1), and all the other applications.

Figure 10 shows the performance results of the Linux scheduler, SBMP-PP and *SBMP-CD* which utilizes Core Donation technique along with SBMP-PP. The average ANTT among the workloads of the Linux scheduler, SBMP-PP and SBMP-CD are 2.06, 1.68 and 1.60, respectively. SBMP-CD shows the best performance on average across the workloads. Because the workloads are composed of applications which have low CPU utilization, the Linux scheduler has the advantage of effectively utilizing the CPUs by assigning ready-to-execute threads one after another for some workloads. However, SBMP-CD performs better than the Linux scheduler by utilizing the CPU time given by the donor applications. This is well confirmed by comparing SBMP-PP against SBMP-CD, which shows that SBMP-CD achieves better or at least comparable performance over SBMP-PP. This shows that the idea of donors giving the CPU time to donees without interfering donor's threads gives performance improvement. Although ANTT difference between SBMP-PP and SBMP-CD is not so large compared to other results (Linux and SBMP-base in Figure 8, and SBMP-base and SBMP-pp in Figure 9), we believe that by having more number of cores on the system and broader optimization space will widen this gap between SBMP-PP and SBMP-CD. Also, another optimization to be considered is that a donor having more than one donees at the same time, which is left for future work.

5.4 Overall Performance with All Programs

Figure 11 presents the ANTT comparison of all the schedulers for all 70 workloads we have evaluated. The figure shows the workloads on the x-axis and the ANTT on the y-axis. We present the curves independently sorted for each scheduler. The overall average ANTT for the Linux, SBMP-base, SBMP-PP and SBMP-CD schedulers are 1.83, 1.99,

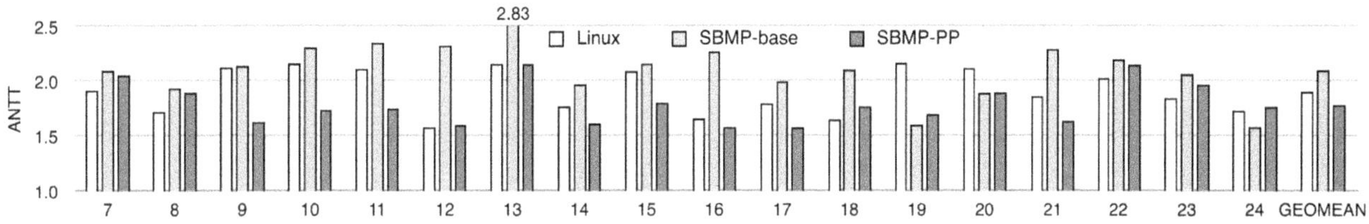

Figure 9: ANTT of Linux and SBMP-PP schedulers for applications with multiple phases.

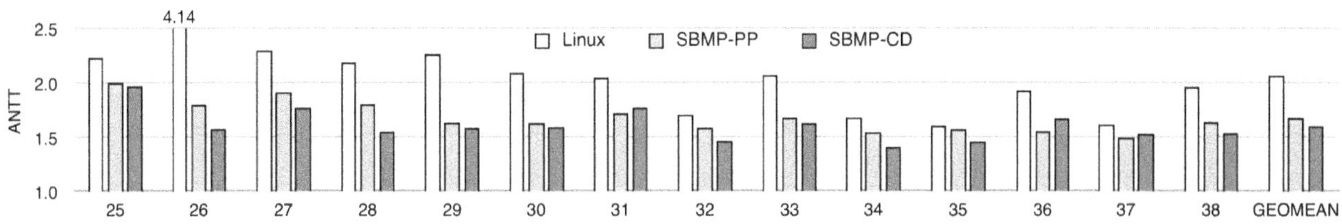

Figure 10: ANTT of Linux and SBMP-CD schedulers for applications with low CPU utilization.

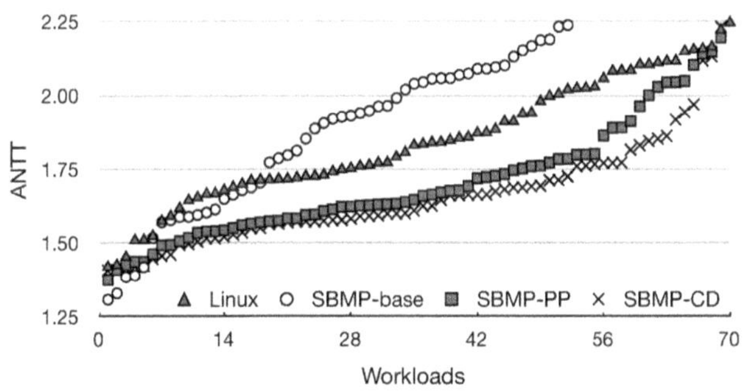

Figure 11: ANTT of all workloads.

1.70 and 1.65, respectively. As can be seen from the figure, SBMP-base scheduler shows the worst performance, and shows 8% degradation against the Linux scheduler. Interestingly, the lowest ANTT values are achieved by SBMP-base, showing the superiority of it when there is only a single phase within the applications. By adding the capability of phase prediction and adaptation to SBMP-base, performance significantly improves and outperforms the Linux scheduler for 8%. Finally, SBMP-CD shows better ANTT over SBMP-PP for 3%, which can clearly seen from the right hand side of figure.

6. RELATED WORK

Scheduling for multiprogrammed multi-threaded applications: The work most close to ours is the HOLISYN schedulers by Bhadauria and McKee [3]. The base concept of applying dynamic space-sharing for applications that do not scale is the same, however, they aim at dealing with scalability limitation caused by hardware resource contention, and the optimization target of their work is energy delay product, and therefore the policy of deciding the number of cores to allocate differs from our work. Our technique considers the scalability of a program limited by the software nature by predicting its scalability, and evaluated with a 48-core system to show the effectiveness. Dynamic space-sharing techniques are well studied in the HPC area [10, 25], and approaches to dynamically adjust the scalability of a program is also examined [9]. Recent work called Thread Tailor [16] proposes a dynamic compilation system that can automatically adjusts the number of threads by combining multiple threads together.

Avoiding contention through scheduling: OS scheduling approaches to avoid contention in multicore processors have been studied as well [12, 22, 30]. Contention in shared resources other than LLC such as the memory controller, prefetcher or the memory bus is also a big cause of performance degradation. In some study, LLC miss rate is shown to be a good indicator of shared resource intensiveness and sensitiveness [30]. A cache model which predicts the performance impact of process-to-core assignment is used in a user level scheduler to improve performance [2]. Our work differs from these studies in several ways but the most important point is that we target multi-threaded applications while they concentrate on single-threaded applications.

NUMA aware systems: Recently, several work have focused on optimizing process scheduling on NUMA systems by taking the physical locations of cores, LLC, and memory controller into account. A simple model proposed to characterize the local and remote memory system performance of NUMA system has been evaluated [20]. In NUMA systems, even when LLC competing threads are on the same die, the optimal scheduling might not be separating these threads apart because a thread being migrated will incur higher latency for memory accesses [6, 19]. The shared resource contention as well as data locality should be considered together to find the optimal scheduling. Our platform is also a NUMA and NUCA system, however, SBMP scheduler has not focused on thread migration to reduce shared resource contention. SBMP scheduler applies a centralized thread assignment which minimizes the shared resource contention at the memory hierarchy in nature. However, we have not evaluated throughly by considering NUMA characteristics and we believe there is still room left for optimization. Those are left for future work.

7. CONCLUSIONS AND FUTURE WORK

In this work, we investigate the OS scheduling for the manycore era where various parallel applications with diverse scalability are co-scheduled. Traditional OS scheduler maintains fairness by giving fair amount of CPU time to each thread or process, however we believe that there are two key factors that the scheduler has to be concerned: scalability and CPU utilization. We have shown that scalability of applications should be taken into account to achieve high system performance, where the key idea is to allocate the appropriate amount of shared resources to programs according to their scalability, in order to maintain high system performance. We have proposed a technique to dynamically predict the scalability of the program, as well as a sophisticated phase recognition technique. We have also found that CPU utilization of multi-threaded applications have diverse characteristics, and proposed *Core Donation* technique which tries to maximize the CPU utilization of the system while still keeping the scalability into account.

We have built a prototype SBMP scheduler and compared the performance with the Linux scheduler for variety of workloads. SBMP scheduler shows higher system performance compared to the Linux scheduler, indicating each optimization technique presented in the paper is quite effective. We have not done any optimizations to avoid shared resource contention, and there might be better scheduling when carefully considering the NUCA and NUMA architecture characteristics in detail. Exploration of the scheduler on NUCA and NUMA architectures are left for future work.

8. ACKNOWLEDGMENTS

This research was supported in part by New Energy and Industrial Technology Development Organization, and JSPS Grant-in-Aid for Challenging Exploratory Research (22650008).

9. REFERENCES

[1] G. Amdahl. Validity of the single processor approach to achieving large scale computing capabilities. In *AFIPS '67 (Spring)*, 1967.

[2] M. Banikazemi et al. PAM: a novel performance/power aware meta-scheduler for multi-core systems. In *SC '08*, 2008.

[3] M. Bhadauria and S. McKee. An approach to resource-aware co-scheduling for CMPs. In *ICS '10*, 2010.

[4] C. Bienia. *Benchmarking modern multiprocessors.* PhD thesis, Princeton University, 2011.

[5] S. Blagodurov et al. Contention-aware scheduling on multicore systems. *ACM Transactions on Computer Systems (TOCS)*, 28(4), 2010.

[6] S. Blagodurov et al. A case for NUMA-aware contention management on multicore systems. In *USENIXATC '11*, 2011.

[7] R. Cochran et al. Pack & Cap: adaptive DVFS and thread packing under power caps. In *MICRO 44*, pages 175–185. ACM Request Permissions, Dec. 2011.

[8] J. Corbalán et al. Performance-driven processor allocation. In *OSDI '00*, 2000.

[9] J. Corbalán et al. Improving Gang Scheduling through job performance analysis and malleability. In *ICS '01*, 2001.

[10] J. Corbalán et al. Performance-driven processor allocation. *IEEE Transactions on Parallel and Distributed Systems*, 16(7):599–611, 2005.

[11] S. Eyerman and L. Eeckhout. System-level performance metrics for multiprogram workloads. *IEEE Micro*, 28(3):42–53, 2008.

[12] A. Fedorova et al. Improving performance isolation on chip multiprocessors via an operating system scheduler. In *PACT '07*, 2007.

[13] P. Hargrove and J. Duell. Berkeley lab checkpoint/restart (BLCR) for linux clusters. *Journal of Physics: Conference Series*, 46:494, 2006.

[14] J. Huh et al. Exploring the Design Space of Future CMPs. In *PACT '01*, 2001.

[15] R. Knauerhase et al. Using OS observations to improve performance in multicore systems. *IEEE Micro*, 28(3), 2008.

[16] J. Lee et al. Thread tailor: dynamically weaving threads together for efficient, adaptive parallel applications. In *ISCA '10*, 2010.

[17] J. Lin et al. Gaining insights into multicore cache partitioning: Bridging the gap between simulation and real systems. In *HPCA '08*, pages 367–378, 2008.

[18] K. Lun et al. Balancing thoughput and fairness in SMT processors. In *ISPASS '01*, 2001.

[19] Z. Majo and T. Gross. Memory management in NUMA multicore systems: trapped between cache contention and interconnect overhead. In *ISMM '11*, 2011.

[20] Z. Majo and T. Gross. Memory system performance in a NUMA multicore multiprocessor. In *SYSTOR '11*, 2011.

[21] C. Pheatt. Intel® threading building blocks. *Journal of Computing Sciences in Colleges*, 23(4), 2008.

[22] K. Pusukuri et al. FACT: a framework for adaptive contention-aware thread migrations. In *CF '11*, 2011.

[23] M. Qureshi and Y. Patt. Utility-based cache partitioning: a low-overhead, high-performance, runtime mechanism to partition shared caches. In *MICRO 39*, 2006.

[24] K. Sankaralingam et al. Exploiting ILP, TLP, and DLP with the polymorphous TRIPS architecture. In *ISCA '03*, 2003.

[25] C. Severance and R. Enbody. Comparing Gang Scheduling with dynamic space sharing on symmetric multiprocessors using automatic self-allocating threads (ASAT). In *IPPS '97*, 1997.

[26] A. Snavely and D. Tullsen. Symbiotic jobscheduling for a simultaneous multithreaded processor. In *ASPLOS-IX*, 2000.

[27] M. Taylor et al. The raw microprocessor: a computational fabric for software circuits and general-purpose programs. *IEEE Micro*, 22(2), 2002.

[28] J. Weinberg and A. Snavely. User-guided symbiotic space-sharing of real workloads. In *ICS '06*, 2006.

[29] S. Zhuravlev et al. Addressing shared resource contention in multicore processors via scheduling. In *ASPLOS '10*, 2010.

[30] S. Zhuravlev et al. AKULA: a toolset for experimenting and developing thread placement algorithms on multicore systems. In *PACT '10*, 2010.

Optimizing Datacenter Power with Memory System Levers for Guaranteed Quality-of-Service *

Kshitij Sudan
University of Utah
kshitij@cs.utah.edu

Sadagopan Srinivasan
Intel Corporation
sadagopan.srinivasan@intel.com

Rajeev Balasubramonian
University of Utah
rajeev@cs.utah.edu

Ravi Iyer
Intel Corporation
ravishankar.iyer@intel.com

ABSTRACT

Co-location of applications is a proven technique to improve hardware utilization. Recent advances in virtualization have made co-location of independent applications on shared hardware a common scenario in datacenters. Co-location, while maintaining Quality-of-Service (QoS) for each application is a complex problem that is fast gaining relevance for these datacenters. The problem is exacerbated by the need for effective resource utilization at datacenter scales. In this work, we show that the memory system is a primary bottleneck in many workloads and is a more effective focal point when enforcing QoS. We examine four different memory system levers to enforce QoS: two that have been previously proposed, and two novel levers. We compare the effectiveness of each lever in minimizing power and resource needs, while enforcing QoS guarantees. We also evaluate the effectiveness of combining various levers and show that this combined approach can yield power reductions of up to 28%.

Categories and Subject Descriptors

C.0 [**GENERAL**]: System architectures, Hardware/software interfaces; C.4 [**PERFORMANCE OF SYSTEMS**]: Design studies; B.8.2 [**HARDWARE**]: Performance Analysis and Design Aids

Keywords

Quality-of-Service, datacenter power consumption, memory system architectures, Service Level Agreements (SLAs), datacenter management, application co-location or consolidation, cloud computing.

*This work was supported in parts by NSF grants CCF-0811249, CCF-0916436, NSF CAREER award CCF-0545959, and the University of Utah.

PACT'12, September 19–23, 2012, Minneapolis, Minnesota, USA.

1. INTRODUCTION

Large datacenter facilities hosting customer applications provide performance guarantees as dictated by service level agreements (SLAs). With recent advances in cloud computing services, Quality-of-Service (QoS) guarantees are now an integral component of these SLA agreements. Customers are guaranteed the level of performance as defined by the resources they pay for. For example, customers "rent" CPU hours, RAM capacity, storage capacity, network bandwidth, etc. Each customer server is then an instantiation of a virtual machine (VM) with these allocated resources. Each VM in turn is hosted on a server and often co-located with other VMs. While co-locating different VMs on the same hardware, the service providers make sure that QoS guarantees are not violated by the co-location schedule. This typically leads to conservative schedules that do not necessarily make the most efficient use of the hardware resources.

Co-location of applications is not a new technology [11]. However, co-location in datacenters has been significantly boosted by recent advances in VM performance [3], and the ability migrate VMs across servers [5, 31]. Owing to the scale of these datacenters, efficient hardware utilization is a critical design point. Co-location of VMs/applications to increase server utilization is fast becoming the preferred approach to maximize utilization at these datacenters. For datacenters hosting customer applications instead of VMs, application co-location across servers is the equivalent of VM co-location. Application and VM migration has been extensively researched in the past [18, 27] and well known mechanisms for migration exist [9, 32]. To simplify the discussion (and subsequent evaluation) from here on, we will discuss our proposals in terms of co-located applications only.

A major concern while co-locating applications is whether any of the simultaneously executing applications on a server will violate their QoS guarantees. It is not acceptable to have a breach of QoS guarantee even if the server utilization improves. As a result, applications are typically scheduled conservatively leading to resource under-utilization [8]. This is an important problem for large datacenters where efficient use of hardware is a primary goal for profitable operation. In this work, we provide a framework that maximizes resource utilization, while maintaining QoS guarantees.

A typical server consolidation framework [1, 30] is expected to incorporate several complex features, most notably, to begin tasks on an appropriate server, to monitor the execution of programs, and to take corrective action if an application threatens to not meet QoS constraints. In this evaluation, we will not model the dynamic adaptation aspects of the above framework, especially since simulators limit our ability to observe behavior for longer than a few seconds. We will instead focus on the process of starting a series of new tasks and identifying the maximum level of server consolidation that can be achieved. In other words, we will attempt to co-schedule N applications on to S servers, and devise techniques that allow us to minimize S, while ensuring that QoS guarantees are preserved. This allows us to power down as many servers as possible to reduce overall power[1].

In our evaluation, we attempt to incrementally pack each program on to an existing powered-up server. If this assignment disrupts the QoS guarantees for some of the applications (*sufferers*) on that server, we attempt to change various micro-architectural priorities to allow the sufferers to boost their throughput and meet their QoS constraint. We consider a number of such micro-architectural priority mechanisms and apply them incrementally until QoS is achieved or we exhaust all available mechanisms. In case of the latter, the suffering applications are then moved to a newly powered-up server. The ultimate metric of interest is the number of servers S activated after all the N programs have been successfully assigned, as to a first order, this has the biggest impact on overall power consumption.

We consider four different micro-architectural priority mechanisms in this work. In essence, each of these mechanisms allows restricting the resources allocated to non-suffering applications. By restricting resources of non-sufferers, more resources are available exclusively to sufferers to meet their QoS guarantees. With such a scheme, the suffering application(s) can meet its QoS constraint while hopefully not causing other applications to miss their constraints. Two of these mechanisms (b, c) have been proposed in prior work: (b) bandwidth priority [14] allocates memory bandwidth among competing programs by setting priorities in the memory controller scheduler, and (c) CacheScouts [33] can be used to allocate shared cache capacity among competing applications. The other two mechanisms (o, p) are being considered here for the first time: (o) open vs. closed page DRAM row buffer policy, where closed-page policy is employed for the non-suffering application, while open-page policy is employed for others, (p) prefetch, where aggressive memory prefetch is performed for the suffering application, while taking some bandwidth away from other applications.

We select these memory system levers because the memory system is known to be a major performance bottleneck in datacenters [4, 15, 16] and the memory system provides a rich set of options when varying application priority. Our study focuses on understanding the relative merits of these four mechanisms. We also attempt to understand how combinations of these mechanisms behave.

2. SHARED-RESOURCE PERFORMANCE

In this section we first present the impact of resource conflicts among concurrently executing applications on a chip multi-processor. Figure 1 shows the impact of co-locating applications on the same server. For this experiment, each

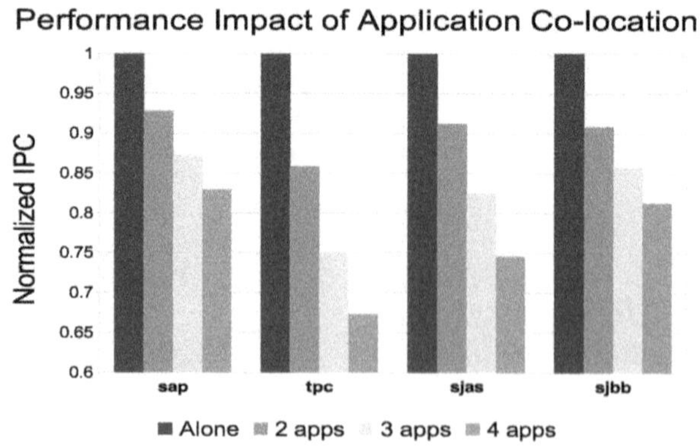

Figure 1: Impact on application performance due to co-location.

application was first run on a 4-core server alone, and then with one other application, two other applications, and finally all four applications were run together. The system configuration is listed in Table 1. These results show that for enterprise class applications, performance degradation due to resource contention can vary from 17% (sap) to 33% (tpc) when all the cores of the CMP are utilized.

This degradation in performance is due to resource contention at various levels of the CMP. Fig. 2 shows the contention for L2 cache and impact on prefetcher's usefulness due to more than one application executing simultaneously on the 4-core server. Fig. 2(a) shows the change in L2 hit-rate. The L2 hit-rates reduce significantly for all application mixes due to higher conflict misses in the shared cache. Similarly, the usefulness of cache lines prefetched into the L2 also decreases as shown by Fig. 2(b). Most of this reduction in usefulness is due to the eviction of prefetched lines from the cache before they are accessed by the CPU.

Similarly, Figure 3 shows the impact of application interference on total DRAM access cycles and DRAM row-buffer hit-rates. DRAM access cycles are counted only when the out-of-order core is stalling on a DRAM request. Fig. 3(a) shows that the number of DRAM cycles increases when more applications are executing because of an increase in queuing delays and DRAM service time. The decrease in row-buffer hit-rates shown in Fig. 3(b) contributes to this increase in DRAM access cycles. The row-buffer hit-rates in Fig. 3(b) are reduced when more than one application is executing because the CPU is now generating conflicting DRAM access requests from different applications.

3. HIGH-LEVEL QOS FRAMEWORK

To set the right context for our proposed mechanisms, we first describe the high-level overview of a QoS framework in future servers. Much of this framework is derived from existing designs [1, 10, 13, 23, 28, 30]. We will refer to this framework as the *High-Level Manager* or *HLM*. The SLAs serve as inputs to the HLM, specifying the expected performance metric (say, throughput, or IPC) for each application. The HLM executes in privileged mode and follows a "measure-check-reorganize" cycle to enforce QoS:

- "measure" refers to hardware performance counters that track the current performance level for each application.

[1]It is almost always more power-efficient to overload a few servers than to distribute load across many servers because of leakage and other constant power delivery overheads [16, 25].

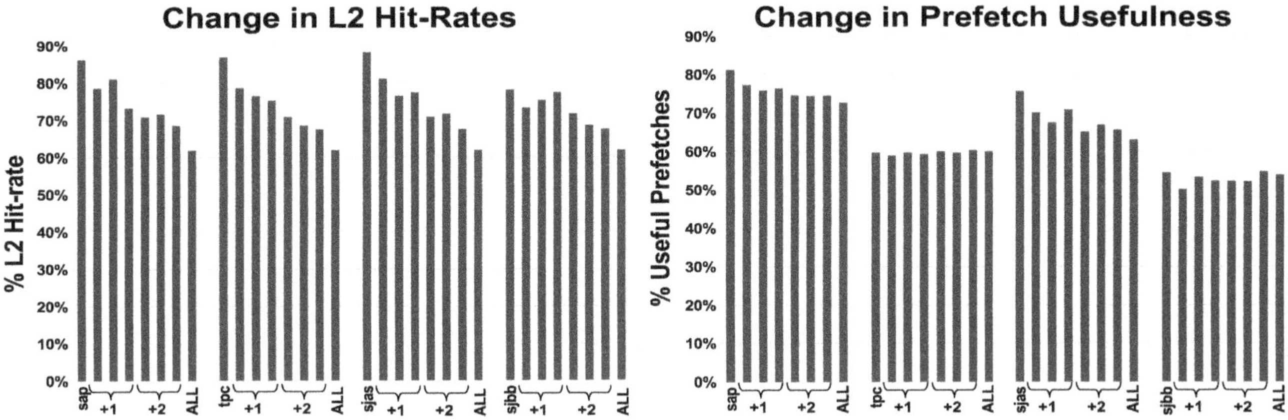

(a) Change in L2 cache hit-rate due to application interference.

(b) Change in usefulness of prefetched entries due to interference.

Figure 2: Impact of application interference on L2 hit-rate and prefetcher usefulness.

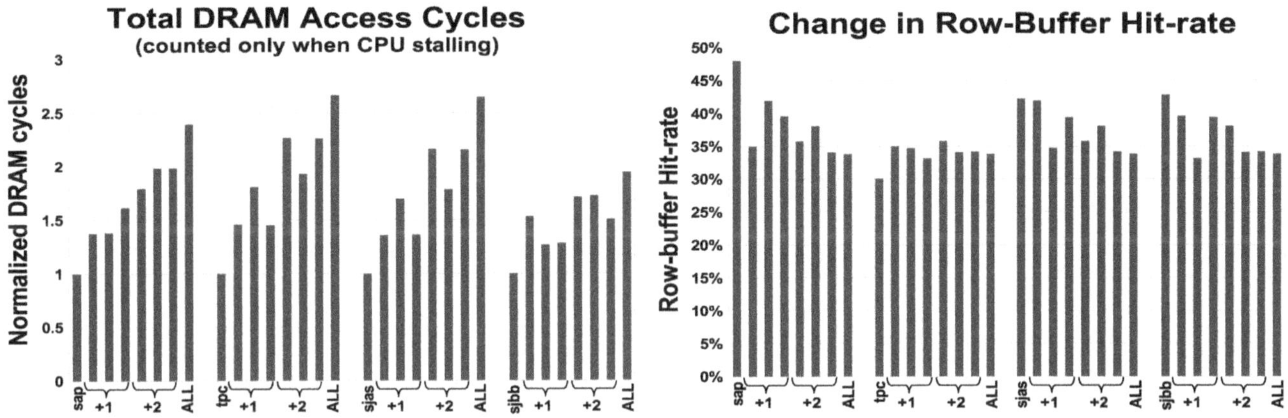

(a) Increase in total cycles spent accessing DRAM due to interference.

(b) Change in DRAM row-buffer hit-rate due to interference.

Figure 3: Impact of application interference on DRAM access cycles and row-buffer hit-rate.

- "check" refers to the HLM reading these performance counters at periodic intervals (referred to as *epochs*) and ensuring that QoS guarantees are being met, or if there is room to improve server utilization.
- "reorganize" refers to the HLM generating a new co-location schedule and performing application migration to meet QoS guarantees or improve server utilization.

When a new task arrives, the HLM attempts to schedule it on one of the already-active servers. Obviously, it is intractable for the HLM to evaluate every possible schedule to determine a power-optimal co-location. The HLM therefore relies on heuristics. In our evaluation, we consider two heuristics: (i) Low Load First (LLF): The new task is scheduled on the least loaded server. If QoS constraints are not met, the new task is migrated to a newly powered-up server. (ii) Heavy Load First (HLF): The new task is first scheduled on the most highly loaded server. If QoS is not achieved, the new task is migrated to the next highly loaded server, and so on. If no existing server can host the new task, it is moved to a newly powered-up server. The HLF policy may incur higher migration overheads, but it increases the likelihood that some lightly loaded server will exist to accommodate a resource-intensive task that may show up. More sophisticated task assignment policies may prune the search space by using pre-computed profiles of the application to help rule out some servers that may not have a light enough load.

Now consider the process of a new task assignment in more detail. After the new task is assigned to the least loaded server (in an LLF policy), we allow a few epochs to go by and then measure performance over the next few epochs. If QoS is not being met for some subset of applications on the server (referred to as the *sufferers*), we attempt to boost their performance by employing our micro-architectural priority levers to *non-suffering* applications. One lever is applied at a time and performance is measured for a few epochs. If QoS failure continues, more levers are applied. Some levers can have parameters associated with them that determine the extent of resource constriction for a non-sufferer. We limit ourselves to parameters that afford three different priority levels for any lever – low, medium, high. When activating a new lever, we first use the low priority level before mov-

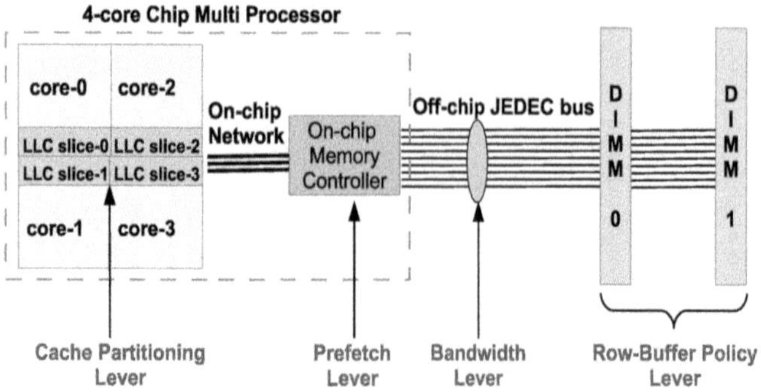

Figure 4: Memory Hierarchy Levers.

ing to medium and high. If we apply a lever change (say, we move from lever-a-low to lever-a-medium) and a hitherto non-suffering application joins the list of sufferers, we immediately cancel that lever change and move to the next item in the list of levers (lever-b-low). Once all the levers are exhausted for all non-suffering applications and QoS guarantees are still not achieved for suffering applications, we simply cancel all levers and move the new task to another server (either a new server (LLF) or the next highly loaded server (HLF)).

In summary, there are aspects of the HLM that are beyond the scope of this paper and are not modeled in our simulation framework (including re-assignment on phase changes, handling disruptions with conservative guarantees, LVT curves, etc.). The following aspects are modeled in the simulator:

- An input SLA specifies N tasks and corresponding QoS specifications. The QoS specification for each task is expressed as a number between 0 and 1, where 1 denotes the throughput of the task (represented by instructions per cycle or IPC) when it executes by itself on an unloaded server.
- Every few epochs, a new task from this list is selected for co-location. It is assigned to an existing server using either LLF or HLF.
- After some warm-up, measurements are taken over subsequent epochs to see if QoS guarantees are being met. If yes, then appropriate co-scheduling is achieved for the new task. Now wait till a new task is admitted.
- If QoS guarantees are not being met for some suffering applications, progressively move through the available set of levers. A lever can potentially have different strength levels. Levers (and their levels) are applied only if they do not introduce new applications into the list of sufferers.
- If all the levers fail to provide QoS, we move the new task to the next server (a newly powered-up server for LLF and the next highly loaded server for HLF).
- Once all tasks have been scheduled, the number of powered-up servers S represents the "goodness metric" for the server consolidation process.

4. MEMORY HIERARCHY LEVERS

Having described the overall QoS framework, we now turn our attention to the micro-architectural levers that allow us to prioritize a set of applications over other co-scheduled applications. These levers are employed when a set of applications (sufferers) are unable to meet their QoS constraints. The one common theme in all of these levers is that they introduce a trade-off between co-scheduled applications, *i.e.*, applying a lever for an application constricts the resources available to it, thereby boosting the performance of a *suffering* application by allocating more resources for its exclusive use. The levers considered in this study are shown in Figure 4. We first describe the two memory hierarchy levers (b and c) that have been employed in prior work.

- **(b) Bandwidth management:** We employ the priority mechanisms introduced by Iyer et al. [14] to provide higher memory bandwidth for suffering applications. With this lever, memory requests are scheduled by the memory controller based on priority ratios set by the HLM. If the HLM has set a priority ratio of 4:3, 4 high priority transactions for suffering applications are handled before 3 low priority transactions for non-sufferers. This is referred to as a bandwidth differential scheme. These priorities are implemented within the memory controller and the baseline memory controller uses the First-Ready-First-Come-First-Served (FR-FCFS [26]) scheduling policy that takes advantage of open rows in DRAM. When the bandwidth lever is applied, the scheduling policy becomes Priority-First-FR-FCFS, where we first apply the above bandwidth differential constraint before using FR-FCFS to select among remaining candidates. The strength of this lever is easily set by picking different bandwidth differential ratios.
- **(c) Cache allocation within the shared LLC:** To control the amount of shared cache capacity an application can use exclusively, we use the CacheScouts [33] mechanism. When this lever is employed, it acts to limit the cache capacity allocated to a given core. It does so by restricting the core to only occupy a maximum of N ways in any given cache set. When this core suffers a cache miss, if the number of lines occupied by the core in the incoming cache line's set is less than N, then the LRU line from the entire set is evicted. If however the core already occupies N lines in the set, then the LRU line among these N lines is evicted. The value of N depends on the applied level of this lever. If a core's cache capacity allocation is not being constrained by this lever, it evicts the LRU line from the incoming cache line's set, irrespective of the owner CPU.

Next, we discuss the two new memory-system levers:

- **(o) Open vs. closed page DRAM row buffer management policy:** Dynamically varying the row-buffer management policy can aid in QoS enforcement by allowing a new degree of control over access latency for DRAM requests. If an application is to be prioritized, we can prioritize it over the other by letting it use an open-row policy. This improves performance for the preferred application, while other applications are forced into using closed-row. Closing the row early for non-preferred applications also speeds up the next access from the preferred application. This lever can

CMP Parameters			
ISA	x86-64 ISA	CMP size	4-core
L1 I-cache	128KB/2-way, private, 1-cycle	L1 D-cache	128KB/2-way, private, 1-cycle
L2 Cache	2 MB, 16-way, shared, 20-cycle	L1 and L2 Cache line size	64 Bytes

DRAM Parameters	
DRAM Device Parameters	Micron MT47H64M8 DDR2-800 Timing parameters [17], t_{CL}=t_{RCD}=t_{RP}=20ns(4-4-4 @ 200 MHz) 4 banks/device, 16384 rows/bank, 512 columns/row, 32 bits/column, 8-bit output/device
DIMM Configuration	8 Non-ECC un-buffered DIMMs, 1 rank/DIMM, 64 bit channel, 8 devices/DIMM
DIMM-level Row-Buffer Size	32 bits/column × 512 columns/row × 8 devices/DIMM = 8 KB/DIMM
Active row-buffers per DIMM	4 (each bank in a device maintains a row-buffer)
Total DRAM Capacity	512 MBit/device × 8 devices/DIMM × 8 DIMMs = 4 GB

Table 1: Simulator parameters.

Application	LLC MPKI	DRAM access/Kilo-Inst
sap	1.91	3.71
tpc	8.23	13.25
sjas	4.77	9.49
sjbb	3.33	4.79

Table 2: Benchmark Properties. DRAM accesses include LLC misses and writebacks

Simulated Workload Mixes	
Application	Workload Mix
Memory Intensive Mix (MI)	replicated copies of *tpc*
Balanced Mix (B)	replicated copies of *tpc, sap, sjas, sjbb*
Non-Memory Intensive Mix (NMI)	replicated copies of *sap*

Generating SLA Guarantees	
SLA level	Fraction of baseline IPC
Relaxed	Random number between [0.66, 0.77]
Medium	Random number between (0.77, 0.88]
Aggressive	Random number between (0.88, 1.0]
Mix	Random number between [0.66, 1.0]

Table 3: Simulated Workload Mixes and SLA Guarantees.

be implemented with minor modifications to the memory controller architecture. The modification involves a small table at the memory controller which contains the process-ID and current row-buffer policy for each application executing on the CPU. This table is populated by the OS with inputs from the HLM. A page can also be closed after a timer expires and different levels of this lever can be implemented by using different timer values.

- **(p) Prefetch request scheduling:** We propose aggressive prefetch from DRAM as another lever. Whenever DRAM accesses are prefetched for an application, it introduces a trade-off since these applications now use more than their share of memory bandwidth to boost their performance. This lever is different than changing the DRAM bandwidth allocation since multiple prefetch requests are issued only when this lever is employed. This lever can be combined with the memory bandwidth lever to prevent low-priority applications from getting starved. We assume an integrated stream buffer plus memory controller. The operation of this integrated prefetch unit and memory controller is quite simple: if the access stream has locality and this lever is employed, the stream buffer issues prefetch requests for the next few cache lines after the current request. Low/medium/high versions of this priority mechanism can be constructed by tuning the threshold to detect streaming behavior and by issuing prefetches for fewer or more subsequent cache lines.

Most of the proposed hardware modifications are to the memory controller. Our design adds limited logic to adjust bandwidth priorities and adds more checks when scheduling accesses. The stream prefetcher has also been augmented. In addition to these changes, most requests must carry a process-ID as they propagate through the memory hierarchy. This allows the above levers to be employed only when applicable. The HLM relies on already existing hardware counters [2, 12] to track the relevant metrics in the SLA (IPC throughput for our evaluation).

5. RESULTS

5.1 Methodology

To evaluate our proposals we use a trace-based simulator that processes traces collected from a real system. We focus only on single-threaded multi-programmed workloads to simplify the simulation. The simulator models an out-of-order CPU and models the execution of multi-programmed workloads on a Chip-Multiprocessor (CMP) platform. We model the memory hierarchy (including the memory controller and the DRAM sub-system) in detail and the parameters for the hierarchy are listed in Table 1.

The workloads chosen to simulate the system are the four enterprise benchmarks — *tpc, sap, sjas, sjbb*. The memory utilization metrics for these applications are listed in Table 2. A *job list* is used to denote the total number of jobs simulated for one experiment, and the order of applications admitted to the simulated datacenter. This job list is created by replicating the benchmarks traces an appropriate number of times. Specific *workload mixes* are created that signify the memory behavior of the job list. Job lists with three different memory access behaviors are used for our simulations and are listed in Table 3. When replicating for number of jobs greater than 4, the order of application admittance to the job pool was also randomized.

Finally, the customer specified input SLA guarantees are generated using a random number generator that specifies the fraction of IPC as the customer demanded QoS guarantee. We experimented with randomly generated SLAs between [0.66, 1] range - 0.66 signifying SLA guarantee equal to 66% of baseline IPC, and 1 signifying 100% of baseline performance of the application when executing alone on a 4-core CMP with parameters listed in Table 1. We did not consider SLA guarantees below 66% of baseline IPC because it is fairly easy for applications to meet this guarantee even when running with 3 other applications. Note that the choice of

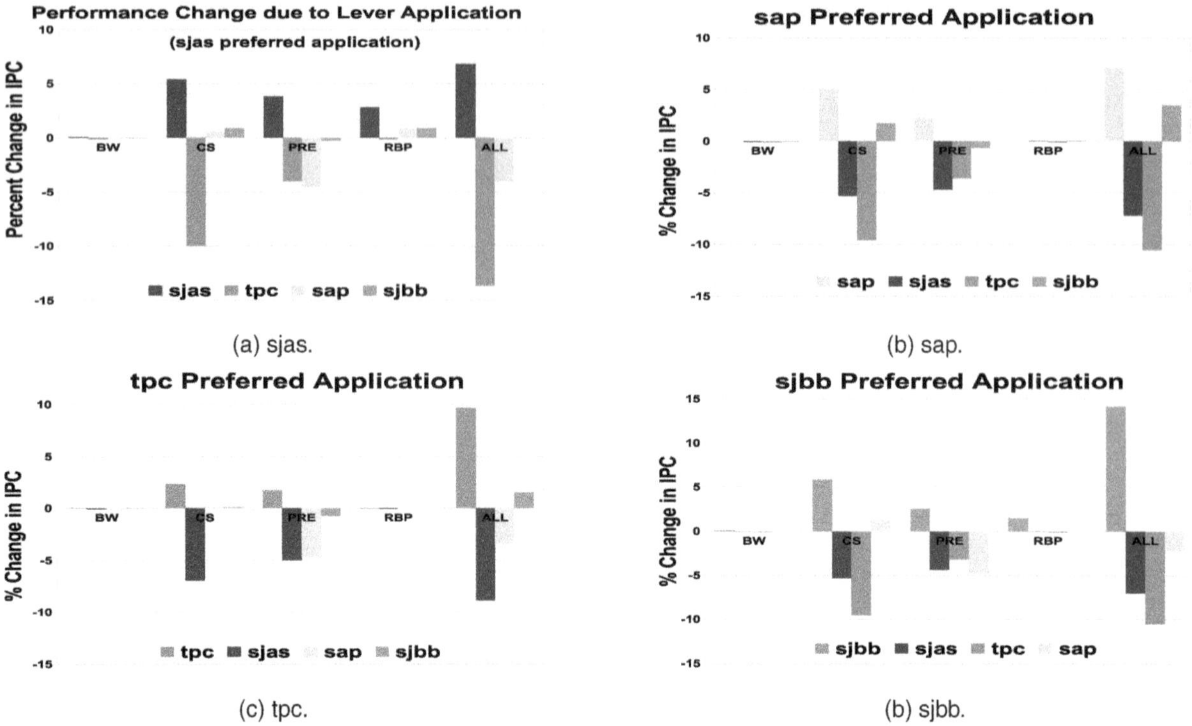

(a) sjas. (b) sap. (c) tpc. (b) sjbb.

Figure 5: Impact of individual lever application on application IPC.

using IPC as a metric for performance does not have any impact on the results. Any other performance metric, like transactions-per-second, can be used in place of IPC.

As listed in Table 3, four different SLA ranges are generated. Each range is meant to represent the application performance the customer expects. These guarantees are combined with the three workload mixes also listed in Table 3 to create one workload-SLA mix. There are thus a total of 12 such pairs (3 workload-mixes x 4 SLA guarantees). These 12 pairs represent various application mixes in terms of their memory intensiveness and SLA guarantees.

The power model for our work uses the following relation between the server utilization and total number of activated servers:

*Total power = num servers * (constant power draw + server utilization * (Watts/utility))*

The $(Watts/utility)$ metric was obtained from Raghavendra et al.'s work [25] for a 2 GHz processor frequency (see Fig. 5 for Server B on page 5 [25]). This is essentially the slope of the line representing the 2 GHz frequency curve in the figure. Such data is consistent with that seen in other work [16]. Meisner et al. [16] show that a lightly loaded server consumes 270 W while a fully active server consumes 450 W. This data is the rationale behind the premise in Section 1 that it is better to consolidate applications to create few highly loaded servers than to create many lightly loaded servers.

5.2 Effectiveness of Levers in Controlling Application IPC

In this section we show results for how effective each lever is when employed to constrict resources for the non-suffering application on a server, and the corresponding increase in a suffering application's IPC. Fig. 5 shows the change in IPC of applications on a 4-core CMP server when different levers are employed. The first application is always the preferred application (the *suffering* application) and the other applications have their resources constricted by lever application. The X-axis shows the four different levers and when ALL levers are applied simultaneously. The Y-axis plots the percent change in IPC compared to the baseline when the application is executing alone on the CMP. As can be seen, the first application always shows improved IPC over baseline, while other three applications show reduction in IPC.

From these results, it can be observed that each lever (except BW) is able to change the IPC of applications to varying degrees. CS lever has the most impact followed by PRE lever, and then by RBP lever. This is to be expected since cache capacity is the most critical shared resource impacting performance. There is little change in IPC with BW lever because the benchmark applications do not saturate the provisioned system bandwidth. We expect other applications which consume more bandwidth than the current applications to show significant change in IPC with the BW lever. In Section 5.3 we provide sensitivity results for the bandwidth lever by artificially reducing system bandwidth. Another important trend to note is that when all levers are used collectively (ALL lever), the impact on IPC is cumulative of each lever's individual impact.

This trend of cumulative impact is examined in detail in Fig. 6(a) and (b) which show change in IPC when two, and three levers are employed respectively. It shows that lever application results in an additive impact on performance. Therefore, applying the levers in succession can improve sufferer application's IPC by progressively reducing available resources for the non-suffering applications. For these experiments, different lever combinations were applied to the

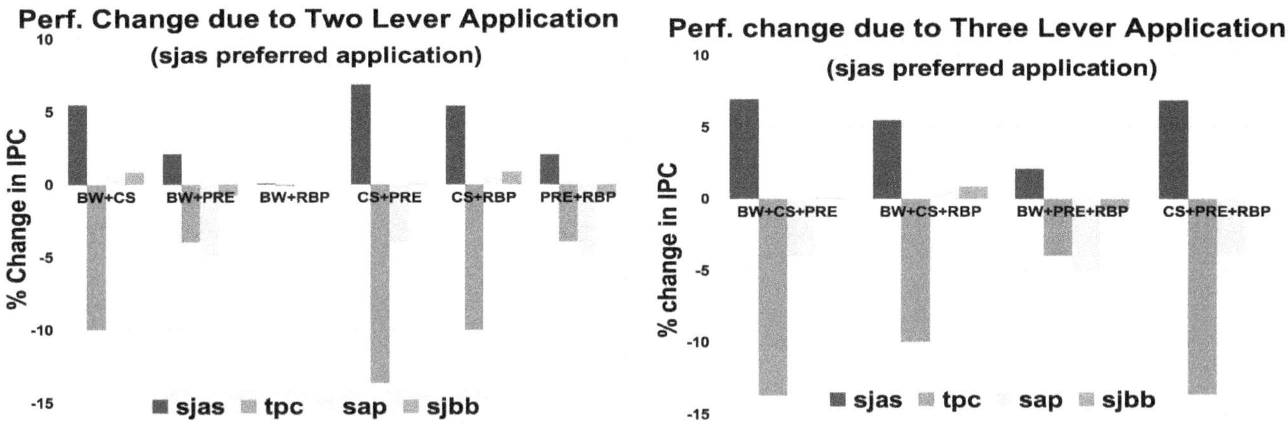

(a) Applying 2 levers simultaneously.

(b) Applying 3 levers simultaneously.

Figure 6: Impact of two and three simultaneous lever application on application IPC.

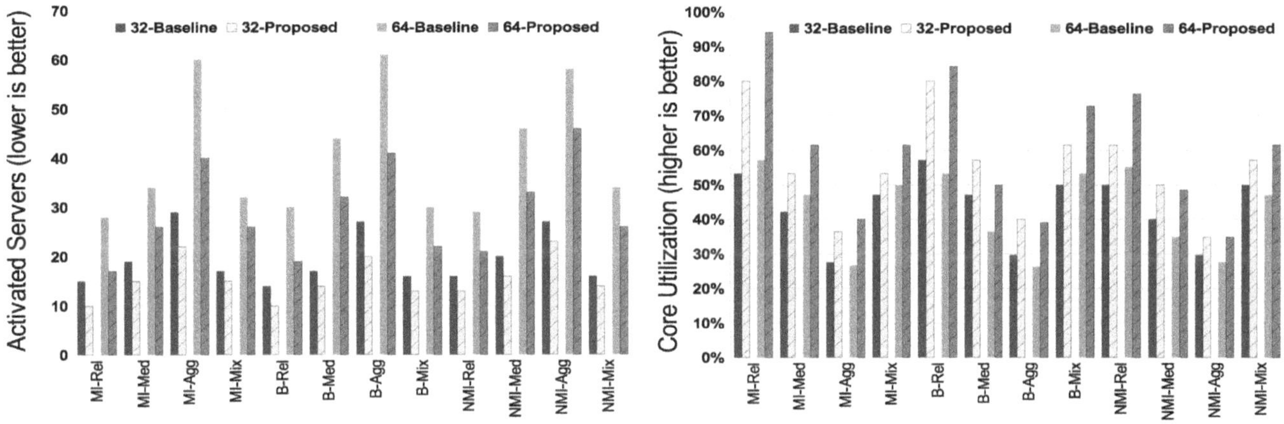

(a) Total servers activated.

(b) Activated core utilization.

Figure 7: Number of servers required, and percent of activated cores utilized with HLF policy.

applications, and as before, the first application is preferred. We show results only for *sjas* since other applications show similar trends.

5.3 Activated Servers

In this section we study the impact of our proposed scheme on the metric of interest — N, the number of servers required. For these experiments, we varied the jobs allocated to the servers by creating workload mixes using the four applications. With these we try to understand the impact of workload mix, job list length, and SLA aggressiveness on the number of servers needed to execute all the applications while meeting their QoS. We compare our proposed results to a baseline, un-optimized system with no QoS levers.

Fig. 7 plots the number of activated servers and core utilization for the baseline and proposed schemes for the 12 workloads (3 benchmark mixes x 4 classes of SLAs). The job length is configured to 32, or 64 total jobs for these experiments. Core utilization shows what fraction of cores are being used among all the activated servers. This can be seen as a metric to measure the density of a co-location schedule with higher being better.

It can be seen that fewer servers need to be activated, and the utilization of activated cores increases when using the proposed scheme. Fig. 7(b) shows that the average core utilization for baseline is quite low — 43.6% and 42.9% for job length of 32 and 64 respectively. This shows that there is a heavy under utilization of the activated servers for the baseline system. With the proposed scheme the average core utilization increases to 55.4% and 60.4% respectively. These increases in utilization might seem small, but when multiplied by millions of cores at a typical datacenter, the efficiency gains are tremendous. Also, with the proposed scheme and longer job lengths, the core utilization will increase further due to reasons explained shortly.

To better understand the trends in Fig. 7, Fig. 8 re-plots the same data in a different way. Fig. 8(a) and 8(b) plot the percent reduction in activated servers and percent improvement in core utilization compared to the baseline. As the memory intensity of applications reduces from left to right, the improvements in core utilization and activated servers decreases. This is to be expected because the levers constrict memory resources and therefore have highest impact on memory intensive applications. For job length of 64, the average reduction in percent of activated servers for MI mix

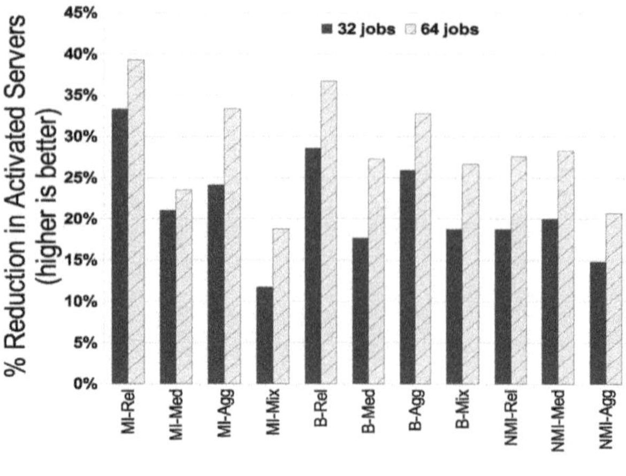

(a) Percent reduction in number of servers ordered w.r.t workload mix.

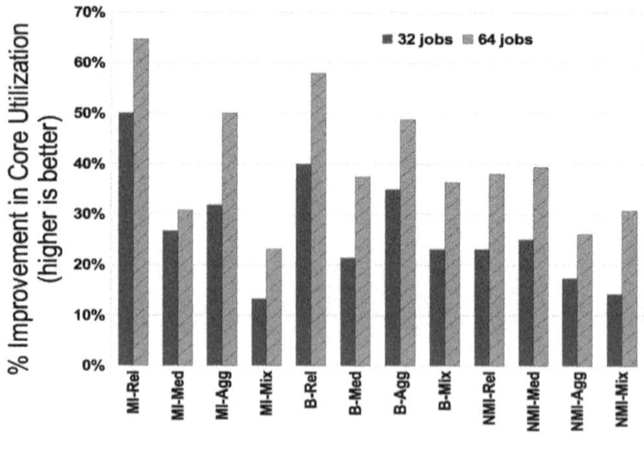

(b) Percent improvement in activated cores utilization ordered w.r.t. workload mix.

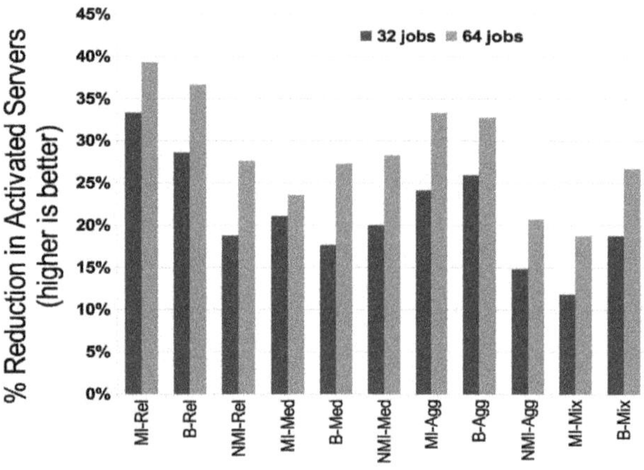

(c) Percent reduction in server activation, ordered w.r.t. SLA aggressiveness.

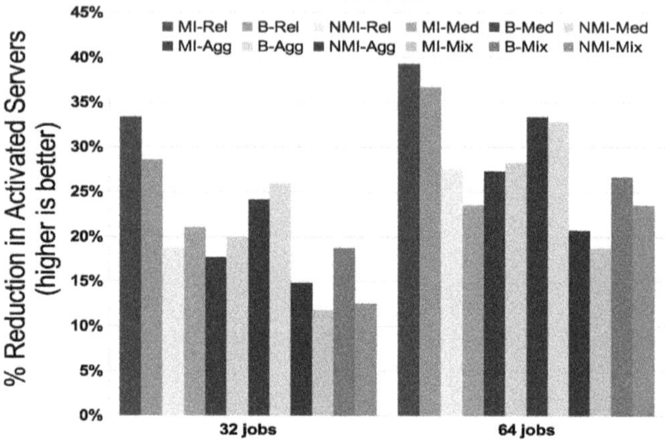

(d) Percent reduction in server activation, ordered w.r.t. job list length.

Figure 8: Number of servers required, and percent of activated cores utilized with HLF policy.

is 30.8%, for Balance mix (B) is 28.7% and for NMI mix is 25%. With large datacenter installations, it is expected that the aggregate workload mix would resemble something like the Balanced mix in our simulations. Balanced mix shows improvements within 2% of MI mix.

Fig. 8(c) and Fig. 8(d) present the same data as in Fig. 7(a) but arranged differently to show how number of activated servers changes with respect to SLA aggressiveness and job list length. For Fig. 8(c), the SLA guarantees get more aggressive from left to right on the X-axis, and improvements also reduce. With more aggressive SLA, each application demands more resources. As a result, the ability to find applications that can be co-scheduled decreases resulting in reduced improvements.

In Fig. 8(d), when improvements are ordered with respect to length of the job list, a trend of improved performance emerges for longer job lists. This occurs due to the possibility of finding applications with a more diverse set of QoS requirements in a longer job list. We also experimented with job list lengths of 4, 8, and 16, and observed this trend of greater performance improvements with longer job lists in all our experiments.

Fig. 9 shows the percent reduction in power for the proposed scheme compared to the baseline. With increased improvements in server consolidation it shows that the total system power reduces in line with the improved consolidation for longer job lists. The average reduction in power for job list length of 32 is 20.5%, and 28.1% for list length of 64.

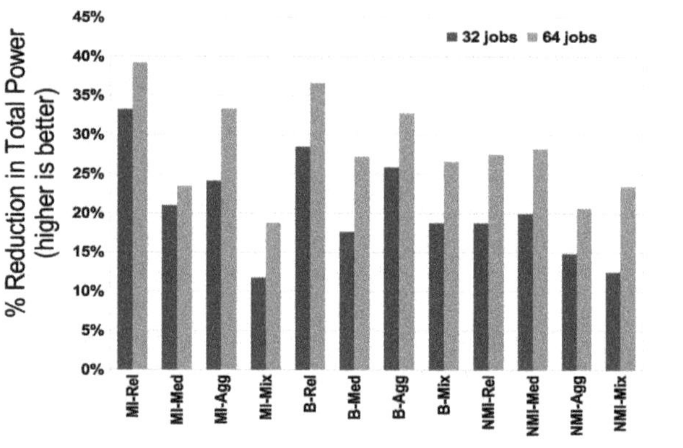

Figure 9: Percent reduction in total power.

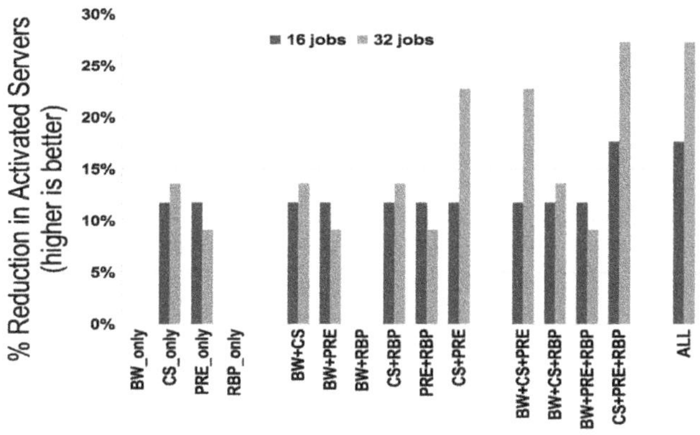

Figure 10: Improvement in activated servers when applying different combination of levers.

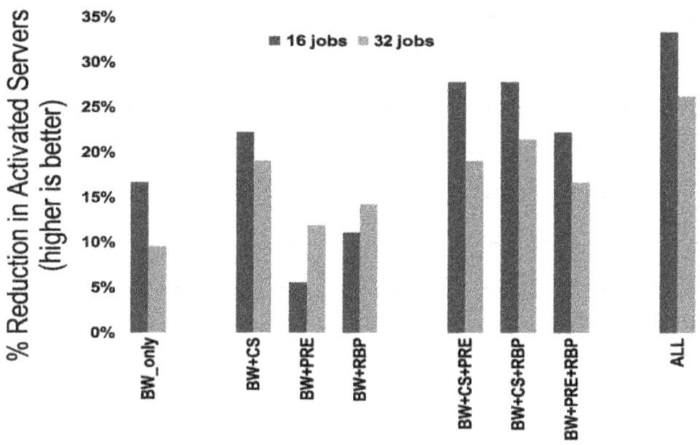

Figure 11: Sensitivity analysis for BW lever.

Fig. 10 shows the improvement in the number of activated servers compared to the baseline while applying varying number, and, varying combination of levers. Only the Balanced-Medium workload-SLA combination is shown in the graph for clarity. It can be observed that BW and RBP lever by themselves show no improvement. This is due to the fact that in our configured system, bandwidth is heavily under utilized. For the remaining combination of levers, we see a cumulative improvement in core utilization as expected. This graph can be correlated with Fig. 6 that shows that for our simulated workloads, the CS+PRE+RBP combination achieves all the improvements by managing the non-sufferer application's IPC and thus improving co-location density.

We expect the BW lever to be much more effective where the application performance is constricted by the aggregate system bandwidth. To perform a sensitivity analysis for the BW lever, we artificially reduced the system bandwidth by $4X$ and performed the same experiment as in Fig. 10, but only with lever combinations involving the BW lever. Fig. 11 shows that the BW lever is indeed effective at reducing the number of activated servers.

We also experimented with the Least-Loaded-First (LLF) job allocation policy described in Section 3. There were minor differences in the number of activated servers compared to the HLF policy. We do not present those results here due to space constraints.

6. RELATED WORK

Enforcing QoS guarantees has been an active area of research. The focus of most of the past work has been on making sure that no shared resource is exclusively over-consumed by a single application in the presence of other simultaneously executing applications. Some proposals like [8, 13, 14, 20, 33] have advanced frameworks that aim at improving overall throughput while enforcing these QoS guarantees. Each proposal has a different mechanism to enforce QoS at the architectural level, but they all are either at the shared cache level [33], or at the main memory bandwidth level [14]. Iyer et al. [14] propose a QoS enabled memory architecture that allocates shared cache capacity and memory bandwidth based on input from the operating environment. Guo et al. [8] use micro-architectural techniques that steal excess resources from applications while still enforcing QoS guarantees. They primarily focus on specification of QoS targets and the resulting job admission policy.

Another body of work [19, 21, 22] aims at improving resource utilization while providing QoS guarantees. These schemes enforce constraints at the DRAM request scheduling stage at the memory controller by modifying the order in which DRAM access commands are serviced. Nesbit et al. [21] propose "Private Virtual Time Memory System" for each thread to ensure each thread gets its allocated share of bandwidth irrespective of the system load. Rafique et al. [24] propose a simpler mechanism for fair allocation of bandwidth while avoiding bandwidth waste. Both these mechanisms only partition available memory bandwidth and do not mention how other resources interplay with such mechanisms. Mutlu and Moscibroda [19] make a critical observation that for chip multi-processor systems, inter-thread interference can introduce significant performance degradation. Their scheduler ensures that priority for open rows doesn't starve requests for closed rows.

The same authors improve upon their scheme by introducing "parallelism-aware batch scheduling" [22]. The idea is to process all possible DRAM requests in parallel for a thread (i.e., servicing requests which exhibit bank level parallelism), and in batches to provide QoS. These contributions are complementary to our proposal and would fall under the umbrella of memory controller levers (lever-(b) in our study). Ebrahimi et al. [6] show that to improve fairness in a CMP system, one needs to throttle the cores by limiting the requests they inject into the memory system. This differs from our proposal because we are not aiming at fairness of all executing applications on the CMP, instead we leverage the asymmetry among the application SLA guarantees to extract maximum resource usage from the server. The same authors also show in [7] that the prefetch requests can degrade system performance unless they are co-ordinated with other resource management policies. This aligns with our work as we show in Section 5 that the PRE lever is more effective when combined with other levers.

Recent work by Tang et al. [29] shows that for datacenter workloads, there is significant resource contention at all levels of the memory hierarchy. They do not consider interference at the DRAM level, but make the same conclusions as in Section 2 about interference at the last-level cache. Their work demonstrates the impact of application interference within caches on datacenter application performance. Their work differs from our proposal because we argue for implementing architectural levers that will help extract the maximum machine resource utilization while maintaining QoS for individual applications. We also show that there needs to be a co-ordinated approach while exercising these levers to achieve high co-location density.

7. CONCLUSIONS

Server consolidation at datacenters is essential for reducing power needs. In terms of power, it is beneficial to execute as many applications as possible on a single server. However, this runs the risk that some applications may not meet their QoS guarantees. To address this problem we study micro-architectural levers to improve co-location density. This work introduces two new levers: a row buffer management policy, and a prefetch lever, and two levers that have been previously proposed: cache and bandwidth allocation. We show that the effects of applying these levers is cumulative. The application of these levers can reduce the number of activated servers by up to 39%, resulting in a power reduction of up to 28%. Much future work remains in developing robust HLM features that can take advantage of these and additional micro-architectural levers.

8. REFERENCES

[1] Amazon Web Services. Amazon CloudWatch, Retrieved Oct. 2009.

[2] AMD Inc. BIOS and Kernel Developer's Guide for AMD Athlon 64 and AMD Opteron Processors, Retrieved Oct. 2009.

[3] P. Barham, B. Dragovic, K. Fraser, S. Hand, T. Harris, A. Ho, R. Neugebauer, I. Pratt, and A. Warfield. Xen and the Art of Virtualization. In *Proceedings of SOSP*, 2003.

[4] L. Barroso and U. Holzle. *The Datacenter as a Computer: An Introduction to the Design of Warehouse-Scale Machines.* Morgan & Claypool, 2009.

[5] C. Clark, K. Fraser, S. Hand, J. G. Hansen, E. Jul, C. Limpach, I. Pratt, and A. Warfield. Live Migration of Virtual Machines. In *Proceedings of NSDI*, 2005.

[6] E. Ebrahimi, C. J. Lee, O. Mutlu, and Y. N. Patt. Fairness via Source Throttling: A ConïňĄgurable and High-Performance Fairness Substrate for Multi-Core Memory Systems. In *Proceedings of ASPLOS*, 2010.

[7] E. Ebrahimi, C. J. Lee, O. Mutlu, and Y. N. Patt. Prefetch-Aware Shared-Resource Management for Multi-Core Systems. In *Proceedings of ISCA*, 2011.

[8] F. Guo, Y. Solihin, L. Zhao, and R. Iyer. A Framework for Providing Quality of Service in Chip Multi-Processors. In *Proceedings of MICRO*, 2007.

[9] S. Hacking and B. Hudzia. Improving the Live Migration Process of Large Enterprise Applications. In *Proceedings of Workshop on Virtualization Technologies in Distributed Computing*, 2009.

[10] IBM Corporation. IBM Systems Director.

[11] IBM Corporation. IBM: z/VM Operating System.

[12] Intel Corporation. Intel 64 and IA-32 Architectures Software Developer's Manual Volume 3B: System Programming Guide, Part 2, Retrieved Oct. 2009.

[13] R. Iyer, R. Illikkal, L. Zhao, , D. Newell, and J. Moses. Virtual Platform Architectures: A Framework for Efficient Resource Metering in Datacenter Servers. Poster Session at SIGMETRICS, 2009.

[14] R. Iyer, L. Zhao, F. Guo, R. Illikkal, D. Newell, Y. Solihin, L. Hsu, and S. Reinhardt. QoS Policies and Architecture for Cache/Memory in CMP Platforms. In *Proceedings of SIGMETRICS*, 2007.

[15] K. Lim, J. Chang, T. Mudge, P. Ranganathan, S. Reinhardt, and T. Wenisch. Disaggregated Memory for Expansion and Sharing in Blade Servers. In *Proceedings of ISCA*, 2009.

[16] D. Meisner, B. Gold, and T. Wenisch. PowerNap: Eliminating Server Idle Power. In *Proceedings of ASPLOS*, 2009.

[17] Micron Technology Inc. *Micron DDR2 SDRAM Part MT47H64M8*, 2004.

[18] D. Milojičić, F. Douglis, Y. Paindaveine, R. Wheeler, and S. Zhou. Process Migration. *ACM Computing Surveys*, 32(3), 2000.

[19] O. Mutlu and T. Moscibroda. Stall-Time Fair Memory Access Scheduling for Chip Multiprocessors. In *Proceedings of MICRO*, 2007.

[20] K. Nesbit, J. Laudon, and J. E. Smith. Virtual private caches. In *Proceedings ISCA*, 2007.

[21] K. J. Nesbit, N. Aggarwal, J. Laudon, and J. E. Smith. Fair Queuing Memory Systems. In *Proceedings of MICRO*, 2006.

[22] O. Mutlu and T. Moscibroda. Parallelism-Aware Batch Scheduling - Enhancing Both Performance and Fairness of Shared DRAM Systems. In *Proceedings of ISCA*, 2008.

[23] P. Padala, K. G. Shin, X. Zhu, M. Uysal, Z. Wang, S. Singhal, A. Merchant, and K. Salem. Adaptive Control of Virtualized Resources in Utility Computing Environments. In *Proceeding of EuroSys*, 2007.

[24] N. Rafique, W. Lim, and M. Thottethodi. Effective Management of DRAM Bandwidth in Multicore Processors. In *Proceedings of PACT*, 2007.

[25] R. Raghavendra, P. Ranganathan, V. Talwar, Z. Wang, and X. Zhu. No "Power" Struggles: Coordinated Multi-level Power Management for the Data Center. In *Proceedings of ASPLOS*, 2003.

[26] S. Rixner, W. Dally, U. Kapasi, P. Mattson, and J. Owens. Memory Access Scheduling. In *Proceedings of ISCA*, 2000.

[27] J. Smith. A Survey of Process Migration Mechanisms. *SIGOPS Operating Systems Review*, 22(3):28–40, 1988.

[28] S. Srikantaiah, A. Kansal, and F. Zhao. Energy aware consolidation for cloud computing. In *Proceedings of HotPower - Workshop on Power Aware Computing and Systems*, 2008.

[29] L. Tang, J. Mars, N. Vachharajani, R. Hundt, and M. L. Soffa. The Impact of Memory Subsystem Resource Sharing on Datacenter Applications. In *Proceedings of ISCA*, 2011.

[30] VMware Inc. VMware vCenter, Retrieved Oct. 2009.

[31] VMware Inc. VMware VMotion, Retrieved Oct. 2009.

[32] C. Wang, F. Mueller, C. Engelmann, and S. L. Scott. Proactive Process-Level Live Migration in HPC Environments. In *Proceedings of Supercomputing*, 2008.

[33] L. Zhao, R. Iyer, R. Illikkal, J. Moses, S. Makineni, and D. Newell. CacheScouts: Fine-Grain Monitoring of Shared Caches in CMP Platforms. In *Proceedings of PACT*, 2007.

Evaluation of Blue Gene/Q Hardware Support for Transactional Memories

Amy Wang
IBM Toronto Software Lab.
Markham, ON, Canada
aktwang@ca.ibm.com

Matthew Gaudet
Dep. of Computing Science
University of Alberta
Edmonton, AB, Canada
mgaudet@ualberta.ca

Peng Wu
IBM Research
Yorktown, NY, USA
pengwu@us.ibm.com

José Nelson Amaral
Dep. of Computing Science
University of Alberta
Edmonton, AB, Canada
jamaral@ualberta.ca

Martin Ohmacht
IBM Research
Yorktown, NY, USA
mohmacht@us.ibm.com

Christopher Barton
IBM Toronto Software Lab.
Markham, ON, Canada
kbarton@ca.ibm.com

Raul Silvera
IBM Toronto Software Lab.
Markham, ON, Canada
rauls@ca.ibm.com

Maged Michael
IBM Research
Yorktown, NY, USA
magedm@us.ibm.com

ABSTRACT

This paper describes an end-to-end system implementation of the transactional memory (TM) programming model on top of the hardware transactional memory (HTM) of the Blue Gene/Q (BG/Q) machine. The TM programming model supports most C/C++ programming constructs on top of a best-effort HTM with the help of a complete software stack including the compiler, the kernel, and the TM runtime.

An extensive evaluation of the STAMP benchmarks on BG/Q is the first of its kind in understanding characteristics of running coarse-grained TM workloads on HTMs. The study reveals several interesting insights on the overhead and the scalability of BG/Q HTM with respect to sequential execution, coarse-grain locking, and software TM.

Categories and Subject Descriptors

B.8.0 [**Hardware**]: Performance and Reliability—*general*; C.1.4 [**Computer Systems Organization**]: Processor Architectures—*parallel architectures*; D.1.3 [**Software**]: Programming Techniques—*concurrent programming, parallel programming*

General Terms

Design, Measurement, Performance

Keywords

Hardware Transactional Memories, Programming Model, Runtime System, Software Support

1. DELIVERING THE PROMISED TRANSACTIONAL MEMORY SIMPLICITY

Transactional memory (TM) was proposed more than twenty years ago as a hardware mechanism to enable atomic operations on an arbitrary set of memory locations [13, 20]. The target applications for TM are those with concurrent computations where it is not possible to determine, until runtime, which specific computations will result into conflicting accesses to memory.

Given the high cost of implementing TM in hardware, the research community developed several implementations of software transactional memory (STM) [7, 9, 18, 19] and conducted simulation-based studies of hardware transactional memory (HTM) [1, 2, 17]. An early implementation of HTM was never distributed commercially [6]. For the HTM by Azul, there is little public disclosure on the implementation and no performance study of the TM support [5]. The specification of a hardware extension for TM in the AMD64 architecture has yet to be released in hardware [4]. It is only recently that IBM [12] and Intel [14] disclosed that they are releasing implementations of HTM.

This paper makes three important contributions. First, it provides a detailed description of the BG/Q HTM implementation and quantifies its major sources of overheads. One of the main pain points of STMs is the high overhead incurred to start and commit a transaction and to instrument and monitor memory references inside a transaction [3]. While it is widely expected that such overheads be significantly reduced in an HTM, one of the surprising findings of this performance study is that, the BG/Q HTM overhead, while much smaller than that of STM's, is still non-trivial. The causes of HTM overheads are also very different from those of STM's. For instance, BG/Q TM maintains speculative states in the L2 cache. This allows for transactions with a large memory footprint, the price to pay, however, is the overhead, where the L1 cache is either bypassed during a transaction or flushed upon entry to a transaction. The loss of cache locality is the dominant cause of BG/Q TM overhead.

Second, the paper conducts a thorough evaluation of the STAMP benchmark suite [16] running on BG/Q TM and in comparison with sequential execution, OpenMP critical, and TinySTM [10]. By comparing the performance of alternative concurrency implementations of the same benchmark with respect to sequential execution baseline, we try to answer the question of how effective BG/Q TM is to improve performance. The performance study leads us to divide typical concurrent applications into three categories. There are applications that are suitable for BG/Q-style HTM, where significant performance improvements can be achieved with very low programming effort. Such applications usually use medium to large transactions that fit in the capacity of BG/Q HTM and exhibit low abort ratios. On the other hand, applications that scale well with conventional locking should use neither STM nor BG/Q TM as both incur larger single-thread overhead. Furthermore, applications using very small transactions but with abundant optimistic concurrency may be better suited for STM because the single-thread overhead of an STM system may be compensated by the additional scalability it enables.

Third, we describe how the best-effort HTM support in BG/Q can be complemented with a software stack that includes the kernel, the compiler, and the runtime system to deliver the simplicity of a TM programming model. The HTM support in BG/Q is best effort because some program-level transactions may never succeed in executing on BG/Q HTM due to the bounded capacity for transactional reads and writes. In terms of programmability, HTM is a clear win over STM. The latter often requires annotations and instrumentation of all codes that can potentially be invoked in a transactional execution. In terms of performance, there is also a noticeable programming difference between codes manually instrumented for STM and those using BG/Q TM. For example, the STM version of the STAMP benchmark is heavily privatized to minimize instrumented memory accesses, whereas the BG/Q TM version of the codes requires only block annotation of transactional codes. As a result, on the two benchmarks that trigger capacity overflow in a single-thread BG/Q TM execution, the STM version performs well and with extremely low overhead because the amount of instrumented states are dramatically reduced by manual instrumentation.

The rest of the paper is organized as follows. Section 2 describes the hardware support for transactional memory in BG/Q. Section 3 describes the TM programming model. And Section 4 describes the extension to the XL compiler, the runtime system, and the kernel to support the TM programming model. The performance study using the STAMP benchmark suite is presented in Section 5. We discuss related work in Section 6 and conclude in Section 7.

2. HARDWARE TRANSACTIONAL MEMORY IMPLEMENTATION IN BG/Q

In BG/Q, each compute chip has 16 A2 processor cores, each core can run four hardware Simultaneous Multi-Threaded (SMT) threads. A core has a dedicated 16K-byte level-1 (L1) cache that is 8-way set-associative with a cache line size of 64-byte and a 2K-byte prefetching buffer. All 16 cores share a 32M-byte level-2 (L2) cache with a cache line size of 128-byte.

As one of the first commercial implementations of HTM, BG/Q provides the following hardware mechanisms to support transactional execution:

- **Buffering of speculative states.** Stores made during a transactional execution constitute *speculative states*. In BG/Q, speculative states are buffered in the L2 cache and are only made visible (atomically) to other threads after a transaction commits.

- **Conflict detection.** Under the transactional execution mode, the hardware detects read-write, write-read, or write-write conflicts among concurrent transactions or when a transactional access is followed by a non-transactional write to the same address. When a conflict is detected, the hardware sends interrupts to transactional threads involved in the conflict. A special conflict register is flagged to record various hardware events that cause a transaction to fail.

2.1 Hardware Support for Transactional Execution in L2

BG/Q's hardware support for transactional execution is implemented primarily in the L2 cache, which serves as the point of coherence. The L2 cache is divided into 16 slices, where each slice is 16-way set-associative. To buffer speculative states, the *multi-versioned* L2 cache can store multiple versions of the same physical memory line, each version occupies a different L2 way. BG/Q uses a pre-existing core design and therefore there is no hardware modification to support transactional execution in L1.

Upon a transactional write, the L2 allocates a new way in the corresponding set for the write. A value stored by a transactional write is private to the thread. It is made visible to other threads when a transaction commits and is discarded upon a transaction abort.

In addition, the L2 directory records, for each access, whether it is read or written, and whether it is speculative. For speculative accesses, it also tracks which thread has read or written the line by recording the speculation ID used by the thread to activate speculation. This tracking provides the basic bookkeeping to detect conflicts among transactions and between transactional and non-transactional memory operations.

The hardware uses unique speculative IDs to associate a memory operation with a transaction. BG/Q provides 128 speculative IDs for transactions. If a program runs out of IDs then the start of a new transaction blocks until an ID becomes available. The L2 examines, at predetermined intervals, lines whose speculation ID has either been invalidated or committed. When all the lines associated with an invalidated ID are marked as invalid, or when lines associated with a committed ID are merged with the non-speculative state, the speculation ID is reclaimed and made available again. This process is called *ID scrubbing*. The interval between two starts of the scrubbing process is the *scrubbing interval*. The default scrubbing interval is 132 cycles but it can be altered by the runtime via a system call. Setting this interval too high may lead to the blocking of new transactions. Setting it too low may cause the scrubbing activity to interfere with the normal operation of the L2 cache.

The buffering of speculative states in the L2 requires cooperation from components of the memory subsystem that are closer to the pipeline than the L2, namely, the L1 cache. BG/Q supports two transactional execution modes for proper interaction between the L1, the L1 prefetcher (L1P) and the L2, each with a different performance consideration. From herein L1 refers to both L1 and L1P unless otherwise stated. The main difference between the two modes is in how the L1 cache keeps a speculative thread's writes invisible to the other three SMT threads sharing the same L1.

- **Short-running mode (via L1-bypass).** In this mode, when a TM thread stores a speculative value, the core evicts the line from the L1. Subsequent loads from the same thread have to retrieve the value from that point on from L2. If the L2 stores multiple values for the same address, the L2 returns the thread-specific data along with a flag that instructs the core to place the data into the register of the requesting thread, but to not store the line in the L1 cache. In addition, for any transactional load served from the L1, the L2 is notified of the load via an L1 notification. The notification from L1 to L2 goes out through the store queue.

- **Long-running mode (via TLB aliasing).** In this mode, speculative states can be kept in the L1 cache. The L1 cache can store up to 5 versions, 4 transactional ones for each of the 4 SMT threads, and one non-transactional. To achieve this, the software creates an illusion of versioned address space via Translation Lookaside Buffer (TLB) aliasing. For each memory reference by a speculative thread some bits of the physical address in the TLB are used to create an aliased physical address by the Memory Management Unit (MMU). Therefore, the same virtual address may be translated to 4 different physical addresses for each of the 4 SMT TM threads at the L1 level. However, as the load or store exits the core, the bits in the physical address that are used to create the alias illusion are masked out because the L2 maintains the multi-version through the bookkeeping of speculation ID. In this mode the L1 cache is invalidated upon entering the transaction because there is no L1 notification to the L2 on an L1 hit. The invalidation of the L1 cache makes all first TM accesses to a memory location visible to the L2 as an L1 load miss.

These two modes are designed to exploit different locality patterns. By default, an application runs under the long running mode. One can specify an environment variable to enable the short-running mode before starting an application. The main drawback of the short-running mode is that it nullifies the benefit of the L1 cache for read-after-write access patterns within a transaction. Thus it is best suited for short-running transactions with few memory accesses. The long-running mode, on the other hand, preserves temporal and spatial locality within a transaction, but, by invalidating L1 at the start of a transaction, prevents reuse between code that run before entering the transaction and code that run within the transaction or after the transaction ends. Thus, this mode is best suited for long-running transactions with plenty of intra-transaction locality.

2.2 Causes of Transactional Execution Failures

BG/Q hardware supports bounded, best-effort, transactional execution. While the entire instruction set is allowed in transactional execution, a transaction may fail in the following scenarios:

- **Transactional conflicts** are detected by the hardware at the L2 cache level as described earlier. In the short-running mode conflicts are detected at a granularity of 8 bytes if no more than two threads access the same cache line, or 64 bytes otherwise. In the long-running mode the granularity is 64 bytes and can degrade depending on the amount of prefetching done by a speculative thread.
- **Capacity overflow** cause a transaction to fail when the L2 cache cannot allocate a new way for a speculative store. By default, the L2 guarantees 10 ways to be used for speculative storage without an eviction. Therefore, up to 20M-bytes (32M*10/16) of speculative state can be stored in the L2. A set may contain more than 10 speculative ways if the speculative ways have not been evicted by the Least Recently Used (LRU) replacement policy. In practice, however, capacity failures may occur at a much smaller speculative state footprint by exhausting the way limitation within a set.
- **Jail mode violation (JMV)** occur when the transaction performs *irrevocable actions*, that is, operations whose side-effects cannot be reversed, such as writes to device I/O address space. Irrevocable actions are detected by the kernel under a special mode called the *jail mode*, which will send a JMV interrupt to the owner thread of the event.

3. TRANSACTIONAL MEMORY (TM) PROGRAMMING MODEL

BG/Q provides a simple TM programming model based on an abstraction called *transactions*. Transactions are single-entry/single-exit code blocks denoted by `#pragma tm_atomic` annotations. Any computation is allowed in a transaction. The only constraint is that the boundary of a transaction must be statically determinable in order for the compiler to insert proper code to end a transaction. As a result, control-flow constructs that may exit a transactional block may result in a compile- or run-time error. Similarly, exceptions thrown by a transaction are unsupported.

The semantics of a transaction is similar to that of a critical section or that of relaxed transactions as defined in [11]. In a multi-threaded execution, transactions appear to execute sequentially in some total order with respect to other transactions. Specifically, operations inside a transaction appear not to interleave with any operation from other (concurrent) transactions. The specification of transactional code region is orthogonal to the threading model such as the use of OpenMP or Pthreads.

Two transactions are nested if one transaction is entirely inside the other transaction. Nested transactions in BG/Q are *flattened*: the entire nest commits at the end of the outermost level of nesting. A failed nested transaction rolls back to the beginning of the outermost nesting level. The nesting support is implemented purely in software, specifically in the TM runtime.

```
#pragma tm_atomic
{
    a[b[i]] += c[i];
}
```

Figure 1: Transaction in kmeans expressed in BG/Q TM annotation.

Figure 1 shows a transaction code expressed by BG/Q TM annotations. This simple programming interface may enclose complex and large transaction regions.

4. SOFTWARE SUPPORT FOR TM PROGRAMMING MODEL

While the BG/Q HTM is bounded and can fail a transactional execution in various ways, a transaction, as defined by the programming model, can be arbitrarily large and is guaranteed to eventually succeed. The TM software stack, developed to bridge the gap between the TM programming model and the TM hardware implementation, includes a transactional memory run-time system and extensions to the kernel and the compiler.

The main component of the TM software stack is the TM runtime. The description of the state transition flow managed by the TM runtime to execute a transaction will refer to the letters that appear in Figure 2.

4.1 Saving and Restoring of Register Context

In BG/Q TM, register checkpointing is done by the software in ⓐ. A straightforward way to save and restore the register context is to use the system `setjmp` and `longjmp` routines [21]. The system `setjmp` routine typically saves all registers into the context buffer and the corresponding `longjmp` routine restores the context by restoring all of these registers. Since the `setjmp` overhead is incurred every time a transaction is entered, the context-save overhead can be significant for small transactions. Therefore, the BG/Q runtime is specially optimized to reduce this overhead. Since rolling back a transaction is equivalent to performing a `longjmp` to the start of the transaction, three registers need to be restored in order to perform the `longjmp` and to establish the minimal context. The registers are the current value of the stack pointer, the global offset table (GOT) pointer – to a table that holds addresses for position-independent code, and a pointer to the first instruction of the register-restore code, which is placed immediately before the start of the transaction. These three registers, which comprise the minimal context information, are passed to the runtime and the runtime passes them down to the kernel because both the runtime and the kernel can rollback a transaction. The analysis to determine which other registers require saving and restoring is left to the compiler. The compiler uses live-range analysis to determine the set of live registers that are modified inside the transaction, to identify the registers that need to be saved and restored.

4.2 Managing Transaction Abort and Retry

The TM runtime activates a hardware transactional execution by writing to a memory-mapped I/O location. When the execution reaches the end of the transaction, it enters the TM runtime routine that handles transaction commit in ⓓ. The TM runtime attempts to commit the transaction. If the commit fails, the transaction is retried. If commit fails for

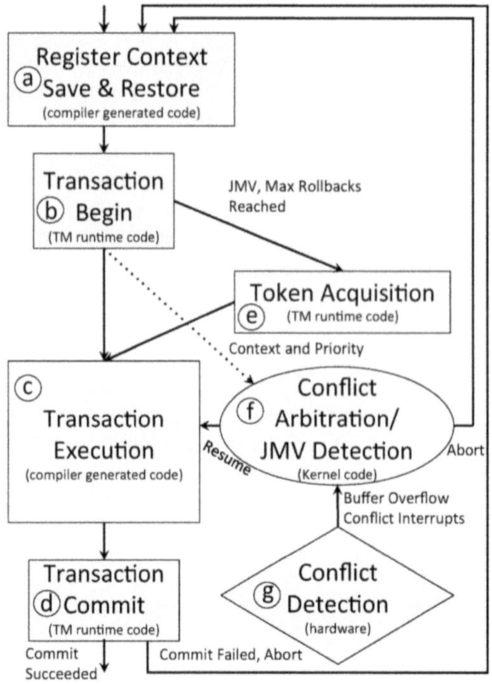

Figure 2: Transactional Memory Execution Overview

a transaction T_A because of conflict with a transaction T_B, the runtime invalidates the speculation ID associated with T_A causing the hardware to clear the conflict register of T_B. Therefore, T_B now has a chance to commit successfully.

Capacity overflow and JMV prevent the thread from further execution, thus the transaction failure must be handled immediately. For JMV, the kernel invalidates the current transaction and invokes the restart handler. The restart handler *sends* the thread back to the start of the failing transaction.

For capacity overflow, the hardware invalidates the transaction and an interrupt is triggered in ⓖ. For conflict-induced transactional failures, the runtime can configure the hardware to trigger a conflict interrupt for *eager* conflict detection in ⓖ as well. This is the default setting of the runtime. Alternatively, conflict interrupts can be suppressed and conflicts are then handled *lazily* when the execution reaches the end of the transaction. A transactional failure due to capacity overflow is retried in the same way as conflict-induced failures because capacity overflow may be a transient failure.

In the eager detection scheme, once the hardware triggers an interrupt, the interrupt handler in the kernel performs *conflict arbitration* by comparing the starting time of the conflicting threads and favours the survival of an older thread. When a transaction is started, the current time is recorded through a read of the timebase register and passed by the runtime to the kernel, which is used as the priority value during conflict resolution.

4.3 Sandboxing of Speculative Execution

System resources must be protected from being corrupted by a transaction that may later get aborted. BG/Q uses a *sandbox*, called *jail mode* to confine transactional executions and prevent speculative accesses to memory-mapped I/O space. These accesses include the ones for starting and stopping hardware transactional execution and the Direct-Memory Access (DMA) engine start operation. In jail mode, transactional accesses to protected TLB entries generate an access-violation exception called *Jail-Mode Violation* detected in ⓕ. Jail mode is entered and exited via system calls inside the `tm_begin` and `tm_end` runtime routines. By default, all transactions are executed in jail mode.

A second aspect of BG/Q sandboxing, which is orthogonal to the jail-mode, is that the interrupt handler in the kernel is, by default, capable of checking whether the triggering thread is speculative or not. System-level side effects of speculative execution, such as TLB misses, divide-by-zero and signals triggered by program fault cause the interrupt handler to invalidate the current speculation and invoke the restart handler.

4.4 Ensuring Forward Progress via Irrevocable Mode

The TM programming model supports transactions of arbitrary size and with any computation including irrevocable ones. However, not all transactions expressed by the programming model can execute successfully by the underlying best-effort HTM. Therefore, one main functionality of the TM software stack is to ensure that a transaction eventually succeeds.

Such guarantee is provided by judiciously retrying failed transactions in a special mode called the *irrevocable mode*. Under the irrevocable mode, a transaction executes non-speculatively and can no longer be rolled back. To execute in the irrevocable mode, a thread must acquire the *irrevocable token*, that is associated with all `tm_atomic` blocks in the program. Interference of the irrevocable token with user-level locking may cause deadlock. Token acquisition in ⓔ is implemented using special BGQ L2 atomics. In essence, transactions executing under the irrevocable mode are serialized and the `tm_atomic` blocks behave like unnamed critical sections. It is however possible that there are concurrent speculative transactions and a transaction running in the irrevocable mode at the same time.

When a hardware transactional execution failure or a JMV exception occurs in ⓓ, the TM runtime determines how to retry the transaction. When the cause of a hardware transaction failure is transient, for example, due to a conflict, the TM runtime may retry transactional execution a few times before switching to the irrevocable mode. However, when a transactional execution failure is likely persistent, for example, due to a JMV, the TM runtime retries the transaction in the irrevocable mode.

4.5 Runtime Adaptation

The runtime employs a simple adaption scheme: it retries a failing transaction a fixed number of times before switching into irrevocable mode. After completion of the transaction in irrevocable mode, the runtime computes the serialization ratio of the executing thread. If the serialization ratio is above a certain threshold, the runtime records this transaction into a hash table. This hash table tracks *problematic* transactions. Once a transaction is entered into the hash table, its next execution will be speculative. Upon failing, it immediately switches into the irrevocable mode.

Benchmark	Running Options
bayes	-v32 -r4096 -n10 -p40 -i2 -e8 -s1
genome	-g16384 -s64 -n16777216
intruder	-a10 -l128 -n262144 -s1
kmeans_low	-m40 -n40 -t0.00001 -i ⟨input⟩[1]
kmeans_high	-m15 -n15 -t0.00001 -i ⟨input⟩[1]
labyrinth	-i inputs/random-x512-y512-z7-n512.txt
ssca2	-s20 -i1.0 -u1.0 -l3 -p3
vacation_low	-n2 -q90 -u98 -r1048576 -t4194304
vacation_high	-n4 -q60 -u90 -r1048576 -t4194304
yada	-a15 -i inputs/ttimeu1000000.2

Table 1: STAMP Benchmark Options

This scheme allows a *problematic* transaction to have a single rollback. The amount of time that a transaction remains in the hash table is controlled via a runtime parameter.

5. EXPERIMENTAL RESULTS

This evaluation runs the STAMP benchmark suite [16] on a single 16-core, 1.6 GHz, compute node of a production BG/Q machine. We choose STAMP as our evaluation target because it is most widely used TM benchmark with largely coarse-grain transactions. The binaries are compiled by a prototype version of the IBM XL C/C++ compiler with the option of `-O3 -qhot -qsmp=omp -qtm`. The study reports the mean of five runs with an error bar. In the absence of more information, the measurements are assumed to be normally distributed. Thus, the length of the error bar is four standard deviations, two above and two below the mean, to approximate 95% confidence.

The baseline for speedups is always a sequential, non-threaded, version of the STAMP benchmark run with the 1-thread input. Table 1 shows that the large input, which is intended for runs on real hardware, is used. The comparison against Software Transactional Memories (STMs) uses TinySTM 1.0.3 [9].

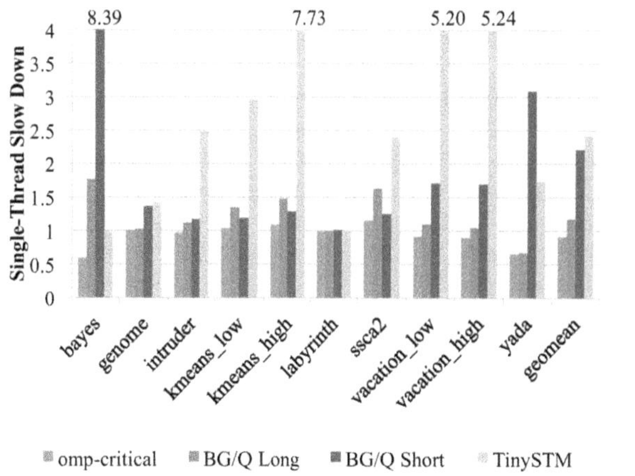

Figure 3: Relative execution time of OMP-Critical, BG/Q TM, and TinySTM over sequential version.

[1]Input for `kmeans` is `inputs/random-n65536-d32-c16.txt`.

5.1 Single-thread TM performance

This section evaluates the overhead of TM execution running on a single-thread. Figure 3 shows the slow down of single-thread BG/Q TM under the short- and long-running modes relative to that of the sequential code. There is no noticeable run-to-run variations in performance for this experiment. For BG/Q TM, `TM_BEGIN` and `TM_END` macros of the STAMP benchmarks are replaced by BG/Q pragma annotation. Likewise, for `omp-critical`, the macros are replaced by `omp critical` pragma. TinySTM, uses the STM version of the benchmarks with extensive privatization to minimize instrumented states. Table 2 shows the number of L1 misses per 100 instructions as well as instruction path lengths, which is the number of instructions executed, collected by hardware performance monitor.

The long-running mode incurs less overhead than the short-running mode for all STAMP benchmarks except for `ssca2` and `kmeans`, which have very small transactions (see Section 5.1.1).

Even using the best performing mode for each application, BG/Q TM still incurs noticeable overhead over the sequential version. The overhead comes primarily from increases in L1 cache misses, but, for some benchmarks, also from path length increases.

The relative speedup of the long-running mode over the sequential version in some benchmarks is the artifact of outlining `OMP` regions, which leads to reduced register pressure and allows the compiler to generate better code. Similar single-thread speedups are also observed on some `omp-critical` versions of the benchmarks.

The rest of the section explains in details the root causes of BG/Q TM overhead.

5.1.1 Cache performance penalty

One of the most dominant BG/Q TM runtime overhead is caused by the loss of L1 cache support due to the L1 flush and bypass needed for the bookkeeping of transactional state in L2. This observation is born by the number of L1 cache misses in short- and long-running modes relative to that of the sequential version. For instance, the three-fold slowdown for `yada` (Figure 3) in short-running mode is caused by 5 times as many L1 misses as the sequential version (Table 2). Similarly, the eight-fold slowdown for `bayes` is caused mainly by the 12× increase in L1 misses. Note that the L2 cache and L1P buffer load latencies are 13x and 5x higher than L1 load latency.

Under the long-running mode, L1 is flushed upon entering the transaction thus destroying any reuse between code before the transaction and code after the transaction. The locality penalty can be severe for small transactions with few memory accesses or little reuse. As shown in Table 2, the long-running mode suffers less L1 misses than the short-running mode for all but `ssca2` and `kmeans`. For `ssca2`, the short-running mode works well because the transactions mostly implement single-address atomic updates. For `kmeans`, both short- and long-running mode cause significant increase in the number of L1 misses because locality exists both within a transaction and across transactional boundaries.

While the long-running mode preserves more locality than the short-running mode for applications with not-so-small transactions, we still observe 15% to 38% increase in L1 misses compared to the sequential version.

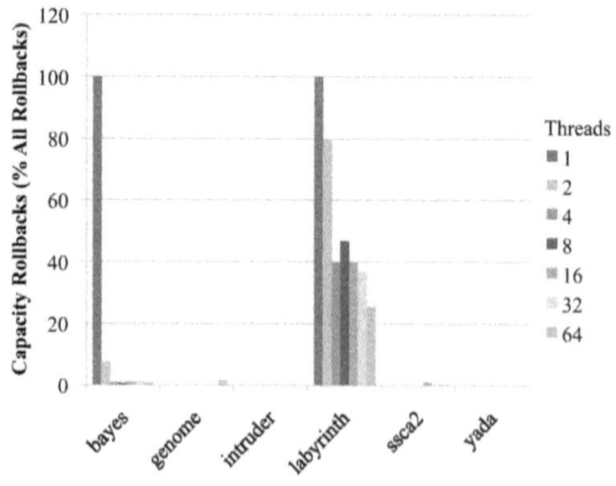

Figure 4: Percentage of rollbacks caused by capacity overflow

5.1.2 Capacity overflow

Compared to STMs, one main disadvantage of a best-effort HTM is the bounded size of speculative states. Figure 4 shows the percentage of rollbacks caused by capacity overflow in relation to the total number of rollbacks experienced by each benchmark for various number of threads. Two of the STAMP benchmarks experience capacity overflow under single-thread TM execution. In `labyrinth`, capacity overflow is persistently triggered in one of its two main transactions, which unconditionally copies a global grid of 14M bytes inside the transaction. As a result, the most important transactions of `labyrinth` (accounting for 50% transactions) are executed in the irrevocable mode, resulting in a TM performance similar to `omp-critical`. For `bayes`, only 3% of the transactions trigger capacity overflow. However, due to the low serialization ratio, each failed transaction is retried 10 times before switching to the irrevocable mode, resulting in a significant (55%) increase in path length. This problem is not observed on `labyrinth` because the runtime adaptation is able to quickly limit the number of retries for consecutively failed transactions.

As shown in Figure 4, except for `labyrinth` and `bayes` which are known to exhibit large transactional footprint, capacity overflow on BG/Q is insignificant for most of the STAMP benchmark. At thread-counts above 16, `genome`, `intruder`, `ssca2` and `yada` experience some capacity overflow because of the shared speculative state, however never more than 2% of transaction rollbacks are caused by capacity overflow. The percent of executed transactions which experience capacity overflow in `bayes` and `labyrinth` decreases as the thread count increases because transactional conflicts become the leading cause of aborts.

5.1.3 Transaction enter and exit overhead

The basic overhead of entering and exiting a transaction comes from several sources: 1) saving of register contexts, 2) obtaining a spec ID, 3) the latency to write to memory-mapped I/O to start or commit a transaction, 4) the system calls to turn on and off kernel sandboxing, 5) additional runtime bookkeeping.

We measured the single-thread overhead of entering and

Benchmark	# L1 misses per 100 instr. (thread=1)			Instr. path length relative to serial (thread=1)		
	sequential	BG/Q Short	BG/Q Long	omp critical	BG/Q Short	BGQ Long
bayes	0.6	8.1	0.7	87 %	155 %	156 %
genome	0.6	1.6	0.7	99 %	101 %	101 %
intruder	0.8	1.5	1.3	97 %	102 %	104 %
kmeans_low	0.1	0.3	2.7	101 %	105 %	106 %
kmeans_high	0.1	0.7	3.2	103 %	110 %	113 %
labyrinth	0.9	1.0	1.2	100 %	100 %	101 %
ssca2	1.0	0.7	1.3	96 %	109 %	111 %
vacation_low	1.5	6.2	2.4	88 %	92 %	93 %
vacation_high	1.7	7.0	2.4	88 %	91 %	92 %
yada	1.5	7.2	0.8	101 %	90 %	90 %

Table 2: Hardware performance monitor stats for the STAMP benchmarks.

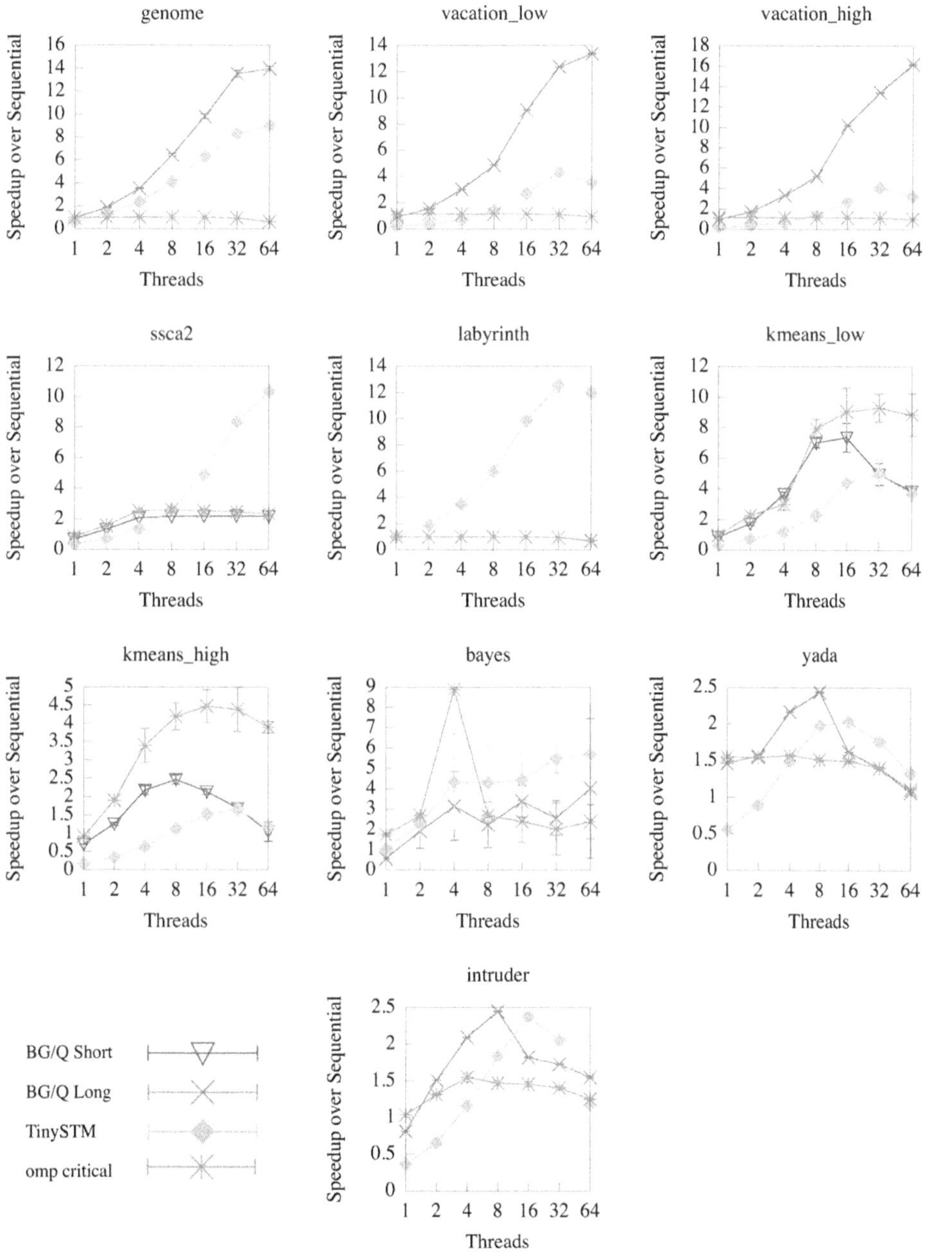

Figure 5: Speedup over sequential for upto 64 threads.

exiting a transaction that implements a single atomic update. While this overhead for both BG/Q TM and TinySTM is in the order of hundreds of cycles, the overhead for BG/Q TM is smaller, about 44% of the TinySTM overhead for short-running mode, and 76% for long-running mode. Long-running mode has higher overhead because accesses to internal TM run-time data structures before and after transaction execution also suffer from L1 misses due to the L1 cache invalidation.

The transaction enter and exit overhead is also reflected in increases of instruction path length. As shown in Table 2, `ssca2` and `kmeans` experience the most path length increase under BG/Q TM (11% for Ĕscans) due to the small size of its transactions.

5.2 HTM Scalability

Figure 5 shows the speedup of BG/Q TM relative to the sequential code for up to 64 threads. The rest of the experiments use long-running mode for all STAMP benchmarks except for `kmeans` and `ssca2` because short-running mode is only beneficial for very small transactions. In `kmeans` short-running mode can be up to 50% faster then long-running mode. In the experiments, each thread is bound to a different core on a round-robin breadth-first fashion.

Table 3 shows two metrics computed from transaction-execution statistics collected by the TM runtime:

- *Serialization ratio* is the percentage of committed transactions that were executed in the irrevocable mode. It is an indicator of the degree of concurrency in the TM execution.
- *Abort ratio* is the percentage of executed transactions that are aborted. It indicates the amount of wasted computation in the TM execution.

Both metrics reflect the combined effects of optimistic concurrency inherent to the program, hardware conflict detection granularity, and the retry adaptation of the TM runtime. A generally preferred scenario for TM is for an application to have both low serialization ratio and low abort ratio. A TM execution with both high serialization and high abort ratio is likely to show low scalability and even absolute performance slowdown. The lower abort ratio at higher number of threads, in Table 3, for some benchmarks (`labyrinth`, `kmeans`, and `vacation`) is counter intuitive. However, aborts caused by conflicts are highly dependent on the start and commit timing for the various transactions and therefore changing the number of threads may change this ratio in unexpected ways.

We first look at the relative speedup of TM execution and classify the benchmarks into several categories:

- **Effective HTM.** `Genome` and `vacation` exhibit good speedup and low serialization ratio. Note that performance boost beyond 16 threads comes from SMT threads multiplexing on the processor pipeline and hiding in-order processor stalls.
- **Spec-ID bottleneck.** Despite zero abort and serialization ratios, `ssca2` scales only up to 4 threads. This is because short and frequent transactions lead the system to quickly run out of spec-IDs, which blocks on spec-ID request until after some spec-IDs are recycled. BG/Q TM has 128 spec IDs that need to be recycled, based on the scrub interval, before being reassigned to new transactions. Figure 6 shows a sensitivity study on the impact of scrub interval on the performance of `ssca2`. With a scrub setting above 34, `ssca2` runs out of IDs and transactions are blocked waiting for an ID. And the scalability improves with lower intervals.

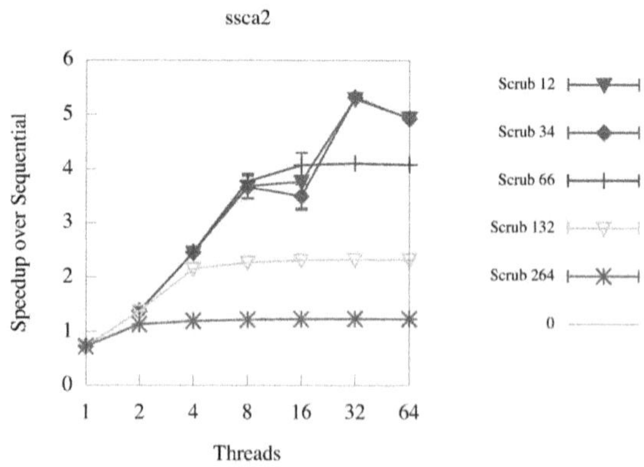

Figure 6: Effect of varying scrub intervals for ssca2.

- **Contention bottleneck.** For `yada`, `bayes`, `intruder`, and `kmeans`, high serialization ratio at higher thread counts is the main bottleneck for scalability. The high serialization ratio is directly caused by the significant increase in aborts. Note that `bayes` exhibits high variability in the execution time because its termination condition depends on the order of its transactions commit.
- **Capacity bottleneck.** Due to the capacity problem (see Section 5.1.2), the main transactions of `labyrinth` are always executed in irrevocable mode and serialized with the irrevocable token. In the end, HTM execution exhibits no scaling and performs very close to naive locking.

5.3 Comparing against OMP-Critical and TinySTM

Using OMP critical (i.e. a big-lock) and using an STM represent the two end points of the spectrum of concurrency implementation. Big-locks have the lowest single-thread overhead, but are more likely to become a locking bottleneck. While STM has the best relative scaling (with respect to single-thread STM), but often exhibits the worst single-thread overhead.

The BG/Q TM fits in between these two ends both in terms of single-thread overhead and relative scalability. This is exactly what we observe. As shown in Figure 5 the scalability curves of `omp-critical` are mostly flat except for `kmeans` which suffers from little contention on a single big lock. When `omp-critical` scales (`kmeans`), it performs the best among the three because it has the lowest overhead. TinySTM, on the other hand, exhibits the best relative scalability with respect to single-thread TinySTM. Comparing BG/Q TM against TinySTM, we make the following observations:

Benchmark	Serialization ratio (# threads)							Abort ratio (# threads)						
	1	2	4	8	16	32	64	1	2	4	8	16	32	64
bayes	3 %	4 %	53 %	64 %	85 %	84 %	84 %	23 %	39 %	50 %	55 %	62 %	73 %	73 %
genome	0 %	0 %	0 %	0 %	1 %	0 %	1 %	0 %	0 %	4 %	5 %	13 %	13 %	18 %
intruder	0 %	0 %	1 %	19 %	58 %	63 %	66 %	0 %	3 %	24 %	53 %	56 %	59 %	59 %
kmeans_low	0 %	0 %	0 %	1 %	7 %	19 %	82 %	0 %	0 %	3 %	21 %	59 %	65 %	59 %
kmeans_high	0 %	0 %	2 %	11 %	62 %	81 %	88 %	0 %	1 %	26 %	53 %	57 %	58 %	57 %
labyrinth	50 %	50 %	50 %	72 %	89 %	94 %	89 %	34 %	55 %	68 %	59 %	59 %	62 %	67 %
ssca2	0 %	0 %	0 %	0 %	0 %	0 %	0 %	0 %	0 %	0 %	0 %	0 %	0 %	0 %
vacation_low	0 %	0 %	0 %	0 %	0 %	0 %	0 %	0 %	15 %	8 %	8 %	17 %	26 %	20 %
vacation_high	0 %	0 %	0 %	0 %	0 %	0 %	0 %	0 %	12 %	6 %	8 %	14 %	28 %	22 %
yada	0 %	5 %	7 %	11 %	41 %	53 %	53 %	0 %	39 %	43 %	49 %	49 %	52 %	52 %

Table 3: Percentage of irrevocable and aborted transactions in BG/Q TM execution.

- **Effective HTM.** For `genome` and `vacation`, BG/Q TM has both a steeper and a longer ascending curve than TinySTM does. This is because, for these benchmarks, BG/Q TM does not suffer from any HTM-specific scaling bottlenecks. In addition, the lower overhead of BG/Q TM likely reduces the window of overlap among concurrent transactions.

- **Spec-ID and capacity bottleneck.** For `ssca2` and `labyrinth`, BG/Q TM peaks much earlier than TinySTM due to HTM-specific scaling bottlenecks.

- **Effective STM via privatization.** The good scaling of `labyrinth` and `bayes` on TinySTM is the result of a STM programming style that relies heavily on privatization and manual instrumentation. On the only two benchmarks with capacity overflow during a single-thread BG/Q TM execution, the STM codes incur no single-thread overhead because instrumented states are aggressively reduced to a tiny fraction of the actual footprint of the transactions.

- **Contention bottleneck.** For the rest of the benchmarks, BG/Q TM has a steeper ascending curve initially, but often peaks at a lower thread count and descends more rapidly afterwards in comparison to TinySTM. This may be explained by the bounded hardware implementation and the coarser granularity of conflict detection in BG/Q TM.

6. RELATED WORK

Despite of many HTM proposals in the literature, only two other real HTM implementations exist today, including the Rock processor [8] and the Vega Azul system [5]. While all three are best-effort HTMs, their design points differ drastically. Table 4 compares the key characteristics of the three systems in detail. The recently announced Intel's Haswell implementation of TSX is not included in Table 4 because that level of information is not yet available.

Both Rock HTM and Vega from Azul have small speculative buffers, compared to BG/Q's 20Mbytes of speculative states. Rock imposes many restrictions on what operations can happen in a transaction excluding function calls, divide, and exceptions. Rock also restricts the set of registers that functions may save/restore to enable the use of save/restore instructions that use register windows [8]. In contrast, in BG/Q, the entire instruction set architecture is supported within a transaction and register save/restore are a responsibility of the compiler and never cause transaction failure.

HTM	BG/Q	Rock	Azul
Buffer capacity	20MB	32 lines	16 KB
Speculative buffer	L2	L2 cache	L1
Register save/restore	no	yes	no
Unsupported ISA	none	div, call, sync	none
Conflict detection	8-64B	n/a	32B
User-level abort	no	n/a	yes

Table 4: Basic features of real HTM implementations.

The method presented in this paper to build a software system to offer guarantee of forward progress on top of a best-effort HTM is an elegant solution that does not require that TM programmers provide an alternative code sequence for transaction rollbacks. Similar methods have been used before [5, 8] and should be useful for upcoming HTM systems [14, 15].

The TM system in Azul deals with more expensive transaction entry/exit operations by restricting speculation to contended locks that successfully speculate most of the time. Azul also avoids speculation on rollbacks. A transaction that has failed once is always executed non-speculatively. This is a contrast to the adaptive retry system described in this paper.

7. CONCLUSION

This detailed performance study of one of the first commercially available HTM systems has some surprising findings. Even though the single-thread overhead is reduced in comparison with STM implementations, it is still significant. The use of L2 to support TMs is essential to enable a sufficiently large speculative state. However, for many TM applications recovering the lower latency of L1 for reuse inside a transaction, through the use of long running mode in BG/Q, is critical to achieve performance. An end-to-end solution that delivers a programming model that supports the entire ISA delivers the simplicity promised by TMs.

Acknowledgments

The BG/Q project has been supported and partially funded by Argonne National Laboratory and the Lawrence Livermore National Laboratory on behalf of the U.S. Department of Energy, under Lawrence Livermore National Laboratory subcontract no. B554331. The evaluation study reported in this paper was partially funded by the the IBM Toronto Centre for Advanced Studies and by grants from the Natural Sciences and Engineering Research Council of Canada. Thanks to Wang Chen for diligently managing the release of this paper through IBM legal process.

Trademarks

8. REFERENCES

[1] J. Bobba, K. Moore, H. Volos, L. Yen, M. D. Hill, M. M. Swift, and D. A. Wood. Performance pathologies in hardware transactional memory. In *International Conference on Computer Architecture (ISCA)*, pages 81–91, San Diego, CA, USA, 2007.

[2] C. C. S. Ananian, K. Asanovic, B. Kuszmaul, C. Leiserson, and S. Lie. Unbounded transactional memory. In *High-Performance Computer Architecture (HPCA)*, pages 316–327, San Francisco, CA, USA, February 2005.

[3] C. Cascaval, C. Blundell, M. Michael, H. W. Cain, P. Wu, S. Chiras, and S. Chatterjee. Software transactional memory: Why is it only a research toy? *Communications of the Association for Computing Machinery*, 51(11):40–46, November 2008.

[4] J. Chung, L. Yen, S. Diestelhorst, M. Pohlack, M. Hohmuth, D. Christie, and D. Grossman. ASF: AMD64 extension for lock-free data structures and transactional memory. In *Intern. Symposium on Microarchitecture (MICRO)*, pages 39–50, Atlanta, GA, USA, December 2010.

[5] C. Click. Azul's experiences with hardware transactional memory. In *HP Labs' Bay Area Workshop on Transactional Memory*, 2009.

[6] S. C. R. Cypher, M. Ekman, M. Karlsson, A. Landin, S. Yip, H. Zeffer, and M. Tremblay. Simultaneous speculative threading: a novel pipeline architecture implemented in sun's rock processor. In *International Conference on Computer Architecture (ISCA)*, pages 484–495, Austin, TX, USA, 2009.

[7] L. Dalessandro, M. F. Spear, and M. L. Scott. NOrec: Streamlining STM by abolishing ownership records. In *Principles and practice of parallel programming*, pages 67–78, Bangalore, India, January 2010.

[8] D. Dice, Y. Lev, M. Moir, and D. Nussbaum. Early experience with a commercial hardware transactional memory implementation. In *Architectural Support for Programming Languages and Operating Systems (ASPLOS)*, pages 157–168, Washington, DC, USA, March 2009.

[9] P. Felber, C. Fetzer, P. Marlier, and T. Riegel. Time-based software transactional memory. *IEEE Transactions on Parallel and Distributed Systems*, 21(12):1793–1807, December 2010.

[10] P. Felber, C. Fetzer, and T. Riegel. Dynamic performance tuning of word-based software transactional memory. In *Principles and practice of parallel programming*, pages 237–246, Salt Lake City, UT, USA, February 2008.

[11] T. M. S. D. Group. Draft specification of transactional language constructs for C++ (version 1.1), 2012.

[12] R. Haring, M. Ohmacht, T. Fox, M. Gschwind, D. Satterfield, K. Sugavanam, P. Coteus, P. Heidelberger, M. Blumrich, R. Wisniewski, A. Gara, G.-T. Chiu, P. Boyle, N. Chist, and C. Kim. The ibm blue gene/q compute chip. *IEEE Micro*, 32(2):48–60, March-April 2012.

[13] M. Herlihy and J. E. Moss. Transactional memory: Architectural support for lock-free data structures. In *International Conference on Computer Architecture (ISCA)*, pages 289–300, San Diego, CA, USA, May 1993.

[14] Intel Corporation. *Intel Architecture Instruction Set Extensions Programming Reference*, 319433-012 edition, February 2012.

[15] D. Kanter. Analysis of Haswell's transactional memory. http://www.realworldtech.com/page.cfm?ArticleID=RWT021512050738&p=1, February 2012. Real World Technologies.

[16] C. C. Minh, J. Chung, C.Kozyrakis, and K. Olukotun. STAMP: Stanford transactional applications for multi-processing. In *International Symposium on Workload Characterization (IISWC)*, pages 35–46, Seattle, WA, USA, September 2008.

[17] C. C. Minh, M. Trautmann, J. Chung, A. McDonald, N. Bronson, J. Casper, C. Kozyrakis, and K. Olukotun. An effective hybrid transactional memory system with strong isolation guarantees. In *International Conference on Computer Architecture (ISCA)*, pages 69–80, San Diego, CA, USA, 2007.

[18] B. Saha, A.-R. Adl-Tabatabai, R. L. Hudson, C. C. Minh, and B. Hertzberg. McRT-STM: A high performance software transactional memory system for a multi-core runtime. In *Principles and practice of parallel programming*, pages 187–197, New York, NY, USA, January 2006.

[19] M. F. Spear, M. M. Michael, and C. von Praun. RingSTM: scalable transactions with a single atomic instruction. In *ACM Symp. on Parallelism in Algorithms and Architectures (SPAA)*, pages 275–284, Munich, Germany, June 2008.

[20] J. M. Stone, H. S. Stone, P. Heidelberger, and J. Turek. Multiple reservations and the Oklahoma update. *IEEE Parallel & Distributed Technology (PDT)*, 1(4):58–71, November 193.

[21] C. Wang, W.-Y. Chen, Y. Wu, B. Saha, and A.-R. Adl-Tabataba. Code generation and optimization for transactional memory constructs in an unmanaged language. In *Code Generation and Optimization (CGO)*, pages 34–48, San Jose, CA, USA, March 2007.

Making Data Prefetch Smarter: Adaptive Prefetching on POWER7

Víctor Jiménez
Barcelona Supercomputing Center
Barcelona, Spain
victor.javier@bsc.es

Roberto Gioiosa*
Pacific Northwest National Laboratory
Richland, WA, USA
roberto.gioiosa@pnnl.gov

Francisco J. Cazorla
Spanish National Research Council and Barcelona Supercomputing Center
Barcelona, Spain
francisco.cazorla@bsc.es

Alper Buyuktosunoglu
IBM T. J. Watson Research Center
Yorktown Heights, NY, USA
alperb@us.ibm.com

Pradip Bose
IBM T. J. Watson Research Center
Yorktown Heights, NY, USA
pbose@us.ibm.com

Francis P. O'Connell
IBM Systems and Technology Group
Austin, TX, USA
oconnell@us.ibm.com

ABSTRACT

Hardware data prefetch engines are integral parts of many general purpose server-class microprocessors in the field today. Some prefetch engines allow the user to change some of their parameters. The prefetcher, however, is usually enabled in a default configuration during system bring-up and dynamic reconfiguration of the prefetch engine is not an autonomic feature of current machines. Conceptually, however, it is easy to infer that commonly used prefetch algorithms, when applied in a fixed mode will not help performance in many cases. In fact, they may actually degrade performance due to useless bus bandwidth consumption and cache pollution. In this paper, we present an adaptive prefetch scheme that dynamically modifies the prefetch settings in order to adapt to the workload requirements. We implement and evaluate adaptive prefetching in the context of an existing, commercial processor, namely the IBM POWER7. Our adaptive prefetch mechanism improves performance with respect to the default prefetch setting up to 2.7X and 30% for single-threaded and multiprogrammed workloads, respectively.

Categories and Subject Descriptors

C.4 [**Performance of Systems**]: Design studies; D.2.8 [**Software Engineering**]: Metrics—*Performance measures*; B.3.m [**Memory Structures**]: Miscellaneous

General Terms

Algorithms, Measurement, Performance

Keywords

Adaptive system, prefetching, performance

1. INTRODUCTION

Hardware data prefetch is a well-known technique to help alleviate the so-called *memory wall* problem [31]. Many general purpose server-class microprocessors in the field today rely on data prefetch engines to improve performance for memory-intensive workloads. Some prefetch engines allow the user to change some of their parameters. In commercial systems, however, the hardware prefetcher is typically enabled in a default configuration during system bring-up, and dynamic reconfiguration of the prefetch engine is not an autonomic feature of current machines. Nonetheless, commonly used prefetch algorithms, when applied in a fixed, non-adaptive mode will not help performance in many cases; and, in fact, they may actually degrade it due to useless bus bandwidth consumption and cache pollution. In this paper, we present an adaptive prefetch scheme that dynamically adapts the prefetcher configuration to the running workload, aiming to improve performance. We use the IBM POWER7 [27] as the vehicle for this study, since: (i) this represents a state-of-the-art high-end processor, with a mature data prefetch engine that has evolved significantly since the POWER3 time-frame; and (ii) this product provides facilities for accurate measurement of performance metrics through a user-visible performance counter interface.

POWER7 contains a programmable prefetch engine that is able to prefetch consecutive data blocks as well as those separated by a non-unit stride [27]. The processor system is provided to customers with a default prefetch setting that is targeted to improve performance for most applications. However, if needed, the user can manually override the default setting via the operating system. The user can specify some parameters such as the prefetch depth and whether strided prefetch and prefetch for store operations should

*This work was done while the author was at BSC.

be enabled or not. Workloads present different sensitivities to changing the prefetch configuration, even within the class of scientific-engineering applications that are generally amenable to data prefetch. While the optimal prefetch setting (if known) can lead to a significant performance improvement, the corollary to this, as we show later in this paper, is that blindly setting a configuration may reduce performance.

Overall, the main contributions of the paper are:

- We first provide a motivation for adaptive prefetching, showing how the different prefetch configurations in POWER7 affect the performance for several workloads. To that end, we use the SPEC CPU2006 benchmark suite [14].
- We present a runtime-based adaptive prefetch mechanism capable of improving performance via dynamically setting the optimal prefetch configuration, without the need for a priori profile information. We evaluate the performance benefits of adaptive prefetching. Our adaptive scheme increases performance up to 2.7X and 30% compared to the default prefetch configuration for single-threaded and multiprogrammed workloads, respectively.
- We also study the implementation of such an adaptive prefetch scheme within the OS kernel. By implementing our adaptive mechanism into the Linux kernel, we have observed similar performance improvements to those obtained by the userspace implementation.

This paper is organized as follows: Section 2 provides background for reading the paper. Section 3 describes the POWER7 processor, providing information on the different knobs that control the prefetcher. It also characterizes the effect of the different knobs on performance. Section 4 describes the methodology that we use in this paper. Section 5 shows the implementation of an adaptive prefetch mechanism and evaluates its impact on performance. Section 6 shows a possible OS-based implementation. Finally, Section 7 presents the conclusions of this paper.

2. RELATED WORK

There is a significant record of past research in data prefetch (e.g., [5, 18, 24]). Most of the initial proposals were based on sequential prefetchers. They prefetch sequential memory blocks relying on the fact that many applications exhibit spatial locality. Although sequential prefetchers work effectively in many cases, there are applications with non-sequential data access patterns that do not benefit from sequential prefetching. That motivated the research on more complex prefetchers that try to capture the non-sequential nature of these applications. Prefetch techniques targeting pointer-based applications have been studied in [12, 26, 32]. Joseph and Grunwald study Markov-based prefetchers in [17]. Solihin et al. used a user-level memory thread in order to prefetch data, delivering significant speedups even for applications with irregular accesses [28]. Yet, most of these prefetch designs have not been implemented in a real processor. Limit studies and prefetch analytical models have been presented in [13, 29].

With the advent of CMP processors, interaction between threads is taken into account when designing a prefetch system. Ebrahimi et al. [11] and Lee et al. [19] study the effect of thread-interaction on prefetch and propose techniques to design prefetch systems that improve throughput and/or fairness. Liu and Solihin study the impact of hardware prefetching and bandwidth partitioning in CMPs [21].

Although there are lots of studies on prefetching based on simulators, there are very few works that deal with hardware-based measurement and characterization. Wu and Martonosi characterize the prefetcher of an Intel Nehalem processor and provide a simple algorithm to dynamically control whether to turn the prefetcher on or off [30]. However, their study is solely oriented towards reducing intra-application cache interference without taking actual system performance. Liao et al. construct a machine learning model that dynamically modifies the prefetch configuration of the machines in a data center (based on Intel Core2 processors) [20]. They improve performance for some applications by enabling/disabling prefetch. In our case, however, the POWER7 processor not only allows us to enable/disable the prefetch, but it exposes a set of knobs to fine tune prefetch configuration.

There are other examples of adaptive mechanisms for controlling thread execution rate. For instance, different instruction fetch policies in the context of SMT processors are studied in [8, 9] to increase throughput and/or provide quality of service (QoS). Similarly, Boneti et al. [6] explore the usage of the dynamic hardware priorities present in IBM POWER5 processor for controlling thread resource balancing and prioritization. Qureshi and Patt [25] study the problem of last-level cache partitioning between multiple applications for improving throughput. Moreto et al. [23] present a similar technique but focus on achieving QoS for the co-running applications.

3. THE POWER7 PROCESSOR

The IBM POWER7 [27] processor is an eight-core chip where each core can run up to four threads. Each core contains two 32KB L1 caches (for instructions and data), plus a 256KB L2 cache. The processor contains an on-chip 32MB L3 cache. Each core has a private 4MB portion of the L3 cache, although it can access the rest of portions from other cores (with higher latency). A core can switch between single-thread (ST), two-way SMT (SMT2), and four-way SMT (SMT4) execution modes.

3.1 POWER7 Prefetcher

POWER7's prefetcher [2, 7, 15] is programmable and allows the user to set different parameters (knobs) that control its behavior: i) *prefetch depth*, how many lines in advance to prefetch, ii) *prefetch on stores*, whether to prefetch store operations, and iii) *stride-N*, whether to prefetch streams with a stride larger than one cache block. The prefetcher is controlled via the data stream control register (DSCR). The Linux kernel exposes the register to the user through the sys virtual filesystem [22], allowing the user to set the prefetch setting on a per-thread basis.

Table 1a describes the possible prefetch configurations and introduces the notation that will be used throughout the paper. The prefetch depth can take values from 2 (*shallowest*) to 7 (*deepest*). Additionally, there are two special values that can be used: 001b (O) and 000b (D). The former disables the prefetcher, while the latter is the system-predefined default depth. In POWER7 the default depth corresponds to depth 5 (*deep*) [3], being automatically selected when the

Table 1: Notation used in this paper for referring to prefetch configurations. We use tags (W/S) to indicate whether *prefetch on stores* (W) or *stride-N* (S) are enabled. Prefetch depth can be *default* (D) or any value in the range 2-7 (*shallowest-deepest*). The special configuration where depth is 001 turns off the prefetcher (O). Table 1b shows some examples with this notation.

(a) Notation

Shortname	DSCR value	Description
O	xx001	Off (prefetch disabled)
D	xx000	Default depth
2	xx010	Shallowest
3	xx011	Shallow
4	xx100	Medium
5	xx101	Deep
6	xx110	Deeper
7	xx111	Deepest
W	x1xxx	Prefetch on stores
S	1xxxx	Stride-N

(b) Examples

Shortname	Depth	Prefetch on stores	Stride-N
D	Default	No	No
WD	Default	Yes	No
SD	Default	No	Yes
SWD	Default	Yes	Yes
S2	Shallowest	No	Yes
S3	Shallow	No	Yes
7	Deepest	No	No
S7	Deepest	No	Yes
SW7	Deepest	Yes	Yes

system boots. *Prefetch on stores* (W) and *stride-N* (S) can only be enabled or disabled (they are disabled in the default configuration). Therefore, the default configuration corresponds to configuration 5 (using our notation). Every knob in the prefetch can be independently configured. Table 1b shows some examples of the possible combinations that can be done by setting values for each prefetch knob. Additionally, it shows how the shortnames that we use along the paper are constructed.

3.2 Impact of Prefetch Settings

In the previous section we have presented the design of the prefetch engine in the POWER7, describing the different available settings. In this section we look at the effect of using settings different from the default one, motivating the need for an adaptive prefetch mechanism.

Figure 1 shows the performance of all the benchmarks in the SPEC CPU2006 suite running in single thread mode under several prefetch settings. We use the default prefetch configuration (D) as the baseline to normalize IPC. Prefetching affects workloads in different ways, depending on their nature. Some experience a significant speedup when prefetch is used, while others are totally insensitive. We classify the benchmarks in four different groups, according to the way prefetch affects their performance when running in single-thread mode on our POWER7 system (Table 2 contains the exact classification for all the SPEC CPU2006 benchmarks): i) *prefetch-insensitive (PI)*; this type of benchmark is insensitive to prefetch. It does not suffer any significant performance variation no matter whether prefetch is enabled or not. Additionally, the various configurations (e.g., depth, stride-N and prefetch-on-stores) do not affect its performance (e.g., sjeng and gamess), ii) *prefetch-friendly (PF)*; enabling prefetch positively affects the performance

Table 2: Benchmark classification based on how their performance is affected by prefetch when running in single-thread mode.

Classes	Benchmarks		
Prefetch-insensitive	perlbench gromacs povray tonto	bzip2 namd sjeng astar	gamess gobmk h264ref xalancbmk
Prefetch-friendly	gcc dealII GemsFDTD sphinx3	zeusmp calculix lbm	cactusADM hmmer wrf
Config-sensitive	bwaves leslie3d	mcf soplex	milc libquantum
Prefetch-unfriendly	omnetpp		

of the benchmarks in this group. However, they are not affected when the prefetch setting is varied (e.g., zeusmp and cactusADM), iii) *config-sensitive (CS)*; for the benchmarks in this group the performance also increases when prefetch is enabled. Moreover, changing the prefetch configuration affects their performance too (e.g., enabling stride-N improves the performance with respect to the default configuration; this is the case for mcf and milc), and iv) *prefetch-unfriendly (PU)*; for this type of benchmark, enabling prefetch negatively affects its performance (e.g., omnetpp).

Overall, as results in Figure 1 show, an adaptive prefetch mechanism could tune the prefetch for every particular benchmark in order to find the prefetch configuration that leads to its optimal performance.

4. METHODOLOGY

We use an IBM BladeCenter PS701 to conduct all the experiments, including the ones in the previous section. This system contains one POWER7 processor running at 3.0 GHz and 32 GB of DDR3 SDRAM running at 800 MHz. The operating system is SUSE Linux Enterprise Server 11 SP1. We use the IBM XL C/C++ 11.1 and IBM XL Fortran 13.1 compilers to compile all the SPEC CPU2006 benchmarks. We disable compiler-generated prefetch instructions in order to avoid interactions between these instructions and the hardware prefetcher. For collecting information from the performance counters we use *perf*, the official implementation in the mainstream Linux kernel [1].

5. ADAPTIVE PREFETCHING

In Section 3.2 we have seen that different applications derive maximum performance benefit from different prefetch settings. In that approach, a user needs to profile applications prior to running them in order to determine the best prefetch setting for each application. We refer to this method as the *best static configuration* approach or, simply, the static approach. In this approach, a priori profiling yields the optimal prefetch configuration for a given application, and all future runs of this application would use this optimal configuration to achieve its efficiency target. Note that in this approach, the prefetch configuration is statically fixed for the duration of the application run. A truly dynamic adaptation of the data prefetch algorithm presents the promise of two potential benefits: (i) users would be able to avoid the per-application profiling step; and, (ii) dynamic phase changes within the same application would trigger adaptation of the prefetch parameters in order to further maximize the targeted efficiency metric.

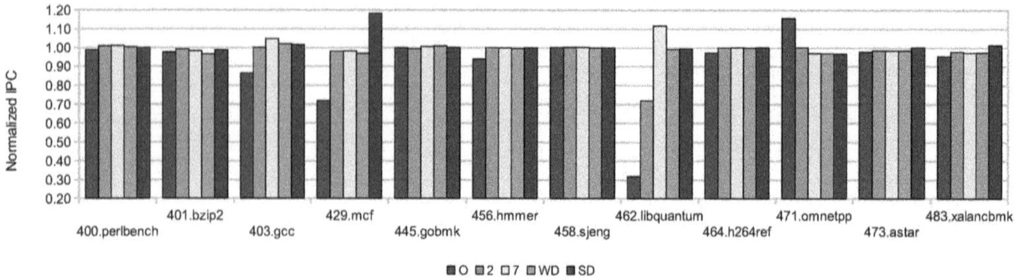

(a) SPECINT

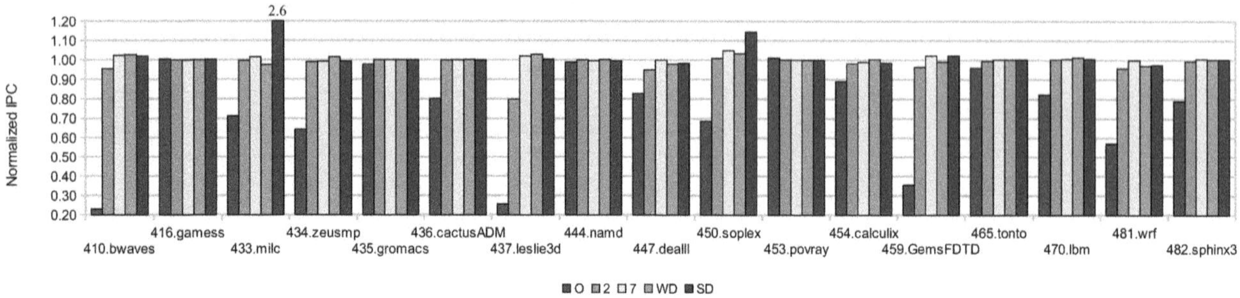

(b) SPECFP

Figure 1: Effect of prefetch on performance for single-threaded runs. Multiple prefetch configurations are used in order to show the effect of each prefetch knob: depth (2-7), prefetch on stores (WD), and stride-N (SD) – refer to Table 1 for notation on prefetch configurations.

5.1 Basic Adaptive Algorithm

Algorithm 1 Base adaptive prefetch algorithm.

```
1: for all t in threads do
2:    for all ps in pref_settings do
3:       set_prefetch(cpu(t), ps)
4:       wait T_e ms
5:       ipc[ps] = read_pmcs()
6:    end for
7:    best_ps = arg max_ps(ipc)
8:    set_prefetch(cpu(t), best_ps)
9: end for
10: wait T_r
```

Algorithm 1 contains two configurable parameters, T_s and T_r. The former specifies the interval length to be used during the exploration phase (line 4). The latter is the amount of time that the best settings found during the exploration phase will be used before a new exploration phase starts (line 10). In our implementation we use the interval lengths $T_e = 10ms$ and $T_r = 100ms$. This granularity is a good compromise between adaptability and overhead. It is actually a typical value for sampling-based approaches in the OS and runtime realms [16]. For instance, the Linux kernel allows the user to choose the granularity of the timer tick from 1 ms up to 10 ms. A finer granularity would introduce a significant overhead in the system.

This first algorithm is the base for the other two presented in this paper. It, however, suffers from two potential problems: the effect of phase changes and the impact of "inefficient" prefetch settings (for a particular workload). Next, we examine and present solutions for these two problems.

5.2 Impact of Phase Changes

It is well-known that applications present phases during their execution [10]. They actually present phases at different levels, ranging from the microsecond to the millisecond level (some phases may even last for some seconds). Our adaptive mechanism periodically samples performance for different settings, attempting to find the best setting for that particular interval. We must, however, take care of possible phase changes that may occur between different samples in the exploration phase. Otherwise, we could attribute a performance change to the effect of a given prefetch setting when the real reason is an underlying phase change between measurements.

In order to alleviate this problem we use a moving average buffer (MAB) [4] that keeps the last m IPC samples for every prefetch setting and process under control of the adaptive prefetch runtime. We then compare the performance of prefetch settings by using the mean of the values in the buffer, instead of using individual measurements. We evaluate the effect of using buffers of different sizes on the IPC variability between consecutive samples. Figure 2 shows the normalized IPC variability as we increase the buffer size from 1 (i.e., no buffer is used) up to 32 positions. IPC variability is computed with the following equation:

$$variability = \frac{1}{n-1}\sum_{i=1}^{n-1}|IPC_{i+1} - IPC_i| \quad (1)$$

where IPC is an array with all the n IPC samples for a given workload execution. Variability is then normalized to the average IPC for every workload. For clarity reasons the figure is split into two. Figure 2a contains the results for SPEC INT benchmarks and Figure 2b does so for SPEC FP benchmarks. As it can be seen in the figure, most of the benchmarks present a small to moderate variation when MAB is not used. A few of them (bzip2, perlbench, wrf and GemsFDTD), however, have quite a high variation. As an example, let us examine bzip2. The average IPC variability between consecutive samples is 30% when MAB is not used. As the buffer size increases the variability is reduced, reaching 2% for a buffer containing the last 32 samples. By using a moving average buffer, we are able to significantly reduce

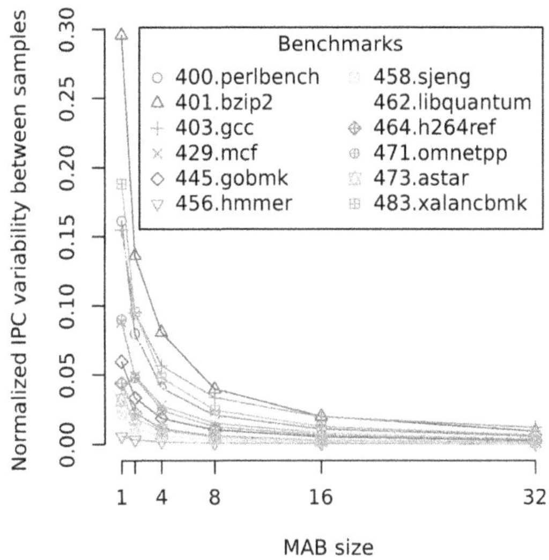

(a) SPEC INT

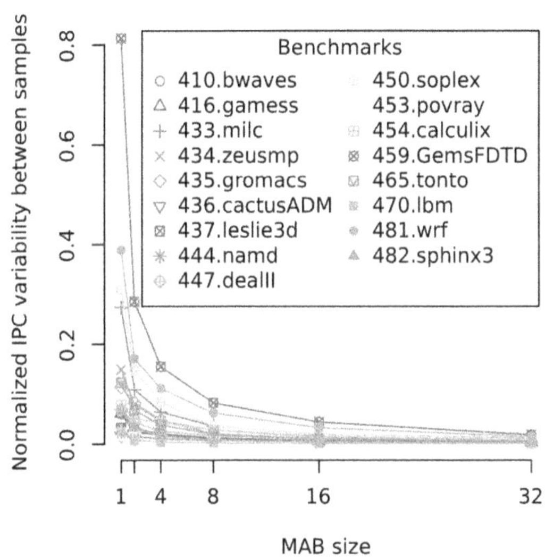

(b) SPEC FP

Figure 2: Effect of changing the buffer size on inter-sample IPC variability. IPC variability (see Equation 1) is normalized to the average IPC for each benchmark.

the impact that phase changes may have on the exploration phase of the adaptive prefetch mechanism.

Algorithm 2 Adaptive prefetch with MAB

1: **for all** t in $threads$ **do**
2:   **for all** ps in $pref\_settings$ **do**
3:     set_prefetch(cpu(t), ps)
4:     wait T_e ms
5:     push($ipc\_mab[t, ps]$, read_pmcs())
6:     $ipc\_mean[ps]$ = mean($ipc\_mab[t, ps]$)
7:   **end for**
8:   $best\_ps = arg\, max_{ps}(ipc\_mean)$
9:   set_prefetch(cpu(t), $best\_ps$)
10: **end for**
11: wait T_r

Algorithm 2 presents the new version of the algorithm, using the moving average buffer. The algorithm is very similar to the one presented in the previous section. The only differences are on lines 5, 6 and 8, where the buffer is actually used. The operation of pushing a new sample into the buffer (line 5) is implemented using a circular buffer. Thus, when the buffer is full and a new sample is added, the oldest one is removed from the buffer.

5.3 Impact of "Inefficient" Prefetch Settings

The base adaptive prefetch algorithm iterates along a set of prefetch settings during the exploration phase. After the exploration phase is over, the runtime lets the threads run for a certain amount of time with the best setting found. Depending on the workload, there could be a significant performance variation between the different settings used in the exploration phase. For instance, for bwaves, disabling the prefetch reduces its performance by 78% with respect to the best setting. Such a significant slowdown may actually impact overall performance if the exploration phase is executed too often. Therefore, for this particular workload disabling prefetch would be an inefficient prefetch setting (it is important to mention that an inefficient setting for one workload may be the best one for another workload; thus settings' efficiency is workload-dependent).

In order to quantify the effect of inefficient settings, we model the expected performance, $\widehat{IPC}$, based on the ratio of exploration and running phases' length. We use the following equation for the model:

$$\widehat{IPC} = \sum_{i=1}^{n} \frac{L_e}{L_t} \times IPC_i + \frac{L_r}{L_t} \times \max_i(IPC_i) \qquad (2)$$

where L_e and L_r are the lengths of the exploration and running phases, respectively, and $L_t = L_e + L_r$. IPC is a set containing the average IPC values for each prefetch setting for a given workload.

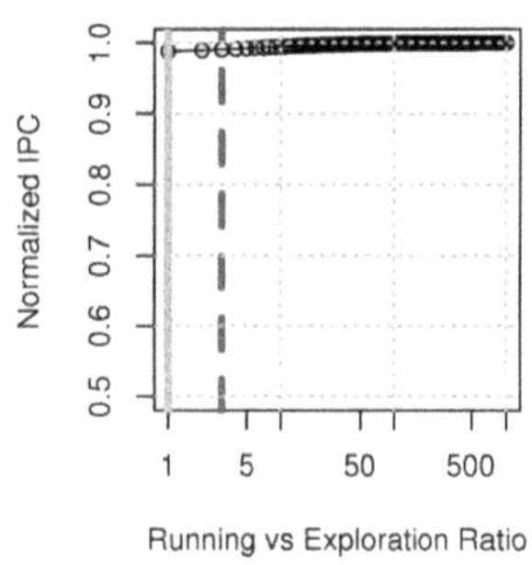

(a) perlbench

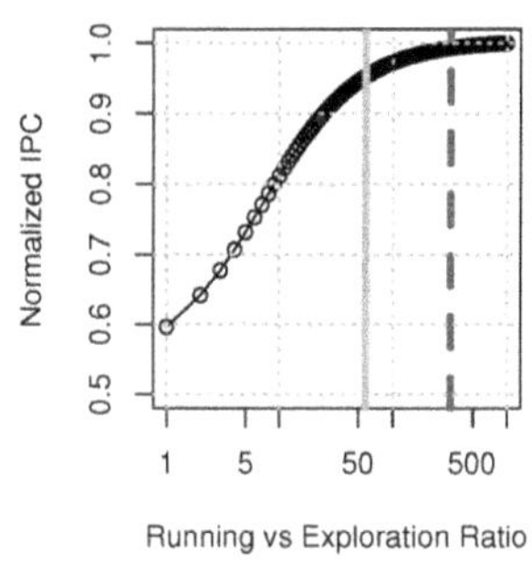

(b) milc

Figure 3: Effect of exploration/running ratio on expected performance. Values are normalized to the maximum values observed for each workload (i.e., $max_i(IPC_i)$).

Figure 3 shows the expected performance for two different types of workloads as the ratio L_r/L_e increases. The solid-green vertical line determines the running-exploration ratio such that the expected performance is within 5% of the best achievable performance (i.e., if there is no exploration phase and the best prefetch setting is used during all the interval). The dashed-blue vertical line is equivalent to the previous one, but it marks the point where the expected performance is within 1% of the best achievable performance. We use two benchmarks, perlbench and milc, to construct an illustrative example. The results for all the other SPEC CPU2006 benchmarks are similar to either one of these two.

Figure 3a shows the results for perlbench. This workload is mostly insensitive to prefetching and, thus, the expected performance follows a very flat curve. In order not to lose more than 1% of performance, it suffices with setting a running phase four times longer than a single exploration interval. For these types of workloads, since they do not really suffer from inefficient prefetch settings, the running-exploration ratio is not so important. This totally changes for a different type of workload such as milc. Figure 3b shows the results for this workload. In this case the curve is not flat anymore. Indeed if we are not willing to pay a performance drop bigger than 5% we must use a running phase at least 50 times longer than a single exploration interval. For a tighter 1% bound, the ratio would increase up to approximately 400. Using such a large value for all the possible workloads would imply a drastic reduction in the number of times that an exploration phase is triggered. Thus, the adaptability of our mechanism would be significantly reduced.

In order to avoid this issue we decided to introduce a new feature in our adaptive prefetch scheme. This feature removes inefficient prefetch settings from the set containing all the settings to be tried during the exploration phase. We call this feature *prefetch setting dropping*. Settings are "dropped" for a certain amount of time based on their inefficiency and then, they are considered again to be selected in a future exploration phase. The exact number of iterations, IT_i, that a given setting, i, will be dropped is given by the following equation:

$$IT_i = DF \times |MAB| \times \left(\frac{max_i(IPCi)}{IPC_i} - 1 \right) \quad (3)$$

where DF is the *drop factor*, $|MAB|$ is the size of the moving average buffer and the last term is a measure of the slowdown experienced when using setting i. If the performance for setting i is equal to the best performance observed, the last term becomes zero and the setting is actually not dropped at all, so it will be used in the next exploration phase. The slowdown term in the last equation penalizes inefficient settings proportionally to the measured slowdown. Thus, settings that significantly deviate from the best setting's performance will be penalized more than the others. The equation drops settings proportionally to the size of the moving average buffer too. After a setting is dropped, its MAB is reset, because by the time the setting is included again in the exploration phase, the contents of the buffer may not be valid anymore. Moreover, the adaptive mechanism does not give a prediction for a setting until its associated buffer is full (doing so would be equivalent to not using a buffer). Therefore, $|MAB|$ exploration phases are necessary before the algorithm can decide whether a prefetch setting that has just been reconsidered again for inclusion continues to be an inefficient setting and, consequently, must be dropped once more. The bigger the size of the moving average buffer, the more potentially harmful effect that an inefficient setting may have. Thus, Equation 3 includes a term that drops settings proportionally to the size of the moving average buffer.

In Equation 3 the drop factor, DF, is the only parameter that the adaptive prefetch mechanism's designer or the end-user must select a value for. Its value will depend on the workloads that the end-user will ultimately execute on the system. We believe, however, that it is possible to select a default value for that parameter, based on mathematical performance modeling and empirical analysis. We use a similar approach as we did to determine the effect of the exploration-execution ratio on performance. In this case, we model the effect of changing the drop factor on the expected performance. We use the following equation to model the impact on performance of different drop factor values for the case of two prefetch settings:

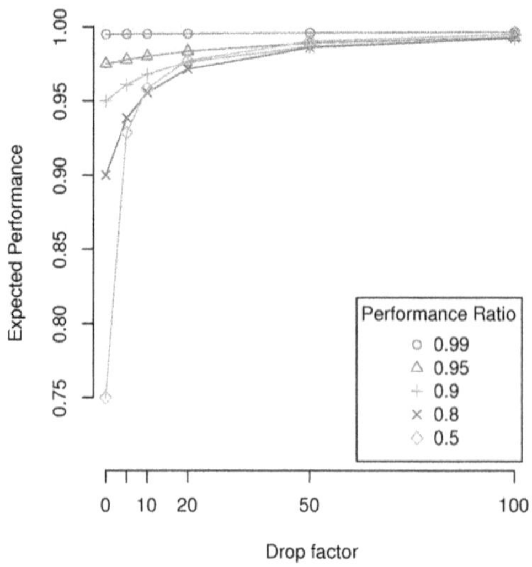

Figure 4: Effect of drop factor on expected performance. Values are normalized to the best possible performance.

$$\widehat{IPC_i} = \frac{t_1}{T} \times IPC_{best} + \frac{t_2}{T} \times \alpha IPC_{best} \quad (4)$$

where t_1 and t_2 correspond to the amount of time that setting one and two are respectively selected. Their values are $|MAB| + IT_i$ and $|MAB|$, respectively. Finally, T is the total interval time ($t_1 + t_2$) and α is the reduction in performance of setting two compared to the first one. Figure 4 shows normalized expected performance for several drop factor values, for the case of two prefetch settings. One of the settings corresponds to the best setting in a given interval (performance = 1.0). We include results for different performances (α) for the second setting, ranging from 1% to 50% slowdown.

As it can be observed in Figure 4, settings that are close to the best one do not reduce performance significantly and, thus, they do not need to be dropped for a long time (if at all). As the performance of the second setting decreases, the impact on performance becomes much more noticeable. For instance, if the performance for the second setting is 50% compared to the best setting, not using the dropping feature would lead to an estimated overall performance of 75% compared to when just the best setting is used. As the drop factor increases, the impact of inefficient settings clearly reduces and the expected performance tends to converge to the performance obtained with the best prefetch setting.

Algorithm 3 presents the latest version of the adaptive prefetch mechanism, both including the moving average buffer and the dropping feature. As it can be seen there is no running phase in this algorithm. The running phase is not necessary anymore since the dropping feature removes inefficient settings, thus, allowing us to perform a continuous exploration. Before trying a prefetch setting, the algorithm decrements the number of drop iterations for that setting, and it only actually considers the setting if it is not dropped

Algorithm 3 Adaptive prefetch with MAB and inefficient setting dropping.

```
1: for all t in threads do
2:   for all ps in pref_settings do
3:     drop_iter[t, ps] = max(0, drop_iter[t, ps] − 1)
4:     if drop_iter[t, ps] = 0 then
5:       set_prefetch(cpu(t), ps)
6:       wait T_e ms
7:       push(ipc_mab[t, ps], read_pmcs())
8:       ipc_mean[ps] = mean(ipc_mab[t, ps])
9:     end if
10:  end for
11:  best_ps = arg max_ps(ipc_mean)
12:  set_prefetch(cpu(t), best_ps)
13:  for all ps in pref_settings do
14:    SL = (ipc_mean[best_ps]/ipc_mean[ps] − 1)
15:    drop_iter[t, ps] = DF × |MAB| × SL
16:  end for
17: end for
```

(lines 3-4). In lines 13-16 the algorithm computes the number of iterations that inefficient settings will be dropped. We select $DF = 100$ based on the previous analysis and on empirical evaluation, obtaining good performance for all the benchmarks both for single-threaded and multiprogrammed workloads, as we will see in the next section.

5.4 Results

In this section we evaluate the performance benefits of using adaptive prefetching. We use both single-threaded workloads as well as multiprogrammed workloads composed of random SPEC CPU2006 benchmark pairs.

5.4.1 Single-Threaded Workloads

Figure 5 shows the results for single-threaded workloads. We present results for all the SPEC CPU2006 benchmarks. The performance values are normalized to the ones obtained with the default prefetch configuration. As can be seen in the figure, many of the benchmarks do not experience any performance variation. That is especially true for prefetch-insensitive workloads. In that case, neither the best static nor the adaptive approaches improve performance. It is important to notice that while the first and the second algorithm may experience a performance decrease compared to the default configuration (due to, for instance, inefficient settings), that is not the case for the third algorithm. Algorithm 3 does not perform worse than the default configuration for any of the benchmarks. That is an important observation, since otherwise it may not be "safe" to unconditionally enable adaptive prefetching.

We can observe the effect of the moving average buffer especially in the case of GemsFDTD. This benchmark is the one that suffered the most from inter-sample variability (see Figure 2). By using a MAB we can reduce the impact of IPC variability between samples and improve performance.

If we look at config-sensitive workloads we observe that adaptive prefetching performs nearly as good as the best static approach. SPEC CPU2006 benchmarks present little variability in terms of which prefetch setting they most benefit from along their execution. Because of this, it is typically not possible for dynamic prefetching to beat the static approach (we look at this in more detail in Section 5.4.3). The speedups obtained with the adaptive scheme are, however, very significant (in the order of 15% for mcf, soplex and libquantum). In the case of milc we observe a large speedup of 2.7X. While all those workloads benefit from prefetch and they see their performance increased when the right setting is selected for them, omnetpp behaves in a completely different way, and it actually benefits from disabling the prefetch. By profiling this benchmark we have seen that it spends a significant percentage of its execution time traversing a heap. A heap is a tree-like data structure and when traversing it, accesses between nodes are separated by a variable stride. This access pattern is very difficult for a sequential prefetch, even if stride-N is enabled. In fact, prior research already showed that omnetpp does not benefit from prefetch [12, 19]. When prefetch is disabled during all the execution (static approach), performance for omnetpp increases 17%. Adaptive prefetching detects that and turns off prefetch most of the time, significantly improving performance too.

Overall, these significant speedups, together with the fact that performance does not decrease when compared to the default configuration, converts adaptive prefetching in a very useful mechanism to improve performance for memory intensive workloads.

5.4.2 Multiprogrammed Workloads

In this section we compare adaptive prefetching against the default configuration and the static approach for multiprogrammed workloads. Since, as we have seen in the previous section, the performance for Algorithm 3 is much better than the other two, in this section we only show results for the third algorithm. The results in Figure 6 are normalized to the case where all the benchmarks run with the default prefetch setting. We construct random pairs in such a way that all the benchmark types listed in Table 2 are represented. Each workload is composed of eight threads, four from a benchmark class and four from the other class. Each thread runs on a different core. We show results for five random workloads for each class combination except for PF-CS and CS-CS where we use ten random workloads since the result space and the performance variability are larger for these combinations. For PU-PU there is only one result, since there are only two benchmarks in PU class.

Looking at the results we observe that, as it was the case with single-threaded workloads, there is not too much difference in performance for workloads composed of prefetch-insensitive or prefetch-friendly benchmarks (PI-PI, PI-PF or PF-PF classes). For config-sensitive workloads, however, we observe very significant speedups (over 10%) for some pairs. Throughput goes up to 30% for the pair omnetpp-milc. In this case the adaptive mechanism disables prefetch for omnetpp and enables stride-N for milc, boosting the performance of both workloads. It is also important to notice that virtually in no case the performance achieved by the adaptive prefetch mechanism is lower than the baseline (using default prefetch for all the threads). The only two cases where this happens are for the pairs GemsFDTD-milc (in PF-CS class) and libquantum-milc (in CS-CS class). The reason for these results is the small absolute IPC for milc. When it runs together with other higher-IPC benchmarks, the total throughput may not increase that much (it may actually decrease) when using the adaptive approach. If we look at the individual IPC values, however, the results show that the adaptive mechanism actually improves performance. Let us examine the GemsFDTD-milc case in more detail. For that pair, adaptive prefetching worsens total throughput 4%

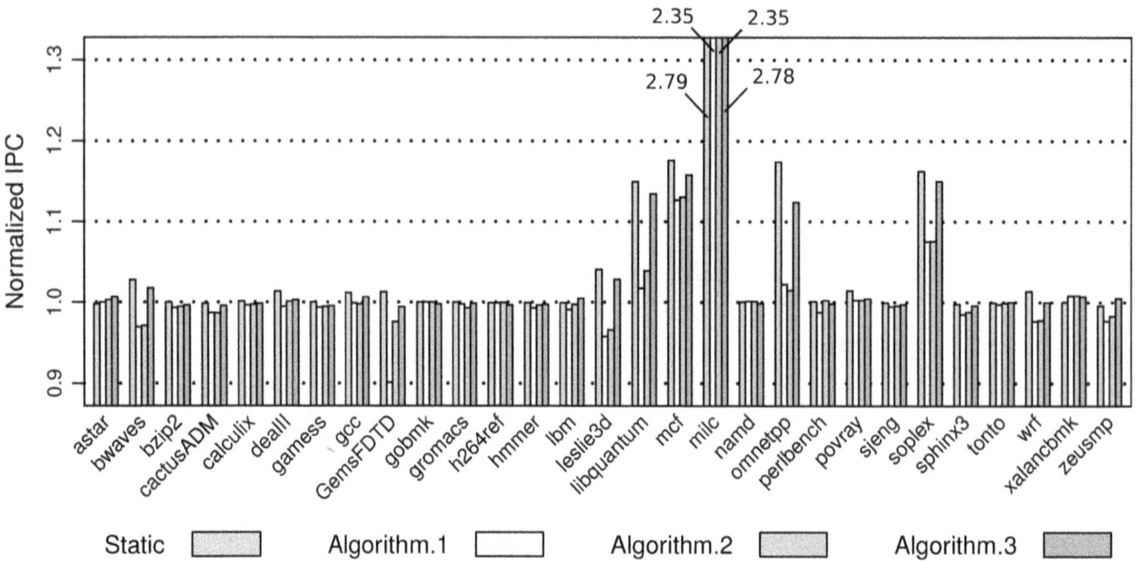

Figure 5: Results for single-threaded workloads normalized to the ones obtained with the default prefetch configuration.

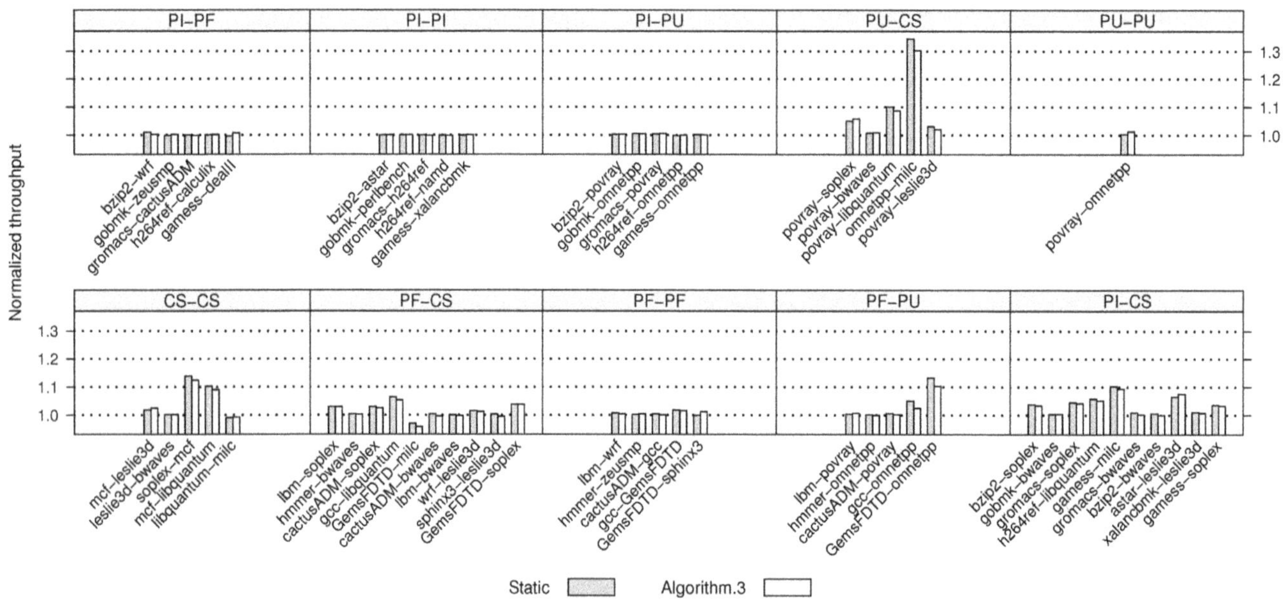

Figure 6: Performance results for both the static and adaptive approaches for mixed-workloads. Each workload is composed of two different benchmarks from different classes (PI=prefetch-insensitive, PF=prefetch-friendly, PU=prefetch-unfriendly, CS=config-sensitive). Four copies of each benchmark are run at the same time. Results are normalized to the ones obtained with default prefetching.

compared to the baseline. When using the baseline the IPC values are 0.61 and 0.18 for GemsFDTD and milc, respectively. Adaptive prefetching selects different prefetch settings, and the IPC values change to 0.37 and 0.34 for the same benchmarks. These results show that GemsFDTD suffers a 35% slowdown, but the speedup for milc is almost 2X, easily compensating the slowdown for GemsFDTD. In addition to throughput, we have used other metrics such as the harmonic speedup in order to obtain performance measurements that combine both throughput and fairness between threads in each pair. Our results show that the adaptive mechanism always obtain a better performance compared to the baseline when using the harmonic speedup metric.

We observe that the static approach always obtains a performance equal or slightly higher than the adaptive one. As we pointed out in the previous section, virtually no SPEC CPU2006 benchmark benefits the most from more than a single prefetch setting. In such a case, the static approach always obtains the best possible performance. With our adaptive scheme, however, the user gets the benefit of autonomic performance boost across all workloads (compared to the default configuration), without the need to invest into a priori characterization of each and every workload.

5.4.3 Composite Workloads

As shown in the previous sections our adaptive scheme is

able to find, without user intervention, the best prefetch setting for all SPEC CPU2006 benchmarks with similar performance speedups to the best static approach. For an application that benefits from multiple "best" prefetch settings over its full execution period, however, the dynamic approach generally performs better. We use the term *intra-workload prefetch setting sensitivity* to refer to the degree of potential improvement that applications may have due to benefiting from multiple prefetch settings within their execution. In the previous sections we have pointed out that a single SPEC CPU2006 benchmark does not benefit from multiple prefetch settings, thus they have a low intra-workload prefetch setting sensitivity.

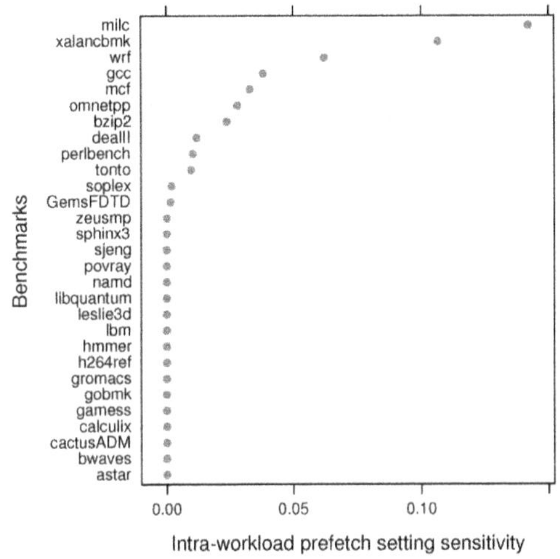

Figure 7: Intra-workload prefetch setting sensitivity for all the SPEC CPU2006 benchmarks.

Figure 7 shows the sensitivity for all the benchmarks. We compute the sensitivity as the ratio of time where a prefetch setting different from best static setting obtains a better performance compared to the best static one. The figure shows that most benchmarks present a very low sensitivity (under 5%). The only three benchmarks with relatively higher sensitivity, however, only experience a slight increase in their performance during less than 15% of their execution. Therefore, we conclude that SPEC CPU2006 benchmarks do not present a high intra-workload prefetch setting sensitivity.

It is, however, conceptually easy to imagine the existence of applications that would benefit from different prefetch settings during their execution. For instance, a scientific application that retrieved a large amount of data from the Internet, uncompressed the data and finally processed it, would have three very different macro-phases. Moreover, each one of these phases may benefit from a different prefetch setting. In such a scenario, the best static approach could definitely perform worse than a dynamic mechanism.

Table 3: Performance increase for adaptive prefetching compared to the static approach for composite workloads.

Workload	IPC speedup (%)
bwaves-omnetpp	9.1
mcf-omnetpp	8.9
milc-omnetpp	10.5
libquantum-omnetpp	7.7

In order to demonstrate the potential benefits of an adaptive scheme compared to a static one, we construct some *composite workloads* by stitching together two SPEC CPU2006 benchmarks, one running after the other. Table 3 shows the speedup obtained by adaptive prefetching compared to the best static approach. As we can observe, there are significant performance improvements for workloads with a higher intra-workload prefetch setting sensitivity. As these results show, the adaptive prefetch mechanism is able to find the best prefetch setting for each of the macro-phases, thus increasing performance compared to a static approach.

6. OS-BASED IMPLEMENTATION

The presented implementation of the adaptive prefetch is based on a user-level runtime. Compared to an OS implementation, a user-level runtime provides the maximum flexibility and portability. An OS-based implementation would provide several advantages, though. For instance, the overhead for reading performance counters as well as for changing the DSCR register would be reduced, since it would not be necessary to change the privilege mode to do so.

Therefore, besides evaluating the runtime-based mechanism, we studied the implementation of adaptive prefetch within the Linux OS. For that purpose, we have actually implemented OS-based adaptive prefetch algorithms similar to the runtime-based ones.

Algorithm 4 OS-based implementation of Algorithm 1

```
1: ct = get_current_running_thread()
2: if mode = EXPLORATION then
3:    perf[ct, curr_ps[ct]] = read_ipc()
4:    if curr_ps[ct] ≠ last_ps() then
5:       curr_ps[ct] = next_ps(curr_ps[ct])
6:       set_dscr(ct, curr_ps[ct])
7:    else
8:       best_ps = arg max_ps(perf[ct])
9:       set_dscr(ct, best_ps)
10:      run_quantum[ct] = RUN_QUANTUM
11:      mode = RUNNING
12:   end if
13: else if mode = RUNNING then
14:   run_quantum[ct] = run_quantum[ct] − 1
15:   if run_quantum[ct] = 0 then
16:      curr_ps[ct] = first_ps()
17:      set_dscr(ct, curr_ps[ct])
18:      mode = EXPLORATION
19:   end if
20: end if
```

We rely on the *timer interrupt* in order to divide the execution of threads into intervals containing exploration and running phases. At each timer interrupt a reference to the thread running on the current context is first obtained (see Algorithm 4). Then the behavior of the algorithm depends on the current phase: i) If the exploration phase is active, the performance for the current prefetch setting (*curr_ps*) is recorded and the next setting is selected (lines 5-6). In case no more settings are available, the algorithm starts the running phase, after selecting the best setting found during the exploration phase (lines 8-11). ii) If the running phase is active, the running quantum is first reduced (line 14). That quantum determines how long a running phase will be. A larger value will reduce the effect of inefficient prefetch settings at the expense of a coarser adaptability.

Using OS-based algorithms we have observed similar results to the ones obtained at user-level. These promising results encourage us to further pursue this path. We leave, however, the exploration of other OS-based adaptive schemes as future work.

7. CONCLUSIONS

Prefetch engines in current server-class microprocessor are getting more and more sophisticated. The IBM POWER7 processor contains a programmable hardware data prefetcher, allowing the user to control different knobs in order to adapt the prefetcher to workload requirements. In this paper we present an adaptive prefetch mechanism capable of boosting performance by leveraging on these knobs. We evaluate its impact on performance for single-threaded and multiprogrammed workloads, showing that significant speedups can be obtained with respect to the default prefetch setting. We compare the adaptive scheme to an approach where applications are first profiled and the best prefetch setting found is used for future executions. Our dynamic approach, however, frees users from profiling every application in order to find the best static prefetch setting.

Although we use POWER7-specific measurements and analysis in this paper, the basic insights gleaned generally also apply to other (non-POWER) systems that use programmable hardware data prefetch engines.

8. ACKNOWLEDGMENTS

This work was supported by a Collaboration Agreement between IBM and BSC. It has also been supported by the Ministry of Science and Technology of Spain under contract TIN-2007-60625 and grant JCI-2008-3688. We also acknowledge Ramon Bertran and Lluís Vilanova for developing data processing tools that significantly simplified handling all the experimental data necessary for this paper.

9. REFERENCES

[1] Performance Counters for Linux. `https://perf.wiki.kernel.org`.

[2] Power ISA^{TM} Version 2.06 Revision B. `https://www.power.org/resources/downloads/PowerISA_V2.06B_V2_PUBLIC.pdf`.

[3] J. Abeles et al. Performance Guide for HPC Applications on IBM POWER 755 System. `https://www.power.org/events/Power7/Performance_Guide_for_HPC_Applications_on_Power_755-Rel_1.0.1.pdf`.

[4] B. Abraham and J. Ledolter. *Statistical Methods for Forecasting*. Wiley series in probability and mathematical statistics: Applied probability and statistics. Wiley, 1983.

[5] J. L. Baer and T. F. Chen. An Effective On-Chip Preloading Scheme To Reduce Data Access Penalty. In *Proc. ACM/IEEE Conf. Supercomputing*, SC, pages 176–186, 1991.

[6] C. Boneti, F. J. Cazorla, R. Gioiosa, A. Buyuktosunoglu, C. Y. Cher, and M. Valero. Software-Controlled Priority Characterization of POWER5 Processor. In *Proc. 35th Int'l Symp. Comp. Arch.*, ISCA, pages 415–426, 2008.

[7] H. W. Cain and P. Nagpurkar. Runahead Execution vs. Conventional Data Prefetching in the IBM POWER6 Microprocessor. In *Proc. Int'l Symp. Perf. Analysis of Systems Software*, ISPASS, pages 203–212, 2010.

[8] F. J. Cazorla et al. Predictable Performance in SMT Processors: Synergy between the OS and SMTs. *IEEE Trans. Comput.*, 55(7):785–799, July 2006.

[9] S. Choi and D. Yeung. Learning-Based SMT Processor Resource Distribution via Hill-Climbing. In *Proc. 33rd Int'l Symp. Comp. Arch.*, ISCA, pages 239–251, 2006.

[10] P. J. Denning. The Working Set Model for Program Behavior. *Commun. ACM*, 11(5):323–333, May 1968.

[11] E. Ebrahimi, C. J. Lee, O. Mutlu, and Y. N. Patt. Prefetch-Aware Shared Resource Management for Multi-Core Systems. In *Proc. 38th Int'l Symp. Comp. Arch.*, ISCA, pages 141–152, 2011.

[12] E. Ebrahimi, O. Mutlu, and Y. N. Patt. Techniques for Bandwidth-Efficient Prefetching of Linked Data Structures in Hybrid Prefetching Systems. In *Proc. 15th Int'l Symp. High Perf. Comp. Arch.*, HPCA, pages 7–17, 2009.

[13] P. G. Emma, A. Hartstein, T. R. Puzak, and V. Srinivasan. Exploring the limits of prefetching. *IBM J. R&D*, 49(1):127–144, January 2005.

[14] J. L. Henning. SPEC CPU2006 Benchmark Descriptions. *SIGARCH Comp. Arch. News*, 34(4):1–17, September 2006.

[15] I. Hur and C. Lin. Memory Prefetching Using Adaptive Stream Detection. In *Proc. 39th Int'l Symp. on Microarchitecture*, MICRO, pages 397–408, 2006.

[16] C. Isci, A. Buyuktosunoglu, and M. Martonosi. Long-Term Workload Phases: Duration Predictions and Applications to DVFS. *IEEE Micro*, 25(5):39–51, September 2005.

[17] D. Joseph and D. Grunwald. Prefetching using Markov Predictors. In *Proc. 24th Int'l Symp. Comp. Arch.*, ISCA, pages 252–263, 1997.

[18] N. P. Jouppi. Improving Direct-Mapped Cache Performance by the Addition of a Small Fully-Associative Cache and Prefetch Buffers. In *Proc. 17th Int'l Symp. Comp. Arch.*, ISCA, pages 364–373, 1990.

[19] C. J. Lee, O. Mutlu, V. Narasiman, and Y. N. Patt. Prefetch-Aware DRAM Controllers. In *Proc. 41st Int'l Symp. Microarch.*, MICRO, pages 200–209, 2008.

[20] S. W. Liao et al. Machine Learning-Based Prefetch Optimization for Data Center Applications. In *Proc. Int'l Conf. High Perf. Comp. Networking, Storage and Analysis*, SC, pages 1–10, 2009.

[21] F. Liu and Y. Solihin. Studying the Impact of Hardware Prefetching and Bandwidth Partitioning in Chip-Multiprocessors. In *Proc. Int'l Conf. Measur. and Model. of Comp. Sys.*, SIGMETRICS, pages 37–48, 2011.

[22] P. Mochel. The sysfs Filesystem. *Proc. Annual Linux Symp.*, 2005.

[23] M. Moreto, F. J. Cazorla, A. Ramirez, R. Sakellariou, and M. Valero. FlexDCP: a QoS Framework for CMP Architectures. *SIGOPS Oper. Syst. Rev.*, 43(2):86–96, April 2009.

[24] S. Palacharla and R. E. Kessler. Evaluating Stream Buffers as a Secondary Cache Replacement. In *Proc. 21st Int'l Symp. Comp. Arch.*, ISCA, pages 24–33, 1994.

[25] M. K. Qureshi and Y. N. Patt. Utility-Based Cache Partitioning: A Low-Overhead, High-Performance, Runtime Mechanism to Partition Shared Caches. In *Proc. 39th Int'l Symp. Microarch.*, MICRO, pages 423–432, 2006.

[26] A. Roth, A. Moshovos, and G. S. Sohi. Dependence Based Prefetching for Linked Data Structures. In *Proc. 8th Int'l Conf. Arch. Support for Prog. Lang. and Operat. Sys.*, ASPLOS, pages 115–126, 1998.

[27] B. Sinharoy et al. IBM POWER7 multicore server processor. *IBM J. R&D*, 55(3):1–29, May-June 2011.

[28] Y. Solihin, J. Lee, and J. Torrellas. Using a User-Level Memory Thread for Correlation Prefetching. In *Proc. 29th Int'l Symp. Comp. Arch.*, ISCA, pages 171–182, 2002.

[29] V. Srinivasan et al. A prefetch taxonomy. *IEEE Trans. Comp.*, 53(2):126–140, February 2004.

[30] C. J. Wu and M. Martonosi. Characterization and Dynamic Mitigation of Intra-Application Cache Interference. In *Proc. Int'l Symp. Perf. Analysis of Systems and Software*, ISPASS, pages 2–11, 2011.

[31] W. A. Wulf and S. A. McKee. Hitting the Memory Wall: Implications of the Obvious. *SIGARCH Comp. Arch. News*, 23:20–24, March 1995.

[32] C. L. Yang and A. R. Lebeck. Push vs. Pull: Data Movement for Linked Data Structures. In *Proc. 14th Int'l Conf. Supercomputing*, ICS, pages 176–186, 2000.

Enhancing Performance Optimization of Multicore Chips and Multichip Nodes with Data Structure Metrics

Ashay Rane
Texas Advanced Computing Center
The University of Texas at Austin
ashay.rane@tacc.utexas.edu

James Browne
Department of Computer Science
The University of Texas at Austin
browne@cs.utexas.edu

ABSTRACT

Program performance optimization is usually based solely on measurements of execution behavior of code segments using hardware performance counters. However, memory access patterns are critical performance limiting factors for today's multicore chips where performance is highly memory bound. Therefore diagnoses and selection of optimizations based only on measurements of the execution behavior of code segments are incomplete because they do not incorporate knowledge of memory access patterns and behaviors. This paper presents a low-overhead tool (MACPO) that captures memory traces and computes metrics for the memory access behavior of source-level (C, C++, Fortran) data structures. It also presents a complete process for integrating code segment-based and memory access pattern measurements and analyses for performance optimization specifically targeting multicore chips and multichip nodes of clusters. MACPO explicitly targets the measurement and metrics important to performance optimization for multicore chips. MACPO uses more realistic cache models for computation of latency metrics than those used by previous tools. Evaluation of the effectiveness of adding memory access behavior characteristics of data structures to performance optimization was done on subsets of the ASCI, NAS and Rodina parallel benchmarks and one application program from a domain not represented in these benchmarks. Adding memory behavior characteristics enabled easier diagnoses of bottlenecks and more accurate selection of appropriate optimizations than with only code centric behavior measurements. The performance gains ranged from a few percent to 38 percent.

Categories and Subject Descriptors

C.4 [**Computer Systems Organization**]: Performance of Systems

General Terms

Performance

Keywords

performance, optimization, memory, data structures

1. INTRODUCTION

Performance optimization requires detailed characterization of the causes of and remedies for performance bottlenecks. Out of the four subtasks of performance optimization (measurement, diagnosis of bottlenecks, selection of effective optimizations, and implementation of optimizations), the measurement, diagnosis and selection of effective optimizations subtasks have, to date, largely focused on code centric measurements, which associates resource use with code segments such as functions or loops. Because memory is much slower than processors, a full understanding of the memory access patterns of important data structures is critical to accurate diagnosis of performance bottlenecks and selection of performance optimizations. A complete approach to performance optimization must therefore combine code-centric and data structure-centric measurements and analyses with code-segment local scope. Understanding memory access patterns becomes even more important for optimization of execution on multicore chips which share memory access paths such as L3 caches and chip-local memory across processing cores. Data structure-oriented measurement and analysis are also important for identifying code segments which can execute efficiently on the SIMT/SIMD accelerators, which are commonly being associated with multicore chips in computation nodes. Several excellent code segment-centric measurement and analysis tools are available. Some tools for data structure access-centric measurement and analyses are also available. However, none of the available tools for measurement of data structure access patterns and latencies provided the required data for full support of performance optimization for multicore chips. Therefore a major requirement for our goal was a data structure access behavior measurement and analysis tool which operates at the resolution of loops and functions. This paper presents the design, implementation and application of such a tool (MACPO, Memory Access Centric Performance Optimization) for measurement and analysis of data structure access patterns and latencies which provides the specific data needed for performance optimization of multicore chips. The paper also specifies and illustrates a complete process for combining code-centric and data structure-centric measurements and analyses for performance optimization for multicore chips and multichip nodes of cluster systems.

The process is implemented and illustrated by combining the measurements and analyses of the MACPO tool with the diagnostic and optimization capabilities of PerfExpert [6,13,27] which is based on code segment-based resource use measurements.

The contributions and innovations in this paper include:

1. An efficient, low-overhead and easy to use tool which resolves measurements onto data structure behavior on code segments, including extensions to incorporate the requirements for performance optimization for multicore chips and multichip nodes

2. A systematic process for combining code segment centric and data structure-centric execution behavior measurements for performance bottleneck diagnosis and identification of optimizations

3. Illustrations of the complete performance optimization process incorporating data structure memory access behaviors including both substantial application codes and examples from standard parallel benchmarks.

The case studies include illustration of the additional diagnostic and optimization capabilities afforded by the data structure behavior measurements. In many cases, adding memory behavior characteristics of data structures enabled easier diagnoses of bottlenecks and more accurate selection of appropriate optimizations than with only code centric behavior measurements.

The rest of the paper is organized as follows. Section 2 covers related research and tools but focuses mainly on previous work on data structure-centric measurement. Section 3 lists the key innovations in this work. Section 4 describes the design and implementation of the MACPO tool. Sections 5 and 6 describe and illustrate the complete analyses with the results of applying these analyses to eight codes. Section 7 recaps the content and suggests conclusions which can be drawn from this research. Section 8 describes future research directions including application to identification of code segments which will execute efficiently on SIMD accelerators such as GPGPUs.

2. RELATED WORK

We limit related work coverage to tools and systems for data structure measurement and behavior analysis and the use of data structure measurements in performance optimization. There are several previous or existing tools which focus on measurement and analysis of memory behaviors. All have some limitations with respect to comprehensive support for effective and efficient performance optimization for multicore chips and multichip nodes. In [16], the authors present an approximation to reuse distance analysis that takes $O(log\ log\ M)$ time for processing every memory reference, where M is the number of unique memory references made by the program. However, their solution only applies to single-core reuse distance calculation. We extend their reuse distance calculation to allow modeling of multicore reuse distances. A probabilistic model for determining the concurrent reuse distance based on the data locality of standalone programs is described in [19]. This approach does not take into consideration interactions between threads arising in a non-simulated environment. Schuff et al. demonstrate a technique in [25, 26] for modeling multicore reuse distances however due to a restricted cache model, their method does not take into account multiple levels of cache. Their approach suffers from over-estimation of penalties from multicore interactions and it does not appear to scale as the number of threads grows. Chameleon [29] incorporates memory trace collection using the PIN dynamic binary instrumentation tool [24], as does [25]. Chameleon is built with the objective of generating and replaying synthetic traces to evaluate cache architectures. TAXI [28] is an X86 simulation environment that collects traces using the Bochs [21] simulator but it does not include the high-level trace analyses (estimated cycles per accesses, access strides, NUMA & cache conflicts). All of the above-mentioned approaches, with the exception of [16] for which there is little information regarding the implementation, use either simulators or PIN. Simulators may not precisely model real-life scenarios such as cache thrashing and prefetching. The use of simulators often greatly increases the time to obtain the results because of the software emulation of instructions. PIN has a wide user base because of its ease of use. However, relating source-level data structures with trace analysis using PIN requires that the binary contain debug information (-g compilation flag), which may introduce some degree of perturbation of memory access patterns [2,3] during program execution. ThreadSpotter [9] is a commercial tool that runs analyses on memory traces without requiring source-level instrumentation. However, to be able to relate measurements back to source code, the binary has to be compiled with debug information. Instead, as described later in Section 4, we instrument our code using LLVM [20] in such a way that the debug information is not required to be present in the binary. Since the instrumented code is compiled to native code, the binary can be run directly on the target platform. SLO, as described in [11, 12] uses a modified version of GCC to instrument programs to collect information about runtime reuse paths and analyze them for locality. Based on the analysis, SLO suggests source code optimizations. However, SLO restricts itself to reuse distance analysis. MACPO, in addition to reuse distance analysis, computes the other metrics needed for complete performance optimization such as average latency for source code data structures, conflicts at the cache and package levels and strides in accesses. Using Instruction Based Sampling (IBS) [15] in AMD processors, Liu and Mellor-Crummey [22] monitor latency of load and store instructions and attribute these to source-level data structures. Their approach has significantly low overhead as compared to most other approaches. However, the only metric available to the user to tune his or her code is the latency of accessing the data structure, which in reality is the symptom but not the cause of the degradation. Itzkowitz, et.al. [18] also profiled memory access characteristics using performance counters. However the value of performance counters in diagnosing the cause of the memory latency is limited; for instance level-3 cache misses could imply (without certainty) large working set size, exceeding memory bandwidth, cache thrashing, etc. Although these are useful metrics, these require that the programmer understand both the source code and the execution environment to identify the true cause of the latency (strided access, cache line invalidation, etc.).

3. INNOVATIONS

This section amplifies the three bullets in the Introduction on the contributions of this paper. It gives details of the measurement and analysis processes which differentiate

MACPO from previous data structure access behavior tools. The last subsection specifies how the code-centric and data-centric measurements and analyses are synergistically combined.

3.1 Low-overhead, code segment-local data structure access behavior measurement

The MACPO tool relates trace information collected about the program back to source-level (C, C++, Fortran) data structures, along with its location in the source code (file name and line number), without requiring the binary to be compiled with debug information (-g compilation flag). This makes it possible to incorporate the memory access behavior of each data structure separately in the diagnosis of bottlenecks and selection of optimizations. Source-level information is obtained during the instrumentation process. MACPO has been designed to keep the overhead of instrumentation low. MACPO collects data only on the data structures in those code segments which have been identified as performance bottleneck. We employ various techniques such as periodically disabling the instrumentation and spacing out the "windows" of instrumentation asymmetrically, whenever possible using atomic data structures instead of locks, etc. Also, MACPO only instruments arrays, unions and structures unlike tools that instrument all memory accesses. While a precise comparison is not possible, we believe MACPO has a measurement overhead of an order of magnitude lower compared to most other tools that use instrumentation [9,25,29], that is, about 2-6x for MACPO (as compared to the average slowdown of 30x for the fastest existing tool [25] according to our survey). We believe that this overhead can be further reduced by employing non-blocking IO operations.

3.2 Use of more accurate cache models

Previous reuse distance-based analyses in most other tools almost universally assume that caches are fully associative. MACPO uses a probabilistic model of set-associative caches based on [23] and incorporates models of each level of cache in the architecture including whether it is private to a core or shared. Incorporating latencies of the individual caches allows a more accurate analysis. As an example, using information about sharing of caches and latencies makes it possible to include the effects of cache thrashing into the memory analysis. This information also makes it possible to answer questions such as what percentage of memory accesses were likely served from the individual caches or how many memory requests were for local memory and how many for remote memory, which can be very helpful in tuning programs on NUMA configurations.

3.3 Multicore reuse distance calculation with low book-keeping overhead

Modeling the reuse distance in the MACPO tool is performed using a technique similar to that described in [16]. However, the idea is adapted for multicore cases by maintaining time-stamps for each cache. This results in $O(M)$ storage for every cache but maintains $O(N \cdot logM)$ time for reuse distance calculation, where N is the number of accesses and M is the number of unique cache lines that were accessed. Depending on the cache that is referenced, the appropriate counter is chosen for finding the reuse distance.

3.4 Stride calculation

The calculation of dominant strides for the program data structures, although simple, is very effective in quickly identifying cases of inefficient data layout. The difference in the address of the last access and the most recent access for each data structure is used for the stride calculation.

3.5 Performance optimization process

The general procedure adopted for tuning all applications using PerfExpert and MACPO is outlined below. Depending on the complexity of the problem, we often found it useful to repeat the entire process. For all codes we first ran PerfExpert on them. PerfExpert identifies the code segments which are performance bottlenecks in the code. It also aggregates various performance counter-based measurements to yield high-level metrics such as cycles spent in data accesses per executed instruction. Information about architectural parameters including memory access latencies is collected during the installation of PerfExpert and is used while calculating the high-level metrics. PerfExpert evaluates program performance on the basis of Local Cycles Per Instruction (LCPI), which is essentially a per-category metric of the cycles per instruction. For instance, the data access LCPI represents the cycles spent by the code segment in data accesses for each of its instructions. This data access LCPI is further divided into the LCPI arising from accessing each level of the data caches (L1, L2 and possibly L3). Programs exhibiting high data access LCPI may be suffering from problems like cache thrashing, capacity misses, etc. Apart from using the data access LCPI, we also consider the data translation look-aside buffer (TLB) LCPI (CPU cycles spent in accessing the data TLB for every instruction in the code segment). Such programs may include data structures that are accessed with long or irregular strides. Once functions that showed poor memory access behaviors were identified, we instrumented these functions using MACPO. Information obtained from the various analyses built in MACPO was combined to manually devise optimizations. 'NUMA hit ratios' and 'cycles per accesses' gave insight into problems arising from multi-threading. High 'stride' values generally indicated inverted loops. Although high 'reuse distances' directly indicates poor locality, correcting this problem usually required understanding the source code in detail. To verify if the change in the application source code indeed improved the total running time of the application, we ran un-instrumented versions of both pre-optimization and post-optimization codes using the Intel 11.1 compiler. The MACPO metrics and the running time for both naïve and optimized versions of the code are shown when discussing the results in Section 6.

4. DESIGN, IMPLEMENTATION AND VALIDATION

In this section, we describe the processes for measurement, generation of metrics, discovering optimizations using MACPO, the limitations of the measurements and validation of the measurements.

4.1 Instrumentation

Capturing data structure access patterns begins with intercepting memory accesses made by the program. There are various ways of solving this problem. We chose compiler-based instrumentation over simulation or binary instrumentation for the following reasons:

1. Compile-time instrumentation enables greater control over the instrumentation process (e.g. only instrumenting specific arrays) because we can operate on the intermediate representation (IR) generated by the compiler prior to the machine-code generation phase.

2. Binary instrumentation tools deal with individual machine instructions. It can be difficult to correlate multiple instructions to loop structures, boundaries and data structure-related operations such as typecasting.

3. The binary generated from compile-time instrumentation runs directly on the target architecture. On the other hand, simulators for complex multicore architectures may not be complete enough to capture advanced hardware optimization techniques (for instance, branch prediction, prefetching). Using simulators has the additional drawback of greatly increasing the time required to obtain results.

Considering these factors, we chose to use the LLVM compiler infrastructure. We added a separate compiler pass in LLVM's extensible framework to implement our instrumentation.

The instrumentation process has the following steps:

1. **Eliminate scalar variables from being instrumented:** Runs the '-mem2reg' pass which promotes local stack variables (other than structs, unions and arrays) to SSA registers, thus leaving non-scalar types, global variables and heap-allocated memory intact for further processing

2. **Run our compiler pass:** This inserts calls to a statically linked library before every access to an array, structure or union in the specified function(s)

3. **Remove debug information:** Runs the '-strip' pass on the IR to remove debug information from the program.

The call in (2) to the runtime library has the prototype:

```
void recordMemoryAccess(
        var_number, address,
        read/write access, file_number,
        line_number);
```

The `var_number`, `file_number` and `line_number` fields are used to relate the address to a location in the source code. The type of access (`read/write`) is used in estimating the latency of serving the memory request. The transformed IR is then compiled to native (x86) code to produce the executable binary.

4.2 Trace collection and analysis

Execution of the instrumented program generates a trace of memory addresses for the portions of the code that were instrumented. These logs are analyzed offline to minimize perturbations in program execution which would result from an online analysis. Most programs of interest for performance optimization are long running applications that typically have repeating patterns. We leverage this to lower overhead by capturing "snapshots" or windows of program execution instead of the entire program behavior from start to finish. Note that metrics from each of the snapshots could have been collected from different invocations to the same function and hence each of the snapshots have to be processed independently. To try and make these snapshots capture the program behavior during its various phases, the time for which the instrumentation is disabled is changed throughout the program's duration and is made to follow the Fibonacci number sequence $(1, 1, 2, 3, 5, 8, 13, 21, \cdots)$. The result is that the number of snapshots does not increase linearly with the running time. This has another advantage of reducing the size of the trace logs in comparison with a full-program trace recording.

4.3 Accuracy of measurements and validation

Instrumentation necessarily modifies the execution behavior of the program. We have been very careful to minimize this perturbation and to test the computed metrics for accuracy.

Instrumentation changes the program behavior: Through compile-time instrumentation, the program performs additional tasks like book-keeping and disk IO for writing logs to a file. Instrumentation at the level of the compiler IR makes it certain that the memory address traces recorded by the instrumentation are the same (relative to base addresses) as will have been generated by the uninstrumented binary. This ensures that the stride and reuse distance metrics should be the same for both the instrumented and un-instrumented programs. The instrumentation does impact both register use and cache use and, of course, increases the running time of the program. However this change does not influence the MACPO measurements because the instrumentation records only the memory references made by the user's source code and not those made by the instrumentation itself. We observed that the instrumented binary ran between 1.2 to 5.5 times slower (Table 1) than the un-instrumented binary. We are able to reduce the overhead and the amount of generated trace information from instrumentation by sampling, by periodically disabling the instrumentation, whenever possible using atomic data structures instead of locks, limiting the collected entries to 1 million per sampling interval and using the '-mem2reg' LLVM pass to eliminate scalar variables from being instrumented. Sampling windows are triggered using `SIGPROF` and are "active" till either the sampling buffer is full or till the sampling period (250ms) is over, whichever occurs first.

To estimate variability in output metrics, we ran the applications multiple times and with different numbers of threads. The computed metrics showed less than 10% percent variation. The sampling rates were varied as were the sizes of the data structures (and thus the running time of the program) to determine sampling rates sufficient to insure accurate measurement in nearly all cases. Additionally the reuse distances and strides computed by MACPO are consistent with those derived manually for simple code examples.

Instrumentation breaks certain compiler optimizations: Typically, optimizations like loop vectorization can no longer be applied after instrumentation because of the newly inserted function calls. As the instrumentation pass operates on the IR, it needs to be run before the code gen-

Table 1: Running time of instrumented code

Application	Running time
SRAD	2.75x
Back Propagation	1.25x
LU	3x
BT	4.66x
Sweep3D	5.52x

eration phase. To ensure that the instrumentation causes minimum possible hindrance to the applicable compiler optimizations, we run the instrumentation pass just before the machine code generation phase. This implies that only those optimizations that are applied after IR generation may not be compiled into the instrumented program.

5. ANALYSES

The analyses built into MACPO operate at the resolution of cache line sizes (usually 64-bytes chunks) instead of a single byte- or word-resolution. We term our resulting analyses as "physical" reuse distance and "physical" strides as these values give a true account of the hardware. We distinguish these physical measurements from the "logical" measurements that refer to the source code data types to determine reuse distance and strides.

MACPO records the complete 64-bit memory address for each reference to the data structures together with the `read` or `write` tag and the ID of the core making the reference. It is thus possible to compute the logical reuse distances and strides at the byte or word resolution. However, we have chosen to have MACPO compute reuse distances and strides in terms of the size of a physical fetch from memory (usually the size of the cache lines in the architecture) since this more accurately reflects the cost for satisfying the reference to a memory address.

To illustrate, consider the following code fragment:

```
long i, a[16];
...
for (i=0; i<16; i++)
    a[i] = a[i]*10;
```

Looking at the source code, one can infer that the (logical) stride for the array `a` is 1. For this case, lets assume that each long integer consumes 8 bytes and that the size of the cache line is 64 bytes. Hence a single cache line can pack up to 8 long integers in one cache line.

Thus while executing the above code the hardware would see the memory references as a single one (`a[0]`) followed by 7 accesses to the same cache line (`a[1]`, `a[2]`, `a[3]`, `a[4]`, ..., `a[7]`) and one again (when the code accesses the first `long`, `a[8]`, in the next 64-byte chunk which causes another fetch from memory). Modeling at such a resolution of cache lines works closely in tandem with the functioning of the architecture and hence gives a realistic picture of the performance of the application.

The different analyses that we have built into MACPO are sketched below. We relate each of the following metrics to source-level data structures.

Figure 1: Example cache organization for memory access streams shown in Tables 2 and 3

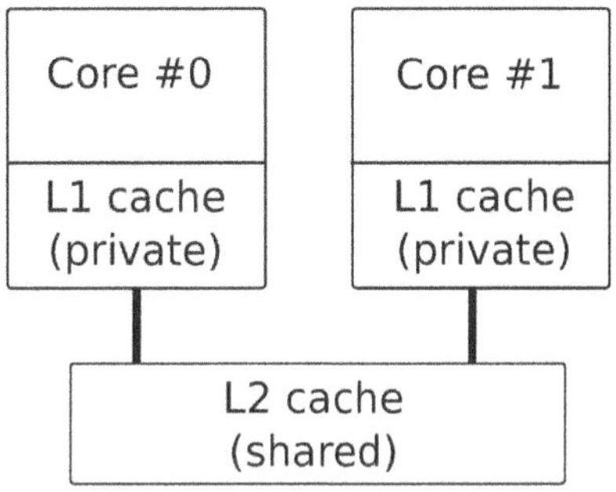

5.1 Multicore reuse distance analysis

Reuse distance is a measure of the number of unique memory accesses made by a program between accesses to a given memory location. The definition of reuse distance changes slightly in the context of multiple cores to account for shared or private references to data items. Also, as explained earlier, MACPO computes reuse distances at a coarser resolution (cache line size) instead of byte- or word-size. As an example consider a stream of references (Table 2) made by two processing cores with a two-level cache organization shown in Figure 1. Here, since neither core references any common data, the reuse distance for data '`a`' for core #1 would be based on all references made by core #1 only. Thus the reuse distance would be based on the number of data references seen by the L1 cache of core #1. Consequently, the reuse distance for '`a`' is 2. However, if both cores performed writes to any common data, then the reuse distance calculation cannot consider the streams of each core in isolation. Consider the case in Table 3, that differs in the core that accessed '`a`' for the second time. In this case, the reference to data '`a`' made by core #2 will cause the fetch to be performed from the cache that is common to both core #1 and core #2. Consequently, MACPO, which records the core which made the reference, computes the reuse distance for '`a`' to be 4.

5.2 Non-Uniform Memory Access (NUMA) hit ratios

On machines that have memory affinity enabled, there can be a significant penalty arising from naïve patterns of allocation and reference of data structures. Threads from a different processor package may incur a high latency from remote fetches while accessing the same memory. References by a thread/process executing on one processor package to a memory location attached to a different processor package

Table 2: Memory access stream with no conflicting accesses

Data	**a**	b	c	b	d	e	**a**
Core#	**1**	2	1	2	2	1	**1**

Table 3: Memory access stream with conflicting accesses

Data	**a**	b	c	b	d	e	**a**
Core#	**1**	2	1	2	2	1	**2**

are called NUMA accesses [4]. Using the `CPUID` instruction [17], the memory addresses being written to the log are tagged with the ID of the core making the memory access request. During the measurement phase we record the core ID, and thus the package, that made the last request for any given cache line. If it was found that the last request to the cache line originated from a different processor package, we classify this request as a NUMA access. In summary, if a write operation is being performed on a remotely-homed memory location, then we classify that access as a NUMA access. This metric can be extended to measure the approximate conflicts among cores within a processor package.

5.3 Cycles per access

Reuse distance represents program behavior but does not take into account latencies arising from conflicting accesses to memory from different cores. The most common case is cache thrashing (two or more cores, each with a private cache, repeatedly accessing the same memory location, thus invalidating other core's cache line), where the reuse distance could be low but the penalty of accesses is high. We therefore decided to model latencies separately from reuse distances. Estimating cycles for memory accesses is derived from the reuse distance analysis, the NUMA hit ratio analysis and from architectural parameters such as cache organization, sizes and latencies. The reuse distance analysis tells us how many unique cache lines were accessed in between accesses to the same data item. Assuming a probabilistic model of set-associative caches [23], we can then estimate whether a given memory access would still be served out of L1 or would overflow the size of the cache, resulting in the memory access being served out of a higher (L2 or possibly L3) level of cache. On a NUMA miss, we associate the remote fetch latency with the memory access. Actual latencies to each cache line are them summed up and divided by the number of requests to yield the average cycles per access.

5.4 Access strides

Programs that have unit strides or small stride values generally execute faster than programs that have long or irregular access strides. This is because the hardware prefetchers can recognize patterns in data accesses and bring data into caches before it is referenced, thus reducing data access penalty. Virtual address to physical address translation can also be serviced more efficiently (using TLBs) when the code exhibits unit strides. Since we have an association between the memory address requested and the source data structure name, we can, for each data structure and thread, keep track of the differences in last requested address and the currently requested address, which is used as the stride value.

6. RESULTS

To evaluate the effectiveness of using MACPO and PerfExpert, we used programs from three benchmark suites: NAS Parallel Benchmarks (size `B`) [10], ASCI Sweep3D benchmark [8] and the OpenMP benchmarks from the Rodinia benchmark suite [14]. We also included a standalone application, a 2D Lattice Boltzmann solver, in the codes that were measured. Four codes (Sweep3D, NAS Block Tridiagonal, NAS LU Symmetric Gauss-Seidel and Lattice Boltzmann) are MPI codes whereas the remaining (Particle Filter, Needleman-Wunsch, Back Propagation and SRAD) are multi-threaded programs that use OpenMP. In all cases, understanding the cause of the degradation and tuning the code simply based on code segment-based measurements was difficult due to the following two main reasons:

1. Counter-based measurements were helpful in discovering the problems but not the causes

2. Code segments commonly used multiple data structures making it difficult to determine the exact bottleneck data structure

For half of the codes, we found the data from MACPO to be critical to characterizing the causes of the performance bottlenecks and devising optimizations. These optimizations included non-trivial optimizations such as changing the OpenMP loop chunk size, discovering a bad algorithm and changing it, partial loop fusion and in another case, loop fission. For the balance of the codes, information from MACPO was useful in quickly determining the cause of the problem and hence the optimization but the MACPO analysis was not critical to discovering the optimization.

The experiments were done on two architecturally different machines. Programs from the Rodinia benchmark suite were run using 8 threads on Longhorn [5], which is comprised of dual quad-core Intel Nehalem chips. Each node has 48 GB of main memory. Each of the 8 cores have 32 KB level 1 data and instruction caches. A unified level 2 cache of size 256 KB is shared between two cores while a unified level 3 cache of size 8 MB is shared by four cores. The Lattice Boltzmann solver, the ASCI Sweep3D benchmark and programs from the NAS parallel benchmarks were measured using 8 threads and tuned on Ranger [7]. Each node of Ranger consists of four quad-core AMD Barcelona processors and contains 32 GB of main memory. Each core has its private L1 data and instruction caches of size 64 KB each. Unlike the Intel Nehalem processor, AMD Barcelona processor supports a per-core unified L2 cache of size 512 KB. The L3 cache (2 MB) is per-socket and is therefore shared among the four cores [1]. The choice of selecting a particular machine for any program was purely random. For brevity, we

```
variable: CDF (avg_dist: 3.85, count: 524174, avg_cpa: 78.53, numa_hit_ratio: 52.38)

  dist  cpa  use ln#  reuse ln#    count     file:
     0  150        0        290    17010   ex_particle_OPENMP_seq.c
     1  250      290        290   129964   ex_particle_OPENMP_seq.c
     1    4      290        290   328165   ex_particle_OPENMP_seq.c

variable: matrix (avg_dist: 0.37, count: 50996, avg_cpa: 95.25, numa_hit_ratio: 100.00)

  dist  cpa  use ln#  reuse ln#    count     file:
     1    4      185        185    19122   ex_particle_OPENMP_seq.c
     0  150        0        185    31874   ex_particle_OPENMP_seq.c
```

Figure 2: Excerpt of trace analysis output for naïve version of Particle Filter code

include part of the MACPO output for one of the programs (Particle Filter) in Figure 2.

6.1 Codes for which MACPO data was critical

6.1.1 ASCI Sweep3D

The Sweep3D benchmark is part of the ASCI benchmark suite and solves the 3D Cartesian geometry discrete ordinates neutron transport problem. PerfExpert showed that most of the data access LCPI (3.7) was arising from L1 accesses (2.9). The code in question was a loop with its body of the form:

```
do i = 1, it
  flux(i,j,k,2) = ...
  flux(i,j,k,3) = ...
  flux(i,j,k,4) = ...
enddo
```

MACPO showed a very high dominant stride (3906 cache lines) for the **flux** data structure. The strided accesses either forced the compiler to not vectorize the loop or caused the processor to read data from memory (instead of it prefetching them). We thus split the loop into three loops, each containing a single statement. Apart from having the intended effect of accessing the array using unit strides, this also caused the compiler to vectorize the loops. The optimized code reduced the dominant stride to 1, reduced the data access LCPI to 2.6 (with 1.8 as the L1 access LCPI) and caused the total running time to decrease by 24%.

6.1.2 NAS LU Symmetric Gauss-Seidel

This code is a non-linear PDE solver. The LU code uses a symmetric successive over-relaxation solver kernel. PerfExpert showed both data accesses and data TLB to be a problem. PerfExpert also showed that the last level cache contributes the most to the data access LCPI value. Data structure analysis showed that the reuse distances for two arrays (**flux** and **u**) were high (approximately 15 and 11 cache lines respectively). We found that a few of the loops that used these arrays could be fused, thus promoting greater reuse. Measurements on the revised code showed that the reuse distance for **flux** and **u** reduced to 11 and 8 cache lines respectively. Post optimization, the running time for the code was reduced by 8%.

6.1.3 Particle Filter

The Particle Filter code tracks an object across video frames. For this code, as shown briefly in Figure 2, we noticed that two data structures (**CDF** and **matrix**) had very high estimated cycles per access (78, 95 respectively). For **matrix**, it was reported that a majority of the accesses were not being fetched from the L1 cache and that this data structure did not use unit strides. For the other data structure (**CDF**), we saw the NUMA hit ratio to be about 50% (indicating that remote fetches probably contributed to the latency). The code in question has all threads performing a linear search over a single large sorted array. To make each core operate on separate portions of the array without significant refactoring of the code, the code was changed to keep track of the successful search index from the previous iteration. The resulting analysis showed that cycles per accesses for **matrix** dropped to 13 while the number of accesses to **CDF** dropped to an insignificant number. On large inputs (40K particles), this resulted in the entire program taking about a quarter of its original running time.

6.1.4 Needleman-Wunsch

This code is a parallel implementation of a dynamic programing solution. In this code, iterations (size of the diagonal) are distributed equally among the cores by the OpenMP runtime. PerfExpert showed that the L1 data access LCPI was high but unlike most other codes, there were fewer last level cache misses. This eliminated capacity misses from the possible causes of the problem. Memory analysis showed that access to the **input_itemsets** array was becoming a problem (reuse distance as high as 13 cache lines). Combining the information that L1 cache access LCPI was high and that all threads access the same array in a loop, one can infer that the multicore reuse distance for this array is affected by simultaneous use by different cores, thus causing contention among processors. To reduce this distance we focused on increasing the affinity between each core and its data. With the objective of ensuring that shuffling of data among cores does not occur too often, we increased the OpenMP chunk size of the iteration distribution to 32. This results in at least 32 consecutive iterations being assigned to a single core, thus increasing reuse within a single cache. The optimized code shows about 4% improvement and the reuse distance for the data structure is decreased from 13 cache lines to 9 cache lines.

6.2 Codes for which MACPO data was not critically important

For the analyses discussed in this section, code centric performance counter measurements enabled identification of appropriate optimizations.

6.2.1 NAS Block Tridiagonal

The Block Tridiagonal code is another non-linear Partial Differential Equation (PDE) solver written in Fortran. This code includes three main routines [`x_solve()`, `y_solve()`, `z_solve()`] that together take about 40% of the total time. All three of them, especially `z_solve()`, have particularly bad data access LCPI values with the last level cache contributing most to the data access LCPI. Data structure analysis showed that two arrays (`fjac` and `njac`) had a reuse distance of about 9 cache lines but were accessed with a unit stride. Similarly another array (`lhs`) had a reuse distance of about 7 cache lines. Inspecting the code showed that in each iteration of the loop body, all three arrays were accessed in a way that the most frequently changing index was not the first one. Changing the data layout reduced the reuse distance for all arrays to 4 cache lines and the running time decreased by 13%.

6.2.2 Lattice Boltzmann

This Fortran code is an MPI-parallel two dimensional Lattice Boltzmann solver for the Navier-Stokes equation. Running PerfExpert on this code showed last level cache misses contributing about a third of the data access LCPI. For the same routine, through data structure measurements, we found that one of the arrays (`f`) had a relatively high reuse distance (7 cache lines). Moreover, MACPO reported that this array was often (about 2,700 times) being accessed with a stride of 2 cache lines. Inspecting the code revealed the multiple elements of this array were being accessed in the loop body in the following form:

```
... = f(i,j,0,now) + f(i,j,1,now) +
      f(i,j,2,now) + ...
```

The index that changes with each access to the array is not the first one hence we were seeing non-zero stride values. Modifying the code so that the first index changed most often caused MACPO to report unit strides with reuse distance dropping from 7 cache lines to 6 cache lines. The running time reduced by 13%.

6.2.3 Back Propagation

This machine learning code is used to determine weights in a layered neural network. Through performance counters, we learned that L1 and L2 accesses dominated the data access LCPI. The L2 miss LCPI was low indicating few capacity misses. Trace analysis on this code showed high cycles per access (64) and relatively high reuse distances (5 cache lines) for two arrays (`w`, `oldw`). Inspection of the code showed that the arrays were being accessed in a strided manner. Such an access pattern affects the processor's ability to prefetch data into the cache. The code in question is a doubly-nested loop in C, similar to the code shown below:

```
loop i = 1 to n
  loop j = 1 to n
    array[j,i] = ...
```

Assuming that program correctness is maintained, a better way to rewrite the same code is by inverting the two loops. Such an inversion for the loop in the Back Propagation code reduced the cycles per access to 5, reuse distance to 2 cache lines and the code showed 17% improvement in total time.

6.2.4 SRAD (Speckle Reducing Anisotropic Diffusion)

SRAD uses Partial Difference Equations for ultrasound imaging. PerfExpert showed that the LCPI for TLB accesses was significantly high. This suggested frequent accesses with long strides. We also noticed that the `image` array had a high reuse distance (21 cache lines) and a high access latency (20 cycles). Stride analysis showed that this array was accessed with an average stride of 32 cache lines. Code inspection showed that the loops were inverted, causing strided accesses to the data structures. Changing the loop order reduced the reuse distance to 1 cache line and access penalty to 13 cycles, ultimately reducing the total time by 38%.

7. CONCLUSIONS

We described the design, implementation and innovations of the MACPO tool which specifically targets generation of the memory access characteristics of data structures required for performance optimization for multicore chip and multichip node execution. We described a process for performance optimization which integrates code-centric measurement with measurements and analyses of data structure memory access characteristics. Illustrations of the enhanced process demonstrate the value of integrating code-centric and data structure-centric analyses and specifically demonstrate the additional capabilities for diagnosis and selection of optimizations enabled by adding data structure-centric analyses to the performance optimization process.

8. FUTURE WORK

Knowledge of the memory access patterns and resolving the cost of data accesses to data structures has a significant role to play in the future of performance optimization. We plan to incorporate this knowledge into the optimization component of PerfExpert [27]. For example, reuse and stride data can be used to automate selection of the optimal tile/block size for loop tiling. An important performance optimization may be mapping of code segments to accelerators which execute in SIMT/SIMD parallelism. The process which combines code segment centric and data structure memory behavior centric measurements can be extended to determine code segments that can readily be converted to execute in SIMT/SIMD mode. The critical properties which can be readily determined from multicore chip/multicore node execution include absence of divergent branches, scalable SPMD parallelism, small and regular access strides and high reuse factors for the data structures in the code segments. Additionally the data from MACPO can guide translation from C, C++ or Fortran to accelerator languages such as CUDA or OpenCL.

9. ACKNOWLEDGEMENTS

This work is funded in part by the National Science Foundation under OCI award #0622780.

10. REFERENCES

[1] AMD Barcelona Processor Cache Architecture. http://developer.amd.com/documentation/articles/pages/8142007173.aspx.

[2] GCC 4.6.2 manual. http://gcc.gnu.org/onlinedocs/gcc-4.6.2/gcc/.

[3] Intel C Compiler Manual. http://software.intel.com/sites/products/documentation/hpc/compilerpro/en-us/cpp/lin/compiler_c/copts/common_options/option_fp_lcase.htm.

[4] Linux support for NUMA hardware. http://lse.sourceforge.net/numa/faq/.

[5] Longhorn User Guide. http://www.tacc.utexas.edu/user-services/user-guides/.

[6] PerfExpert. http://www.tacc.utexas.edu/perfexpert.

[7] Ranger User Guide. http://www.tacc.utexas.edu/user-services/user-guides/.

[8] The ASCI Sweep3D Benchmark Code. DOE Accelerated Strategic Computing Initiative. http://www.c3.lanl.gov/pal/software/sweep3d/sweep3d_readme.html.

[9] ThreadSpotter. http://www.roguewave.com/.

[10] D. H. Bailey, E. Barszcz, L. Dagum, and H. D. Simon. NAS Parallel Benchmark Results 3-94. *Proceedings of the Scalable High Performance Computing Conference*, pages 386–393, 1992.

[11] K. Beyls and E. D'Hollander. Discovery of locality-improving refactorings by reuse path analysis. *High Performance Computing and Communications*, pages 220–229, 2006.

[12] K. Beyls and E. H. D'Hollander. Refactoring for Data Locality. *Computer*, 42(2):62–71, 2009.

[13] M. Burtscher, B. D. Kim, J. Diamond, J. Mccalpin, L. Koesterke, and J. Browne. PerfExpert : An Easy-to-Use Performance Diagnosis Tool for HPC Applications. In *Computer*, pages 1–11. IEEE, 2010.

[14] S. Che, M. Boyer, J. Meng, D. Tarjan, J. W. Sheaffer, S.-H. Lee, and K. Skadron. Rodinia: A benchmark suite for heterogeneous computing. *2009 IEEE International Symposium on Workload Characterization IISWC*, 2009(c):44–54, 2009.

[15] J. Dean, J. E. Hicks, C. A. Waldspurger, W. E. Weihl, and G. Chrysos. ProfileMe: hardware support for instruction-level profiling on out-of-order processors. *Proceedings of 30th Annual International Symposium on Microarchitecture*, pages 292–302, 1997.

[16] C. Ding and Y. Zhong. Predicting whole-program locality through reuse distance analysis. In *Proceedings of ACM SIGPLAN Conference on Programming Language Design and Implementation*, 2003.

[17] Intel. Intel Processor Identification and the CPUID Instruction. *Journal On The Theory Of Ordered Sets And Its Applications*, (August), 2009.

[18] M. Itzkowitz, B. J. N. Wylie, C. Aoki, and N. Kosche. Memory profiling using hardware counters. In *In Supercomputing Conference (SC*, pages 17–30, 2003.

[19] Y. Jiang, E. Zhang, K. Tian, and X. Shen. Is Reuse Distance Applicable to Data Locality Analysis on Chip Multiprocessors? In *Compiler Construction*, pages 264–282. Springer, 2010.

[20] C. Lattner and V. Adve. LLVM: A compilation framework for lifelong program analysis & transformation. *International Symposium on Code Generation and Optimization 2004 CGO 2004*, (c):75–86, 2004.

[21] K. Lawton. Bochs IA-32 Emulator Project, 2004.

[22] X. Liu and J. Mellor-Crummey. Pinpointing Data Locality Problems Using Data-centric Analysis. *CGO*, pages 171–180, 2011.

[23] G. Marin. Scalable cross-architecture predictions of memory hierarchy response for scientific applications. In *In Proceedings of the Symposium of the Las Alamos Computer Science Institute, Sante Fe*, 2005.

[24] V. J. Reddi, A. Settle, D. A. Connors, and R. S. Cohn. PIN: a binary instrumentation tool for computer architecture research and education. *Computer Architecture*, 2004.

[25] D. L. Schuff, M. Kulkarni, V. S. Pai, and W. Lafayette. Accelerating Multicore Reuse Distance Analysis with Sampling and Parallelization. *Measurement*, pages 53–63, 2010.

[26] D. L. Schuff, B. S. Parsons, and V. S. Pai. Multicore-aware reuse distance analysis. *Measurement*, page 8 pp., 2010.

[27] O. A. Sopeju, M. Burtscher, A. Rane, and J. Browne. AutoSCOPE : Automatic Suggestions for Code Optimizations using PerfExpert. *International Conference on Parallel and Distributed Processing Techniques and Applications*, 2011.

[28] S. Vlaovic and E. S. Davidson. *TAXI: Trace Analysis for X86 Interpretation*. PhD thesis, University of Michigan, 2002.

[29] J. Weinberg and A. Snavely. Chameleon: A framework for observing, understanding, and imitating the memory behavior of applications. In *PARA08: Workshop on State-of-the-Art in Scientific and Parallel Computing, Trondheim, Norway*. Citeseer, 2008.

Compiling to Avoid Communication

Kathy Yelick
University of California at Berkeley
Lawrence Berkeley National Laboratory

ABSTRACT

Future computing system designs will be constrained by power density and total system energy, and will require new programming models and implementation strategies. Data movement in the memory system and interconnect will dominate running time and energy costs, making communication cost reduction the primary optimization criteria for compilers. Communication cost can be divided into latency costs, which are per communication event, and bandwidth costs, which grow with total communication volume.

Latency can be reduced by a number of techniques, including message aggregation, reducing software overhead of messaging, and overlapping communication with computation or with other communication events. While these techniques have been studied extensively, there are still many open challenges in automating these techniques in the context of explicitly parallel programs. I will describe some of the history of this work, and the program analysis challenges related to keeping a simple semantic model for programmers.

Bandwidth reduction requires more substantial algorithmic transformations, although some techniques, such as loop tiling, are well known. These can be applied as hand-optimizations, through code generation strategies in autotuned libraries, or as fully automatic compiler transformations. Less obvious techniques for communication avoidance have arisen in developing algorithms that are provably communication-optimal, the so-called "2.5D" algorithms in dense linear algebra. I will describe how these ideas generalize to other loop nests and some initial thoughts on automating such transformations.

Categories and Subject Descriptors

C.4 [**Performance of Systems**]: Performance attributes; D.3.3 [**Language Constructs and Features**]: Concurrent programming structures.

Keywords

Compiler, Communication, Autotuning, Latency, Bandwidth.

BIO

Kathy Yelick is the Associate Laboratory Director for Computing Sciences at Lawrence Berkeley National Laboratory. She is also a Professor of Electrical Engineering and Computer Sciences at the University of California at Berkeley. She co-invented the UPC and Titanium languages as well as techniques for self-tuning sparse matrix kernels, and has published over 100 technical papers. She earned her Ph.D. in EECS from MIT and has been a professor at UC Berkeley since 1991 with a joint appointment at LBNL since 1996. She has received multiple research and teaching awards and is a member of the California Council on Science and Technology and the National Academies Computer Science and Telecommunications Board.

PACT'12, September 19–23, 2012, Minneapolis, Minnesota, USA.
ACM 978-1-4503-1182-3/12/09.

Visualizing Transactional Memory

Justin E. Gottschlich
Intel Corporation
Programming Systems Lab
justin.e.gottschlich@intel.com

Maurice P. Herlihy
Brown University
Dept. of Computer Science
herlihy@cs.brown.edu

Gilles A. Pokam
Intel Corporation
Programming Systems Lab
gilles.a.pokam@intel.com

Jeremy G. Siek
University of Colorado-Boulder
Dept. of Electrical and Computer Engineering
jeremy.siek@colorado.edu

ABSTRACT

This paper presents *TMProf*, a transactional memory (TM) profiler, based on three visualization principles. These principles are *(i)* the precise graphical representation of transaction interactions including cross-correlated information and source code, *(ii)* visualized soft real-time playback of concurrently executing transactions, and *(iii)* dynamic visualizations of multiple executions. We describe how these principles break new ground and create new challenges for TM profilers.

We discuss our experience using TMProf with InvalSTM, a state-of-the-art software TM, and show how TMProf's feedback led to the design of two new contention managers (CMs). We demonstrate the performance benefits of these CMs, which generally led to improved performance as the amount of work and threads increase per benchmark. Our experimental results show that iBalanced, one of our newly designed CMs, can increase transaction throughput by nearly 10× over iFair, InvalSTM's previously best performing CM.

Categories and Subject Descriptors: D.1.3 [Concurrent Programming]: Parallel programming; D.1.7 [Visual Programming]; D.2.8 [Metrics]: Performance measures.

General Terms: Algorithms, Measurement, Performance

Keywords: Transactional Memory, Visualization, Profiler

1. INTRODUCTION

With the announcement of upcoming hardware transactional memory (HTM) support in Intel's Haswell and IBM's Blue Gene/Q processors, tools that help programmers write correct and efficient transactional memory (TM) programs are now more important than ever [1, 27]. Programs that use TM, like any other class of programs, need effective profilers. While many profiling tasks are common to all software systems, TM-based systems present unique profiling challenges [29, 32]. In particular, if two transactions access the same data object, and at least one access is a write, then the transactions *conflict* [25, 30]. Such conflicts can have a substantial impact on system performance [14]. In some TM implementations, conflicts are detected lazily, causing transactions that conflict to be *aborted*, that is, rolled back and restarted. In others, conflicts are detected eagerly, causing some transactions to block waiting for conflicting transactions to finish. No matter how conflicts are resolved, a TM profiler should help programmers understand how and when conflicts occur and provide insight into how they can be managed to improve a program's performance. [1]

Profilers for single-threaded programs generally capture at least the following two performance metrics: *(i)* the total execution time spent inside a function and *(ii)* the number of times the function is executed [13]. When these metrics are used together, programmers can generally resolve most single-threaded performance bottlenecks. If similar metrics were used for multi-threaded TM programs, a TM profiler might track *(i)* the total execution time per transaction and *(ii)* the number of times each transaction is executed. Unfortunately, these metrics alone have limited utility in TM profiling because they do not capture key pieces of contextual information.

For example, only considering a transaction's total execution time does not isolate the effects of *transactional interference*, those conflicting transactions that execute concurrently causing at least one transaction to abort or stall. It is important to capture the effects of transactional interference because such information quantifies the amount of time a transaction's execution has, or has not, been impacted by conflicting transactions. Furthermore, only considering the number of times a transaction has executed (i.e., committed) will not include the number of times it was previously aborted. Understanding aborted transactional data can shed light on the type and potency of optimizations for transactions.

To address these and other issues with single-threaded profilers, TM profiler and optimizer research has emerged with a central focus on how aborts impact performance. Lev's and Zyulkyarov et al.'s TM profiling research provides various facilities to track and quantify aborts [24, 38], while Chakrabarti et al.'s TM optimizer automatically reduces the

[1] An alternative to programmers using profiling data to improve a TM program's performance is to use a system that automatically switches to the most efficient software TM, from a given set, based on the program's execution pattern [36].

PACT'12, September 19–23, 2012, Minneapolis, Minnesota, USA.

number of aborts produced by an execution by utilizing the information generated in its run-time abort graph [5]. In addition to the reasons described above, these works observe that aborts represent the most obvious form of wasted work and therefore are a natural target for optimization.

1.1 Overview of TMProf

Like these works, the profiler we present in this paper, *TMProf*, provides specific techniques to track and quantify aborts. Yet, unlike them, TMProf can help programmers understand the importance of aborts (and commits) with precise cross-correlated information. This information distills how aborts and commits in one thread influence the forward progress of transactions in another. In Section 2, we illustrate how the right type of abort at the right time can improve performance, rather than degrade it, and how visualizations reduce the challenge of identifying such behavior. We extend this notion in Section 4 to demonstrate how certain commits can degrade performance rather than improve it. We then use these techniques together with TMProf's visualizations to find new contention management (CM) strategies.

In addition to cross-correlated abort and commit information, TMProf provides a visualized playback feature that replays the program's execution in soft real-time [4]. TMProf's playback feature conveys the complex interactions between transactions as they unfold in time and presents the effects of such interactions in the broader context of the program's complete execution. With such playback, a programmer can track transactional interference amongst transactions in specific phases of the program and understand how such interference impacts the immediate and long-term forward progress of the execution.

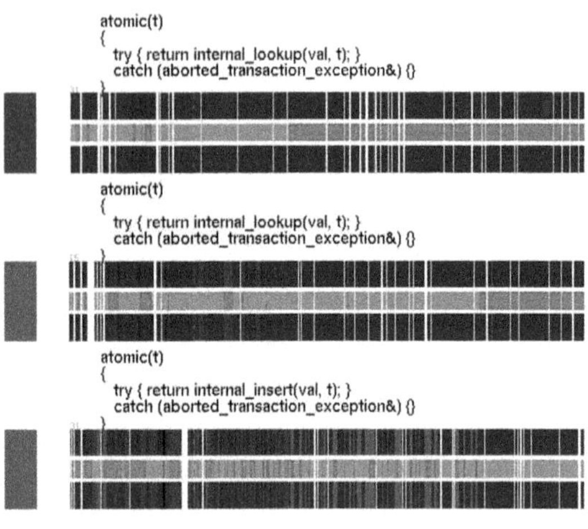

Figure 1: Using TMProf to Replay an Execution.

TMProf's visualizations are also dynamic and can display as many complete program executions as are necessary to understand and analyze a specific behavior. A visualization displaying a single execution shows how transactions interact across several threads. A visualization displaying multiple executions of the same program illustrates how a change to the program has impacted its performance and the reason(s) for such a difference. TMProf can also display the transactional source code associated with any number of visualized executions, as shown in Figure 1, where each thread is represented as a horizontal bar and the various colors identify conflicts between transactions.

Providing TMProf's visualization functionality does not come without cost and these costs create new challenges in both the data collection and the visual representation aspects of the system. Like the works of Chakrabarti et al. [5], Lev [24], and Zyulkyarov et al. [38], TMProf must gather enough data to provide meaningful profiling information without incurring a *probe effect*, where a program's behavior is unintentionally altered by an external system that is analyzing it [9]. Minimizing the likelihood of a probe effect requires a trade-off between the amount of data gathered and the profiler's precision. Yet, unlike prior TM profiler research, TMProf must perform full execution traces because it provides cross-correlation information rendered across *entire* executions. Moreover, TMProf's execution playback functionality requires precise back-end timing data collection for near real-time playback. Gathering this data increases the data density per transaction and, therefore, the likelihood of a perturbation of the recorded program's execution, as well as increasing the computational workload during TMProf's front-end visualization.

For the remainder of this paper, we gradually explore TMProf's visualization capabilities, the challenges that were overcome to support its functionality, and the TM optimizations we constructed based on its feedback. This paper makes the following technical contributions.

1. We present TMProf, a TM profiler that provides *(i)* graphical representation of transaction-level interactions including cross-correlated information and transactional code, *(ii)* visualized soft real-time playback of concurrently executing transactions, and *(iii)* dynamic visualizations of multiple TM executions (Section 2).

2. We present the challenges we encountered building TMProf and the unique design and implementation decisions we made to overcome them (Section 3).

3. We present a case study using TMProf, including the algorithmic details of the CMs we built using TMProf's visualizations (Section 4).

4. We provide 8- to 24-threaded benchmarks that demonstrate the benefits of the CM optimizations we built yielding nearly a 10× scalable improvement over InvalSTM's previously most efficient CM [12] (Section 4).

2. VISUALIZATION

Profiling parallel programs is much more challenging than profiling sequential programs. For multithreaded programs, shared-memory synchronization is a principal source of latency [2, 22]. For TM programs, synchronization costs may be even more substantial, because conflicts can cause longer waits or transaction aborts [14]. In general, reducing conflicting data accesses enhances concurrency and reduces the need to abort and restart transactions. One of the most important functions of a TM profiler is thus to capture and convey how transactions interact, with the goal of helping the developer understand and reduce conflicts. *This observation implies that an effective TM profiler should be primarily visual, because graphical representation is the best way to convey complex interactions unfolding in time.*

Figure 2 shows a four-threaded TM execution as presented by TMProf. Each horizontal bar represents a single thread.

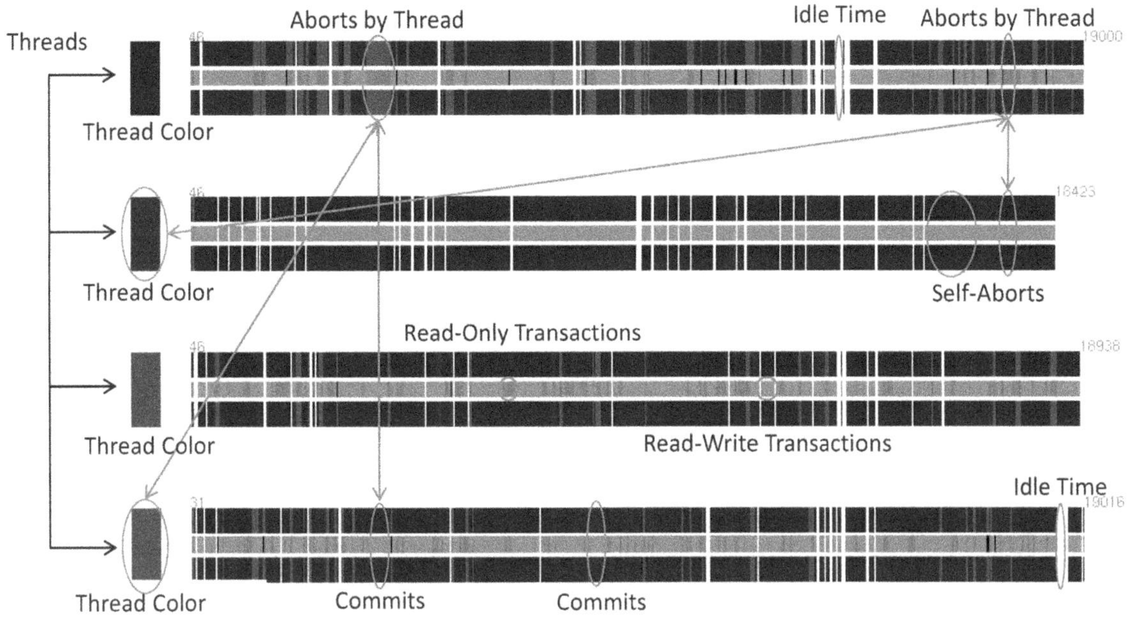

Figure 2: An Example of TMProf's Visualization.

The numbers to the left and right of each thread indicate the thread's respective starting and ending times in milliseconds. Each thread has three bar segments: two outer and one inner. The outer segments indicate if the transaction was committed (green) or aborted (some other color). The inner segment indicates the transaction type when it was committed or aborted: green indicates read-only transactions, grey indicates transactions that both read and write, and black indicates write-only transactions.

At startup, TMProf assigns a unique color to each thread, which is indicated by the rectangle to the left of the thread's execution. When a transaction is aborted, it is assigned either a blue color, which indicates the transaction was self-aborted, or a thread's color, which indicates that the corresponding thread caused the transaction to abort due to a conflict.

2.1 Transaction Interference

Perhaps the most important function of a TM profiler is its ability to provide a clear and precise picture of how and why transactions abort. Because aborted transactions represent wasted work, they are a natural target for optimization [37]. Understanding why transactions abort requires an understanding of how their data accesses conflict [18]. Once the nature of the conflicts is understood, the developer can attempt to change or reduce conflicts, perhaps by restructuring the data, changing transaction functionality, or modifying the TM system or its contention manager (CM) [15, 33, 35]. To achieve this kind of understanding, each of the prior works from Chakrabarti et al. [5], Lev [24], and Zyulkyarov et al. [38] provide unique facilities to track aborts.

TMProf introduces advanced cross-correlation abort and commit tracking facilities which complement the existing ones provided by prior research. TMProf's cross-correlation feature visually conveys how aborts and commits improve or degrade the overall performance of the program. To demonstrate this, consider the execution shown in Figure 3. In this example, each thread performs an equal number of inserts on a shared linked list and the CM strategy is designed so a committing transaction always aborts conflicting inflight transactions.

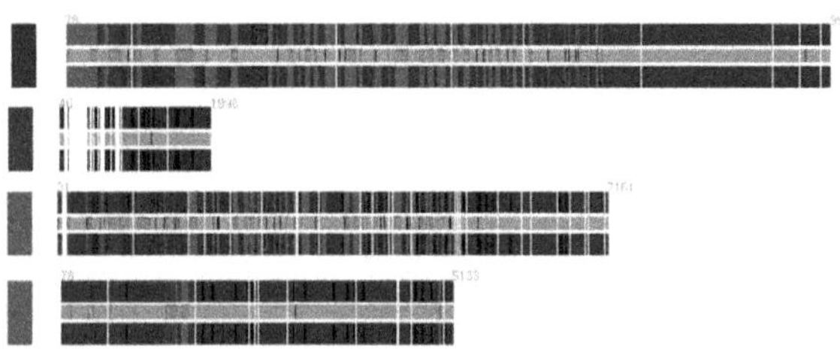

Figure 3: 4-Threaded Linked List Benchmark.

The transactions of the thread second from the top suffer almost no aborts because its transactions insert items near the front of the linked list. Its transactions are shorter running and reach their commit phase sooner than the other transactions and its total execution time reflects this, which is almost 5× faster than the slowest thread. The top-most thread's transactions suffer numerous aborts because its transactions insert items at the tail of the linked list. Its transactions run longer than others, making them susceptible to aborts by other committing transactions.

When considered in isolation, each thread's behavior performs exactly as it should to keep aborts to a minimum. If the goal is to minimize the total number of aborts, the TM's behavior is close to optimal. Yet, by viewing TMProf's visualization of the program, one can immediately determine that an optimally low number of aborts is not necessarily what will make this program execute more efficiently. Instead, improved performance will likely come from more balanced execution times across all threads, which may mean having a disproportionately large number aborts for the fastest executing thread, which can improve the efficiency of the slowest executing thread by reducing its aborts.

This example illustrates the importance of understanding aborts and commits within the context of an entire program's execution. While it may seem generally reasonable to reduce aborts in an attempt to improve performance because they represent wasted work, when universally applied, such an approach may counterintuitively degrade performance, as shown in Figure 3, resulting in a notable disparity in execution time between threads.

2.2 Execution Playback

Multithreaded execution playback can be performed online or offline. An online playback system, such as Patil et al.'s PinPlay [31] or Lev's T-PASS [24], replays an execution by re-executing the original program, instruction by instruction. These systems also include complex logic for correct multithreaded replay, which when combined their instruction-by-instruction playback, can reduce replay speeds by upwards of 100× compared to a normal execution. Offline playback systems, such as TMProf, replay an execution by simulating certain aspects of the recorded execution using logged information that was generated during the original execution [7]. While offline replayers do not re-execute each instruction, and, therefore, have limitations of the program state they can reproduce, they have the advantage of being able to simulate aspects of the original execution at various speeds, which can be instrumental in identifying and resolving performance bottlenecks.

TMProf supports forward and reverse playback control, pause, and user-controllable playback rates (from 0.0001× to 1000× normal execution speed). Although we cannot demonstrate TMProf's playback functionality within this paper, a recorded demonstration of its playback functionality can be downloaded at http://tinyurl.com/7v5oj47 and viewed in any media software player compatible with AVI recordings. TMProf has been optimized so that it can manage the soft real-time playback of roughly a hundred threads at a time. In our experiments, however, we have found that replaying just a few threads, more than two but less than eight, provides enough detail of program contention to create optimizations that scale to dozens of threads.

2.3 Dynamic Visualizations

The work of Lev [24] and Zyulkyarov et al. [38] provides functionality to analyze and inspect a multithreaded TM execution from different visual viewpoints. We extend these techniques in TMProf by enabling full program executions to be visually compared to each other in a side-by-side fashion. Such side-by-side comparisons are useful because they provide the programmer with immediate feedback on how optimizations have impacted the dynamic behavior of the transactions, such as their throughput and interaction with one another. Figure 4 shows two side-by-side executions. TMProf also supports executions to be overlaid on top of each other with minimal loss of visual integrity. [2]

Once a TM profiler supports the visualization of multiple executions and execution playback, a fixed representation of the visualizations may be insufficient for a programmer to gain a comprehensive understanding of the execution(s) [23]. Instead, rendering of such complex visualizations should be

[2] Because transparency effects do not transfer well to paper, we do not show any example displays here.

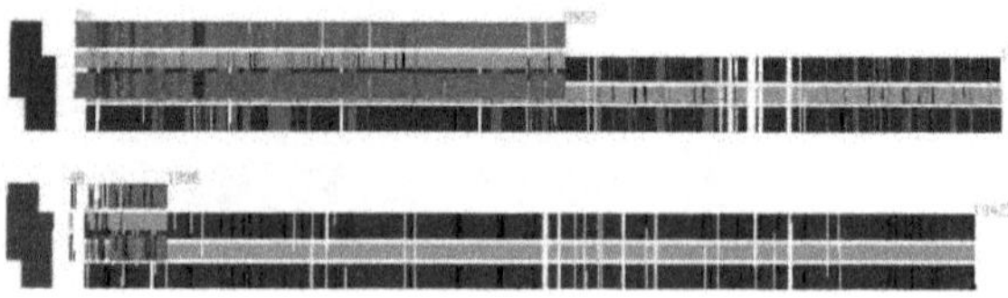

Figure 4: TMProf Overlaying Two Executions.

fluid, that is, they should change, dynamically, based on the user's needs. TMProf handles this by providing dynamic visualizations where the user can move, rotate, and change the visual representation of the scene. These features are important for detailed program inspection as we discuss in Section 4, which may be difficult to achieve from a fixed visualization such as those found by Zyulkyarov et al.'s TM profiler [38].

3. DESIGN AND OVERHEAD

Although TMProf can be used with any TM, its abort tracking system is particularly useful for TMs that use some form of *invalidation*, a conflict detection strategy where one active transaction aborts or stalls other active transactions [17, 10]. This is because such a system can generally capture information about which transactions conflict with others. Once this information is collected, it can be viewed in the context of TMProf's transactional interference visualization. TMs that use *validation*, where a transaction checks its own memory for conflicts with previously committed transactions, may be less useful for TMProf because in these systems information detailing which transaction caused another transaction to abort may not be available. Without such information, TMProf cannot visualize the correlation of conflicts between transactions.

Herlihy and Moss's original HTM is an example of an invalidation-based system, which uses a snoop-based cache coherence invalidation mechanism [21]. Software TMs (STMs) that use invalidation include RSTM's mixed invalidation [34], DSTM and DSTM2's eager write-write conflict detection [20, 19], Fraser and Harris's OSTM which uses lazy write-write conflict detection [8], and InvalSTM which uses full invalidation [12]. Furthermore, any TM that uses a CM to manage transactional conflicts can benefit from TMProf. The justification for each abort will be captured in TMProf's data gathering phase and then displayed by its visualization, providing cross-correlated transactional interference information, which can then be used to optimize the program or TM system.

3.1 No Sampling

A common problem associated with profilers, regardless of their single or multithreaded nature, is the computational and spatial overhead they introduce when gathering execution data [3, 7]. This overhead is sometimes referred to as *intrusion overhead*, because the external system's intrusion increases the execution time of the program it is analyzing [26]. In an attempt to minimize the impact of intrusion overhead many profilers use *sampling*, where a subset of program's execution is analyzed to estimate the behavior of the entire program. Sampling can reduce both the amount of time the program's execution is perturbed and the spatial impact of recording data, both of which can reduce the likelihood of a probe effect [3, 9]. For these and other reasons, Chakrabarti et al.'s [5] TM optimizer and Lev's [24] TM profiler use sampling. Zyulkyarov et al.'s profiler supports sampling, but they do not use it [38].

Unfortunately, because TMProf's visualization and replay features require complete execution traces, it cannot use sampling. If sampling were used, TMProf's execution traces would contain gaps resulting in incomplete visualizations. Furthermore, TMProf would be unable to provide its cross-correlated transaction interference feature, because not all transaction interactions would be captured. This places TMProf in a unique design space when compared to prior works that perform sampling. However, just as the prior systems of Chakrabarti et al., Lev, and Zyulkyarov et al., must minimize their intrusion overhead and probe effect, so too must TMProf, otherwise its resulting reports might be misleading. We explain how TMProf achieves this in the following sections.

3.2 Begin and End Events

To make TMProf practical, it does not track transactional memory accesses as is done in prior works [5, 24, 38]. Although such additional data would provide TMProf with more exhaustive execution information, we believe it would exceed limitations in both TMProf's graphical front-end and its data collection back-end. A data collection system that tracks transactional read, write, and opacity validation [16] events has an $O(N)$ space complexity, where N is the number of read and write elements per transaction, and, usually, an $O(N^2)$ or $O(N)$ time complexity if opacity read validations are tracked or not, respectively.

To reduce this complexity, TMProf limits its data collection to begin and end transactional events, as shown in Figure 5. Transactions generally begin in the same fashion, but end with either a commit or an abort. In Figure 5 we label these *end actions* (EA) as EA_N, where N is a unique identifier for the transaction. By only tracking begin and end events, TMProf's space and time overhead for both its data collection back-end and its graphical front-end is reduced to $O(1)$ per transaction.

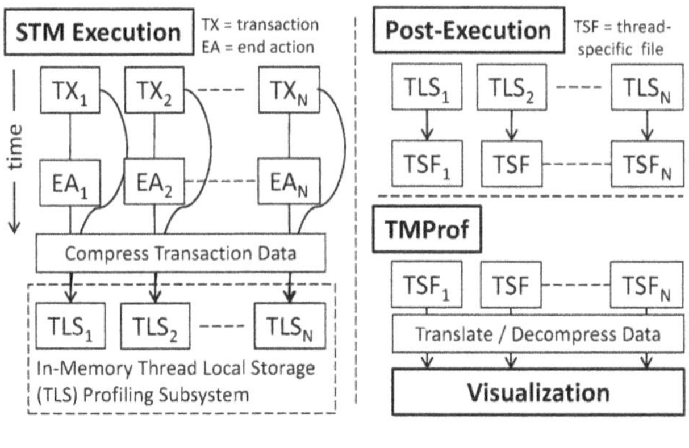

Figure 5: TMProf's High-Level Design.

To demonstrate the impact this has on TMProf's graphical front-end, consider Figure 6, which shows the number of polygons needed to display various events. For 64-threaded visualizations, with 16,384 transactions per thread and 32 reads and 1 write per transaction, displaying read, write, and opacity events requires three orders of magnitude more polygons than only displaying begin and end events. If opacity events are ignored, displaying only read and write events requires roughly an order and a half of magnitude, about 34×, more polygons than displaying only begin and end events. Because TMProf supports soft real-time playback, some percentage of these polygons, based on the current replay point and the user's chosen dynamic display, must be displayed roughly 30× per second so the visualizations are perceived as occurring in real-time. For these reasons, having TMProf display begin and end events, seems to align well with its soft real-time playback requirement.

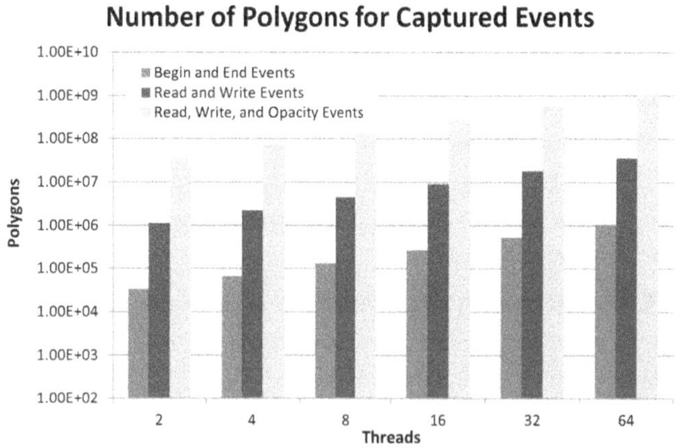

Figure 6: TMProf's Data Representation Overhead.

3.2.1 *Haswell's Restricted Transactional Memory*

An additional advantage of using begin and end events is their direct mapping to the Restricted Transactional Memory (RTM) instructions in Intel's upcoming Haswell processor [1]. Although we have not yet tested TMProf with Haswell, as it is not yet available, the Transactional Synchronization Extensions (TSX) instructions of Haswell's RTM – XBEGIN, XEND, and XABORT – map directly to TMProf's begin transaction, commit transaction, and abort transaction events. As such, it is our belief that TMProf will integrate well with Haswell's RTM. We plan to integrate TMProf with Haswell as soon as it becomes available.

3.3 Space and Time Optimizations

To further reduce TMProf's intrusion overhead, it uses thread local storage (TLS) and the thread-level parallelism that already exists in the multithreaded executions that it analyzes [28]. Although not novel, with TLS and a sufficient number of available cores, TMProf can concurrently gather execution data for any number of threads without introducing additional serialization. This is important in reducing intrusion overhead and limiting program perturbation.

TMProf also uses in-memory stream buffers when gathering execution data to reduce the computational latency associated with non-volatile I/O storage. Although in-memory buffers have the advantage of reducing time overhead, they introduce space overhead. To reduce this overhead, TMProf uses a hash-based compression algorithm that encodes a transaction with a unique identifier the first time it is encountered. When the same transaction is subsequently executed, the in-memory representation of that transaction is reduced to a single identifier (32-bits in TMProf's current implementation). TMProf uses an additional byte for the transaction event type and a 32-bit segment for the time of the event. For commit events one additional byte is needed to capture the type of transaction (i.e., read, write, or read and write). Abort events use an extra 32-bits to capture the unique thread identifier that caused the transaction to abort, which can be reduced to 8-bits for most practical purposes.

When a thread terminates, TMProf transfers the in-memory transactions of that thread to a thread-specific trace file, as shown in Figure 5. [3] In TMProf's initial design, it decompressed each transaction that was stored in the in-memory buffers before writing them to their appropriate trace file. However, this resulted in unacceptably large trace files. In the current design, all in-memory transactions remain compressed in their respective trace files. These files are then decompressed during the startup of TMProf's graphical front-end, which reduced the trace file sizes by $\approx$ 80% to 95% depending on the code size associated with the transactions, number of unique transactions, and frequency in which transactions were invoked.

3.4 Intrusion Overhead

Figure 7 displays TMProf's intrusion overhead for the microbenchmarks we discuss in Section 4. These microbenchmarks are linked list, hash table, red-black tree, and 1-writer / N-readers. We list TMProf's intrusion overhead only for 4-threaded instances of these benchmarks because the optimizations discussed in Section 4 were found by profiling 4-threaded versions of the respective workloads.

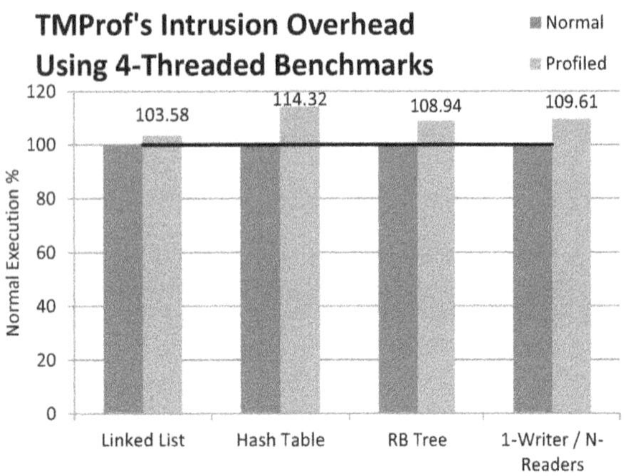

Figure 7: TMProf's Data Collection Overhead.

In each benchmark, with the exception of the 1-writer / N-readers, each thread populates its shared container with 4096 nodes. For the 1-writer / N-readers benchmark, one thread performs tail insertion to a shared linked list, while the other three threads perform iterative lookups on it. TMProf incurs 3.58%, 14.32%, 8.94%, and 9.61%, intrusion overhead for the linked list, hash table, red-black tree, and 1-writer / N-reader benchmarks, respectively.

Chakrabarti et al.'s TM optimizer, which uses sampling to gather profiling data, has an intrusion overhead percentage that ranges from 14.1% to 21.1% for STAMP benchmarks using 16-threaded executions [5]. Zyulkyarov et al.'s TM profiler, which captures read and write set sizes and begin and end events for every transaction and the address of conflicting memory locations for aborted transactions, has an intrusion overhead that ranges from -2.2% to 252% for STAMP benchmarks using 4-threaded executions [38]. Lev does not report intrusion overhead introduced by his profiler [24].

It is important to note that there are many factors that could lead to substantial differences in the intrusion overhead between TMProf and Chakrabarti et al.'s RAG optimizer and Zyulkyarov et al.'s TM profiler, such as, benchmarks analyzed, number of threads used, sampling versus tracing, processor configuration, and run-time events captured. Therefore, it would be inappropriate for us to make any claims about TMProf's intrusion overhead compared to these works. With that said, we include Chakrabarti et al.'s optimizer and Zyulkyarov et al.'s profiler overhead numbers to demonstrate that TMProf is competitive with them.

4. OBSERVATIONS AND EXPERIMENTS

Regardless of the features a profiler provides, its intrusion overhead, or the data it collects, the measure of a profiler's true utility comes from its ability to help programmers optimize programs. In this section, we present several examples of such cases using TMProf. Although the figures in this section do not include TMProf's transactional source code feature, where the code associated with each transaction's visualization is shown along side it, we would like to note that we relied, heavily, on this feature during our experimental analysis, as it helped us determine which transactions were conflicting and, consequently, how we could build optimizations that would efficiently manage such conflicts.

4.1 Experimental Overview

In our prior work developing InvalSTM, we found that CMs would be a natural target area for future optimizations. This is because InvalSTM provides a CM with more information (i.e., knowledge) than is generally available in TMs that do not use full invalidation [10, 11]. In this section, we show how TMProf helped us identify ways to more efficiently manage contention, leading to the construction of more efficient CMs. We describe how TMProf guided us to the construction of each CM, their algorithmic details, and the experiments we used to demonstrate each CM's scalability and generality, or lack thereof. We used InvalSTM, a state-of-the-art STM that is competitive with TL2 [6], as our baseline system and the iFair CM, which is InvalSTM's best performing CM [12]. All experiments were run on a 24-way Intel Xeon X5650 running at 2.67GHz.

We profiled the same benchmarks used in the initial InvalSTM study: *(i)* 1-writer / N-readers, *(ii)* linked list, *(iii)*, hash table, and added a *(iv)* red-black tree (RBtree) benchmark. For all benchmarks, except the 1-writer / N-readers benchmark (details forthcoming) each thread populates the same shared container using a non-overlapping range of incrementing values. Once a thread has inserted all of its values, it performs lookup operations on the inserted values as a sanity check. We also added remove operations for each element inserted after the sanity check had been performed. Each of these operations, insert, lookup, and remove, were programmed as individual transactions.

[3]These files are thread-specific so multiple files can be concurrently populated with trace data.

(a) iFair CM. (b) Bottom two iFair threads. (c) threadFair CM.

Figure 8: 1-Writer / N-Readers Visualized in TMProf.

4.2 The iFair CM

To understand how we derived our optimized CMs from TMProf's visualizations, we must first provide a brief outline of iFair. In general, iFair aims to limit wasted work by minimizing aborts and enabling transactions with large read and write sets to commit. Each transaction is given a dynamic priority that is increased each time it is aborted and a weighted average value, V, that is based on its dynamic priority multiplied by the number of reads and writes it has performed. Writes are given a greater weight than reads because they require more work to perform. When conflicts are resolved at commit-time, the only time they are resolved with InvalSTM, a committing transaction's V is compared against all of the other transactions with which it conflicts. If the committing transaction's V is greater than the sum of the conflicting transactions' V, it is permitted to commit, aborting the conflicting transactions. Otherwise, it aborts. iFair ensures no transaction starves by increasing the transaction's dynamic priority each time it is aborted. We call iFair a *transaction-level fair* CM, because it attempts to achieve fairness with respect to individual transactions. For example, if transaction T_1 is aborted by transaction T_2, T_1's priority is subsequently increased and is therefore less likely to be aborted by future transactions. Once a transaction successfully commits, its dynamic priority is reset to 1.

4.3 The threadFair CM

We began our experiments by analyzing the behavior of iFair using the 1-writer / N-readers benchmark, where one thread writes to a shared container and the other N threads read values from it. When contention arises, it is always with the writer transaction, because read-only transactions cannot conflict with one another. As shown in Figure 8(a), highlighted by the red rectangles, the number of aborts is reasonably low. This means that, in practice, the reader transactions are unlikely to simultaneously access the same location as the writer transaction. Therefore, it is unlikely that iFair can be optimized by reducing aborts, at least for this benchmark. Yet, because reducing aborts is the most common way to optimize TMs [5], such approaches have little opportunity for optimization here.

By analyzing TMProf's visualization of the 1-writer / N-readers benchmark using iFair, as depicted in Figure 8(a), we were able to make the following observations. [4] First, we noticed that the writer thread, the top-most thread, completes its execution $\approx 40\%$ sooner than the other threads. Second, all aborts occurred in the reader threads. Third, by successively playing, rewinding, and replaying at slower rates, we were able to determine that, in many cases, aborts in the reader threads (the bottom three threads of Figure 8(a)) come in successive waves. We would not have observed this without TMProf's playback feature, because when such self-aborts occur, they cannot be seen from a static view. This is because a static view provides no way to distinguish when a self-abort is a single, long running transaction or a grouping of multiple, short running ones.

From these observations, we tried to imagine how to build a more efficient CM. From our first observation, it seemed clear that a more efficient CM would extend the execution time of the writer thread to shorten the execution time of the reader threads. It seemed that we could achieve this by using the information we found from our second observation, which illustrated that all aborts originated from the reader threads. Moving those aborts to the writer thread would likely increase the writer thread's overall execution time, subsequently reducing the readers' execution time. Our third, and most important observation, provided the clue that iFair's transaction-level fairness, where the priority of a transaction is increased each time it is aborted, did not have any meaningful impact in this benchmark. This is because the reader transactions were aborted in succession, which iFair's transaction-level fairness was supposed to mitigate. Therefore, an alternative fairness mechanism would be needed. To fix this behavior, we would need to rely on something other than iFair's weighted V to balance the execution.

From these conclusions, we built the threadFair CM, which performs *thread-level fairness*, an algorithm that enables transaction T_1 to abort transaction T_2 only if T_1's *thread* has fewer commits than T_2's *thread*. To correct the behavior we saw in our third observation with iFair's V, threadFair provides no weighted value for a transaction. This guarantees that thread-level fairness will be respected by the writer transactions, preventing them from unfairly aborting other transactions.

Algorithm 1 describes threadFair in pseudocode. It returns true when the committing transaction, *commitTx*, is permitted to abort the set conflicting transactions, *conflicts*,

[4] Due to limited space, we shrunk TMProf's visualizations and used red rectangles to highlight the aborts in Figure 8. Note: this problem is specific to presenting TMProf in a paper, and is not a problem with the tool itself.

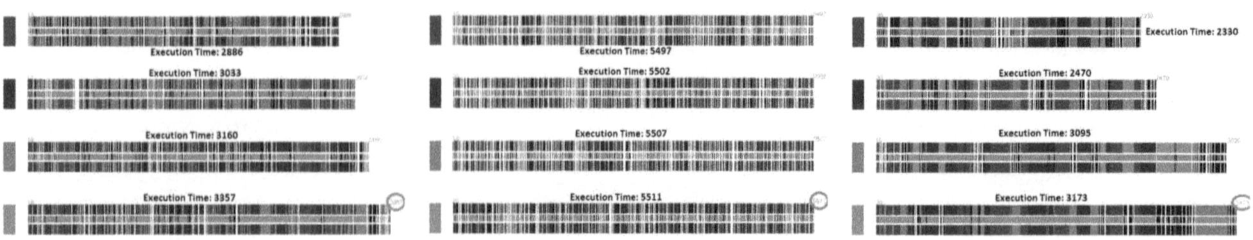

(a) iFair CM. (b) threadFair CM. (c) iBalanced CM.

Figure 9: Red-Black Tree Visualized in TMProf.

otherwise it aborts *commitTx*. *NextTx* returns a pointer to the next transaction in a set of transactions that are passed to it in the first parameter, returning NULL when the end of the set has been reached. If NULL is supplied, it begins iteration over the set. The *commits*() function returns the total number of commits for the thread. The *commitTx.sleep*(S) puts *commitTx*'s thread to sleep for S milliseconds after it is aborted.

Algorithm 1 The threadFair Contention Manager

```
procedure THREADFAIR(Transaction *commitTx, TransactionSet conflicts)
    boolean canAbort = true
    Transaction *tx = NULL
    loop
        tx = NextTx(conflicts, tx)
        if (tx ≡ NULL) then
            break
        if (commits(commitTx) > commits(tx)) then
            canAbort = false; *commitTx.sleep(S); break
    return canAbort
```

TMProf's visualization of threadFair, shown in Figure 8(c), successfully illustrates our assumptions about the how to improve the CM performance of the 1-writer / N-readers benchmark. The visualization shows *(i)* the writer thread's time is increased in favor of shortening the reader threads, *(ii)* aborts are moved from the reader threads to the writer thread, and *(iii)* using thread-level fairness, rather than transaction-level fairness, keeps the threads' overall progress closer together. Figures 8(a) and 8(c), show that threadFair (12443ms) yields a 6.6% performance improvement over iFair (13264ms). In Figure 10, we applied threadFair to 8-, 16-, and 24-threaded 1-writer / N-readers workloads and found that it scales well. For example, in the 24-threaded 1-writer / N-readers benchmark, threadFair, labeled "thread", outperforms iFair by upwards of 2.14×, a notable margin for a state-of-the-art STM.

4.4 The iBalanced CM

The first observation we made after creating threadFair is that while it performs well for the 1-writer / N-readers benchmark, it does not yield the same performance benefits for other benchmarks, as shown in Figure 9 which visualizes a 4-threaded RBtree. To begin to understand why, we explored threadFair's RBtree execution using TMProf's replay functionality. This led to a second observation: a substantial number of aborts, across all threads, were self-aborts (i.e., blue horizontal bars). We were unable to see this behavior using TMProf's static view because, *(i)* with a static view aborts are blended together, making it challenging to visually disambiguate one transaction's color from another; *(ii)* in playback mode, each thread's most recent transaction is displayed with a whitespace to its right, making its color easier to discern; and *(iii)* in playback mode, our concentration stayed fixed on the active transaction, making it easier to comprehend the events as they occur in sequence. We believe these reasons further reinforce the importance of TMProf's playback functionality.

Our third and final observation required almost all of TMProf's functionality. In short, we aimed to determine if self-aborts from one thread resulted in subsequent commits for the in-flight transactions of the other threads. If we could observe this behavior it would tell us if self-aborts resulted in some form of forward progress. Attempting this required control of several of TMProf's features.

First, we reduced the playback rate of the execution to no greater than $10^{-3}\times$ the normal execution speed, which allowed us enough time to pause the execution as soon as a specific transaction completed, but before the next transaction appeared. We then began execution playback. When the transaction we were interested in self-aborted, we paused the execution and zoomed-in to ensure it was a self-abort. Once we verified the self-abort, we zoomed out to see all threads, enabling us to see the next transaction's outcome. We resumed playback, paused it as soon as the next transaction appeared, and then zoomed in to see if the transaction committed.

Using this approach, we were able to determine the exact behavior of the other in-flight transactions once one of them was self-aborted. [5] What we found, we believe, was the principle reason behind threadFair's degraded performance. In short, throughout the execution when one transaction was self-aborted it was generally *not* the case that at least one subsequent transactions committed from the other threads. This means that threadFair was unnecessarily aborting a transaction at commit-time in favor of another in-flight transaction that subsequently did not commit, resulting in no forward progress. We tried to observe the same behavior in the iFair execution, but found that because self-aborts were rare, it did not contain such behavior.

By combining these observations, most especially the latter, we built the iBalanced CM. The essence of iBalanced is to combine the best pieces of threadFair and iFair to create a more efficient CM. From threadFair, we lifted thread-level fairness, because it helps ensure that threads have reduced

[5] We could determine the other transactions were in-flight because their thread's progress was shorter than the self-aborted transaction, meaning a transaction was currently in-flight when the first transaction self-aborted.

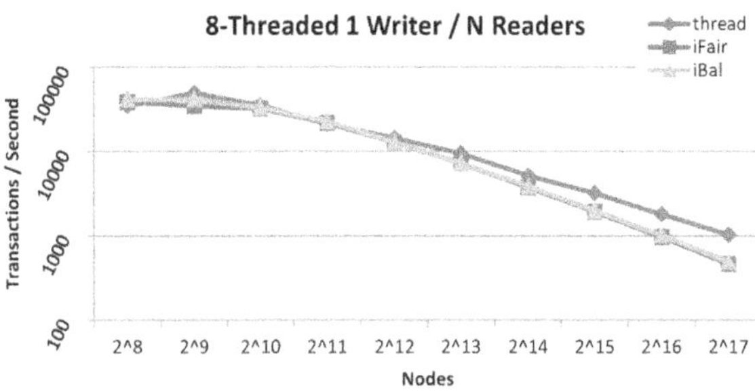

(a) 8-Threaded 1-Writer / N-Readers Benchmark.

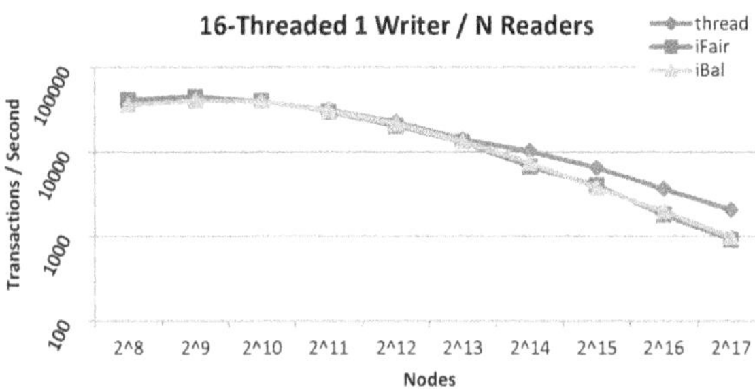

(b) 16-Threaded 1-Writer / N-Readers Benchmark.

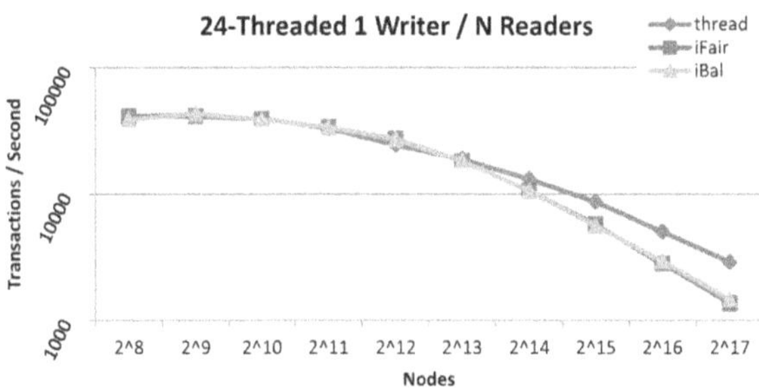

(c) 24-Threaded 1-Writer / N-Readers Benchmark.

Figure 10: 1-Writer / N-Readers Benchmarks.

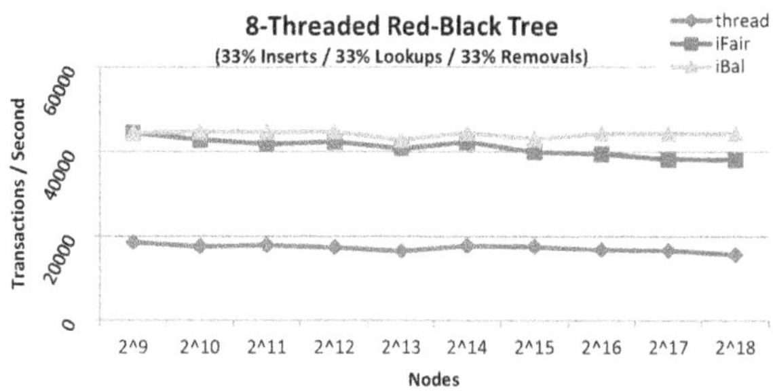

(a) 8-Threaded Red-Black Tree Benchmark.

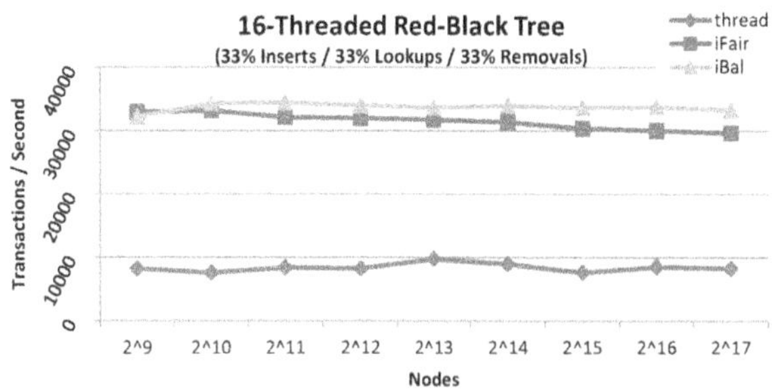

(b) 16-Threaded Red-Black Tree Benchmark.

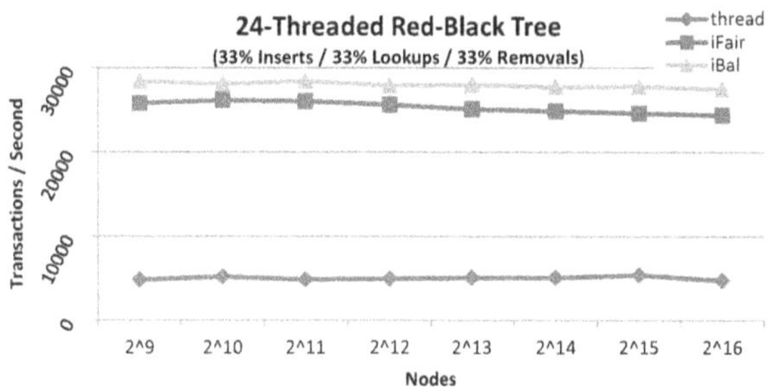

(c) 24-Threaded Red-Black Tree Benchmark.

Figure 11: Red-Black Tree Benchmarks.

variation in their total execution time, helping eliminate obvious critical paths (see Figure 3). From iFair, we lifted the goal of minimizing self-aborts at commit-time, such as ensuring a transaction with the most reads or writes commits, because such transactions represent forward progress if permitted to commit. However, instead of comparing a committing transaction's reads or writes against the sum of all other in-flight transactions (iFair's V), we only require the committing transaction have the largest read or write set, overall, which decreases the likelihood of self-aborts. We also introduced new predicates, not originally part of iFair, that we found by analyzing TMProf's visualizations, such as when a transaction is in its commit phase and its thread has the fewest commits of any conflicting transaction that it should be allowed to commit regardless of the transactions it may abort. When any of these new predicates are satisfied, they guarantee a transaction will commit.

The iBalanced algorithm is shown in Algorithm 2. WC, RC, FCC, and SC represent constant multipliers for a committing transaction's write set, read set, fewest commits, and set size, respectively. These multipliers control the importance of each characteristic, where a higher multiplier value denotes more importance and a lower multiplier value, with 1 being the lowest, denotes less. For our experiments, we found $WC = 3$, $RC = 1$, $FCC = 3$, and $SC = 3$, yield the best general performance. Functions $reads()$ and $writes()$ return the number of elements a transaction has read and written, respectively. The $prio()$ function returns the transaction's priority, which is incremented each time the transaction is aborted and reset to 1 when it commits.

TMProf's visualization of the RBtree benchmark (Figure 9) shows iFair outperform threadFair by 61.4%. It also shows iBalanced outperform threadFair by 73.7% and iFair by 5.8%. When using iBalanced in the same benchmark with more threads and larger workloads (including remove operations), as shown in Figure 11, it performs $\approx$ 10% faster than iFair except for small-sized workloads. Although this margin is small, it demonstrates that, in this case, iBalanced chooses a more optimal set of transactions to abort than iFair, thereby improving performance.

4.5 Linked List and Hash Table

For the linked list benchmark, shown in Figure 12, iBalanced outperforms iFair by upwards of 9.28× and threadFair by upwards of 15.84×. The key reason for iBalanced's modest performance improvement over the other CMs in this

Algorithm 2 The iBalanced Contention Manager

```
procedure IBAL(Transaction *commitTx, TransactionSet conflicts)
    Transaction *c = commitTx, *tx = NULL
    integer setSize = (writes(c) * (prio(c) + WC)) + (reads(c) * (prio(c) + RC))
    integer abortPrio = 0, abortSetSize = 0, highestPrio = 0
    boolean mostReads = true, mostWrites = true
    boolean fewestCommits = true, canAbort = false
    loop
        tx = NextTx(conflicts, tx)
        if (tx ≡ NULL) then
            break
        if (commits(tx) < commits(c)) then
            fewestCommits = false
        if (reads(tx) > reads(c)) then
            mostReads = false
        if (writes(tx) > writes(c)) then
            mostWrites = false
        if (prio(tx) > highestPrio) then
            highestPrio = prio(tx)
        abortSetSize + = writes(tx) + reads(tx)
        abortPrio + = prio(tx)
    integer p = prio(c)
    if (fewestCommits) then
        p = p * FCC
        setSize = setSize * SC
    if (p ≥ highestPrio) then
        canAbort = true
    if (mostReads ∨ mostWrites ∨ fewestCommits) then
        canAbort = true
    if (setSize ≥ abortPrio + abortSetSize) then
        canAbort = true
    return canAbort
```

benchmark is that iBalanced significantly reduces aborts for transactions that have already executed a notable amount of work, thereby reducing the critical path of an execution. Reducing aborts for large transactions is a vital characteristic for improving the efficiency of the linked list benchmark, as explained in the Section 2.1 and shown in Figure 3, because workloads can be highly disjoint for different threads. Even though iFair performs upwards of 3× faster than TL2 for this benchmark, iBalanced's performance demonstrates that reducing the critical path (the longest executing thread) can result in a substantial wasted work savings.

For the hash table benchmark, shown in Figure 13, iBalanced outperforms iFair by upwards of 2.05× and threadFair by upwards of 3.27×. iBalanced achieves this performance benefit for the same reason it outperforms the other CMs for linked list benchmark. However, the performance benefits for the hash table benchmark are not as notable, because the initial insert operations on the hash table are, at least initially, highly parallel (i.e., no conflicts). Once the buckets of the hash table reach a certain threshold, however, transactions begin to conflict and iBalanced's more optimal choice of transactional aborts and commits results in improved performance over iFair.

4.6 Revisiting 1-Writer / N-Readers

For our RBtree, linked list, and hash table experiments, iBalanced is more efficient than iFair and threadFair. However, it is not more efficient than threadFair for the 1-writer / N-readers benchmark, where threadFair outperforms both iFair and iBalanced. This is due to threadFair's algorithmic design being an excellent match for exploiting the concurrency of the 1-writer / N-readers benchmark. Because of this, we believe threadFair is a realistic CM candidate for

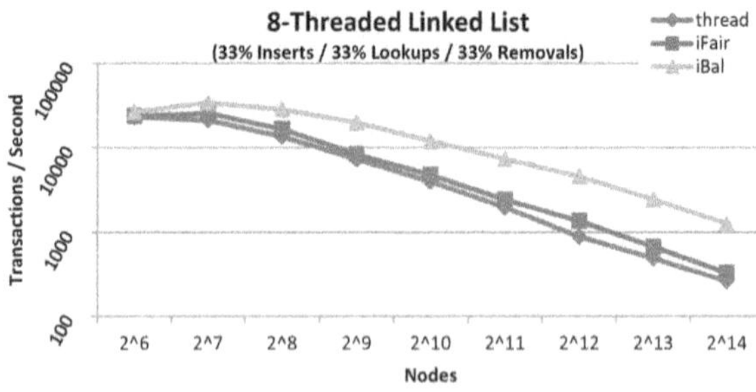

(a) 8-Threaded Linked List Benchmark.

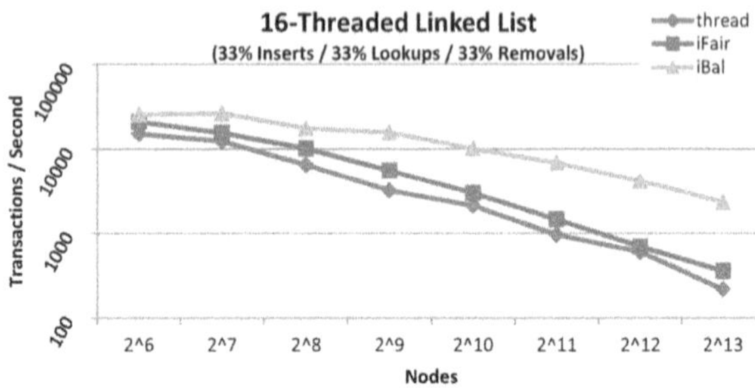

(b) 16-Threaded Linked List Benchmark.

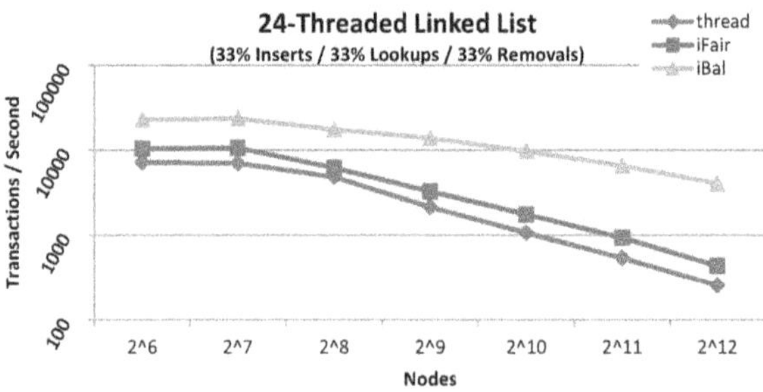

(c) 24-Threaded Linked List Benchmark.

Figure 12: Linked List Benchmarks.

certain TM use cases, especially those that have an even, or close to even, distribution of work across all threads.

Even though iBalanced does not perform as well as threadFair for the 1-writer / N-readers benchmark, it does perform as well or better than iFair, InvalSTM's previously best-performing CM, for all of the benchmarks we analyzed. Furthermore, iBalanced's efficiency rate over iFair tends to improve on each benchmark as the benchmarks scale to a greater number of threads and larger workloads.

4.7 Other Usages

Parallel programmers can also use TMProf for application-level optimizations, rather than TM-specific ones. For instance, performance bottlenecks can be identified by utilizing TMProf's cycle information shown during playback or by considering visualized contention across an entire execution. One can then zoom into these bottleneck-regions to understand their cause, and, eventually resolve them. For this paper, however, we did not explore application-level optimizations because, unlike InvalSTM itself, there has been no prior effort to optimize the benchmarks used in this section. Therefore, any benchmark optimizations we would

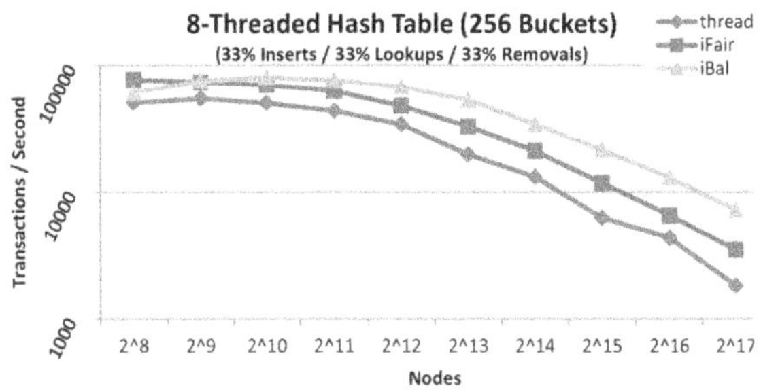

(a) 8-Threaded Hash Table Benchmark.

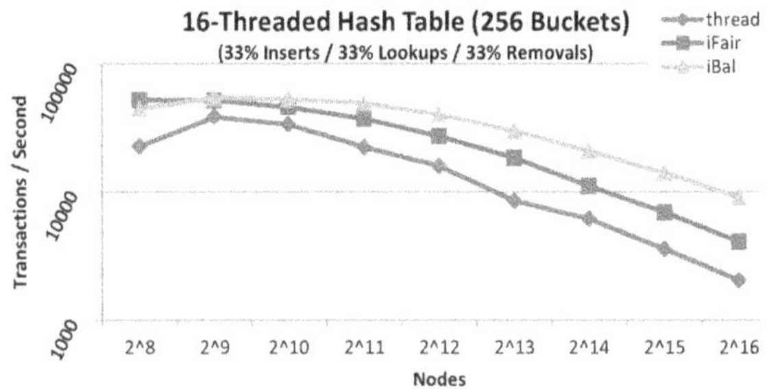

(b) 16-Threaded Hash Table Benchmark.

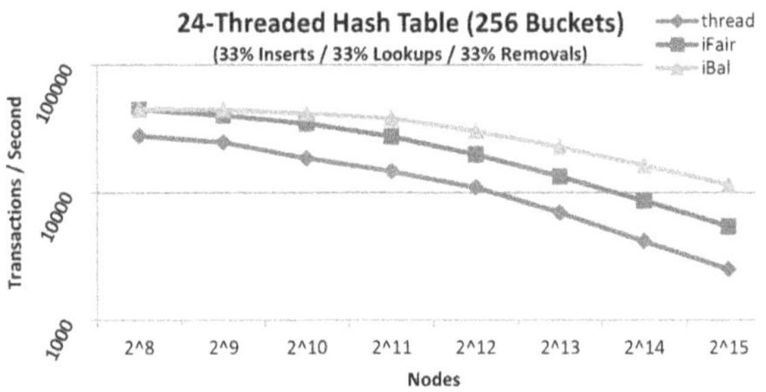

(c) 24-Threaded Hash Table Benchmark.

Figure 13: Hash Table Benchmarks.

have found would demonstrate little in terms of the utility and practicality of TMProf.

5. CONCLUSION

This paper presented TMProf, a transactional memory (TM) profiler based on three visualization principles that extend the current state of TM profilers and optimizers. These principles are *(i)* the precise graphical representation of transaction interactions including cross-correlation information and transaction source code, *(ii)* visualized soft real-time playback of concurrently executing transactions, and *(iii)* dynamic visualizations of multiple executions.

We described our experience using TMProf and showed how TMProf's feedback led to the design of two new CMs. We illustrated how these CMs generally led to increased transaction throughput as the threads and size of the workloads increased. Our experimental results showed that iBalanced, one of our newly designed CMs, can increase transaction throughput by nearly 10× over iFair, InvalSTM's previously best performing CM, and is the new best-performing CM for InvalSTM for our studied experiments.

The key contribution of this paper was to demonstrate that, due to the complexity of TM, textual representations of such programs are insufficient for profiling, especially because such representations do not clearly illustrate contention amongst transactions. Instead, we proposed that a TM profiler should be primarily visual, as graphical representation is the best way to convey complex interactions that unfold over time. Furthermore, we argued that such a visualized TM profiler should include execution playback functionality so that the results of transactional conflict mitigation can be observed over the course of the entire execution.

6. ACKNOWLEDGEMENTS

We would like to thank the anonymous reviewers for their insightful suggestions. We also sincerely appreciate the feedback offered by Ferad Zyulkyarov, which helped us improve the technical correctness of the paper. Finally, we thank Lori Peek for her numerous edits across several revisions of this paper. Any remaining errors that exist in this paper are our own.

7. REFERENCES

[1] Intel architecture instruction set extensions programming reference, chapter 8: Transactional synchronization extensions. 2012.

[2] G. M. Amdahl. Validity of the single processor approach to achieving large scale computing capabilities. In *SJCC*, 1967.

[3] J. M. Anderson, L. M. Berc, J. Dean, S. Ghemawat, M. R. Henzinger, S.-T. A. Leung, R. L. Sites, M. T. Vandevoorde, C. A. Waldspurger, and W. E. Weihl. Continuous profiling: where have all the cycles gone? *ACM Trans. Comput. Syst.*, 15:357–390, November 1997.

[4] S. A. Brandt, S. Banachowski, C. Lin, and T. Bisson. Dynamic integrated scheduling of hard real-time, soft real-time and non-real-time processes. In *RTSS*, 2003.

[5] D. R. Chakrabarti, P. Banerjee, H.-J. Boehm, P. G. Joisha, and R. S. Schreiber. The runtime abort graph and its application to software transactional memory optimization. In *CGO*, April 2011.

[6] D. Dice, O. Shalev, and N. Shavit. Transactional locking II. In *DISC*, pages 194–208, 2006.

[7] E. Duesterwald and V. Bala. Software profiling for hot path prediction: less is more. In *ASPLOS*, 2000.

[8] K. Fraser and T. Harris. Concurrent programming without locks. *ACM Trans. Comput. Syst*, 25(2), 2007.

[9] J. Gait. A probe effect in concurrent programs. *Softw., Pract. Exper.*, 16(3):225–233, 1986.

[10] J. E. Gottschlich and D. A. Connors. Extending contention managers for user-defined priority-based transactions. In *EPHAM*, Apr 2008.

[11] J. E. Gottschlich, J. G. Siek, and M. Vachharajani. Proving conflict serializability for full invalidation. In *WTTM*, September 2010.

[12] J. E. Gottschlich, M. Vachharajani, and J. G. Siek. An efficient software transactional memory using commit-time invalidation. In *CGO*, April 2010.

[13] S. L. Graham, P. B. Kessler, and M. K. Mckusick. Gprof: A call graph execution profiler. In *Proceedings of the Symposium on Compiler construction*, 1982.

[14] R. Guerraoui, M. Herlihy, and B. Pochon. Polymorphic contention management. In *DISC*. LNCS, 2005.

[15] R. Guerraoui, M. Herlihy, and B. Pochon. Toward a theory of transactional contention managers. In M. K. Aguilera and J. Aspnes, editors, *PODC*, pages 258–264. ACM, 2005.

[16] R. Guerraoui and M. Kapalka. On the correctness of transactional memory. In *SPAA*, pages 175–184, New York, NY, USA, 2008. ACM.

[17] T. Harris, J. R. Larus, and R. Rajwar. *Transactional Memory, Second Edition.* Morgan and Claypool, 2010.

[18] T. Harris, M. Plesko, A. Shinnar, and D. Tarditi. Optimizing memory transactions. *ACM SIGPLAN Notices*, 41(6):14–25, June 2006.

[19] M. Herlihy, V. Luchangco, and M. Moir. A flexible framework for implementing software transactional memory. In *OOPSLA*, pages 253–262, New York, NY, USA, 2006. ACM.

[20] M. Herlihy, V. Luchangco, M. Moir, and I. William N. Scherer. Software transactional memory for dynamic-sized data structures. In *PODC*, 2003.

[21] M. Herlihy and J. E. B. Moss. Transactional memory: Architectural support for lock-free data structures. In *ISCA*. May 1993.

[22] M. Herlihy and N. Shavit. *The Art of Multiprocessor Programming.* Elsevier, Inc., 2008.

[23] T. Kühl, K. Scheiter, P. Gerjets, and J. Edelmann. The influence of text modality on learning with static and dynamic visualizations. *Comput. Hum. Behav.*, January 2011.

[24] Y. Lev. *Debugging and Profiling of Transactional Programs.* PhD thesis, Brown University, 2010.

[25] N. A. Lynch, M. Merritt, W. E. Weihl, and A. Fekete. *Atomic Transactions: In Concurrent and Distributed Systems.* Morgan Kaufmann Publishers Inc., San Francisco, CA, USA, 1993.

[26] A. D. Malony and S. S. Shende. Overhead compensation in performance profiling. In *Euro-Par*, 2004.

[27] R. Merritt. IBM plants transactional memory in CPU. *EE Times*, 2011.

[28] T. Moseley, A. Shye, V. J. Reddi, D. Grunwald, and R. Peri. Shadow profiling: Hiding instrumentation costs with parallelism. In *CGO*, 2007.

[29] V. Pankratius and A.-R. Adl-Tabatabai. A study of transactional memory vs. locks in practice. In *SPAA*, 2011.

[30] C. Papadimitriou. *The theory of database concurrency control.* Computer Science Press, Inc., New York, NY, USA, 1986.

[31] H. Patil, C. Pereira, M. Stallcup, G. Lueck, and J. Cownie. Pinplay: a framework for deterministic replay and reproducible analysis of parallel programs. In *CGO*, 2010.

[32] D. E. Porter and E. Witchel. Understanding transactional memory performance. In *ISPASS*. 2010.

[33] W. N. Scherer and M. L. Scott. Advanced contention management for dynamic software transactional memory. In *PODC*, 2005.

[34] M. F. Spear, L. Dalessandro, V. Marathe, and M. L. Scott. A comprehensive strategy for contention management in software transactional memory. In *PPoPP*, 2009.

[35] M. F. Spear, V. J. Marathe, W. N. Scherer III, and M. L. Scott. Conflict detection and validation strategies for software transactional memory. In *DISC*, Sep 2006.

[36] Q. Wang, S. Kulkarni, J. Cavazos, and M. Spear. A transactional memory with automatic performance tuning. *ACM Trans. Archit. Code Optim.*, 8(4), Jan. 2012.

[37] F. Zyulkyarov, T. Harris, O. S. Unsal, A. Cristal, and M. Valero. Debugging programs that use atomic blocks and transactional memory. In *PPoPP*, 2010.

[38] F. Zyulkyarov, S. Stipic, T. Harris, O. S. Unsal, A. Cristal, I. Hur, and M. Valero. Discovering and understanding performance bottlenecks in transactional applications. In *PACT*, 2010.

Sandboxing Transactional Memory*

Luke Dalessandro and Michael L. Scott
University of Rochester
Department of Computer Science
{luked,scott}@cs.rochester.edu

ABSTRACT

Correct transactional memory systems (TMs) must address the possibility that a speculative transaction may read mutually inconsistent values from memory and then perform an operation that violates the underlying language semantics. TMs for managed languages can leverage type safety, just-in-time compilation, and fully monitored exceptions to *sandbox* transactions, isolating the rest of the system from damaging effects of inconsistent speculation. In contrast, TMs for unmanaged languages that lack these properties typically avoid erroneous behavior by *validating* a transaction's view of memory incrementally after each read operation.

Recent results suggest that performing validation *out-of-band* can increase performance by factors of 1.7× to 5.2× over incremental validation, but allowing a transaction's main computation to progress in parallel with validation introduces periods in which inconsistent speculative execution may violate language semantics. Without sandboxing—which some authors have suggested is not possible in unmanaged languages—programmers must manually annotate transactions with validation barriers whenever inconsistency might lead to semantic violations, an untenable task.

In this work we demonstrate that sandboxing for out-of-band validation is, in fact, possible in unmanaged languages. Our implementation integrates signal interposition, periodic validation, and a mix of static and dynamic instrumentation into a system comprising the LLVM-based Dresden TM compiler and the RSTM runtime. We show that these mechanisms introduce negligible overhead, thus extending the results of out-of-band validation to POSIX programs without requiring manual annotation. Furthermore, we establish sandboxing as a technique that can complement, or replace, incremental validation in any TM that keep speculatively written values in a private buffer.

*This work was supported in part by the National Science Foundation under grants CCR-0963759, CCF-1116055, and CNS-1116109.

PACT'12, September 19–23, 2012, Minneapolis, Minnesota, USA.

Categories and Subject Descriptors

D.1.3 [**Programming Techniques**]: Concurrent Programming—*Parallel Programming*; D.3.4 [**Programming Languages**]: Processors—*Run-time environments*

Keywords

Transactional memory, validation, sandboxing, opacity

1. INTRODUCTION

Transactional Memory (TM) [16, 18] raises the level of abstraction for synchronization, allowing programmers to delimit operations that need to execute atomically without specifying *how* that atomicity is to be achieved. The underlying system then attempts to execute atomic sections of separate threads concurrently whenever possible, typically by means of speculation.

Speculative transactions are said to *commit* at the end of their execution; others *abort*, roll back, and try again. All speculation-based TM systems require a mechanism to detect and resolve conflicts between transactions, ensuring that they commit only as part of a global serialization order. Additionally, committed transactions must obey the semantics of the source programming language.

A speculative transaction becomes inconsistent when it reads a pair of values that were never simultaneously valid in the execution history defined by the program's committed transactions. To ensure overall program correctness, at least in the general case, a TM must force inconsistent transactions to abort. To this end, transactions in software TM runtimes (STM) typically *validate* by double-checking their read sets, and abort in the event of inconsistency.

STM runtimes for managed languages like Java and C# [2, 17], as well as systems based on dynamic binary instrumentation [24], validate transactions before they commit, leveraging type safe, just-in-time compilation, and managed exceptions to *sandbox* speculative transactions and protect the system from the effects of inconsistent execution.

In unmanaged languages—where some authors have implied sandboxing is impossible [22], several historical TM systems depended on explicit programmer-inserted validation for correct execution [12, 15, 18, 28], a strategy that has been discarded as difficult and error prone. Modern TMs for unmanaged languages validate *incrementally* [19]—after every transactional read operation—a technique that has been formalized as the theory of *opacity* [13, 14]. Minor relaxations of opacity [31] and optimizations to dynamically elide redundant checks [8, 27, 32] can significantly reduce the frequency and overhead of validation. In the worst case, however, validation remains a problem quadratic in the number of transactional read operations, a cost paid on the transaction's critical path.

Recent work by Casper et al. [3] and Kestor et al. [20] suggests that moving validation off of the critical path and performing it *out-of-band*—in parallel with the "real work" of the transaction—can result in performance improvements of 1.7× and 1.8×–5.2× respectively. Naive out-of-band validation, however, allows inconsistent speculative transactions ("zombies") to execute erroneous operations that result in visible violations of the semantics of the source programming language. Casper et al. and Kestor et al. echo historical techniques and require the programmer to manually annotate any operation within a transaction that may violate language semantics if performed by a zombie.

In the extreme, the programmer has the option of annotating every read—essentially restoring the validations that would be performed by an opaque system. Anything shy of this, however, requires reasoning about the potential effect of data races—a task we consider untenable. We believe the more attractive option, even in the context of an unmanaged language, is to rely on the compiler and runtime to protect the programmer from zombie execution by automatically suppressing the effects of dangerous operations—those whose behavior cannot be guaranteed to be invisible to other threads—until the transaction is known to be consistent. A complete characterization of dangerous operations is tricky (see Section 2.1); at the very least we must guard against faults and against stores to incorrectly computed addresses.

To the best of our knowledge, no previous project has carefully explored the feasibility of such sandboxing in unmanaged languages; however, its capacity to eliminate control dependencies between validation and most operations in the rest of the transaction makes it a compelling study.

Sandboxing is appealing for a number of reasons in addition to out-of-band validation. It offers the opportunity to relax the coupling in hardware TM systems between conflict detection in the memory hierarchy and execution in the processor core: precise, immediate notification of transaction conflicts would not be needed if the compiler always generated a "TM fence" before each dangerous instruction [4]. Given that dangerous operations (i.e., those that may result in errant behavior when executed inconsistently) tend to be much less common than transactional loads, it has the potential to reduce the validation overhead in TM implementations that perform in-line validation. Spear et al. [29] also suggests that it can serve as a solution to the privatization problem in some circumstances.

In this paper we show that transactional sandboxing is possible in POSIX-compliant C programs, and is practical both for TM systems that validate out-of-band and for lazy-versioning TMs in general. This result strongly suggests that the performance results reported by Casper et al. and Kestor et al. are valid for all programs—not just those that have been manually annotated for safety. More broadly, our results unlock a wide and previously proscribed design space for TM development.

In Section 2 we characterize potentially dangerous operations for zombie transactions in POSIX-compliant C. We also explore the interaction of sandboxing and several common STM algorithms. In Section 3 we describe our sandboxing implementation, including the algorithms used to instrument dangerous instructions and the algorithm-independent machinery used to address infinite loops and faults. We evaluate the overhead of this infrastructure for out-of-band validation TMs in Section 4. We extend the evaluation to systems with in-line validation in Section 5, by presenting and evaluating a "maximally lazy" sandboxed STM based on the open-source RSTM framework [25]. Finally, we conclude in Section 6.

2. SANDBOXING PRAGMATICS

We assume a semantics in which transactions are *strictly serializable* (SS): they appear to execute atomically in some global total order that is consistent with program order in every thread; further, each transaction is globally ordered with respect to preceding and following nontransactional accesses of its own thread. Given an SS implementation, one can prove that every data-race-free program is *transactionally sequentially consistent* (TSC) [5, 30]: its memory accesses will always appear to occur in some global total order that is consistent with program order and that keeps the accesses of any given transaction contiguous. These semantics are an idealized form of those of the draft transactional standard for C++ [1].

In contrast to opacity, which requires aborted transactions to observe the same consistency constraints as successful ones, aborted transactions play no role in SS. In principle, a transaction that is going to abort may do anything at all, provided the resulting history of committed transactions is still SS. In an implementation adhering to these semantics, sandboxing must ensure the isolation of *zombie transactions*, which have performed a speculative read that cannot be explained by any serial execution [18], but it need not restrict the internal behavior of such transactions beyond this isolation constraint.

2.1 Dangerous Operations

We say that an operation is *dangerous* if its execution in a zombie transaction may allow the user to observe an execution that is not SS. Here we enumerate what we believe to be a complete list of dangerous operations (a formal proof of completeness is deferred to future work). Section 3 details the concrete sandboxing mechanisms that we implement.

In-place Stores.

Zombie transactions that perform a store in-place (to a native address rather than a private buffer), are a primary concern for a sandboxing runtime. Reading such an inconsistently written value, or a stale value if the write was to an incorrect address, may constitute a data race, violate the sequential language semantics, or even result in execution of arbitrary code. In-place stores may target shared or private locations (e.g., the stack), and may be either instrumented (e.g., in an eager, in-place STM) or uninstrumented (e.g., if the compiler or programmer has concluded that there is no TSC execution in which a particular store can be part of a race).

In-place stores that cannot be proven consistent must be preceded by a run-time validation check.

Indirect Branches.

An inconsistent indirect branch may lead to an unprotected in-place store, or to executable data that *looks like* one. Compilers use such branches to implement virtual function calls, large **switch** statements, computed **goto**s, and **return**s. Fortunately, STM implementations already perform run-time mapping of native function pointers to their transactional clones' addresses. A successful lookup implies that the target will have proper sandboxing instrumentation. If a clone is not found, then the transaction will switch to *serial-irrevocable* execution, which precludes roll-back. This transition includes an embedded validation. These observations imply that, as long as we protect the integrity of the stack, no new mechanism is required to sandbox indirect calls.

Faults.

The sandboxing runtime must distinguish faults (hardware exceptions) that occur due to inconsistent execution from those that would have occurred in some TSC execution of the program, and prevent inconsistent signals from becoming visible to the programmer. In a POSIX-compliant C/C++ implementation, such faults are encoded as synchronous signals. Olszewski et al. [24] suggest either containing inconsistent signals inside the operating system by making the kernel transaction-aware, or relying on user-space signal handling to suppress inconsistent signals once received. They implemented the first option; we will use the second (Section 3.2).

Infinite Loops and Recursion.

A zombie transaction may enter into an infinite loop or infinite recursion due to inconsistent execution. These may not be a concern if validation is performed continually and out-of-band, and reported to the transaction thread via asynchronous interrupt. Some out-of-band systems, however (including those of Casper et al. and Kestor et al.), require the transaction thread to poll for notifications, and any systems with in-line validation similarly requires an active mechanism to detect and recover from an inconsistent infinite loop or recursion. (Exhaustion of stack space is a synchronous event that can, with care, be treated as any other fault.)

Previous systems have instrumented loop back edges with a check to force periodic validation [24, 28]. This approach adds overhead that can be expensive for tighter loops, and pollutes hardware resources like branch predictors. We use an alternative approach in which timers force the STM to validate periodically. This avoids common-case overhead, and the timer period can be sufficient long that applications that do not suffer from inconsistent infinite loops pay very little overhead. If infinite loops are common, however, timer-based validation may be slow to detect the problem. We could imagine a hybrid approach in which hot-patch locations are left on loop back edges so that polling code can be injected into loops that show a high probability of infinite looping.

TM Commit.

Many opaque TM algorithms allow read-only transactions to commit without validating, under the assumption that they were correct as of the validation performed at their last read operation. This assumption isn't valid in a sandboxed TM, which must validate again at commit if any shared locations have been read since the most recent previous validation. In a hardware TM system (not considered here) commit instructions would likewise need sandboxing [4]. This said, end-of-transaction validation imposes no additional penalty on systems with out-of-band validation: these always synchronize with the validation entity at commit.

Waivered Code Regions.

TM APIs may allow programmers to specify that certain *waivered* code regions should run without instrumentation. Because these regions may perform arbitrary actions, they require pre-validation.

System and Library Calls.

Many system calls are incompatible with optimistic transactional execution. We expect that TM systems will force transactions to become irrevocable—as suggested by the draft C++ TM proposal [1]—before performing a system call. This already entails validation so we do not consider system calls to be dangerous. Library calls may be compiled to be transactional, and in such case they must be compiled in a manner compatible with zombie execution.

We have found that a smart compiler like the DTMC [11] will occasionally allow a library call, e.g., abort, to occur without becoming irrevocable first. If we do not have direct control of this behavior we must detect and instrument such calls.

2.2 Impact on existing STM algorithms

The immediate impact of sandboxing is that TL2 and its derivatives [6, 7, 8, 21] no longer require post-read validation. Omitting this validation eliminates an ordering constraint in the read barrier in exchange for the possibility of wasted work—continued execution in a transaction that is doomed to abort. Sandboxing also allows these systems to tolerate *privatization* violations without additional barriers [29]. Unfortunately, sandboxing reduces the value of TinySTM-style timestamp extension [26], as a zombie transaction will probably have already used an inconsistent value by the time it tries to validate. We address this issue more thoroughly in Section 5.1 as we develop our prototype sandboxed STM.

3. SANDBOXING INFRASTRUCTURE

Our sandboxing infrastructure consists of the three main components: LLVM-based instrumentation for run-time taint tracking and pre-validation of dangerous operations, POSIX signal interposition and chaining, and timer-based periodic validation.

3.1 LLVM-based Instrumentation

LLVM provides several benefits that make it suitable for sandboxing: (1) it explicitly encodes the dangerous operations that we need to consider without exposing the analysis to low-level details such as stack manipulation; (2) the publicly available Dresden Transactional Memory Compiler (DTMC) and its Tanger instrumentation pass [11] produce instrumented LLVM IR that is ready for analysis and instrumentation; and (3) LLVM's link-time-optimization functionality allows us to perform whole-program analysis and instrumentation, which can result in less conservative instrumentation.

In principle, the only operations of concern are those detailed in Section 2.1. In our current work we assume an *out-of-place* STM system, which keeps speculatively written values in a *redo log* and moves them to regular memory on commit. For an in-place STM (one that keeps an *undo log* of old values to restore on abort), we would need to treat speculative stores as dangerous operations; we leave this for future work.

In practice, we have little direct control over how LLVM's code generator uses the stack. To guarantee the safety of stack-relative addressing, we instrument anything that may update the stack structure in a potentially inconsistent way. Specifically, we instrument allocas if they may be executed on an inconsistent control path, or if their **size** parameter may be inconsistent. A benefit of aggressively protecting the consistency of the stack is that **return** instructions—technically indirect branches, but not normally mapped by the STM runtime (Section 2)—are not dangerous because the return address on the stack cannot have been corrupted.

Our goal is to instrument all dangerous operations that will execute in an inconsistent context. Identifying such contexts precisely is an information-flow-tracking problem reminiscent of *taint* analysis [35, pp. 558ff], where the values produced by transactional reads are taint sources and the operands of dangerous instructions are taint sinks. Precise taint tracking at compile time is challenging in the presence of aliasing and context sensitivity. We currently employ conservative dynamic tracking and simple static barrier elimination; our evaluation finds that these are mostly adequate.

We start by dynamically maintaining a single-bit taint flag. We extend the STM read barrier to set the flag, and we instrument every dangerous operation with a *validation barrier* that checks the flag and, if it is set, clears it and invokes STM-system-specific validation. Dynamic taint tracking trivially satisfies our requirement that no dangerous operation is performed inconsistently. While the overhead of dynamically checking the flag is small in the common case (a function call, thread-local access, and branch) we would still like to statically eliminate as many redundant barriers as possible.

We currently perform a single static optimization, which we term straight-line redundant validation elimination (SRVE). It exploits the observation that a consistent transaction remains consistent until it performs a transactional read. SRVE tracks the possibility of taint statically, at the basic block level. It initializes each basic block as "possibly inconsistent," and then scans forward. When SRVE encounters a dangerous operation in a possibly inconsistent state, it inserts a validation barrier and changes the state to "consistent." When SRVE encounters a transactional read or function call (SRVE is not context sensitive) it reverts to "possibly inconsistent":

```
SRVE_instrument(BasicBlock bb)
  bool consistent = false;
  foreach Instruction i in bb
    if i is STM_read
      consistent = false
    else if i is function call
      consistent = false
    else if i is dangerous
      if not consistent
        instrument(i)
        consistent = true
```

SRVE is conservative in initializing each basic block as possibly inconsistent. Global analysis could be used to identify basic blocks that are sure to be consistent on entry, but our results have not yet shown the need: SRVE eliminates many of the redundant validation barriers in our benchmarks, and dynamic taint tracking (which remains in place) eliminates most of the work for dynamically redundant barriers that precede any transactional read in their respective basic blocks.

3.2 POSIX Signal Chaining and Validation

We suppress delivery of inconsistent signals using only user space mechanisms. We provide custom signal handlers for all potential faults. These perform validation, and abort if the signal was generated by zombie execution. Otherwise, they forward the signal to a *chained* user handler if one exists, or perform the default action for that signal if it does not. We arrange for any dynamically installed user handlers to fall behind our custom handlers, using libdl-based interposing on signal and sigaction, in a manner reminiscent of the interposition and chaining in Java's libjsig [33] library. We interpose on pthread_sigmask as well in order to restore the correct state during an abort.

We only need to sandbox the synchronous signals distinguished by the libc reference manual [34] as *program error signals*. The remaining signals are asynchronous notifications of events that the program has asked to, or needs to, know about. We believe that user (or default) handlers for these asynchronous signals can be run without regard for the current transactional state of the interrupted execution. These signal handlers are effectively independent threads of execution and thus must be properly synchronized and will be protected from potential zombies with standard transactional mechanisms.

While the details of our signal system are quite complex, they accomplish a straightforward goal: masking out signals that reflect faults in inconsistent transactions, without any kernel assistance, and in a manner that otherwise preserves all standard signal semantics.

3.3 Timer-based Periodic Validation

We guard against inconsistent infinite loops and infinite recursion by installing a timer that triggers periodic validation. This technique is a compelling choice in RSTM [25], which allows dynamic adaptation among numerous STM algorithms, most of which are opaque. Instrumenting loop back edges statically would force those algorithms to pay the back-edge overhead needlessly.

The user application may attempt to use the process-wide POSIX timer functionality, so we must be prepared to interpose on timer-based routines, multiplex library timers with client timers, and use the signal chaining infrastructure described above if required.

Our handler leverages an existing RSTM *epoch* mechanism to detect transactions that have made progress since the last timer event, and uses pthread_kill to trigger validation in those that have not. If all threads have made progress, we reduce the frequency of future validation interrupts. If an interrupted thread detects that it is in an inconsistent infinite loop, we increase the frequency of future interrupts. We set upper and lower bounds on timer frequency at 100Hz and 1Hz, respectively. We also provide a low overhead mechanism to enable and disable timer-based validation on a per-thread basis; this can be used to protect critical, non-reentrant, STM library code, as well as to suppress timer-based aborts during waivered code execution.

4. BASIC SANDBOXING OVERHEAD

Section 3 presents the three components of our sandboxing infrastructure. Though we have yet to develop a formal proof of safety, we believe that these components demonstrate the feasibility of sandboxing in an unmanaged language. Here we examine the cost of our mechanisms to show that sandboxing is a *practical* alternative to (error prone) programmer annotation for use in an out-of-band validation TM.

4.1 Experimental Setup

We run our experiments on a dual-socket system equipped with two 6-core Intel Xeon E5649 processors running Linux 2.6.34. STM runtimes are based on a development version of RSTM, compiled into a highly optimized archive library with gcc-4.7.2, and linked into the benchmarks as native 64-bit libraries. Benchmarks that require sandboxing are compiled using a research version of the DTMC compiler that is compatible with LLVM-2.9. Instrumentation for dangerous operation pre-validation is generated using a custom LLVM pass implementing the SRVE algorithm (Section 3.1).

RSTM provides a set of microbenchmarks that allow us to focus on instrumentation overhead. Specifically, we use the *set* microbenchmark, which performs repeated inserts, lookups, and deletes in sets implemented as lists, hashtables, and red-black trees. This microbenchmark has no dangerous operations, aside from read-only STM_commit operations, but does suffer from inconsistent infinite loops and segmentation faults.

We also use applications from the *STAMP* benchmark suite [23]. STAMP is manually instrumented using a macro-based API that relies heavily on implicitly waivered code, without which the read sets of transactions in many of the included applications get to be so large that the transactions will not terminate. We have added the DTMC equivalent of explicit code waivers where possible to permit us to run the standard test configurations; the results, however, are not directly comparable with other published STAMP results. Our results include the cost of pre-validation and special timer handling for waivered code (Section 3). Conversely, STAMP performs manual checks for inconsistent results. We elide those checks, as they are not necessary in our opaque STMs, and are redundant given sandboxing.

We have been unable to successfully apply transactional waivers to bayes or intruder, and yada results are unreliable, so these three benchmarks are not included in our analysis.

4.2 Results & Analysis

Our signal interposition and chaining implementation consists of a small amount of additional code for each interposed signal handler invocation, including an extra indirect branch and a synchronization operation. Measurements on our Xeon test platform show that this approximately doubles the cost of native signal delivery. While this might in principle impact the performance of an application that depends on the efficiency of small, synchronous signal handlers, we could not measure a negative effect on any of the applications that we tested. In the same vein, an application that is designed to field a large number of signals *during* transactional execution may experience additional overhead from the validation we perform before delivering such signals. In our applications, however, we observed that all synchronous signals that occur in transactions were segfaults resulting from zombie execution.

For programs that use timers, timer-based validation requires SIGALRM and related system call interposition, as well as related multiplexing and demultiplexing code. This could add overhead in applications that depend on the performance of high-frequency timers, but we could not measure an impact on our applications.

Finally, we must consider the cost of the instrumentation for pre-validation of dangerous operations. Pre-validation consists of a lookup and branch on the thread-local taint bit (Section 3.1). This represents real overhead relative to the dangerous operation, which is typically an alloca or a simple store, and can impact the overall performance of a TM system if dangerous operations are common. Of the benchmarks that we tested, only STAMP's labyrinth and genome benchmarks perform substantial numbers of dangerous operations. In each case, these consist of expensive waivered computations that dominate the cost of pre-validation.

These sandboxing mechanisms are entirely thread-local overhead. As such, these results lead us directly to the conclusion that sandboxing is a viable replacement for manual annotation in out-of-band validation TMs, and that the results of Casper et al. and Kestor et al. should hold for general programs.

5. SANDBOXING IN GENERAL

Section 4 evaluated the practicality of sandboxing in the context of out-of-band validation, finding that it effectively replaces manual annotation as a means of ensuring strict serializability. We would like to show that similar results hold for generic buffered update TMs, with in-line validation. To do so we must account more fully for the potential performance degradation resulting from "wasted work" that a zombie transaction performs between the time that it becomes inconsistent and the time that it aborts. With out-of-band validation, wasted work occurs only in systems that poll for notification, and then only in infinite loops and recursions that contain no shared memory accesses (and thus no polling operations). With in-line validation, large amounts of wasted work can, at least in principle, occur in any long-running transaction that performs no dangerous operations (and thus no validations prior to commit).

In order to establish that wasted work is not a problem in practice for buffered update TMs, we develop and test a novel, "maximally lazy" sandboxed STM algorithm that is designed to detect inconsistency as slowly as possible without violating strict serializability.

5.1 Maximally-Lazy Sandboxed STM

Our *maximally lazy STM* descends from the time-based algorithms of Dice et al.'s TL2 [8], Felber et al.'s TinySTM [10], and Dragojević et al.'s SwissTM [9] in their buffered-update forms. It manages concurrency control by mapping individual words of memory to entries in a large table of versioned locks (called ownership records, or *orecs*). Version numbers are taken from a global counter (clock) that is incremented by writer transactions during their commit; the value in an orec indicates the logical time of the most recent update of any word mapping to that orec.

A representative time-based read barrier appears as STM_read_opaque in Figure 1. It identifies and inspects the appropriate orec (Lines 4–7), performs at least one memory

```
1  STM_read_opaque(addr)
2      if addr in write_buffer
3          return value from write_buffer
4      compute orec guarding addr
5      read orec as o1
6      if o1 is locked
7          restart STM_read_opaque
8      FENCE
9      read addr as val
10     FENCE
11     read orec as o2
12     if o2 is locked
13         restart STM_read_opaque
14     if o2 > my_start_time
15         validate
16         set my_start_time to o1
17         restart STM_read_opaque
18     log orec in read_log
19     return val

21 STM_read_sandboxed(addr)
22     if addr in write_buffer
23         return value from write_buffer
24     log addr in read_log
25     read addr as val
26     return val

28 STM_validate_sandboxed()
29     read global time as snapshot
30     for addr in read_log
31         compute orec guarding addr
32         read orec as o
33         while o is locked
34             wait
35         if o > my_start_time
36             abort
37     set my_start_time to snapshot
```

Figure 1: An example read barrier for an opaque STM, and the corresponding sandboxed read/validate decomposition used in our maximally lazy STM.

fence, and validates before returning (Lines 11–17). The use of time-based version numbers provides an opportunity to avoid validation overhead in the absence of recent writes to addr (Line 14) and, in some systems, in the absence of concurrent writer commits (not shown).

Sandboxing allows us to safely return an inconsistent value, and thus to delay both orec identification and validation—in the extreme, until just prior to performing a dangerous operation. Delaying in turn eliminates the need for strong ordering between the reads of an address and its corresponding orec, thereby exposing additional compiler and pipeline parallelism. Psuedocode for this relaxation appears in Figure 1.

Note that we continue to use TinySTM-style timestamp extension, updating my_start_time on a successful validation; however, where TinySTM can recover from reading an inconsistent value, we cannot. TinySTM can validate and re-execute the inconsistent read based on a newly extended my_start_time before returning from STM_read_opaque (Figure 1, Lines 16–17). By contrast, STM_read_sandboxed will return the inconsistent value, which may then be used in the client code, dooming the transaction. We can, however, extend our timestamp after a successful validation (Figure 1, Line 37).

Not shown in Figure 1, but described in Section 2.1, is that the STM_commit_sandboxed routine must validate at the end of a read-only transaction—a validation that its opaque precursors may elide.

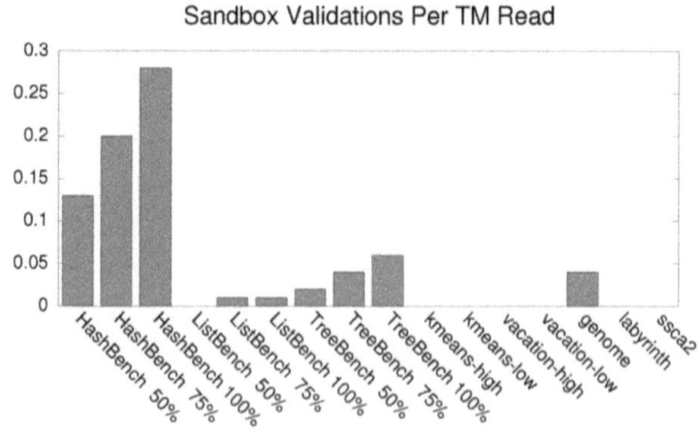

Figure 2: The number of dynamic pre-validation barriers that are executed relative to the number of STM read barriers in our maximally lazy STM. This includes pre-validation of read-only STM_commit_sandboxed routines. The suffixes on microbenchmark names indicate the percentage of read-only transactions in the particular execution.

The cost of STM_read plays a key role in overall transaction latency, since reads are the most common transactional operation. The STM_read_sandboxed barrier performs the minimum possible instrumentation for a buffered-update STM, and thus we expect it to have low overhead. At the same time, it makes long-running zombie transactions possible, and introduces the specter of a decrease in scalability due to potential wasted work, as desired for testing.

5.2 Results and Analysis

Using the same experimental setup as described in Section 4.1, we compare the maximally-lazy, sandboxed STM of Section 5.1 (*Sandbox*) to the *Opaque* counterpart from which it was derived, available as *OrecELA* in the freely available RSTM suite [25]. *Opaque* ensures that a transaction that is doomed to abort discovers this fact as soon as possible by validating each instrumented STM read operation.

Pre-validation Overhead.

Sandbox trades *Opaque's* post-validation of read operations for pre-validation of dangerous operations. We can estimate the impact of the trade simply by looking at the ratio of validations between the two implementations. Intuitively, we expect to eliminate more validations than we introduce; Figure 2 confirms this expectation. In the absence of wasted work, this reduction in the number of validation checks should benefit performance. The RSTM microbenchmarks ("HashBench") have the highest ratios; these reflect the additional validations required at the end of read-only transactions, which in these applications are both numerous and short. Note that the ratios of Figure 2 are suggestive of performance but do not fully determine it: they capture the number of instrumentation points, but not their actual cost (these depend on details of the STM back end).

RSTM set benchmarks.

Figure 3 compares the throughput of the three RSTM microbenchmarks. For these we report results using only one of the two processors: the frantic rate at which transactions are executed in the microbenchmarks causes RSTM's global

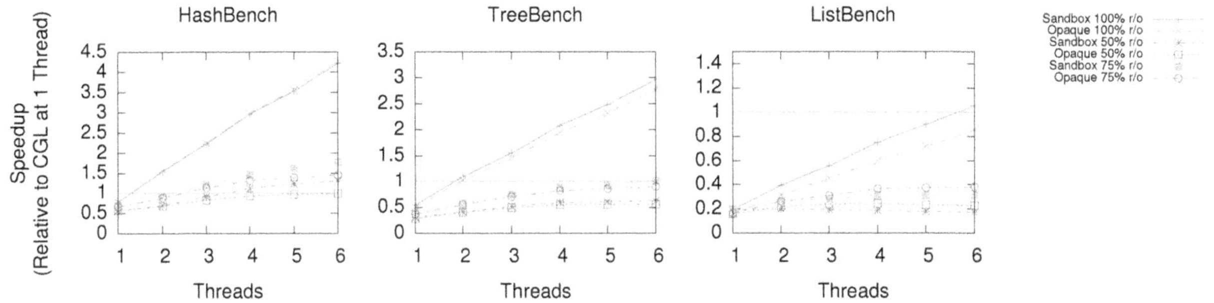

Figure 3: Our maximally lazy STM compared to an equivalent opaque STM on the RSTM set microbenchmarks. Lines are labeled with the percentage of read-only transactions that are performed. Throughput is shown as speedup relative to coarse-grained-lock throughput at 1 thread for the respective read ratio.

commit counter to become an unacceptable bottleneck once cross-chip communication is required.

Lines are labeled with the percent read-only transactions that they perform. This number is important, as *Sandbox* performs a commit-time validation for read-only transactions that *Opaque* does not. The results of these tests are encouraging and consistent with our expectations given Figure 2. The relative number of validation barriers is a good predictor of a reduction in the overhead of *Sandbox*, and we see few ill effects from wasted work.

The hashtable set consists of tiny, CPU-bound transactions, where the cost of validation is quite low. *Sandbox* suffers from negligible wasted work in this case, and thus its performance relative to *Opaque* is entirely predictable. Read-only performance is indistinguishable, and as writers become more common, *Opaque* transactions must validate more frequently than their *Sandbox* counterparts, resulting in slightly less scalable performance.

The tree-based benchmark contains longer, larger transactions, as well as cases where rotation provides large asymmetries. The linked structure is an interesting test of our sandboxing infrastructure as it suffers from both inconsistent SEGFAULTs and infinite loops. *Sandbox*'s reduced validation overhead results in an advantage for read-only execution, but its inability to perform in-barrier timestamp extension (Figure 1, Lines 14–17) results in more frequent aborts as writers become more common.

The list microbenchmark evaluates performance for large transactions. Large, non-conflicting transactions are an ideal workload for *Sandbox*, which simply performs a single validation barrier at commit time, while *Opaque* must execute a barrier for each node read during the search. This results in substantially less overhead for *Sandbox*, as well as better scalability when conflicts are infrequent. On the other hand, writer transactions trigger high abort rates that *Opaque* tolerates better due to its early conflict detection. *Sandbox* suffers from large amounts of wasted work in this case. It must be noted that neither runtime performs well in this common-conflict setting, but RSTM's ability to dynamically adapt between opaque and sandboxed execution (not exploited in these experiments) may prove a valuable feature.

STAMP Benchmarks.

RSTM's microbenchmarks are intended as a stress test for STM systems: their performance depends almost entirely on the STM infrastructure. On the other hand, STAMP's large scale and reliance on waivered execution means that performance is much less sensitive to details of the STM algorithm (though still heavily dependent on abort rates). Figure 3 shows results on five of the eight STAMP benchmarks as described in Section 4.1. RSTM's bottlenecks are not a factor with more reasonable rates of transactional execution, so we test *Opaque* and *Sandbox* using native Linux scheduling out to the full 12 cores of the machine.

STAMP's large transactions raise the specter of reduced scalability due to wasted work, but we see no evidence of this in the results, where *Opaque* and *Sandbox* are generally very well matched. *Sandbox* outperforms *Opaque* at one thread due to its lower overheads and continues to perform well out to 12 threads in most cases. *Sandbox* suffers a somewhat higher abort rate than *Opaque* due to its reduced ability to do timestamp extension. This manifests as lower performance in labyrinth, whose enormous transactions lead to a very high abort penalty.

Overall, the performance of *Sandbox* is at least on par with that of *Opaque* when parallelism is available, and often slightly better. This result demonstrates that, for the applications that we test, wasted work is unlikely to negatively impact performance. As such, it is reasonable to conclude that our sandboxing infrastructure is a viable option for validation in buffered update TMs in general.

6. CONCLUSIONS

We have shown that sandboxed STM in an unmanaged language is both possible and practical. Our results with maximally lazy sandboxing further suggest that wasted work is unlikely to be a real-world problem. Given the appeal of out-of-band validation for both hardware and software TM, we conclude that sandboxing is a promising avenue toward increased performance in future TM systems. Our work should enable researchers to explore this design space without concern.

Future Work.

Our general notion of dangerous operations and sandboxing semantics must be formalized to prove that we have not overlooked any cases where instrumentation is necessary. At the same time, formalization is likely to ignore certain practical interactions between the program and the system —operating system accounting, performance counters, debugging, etc.—in which zombie execution may be visible.

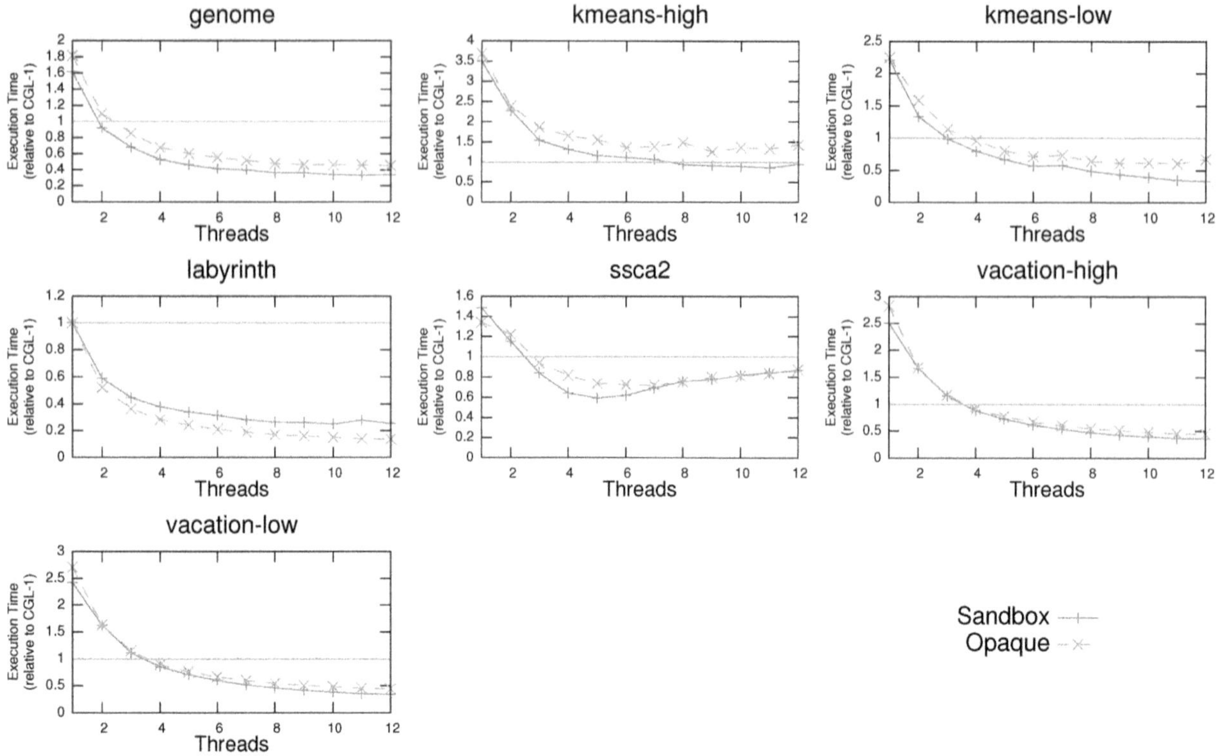

Figure 4: Our lazy STM compared to an equivalent opaque STM for five STAMP benchmarks. Throughput is shown as execution time relative to that of coarse-grained-lock at 1 thread.

Working in the context of these interactions remains a topic of research.

The results presented here should be considered indicative of likely performance only for buffered-update STMs, in which transactional writes are not considered dangerous. For in-place systems, the number of sandboxing validation barriers will be substantially larger. The performance of sandboxing in such a setting will be more strongly contingent on the quality of the pre-validation instrumentation algorithm.

Along this line, there is a clear opportunity to implement more expensive static analysis to attempt to eliminate always-redundant instrumentation on dangerous operations. This could include full information-flow tracking as well as potential code cloning and specialization to partition occasionally-redundant instrumentation points into always-redundant and necessary pairs.

And of course, we encourage researchers to aggressively explore the space of concurrent-validation TM, both in software and in hardware.

Acknowledgments.

Our thanks to: Patrick Marlier for his help in understanding the DTMC/TinySTM code base, as well as his implementation of the DTMC shim for RSTM used in our evaluation; Michael Spear for his assistance in the development of our sandboxed STM, as well as contributing some text and pseudocode in Section 5.1; Martin Nowak for his help in delivering a DTMC compiler compatible with LLVM-2.9; and Gökçen Kestor for her assistance with benchmarking. Finally, we thank our reviewers for their careful reading of our original draft and their resulting valuable advice.

References

[1] Draft Specification of Transaction Language Constructs for C++. Version 1.0, IBM, Intel, and Sun Microsystems, Aug. 2009.

[2] A.-R. Adl-Tabatabai, B. T. Lewis, V. Menon, B. R. Murphy, B. Saha, and T. Shpeisman. Compiler and Runtime Support for Efficient Software Transactional Memory. *SIGPLAN 2006 Conf. on Programming Language Design and Implementation*, June 2006.

[3] J. Casper, T. Oguntebi, S. Hong, N. G. Bronson, C. Kozyrakis, and K. Olukotun. Hardware Acceleration of Transactional Memory on Commodity Systems. *16th Intl. Conf. on Architectural Support for Programming Languages and Operating Systems*, Mar. 2011.

[4] L. Dalessandro, F. Carouge, S. White, Y. Lev, M. Moir, M. L. Scott, and M. F. Spear. Hybrid NOrec: A Case Study in the Effectiveness of Best Effort Hardware Transactional Memory. *16th Intl. Conf. on Architectural Support for Programming Languages and Operating Systems*, Mar. 2011.

[5] L. Dalessandro, M. L. Scott, and M. F. Spear. Transactions as the Foundation of a Memory Consistency Model. *24th Intl. Symp. on Distributed Computing*, Sept. 2010. Earlier but expanded version available as TR 959, Dept. of Computer Science, Univ. of Rochester, July 2010.

[6] D. Detlefs. Unpublished manuscript, 2007.

[7] D. Dice and N. Shavit. TLRW: Return of the

Read-Write Lock. *4th ACM SIGPLAN Workshop on Transactional Computing*, Feb. 2009.

[8] D. Dice, O. Shalev, and N. Shavit. Transactional Locking II. *20th Intl. Symp. on Distributed Computing*, Sept. 2006.

[9] A. Dragojević, R. Guerraoui, and M. Kapałka. Stretching Transactional Memory. *SIGPLAN 2009 Conf. on Programming Language Design and Implementation*, June 2009.

[10] P. Felber, T. Riegel, and C. Fetzer. Dynamic Performance Tuning of Word-Based Software Transactional Memory. *13th ACM Symp. on Principles and Practice of Parallel Programming*, Feb. 2008.

[11] P. Felber, E. Rivière, W. M. Moreira, D. Harmanci, P. Marlier, S. Diestelhorst, M. Hohmuth, M. Pohlack, A. Cristal, I. Hur, O. S. Unsal, P. Stenström, A. Dragojevic, R. Guerraoui, M. Kapalka, V. Gramoli, U. Drepper, S. Tomić, Y. Afek, G. Korland, N. Shavit, C. Fetzer, M. Nowack, and T. Riegel. The Velox Transactional Memory Stack. *IEEE Micro*, 30(5): 76–87, Sept.-Oct. 2010.

[12] K. Fraser. Practical Lock-Freedom. Ph. D. dissertation, UCAM-CL-TR-579, Computer Laboratory, Univ. of Cambridge, Feb. 2004.

[13] R. Guerraoui and M. Kapałka. On the Correctness of Transactional Memory. *13th ACM Symp. on Principles and Practice of Parallel Programming*, Feb. 2008.

[14] R. Guerraoui and M. Kapałka. *Principles of Transactional Memory.* Morgan & Claypool, 2010.

[15] T. Harris and K. Fraser. Language Support for Lightweight Transactions. *OOPSLA 2003 Conf. Proc.*, Oct. 2003.

[16] T. Harris, J. R. Larus, and R. Rajwar. *Transactional Memory.* Synthesis Lectures on Computer Architecture. Morgan & Claypool, 2nd edition, 2010.

[17] T. Harris, M. Plesko, A. Shinnar, and D. Tarditi. Optimizing Memory Transactions. *SIGPLAN 2006 Conf. on Programming Language Design and Implementation*, June 2006.

[18] M. Herlihy and J. E. Moss. Transactional Memory: Architectural Support for Lock-Free Data Structures. *20th Intl. Symp. on Computer Architecture*, May 1993. Expanded version available as CRL 92/07, DEC Cambridge Research Laboratory, Dec. 1992.

[19] M. Herlihy, V. Luchangco, M. Moir, and W. N. Scherer III. Software Transactional Memory for Dynamic-sized Data Structures. *22nd ACM Symp. on Principles of Distributed Computing*, July 2003.

[20] G. Kestor, R. Gioiosa, T. Harris, O. S. Unsal, A. Cristal, I. Hur, and M. Valero. STM^2: A Parallel STM for High Performance Simultaneous Multithreading Systems. *2011 Intl. Conf. on Parallel Architectures and Compilation Techniques*, Oct. 2011.

[21] V. J. Marathe, M. F. Spear, and M. L. Scott. Scalable Techniques for Transparent Privatization in Software Transactional Memory. *2008 Intl. Conf. on Parallel Processing*, Sept. 2008.

[22] V. Menon, S. Balensiefer, T. Shpeisman, A.-R. Adl-Tabatabai, R. L. Hudson, B. Saha, and A. Welc. Practical Weak-Atomicity Semantics for Java STM. *20th ACM Symp. on Parallelism in Algorithms and Architectures*, June 2008.

[23] C. C. Minh, J. Chung, C. Kozyrakis, and K. Olukotun. STAMP: Stanford Transactional Applications for Multi-Processing. *2008 IEEE Intl. Symp. on Workload Characterization*, Sept. 2008.

[24] M. Olszewski, J. Cutler, and J. G. Steffan. JudoSTM: A Dynamic Binary-Rewriting Approach to Software Transactional Memory. *16th Intl. Conf. on Parallel Architectures and Compilation Techniques*, Sept. 2007.

[25] Reconfigurable Software Transactional Memory Runtime. Project web site. `code.google.com/p/rstm`.

[26] T. Riegel, C. Fetzer, and P. Felber. Time-based Transactional Memory with Scalable Time Bases. *19th ACM Symp. on Parallelism in Algorithms and Architectures*, Jun 2007.

[27] T. Riegel, C. Fetzer, and P. Felber. Snapshot Isolation for Software Transactional Memory. *1st ACM SIGPLAN Workshop on Transactional Computing*, June 2006.

[28] B. Saha, A.-R. Adl-Tabatabai, R. L. Hudson, C. C. Minh, and B. Hertzberg. McRT-STM: A High Performance Software Transactional Memory System for a Multi-Core Runtime. *11th ACM Symp. on Principles and Practice of Parallel Programming*, Mar. 2006.

[29] M. F. Spear, V. J. Marathe, L. Dalessandro, and M. L. Scott. Privatization Techniques for Software Transactional Memory (brief announcement). *26th ACM Symp. on Principles of Distributed Computing*, Aug. 2007. Extended version available as TR 915, Dept. of Computer Science, Univ. of Rochester, Feb. 2007.

[30] M. F. Spear, L. Dalessandro, V. J. Marathe, and M. L. Scott. Ordering-Based Semantics for Software Transactional Memory. *12th Intl. Conf. on Principles of Distributed Systems*, Dec. 2008.

[31] M. F. Spear, M. M. Michael, M. L. Scott, and P. Wu. Reducing Memory Ordering Overheads in Software Transactional Memory. *Intl. Symp. on Code Generation and Optimization*, Mar. 2009.

[32] M. F. Spear, V. J. Marathe, W. N. Scherer III, and M. L. Scott. Conflict Detection and Validation Strategies for Software Transactional Memory. *20th Intl. Symp. on Distributed Computing*, Sept. 2006.

[33] `libjsig`: Java™ RFE 4381843. Online documentation. `docs.oracle.com/javase/1.5.0/docs/guide/vm/signal-chaining.html`.

[34] The GNU C Library. Online documentation. `www.gnu.org/s/hello/manual/libc/index.html`.

[35] L. Wall, T. Christiansen, and J. Orwant. *Programming Perl.* O'Reilly Media, Third Edition, 2000.

Transactional Prefetching: Narrowing the Window of Contention in Hardware Transactional Memory

Anurag Negi† Adrià Armejach*‡ Adrián Cristal*◇ Osman S. Unsal* Per Stenstrom†
†Chalmers University of Technology *Barcelona Supercomputing Center
‡Universitat Politècnica de Catalunya ◇IIIA - CSIC - Spanish National Research Council
{negi, per.stenstrom}@chalmers.se
{adria.armejach, adrian.cristal, osman.unsal}@bsc.es

ABSTRACT

Memory access latency is the primary performance bottleneck in modern computer systems. Prefetching data before it is needed by a processing core allows substantial performance gains by overlapping significant portions of memory latency with useful work. Prior work has investigated this technique and measured potential benefits in a variety of scenarios. However, its use in speeding up Hardware Transactional Memory (HTM) has remained hitherto unexplored. In several HTM designs transactions invalidate speculatively updated cache lines when they abort. Such cache lines tend to have high locality and are likely to be accessed again when the transaction re-executes. Coarse grained transactions that update several cache lines are particularly susceptible to performance degradation even under moderate contention. However, such transactions show strong locality of reference, especially when contention is high. Prefetching cache lines with high locality can, therefore, improve overall concurrency by speeding up transactions and, thereby, narrowing the window of time in which such transactions persist and can cause contention. Such transactions are important since they are likely to form a common TM use-case. We note that traditional prefetch techniques may not be able to track such lines adequately or issue prefetches quickly enough. This paper investigates the use of prefetching in HTMs, proposing a simple design to identify and request prefetch candidates, and measures performance gains to be had for several representative TM workloads.

Categories and Subject Descriptors

C.1 [**Processor Architectures**]: Parallel Architectures

Keywords

hardware transactional memory, multicores, prefetching

PACT'12, September 19–23, 2012, Minneapolis, Minnesota, USA.

1. INTRODUCTION

The ever-widening disparity between the speed at which a processor core can process data and the speed at which the memory hierarchy can supply it has led to a myriad of techniques that aim at overlapping data access latency with some form of useful work. Prefetching is one such technique where, by predicting memory references likely to occur in the near future, data is fetched into structures close to the core before its needed. Various prediction techniques have been employed, targeting frequently encountered patterns in memory references. However, Hardware Transactional Memory (HTM) [13] presents a scenario where a new form of prefetching may be invoked that complements and, in certain scenarios, allows more effective latency hiding than standard techniques.

Several implementations of HTM [9, 6, 25, 19, 18] use first-level caches to isolate speculative state, preserving a consistent state by pushing clean (old) cache lines to second-level caches and beyond. Transactions execute speculatively and any data races detected by the HTM system are typically resolved by forcing one or more of the conflicting transactions to abort. When a transaction aborts speculative state must be discarded and the transaction must be re-executed. To do so, all speculatively modified lines in the first-level cache are invalidated. Subsequent references to such lines during re-execution will miss in the first-level cache and retrieve a clean version of the line from deeper levels of the memory hierarchy. Thus, data transfer latencies delay transactional execution. In scenarios with moderate to high contention this can result in extended transaction execution times, application slow-down and a higher probability of contention. We observe that while a technique like runahead execution [8, 16] could be advantageous here, the hardware requirements for runahead execution and transactional execution are similar (support for checkpointing and dependency tracking) and thus would need to be duplicated in hardware.

In this study we investigate potential gains to be had when lines in the write-set – *the set of speculatively updated cache lines* – of a transaction are prefetched when it begins execution. These lines are highly likely to be referenced again when an aborted transaction re-executes. Interestingly, high contention typically implies high locality of reference. Moreover, in Section 2 we show that this locality of reference is not limited to re-executions of a particular transaction invocation and persists even when a new invocation of the transaction occurs. These observations have motivated the design of hardware prefetching mechanisms described in this paper. These mechanisms are able to track important write-set lines and are brought into play upon aborts and new transaction starts to prefetch lines that would be required by the transaction during its execution.

The benefits from prefetching write-set lines are expected to be most noticeable in lazy versioning systems like TCC [9, 6]. This is so because, unlike eager versioning designs, they do not restore clean values when speculation fails, and rely upon deeper levels of the memory hierarchy to provide consistent data. However, eager versioning designs like LogTM[26] will benefit from prefetches that are initiated when a new instance of a transaction first begins. In this case a part of the write-set may not be present in the cache when the transaction starts execution, particularly when the contention is high. This effect not only improves execution times but also narrows the window of contention improving concurrency overall.

The rest of this paper is organized as follows. Section 2 shows strong evidence of the locality of reference that exists between multiple invocations of a given transaction for a variety of transactional workloads. This also motivates the hardware structures which are described in detail in Section 3. Section 3 also describes the operation of the prefetch mechanism. Section 4 presents potential performance gains that can be achieved when such prefetching is enabled. We evaluate several transactional prefetching configurations based on the design presented in Section 3, including an idealized variant. Section 5 puts our contributions in perpective of prior work done in prefetching and HTM.

2. MOTIVATION

To make a case for prefetching in transactions we have investigated the behavior of several workloads in the STAMP benchmark suite [5]. The goal of this analysis was to quantify the locality of reference that exists in write-sets across different invocations of the same atomic block or transaction. We recorded all stores issued by each transaction from one thread of each application, tracking the number of transaction invocations that reference each distinct cache line address. We then ranked accessed locations on the basis of frequency of such references for all invocations of each transaction. We choose to concentrate on write-sets for two reasons – first, such lines are likely to get invalidated due to coherence actions or aborts and, second, the read-modify-write nature of common transactions results in a significant overlap with the read-set. The non-overlapping part of the read-set typically sees less contention and is, therefore, likely to be found in the private cache hierarchy.

Figure 1 presents several plots (one for each workload included in the study) that show the number of distinct addresses that can cover a certain fraction of the total number of memory references generated by all invocations of a certain transaction over the duration of the application. For each plot the x-axis is in logarithmic scale and shows the number of distinct addresses, N. The y-axis plots cumulative reference count, C, (for the N most frequently referenced addresses) normalized to the total number of references issued. In other words, if we can track and prefetch a certain number, N, of the most frequently referenced addresses then we can potentially satisfy a fraction, C, of stores in transactions. Moreover, it can be inferred from the read-modify-write behavior of common transactions that these prefetches would also satisfy a significant portion of loads issued by the transaction.

Some transactions have almost no locality of reference, like Tx2 from kernel 1 in SSCA2, a workload with little contention. The linear rise (note that the x-axis is logarithmic) in cumulative reference count is indicative of this fact. A similar case occurs in Labyrinth, where concurrency is limited but the nature of work results in the different invocations of the same transaction updating very different locations. However, for applications like Intruder, Genome, Kmeans and Yada one notices saturation or very low growth in cumulative reference count beyond 16 or 20 addresses, indicating strong locality of reference.

The optimistic nature of TM usually provides good performance when workloads have little contention. However, when contention is high overheads of managing and restoring speculative state grow and increase application execution times. Therefore, to improve HTM design one must aim at minimizing overheads when running applications with moderate to high contention. Besides direct improvements in transaction execution times, prefetching data can potentially improve overall concurrency by narrowing the window of contention for transactions. Figure 2 shows a very simplified view of how this might occur. We view a conflicting access as an event that can occur with equal likelihood at any point during the lifetime of a thread which might intermittently execute transactions. In such a case the probability of contention for the transaction can be represented by the time the thread spends executing the transaction expressed as a fraction of its lifetime. It can be seen that shortening the duration of a transaction reduces the probability of encountering a conflict. Moreover (not shown in the figure) this reduced probability also results in fewer aborts and consequent re-executions (which degrade overall contention even further). This results in fewer conflicting accesses being generated in the system.

Prior work [17] has found that containing transactional stores in dedicated hardware buffers can mitigate overheads associated in reading back lines invalidated on an abort. However, our prefetching technique provides improvements in performance for fresh transaction invocations as well.

As single-thread performance growth stagnates, running applications with inherently limited parallelism in a multi-threaded fashion will be a natural recourse to extract maximum benefit from core count scaling. For such applications in our study (Genome, KMeans, Yada, Intruder) we see that significant locality of reference exists. If we track the 16 most frequently accessed addresses for each transaction we can typically cover more than 60% of the references issued.

3. DESIGN

We subdivide the design into three components – the first which infers locality, the second which manages prefetches and the third which trims prefetch lists. The subsections below describe the structure and behavior of each component. These components are instantiated for each core in a chip-multiprocessor.

3.1 Inferring locality

To decide which cache line addresses are most suitable for prefetching one must first get a measure of the associated locality. The key problem that arises when one attempts to track locality traits of arbitrary memory locations is that

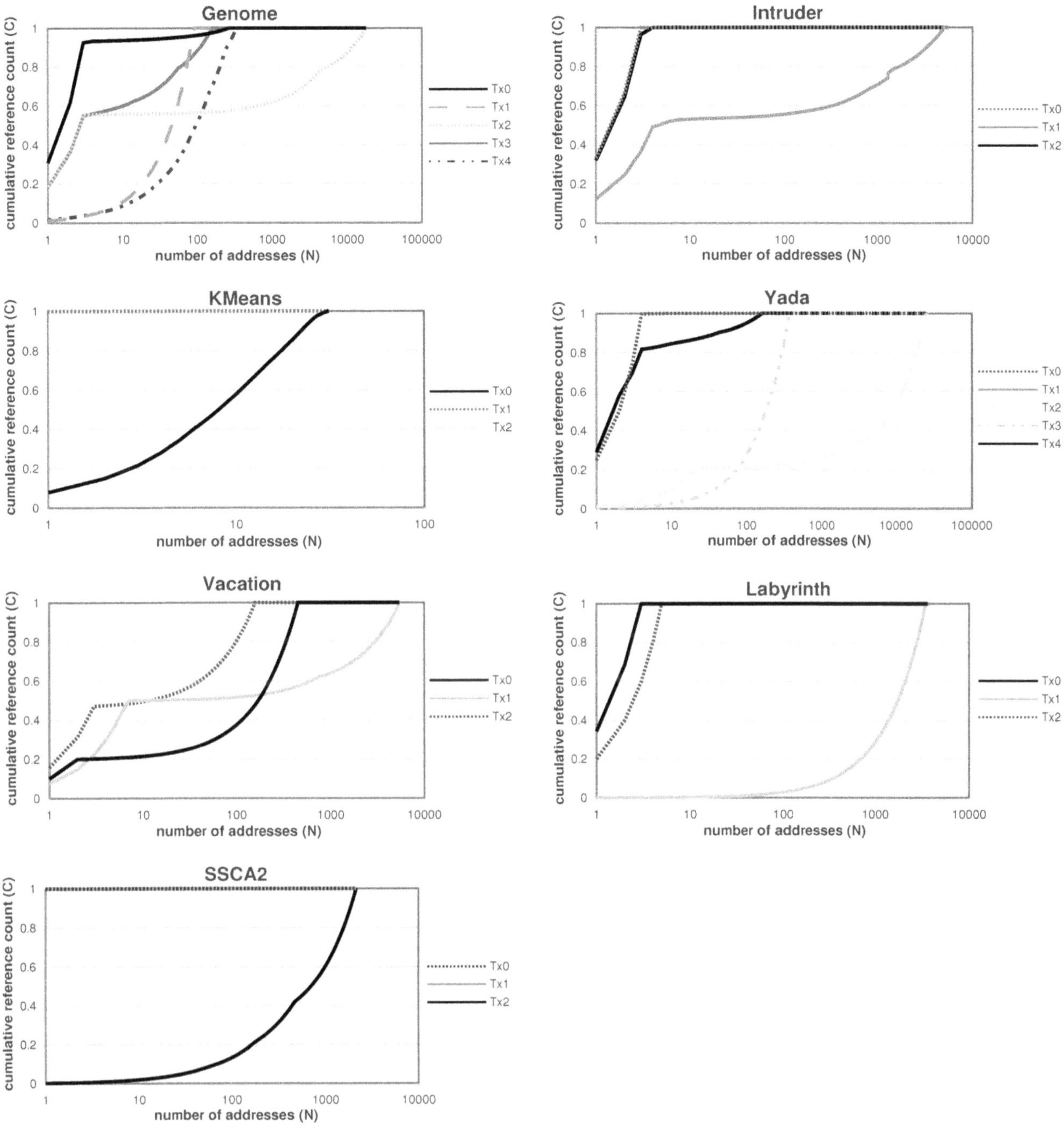

Figure 1: Locality of reference across transaction invocations.

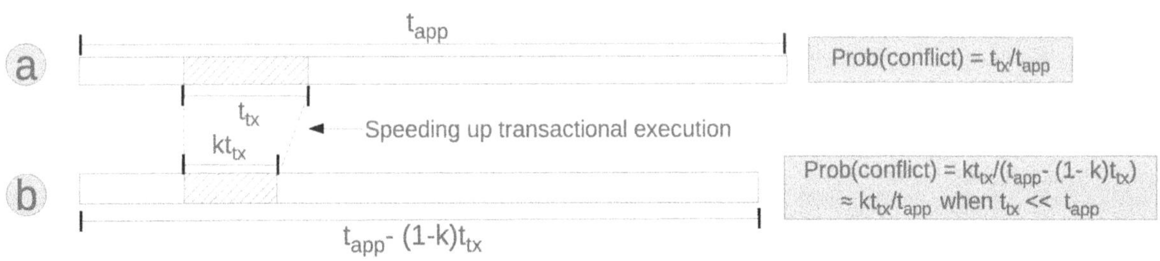

Figure 2: Narrowing the window of contention: effect on conflict probabilities.

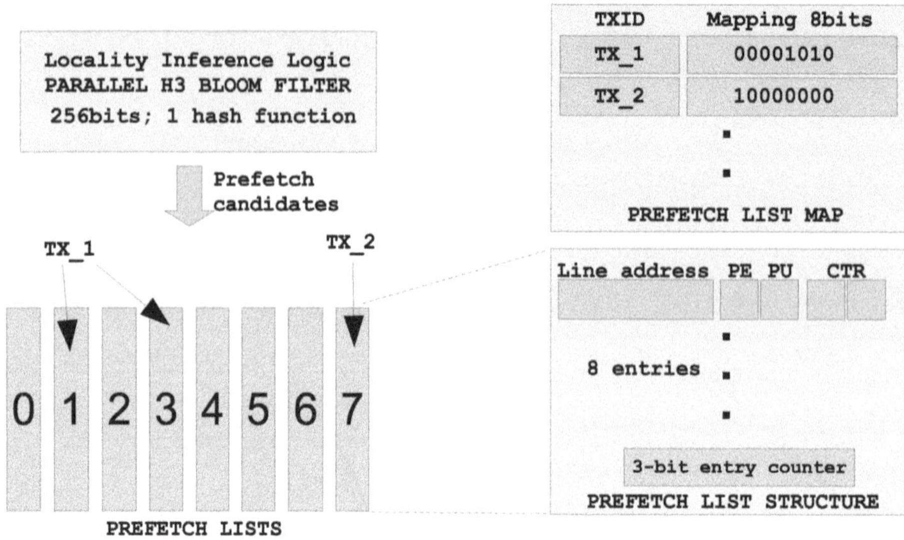

Figure 3: Transactional Prefetching: Key components.

of maintaining a history of memory references until there is enough to infer useful behavioural characteristics. While the history is being recorded there might not be any notion of relative importance of different addresses, resulting in seemingly very large storage requirements or extremely long delays in making inferences. A trade-off must be made that keeps the design simple yet responsive. We choose to do so by employing one or two bloom filters [3] to track memory access history for one or more invocations in the past. Performance evaluations presented later will show performance differences between designs with one and two bloom filters. The single filter design uses a two-step iterative refinement mechansim to learn high-locality cache line addresses one transaction at a time. The two-filter design (described later in Section 4.3) uses a 3-step mechanism using the bloom filters in a ping pong fashion.

When employing a single-bloom filter, two invocations of a transaction are required to learn prefetch candidates. Figure 3 shows the key elements of the proposed mechanism. During the first invocation, cache line addresses in the write set are added to the bloom filter. During the second invocation, cache line addresses targeted by stores are checked for presence in the bloom filter. If a positive match is found the address is added to one of the prefetch candidate lists. Either free lists are used or the lists allocated to the least recently invoked transaction are freed, as explained in Section 3.2.

Locality inference is not initiated for transactions as long as they have prefetch resources allocated to them. Training is aborted if two invocations of another transaction are seen and a watchdog timer has been triggered. This prevents seldom executed transactions from permanently blocking access to locality inference structures. We employ parallel bloom filters employing high-quality H3 hash functions, which have been found, in prior work [22], to be suitable for hardware implementation. The evaluation includes results for both real and perfect bloom filters. Note that the performance (false-positive rate) of these filters is not as critical to performance as when using such filters for conflict detection.

3.1.1 Training in parallel

It is conceivable that the bloom filters can be used to train on more than one transaction simultaneously. This would involve inserting *(address, transaction id)* tuples instead of just addresses into the bloom filters. Since it is non-trivial to selectively delete entries from a bloom filter, such a design must consider the cost of false positives, transaction invocation frequencies and overall responsiveness. We do not study the concept further in this work.

3.2 Managing prefetches

Prefetch candidates produced through locality inference are stored in one or more of several prefetch lists. For the purposes of this study we have 8 lists, 8 entries each. Thus we can support 8 distinct transactions or atomic blocks. If there are fewer transactions which require more than 8 prefetch entries, two or more lists can be chained together. This is managed by the Transactional Prefetch List Map (TPLM), as shown in Figure 3. This is a structure with 8 entries. Each entry contains a TXID (transaction identifier) field and an 8-bit map with high bits indicating prefetch lists allocated to the transaction. Chaining lists together provides flexibility in dealing with transactions of different sizes. When more than 8 transactions exist or no prefetch lists are available we employ an LRU scheme to release resources for the least recently invoked transaction. Prefetches are issued when a transaction begins and has prefetch lists associated with it. In our experiments with lazy conflict resolution designs, it is safe to not regard prefetches as transactional accesses.

Each entry in the prefetch list contains the cache line address, a PE (prefetch enable) bit, a PU (Prefetch Useful) bit and a 2-bit counter. The PE bit is set when the corresponding line is invalidated or evicted from the cache or when a transactional store updates it. Lines with PE bit set to 0 are not prefetched. Transactional commits reset all PE bits. PE bits are also reset when a cache line fill occurs and a transactional update to the line has not yet been issued. All PU bits are reset when a transaction begins. The PU bit

Cores	32 in-order 2GHz Alpha cores, 1 IPC
L1 Caches	32KB 4-way, 64B lines, 1-cycle hit
Bloom filter	256-bit, parallel H3, 1 hash function
L2 Cache	1MB/bank 8-way, 64B lines, 10-cycle hit
Memory	4GB, 150-cycle latency
Interconnect	2D mesh, 2 cycles per hop
Directory	full-bit vector sharers list, 10-cycle directory latency

Table 1: Simulation parameters.

Benchmark	Input parameters
Genome	-g4096 -s128 -n524288
Intruder	-a10 -l32 -n8192 -s1
KMeans	-m15 -n15 -t0.05 -i n32768-d24-c16
Labyrinth	-i random-x96-y96-z3-n384.txt
SSCA2	-s13 -i1.0 -u1.0 -l3 -p3
Vacation	-n8 -q40 -u90 -r1048576 -t32768
Yada	-a20 -i ttimeu10000.2

Table 2: Evaluated STAMP benchmarks and input parameters.

is set when a transactional store targets the corresponding cache line, indicating that the address still retains locality.

3.3 Trimming prefetch lists and transactions

The two bit counter for each prefetch candidate is set to 4 when the entry is first created. On transaction commits the counter is decremented for all entries in the prefetch list for which PU bit is not set. If this counter reaches 0 the line is not prefetched any more. If all entries for a certain transaction have counts set to 0, the resources (prefetch lists and TPLM) are released for use by other transactions. This is easily achieved by associating a 3-bit counter with each prefetch list. It tracks the number of active prefetch candidates in the list. It is incremented when entries are added to the prefetch list after training and decremented every time a prefetch candidate is trimmed. When the counter is decremented to zero the corresponding bit in the list allocation bit-map in the TPLM is reset. When all bits in the list allocation bit map of a transaction are set to zero, the entry can be reused. The next invocation of such a trimmed transaction will be eligible for locality inference, when prefetch lists will be rebuilt.

4. EVALUATION

In this section we evaluate the performance of transactional prefetching. We use as baseline Scalable-TCC, a state-of-the-art lazy HTM system. We first describe the simulation environment that we use, then we present our preliminary results.

4.1 Simulation Environment

For the evaluation we use M5 [2], an Alpha 21264 full-system simulator. We modify M5 to faithfully model the Scalable-TCC proposal to operate in a chip multi-processor (CMP) with private L1 caches and a banked L2 cache. The design is configured to avoid rare overflows of transactional data from private caches. These are handled using a special overflow buffer. In our experiments only a few such events are noticed. Scalable-TCC has an always-in-transaction approach and employs lazy conflict detection and resolution at commit time, transactional updates are kept in private buffers (caches) to maintain isolation. Note that the prefetch mechanism is invoked only for transactions defined in the application source code. Table 1 summarizes the system parameters that we use, with one level of private cache and a 2D mesh network connecting the shared L2 banks, resembling the Scalable-TCC proposal. Our proposed transactional prefetching scheme is implemented on top of the baseline HTM. This detailed simulation model , denoted as TP (Transactional Prefetching), employs one 256-bit H3 bloom filter. In addition, we also simulate an idealized model that at the beginning of a transaction prefetches all the lines that have been speculatively written by that transaction in the past. These prefetches are considered to be serviced instantaneously. We name this model PA (Prefetch All).

We use the STAMP benchmark suite [5] to evaluate our proposal. Table 2 lists the evaluated workloads and input parameters. We exclude the application Bayes from our evaluation, because this application has non-deterministic exiting conditions leading to severe load imbalance between threads, which makes comparison between different systems inconclusive.

4.2 Performance Results

Figure 4 shows the execution time breakdown for the HTM systems that we evaluate, namely Scalable-TCC (S), Transactional Prefetching (TP), and Prefetch All (PA). The results in Figure 4 are normalized to Scalable-TCC 32-threaded executions, and they are split into six parts, namely Barrier, Commit, Useful, StallCache, Wasted, and WastedCache. The component, Useful, is defined as one cycle per instruction plus the number of memory accesses per instruction multiplied by the L1D hit latency; the component, StallCache, is defined as the time spent waiting for an L1D cache miss to be served. Analogously, for aborted transactions we define Wasted and WastedCache.

Intruder shows remarkable improvement when prefetching is enabled (a speedup of more than 30%). It is a highly contended application exhibiting significant locality across various transaction invocations. In this scenario prefetching data results in substantial shortening of transaction lifetimes. The components, StallCache and WastedCache, show major reductions, as can be seen in Figure 4. We highlight this application because in our opinion it is an important workload that is representative of applications with limited concurrency. Such multithreaded applications will gain importance as parallelization is expected to become the only source of performance scaling.

Genome shows moderate contention and a significant amount of locality for most transactions (see Figure 1). It shows two distinct phases during execution – a short early high contention phase followed by a longer phase with low to moderate contention. The benefits of prefetching accrue in the first phase, yielding an 16% improvement over the baseline.

Yada is another application with moderate contention (see Figure 1). Prefetching lines improves performance, though not by much (3%). One of the reasons for this is limited tracking resources at the prefetcher. Yada has large transactions, and the number of prefetched addresses constitutes a small fraction of the memory references generated.

Vacation has large transactions, there is very little con-

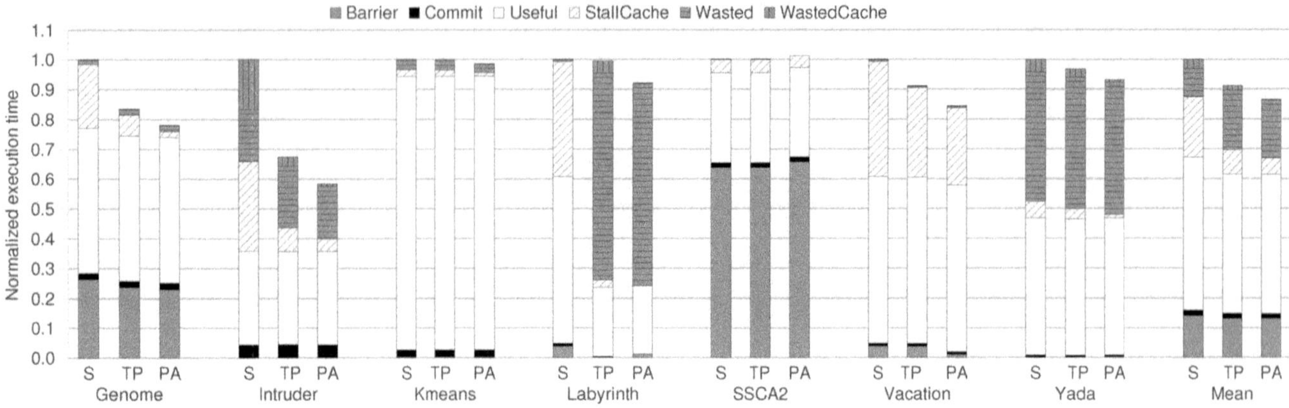

Figure 4: Normalized execution time breakdown for 32 threads.
S — Scalable-TCC; **TP** — Transactional Prefetching; **PA** — Prefetch All

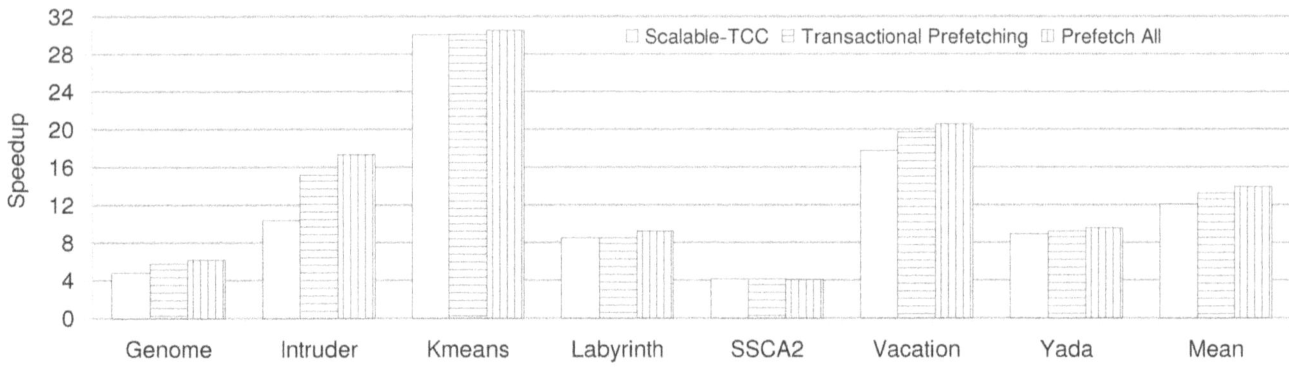

Figure 5: Scalability for 32 threaded workloads.

Benchmark	%Useful	%Trimmed	%Cache improv.	Prefetches per Commit
Genome	92.88	81.36	60.07	0.02
Intruder	99.87	11.11	64.55	4.28
KMeans	41.64	99.54	1.55	0.2
Labyrinth	100.00	0.00	82.74	2.27
SSCA2	0.00	99.49	0.00	0
Vacation	98.04	14.66	14.74	0.03
Yada	98.97	38.64	36.66	2.26
Mean	88.56	40.88	37.19	1.3

Table 3: Statistics of Transactional Prefetching for evaluated workloads.

Legend: **%Useful** — Percentage of useful prefetches compared to issued prefetches; **%Trimmed** — Percentage of trimmed entries compared to added in prefetch lists; **%Cache improvement** — Percentage improvement of total cache service time compared to Scalable-TCC; **Prefetches per commit** – Average number of prefetches issued per committed transaction.

tention and transactions are read dominant. The dominant transaction (shown as Tx1 in Figure 1) has good locality of reference and the TP configuration is able to take advantage of this, yielding an improvement of about 15% over the baseline (as seen in Figure 6).

KMeans exhibits short phases with some degree of locality. This is evident from the number of trimmed and useful prefetches as shown in Table 3. However, transactions do not appear to have a dominant effect on execution time in this application. We, therefore, do not notice any appreciable deviation in execution times across various configurations.

SSCA2 is a highly concurrent application with little contention and almost no locality across transactions(see Figure 1). Hence, prefetching is not expected to play a role here, and as shown in Table 3 our proposed prefetch mechanism issues just 35 prefetches spread over more than 100,000 transaction invocations. Moreover, these prefetches get trimmed from the lists rapidly (as indicated by the high (99.49%) percentage of trimmed prefetches, see Table 3). Though

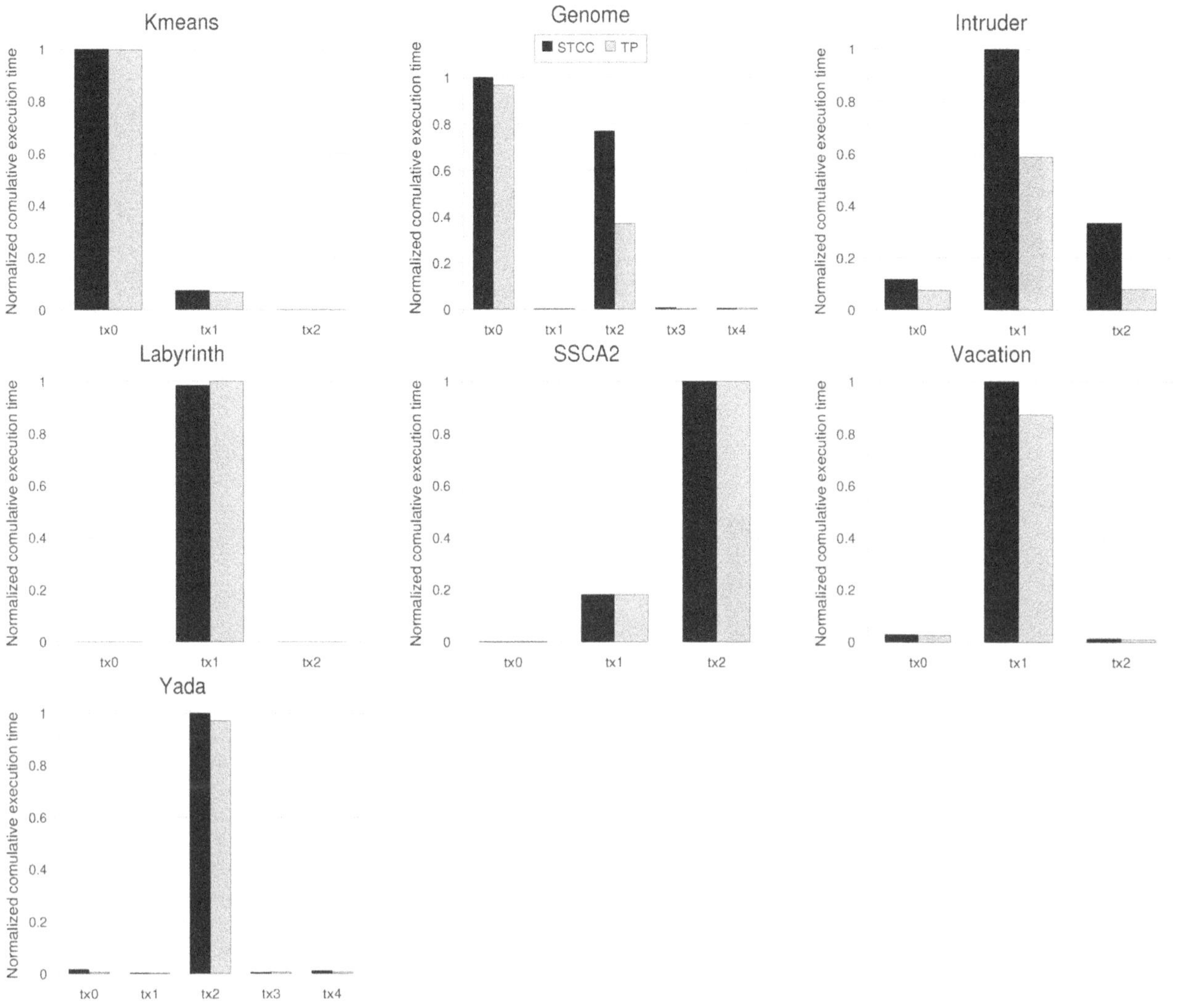

Figure 6: Impact on transaction execution times

Labyrinth repeatedly accesses a large set of addresses, it executes a very small number of transactions (less than ten instances of each defined transaction), leading to negligible performance gains for the TP configuration. Moreover, due to Labyrinth's lack of parallelism and sensitivity to transaction interleaving, some configurations exhibit increased contention and therefore more wasted work, as can be seen in Figure 4.

Figure 5 shows the scalability chart for the evaluated workloads using 32 threads on 32 cores. Intruder has a remarkable boost in scalability reaching 15.3× with TP, a promising result for an application that is known to have difficulties to scale. Noticeable improvements can be also seen in Genome, KMeans, Vacation and Yada, while applications like SSCA2 and Labyrinth remain flat due to their transactional characteristics.

Overall, as shown in Table 3 our transactional prefetching mechanism successfully infers locality from the evaluated workloads, achieving more than 90% utilization of issued prefetches for all applications except KMeans, where locality is high, but appears in short phases. Moreover, our design is able to detect scenarios where prefetching is not useful, for example in applications like SSCA2, and does not issue useless prefetches for such scenarios. In general, as can be observed in Table 3, if the usefulness of prefetches is low then the number of issued prefetches per committed transaction is rather small as well.

Figure 6 shows relative cumulative execution times for each transaction defined in code. Only successful commits have been considered. From these numbers it is possible to estimate the impact of transactional prefetching. For each transaction, two bars are shown – the left one corresponds to execution time seen with the baseline design and the right one corresponds to execution time with prefetching enabled. It is instructive to compare these numbers to those shown in Figure 1. We can see that applications which show high locality (Genome, Intruder, Yada, Vacation) also see an improvement in execution times. The improvement moreover is proportional to the degree of locality seen – for example, in Intruder most transactional accesses target only a few addresses and hence, we see a larger improvement than that seen in Yada. SSCA2 and Kmeans do not show much improvement since there is little locality.

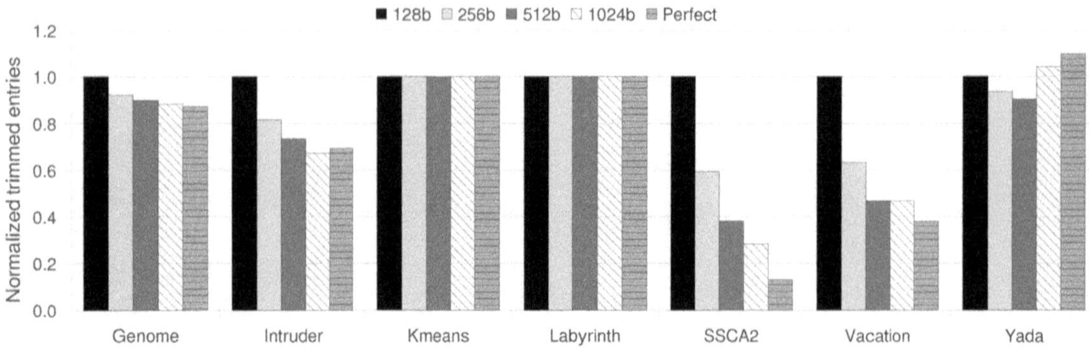

Figure 8: Impact of bloom filter size on trimmed entries.

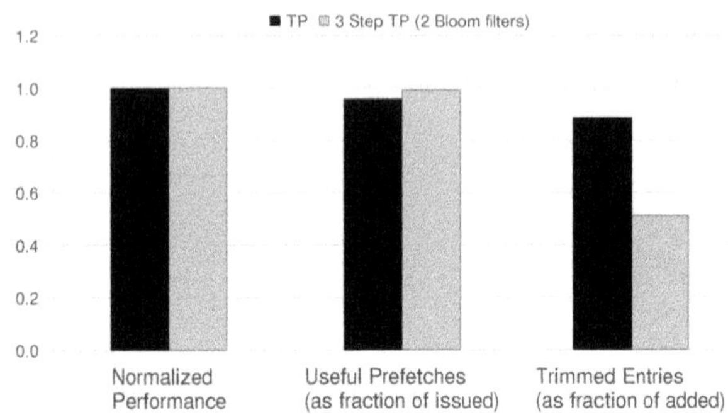

Figure 7: Impact of the 2-filter 3-step approach.

4.3 Two Filter Approach

More accurate learning of prefetch candidates can be performed by employing two bloom filters in a ping-pong fashion. We test this approach by using a 3-step interative refinement design. The first step inserts write-set cache line addresses in one (BFx) of the two filters (BFx and BFy). The next invocation of the transaction triggers the second step wherein written lines that are found in BFx are inserted in BFy. The third invocation starts the final step of the learning process, filling prefetch candidate lists based on written lines that are found in BFy. As before, we train one transaction at a time, releasing training resources on completion. This approach enables more accurate learning at the cost of responsiveness (it takes longer to train). Figure 7 shows how this approach compares against the single filter approach in terms of overall performance and the fraction of useful and trimmed prefetches. Although there is no appreciable difference in performance the two filter approach generates more accurate prefetches, as indicated by a larger fraction of useful prefetches and fewer trims.

4.4 Sensitivity Analysis

Bloom filter configuration has little impact of performance of transactional workloads. We varied bloom filter sizes, ranging from 128 bits to 1024 bits and also implemented perfect signatures. There is remarkable consistency in execution times across different filter configurations. This is because few additional prefetches arising from increased false positives with small bloom filter sizes have negligible impact on performance and are quickly trimmed from prefetch lists. Figure 8 shows that smaller filters result in more trimmed entries. However, in the case of Yada, variations in behavior induced by transaction interleaving cause minor deviation in the number of trimmed entries (with a 2% spread in execution times).

5. RELATED WORK

Although the first proposal by Herlihy and Moss [11] appeared in 1993, research in TM gained momentum with the introduction of multicore architectures. Two early HTM proposals, TCC [10] and LogTM [26], explore two very different points in the HTM design space. TCC defines a lazy conflict resolution design where transactions execute speculatively until one tries to commit its results and causes the re-execution of any concurrent conflicting transaction. LogTM describes an eager conflict resolution design that employs coherence to detect conflicts as soon as they occur and are resolved by asking the requester to retry (with a way to break occasional deadlocks through software intervention). Since then a lot of work has been done targeting a host of different issues that arise when transactional applications run on multicores. Bobba et al. [4] categorized pathologies that can arise in fixed policy HTM designs and degrade scalability and performance. The paper pointed out performance bottlenecks that can arise out of limited commit bandwidth in lazy conflict resolution designs and overheads due to excessive aborts in eager resolution designs. Several designs since then have targeted improved scalability in lazy conflict resolution systems through various means – making write-set commits more fine-grained [6, 20, 21] and ensuring conflicting transactions do not interfere with an on-going commit [25, 18]. Others have attempted to reduce abort overheads in both eager and lazy conflict resolution systems – by allowing eager systems to utilize deeper levels of the memory hierarchy to buffer old values [14] and by having caches with special SRAM cells that can store two versions of the same line simultaneously [1]. Yet others have attempted to incorporate the best of both eager and lazy policies in one design – at the granularity of application phases [19], at the granularity of transactions [15] , and at the granularity of cache lines [24]. There exist studies that have attempted to insulate the coherent cache hierarchy from adverse effects of repeated aborts [17]. These varied attempts at reducing overheads involved in shared data accesses by cooperating threads have motivated the design effort in this work. This paper, however, presents a study and design that is largely orthogonal to the various design approaches discussed above. It uses the fact that transactions show locality of reference which can be utilized to improve the speed at which they can complete updates to shared data, thereby improving speed and reducing contention.

Several prior studies have developed ideas regarding cache line prefetching [12, 23] and investigated various prefetching schemes based on detecting cache-miss patterns in non-transactional workloads. This paper, unlike prior work, describes a scheme that does not rely upon the existence of a simple pattern (like a stride) in the memory reference stream. It can learn arbitrary sets of cache line addresses as long as they show locality of reference across multiple invocations of the same section of code. Thus, this proposed technique is expected to be complementary to others. Moreover, with this technique prefetches can be issued earlier than in other techniques. Chou et. al [7] present epoch-based correlation prefetches which utilize special hardware and software support structures to detect prefetch trigger events and manage prefetch candidates. Our work presents a simpler, less expensive interface to manage and trigger prefetches using low complexity per-core hardware.

6. CONCLUSIONS AND FUTURE WORK

This paper highlights the importance of prefetching data in the new context of hardware transactional memory. Since transactions are used to annotate parts of multithreaded algorithms where concurrent tasks share information, it is important that they run as fast as possible to improve overall scalability of the application. Moreover transactions are clearly demarcated sections of code and thus can be targeted by techniques, such as the one proposed in this paper, that attempt to utilize any locality of reference that may exist within such codes. Our technique, using relatively modest hardware support shows improvements for most transactional workloads we have analyzed, with substantial gains of upto 35% under high contention (for intruder).

In the future we would like to enhance this technique and apply it to other scenarios to accelerate generic blocks of code that exhibit high locality of reference across invocations. We feel that critical sections and synchronization operations could also benefit from such prefetching. The observation that high contention is indicative of high locality makes this technique potentially advantageous in mitigating the impact of data-sharing bottlenecks in multithreaded applications. We also wish to study interactions when this technique is combined with other forms of prefetching, using the insights so acquired to develop synergistic techniques that further improve the design to speed up both transactional and non-transactional code.

Acknowledgements

This paper is the result of a research collaboration between Chalmers University of Technology and Barcelona Supercomputing Center (BSC) made possible through a collaboration grant to Adria Armejach by the European HiPEAC Network of Excellence. Anurag Negi's work at Chalmers is supported by grants from the Swedish Foundation for Strategic Research (SSF) under the SCHEME project. Adrià's work is supported by the agreement between the Barcelona Supercomputing Center and Microsoft Research, by the Ministry of Science and Technology of Spain and the European Union under contracts TIN2007-60625 and TIN2008-02055-E.

7. REFERENCES

[1] A. Armejach, A. Seyedi, R. Titos-Gil, I. Hur, O. S. Unsal, A. Cristal, and M. Valero. Using a reconfigurable L1 data cache for efficient version management in hardware transactional memory. In *PACT '11: Proc. 20th International Conference on Parallel Architectures and Compilation Techniques*, 2011.

[2] N. Binkert, R. Dreslinski, L. Hsu, K. Lim, A. Saidi, and S. Reinhardt. The M5 simulator: Modeling networked systems. *IEEE Micro*, 2006.

[3] B. H. Bloom. Space/time trade-offs in hash coding with allowable errors. *Commun. ACM*, 13:422–426, July 1970.

[4] J. Bobba, K. E. Moore, L. Yen, H. Volos, M. D. Hill, M. M. Swift, and D. A. Wood. Performance pathologies in hardware transactional memory. In *Proceedings of the 34th Annual International Symposium on Computer Architecture*, June 2007.

[5] C. Cao Minh, J. Chung, C. Kozyrakis, and K. Olukotun. STAMP: Stanford transactional applications for multi-processing. In *Proceedings of The IEEE International Symposium on Workload Characterization*, Sep 2008.

[6] H. Chafi, J. Casper, B. D. Carlstrom, A. McDonald, C. C. Minh, W. Baek, C. Kozyrakis, and K. Olukotun. A scalable, non-blocking approach to transactional memory. In *Proceedings of the 13th International Symposium on High-Performance Computer Architecture*, 2007.

[7] Y. Chou. Low-Cost Epoch-Based Correlation Prefetching for Commercial Applications. In *40th Annual IEEE/ACM International Symposium on Microarchitecture, 2007*, pages 301 –313, dec. 2007.

[8] J. Dundas and T. Mudge. Improving data cache performance by pre-executing instructions under a cache miss. In *In Proceedings of the 1997 International Conference on Supercomputing*, pages 68–75, 1997.

[9] L. Hammond, B. D. Carlstrom, V. Wong, M. Chen, C. Kozyrakis, and K. Olukotun. Transactional coherence and consistency: Simplifying parallel hardware and software. *IEEE Micro*, 24(6), Nov-Dec 2004.

[10] L. Hammond, V. Wong, M. Chen, B. D. Carlstrom, J. D. Davis, B. Hertzberg, M. K. Prabhu, H. Wijaya, C. Kozyrakis, and K. Olukotun. Transactional memory coherence and consistency. In *Proceedings of the 31st International Symposium on Computer Architecture*, June 2004.

[11] M. Herlihy and J. E. B. Moss. Transactional memory: Architectural support for lock-free data structures. In *Proceedings of the 20th Annual International Symposium on Computer Architecture*, May 1993.

[12] N. P. Jouppi. Improving direct-mapped cache performance by the addition of a small fully-associative cache and prefetch buffers. In *Proceedings of the 17th annual International Symposium on Computer Architecture*, ISCA '90, pages 364–373, 1990.

[13] J. R. Larus and R. Rajwar. *Transactional Memory*. Morgan & Claypool, 2006.

[14] M. Lupon, G. Magklis, and A. Gonzalez. FASTM: A log-based hardware transactional memory with fast abort recovery. In *Proceedings of the 18th International Conference on Parallel Architectures and Compilation Techniques*, Sept. 2009.

[15] M. Lupon, G. Magklis, and A. González. A dynamically adaptable hardware transactional

memory. In *In Proc. of 43rd Annual IEEE/ACM International Symposium on Microarchitecture*, Dec 2010.

[16] O. Mutlu, J. Stark, C. Wilkerson, and Y. N. Patt. Runahead execution: An alternative to very large instruction windows for out-of-order processors. In *In HPCA-9*, pages 129–140, 2003.

[17] A. Negi, R. Titos-Gil, M. E. Acacio, J. M. Garcia, and P. Stenstrom. Eager Meets Lazy: The impact of write-buffering on hardware transactional memory. *International Conference on Parallel Processing (ICPP)*, pages 73–82, 2011.

[18] A. Negi, R. Titos-Gil, M. E. Acacio, J. M. Garcia, and P. Stenstrom. π-TM: Pessimistic Invalidation for Scalable Lazy Hardware Transactional Memory (poster). In *Parallel Architectures and Compilation Techniques (PACT) 2011*, Oct. 2011.

[19] A. Negi, M. Waliullah, and P. Stenstrom. LV*: A low complexity lazy versioning HTM infrastructure. In *Proc. of the Intl. Conference on Embedded Computer Systems: Architectures, Modeling, and Simulation (IC-SAMOS 2010)*, pages 231–240, July 2010.

[20] S. H. Pugsley, M. Awasthi, N. Madan, N. Muralimanohar, and R. Balasubramonian. Scalable and reliable communication for hardware transactional memory. In *PACT '08: Proc. 17th international conference on Parallel architectures and compilation techniques*, pages 144–154, Oct. 2008.

[21] X. Qian, W. Ahn, and J. Torrellas. Scalablebulk: Scalable cache coherence for atomic blocks in a lazy environment. In *In Proc. of the 43rd Annual IEEE/ACM International Symposium on Microarchitecture, MICRO 2010*, pages 447–458, 2010.

[22] D. Sanchez, L. Yen, M. D. Hill, and K. Sankaralingam. Implementing signatures for transactional memory. In *Proceedings of the 40th Annual IEEE/ACM International Symposium on Microarchitecture*, 2007.

[23] T. Sherwood, S. Sair, and B. Calder. Predictor-directed stream buffers. In *Proceedings of the 33rd annual ACM/IEEE International Symposium on Microarchitecture*, MICRO 33, pages 42–53, 2000.

[24] R. Titos-Gil, A. Negi, M. E. Acacio, J. M. García, and P. Stenstrom. ZEBRA: a data-centric, hybrid-policy hardware transactional memory design. In *Proceedings of the international conference on Supercomputing*, ICS '11, 2011.

[25] S. Tomić, C. Perfumo, C. Kulkarni, A. Armejach, A. Cristal, O. Unsal, T. Harris, and M. Valero. EazyHTM: eager-lazy hardware transactional memory. In *Proceedings of the 42nd Annual IEEE/ACM International Symposium on Microarchitecture*, Dec. 2009.

[26] L. Yen, J. Bobba, M. M. Marty, K. E. Moore, H. Volos, M. D. Hill, M. M. Swift, and D. A. Wood. LogTM-SE: Decoupling hardware transactional memory from caches. In *Proceedings of the 13th International Symposium on High-Performance Computer Architecture*, Feb. 2007.

RISE: Improving the Streaming Processors Reliability Against Soft Errors in GPGPUs

Jingweijia Tan, Xin Fu
Department of Electrical Engineering and Computer Science
University of Kansas
Lawrence, KS 66045 USA
{jtan, xinfu}@ittc.ku.edu

ABSTRACT

With hundreds of cores integrated into a single chip, the general-purpose computing on graphic processing units (GPGPUs) provide high computing power to accelerate parallel applications. However, they are prone to manifest high soft-error vulnerability due to the lack of fault detection and tolerance. Especially, streaming processors become the reliability hot-spot in GPGPUs. This paper explores two opportunistic soft-error detection techniques to cost-effectively improve the streaming processors reliability. Observing that the streaming processors are not fully utilized during the branch divergence and pipeline stalls caused by the long latency operations, we propose to Recycle the streaming processors Idle time for Soft-Error detection (RISE) and obtain the good fault coverage with negligible performance degradation. RISE is composed of full-RISE and partial-RISE. Full-RISE selectively triggers the redundancy for a set of warps so that leverages the fully idled streaming processors during the pipeline stall time for the error detection. Partial-RISE performs the redundancy for a number of threads in certain warps using the partially idled streaming processors during the branch divergence. Our experimental results show that RISE shows strong capability in improving the SPs soft-error reliability by 43% with negligible (e.g. 4%) performance loss.

Categories and Subject Descriptors

B.8.1 [**Performance and Reliability**]: Reliability, Testing, and Fault-Tolerance; I.3.1 [**Computer Graphics**]: Hardware Architecture – *Graphics processors*

General Terms

Performance, Reliability

Keywords

GPGPU, Reliability, Soft Errors, Streaming multiprocessors

1. Introduction

Modern graphic processing unit (GPU) supports thousands of concurrent threads and provides remarkably higher throughput than CPU for parallel applications. In addition, the programming models (e.g. NVIDIA CUDA [1], AMD Stream [2], OpenCL[3]) facilitate the development of data parallel applications on GPU. With their strong computing power and improved programmability, the General-Purpose Computing on GPUs (GPGPUs) emerge as a highly attractive platform for a wide range of HPC applications exhibiting intensive data-level or thread-level parallelism. This extensive usage of GPGPU makes reliability a critical concern. Traditionally, the dominant workloads on GPUs are graphic processing applications which can effectively mask errors and have relaxed request on computation correctness. The error detection and fault tolerance on GPUs receive little attention. However, the newly adopted HPC applications, such as the scientific computing, financial application and medical data processing, have rigorous requirements on execution correctness. For example, in the GPGPU application computing a correlation function [4], 1% of value errors in any of the program output elements is treated as a silent data corruption (SDC) error and cannot be tolerated.

Soft errors, also called transient faults or single upset events, are failures caused by high-energy neutron or alpha particle strikes in integrated circuits. These faults are said to be "soft" in contrast to hard-faults which are permanent in the device. Soft errors may silently corrupt the data and lead to erroneous computation results. Soft error rate (SER) has been predicted to increase exponentially with the shrinking of feature sizes and growing integration density [5, 6], and GPGPUs with hundreds of cores integrated in a single chip are prone to suffer severe soft error attacks. For examples, [7] has already observed eight soft errors in a 72-hour run of testing program on 60 NVIDIA GeForce 8800GTS 512. [8] finds that the silent data corruption ratio in commodity GPU is 16~33%, while the ratio is smaller than 2.3% in CPUs which have comparatively developed fault tolerance techniques. The increasing SER becomes the major obstacle to current and future GPGPU design.

There are several parallel streaming processors (SPs) in each GPGPU core. They perform the fundamental computing operations, and play an important role in exploiting the parallel computing. In the GPGPU with thousands of parallel threads, SPs execute numerous instructions and expose them to neutron and alpha particle strikes, leading to the high SER. We evaluate the SPs soft-error vulnerability by computing its architecture vulnerability factor (AVF) which estimates the possibility that a transient fault in the structure will produce incorrect computation output, and find that the AVF is 53% on average (detailed description on AVF can be found in Section 4). In addition, as the key and representative combinational logic-based structure in the GPGPU, SPs occupy a large fraction of the chip area, the SER of SPs becomes the major contributor to the overall SER of the GPGPU processor. Effectively protecting SPs becomes the essential first step to build the resilient GPGPU architecture.

To overcome the reliability challenge, duplication [9] is the well-known classical technique: all instructions can be redundantly executed in the SPs and two copies are compared for soft-error detection. However, the simple duplication will lead to high performance penalty. Based on our experiments on various benchmarks, we found that on average, the full redundancy results in 58% performance degradation. The high computing throughput is the critical feature provided by GPGPUs. In general, substantially sacrificing the performance to achieve the perfect error coverage is not an efficient solution to the reliability issue in GPGPUs. A good trade-off between performance and reliability is more acceptable and desirable in future commodity GPGPU design.

GPGPU exploits thread-level parallelism (TLP) by grouping a number of threads into a warp which simultaneously executes the same instruction from each thread, warp are interleaved at cycle-by-cycle basis to hide the latency caused by the data dependence between consecutive instructions from a single warp. However, SPs are unused when all warps stall in the pipeline due to the long latency operations (e.g. off-chip memory access). In addition, threads in the same warp may direct to different paths at a branch, they execute sequentially in the diverged warp and partial SPs in the GPU core become idle [10]. We investigate a large set of GPGPU benchmarks, and find that on average, all SPs in a GPU core are idle during 35% of the total execution time, and the case that the SPs are partially idle appears in 11% of the execution time. The large fraction of the SPs idle time provides great opportunities to trigger the partial redundancy and trade-off little performance degradation for maximal reliability improvement. In this paper, we propose RISE (Recycling the streaming processors Idle time for Soft-Error detection) which intelligently leverages the under-utilized SPs to perform the redundancy.

The contributions of this work are as follows:

- We propose full-RISE that effectively re-uses the *fully* idled SPs in the GPU core caused by the long-latency memory accesses and the load imbalance among cores for soft-error detection. Full-RISE is composed of the request pending aware Full-RISE (RP-FRISE) and idle streaming multiprocessors (SMs) aware Full-RISE (IS-FRISE). RP-FRISE predicts the warp stall time for its next off-chip memory access and appropriately delays the warp progress via the redundant execution, therefore, successfully recycles the stall time for redundancy without degrading the performance. IS-FRISE estimates the load imbalances among cores, and smartly triggers the redundancy in cores which are predicted to execute fewer threads.
- We propose partial-RISE that redundantly executes a number of threads from a warp by combining their execution with the diverged warp, therefore utilizes the *partially* idled SPs during the branch divergence for reliability optimization.
- Our experiments show that both full-RISE and partial-RISE are capable of optimizing the SPs soft-error robustness substantially with negligible performance penalty. As the integration of the two techniques, RISE is able to enhance the SPs vulnerability by 43% with only 4% performance loss. Based on our sensitivity analysis, RISE is also applicable to GPU architecture designs with various performance optimization schemes.

The rest of this paper is organized as follows: Section 2 provides background on state-of-the-art GPGPU architecture. Section 3 presents our full-RISE and partial-RISE techniques. Section 4 describes our experimental methodologies. Section 5 evaluates the proposed techniques. We discuss the related work in Section 6, and conclude the paper in Section 7.

2. Background: General-purpose computing on graphic processing units (GPGPU) architecture

Figure 1(a) shows an overview of the state-of-the-art GPU Architecture [1]. It consists of a scalable number of in-order streaming multiprocessors (SM) that can access to multiple memory controllers via an on-chip interconnection network. Figure 1(b) illustrates a zoom-in view of the SM. It contains the warp scheduler, register files, streaming processors (SPs), constant and texture caches, and shared memory. In addition to CPU main memory, the GPU device has its own off-chip external memory (e.g. global memory) connected to the on-chip memory controllers. Some high-end GPUs also have L2 cache (shown as dotted line in Figure 1), and error-checking-correction unit for both on-chip and off-chip memory [11].

In this paper, we study the NVIDIA CUDA programming model but some of the basic constructs will hold for most GPU programming models. In CUDA, the GPU is treated as a co-processor that executes highly-parallel kernel functions launched by the CPU. The kernel is composed of a grid of light-weighted threads; a grid is divided into a set of blocks (referred as cooperative thread arrays in CUDA); each block is composed of hundreds of threads. Threads are distributed to the SMs at the granularity of blocks, and threads within a single block communicate via the shared memory and synchronize at a barrier if desired. Per-block resources, such as registers, shared memory, and thread slots in an SM are not released until all the threads in the block finish execution. More than one block can be assigned to a single SM if resources are available.

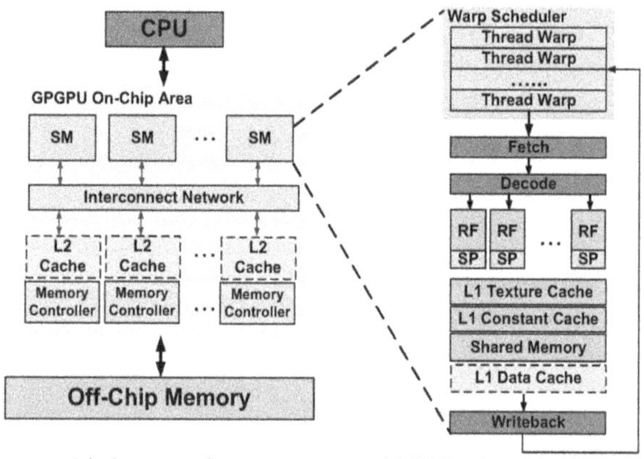

(a) An overview **(b) SM microarchitecture**

Figure 1. General-Purpose Computing on Graphic Processing Units (GPGPU) architecture

Threads in the SM execute on the single-program multiple-data model. A number of individual threads (e.g. 32 threads) from the same block are grouped together, called warp. In the pipeline, threads within a warp execute the same instruction but with different data values. Figure 1(b) also presents the details of SM microarchitecture. Each warp has a dedicated slot in the scheduler which records the warp ID (WID), active mask describing the active threads in the warp, and a single PC.

At every cycle, a ready warp is selected by the scheduler to feed the pipeline. The execution of a branch instruction in the warp may cause warp divergence, threads in a diverged warp have to execute in serial fashion which greatly degrades the performance. In the pipeline, a long latency off-chip memory access from one thread would stall all the threads within a warp, and the warp cannot proceed until all the memory transactions complete. The load/store requests issued by different threads can get coalesced into fewer memory requests according to the access pattern.

3. RISE: Recycling the Streaming Processors Idle Time for Soft-Error Detection

In this section, we propose to intelligently Recycle the stream processors Idle time for Soft-Error detection (RISE). It leverages the SPs idle time to execute the redundant threads and substantially improve the SPs reliability with negligible performance loss. We present the full-RISE and partial-RISE in Section 3.1 and 3.2, respectively.

When implementing the redundant multithreading technique in CPUs, the main and redundant threads share the pipeline resources, no extra hardware resources are required to support the redundant thread. However, every parallel thread in GPGPU has statically allocated resources including the register files and on-chip shared memory. Those per-thread resources have to be double-sized to successfully launch the main and redundant threads simultaneously into the GPU core, which leads to extremely high resource usage and power consumption [12]. In order to avoid this high overhead, the redundant thread in our study will use the same per-thread resources with the main thread. In other words, the redundant thread follows the main thread immediately, they interleave at the instruction-by-instruction basis and execute at the same speed.

In this study, we focus on the single-bit error model which has the first order impact on the failure rate in processors [35]. Note that SPs will operate the computations from main and redundant threads in two consecutive cycles, our technique is sufficient to detect the single-bit errors in SPs. Moreover, it is also able to catch the multiple-bit errors occurring simultaneously in the SPs resulting from either single upset event or multiple, independent upsets. The particle-strikes which could last for more than a cycle in a single bit are not considered in this paper.

3.1 Full-RISE

In previous work, the opportunistic transient-fault detection in CPUs has been proposed by Gomma et al. [13]. It keeps the progress difference between the main and redundant threads, and triggers the redundant thread when the main thread stalls for the long-latency operations. Therefore, the redundant thread can efficiently leverage the under-utilized pipeline resources to perform the redundancy without degrading the performance. However, the technique is not applicable to the SPs soft-error detection in GPGPUs since both main and redundant threads in GPUs have to keep the same progress (as we described above), and they stall at the same time. A novel technique is desired to intelligently trigger the redundant thread ahead of the pipeline stalls in the SM. In this subsection, we propose Full-RISE which is composed of two methodologies: request pending aware full-RISE and idle SMs aware full-RISE.

3.1.1. Request Pending Aware Full-RISE

3.1.1.1. The Observation on Resource Contentions among Memory Requests

In CUDA programming model, all threads in a kernel execute the same code. Moreover, warps in the GPU SM interleave at cycle-by-cycle basis and exhibit similar execution progress. When one warp sends out a request for the off-chip memory access, other warps are likely to issue the requests at approximately the same time. The sudden burst of the memory requests will cause the congestion in the interconnect network and the memory controller, leading to the severe resource contentions. Especially, the input buffer in the memory controller will be quickly filled up by the requests. Generally, the out-of-order (OoO) first-ready first-come first-serve scheduling policy is applied in the memory controller. It grants higher priority to the requests which hit an open row in the DRAM, and save the time spent on precharge and activation to open a new row. However, its impact on alleviating the request congestion is ambiguous since a limited number of requests (e.g. only one) can be serviced at a time, and most requests are experiencing the long waiting time.

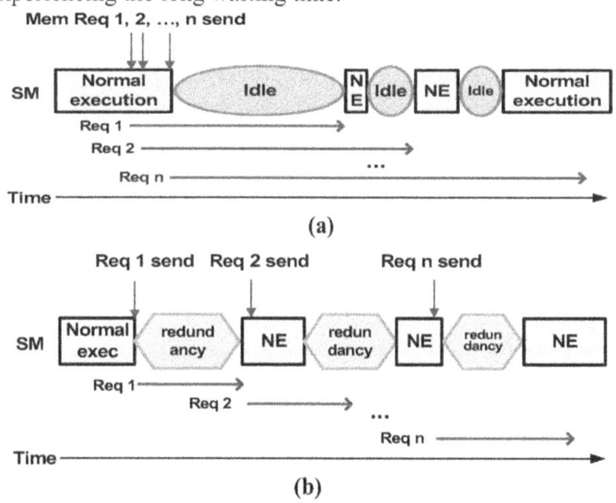

Figure 2. SPs idle time (a) caused by resource contentions among memory requests, and (b) recycled for partial Redundancy (NE: normal execution)

Figure 2 shows a case observed in a CUDA benchmark - *BP*. A large number of memory requests from the SM are routed to the memory controller in a short period. Due to the serious resource contentions, the off-chip memory access takes up to thousands of cycles. Correspondingly, the SM suffers extremely long pipeline stall, and SPs remain idle (as shown in Figure 2(a)). Instead of sending the memory requests at similar time and stalling afterwards for a long period, warps can run at slower pace which prolongs their requests issues (e.g. req2 ~ reqn in Figure 2(b)) and avoids the possible resource contentions, therefore, their requests are serviced without any delay in the input buffer. Due to the dramatically reduced memory operation latency, the total warp execution time still keeps the same or even decreases. This provides the great opportunity for temporal redundancy, whose negative effect on performance can just be positively used to postpone the warp execution progress and their requests issue time. The SPs idle time caused by the request pending in the memory controller (highlighted with red color in Figure 2(a)) is successfully recycled for the redundancy (highlighted with green color in Figure 2(b)). Note that the redundant and normal executions are interleaved at cycle level. We mark the redundancy separately from the normal execution in Figure 2(b) for the easy understanding of the impact of redundancy. By running a large number of benchmarks, we observe that the request pending contributes to 65% of the time that all SPs in the SM are free. It implies that the SPs soft-error reliability can be substantially improved with no performance penalty.

3.1.1.2. The Concept of Request Pending Aware Full-RISE

As discussed above, the partial redundancy (relative to the full redundancy) can be treated as the knob to control the warp progress. It has to be carefully tuned: the over adjustment will result in the excessive redundancy and unnecessarily delay, consequentially, degrades the performance significantly; on the other hand, the insufficient adjustment cannot effectively leverage the SPs idle time for reliability enhancement. Moreover, different warps should spend different amount of time on redundancy in order to separate their memory requests. In one sentence, the warp progress should well adapt to its memory access pattern to achieve the optimal SPs soft-error robustness. Obviously, statically determining the period of performing the partial redundancy fails to meet the goal since workloads have various memory access patterns. In this study, we propose RP-FRISE, as the abbreviation of request pending aware full-RISE, which dynamically tunes the knob (i.e. partial redundancy) per warp and recycles the SPs idle time to maximize the error coverage in SPs.

Since the major resource contentions occur in the memory controller, the request waiting time in the input buffer is a good indicator to the necessity of slowing down the warp. A long waiting time implies a serious resource contention, the warp which issues the request should have been delayed. While a short waiting time means that the request is issued appropriately, postponing the warp progress may degrade the performance. In the ideal case, a memory request gets serviced once it arrives at the memory controller: the period that allows a warp to perform the redundant execution should be equal to its request waiting time. In RP-FRISE, we use the previous request pending time to predict the delay in the following memory transaction and tune the partial redundancy in the warp.

Note that the warp progress has already been postponed somehow when finishing the previous memory access, further slowing it down as the same amount of the previous request waiting time may serious prolong the warp computation. An example is shown in Figure 3 to illustrate the challenge: warp0 and warp1 exhibit different execution progress after the first memory access, and their following memory requests have less interference. Using the previous request waiting time leads to excessive redundancy and degrades the performance. On the other hand, although warps run at different rate after the long latency memory access, the interference is still severe. Figure 4 demonstrates the case. When the second memory request is issued from warp0, it interferes with the unfinished memory access from warp1 and the waiting time increases. The extended memory access in warp0 further affects the warp1, and setting the redundancy time as the preceding request waiting time for warp1 is appropriate. Note that warp1 may not delay as long as the scheduled redundancy time even performing the full redundancy for the computation between its two memory accesses (highlighted by the pink color in Figure 4). In that case, it will be stalled after finishing the redundancy due to the interference with warp0. Therefore, the required redundancy time still accurately predicts the necessary delay in warp1. As can be seen from Figures 3 and 4, generally, the excessive redundancy occurs when the kernel is more computation-intensive and the time spent on the normal computation alleviates the memory contentions among threads. While the short normal computation in the memory-intensive kernel cannot effectively separate the memory requests, a longer redundant execution is desired.

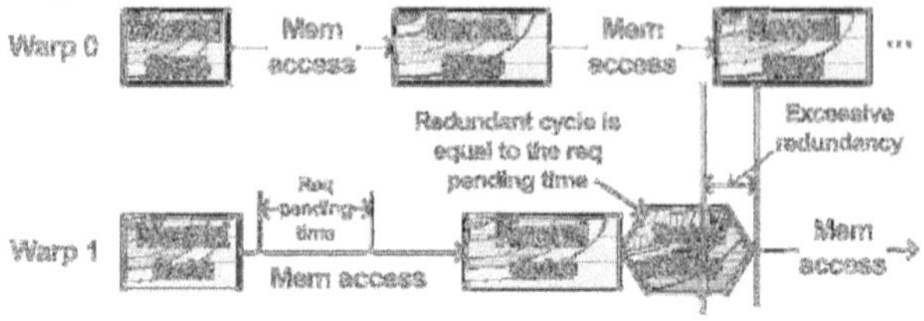

Figure 3. An Example of the Excessive Redundancy

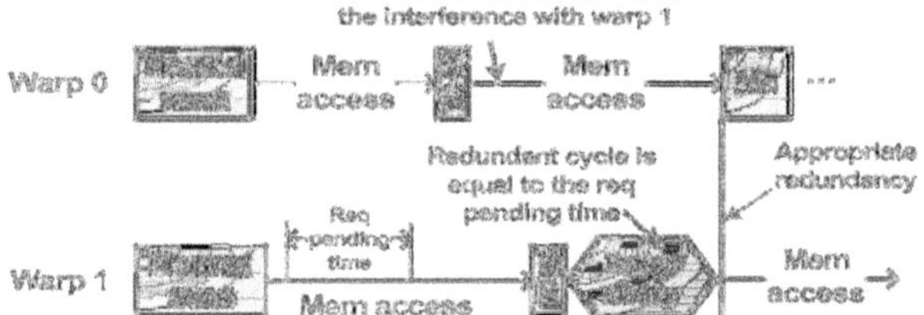

Figure 4. An Example of the Appropriate Redundancy

In our study, we sample the memory access latency periodically when running a kernel, and use it to adjust the amount of cycles that the warp executes the redundant threads. Eq.1 describes the analytical model to dynamically determine the redundancy cycles (represented by RC) in the warp based on its previous request pending time (represented by T_P) and the latest sampled memory access latency (represented by T_{acc_lat}).

$$RC = \begin{cases} 0, & \text{if } T_P \le T_{thr\_pend} \\ \left\lceil \dfrac{T_{acc\_lat}}{T_{ref\_lat}} \times T_P \right\rceil, & \text{if } T_{acc\_lat} < T_{ref\_lat},\ T_P > T_{thr\_pend} \\ T_P, & \text{if } T_{acc\_lat} \ge T_{ref\_lat},\ T_P > T_{thr\_pend} \end{cases} \qquad \text{Eq.1}$$

where T_{thr_pend} is the threshold of the request pending time. It is possible that the previous memory access is over delayed by the redundancy, the improper delay (implied in the prior request pending time) cannot further propagate to the following execution. T_{thr_pend} plays an important role to filter it out. Only when T_P is longer than T_{thr_pend}, the warp redundancy would be enabled, otherwise, it is disabled to maintain the performance. T_{ref_lat} is the referred memory access latency describing the memory access time with moderate resource contentions. When T_{acc_lat} is higher than T_{ref_lat}, it implies that the kernel currently exhibits the memory-intensive characteristics and the aggressive redundancy (i.e. directly setting the redundancy cycles as the request pending time) should be applied. To the contrary, a lower T_{acc_lat} means that the kernel involves heavier computation, the redundancy period should be scaled down according to the ratio of T_{acc_lat} to T_{ref_lat}.

Recall that threads in a warp execute the same instruction, triggering the redundancy at the warp level becomes the first choice in RP-FRISE. However, all threads in the block have to synchronize at barriers if exist, large progress difference among warps belonging to the same block will extend the faster warps' waiting time at the barrier and hurt performance. Additionally, GPGPU programmers are encouraged to make consecutive threads access consecutive memory locations, warps in a block tend to show the strong spatial locality [1, 14]. The memory requests issued by those warps are likely to be directed to the same row in the DRAM, called row locality [10]. When they are sent out simultaneously, the pending time in the input buffer of the memory controller tends to be similar under the out-of-order memory scheduling policy. On the other hand, it will even take longer time to complete the memory transactions if issued separately, because the row locality among warps is broken and the row switches more frequently. In order to maintain the performance, RP-FRISE performs the block level redundancy. Since the redundant time is computed on the basis of memory request, a single warp may have more than one option on setting the redundancy cycles, and there are numerous choices when extending to a block. In RP-FRISE, the redundancy time will be incorporated into the response packet from the memory to the SM. To a block, the first arrived packet after it finishes the previous assigned redundant execution sets the new redundancy cycles, which should be applied to all its warps.

3.1.2. Idle SMs Aware Full-RISE

While a kernel is launched into the GPU, its blocks may not be even distributed across the SMs. A number of SMs are free when approaching the end of the kernel execution, and they have to wait for other busy SMs to finish their tasks. In other words, the SPs become idle when no more blocks can be assigned to the SM. We found that this case contributes to 35% of the time that all SPs are free in the SM. Those free SPs can be leveraged for redundant execution. One straightforward method is to redundantly execute the blocks which are currently running in other SMs. It will cause the challenges for memory synchronization between the original and redundant blocks and introduce more memory transactions from the redundant blocks.

Instead of implementing the redundancy when the SM is free, we propose to do it at the beginning of the kernel execution so that the SMs execution time is aligned and the SPs idle time is effectively recycled for redundancy. This technique is named as IS-FRISE, as the abbreviation of idle SMs aware Full-RISE. Based on the information obtained during the kernel launch process (e.g. the total number of blocks, the maximum concurrent blocks a single SM supports when running the specific kernel), a simple calculation is done to roughly estimate the total number of blocks assigned to each SM through the entire kernel execution ignoring the possible memory access delay. We conservatively assume that there is only one block difference among SMs, and divide the block quantity by the number of SMs. If there is a remainder, we expect that some SMs may be free at the end of the kernel execution, and the remainder determines the quantity of SMs (which are randomly selected among all the SMs) running an additional block. Once the kernel is launched, the full redundancy is applied to one of the currently executed blocks in SMs which are predicted to run fewer blocks, thus, the total loads including the redundancy are balanced across SMs and performance remains the same. Note that the load imbalance among SMs can be larger than one block since faster SMs will take more blocks, but predicting a large load difference is likely to cause the overestimate of the SMs idle time which leads to the aggressive redundancy and hurt the performance.

When integrating the two full-RISE techniques simultaneously, some blocks may perform the redundancy twice which is a waste of resources. Considering that IS-FRISE only takes in effect on a small set of blocks, the redundant execution scheduled by RP-FRISE on those blocks will be ignored. Although there is an overlapped effect between the two techniques, their positive interaction minimizes the potential of excessive redundancy in RP-FRISE. Recall that RP-FRISE depends on the previous request pending time to determine the redundancy cycles for the following execution, it loses the opportunities to perform redundant execution before the blocks issue their first memory requests. The memory contentions among the first memory transactions tend to be severe. Using the first request's pending time for redundancy cycles calculation would over delay the block progress, and this negative effect is likely to propagate towards the end of the kernel execution. IS-FRISE triggers the full redundancy on certain blocks at the very beginning of the kernel execution, it differentiates the block progress across SMs and mitigates the resource contentions even before the first memory requests, hence, effectively reduces the possibility of the unnecessary redundancy.

3.1.3. The Implementation of Full-RISE

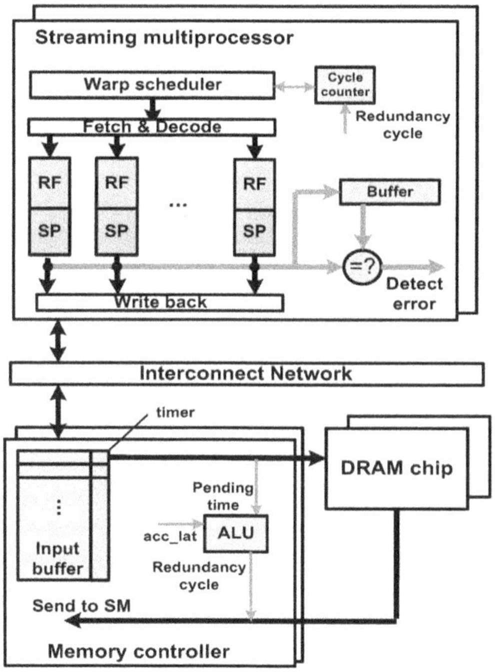

Figure 5. The Implementation of Request Pending aware Full-RISE

Figure 5 shows the implementation of the request pending aware full-RISE in the GPGPU architecture. In the memory controller, a timer is attached to each input buffer entry, and an arithmetic logic unit (ALU) is added to calculate the redundancy cycles (in our study, we assume that only one request is serviced at a time, and one ALU is sufficient to perform the calculation). When a memory request is written into the input buffer, the timer is set as zero and automatically increments every cycle, it records the request pending cycles which will be sent to the ALU when the request is issued out for DRAM access. The sampled memory access latency, threshold pending time and referred access latency are used as the inputs to the ALU as well. Its output is combined with the response packet and sent back to the SM. Considering that ALU operation has to be done per memory request, and the major computation in it is the division (as shown in Eq.1.) which lasts for tens of cycles, we set the referred access latency as 2 to power of n and translate the division into logical shift. It will operate based on the product of the average access latency and the pending time. We performed the detailed sensitivity analysis on the referred access latency, and found that RP-FRISE achieves optimal trade-off between reliability and performance when setting it as 2^7=128 cycles. Note that the redundancy time computation occurs in parallel with the data access in DRAM, it does not introduce any extra delay to the critical path in the memory controller.

As Figure 5 shows, each block in the SM is allocated a cycle counter which keeps the redundancy cycles. The amount of counters per SM is determined by the maximum number of concurrent blocks an SM supports (e.g. 8 in our default configuration). When a response packet arrives at the SM, we can find out its corresponding cycle counter based on the warp it returns to. If the counter is larger than zero, it implies that the block is already under the redundancy mode, the new redundancy time (in cycles) will be ignored. Otherwise, it is multiplied by the number of warps in the block, and the result will be written into the counter, which implies the desired total amount of redundancy cycles applied to all warps in the block. In this study, instead of controlling each warp in a block to spend the same amount of time in redundancy mode, we apply a relaxed mechanism to manage the total redundancy cycles at the block level. When a ready warp is selected to feed the pipeline, the counter is accessed, a larger-than-zero value suggests a redundant execution. The warp will remain in the warp scheduler and be granted a high issue priority to ensure that the same redundant warp is executed in the following cycle. Meanwhile, the counter decreases by one. During the write back stage, the SPs outputs of the original warp are written into the destination registers and an attached buffer; while the redundant warp's outputs will skip the write operation, and directly compare with the data just written into the buffer for the error detection. A mis-match will raise the recovery signal. The warp PC will be fetched again to start additional redundant execution, three copies' comparison will correct the error and resume the warp computation.

The idle SMs aware full-RISE requires modulo operation to determine the number of SMs running fewer blocks. A simple AND logic operation can compute out the remainder. It performs simultaneously with the kernel launch process, and no extra delay is introduced to the normal kernel execution. When combining the two full-RISE mechanisms, the block with full redundancy selected by the IS-FRISE will set its counter as one and disable the value decrease function until it finishes, ensuring the full redundant execution for its warps.

As can be seen in Figure 5, the major hardware added into the memory controller includes the unit performing simple integer arithmetic and logic operations, and a number of 10-bit timers (we set the maximum request pending time as 1024 cycles), it causes around 3% area overhead to the memory controller. In the SM, the added hardware contains 8 cycle counters, thirty-two 32-bit buffers for warp outputs (the SM pipeline width is 32 in the default configuration, each SP output 32-bit value), and some combinational logics, totally resulting in 1% area overhead to the SM.

3.2 Partial-RISE

3.2.1. The Concept of Partial-RISE

When the warp diverges at the branch instruction, several SPs in the SM are idle. In the workload encountering frequent branch divergences, SPs are partially free in majority of the time. For instance, the case occurs during 52% of the total kernel execution time in a CUDA benchmark - *HS*. Unfortunately, full-RISE fails to leverage such large portion of SPs idle time for reliability optimization due to its nature of performing the redundancy via using all SPs. In this subsection, we propose partial-RISE which intelligently combines the redundant threads into the diverged warp to utilize the partially idled SPs, thus, improves the SPs error coverage and maintains the performance.

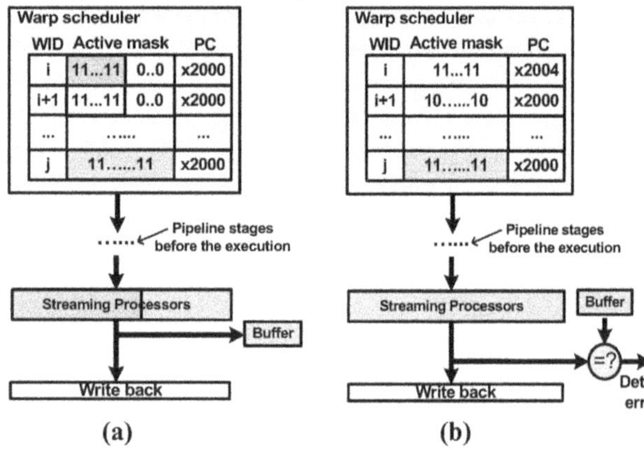

Figure 6. An Example of Partial-RISE

As described in Section 3.1, GPGPU has the unique microarchitecture characteristic (e.g. warps interleave at cycle level, and all threads execute the same code), and typically, there are numerous warps in the SM warp scheduler. When a ready warp is issued into the pipeline, it is highly possible that another ready warp sharing the same PC is sitting in the scheduler. Similarly, the diverged ready warp can usually find another ready warp (not necessarily diverges), and both are going to perform the same operation in SPs. A number of threads from a warp with the same PC can join the execution of the diverged warp. Therefore, the warp is partially protected as the idle SPs in the diverged warp are effectively utilized to execute the redundant threads for it. Moreover, the warp will be issued in the following cycle so that both main and redundant threads output can be compared immediately for the error detection. We name this technique as partial-RISE. Figure 6 demonstrates an example of it. In Figure 6(a), at cycle *m*, the warp *i* and *j* have the same PC, and the active mask shows that warp *i* diverges. When it is issued into the pipeline, threads from warp *j* will take the free slots in warp *i* based on its active mask. When the outputs of warp *j* are available, they will be sent to the buffer instead of writing to the registers. During the cycle *m*+1(shown in Figure 6(b)), warp *j* is issued, it outputs are compared with the data saved in the buffer in previous cycle.

Finding the warp with the same PC is critical to partial-RISE. We investigate various benchmarks, and Figure 7 plots the ratio of the number of cycles that at least one ready warp has the identical PC with the currently issued diverged warp to the total warp divergence cycles (shown as the red bars). The round-robin policy is applied for the warp scheduling. The benchmarks with quite few branch divergences are not shown in the figure since the partial-RISE is rarely triggered in that case. As it demonstrates, in more than half of the time, the diverged warp has the opportunity to combine with another warp by searching across the warp scheduler. However, the two warps are likely to use the SP and registers belonging to the same lane and encounter the lane conflict. It becomes the major obstacle to partial-RISE. As shown in Figure 6(a), although warp *i*+1 has the identical PC with warp *i*, partial-RISE cannot be used as both them have the same active mask. Figure 7 also shows the possibility that a diverged warp can be combined with another warp without lane conflict (shown in the yellow bars). As can be seen, it decreases significantly down to 16%, and even becomes zero in some benchmarks (e.g. *BP*, *SLA*, and *ST3D*). Since threads in a warp are independent but their operations are the same, there is no requirement to bind a thread to a certain lane. We propose to randomly shuffle the threads while sending them to the SMs, it will be performed in parallel with the kernel launch process and no extra delay to the entire kernel execution. By doing that, the possibility of lane conflicts between two warps decreases and partial-RISE can be triggered more frequently. The black bar in Figure 7 shows that re-arranging threads successfully brings the possibility of finding a ready warp with the same PC back to 48%.

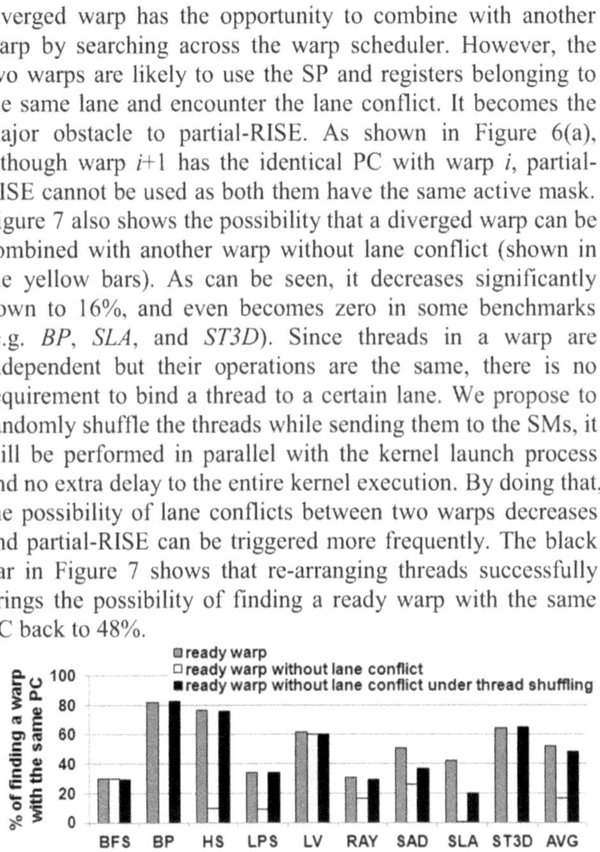

Figure 7. Possibility that a Diverged Warp Finding a Warp with Identical PC

Recently, several mechanisms (e.g. the dynamic warp formation [15], thread block compaction [16], the large warp microarchitecture (LWM) [10]) have been proposed to improve the efficiency of branch handling. Take the LWM as an example, it implements larger warp so that the sub-warps can be formed from the active threads in a large warp, and when they are executed in the pipeline, the SPs idle time reduces under branch divergences. One possible concern is that partial-RISE has trivial benefit for reliability enhancement when LWM is applied in the GPU. This is not the case. A large warp contains much smaller number of threads (e.g. 256) compared to the entire warp scheduler. It is unable to find active threads out of the warp, and it does not provide any mechanism to avoid the lane conflicts. LWM does not always fully utilize the idled SPs during branch divergences. While partial-RISE searches warps across the entire scheduler, and is equipped with the thread shuffling technique, it can efficiently use those idled SPs in LWM for redundant execution. We observe that partial-RISE takes in effect in 20% of the time when LWM fails to fully utilize the SPs.

In some benchmarks (e.g. *NN*, *NW*), the block contains few threads (e.g. 16) so that it has only one warp and all threads in that warp cannot fill up the SIMT pipeline width. Since several lanes keep idle through the entire kernel execution, partial-RISE will perform the intra-warp duplication which leverages those idle lanes to provide the spatial redundancy for some threads contained in the warp.

3.2.2. The Implementation of Partial-RISE

In the SM pipeline, when the warp enters to the final pipeline stage (i.e. write back stage), its PC and active mask are updated, and its status turns to be ready for issue in the following cycle. To implement the partial-RISE technique, a comparator is attached to each warp entry in the warp scheduler. While updating the warp status, its PC (active mask) will be compared with other ready warp PCs (active masks) in the scheduler to seek a warp for joined execution. The comparison is executed along with the write back stage, and no impact to the critical path delay. If succeeds, the scheduler will be notified to issue the diverged warp and threads from its matched warp simultaneously in the next cycle, followed by the normal issue of the matched warp. Partial-RISE will re-use the hardware (e.g. buffer, comparator) in Full-RISE to perform the error detection. In total, partial-RISE leads to additional 1% area overhead to the SM equipped with full-RISE.

3.3 RISE: Putting It All Together

Since Full-RISE and Partial-RISE target to recycle the SPs idle time caused by two different cases for reliability improvement, they can be integrated into RISE. While implementing RISE, the warp under the redundancy mode due to the full-RISE will not be considered in partial-RISE. Although full-RISE differentiates the block execution progress, it does not degrade the efficiency of partial-RISE in finding appropriate warp for redundancy. We find that the partial-RISE trigger time even increases by 2% when combined with full-RISE. It is because that the row locality leads to the similar redundancy cycles, and consequently, similar progress among blocks in the same SM under full-RISE, and the block progress difference generally happens at the SM level.

4. Experimental Setup

We use architecture vulnerability factor (AVF) [17] to evaluate the error coverage of our proposed RISE. A hardware structure's AVF refers to the probability that a transient fault in that hardware structure will result in incorrect program results. Therefore, the AVF, which can be used as a metric to estimate how vulnerable the hardware is to soft errors during program execution, is determined by the processor state bits required for architecturally correct execution (ACE). The structure's AVF in a given cycle is the percentage of ACE bits that the structure holds, and its overall AVF during program execution is the average AVF at any point in time. We apply the methodology proposed by Mukherjee et al. [17] to identify the ACE bits and their residency time in the structure and compute the AVF of GPGPU microarchitecture structures. We build our vulnerability estimation framework based on the

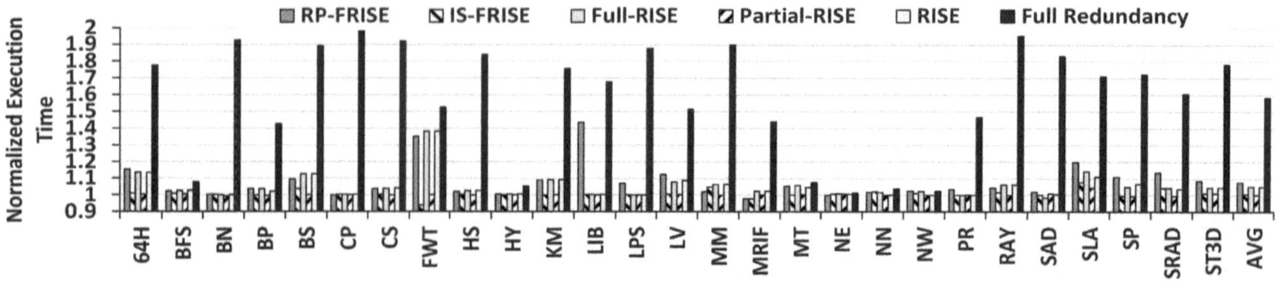

(a) Normalized Execution Time

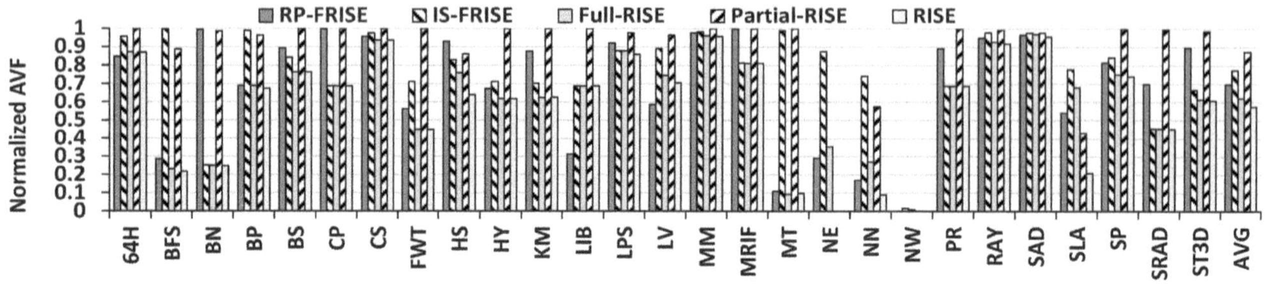

(b) Normalized AVF of Streaming Processors

Figure 8. The normalized (a) Execution Time and (b) SPs' AVF under IS-FRISE, RP-FRISE, Full-RISE, Partial-RISE, RISE, and Full Redundancy techniques

cycle-accurate, open-source, and publicly available simulator GPGPU-Sim [18], and obtain the GPGPU reliability and performance statistics. Our baseline GPGPU configuration is set as follows: there are 28 SMs in the GPU, SM pipeline width is 32, warp size is 32, each SM supports 1024 threads and 8 blocks at most, each SM contains 16K 32-bit registers, 16KB shared memory, 8KB constant cache, and 64KB texture cache, the warp scheduler applies the round robin scheduling policy, the immediate post-dominator reconvergence [19] is used to handle the branch divergences; the GPU includes 8 DRAM controllers, each controller has a 32-entry input buffer, and applies out-of-order first-ready first-come first-serve scheduling policy; the interconnect topologies is Mesh, and the dimension order routing algorithm is used in the interconnect. We collect a large set of available GPGPU workloads from Nvidia CUDA SDK [20], Rodinia Benchmark [21], Parboil Benchmark [4] and some third party applications. The workloads show significant diversity according to their kernel characteristics, divergence characteristics, memory access patterns, and so on.

5. Evaluation

5.1 Effectiveness of RISE

To better analyze the technique effectiveness, we classify the benchmarks into four categories based on their workload characteristics. The first category includes memory-intensive benchmarks such as *64H, BFS, BP, HY, LIB, LV, MT, NE, NN, NW, PR,* and *SLA*. The second category contains benchmarks which cause load imbalance across SMs in our baseline GPGPU configuration, they are *BN, CP, FWT, HY, KM, LV, MRIF, NW, PR, SLA, SP, SRAD,* and *ST3D*. The third category includes benchmarks usually utilizing partial SPs (caused by the frequent branch divergences or the partially full warps) such as *BFS, BP, HS, LPS, LV, NN, NE, NW, SAD, SLA,* and *ST3D*. The last category includes the computation-intensive benchmarks such as *BS, CS, MM,* and *RAY*. Note that the categories described above are not exclusive (i.e. one benchmark can be classified into different categories).

Figure 8 shows the (a) execution time and (b) the AVF of streaming processors when running various benchmarks under the impact of IS-FRISE, RP-FRISE, Full-RISE, Partial-RISE, and RISE, respectively. The execution time of full redundancy is demonstrated in Figure 8(a) as well for comparison. As can be seen, on average, it results in 58% performance degradation. Since the full redundancy achieves 100% error coverage (i.e. AVF is zero), its results are not shown in Figure 8(b). We present the averaged results across SMs, and the results are normalized to the baseline case without any optimization. As Figure 8 shows, RP-FRISE exhibits strong capability in improving the SPs soft-error vulnerability with little performance loss when executing the memory-intensive benchmarks (classified as the first category). Take the *MT* as an example, the SPs' AVF decreases by 90% with only 4% performance penalty. It implies that the redundancy cycles are properly set by RP-FRISE and the SPs idle time in the baseline cases is effectively recycled for redundant execution. One may notice that the AVF reduction under RP-FRISE is less obvious in *PR*, although the warps spend 17% of the execution time in waiting for the memory transactions. It is because their memory requests have already well separated during the execution, the memory access latency is generally short, and the pipeline only stalls couple of cycles for the memory transaction. Postponing the warp progress would easily hurt the performance substantially, therefore, RP-FRISE is seldom triggered. While improving the SPs' AVF, RP-FRISE degrades performance in some benchmarks such as *FWT, LIB,* and *SLA*. Because RP-FRISE uses the last request pending time to predict the next request waiting time and determine the redundancy cycles correspondingly, its prediction accuracy is affected when the next memory access pattern differs greatly from the last one. As a result, the excessive redundancy is applied which hurts the performance. On average across the

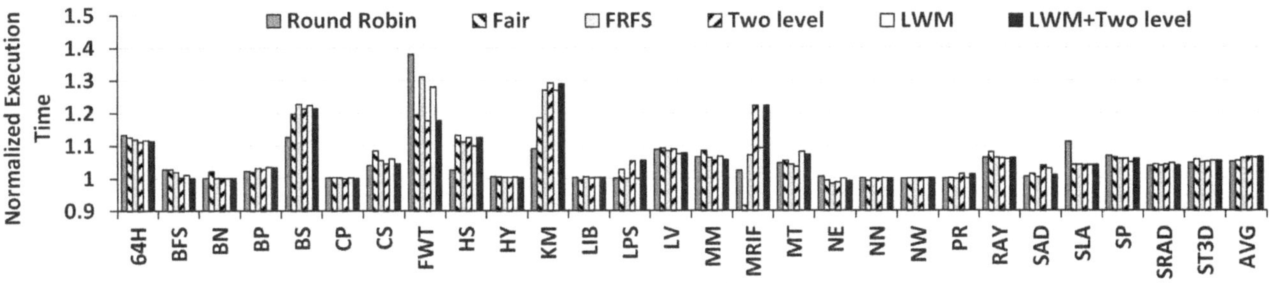

(a) Normalized Execution Time

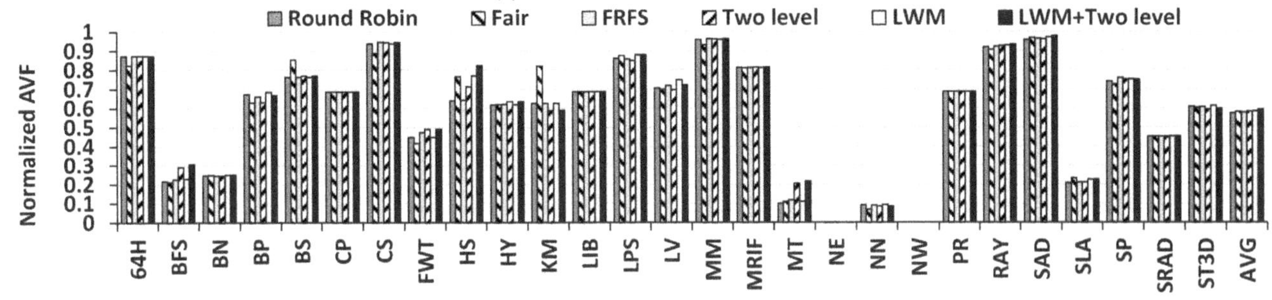

(b) Normalized AVF of Streaming Processors

Figure 9. The normalized (a) Execution Time and (b) SPs' AVF under Various Scheduling Policies and Performance Optimizations

benchmarks in the first category, RP-FRISE enhances the SPs soft-error robustness by 57% with 8% performance loss.

The impact of IS-FRISE on improving the SPs' error coverage is impressive in benchmarks belonging to the second category. For example, the SPs free time caused by the imbalanced block distribution is completely recycled for redundancy in *BN* and the AVF decreases 75% with 0.1% performance loss. Recall that IS-FRISE conservatively assumes one block difference among SMs to maintain the kernel execution time, while the difference is larger in some benchmarks (e.g. *LV*). In the GPU, a block is assigned once there is an empty slot in certain SM. It is possible that an SM commits multiple blocks at similar time and the remaining unexecuted blocks are all allocated to it. Although other SMs finish the block execution in the very near future, they have to remain idle till the kernel completes. In that case, IS-FRISE does not fully leverage the idle SPs to perform redundancy. Monitoring and predicting the block progress in each SM and dynamically controlling the number of redundant blocks may lead to better reliability improvement, but it induces complicated hardware design which should be avoided. On average across benchmarks in the second category, IS-FRISE reduces SPs' AVF 37% with no performance loss. Note that the load imbalance of a benchmark is related to the GPU configuration (e.g. number of SMs), it may not be an issue when configuring the machine differently, but meanwhile, another set of benchmarks may encounter this problem. Therefore, IS-FRISE is applicable to various GPU architecture designs. As the combination of RP-FRISE and IS-FRISE, Full-RISE keeps their positive effects on optimizing the soft-error robustness substantially, and more important, their interaction effectively mitigates the performance penalty caused by the RP-FRISE. As Figure 8 shows, Full-RISE improves SPs AVF 39% with 4% performance loss on average across all investigated benchmarks.

The major benefit of Partial-RISE is observed in benchmarks classified into the third category. As shown in Figure 8, on average across benchmarks in the third category, it reduces SPs AVF by 32% without any performance penalty. Finally, when putting all together, RISE integrates the benefit of all the proposed techniques by achieving 43% SPs soft-error reliability enhancement and minimizes (only 4%) the performance loss. In the computation-intensive benchmarks, the effect of RISE is less impressive due to the limited SPs idle time. Note that, RISE optimizes the SPs vulnerability via redundancy, the SPs AVF does not migrate to any other microarchitecture structures.

5.2 Sensitivity Analysis

Various techniques have been proposed on warp scheduling and warp formation to improve the GPGPU throughput, such as Fair which issues the instruction for the warp with minimum number of instructions executed [22], First-Ready First-Served (FRFS), large warp microarchitecture (LWM), and two-level round-robin warp scheduling that effectively hides long memory access latency and improves the SPs utilization [10]. Figure 9 shows (a) the execution time and (b) SPs' AVF under RISE when those optimization schemes are enabled. Results are normalized to the baseline case with the corresponding optimizations, respectively. The results obtained when using the default scheduling policy (i.e. Round Robin) is also shown in the figure for comparisons. As it shows, the effectiveness of RISE is not affected when running with different schemes: on average, the SPs AVF reduction keeps around 42% with 6% performance loss. Take the scheme of LWM+two_level as an example, it reduces the SPs idle time to some degree to shrink the kernel execution time, one would expect that it largely diminishes the opportunities to trigger RISE. However, this only occurs in a limited number of benchmarks (i.e. *BFS, HS, MT*) which shrinks the reliability optimization by around 12%. As we described in Section 3.2.1., LWM only finds active threads in the warp scope and cannot avoid the lane conflicts, it leaves sufficient room for Partial-RISE in RISE to further use the partially idled SPs for redundant execution. Moreover, the two-level round robin scheduling cannot totally avoid the memory contentions and the load imbalance across SMs, therefore, the Full-RISE in RISE can be frequently triggered to recycle the SPs free time for reliability enhancement.

6. Related Work

There have been various studies on protecting CPUs via software/hardware-based duplication. For instance, Qureshi et al. [34] appropriately trigger redundant threads to minimize performance loss and provide full soft error coverage for the entire pipeline. Slick [23] avoids the redundancy for results predictable instructions to improve the performance when running redundant multithreading. Feng et al. [24] leverage the symptom based detection and selective instruction duplication to minimize user-visible failures induced by soft errors. Sun et al. [25] combine the C-element based error detection techniques with idle resources exploited in functional units at the circuit level to improve their fault tolerance capability. However, they mainly target on CPUs and largely ignore the GPGPU architecture.

Soft-errors on GPU have been investigated in [26 ~ 28], and recovered via redundancy and checkpointing [9, 29 ~ 32]. For example, Sheaffer et al. [30] explore the concept of the sphere of replication on GPGPU processors, and present a hardware redundancy-based approach to create a reliable GPU with no performance loss. Dimitrov [31] investigate three software approaches to perform redundant execution for GPGPU reliability. Maruyama et al. [9] propose a high-performance software framework to enhance GPU with DRAM fault tolerance. It leverages light-weight data coding for error detection and checkpointing for recovery. Solano-Quinde et al. [32] propose an application-level checkpoint scheme for GPGPU systems, and explore the computation-communication overlapping to reduce the checkpoint overhead. In our study, we exploit the SPs idle time and recycle it to perform the redundancy for error detection to maximize the SPs reliability with little performance loss. Recently, Nathan et al. [33] develop Argus-G, it implements control flow, dataflow and computation checkers in the SPs for low cost error detection. Yim et al. [8] strategically places customized error detectors in the source code of GPU applications to tolerate errors. Both the two schemes are orthogonal to our proposed techniques.

7. Conclusions

With their strong computing power and improved programmability, GPGPUs emerge as highly-efficient devices for a wide range of parallel applications. Meanwhile, GPGPU with hundreds of cores integrated in a single chip are highly vulnerable to the soft error strikes. Especially, streaming processors play an important role to exploit the data parallelism and are becoming the vulnerability hot-spots in GPUs. This work explores the first essential step to optimize the SPs soft-error robustness. We propose RISE to effectively recycle the SPs idle time for soft-error detection. RISE is composed of full-RISE and partial-RISE. Full-RISE exploits the fully idled SPs caused by the long-latency memory transactions and imbalanced load assignment among GPU cores, and uses them to perform the redundant execution and enhance the SPs reliability. Partial-RISE combines the redundant execution of a number of threads from a warp with a diverged warp to recycle the SPs idle time during the branch divergence for their reliability optimization. Experiment results show that RISE reduces the SPs AVF by 43% with only 4% performance loss. Our sensitivity analysis also shows that RISE is applicable to GPUs with various performance optimization mechanisms.

Acknowledgement

This work is supported by the National Science Foundation under Award No. EPS - 0903806 and matching support from the State of Kansas through the Kansas Board of Regents.

References

[1] NVIDIA. CUDA Programming Guide Version 3.0., Nvidia Corporation, 2010.
[2] Advanced Micro Devices, Inc. AMD Brook+. http://ati.amd.com/technology/streamcomputing/AMD-Brookplus.pdf.
[3] Khronos. Opencl – the open standard for parallel programming of heterogeneous systems. http://www.khronos.org/opencl/
[4] Parboil Benchmark suite. URL: http://impact.crhc.illinois.edu/ parboil.php.
[5] N. Wang and S. Patel, ReStore: Symptom Based Soft Error Detection in Microprocessors, In Proceedings of DSN, 2005.
[6] C. Weaver, J. Emer, S. Mukherjee, and S. Reinhardt, Techniques to reduce the soft error rate of a high-performance microprocessor, In Proceedings of ISCA, 2004.
[7] N. Maruyama, A. Nukada, and S. Matsuoka, A High Performance Fault-Tolerant Software Framework for Memory on Commodity GPUs, In Proceedings of IPDPS, 2010
[8] K. Yim and R. Iyer. Hauberk: Lightweight silent data corruption error detectors for gpgpu. In Proceedings of the 17th Humantech Thesis Prize (Also in IPDPS 2011), 2011.
[9] S.K. Reinhardt, and S.S. Mukherjee, Transient Fault Detection via Simultaneous Multithreading, In Proceedings of ISCA, 2000.
[10] V. Narasiman, C. J. Lee, M. Shebanow, R. Miftakhutdinov, O. Mutlu, and Y. N. Patt. Improving GPU Performance via Large Warps and Two-Level Warp Scheduling. In Proceedings of MICRO, 2011.
[11] Nvdia's Next Generation CUDA™ Compute Architecture: Fermi™, http://www.nvidia.com/content/PDF/fermi_white_papers/NVIDIA_Fermi_Compute_Architecture_Whitepaper.pdf
[12] X Yang, et. al., TH-1: China's first petaflop supercomputer, Frontiers of Computer Science in China, 2010.
[13] M. A. Gomaa and T. N. Vijaykumar, Opportunistic Transient-Fault Detection, In Proceedings of ISCA, 2005.
[14] D. Kirk and W. W. Hwu. Programming Massively Parallel Processors: A Hands-on Approach. Elsevier Science, 2010.
[15] W. W. L. Fung, I. Sham, G. Yuan, and T. M. Aamodt, Dynamic Warp Formation and Scheduling for Efficient GPU Control Flow, In Proceedings of MICRO, 2007.
[16] W. W. L. Fung and T. Aamodt. Thread Block Compaction for Efficient SIMT Control Flow. In Proceedings of HPCA, 2011.
[17] S. S. Mukherjee, C. Weaver, J. Emer, S. K. Reinhardt, and T. Austin, A Systematic Methodology to Compute the Architectural Vulnerability Factors for a High-Performance Microprocessor, In Proceedings of MICRO, 2003.
[18] A. Bakhoda, G.L. Yuan, W. W. L. Fung, H. Wong, Tor M. Aamodt, Analyzing CUDA Workloads Using a Detailed GPU Simulator, In Proceedings of ISPASS, 2009.
[19] S. S.Muchnick. Advanced Compiler Design and Implementation. Morgan Kaufmanns, 1997.
[20] http://www.nvidia.com/object/cuda_sdks.html
[21] S. Che, M. Boyer, J. Meng, D. Tarjan, J. Sheaffer, S. Lee, and K. Skadron. Rodinia: A Benchmark Suite for Heterogeneous Computing, In Proceedings of IISWC, 2009.
[22] N. B. Lakshminarayana, H. Kim, Effect of Instruction Fetch and Memory Scheduling on GPU Performance, Workshop on Language, Compiler, and Architecture Support for GPGPU, 2010.
[23] A. Parashar, A. Sivasubramaniam, S. Curumurthi, SlicK: Slice-based Locality Exploitation for Efficient Redundant Multithreading, In Proceedings of ASPLOS, 2006.
[24] S. Feng, S. Gupta, A. Ansari, and S. Mahlke, Shoestring: probabilistic soft error reliability on the cheap, In Proceedings of ASPLOS, 2010.
[25] Y. Sun, S. Li, M. Zhang, C. Song, Exploiting Idle Resources for Reducing SER of Microprocessor Functional Units, In Proceedings of ICCET, 2010.
[26] I. Haque and V. Pande. Hard Data on Soft Errors: A Large-Scale Assessment of Real-World Error Rates in GPGPU. In Proceedings of CCGrid, 2010.
[27] G. Shi, J. Enos, M. Showerman, and V. Kindratenko. On Testing GPU Memory for Hard and Soft Errors. In Proceedings of SAAHPC, 2009.
[28] J. Tan, N. Goswami, T. Li, and X. Fu, Analyzing Soft-Error Vulnerability on GPGPU Microarchitecture, In Proceedings of IISWC, 2011.
[29] N. Maruyama, A. Nukada, and S. Matsuoka. Software-Based ECC for GPUs. In Proceedings of SAAHPC, 2009.
[30] J. Sheaffer, D. Luebke, and K. Skadron, A Hardware Redundancy and Recovery Mechanism for Reliable Scientific Computation on Graphics Processors, In Proceedings of Graphics Hardware 2007.
[31] M. Dimitrov, M. Mantor, and H. Zhou, Understanding Software Approaches for GPGPU Reliability, The 2nd workshop on General-Purpose Computation on Graphics Processing Units (GPGPU-2), 2009.
[32] L. Solano-Quinde, B. Bode, and A. Somani, Coarse Grain Computation-Communication Overlap for Efficient Application-Level Checkpointing for GPUs, In Proceedings of International Conference on Electro/Information Technology (EIT), 2010.
[33] R. Nathan, D. J. Sorin, Argus-G: A Low-Cost Error Detection Scheme for GPGPUs, Workshop on Resilient Architectures (WRA), 2010.
[34] M. K. Qureshi, O. Mutlu, Y. N. Patt, Microarchitecture-Based Introspection: A Technique for Transient-Fault Tolerance in Microprocessors, In Proceedings of DSN, 2005.
[35] S.S.Mukherjee, J. Emer, and S.K.Reinhardt, The Soft Error Problem: An Architectural Perspective, In Proceedings of HPCA, 2005.

Chrysalis Analysis: Incorporating Synchronization Arcs in Dataflow-Analysis-Based Parallel Monitoring

Michelle L. Goodstein[1], Shimin Chen[2], Phillip B. Gibbons[3], Michael A. Kozuch[3], Todd C. Mowry[1]
[1]Carnegie Mellon University [2]HP Labs China [3]Intel Labs Pittsburgh
mgoodste@cs.cmu.edu, shimin.chen@hp.com,
{phillip.b.gibbons, michael.a.kozuch}@intel.com, tcm@cs.cmu.edu

ABSTRACT

Software *lifeguards*, or tools that monitor applications at runtime, are an effective way of identifying program errors and security exploits. Parallel programs are susceptible to a wider range of possible errors than sequential programs, making them even more in need of online monitoring. Unfortunately, monitoring parallel applications is difficult due to *inter-thread data dependences*. In prior work, we introduced a new software framework for online parallel program monitoring inspired by dataflow analysis, called Butterfly Analysis. Butterfly Analysis uses bounded windows of uncertainty to model the finite upper bound on delay between when an instruction is issued and when all its effects are visible throughout the system. While Butterfly Analysis offers many advantages, it ignored one key source of ordering information which affected its false positive rate: explicit software synchronization, and the corresponding high-level happens-before arcs.

In this work we introduce *Chrysalis Analysis*, which extends the Butterfly Analysis framework to incorporate explicit happens-before arcs resulting from high-level synchronization within a monitored program. We show how to adapt two standard dataflow analysis techniques and two memory and security lifeguards to Chrysalis Analysis, using novel techniques for dealing with the many complexities introduced by happens-before arcs. Our security tool implementation shows that Chrysalis Analysis matches the key advantages of Butterfly Analysis—parallel monitoring, no detailed inter-thread data dependence tracking, no strong memory consistency requirements, and no missed errors—while significantly reducing the number of false positives.

Categories and Subject Descriptors

F.3.2 [**Logics & Meanings of Programs**]: Semantics of Programming Languages—*Program Analysis*; D.1.3 [**Programming Techniques**]: Concurrent Programming—*Parallel Programming*; D.2.5 [**Software Engineering**]: Testing and Debugging—*Monitors*

Keywords

Data Flow Analysis, Parallel Programming, Dynamic Program Monitoring, Vector Clocks, High-Level Synchronization

PACT'12, September 19–23, 2012, Minneapolis, Minnesota, USA.

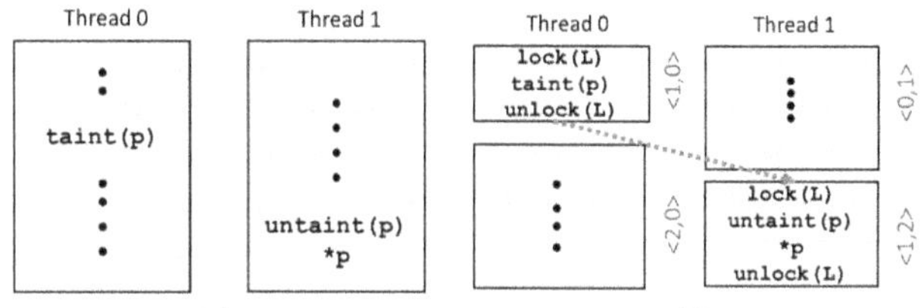

Figure 1: (a) Butterfly Analysis ignores synchronization arcs (such as from locks), and hence views the `taint(p)` and `*p` as racing if they are close in time, even if the source code resembles (b). (b) Chrysalis Analysis eliminates such false positives by dynamically capturing explicit synchronization arcs. (Note that `[un]taint(p)` indicates an application operation that would cause the lifeguard to [un]set the "tainted" metadata value for p.)

1. INTRODUCTION

To help programmers identify software bugs, a number of powerful tools have been developed for recognizing incorrect behaviors (e.g., memory [15], security [16], and concurrency [17] bugs) by performing sophisticated analysis of the dynamic execution path at run-time. These dynamic tools (aka *"lifeguards"*) are typically implemented using either dynamic binary instrumentation (e.g., Valgrind [14], Pin [11], or DynamoRio [3]) or with hardware-assisted logging [4].

Lifeguards often analyze program execution at the instruction level by maintaining shadow state (*metadata*) for program memory and register locations [14]. Examples of lifeguards discussed throughout this paper include ADDRCHECK [13] and TAINTCHECK [16]. ADDRCHECK ensures that every memory access in the monitored application touches a properly allocated region of memory by intercepting calls to library routines such as `malloc` and `free` to maintain metadata state, and checking the state on every memory access. TAINTCHECK detects security exploits due to memory overwrites by tagging as *tainted*, in its metadata, any application memory locations corresponding to unverified input data, tracking the propagation of tainted data through the application, and checking that tainted data is not used in indirect jump targets, system call arguments, and other critical operations.

Parallel Monitoring via Butterfly Analysis. A key challenge in extending lifeguards such that they can find bugs in *parallel* software is dealing with *inter-thread data dependences* [9, 24]. In contrast to proposals for hardware-assisted solutions [24], our recent work introduced "Butterfly Analysis" [9] as a *software-only* solution. Butterfly Analysis avoids depending upon capturing a precise interleaving of events across threads (which is impractical to capture on modern machines) and instead, uses a new form of

Table 1: Comparison of Parallel Program Monitoring Solutions

	Implementation requirements		Analysis supports	Monitoring precision	
	Hardware support	Inter-thread dependence tracking	Weak models of consistency	General programs	Data-race-free programs
ParaLog [24]	Yes	Yes	TSO only	high	high
Chrysalis Analysis	*No*	*No*	*Yes*	*good*	*high*
Butterfly Analysis [9]	No	No	Yes	fair	fair

dataflow-style analysis (inspired by *interval analysis* [21]) that automatically reasons about *bounded windows of uncertainty*. Such windows capture the fact that on modern machines there is an upper bound on the delay between when an instruction is issued and when all its effects are reflected system-wide. Thus, uncertainty concerning the relative ordering among events on different threads is limited to instructions issued within a bounded window of time of each other. In order to avoid considering a combinatorial explosion of potential orderings, Butterfly Analysis instead performs a new form of "closure" operation across sliding windows of uncertainty.

False Positives in Butterfly Analysis. While the dataflow-based approach of Butterfly Analysis offers many advantages (including a theoretically sound framework with no missed errors), one of the limitations of the original framework was that it ignored explicit software synchronization. Because Butterfly Analysis considers all possible instruction interleavings within each window of uncertainty, lifeguards can conservatively report an error based on a hypothetical ordering that can never arise due to synchronization operations. In Figure 1, for example, because the ordering `untaint(p)`, `taint(p)`, `*p` cannot be ruled out under Butterfly Analysis, a lifeguard would report the dereference of a possibly tainted pointer. Such *false positives* represent an additional burden on the application developer as error reports must be analyzed, true errors may be missed if they are lost in a large number of false positive messages, and developers may abandon the tool if the work required to process the false reports exceeds the tool's benefits.

Chrysalis Analysis: Adding Happens-Before Arcs to Butterfly Analysis. In this paper, we propose and evaluate *"Chrysalis Analysis,"* which is an extension of Butterfly Analysis that takes into account the dynamic happens-before constraints resulting from explicit software synchronization, thereby reducing the number of erroneous false positives, as illustrated in Figure 1(b). Integrating happens-before relationships into the Butterfly Analysis framework while retaining the elegance and efficiency of the original framework was a major challenge, due to the irregularities that this introduced, as will be described in detail in Section 3. This required generalizing the dataflow analysis mechanisms in the original framework (which were based on simple sliding windows spanning all the threads) to handle all the complexities introduced by partial orderings induced by happens-before arcs between pairs of threads.

Related Work. This work significantly extends our previous work on Butterfly Analysis [9], which we will review in more detail later in Section 2, making use of vector clocks to track synchronization events. Vector clocks [1, 5, 19] have been used in a number of data race detectors [2, 7, 8, 12, 18, 26]. For example, Flanagan and Freund proposed *FastTrack* [8], which primarily uses a compact representation to detect data races but still uses vector clocks to track `lock` and `unlock` operations. *FastTrack* achieves precision similar to full vector-clock based methods and performance similar to LockSet [17]. Muzahid *et al.* [12] divide thread execution into epochs to form a data race detector based on signatures, and use vector clocks to determine happens-before relationships. In contrast, Chrysalis Analysis is not simply a data race detector, but a general dataflow analysis framework for implementing a broad range of sophisticated lifeguards.

Prior work in adapting lifeguards to parallel applications falls into two categories: *synchronous* frameworks, where lifeguard metadata values are updated immediately when triggering application operations are encountered, and *non-synchronous* frameworks, where the metadata values are updated more lazily. The primary challenge with synchronous approaches (e.g., binary instrumentation [3, 11, 14]) is ensuring that the lifeguard metadata is updated atomically with the application data. Synchronous examples include Chung *et al.* [6], which relies on transactional memory and exhibits significant performance slowdowns, and FlexiTaint [22], which requires extensive hardware support. Non-synchronous approaches, such as Kannan [10] and ParaLog [24], focus on enabling a parallel lifeguard to reproduce the order of application events. While these designs provide good monitoring fidelity, they require hardware to monitor cache coherency and are unable to handle memory-ordering models weaker than TSO [20].

Table 1 compares Chrysalis Analysis with Butterfly Analysis and ParaLog [24]. Compared to ParaLog, Chrysalis Analysis does not require special hardware support or a mechanism for tracking inter-thread memory dependences, and it can also handle weak memory consistency models. Compared to Butterfly Analysis, Chrysalis Analysis offers improved precision by not reporting errors that are precluded by software synchronization. In fact, when monitoring data-race-free parallel programs, the precision of Chrysalis Analysis should be comparable to ParaLog (because all valid orderings are accurately captured via happens-before arcs).[1] There is a trade-off, though, in obtaining this improved precision, as Chrysalis Analysis is somewhat slower than Butterfly Analysis.

Contributions. This paper makes the following contributions:

- We propose *Chrysalis Analysis*, which builds upon Butterfly Analysis to model the *happens-before* arcs from explicit synchronization, thereby increasing precision. While Butterfly Analysis supported only a very simple and regular concurrency structure of sliding windows across all threads, Chrysalis Analysis supports an arbitrarily irregular and asymmetric acyclic structure within such windows (making the analysis problem considerably more challenging).
- We present (sound) formalizations in the Chrysalis Analysis framework for reaching definitions, available expressions, and two well-studied lifeguards.
- In contrast to our prior work [9], we implemented a far more challenging lifeguard (TAINTCHECK, requiring not only dataflow analysis but also *inheritance* analysis whereby a single instruction is itself a transfer function) in both the Butterfly and Chrysalis Analysis frameworks to evaluate their precision.
- Our experimental results demonstrate a factor of 17.9x reduction in the number of false positives, while slowing down the lifeguard by an average of 1.9x.

2. BACKGROUND: BUTTERFLY ANALYSIS

Butterfly Analysis [9] is a parallel dataflow analysis framework supporting lifeguard analysis of parallel applications. Unlike traditional dataflow analysis, which performs static analysis on control flow graphs, Butterfly Analysis analyzes *dynamic* execution traces of instructions on different threads.

[1] We assume explicit synchronization such as locks and barriers (tracked by Chrysalis Analysis) are used to prevent races.

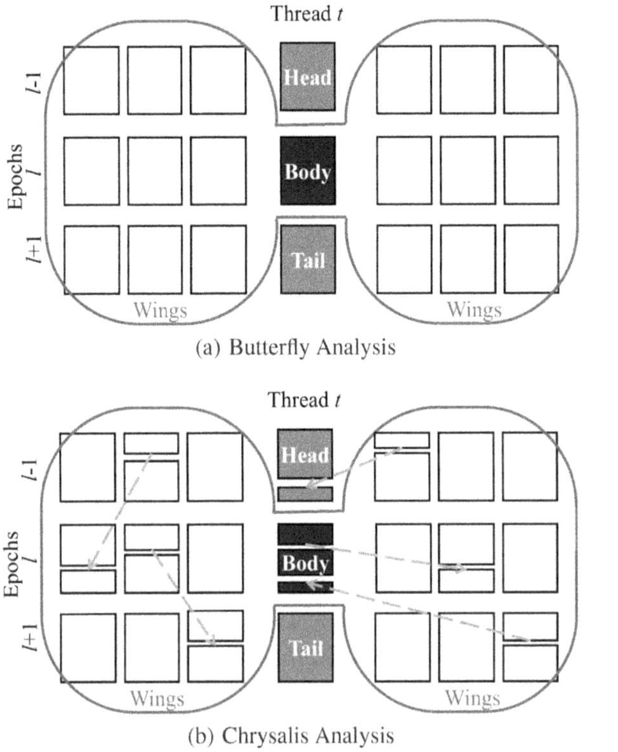

Figure 2: (a) Butterfly Analysis divides thread execution into *epochs*. A *block* is a thread-epoch pair. (b) Chrysalis Analysis incorporates high-level synchronization events by dividing blocks into *subblocks* based on the happens-before arcs (shown as dashed arrows) resulting from such events.

Insights and Structure of Butterfly Analysis. Butterfly Analysis is based on the observation that modern systems have only a finite amount of buffering. Even taking into account memory access latency, and store reorder buffer sizes, if two instructions are issued sufficiently "far apart" (meaning many instructions issued between them) then they could not have both been buffered within the system simultaneously. Butterfly Analysis leverages this observation *to extract a partial order of a parallel application's events without monitoring detailed inter-thread data dependence traffic.*

Butterfly Analysis achieves this goal by dividing execution time into epochs. The interval between issuing epoch boundaries is constructed to account for the reorder buffer, store buffer, memory latency and skew in delivering notice of an epoch change. Epoch boundaries are communicated to cores, using either a software-only token ring combined with a memory fence or a simple piece of hardware. Note that epoch boundaries need not be established instantaneously—the sole requirement is a guaranteed maximum skew among the times a given epoch boundary is established at every core.

Note that by construction, two instructions in *non-adjacent epochs* (i.e., epochs which do not share an epoch boundary) cannot interleave. This follows from how epochs are defined: instructions in non-adjacent epochs were already implicitly ordered by the system, as the earlier instruction must have committed, with any related store draining from the store buffer, before the later instruction was even issued. In Figure 2(a), instructions in epoch $l-1$ must all have committed with any related store draining before any instruction in epoch $l+1$ is issued. This motivates the use of a 3-epoch sliding window in Figure 2(a); instructions separated by an epoch or more are automatically ordered.

On the other hand, instructions in *adjacent* epochs, i.e., epochs that share an epoch boundary, are assumed to be potentially concurrent when they are not in the same thread. For example, in Figure 2(a), epochs $l-1$ and l are adjacent, as are epochs l and $l+1$. Figure 2(a) depicts *blocks*[2] of instructions for three epochs across seven threads, summarizing the potential concurrency with instructions by thread t in epoch l (labeled the **body** of the "butterfly"). Instructions in the body of the butterfly are concurrent with instructions in the **wings**, but ordered with respect to the **head** and **tail**, as intra-thread data dependences are still respected. In reality, epoch boundaries will be staggered due to skew in delivery latency, and blocks will be of somewhat varying sizes.

Two-Pass Lifeguard Analysis. Analysis proceeds one epoch at a time, using a sliding window of three epochs. Lifeguard threads, one per application thread, execute in parallel and lag at least two epochs behind the application threads. Unlike traditional dataflow analysis, Butterfly Analysis maintains global state to summarize earlier epochs that are no longer within the window. The *Strongly Ordered State (SOS)* represents the global metadata resulting from all instructions *executed at least two epochs prior* to epoch l. Each lifeguard thread operating on a butterfly also knows that the *head* has already executed relative to the *body* for its application thread (Figure 2(a)), and augment the SOS with this additional, locally known information to form their thread's *Local Strongly Ordered State (LSOS)*.

Analysis for a given epoch proceeds in two passes. In the first pass, each lifeguard thread performs dataflow analysis using only local events, and produces a summary or SIDE-OUT of lifeguard-relevant events. In the next phase, lifeguard threads compute the *meet* of these summaries to create the SIDE-IN. In the second pass, dataflow analysis is repeated, this time including the SIDE-IN, and lifeguard checks are performed. Finally, a summary of the entire epoch's execution is created, and used to update the SOS.

The events the dataflow analysis will track, the meet operation, the metadata format, and the checking algorithm are all specified by the lifeguard writer. Tolerating uncertainty introduces imprecision into the dataflow analysis. Our prior paper [9] proved that Butterfly Analysis does not miss any errors (zero *false negatives*), but it sacrifices precision in the form of *false positives* arising from the lack of a relative ordering among events within a sliding window.

3. OVERVIEW OF CHRYSALIS ANALYSIS

In this section, we introduce Chrysalis Analysis. We begin by motivating the utility of our analysis using simple examples, as well as showcasing the challenges we faced in generalizing Butterfly Analysis. Then, we introduce the new primitives that enable Chrysalis Analysis. Finally, we illustrate some of the major challenges in generalizing Butterfly Analysis to produce Chrysalis Analysis, namely maintaining global state and updating local state.

3.1 Adding Happens-Before Arcs: A Case Study

We begin with a few examples that illustrate the utility of our new primitives as well as the challenges that lie ahead.

Consider Figure 3(a). This shows a single thread's execution, where in one block it issues (an instruction that serves to) `untaint(p)` and in the next `*p`. Any single-threaded analysis will conclude that at the point where `*p` is dereferenced, `p` is untainted because only one thread was executing and that thread untainted `p` prior to dereferencing it as a pointer.

Now consider Figure 3(b). Here, we see Thread 1 issuing `untaint(p);` `unlock(L)`. After Thread 1 unlocks `L`, Thread 0 is the next thread to

[2] A block is specified by an epoch-thread tuple (l, t).

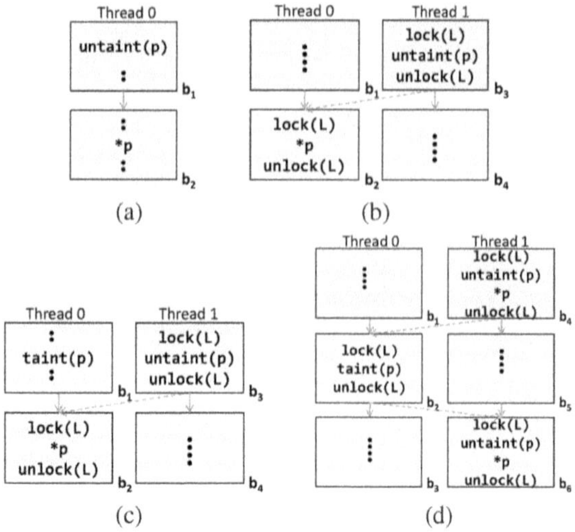

Figure 3: TAINTCHECK examples for dereferencing a pointer p. (a) In single-threaded execution, respect of intra-thread dependences implies p is untainted. (b) The synchronization between Thread 1 and Thread 0 means block b_3 executes before block b_2. Since b_1 does not assign to p, p is untainted. This is a win for Chrysalis Analysis. (c) Similar to (b), but now Thread 0 issues `taint(p)` in b_1 concurrently with b_3. Conservative analysis means p must be treated as tainted. (d) Another win for Chrysalis Analysis. Each dereference of p in b_4 and b_6 is guaranteed to only see p as untainted.

acquire L (`lock(L)`) and then issues $*$p. In this case, the happens-before relationship is not due to intra-thread data dependences but rather the synchronization on lock L. However, from the perspective of a lifeguard monitoring this program, Thread 1 issued `untaint(p)` before Thread 0 issued $*$p; since no instructions in Thread 0 prior to $*$p conflict, this analysis should be identical to case (a). This is true for Chrysalis Analysis, but not Butterfly Analysis.

Finally, consider Figure 3(c), which contains a data race. Thread 1 is still untainting p and releasing lock L immediately before Thread 0 dereferences p. However, we also see that block b_1 in Thread 0, prior to issuing `lock(L)` in block b_2, issued `taint(p)` without holding lock L. To know whether the dereference of p is safe in Thread 0, the analysis needs to know whether p was tainted at the program point immediately prior. It knows that two things happened before the dereference: p was tainted by Thread 0, and p was untainted by Thread 1. However, *the ordering between these two operations remains unknown!* Figure 3(c) illustrates that extra happens-before information is not a panacea for all causes of imprecision. In this case, the lifeguard must behave conservatively, since the analysis cannot determine whether the `taint(p)` occurs before or after the `untaint(p)`.

While incorporating happens-before arcs can significantly improve precision, it spoils the key ingredient underlying Butterfly Analysis, namely, that the simple "butterfly" of Figure 2(a) captured all the ordering information known to the lifeguard. Each of the steps in Butterfly Analysis' two-pass analysis exploits this regular structure in a fundamental way; and with happens-before arcs, this regularity no longer exists (see Figure 2(b)). Including additional partial ordering information, while making the analysis more precise, also makes the analysis much more difficult!

3.2 Maximal Subblocks

Consider again Figures 3(b) and (c). In both cases, what allowed us to analyze these figures was the fact that the traces were divided at each `lock` or `unlock` call. This allowed us to reason that an entire section of the trace *happened before* another section. This motivates the following definition, based on the synchronization events currently tracked by our analysis. An execution trace for a thread is partitioned into *maximal subblocks* (*subblocks* for short) by breaking the trace (i) after the last instruction of an epoch, (ii) after each `send`, `unlock`, or `barrier-wait` call, and (iii) whenever the following instruction is a `receive` or `lock` call.[3] This subdivision enables us to reason that entire maximal subblocks must have occurred before, after, or concurrent with other maximal subblocks. Note that the maximal subblocks are precisely the irregularity mentioned earlier. The number and size of maximal subblocks per thread, and per epoch, is based on the frequency and types of synchronization used by the application. This is illustrated in Figures 1(b) and 2(b).

Despite the introduction of subblocks, for ease of comparison, we will adopt the notation of Butterfly Analysis by referring to instructions based on their offset within blocks. Namely, (l, t, i) refers to the ith instruction in epoch l of thread t's trace.

Next, we discuss how to determine, given two subblocks, b and b', if b executed before, after, or concurrent with b'.

3.3 Testing Ordering Among Subblocks

To test ordering between maximal subblocks, each maximal subblock b has an associated vector clock $v(b)$. Vector clocks have been used in many other works [1, 2, 5, 8, 19]; they are a natural distributed clock primitive. We are using them here to label individual subblocks based on synchronization events and epoch boundaries.[4] The addition of vector clocks and subblocks transforms the Butterfly Analysis diagram, shown in Figure 1(a), into Figure 1(b).

We modify the standard vector clock algorithm slightly. Let n be the number of threads. If $v(b)[i]$ is the ith position in vector clock $v(b)$, then for $0 \le i < n$ we initially set $v(b)[j] = 1$ if $j = i$ and $v(b)[j] = 0$ otherwise. For example, the second thread in a 3-thread system would begin with vector clock $< 0, 1, 0 >$. Consider a `send` (equivalently, `unlock L`) from thread j to thread k. If v_j is thread j's current vector clock and v_k is thread k's current vector clock, then thread j will first bind v_j to v_{send}, which k will later receive. Then, $v_j[j]$ is incremented, and a new maximal subblock begins in thread j. When thread k processes the associated `receive` (equivalently, `lock L`), it will set $v_k[i] = \max\{v_{\mathsf{send}}[i], v_k[i]\}$ for $0 \le i < n$ and then increment $v_k[k]$. The `receive` instruction in thread k begins a new maximal subblock.

On a barrier wait (assuming all n threads participate) let

$$\forall i, 0 \le i < n, v_{bar}[i] = v_i[i].$$

Then, thread j updates its vector clock to be:

$$\forall i \ne j, v_j[i] = v_{bar}[i], \quad v_j[j]{+}{+}$$

This is easily extended to work for a barrier of $n' < n$ threads: Update $v_j[i]$ only if both threads i and j were among the n' threads participating in the barrier.

It makes sense to include ordering information that Butterfly Analysis provides. After the second epoch, we can update vector clocks at epoch boundaries, since the ordering is always known

[3]In the special case where the first instruction of an epoch is a `receive` or `lock` call, the first maximal subblock is considered empty and the second maximal subblock begins with the `receive` or `lock`, respectively.

[4]We make the typical assumption that, even on relaxed memory consistency models, synchronization events such as `lock`, `unlock` and `barrier-wait` always carry an associated memory fence. Such a fence implies, for example, that all the effects of instructions before an `unlock` complete before the lock is released.

when instructions are separated by at least an epoch. Epoch l treats a snapshot of the vector clocks available at the end of epoch $l-2$ as a barrier (call them v^*_{bar}). While v^*_{bar} is calculated the same as v_{bar}, the update rule differs slightly:

$$\forall i \neq j, v_j[i] = \max\{v^*_{bar}[i], v_j[i]\}, \quad v_j[j]{+}{+}$$

We can compare two vector clocks, v and v', by comparing their components. Vector clock v *happens before* vector clock v' if $\forall i, v[i] \leq v'[i] \wedge \exists j$ s.t. $v[j] < v'[j]$. We indicate this relationship using $v < v'$ or equivalently, $v' > v$. If $v \nless v'$ and $v' \nless v$, then v and v' label *concurrent* maximal subblocks; we will denote this as $v \sim v'$.

We will use this terminology loosely. For instance, if (l, t, i) is an instruction in maximal subblock b, then we might talk about $v(l, t, i)$ or $v(b)$, which are equivalent vector clocks.

3.4 Reasoning About Partial Orderings

Some new complexities arise when trying to reason about all the partial orderings which are consistent with Chrysalis Analysis. For instance, there can be an upwards arc from epoch $l+1$ into epoch l, where a subblock in epoch $l+1$ happens before a different subblock in epoch l. This is illustrated in Figure 2(b), where the last subblock in the body happens after a subblock in the rightmost thread in the wings. Once all the instructions in epoch l have executed, we also know that some of the instructions in epoch $l+1$ have also executed, because there exists a maximal subblock in epoch l which happens after a maximal subblock in epoch $l+1$. We call l^+ the **extended epoch of** l, and define it to include all instructions in epoch l, as well as all instructions $(l+1, t, i)$ in epoch $l+1$ for which there is some subblock b in epoch l where $v(l+1, t, i) < v(b)$.

We introduce the concept of a *valid vector ordering*, which extends Butterfly Analysis' *valid ordering* to incorporate happens-before arcs. A valid ordering is any total sequential ordering of instructions consistent with both the intra-thread dependences and the ordering of instructions in non-adjacent epochs. This is too broad a set of orderings for Chrysalis Analysis to use because it includes orderings that violate the happens-before arcs captured by our vector clocks. To capture the more restricted set of orderings, we define valid vector orderings:

DEFINITION 3.1. *O_l is a **valid vector ordering (VVO)** if:*

- BACKWARDS COMPATIBLE
  O_l restricted to epochs $[0, l]$ and ignoring happens-before arcs is a valid ordering.
- INCLUDES ALL INSTRUCTIONS THROUGH EPOCH l^+
  All instructions from epochs 0 to l are included, as well as those instructions from epoch $l+1$ that belong to l^+, with no instructions from epochs $> l+1$ included.
- RESPECTS HAPPENS-BEFORE
  If $v(l, t, i) < v(l', t', i')$, instruction (l, t, i) appears before instruction (l', t', i') in O_l.

3.5 Challenge: Maintaining Global State

As in Butterfly Analysis, Chrysalis Analysis requires global state because the analysis only proceeds over a sliding window of execution. Butterfly Analysis made simplifying assumptions that allowed it to symmetrically reason about each butterfly in parallel. For instance, consider the traces depicted in Figure 3(d). In Butterfly Analysis, the dashed happens-before arcs (from synchronization) are ignored. Suppose this all occurred within the same epoch l. Both subblocks b_4 and b_6 would conservatively reason that `p` was tainted before the dereference, as it was possible that the `taint(p)` occurred between the `untaint(p)` and `*p`. However, that `taint(p)` is issued only once, whereas Thread 1 issues `untaint(p)` twice! It was impossible for both dereferences of `p` to be against a tainted pointer, and also have `p` tainted at the end of epoch l. However, Butterfly Analysis would have summarized this epoch with `p` tainted.

Once Chrysalis Analysis adds the happens-before (dashed) arcs in Figure 3(d), it is clear not only that each `*p` is to untainted data, but also that at the end of the epoch, `p` is untainted. This requires epoch-level summarization to consider the happens-before arcs. Summarizing an "epoch" in Chrysalis Analysis will also mean summarizing the extended epoch. Suppose alternatively that subblocks b_2 and b_3 were instead in epoch $l+1$, while all other subblocks were in epoch l as before; b_2 now belongs to l^+, and we still conclude that after all instructions in l^+ have executed, `p` is untainted and we update the global state (SOS) accordingly.

3.6 Challenge: Updating Local State

Once again, consider Figure 3(d). As stated earlier, the second pass for Butterfly Analysis was entirely in parallel, because there were no additional happens-before arcs. Chrysalis Analysis wishes to improve on this imprecision. As the second pass of the analysis proceeds, at each entry point to a new maximal subblock Chrysalis Analysis must wait for all of its direct parents (those subblocks with a happens-before arc pointing to it) to finish their second pass before beginning. This makes the analysis aware, for example, that b_2's taint of `p` was prior to b_6, and hence b_6's subsequent issue of `untaint(p)` made `*p` safe.

To do this analysis correctly, it is important to note that each direct parent takes on a role analogous to the head in Butterfly Analysis. However, now we can have multiple "heads", arising either due to explicit synchronization or intra-thread sequential semantics. The parents are unlikely to be ordered themselves. Just as in Figure 3(c), we will need to conservatively reason about instructions that executed prior to a subblock. This will lead to our treating the local state (LSOS) more as a dataflow problem and less as pure state. We will conduct a "meet" at subblock entry points of the incoming GEN and KILL sets we define in the sections that follow.

4. REACHING DEFINITIONS

In this section, we will show how to extend Reaching Definitions, a classical dataflow analysis problem, to Chrysalis Analysis. We will begin by showing how to define generating and killing definitions at the instruction, subblock and epoch level, as well as showing how to compute the Side-In and Side-Out primitives. Then we will show how to update both the Strongly Ordered State (SOS) and the Local Strongly Ordered State (LSOS), and present the two-pass algorithm for reaching definitions. Throughout the section, we will prove key properties of our definitions, showing that Chrysalis Analysis will not "miss an error" (meaning, it will never claim a definition d does not reach a program point p when there was a way for that to happen). Later in Section 5 we will give an example lifeguard, TAINTCHECK, based on reaching definitions. Extensions of Chrysalis Analysis to Available Expressions, another classical dataflow analysis problem, and ADDRCHECK, a memory lifeguard, appear in Appendices A and B, respectively.

4.1 Gen and Kill equations

We begin by defining GEN and KILL at all granularities, represented by $\mathcal{G}$ and $\mathcal{K}$, respectively.

Instruction-Level. Let $\mathcal{G}_{l,t,i} = \{d\}$ if (l, t, i) generates d. Let $\mathcal{K}_{l,t,i} = \{d | (l, t, i) \text{ kills } d\}$.

Maximal Subblock-Level. We often wish to refer to a maximal subblock b as $(l, t, (i, j))$, meaning it is composed of instructions (l, t, i) through (l, t, j). If $b = (l, t, (i, j))$ then:

$$\mathcal{G}_b = \mathcal{G}_{l,t,(i,j)} = \mathcal{G}_{l,t,j} \cup (\mathcal{G}_{l,t,(i,j-1)} - \mathcal{K}_{l,t,j})$$
$$\mathcal{K}_b = \mathcal{K}_{l,t,(i,j)} = \mathcal{K}_{l,t,j} \cup (\mathcal{K}_{l,t,(i,j-1)} - \mathcal{G}_{l,t,j})$$

with $\mathcal{G}_{l,t,(i,i)} = \mathcal{G}_{l,t,i}$ and $\mathcal{K}_{l,t,(i,i)} = \mathcal{K}_{l,t,i}$ as base cases to the recursion. These are the standard flow equations for GEN and KILL, defined now over maximal subblocks.

Side-Out and Side-In (Per Subblock). In generalizing Butterfly Analysis' treatment of Side-Out and Side-In, we must take into account the additional information provided by the vector clocks. It now makes sense to consider Side-Out and Side-In per maximal subblock b, rather than per block (l, t). In the event that there are no happens-before arcs, the subsequent equations are equivalent to the original Butterfly Analysis equations for Side-Out and Side-In. For maximal subblocks b and b', where $b = (l, t, (j, k))$, the new equations for GEN-SIDE-OUT and GEN-SIDE-IN are:

$$\text{GEN-SIDE-OUT}_b = \bigcup_{j \le i \le k} \mathcal{G}_{l,t,i}$$
$$\text{GEN-SIDE-IN}_b = \bigcup_{\{b' | v(b') \sim v(b)\}} \text{GEN-SIDE-OUT}_{b'}$$

Epoch-Level. We will define three useful sets, AFTER, MB and NBEFORE, and use them to define $\mathcal{G}_l$ and $\mathcal{K}_l$ for an epoch l. If b is a maximal subblock in l^+ (the extended epoch of l), then:

$$\text{MB}_l = \{b | b \text{ is a maximal subblock in epoch } l\}.$$
$$\text{AFTER}_b = \{b' | b' \in \text{MB}_{l^+} \text{ and } v(b) < v(b')\}$$
$$\text{NBEFORE}_b = \{b' | b' \in (\text{MB}_{l-1} \cup \text{MB}_{l^+}) \wedge (v(b) \sim v(b') \vee v(b) < v(b'))\}$$
$$\mathcal{G}_l = \bigcup_{\{b | b \in \text{MB}_{l^+}\}} \left(\mathcal{G}_b - \bigcup_{b' \in \text{AFTER}_b} \mathcal{K}_{b'}\right)$$
$$\mathcal{K}_l = \bigcup_{\{b | b \in \text{MB}_{l^+}\}} \left(\mathcal{K}_b - \bigcup_{\{b' | b' \in \text{NBEFORE}_b\}} \mathcal{G}_{b'}\right)$$

LEMMA 1. *If there exists a valid vector ordering (VVO) O_l of the instructions in l^+ such that $d \in \mathcal{G}(O_l)$ then $d \in \mathcal{G}_l$.*

PROOF. $d \in \mathcal{G}(O_l)$ implies that there exists an instruction (l, t, i)[5] in the total order O_l such that (l, t, i) generates d and no subsequent instruction kills d. Let b be the maximal subblock containing (l, t, i). By the definition of VVO, there is no instruction (l', t', i') that kills d such that either $v(l, t, i) < v(l', t', i')$ or (l, t, i) is before (l', t', i') in the same block b. Thus, $d \in \mathcal{G}_b$ (by construction) and $d \notin \bigcup_{b' \in \text{AFTER}_b} \mathcal{K}_{b'}$, implying $d \in \mathcal{G}_l$. □

LEMMA 2. *If $d \in \mathcal{K}_l$, then no valid vector ordering O of the instructions in epochs $l - 1$ through l^+ exists such that $d \in \mathcal{G}(O)$.*

PROOF. If $d \in \mathcal{K}_l$, then by definition there exists a maximal subblock b such that $d \in \mathcal{K}_b$ and for all maximal subblocks b' such that $v(b) \sim v(b')$ or $v(b) < v(b')$, $d \notin \mathcal{G}_{b'}$. Let (l, t, k) be the last instruction in b that kills d; $d \in \mathcal{K}_b$ implies that no instruction in b after (l, t, k) generates d. (Due to data dependences, kills and generates of d are strictly ordered within a subblock.)

Consider any VVO O of the instructions in epochs $l - 1$ through l^+. By the definition of VVO, the only instructions following (l, t, k) in O that can kill or generate d are those belonging to any maximal subblock b' that is concurrent or occurs strictly after b. As argued above, $d \notin \mathcal{G}_{b'}$, implying either (i) b' never generates d or (ii) any generation of d in b' is followed by a subsequent kill of d also in b', which would be reflected in O. Thus, any generation of d in O either occurs strictly before (l, t, k), or else is followed by a kill of d; either way, d does not reach the end of O. Hence, $d \notin \mathcal{G}(O)$. □

[5]Actually, the instruction must exist in l^+, not just in l. For simplicity of exposition, we chose to use l.

4.2 Strongly Ordered State

As in Butterfly Analysis, Chrysalis Analysis uses the epoch-level summaries $\mathcal{G}_l$ and $\mathcal{K}_l$ to compute the Strongly Ordered State (SOS). This equation is unchanged from Butterfly Analysis; all the changes are in the generalization of $\mathcal{G}_l$ and $\mathcal{K}_l$.

$$\text{SOS}_0 = \text{SOS}_1 = \varnothing$$
$$\text{SOS}_l = \mathcal{G}_{l-2} \cup (\text{SOS}_{l-1} - \mathcal{K}_{l-2}) \; \forall l \ge 2$$

The following theorem proves that if there exists any VVO such that a definition d reaches the end of l epochs, then it will be in SOS_{l+2}.

THEOREM 3. *If there exists a valid vector ordering O_l of the instructions in epochs $[0, l^+]$ such that $d \in \mathcal{G}(O_l)$ then $d \in \text{SOS}_{l+2}$.*

PROOF. Our proof will proceed by induction on l. In the base case of $l = 0$, we have $\text{SOS}_{l+2} = \mathcal{G}_0$ by an application of Lemma 1. Now assume that the lemma is true for all $l < k$, and show for $l = k$. Suppose $d \in \mathcal{G}(O_l)$. As in Lemma 1, by the definition of VVO, there exists an instruction $(\tilde{l}, \tilde{t}, \tilde{i})$ in O_l generating d such that no subsequent instruction kills d. In particular, $\forall (l', t', i')$ where $v(\tilde{l}, \tilde{t}, \tilde{i}) < v(l', t', i')$, $d \notin \mathcal{K}_{l',t',i'}$. There are two cases:

$\tilde{l} \ge l$: Let b be the maximal subblock containing instruction $(\tilde{l}, \tilde{t}, \tilde{i})$. No subsequent instruction in b can kill d. Thus, $d \in \mathcal{G}_b$ and b belongs to l^+, which implies $d \in \mathcal{G}_l$. Hence, $d \in \text{SOS}_{l+2}$ by definition.

$\tilde{l} < l$: Because, as argued above, there is no kill ordered after $(\tilde{l}, \tilde{t}, \tilde{i})$, we have that $d \notin \mathcal{K}_l$ and there exists a VVO O_{l-1} of the instructions in epochs $[0, (l-1)^+]$ such that $d \in \mathcal{G}(O_{l-1})$. Applying the inductive hypothesis, we have that $d \in \text{SOS}_{l+1}$. Thus, $d \in \text{SOS}_{l+1} - \mathcal{K}_l$, implying $d \in \text{SOS}_{l+2}$.

□

4.3 Local Strongly Ordered State

Once we have computed the SOS, the next step is to calculate the Local Strongly Ordered State (LSOS). As mentioned in Section 3.6, we face a few challenges in generalizing Butterfly Analysis' LSOS update rule. Butterfly Analysis proposed an equation for calculating the LSOS from the body (block (l, t)) based on the SOS, and the $\mathcal{G}$ and $\mathcal{K}$ from the head (block $(l - 1, t)$):

Butterfly Analysis: $\text{LSOS}_{l,t} = \mathcal{G}_{l-1,t} \cup (\text{SOS}_l - \mathcal{K}_{l-1,t}) \cup \{d | d \in \text{SOS}_l \wedge d \in \mathcal{K}_{l-1,t} \wedge \exists t' \neq t \text{ s.t. } d \in \mathcal{G}_{l-2,t'}\}$

This rule took advantage of a specialized structure that does not hold in Chrysalis Analysis. First, there was only one head, or direct predecessor, for any block, so $\mathcal{G}_{l-1,t}$ and $\mathcal{K}_{l-1,t}$ are easily directly referenced. Second, removing a definition $d \in \mathcal{K}_{l-1,t}$ from SOS_l was incorrect if another thread t' had actually generated d in epoch $l - 1$ or $l - 2$; only $l - 2$ had to be directly added back in, because everything in epoch $l - 1$ was part of the $\text{GEN-SIDE-IN}_{l,t}$. The union of the final set fixed the accuracy of the LSOS, but at the price of a deviation from the standard OUT $=$ GEN $\cup$(IN $-$ KILL) formulation.

Chrysalis Analysis must anticipate the possibility of a more generalized structure, where subblocks have multiple direct parents, which may all execute before a particular subblock b, but not necessarily be totally ordered amongst themselves. This is illustrated in Figure 3(c), where b_1 and b_3 both occur before b_2 but the taint status of p is uncertain (conservatively, tainted) before b_2. Dataflow analysis provides a natural way of handling such effects: the meet operator.

Our solution for Chrysalis Analysis will involve representing the local differences applied to the SOS as transfer functions. We will use $\text{IN}^{\mathcal{G}}$ and $\text{OUT}^{\mathcal{G}}$ for GEN difference, and $\text{IN}^{\mathcal{K}}$ and $\text{OUT}^{\mathcal{K}}$ for KILL. Furthermore, we will present a way of calculating the LSOS from the SOS that will use the OUT = GEN$\cup$(IN − KILL) structure, where IN = SOS_l and OUT = LSOS_b, without involving extra sets.

The rest of the section focuses on the program point immediately before a maximal subblock b. For instructions on the "interior" of b, we can use standard dataflow analysis techniques to update the intermediate state, *i.e.*, $\text{LSOS}_{l,t,i+1} = \mathcal{G}_{l,t,i} \cup (\text{LSOS}_{l,t,i} - \mathcal{K}_{l,t,i})$. We only require a more general solution to the entry points of maximal subblocks. The meet operator ($\sqcap$) for reaching definitions in Chrysalis Analysis is union ($\bigcup$).

LSOS: Representing GEN As Transfer Functions.

The LSOS transfer functions focus on the sliding window of epochs $l-1$ through $l+1$. Let $\text{MB}_{[l_1,l_2]} = \bigcup_{l_1 \le l_i \le l_2} \text{MB}_{l_i}$. Then, we define $\text{HB}(b)$:

$$\text{HB}(b) = \{b' | v(b') < v(b) \text{ where } \left(b' \in \text{MB}_{[l-1,l+1]}\right) \vee \left(b' \in \text{MB}_{l-2} \wedge \exists b'' \in \text{MB}_{l-1} \text{ such that } v(b'') < v(b')\right)\}$$

for maximal subblocks b and b'. Note that this captures all maximal subblocks b' that happen before b and are within the 3 epoch sliding window, as well as including those subblocks in epoch $l-2$ that have predecessors in epoch $l-1$.

For the LSOS, we define $\mathcal{G}_b$ and $\mathcal{K}_b$ to be the standard dataflow formulations of $\mathcal{G}$ and $\mathcal{K}$ over a maximal subblock b, restricted to the sliding window of epochs $l-1$ through $l+1$. Define pred(b) to be the set of maximal subblocks $b' \in \text{HB}(b)$ such that either (i) b' is the immediate predecessor of b in thread t or (ii) the first instruction of b receives a send from (equivalently, locks an unlock by) the last instruction of b'. Barriers are an all-to-all send/receive. Then we can define the OUT and IN formulas for GEN:

$$\text{OUT}^{\mathcal{G}}_b = \mathcal{G}_b \cup (\text{IN}^{\mathcal{G}}_b - \mathcal{K}_b)$$

$$\text{IN}^{\mathcal{G}}_b = \begin{cases} \varnothing & \text{if } b \text{ is a thread's 1st subblock at level } l-1 \\ \sqcap_{b' \in \text{pred}(b)} \text{OUT}^{\mathcal{G}}_{b'} & \text{otherwise} \end{cases}$$

The following establishes the correctness of this formulation:

LEMMA 4. *If there exists a valid vector ordering O of the instructions in $\text{HB}(b)$ such that $d \in \mathcal{G}(O)$ then $d \in \text{IN}^{\mathcal{G}}_b$.*

PROOF. Suppose $\text{HB}(b)$ is not empty and $d \in \mathcal{G}(O)$. As in earlier proofs, the definition of VVO implies that there exists in O an instruction (l', t', j') that generates d in a maximal subblock b', such that no subsequent instruction kills d, and in particular, $\forall$ maximal subblocks $\tilde{b} \in \text{HB}(b)$ with $v(b') < v(\tilde{b})$, we have $d \notin \mathcal{K}_{\tilde{b}}$. It follows that $d \in \mathcal{G}_{b'}$, and hence $d \in \text{OUT}^{\mathcal{G}}_{b'}$. Moreover, since $d \notin \mathcal{K}_{\tilde{b}}$ and $\tilde{b}$ is not the first subblock for its thread at level $l-1$, we have that $d \in \text{OUT}^{\mathcal{G}}_{\tilde{b}}$ for all such $\tilde{b}$.

If $b' \in \text{pred}(b)$, then by the definition of $\text{IN}^{\mathcal{G}}_b$ and the fact that b is not the first subblock for its thread at level $l-1$, we have $d \in \text{IN}^{\mathcal{G}}_b$. If $b' \notin \text{pred}(b)$, then $b' \in \text{HB}(b)$ implies that there exists a $\tilde{b} \in \text{pred}(b)$ such that $v(b') < v(\tilde{b})$. As argued above, $d \in \text{OUT}^{\mathcal{G}}_{\tilde{b}}$, and hence $d \in \text{IN}^{\mathcal{G}}_b$. □

$\text{IN}^{\mathcal{G}}_b$ captures the set of local GEN differences to reflect in the LSOS at the entry point to b, i.e., definitions from instructions that executed before b but may not be in the SOS.

LSOS: Representing KILL As Transfer Functions.

The formula for $\text{OUT}^{\mathcal{K}}_b$ is similar to the formula for $\text{OUT}^{\mathcal{G}}_b$:

$$\text{OUT}^{\mathcal{K}}_b = \mathcal{K}_b \cup (\text{IN}^{\mathcal{K}}_b - \mathcal{G}_b).$$

Recall that the meet function $\sqcap$ is still union, even though we are combining kill sets.

In defining $\text{IN}^{\mathcal{K}}_b$, it helps to have the following set:

$$\text{DEL-INK}_{b'} = \{b'' | (v(b'') \sim v(b')) \vee ((v(b') < v(b'')) \wedge (v(b) \not< v(b'')))\}$$

$$\text{IN}^{\mathcal{K}}_b = \begin{cases} \varnothing & \text{if } b \text{ is a thread's 1st subblock at level } l-1 \\ \sqcap_{b' \in \text{pred}(b)} (\text{OUT}^{\mathcal{K}}_{b'} - \\ \quad (\cup_{b'' \in \text{DEL-INK}_{b'}} \text{GEN-SIDE-OUT}_{b''})) & \text{otherwise} \end{cases}$$

LEMMA 5. *If $d \in \text{IN}^{\mathcal{K}}_b$ then $\forall$ valid vector orderings O composed solely of all instructions from maximal subblocks b' such that $v(b') < v(b)$, $d \notin \mathcal{G}(O)$.*

PROOF. If $d \in \text{IN}^{\mathcal{K}}_b$ then $\exists b' \in \text{pred}(b)$ such that $d \in \text{OUT}^{\mathcal{K}}_{b'}$ and $\forall b''$ such that b'' is concurrent with b' or b'' occurs after b' but not after b, $d \notin \text{GEN-SIDE-OUT}_{b''}$.

Consider any O, restricted to subblocks that occur before b. It must have a nonempty suffix S beginning with an instruction (l', t', i') that is the last kill of d in b'. By the definition of VVO, the remaining instructions in S must either be concurrent with b' or happen after—precisely the set encapsulated by $\text{DEL-INK}_{b'}$. By construction, if $d \in \text{OUT}^{\mathcal{K}}_{b'} - (\bigcup_{b'' \in \text{DEL-INK}_{b'}} \text{GEN-SIDE-OUT}_{b''})$ then $d \notin \text{GEN-SIDE-OUT}_{b''}$ for all $b'' \in \text{DEL-INK}_{b'}$, meaning no later instruction in S can define d. Thus, since $d \in \mathcal{K}(S)$ for a nonempty suffix S implies $d \in \mathcal{K}(O)$, we have that $d \notin \mathcal{G}(O)$. □

Creating LSOS. We now have all the building blocks we need to adjust the formula for calculating LSOS at subblock entry points. If $b = (l, t, (i, j))$ is a maximal subblock, let LSOS_b indicate the LSOS at the entry to block b, namely, $\text{LSOS}_{l,t,i}$. Then $\text{LSOS}_b = \text{IN}^{\mathcal{G}}_b \cup (\text{SOS}_l - \text{IN}^{\mathcal{K}}_b)$.

THEOREM 6. *If $\exists$ a valid vector ordering O of the instructions from epochs $[0, (l-2)^+]$ and $\text{HB}(b)$ such that $d \in \mathcal{G}(O)$, then $d \in \text{LSOS}_b$.*

PROOF. The proof follows from a straightforward extension of Lemma 4. Instead of limiting ourselves to an ordering of instructions in $\text{HB}(b)$, we consider all instructions from epochs $[0, (l-2)^+]$ and $\text{HB}(b)$. Then if the instruction (l', t', i') generating d has $l' > l-2$, Lemma 4 dominates. Otherwise, it is still the case the d is not in a later kill set (represented by $\text{IN}^{\mathcal{K}}_b$). If we restrict the ordering to the first $[0, (l-2)^+]$ epochs, this is the same as the proof that $d \in \text{SOS}_l$ (Theorem 4.2), so $d \in \text{SOS}_l - \text{IN}^{\mathcal{K}}{}_b$. □

4.4 In and Out Functions

We now consider what each instruction will compute for its IN and OUT functions. For an instruction (l, t, i) that belongs to maximal subblock $b = (l, t, (j, j'))$:

$$\text{IN}_{l,t,i} = \text{GEN-SIDE-IN}_b \bigcup \text{LSOS}_{l,t,i}$$
$$\text{OUT}_{l,t,i} = \mathcal{G}_{l,t,i} \bigcup (\text{IN}_{l,t,i} - \mathcal{K}_{l,t,i})$$

4.5 Applying the Two-Pass Algorithm

Reaching Definitions in Chrysalis Analysis, like in Butterfly Analysis, is implemented as a two-pass algorithm. In the first pass, $\mathcal{G}_b$, $\mathcal{K}_b$ and GEN-SIDE-OUT_b are calculated. Once all threads finish the first pass, the second pass can begin. The second pass must respect the happens-before arcs; if subblock b' in thread t' is an immediate predecessor of subblock b in thread t, thread t cannot calculate $\text{IN}^{\mathcal{G}}_b$ or $\text{IN}^{\mathcal{K}}_b$ until the second pass of b' has completed and $\text{OUT}^{\mathcal{G}}_b$ and $\text{OUT}^{\mathcal{K}}_b$ are available. This means the $LSOS_b$ cannot be computed until just before the start of the second pass for subblock b. Once all threads have completed the second pass, it is safe to update the SOS.

5. TAINTCHECK

As in Butterfly Analysis, we build the Chrysalis Analysis extension of TAINTCHECK on top of reaching definitions. TAINTCHECK presents a unique challenge, as it incorporates not only dataflow but also *inheritance*. Instead of definitions, expressions, or addresses, a particular $\mathcal{G}_{l,t,i}$ is actually a transfer function. An instruction can either taint a memory location x, untaint a memory location x, be a unary operation on some location a or a binary operation on locations a and b. More formally, as in Butterfly Analysis, define $\mathcal{G}_{l,t,i}$ as:

$$\mathcal{G}_{l,t,i} = \begin{cases} (x_{l,t,i} \leftarrow \bot) & \text{if } (l,t,i) \equiv \texttt{taint}(x) \\ (x_{l,t,i} \leftarrow \top) & \text{if } (l,t,i) \equiv \texttt{untaint}(x) \\ (x_{l,t,i} \leftarrow \{a\}) & \text{if } (l,t,i) \equiv x := \texttt{unop}(a) \\ (x_{l,t,i} \leftarrow \{a,b\}) & \text{if } (l,t,i) \equiv x := \texttt{binop}(a,b) \end{cases}$$

When $x := \texttt{unop}(a)$, we say x *inherits (metadata) from* a and likewise $x := \texttt{binop}(a,b)$ indicates x *inherits (metadata) from* a *and* b. We use the set $S = \{\top, \bot, \{a\}, \{a,b\} | a, b \text{ are memory locations}\}$ to represent the set of all possible right-hand values in our mapping. We will also utilize the function `loc()` that given (l,t,i) returns x, where x is the destination location in instruction (l,t,i). As in Butterfly Analysis, $\mathcal{K}_{l,t,i}$ takes the form:

$$\mathcal{K}_{l,t,i} = \{(x_{l,t,j} \leftarrow s) | s \in S, j < i, \texttt{loc}(l,t,j) = \texttt{loc}(l,t,i)\}$$

$\mathcal{G}_b, \mathcal{K}_b$, GEN-SIDE-OUT$_b$ and GEN-SIDE-IN$_b$ all follow the reaching definitions template, but now track transfer functions instead of actual states. However, the LSOS and SOS still need to be states, as in reaching definitions. In general, we would like GEN to track $\bot$ and KILL to track $\top$. To convert between transfer functions and actual metadata, Butterfly Analysis introduced a `resolve`, or checking, algorithm: `resolve`(m,l,t,i) takes a memory location m which is the destination of instruction (l,t,i) and returns either $\top$ or $\bot$.

Resolving Transfer Functions to Taint Metadata. TAINTCHECK requires resolving potential inheritance relationships when the ordering between concurrent instructions is unknown. Our previous work [9] introduced an algorithm for "resolving" inheritance by recursively evaluating transfer functions in the wings, subject to two termination conditions: one for sequential consistency and one for relaxed memory models. The addition of vector clocks naturally prunes the search space any taint resolution algorithm has to explore: we associate the vector clock with each predecessor and verify that the current path of vector clocks is a VVO. The `resolve` algorithm is shown in Algorithm 1. Our `resolve` algorithm takes an input a tuple (m,l,t,i) and a set T of transfer functions, and returns the taint status of m at instruction (l,t,i). For brevity within `resolve`, `loc`(y_i) will refer to the destination of the instruction associated with y_i.

We define a *proper predecessor* of $x_{l,t,i} \leftarrow s$ to be any $y_{l',t',i'} \leftarrow s'$ such that $\texttt{loc}(l',t',i') \in s$, $s \in S$ and $v(l,t,i) \not< v(l',t',i')$.

The sequential consistency and relaxed memory consistency models termination conditions[6] are maintained. Now, `resolve` will only replace a predecessor $y_j \leftarrow s$ with a new predecessor $y_{j'} \leftarrow s'$ if, using vector clocks, the instruction associated with $y_{j'}$ *does not occur after* the instruction associated with y_j.

[6]The sequential consistency termination condition required ensuring that a sequence of proper predecessor replacement operations, when restricted to a single thread, only allowed replacement if the associated instruction occurred earlier within the thread; the relaxed memory consistency termination condition disallowed a predecessor to eventually be replaced by itself [9].

Algorithm 1 TAINTCHECK `resolve`(m,l,t,i)

Input: $m, (l,t,i), T$
Initialize $P(m,l,t,i)$ as the list of proper predecessors of $(x_{l,t,i} \leftarrow s)$ from T: $\{(y_0 \leftarrow s_0), \ldots, (y_k \leftarrow s_k)\}$, where $\texttt{loc}(y_i) \in s$.
for all $(y_j \leftarrow s_j) \in P(m,l,t,i)$ **do**
  if $s_j = \bot$ **then**
    Terminate with the rule $(x_{l,t,i} \leftarrow \bot)$.
  else if $s_j = \top$ **then**
    Remove the $(y_j \leftarrow \top)$ from $P(m,l,t,i)$, and continue
  Add the proper predecessors $(y'_{i'} \leftarrow s'_{i'}) \in T$ of $(y_j \leftarrow s_j)$ to $P(m,l,t,i)$, subject to a termination condition and verification that following these new arcs does not violate VVO rules.
Postcondition: Either $(x_{l,t,i} \leftarrow s)$ converges to $(x_{l,t,i} \leftarrow \bot)$, or $P(m,l,t,i)$ becomes empty. If $P(m,l,t,i)$ is empty, conclude $(x_{l,t,i} \leftarrow \top)$.

Converting Transfer Functions Into Metadata. We will use the function LASTCHECK(x,b), introduced in Butterfly Analysis, which represents the last taint status returned when resolving the metadata of location x in subblock b, modified to summarize a subblock b instead of a block (l,t). If x was the destination for an instruction in subblock b, then LASTCHECK(x,b) will return $\top$ or $\bot$; otherwise, it returns $\varnothing$. This serves as a proxy for $\mathcal{G}_b$ or $\mathcal{K}_b$ whenever we require states, not transfer functions.

Extracting GEN-SIDE-OUT into State. We introduce a new set DIDTAINT$_b$ for a maximal subblock b, which includes memory location m if there exists an instruction (l,t,i) contained within b for which m was the destination, and $\texttt{resolve}(m,l,t,i)$ returned $\bot$. More formally:

DIDTAINT$_b$ $= \{m | \exists (l,t,v), i \le v \le j, m = \texttt{loc}(l,t,v) \wedge \texttt{resolve}(m,l,t,v) \leftarrow \bot\}$

If the `resolve` function for a location m ever returns $\bot$, $m \in$ DIDTAINT$_b$. This set is now used in place of the GEN-SIDE-OUT whenever we need an actual state versus transfer functions.

At this point, we have almost completed the adaptation of TAINTCHECK into Chrysalis Analysis. We have $\mathcal{G}_b, \mathcal{K}_b$, GEN-SIDE-OUT and GEN-SIDE-IN, and when necessary can move between transfer functions and actual states.

Complications: Calculating $\text{IN}_b^{\mathcal{K}}$. One complication arises that was not an issue for Butterfly Analysis. Butterfly Analysis had a special case for updating the LSOS, which used the head. Because the head always executed before the body, LASTCHECK for the head was always available. In Section 4.3, our generalization of the update rules for the LSOS requires access to GEN-SIDE-OUT$_b$ as states, not transfer functions. We require them before we begin the second pass over subblock b, but they are not guaranteed to be available until after each thread completes its entire second pass. Recall the equations:

$$\text{DEL-INK}_{b'} = \{b'' | (v(b'') \sim v(b')) \vee ((v(b') < v(b'')) \wedge (v(b) \not< v(b'')))\}$$

$$\text{IN}_b^{\mathcal{K}} = \prod_{b' \in \text{pred}(b)} \left(\text{OUT}_{b'}^{\mathcal{K}} - \left(\bigcup_{b'' \in \text{DEL-INK}_{b'}} \text{GEN-SIDE-OUT}_{b''} \right) \right)$$

At first, it seems paradoxical. However, the situation is salvageable after making a key observation. If $b'' \in$ DEL-INK$_{b'}$ and $v(b'') \not< v(b)$, then $v(b'') \sim v(b)$. (To see this, suppose instead that $v(b'') > v(b)$. Because $b' \in \text{pred}(b)$, we have $v(b') < v(b)$, which implies $v(b') < v(b'')$. But then by the definition of DEL-

INK, $v(b) \not< v(b'')$, a contradiction.) In other words, when we first need to calculate $\text{IN}_b^{\mathcal{K}}$ before the second pass over block b, if not all of the actual $\text{DIDTAINT}_{b''}$ are available, at least the transfer functions are; and we will use them in the `resolve` process. As long as our `resolve` process is accurate, our second pass will still be accurate.

However, there is another use of $\text{IN}_b^{\mathcal{K}}$ and $\text{OUT}_b^{\mathcal{K}}$, namely, seeding the next epoch's initial $\text{IN}^{\mathcal{K}}$ for the same thread. To fix this, we make a second observation: All of the subblocks in epoch l^+ had correct and complete DIDTAINT sets available once their second pass was completed. Starting from the initial seed values of $\text{IN}^{\mathcal{K}}$ for the first subblock of epoch l in each thread, we can recompute $\text{IN}^{\mathcal{K}}$ and $\text{OUT}^{\mathcal{K}}$ for all subblocks so that the next sliding window can proceed. While not every subblock from epoch $l+1$ will have a DIDTAINT set ready, all subblocks (and their GEN-SIDE-OUT) in epoch $l+1$ remain available in the next sliding window.

Updating State. Once we have LASTCHECK_b and DIDTAINT_b as the state proxies for $\mathcal{G}_b$, $\mathcal{K}_b$, GEN-SIDE-OUT_b and GEN-SIDE-IN_b, we can calculate $\mathcal{G}_l$, $\mathcal{K}_l$ and SOS_l, using the same SOS update rules as reaching definitions. With $\text{IN}_b^{\mathcal{K}}$, $\text{OUT}_b^{\mathcal{K}}$, $\text{IN}_b^{\mathcal{G}}$ and $\text{OUT}_b^{\mathcal{G}}$, we can compute the LSOS.

THEOREM 7. *If* `resolve` *returns* $(x_{l,t,i} \leftarrow \top)$, *then there is no valid vector ordering of the instructions in epochs* $[0, (l+1)+]$ *such that* x *is* $\bot$ *at instruction* (l, t, i).

PROOF SKETCH. Suppose there were a VVO such that $x_{l,t,i} \leftarrow \bot$ at instruction (l, t, i). This implies a finite sequence of transfer functions $\hat{f}$ such that the associated instructions in order would (a) taint x and (b) obey all vector orderings. Our `resolve` algorithm will follow all valid vector orderings, so it would have discovered the $x_{l,t,i} \leftarrow \bot$ and returned $\bot$, a contradiction. □

It follows that any error detected by the original TAINTCHECK on a valid execution ordering for a given machine (with a memory model that at least obeys intra-thread dependences and supports cache coherence) will also be flagged by Chrysalis Analysis.

6. EVALUATION AND RESULTS

We now present our preliminary experimental evaluation of TAINTCHECK comparing the precision and performance of our TAINTCHECK implementation in Chrysalis Analysis to our implementation in Butterfly Analysis. Both the Chrysalis Analysis and Butterfly Analysis implementations of TAINTCHECK are new for this work.

6.1 Experimental Setup

Chrysalis Analysis, like Butterfly Analysis, is general purpose and can be implemented using a variety of dynamic analysis frameworks, including those based on binary instrumentation [3, 11, 14]. We built Chrysalis Analysis on top of the *Log-Based Architectures* (LBA) framework [4]. In LBA, every application thread is monitored by a dedicated lifeguard thread running on a core distinct from the application; as the application executes, a dynamic instruction trace is captured and transported to the lifeguard through a log that resides in the last-level on-chip cache. LBA itself is modeled using the Simics [23] full-system simulator.

We implemented a word-granularity version of TAINTCHECK in both Chrysalis and Butterfly Analyses. Some conservative assumptions were made in the `resolve` algorithm, such as setting a threshold for how many predecessors (set at 1024) we will follow before cutting off the `resolve` algorithm and conservatively tainting the destination. We tested our implementation on four Splash-2 benchmarks [25], shown in Table 2, where we synthetically tainted the benchmarks' input data. We tested two different configurations for both Butterfly and Chrysalis Analysis, shown in Table 3. To capture happens-before arcs, we leveraged the wrapper for shared library calls used by LBA [4] and generated vector clocks on the producer side, which were communicated to the lifeguard cores via the log.

Table 2: Splash-2 [25] benchmarks used in evaluation

Benchmark	Inputs
BARNES	512 bodies
FFT	$m = 14$ (2^{14} sized matrix)
FMM	512 bodies
LU	Matrix size: 128×128, $b = 16$

Table 3: Simulator Parameters used in evaluation

Simulation Parameters	
Cores	{4, 8} cores
Application/Lifeguard	{2/2, 4/4} Threads
L1-I, L1-D	64KB
L2	{2MB, 4MB}
Epoch boundaries	Insert every 8K instructions/thread (on average)[7]

Table 4: Potential errors reported by our lifeguard. Two configurations are shown, each with a Butterfly and Chrysalis implementation.

	4-core		8-core	
	Butterfly	Chrysalis	Butterfly	Chrysalis
BARNES	13	1	38	0
FFT	3	0	9	0
FMM	62	0	93	12
LU	5	0	10	0
Total	83	1	150	12

Our prior work on Butterfly Analysis [9], focusing on ADDRCHECK[8] as a lifeguard, assumed pointers to memory in the benchmarks tested were properly allocated and thus any reported errors were false positives. In contrast, our new TAINTCHECK tool reports *potential errors*. Due to the introduction of synthetic tainting, true positives are possible if taint flows from a synthetically tainted address to a jump target, for example. Accordingly, we treat the total number of potential errors reported as a ceiling for false positives encountered. The reduction in potential errors in our results comparing the Butterfly and Chrysalis precision numbers is entirely due to Butterfly reporting false positives due to the lack of happens-before arcs. The current Chrysalis implementation can only report potential errors, and not distinguish between false and true positives.

6.2 Results

The primary motivation for Chrysalis Analysis was improved precision relative to Butterfly Analysis. As shown in Table 4, precision in TAINTCHECK improved significantly compared to Butterfly Analysis for all benchmarks and both configurations (4- and

[7] We used LBA to generate and communicate epoch boundaries, inserting epoch boundaries after hn instructions had been executed by the entire application, where n is the number of application threads; h was set at 8K for these experiments.

[8] The extension of ADDRCHECK to Chrysalis Analysis appears in Appendix B.

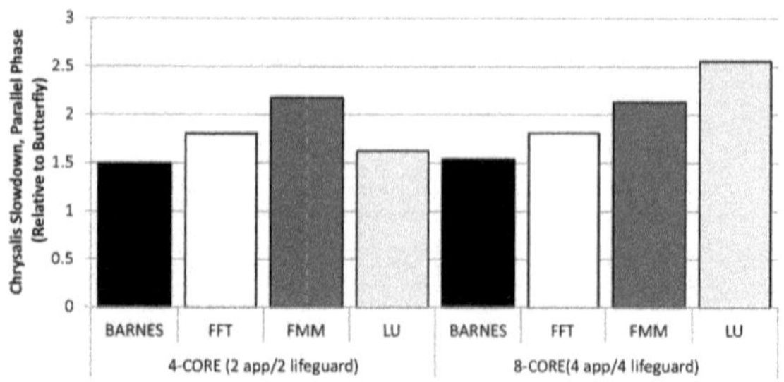

Figure 4: Chrysalis Analysis, normalized to Butterfly Performance.

8-core). Some false positives were possible in our implementation of TAINTCHECK as we made several conservative decisions in both the Chrysalis and Butterfly Analysis implementations, such as fixing a threshold for exploring predecessors in `resolve`, tracking taint status at word (instead of byte) granularity, and using synthetic tainting. Conservative decisions made in situations such as Figure 1(c), when there is not enough ordering information to precisely determine taint status, could also lead to a memory address being falsely tainted.

For the 4-core configuration, Chrysalis Analysis reports only one potential error across all benchmarks, on the BARNES run. The equivalent Butterfly Analysis 4-core BARNES run has 13 potential errors. On the 8-core configuration, the only Chrysalis Analysis run to report potential errrors is FMM. Its Butterfly Analysis counterpart has 93 potential errors, compared to 12 for Chrysalis, approximately a 7.8x reduction in false positives. The potential errors in the 8-core Chrysalis FMM run correspond primarily to starting and exiting a thread as well as `pthread_mutex_lock`. Note that the implementation of the high-level synchronization primitives that we capture cannot themselves be protected by the same high-level synchronization, so we may miss some arcs that would prevent races. *Over all benchmarks and configurations, Chrysalis Analysis improved precision by a factor of 17.9x relative to Butterfly Analysis.*

Next, we examine the performance overheads of Chrysalis Analysis relative to Butterfly Analysis. Across all benchmarks, the slowdowns range from 1.5x to less than 2.6x. Over all benchmarks and configurations, the geometric mean slowdown is approximately 1.9x. This is not an unreasonable tradeoff; an average of less than two-fold slowdown in exchange for a drastic improvement in precision. For BARNES, FFT, and FMM, the slowdowns remain fairly constant when comparing the 8-core configuration to the 4-core configuration, indicating that the Chrysalis Analysis implementation is scaling at the same rate as the Butterfly Analysis tool. There is an increase in overhead for the 8-core LU, but even in this case its overheads are still less than 2.6x.

Because our prototype of Chrysalis Analysis was intended to be a proof-of-concept rather than a highly tuned piece of software, we believe that the results shown in Figure 4 are conservative.

7. CONCLUSION

To retain the advantages of Butterfly Analysis while reducing the number of false positives, we have proposed and evaluated *Chrysalis Analysis*, which incorporates happens-before information from explicit software synchronization. Our implementation of the TAINTCHECK lifeguard demonstrates that Chrysalis Analysis reduces the number of false positives by 17.9x while increasing lifeguard overhead by an average of 1.9x.

Future work will focus on isolating actual errors from possible errors (where not enough information is known), further reducing false positives, and optimizing the implementation to reduce its overheads.

8. ACKNOWLEDGMENTS

This research was funded in part by the Intel Science and Technology Center for Cloud Computing, an Intel PhD Fellowship and by a grant from the National Science Foundation. The second author contributed to this work while with Intel Labs Pittsburgh.

References

[1] R. Baldoni and M. Klusch. Fundamentals of Distributed Computing: A Practical Tour of Vector Clock Systems. *IEEE Distributed Systems Online*, 3, February 2002.

[2] M. D. Bond, K. E. Coons, and K. S. McKinley. PACER: Proportional Detection of Data Races. In *PLDI*, 2010.

[3] D. Bruening. *Efficient, Transparent, and Comprehensive Runtime Code Manipulation*. PhD thesis, MIT, 2004.

[4] S. Chen, M. Kozuch, T. Strigkos, B. Falsafi, P. B. Gibbons, T. C. Mowry, V. Ramachandran, O. Ruwase, M. Ryan, and E. Vlachos. Flexible Hardware Acceleration for Instruction-grain Program Monitoring. In *ISCA*, 2008.

[5] M. Christiaens and K. De Bosschere. Accordion Clocks: Logical Clocks for Data Race Detection. In *Euro-Par 2001 Parallel Processing*, 2001.

[6] J. Chung, M. Dalton, H. Kannan, and C. Kozyrakis. Thread-Safe Dynamic Binary Translation using Transactional Memory. In *HPCA*, 2008.

[7] C. Flanagan and S. N. Freund. Adversarial Memory for Detecting Destructive Races. In *PLDI*, 2010.

[8] C. Flanagan and S. N. Freund. FastTrack: Efficient and Precise Dynamic Race Detection. In *PLDI*, 2009.

[9] M. L. Goodstein, E. Vlachos, S. Chen, P. B. Gibbons, M. A. Kozuch, and T. C. Mowry. Butterfly Analysis: Adapting Dataflow Analysis To Dynamic Parallel Monitoring. In *ASPLOS*, 2010.

[10] H. Kannan. Ordering Decoupled Metadata Accesses in Multiprocessors. In *MICRO*, 2009.

[11] C.-K. Luk, R. Cohn, R. Muth, H. Patil, A. Klauser, G. Lowney, S. Wallace, V. J. Reddi, and K. Hazelwood. Pin: Building Customized Program Analysis Tools with Dynamic Instrumentation. In *PLDI*, 2005.

[12] A. Muzahid, D. Suárez, S. Qi, and J. Torrellas. SigRace: Signature-Based Data Race Detection. In *ISCA*, 2009.

[13] N. Nethercote. *Dynamic Binary Analysis and Instrumentation*. PhD thesis, U. Cambridge, 2004. http://valgrind.org.

[14] N. Nethercote and J. Seward. Valgrind: A Framework for Heavyweight Dynamic Binary Instrumentation. In *PLDI*, 2007.

[15] N. Nethercote and J. Seward. Valgrind: A Program Supervision Framework. *Electronic Notes in Theoretical Computer Science*, 89 (2), 2003.

[16] J. Newsome and D. Song. Dynamic Taint Analysis for Automatic Detection, Analysis, and Signature Generation of Exploits on Commodity Software. In *NDSS*, 2005.

[17] S. Savage, M. Burrows, G. Nelson, P. Sobalvarro, and T. Anderson. Eraser: A Dynamic Race Detector for Multi-threaded Programs. *ACM Transactions on Computer Systems*, 15(4), 1997.

[18] K. Serebryany and T. Iskhodzhanov. ThreadSanitzer - Data Race Detection in Practice. In *WBIA*, 2009.

[19] M. Singhal and A. Kshemkalyani. An efficient implementation of vector clocks. *Inf. Process. Lett.*, 1992.

[20] SUN Microsystems, Inc. The SPARC Architecture Manual, 1991. version 8.

[21] R. E. Tarjan. Fast Algorithms for Solving Path Problems. *Journal of the ACM*, 28(3), 1981.

[22] G. Venkataramani, I. Doudalis, Y. Solihin, and M. Prvulovic. FlexiTaint: A Programmable Accelerator for Dynamic Taint Propagation. In *HPCA*, 2008.

[23] Virtutech Simics. http://www.virtutech.com/.

[24] E. Vlachos, M. L. Goodstein, M. A. Kozuch, S. Chen, B. Falsafi, P. B. Gibbons, and T. C. Mowry. ParaLog: Enabling and Accelerating Online Parallel Monitoring of Multithreaded Applications. In *ASPLOS*, 2010.

[25] S. C. Woo, M. Ohara, E. Torrie, J. P. Singh, and A. Gupta. The SPLASH-2 Programs: Characterization and Methodological Considerations. In *ISCA*, 1995.

[26] Y. Yu, T. Rodeheffer, and W. Chen. RaceTrack: Efficient Detection of Data Race Conditions via Adapative Tracking. In *SOSP*, 2005.

APPENDIX

A. AVAILABLE EXPRESSIONS

The adaptation of Available Expressions to Chrysalis Analysis proceeds in a similar manner to Reaching Definitions, with the roles of $\mathcal{G}$ and $\mathcal{K}$ reversed. We will show the equations for $\mathcal{G}$ and $\mathcal{K}$ at all granularities, or state when they are equivalent to Reaching Definitions. Due to the strong similarity, when proofs are equivalent up to refactoring $\mathcal{G}$ and $\mathcal{K}$, references to the corresponding proofs are provided instead of duplicating them.

A.1 Gen and Kill equations

Instruction Level. Let $\mathcal{G}_{l,t,i} = \{e\}$ if instruction (l, t, i) generates expression e. Let $\mathcal{K}_{l,t,i} = \{e|(l, t, i) \text{ kills } e\}$ (e.g., (l, t, i) may redefine e's terms).

Maximal Subblock-Level. The equations for dataflow at the maximal subblock level are equivalent to those of Reaching Definitions.

Kill-Side-Out/Kill-Side-In. We define KILL-SIDE-OUT$_b$, the analog of GEN-SIDE-OUT$_b$ in Reaching Definitions. As in Reaching Definitions, we now have KILL-SIDE-OUT$_b$ and KILL-SIDE-IN$_b$ at the maximal subblock level. For maximal subblock $b = (l, t, (j, k))$:

$$\text{KILL-SIDE-OUT}_b = \bigcup_{j \le i \le k} \mathcal{K}_{l,t,i}$$
$$\text{KILL-SIDE-IN}_b = \bigcup_{\{b'|v(b') \sim v(b)\}} \text{KILL-SIDE-OUT}_{b'}$$

Epoch-Level. In defining the epoch-level sets necessary for Available Expressions, we reuse the sets MB$_l$, AFTER$_b$, and NBEFORE$_b$ defined in Section 4.1. For an epoch l and maximal subblocks $b \in \text{MB}_{l^+}$, the epoch-level summaries are:

$$\mathcal{K}_l = \bigcup_{\{b|b \in \text{MB}_{l^+}\}} \left(\mathcal{K}_b - \bigcup_{b' \in \text{AFTER}_b} \mathcal{G}_{b'}\right)$$
$$\mathcal{G}_l = \bigcup_{\{b|b \in \text{MB}_{l^+}\}} \left(\mathcal{G}_b - \bigcup_{\{b'|b' \in \text{NBEFORE}_b\}} \mathcal{K}_{b'}\right)$$

Once more, the roles of $\mathcal{K}$ and $\mathcal{G}$ are reversed compared to Reaching Definitions. This correspondence is evident in the correctness results we obtain for available expressions. The proofs to Lemmas 8 and 9 are quite similar to those of Lemmas 2 and 1, respectively, with the roles of $\mathcal{G}$ and $\mathcal{K}$ reversed. They are provided for completeness.

LEMMA 8. *If $e \in \mathcal{G}_l$ then $\forall$ valid vector orderings O of the instructions in $l-1$ through l^+, $e \in \mathcal{G}(O)$.*

PROOF. Suppose $e \in \mathcal{G}_l$. Then there must exist an instruction (l, t, k) in a maximal subblock b such that $e \in \mathcal{G}_b$ and for all subblocks b' such that $v(b) \sim v(b')$ or $v(b) < v(b')$, $e \notin \mathcal{K}_{b'}$. This follows from $e \in \mathcal{G}_l$. Consider any VVO O.

Consider the *suffix* of O beginning with instruction (l, t, k). By definition of VVO, the only instructions that can follow (l, t, k) are other instructions in b (while respecting data dependences), and instructions belonging to any maximal subblock b' which is concurrent with or strictly after b. We have shown that for such b', $e \notin \mathcal{K}_{b'}$, implying either b' never kills e or any kill of e in b' is followed by a subsequent generate of e also in b'. Applying the definition of VVO, if a generate of e in b' is followed by a kill of e in b', this would be reflected in O. In particular, it is also reflected in the suffix beginning with (l, t, k). Thus, for the suffix of O beginning with (l, t, k), if e is killed at all, it is guaranteed to be followed by a generate of e. So any kill of e in O either occurs strictly before (l, t, k) or else is followed by a generate of e. Either way, e reaches the end of O, thus $e \in \mathcal{G}(O)$. □

LEMMA 9. *If $\exists$ a valid vector ordering O of the instructions in l^+ such that $e \in \mathcal{K}(O)$ then $e \in \mathcal{K}_l$.*

PROOF. First, there must exist an instruction (l, t, i) in O such that (l, t, i) kills e and no subsequent instruction in O generates e. This follows from $e \in \mathcal{K}(O)$. This implies there is no instruction (l', t', i') such that $e \in \mathcal{G}_{(l',t',i')}$ and $v(l, t, i) < v(l', t', i')$ (by definition of VVO). Then let b be the maximal subblock containing (l, t, i). We know that $e \in \mathcal{K}_b$ (by construction) and that $e \notin \bigcup_{b' \in \text{AFTER}_b} \mathcal{G}_{b'}$, so $e \in \mathcal{K}_l$. □

A.2 Strongly Ordered State

The equation for computing SOS$_l$ is unchanged from Reaching Definitions (Section 4.2); the differences are captured in the new equations for $\mathcal{G}_l$ and $\mathcal{K}_l$. However, the correctness result we prove varies slightly compared to Reaching Definitions, reflecting the differences between showing the existence of an interleaving where a property holds (Reaching Definitions) and showing that a property holds across all interleavings (Available Expressions).

THEOREM 10. *If $e \in \text{SOS}_{l+2}$ then for all valid vector orderings O_l of instructions in epochs $[0, l^+]$, $e \in \mathcal{G}(O_l)$.*

PROOF. Our proof will proceed by induction on l. In the base case of $l = 0$, we have $e \in \text{SOS}_2 = \mathcal{G}_0$. Applying Lemma 8 proves the base case. Now assume the lemma is true for all $l < j$, and show for $l = j$. Suppose $e \in \text{SOS}_{l+2}$. Then either $e \in \mathcal{G}_l$ or $e \in \text{SOS}_{l+1} - \mathcal{K}_l$.

$e \in \mathcal{G}_l$: We need a slight generalization of Lemma 8. Consider any VVO O_l of epochs $[0, l^+]$. Again, there exists an instruction (l, t, k) in a maximal subblock b, $e \in \mathcal{G}_{l,t,k}$, such that $\forall b'$ where $v(b) \sim v(b')$ or $v(b) < v(b')$, $e \notin \mathcal{K}_{b'}$. We again consider the suffix of O_l beginning at (l, t, k), and reach the same conclusion as Lemma 8. So $e \in \mathcal{G}(O_l)$.

$e \in \text{SOS}_{l+1} - \mathcal{K}_l$: Both $e \in \text{SOS}_{l+1}$ and $e \notin \mathcal{K}_l$ hold. Consider any VVO O_l of epochs $[0, l^+]$. Let O' be the restriction of O_l to epochs $[0, (l-1)^+]$. Applying the inductive hypothesis, we know that $e \in \mathcal{G}(O')$. There must be some instruction (l', t, k) in O' such $e \in \mathcal{G}_{l',t,k}$ and no instruction after (l', t, k) in O' kills e. We now return to O_l, and consider the suffix of O_l beginning with (l', t, k). The difference in the two suffixes must be solely made up of instructions from l^+.

By the contrapositive of Lemma 9, we know that no VVO O'' of instructions in l^+ can kill e. It follows that no suffix of O'' can kill e. Integrating a suffix of O'' which does not kill e with the suffix of O' beginning with (l', t, k) (also composed of instructions which do not kill e) cannot kill e, so the suffix beginning at (l', t, k) in O_l must generate e; thus $e \in \mathcal{G}(O_l)$.

□

A.3 Local Strongly Ordered State

LSOS: Representing KILL As Transfer Functions. The $\text{OUT}_b^{\mathcal{K}}/\text{IN}_b^{\mathcal{K}}$ sets in Available Expressions strongly correspond to $\text{OUT}_b^{\mathcal{G}}/\text{IN}_b^{\mathcal{G}}$ in Reaching Definitions. As in Reaching Definitions, the meet operator ($\sqcap$) for Available Expressions is union($\cup$). These represent the expressions which should be killed in the LSOS_b as compared to the SOS_l.

$$\mathrm{OUT}_b^{\mathcal{K}} = \mathcal{K}_b \cup (\mathrm{IN}_b^{\mathcal{K}} - \mathcal{G}_b)$$

$$\mathrm{IN}_b^{\mathcal{K}} = \begin{cases} \varnothing & \text{if } b \text{ is a thread's 1st subblock at level } l-1 \\ \bigsqcap_{b' \in \mathrm{pred}(b)} \mathrm{OUT}_{b'}^{\mathcal{K}} & \text{otherwise} \end{cases}$$

In our correctness result, we reuse the notation $\mathrm{HB}(b)$ as defined in Section 4.3.

LEMMA 11. *If $\exists$ a valid vector ordering O of the instructions in $\mathrm{HB}(b)$ such that $e \in \mathcal{K}(O)$ then $e \in \mathrm{IN}_b^{\mathcal{K}}$.*

The proof for Lemma 11 is essentially identical to Lemma 4, with the roles of $\mathcal{K}$ and $\mathcal{G}$ reversed.

LSOS: Representing GEN As Transfer Functions. The $\mathrm{IN}_b^{\mathcal{G}}/\mathrm{OUT}_b^{\mathcal{G}}$ sets in Available Expression strongly correspond to $\mathrm{IN}_b^{\mathcal{K}}/\mathrm{OUT}_b^{\mathcal{K}}$ in Reaching Definitions. These represent the expressions which should be added to the LSOS_b as compared to SOS_l.

$$\mathrm{OUT}_b^{\mathcal{G}} = \mathcal{G}_b \cup (\mathrm{IN}_b^{\mathcal{G}} - \mathcal{K}_b)$$

$$\text{DEL-ING}_{b'} = \{b'' | (v(b'') \sim v(b')) \vee ((v(b') < v(b'')) \wedge (v(b) \not< v(b'')))\}$$

$$\mathrm{IN}_b^{\mathcal{G}} = \begin{cases} \varnothing & \text{if } b \text{ is a thread's 1st subblock at level } l-1 \\ \bigsqcap_{b' \in \mathrm{pred}(b)} (\mathrm{OUT}_{b'}^{\mathcal{G}} - \\ \quad (\cup_{b'' \in \text{DEL-INK}_{b'}} \text{KILL-SIDE-OUT}_{b''})) & \text{otherwise} \end{cases}$$

LEMMA 12. *If $e \in \mathrm{IN}_b^{\mathcal{G}}$ then $\forall$ valid vector orderings O composed solely of all instructions from maximal subblocks b' such that $v(b') < v(b)$, $e \in \mathcal{G}(O)$.*

The proof for Lemma 12 is essentially identical to the proof of Lemma 5, with the roles of $\mathcal{G}$ and $\mathcal{K}$ reversed.

Creating LSOS. As with the SOS, the equation for the LSOS is unchanged compared to Reaching Definitions: $\mathrm{LSOS}_b = \mathrm{IN}_b^{\mathcal{G}} \cup (\mathrm{SOS}_l - \mathrm{IN}_b^{\mathcal{K}})$. The differences have been folded into the equations for $\mathrm{IN}_b^{\mathcal{G}}$ and $\mathrm{IN}_b^{\mathcal{K}}$.

THEOREM 13. *If $e \in \mathrm{LSOS}_b$, then $\forall$ valid vector orderings O of the instructions from epochs $[0, (l-2)^+]$ and $\mathrm{HB}(b)$, $e \in \mathcal{G}(O)$.*

PROOF. Suppose $e \in \mathrm{LSOS}_b$. Then either $e \in \mathrm{IN}_b^{\mathcal{G}}$ or $e \in \mathrm{SOS}_l - \mathrm{IN}_b^{\mathcal{K}}$.

$e \in \mathrm{IN}_b^{\mathcal{G}}$: Then $e \in \mathcal{G}(O)$ by application of Lemma 12.

$e \in \mathrm{SOS}_l - \mathrm{IN}_b^{\mathcal{K}}$: In this case, $e \in \mathrm{SOS}_l$ and $e \notin \mathrm{IN}_b^{\mathcal{K}}$. Applying Theorem 10, we know that for every VVO O' of instructions in epochs $[0, (l-2)^+]$, $e \in \mathcal{G}(O')$. The contrapositive of Lemma 11 implies that no VVO composed solely of instructions in $\mathrm{HB}(b)$ will kill e. Finally, we note that if a sequence of instructions does not kill an expression e, then interleaving that sequence of instructions with an O' which generates e (while maintaing all properties of a VVO) must still generate e. Thus, $e \in \mathcal{G}(O)$.

□

Applying the Two-Pass Algorithm. Available Expressions is also implemented as a two pass algorithm. In the first pass, $\mathcal{G}_b$, $\mathcal{K}_b$ and KILL-SIDE-OUT_b are calculated. When all threads complete the first pass, threads begin the second pass. During the second pass, threads wait for their predecessors b' to compute $\mathrm{OUT}_{b'}^{\mathcal{G}}$ and $\mathrm{OUT}_{b'}^{\mathcal{K}}$ so they can compute the $\mathrm{IN}_b^{\mathcal{G}}$, $\mathrm{IN}_b^{\mathcal{K}}$ and ultimately LSOS_b. The KILL-SIDE-IN_b can be computed on demand during the second pass. Finally, after all threads complete the second pass, the SOS is updated.

B. ADDRCHECK

As in Butterfly Analysis, we model ADDRCHECK on available expressions. Allocations will "generate" the memory location "expression", and deallocations kill such "expressions". Let $\mathcal{G}_{l,t,i} = \{m\}$ if and only if instruction (l,t,i) allocates memory location m and otherwise $\varnothing$. Likewise, $\mathcal{K}_{l,t,i} = \{m\}$ if and only if instruction (l,t,i) deallocates memory location m and otherwise $\varnothing$. $\mathcal{G}_b$, $\mathcal{K}_b$, $\mathcal{G}_l$, $\mathcal{K}_l$, $\mathrm{IN}_b^{\mathcal{G}}$, $\mathrm{IN}_b^{\mathcal{K}}$, SOS and LSOS all take their form from the Available Expressions template. In addition, ADDRCHECK tracks a unified read/write set called ACCESS.

We extend the two modes of checking, local and isolation, introduced by Butterfly Analysis. Local checking verifies that any address that was accessed or deallocated in a thread's maximal subblock was locally allocated at the start of the subblock; it also verifies that any address that was allocated in a thread's maximal subblock was locally deallocated at the start of the subblock. Isolation checking ensures that these local checks do not miss interference by another thread; for example, if Thread 1 believes address m to be locally allocated, but was unaware it had been recently freed by Thread 2.

Local Checks. As in Butterfly Analysis, local checks are resolved via LSOS lookups. The formulas for the LSOS generalize in the same ways the formulas for available expressions were generalized.

Isolation Checks and Summaries. Isolation checks again utilize a *summary*, which is now for a maximal subblock b instead of a block (l,t). A summary is represented as $s_b = (\mathcal{G}_b, \mathcal{K}_b, \mathrm{ACCESS}_b)$, where ACCESS_b contains all addresses that subblock b read or wrote.

We create a "side-in" summary:

$$S_b = (\bigcup_{\{b' | v(b') \sim v(b)\}} \mathcal{G}_{b'}, \bigcup_{\{b' | v(b') \sim v(b)\}} \mathcal{K}_{b'}, \bigcup_{\{b' | v(b') \sim v(b)\}} \mathrm{ACCESS}_{b'}).$$

To verify isolation, we check that the following set is empty:

$$((s_b.\mathcal{G}_{l,t} \cup s_b.\mathcal{K}_{l,t}) \bigcap (S_b.\mathcal{G}_{l,t} \cup S_b.\mathcal{K}_{l,t})) \bigcup (s_b.\mathrm{ACCESS}_{l,t} \bigcap (S_b.\mathcal{G}_{l,t} \cup S_b.\mathcal{K}_{l,t})) \bigcup (S_b.\mathrm{ACCESS}_{l,t} \bigcap (s_b.\mathcal{G}_{l,t} \cup s_b.\mathcal{K}_{l,t}))$$

and otherwise flag an error.

THEOREM 14. *Any error detected by the sequential ADDRCHECK on a valid vector ordering O for a given machine will also be flagged by Chrysalis Analysis.*

PROOF SKETCH. The correctness proof follows the lines of the corresponding proof in the Butterfly Analysis paper [9]. Observe that ADDRCHECK detects errors based on a pairwise interactions between operations (i.e., allocations, accesses and frees). Suppose there was an execution E such that a sequential ADDRCHECK would have caught an error on memory location x. Represent this execution as E, with $E|x$ the execution restricted to operations utilizing x. By the assumptions of Chrysalis Analysis, a VVO O must exist such that $O|x$, is equivalent to $E|x$. Since Chrysalis Analysis will take O into account, it will also catch the error. □

Probabilistic Diagnosis of Performance Faults in Large-Scale Parallel Applications *

Ignacio Laguna†, Dong H. Ahn§, Bronis R. de Supinski§, Saurabh Bagchi†, Todd Gamblin§

†Purdue University, School of Electrical and Computer Engineering, West Lafayette, IN 47907
{ilaguna, sbagchi}@purdue.edu

§Lawrence Livermore National Laboratory, Computation Directorate, Livermore, CA 94550
{ahn1, bronis, tgamblin}@llnl.gov

ABSTRACT

Debugging large-scale parallel applications is challenging. Most existing techniques provide mechanisms for process control but little information about the causes of failures. Most debuggers also scale poorly despite continued growth in supercomputer core counts. Our novel, highly scalable tool helps developers to understand and to fix performance failures and correctness problems at scale. Our tool probabilistically infers the least progressed task in MPI programs using Markov models of execution history and dependence analysis. This analysis guides program slicing to find code that may have caused a failure. In a blind study, we demonstrate that our tool can isolate the root cause of a particularly perplexing bug encountered at scale in a molecular dynamics simulation. Further, we perform fault injections into two benchmark codes and measure the scalability of the tool. Our results show that it accurately detects the least progressed task in most cases and can perform the diagnosis in a fraction of a second with thousands of tasks.

Categories and Subject Descriptors

D.2.5 [**Software Engineering**]: Testing and Debugging—*Distributed debugging, Debugging aids*

General Terms

Reliability, Performance

1. INTRODUCTION

Debugging errors and abnormal conditions in large-scale parallel applications is difficult. While High Performance Computing (HPC) applications have grown in complexity and scale, debugging tools have not kept up. Most tools cannot scale to the process counts of the largest systems. More importantly, most tools provide little insight into the causes of failures. The situation is particularly challenging for performance faults (e.g., slow code regions) and correctness problems (e.g., deadlocks), which may manifest in different code or on a different process from their causes.

We present a framework that provides insight into performance faults in large-scale parallel applications[1]. Our framework identifies the *least progressed (LP)* task (or tasks) probabilistically in parallel code by using a Markov Model (MM) as a lightweight, statistical summary of each task's control-flow history. MM states represent MPI calls and computation, and edges represent state transitions (i.e., transfer of control between two code regions). This model lets us associate faults with code locations. However, in parallel applications, faults may lie on separate tasks from their root causes, so we introduce *progress dependence* to diagnose performance faults in parallel applications. We create a *progress dependence graph* (PDG) to capture wait chains of non-faulty tasks that depend on the faulty task to progress. We use these chains to find the LP task in parallel. Once we find the LP task, we apply program slicing [35] on the task's state to identify code that may have caused it to fail. We implement this framework as an extension to the *AutomaDeD* (Automata-based debugging for dissimilar parallel tasks) tool [9, 23].

To ensure scalability, we use a novel, fully distributed algorithm to create the PDG. Our algorithm uses minimal per-task information, and it incurs only slight runtime overhead for the applications we tested. Our implementation of *AutomaDeD* is non-intrusive, using the MPI profiling interface to intercept communication calls, and it does not require separate daemons to trace the application as other tools do (e.g., TotalView [26], STAT [5]).

This paper makes the following contributions:

- The concept of progress dependence between tasks and its use for diagnosing performance faults;
- A scalable, distributed, probabilistic algorithm to create a PDG and to discover the LP task;
- A practical way to apply backward slicing to find the

*This material is partly based upon work supported by the National Science Foundation under Grant No. CNS-0916337. (LLNL-PROC-548642)

[1]A failure is a deviation from specification, while a fault may cause failures. A hang is a failure, while a fault is a code segment that sends an incorrect message.

PACT'12, September 19–23, 2012, Minneapolis, Minnesota, USA.

Sample code

```
10 // Computation code ...
11 MPI_Bcast(.., MPI_COMM_WORLD);
12 // ...
13 if (...) {
14   // ...
15   MPI_Reduce(..., comm_1);
16   // ...
17   MPI_Barrier(comm_1);
18 } else {
19   //...
20   MPI_Bcast(..., comm_2);
21 }
22 // ...
```

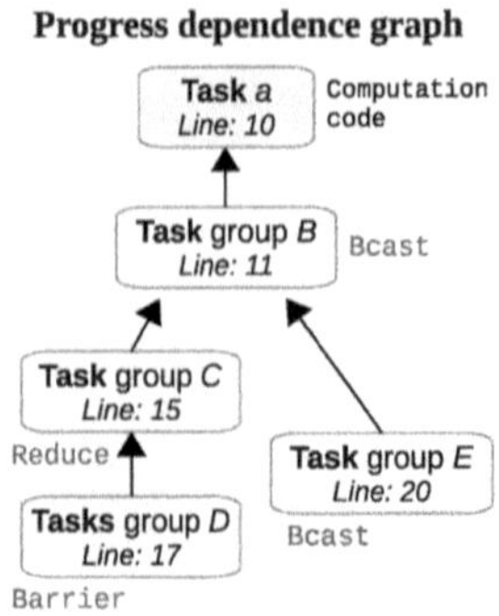

Figure 1: Progress dependence graph example.

origin of a fault from the state of the LP task in a faulty execution.

We evaluate *AutomaDeD* by performing fault injections on AMG2006 and LAMMPS, two of the ASC Sequoia benchmarks. *AutomaDeD* finds a faulty task in a fraction of a second on up to 32,768 tasks. *AutomaDeD* accurately identifies the LP task 88% of the time, with perfect precision 86% of the time. We show that *AutomaDeD* can diagnose a difficult bug in a molecular dynamics code [28] that manifested only with 7,996 or more processes. *AutomaDeD* quickly found the fault — a sophisticated deadlock condition.

The rest of the paper is organized as follows. Section 2 presents an overview of our approach and Sections 3 and 4 detail our design and implementation. Section 5 presents our case study and fault injection experiments.

2. OVERVIEW OF THE APPROACH

2.1 Progress Dependence Graph

A *progress-dependence graph* (PDG) represents dependencies that prevent tasks from making further execution progress at any given time. It facilitates pinpointing performance faults that cause failures such as program stalls, deadlocks and slow code regions, and in performance tuning the application (e.g., by highlighting tasks with the least progress).

A PDG starts with the observation that two or more tasks must execute an MPI collective in order for (all of) them to move forward in the execution flow. For example, `MPI_Reduce` is often implemented in MPI using a binomial tree for short messages [30]. Since the MPI standard does not require collectives to be synchronized, some tasks could enter and leave this state — the `MPI_Reduce` function call — while others remain in it. Tasks that only send messages in the binomial tree enter and leave this state, while tasks that receive (and later send) messages block in this state until the corresponding sender arrives. These blocked tasks are *progress dependent* on other (possibly delayed) tasks.

This definition formalizes progress dependence: *Let the set of tasks that participate in a collective operation be* X. *If a task subset* $Y \subseteq X$ *has reached the collective operation while another task subsets* $Z \subseteq X$, *where* $X = Y \cup Z$ *has not yet reached it at time* t *such that the tasks in* Y *blocked at* t *waiting for tasks in* Z *then* Y *is progress-dependent on* Z, *which we denote as* $Y \xrightarrow{pd} Z$.

Figure 1 shows an example PDG in which task a blocks in (computation code) line 10. Task a could block for many reasons, such as a deadlock due to incorrect thread-level synchronization. As a consequence, a group of tasks B block in `MPI_Bcast` in line 11 while other tasks proceed to other code regions — tasks group C, D and E block in code lines 15, 17, and 20. No progress-dependence exists between groups C and E because they are in different execution branches.

Point-to-Point Operations: In blocking point-to-point operations such as `MPI_Send` and `MPI_Recv`, the dependence is only on the peer task, which we formalize as: *If task* x *blocks when sending (receiving) a message to (from) task* y *at time* t *then* x *is progress dependent on* y, *i.e.*, $x \xrightarrow{pd} y$. This definition also applies to nonblocking operations such as `MPI_Isend` and `MPI_Irecv`. The main difference is that the dependence does not apply directly to the send (or receive) operation, but to the associated completion (e.g., a wait or test operation). If a task x blocks on `MPI_Wait`, for example, we infer the task y, on which x is progress dependent, from the request on which x waits. Similarly, if x spins on a test, for example by calling `MPI_Test`, we infer the peer task on which x is progress dependent from the associated request. On the receiving end, we can also infer the dependence from other test operations such as `MPI_Probe` or `MPI_Iprobe`. In any case, we denote the progress dependence as $x \xrightarrow{pd} y$.

PDG-Based Diagnosis: A PDG can intuitively pinpoint the task (or task group) that originates a performance failure. In Figure 1, task a can be blamed for originating the program's stall since it has no progress dependence on any other task (or group of tasks) in the PDG. It is also the least progressed (LP) task.

From the programmer's perspective, the PDG provides useful information in debugging and performance tuning. First, given a performance failure such as the one in Figure 1, the PDG shows where to focus attention, i.e., the LP task(s). Thus, debugging time is substantially reduced, as the programmer can focus on the execution context of one (or a few) task(s) rather than on possibly thousands of tasks. Second, we can efficiently apply static or dynamic bug-detection methods based on the LP task(s) state. *AutomaDeD* applies slicing [35] using the state of the LP task as initial criterion, which substantially reduces the search space of slicing when compared to slicing the execution context of each task (or representative task group) separately and then combining this information to find the fault.

PDG Versus Other Dependency Graphs: A PDG is different from the dependency graph used in MPI deadlock detection [17, 18, 32]. A PDG hierarchically describes the execution progress of MPI tasks. It addresses questions such as: Which task has made the least progress? Which tasks does the LP task prevent from making progress? In contrast, knots in traditional dependency graphs can detect real and potential deadlocks. We do not detect deadlocks by checking for knots in a PDG. However, since a PDG combines dependencies arising from MPI operations, it can indicate that a deadlock caused a hang. Performance failures are a superset of hangs; deadlocks or other causes can lead to hangs. Our case study with a real-world bug in Section 5.1 shows an example in which we use a PDG to identify that a deadlock was the root-cause of a hang.

2.2 Workflow of Our Approach

Figure 2 shows the steps in *AutomaDeD* to diagnose performance problems. Steps 1–3 are distributed while steps 4–6 are performed in a single task.

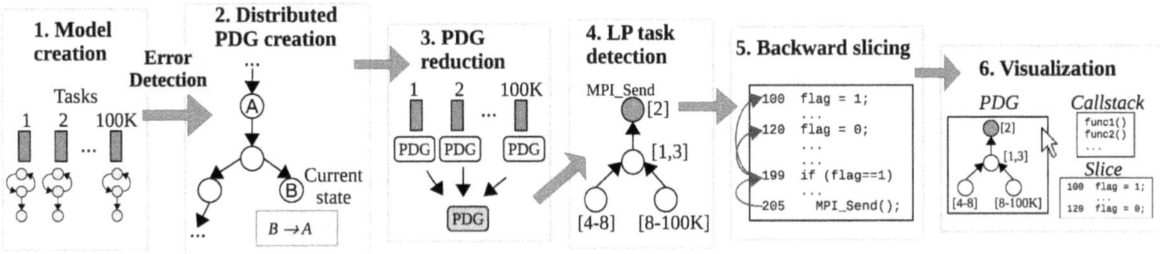

Figure 2: Overview of the diagnosis work flow.

(1) Model creation. *AutomaDeD* captures per-MPI-task control-flow behavior in a Markov model (MM). MM states correspond to two code region types: *communication* regions, i.e., code executed within an MPI function; and *computation* regions, i.e., code executed between two MPI functions. Other work uses similar Markov-like models (in particular semi-Markov models) to find similarities between tasks to detect errors [9, 23]. Our novel framework instead uses MMs to summarize control-flow execution history. No prior work to our knowledge uses MMs to infer progress dependencies.

(2) Distributed PDG creation. When a system detects a performance fault (either *AutomaDeD* or a third-party system), *AutomaDeD* uses a distributed algorithm to create a PDG in each task. First, we use an all-reduce over the MM state of each task, which provides each task with the state of all other tasks. Formally, if a task's local state is s_{local}, this operation provides each task with the set $S_{\text{others}} = s_1, \ldots, s_j, \ldots, s_N$, where $s_j \neq s_{\text{local}}$. Next, each task probabilistically infers its own local PDG based on s_{local} and S_{others}.

(3) PDG reduction. Our next distributed step reduces the PDGs from step (2) to a single PDG. The reduction operation is the union of edges in two PDGs, i.e., the union (in each step of the reduction) of progress dependencies.

(4) LP task detection. Based on the reduced PDG, we determine the LP task and its state (i.e., call stack and program counter), which we use in the next step.

(5) Backward slicing. We then perform backward slicing using Dyninst [3]. This step finds code that could have led the LP task to reach its current state.

(6) Visualization. Finally, *AutomaDeD* presents the program slice, the reduced PDG and its associated information. The user can attach a serial or parallel debugger to the LP task based on the PDG. The slice brings the programmer's attention to code that affected the LP task, and allows them to find the fault.

3. DESIGN

3.1 Summarizing Execution History

A simple approach to save the control-flow execution history directly might build a control-flow graph (CFG) based on executed statements [20]. Since large-scale MPI applications can have very large CFGs, *AutomaDeD* instead captures a compressed version of the control-flow behavior using our MM with communication and computation states. The edge weights capture the frequency of transitions between two states. Figure 3 shows how *AutomaDeD* creates MMs at runtime in each task. We use the MPI profiling interface

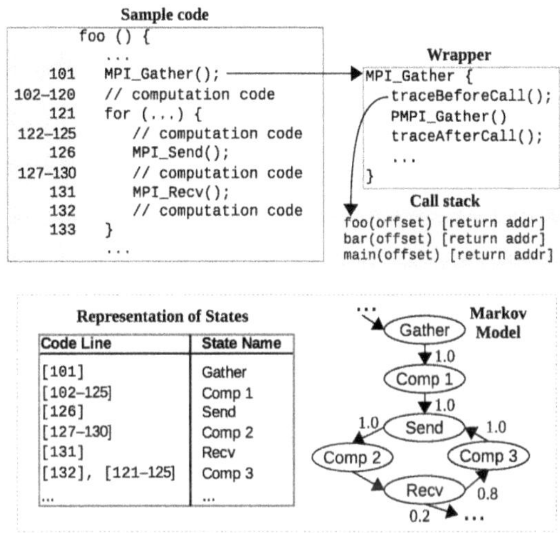

Figure 3: Markov model creation.

to intercept MPI routines. Before and after calling the corresponding PMPI routine, *AutomaDeD* captures information such as the call stack, offset address within each active function and return address. We assume that the MPI program is compiled using debugging information so that we can resolve function names.

3.2 Progress Dependence Inference

In this section, we discuss how we infer progress dependence probabilistically from our MMs. We restrict the discussion to dependencies that arise from collective operations, since dependencies from point-to-point operations do not require our probabilistic analysis. For example, if task t_i is waiting for another task in `MPI_Recv`, *AutomaDeD* uses the parameters of the MPI call to determine on which task t_i is progress-dependent. In cases when a task blocks in `MPI_Wait`, for example when using non-blocking operations, *AutomaDeD* uses request handlers to identify the matching progress-dependence task. We cannot infer progress dependence for `MPI_ANY_SOURCE`, in which case *AutomaDeD* omits this progress-dependence edge, which reflects the probabilistic nature of our approach.

AutomaDeD probabilistically infers progress dependence between a task's local state and the states of other tasks. Intuitively, our MM models the probability of going from state x to state y via *some* path $x \rightsquigarrow y$. If a task t_x in x must eventually reach y with high probability then we can determine that a task t_y in state y could be waiting for t_x in which case we infer that $y \xrightarrow{pd} x$ (for simplicity, we represent progress dependencies in terms of task states).

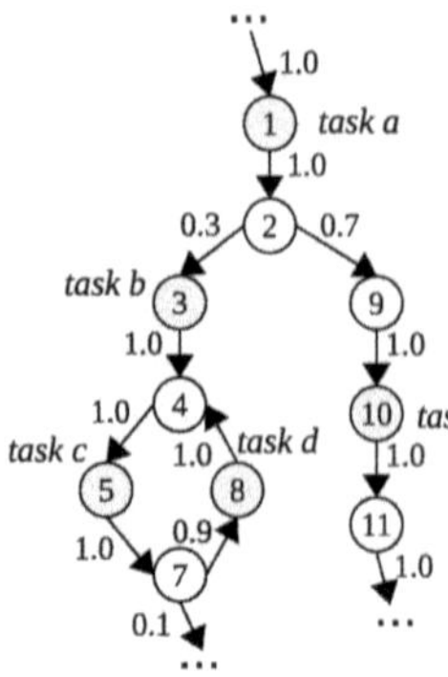

Figure 4: Sample MM with five blocked tasks.

Table 1: Dependence based on path probabilities.

$P(i,j)$			$P(j,i)$				
0	$0 < P < 1$	1	0	$0 < P < 1$	1	Dependence?	Type
✓			✓			No	
✓				✓		Yes	$t_i \xrightarrow{pd} t_j$
✓					✓	Yes	$t_i \xrightarrow{pd} t_j$
	✓		✓			Yes	$t_i \xleftarrow{pd} t_j$
	✓			✓		?	
	✓				✓	Yes	$t_i \xrightarrow{pd} t_j$
		✓	✓			Yes	$t_i \xleftarrow{pd} t_j$
		✓		✓		Yes	$t_i \xleftarrow{pd} t_j$
		✓			✓	?	

Figure 4 illustrates how we infer progress dependence from our MMs. Five tasks (a, b, c, d and e) are blocked in different states (1, 3, 5, 8, and 10 respectively). To estimate the progress dependence between task b and task c, we calculate that the path probability $P(3,5)$, the probability of going from state 3 to state 5 over all possible paths, which is 1.0. Thus, *task c is likely to be waiting for task b, since according to the observed execution, if a task is in state 3 it always must reach state 5.* To estimate progress dependence more accurately, we consider the possibility of loops and evaluate the backward path probability $P(5,3)$, which in this case is zero. Thus, task c cannot reach task b, so we can consider it to have progressed further than task b so $c \xrightarrow{pd} b$.

Resolving conflicting probability values. When a backward path probability $P(j,i)$ is zero, a task in state j has made more progress than a task in state i. However, if the forward path probability $P(i,j)$ is 1.0 and the backward path probability is nonzero then the task in state j might return to i. For example, for tasks d and c in Figure 4, $P(8,5) = 1.0$ but $P(5,8) = 0.9$. In this case, task d must eventually reach state 5 to exit the loop so we estimate that $c \xrightarrow{pd} d$; our results demonstrate that this heuristic works well in practice.

The dependence between task b and task e is null, i.e., no progress dependence exists between them. They are in different execution branches so the forward and backward path probabilities between their states, i.e., $P(3,10)$ and $P(10,3)$, are both zero. The same holds for the dependencies between task e and task c or d.

General progress dependence estimation. To estimate the progress dependence between tasks t_i and t_j in states i and j, we calculate two path probabilities: (i) a forward path probability $P(i,j)$; and (ii) a backward path probability $P(j,i)$. A path probability is the likelihood of going from one state to another over all possible paths. We use Table 1 to estimate progress dependencies. If both probabilities are zero (i.e., the tasks are in different execution branches), no dependence exists between the tasks. When one probability is 1.0 and the other is less than 1.0, the first *predominates* the second. Therefore, the second probability determines the dependence. For example, if the second is $P(j,i)$ we determine $t_j \xrightarrow{pd} t_i$ since execution goes from i to j. If one probability is zero and the second is nonzero, then the second predominates the first. Therefore, the first probability determines the dependence. For example, if the first is $P(i,j)$ we determine $t_i \xrightarrow{pd} t_j$ because execution could go from j to i but not from i to j.

We cannot determine progress dependence for two cases: when both probabilities are 1.0; and when both probabilities are in the range $0.0 < P < 1.0$. The first case could happen when two tasks are inside a loop and, due to an error, they do not leave the loop and block inside it. In this case both backward and forward path probabilities are 1.0, so it is an undefined situation. The probabilities in the second case simply do not provide enough information to decide. For these cases, *AutomaDeD* marks the edges in the PDG as undefined so that the user knows that the relationship could not be determined. These cases occur infrequently in our experimental evaluation. When they do, the user can usually determine the LP task by looking at tasks that are in one group or cluster. Section 5 gives examples of how the user can resolve these cases visually.

```
Input: mm (Markov model), closure (transitive closure
of the mm), statesSet (set of states)
Output: depMatrix (PDG adjacency-matrix representation)

progressDependenceGraph() { /* Builds PDG */
  State localState ← getLocalState(mm)
  for each State s in statesSet
    if s is not localState {
      d ← dependence(localState , s)
      depMatrix[localState , s] ← d
    }
}

/* Calculates dependence between two states */
dependence(State src , State dst) {
  p ← probability(src , dst)
  d ← dependenceBasedOnTable(p)
  return d
}

/* Calculates reachability probability */
probability(State src , State dst) {
  p ← 0
  if src can reach dst in closure {
    for each Path p between src and dst
      p ← p + pathProbability(src , dst)
  }
  return p
}
```

Figure 5: Algorithm to create the PDG.

Algorithm. Figure 5 shows our local PDG construction algorithm, which takes an MM and *statesSet*, the states of all other tasks as input. We compute the dependency between the local state and *statesSet*. We represent dependencies as integers (0: no dependence; 1: forward dependence; 2: backward dependence; 3: undefined). We save the PDG in an adjacency matrix. The function `dependence` determines

Table 2: Some examples of dependence unions.

No	Task x	Task y	Union	Reasoning	OR operation
1	$i \rightarrow j$	null	$i \rightarrow j$	first dependence dominates	$1 + 0 = 1$
2	$i \rightarrow j$	$i \rightarrow j$	$i \rightarrow j$	same dependence	$1 + 1 = 1$
3	$i \leftarrow j$	$i \leftarrow j$	$i \leftarrow j$	same dependence	$2 + 2 = 2$
4	$i \rightarrow j$	$i \leftarrow j$	$i?j$	undefined	$1 + 2 = 3$
5	null	null	null	no dependence	$0 + 0 = 0$

dependencies based on all-path probabilities (calculated in `probability`) and Table 1 (captured in `dependenceBasedOnTable`).

The overall complexity of the algorithm is $O(s \times (|V| + |E|))$, where s is the number of states in *statesSet*, and $|V|$ and $|E|$ are the numbers of states and edges of the MM. In practice, the MMs are sparse graphs in which $|E| \approx |V|$, so the complexity is approximately $O(s \times |E|)$.

Comparison to postdominance. Our definition of progress dependence is similar to the concept of postdominance [12] in which a node j of a CFG postdominates a node i if every path from i to the *exit* node includes j. However, our definition does not require the *exit* node to be in the MM (postdominance algorithms require it to create a postdominator tree). Since a fault could cause the program to stop in any state, we are not guaranteed to have an exit node within a loop. Techniques such as assigning a dummy exit node to a loop do not work in general for fault diagnosis because a faulty execution makes it difficult (or impossible) to determine the right exit node. In order to use postdominance theory, we could use static analysis to find the exit node and map it to a state in the MM. However, our dynamic analysis approach is more robust and should provide greater scalability and performance.

4. SCALABLE PDG-BASED ANALYSIS

AutomaDeD is implemented in C++ and uses the Boost Graph Library [2] for graph-related algorithms such as depth-first search. In this section, we focus on the implementation details that ensure scalability.

4.1 Error Detection

We assume that a performance problem has been detected, for example, because the application is not producing the expected output in a timely manner. The user can then use *AutomaDeD* to find the tasks and the associated code region that caused the problem. *AutomaDeD* includes a timeout detection mechanism that can trigger the diagnosis analysis, and it can infer a reasonable timeout threshold (based on the mean time and standard deviation of state transitions). The user can also supply the timeout as an input parameter. Our experiments with large-scale HPC applications found that a 60 second threshold is sufficient.

4.2 Distributed Inference of the PDG

Helper thread. *AutomaDeD* uses a helper thread to analyze the MM (that is built in the main thread). The core of the dependence inference, Steps 2–3 in Figure 2, is distributed while only one task (MPI rank 0 by default) performs the inexpensive operations in Steps 4–6. *AutomaDeD* uses `MPI_THREAD_MULTIPLE` to initialize MPI so that multiple threads can call MPI. On machines that do not support threads, such as BlueGene/L, we save all MMs to the parallel file system when we detect an error. *AutomaDeD* then reads these MMs for analysis in a separate MPI program.

Distributed algorithm. The following steps provide more detail of Steps 2–3 in the workflow:
(1) We first perform a reduction over the current state of all tasks to compute the *statesSet* of all tasks.
(2) We next broadcast *statesSet* to all tasks.
(3) Each task uses the algorithm in Figure 5 to compute its local PDG from its local state and *statesSet*.
(4) Finally, a reduction of the local PDGs calculates the union of the edges (forward or backward). Table 2 shows examples of some union results. In case 1, a dependence is present in only one task so the dependence predominates. In cases 2 and 3, the dependencies are similar so we retain it. In case 4, they conflict so the resulting dependence is undefined. We efficiently implement this operator using bitwise `OR` since we represent dependencies as integers.

We cannot use `MPI_Reduce` for our reduction steps (for example, tasks can contribute states of different sizes) so we implement custom reductions that use binomial trees. These operations have $O(\log p)$ complexity where p is the number of tasks. Assuming a scalable broadcast implementation, the overall complexity is also $O(\log p)$. Our algorithm can therefore scale to the task counts found on even the largest HPC systems.

4.3 Determination of LP Task

We compute the LP task (or task group) from the reduced PDG. *AutomaDeD* first finds nodes with no outgoing edges based on dependencies from collectives and marked them as LP. If more than one node is found, *AutomaDeD* discards nodes that have point-to-point dependencies on other non-LP tasks in different branches. Since *AutomaDeD* operates on a probabilistic framework (rather than on deterministic methods [5]), it can incorrectly pinpoint the LP task, although such errors are rare according to our evaluation. However, in most of these cases, the user can still determine the LP task by visually examining the PDG (by looking for nodes with only one task).

4.4 Guided Application of Program Slicing

Background. Program slicing transforms a large program into a smaller one that contains only statements that are relevant to a particular variable or statement. For debugging, we only care about statements that could have led to the failure. However, message-passing programs complicate program slicing since we must reflect dependencies related to message operations.

We can compute a program slice statically or dynamically. We can use static data and control flow analysis to compute a static slice [35], which is valid for all possible executions. Dynamic slicing [22] only considers a particular execution so it produces smaller and more accurate slices for debugging.

Most slicing techniques that have been proposed for debugging message-passing programs are based on dynamic slicing [21, 25, 27]. However, dynamically slicing of a message-passing program usually does not scale well. Most proposed techniques have complexity at least $O(p)$. Further, the dynamic approach suffers high costs to generate traces of each task (typically by code instrumentation) and to aggregate those traces centrally to construct the slice. Some approaches reduce the size of dynamic slices by using a global predicate rather than a variable [25, 27]. However, the violation of the global predicate may not provide sufficient information to diagnose failures in complex MPI programs.

We can use static slicing if we allow some inaccuracy. However, we cannot naively apply data-flow analysis (which slicing uses) in message-passing programs [29]. For example, consider the following code fragment:

```
1 program() {
2   ...
3   if (rank == 0) {
4     x = 10;
5     MPI_Send(...,&x,...);
6   } else {
7     MPI_Recv(...,&y,...);
8     result = y * z;
9     printf(result);
10    ...
```

Traditional slicing on `result` in line 9 identifies statements 7, 8, and 9 as the only statements in the slice, but statements 3–9 should be in the slice. Statements 4-5 should be in the slice because the value x sent is received as y which obviously influences z. Thus, we must consider the SPMD nature of the program in order to capture communication dependencies. The major problem with this *communication-aware slicing* is the high cost of analyzing a large dependence graph [29] to construct a slice based on a particular statement or variable. Further, the MPI developer must decide on which tasks to apply communication-aware static slicing since applying it to every task is infeasible at large scales.

Approach. *AutomaDeD* progressively applies slicing to the execution context of tasks that are representative of behavioral groups, starting with the groups that are most relevant to the failure based on the PDG. *AutomaDeD* uses the following algorithm:

(1) Initialize an empty slice S.

(2) Iterate over PDG nodes from the node corresponding to the LP task to nodes that depend on it, and so on to the leaf nodes (i.e., the most progressed tasks).

(3) In each iteration i, $S = S \bigcup s_i$ where s_i is the statement set produced from the state of a task in node i.

This slicing method reduces the complexity of manually applying static slicing to diagnose a failure. The user can simply start with the most important slice (i.e., the one associated with the LP task) and progressively augment it by clicking the "next" button in a graphical interface, until the fault is found.

5. EVALUATION

We demonstrate how *AutomaDeD* diagnose a difficult bug in a molecular dynamics program that manifested only at large scale. We also perform 280 experiments to evaluate *AutomaDeD* in a controlled setting: 50 fault injection experiments; 160 slowdown and memory usage experiments; and 70 scalability experiments. The next sections provide the experimental settings and main results.

5.1 Case Study

An application scientist challenged us to locate an elusive error in ddcMD, a parallel classical molecular-dynamic code [28]. The bug manifested as a hang that emerged intermittently only when run on Blue Gene/L with 7,996 MPI tasks. Although he had already identified and fixed the error after significant time and effort, he hoped that we could provide a technique that would not require tens of hours. In this section, we present a blind case study, in which we were supplied no details of the error, that demonstrates *AutomaDeD* can efficiently locate the origin of faults.

Figure 6 shows the result of our analysis. Our tool first detects the hang condition when the code stops making progress, which triggers the PDG analysis to identify MPI task 3,136 as the LP task — *AutomaDeD* first detects tasks 3,136 and 6,840 as LP tasks and then eliminates 6,840 since it is point-to-point dependent on task 0, a non-LP task, in the left branch. The LP task in the `a` state, causes tasks in the `b` state that immediately depend on its progress to block, ultimately leading to a global stall through the chain of progress dependencies. This analysis step reveals that task 3,136 stops progressing as it waits on an `MPI_Recv` within the `Pclose_forWrite` function. Once it identifies the LP task, *AutomaDeD* applies backward slicing starting from the `a` state, which identifies `dataWritten` as the data variable that most immediately pertains to the current point of execution. Slicing then highlights all statements that could directly or indirectly have affected its state.

The application scientist verified that our analysis precisely identified the location of the fault. ddcMD implements a user-level, buffered file I/O layer called `pio`. MPI tasks call various `pio` functions to move their output to local per-task buffers and later call `Pclose_forWrite` to flush them out to the parallel file system. Further, in order to avoid an I/O storm at large scales, `pio` organizes tasks into I/O groups. Within each group, one writer task performs the actual file I/O on behalf of all other group members. A race condition in the complex writer nomination algorithm — optimized for a platform-specific I/O forwarding constraint — and overlapping consecutive I/O operations causes the intermittent hang. The application scientist stated that the LP task identification and highlighted statements would have provided him with critical insight about the error. He further verified that a highlighted statement was the bug site.

More specifically, on Blue Gene/L, a number of compute nodes perform their file I/O through a dedicated I/O node (ION) so `pio` nominates *only one* writer task per ION. Thus, depending on how MPI tasks map to the underlying IONs, an I/O group does not always contain its writer task. In this case, `pio` instead nominates a non-member task that belongs to a different I/O group. This mechanism led to a condition in which a task plays dual roles: a non-writer for its own I/O group and the writer for a different group.

Figure 6 shows the main loop of a writer. To receive the file buffer from a non-writer, the group writer first sends a request to each of its group members to send the file buffer via the `MPI_Send` at line 317. The group member receives that request via the `MPI_Recv` at line 341 and sends back the buffer size and the buffer. As shown in the loop, a dual-purpose task has an extra logic: it uses `MPI_Iprobe` to test whether it must reply to its non-writer duty while it performs its writer duty. The logic is introduced in part to improve performance. However, completing that non-writer duty frees its associated writer task to move on from MPI blocking communications. The hang arises when two independent instances of `pio` are simultaneously processing two separate sets of buffers. This pattern occurs in the application when a small data set is written immediately after a large data set. Some tasks can still be performing communication for a large data set while others work on a small set. Because the MPI send/recv operations use tags that are fixed at compile time, messages from a small set could be confused for those for a large set of `pio` and vice-versa,

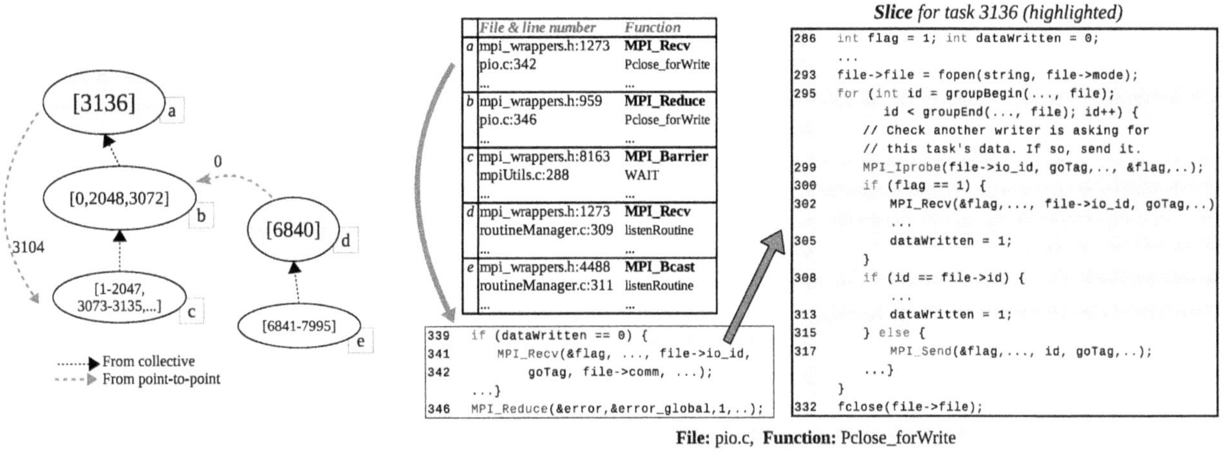

Figure 6: Output for ddcMD bug.

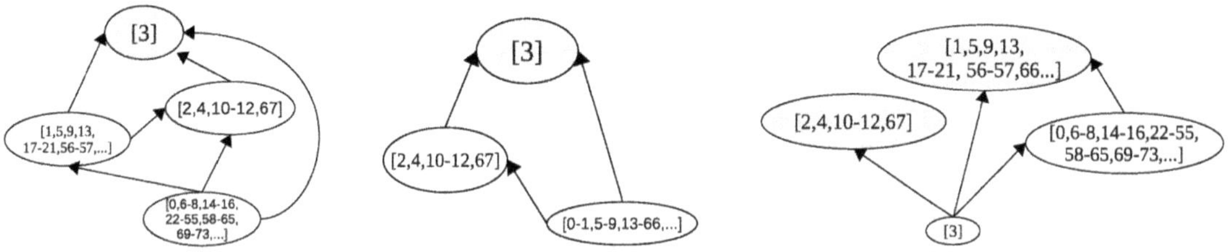

(a) hypre_ParVectorCopy (b) hypre_CSRMatrixMatvec (c) MPI_Irecv

Figure 7: Examples of PDGs indicating LP tasks (highlighted) for AMG2006. Errors are injected in task 3.

leading to a condition in which a task could hang waiting for a message that was intercepted by a wrong instance.

This error only arose on this particular platform because the dual-purpose condition only occurs under Blue Gene's unique I/O forwarding structure. We also theorize that the error emerges only at large scales because this scale increases the probability that the dual-purpose assignments and simultaneous `pio` instances occur. The application scientist had corrected the error through unique MPI tags in order to isolate one `pio` instance from another.

5.2 Fault injections

Applications. To evaluate *AutomaDeD*, we inject faults into two Sequoia benchmarks: AMG2006 and LAMMPS [1]. These codes are representative of large-scale HPC production workloads. AMG2006 is a scalable iterative solver for large structured sparse linear systems. LAMMPS is a classical molecular dynamics code. For AMG-2006, we use the default 3D problem (test 1) with the same size in each dimension. For LAMMPS, we use "crack", a crack propagation example in a 2D solid.

Injections. We inject a local application hang by making a randomly selected process suspend execution for a long period to activate the timeout error detection mechanism in *AutomaDeD*. We use Dyninst [3] to inject the fault into the application binaries as a sleep call at the beginning of randomly selected function calls (20 user, 5 MPI). Our injector first profiles a run of the application so that we randomly choose from functions that are used during the run. This ensured that all injections resulted in errors. We use a higher proportion of user function calls because more user functions than MPI functions are used at runtime. These function calls capture a wide range of program behaviors including calls inside complex loops as well as ones at the beginning or end of the program. We perform all fault-injection experiments on a Linux cluster with nodes that have six 2.8 GHz Intel Xeon processors and 24 GB of RAM. We use 1,000 tasks in each experiment.

Coverage results. We use three metrics to evaluate diagnosis quality: *LPT detection recall*, the fraction of cases in which the set of LP tasks that *AutomaDeD* finds includes the faulty task; *isolation*, the fraction of cases in which the faulty task is not detected but it is the only task in a PDG node (i.e., a singleton task); and *imprecision*: the percentage of the total number of tasks in the LP task set that *AutomaDeD* finds that are not LP tasks; we should have only one task in the set since we inject in a single task. Figure 7(a)-(b) shows two cases of correct LPT detections, which should have only the one task into which we inject the error for these experiments. A singleton task appears suspicious to a user so we consider isolation as semi-successful. Figure 7(c) shows an example of isolation — the PDG isolates faulty task {3} (although *AutomaDeD* failed to select it as the LP task).

AutomaDeD detects the LP task accurately most of the time (for AMG2006, all 20 user calls and 2 MPI calls; for LAMMPS, 19 user calls and 3 MPI calls). *AutomaDeD* isolates the LP task in all cases that it is not detected.

AutomaDeD has low imprecision: 43 (out of 50) injections resulted in no incorrect tasks in the LP set, i.e., *AutomaDeD* incorrectly flagged the LP task only 7 times. In these 7 cases, *AutomaDeD* can detect the faulty task by finding the isolated task in the PDG. Only one AMG2006 case gives high imprecision (0.99) since progress dependencies are undetermined (and the PDG had only one node). Three remaining cases had low imprecision of 0.01 to 0.05. LPT detection

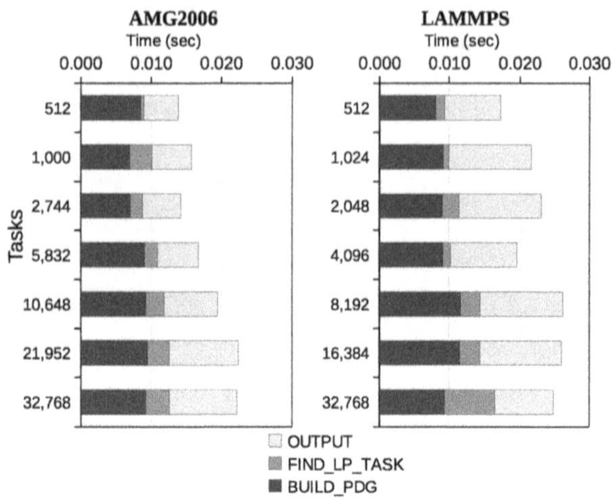

Figure 8: Time to perform distributed analysis (steps 2–4 in workflow) on BlueGene/P.

recall is higher for user calls than MPI calls because if a task blocks in a computation region, the remaining tasks are likely to block in the next communication region, which follows the computation region in our MM with probability one and, thus, *AutomaDeD* is likely to detect the dependence. Alternatively, if a task blocks in a communication region, the other tasks likely block in another communication region, which is necessarily not an adjacent MM state so *AutomaDeD* has a lower probability of finding the LP task. Nonetheless, *AutomaDeD* isolates the faulty task in all cases that it does not correctly detect the LP task.

5.3 Performance

Scalability We run AMG2006 and LAMMPS with up to 32,768 MPI tasks on an IBM BlueGene/P and measure the time for *AutomaDeD* to perform the distributed part of its analysis (i.e., Steps 2–4 in its workflow). In each code, we inject an error close to its final execution phase in order to have the largest possible MM (to stress *AutomaDeD* with the largest input graph). We used BlueGene/P's SMP mode in which each node has one MPI task with up to four threads.

Figure 8 shows the results of these experiments. In each run, we measure three main steps: `BUILD_PDG` (Steps 2 and 3); `FIND_LP_TASK` (the first part of Step 4 in which the helper thread identifies the LP task); `OUTPUT` (the second part of Step 4, which post-processes the final PDG). In `OUTPUT`, *AutomaDeD* eliminates duplicate edges in the PDG that may result from the distributed merge processing of PDGs. It also groups MPI task ranks into ranges of the form [x–y] and adds these ranges to the corresponding PDG nodes. Figure 8 shows that `FIND_LP_TASK` contributes the least to the analysis overhead. Intuitively, finding the LP task is simple once we have built the PDG. `BUILD_PDG` is the core of the analysis and, so, accounts for the most overhead. However, in practice PDGs tend to be small (i.e., usually 2–10 different states) because our approach builds them probabilistically using Markov models. Thus, they do not impose intractability problems for *AutomaDeD* to analyze them and to find the LP task. Our results demonstrate the scalability of *AutomaDeD*. The distributed analysis takes less than a second on up to 32,768 MPI tasks. The low cost of this analysis

Table 3: Slowdown and proportional increase in memory usage.

Benchmark	Slowdown	Memory-usage Increase
LAMMPS	1.59	6.11
AMG2006	1.46	10.36
BT	1.08	3.75
SP	1.67	5.14
CG	1.14	2.21
FT	1.05	1.01
LU	1.39	5.37
MG	1.04	1.04

suggests that we can trigger it at multiple execution points with minimal impact on the application run.

Slowdown and memory usage. Table 3 shows application slowdown and *AutomaDeD* memory usage for AMG-2006, LAMMPS, and six NAS Parallel benchmarks: BT, SP, CG, FT, LU and MG [7]. We omit EP because it performs almost no MPI communication and IS because it uses MPI only in a few code locations. Since their MPI profiles produce small MMs, monitoring at the granularity of MPI calls does not suit these applications. Slowdown is the ratio of the application run time with *AutomaDeD* to the run time without it. Memory usage shows the proportional increase in program heap usage when we use *AutomaDeD* (i.e., *increase = (memory-with-tool)/(memory-without-tool)*). Since *AutomaDeD* operates as a linked library, its memory usage increases the memory usage of the tasks themselves. Since tasks can have different memory usage (depending on their behavior), we used the task with the highest memory usage to calculate the increase. *AutomaDeD* incurs little slowdown – the worst is 1.67 for SP – because the overhead is primarily the cost of intercepting MPI calls and updating the MM, steps that we have highly optimized. For example, to optimize MM creation, we use efficient C++ data structures and algorithms such as associative containers and use pointer comparisons (rather than string-based comparisons) to compare states. Memory usage is moderate for most benchmarks; the largest is AMG2006 (10.36), which has many (unique) states in its execution. The factor that most affects slowdown is the number of MPI calls from different contexts since this increases the number of states that *AutomaDeD* creates. Benchmarks with slowdown of 1.3 (or more) call MPI routines from different contexts more often than the others. Applications with higher slowdown (AMG2006, LAMMPS, SP and LU) also exhibit higher *AutomaDeD* memory use due to the number of states.

6. RELATED WORK

The traditional debugging paradigm [6, 15, 26] of interactively tracking execution of code lines and inspecting program state does not scale to existing high-end systems. Recent efforts have focused on the scalability of tools that realize this paradigm [6, 10]. Ladebug [8] and the PTP debugger [34] also share the same goal. While these efforts enhanced debuggers to handle increased MPI concurrency, root cause identification is still time consuming and manual.

Parallel profiling tools such as Slack [19] and PGPROF [31] identify performance bottlenecks in parallel programs so that runtime can be reduced. These tools provide the time spent in each procedure within (critical) paths while *AutomaDeD* automates the analysis to find the task(s) and code regions in which a performance fault or a correctness problem manifests itself. Unlike *AutomaDeD*, the profilers do not address scalability issues such as the cost of aggregating profiling traces from a large number of MPI tasks.

Automated root-cause analysis tools target general coding errors in large-scale scientific computing. Research work includes probabilistic tools [9, 13, 23, 24] that detect errors through deviations of application behavior from a model. AutomaDeD [23] and Mirgorodskiy et al. [24] monitor the application's timing behaviors and focus the developer on tasks and code regions that are unusual. Other tools target specific error types, such as memory leaks [16] or MPI coding errors [13, 14, 17, 18, 32]. These tools are complimentary to *AutomaDeD* as they can detect a problem and trigger *AutomaDeD*'s diagnosis mechanisms.

Assertion-based debugging also targets reduced manual effort. Recent work addressed scalability of parallel assertion-based debugging [11] but does not suit localization of performance faults. Differential debugging [4] provides a semi-automated approach to understand programming errors; it dynamically compares correct and incorrect runs. While these techniques have been applied at small scales [33], the time and scale expenses are likely prohibitive at large scales.

The closest prior work to *AutomaDeD* is STAT [5], which provides scalable detection of task behavioral equivalence classes based on call stack traces. Its temporal ordering relates tasks by their logical execution order so a developer can identify the least- or most-progressed tasks. However, STAT primarily assists developers in the use of traditional debuggers while *AutomaDeD* detects abnormal conditions and locates the fault automatically.

Others have explored program slicing in MPI programs to locate code sites that may lead to errors. To provide higher accuracy, most techniques use dynamic slicing [21, 25, 27]. These tools tend to incur large runtime overheads and do not scale. Also, techniques must include communication dependencies into data-flow analysis, which is also expensive, to avoid misleading results. *AutomaDeD* uses other information to limit the use of slicing in order to limit overhead.

7. CONCLUSIONS

Our novel debugging approach can diagnose faults in large-scale parallel applications. By compressing historic control-flow behavior of MPI tasks using Markov models, our technique can identify the least progressed task of a parallel program by inferring probabilistically a progress-dependence graph. We use backward slicing to pinpoint code that could have led to the unsafe state. We design and implement *AutomaDeD*, which diagnoses the most significant root-cause of a problem. Our analysis of a hard-to-diagnose bug and fault injections in three representative large-scale HPC applications demonstrate that *AutomaDeD* identifies these problems with high accuracy, where manual analysis and traditional debugging tools have been unsuccessful. The distributed part of the analysis is performed in a fraction of a second with over 32 thousand tasks. The low analysis cost allows its use multiple times during program execution.

Our work and results suggest future directions that can be explored, including: (1) using additional features in the Markov models, such as transition counters, to infer dependencies with more accuracy between complex loop iterations; (2) measuring the accuracy of program slicing in identifying the location of faults at a granularity of code lines.

8. ACKNOWLEDGMENTS

The authors thank David Richards of Lawrence Livermore National Laboratory for helping us to conduct the blind study on ddcMD and to validate the results.

9. REFERENCES

[1] ASC Sequoia Benchmark Codes. `https://asc.llnl.gov/sequoia/benchmarks/`.

[2] Boost C++ libraries. `http://www.boost.org/`.

[3] DynInst - An Application Program Interface (API) for Runtime Code Generation. `http://www.dyninst.org/`.

[4] D. Abramson, I. Foster, J. Michalakes, and R. Sočič. Relative Debugging: A New Methodology for Debugging Scientific Applications. *Communications of the ACM*, 39(11):69–77, 1996.

[5] D. H. Ahn, B. R. D. Supinski, I. Laguna, G. L. Lee, B. Liblit, B. P. Miller, and M. Schulz. Scalable Temporal Order Analysis for Large Scale Debugging. In *SC '09*, 2009.

[6] Allinea Software Ltd. Allinea DDT - Debugging tool for parallel computing. `http://www.allinea.com/products/ddt/`.

[7] D. Bailey, J. Barton, T. Lasinski, and H. Simon. The NAS Parallel Benchmarks. RNR-91-002, NASA Ames Research Center, Aug. 1991.

[8] S. M. Balle, B. R. Brett, C. Chen, and D. LaFrance-Linden. Extending a Traditional Debugger to Debug Massively Parallel Applications. *Journal of Parallel and Distributed Computing*, 64(5):617–628, 2004.

[9] G. Bronevetsky, I. Laguna, S. Bagchi, B. de Supinski, D. Ahn, and M. Schulz. AutomaDeD: Automata-Based Debugging for Dissimilar Parallel Tasks. In *IEEE/IFIP Conference on Dependable Systems and Networks (DSN)*, pages 231 –240, 2010.

[10] J. DelSignore. TotalView on Blue Gene/L. Presented at "Blue Gene/L: Applications, Architecture and Software Workshop", Oct. 2003.

[11] M. N. Dinh, D. Abramson, D. Kurniawan, C. Jin, B. Moench, and L. DeRose. Assertion based parallel debugging. In *IEEE/ACM International Symposium on Cluster, Cloud and Grid Computing (CCGRID)*, pages 63–72, 2011.

[12] J. Ferrante, K. J. Ottenstein, and J. D. Warren. The program dependence graph and its use in optimization. *ACM Trans. Program. Lang. Syst.*, 9(3):319–349, July 1987.

[13] Q. Gao, F. Qin, and D. K. Panda. DMTracker: Finding Bugs in Large-scale Parallel Programs by Detecting Anomaly in Data Movements. In *ACM/IEEE Supercomputing Conference (SC)*, 2007.

[14] Q. Gao, W. Zhang, and F. Qin. FlowChecker: Detecting Bugs in MPI Libraries via Message Flow Checking. In *ACM/IEEE Supercomputing Conference (SC)*, 2010.

[15] GDB Steering Committee. GDB: The GNU Project Debugger. `http://www.gnu.org/software/gdb/documentation/`.

[16] S. C. Gupta and G. Sreenivasamurthy. Navigating C̈in a L̈eakyB̈oat? Try Purify. *IBM developerWorks*, 2006.

[17] W. Haque. Concurrent deadlock detection in parallel programs. *International Journal of Computers and Applications*, 28:19–25, January 2006.

[18] T. Hilbrich, B. R. de Supinski, M. Schulz, and M. S. Müller. A graph based approach for mpi deadlock detection. In *International conference on Supercomputing (ICS)*, pages 296–305, 2009.

[19] J. Hollingsworth and B. Miller. Parallel program performance metrics: a comparison and validation. In *Proceedings of Supercomputing '92.*, pages 4 –13, Nov 1992.

[20] M. Kamkar and P. Krajina. Dynamic slicing of distributed programs. In *International Conference on Software Maintenance*, pages 222 –229, oct 1995.

[21] M. Kamkar, P. Krajina, and P. Fritzson. Dynamic slicing of parallel message-passing programs. In *Proceedings of the Fourth Euromicro Workshop on Parallel and Distributed Processing, 1996. PDP '96.*, pages 170 –177, jan 1996.

[22] B. Korel and J. Laski. Dynamic slicing of computer programs. *Journal of Systems and Software*, 13(3):187–195, Dec. 1990.

[23] I. Laguna, T. Gamblin, B. R. de Supinski, S. Bagchi, G. Bronevetsky, D. H. Anh, M. Schulz, and B. Rountree. Large scale debugging of parallel tasks with automaded. In *ACM/IEEE Supercomputing Conference (SC)*, pages 50:1–50:10, 2011.

[24] A. V. Mirgorodskiy, N. Maruyama, and B. P. Miller. Problem Diagnosis in Large-Scale Computing Environments. In *ACM/IEEE Supercomputing Conference (SC)*, New York, NY, USA, 2006. ACM.

[25] J. Rilling, H. Li, and D. Goswami. Predicate-based dynamic slicing of message passing programs. In *Second IEEE International Workshop on Source Code Analysis and Manipulation*, pages 133 – 142, 2002.

[26] Rogue Wave Software. TotalView Debugger. `http://www.roguewave.com/products/totalview.aspx`.

[27] G. Shanmuganathan, K. Zhang, E. Wong, and Y. Qi. Analyzing message-passing programs through visual slicing. In *International Conference on Information Technology: Coding and Computing (ITCC)*, volume 2, pages 341 – 346 Vol. 2, april 2005.

[28] F. H. Streitz, J. N. Glosli, M. V. Patel, B. Chan, R. K. Yates, B. R. de Supinski, J. Sexton, and J. A. Gunnels. Simulating solidification in metals at high pressure: The drive to petascale computing. *Journal of Physics: Conference Series*, 46(1):254, 2006.

[29] M. Strout, B. Kreaseck, and P. Hovland. Data-flow analysis for mpi programs. In *International Conference on Parallel Processing (ICPP)*, pages 175 –184, aug. 2006.

[30] R. Thakur, R. Rabenseifner, and W. Gropp. Optimization of collective communication operations in mpich. *International Journal of High Performance Computing Applications*, 19:49–66, 2005.

[31] The Portland Group. PGPROF Graphical Performance Profiler. `http://www.pgroup.com/products/pgprof.htm`.

[32] J. S. Vetter and B. R. de Supinski. Dynamic software testing of mpi applications with umpire. In *ACM/IEEE Supercomputing Conference (SC)*, 2000.

[33] G. Watson and D. Abramson. Relative Debugging for Data-Parallel Programs: A ZPL Case Study. *IEEE Concurrency*, 8(4):42–52, 2000.

[34] G. Watson and N. DeBardeleben. Developing Scientific Applications Using Eclipse. *Computing in Science & Engineering*, 8(4):50–61, 2006.

[35] M. Weiser. Program slicing. In *Proceedings of the 5th International Conference on Software Engineering*, pages 439–449, 1981.

Top500 Versus Sustained Performance – the Top Problems with the TOP500 List – And What to Do About Them

William Kramer
National Center for Supercomputing Applications
University of Illinois
1205 W Clark Street
Urbana, Illinois 61821
217 333-6260
wtkramer@illinois.edu

ABSTRACT
A popular U.S. talk show host uses "top 10" lists to critique events and culture every night. Our HPC industry is captivated by another list, the TOP500 list, as a way to track HPC systems' performance based on FLOPS/S assessed by a single, long-lived benchmark—Linpack. The TOP500 list has grown in influence because of its value as a marketing tool. It simplistically, but unrealistically, describes performance of HPC systems. The proponents have advocated for the TOP500 list for different reasons at different times. This paper critiques the Top 10 problems with the TOP500 list and provides suggestions on how to correct those shortcomings. It discusses why the TOP500 list is limiting the impact of HPC systems on real problems and other metrics that may be more meaningful and useful to represent the real effectiveness and value of HPC systems.

Categories and Subject Descriptors
C.4 [**Computer Systems Organization**]: Performance Of Systems - *Measurement techniques; Reliability, availability, and serviceability*

General Terms
Measurement, Performance, Economics.

Keywords
Performance, Performance, Linpack, Top500, PERCU, Benchmarks, System Evaluation, Supercomputing, HPC.

1. BACKGROUND
The TOP500 list was introduced almost 20 years ago as a way of classifying computer performance. The list is based on the floating point computational performance assessed by a single benchmark, Linpack. It has grown in influence because it has become a marketing tool and a simplistically described measurement of performance for high-performance computers. The proponents of the list advocate its importance. At first it was presented as an important distinguisher of the performance of different systems and an indicator of the amount of scientific and/or engineering work particular systems could accomplish. In later years, the advocates have admitted its shortcomings, but shifted to extolling the historic value of the list and its ability to project future trends in high-performance computing.

1.1 The Linpack benchmark
The widely discussed Linpack benchmark [1] that is used to determine the TOP500 List [2][3] is a single test that solves Ax=b where matrix A is a dense linear matrix. Linpack uses Gaussian elimination with partial pivoting. For matrix A, that is size M x M, Linpack requires 2/3 M^3 + $2M^2$ operations. The latest Linpack benchmark implementation, HPL [4], can run on any number of processors, but uses weak scaling to achieve higher performance. In order to provide enough work to each processor, the size of the A matrix has to increase, not only taking more memory, but increasing the wall clock time of the run. Linpack is the only metric the TOP500 uses to assess system performance.

2. THE TOP 10 PROBLEMS WITH THE TOP500 APPROACH
While initially providing interesting information, for a long time, unfortunately, the Top500 list has done more harm than good to the high-performance computing community for the following reasons, which are presented in reverse order of importance as David Letterman does on his Late Show.

2.1 Number 10: The Linpack benchmark serves only one of the four purposes of a good benchmark.
Effective benchmark tests should serve four purposes in one implementation. Benchmark tests are representative approximations of the real work a computer system can accomplish. In other words, benchmark tests estimate the potential of computer systems to solve a set of real world problems. Benchmark tests are made up of computer programs (codes) and one or more input data sets that state a problem the program is to solve. One set of computer codes can exhibit different behavior based on the problem being solved and the parameters involved. Each purpose of the benchmark tests influences the selection and the characteristics of the benchmarks as well. The four purposes of benchmarks are:

1. Evaluation and/or selection of a system from among its competitors.
2. Validating that the selected system works as expected once it is built and/or arrives at a site.

3. Assuring the system performance stays as expected throughout the systems lifetime (e.g. after upgrades, changes, and regular use.)
4. Helping guide future system designs.

The TOP500 Linpack test, as the Top500 requires it to be run, does not serve any of the above purposes well. In fact the Top500 test is not able to serve purpose #3 at all because of the long run times required. For reasons discussed in the following sections, Linpack is seldom very effective in distinguishing between systems either. This is because most modern processors are designed to support cache-friendly, dense matrix algorithms. Indeed, the efficiency of all the systems on the most recent TOP500 list only varied by a modest amount that can be examined with other less intrusive tests.

In a limited way, Linpack can validate whether a system meets performance expectations at time of arrival (purpose #2), but is not efficient in doing so. The limitation of Linpack for this purpose is due to it correlating very well with peak performance. But there are many (even most) applications whose performance does not correlate with Linpack. Further, running Linpack at scale takes very long run times to achieve expected performance, as discussed below.

Linpack also has little to add to future architectural improvements, except possibly as a regression test to insure architectures continue to do well with dense, cache-friendly computations. But this regression test can be achieved by much simpler and less time-consuming tests, such as DGEMM running on a node. Since Linpack only partially addresses purposes #1 and #2, and does not address purposes #3 or #4, it is a not a useful indicator of how well as system is able to process work.

2.2 Number 9: The TOP500 list disenfranchises many important application areas.

Linpack solves a set of dense linear equations, yet many if not most applications involve algorithms that are not well represented by dense matrix solvers. Figure 1 shows a collection of scientific disciplines and the algorithms that were in use by informed applications in science domains at the National Energy Research Scientific Computing Center between 1996 and 2008 [5]. Table 2 is a similar summary of analysis of the applications used by 26 science teams with initial allocations on the NSF Blue Waters system [6]. The methods, or motifs, across the top of the charts directly relate to system architectural features. In assessing these and similar requirements analysis, well-balanced systems are required for most science applications.

These tables demonstrate that high-end computation involves much more than a single method, even within a single science domain. While dense linear algebra plays a role in problem solving, that role has significantly diminished as new computational methods evolve. Methods such as sparse linear algebra and adaptive mesh refinement have become increasingly important components in the computational scientist's toolkit but do not correlate to Linpack performance. Furthermore, computer architectures have changed over the past 15 years. When Linpack was introduced, vector processors and high-bandwidth memory systems dominated the HPC world. As shown in the table, dense methods are only one of many algorithmic methods in use today. All science disciplines use multiple methods, if not in one application, then in different applications to pursue science goals in each area.

Science areas	Multi-physics, Multi-scale	Dense linear algebra (DLA)	Sparse linear algebra (SLA)	Spectral Methods (FFT)s (SM-FFT)	N-Body Methods (N-Body)	Structured Grids (S-Grids)	Unstructured Grids (U-Grids)	Data Intensive
Nanoscience	X	X	X	X	X	X		
Chemistry	X	X	X	X	X			
Fusion	X	X	X			X	X	X
Climate	X		X	X		X	X	X
Combustion	X		X			X	X	X
Astrophysics	X	X	X	X	X	X	X	X
Biology	X	X					X	X
Nuclear		X	X		X			X
System Balance Implications	General Purpose balanced System	High Speed CPU, High Flop/s rate	High Performance Memory	High Interconnect Bisection bandwidth	High Performance Memory	High Speed CPU, High Flop/s rate	Irregular Data and Control Flow	High Storage and Network bandwidth

Table 1. This table indicated significant algorithmic methods in use for different science areas. System architectural features are also indicated according the algorithmic method. The TOP500 metric corresponds only to one architectural feature since it is dominated by dense linear algebra.

Science Area	Number of Teams	Codes	Structured Grids	Unstructured Grids	Dense Matrix	Sparse Matrix	N-Body	Monte Carlo	FFT	Significant I/O
Climate and Weather	3	CESM, GCRM, CM1, HOMME	X	X		X		X		
Plasmas/ Magnetosphere	2	H3D(M), OSIRIS, Magtail/UPIC	X				X		X	X
Stellar Atmospheres and Supernovae	2	PPM, MAESTRO, CASTRO, SEDONA	X			X		X		X
Cosmology	2	Enzo, pGADGET	X			X	X			
Combustion/ Turbulence	1	PSDNS	X						X	
General Relativity	2	Cactus, Harm3D, LazEV	X			X				
Molecular Dynamics	4	AMBER, Gromacs, NAMD, LAMMPS			X		X		X	
Quantum Chemistry	2	SIAL, GAMESS, NWChem			X	X	X	X		X
Material Science	3	NEMOS, OMEN, GW, QMCPACK			X	X	X	X		
Earthquakes/ Seismology	2	AWP-ODC, HERCULES, PLSQR, SPECFEM3D	X	X			X			X
Quantum Chromo Dynamics	1	Chroma, MILC, USQCD	X		X	X	X		X	
Social Networks	1	EPISIMDEMICS								
Evolution	1	Eve								
Computer Science	1			X	X	X			X	X

Table 2. Table showing the analysis of codes used by 26 science teams with initial allocations on the Blue Waters sustained petascale system. Note many teams use more than one application to achieve their science goals.

The TOP500 metric only deals with dense linear systems and gives no insight as to how well a system works for most of the algorithmic methods (and hence applications) in use today.

2.3 Number 8: There is no relationship between the TOP500 ranking and user productivity or system usability for real application workloads.

The TOP500 list does not indicate whether the systems listed are usable or productive. In a number of cases, systems have been listed while being assembled at factories rather than when installed at their host facilities, leaving a gap of months between when a system is listed and when it is usable by scientists and engineers. Even if the system is installed before being listed, it does not mean the system is usable or productive. To demonstrate the disconnect between the ranking and how effective a system is for a real workload, Figure 1 shows a comparison of the Linpack rating for systems procured and installed at NERSC and the NERSC Sustained System Performance [7] metrics for a 14-year period. The SSP has been shown to be a reasonable representation of the actual NERSC workload that covers almost all science disciplines and hundreds of applications [8]. As shown in Figure 1, there is an increasing discrepancy between the actual sustained performance and both the peak and Linpack performance across a number of systems and architectures.

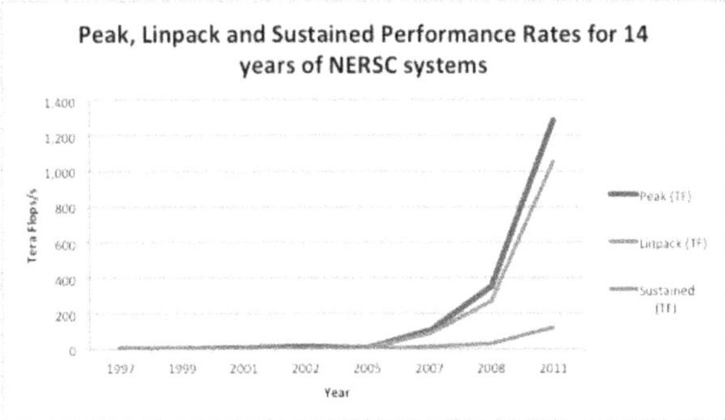

Figure 1. Comparison of NERSC SSP to Linpack performance over a 14-year period shows Linpack greatly misrepresents the real performance one can expect from a computer system.

In another view of the same data, Figure 2 compares the reported Linpack performance with the reported average sustained application performance using between six and eight applications and multiple input sets. The observer can see that sustained performance bears little correlation to Linpack performance.

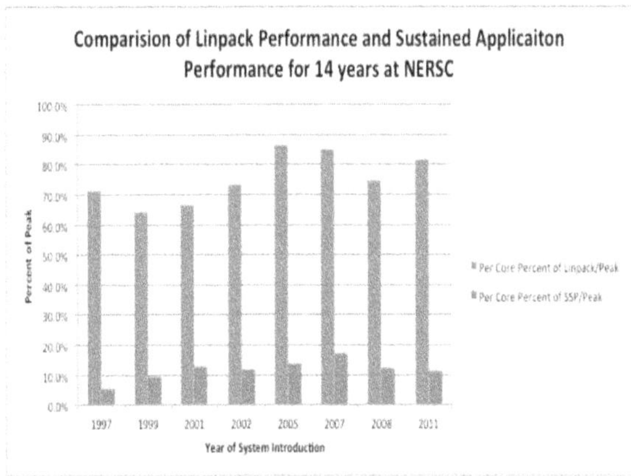

Figure 2. Comparison of Linpack performance and average sustained application performance for 8 systems over 14 years at NERSC

The results seen for NERSC-5 are aligned with the results seen using the similar versions of the tools for the DOD Modernization Program TI-05 evaluation and acquisition [9] which reports:

- simple tests are inadequate for predicting or assessing application performance on systems, with Linpack being the poorest simple test studied;
- combining simple tests with optimized weights also is inadequate for meaningful application performance prediction;
- convolving application traces with metrics derived from a specific set of simple tests (the PMaC methodology) can predict performance of applications to about 80% accuracy for the same system (no comment is made for similar but not identical systems); and
- acquiring the application-specific traces is "painful." It is noted that PMAC has since abandoned this version of the framework and has moved to a new framework for performance prediction [10] that recently reported predictions with 90% accuracy on a limited set of applications for the same system as was instrumented.

2.4 Number 7: The Linpack performance test is dominated by single-core, dense linear algebra peak performance.

Over the 16 years of the lists being reported, Linpack results have tracked the peak performance of the systems with only a few exceptions. Figure 3 shows the ratio of the reported Linpack performance (R_{max}) to peak performance (R_{peak}) for the #1 system for each list. It also shows the average ratio across all years.

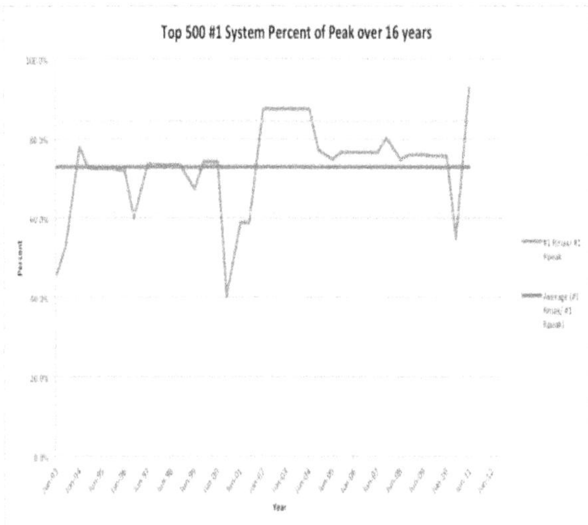

Figure 3. The 16-year comparison of system peak speed (R_{peak}) to measured Linpack rates (R_{max}) for the number 1 system on the list. The figure shows only a few times when there are any significant deviations, which are mostly explained by other causes.

There are only a few places where the ratios show a move away from the long-term average. In the first two lists, this difference is probably sites starting to pay attention to the implementation of their submitted times once they realized others would notice. The next difference in June 1996 is due to a new system that may have had limited tuning time. The next major difference in June 1999 is informative. It is the ASCI Red Storm system, which was also number 1 on the November 1998 list with improved R_{max}, probably due to additional tuning. The changes in November 2000 and June 2001 are both the ASCI White system at Lawrence Livermore National Laboratory, but with a percent of peak improvement of almost 50% in between the two lists. In this case, the low initial performance was good enough to claim the top spot on the list in November 2000 when the system was not complete, but the system's performance got much better before it went into service. Obviously the improvement in 2002 was the Earth Simulator, which was not only a case of vector vs. RISC system but also had very significantly more funding than any other system ever on the list. The improvement in June 2006 was the Los Alamos National Laboratory's Roadrunner system with a specialized, but limited use, Cell architecture, and November 2010 #1 on the list was again a specialized system with accelerators.

2.5 Number 6: The TOP500 metric has not kept up with changing algorithmic methods.

Today, computational scientists have to deal with massive parallelism using computational nodes that are often under-provisioned with memory and memory bandwidth. Therefore, computational methods have evolved significantly since Linpack represented the majority of methods used to solve problems.

The effectiveness of a metric for assessing delivered performance is founded on its accurate mapping to the target workload. A static benchmark suite will eventually fail to provide an accurate means for assessing systems. Several examples, including Linpack, show that over time, fixed benchmarks become less of a discriminating factor in predicting application workload performance. This is because once a simple benchmark gains traction in the community; system designers customize their designs to do well on that benchmark. The Livermore Loops, SPEC [11], Linpack, NAS Parallel Benchmarks (NPB) [12], etc. all have had this issue. It is clear Linpack now tracks peak performance in the large majority of cases.

Simon and Strohmaier [13] showed, through statistical correlation analysis, that within two Moore's Law generations of technology and despite the expansion of problem sizes, only three of the eight NPBs remained statistically significant distinguishers of system performance. This was due to system designers making systems that responded more favorably to the widely used benchmark tests with hardware and software improvements.

Thus, long-lived benchmarks should not be a goal except possibly as regression tests to make sure improvements they generate stay in the design scope. There must be a constant introduction/validation of the "primary" tests that will drive the features for the future, and a constant "retirement" of the benchmarks that are no longer strong discriminators. On the other hand, consistency of methodology and overlapping of benchmark generations are useful so there can be comparison across generations of systems. Consequently, the metrics that continue to evolve to stay current representative with of current workloads and future trends by changing both the application mix and the problem sets in a coordinated manner have shown to be useful over longer periods. The NAS Parallel Benchmarks partially addressed this by providing multiple size versions (Class A thru E) so as systems scaled to higher core counts there was some relevancy. Other tests, such as the NERSC Sustained System Performance test, SPEC, and the DOD Technology Insertion [14] benchmarks do a reasonable job of introducing new applications and methods, while at the same time correlating new versions to past versions. It is possible to compare the different measures so long-running trends can be tracked.

This lack of relevance to current methods will get worse for Linpack as we move from petascale to exascale. Linpack, and therefore the Top500, is highly parallelizable, particularly in the weak scaling mode, due to the static properties of the problem. So using this relatively simplistic measure may overlook or minimize issues with the upcoming "massive parallelism" systems to be developed in the next decades.

2.6 Number 5: The TOP500 measure takes too long to run and does not represent strong scaling.

The latest Linpack benchmark implementation, High Performance Linpack (HPL), can run on any number of processors, but in order to provide enough work to each processor, the size of the A matrix has to increase, not only taking more memory, but increasing the wall clock time of the run more than linearly. This is *memory-constrained scaling* "which is attractive to vendors because such speed ups are high" [15]. In order to keep scaling high, as much work per processor as possible has to be loaded into the system's memory. The amount of memory used grows at $O(N^2)$; the run time to do the work grows at $O(N^3)$. So for a system such as the NERSC Cray XT-4 with ~39,000 cores and ~80 TB of aggregate memory, a single run of Linpack may take 17-20 hours on the entire system. On large systems today, Linpack takes multiple days, and multiple tuning runs are typically done to achieve high list rankings. While few sites admit the time used for Top500 results, informal statements indicate it often takes weeks of dedicated system time for a submitted ranking run.

To address this specific issue, Dongarra recently suggested modifications to the TOP500 run rules to allow entries that do not complete the entire calculation [16]. This will make the run time needed for an entry shorter, but also have impact on the expressed performance. Furthermore, it lowers the probability the Linpack run will detect any abnormality in the system (e.g. incorrect answers) but is likely to allow people to post results for systems above tens of Petaflops.

2.7 Number 4: The TOP500 is dominated by who has the most money to spend–not what system is the best.

The TOP500 list's proponents represent it as an important indicator that is useful for historical purposes and its ability to predict the future of HPC technology. However, the dominant factor for list performance is who has the most funding to spend, followed by Moore's Law. Figure 4 is the typical historical graphic showing the Top500 number 1 and number 500 systems, with a new line showing known U.S. government spending in HPC over the same time period [17]. The funding is adjusted for inflation as reported by the Consumer Price Index [18]. While the speeds documented in the list are indeed increasing, it is clear that a major contributor to the increased speeds reported is the increased funding available for HPC systems.

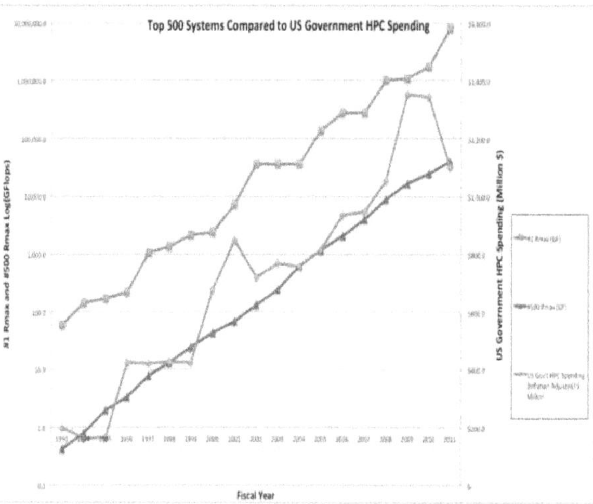

Figure 4. Linpack reported results compared with U.S. government funding for the 19-year period

This chart shows that a major contributing factor to the increases in performance on the Top500 is increases increased U.S. government funding. The U.S. government funding is representative of funding increases for other governments. For example, it is well documented that the Japanese government devoted significant resources to HPC over this time period as well, at times surpassing the U.S. investments. Indeed, list sponsors sometimes tout the fact that the list increases faster than Moore's Law [19] would predict, but this figure clearly shows that funding increases contribute to that, and in fact, the list is increasing more slowly than Moore's Law acceleration once the funding is factored in.

2.8 Number 3: The TOP500 provides little historical value.

Recently, while people acknowledge the lack of correlation with real workloads, the Top500 list is defended as having historical value to show changes over time for HPC systems. While there may be some historical value for such information, such as the number of systems by vendor or geographic region, most of the historical insights can come from other information that is more meaningful. Since the list convolves multiple factors, predominately how much money is available for HPC purchases and Moore's law, the list does nothing to resolve the influences of other respective components. Both of the two main factors are clearly available from other sources.

Another attribute of the list that can lead to historic misinformation is that there is no correlation between being able to list a system on the Top500 and having it available to perform its mission of running science and engineering applications. Systems have been known to be listed even though they are still in their factory bring up and not close to being shipped and installed. Other systems listed have been engineering prototypes that are never intended for production use. This gives the appearance of an acceleration of performance that is not reality.

2.9 Number 2: The TOP500 encourages organizations to make poor choices.

There have been notable examples of systems being ill-configured in order to increase the ranking on the Top500 list, leaving organizations with systems that are imbalanced and less efficient for their application workloads. Repeatedly, storage capacity and bandwidth and memory capacity are sacrificed in order to increase the number of peak (and therefore Linpack) flops in a system. In these cases–which include some very large systems–it is often the case that the types of applications that can be run are limited.

Also, the goal of listing a system can be so important to organizations that they may actually defer any use of the system. The modest example is that runs of the Linpack code take days to complete and often require multiple trials to tune–costing sites weeks of non-productive time. But occasionally more significant issues arise, such as occurred with the "System X" listed as number 3 on the November 2003 list[1]. After publication, it was disclosed that the system was unable to run any other application because it had memory without error-correcting hardware and could not be trusted to produce correct answers. Furthermore, the system had numerous Linpack runs, not for tuning, but to get a single correct result. System X was completely disconnected and almost all parts replaced with entirely different parts that took a year to put into place. Hence, System X did no useful work for approximately one year but still holds its place as the number 3 highest-performing system at the time to this day. The desire to gain a notable list rank meant the organization had no recourse to pursue their science and engineering work for this time.

[1] Private communication with Dr. Wu Feng during presentation at LBNL, January 2004.

2.10 Number 1: The TOP500 gives no indication of the cost of value of a system.

The Number 1 issue of the Top500 is that is gives no indication of the cost or value of the systems it lists. Hence, there is no way to compare different system architectures or implementations since the dominant factor in performance and list ranking is how much money was spent. While the exact cost of the Earth Simulator was never fully documented in public, indications are it cost substantially more than other contemporary systems. Indeed, using NEC list pricing for equivalent parts at the time, the Earth Simulator added up to well over $1 billion. The next-ranked systems cost five to 10 times less. Similar situations exist throughout the history of the list where high positions on the list can be "bought" if an organization has sufficient funding.

Value is the ratio of the amount of work a system can do to the cost of the system. Even if Linpack were an accurate measure of the amount of real work a system is capable of, without an expression of cost listed alongside the performance metric it is impossible to understand the relative value of the systems. Without the ability of assessing value, it is not meaningful to discuss comparisons of systems either within a particular list or across lists.

One defense used for not requiring any cost information is that different discounting is used and/or the actual cost is not possible to know for all systems at high accuracy. While it is unrealistic to have an exact cost figure for all systems, it is misleading to say that gathering information is impossible and hence should not be attempted. For example, many press releases about new systems, a cost figure is given, and many procurement documents provide the estimated available funds. Furthermore, an existence proof that gathering cost data is possible is in place because the original NAS parallel benchmark rules [20] were specific that a system would not be listed unless a cost estimate was provided for that system–and the NPBs were highly successful in capturing meaningful performance information for many years.

3. RECOMMENDATIONS FOR IMPROVEMENTS

Recommendations to improve the state of HPC system comparisons over time separate into two classes. *Evolutionary* improvements are meaningful improvements that can be made within the context of the current list structure that do not require major effort. *Revolutionary* improvements are major restructuring that will result in new methods to assess systems and community progress. These improvements address one or more of the issues discussed above.

3.1 Evolutionary Improvements

The most important, immediate improvements are listed below.

3.1.1 Require cost data for every system listed

Require all list submissions provide a system cost along with the Linpack run submission. The cost estimate can be flexible, as it was in the NAS Parallel Benchmark. It could be the actual cost paid or a cost estimated from pricing tables (e.g. U.S. government GSA contracts) or other methods. For the latter, it may be that large system units are not listed, but smaller ones are so there would be some proration. At the worst, a component-wise estimate can be done as discussed above for the Earth Simulator.

It is not necessary to have the cost data as precise as the performance run, but having even roughly comparable cost data would begin to allow comparisons of value. Furthermore, it would provide additional historical relevance of the list since then the community has readily available information about changing investments in HPC.

This improvement is similar to the change in the list managers made recently to request (and possibly eventually require) energy consumption information associated with the performance information. The measurement method for energy consumption is not proscribed, but it is useful data to have. The positive experience with this (and the growth of new comparative metrics such as the Green 500 list) show some variation in costing calculations can be tolerated while still being very meaningful.

3.1.2 Do not allow a system to be listed until it is fully accepted and performing its mission

Often, one of the very first things a site does is run the Linpack test for submission to the list. A system may spend six to 12 months before it is in real production service. So the list gives an unrealistic perspective of how much computing capability is being delivered to the community.

It is more realistic to require that any ranked system actually be doing its intended work before listing the system. This could mean requiring the submitter to verify it is in production use or requiring some verification of meaningful scientific results being accomplished along with the data of the Linpack run.

3.1.3 Require a complete description for every system listed

Require sites to fully specify their system capacities and feeds. For example, the amount and speed of memory and the amount and speeds of the I/O subsystems should be recorded for all entries. This improvement would allow assessment of how well balanced a system is and would reflect the investment strategy for a system. It would also document how different types of components influence the performance results.

3.1.4 Move from weak scaling to strong scaling Linpack

The weak scaling approach of Linpack, essentially requiring more and more work to be performed to achieve a certain level of performance, makes the metric less meaningful. While in the past many applications did increase the amount of work they performed as system size and performance increased, that option is less practical as we move to the future. Systems are moving into a time when parallelism will dominate, but system bottlenecks such as memory capacity will not increase as quickly, making strong scaling dramatically more important than in the past. Hence a simple improvement is for the list to set levels of problem size that are independent of system scale. The NAS Parallel Benchmarks has introduced five classes of problems over time so that there is enough work in the problem set, and the Top500 criteria should follow a similar approach.

3.2 Revolutionary Improvements

Revolutionary approaches are to make major modifications and/or entirely replace the Top500 with a new list(s) that is much more realistically aligned with application performance.

3.2.1 Align the metric to best practices in benchmarking

There are attributes of any benchmark and metric that are generally agreed upon. Combining the criteria from [21] and [22] provides the following list of good attributes performance measurement should have.

- Proportionality—a linear relationship between the metric used to estimate performance and the actual performance observed by the workload. In other words, if the metric increases by 20%, then the real performance of the system should be expected to increase by a similar proportion.
  - A scalar performance measure for a set of benchmarks expressed in units of time should be directly proportional to the total time consumed by the benchmarks.
  - A scalar performance measure for a set of benchmarks expressed as a rate should be inversely proportional to the total time consumed by the benchmarks.
- Reliability—if the metric shows System A is faster than System B, it would be expected that System A outperforms System B in a real workload represented by the metric.
- Consistency—the definition of the metric is the same across all systems and configurations.
- Independence—the metric is not influenced by outside factors such as a vendor putting in special instructions that just impact the metric and not the workload.
- Ease of use—so the metric can be used by more people and/or more frequently.
- Repeatability—running the test for the metric multiple times should produce close to the same result.

While the Top500 metric does have some of these attributes, it misses several others. Whatever new approach is adapted should improve the ability for the metric to have all these attributes and also be more closely aligned to the spirit of these attributes. Furthermore, it would be beneficial if the metrics could meet the goals of any benchmark in representing an evolving workload and covering all the purposes of benchmarks discussed in section 2.1 above.

3.2.2 Aggregate the HPCC metrics into a single value

Dongarra's HPCC tests [23] are an attempt to provide a more general view of a system and its ability to perform on a wider range of applications. While each year individual measures are recorded and "winners" announced, this approach has never replaced the single metric Top500 list because it is harder to issue press releases or make simplified claims by using four values rather than one. However, there is no reason most of the HPCC measures cannot be generalized into a single composite measure. While each test assesses different characteristics, with the exception of *randomring* latency, the tests all have one thing in common: They do a certain amount of work in a given time period and the work unit is encapsulated in some activity, be the activity a floating-point operation or moving data from one location to another. Therefore, each test has a given amount of work to be done represented by the total number of reference actions that have to be carried out to complete the test. If the number of actions is deterministic, then the difference between two rates is only the wall clock time it takes to carry out all those actions. Hence, an appropriate composite function (see PERCU reference for a discussion of appropriate compositing functions) can result so that time-to-solution for each test is the only variable. As everyone agrees, time-to-solution is the only real measure of performance. Making this improvement will provide the community with a single "actions/second" measure more representative of realistic system use.

3.2.3 *Individualized rankings*

Given enough data—such as the HPCC values and perhaps a few others, such as I/O and perhaps a deterministic random access, represented by the Graph500 test—it would be possible to create meaningful customized rankings. For example, one could set weights and create a custom listing—the top 500 machines for the workload in which a community is interested. This improvement would help our community get away from the mass-market rankings and promote personalized rankings that are really useful.

3.2.4 *Weighted composite of actions*

Combining improvements 2 and 3 may be a straightforward way to greatly improve the realism of a single metric without tremendous effort. As a thought experiment, assume there are three measures (from the HPCC or others tests): one for an arithmetic operation for a quantum of values, one for moving a quantum of data between memory locations, and one for moving a quantum of data across the interconnect. Call these actions A_1, A_2, and A_3. Each test would have a deterministic number of actions it carries out, represented as Na_1, Na_2, and Na_3, and the measurement of the time it takes to complete the amount of actions, shown as t_1, t_2 and t_3. Then the rate of actions is $\Phi(Na_1/t_1, Na_2/t_2, Na_3/t_3)$ where Φ is a composite function such as the geometric mean. Since Na_{1-n} are deterministic, the only variables are the times to completing the work, giving this approach the proportional and other properties discussed above.

Good rates for some actions may be necessary, but not sufficient for achieving good overall performance. For example, for large-scale applications, flops/s are no longer the bottleneck ("flops are free"), but memory bandwidth and interconnect bandwidth often are. In the future, the shift of the bottleneck will be more true since moving data will dominate the use of energy within systems.

So, one can use a weighted composite function, with weights w_1, w_2 and w_3. Since systems today may have 100 to 1,000 more flops than interconnect bandwidth and 10 to 100 times more flops than memory bandwidth, it is possible to use 1, 10 and 100 for the weighting factors. Using weights, particularly with some study matching the best weights to workloads, could provide a more realistic single indicator for real (sustained) performance than just a Linpack value.

3.2.5 *Create a new, meaningful suite of benchmarks*

Many of the benchmark suites that are held in high regard (Livermore Loops [24], NPBs, SPEC) over time are suites of pseudo and/or full applications. While the best case for any benchmark is to be a statistically representative sample of real workload, in realty, this is not possible for community tests. Mashey [25] labels the Workload Characterization Analysis (WCA), a statistical study of all the applications in a workload, including their frequency of invocation and their performance. WCA is equivalent to the methodology outlined in [26]. This type of analysis provides a statistically valid random sampling of the workload. Of course, WCA takes a lot of effort and is rarely done for complex workloads. WCA also cannot be done with standard benchmark suites such as NPB or SPEC. While such suites may be related to a particular workload, by definition they cannot be random samples of a workload. The Workload Analysis with Weights (WAW) is possible after extensive WCA because it requires knowledge of the workload population. It can predict workload behavior under varying circumstances but still is not possible for broad community measures. For the goals of cataloguing a wide range of workloads, WAC and WAW are impracticable. The other type of analysis is the SERPOP (Sample Estimation of Relative Performance of Programs) method. In this category, a sample of a workload is selected to represent a workload. However, the sample is not random and cannot be considered a statistical sample. SERPOP methods occur frequently in performance analysis and reflect very meaning measures that span individual communities.

Many common benchmark suites—including SPEC, TCP and NPB, as well as many acquisition test suites—are SERPOP. In SERPOP analysis, the workload should be related to SERPOP tests, but SERPOP does not indicate the frequency of usage or other characteristics of any individual workload.

4. A COMMUNITY CALL TO ARMS

The community desperately needs a new, comprehensive SERPOP metric for HPC systems, particularly when extreme architectures will be evolving in the face of many technology constraints. Several SERPOP metrics exist and are in use today, such as the NERSC SSP test series, the DOD Technology Insertion benchmark series, and the NSF/Blue Waters SPP test [27]. While none represent every possible workload component, all are much more representative of real workloads than Linpack. So, any such SERPOP test would be more useful than Linpack.

It is time the HPC community stop apologizing for a poor and misleading metric that we claim we have to run and post. It is clear much better measures can do a much better job in representing the important advances of HPC technology and investment while better representing the end purpose of our systems and programs. So, this paper ends by asking all community segments system vendors, facility managers, funding stakeholders, and the press—to resist using measures that are grossly flawed.

Rather, we should insist in immediate evolutionary improvements while, in a very timely manner, moving to implement revolutionary improvements. It should be our shared goal that in November 2013, the 20th anniversary of the first release of the Top500 list, an entirely re-engineered metric is in place to guide our discussions, investment strategies and to record the amazing accomplishments of a vibrant segment of computing.

5. ACKNOWLEDGEMENTS

First, the author wishes to thank the four originators of the Top500 list, Jack Dongarra, Hans Meuer, Horst Simon, and Erich Strohmaier, for providing many years of data and insight. While this paper points out issues that have developed over time with the Top500 list it does not in any way indicate ill will or lack of respect for the accomplishment of creating the Top500 list. The author also wants to anonymously thank the community members for the thoughts and ideas on this topic. Finally, all comments are those of the author alone and do not represent any formal view of the organizations with which he has been or is associated.

6. REFERENCES

[1] Dongarra, Jack. *Performance of Various Computers Using Standard Linear Equations Software.* Computer Science , University of Tennessee, Knoxville TN, 37996: University of Tennessee, 1985

[2] Top 500 List. 1993-2012. http://www.top500.org (accessed 2012).

[3] http://www.netlib.org/Linpack

[4] Linpack Download. 2008. http://www.netlib.org/LINPACK (accessed 2008).

[5] Kramer, William T.C., *PERCU Results in a Reawakened Relationship for NERSC and Cray*, Cray User Group (CUG 2007) Conference, Seattle, WA, May 2007.

[6] Kramer, William. Blue Waters – A Super System for Super Challenges. *Proceedings of the Cray User Group, Stuttgart*, Germany, April 29-May3, 2012.

[7] NERSC SSP Project. *NERSC Projects*. http://www.nersc.gov/projects/ssp.php (accessed 2011).

[8] Kramer, William. *PERCU: A Holistic Method for Evaluating High Performance Computing Systems*, A Dissertation, University of California Berkeley, October 2008. http://www.eecs.berkeley.edu/Pubs/TechRpts/2008/EECS-2008-143.pdf

[9] Carrington, Laura, M. Laurenzano, Allan Snavely, Roy Campbell, and Larry Davis. How Well Can Simple Metrics Represent the Performance of HPC Applications? *SC 05 - The High Performance Computing, Storage, Networking and Analysis Conference 2005.* Seattle, WA: Association of Computing Machinary (ACM), 2005.

[10] Tikir, M., L. Carrington, E. Strohmaier, and A. Snavely. A Genetic Algorithms Approach to Modeling the Performance of Memory-bound Computations. *Proceedings of SC07.* Reno, NV: Association of Computing Machinery (ACM), 2007.

[11] SPEC Benchmarks. 2000. http://www.spec.org (accessed 2008).

[12] Bailey, David H., and el.al. The NAS Parallel Benchmarks. *Intl. Journal of Supercomputer Applications* vol 5, no. 3 (Fall 1991): 66-73.

[13] Simon, Horst, and Erich Strohmaier. *Statistical Analysis of NAS Parallel Benchmarks and LINPACK Results.* Vol. 919, in *Lecture Notes In Computer Science*, edited by Bob Hertzberger and Guiseppe Serazzi, 626 - 633. London: Springer-Verlag, 1995.

[14] High Performance Technology Insertion 2006 (TI-06). *DOD Modernization Program.* 2005. http://www.fbodaily.com/archive/2005/05-May/08-May-2005/FBO-00802613.htm (accessed 2005).

[15] Culler, David E., and Jaswinder Pal Singh. *Parallel Computer Architecture: A Hardware/Software Approach.* First. Edited by Denise P.M. Penrose. San Francisco, CA: Morgan Kaufmann Publishers, Inc., 1999.

[16] Dongarra, Jack, *Reduced Linpack to Keep the Run Time Manageable for Future TOP500 Lists*, invited talk, International Supercomputing Conference, ISC 12, Homburg, Germany, June 17-21, 2012

[17] The Networking and Information Technologies Research and Development Program, Supplement to the President's Budget FY1993 to FY 2013, http://www.nitrd.gov/pubs/2013supplement/FY13NITRDSupplement.pdf

[18] Consumer Price Index – Bureau of Labor Statistics. www.bls.gov/cpi/, (Accessed April 2012)

[19] Moore, Gordon E., Cramming more components onto integrated circuits. *Electronics Magazine*, 1965.

[20] Saini, Subach and David Bailey, *NAS Parallel Benchmark Results (Version 1.0) 11-96.* NAS Technical Report 96-18, Nasa Ames, tables 13-17. http://www.nas.nasa.gov/assets/pdf/techreports/1996/nas-96-018.pdf - other data is available in similar reports.

[21] Smith, J. E. Characterizing Computer Performance with a Single Number. *Communications of the ACM* (Association of Computing Machinery) 31, no. 10 (October 1988): 1202-1206.

[22] Lilja, David. *Measuring Computer Performance: A Practitioner's Guide.* Cambridge University Press, 2000.

[23] Dongarra, Jack. *Performance of Various Computers Using Standard Linear Algebra Software in a Fortran Environment.* HPCC. http://www.netlib.org/benchmarks/performance.ps (accessed 2012).

[24] McMahon, F. *The Livermore Fortran Kernels: A computer test of numerical performance range.* Technical Report , Lawrence Livermore National Laboratory, Livermore, CA: University of California, 1986.

[25] Mashey, John R. War of the Benchmark Means: Time for a Truce. *ACM SIGARCH Computer Architecture News* (Association for Computing Machinery) 32, no. 4 (September 2004).

[26] Bucher, Ingrid, and Joanne Martin. *Methodology for Characterizing a Scientific Workload.* Technical Report, Los Alamos, NM 87545: Los Alamos National Laboratory, 1982

[27] Gregory H. Bauer, Torsten Hoefler, William T. Kramer and Robert A. Fiedler. Analyses and Modeling of Applications Used to Demonstrate Sustained Petascale Performance on Blue Waters, *Proceedings of the Cray User Group*, Stuttgart, Germany, April 29-May3, 2012

Practically Private: Enabling High Performance CMPs Through Compiler-assisted Data Classification

Yong Li
Department of ECE
University of Pittsburgh
Pittsburgh, PA, 15261
yol26@pitt.edu

Rami Melhem
Department of CS
University of Pittsburgh
Pittsburgh, PA, 15260
melhem@cs.pitt.edu

Alex K. Jones
Department of ECE
University of Pittsburgh
Pittsburgh, PA, 15261
akjones@pitt.edu

ABSTRACT

State-of-the-art chip multiprocessor (CMP) proposals emphasize optimization to deliver computing power across many types of applications. Potentially significant performance improvements that leverage application specific characteristics such as data access behavior are missed by this approach. In this paper, we demonstrate that using fairly simple and inexpensive static analysis, data can be classified into private and shared. In addition, we develop a novel compiler-based approach to speculatively detect a third classification: *practically private*. We demonstrate that practically private data is ubiquitous in parallel applications and leveraging this classification provides opportunities to benefit performance. While this proposed data classification scheme can be applied to many micro-architectural constructs including the TLB, coherence directory and interconnect, we demonstrate its potential through an efficient cache coherence design. Specifically, we show that the compiler-assisted mechanism reduces an average of 46% coherence traffic and achieves up to 13%, 9%, and 5% performance improvement over shared, private, and state-of-the-art NUCA-based caching, respectively depending on scenarios.

Categories and Subject Descriptors

B.3 [**Hardware**]: Memory Structures; D.3.4 [**Programming Languages**]: Processors—*Compilers, Optimization*

General Terms

Design, Experimentation, Performance

Keywords

Data Parallel, Multi-threaded Applications, Compilers, Cache Coherence

1. INTRODUCTION

Chip multiprocessors (CMPs) have become a popular class of computer architectures to harness the incredible number of transistors possible within a single die. While many effective improvements to CMPs have been proposed, many optimization opportunities are lost unless specific characteristics of the application(s) running on the system can be leveraged. In particular, the lack of information about characteristics of a running application such as data access patterns, communication behavior, memory usage, etc., typically results in a more generic but less efficient method for utilizing on-chip caches, interconnect and coherence directories. Thus, it is critical to design architectures that are aware of application behavior, as proposed recently in the research literature [1, 2, 3, 4].

To determine relevant application behavior, we have studied various parallel benchmarks and found that many multi-threaded applications, such as those from the SPLASH-2 [5] and PARSEC [6] benchmark suites, exhibit regular data access behavior that can be discovered statically. For example, in these benchmarks stack accesses are predominantly local/private and data in the text segment can be largely classified as shared. Static global and dynamically allocated objects are typically an application dependent mixture of private and shared data. However, this mix can often be understood by studying how and where data objects are declared/allocated and used in the source code. For example, data-parallel applications typically allocate objects dynamically within a particular working thread and these objects are accessed by that thread with minimal sharing with other threads.

In this paper we present compiler analysis techniques to distinguish between private and shared style data accesses. To reduce the compilation complexity and avoid NP-complete compiler analyses, we introduce a new data classification called *practically private*. We call data practically private when the compiler cannot easily prove that the memory is accessed privately (e.g., exclusively by one thread/core) but speculatively determines that private access is highly probable and any sharing is minimal. Our data classification promotes access proximity for practically private data, which would in fact be treated as shared in many run time schemes. Moreover, the proposed classification is helpful in designing a more efficient coherence protocol that distinguishes practically private versus shared data, which have remarkably distinct sharing behavior and thus incurring significantly different coherence complexities. We demonstrate that practically private data is ubiquitous across a variety of applications and a high percentage of practically private data is dominated by local accesses. Finally, we provide a case study of a system that utilizes the page-table as a conduit to communicate application specific behavior information to the runtime system and a cache coherence protocol that leverages this application behavior information to

PACT'12, September 19–23, 2012, Minneapolis, Minnesota, USA.
Copyright 2012 ACM 978-1-4503-1182-3/12/09 ...$10.00.

reduce coherence traffic and improve performance. In particular, this paper makes the following contributions:

- We introduce *practically private*, a novel data classification that represents an important category of data access behavior for a variety of multi-threaded applications. Our experiments on 11 benchmarks show that more than half of data accesses are practically private.
- We present a compiler methodology and implementation based on the SUIF Sharlit framework [7] to perform data classification. Using profiling to verify the compiler-based data classification, we demonstrate that more than 65% of practically private data blocks are actually private and up to an additional 20% are mostly private (shared infrequently, with only one other core).
- We describe a customized memory allocator to store and pass the compiler identified classification information to the underlying architecture.
- Finally, we developed an efficient cache organization and specialized coherence protocol that demonstrate the usage of the proposed data classification for CMP performance improvement. Our data classification aware cache reduces coherence traffic by 46%. It achieves an 13% performance improvement over a static non-uniform access cache (S-NUCA) in which data is placed in an interleaved manner determined by the data's physical address, an 9% improvement over private caches, and a 5% improvement over the state-of-the-art runtime classification-based cache depending on scenarios.

The rest of the paper is organized as follows: Section 2 describes related efforts for utilizing data classification or access pattern analysis to optimize CMP performance. Section 3 introduces our compiler analysis technique for data classification and identification. In Section 4, we describe a case study system in which the compiler analysis is utilized. We examine the effectiveness of the compiler for identifying private, practically private and shared data and demonstrate the performance gain of our compiler-assisted case study system in Section 5. Finally, we draw some conclusions and describe on-going and future work directions of this effort in Section 6.

2. RELATED WORK

A number of prior efforts have attempted to utilize application data access characteristics to optimize different hardware components of CMPs such as caches, interconnects, coherence directories, etc.

In reactive NUCA (R-NUCA) [1], data accesses are classified as private, shared, and read-only at the page granularity. Data is assumed to be private until a second core accesses the data (signaled by a translation look-aside buffer (TLB) miss). Data lines from private pages are cached locally to improve access latency while lines from shared pages are cached using S-NUCA style [8, 9] (i.e., distributed shared data placement) to improve capacity.

Another relevant effort is Jin and Cho's software oriented shared (SOS) cache management [2]. They classify data accesses to a range of memory locations (returned by a memory allocation function such as `malloc()`) into several categories such as Even Partition, Scattered, Dominant Owner, Small-Entity, and Shared. Applications are profiled and memory accesses are matched to one of the above categories. Hints are provided to the memory allocation functions based on the matched access patterns. Pages within the memory ranges are placed to cache tiles indicated by these hints.

R-NUCA and SOS are techniques that leverage execution history and profiling to detect the data access pattern. In addition, they work at the operating system (OS) page granularity, which has higher probability of one data access pattern being polluted by another compared with a finer granularity structure such as a cache line or data-structure element.

Cuesta et al. [3] recently presented an efficient cache coherence directory based on a runtime data classification scheme similar to the one used in R-NUCA. The proposed scheme saves 57% of the coherence directory entries by distinguishing shared data blocks from private ones and maintaining directory entries for only the shared data blocks. When the classification of a data page experiences a transition from private to shared, as detected by the OS, a coherence recovery process is invoked to recover the coherence states.

Some application behavior has great impact on interconnect, as explored in Shao et al.'s work [4]. In this work the communication pattern of message passing applications is extracted statically to guide an optical circuit-switching interconnect configuration to minimize runtime circuit establishment overhead.

In the above research efforts, data classification and pattern detection can be helpful in many scenarios. In this paper, we present a lightweight compile-time data access analysis that utilizes a novel data classification including practically private data. We do not rely on expensive and conservative analysis techniques with limited practical application and avoid the need for running and profiling programs, which can result in misleading results due to the workload. Additionally, by completing the analysis at compile-time, we can avoid data classification pollution due to the relative coarse granularity of pages by guiding the memory allocator to group data classifications together within pages. Our proposed data classification technique can be applied to improve the performance of different on-chip components including caches, TLBs, directories, interconnects, etc.

3. DATA CLASSIFICATION

A study of multi-threaded code from a variety of program domains such as scientific computing, multimedia, image processing and financial processing reveals that data structures can be used in quite different ways. We also observe that the way data is usually used by multiple threads can be implied by information such as where in the virtual memory space the data is allocated and how the references of data are handled. For example, instructions and globally allocated data such as synchronization structures are typically shared by all threads. In contrast, stack and heap objects allocated within a thread usually have very few sharers. From the system performance point of view, the access characteristics of these data objects are so different that each of them should be treated using a customized design. This section describes our approach to classify and identify the data classification at compile time. Since a variety of multi-threaded benchmarks feature extensive usage of dynamic memory allocation for managing computed data, we concentrate on analyzing data blocks allocated through memory allocators such as `malloc()`. The analysis approach can be extended to other memory allocation routines such as `new`.

3.1 Data Classification Motivation

Understanding the data access behavior in multi-threaded programs is essential to deliver high performance on CMPs.

Parallel applications tend to exhibit flexible and diverse data access patterns. This poses a challenge for compiler to detect and describe these patterns. However, our study shows that there are several representative patterns/classifications that exist in a variety of parallel applications and they dominate the entire program execution. Consider Figure 1. The code in Figure 1(a) computes the product of matrix a and vector b and stores the result in x. Figure 1(b) shows a typical parallelized version of the same problem using POSIX threads, assuming the number of available threads is 4 ($PROCS$ = 4). Both the source code and the illustration in Figure 1(b) imply a clear data classification: a and x are partitioned across the 4 threads and thus can be classified as private while b should be classified as shared since it is entirely shared by all threads. We will revisit this example in more detail in Section 3.2 and elaborate on how such a data classification can be formally identified from source code.

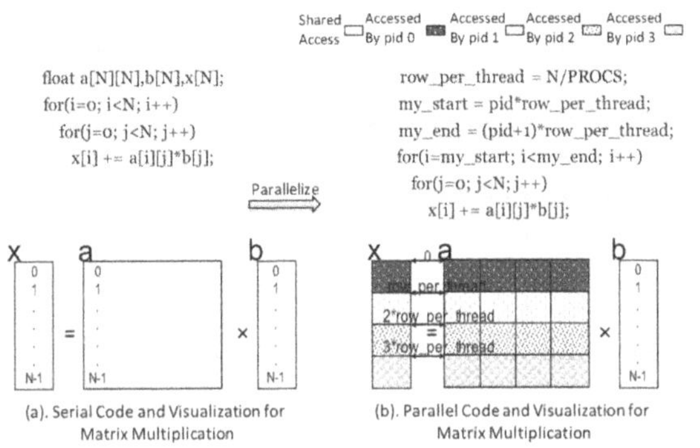

Figure 1: Serial and parallel computation for matrix multiplication

Generally, the classification of data must meet certain criteria to improve data access latency, save coherence directory or reduce network traffic, in particular:

- Different classifications within an application exhibit remarkable disparity in terms of locality, storage requirements, and access latency and as such must be treated differently.
- Classifications are practical for the compiler to identify.
- Classifications are representative for a wide spectrum of parallel applications.

A straightforward method is to classify data blocks into two distinct access categories: private versus shared, as shown in the above example. Private data is accessed by only one processor and thus is suitable to be placed locally to reduce access latency and promote locality. Coherence directory size can also be reduced by eliminating entries for private data [3]. Conversely, shared data is accessed by more than one processor and should be optimized using different methods than private data. Shared data can be placed at a fixed location indexed by its address or at the "center of gravity" of its requesters [10] to reduce coherence traffic, save directory entries and simplify searching of data, especially when the data exhibits frequent/heavy sharing.

As a compiler-assisted data classification approach, our analyses must remain conservative when identifying private data to guarantee correctness. Unfortunately, complicated and NP-complete compiler analyses (e.g., data reuse analysis, data disambiguation, etc.) are usually involved to guarantee data to be private to a particular thread. Sometimes it is even impossible to ensure data privacy due to a lack of runtime information. To avoid this complication and expensive analyses, we extend our classification to include a third category: *practically* private data. Our classification is described as follows:

- **Private:** In multi-threaded applications, a data block (returned by `malloc()`) is defined to be *private* if every element in it is accessed by only one thread in the parallel program section. This is the case when multiple threads in the program partition a data block exclusively without overlap.
- **Practically Private:**

  For data that appears to be private but is not provably so from our compiler analysis, we call this data *practically* private. There are two scenarios that this classification covers and the same analysis discovers and optimizes our system for both. First, data that is *probably* private can practically be treated as private. Probably private data is frequently entirely private at runtime, as depicted in Figure 2(a), but we must take safeguards to deal with cases when sharing occurs. Second, if the practically private data is not entirely private, typically it is still *mostly* private, as illustrated in Figure 2(b) and Figure 2(c). Figure 2(b) indicates spatial mostly private data where each thread operates on largely exclusive data regions with shared boundaries. Figure 2(c) illustrates temporal mostly private data on which multiple threads operate exclusively at most of the time (e.g., data is shared only at the beginning or the end when threads are forked/joined). Typically mostly private data has a low degree of sharing in terms of sharers and frequency of sharing, making it suitable for private treatment in practice.
- **Shared:** This is the default classification when a data block can neither be classified as private nor practically private.

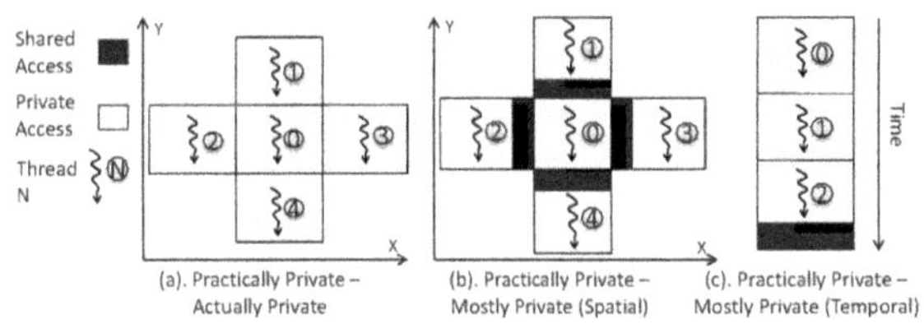

Figure 2: Different scenarios for practically private data

3.2 Data Classification Detection

In order to detect data classification for dynamic memory allocations, we use a structure called a *reference list* to keep track of all the pointers that may point to a particular memory block. Initially, a reference list is created at each call site of `malloc()` and the return address is added into the reference list. Reference list updates utilize data flow analysis that traverses the CDFG (control and data flow graph) of the analyzed program as follows: Let s be a statement node in the CDFG, $succ(s)$ be the list of the immediate successor nodes of s, $pred(s)$ be the list of the immediate predecessor nodes of s, $In(s)$ be the reference list state before executing s and $Out(s)$ be the state after executing s. Each statement s in the program has two effects on $In(s)$ and $Out(s)$: *Gen* and

Kill. *Gen* generates a new reference list or adds a pointer in an existing reference list, depending on the format of *s*. *Kill* removes a reference list or a pointer within it. For example, the statement $a = malloc()$ has the *Gen* function of creating a reference list with a in it and the *Kill* function of removing a from its current reference list. Likewise, the statement $b = a$ generates b for the reference list that contains a and kills b from its current reference list.

The data flow equation for updating the reference list can be derived based on the above notions:

$$Out(s) = Gen(s) \bigcup (In(s) - Kill(s)) \quad (1)$$

$$In(s) = \bigcup_{s\prime \epsilon pred(s)} Out(s\prime) \quad (2)$$

To illustrate the operation of this analysis, consider the example shown in Figure 3. The sample code on the left allocates data using `malloc()` and accesses the allocated data after multiple threads are forked. The analysis begins by constructing a control flow graph (CFG). As the CFG is being traversed, `malloc()` routines and pointer assignments are detected. Using the *Gen*/*Kill* functions and data flow equations, reference lists are created and updated, as shown on the right hand side in Figure 3. Initially, the reference list set is empty. At the first `malloc()` call site (labeled as *malloc*1()), x is added into the reference list as a pure pointer. The next assignment $A = x$ adds A into the reference list that contains x. When x is reassigned by a second `malloc()` x is removed from the reference list with A and a new reference list is created to which B is added with the succeeding assignment statement. When the conditional branch is encountered, C is added into both reference lists.

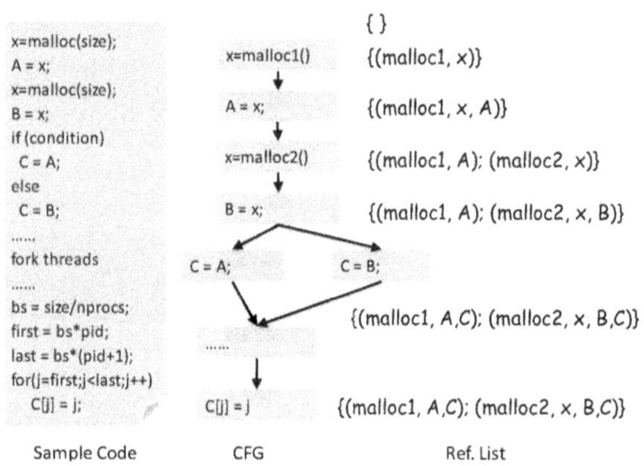

Figure 3: Pointer analyses example for data classification

The classification of a data block is strongly implied by the pointer dereference features. One of such important features for the compiler to discover is pointer dereference (array access) with *Thread-Identifying Variables* [11]. Thread-Identifying variables (TI variables) are thread-local variables which have unique values for different threads of execution. Typically, these variables are used to determine which memory blocks and in some cases which portion of the memory block the thread will access. The compiler must identify which variables in the program are TI variables in order to determine how the pointers in the reference lists are dereferenced and used by each of the threads.

In POSIX threads, one common method to assign values to TI variables is to pass different values to each of the parallel threads as function arguments during thread creation, as shown in Figure 4 (a). For other parallel programming interfaces such as OpenMP, each thread is internally assigned with an ID number, which can be returned by calling a specific function (e.g., `OMP_GET_THREAD_NUM()`). The thread ID numbers are also TI variables and can be recognized by keeping track of the specific function calls for a particular programming interface.

Another method for populating TI Variables is when multiple threads try to access and modify a global variable under the protection of a mutex as illustrated in Figure 4 (b). This type of code is much more difficult for a compiler to analyze. If the code uses this or any other subtle methods to specify TI variables we require the user to include a directive to assist the compiler in determining TI variables for analysis. In the example, **`#pragma TIV pid`** specifies **`pid`** as a TI variable.

Note that variables derived from other TI variables, either through calculation or assignment, are also TI variables. Once the basic TI variables are identified using the above methods, all other TI variables can be detected by performing a data flow analysis similar to the reaching definition problem.

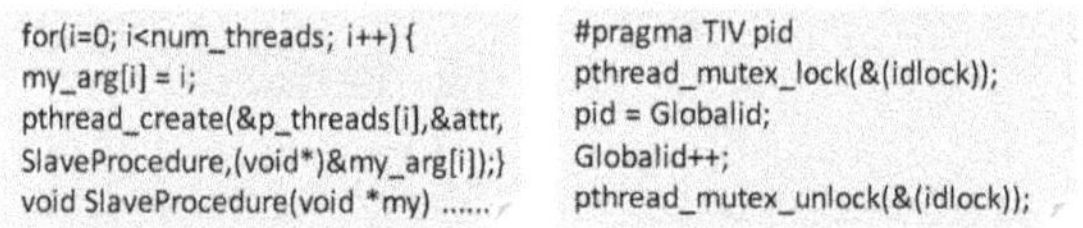

(a). Identifying TI variables passed as parameters.

(b). Identifying TI variables using directives

Figure 4: Identifying TI variables

Given the notions of reference list and TI variables, we introduce the data classifying rules as follows:

- **Determine Private Data:** Data can be assured to be private if all the pointers in the associated reference list are of local scope (i.e., pointers are never passed to global pointers or other threads).
- **Determine Practically Private Data:** Data on the stack is classified into this category. Heap data blocks are also identified as practically private if at least one pointer in the reference list is of global scope (i.e., the pointer is global or passed to other threads) and that pointer is dereferenced with a TI variable. Typically, this indicates that these data blocks are probably private. In many embarrassingly parallel applications, probably private is actually private when the global data blocks are exclusively partitioned among multiple threads by TI variables. Even if the practically private data blocks are not actually private, it is likely that they are mostly private, as the cases in many particle interaction simulation programs where small amount of data is shared among neighboring processing nodes (please refer to Figure 2).
- **Determine Shared Data:** Data that can not be identified as belonging to the above two categories is classified as shared.

As we can see from the above rules, detecting private data is conservative, since any pointer in the reference list that implies shared or practically private classification will overwrite the ones that imply private classification. Determining practically private however, is aggressive. The data classifying rules are designed as such to maximally expose optimization opportunities while guaranteeing correctness. This is also revealed from Algorithm 1, as will be described in Section 3.3.

Algorithm 1: Data classification routine on graph $G(V, E, r)$

```
for each node b_i ∈ V do
  if b_i is an array access or pointer dereference then
    get the array base A and the offset o;
    get a list L of malloc() associated with A based on
    the reference list;
    for each element e_i ∈ L do
      if e_i has been classified as shared then
        if A is of global scope && o is TI variable then
          overwrite the data classification of e_i with
          practically private;
        else
          /* private does not overwrite shared */
          do nothing (stay shared);
        end if
      else if e_i has been classified as private then
        if A is of global scope && o is non-TI variable
        then
          overwrite the data classification of e_i with
          shared;
        else if A is of global scope && o is TI variable
        then
          overwrite the data classification of e_i with
          practically private;
        else
          /* A is of local scope */
          do nothing (stay private);
        end if
      else
        /* e_i has not been classified yet */
        if A is of global scope && o is non-TI variable
        then
          classify e_i as shared;
        else if A is of global scope && o is TI variable
        then
          classify e_i as practically private;
        else
          /* A is of local scope */
          classify e_i as private;
        end if
      end if
    end for
  else
    continue;
  end if
end for
mark unclassified memory allocations as shared;
```

Given the data classification methodology described so far, let us now revisit the example shown in Figure 1 (b). Without loss of generality, we shall assume that all the matrices are globally declared (we can not identify them as private). We first note that the variable *pid* is a TI variable. Since both *my_start* and *my_end* are expressions of *pid*, they are also identified as TI variables using forward data flow analysis. Variables *my_start* and *my_end* further serve as loop bounds, making the index i a TI variable. Since the pointers a and x are accessed with the index i, matrices a and x are thus classified as practically private based on the data classification rules introduced above. Similarly, b is classified as shared. In this example, we can see that our data classification scheme does not identify matrices a and x as private data. This conservatism is to guarantee correctness in the presence of complicated pointer usage, which makes global data difficult to be assured private. Furthermore, we expect treating private data as practically private will not significantly degrade performance.

3.3 Implementation

We use SUIF [12] to implement the necessary compiler analyses for the proposed data classification. SUIF provides a framework called Sharlit [7] to facilitate the implementation of data flow analyses. Sharlit first constructs a reduced flow graph for the source program based on an extension of Tarjan's fast path algorithm [13]. It then uses an iterator to traverse the reduced graph, calling user specified flow functions (e.g., the *Kill* and *Gen* functions described in Section 3.2) and applying meet rules (e.g., Eqs. (1) and (2)) at path joints, until solutions (e.g., reference lists and TI variables) are found. After the iterative process is complete, reference lists are attached to the nodes where pointers are dereferenced (e.g., array accesses). In addition, every variable is identified either as TI or non-TI variable. The flow graph is then traversed in another pass during which an action routine that checks the data classification rules at the array access points, such as $C[j]$ in Figure 3, is called at every node. The algorithm for the action routine is summarized in Algorithm 1, assuming $G = (V, E, r)$ is a directed graph with nodes V, edges E, and a entry node r.

4. CASE STUDY: A DATA CLASSIFICATION AWARE CMP ARCHITECTURE

The performance of CMPs is largely limited by the latency of data accesses, which is highly dependent on the organizations of its memory caches connected using on-chip interconnect. As the number of cores in CMP systems increases, the latency of the interconnect is becoming an even greater bottleneck. As a result, elimination of remote data accesses and localization of communication have been demonstrated to be crucial to the performance improvement [14]. A number of architectural techniques have been proposed to achieve this goal [15, 16, 17, 18, 19]. In general, these techniques aim at a compromise between the two basic cache organizations, namely the static non-uniform cache architectures (S-NUCA) [8, 9][1] and the per-core private cache architectures [20]. The goal is promoting data proximity while efficiently utilizing the entire cache capacity with minimal coherence overhead. In this section we provide a case study of a CMP architecture that leverages the proposed data classification technique and utilizes this to optimize the design of on-chip last level caches to achieve this goal.

4.1 Customized Memory Allocator

For the underlying architecture to be data-classification-aware, we employ a modified memory allocator to store and pass the compiler instrumented classification information to the runtime system. Existing memory allocators such as `malloc()` obtain the starting address of the heap from the operating system (OS) for the requested data block and maintain a list to keep track of allocated as well as free memory blocks in virtual heap space. The newly allocated

[1] In this paper we use the terms S-NUCA and distributed shared caches interchangeably

block is filled with some useful information in its first few bytes such as the size and pointer to the next block. This information is necessary to maintain the list. The memory allocator also optimizes the allocated blocks by reducing memory fragmentation through mechanisms such as eight-byte alignment, splitting and coalescing blocks, etc.

A similar mechanism can be used to provide support for efficient sharing of information between the compiler and architecture. To inform the hardware of the data classifications identified by the compiler, we extend the prototype of `void *malloc(size_t size)` to: `void *malloc(size_t size, classification_t cls)`. The `size` parameter is retained from the original version of `malloc()` and is the size of the requested data block. The second parameter `cls` is automatically filled by the compiler with the data classification. The memory allocator adds this classification parameter to the record associated with the newly allocated memory block in addition to other parameters. In our modified `malloc()` we also extend the memory allocator to aggregate blocks with the same classification and to keep them page aligned. In other words, data blocks with different classifications are not permitted to be allocated within the same page.

4.2 Data Classification Aware Caching

This section describes how the data classification can be utilized by designing an CMP architecture with supporting caching policies.

4.2.1 Architecture and Cache Organization

Figure 5 depicts how the identified data classification information can be utilized in a typical CMP microarchitecture in which each node has a processing core, caches, TLBs, etc. L1 instruction and data caches are local and private to each core. Physically, the L2 is tiled and distributed. Logically, it could be either private to its local node or shared among all nodes, depending on the data classification of the served L2 data block. To support caching both private and shared data, each cache block (in both L1 and L2) is augmented with an additional two-bit field, *class*, indicating its data classification. The *class* field of each cache block is filled with the classification information from the corresponding TLB entry during the address translation process. Whenever a cache block needs to be searched, placed or written back, the cache controller consults the *class* field before communicating with the corresponding nodes. This creates an illusion that both private and shared cache blocks are respected in their favored cache organizations, private and shared caches, respectively.

As in a distributed shared cache, an in-cache directory [21] is used to maintain the L1 coherence using the MESI protocol. Another on-chip sparse directory [21] is provided to handle the L2 coherence for only the practically private data. This saves significant directory entries, compared to the traditional private cache organization in which each datum requires a coherence directory entry.

In particular, the placement and search policy after an L1 miss is described as follows:

- **Private:** For a private access, we directly check the local L2 cache bank. Upon a miss the data is directly obtained from main memory and added to the cache as if it were a private L2 scheme. Because the private data is only accessed locally, there is no need to maintain any cache coherence information in the distributed directory, which saves considerable overhead.
- **Practically Private:** Practically private data is likely to be accessed as private data, thus the local core would retrieve the data from the local cache tile. However, because it is not guaranteed to be private it may be accessed by other cores. To ensure correctness and promote locality at the same time, we place data of this category within the local cache tile of the requester (e.g., first touch access), and adopt the MESI protocol to maintain coherence, as performed in a traditional private cache organization. For data that is shared by two or more cores this can result in replication and reduced overall cache capacity. However, because the compiler has determined this is practically private we expect this type of sharing to be infrequent and not significantly harm overall capacity.
- **Shared:** Shared data is statically distributed throughout all the cache tiles as a function of its physical address. This keeps a unique copy at a fixed location to maximize effective cache capacity, simplify data search and avoid the need to keep coherence at the L2 level. Each shared cache line in L2 is associated with an entry in the in-cache directory to maintain the L1 coherence.

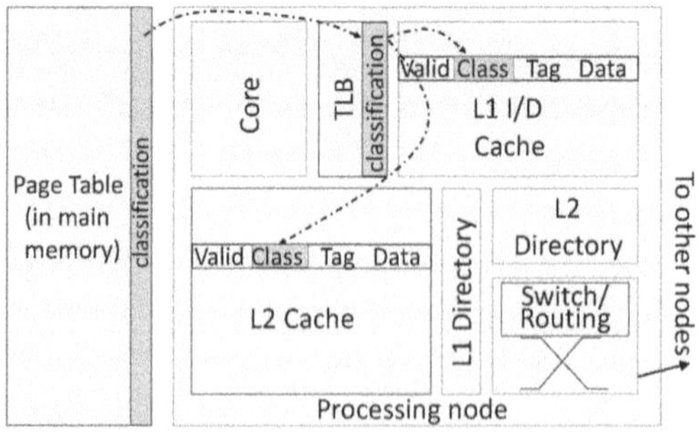

Figure 5: Architecture organization for data classification aware caching

Considering the interferences among cache blocks with distinct classifications, the placement, eviction and coherence problems need to be carefully handled so that cache blocks of all types are respected. To illustrate the proposed scheme, we show a number of examples in Figure 6, where the classification of a cache block or memory request is indicated by its fill color and the MESI state is represented as a letter within a parentheses attached with the cache block. We use dashed and solid lines to distinguish the eviction (including replacement, write back, directory notification, etc) and data lookup (including data search, directory lookup, data reply, etc), respectively. The examples illustrate where the requested data is fetched, omitting MESI state changes, upon a local L1 miss for various data classification scenarios.

Figure 6(a) illustrates a *requester* issuing a practically private memory request which misses in its local cache (L1 and L2) and fetches the block from the owner's L2 after evicting the shared *victim1* in the (M) state and the shared *victim2* in the (S) state. To accomplish this (1) the *requester* chooses *victim1* for replacement and (2) because *victim1* has shared classification, writes back to *victim1's* home, which is determined by *victim1's* physical address. At step (3), the local L2 is probed for the requested block since the request is practically private. Upon an L2 miss, *victim2* is selected for replacement. Because *victim2* is shared, the block and all its sharers are evicted at step (4). After the eviction, the directory at the home node of the originally requested data is searched in step (5) and the message is forwarded to the owner in step (6). We refer to the owner as the node that

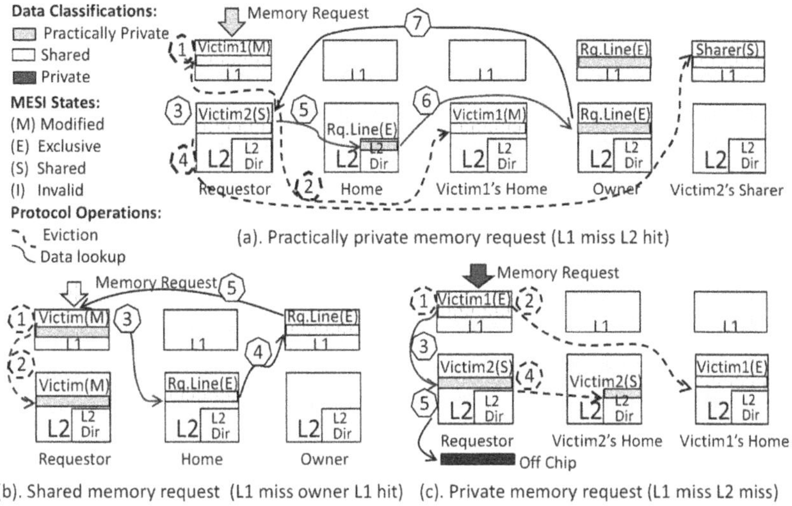

Figure 6: Examples of data flow and coherence protocol for different data classifications

has the only valid copy of the requested block with an (E) or (M) state. Any cache can be the owner if the directory indicates the block is in the (S) state. Finally, step (7) returns the requested block to the requester. The coherence states are updated to (S) upon a read, to (M) and (I) as appropriate upon a write.

Figure 6(b) explains the situation when a shared memory request replaces a practically private block in (M) state and then obtains the block from the owner's L1. Steps (1) and (2) show the victim replacement and write back. Since the request is shared, the home node is checked in step (3) and the in-cache directory indicates the owner has the only valid copy in its L1 in step (4). Step (5) returns the block to the requester. If the requested block is (M) or (S) in the in-cache directory, the block can be directly returned to requester without step (4).

In Figure 6(c), a private memory request replaces the shared *victim1* in the (E) state determined in step (1), resulting in an in-cache directory update (step (2)). Since the request is private, the block is either in the local L2 or off-chip. A miss in L2 will trigger an access to main memory. In this example, a practically private *victim2* in the (S) state is replaced (step (3))and the distributed directory at *victim2's* home is notified to make necessary changes (e.g., remove the *victim2* as a sharer) in step (4). Finally at step (5), the requested line is fetched from main memory and placed in the local L2 bank.

5. EVALUATION

In this section, we examine the compiler-classified data access modes and their use in a case study of classification-aware cache organization in a CMP. We first study the accuracy of our compiler-based data classification approach by comparing its results with classification based on run-time profiling. Second our case study examines how the classification aware CMP performs compared with two baseline cache organizations, distributed shared and private, and a state-of-the-art, runtime page-level data classification mechanism R-NUCA[2] [1] (see Section 2).

To conduct our experiments, we use Wind River Simics [22] as our simulation environment and implemented the relevant caching schemes within it. As previously mentioned, for R-NUCA we focused on the features relevant to the comparison, namely the classification of data as shared or private at the page level. The target architecture is a tiled CMP consisting of 16 SPARC 2-way processors laid out as a 4×4 mesh. The network contention due to data and control messages is modeled using a FIFO link reservation mechanism. The detailed architecture parameters are presented in Table 1.

Processor	16 SPARC cores, 2G Hz, 2 issue width
Operating System	64-bit Solaris 10
L1 Cache	32KB/core, 4-way associative, 64B block size, 1-cycle hit latency, write-back
L1 Coherence	MESI protocol
L1 Directory	L2 in cache directory, 3-cycle hit latency
L2 Cache	8/16M, 32-way associative, 64B block size, 5-cycle hit latency, write-back
L2 Coherence	customized protocol (based on MESI, data-classification aware, see Figure 6)
L2 Directory	sparse directory, 3-cycle hit latency
Network	4x4 mesh, packet switching, X-Y routing
Main Memory	4GB, 150-cycle latency

Table 1: Architecture configurations

Benchmark	Shared-averse(16M)	Private-averse(8M)
BLACKSCHOLES	20000 options;	200000 options;
SWAPTIONS	64 swaptions;	512 swaptions;
BARNES	524288 particles;	1048576 particles;
OCEAN	1026x1026 matrix;	2050x2050 matrix;
RADIX	10485760 radix;	104857600 radix;
STREAMCLUSTER	1024 data points;	1024 data points;
FFT	2^26 even integers;	2^26 even integers;
CHOLESKY	input file *tk23.O*;	input file *tk29.O*;
RAYTRACE	input file *teapot*;	input file *car*;
PBZIP	35 kilo bytes ;	100 kilo bytes;
WATER-SPATIAL	3000 molecules;	27000 molecules;

Table 2: Simulation Configurations

We selected benchmarks from the SPLASH-2 [5] and PARSEC [6] suites listed in Table 2. As the size of the dataset can bias the results toward a particular type of cache, one that

[2]We simulate only the data access classification component of R-NUCA as the code page replication and clustering component is orthogonal to data classification and can be applied to many caching schemes including ours.

favors private (i.e., a small dataset/working that can easily fit into the cache even with significant replication) and one that favors shared (a larger dataset/working set where cache capacity is at a premium). However, the problem size of our simulations was limited due to the intractably long simulation times of large workloads. Thus, to simulate these two conditions, we use two configurations, shared-averse and private-averse, with each configuration/workload enumerated in Table 2. In the shared-averse configuration, the aggregate L2 cache capacity is configured as 16M and the smaller of two workloads is selected. This favors private caches as the application can still remain relatively cache bound even if a lot of data replication occurs. To simulate a private-averse system we reduced the cache size to 8M bytes to make the overall capacity a bigger factor and used the largest possible workload (all other system parameters for shared-averse and private-averse configurations are the same, as shown in Table 1).

5.1 Compiler-based Data Classification

To demonstrate the data-classification capability of the compiler analysis, we show in Figure 7, the percentage of data accesses in each category during the application execution (running with shared-averse configuration). Except for FFT, which is dominated by shared accesses, typically a significant amount of the accesses are private.

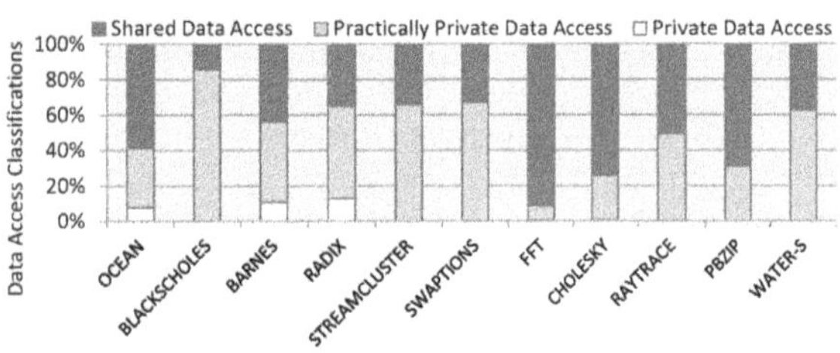

Figure 7: Percentage of accesses classified by the compiler as shared, practically private, and private

To determine the effectiveness of our classification we examined the accuracy of data classified as practically private. Figure 8 shows the actual sharing behavior at run-time for the data that is identified as practically private. More than 65%, on average, of all data identified at compile time as practically private were accessed privately. There is also a significant portion of the data that has only two sharers.

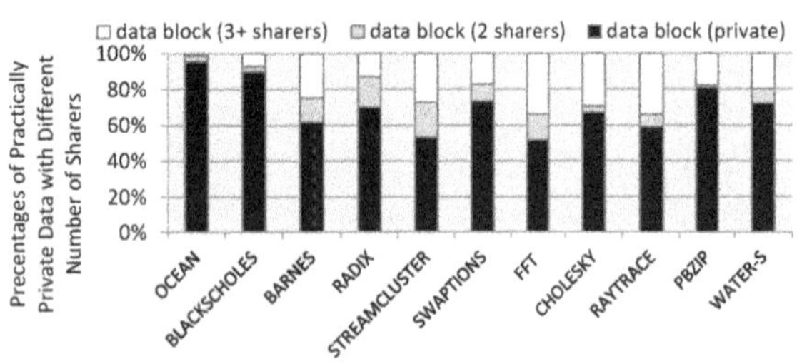

Figure 8: Proportions of data blocks classified as practically private that are accessed by one core (private), two cores, or three or more cores

5.2 Effect on Coherence Traffic

Traditional coherence protocol such as MESI incurs large volume of coherence messages, especially for heavily accessed data with numerous sharers. This impedes the scaling of future many-core CMPs. Our technique significantly reduces the number of coherence messages since it only maintains the coherence for data identified as practically private data, which likely to have no or small number of sharers. Figure 9 reports the percentage of reduced coherence traffic compared with private caches with MESI protocol. Adopting practically private concept eliminates from 11% to 78% of the coherence traffic. On average, coherence traffic is reduced by 46% using the proposed data classification.

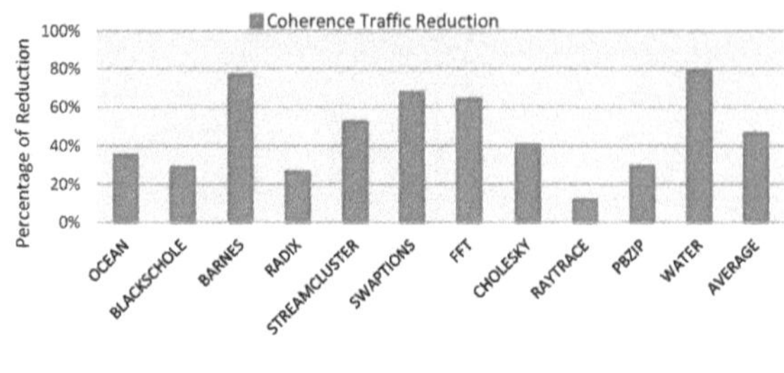

Figure 9: Percentage of coherence traffic reduced compared to private caches

5.3 Performance Evaluation

To evaluate the performance of the designed caching scheme that uses compiler-based data classification (we hereafter refer to our scheme as PSP, which stands for private, shared and practically private data classification), we compare our approach with distributed shared [8], private [20] and R-NUCA [1] caches in terms of cache miss rate, average memory access latency and speedup.

5.3.1 Miss Rate

Figures 10 and 11 show the L2 cache miss rate for shared-averse and private-averse configurations, respectively (each normalized to the distributed shared cache). In general, distributed shared caches have the lowest miss rate because replication is not allowed and as such the cache capacity is used most effectively. Conversely, in the private cache organization, multiple cache blocks become replicated and consume more capacity, typically resulting in a higher miss rate. Somewhat surprisingly, R-NUCA has an undesirable miss rate due to its page re-classification mechanism. When a page initially classified as private is re-classified as shared, all the cache blocks within the page that have been cached must be invalidated, resulting in a higher miss rate.

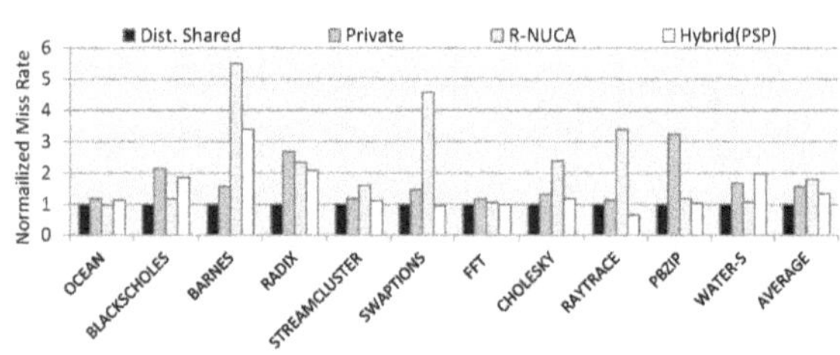

Figure 10: Miss rate for shared-averse configuration

The miss rate of the proposed PSP is typically in the middle and often approaches the better of the two baseline caching schemes based on the conditions. For shared-averse, PSP is better than shared and approaches the quality of private. For private averse, PSP is better than private and approaches the quality of shared.

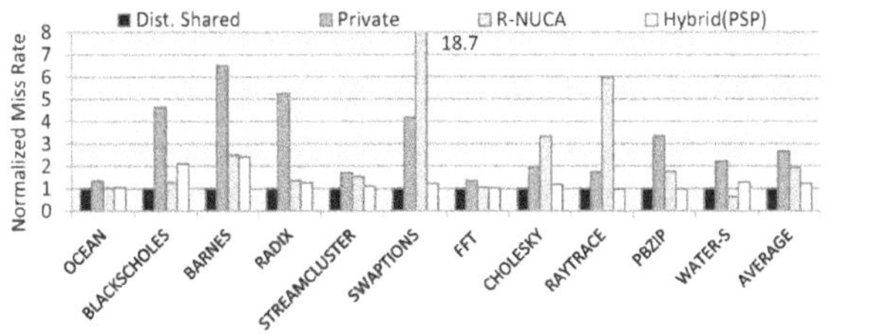

Figure 11: Miss rate for private-averse configuration

We believe this is due to a fundamental advantage of our PSP scheme. For practically private data that is mostly private (e.g., has a small number of sharers) PSP allows replication which keeps data local to each core that accesses it without increasing cache utilization dramatically. For data that is heavily shared, PSP keeps a single copy of the data for all sharers for effective use of cache capacity. Conversely, R-NUCA places all shared data, even infrequently shared data into the shared location creating higher access latency. Additionally, unlike PSP, private cache miss rates are more sensitive to the working set due to data replication regardless of the number of sharers. This results in poorer utilization of capacity when space is at a premium.

5.3.2 Latency

Average memory access latencies of all relevant schemes are reported in Figures 12 and 13. Data access latency is affected by both miss rate and on a hit, the distance that must be traversed to retrieve the data from a potentially remote tile. In distributed shared caches, most data is stored in a remote tile from the core that heavily accesses it, resulting in a higher latency, especially in the shared-averse configuration. In contrast, private caching absorbs all the data to the local tile and thus has a lower hit latency because off tile cache accesses are minimized. This is true especially when the working set size does not exceed the cache capacity, as shown in Figure 12 for a shared-averse configuration. As the cache capacity is pressured by increasing working load, the latency is dominated by off-chip misses and the performance begins to degrade, as demonstrated in Figure 13.

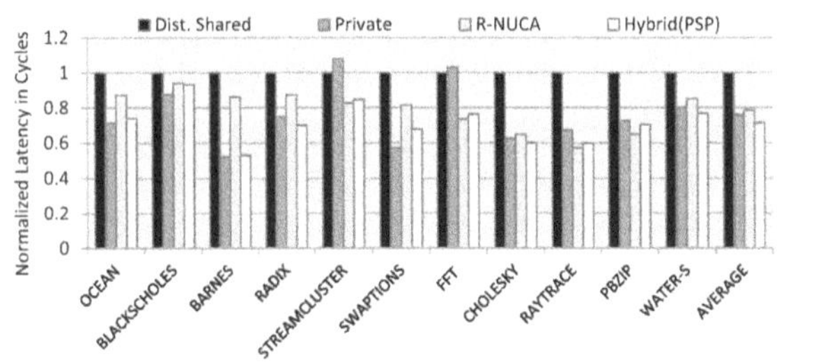

Figure 12: Average memory access latency for shared-averse configuration

R-NUCA also suffers partly from high access latency similar to distributed shared caches when the pages are classified as shared, although it reduces the access latency when pages are initially accessed locally or remain private to a particular processor. Another problem of R-NUCA data classification is the page granularity makes it impossible to optimize smaller memory blocks. One byte of shared access in a private page results in the whole page being re-classified as shared. Additionally, R-NUCA is an "all-or-nothing" approach. For a single access by another core the page is classified as shared even if this is a uncommon or one time occurrence (e.g., data initialized by main thread but used by another working thread) and a private style scheme will still save considerable data access latency.

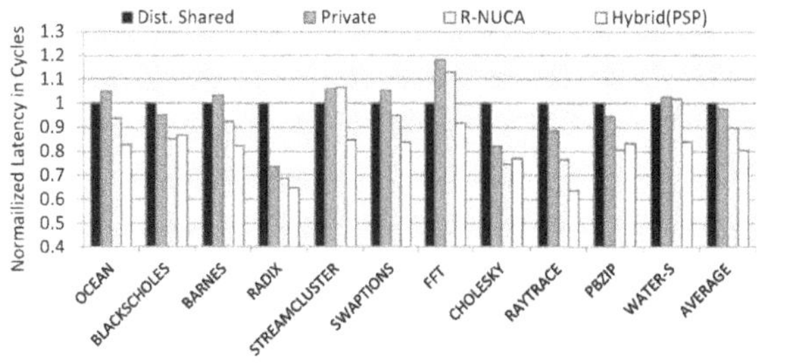

Figure 13: Average memory access latency for private-averse configuration

Our compiler-assisted caching addresses these problems through customized placement policies for classified data, packing a page with data of the same classification, and for tolerating a stray shared access in a practically private configuration. In the shared-adverse configuration, PSP reduces memory latency for distributed shared, private and R-NUCA by 29%, 6% and 9%, respectively. In private-adverse configuration, the corresponding latency reductions are 20%, 18% and 10%.

5.3.3 Performance Improvement

From Figure 14 we can see that in shared-adverse configuration our scheme, PSP, outperforms distributed shared caches by 13% and still provide noticeable gains over private (3%) and R-NUCA (5%). These gains are from keeping the data local to the core(s) that leverage it as well as the coherence traffic reduction. R-NUCA's performance suffers from a lot of practically private data being categorized as shared and requiring longer access latency than PSP. Figure 15 indicates that for large working set sizes (private-adverse configuration), PSP outperforms shared, private and R-NUCA caches by 10%, 9% and 5%, respectively.

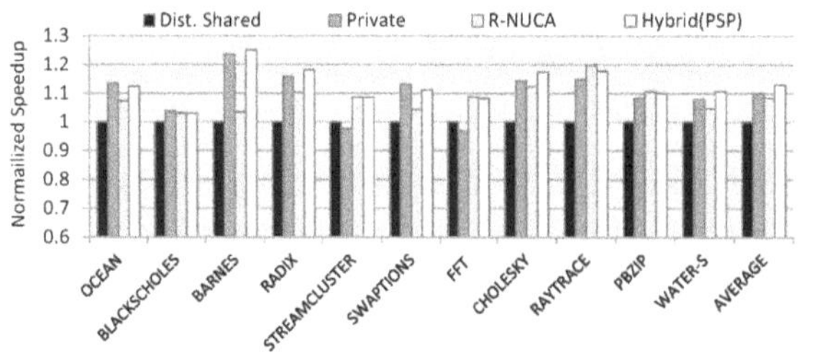

Figure 14: Speedup for shared-averse configuration

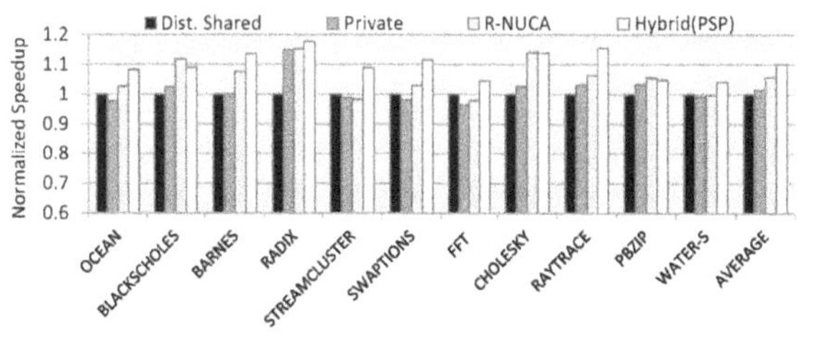

Figure 15: Speedup for private-averse configuration

6. CONCLUSION

In this paper we have presented a compiler-assisted data classification scheme that can help improve CMP performance in many scenarios. We introduce a data classification of "practically private" to capture important application characteristics while significantly reducing data classification complexity and overhead. To demonstrate the utilization of the introduced classification, we have proposed a cache that uses a hybrid of private and S-NUCA caching directed by the compiler data classification. Comparing with other cache mechanisms, in particular R-NUCA in addition to traditional private and shared caches, our cache scheme is unique as it utilizes the data classification available at compile time, thus, eliminating the need for potentially expensive runtime monitoring and profiling. Through the data-classification-aware cache organization we can achieve up to 13%, 9% and 5% performance improvements over shared, private and R-NUCA caching, respectively. Future directions for this work include expanding our analysis to determine the weight of private access for shared or practically private data classifications. We also plan to explore a more aggressive compiler analysis based on data partitioning within data blocks from `malloc()`.

7. ACKNOWLEDGEMENT

This work is supported by NSF award CCF-1064976.

8. REFERENCES

[1] N. Hardavellas, M. Ferdman, B. Falsafi, and A. Ailamaki, "Reactive NUCA: near-optimal block placement and replication in distributed caches," in *Proceedings of the 36th annual international symposium on Computer architecture*, ser. ISCA '09. New York, NY, USA: ACM, 2009, pp. 184–195.

[2] L. Jin and S. Cho, "SOS: A software oriented distributed shared cache management approach for chip multiprocessors," in *Intl Conference on Parallel Architectures and Compilation Techniques PACT*, 2009.

[3] B. A. Cuesta, A. Ros, M. E. Gómez, A. Robles, and J. F. Duato, "Increasing the effectiveness of directory caches by deactivating coherence for private memory blocks," in *Proceedings of the 38th annual international symposium on Computer architecture*, ser. ISCA '11. New York, NY, USA: ACM, 2011, pp. 93–104.

[4] S. Shao, A. K. Jones, and R. Melhem, "Compiler techniques for efficient communications in circuit switched networks for multiprocessor systems," *IEEE Transactions on Parallel and Distributed Systems (TPDS)*, vol. 14, no. 1, pp. 331–345, 2008.

[5] J. M. Arnold, D. A. Buell, and E. G. Davis, "Splash 2," in *Proceedings of the ACM Symposium on Parallel Algorithms and Architectures*. New York, NY, USA: ACM, 1992, pp. 316–322.

[6] C. Bienia, S. Kumar, J. P. Singh, and K. Li, "The parsec benchmark suite: Characterization and architectural implications," Princeton University, Tech. Rep. TR-811-08, January 2008.

[7] S. W. K. Tjiang and J. L. Hennessy, "Sharlit—a tool for building optimizers," in *PLDI '92: Proceedings of the ACM SIGPLAN 1992 conference on Programming language design and implementation*. New York, NY, USA: ACM, 1992, pp. 82–93.

[8] C. Kim, D. Burger, and S. W. Keckler, "Nonuniform cache architectures for wire-delay dominated on-chip caches," *IEEE Micro*, vol. 23, no. 6, pp. 99–107, 2003.

[9] ——, "An adaptive, non-uniform cache structure for wire-delay dominated on-chip caches," in *Proceedings of the 10th International Conference on Architectural Support for Programming Languages and Operating Systems*, 2002.

[10] M. Hammoud, S. Cho, and R. G. Melhem, "Cache equalizer: a placement mechanism for chip multiprocessor distributed shared caches," in *Proceedings of the 6th International Conference on High Performance and Embedded Architectures and Compilers*, ser. HiPEAC '11. New York, NY, USA: ACM, 2011, pp. 177–186.

[11] Y. Li, A. Abousamra, R. Melhem, and A. K. Jones, "Compiler-assisted data distribution for chip multiprocessors," in *PACT '10: Proceedings of the 19th international conference on Parallel architectures and compilation techniques*. New York, NY, USA: ACM, 2010, pp. 501–512.

[12] R. P. Wilson, R. S. French, C. S. Wilson, S. P. Amarsinghe, J. M. Anderson, S. W. K. Tjiang, S. W. Liao, C. W. Tseng, M. W. Hall, M. s. Lam, and J. L. Hennessy, "SUIF: An infrastructure for research on parallelizing and optimizing compilers," in *SIGPLAN Notices*, 1994.

[13] R. E. Tarjan, "Fast algorithms for solving path problems," *J. ACM*, vol. 28, pp. 594–614, July 1981.

[14] A. Abousamra, R. Melhem, and A. K. Jones, "Winning with pinning in NoC," in *Proceedings of IEEE Hot Interconnects*, 2009.

[15] Z. Chishti, M. D. Powell, and T. N. Vijaykumar, "Optimizing replication, communication, and capacity allocation in cmps," in *ISCA*, 2005, pp. 357–368.

[16] H. Dybdahl and P. Stenstrom, "An adaptive shared/private NUCA cache partitioning scheme for chip multiprocessors," in *Proceedings of International Symposium on High Performance Computer Architecture*, 2007.

[17] J. Chang and G. S. Sohi, "Cooperative caching for chip multiprocessors," in *The 33rd International Symposium on Computer Architecture*, 2006.

[18] M. Zhang and K. Asanovic, "Victim replication: Maximizing capacity while hiding wire delay in tiled chip multiprocessors," in *32nd Annual International Symposium on Computer Architecture*, 2005.

[19] P. Kongetira, K. Aingaran, and K. Olukotun, "Niagara: A 32-way multithreaded sparc processor," *IEEE Micro*, vol. 2, no. 25, pp. 21–29, 2005.

[20] J. A. Brown, R. Kumar, and D. M. Tullsen, "Proximity-aware directory-based coherence for multi-core processor architectures," in *Proceedings of the ACM symposium on Parallel Algorithms and Architectures*, 2007, pp. 126–134.

[21] J. Zebchuk, V. Srinivasan, M. K. Qureshi, and A. Moshovos, "A tagless coherence directory," in *Proceedings of the 42nd Annual IEEE/ACM International Symposium on Microarchitecture*, ser. MICRO 42. New York, NY, USA: ACM, 2009, pp. 423–434.

[22] P. S. Magnusson, M. Christensson, J. Eskilson, D. Forsgren, G. Hallberg, J. Hogberg, F. Larsson, A. Moestedt, and B. Werner, "Simics: A full system simulation platform," *IEEE Computer*, vol. 35, no. 2, pp. 50–58, February 2002.

Complexity-Effective Multicore Coherence

Alberto Ros
Department of Computer Engineering
University of Murcia, Spain
aros@ditec.um.es

Stefanos Kaxiras
Department of Information Technology
Uppsala University, Sweden
stefanos.kaxiras@it.uu.se

ABSTRACT

Much of the complexity and overhead (directory, state bits, invalidations) of a typical directory coherence implementation stems from the effort to make it "invisible" even to the strongest memory consistency model. In this paper, we show that a much simpler, directory-less/broadcast-less, multicore coherence can outperform a directory protocol but without its complexity and overhead. Motivated by recent efforts to simplify coherence, we propose a hardware approach that does not require any application guidance. The cornerstone of our approach is a dynamic, application-transparent, write-policy (write-back for private data, write-through for shared data), simplifying the protocol to just two stable states. Self-invalidation of the shared data at synchronization points allows us to remove the directory (and invalidations) completely, with just a data-race-free guarantee from software. This leads to our main result: a virtually costless coherence that outperforms a MESI directory protocol (by 4.8%) while at the same time reducing shared cache and network energy consumption (by 14.2%) for 15 parallel benchmarks, on 16 cores.

Categories and Subject Descriptors

C.1.2 [**Processor Architectures**]: Multiple Data Stream Architectures (Multiprocessors)—*Parallel processors*; B.3.2 [**Memory Structures**]: Design Styles—*Cache memories*

General Terms

Design, Experimentation, Performance

Keywords

Multicore, simple cache coherence, directory-less protocol, dynamic write policy, self-invalidation, multiple writers

1. INTRODUCTION

"For any given memory location, at any given moment in time, there is either a single core that may write it (and that may also read it) or some number of cores that may read it. ..." [31]

Among several definitions of Cache Coherence (CC), Sorin, Hill, and Wood propose and cite the above for its insight. To satisfy such a definition, coherence protocols react immediately to writes, and invalidate all cached read copies. This is a source of significant complexity. It requires snooping or a directory to constantly track cached copies and send invalidations (or broadcasts). It necessitates additional protocol states for performance (e.g., Exclusive, Owned), which causes an explosion in the number of transient states required to cover every possible race that may arise. For example, the GEMS [24] implementation of the MESI directory protocol –a direct descendant of the SUNfire coherence protocol– requires no less than 30 states.

Complexity translates into cost. Storage is needed for cache-line state, the directory (or dual-ported/duplicate tags for snooping), and the logic required by complex cache and directory controllers. Significant effort has been expended to reduce these costs, especially the storage cost [2, 9, 10, 27], but also verification cost [11, 32]. In terms of performance and power, complex protocols are characterized by a large number of broadcasts and snoops. Here too, significant effort has been expended to reduce or filter coherence traffic [19, 25, 34] with the intent of making complex protocols more power- or performance-efficient. Verification of such protocols is difficult and in many cases incomplete [1].

We take an alternate approach that eliminates the need for directories, invalidations, broadcasts and snoops. Indeed, this approach eliminates the need for almost all coherence state (besides the rudimentary valid/invalid and clean/dirty states). Our approach exploits a typical multicore cache hierarchy organization with private L1(/L2) caches and a shared Last-Level-Cache (LLC). Our motivation is to simplify coherence and practically eliminate the hardware cost (storage and logic), while at the same time achieving improvements in both performance and energy consumption.

Our proposal targets multicore/manycore[1] architectures where the relative cost of coherence is significant compared to the complexity of the cores. This includes many accelerators based on simple cores (e.g., Tilera [6]), standalone GPUs, but also cache-coherent shared virtual memory GPUs coupled to general purpose cores. We do not envision our

[1]In the interest of brevity, we will use the term multicore to describe both.

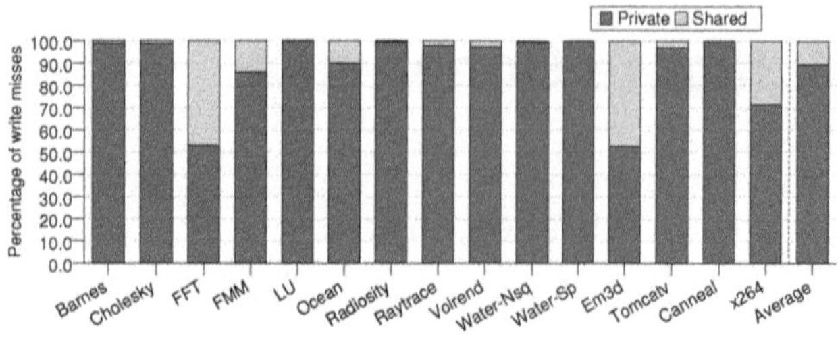

Figure 1: Percentage of write misses in a write-through protocol for both private and shared data

proposal for multicores based on few fat complex cores, where the relative cost of implementing a snooping or directory MESI protocol is not an issue, and such protocols are routinely implemented; nor do we explore workloads where performance is dominated by off-chip memory accesses rendering the on-chip coherence effects negligible (e.g., commercial workloads).

In addition, the focus of our work is the multicore cache hierarchy. Thus, the scope of this paper does not extend to inter-chip implementations which we discuss only briefly in Section 6.1. The well-known and well-understood coherence schemes employed widely today have been developed for multi-chip SMPs or distributed shared memory machines where the trade-offs are markedly different from a multicore cache hierarchy.

Contributions. Our proposal is a simplification of multicore coherence to the bare necessities, but without sacrificing performance or power compared to more sophisticated versions. We achieve this in two steps:

1. We propose a **dynamic write policy**, a very simple albeit novel idea, that simplifies the protocol to just two cache states (Valid/Invalid), eliminates the need to track writers at the (LLC) directory, and eliminates read- indirection through the directory. Significant complexity in current protocols comes from strategies for efficient execution of sequential applications (e.g., the E state in MESI) or optimizations to avoid memory (e.g., the O state in MOESI) largely ignoring that in multicores there is an LLC between the cores and memory. A simple Write-Through policy to the LLC would obviate almost all coherence states (even the M state) but it is not acceptable as it sacrifices performance. The observation, however, that drives our approach is that most write misses (around 90%) in a write-through protocol actually come from private blocks, as Figure 1 shows. We select between Write-Back and Write-Through to the LLC depending on whether data are private or shared. The distinction between private and shared data is determined dynamically at a page granularity utilizing the page table and the TLBs [12, 15] (Section 3.1).

2. We **selectively flush** shared data from the L1 caches on synchronization points. Our approach is a generalization of *read-only* tear-off copies [19, 21] to all shared data (including writable copies). This step eliminates the need to track readers for invalidation, therefore obviating the need for a directory/broadcast or snoops. Write-throughs are performed by transferring only what is modified (diffs) in a cache-line, allowing multiple simultaneous writers per cache line (as long as their writes constitute false sharing on separate words in a cache line and not a true data race) (Section 3.2).

While write-through protocols and self-invalidation have been proposed separately in the past, we combine them and, for the first time, make them *practical* by applying them dynamically, based on a run-time division of data to shared and private at a page granularity. This leads to the main novel result we report in this paper: a minimal, very simple, virtually costless coherence protocol that does not require any application involvement or guidance. While our work bears some similarity to the work of Choi *et al.* we pursue an application-transparent approach, as opposed to their application-driven approach [11], we arrive at a truly directory-less coherence protocol while they still implement a "registry" in the LLC, and we provide support for synchronization without a directory or invalidations that is lacking in prior work.

Another advantage of our approach is that it is interconnect-agnostic, meaning that our coherence protocol is exactly the same whether implemented over a bus, a crossbar, or a packet-based, point-to-point, NoC. This leads to seamless scaling from low-end to high-end parts or free intermixing of buses and NoCs on the same chip, e.g., in an heterogeneous multicore/manycore chip. In the limited space of this paper we cannot evaluate all the network options, so we limit our discussion to the most general and challenging case of an unordered, packet-based NoC.

There are two implications of our approach. First, the protocol resulting from the second step cannot support Sequential Consistency (SC) for data races. This is because without a directory or broadcasts, a core writing a memory location cannot invalidate any other cores that may be reading this location. This violates the definition of coherence but it is actually an acceptable behavior for a weak consistency memory model [31] (Section 3.4). Thus, our protocol is incoherent for data races but satisfies the definition of coherence for the important class of Data-Race-Free (DRF) programs. Data races are the culprits of many problems in parallel software and the benefits of data-race-free operation are well argued by Choi *et al.* [11]. Thus, similarly to SC for DRF [3], our approach provides Coherency for DRF.

The second implication is that, synchronization instructions (such as T&S or Compare&Swap) which inherently rely on data races, require their own protocol for a correct implementation. We propose an efficient and resource-friendly **synchronization protocol** that works without invalidations (Section 3.3) and in many cases eliminates spinning.

Results. Our approach leads to a very simple cache coherence protocol that requires no directory, no state bits in the caches (other than the standard Valid/Invalid and Dirty/Clean bits), no broadcasts/snoops, nor invalidations, and outperforms a directory protocol by 4.8%, on average for 15 parallel benchmarks on a 16-core architecture with 32KB L1 caches. It minimizes control message traffic by not requiring invalidations or unblock messages, and it minimizes data traffic by sending only cache-line diffs to the LLC from multiple simultaneous writers. Diffs are correctly merged in the cache-lines –in the absence of data-races– thereby solving the false-sharing problem. Our evaluation focus is on a tiled manycore architecture, reflecting our conviction that very simple coherence is especially appealing in this case.

Results show that reductions in traffic and LLC power consumption can lead to energy saving of 14.2%, on average, with respect to a directory protocol.

2. BACKGROUND

2.1 Write-Through Caches and Coherence

A write-through policy for L1 caches has the potential to greatly simplify the coherence protocol [31]. Just two states are needed in the L1 cache (Valid-Invalid) and there is no need for a Dirty/Clean bit (so evictions do not need to write-back). Further, the LLC always holds the correct data so it can immediately respond to requests. This means that there is no indirection for reads and that there is no need to track the writers at the directory. Invalidation is still required, however, and the readers need to be tracked. Alternatively, with a Null Directory in the LLC and Dir_0B protocol [4], or in a bus-based multicore, broadcasts to all the caches are used for invalidation. Unfortunately, because the number of write-throughs far exceeds the number of write-backs, this results in abysmal performance, and significantly increased traffic and power, as we show in Section 5.

2.2 Private vs. Shared Data Classification

Recent work realizes the importance of classifying private and shared data. Some work uses hardware mechanisms for performing this task [16, 29], other rely on the operating system [12, 15, 20], and other on the compiler [22]. The advantage of hardware mechanisms is that they can work at cache-line granularity but can be prohibitive in their storage requirements. On the other hand, the techniques which employ the OS do not impose any extra requirements for dedicated hardware, since they store the information along with the page table entries working at a page granularity. This means that if a single block in the page is shared (or even if two different private blocks within the same page are accessed by different cores) the whole page must be considered as shared, thus, leading to misclassified blocks. Finally, the disadvantage of the compiled-assisted classification is that it is difficult to know at compile time if a variable is going to be shared or not.

On the other hand, different proposals use this classification to reach different goals. Some of them to perform an efficient mapping for non-uniform cache access (NUCA) caches [15, 22]. Others to reduce the number of broadcast required by a snooping protocol [20], or to reduce the size of the directory cache in a directory-based protocol [13, 12]. Finally, similarly to us, Pugsley *et al.* [29] and Hossain *et al.* [16] use the classification for choosing among different behaviors for the coherence protocol but both of these approaches rely on *directory* or *bus invalidation* coherence. Our goal is to simplify coherence. Thus, the most appropriate way of classifying blocks is the one managed by the operating system, due to its simplicity, effectiveness, and lack of extra hardware. It allows us to define two completely isolated protocols for private and shared data that can be verified independently.

2.3 Self-Invalidation

Dynamic self-invalidation and tear-off copies were first proposed by Lebeck and Wood as a way to reduce invalidations in cc-NUMA [21]. The basic idea is that cache blocks can be teared off the directory (i.e., not registered there) as long as they are discarded voluntarily before the next synchronization point by the processor who created them. As the authors note, this can only be supported in a weak consistency memory model (for SC, self-invalidation needs to be semantically equivalent to a cache replacement).

Lebeck and Wood proposed this as an optimization on top of an existing cc-NUMA protocol. Furthermore, they made an effort to restrict its use only to certain blocks through a complex classification performed at the directory. Their design choices reflect the trade-offs of a cc-NUMA architecture: not applying self-invalidation indiscriminately is because misses to the directory are expensive.

Self-invalidation was recently used by Kaxiras and Keramidas in their "SARC Coherence" proposal [19]. They observe that with self-invalidation, writer prediction becomes straightforward to implement. The underlying directory protocol is always active to guarantee correctness. Despite the advantage for writer prediction, their proposal increases the complexity of the base directory protocol with another optimization layer and leaves the directory untouched. Finally, Choi *et al.* use self-invalidation instructions, inserted by the compiler after annotations in the source program, in their application-driven approach [11]. We discuss this further in Section 7.

3. PROTOCOLS

Our approach boils down to two successive steps: i) reduce protocol complexity by making a write-through policy to the LLC practical; ii) eliminate the directory from the LLC and all invalidation (including broadcasts).

3.1 Step 1: Simplifying the Protocol

The centerpiece of our strategy for reducing the complexity of coherence is to distinguish between private and shared data references. For the coherence of the shared data, we rely on the simplicity of a write-through policy. However, the write-through policy does not have to be employed on the private data, for which a write-back policy can be safely used without any coherence support (apart from the one already required for uniprocessors). In the L1 a Dynamic Write-Policy distinguishes between private and shared data guided by page level information supplied by the TLB. Pages are divided into "Private" and "Shared" at the OS level, depending on the observed accesses. Because the resulting protocols have only two states (Valid/Invalid) and we differentiate between private and shared data, we call the overall protocol VIPS (Valid/Invalid – Private/Shared).

We will just dwell on single point: our proposal is minimally intrusive in the design of the core and its local cache. In fact, it leaves the L1 cache unmodified. We assume that each L1 line has the common Valid/Invalid (V) and Clean/Dirty (D) bits and that TLB entries use two bits from the reserved ones to indicate the Private/Shared (P/S bit) status of the page and to lock the TLB entry (L bit) when we are switching from write-back to write-through. The dynamic write policy is implemented outside the L1. The P/S bit of the accessed data controls whether a write-through will take place.

3.1.1 VIPS Protocol: Write-Back for Private Lines

The protocol transactions for private lines are simple, since no effort is expended on maintaining coherence. Figure 2 shows the read (PrRd), write (PrWr), and eviction (WrB)

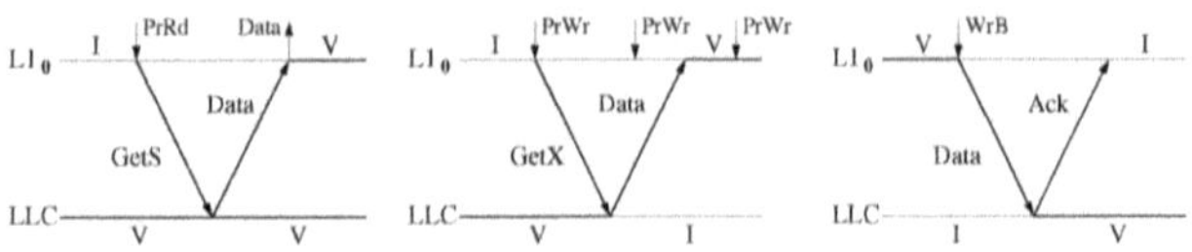

Figure 2: Read (PrRd), write (PrWr), and write-back (WrB) transactions for private lines

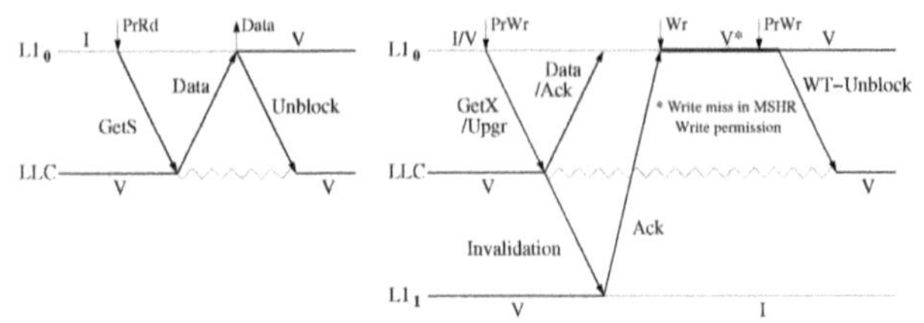

Figure 3: Read (PrRd) and write (PrWr) transactions for shared lines

initiated transactions. For private request the LLC controller does not block the corresponding lines, i.e., there are no transient states. The Write-Back transaction requires an acknowledgment for memory ordering purposes (so that fence instructions can detect its completion) in the corner case when a page changes designation from private to shared after it has been written.

3.1.2 *VIPS Protocol: Write-Through for Shared Lines*

The transactions for shared lines follow a write-through protocol (Figure 3). As in a MESI implementation, the LLC line is blocked both for PrRd and PrWr transactions and requires *Unblock* messages to unblock it. A PrRd transaction that misses in the L1 gets the line and set its state to Valid (Figure 3, left side). PrWr transactions (Figure 3, right side) send a *GetX* to the LLC controller that blocks the line (and gets the data if needed). Copies in other cores are invalidated (with the acknowledgments returning to the writer). When all acknowledgements arrive, the write (*Wr*) is performed. The write-through can be delayed arbitrarily (we call this *Delayed Write-Through*) keeping the LLC line blocked. While the L1 line is in state V and dirty there is still an entry for that line in the MSHR structure and the line can be written repeatedly. The write-through (*WT-Unblock*) clears the L1 dirty bit, unblocks the line, and writes the new data in the LLC. A PrWr on a clean and valid line initiates a write-through anew.

3.1.3 *Transitions Between Write-Back and Write-Through*

A page accessed by a single core starts as private in the page table, so a write-back policy is applied for every requested line within that page. When a second core accesses the same page it notices that it is tagged as private by another core. The first core needs to be interrupted and its TLB entry updated so it can see the page, henceforth, as shared. The write policy of the lines within this page will change from write-back to write-through. Consequently, those lines marked as dirty in the L1 cache for the core being interrupted need to be cleared by means of a write-back transaction. While this is an expensive operation, it is rather rare. The same technique for detecting private and shared pages has been used in recent work and in the interest of space, we will refer the reader to the excellent and detailed descriptions published elsewhere [12, 15].

3.1.4 *Delayed Write-Throughs*

The obvious optimization to any Write-Through cache is to reduce the amount of write-throughs by coalescing as many writes as possible. In the transactions presented above, the write-through can be delayed. In the meantime, the line can be written multiple times by the same core. This corresponds roughly to a MESI "Modified" state, but is strictly transient (exists only from the *GetX* to the write-through that unblocks the LLC line) and *invisible* to transactions from other cores. During that time, the address of the line is in one of the core's MSHRs. We assume that the MSHRs track only addresses and meta-information but do not carry a copy of the data. One simple implementation of the delayed write-through is to augment the MSHRs with a timer that causes the actual write-through to happen a fixed delay after the initial write. Since the delayed write-through is transparent to other cores, this allows our protocol to have the same states as a traditional simple write-through protocol, thus significantly reducing the number of race conditions, and therefore, transient states with respect to a MESI protocol.

3.2 Step 2: Eliminating the Directory

Our next goal is to eliminate the directory. We have already removed the need for tracking the writer in the directory with the private-shared classification and the write-through policy. What is left is to get rid of the need to track the readers of a memory location just to invalidate them later on a write. Self-invalidation serves exactly this purpose [21]: readers are allowed to make unregistered copies of a memory location, as long as they promise to invalidate these copies at the next synchronization point they encounter. Our approach is similar but with a difference: *all* shared data in the L1 caches whether read or written to –not just data brought in as Read-Only, e.g., as in [21] and [19]– are tear-off copies. A core encountering a synchronization point (lock acquire/release, barriers, wait/signal synchronization) flushes its shared data from the L1. Since we flush only shared and not private data, we call this *Selective Flushing*, (SF). Implementing selective flushing incurs very little change to the cache design. Valid bits are guarded by per-line Private/Shared (P/S) bits. The P/S bits are set when a line is brought into the L1. Subsequently a "flush" signal, resets all the valid bits guarded by P/S bits in state Shared. The implementation of the flush is straightforward when valid bits are implemented as clearable flip-flops outside the L1 arrays. As is pointed out in prior work [11, 19, 21], self-invalidation, and by extension selective flushing, implies a weak consistency memory model and only guarantees SC for Data-Race-Free (DRF) programs [3].

However, even with a DRF guarantee the lack of invalidations can cause problems. Consider two concurrent readers, each holding a valid copy of the same cache line. Assume that the two readers decide to write two different words in the cache line –false sharing– without any intervening synchronization. If their write-throughs happen at the granularity of a cache line, they can overwrite each other's new value, leading the system to an incoherent state. LLC blocking does not help in this case, since the two write transactions can be spaced sufficiently apart so they do not overlap.

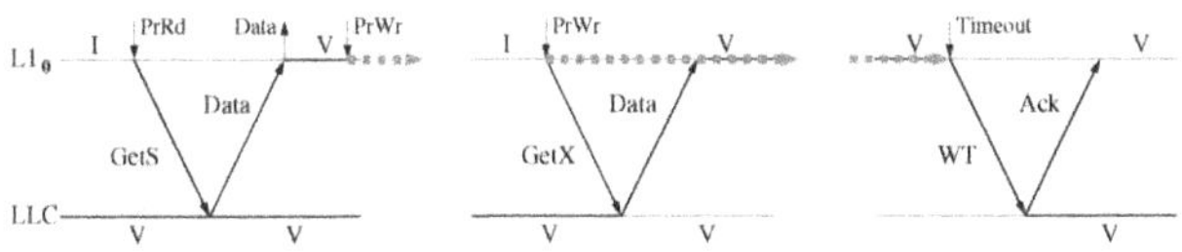

Figure 4: VIPS-M Read (PrRd), write (PrWr), and Delayed Write-through (WT at Timeout) transactions

One solution would be to demand DRF guarantees at the cache-line level but that would place a heavy burden on software. Our solution is to perform write-throughs at a word granularity which has the additional benefit of reducing the amount of data transferred to the LLC.

Write-throughs at a word granularity require per-word dirty bits. This allows multiple concurrent writers on a cache line to write-through to the LLC just the words they modify but no other. Delayed write-throughs send their cache-line diffs which are then merged in the LLC. The important realization here is that immediately seeing the new values written by other writers is not a requirement in a weak consistency memory model –already implied by self-invalidation. We call this protocol Multiple-Writer-Merge and denote it with a simple M suffix: VIPS-M.

An important implication of word granularity for the write-throughs is that it makes blocking of the lines at the LLC controller unnecessary. But this in turn, allows us to equate the protocol for shared, data-race-free data to the protocol for private data. At word granularity, we simplify the write transaction to just a write-through (WT) followed by an acknowledgment (Figure 4, right side). If the line is already valid in the L1 (for example, as a result of a read –Figure 4, left side) an upgrade request (Upgr) is no longer needed, while from an invalid state, a GetX gets the data but does not block the LLC line (Figure 4, middle) which remains valid. Thus, shared-data write transactions become similar to private-data write transactions. Practically all data, whether shared (data-race-free) or private, are handled without any state in the LLC. The main difference is in when dirty data are put back in the LLC. Private data follow a write-back on eviction policy, while shared, data-race-free data follow a delayed (up to a synchronization point or an MSHR replacement) write-through policy. Synchronization data, however, still require a blocking protocol, described below in Section 3.3.

The overhead of the M version is that we need to track exactly what has been modified in each dirty line so we can selectively write back only the modified words to the LLC. One would assume that this means per-word dirty bits for every line in the L1. But per-word dirty bits are needed only for delayed write-throughs and are attached only to the MSHRs. No additional support is needed in the L1 or the LLC –other than being able to update individual words.

3.3 Synchronization Without Invalidation

Synchronization relies on data races. Instructions such as Test&Set or Compare&Swap, race to read-modify-write atomically a memory location if a condition is met (i.e., the "Test" or "Compare" parts). Otherwise, a copy of the memory location allows a core to spin locally in its L1 until the condition is changed by another core. In our approach, because we have no invalidations, a core cannot "signal" a change in the condition to the other cores that might be

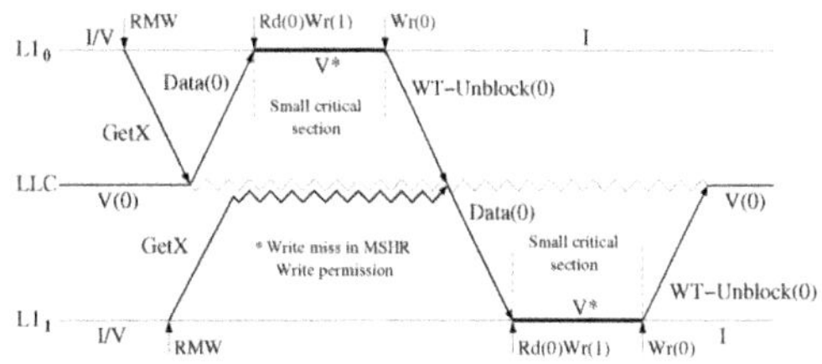

Figure 5: Atomic RMW transactions for shared lines

spinning, endangering forward progress. Therefore, atomic instructions always re-read the LLC copy.

The protocol is shown in Figure 5 for a simple atomic instruction such as Test&Set. Regardless of the existence of an L1 copy, an atomic instruction invariably sends a *GetX* to the LLC. If the line is unblocked, its data are returned to the core, and if the test succeeds, the line is written with a new value (indicating, for example, that a lock is held by a core). Throughout the duration of the read-modify-write the line is blocked by the LLC controller; it is only unblocked by a final write-through. In the interim no other core can complete any transaction on that line (as core 2 in Figure 5). Their requests enter a finite queue (bounded by the number of cores) managed by the LLC controller.

At first sight, bypassing the L1 and re-reading the LLC seems to make spinning very expensive. But this is not always so. By delaying the write-throughs of atomic instructions in the MSHRs, we are delaying the completion of a successful lock acquire. This may seem counter-intuitive but has a significant advantage. The more we delay the write-through of a winning lock acquire the more we reduce the LLC spinning of the other cores that are trying to get the lock at the same time. Other cores are blocked at the LLC controller and cannot even complete the Test part of the Test&Set. In fact, it is quite possible, that for a short critical section, the write-back of the Test&Set can be delayed in the MSHR for the whole duration of the critical section, as shown in Figure 5. The lock release operation which is a simple write on the same lock, coalesces with the delayed write-through of the Test&Set. After the lock release, the delayed write-through must complete immediately to pass the lock to the next core in line. While we can eliminate spinning for short critical sections, in longer ones the write-through of the atomic instruction eventually completes and spinning resumes by the other waiting cores. This spinning in the LLC can increase traffic, so an exponential back off in software is essential to lessen it.

3.4 Putting it All Together: Memory Consistency and Coherence

Let us now return to the definition of coherence by Sorin, Hill, and Wood, called the Single-Writer/Multiple-Reader (SWMR)/Data-Value invariant. The definition (quoted from [31]) has two parts:

- *"For any given memory location, at any given moment in time, there is either a single core that may write it (and that may also read it) or some number of cores that may read it."*
- *"Data-Value Invariant: the value of a memory location at the start of an epoch is the same as the value of the memory location at the end of its last read-write epoch."*

Table 1: SC litmus test

Core C1	Core C2	Comments
S1: x = NEW;	S2: y = NEW;	Initially x = 0, y = 0
L1: r1 = y;	L2: r2 = x;	

A coherence protocol that satisfies this definition is invisible to the underlying memory consistency model [31]. In other words, "correct" coherence cannot weaken a memory model. We use this definition to reason about the behavior of the two proposed protocols with respect to memory models.

Step 1: VIPS protocol. The protocol in Step 1 adheres to the SWMR definition without constraints. Even in the face of data races and/or false sharing, it allows only one writer at a time (because of the invalidation). Similarly to MESI implementations [24], LLC blocking guarantees that values are propagated correctly.[2] It is therefore invisible to the memory consistency model, and thus, can support even the strictest model: SC.

Step 2: VIPS-M protocol. The lack of directory and invalidations in Step 2 leads to a protocol that is incoherent for data races, but adheres to the SWMR definition for data-race-free operation.

It is easy to see how Step 2 violates the SWMR invariant for data races. Consider the following classic example for SC in Table 1. In an SC implementation $r1$ and $r2$ cannot be both 0, after the execution of the code shown for cores $C1$ and $C2$. A coherence protocol adhering to the SWMR/Data-Value invariant cannot change this. However, Step 2 does! Assume that y is cached in $C1$ before the execution of the $C2$ code. Since $C2$ cannot invalidate the cached copy of y, L1 will load 0 into $r1$. Similarly for x in $C2$, resulting in both $r1$ and $r2$ having the value 0, even after both writes have been performed. The single-writer invariant is violated.

However, for DRF operation, VIPS-M does satisfy the coherency definition: i) false sharing does not violate the single writer invariant because write-throughs happen at word granularity; thus there is only one writer per word at a time (otherwise there would be a data race); ii) the data value invariant holds because writes and reads are separated by synchronization, whereupon all shared lines are flushed. Note that on synchronization all outstanding write-throughs are sent immediately to the LLC and fence instructions must wait for the acknowledgments of the write-throughs for DRF lines to guarantee proper memory ordering.

Thus, VIPS-M is invisible to SC for DRF. Similarly to the reasoning of SC for DRF [3], we implement Coherence for DRF. DRF satisfies by itself the single writer multiple reader invariant. All we have to do is to guarantee the Data Value invariant and this is achieved writing-through the correct data, and flushing the L1 at synchronization. This is why in VIPS-M we can equate the protocol for shared DRF data to the protocol for private data.

3.5 Optimizations

So far we have been in the process of de-evolving coherence: we removed most coherence state and the directory. It is therefore important that any optimization we introduce is neutral to complexity and cost. We consider only very simple optimizations that adhere to this principle.

3.5.1 Classification Optimizations

Data classification is not the focus of this paper. We employ a very simple classification scheme that, nevertheless, allows our protocols to outperform more complex protocols. However, some classification optimizations are straightforward in our case.

Self-invalidation can cause needless misses on shared data that have not been modified. Complex techniques to exclude such data have been proposed [21]. In our approach, we simply tag pages as *Read-Only* (RO) if they are not written, and Read-Write (RW) otherwise. A page stars as RO but transitions to RW on the first write (there is no reverse transition). Because the page is shared, all the cores that have a TLB entry must be interrupted and notified of this change. Cache lines belonging to RO pages are spared from self-invalidation. Although a crude approximation to the optimization proposed by Lebeck and Wood, it yields good results and we use it in the evaluation. More sophisticated approaches can be explored in future work (e.g., accounting for thread migration to perform the page classification as suggested by Hardavellas *et al.* [15]).

3.5.2 Relaxing Inclusion Policies

In a MESI protocol, in which the directory information is stored along with the LLC entries, inclusion between the L1 and the LLC is enforced. When a line is evicted from the LLC, the directory information is evicted as well, and all copies in L1 are invalidated to maintaining coherence. In the VIPS protocol, private lines do not require directory information, and therefore we can selectively relax the inclusion policy for them. An exclusive policy for private lines can make better use of the LLC storage, potentially reducing expensive off-chip misses. But, silent conflict evictions of clean L1 copies result in subsequent misses in the LLC. One option is to victimize clean L1 copies into the LLC. This increases traffic but saves latency in L1 conflicts. A middle-of-the-road approach that reduces this traffic is to opt for a non-inclusive policy where data requested by the L1 with read-only permission are also stored in the LLC. This way, evictions of clean lines can be silent both in the L1 and in the LLC. Because the LLC is not stressed by our benchmarks, we have seen that the later approach can reduce traffic requirements. In the VIPS-M protocol inclusion is not required for any line, since we do not have directory information in the LLC. Therefore, the same optimizations for private lines in the VIPS protocol, are applicable to all lines in the VIPS-M protocol.

4. EVALUATION METHODOLOGY

4.1 Simulation and System Configuration

The evaluation of the protocols proposed in this work is carried out with full-system simulation using Virtutech Simics [23] and the Wisconsin GEMS toolset [24]. The interconnection network is modeled using GARNET [5]. We simulate a 16-tile chip multiprocessor (CMP) architecture. The values of the main parameters used for the evaluation are shown in Table 2. Through experimentation we have found that only 16 entries per MSHR are needed to keep shared data as dirty for enough time to avoid most write misses.

[2]An old value cannot be accessed at the LLC if a write-through is in progress. This guarantees, for example, that only the new value of a write-through that started before a synchronization will be visible after the synchronization.

Table 2: System parameters (between brackets: ranges for sensitivity analysis; in bold: main configuration)

Memory Parameters	
Processor frequency	3.0GHz
Block/Page size	64 bytes/4KB
MSHR size/Delay timeout	16 entries/1000 cycles
Split L1 I & D caches	[16KB, **32KB**, 64KB], 4-way
L1 cache hit time	1 (tag) and 2 (tag+data) cycles
Shared unified L2 cache	8MB, 512KB/tile, 16-way
L2 cache hit time	[**2**, 6] (tag) and [**4**, 12] (tag+data) cycles
Memory access time	160 cycles
Network Parameters	
Topology	2-dimensional mesh (4x4)
Routing technique	Deterministic X-Y
Flit size	16 bytes
Data message size	5 flits (if MWM not used)
Control message size	1 flit
Routing time	2 cycles
Switch time	2 cycles
Link time	2 cycles

Likewise, a timeout between 500 and 2000 cycles for the delayed write-throughs (or up to eviction in the MSHR) offers a good compromise between the reduction in the number of extra write-misses and the time the LLC remains blocked. MSHR timeout timers are implemented as cache decay hierarchical counters [18]. Cache latencies, energy consumption, and area requirements are calculated using the CACTI 6.5 tool [26] assuming a 32nm process technology. Likewise, the energy consumption overhead from extra L1 hardware (timers, selective flush support, etc.), is estimated to be a very small part (less than 1%) of the L1 energy.

We evaluate the five cache coherence protocols shown in Table 3. This table summarizes some of their characteristics. The first protocol (Hammer) corresponds to a broadcast-based protocol for unordered networks [28]. Since in this protocol invalidations are sent to all cores, there is no need for a directory. However, this protocol generates a significant amount of traffic, which dramatically increases with the number of cores. The second protocol (Directory) corresponds to a MESI directory-based protocol where the directory information is stored along with the LLC tags. The directory information allows the protocol to filter some traffic, and therefore, save energy consumption. Inclusion between L1 caches and the LLC is enforced in this case. The main advantage of the third protocol (Write-Through) is its simplicity, since it only has two base states for lines in L1 caches (as do our protocols). Although this protocol accelerates read misses by removing their indirection, the write-through policy increases the number of write misses and severely hurts performance. The fourth protocol is our SC protocol (VIPS). It only has two base states, and can relax the inclusion policy for private blocks. Despite being simple it still requires invalidations. Finally, the fifth protocol (VIPS-M) provides SC only for DRF applications. The main characteristic of this protocol is that it completely removes both the need of storing directory information and sending invalidations, as well as the indirection for all cache misses. The absence of a directory reduces the LLC tag area, and allows the protocol to relax the inclusion policy.

4.2 Benchmarks

We evaluate the five cache coherence protocols with a wide variety of parallel applications. *Barnes* (16K particles),

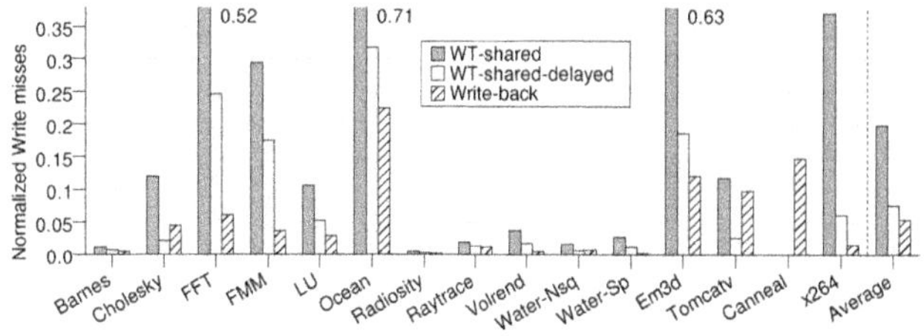

Figure 6: Reduction in write misses due to the private/shared classification and delayed write-through. Write misses have been normalized with respect to the simple write-through policy.

Cholesky (tk16), *FFT* (64K complex doubles), *FMM* (16K particles), *LU* (512×512 matrix), *Ocean* (514×514 ocean), *Radiosity* (room, -ae 5000.0 -en 0.050 -bf 0.10), *Raytrace* (teapot, optimized version that removes unnecessary locks), *Volrend* (head), *Water-Nsq* (512 molecules) and *Water-Sp* (512 molecules) belong to the *SPLASH-2* benchmark suite [33]. *Em3d* (38400 nodes, 15% remote) is a shared-memory implementation of the Split-C benchmark. *Tomcatv* (256 points, 5 time steps) is a shared-memory implementation of the SPEC benchmark. *Canneal* (simsmall) and *x264* (simsmall) are from the PARSEC benchmark suite [7].

To accurately simulate our VIPS-M protocol we have instrumented the synchronization mechanisms (locks, barriers, conditions) used by the benchmarks so they are "visible" by the hardware. Synchronization points are signaled by fences preceding synchronization. In this way, processors can perform the selective flushing on their caches when required. Data accessed by atomic instructions follow the synchronization protocol described in Section 3.3. We simulate the entire applications, but collect statistics only from start to completion of their parallel part.

5. EXPERIMENTAL RESULTS

5.1 Impact on Write Misses

As discussed throughout this paper, the main drawback of a write-through policy is the significant amount of write misses it entails. In this section, we show the ability of both the private/shared classification and the delayed write-throughs to reduce this overhead. Figure 6 shows the number of write-misses for the different mechanisms normalized with respect to a write-through policy (not shown). Since most of the write misses in a write-through protocol come from private blocks (Figure 1), by switching to a write-back policy for private blocks we can save 72.7%, on average, of write misses (first bar). However, if we compare to a write-back policy (third bar), we can see that we still incur extra misses. Although the effectiveness of the private/shared classification in reducing write misses is noticeable, a delayed write-through mechanism is still necessary to be competitive to a write-back policy (a MESI directory protocol in this case). This is shown in the second bar (WT-shared delayed), where the number of write misses is reduced by 90.4%, on average, compared to a write-through protocol, thus making this number close to the one obtained by a write-back policy (94.6%, on average).

Table 3: Evaluated protocols

Protocol	Invalidations	Directory	Indirection	Inclusion	L1 base states	LLC tag area (mm^2)
Hammer	Broadcast	None	Yes	No	5 (MOESI)	0.0501
Directory	Multicast	Full-map	Yes	Yes	4 (MESI)	0.0905
Write-Through	Multicast	Full-map	Only for write misses	Yes	2 (VI)	0.0905
VIPS	Multicast	Full-map	Only for write misses	Only for shared blocks	2 (VI)	0.0905
VIPS-M	None	None	No	No	2 (VI)	0.0501

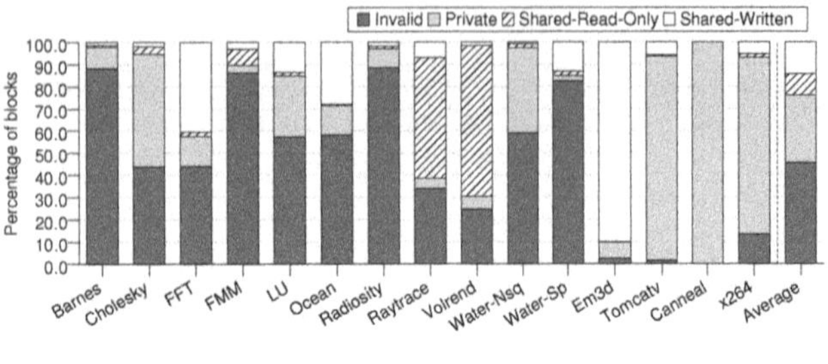

(a) Lines found in the cache upon a selective flushing

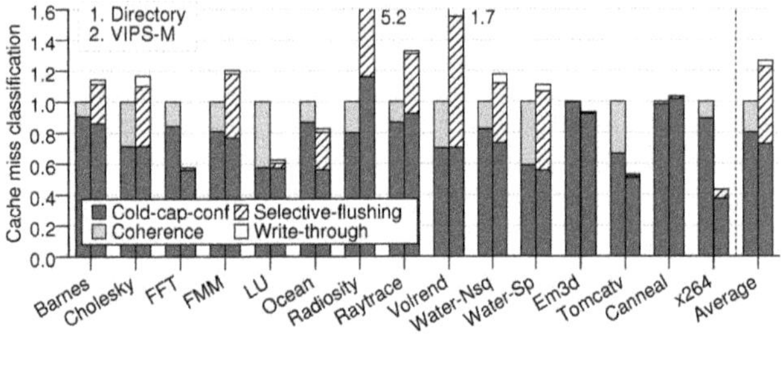

(b) Cache misses normalized w.r.t. *Directory*

Figure 7: Impact of selective flushing

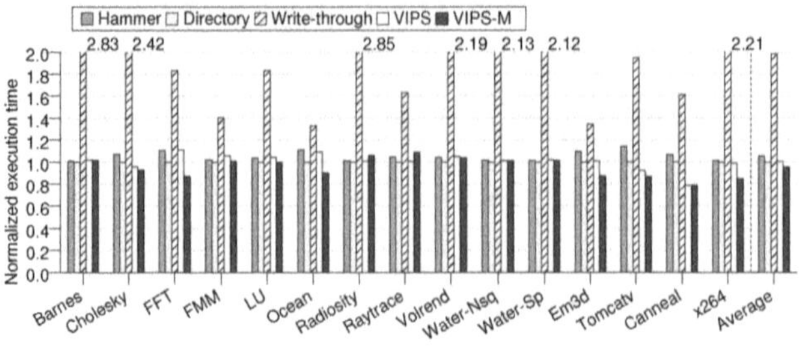

Figure 8: Normalized execution time w.r.t. *Directory*

5.2 Selective Flushing

VIPS-M relies on selective flushing at synchronization points to keep coherence (and provide SC) for DRF applications. We only flush lines whose page is being shared among different cores and modified by at least one of the cores (read-only optimization, Section 3.5.1). As shown in Figure 7a this selective flushing prevents about 73.9%, on average, of valid lines from being evicted from cache. This significantly lessens the number of misses as consequence of self-invalidations. We can also observe that 14.2% of cache lines will be flushed. Most of them are silently invalidated because their copy is clean. This happens for lines brought in the cache as consequence of read misses, or lines that have performed a write-through (synchronization or DRF lines). Dirty lines for which a write-through has not happened will be sent immediately to the LLC. Fence instructions must wait for the acknowledgments of such write-throughs to guarantee proper memory ordering. Frequent synchronization results in parts of the cache already being invalid in the next flush.

Selective flushing prevents significant part of the cache from being needlessly invalidated so it can be competitive to directory invalidations. Figure 7b shows the L1 misses in a directory protocol and in VIPS-M classified by the event that caused them. The percentage of cold, capacity, and conflict misses (*Cold-cap-conf*), slightly decreases in *VIPS-M* due to the lack of write misses for DRF lines. For some applications, e.g., *FFT*, *LU*, *Em3d*, *Tomcatv*, and *x264*, the impact of the selective flushing on the miss rate is negligible. In *FFT* and *LU*, this is because they have only a few barriers, so the selective flushing is not frequent. In *Em3d*, *Tomcatv*, and *x264*, the working set accessed between synchronization points is much larger than the cache size (few invalid lines are flushed, as shown in Figure 7a), thus, after a synchronization point, misses are not due to self-invalidation. On the other hand, applications like *Radiosity* and *Volrend* incur numerous extra misses due to self-invalidation because of frequent locking. This impacts performance and energy consumption as we show in next section. For the remaining applications, the number of misses is comparable in both protocols.

5.3 Performance Results

Figure 8 shows the applications' execution time for the five protocols evaluated in this work (see Table 3). The execution time has been normalized with respect to a directory protocol. The broadcast-based *Hammer* protocol slightly increases application's execution time with respect to *Directory*. The performance of the *Write-through* protocol is prohibitive due to the dramatic increase in the miss rate for writes. But this increase can be lessened if private lines are detected (and their write misses removed) and a delayed write-through mechanism is implemented. As we can observe, the simple VIPS protocol has similar performance to the complex directory protocol. In some applications it is faster, while in other ones slightly slower (but no more than 10%). VIPS-M, despite not having a directory structure at all, is faster in most applications (e.g., *Cholesky*, *FFT*, *Ocean*, *Em3d*, *Tomcatv*, *Canneal*, and *x264*, ranging from 7.7% to 21.5% faster). The exceptions being *Radiosity*, *Raytrace* (15.5% slower), and *Volrend* due to selective flushing. On average over the 15 applications, VIPS-M is 4.8% faster than Directory because of faster writes (no write-misses), faster reads (no directory indirection), and less traffic in the NoC.

Sensitivity Analysis. Figure 10a shows the average performance (over the 15 applications) of the two proposed protocols by varying the L1 cache size from 16KB to 64KB. The performance of VIPS with respect to MESI is not affected significantly by the cache size. However, VIPS-M flushes shared blocks from the L1 upon fence instructions and therefore, larger cache sizes impact its performance more. VIPS-

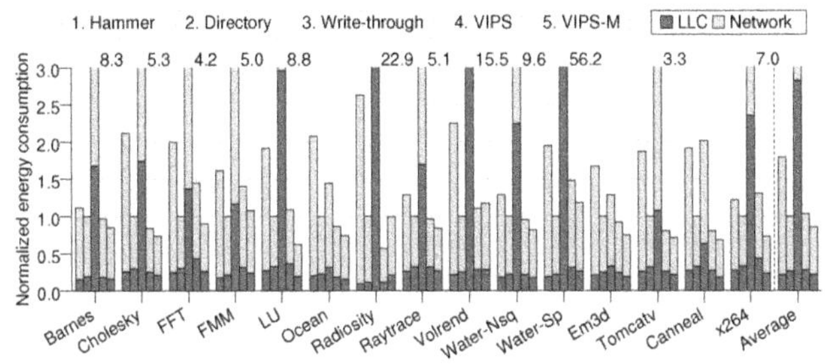

Figure 9: Normalized energy consumption w.r.t. *Directory*

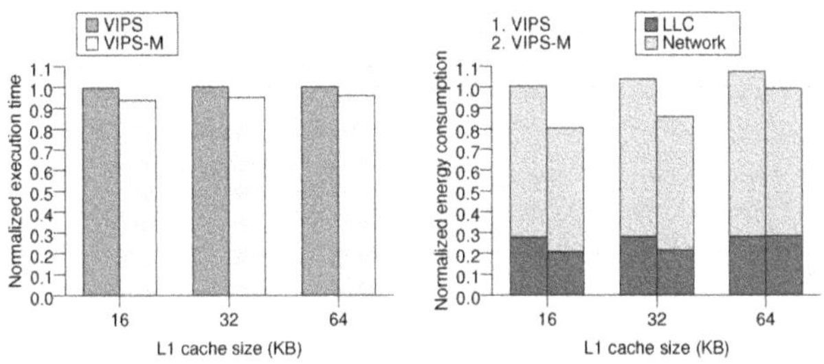

(a) Performance 16KB–64KB L1 (b) Energy 16KB–64KB L1

Figure 10: Sensitivity analysis

M improvements still range from 6.2% (16KB), 4.8% (32KB), to 4.0% for the 64KB L1 cache. We have also studied larger sizes that would approximate private L1/L2 caches. VIPS becomes slightly slower than MESI for large private hierarchies (but less than 3% for 256KB). VIPS-M is still faster than MESI for 128KB caches, but becomes slightly slower (less than 2%) for 256KB caches. Tripling the latency of the LLC (to 12 cycles) does not affect the relative performance of VIPS and VIPS-M to MESI.

5.4 Energy Consumption

Figure 9 shows the energy consumed by the network and the LLC for the applications and protocols evaluated in this work for 32KB L1 caches. Broadcasting invalidations and receiving acknowledgments in *Hammer* leads to a significant increase in the energy consumed by the network (around 1.75× compared to *Directory*). Additional write misses in a write-through protocol result in a dramatic increase in traffic and LLC accesses. As with execution time, the detection of private pages, and the delayed write-throughs help to reduce L1 misses, and therefore, traffic and LLC accesses. Thus, VIPS reduces significantly the consumption when compared with *Write-through*, consuming less than a directory protocol for many applications (e.g., *Barnes*, *Cholesky*, *Radiosity*, *Em3d*, and *Tomcatv*). Finally, although the selective flushing in VIPS-M causes extra L1 misses, thanks to the Multiple-Writer-Merge protocol the amount of data written back into the LLC is significantly reduced, which translates into a reduction in dynamic consumption of 14.2%, on average, with respect to a directory protocol.

Sensitivity Analysis. Figure 10b shows the energy consumption of our protocols varying the cache size (from 16KB to 64KB) with respect to a directory protocol. Our protocols increase their traffic and accesses to the LLC relative to a directory protocol, for larger cache sizes. This is mainly due to two reasons: First, in VIPS and VIPS-M the rate of write-throughs is independent of the cache size (since they are always delayed the same) but in MESI, shared blocks stay longer in larger caches before they are written-back. Second, flushing in VIPS-M affects more lines in larger caches. This is why energy consumption (normalized to Directory) in VIPS-M increases faster than VIPS with cache size.

6. DISCUSSION

There are several issues concerning our proposal that we discuss in this section to argue for its applicability in real-world situations.

6.1 Inter-Chip Coherence

Extending our simple protocol to go beyond a single chip faces a different set of trade-offs. Naïvely, one could extend the same scheme outside the chip: write-backs would have to go through the LLC to the external memory and the entire LLC would need to be flushed of all the shared data on any synchronization. Because of limited bandwidth and high latency outside the chip both of these propositions are prohibitive. Consequently, an invalidation strategy is more appropriate for inter-chip coherence but comes at a cost. Here, we describe in broad strokes this strategy. Only the LLC of each chip needs to be interfaced to an invalidation-based protocol (e.g., MESI or MOESI), with state for LLC blocks and an inter-chip directory, –alternatively, external broadcasts and snooping. The rest of the on-chip cache hierarchy remains the same. Because there is no invalidation for the L1s, even with external invalidations the DRF semantics need to be preserved. Assume, for example, that a write to the memory location A in chip $M1$, invalidates a copy of A in the LLC of chip $M2$. Although the LLC copy in $M2$ is invalidated, there is no way to forward this invalidation to the ($M2$) L1s. There are two cases: either there are copies of A in the L1s or they have been self-invalidated. The former case constitutes a data race if the L1 copies are read. This is forbidden. In the later case, coherence is extended across chips.

6.2 OS, Migration, and Multithreading

OS or thread migration from one core to another can (falsely) tag a private page as shared in our classification scheme. Better classification (possibly with reverse adaptation) or migration-aware classification by the OS itself, as described by Hardavellas *et al.* [15], alleviates these problems. Another issue is the flushing of shared data by the OS. In the implementation for this paper, context switches, system calls, I/O, thread migration, etc., conservatively flush all shared data. This can be optimized by tagging L1 lines as *system* or *user* lines. Similarly, tagging L1 lines with a thread ID and differentiating operations on them, avoids data classification or data flushing problems that may arise due to multithreading.

6.3 Debugging

VIPS-M can be incoherent in the presence of data races which may complicate debugging when a program is malfunctioning. Fortunately, a significant body of work on detecting data races already exists [30]. It is worth mentioning here some of the data-race debugging tools available that do not require any hardware support: *Velodrome*, *RecPlay*, *RaceTrack*, *FastTrack*, *RacerX*, *Eraser*, and *Goldilocks*, among others. With respect to debugging, we believe this is the way to go rather than relying on coherence being continuously present. Furthermore, eliminating the possibility of races at the programming model (e.g., as in DPJ or DRFx) would significantly help debugging.

6.4 Verification

VIPS has similar properties to MESI, only fewer states. Therefore it is easier to verify. In VIPS-M, the protocols for private and shared (DRF) data are nearly identical. There are only two stable states (Valid/Invalid) and two transient states (I–V and V–I) in the L1s and no states at all in the LLC (no blocking). Compared to standard protocols (e.g., MESI), there is a fundamental difference for the transient states: in VIPS-M there are no downgrades, invalidations, or data requests, so its transient states are invisible to the outside world.[3] They exist only in the MSHRs, and only to wait replies from the LLC. VIPS-M is thus simple to verify and significantly easier than MESI which requires extensive state exploration [11].

6.5 Speculation

Although we envision our coherence protocols as a better fit for simple cores, they can also be used to advantage with complex cores that support speculation and dynamic execution. In this case, a new possibility for optimization opens up. Selective flushing in VIPS-M leads to a small number of extra misses compared to a standard directory protocol. These misses are due to self-invalidated cache lines that are reused after synchronization, but without having been modified by any other core in the interim. With speculative execution mechanisms available, one can hide the latency of these misses by performing a Speculative Cache Lookup (SCL) and applying Coherence Decoupling as proposed by Huh *et al.* [17] on top of VIPS-M. Speculative cache lookups in VIPS-M, allow the cores to continue execution with self-invalidated data while the decoupled protocol reloads invalid cache lines with their latest version from the LLC. If the self-invalidated and LLC data differ (i.e., the line has been modified), speculation is squashed. In this case, the cost is just the wasted speculative execution. If, on the other hand, the data are the same (i.e., the line has not been modified), the speculation is verified and the latency of going to the LLC is completely hidden. The benefit of this optimization is obvious: it completely hides any performance penalty from selective flushing, but at the expense of some extra, discarded, speculative execution.

7. RELATED WORK

We have already discussed in passing most of the related work. Here, we will just summarize the similarities and differences with the work closest to ours, the DeNovo work of Choi *et al.* [11]. Relying on disciplined parallelism, Choi *et al.* take a similar approach to simplify coherence. However, in contrast to our approach, they require significant feedback from the application which must define memory regions of certain read/write behavior and then convey and represent such regions in hardware. This requires programmer involvement at the application layer (to define the regions), compiler involvement to insert the proper self-invalidation instructions, an API to communicate all this information to the hardware, and additional hardware near the L1 to store this information.

[3]With respect to verification this makes the treatment of the delayed write-throughs analogous to that of write buffers.

The DeNovo approach still implements a directory ("registry") that tracks the writers (but not the readers), and cleverly hides it in the data array (since LLC data are stale in the presence of a writer). Although the directory storage cost is hidden, there is still directory functionality, and therefore, directory indirection, in the LLC. In our VIPS-M protocol the directory is fully abolished leaving behind a "passive" LLC. We rely on keeping the LLC up-to-date with write-throughs; fresh (non-stale) data are always found in the LLC. This also leads to another difference: the DeNovo approach has directory indirection for reads (to get the new values), but we do not. To eliminate this indirection Choi *et al.* use writer-prediction, as proposed by Kaxiras and Keramidas, and revert to the registry on mispredictions. This adds complexity and cost. Finally, although Choi *et al.* simplify coherence for DRF, they do not address the issue of synchronization races.

The heavy reliance of the DeNovo approach on application involvement –and without having access to the source code annotations for the regions, the same compiler for the self-invalidation instructions, and the API to convey information to the hardware– prevents us from replicating their results for a direct comparison. By inspecting the published results, however, we can make the following observations: i) both approaches are competitive to MESI; ii) DeNovo performs well, but this is to be expected since it has access to much more in-depth information on application behavior –our page classification is coarse-grain in comparison, but completely transparent; iii) their results do not, apparently, include synchronization operations. Overall, we consider the results of the two approaches to be representative of the trade-off between application involvement and application-transparent implementation.

8. CONCLUSIONS

This paper goes contrary to the experience of more than three decades in coherence complexity, and takes us back to before the IBM centralized directory, Censier and Feautrier's distributed directory [8] or Goodman's write-once protocol [14]. Inspired by efforts to simplify coherence and/or reduce directory cost [11, 12, 13, 16, 19] we go a step further and completely eliminate the need for a directory. In a multi-core cache hierarchy, as long as we treat private and shared data separately, we can improve both performance and energy consumption even with the simplest protocol. Our approach is based on a dynamic write policy (Write-Through for shared and Write-Back for private data) and selective flushing of the shared data from the L1 caches upon synchronization. By separating private from shared data at the page level, we minimize the impact of the write-through policy, since many of the write-misses are due to private data.

In the interest of programming clarity and correctness there is a growing consensus that data races should be banned. In our work, we show that in the absence of data races, we can simplify the coherence protocols for shared data to that of private data with just a simple rule of when to write data back to the LLC. The end result outperforms more complex protocols while at the same time consumes less energy. Data races, however, are still pertinent to synchronization operations. In our proposal, we maintain the memory semantics of atomic instructions with a simple synchronization protocol that does not need a directory or invalidations.

9. ACKNOWLEDGMENTS

This work is supported, in part, by the Swedish Research Council UPMARC Linnaeus Centre and the EU HEAP Project FP7-ICT-247615.

10. REFERENCES

[1] D. Abts, S. Scott, and D. J. Lilja. So many states, so little time: Verifying memory coherence in the Cray X1. In *17th Int'l Parallel and Distributed Processing Symp. (IPDPS)*, Apr. 2003.

[2] M. E. Acacio, J. González, J. M. García, and J. Duato. A new scalable directory architecture for large-scale multiprocessors. In *7th Int'l Symp. on High-Performance Computer Architecture (HPCA)*, pages 97–106, Jan. 2001.

[3] S. V. Adve and K. Gharachorloo. Shared memory consistency models: A tutorial. *IEEE Computer*, 29(12):66–76, Dec. 1996.

[4] A. Agarwal, R. Simoni, J. L. Hennessy, and M. A. Horowitz. An evaluation of directory schemes for cache coherence. In *15th Int'l Symp. on Computer Architecture (ISCA)*, pages 280–289, May 1988.

[5] N. Agarwal, T. Krishna, L.-S. Peh, and N. K. Jha. GARNET: A detailed on-chip network model inside a full-system simulator. In *IEEE Int'l Symp. on Performance Analysis of Systems and Software (ISPASS)*, pages 33–42, Apr. 2009.

[6] S. Bell, et al. TILE64^{TM} processor: A 64-core SoC with mesh interconnect. In *IEEE Int'l Solid-State Circuits Conference (ISSCC)*, pages 88–598, Jan. 2008.

[7] C. Bienia, S. Kumar, J. P. Singh, and K. Li. The PARSEC benchmark suite: Characterization and architectural implications. In *17th Int'l Conf. on Parallel Architectures and Compilation Techniques (PACT)*, pages 72–81, Oct. 2008.

[8] L. M. Censier and P. Feautrier. A new solution to coherence problems in multicache systems. *IEEE Transactions on Computers (TC)*, 27(12):1112–1118, Dec. 1978.

[9] D. Chaiken, J. Kubiatowicz, and A. Agarwal. LimitLESS directories: A scalable cache coherence scheme. In *4th Int'l Conf. on Architectural Support for Programming Language and Operating Systems (ASPLOS)*, pages 224–234, Apr. 1991.

[10] G. Chen. Slid - a cost-effective and scalable limited-directory scheme for cache coherence. In *5th Int'l Conf. on Parallel Architectures and Languages Europe (PARLE)*, pages 341–352, June 1993.

[11] B. Choi, R. Komuravelli, and H. Sung, et al. DeNovo: Rethinking the memory hierarchy for disciplined parallelism. In *20th Int'l Conf. on Parallel Architectures and Compilation Techniques (PACT)*, Sept. 2011.

[12] B. Cuesta, A. Ros, M. E. Gómez, A. Robles, and J. Duato. Increasing the effectiveness of directory caches by deactivating coherence for private memory blocks. In *38th Int'l Symp. on Computer Architecture (ISCA)*, pages 93–103, June 2011.

[13] M. Ferdman, P. Lotfi-Kamran, K. Balet, and B. Falsafi. Cuckoo directory: A scalable directory for many-core systems. In *17th Int'l Symp. on High-Performance Computer Architecture (HPCA)*, pages 169–180, Feb. 2011.

[14] J. R. Goodman. Using Cache Memory to Reduce Processor-Memory Traffic. In *10th Int'l Symp. on Computer Architecture (ISCA)*, pages 124–131, June 1983.

[15] N. Hardavellas, M. Ferdman, B. Falsafi, and A. Ailamaki. Reactive NUCA: Near-optimal block placement and replication in distributed caches. In *36th Int'l Symp. on Computer Architecture (ISCA)*, pages 184–195, June 2009.

[16] H. Hossain, S. Dwarkadas, and M. C. Huang. POPS: Coherence protocol optimization for both private and shared data. In *20th Int'l Conf. on Parallel Architectures and Compilation Techniques (PACT)*, Sept. 2011.

[17] J. Huh, J. Chang, D. Burger, and G. S. Sohi. Coherence decoupling: Making use of incoherence. In *11th Int'l Conf. on Architectural Support for Programming Language and Operating Systems (ASPLOS)*, pages 97–106, Oct. 2004.

[18] S. Kaxiras, Z. Hu, and M. Martonosi. Cache decay: Exploiting generational behavior to reduce cache leakage power. In *28th Int'l Symp. on Computer Architecture (ISCA)*, pages 240–251, June 2001.

[19] S. Kaxiras and G. Keramidas. SARC coherence: Scaling directory cache coherence in performance and power. *IEEE Micro*, 30(5):54–65, Sept. 2011.

[20] D. Kim, J. A. J. Kim, and J. Huh. Subspace snooping: Filtering snoops with operating system support. In *19th Int'l Conf. on Parallel Architectures and Compilation Techniques (PACT)*, pages 111–122, Sept. 2010.

[21] A. R. Lebeck and D. A. Wood. Dynamic self-invalidation: Reducing coherence overhead in shared-memory multiprocessors. In *22nd Int'l Symp. on Computer Architecture (ISCA)*, pages 48–59, June 1995.

[22] Y. Li, A. Abousamra, R. Melhem, and A. K. Jones. Compiler-assisted data distribution for chip multiprocessors. In *19th Int'l Conf. on Parallel Architectures and Compilation Techniques (PACT)*, pages 501–512, Sept. 2010.

[23] P. S. Magnusson, M. Christensson, and J. Eskilson, et al. Simics: A full system simulation platform. *IEEE Computer*, 35(2):50–58, Feb. 2002.

[24] M. M. Martin, D. J. Sorin, and B. M. Beckmann, et al. Multifacet's general execution-driven multiprocessor simulator (GEMS) toolset. *Computer Architecture News*, 33(4):92–99, Sept. 2005.

[25] A. Moshovos, G. Memik, B. Falsafi, and A. N. Choudhary. JETTY: Filtering snoops for reduced energy consumption in SMP servers. In *7th Int'l Symp. on High-Performance Computer Architecture (HPCA)*, pages 85–96, Jan. 2001.

[26] N. Muralimanohar, R. Balasubramonian, and N. P. Jouppi. Cacti 6.0. Technical Report HPL-2009-85, HP Labs, Apr. 2009.

[27] B. W. O'Krafka and A. R. Newton. An empirical evaluation of two memory-efficient directory methods. In *17th Int'l Symp. on Computer Architecture (ISCA)*, pages 138–147, June 1990.

[28] J. M. Owen, M. D. Hummel, D. R. Meyer, and J. B. Keller. System and method of maintaining coherency in a distributed communication system. U.S. Patent 7069361, June 2006.

[29] S. H. Pugsley, J. B. Spjut, D. W. Nellans, and R. Balasubramonian. SWEL: Hardware cache coherence protocols to map shared data onto shared caches. In *19th Int'l Conf. on Parallel Architectures and Compilation Techniques (PACT)*, pages 465–476, Sept. 2010.

[30] A. Raza. A review of race detection mechanisms. In *1st International Computer Science Conference on Theory and Applications*, pages 534–543, June 2006.

[31] D. J. Sorin, M. D. Hill, and D. A. Wood. *A Primer on Memory Consistency and Cache Coherence*, volume 6 of *Synthesis Lectures on Computer Architecture*. Morgan & Claypool Publishers, May 2011.

[32] D. Vantrease, M. H. Lipasti, and N. Binkert. Atomic coherence: Leveraging nanophotonics to build race-free cache coherence protocols. In *17th Int'l Symp. on High-Performance Computer Architecture (HPCA)*, pages 132–143, Feb. 2011.

[33] S. C. Woo, M. Ohara, E. Torrie, J. P. Singh, and A. Gupta. The SPLASH-2 programs: Characterization and methodological considerations. In *22nd Int'l Symp. on Computer Architecture (ISCA)*, pages 24–36, June 1995.

[34] H. Zhao, A. Shriraman, and S. Dwarkadas. SPACE: Sharing pattern-based directory coherence for multicore scalability. In *19th Int'l Conf. on Parallel Architectures and Compilation Techniques (PACT)*, pages –, Sept. 2010.

HaLock: Hardware-Assisted Lock Contention Detection in Multithreaded Applications

Yongbing Huang[†‡], Zehan Cui[†‡], Licheng Chen[†‡], Wenli Zhang[†], Yungang Bao[†], Mingyu Chen[†]
[†]State Key Laboratory of Computer Architecture, Institute of Computing Technology,
Chinese Academy of Sciences, Beijing, China
[‡]Graduate University of Chinese Academy of Sciences, Beijing, China
{huangyongbing, cuizehan, chenlicheng, zhangwl, baoyg, cmy}@ict.ac.cn

ABSTRACT

Multithreaded programming relies on locks to ensure the consistency of shared data. Lock contention is the main reason of low parallel efficiency and poor scalability of multithreaded programs. Lock profiling is the primary approach to detect lock contention. Prior lock profiling tools are able to track lock behaviors but directly store profiling data into local memory regardless of the memory interference on targeted programs.

In this paper, we find that the memory interference is non-trivial and can significantly affect programs' execution as thread number increases. To address this problem, we propose a hardware assisted lock profiling mechanism (HaLock) which leverages a specific hardware memory tracing tool (HMTT) to record large amount of profiling data with negligible overhead and impact on even large scale multithreaded programs.

Experimental results show that HaLock incurs only about 14.8% additional L3 cache misses and 34.3% extra memory requests for a lock-intensive workload (bodytrack of PARSEC benchmark) with 512 threads, while the previous state of the art low-overhead approach causes 25.9% additional L3 cache misses and 73.8% additional memory requests. Compared with HaLock's profiling data, we find that the lock behaviors obtained by the state of art lock profiling tools have substantial distortions, resulting in non-negligible inaccuracy problems.

Categories and Subject Descriptors

C.4 **[Performance of systems]**: Measurement techniques, performance attributes; D.1.3 **[Programming techniques]**: Concurrent Programming--Parallel programming

General Terms

Design, Measurement, Performance

Keywords

Multithreading, Lock Contention, Memory Interference, Performance Analysis, HMTT

1. INTRODUCTION

Multithreaded programming is the dominated programming model on shared memory multicores platform. Recent research [23] argues that coherence protocol which is regarded as the primary reason of poor scalability of shared memory architecture, is able to scale well up to even 512-core. Therefore, multithreaded programming will probably still be the most popular programming model for forthcoming many-core machines.

Since multithreaded applications use locks, such as mutex locks of POSIX thread [13] library, to guard the consistency of shared data, lock contention has long been considered as a key impediment to applications' scalability. For instance, Johnson et al. [22] investigate four popular open source databases (Shore, BerkeleyDB, MySQL, and PostgreSQL) on a multicore system, and identify lock contention as the major bottleneck for scaling up to 32 threads. Multithreaded programming relying on locks puts programmers in a dilemma that coarse-grain locks significantly degrade program's performance and scalability due to lock contention but fine-grain locks are error-prone, thus requiring substantial development efforts. Therefore, profiling lock information and diagnosing lock contention are still of great interest. By identifying lock contention hotspots and shortening or removing them, Johnson et al. [22] achieved 2-4 times performance improvement.

Generally, a typical look profiling tool consists of two steps: Firstly, it adopts either instrumentation or performance counter to capture runtime lock information such as thread id, operation types and time information [5, 12, 16]. Some tools may further support advanced functionalities, such as thread filters or source file filters [28]. Obliviously, collecting more information means paying higher cost. Generally, instrumentation has higher cost but is more flexible, while performance counter costs less but collects less information. Secondly, it needs to record the profiling data for offline analysis. To our best knowledge, almost all of the current tools preserve profiling data in local memory buffers or disks [2, 4, 5, 12, 15, 16, 28]. Basically, a profiling tool itself should not significantly affect its target program's execution.

However, writing large amount of data into memory will cause additional cache pollution and extra memory pressures which may significantly perturb the targeted program's runtime behaviors thereby resulting in distorted profiling, especially for memory sensitive applications.

Sampling is an alternative method to reduce the profiling overhead and the runtime interference. However, it is likely to miss small critical sections [11, 16] which are also necessary to be optimized for scalability [19]. But Boyd-Wickizer et al. [11] show that even for very short mutex-lock based critical sections can cause dramatic collapse in the performance of real workloads, when the cores are increasing.

Table 1. Summary of Lock Contention Profiling System

System	Info. Acquisition*	Collection Method	Data Record
HPCToolKit [28]	P.C. & Inst.	Sampling	Memory & Disk
CodeAnalyst[1]	P.C. & Inst.	Sampling	Memory & Disk
VTune (Thread Profiler) [3, 4]	P.C. & Inst.	Sampling	Memory & Disk
Jucprofiler [5]	Inst.	Continuous	Memory & Disk
Lockmeter [12]	Inst.	Continuous	Memory & Disk
LockStat [6]	Inst.	Continuous	Memory
LiMiT [16]	P.C. & Inst.	Continuous	Memory & Disk
HaLock	Inst.	Continuous	HMTT
* P.C is short for Performance Counter, Inst. for Instrumentation			

Table 1 illustrates several prevalent lock profiling tools. All previous tools primarily record profiling data in memory. These approaches work well for small scale of threads but will cause unacceptable memory interferences for dozens of threads which will be common in a many-core system. Our experimental results show that for a current low-overhead lock profiling approach, the additional cache misses increase substantially from 8.7% (8 threads) to 25.9% (512 threads) and the extra memory requests also increase from 15.1% (8 threads) to 73.9% (512 threads).

Since the cache and memory resources per core are decreasing and becoming critical resources with the core number increasing, it makes significant sense to provide a lock detection technique with little memory interference.

In this paper, we propose a hardware assisted lock profiling mechanism (HaLock) to reduce the memory interference of lock profiling.

Basic Idea: As illustrated in Table 1, we gather lock information such as thread id, lock address and lock type via instrumentation. The distinct advantage of HaLock is that it leverages a specific hardware called HMTT [2, 9] to record profiling data. We encode runtime lock information (i.e., thread id, lock address and lock operation type etc.) into specific memory addresses which are reserved for HaLock and are uncacheable to avoid cache pollution. When one lock operation is captured, instead of storing the profiling data in memory as previous tools do, HaLock just issues a one-byte memory read request to an encoded memory address. This specific memory request is monitored by HMTT which is a hardware-software hybrid memory trace toolkit for real systems. HMTT packs each memory address with a timestamp (HMTT's clock cycles) to form one lock operation trace, and finally transmits the trace to another machine via a PCI-e cable.

We implement HaLock in Linux 2.6.32 Kernel and evaluate HaLock on an 8-core SMP system in comparison to the state of the art profiling tool LiMiT which temporarily buffers data in memory and dumps the data into disks afterwards. Experimental results show that for 8 threads HaLock incurs less than 1.2% extra memory requests for multithreaded programs while the overhead of LiMiT is nearly 3.9% on average. Meanwhile, HaLock exhibits much better scalability than LiMiT, and scales well up to 512 threads. Specifically, HaLock incurs only 4.0% additional L3 cache miss and 3.8% extra memory requests for even an extreme lock-intensive workload (bodytrack of PARSEC benchmark [10] exhibiting 4K lock–acquisition operations per second per thread) with 8 threads (14.8% additional L3 cache miss and 34.3% extra memory requests for 512 threads). Furthermore, we observe that the lock behavior collected by HaLock and LiMiT are substantially different. Since HaLock has much less memory interference than LiMiT, the large difference means that current lock profiling tools have non-negligible distortions and inaccuracy problems. Since performance tuning and debugging are essential software development steps, it is worthwhile to call for attention on how to provide efficient and accurate profiling tools. Thus, we argue that hardware-enabled lock profiling mechanism is necessary for forthcoming many-core architecture.

In summary, we make the following contributions:

1) The cache and memory interference of recording profiling data into memory adopted by current lock profiling tools are quantitatively analyzed. And we demonstrate that recording data into memory results in serious memory interference.

2) We propose and implement a hardware assisted lock profiling tool called HaLock which is able to significantly reduce the memory interference and scales well up to hundreds of threads.

3) We reveal that the start of the art lock profiling tools have non-negligible distortions and inaccuracy problems, which implies the necessity of hardware-enabled lock profiling mechanisms for many-core architectures. We also argue that it is worthwhile to pay more attention on how to provide efficient and accurate profiling tools for many-core architectures.

The rest of this paper is organized as follows: Section 2 introduces the background of lock contention detection and shows our motivations for this paper. We describe our mechanism in Section 3. Experiment environment and evaluation results are

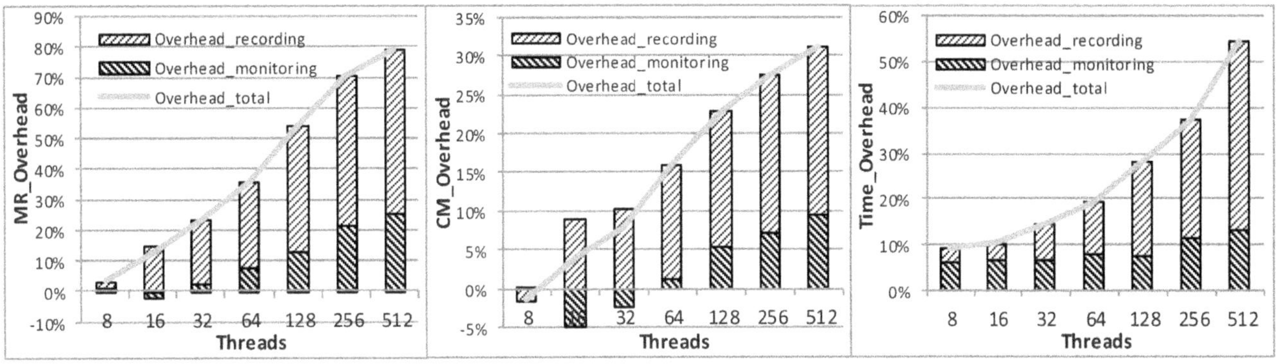

(a) (b) (c)

Figure 1. Profiling overhead of bodytrack program by recording traces through memory.

described and analyzed in Section 4. We summarize the related work in Section 5, and finally conclude this paper in Section 6.

2. BACKGROUND AND MOTIVATIONS

2.1 Lock Profiling Overhead

As illustrated in Table 1, many efforts have already been made on improving profiling accuracy and reducing profiling overhead. Specifically, the overhead of lock profiling depends on three factors as illustrated in the following formula:

$$\boldsymbol{Overhead_{total}} = \boldsymbol{Overhead_{per\_lock\_trace}} * \boldsymbol{Lock\_Trace\_Number_{per\_thread}} * \boldsymbol{Thread\_Number}$$

For $\boldsymbol{Overhead_{per\_lock\_trace}}$, it consists of two phases: 1) monitoring lock information and 2) recording profiling data. Previous researches in Table 1 mainly focus on the first phase, e.g., exploiting performance counter. Nevertheless, for the second phase, almost all of the current tools adopt a straightforward way to record profiling data, i.e., writing data directly into local memory buffers or disks. Sampling techniques is another optimization direction which tries to reduce $\boldsymbol{Lock\_Trace\_Number_{per\_thread}}$, but it is tricky and probably leads to the inaccuracy problem.

Most lock profiling tools claim that they have little overhead (<10%). It is true for small ***Thread_Number***. For example, our experimental results show that the memory overhead of a profiling tool similar to LiMiT is only about 3.9% for 8 threads. But as ***Thread_Number*** keeps increasing in this multicore/many-core era, both $\boldsymbol{Overhead_{per\_lock\_trace}}$ and $\boldsymbol{Lock\_Trace\_Number_{per\_thread}}$ are also influenced, deserving re-evaluation. Intuitively, the total trace number would sharply increase, probably resulting in more memory overhead.

2.2 Challenges of Large Scale Threads

To investigate the impact of the increasing ***Thread_Number*** on lock profiling overhead, we measure and analyze the lock behavior of bodytrack of PARSEC benchmark on an Intel Xeon 8-core machine (details in Section 4). We use an in-house LiMiT-like tool to collect performance metrics (such as cache miss ratio and memory requests) via performance counters, and use the commonly used RDTSC instruction to obtain lock operations' timestamps. Our lock profiling approach also consists of two phase. For the monitoring phase, we instrument bodytrack's binary codes to collect lock information; for the recording phase, we first write profiling data into a memory buffer (64MB) and then dump them into disk when the buffer is full. To facilitate analyzing, we also divide $\boldsymbol{Overhead_{total}}$ into two portions according to the two phases mentioned in Section 2.1, i.e., $\boldsymbol{Overhead_{monitoring}}$ and $\boldsymbol{Overhead_{recording}}$. Thus,

$$\boldsymbol{Overhead_{total}} = \boldsymbol{Overhead_{monitoring}} + \boldsymbol{Overhead_{recording}}.$$

We run the bodytrack benchmark from 8 threads to 512 threads. Figure 1 illustrates the profiling overhead changes in terms of memory requests (***MR_Overhead***), L3 cache miss rate (***CM_Overhead***) and execution time (***Time_Overhead***). According to Figure 1(a), $\boldsymbol{MR\_Overhead_{total}}$ increases substantially from 3.3% (8 threads) to 79.2% (512 threads). This shows that the profiling tools have serious memory interference, which may potentially alter programs' execution behaviors and lead to inaccurate lock behaviors consequently. Figure 1(b) demonstrates the same phenomenon from the view of L3 cache miss.

Generally, execution time is the most straightforward metric of programs' execution behaviors. If we observe $\boldsymbol{Time\_Overhead_{total}}$ shown in Figure 1(c), we can see that the execution time increases sharply with the thread number, and thus can roughly conclude that the execution behaviors of the profiled programs are indeed disturbed. Naturally, the accuracy of current lock profiling tools is doubtful.

Moreover, compared to $\boldsymbol{MR\_Overhead_{total}}$, $\boldsymbol{MR\_Overhead_{monitoring}}$ increases slowly, just from 0.8% (8 threads) to 25.1% (512 threads), which implies that the recording phase becomes dominant of memory interferences with ***Thread_Number*** increasing. $\boldsymbol{CM\_Overhead_{recording}}$ and $\boldsymbol{Time\_Overhead_{recording}}$ also confirm the situation. Thus, we should put more emphasize on the recording phase.

Among current recording methods, bypassing cache [26] seems to be able to eliminate cache pollution but does no help with memory interference. What's more, directly dumping traces into files is too slow that the traces may be dropped when locks are highly contended. Thus, currently there are no appropriate solutions to solve the dilemma of the recording phase.

2.3 Our Goal

According to above analysis, current recording mechanisms suffer from serious cache pollution and memory interferences. In contemporary multicore systems, L3 cache and memory system become critical resources, and then memory interference would result in unpredictable execution behavior variations and inaccuracy profiling results. There have been numerous studies focusing on reducing cache interference and memory interference [17, 18, 25]. It is unacceptable for a profiling tool to cause such serious interferences to its target programs. Thus, we propose a hardware assisted lock profiling mechanism (HaLock) which leverages a specific hardware memory tracing tool (HMTT) to record large amount of profiling data with negligible overhead.

3. HARDWARE ASSISTED LOCK PROFILING MECHANISM (HaLock)

3.1 Overview

3.1.1 Introduction of HMTT

HMTT [2, 9] is a platform independent full system memory trace monitoring system. The system adopts a DIMM-snooping mechanism which uses hardware boards plugged in DIMM slots to track virtual memory reference traces of full systems. Thus it is able to track complete, detail and undistorted traces without altering original programs' behavior. In order to dump full mass memory traces, HMTT utilizes multiple Gigabit Ethernets or PCI-e cables and RAIDs to send and receive mass memory traces respectively, which does not perturb host system's execution at all even when traces are generated at high speeds. That is why we choose HMMT to collect lock traces in our lock profiling approach. Meanwhile, HMTT now supports both DDR2 and DDR3 UDIMM and RDIMM interfaces, and thus has good portability.

3.1.2 Principle

The hardware assisted lock profiling mechanism (HaLock) makes use of HMTT to study lock behaviors of multithreaded programs. As indicated by Section 2, purely software methods of lock profiling may lead to heavy memory interferences with running programs, and consequently derive distorted and inaccuracy lock behaviors. In order to alleviate memory interference, HaLock leverages a hybrid mechanism which combines software-based lock detector and hardware-based trace collector. Figure 2 depicts the framework of HaLock. There are five main steps:

1) HaLock detects lock operations and tracks necessary information such as thread id, lock address, and operation type (Section 3.2.1) in runtime system. Instrumentation is an efficient

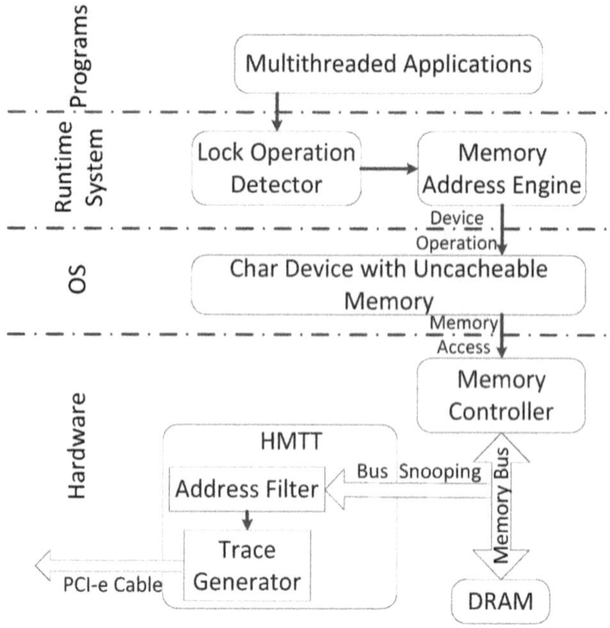

Figure 2. Framework of HaLock.

method to achieve this by modifying the source codes of profiled programs or overlaying dynamic libraries, such as Pthread library for mutex lock. Though time is indispensable for analyzing lock behavior, HaLock resorts to HMTT's hardware clock time.

2) After gathering the required data for each lock operation, HaLock encodes them into a specific memory address by memory address engine (Section 3.2.2). Each part of the memory address has its specific meaning and we can pick out thread id, lock address and operation type from it. Then, memory address engine triggers an access to the memory address by issuing a one-byte memory read instruction and hopes it to be captured by HMTT immediately. In order to eliminate negative cache effects and protect these memory addresses from other processors, a virtual device owing uncacheable physical memory is registered into operating system.

3) HMTT is configured to only capture memory address signals generated by the memory address engine. Once HMTT captures a signal on memory bus, it filters the address and only records predefined memory address. Then, a complete trace is constructed by combining the memory address and HMTT's global clock time.

4) HaLock leverages HMTT to record above traces by sending them to another machine via a PCI-e cable or Ethernet. Under this way, HaLock supports to record even a large amount of traces without utilizing local CPU and memory resource. Thus, it achieves provable, strong guarantees, namely, it eliminates the interference to running programs no matter how large the traces are.

5) Using off-line analysis, HaLock can display the lock contention distribution of different locks among all the threads.

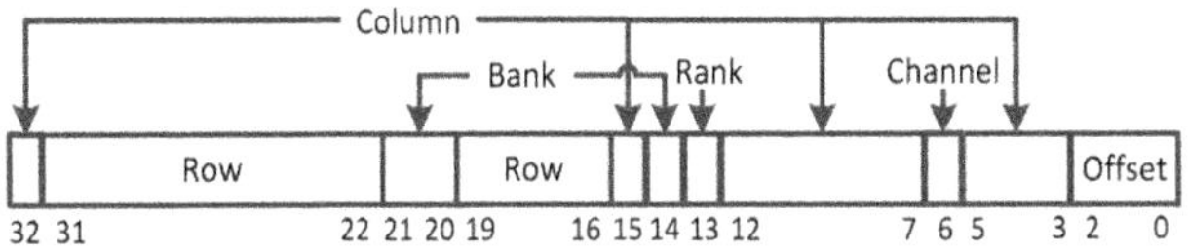

(a) Memory address mapping for dual channels memory

Rsvd #1 (6 bits)	TID (10 bits)	Lock ID (9 bits)	Rsvd #2 (1 bit)	Flag (3 bits)	Rsvd #3 (3 bits)

(b) Address coding format corresponding to (a)

Figure 3. Memory address mapping and its corresponding address coding format of HaLock.

3.1.3 Advantages

HaLock provides *high accuracy* and *strong scalability* (see Section 4). Firstly, while HaLock stores a large amount of lock behavior traces through HMTT, it introduces few extra memory requests unlike previous methods which store traces through local memory. Therefore, HaLock may degrade little programs' performance. Secondly, with the help of global hardware clock provided by HMTT, HaLock does not need to care about clock variants among different cores. In software based tools, if a thread is migrated to another processor during lock operations, the clock difference between two processors may mess up the lock behavior of this thread, such as negative acquisition time and impossible huge hold time. HaLock has two advantages: saving time to read performance counters and eliminating clock inconsistence among multiple processors.

Finally and the most important one, since HaLock has less memory interference, the lock behaviors reflected by it are more convincing and helpful for programs debugging and optimization.

3.2 Runtime System Extensions

3.2.1 Lock Operation Detector

Source and binary instrumentation are both common ways to obtain runtime contexts such as lock operation behaviors. Since this paper focuses on mutex lock, we implement lock operation detector simply by overlaying Pthread library which is transparent to applications and suitable for those applications without source codes such as databases.

We instrument routines that could potentially cause lock contention: pthread_mutex_{lock, trylock, unlock} in the overlaid Pthread library. To override a routine in a dynamically linked program, we use library preloading parameter indicated by LD_PRELOAD environment variable on Linux. When the target program calls one of the overlaid routines, the instrumented version of the routine takes over the execution. The overlaid routine first gathers current thread id and lock address, and then determines the flag for each kind of lock type.

In order to put emphasis on the effects of recording profiling data but not obtaining them, the experiments in Section 4 just obtain basic profiling data by runtime systems. If more profiling data are collected for each lock operation such as calling stacks, data recording phase may cause more serious interference by software based mechanisms and thus HaLock may gain more benefits.

Though this paper aims at analyzing mutex lock, other locks such as spinlock contained in Pthread library can also be monitored by the same technique. As to other lock types beyond Pthread library such as user defined lock, source code instrumentation is an alternative and feasible way.

3.2.2 Memory Address Engine

Since there exists a semantic gap between software trace data and memory bus signals, memory address engine in Figure 2 solves this challenge.

Memory address engine transforms profiling data for a single lock operation into a specific memory address. This procedure consists of two parts: (1) how to distinguish these specific memory addresses from other processes' memory addresses, and trigger them to be immediately captured by HMTT; and (2) how to encode lock addresses, thread identities and lock types in memory address space.

Device with uncacheable memory: We reserve a small amount of continuous physical memory for HaLock by setting "mem" parameter in boot loader. In our experiments, the value of "mem" is 64MB less than the actual total physical memory size. Then, the remained 64MB memory cannot be allocated to any processes by operating system directly, but are accessible by operating system. We utilize above remained memory as the HaLock's specific memory and HMTT can easily distinguish them from other memory addresses.

However, physical memory addresses cannot be directly accessed without corresponding linear addresses mapped in Linux's page tables. The virtual device shown in Figure 2 fills the address transformation gap. All the remained memories are registered into the virtual char device. Insides the char device's operations such as mmap and read, we construct the address mapping from the user's linear addresses to remained physical addresses making use of kernel function "remap_pfn_range". As a result, the memory address engine achieves to trigger access to remained physical address by operating the char device.

In general, memory requests are satisfied by caches firstly, and only memory requests missing caches are sent to memory bus. In order to get rid of the negative of caches and capture the requests by HMTT immediately, all the remained memory addresses are marked as uncacheable in the char device. This feature also eliminates polluting running programs' caches and reduces the memory interference.

Memory address space formats: HaLock's memory region is partitioned into three regions which delegate thread id, lock address and lock type respectively. Obviously, thread id and lock address, which are 32-bit and 64-bit respectively, cannot encode into memory address space directly. To address this issue, we propose a hash table based data transformation approach. In this approach, HaLock's runtime system creates two hash tables for threads and locks respectively. When new locks or threads are detected, the runtime system inserts them into their corresponding hash tables and uses their hash indices to represent them.

Figure 3(b) shows one typical address coding format in our experiments. If we use a 1024-entry hash table for thread id and 512-entry hash table for lock id, their corresponding hash indices are 10 bits and 9 bits respectively. The "Flag" attribute delegates the operation, such as lock, trylock, and unlock. There are three reserved fields. The length of "Rsvd #1" depends on the size of HaLock's region, e.g., 64MB indicating that the high 6 bits are fixed and the lowest 26 bits are available for HaLock; The "Rsvd #3" attribute depends on memory bus width and 3 bits means 8-Byte memory transfer unit. The existence of "Rsvd #2" is determined by the memory address mapping. In our experiment platform, the 6th bit of memory address identifies the memory channel number as illustrated in Figure 3(a). Since one HMTT card can only monitor one memory channel, the channel bit in the memory address must be set to the channel that HMTT is plugged in. The similar reservation fields of "Rsvd #2" are determined by the memory address mappings which vary largely on different platforms.

3.3 Limitation

Since HMTT is essentially a memory trace toolkit for recording profiling data, it is not surprising that there are limitations affiliated to HaLock.

Delayed timestamp: We propose to exploit global hardware clock of HMTT as lock operations' occurrence timestamps. But this clock has some delays caused by memory controllers which usually buffer memory requests for scheduling in order to improve memory efficiency or power [17, 18, 25, 27]. Since the delays are constrained to at most dozens of cycles by the state-of-art scheduling algorithms, the timestamp is still trustworthy.

Memory address space formats: In HaLock's profiling traces, runtime information are encoded into memory addresses. However, available bits in memory address are limited to the size of reserved physical memory and memory address mapping. For instance, in Figure 3, there are totally 22 bits which can be shared by threads offset, lock offset and lock types. Generally, these bits can be enough for most applications. But there might be some extreme cases that more threads and locks are exploited in a program. One solution is to reserve more physical memory for HaLock at the expense of less available memory for targeted programs.

4. EXPERIMENTS

4.1 Methodology

Platform: Our experiments are conducted on Intel Nehalem processors. Table 2 summarizes the architectural parameters. As the bandwidth of PARSEC benchmark is not high, we use only one DIMM for two sockets. Meanwhile, we reserve 64MB memory for HaLock which costs only 1.5% of total memory and does not affect programs execution.

Table 2: Experimental Platform Configuration

Processor	Intel Xeon E5504 (2.0GHz, 32KB L1I and L1D Cache, 256KB L2 Cache, 4MB L3 Cache)
# of processors	2
#of cores	8
Channel	2
DIMM	2
Memory Type	DDR3-800
Memory Size	4GB (64MB Reserved)

Benchmarks: We use a selection of benchmarks from PARSEC Benchmarks. In this work, we only focus on mutex lock of Pthread library. Thus, we choose the programs which on average have many lock operations from PARSEC benchmark. Table 3 lists the benchmarks we use in the following experiments.

Table 3: Benchmark summary

Benchmark	Parallelization Model	Lock Operations per thread per second
bodytrack	data-parallel	4800
facesim	data-parallel	670
streamcluster	data-parallel	1950
vips	data-parallel	55
x264	pipeline	537

Tools: In our experiments, we use hardware performance counter events [8] to evaluate programs' behaviors, such as L3 miss ratio and the number of total memory requests. We utilize TopMC [7] which provides low-overhead access to performance counters including uncore events (i.e. off-chip events) in Nehalem architecture.

Comparisons: In order to show that HaLock can reduce cache misses and memory interferences in recording phase, we compare HaLock with software based mechanisms storing profiling data into memory and disk. In the monitoring phase of all mechanisms, thread id, lock address and lock operation type are collected for each lock operation. Since HaLock exploits HMTT's hardware clock as lock operations' timestamp, we try to use low-overhead, and precise time collecting approaches to ensure fairness in compared mechanisms. Usually, programs use **rdtsc** instruction to obtain time information. LiMiT [16] provides a precise, lightweight mechanism to access on-chip performance counters including each core's accurate clock information. Thus, we compare HaLock with two software based mechanisms which utilize **rdtsc** instruction (RDTSC-Lock) and LiMiT (LiMiT-Lock) to acquire timestamp respectively in our experiments.

4.2 Memory Interferences of Different Lock Profiling Mechanisms

In this subsection, we will evaluate the memory interferences of HaLock, RDTSC-Lock and LiMiT-Lock using the aforementioned programs. For all overhead results in the experiments, we use original programs without any profiling tools as the baselines.

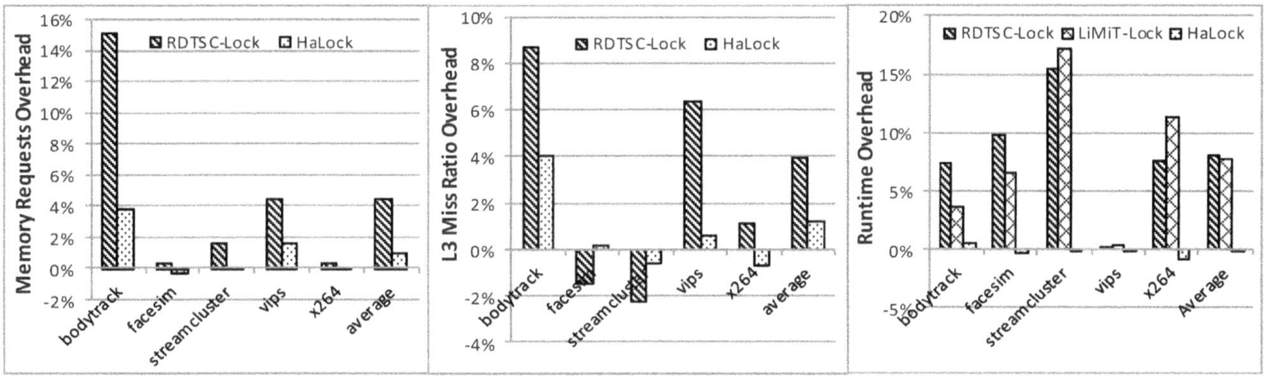

(a) Memory Requests **(b) L3 Miss Ratio** **(c) Overall Runtime**

Figure 4. Memory interference comparison for different lock profiling mechanisms when running multiple PARSEC benchmarks using 8 threads. As LiMiT cannot monitor off-chip events itself, and conflicts with TopMC, the results of LiMiT-Lock are not shown in (a) and (b).

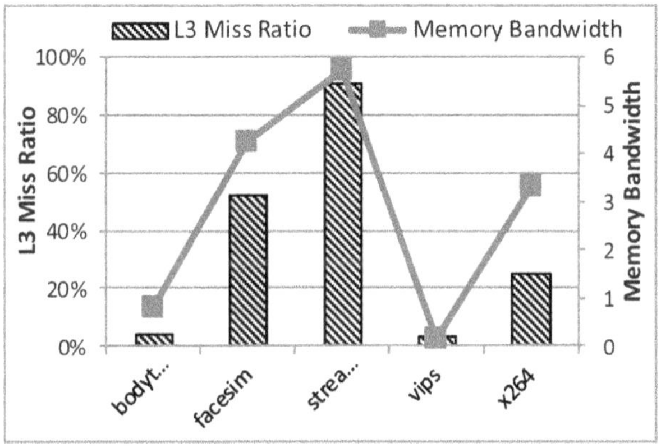

Figure 5. L3 cache miss and memory bandwidth of tested benchmarks.

4.2.1 Memory Interferences for Different Multithreaded Programs

Figure 4 shows the memory interferences and overall behaviors of the different lock profiling mechanisms for different multithreaded programs with 8 threads. In general, HaLock incurs less perturbation than the two other mechanisms for all tested programs.

As shown in Figure 4, HaLock yields only about 1% extra memory requests and 1.2% extra cache misses while RDTSC-Lock results in more than 4.4% extra memory requests and 3.9% extra cache misses on average. For each program, the increased memory requests and changed cache miss ratio incurred by HaLock are less than that incurred by RDTSC-Lock. Since RDTSC-Lock and LiMiT-Lock both use low-overhead instructions (**rdtsc** and **rdpmc** respectively) to gather timestamps without incurring memory requests, the monitoring phase of RDTSC-Lock and LiMiT-Lock are the same as HaLock in terms of memory requests. Thus, the difference shown in Figure 4 attributes to the recording phase.

In the recording phase of RDTSC-Lock, large amounts of profiled data are firstly buffered in memory, which would cause additional cache eviction operations and thus extra memory requests. When the memory buffer are full, these data are dumped into disk and this procedure consumers both memory and buffer cache. However, HaLock only issues a one-byte uncacheable memory request for each lock operation in the whole recording phase. Thus, the memory requests and L3 cache miss ratios shown in Figure 4(a) and 4(b) are lower than RDTSC-Lock.

The memory interference behaviors vary largely for different programs as shown in Figure 4(a). On one hand, the interferences are positively correlated to the lock operation frequency. As the lock operation frequency increases, more memory requests are issued by each profiling tools. Bodytrack has the highest lock operation frequency which means that it has the most potential memory interference. However, the situation seems not suitable for streamcluster which has 1950 operations per second but only 1.67% extra memory requests even for RDTSC-Lock. Besides lock operation frequency, the internal behaviors, such as memory bandwidth and L3 cache miss, of tested programs determine the overall effects of interferences on the other hand. Figure 5 demonstrates the memory bandwidth and L3 cache miss ratio for each tested program. The memory bandwidth of streamcluster is nearly 89% of the total memory bandwidth of our experiment platform. Compared with streamcluster, the memory requests issued by RDTSC-Lock are not so obvious. That's why the memory requests overhead is low for streamcluster though RDTSC-Lock incurs lots of extra memory requests.

The above analysis can also illustrate the cache miss ratio overhead indicated in Figure 4(b). Interestingly, both increased and decreased cache misses exist. The cache miss of tested programs are constrained to three factors: originally cache miss, cache miss of memory requests issued by profiling tools and cache pollution proportion. Generally, the memory requests produced by RDTSC-Lock are sequential, and only one request may be cache miss ideally for each 8 requests. If the tested programs have poor locality and cache pollution is not serious, they may suffer from decreased cache misses, such as facesim and streamcluster, and vice versa.

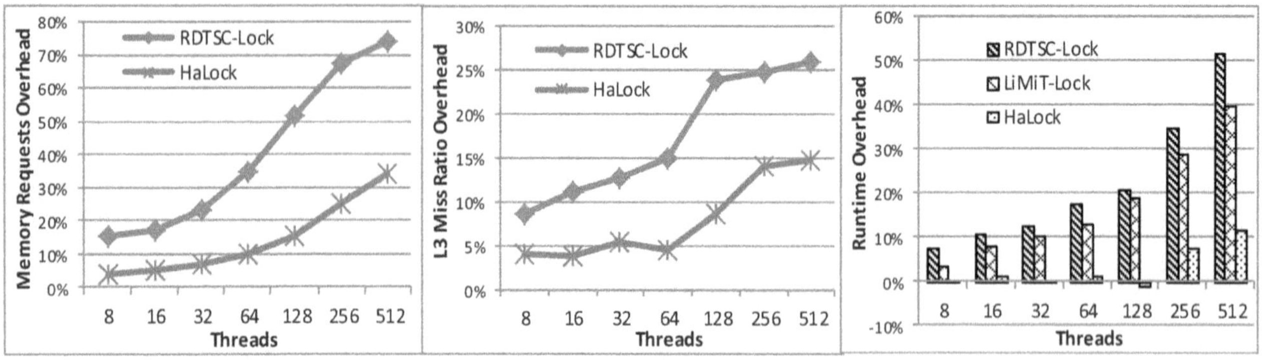

(a) Memory Requests **(b) L3 Miss Ratio** **(c) Overall Runtime**

Figure 6. Memory interference comparison for different lock profiling mechanisms when the thread number increases up to 512.

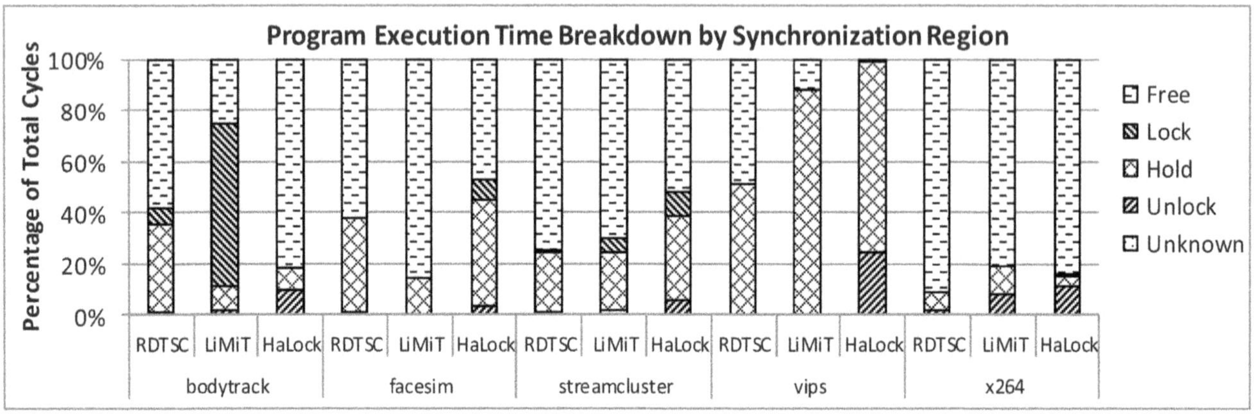

Figure 7. Comparison of lock behaviors collected by different mechanisms for PARSEC benchmarks running with 8 threads.

After studying the memory interference of RDTSC-Lock and HaLock, we can learn the side effects of these interferences in terms of runtime in Figure 4(c). On average, the runtime overheads incurred by RDTSC-Lock and LiMiT-Lock are 8.1% and 7.8% respectively, but HaLock only incurs 0.1% runtime overhead. The results demonstrate that RDTSC-Lock and LiMiT-Lock indeed seriously alter the programs' execution compared to HaLock. Especially for memory intensive programs such as streamcluster, the memory resources become so critical that additional memory interferences of profiling tools can severely change programs' normal execution, increasing up to 17.1% runtime for streamcluster.

Totally, compared with RDTSC-Lock and LiMiT-Lock, HaLock is able to reduce memory interference and just slightly affects programs' execution.

4.2.2 Scalability for Different Lock profiling Mechanisms

As the number of cores continually increases, scalability is significantly important for profiling tools in many-core era. Obviously, lock contention will be exacerbated when thread numbers are increasing in multithreaded programs, and memory interferences would be enlarged for any lock profiling mechanisms. We measure the scalability of each profiling mechanisms running bodytrack from 8 threads to 512 threads in Figure 6.

When bodytrack scales up to 512 threads, HaLock brings about 34.3% additional memory requests, less than half of memory overhead brought by RDTSC-Lock shown in Figure 6(a). The memory interference gap between HaLock and RDTSC-Lock is enlarged as the number of threads increases. Figure 6(b) indicates that L3 cache miss has the same tendency as memory requests. Thus, HaLock has good scalability than other mechanisms. From Figure 6(c), we can conclude that HaLock can actually reduce profiling perturbations on programs' execution behaviors even if thread number increases.

4.3 Lock Behaviors of Programs

In order to demonstrate the importance of memory interference on programs' execution, we use HaLock, RDTSC-Lock and LiMiT-Lock to collect profiling data and compare their results in terms of execution time related to lock operations. Figure 7 illustrates an overview of execution time breakdown by synchronization region for all tested programs. **Free** time is the total cycles when threads are not related to any lock operation; **Lock** and **Unlock** time is the cycles spent in pthread_mutex_lock and pthread_mutex_unlock for all threads respectively; Lock **Hold** time is defined as summation of cycles each thread holds for each lock. We consider those error traces having huge or negative cycles as **Unknown** region. All the time regions shown in Figure 7 are normalized to the total execution cycle for each thread.

We observe that the lock behaviors collected by HaLock, RDTSC-Lock and LiMiT-Lock are substantially different. Firstly, the proportions of profiled region by these mechanisms are varied, and the memory interferences determine the gap size. As shown in Figure 4(a), bodytrack and vips suffer from the most serious memory interferences, and thus their lock behaviors are sharply differed. Take bodytrack as an example, free time is 58.1% of the total cycle obtained by RDTSC-Lock, only 24.6% by LiMiT-Lock, but nearly 81% by HaLock. Secondly, **Unlock** time of all programs measured by HaLock are not negligible while the corresponding time are trivial obtained by LiMiT-Lock and RDTSC-Lock. Since unlock operation requires invoking system calls to awake those threads waiting on the lock and hence traps into interrupt, unlock time should not be as small as shown by LiMiT-Lock and RDTSC-Lock.

Since all the current profiling tools inevitably bring about memory interferences to target programs, we have proved that HaLock has the least memory interferences than current software-based mechanisms in above subsections. Thus, we can conclude that current mechanisms have non-negligible distortions and inaccuracy problems. HaLock can actually provide the most accurate lock behaviors than other current mechanisms.

5. RELATED WORK

Dedicated hardware for memory trace: Various hardware monitors are able to monitor memory trace online. Besides HMTT utilized in this work, other hardware monitors such as BACH [20], SHRIMP [24], Alliant System [14], can also collect memory traces online. BACH utilizes a logic analyzer to interface with host system and buffer the collected traces. When the buffer is full, the host system is halted by an interrupt and the traces are moved out. However, this halting mechanism may alter original behaviors of programs. SHRIMP performance monitor is a hardware monitor with several novel features including multi-dimensional histograms, page tags, histogram categories, and a threshold interrupt mechanism. Torrellas et al. [29] present a similar hybrid hardware/software approach which could potentially be used for lock profiling. However their hardware monitor relied on MIPS buses which were proprietary, and the software implementations are totally different.

Performance tools: There are numerous studies on analyzing lock contention. Almost all of them focus on monitoring phase regardless of how to optimize data recording phase.

IBM's jucprofiler [5] analyzes Java's concurrent locks. It mainly identifies threads' contention time and waiting time caused by contending Java's concurrent locks. The collected information by jucprofiler is quite similar with our work. However, jucprofiler records above information in local memory and local disk. HPCToolkit [28] uses runtime information associated with locks to blame lock holders for the idleness of spinning threads. Thread Profiler [3] measures routines' effective parallelism and distinguishes between interaction effects such as cruise, impact and blocking time of each thread. Lockmeter [12] and LockStat [6] are tools for analyzing locks in a multiprocessor Linux kernel.

Others utilize hardware performance events to assist lock profiling. LiMiT [16] enables precise, lightweight interface to on-chip performance counter which allows precise reading of virtualized counters by one or two orders of magnitude faster than current access techniques. The synchronization characteristics of PARSEC benchmark detected by LiMiT are different from characteristics shown by others performance counter tools which have larger overheads. We compare LiMiT with our approach, and show that their synchronization characteristics are also varied a lot because of overheads in data recording phase. Hardware performance events are also exploited by other tools, such as Inter's VTune [4], AMD's CodeAnalyst [1], ProfileMe [15] and so on.

6. CONCLUSIONS

In this paper, we have studied the memory interferences incurred by current lock profiling tools storing profiling data into memory or disk. Then, we have proposed a hardware assisted lock profiling tool (HaLock) which is able to significantly reduce the memory interferences and scales well up to hundreds of threads by recording all the lock behavior traces through the hardware HMTT.

Experimental results show that HaLock incurs only 3.8% extra memory requests and 4% additional cache miss for even a lock-intensive workload with 8 threads, and has well scalability up to 512 threads. We also illustrated that the start-of-art lock profiling tools such as LiMiT have serious memory interferences and non-negligible inaccuracy problems. Since the synchronization behaviors obtained by LiMiT have big difference from those obtained by HaLock, we argue that hardware-enabled lock profiling mechanism is necessary to analyze lock behaviors.

7. ACKNOWLEDGMENTS

We would like to thank Guangming Tan, Mingyang Chen and other teammates from ASL, ICT, and the anonymous reviewers for useful suggestions and insightful feedbacks. This research is supported by the National Basic Research Program of China (973 Program) under the grant number 2011CB302502 and the National Natural Science Foundation of China (NSFC) under the grant number 60925009, 60903046 and 60921002.

8. REFERENCES

[1] AMD CodeAnalyst. http://developer.amd.com/tools/codeanalyst/pages/default.aspx.

[2] HMTT. http://asg.ict.ac.cn/hmtt/index.html.

[3] Intel Thread Profiler. http://software.intel.com/en-us/articles/using-intel-thread-profiler-for-win32-threads-philosophy-and-theory, August 2007.

[4] Intel VTune Amplifier XE. http://software.intel.com/en-us/intel-vtune.

[5] Jucprofiler. http://www.infoq.com/articles/jucprofiler.

[6] LockStat. http://hub.opensolaris.org/bin/view/Community+Group+dtrace/WebHome.

[7] TopMC. http://asg.ict.ac.cn/projects/topmc/.

[8] Intel 64 and IA-32 Architectures Software Developer's Manual, vol. 3A & 3B, 2011.

[9] Yungang Bao, Mingyu Chen, Yuan Ruan, et al. HMTT: a platform independent full-system memory trace monitoring system. In *ACM SIGMETRICS: International Conference on Measurement and Modeling of Computer Systems*, pages 229-240, 2008.

[10] Christian Bienia, Sanjeev Kumar, Jaswinder PalSingh, and Kai Li. The parsec benchmark suite: Characterization and architectural implications. In *Proceedings of the 17th International Conference on Parallel Architectures and Compilation Techniques*, 2008.

[11] Silas Boyd-Wickizer, M. Frans Kaashoek, Robert Morris, and Nickolai Zeldovich. Non-scalable locks are dangerous. In *Proceedings of the Linux Symposium*, Ottawa, Canada, July 2012.

[12] R. Bryant and J. Hawkes. Lockmeter: Highly-Informative Instrumentation for Spin Locks in the Linux Kernel. In *Proceedings of the 4th Annual Linux Showcase and Conference*, pages 271-282, 2000.

[13] D. R. Butenhof. Programming with POSIX threads. Addison-Wesley Longman Publishing Co., Inc., Boston, MA, USA, 1997.

[14] R. Daigle, C. Xia, and J. Torrellas. Low Perturbation Address Trace Collection for Operating System, Multiprogrammed, and Parallel Workloads in Multiprocessors. *Technical report*, Center for Supercomputing Research and Development, Univ. of Illinois at Urbana-Champaign, Mar. 1996.

[15] Jeffrey Dean, James E. Hicks, Carl A. Waldspurger, William E. Weihl, and George Chrysos. Profileme: hardware support for instruction-level profiling on out-of-order processors. In *Proceedings of the 30th annual ACM/IEEE International Symposium on Microarchitecture*, pages 292-302, 1997.

[16] J. Demme and S. Sethumadhavan. Rapid identification of architectural bottlenecks via precise event counting. In *Proceedings of the 38th International Symposium on Computer Architecture*, pages 353-364, 2011.

[17] Eiman Ebrahimi, Chang Joo Lee, Onur Mutlu, and Yale N. Patt. Fairness via Source Throttling: A Configurable and High-Performance Fairness Substrate for Multi-Core Memory Systems. In *Proceedings of the 15th International Conference on Architectural Support for Programming Languages and Operating Systems*, pages 335-346, 2010.

[18] Eiman Ebrahimi, Rustam Miftakhutdinov, Chris Fallin, Chang Joo Lee, Onur Mutlu, and Yale N. Patt. Parallel Application Memory Scheduling. In *Proceedings of the 44th International Symposium on Microarchitecture*, pages 2011.

[19] Stijn Eyerman and Lieven Eeckhout. Modeling critical sections in amdahl's law and its implications for multicore design. In *SIGARCH Comput. Archit. News*, pages 38:362-370, 2010.

[20] J. K. Flanagan, B. E. Nelson, J. K Archibald, K. S. Grimsrud. BACH: BYU Address Collection Hardware, The Collection of Complete Traces. In *Computer Performance Evaluation '92: Modeling Techniques and Tools*, 1993.

[21] B. Jacob, S. Ng, and D. Wang. Memory systems: Cache, dram, disk. In *Elsevier*, 2008.

[22] R. Johnson, I. Pandis, N. Hardavellas, A. Ailamaki, and B. Falsafi. Shore-MT: A scalable storage manager for the multicore era. In *Proc. 12th International Conference on Extending Database Technology: Advances in Database Technology*, pages 24–35, New York, NY, USA, 2009.

[23] Milo M. K. Martin, Mark D. Hill, Daniel J. Sorin. Why On-Chip Cache Coherence is Here to Stay. In *communications of the ACM*, vol 55, no 7, July 2012.

[24] M. Martonosi, D. W. Clark, and M. Mesarina. The SHRIMP Hardware Performance Monitor: Design and Applications. In *Proceedings of SIGMETRICS Symposium on Parallel and Distributed Tools,* pages 61-69, February 1996.

[25] Onur Mutlu and Thomas Moscibroda. Parallelism-Aware Batch Scheduling: Enhancing both Performance and Fairness of Shared DRAM Systems. In *Proceedings of the 35th International Symposium on Computer Architecture*, pages 63-74, 2008.

[26] N. Qu, X. G. Gou, and X. Cheng. Using Uncacheable Memory to Improve Unity Linux Performance. In Proceedings of the 6th Annual Workshop on the Interaction between Operating Systems and Computer Architecture, pages 27-32, 2005.

[27] S. Rixner. Memory Controller Optimizations for Web Servers. In *Proceedings of the 37th International Symposium on Microarchitecture*, pages 355-366, 2004.

[28] N. R. Tallent, J. M. Mellor-Crummey, and A. Porterfield. Analyzing Lock Contention in Multithreaded Applications. In *Proceedings of the ACM SIGPLAN Symposium on Principles and Practice of Parallel Programming*, pages 269–279, 2010.

[29] Josep Torrellas , Anoop Gupta , John Hennessy. Characterizing the caching and synchronization performance of a multiprocessor operating system, In *Proceedings of the fifth international conference on Architectural support for programming languages and operating systems*, p.162-174, 1992.

Runtime Detection and Optimization of Collective Communication Patterns

Torsten Hoefler
Department of Computer Science
ETH Zurich
Switzerland
htor@inf.ethz.ch

Timo Schneider
University of Illinois
at Urbana-Champaign
Illinois, USA
timos@illinois.edu

ABSTRACT

Parallelism is steadily growing, remote-data access will soon dominate the execution time of large-scale applications. Many large-scale communication patterns expose significant structure that can be used to schedule communications accordingly. In this work, we identify concurrent communication patterns and transform them to semantically equivalent but faster communications. We show a directed acyclic graph formulation for communication schedules and concisely define their synchronization and data movement semantics. Our dataflow solver computes an internal representation (IR) that is amenable to pattern detection. We demonstrate a detection algorithm for our IR that is guaranteed to detect communication kernels on subsets of the graph and replace the subgraph with hardware accelerated or hand-tuned kernels. Those techniques are implemented in an open-source detection and transformation framework to optimize communication patterns. Experiments show that our techniques can improve the performance of representative example codes by several orders of magnitude on two different systems. However, we also show that some collective detection problems on process subsets are NP-hard. The developed analysis techniques are a first important step towards automatic large-scale communication transformations. Our developed techniques open several avenues for additional transformation heuristics and analyses. We expect that such communication analyses and transformations will become as natural as pattern detection, just-in-time compiler optimizations, and autotuning are today for serial codes.

Categories and Subject Descriptors

D.1.3 [**Programming Techniques**]: Concurrent Programming—*Parallel Programming*

General Terms

Performance

Keywords

Collective Operations, Dynamic Optimization, MPI

1. INTRODUCTION

Compiler transformations, such as loop tiling, hoisting, unrolling, or fusion, are well known to improve performance of serial codes. Such transformations are important for performance portability to different architectures and work by transforming the dataflow graph (e.g., in a polyhedral model) without changing the program semantics. As applications move to hundreds of thousands of processors in the next generation computing systems, it is not sufficient to only optimize the serial parts of the computation. In fact, it can be expected that the time to solution will be dominated by communication and it will thus be most important to also optimize those critical communication parts of parallel applications.

Well-known optimizations at the message level, such as pipelining [30], remote direct memory access [24], or message coalescing, have a fundamental limitation: *No matter how powerful, they are no substitute for hand-optimized (collective) communication algorithms.* Consider a blocking broadcast to P processes. For large P, a less optimized binomial tree algorithm will always outperform a highly optimized (but asymptotically slower) linear broadcast.

Similar arguments have been well-studied for serial codes. For example, the performance of hand-tuned routines such as Goto's dense matrix multiplication [10] can hardly be achieved by automatic transformations of the simple three-loop formulation. Instead, kernel recognition is considered as generally beneficial [19]. The recognition is often performed on some representation of the dataflow graph [13] where semantic components are replaced with calls to the optimized kernel routine. *In this work, we extend this idea towards the recognition and replacement of parallel application communication patterns.*

Most of today's large-scale parallel codes are implemented in a message-passing programming model using the Message Passing Interface (MPI) standard [20]. MPI offers a large set of predefined communication patterns called *collective operations*. Many newer programming paradigms, such as PGAS languages [22, 33, 6, 5], declarative parallel languages [17], or annotation-based languages [35, 23] provide a conceptually simpler programming interface and rely on the compiler or the communication layer for optimizations. While some languages offer intrinsics or runtime libraries for several collective operations, many do not support such a specification **at all** moving the burden of pattern recognition to the compiler or forcing the user to hand-code non performance-portable algorithms. The following table shows an exemplary overview of parallel languages and environments and their support for collective operations:

MPI 2.2 [20]	17 collective library calls
UPC 1.2 [33]	8 collective library calls
CAF 2.0 [18]	9 collective intrinsics
CAF (Fortran 2008) [22]	no support for collectives
OpenMP [23]	only reductions
Chapel [6]	compiler support mentioned
XscalableMP [35]	compiler support mentioned

PACT'12, September 19–23, 2012, Minneapolis, Minnesota, USA.

Many languages mention compiler support in publications but it is not implemented yet to the best of our knowledge. Others provide only the most commonly used collective operations. Even MPI which offers arguably the most extensive and mature set of collective operations may not support all variations. A good example is the recently introduced MPI_Reduce_scatter_block, which has been missing in MPI for 15 years and which offers additional optimization opportunities compared to MPI_Reduce_scatter. The optimization framework that we will present could have auto-detected this more restricted collective operation and replaced it with a hand-tuned kernel transparently.

Another issue with today's parallel programs is that many legacy codes use point-to-point patterns instead of collective communications because at some point programmers observed them to be faster than the corresponding MPI collective operation (in one particular MPI implementation). This problem is well known in the MPI community leading to efforts to define self-consistency performance metrics for MPI [16] to prevent it. Other applications implement hand-tuned pipelined communication patterns instead of using MPI optimized collective operations. The most prominent example here is the High Performance Linpack benchmark [8] which is used to rank machines in the top 500 list.

The lack of support for collective operations in many high-level programming models, legacy MPI codes using "manual" collectives, the potential for identifying new important collective communications, and the pipelined collective implementations motivate the *automatic detection and optimization of known communication patterns in parallel programs*. Such a detection scheme would allow all parallel languages (including Chapel and XalableMP) to take advantage of collective semantics and allow them to use highly tuned communication kernels or collective acceleration hardware (cf. Section 1.3).

Pattern detection and optimization could either be carried out during compile time or during run time of the application. Compile time, or static, optimizations have the advantage that their execution time does not influence the overall performance of the applications but it often suffers from *exponential state explosion* [34] and it cannot be applied if the communication structure is *input-dependent*. Run time, or dynamic, optimizations on the other hand can benefit from all information available at runtime. The overheads during runtime are usually offset by the repeated use of the optimized operation. We will show in our experimental section that the number of necessary repetitions needed to offset the optimization costs shrinks with the growing numbers of processes and is often small (e.g., less than 10). Thus, we focus on dynamic optimization in this work.

1.1 A Simple Internal DAG Representation

We use a simple, domain-specific directed acyclic graph (DAG) formulation to represent communications that we call *communication DAG* (cDAG). cDAG allows the DAG specification of operations such as sends, receives and local operations. All cDAG operations form a global graph with local dependencies (edges specifying the order of operations at each process) and remote dependencies (edges specifying dataflow and synchronization between processes).

In the following section, we show an example how well-known compiler transformations can modify a PGAS code to specify a cDAG IR during runtime. However, the focus of this work lies not on generating the IR from application codes (there are too many parallel libraries and languages in use today to tackle such a task in a single article) but rather how a cDAG just-in-time compiler and optimizer can detect communication primitives in the DAG IR and how it can transform the communication graph to use optimized kernels.

1.2 Extracting Communication Graphs

Communication graphs in MPI can be found in the parallel control flow graph of an MPI program (pCFG, [3]), or they can be specified directly as neighborhood collective communications, a functionality proposed for MPI-3.

To demonstrate the applicability to PGAS languages, we use an example from the FT code, the fast Fourier transform kernel from the NAS benchmark suite that was ported to UPC [9]. It includes the following code-fragment:

```
upc_barrier;
for (int i = 0; i < THREADS; i++) {
    upc_memget((dcomplex*)&dst[MYTHREAD].cell[chunk*i],
    &src[i].cell[chunk*MYTHREAD], sizeof(dcomplex) * chunk );
}
upc_barrier;
```

A parallel control flow graph (pCFG) as described in [3] could be used to track the dataflow from one image to another. Dataflow analysis identifies the buffer `dst[MYTHREAD].cell[chunk*i]` as target and `src[i].cell[chunk*MYTHREAD]` as source buffer. The analysis would then replace the data movement with send and receive calls which add edges to the communication DAG. This simple transformation would then result in the following cDAG code:

```
upc_barrier;
cDAG_graph g = cDAG_CreateGraph();
for (int i = 0; i < THREADS; i++) {
    int msgsize = sizeof(dcomplex) * chunk;
    cDAG_Send(g, &src[MYTHREAD].cell[chunk*i], msgsize, i);
    cDAG_Recv(g, &dst[MYTHREAD].cell[chunk*i], msgsize, i);
}
cDAG_Schedule sched = cDAG_CompileGraph(g);
cDAG_Run(sched);
```

We observe that the code's branch structure stays the same which simplifies the compiler analysis needed to perform this step. The function cDAG_CreateGraph() creates a DAG object to which send and receive operations and dependencies between them can be attached (cDAG_Send() and cDAG_Recv() do not communicate data themselves but add the specified communications to the communication graph). cDAG_CompileGraph() performs the online compilation, detection, and transformation of the graph as described later in this paper, and cDAG_Run() executes the optimized schedule. Just like a binary program, a cDAG schedule can be re-used with cDAG_Run() after it has been compiled, so repeated calls of the same loop would not need to rebuild the graph (the code for checking if the graph object already exists is trivial and has been omitted for brevity and clarity). We remark that cDAG is somewhat similar to MPI Datatypes [20] but targets communication patterns instead of memory accesses.

The described analyses and transformations into cDAG graphs use only well-known dataflow-techniques and simple loop splitting to transform the serial code and are outside the scope of this work. We also note that transformations to cDAG can always be done manually or with the help of refactoring tools.

1.3 Optimized Collective Operations

Numerous research groups demonstrated speedups up to several orders of magnitude using optimized algorithms and implementation strategies for collective operations in hundreds of publications, e.g., [31, 4, 25]. In addition to such highly optimized point-to-point patterns, nearly all modern supercomputers and high-performance networks such as Blue Gene/P [15], IBM PERCS [2], InfiniBand ConnectX2 [11], and Portals [29] provide specialized hardware support or even separate networks [15] for collective operations. Such *collective accelerators* provide significant speedup over implementations based on point-to-point messages and can easily be utilized once a supported collective operation is detected.

Implementing collective operations on shared memory systems is also a well-known research topic, e.g., [32]. The best implementations often depend on the details of the cache coherence protocol on a particular architecture and are often not performance-portable. Thus, machine-specific optimizations may provide benefits even for shared memory models such as OpenMP.

1.4 Related Work

Detecting collective operations in point-to-point patterns is an important problem. Most previous works performed the detection *post-mortem* by analyzing traces of the program run. This bears several problems: (1) real traces are often of unmanageable size, (2) on-node data-transformations (e.g., reductions) cannot be captured, and (3) the optimizations cannot be applied dynamically during the program run which is problematic if communication patterns depend on the input data. The fundamental difference between most trace-based analyses and our detection scheme is that we have exact data-dependency information, where trace-based analyses often resort to heuristic approches.

Knüpfer et al. proposed a scheme to detect alltoall, scatter, gather, and broadcast by analyzing point-to-point patterns in message traces [14]. This detection scheme can guide programmers to apply source-code changes. However, the authors mention that their analysis suffers from detecting "pseudo patterns" for some process counts but not for others. While programmers cannot replace such an operation with a collective call, our dynamic optimization scheme is able to optimize this case transparently without user intervention. In addition, Knüpfer's detection scheme is also not suitable to detect if data is forwarded through other processes as commonly done in manually optimized algorithms.

Kranzlmüller et al. investigate the detection of repetitive communication patterns in [26]. Like Knüpfer, they only look at single point-to-point operations in MPI traces such that forwarding of data through proxy processes cannot be detected in this scheme. The same authors discuss how to guide compiler transformations with the trace analysis techniques [28, 27], however, they leave the problem of detecting collective operations open.

We are not aware of any dynamic collective detection scheme. In this work, we propose a scheme that is *guaranteed* to detect collective operations on the full process set in a communication graph. That is, our scheme will detect collective operations, even after arbitrary transformations of the communication graph (e.g., data forwarding through proxy processes). Even though we focus on dynamic optimizations in this paper, the discussed techniques can also be applied statically (post-mortem, trace-based, assuming that the trace contains the whole dataflow including all buffer addresses). We presented some preliminary results of our work as a poster [12].

1.5 Terms and Notation

Let the complete communication and dependency graph of represented as $G = (V, E)$ where the vertex-set V contains the send and receive operations, $S \cup R$. The set of edges $E = D \cup M$ contains the communication edges (we call this *matching set* $M \subseteq S \times R$) and local dependency edges $D \subseteq V \times V$ (this set specifies the order of process-local send/recv operations). We use $|V| = n$, $E = M \cup D$, and $|E| = m$ in our analyses. The set of processes is denoted as P and $|P| = p$.

1.6 Limitations and Contributions

The proposed scheme is limited by the power of the transformations of a parallel code to a cDAG code. The symbolic analysis of pCFGs is often limited by the problem of static message matching [3] and fully automated transformations may not always be possible. Those static compiler transformations are outside the scope of this work. However, user-annotations or manual re-writing to cDAG can also be used to enable our optimizations. Once all concurrent communication operations are expressed in cDAG, our automatic detection and transformation scheme is guaranteed to find and replace all patterns that are semantically equivalent to predefined collective operations.

The key contributions of our work are:

- A specification of synchronization and dataflow semantics for communication DAGs.
- A dataflow propagation algorithm that transforms the communication DAG into an efficient internal representation in time $\mathcal{O}(n \log m)$.
- A classification of MPI collective operations with regards to their level of abstraction and composeability.
- An algorithm for detecting all collective operations in time $\mathcal{O}(n \log n)$.
- A proof that the problem of detecting several collective operations on process subsets in communication graphs is NP-hard.

In general, we demonstrate a flexible approach for dynamic communication optimization of parallel communication graphs. We accompany the theoretical discussion and analysis of the dataflow algorithms with a practical and complete open-source implementation of the analysis and transformation and demonstrate the benefits of applying our scheme to different parallel codes and architectures.

2. DYNAMICALLY DETECTING COLLECTIVE OPERATIONS

First we introduce our running example to explain our notation and detection scheme. Figure 1 shows an optimized alltoall implemented with a butterfly communication pattern [4] on four processes. All previous collective detection schemes would not be able to find the alltoall communication in this pattern. We will use this nontrivial example throughout the paper (Figures 1 to 5) to describe the dataflow propagation and other algorithms.

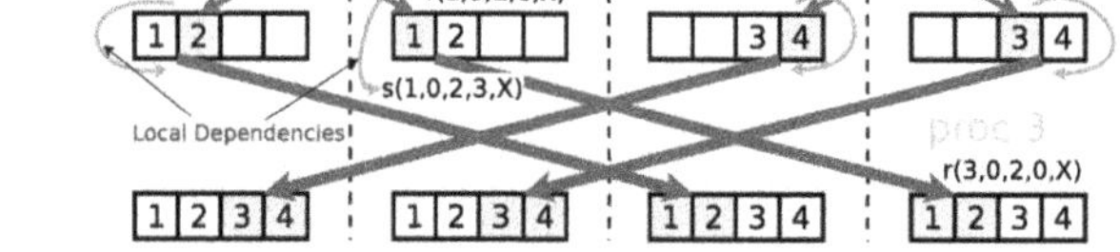

Figure 1: Alltoall with a Butterfly Pattern (p=4)

The send and receive sets (*S* and *R*) contain the send and receive operations and elements in S and R are named $s(\ldots)$ and $r(\ldots)$, respectively. Not all elements of those sets are shown in Figure 1

due to space constraints; Figure 2 contains all elements. Each element of those sets is a tuple with (owner, address, size, peer, address at peer). **The dependency set (*D*)** contains local dependencies (curved arrows) between operations. Dependencies are added by the transformations described in Section 1.2 if there are dependencies in the local control flow graphs between accesses (sends or local operations) to buffers that have been received before. This is illustrated in round 2 of the dissemination algorithm where the send on each rank reads data that was received before, i.e., the send *depends* on the completion of the respective receive. **The matching set (*M*)**, represented by straight arrows in Figure 1, is determined by the local order (specified by D) and send/recv pairs (S/R).
The dataflow propagation and all auxiliary algorithms are *serial*, i.e., we assume that the DAG is communicated (gathered) to a single process to perform the analysis and transformation and is scattered to all processes before execution. We will discuss the overheads of this approach in Section 3.

2.1 The Message Matching Problem

Many **message passing specifications** (e.g., MPI) use tagged communications (or named channels). User-selected tags restrict the valid executions such that only sends and receives with *matching* tags and source arguments generate a flow in the communication graph. Some messaging interfaces allow wildcard matching which can lead to non-deterministic [34] communications. A correct program must allow any matching order for non-determinstic matchings and our algorithm can match messages in one particular order to avoid *state explosion* (cf. [34]).
Applications using either the **one-sided PGAS or shared memory model** specify the remote buffer for each remote access directly and our transformation to cDAG generates a send/recv pair for each access. In this special case, the matching set M can be computed in $\mathcal{O}(1)$ by including all auto-generated send/recv pairs and the following matching algorithm is **not** necessary.
We now discuss an algorithm for generic dynamic matching, i.e., to construct the matching set M from the process-local sets R_i, S_i, and D_i for $0 \le i < p$. The algorithm essentially simulates a parallel execution of the schedule and needs to follow local and remote (send/recv) dependencies to ensure message matches in correct order.
Our algorithm starts to match send and receive operations that have no dependencies (in the Matching Queue MQ). Once a match is established, the operations and their dependencies are removed. Operations for which all dependencies have been removed may be and matched are thus added to MQ. This fix-point algorithm is repeated until it converges. This serial algorithm could be replaced by a symbolic parallel execution with zero-byte messages to record the matching set M, however, our algorithm performs significantly better than sending each message over the network. The complete pseudo-code is shown in the appendix in Algorithm 1.
An example for matching is shown in Figure 2 and 3. Figure 2 shows the initial state in the first iteration. All shaded tuples are in MQ waiting to be activated. Figure 3 shows an intermediate state of the algorithm where the first receive of process 0 is matched. After matching, the dependency is removed and the second send to process 2 is added to MQ (shaded grey). The algorithm continues by picking the next unmatched operation.

Time Complexity of Matching.

Each node is inserted in MQ exactly once and in each fixpoint iteration one node is removed from MQ, forcing convergence after n iterations. Finding the matching target for each node and updating the appropriate sets can be done in time $\mathcal{O}(n \log n)$ using red-black

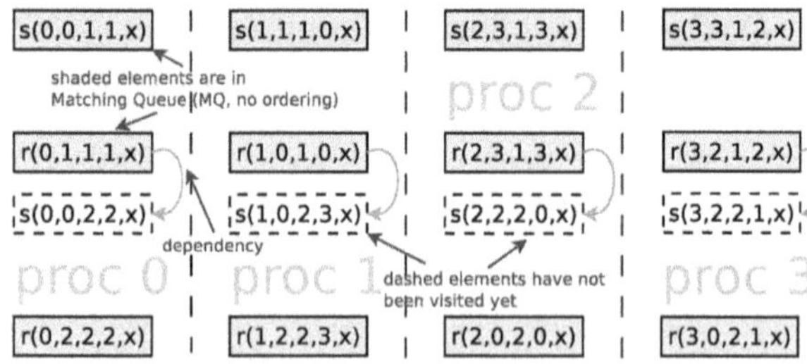

Figure 2: Matching Example, initialization (p=4)

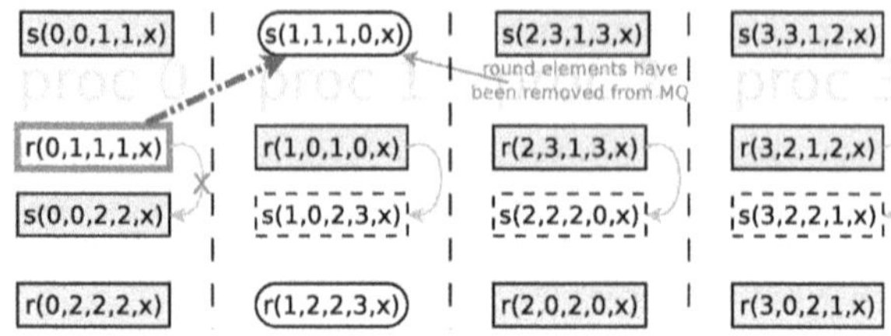

Figure 3: Matching Example, after a few steps (p=4)

trees. While traversing the tree, each of the $|D| < m$ dependencies is removed once and each vertex is traversed once leading to an additional time of $\mathcal{O}(n + m)$. The total cost for the matching algorithm is thus $\mathcal{O}(n \log n + m)$.

2.2 Synchronization and Data Movement Semantics

Every communication has two separable side effects: *synchronization* and *data movement*. Synchronization semantics define for each process from which other processes it receives a message, i.e., it has to wait for. Data movement semantics define how memory locations are changed during the execution of a communication DAG. Both semantics are independent: synchronization can happen without changing remote memory (the best example is a barrier collective operation or simply zero-byte communications) and data movement can happen without synchronization (e.g., one-sided memory accesses).

2.3 Dynamic Dataflow Analysis

Our dataflow propagation computes both semantics: **Synchronization** is captured in the **wait set** W_i, which specifies the processes that process i needs to wait for (synchronize with) before exiting the communication. The wait set W_i for process i can be computed with a (reverse) traversal of the communication and dependency graph $G = (V, E = M \cup D)$ starting at i and adding all reachable processes to W_i. We omitted the detailed algorithm of this simple traversal due to space restrictions.
The more complex **data movement** semantics are expressed as a set of dataflow tuples from all **original sends** S^0 to all **final receives** R^∞. An original send is a send operation that specifies user memory that has not been received from another process and a final receive is a receive that specifies user memory that will not be overwritten as destination. The sets S^0 and R^∞ represents all dataflow semantics of a communication graph. In fact, they form an IR similar to the well-known Static Single Assignment form used for serial compiler transformations (every address is only written once). Thus, we call the resulting representation of the dataflow from S^0 to R^∞ Static Single Transfer (SST; each transfer from a source to a target buffer happens exactly once). The SST form expresses the overall data-movement abstractly and allows to detect (pattern-match) collective operations.

We use a dataflow propagation algorithm to transform our DAG IR into SST form. This fixpoint algorithms propagates the send buffer information along the matched send/receive edges in the graph until they reached the final receives. Like before, each send and receive is specified as a tuple of (owner, start address, size, peer (source or destination), start address at peer). Our algorithm works on a queue of independent sends (sends without incoming dependencies) and propagates the dataflow from the sends to the final receives. As receives are processed in the dataflow, their dependencies are marked as satisfied which may enable new sends to be added to the queue. Figure 4 shows the tuple transformations performed by the dataflow

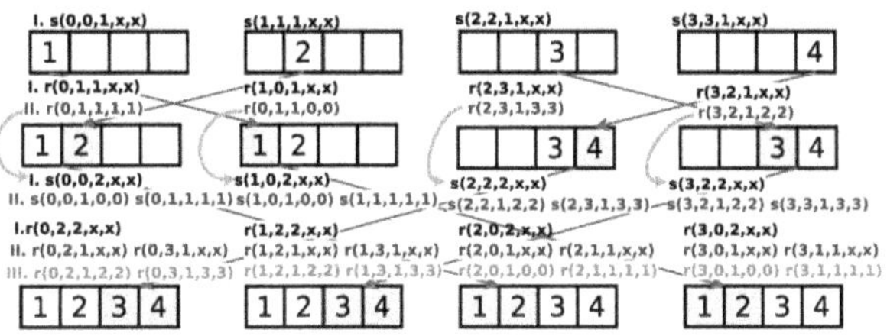

Figure 4: The Dataflow Propagation (p=4)

propagation algorithm. The original tuples are shown in the black lines, marked with *I*. the tuples that are transformed in the first iteration are shown in red and marked with *II*, and the tuples transformed in the second (last) iteration are shown in green, marked with *III*. The dataflow algorithm has to *split* send/recv matches in the second iteration to separate data flows from the local memory and data that was received in the first iteration. If a received buffer is not sent fully or sent to different destinations, we split the backwards dataflow into two separate flows (SST assignments, represented as tuples).

Figure 5 shows the split at process 0 in the first iteration of the dataflow algorithm. Since the two-element message from process 0 to process 2 sends data from local memory (original send) as well as data that was received from process 1, it needs to be split into two SST assignments.

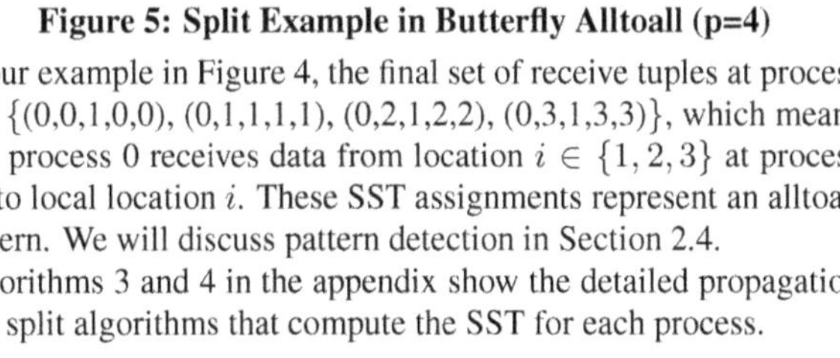

Figure 5: Split Example in Butterfly Alltoall (p=4)

In our example in Figure 4, the final set of receive tuples at process 0 is {(0,0,1,0,0), (0,1,1,1,1), (0,2,1,2,2), (0,3,1,3,3)}, which means that process 0 receives data from location $i \in \{1,2,3\}$ at process i into local location i. These SST assignments represent an alltoall pattern. We will discuss pattern detection in Section 2.4.

Algorithms 3 and 4 in the appendix show the detailed propagation and split algorithms that compute the SST for each process.

Time Complexity of Dynamic Dataflow Analysis.

We analyze the complexity by stating some invariants for the dataflow propagation. Every send or receive will be visited exactly once in the algorithm (data is propagated only forward). Finding a match in the ordered matching set M costs $\mathcal{O}(\log |M|)$. Each split can generate new send/recv vertices. However, a critical observation is that one recv in the input can result in a maximum of two new split send/recv pairs (cf. Figure 5). And every newly generated send/recv pair can again only generate a single split because the communicated memory is consecutive. Thus, there are a maximum of $\mathcal{O}(|V|)$ additional send/recv pairs generated in splits. The total runtime of the propagation algorithm is thus $\mathcal{O}(|V|\log|M|) = \mathcal{O}(n \log m)$.

2.4 Detecting MPI Collective Operations

Each collective data movement operation can be defined as a set of SST assignments (as returned from the dataflow propagation algorithm), for example a broadcast can be defined as $(i, o_i, l, j, o_j)\ 0 \leq j < P, j \neq i$, where i is the root process, s is the length of the message, o_i is the offset at the root process, j are all other (receiving) processes, and o_j the local memory offset at process j.

2.4.1 Collective Data Movement Signatures in SST

We now discuss the signatures for all collective operations that move data. We use the SST tuple notation like before, i.e., (s, o_s, l, r, o_r) means that data of size l is moved from offset o_s at process s to offset o_r at process r. We use r to denote the root process of a collective (if applicable), j and i to denote source and target processes respectively, o_x to denote the local offset for communication originating or terminating at process x, and $o_{x,y}$ to denote local offset for communication from process x to y.

The following table lists the data movement signatures that are used to detect common collective operations:

bcast	$(r, o_r, l, j, o_j)\ 0 \leq j < p, j \neq r$
gather	$(i, o_{i,r}, l, r, o_{r,i})\ 0 \leq i < p, i \neq r$
scatter	$(r, o_{r,j}, l, j, o_j)\ 0 \leq j < p, j \neq r$
allgather	$(i, o_i, l, j, o_{i,j})\ 0 \leq i, j < p, j \neq i$
alltoall	$(i, o_{i,j}, l, j, o_{i,j})\ 0 \leq i, j < p, j \neq i$

This list can easily be extended with any data movement signature. The last condition ($j \neq r$ or $j \neq i$) removes the send-to-self, i.e., local copy, from the detection.

2.4.2 Detection Hierarchy for Collective Operations

The data movement patterns show that MPI's collective operations form a strict hierarchy, i.e., some collective operations can be expressed as a set of others. For example, an alltoall can be expressed with p broadcasts, an allgather can be expressed as p gather operations, or a broadcast can be expressed as a scatter from the same memory location at the root. Collective operations that can be expressed as a composition of other operations offer a higher level of abstraction with higher optimization opportunities [14]. Thus, we establish the following order of collective operations from "highest" to "lowest" abstraction: **allgather** $\succ$ **alltoall** $\succ$ **broadcast** $\succ$ **gather, scatter**.

2.4.3 An Algorithm to Detect Collective Operations

We can now detect collective operations by searching for the data movement signatures from the most abstract to the least abstract operation as defined before. After finding an operation, we remove all tuples that matched this operation and insert a call to the detected operation instead (i.e., remove and replace the communication kernel). We then run the algorithm repeatedly until no operation is detected.

The detailed algorithm is shown in the appendix as Algorithm 5.

Time Complexity.

The number of SST assignments is limited by $\mathcal{O}(n)$ because each send and recv will result in one receive tuple and each send/recv pair can at most generate one new assignment in a split. The tuples

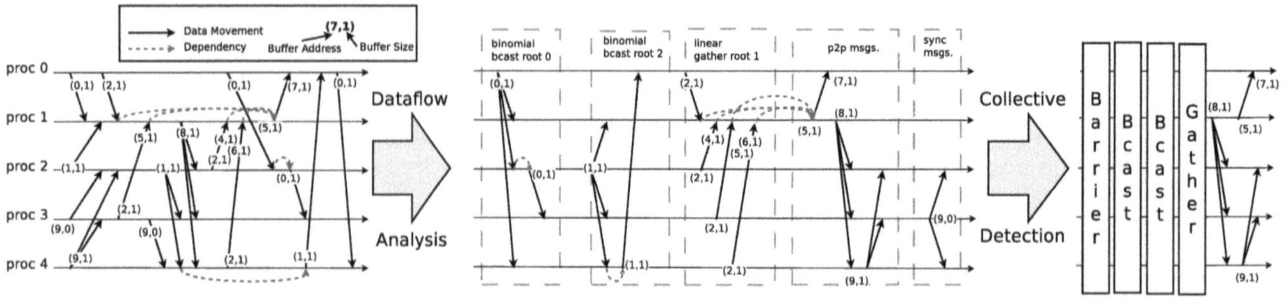

Figure 6: A more complex artificial test graph with 20 messages among five processes

are sorted in $\mathcal{O}(n \log n)$ before the detection. Assuming a constant number of message sizes, each tuple is only considered once in the detection of each algorithm. Thus, the overall time complexity of the detection algorithm is $\mathcal{O}(n \log n)$.

Operations with Noncontiguous Data Access.

Some communication layers (e.g., MPI) offer support for noncontiguous data layouts in send and receive memory. This allows to send data that is scattered in memory within the same collective operation call. The detection algorithm will detect one collective operation for each contiguous block (SST tuple). We can then simply combine all collective operations of the same *shape* (i.e., the same operation and the same root if applicable) into one collective operation with noncontiguous data layouts (e.g., MPI datatypes).

Detecting Vector Collective Operations.

We excluded the vector operations alltoallv, alltoallw, allgatherv, scatterv, gatherv from our previous classification because they can trivially match many SSTs, e.g., a simple send/recv pair can be expressed as gatherv with all counts but one set to zero.

Nevertheless, we can modify our detection algorithm to support vector collectives if we allow arbitrary data-sizes between pairs of processes and define a factor τ which specifies the desired *density* of the collective, i.e., the percentage of edges relative to the non-vector operation that need to exist in the detected vector collective. The vector collective detection is similar to the previous algorithm but only $\tau \cdot p(p-1)$ (allgather, alltoall) or $\tau \cdot (p-1)$ (broadcast, gather, scatter) need to be found to detect a collective vector operation.

Barrier Collectives.

Barrier collectives are an exception because data is neither communicated nor reduced. Thus, the detection based on dataflow cannot detect barrier calls. However, the barrier call will be detected by the synchronization detection and will result in complete wait sets for all processes. In general, any transformation must check if is fulfills the synchronization specified by the wait sets. If it lacks synchronizations, then they can simply be introduced by zero-byte send/recv pairs.

3. EXAMPLES AND EXPERIMENTS

Figure 6 shows a more complex example (one of our unit tests) to demonstrate the capabilities of our detection scheme. The left side shows a communication graph with five participating processes. Each solid arrow represents a message with a send (sendbuf, size) and a receive (recvbuf, size) at the beginning and end. The middle figure shows the result after our detection algorithm and the right shows the optimized graph.

We tested several different detection patterns in order to evaluate correctness and performance of our implementation. We generated simple linear and complex (binomial tree, bruck, dissemination) broadcast, gather, scatter, and alltoall graphs and for different numbers of processes and added p random messages with dependencies. Our implementation detected all collectives and correctly isolated all operations that were part of it. In the following, we provide a performance analysis for detecting a broadcast, implemented as binomial tree on p processes.

3.1 Experimental Environment

Our optimization framework is implemented in C++ and uses MPI as transport layer. We analyzed the performance on multiple parallel systems and present the two systems: (1) Odin, an InfiniBand cluster with quad-core Opteron CPUs and (2) NERSC Hopper, a Cray XE6 with 2.1 GHz AMD MagnyCours CPUs. We used the default C++ compilers on both systems with highest optimization available (g++ 4.1.2 with -O3 on Odin and PGI 11.7 with -fast on Hopper). The complete source code and tests can be downloaded from `http://unixer.de/research/cDAG`.

3.2 Scalability and Performance Analysis

Figure 7(a) shows the runtime of the different parts of the collective detection on Hopper as described before. **Matching** implements a simple depth-first search (DFS) traversal as described in Section 2.1, **Dataflow** is the dataflow propagation algorithm, **Colldetect** is the detection and replacement algorithm, and **Scatter/Gather** represents the communication overhead to gather all the schedules to a single process and distribute (scatter) the optimized schedules back to all processes.

The figure shows measurement results as dots and our performance models as lines. For the broadcast problems, we have $n \approx p \approx m$. Thus, we use $a \cdot p \log(p)$ to represent the runtime of the Dataflow, Matching and Colldetect phases. The used scatter and gather implementations are linear (sending from the root to all processes). For relatively small process counts, the ($\approx$ 100 Bytes) messages are communicated quickly into local eager MPI buffers. Beginning with $\approx$ 2500 processes, those buffers are exhausted and the curve starts the expected linear slope and we use the model $b \cdot p$ to represent the runtime. The performance for large process counts ($>$ 2000) can be accurately represented with the following constants for a and b:

System	a (Dataflow)	a (Matching)	a (Colldetect)	b
Hopper	0.59 μs	0.19 μs	0.15 μs	39 μs
Odin	0.85 μs	0.15 μs	0.13 μs	21 μs

The b factor in the communication is dominating on both systems with 39μs and 21μs per process. For example, the detection and optimization scheme would take $\approx$ 15s on 300.000 cores of a petascale-class machine. The used memory for 300.000 processes is less than 85 MiB (283 Bytes per process). The whole optimization process can be offloaded to a separate core and optimize sched-

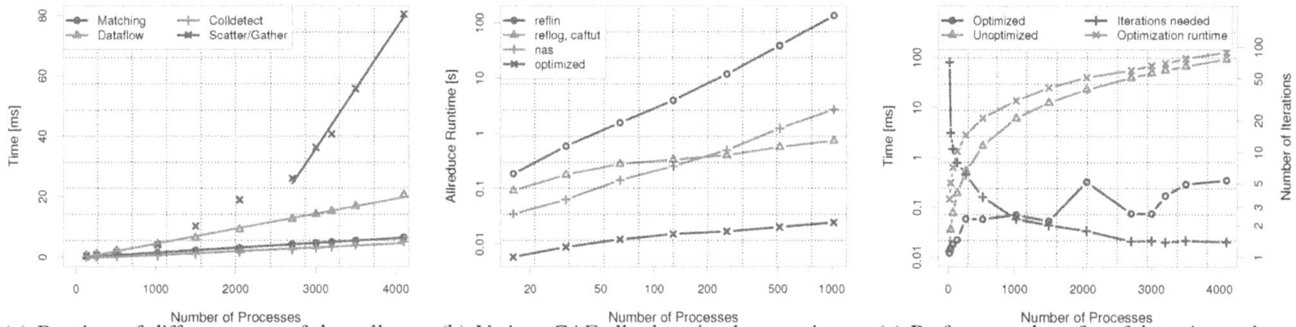

(a) Runtime of different parts of the collective detection for a binomial broadcast

(b) Various CAF allreduce implementations on Hopper and optimized version

(c) Performance benefits of detecting and replacing a linear broadcast

Figure 7: Experimental Results of the cDAG implementation with collective detection enabled

ules while the (unoptimized or partially optimized) communication takes place.

3.3 Microbenchmarks

We now discuss the possible performance gain by detecting and replacing known communication patterns in existing applications. We utilize the patterns that we found in the Co-Array Fortran NAS codes [7], the UPC NAS codes [9], and SPhot, an MPI application from the Sequoia benchmark suite.

First, we investigate the performance of logical allreduce patterns in Co-Array Fortran. We compare six different implementations in order to capture several versions of code that a typical user would implement. The first implementation ("reflin") is a linear reference algorithm from [22] (Section 2.5 "Summing over the co-dimension of a co-array"). The second algorithm ("reflog") is a more complex version with logarithmic complexity of the same algorithm [22] (Section 4.4). The third implementation ("caftut") has identical performance as "reflog" and was given as an example by Numrich in [21]. The fourth implementation ("nas") was extracted from the Co-Array Fortran version of the NAS benchmarks [7]. The last implementation ("optimized") represents an architecture-optimized call to MPI_Allreduce.

Figure 7(b) shows the time to perform 1000 allreduce calls with different number of processes on the Hopper system using the Gemini interconnect that is optimized for PGAS and Co-Array Fortran [1]. We used the Cray PE version 3.1.61 for all experiments. We observe that the different implementations have widely varying and scale-dependent performance characteristics. However, all user implementations are significantly slower than the well optimized "opt" algorithm (more than three orders of magnitude for the linear implementation).

As discussed before, the dynamic optimization comes with an overhead during runtime (cf. Figure 7(a)) and it is important to compare the runtime overhead to the gains of the optimized schedule. In Figure 7(c) compares the naive (as one would do in CAF for example) and the transformed execution of a broadcast on Hopper. It also shows the runtime of the complete detection and transformation (magenta, diagonal crosses) which is just slightly slower than a single linear broadcast. The green line shows how often a schedule needs to be re-executed before our scheme decreases the application runtime. We see that the necessary number of iterations is rapidly decreasing with scale and with $p > 1500$ even two iterations (a single re-use of the schedule) are sufficient to offset the costs of the optimization. On Odin two iterations are beneficial for $p > 1000$.

3.4 Application Benchmarks

In this section, we demonstrate the usefulness of our method on two representative applications, SPhot and NAS/FT. SPhot is part of the Sequoia benchmark suite. It contains a loop which performs a logical gather using point-to-point messages. Our cDAG scheme detected and optimized this communication pattern by replacing it with a call to a vendor-optimized gather call. The observed application improvement ranged from 0.3% to 14.1%.

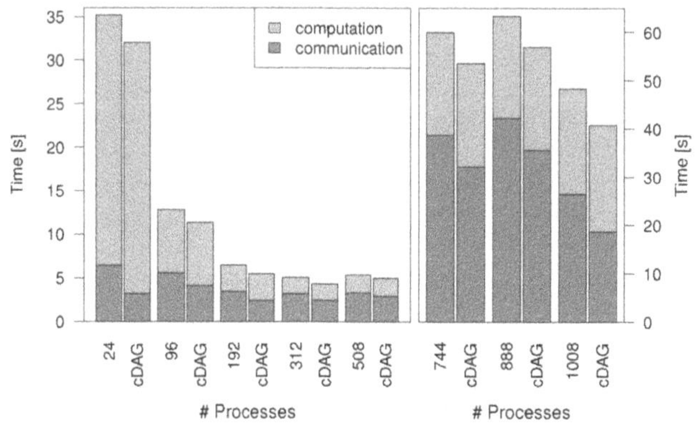

Figure 8: NAS/FT Performance on Hopper

To demonstrate the applicability to PGAS codes, we applied the cDAG scheme to the NAS codes that were ported to UPC [9]. While those codes offer several opportunities to detect and optimize collective patterns, we will focus on the FT (fast Fourier transform) benchmark in the following. The benchmark contains the exact loop and transformation that we showed in the example in Section 1.2. We used the class C FT benchmark up to 508 processes, to scale further we utilized class D (which could not be used for smaller numbers of processes due to memory requirements).

Our scheme replaces the communication in NAS/FT with an optimized version that uses Cray's DMAPP low-level communication API to perform the alltoall. We observe a 29% improvement of the raw communication performance which translated to 16% improvement in overall application performance at 1008 processes.

4. ON DETECTING COLLECTIVES ON PROCESS SUBSETS

We discussed fast algorithms for detecting arbitrary collective operations in arbitrary communication patterns. However, those algorithms only detect operations that are performed on the *complete set of processes*. The problem of detecting collective operations on arbitrary process subsets is also relevant. For example, a pattern where every other process participates in a global broadcast or a pattern where all but one processes perform a global alltoall exchange.

This problem is much harder; we start by showing that the simplified problem of detecting maximum groups with barrier semantics is NP-complete. This makes the general case of detecting collective operations on maximum process subsets NP-complete.

4.1 Finding Maximum Barrier Groups

We say that a set $C \subset P$ has barrier semantics iff the wait sets W_i (cf. Section 2.3) of all $i \in C$ include all processes in C. We define the *single largest barrier* (SLB) problem as follows: Find the largest subset of $C \subset P$ that has barrier semantics and that cannot be extended by another process $p \in P$ such that the set $C \cup \{p\}$ has barrier semantics.

THEOREM 1. *The construction problem of SLB is NP-complete.*

PROOF. First, we show that SLB is in NP: Testing if a subset of processes C of a pattern has barrier semantics can be done by checking if every node in the wait set of all other nodes in C. The wait sets can be established in polynomial time as described in Section 2.3 and the check can be performed in $\mathcal{O}(|C|^2)$.

We show NP-completeness of the SLB problem by showing CLIQUE $\leq_P$ SLB. Let the undirected graph $G = (V, E)$ be the input for CLIQUE. We can now construct a cDAG communication graph $G' = (V', E')$ which has an SLB of size k iff G has a clique of size k. The mapping between elements in V and processes in the cDAG is bijective. For each edge $(u, v) \in E$ add a send and a receive operation to V' so that the process u' mapping to u sends data to the process v' mapping to v, the cDAG contains no dependencies and the matching set E' is such that $(u, v) \in E \Leftrightarrow (u', v') \in E'$. By construction, G' now has a SLB of size k iff G has a clique of size k. □

The barrier problem is the simplest to show NP completeness since no data is communicated. However, adding dataflow in the form of SST does not make the problem simpler. Informally said, the detection of all-collectives (allreduce, alltoall, allgather, etc.) in our SST formulation is likely to be as hard as solving the SLB problem.

4.2 Finding Maximum Subsets of Rooted Collectives

The problem of finding maximum groups for rooted collectives (e.g., scatter, gather, bcast) can be solved in polynomial time in the SST form (Algorithm 3).

The detection algorithm is similar to the collective detection algorithm in Section 2.4.3. For example for broadcast or scatter it simply tests the number of flows of equal size from each process to other processes. The process with the highest number of flows to other processes is root of the largest broadcast or scatter subgroup. The matching nodes can be removed and the algorithm can be applied to find the next largest set. The time to perform this detection is $\mathcal{O}(n \log n)$. Algorithms for all other rooted collectives follow the same principle.

5. DISCUSSION AND FUTURE WORK

In this work we propose a dynamic transformation scheme for communication graphs as first steps towards communication- and network-centric compiler optimizations. We expect this area of research to grow quickly in importance as we are moving towards higher parallelism. Our transformations uses an abstract graph-based representation as input and we developed a set-based single static transfer (SST) representation that represents dataflows from source buffers to target buffers in a distributed memory model. We show that SST is ideally suited for analyses such as the detection of collective operations. We demonstrate fast algorithms for building the SST form and computing synchronization semantics of the input graph.

We introduced a hierarchy of collective operations based on their level of abstraction and composeability. We demonstrated that the algorithms are able to detect collective operations on the full process set on arbitrary subsets of operations in a graph. We proved that finding maximum synchronization groups (e.g., detecting barriers) on arbitrary process subsets is NP-complete. However, we also provide polynomial-time algorithms to detect rooted collectives on largest process subsets. Developing practical heuristics for detecting all-collectives on maximum process subsets is an interesting problem for future work.

Our approach for dynamic communication graph optimization is feasible in practice up to large numbers of processes. Our accurate performance model of the optimization time on 300.000 processes predicts $\approx 15s$ and a memory requirement of 283 Bytes per process.

We demonstrated that PGAS microbenchmark performance can be improved by an order of magnitude over an optimized textbook version and a practical implementation of the NAS benchmarks. We also measured performance improvements of up to 14% for the SPhot application from the ASC Sequoia Benchmark suite and up to 16% for the NAS FT benchmark.

Our work is an important step towards automatic dynamic and static optimization of communication patterns in large-scale computing. Detecting collective operations and replacing them with hardware-accelerated or optimized implementations is comparable to known techniques such as auto-vectorization. More advanced techniques that can be applied in addition to the optimizations proposed in this work, such as automated topology-aware graph tuning and transformations are being developed.

Acknowledgments

This work was supported in part by the DOE Office of Science, Advanced Scientific Computing Research, under award number DE-FC02-10ER26011, program manager Lucy Nowell. This work is partially supported by the Blue Waters sustained-petascale computing project, which is supported by the National Science Foundation (award number OCI 07-25070) and the state of Illinois.

6. REFERENCES

[1] R. Alverson, D. Roweth, and L. Kaplan. The Gemini System Interconnect. In *18th IEEE Symp. on High Performance Interconnects*, 2010.

[2] B. Arimilli et al. The PERCS High-Performance Interconnect. In *Proc. of 18th Symp. on High-Performance Interconnects*, Aug. 2010.

[3] G. Bronevetsky. Communication-sensitive static dataflow for parallel message passing applications. In *Proc. of the 7th IEEE/ACM Intl. Symp. on Code Generation and Optimization*, pages 1–12, 2009.

[4] J. Bruck, C. T. Ho, S. Kipnis, and D. Weathersby. Efficient algorithms for all-to-all communications in multi-port message-passing systems. In *6th ACM Symp. on Par. Alg. and Arch.*, pages 298–309, 1994.

[5] D. Callahan, B. L. Chamberlain, and H. P. Zima. The Cascade High Productivity Language. In *Intl. Workshop on High-Level Par. Progr. Models and Supportive Environments*, pages 52–60, April 2004.

[6] P. Charles, C. Grothoff, V. A. Saraswat, et al. X10: An

object-oriented approach to non-uniform cluster computing. In *Obj. Oriented Prog., Sys., Lang., and Apps.*, 2005.

[7] C. Coarfa et al. An evaluation of global address space languages: co-array fortran and unified parallel c. In *10th Symp. on Princ. and Practice of Par. Progr.*, 2005.

[8] J. J. Dongarra. Performance of various computers using standard linear equations software. *SIGARCH Comput. Archit. News*, 20:22–44, June 1992.

[9] T. El-Ghazawi et al. UPC Implementation of NAS Parallel Benchmark Kernels . Technical report, George Washington University, 2002.

[10] K. Goto and R. Van De Geijn. High-performance implementation of the level-3 blas. *ACM Trans. Math. Softw.*, 35:4:1–4:14, July 2008.

[11] R. L. Graham et al. ConnectX-2 InfiniBand management queues: First investigation of the new support for network offloaded collective operations. *CCGrid*, pages 53–62, 2010.

[12] T. Hoefler and T. Schneider. Communication-Centric Optimizations by Dynamically Detecting Collective Operations. In *Proceedings of the 17th ACM PPoPP'12*, Feb. 2012. (poster paper).

[13] U. Khedker, A. Sanyal, and B. Karkare. *Data flow analysis: theory and practice.* Taylor and Francis, 2009.

[14] A. Knüpfer, D. Kranzlmüller, and W. E. Nagel. Detection of Collective MPI Operation Patterns. In *EuroPVM/MPI.*, volume 3241, pages 259–267. 2004.

[15] S. Kumar et al. The deep computing messaging Framework: Generalized scalable message passing on the BlueGene/P supercomputer. In *Proc. of the 22nd Intl. Conf. on Supercomputing*, pages 94–103, 2008.

[16] J. Larsson Träff, W. D. Gropp, and R. Thakur. Self-consistent mpi performance guidelines. *IEEE Trans. Parallel Distrib. Syst.*, 21:698–709, May 2010.

[17] H.-W. Loidl, P. W. Trinder, K. Hammond, A. Al Zain, and C. A. Baker-Finch. Semi-explicit parallel programming in a purely functional style: GpH. Dec. 2008.

[18] J. Mellor-Crummey, L. Adhianto, W. N. Scherer, III, and G. Jin. A new vision for coarray fortran. In *Proc. of the 3rd Conf. on PGAS Progr. Models*, PGAS '09, pages 5:1–5:9, 2009.

[19] R. Metzger and Z. Wen. *Automatic algorithm recognition and replacement: a new approach to program optimization.* MIT Press, Cambridge, MA, USA, 2000.

[20] MPI Forum. *MPI: A Message-Passing Interface Standard. Version 2.2*, June 23rd 2009. www.mpi-forum.org.

[21] R. W. Numrich. A Co-Array Fortran Tutorial, 2001. Tutorial at ACM/IEEE Supercomputing 2001.

[22] R. W. Numrich and J. Reid. Co-array fortran for parallel programming. *SIGPLAN Fortran Forum*, 17:1–31, August 1998.

[23] OpenMP Architecture Review Board. *OpenMP C and C++ Application Program Interface*, version 1.0 edition, 1998.

[24] S. Pakin. Receiver-initiated message passing over RDMA Networks. In *22nd IEEE Intl. Symp. on Par. and Distr. Proc., IPDPS 2008*, pages 1–12, 2008.

[25] J. Pjesivac-Grbovic, T. Angskun, G. Bosilca, G. E. Fagg, E. Gabriel, and J. J. Dongarra. Performance Analysis of MPI Collective Operations. In *PMEO-PDS workshop*, 2005.

[26] R. Preissl et al. Detecting Patterns in MPI Communication Traces. In *Proc. of 37th Intl. Conf. on Par. Proc.*, 2008.

[27] R. Preissl et al. Using MPI Communication Patterns to Guide Source Code Transformations. In *8th Intl. Conf. on Comp. Science*, 2008.

[28] R. Preissl et al. Transforming MPI source code based on communication patterns. *Future Gener. Comput. Syst.*, 26:147–154, January 2010.

[29] R. E. Riesen et al. *The Portals 4.0 message passing interface*, April 2008. Sandia Natl. Labs, Tech. Rep. SAND2008-2639, April 2008.

[30] A. Rodrigues, K. Wheeler, P. M. Kogge, and K. D. Underwood. Fine-Grained Message Pipelining for Improved MPI Performance. In *Proc. of the 2006 IEEE Intl. Conf. on Cluster Comp.*

[31] P. Sanders, J. Speck, and J. L. Träff. Two-tree algorithms for full bandwidth broadcast, reduction and scan. *Parallel Comput.*, 35:581–594, December 2009.

[32] M. L. Scott and J. M. Mellor-Crummey. Fast, contention-free combining tree barriers for shared-memory multiprocessors. *Int. J. Parallel Program.*, 22:449–481, August 1994.

[33] UPC Consortium. UPC Language Specifications, v1.2. Technical report, Lawrence Berkeley National Laboratory, 2005. LBNL-59208.

[34] A. Vo et al. A scalable and distributed dynamic formal verifier for mpi programs. In *Proc. of Supercomputing 2010*, SC'10, pages 1–10.

[35] XcalableMP Specification Working Group. *Specification of XcalableMP, version 0.7a*, April 2010.

APPENDIX

A. DETAILED ALGORITHMS

The appendix lists all algorithms in pseudo-code to ensure reproducibility.

A.1 Matching Algorithm

This algorithm computes the matching set M from the sets R, S, and D. It assumes that the sets have been collected from all participating processes and are arranged in process-local sets R_i, S_i, and D_i such that $R = \bigcup_{i=1}^{p} R_i$, $S = \bigcup_{i=1}^{p} S_i$, and $D = \bigcup_{i=1}^{p} D_i$.

Algorithm 1: Matching Algorithm

Input: List of cDAG graphs G_i, grouped by process i: a set of receives (R_i), a set of sends (S_i), and a set of dependencies (D_i).
Output: Set of matches (M).

$MQ \leftarrow$ all independent nodes *// unsorted list of nodes*;
$\forall i : AQ_i \leftarrow \emptyset$ *// AQ is a sorted list of nodes*;
while $MQ \neq \emptyset$ **do**
  $a \leftarrow pop(MQ)$;
  // invert type, swap peer and owner:
  $y \leftarrow (\overline{a_{type}}, a_{peer}, a_{owner}, a_{size}, a_{tag})$;
  if $y \in AQ_{a_{peer}}$ **then**
    $AQ_{a_{peer}} \leftarrow AQ_{a_{peer}} \setminus \{y\}$;
    $remove\_deps(a, D_{a_{owner}}, MQ)$;
    $remove\_deps(y, D_{a_{peer}}, MQ)$;
    $M \leftarrow M \cup \{(a, y)\}$;
  else
    $AQ_{a_{owner}} \leftarrow AQ_{a_{owner}} \cup \{a\}$;

The procedure $remove\_deps$ removed all dependencies to matched operations and adds the newly freed operations to the matching queue MQ.

Procedure `remove_deps` (n, P, MQ)

Input: Node n, set of dependencies D, list MQ

forall $(n, x) \in D$ **do**
  $D \leftarrow D \setminus \{(n, x)\}$;
  if $\forall y : (y, x) \notin D$ **then** $MQ \leftarrow MQ \cup \{x\}$

A.2 Dataflow Propagation

The dataflow propagation algorithm works on the full DAG identified by the sets S, R, D, and M. It propagates the send buffers as sources to the receive buffers and uses splitting when incomplete buffers are sent. The result of the propagation algorithm is a static single transfer (SST) form (a set of SST assignments in form of tuples) where each memory location is written exactly once.

Algorithm 3: cDAG Dataflow Propagation Algorithm.

Input: cDAG Graph as set of receives (R), set of sends (S), set of no-ops (N), set of matches ($M \subseteq S \times R$), and set of dependencies ($D \subseteq (\{S, R, N\} \times \{S, R, N\})$.
Output: Updated set of receive dataflow tuples R (SST).

// recv and send tuples: (owner:start:size:peer:sstart);
set all $r \in R$, $s \in S$ to (owner:start:size:NIL:NIL);
$F_R \leftarrow \emptyset$; // finished receives;
$F_S \leftarrow \emptyset$; // finished sends;
$I_S \leftarrow \emptyset$; // independent sends;
find $I_S \subseteq S$ for $\forall s \in I_S \Rightarrow (x, s) \notin D$;
while $|I_S| \neq 0$ **do**
  foreach $s \in I_S$ **do**
    find $r \in R$ for $(s, r) \in M$; // or fail;
    if s_{sstart} = *NIL* **then**
      update r dataflow tuple to (X:X:X:s.owner:s.start);
    else
      update r dataflow tuple to (X:X:X:s.peer:s.sstart);
    remove $(r, *)$ from D;
    $F_R \leftarrow F_R \cup \{r\}$; $F_S \leftarrow F_S \cup \{s\}$;
  remove all no-ops $(n, *)$ from D for $(x, n) \notin D$;
  $A_S \leftarrow \emptyset$; // active sends;
  find A_S for $s \in A_S \Rightarrow s \in S \wedge (x, s) \notin D \wedge s \notin F_S$;
  $I_S \leftarrow \emptyset$; // reset independent sends;
  foreach $a \in A_S$ **do**
    $O_R \leftarrow \emptyset$; // set of receive overlap regions;
    insert each $r \in F_R$ and r_{owner}=a_{owner} that overlaps with region (a_{start},a_{size}) into O_R;
    S_S = split(O_R, a); // splits sends and matching receives;
    $I_S \leftarrow I_S \cup S_S$;
if $(|F_R| \neq |R|) \wedge (|F_S| \neq |S|)$ **then**
  return "unmatched Send/Recv or cycle!"
// collective detection can now be done for receive tuples;

A.2.1 Split

A split is performed when a part of a buffer that was received from a process is sent to another process. The split creates a new dataflow tuple (which will eventually be an SST assignment).

B. COLLECTIVE DETECTION

The collectve detection algorithm finds collective operations in the SST form and removes all tuples that form the collective operation. It can then be replaced by a call to special hardware or an optimized algorithm.

Algorithm 4: Split.

Input: set of overlapping receives O_R and single send s.
Output: Set of split sends S_S, updated sets S, R, M, D as side-effect.

if $|O_R| = 1 \wedge r \in O_r : \wedge(r_{start}, r_{size}) = (s_{start}, s_{size})$ **then**
  $s_{peer} \leftarrow r_{peer}$;
  $s_{sstart} \leftarrow r_{sstart}$;
  return $\{s\}$ // no split necessary (expected case)
sort O_R by start address;
find r for $(s, r) \in M$;
riter $\leftarrow r_{start}$;
dummyops $d_r \leftarrow d_s \leftarrow$ new cDAG no-op;
replace r with d_r in R, D; replace s with d_s in S, D;
remove (s, r) from M;
siter $\leftarrow s_{start}$;
foreach $ir \in O_R$ *(sorted)* **do**
  locrange $\leftarrow$ max(ir_{start},siter) - siter;
  if *locrange* > 0 **then**
    // if we send something that wasn't received;
    send $n_s \leftarrow$ (s_{owner},*siter*,*locrange*,s_{owner},*siter*);
    recv $n_r \leftarrow$ (r_{owner},*riter*,*locrange*,s_{owner},*siter*);
    $S \leftarrow S \cup \{n_s\}$; $S_S \leftarrow S_S \cup \{n_s\}$; $R \leftarrow R \cup \{n_r\}$;
    $D \leftarrow D \cup \{(d_r, n_r)\}$; $D \leftarrow D \cup \{(n_s, d_s)\}$;
    $M \leftarrow M \cup \{(n_s, n_r)\}$;
    siter $\leftarrow$ siter + locrange; riter $\leftarrow$ riter + locrange;
  remrange $\leftarrow$ min(ir_{start}+ir_{size},s_{start}+s_{size}) - siter;
  send $n_s \leftarrow$ (s_{owner},*siter*,*remrange*,ir_{sowner},ir_{sstart});
  recv $n_r \leftarrow$ (r_{owner},*riter*,*remrange*,ir_{sowner},ir_{sstart});
  $S \leftarrow S \cup \{n_s\}$; $S_S \leftarrow S_S \cup \{n_s\}$; $R \leftarrow R \cup \{n_r\}$;
  $D \leftarrow D \cup \{(d_r, n_r)\}$; $D \leftarrow D \cup \{(n_s, d_s)\}$;
  $M \leftarrow M \cup \{(n_s, n_r)\}$;
  siter $\leftarrow$ siter + remrange; riter $\leftarrow$ riter + remrange;

Algorithm 5: Collective Detection.

Input: All dataflow tuples R in STT form.
Output: Detected collectives and remaining tuples in R.

foreach *size s in any tuple* $\in R$ **do**
  $C \leftarrow \emptyset$; // detection set;
  foreach $i = 0..p$ *and* $j = 0..p$ *and* $i \neq j$ **do**
    find tuple $r \in R$ with size s, owner=i, and peer=j;
    if r *exists* **then** $C \leftarrow C \cup \{r\}$
  if $|C| = p(p-1)$ **then**
    if *input bufs for each peer are identical* **then** found alltoall of size s;
    else found allgather of size s;
    $R \leftarrow R \setminus C$; // remove tuples that formed collective;
  $S \leftarrow \emptyset$; // scatter set;
  $G \leftarrow \emptyset$; // gather set;
  foreach r *is peer in any tuple of size s* **do**
    foreach $i = 0..p$ *and* $i \neq r$ **do**
      find tuple $r \in R$ with size s, owner=i, and peer=r;
      if r *exists* **then** $S \leftarrow S \cup \{r\}$ find tuple $r \in R$ with size s, owner=r, and peer=i;
      if r *exists* **then** $G \leftarrow G \cup \{r\}$
  if $|S| = p - 1$ **then**
    if *input buf for each owner is identical* **then** found bcast of size s;
    else found scatter of size s;
    $R \leftarrow R \setminus S$; // remove tuples that formed scatter;
  if $|G| = p - 1$ **then**
    found gather of size s;
    $R \leftarrow R \setminus G$; // remove tuples that formed gather;

Coalition Threading: Combining Traditional and Non-Traditional Parallelism to Maximize Scalability

Md Kamruzzaman
Computer Science and Engineering
University of California San Diego
mkamruzz@cs.ucsd.edu

Steven Swanson
Computer Science and Engineering
University of California San Diego
swanson@cs.ucsd.edu

Dean M. Tullsen
Computer Science and Engineering
University of California San Diego
tullsen@cs.ucsd.edu

ABSTRACT

Non-traditional parallelism provides parallel speedup for a single thread without the need to manually divide and coordinate computation. This paper describes *coalition threading*, a technique that seeks the ideal combination of traditional and non-traditional threading to make the best use of available hardware parallelism. Coalition threading provides up to 2× gains over traditional parallel techniques on individual loops. However, deciding when and to what degree to apply either traditional or non-traditional threading is a difficult decision. This paper provides heuristics for identifying loops that benefit from a combination of traditional and non-traditional parallelism and those that will perform best with a single technique. Using this heuristic, coalition threading provides an average gain of 17% across all the loops and an average speedup of 16.7% for the full applications over traditional parallelism. This performance is within 0.7% of the speedup that an oracle heuristic could attain.

Categories and Subject Descriptors

D.3.4 [**Programming Languages**]: Processors–Optimization

General Terms

Languages, Performance

Keywords

non-traditional parallelism, inter-core prefetching, chip multiprocessors, helper threads, compilers

1. INTRODUCTION

In the past decade, multiprocessor architectures have gone from being the domain of high-end servers and specialized high-performance computing systems, to becoming ubiquitous in every type of computing platform from smart phones to the data center. While these architectures have delivered the potential for scalable, parallel performance, the impact at the application level has been uneven – software parallelism is not nearly as pervasive as hardware parallelism. There are some environments that provide near-infinite parallelism. Other environments and workloads scale poorly or not at all. If we are to continue to provide performance scaling in this era of increasing hardware parallelism, we must scale application performance both in the presence of abundant software parallelism and when that parallelism is harder to find.

Traditional parallel execution techniques involve the programmer, compiler, libraries, or language constructs dividing the computation and memory activity of an application across processing elements to achieve speedup. However, many applications do not naturally allow this type of division of effort and even fewer return perfect performance scaling when they are so divided.

Researchers have proposed several *non-traditional parallelism (NTP)* techniques to provide parallel speedup (several cores or hardware contexts execute a program faster than a single core) without changing the number of logical threads (e.g., pthread or MPI threads) running the computation. Non-traditional parallelism techniques include helper thread prefetching [5, 7, 12, 13, 14, 16], helper thread dynamic recompilation [6, 15, 27, 28], and software data spreading [11]. Speculative multithreading (thread-level speculation) [18, 21, 23] maintains single-thread semantics from a software perspective, but tends to look more like traditional parallelism when running on the hardware.

Previous work demonstrates that non-traditional parallelism is useful when traditional parallelism is not available (i.e., serial code). This paper shows that it is also effective even when traditional parallelism exists. For many loops, the best parallel solution is to apply non-traditional parallelism on top of traditional parallelism rather than using only traditional parallelism. We can exploit this by using a combination of these two types of parallelism that applies different techniques to different parts of an application to increase scalability. We call this combination *coalition threading*, and in this paper we examine, in particular, the combination of traditional parallelism expressed as pthreads and OpenMP constructs, paired with inter-core prefetching (ICP) [12]. ICP uses a helper thread to prefetch data into a local cache on one core, then migrates execution to that core. This technique requires no hardware support and works across cores, sockets, and SMT contexts, so it is applicable to a wide range of current and future parallel microprocessors.

PACT'12, September 19–23, 2012, Minneapolis, Minnesota, USA.

This paper quantifies the benefits of coalition threading on a state-of-the-art multiprocessor, running a range of benchmarks, and describes compiler heuristics that can identify the loops in each benchmark most suited to non-traditional techniques. While coalition threading represents an opportunity for the programmer or compiler to increase parallel speedup and scalability, deciding when to apply each technique is not easy, and making a poor decision can adversely impact performance.

Our results show that coalition threading with ICP can outperform traditional threading in 39% of the 108 loops in eleven applications we studied, chosen to only include those that already saw some benefit from traditional parallelism. By selecting the best threading strategy on a loop-by-loop basis, we demonstrate that coalition threading improves total performance by 17% on average and up to 51% for some applications.

Achieving that level of performance requires that the compiler, programmer, or runtime system be able to determine when to apply each type of parallelism. We find that a standard machine learning technique, linear classification [8], accurately classifies 98% of the loops where the decision is critical and 87% overall. Considering application performance, the heuristic achieves over 99.4% of the performance that an oracle could deliver.

This paper makes the following contributions. It is the first investigation into the effectiveness of combining non-traditional parallelization techniques with traditional parallelization. It demonstrates that a combined approach can as much as double the performance of traditional parallelization alone for particular loops. We show that performance can be highly sensitive to the decision made for each loop. To handle that, this paper develops heuristics that a compiler can easily implement to identify which combination of traditional and non-traditional parallelism will work best.

The remainder of this paper is organized as follows. Section 2 discusses work related to this research. Section 3 describes coalition threading. Section 4 describes our methodology. Section 5 compares the performance of parallelization techniques. Section 6 derives and evaluates heuristics that allow the compiler to accurately identify the best parallel approach, and Section 7 concludes.

2. BACKGROUND AND RELATED WORK

This work combines elements of traditional parallelism and helper thread prefetching. This section describes prior work in these two areas.

Traditional Parallelism.

This research specifically focuses on explicitly programmed parallelism, and a set of applications known to achieve parallel speedup by using Pthreads [19] or OpenMP [4]. Coalition threading, however, could be applied to most forms of traditional parallelism, including mechanisms such as MPI that do not communicate through shared memory.

Non-traditional Parallelism.

Non-traditional parallelism encompasses several existing techniques including helper threads, dynamic compilation, and some types of speculative threading.

Helper threads execute in parallel with the main thread, accelerating the application without necessarily taking over any of the computation [5]. Helper threads can be used to precompute memory addresses for prefetching [5, 6, 7, 10, 12, 13, 14, 15, 16, 25], to precompute branch outcomes [28], and to recompile hot traces in the main thread based on runtime behavior [26, 27]. This work uses helper threads for data prefetching.

Most of the prior work on helper-thread prefetching targets multithreaded (e.g., simultaneous multithreaded, or SMT) processors and executes prefetch code in another SMT context [5, 6, 7, 13, 14, 16, 28]. Other techniques execute helper threads in separate cores in a CMP [10, 12, 15]. All these techniques "distill" the main thread code to include just enough computation to predict future load addresses.

Systems construct helper threads in different ways including hardware-only schemes [6], conventional profile-driven compilers [13], hand-construction [7, 12, 28], and dynamic compilation [15, 27]. This work does not address helper thread creation, but assumes they exist.

This research particularly exploits Inter-Core Prefetching [12], a software technique that uses thread migrations and allows helper thread prefetching on multicores that do not share the lowest level caches. Unlike SMT-based helper threads, ICP can exploit any type of hardware parallelism between cores, sockets, or thread contexts. When applied across cores, it reduces competition for execution resources and private cache space between the main thread and the helper threads.

Other techniques have applied NTP to CMPs. Data Spreading [11] partitions a thread's working set across the system's caches rather than prefetching. Slipstream processors [10] execute a reduced version of the program ahead of the main program in another core to provide fault tolerance and improve performance.

Speculative multithreading [18, 21, 23] straddles the line between traditional and non-traditional parallelism. Most of this work strives to maintain single-thread software semantics, while the hardware executes threads in parallel. A typical example of speculative multithreading would speculatively execute loop iterations from the serial execution across multiple cores or SMT contexts and verify correctness at runtime. Mitosis [21] is a hardware-software approach that extends the concept further by adding helper threads to precompute critical data.

Other Related Work.

Researchers have also improved scalability of parallel code by combining different types of traditional parallelism and by dynamically changing thread behavior. Researchers have proposed hybrid models [17] that combine subsets of Pthreads, OpenMP, and MPI as well as systems that combine multiple forms of parallelism. For example, Gordon, et al. [9] propose a compiler that combines task parallelism, data parallelism, and pipeline parallelism for stream programming. Feedback-driven threading [24] shows, analytically, how to dynamically control the number of threads to improve performance and power consumption. It dynamically measures data synchronization and bus bandwidth usage to modify its threading strategy.

3. COALITION THREADING

Coalition threading augments conventional parallel threads with helper threads to improve performance and scalability. Coalition threading works because many loops (virtually all, if you scale far enough) have limited scalability – non-traditional parallelism can pick up when traditional tails off. In addition, NTP is not bound by the limits of traditional parallelism. Recent work [11, 12] has demonstrated greater than n-fold speedups with n helper threads.

This means that NTP can be a profitable choice even for scalable loops.

In principle, coalition threading will work with many different kinds of helper threads, but we focus on inter-core prefetching [12], a software-only technique that works on any cache coherent system and subsumes other techniques like software data spreading [11], SMT helper thread prefetching [7], and shared cache prefetching [15].

The following section describes ICP and identifies the key issues that arise in coalition threading in general and with ICP in particular. Then we describe the implementation of our coalition threading framework.

3.1 Inter-core prefetching

ICP helper threads prefetch data into their local caches, paving the way for main threads that come behind and perform the program's actual computation. To accomplish this, ICP divides the execution of a loop into multiple *chunks*. The main thread executes the program on one core while a helper thread runs concurrently on another, prefetching a future chunk into the local cache. Once the main thread finishes its chunk, the threads swap cores. The main thread finds the data it needs waiting for it and the helper thread starts prefetching another chunk.

Like other helper-thread prefetchers, inter-core prefetching is most useful when the access pattern is somewhat non-linear (e.g., accessing an array of pointers or multi-dimensional arrays) and there are computations that depend on the accessed data. The hardware prefetcher is ineffective in this case, because there is no predictable pattern. Helper threads, on the other hand, prefetch correctly and stay ahead of the main thread. Our experience shows that most memory-intensive loops meet both criteria and it is possible to extract more than $2\times$ speedup in some cases by using one helper thread for this type of code. However, ICP can still be useful even for regular access patterns that hardware prefetchers excel at, for three reasons. First, the data ICP prefetches is brought into a separate cache, which does not conflict with the main thread's cache. Second, the prefetching puts no pressure on the main thread's memory interface (e.g., miss status holding registers). Finally, ICP's software prefetch threads can fetch across page boundaries (unlike most hardware prefetchers) and the amount of incorrect prefetching is minimal.

The scalability of ICP is very different than traditional parallelism, another reason that the two techniques are synergistic. While in the best case traditional parallelism scales slowly but steadily (e.g., linear speedups), ICP tends to scale quickly then tail off. If a single helper thread (per main thread) can complete its chunk faster than the main thread, one helper thread suffices and there is little or no gain to adding more. But with that single helper thread, it can often get performance that significantly exceeds linear gains. However, if the ratio of computation to memory access is low, we may need multiple helper threads operating in parallel to fully cover the main thread's accesses. In that case, performance continues to scale, to some degree, as we add helper threads.

Unlike other helper thread prefetchers, ICP does all of its work (either main thread execution or helper thread prefetching) on chunk boundaries, where a "chunk" is a set of iterations expected to access a certain amount of data. Chunking provides two advantages. First, it reduces the cost of synchronization and thread migration by only doing them once for a chunk. Second, it prevents helper threads that run faster than the main thread from running too far ahead and evicting prefetched data from the local cache before the main thread uses it. Chunk size determines the level of cache that ICP targets. Smaller chunks that fit in the L1 cache make prefetching the most effective, but results in frequent synchronization that increases total migration overhead. Chunks that target the L2 cache reduce migration overhead, but provide smaller prefetching gains.

The effectiveness of inter-core prefetching also depends on the amount of data overlap between chunks. Write sharing can result in prefetched data being invalidated before use, and read sharing is often correlated with high cache hit rates (in which case ICP is less effective).

3.2 ICP based coalition threading

Our coalition threading implementation uses ICP as the non-traditional component. For clarity, we use the term *par-ICP* to describe ICP implemented on top of traditional parallelism, and applied to each of the original parallel threads. *Seq-ICP* is ICP applied alone, running on top of a single-thread version of an application. Coalition threading refers to choosing the best technique (seq-ICP, par-ICP, or traditional parallelism) for a particular loop or for all the loops in an application.

Par-ICP applies inter-core prefetching to each original or *main* thread. If an application has N main threads and ICP provides M helper threads per main thread we need a total of $T = (N+N\times M)$ hardware contexts. When N is one, we only exploit helper thread parallelism. Likewise when M is zero, the application is running with just traditional parallelism.

Note that the choice for the value of M is critical for parallel code. In prior work, it was assumed that other cores were otherwise idle, and adding more helper threads was close to free. For parallel code, there is typically a high opportunity cost, because even increasing M by one reduces the number of main threads by a factor of $(2+M)/(1+M)$. For example, for a total of 24 threads, we can either have 24 main threads with no helper threads, 12 main threads each with one helper thread, or 8 main threads each with two helper threads. Recall that for ICP, more than one helper thread is only useful when it takes more time to prefetch a chunk than to execute that chunk. Thus, we want our prefetch threads to be as efficient as possible, and to use no more threads than necessary to leave more threads/cores for traditional parallelism. Fortunately, in most cases, ICP achieves nearly all its benefits with M=1.

Several new factors impact the effectiveness of ICP when applied to parallel code, including parallel data sharing and synchronization overhead.

Data sharing (including false sharing) has a stronger negative impact on the effectiveness of par-ICP than it has on seq-ICP. For read sharing, if the main threads share data then so do helper threads, both with each other and with other main threads. Thus, a single cache line can be in many caches. This uses the caches inefficiently and potentially leads to expensive upgrade events when a main thread eventually writes the line. Write sharing is even more critical, because more than one thread can now invalidate the prefetched data a helper thread has accumulated.

Conversely, if access to that shared data is protected by barriers or locks, ICP can be extremely effective. There are several reasons for this. First, synchronization overhead slows down the main thread, making it easier for prefetch threads to keep up. Second, those applications tend to scale poorly, so even if ICP is not helpful at low thread counts, it can be better than traditional parallelism at high thread counts. Third, loops with frequent communication are often vulnerable to load imbalance – in those cases it is often better to make every main thread faster rather than increase the number of main threads.

3.3 Our coalition threading framework

We develop a custom-built source-to-source translator based on Rose [20] to implement coalition threading. Our framework is flexible enough to apply other non-traditional techniques like shared cache prefetching [15] or software data spreading [11]. However, ICP generally outperforms these techniques and so we do not demonstrate them in this paper. The framework supports both OpenMP or pthread code. In the case of OpenMP applications, the framework first converts the OpenMP pragmas into pthread constructs.

Our system decides on a loop-by-loop basis whether and to what extent to apply traditional threading or par-ICP. The framework uses a heuristic to decide the threading technique for each loop and automatically produces code that implements the selected threading technique. The new code generates a *thread group* of $(1 + M)$ threads for each of the original threads.

Threads within a thread group can trade places with one another, but cannot migrate across thread groups. We use a user-space thread migration system to make migration as cheap as possible, as in [12].

The framework uses all $(N + N \times M)$ threads for parallel execution for loops selected for traditional threading. For par-ICP loops, the framework implements ICP within each thread group with one main thread and M helper threads. The framework generates all the code necessary for splitting the loop into chunks and the coordination between main threads and helper threads required for swapping cores within a group. Each main thread provides necessary information (live-ins, chunk id) to the corresponding helper threads to prefetch the right chunk. However, the framework does not automatically create the code that will prefetch data. Instead the framework looks for a callback function associated with a loop that will act as the prefetch function. Generating the callbacks automatically is possible (e.g., as in [13]), but for the applications we study, we construct them by hand.

To maximize prefetching efficiency we introduce two optimizations over the original ICP implementation [12]. First, we use software prefetching instructions instead of regular loads to avoid accidental page faults. Second, we prefetch the chunk in reverse order – iterations that are to be executed last by the main thread are prefetched first by the helper thread. This ensures that the data the main thread will use first will be in the L1 cache even if our prefetch code and chunk size target the L2 cache.

4. METHODOLOGY

This section describes our experimental methodology – the benchmarks that we target and the systems that we use to evaluate coalition threading.

4.1 Evaluation Systems

We use a quad socket, 32-core state of the art AMD Opteron system running Linux 2.6. Table 1 gives more information about the system. We compile all codes using gcc4.1.2 with -O3 optimization level and keep hardware prefetching enabled for all experiments. To measure microarchitectural characteristics like L2 cache misses, we use hardware performance counters.

CPU components	Parameters
CPU model	AMD Opteron 6136 2.4 GHz
Number of cores	Quad-socket 32 cores
Level-1 (L1) cache	64-Kbyte, 3 cycles
Level-2 (L2) cache	512-Kbyte, 15 cycles
Level-3 (L3) cache	6-Mbyte, 50 cycles
Cache to cache transfer latency	120-400 cycles
Memory	60-Gbyte DRAM, 150 cycles
Migration cost	$2 - 5\mu s$

Table 1: Memory hierarchy information and migration cost for the AMD Opteron system used in our experiments.

Benchmark Name	Suite Input used	Loops Evaluated
BT	NAS, B	23
CG	NAS, B	2
LU	NAS, B	14
MG	NAS, C	6
SP	NAS, B	35
Ammp	SpecOMP, Ref	6
Art	SpecOMP, Ref	2
Equake	SpecOMP, Ref	5
Fluidanimate	Parsec, Native	6
Streamcluster	Parsec, Native	2
Graph500	Graph500, 25–5	7

Table 2: Our benchmarks, with the number of loops analyzed.

4.2 Applications

To evaluate coalition threading, we use memory intensive multi-threaded applications from the NAS parallel benchmark suite [2], SpecOMP [1], Parsec [3], and Graph500 [22] workloads. Table 2 summarizes the particular applications and input sizes we use. We did not include SpecOMP benchmarks that were not written in C or C++ code. In addition, we had to exclude a few more benchmarks because Rose could not handle them.

In all, we target 108 loops (Table 2) from 11 applications. All of these 108 loops are programmer-parallelized and they include all the loops that contribute more than 0.5% of the total execution time of the corresponding benchmark when the benchmark executes with one thread.

5. EFFECTIVENESS OF THE DIFFERENT PARALLELIZATION TECHNIQUES

This section measures the effectiveness of coalition threading on a variety of parallel workloads. All the data presented in this section apply for our large 32-core Opteron system.

5.1 Benefits of coalition threading

The usefulness of coalition threading varies on a loop-by-loop basis, so coalition threading for a particular application may include traditional threading for some loops and a combination for others. We will use the term *traditional* when we use only the parallelism as indicated in the parallel programs themselves, seq-ICP means we only apply inter-core prefetching, par-ICP means we

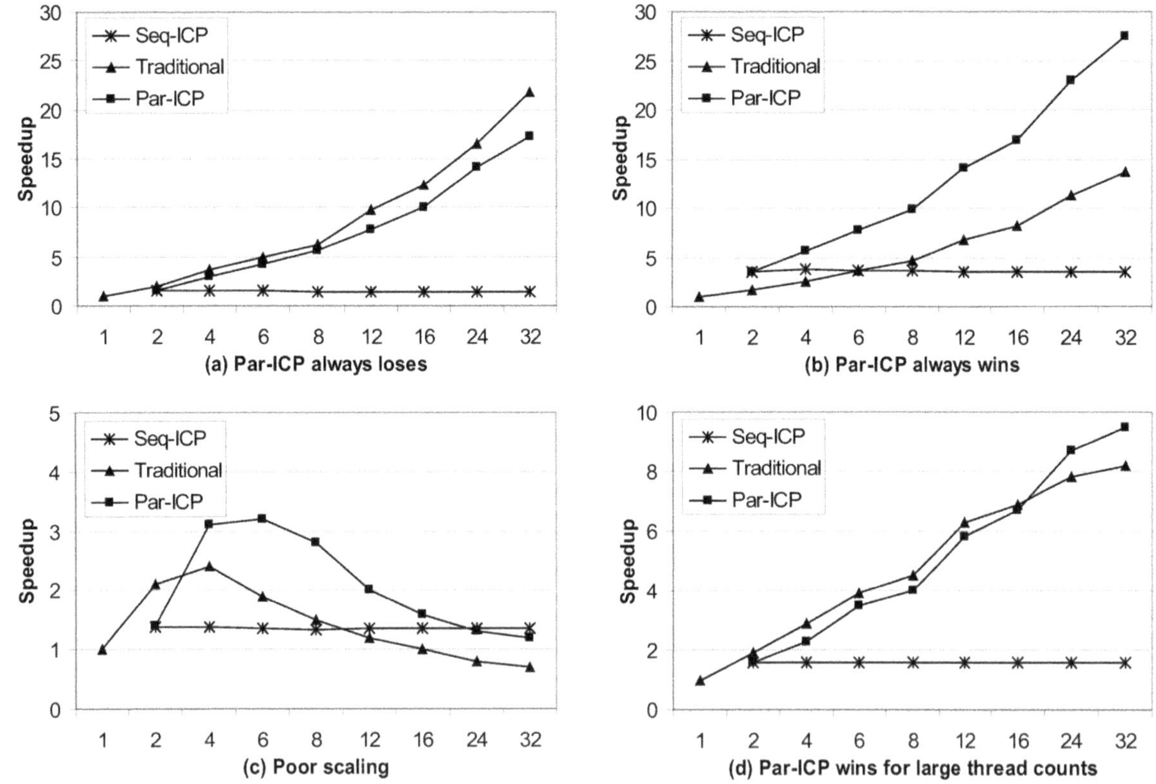

Figure 1: Loops show four different behaviors when we apply seq-ICP, traditional threading, and par-ICP for different thread counts (shown on the x-axis). Most applications contain loops from more than one group. Here, all four loops are from the benchmark *SP*.

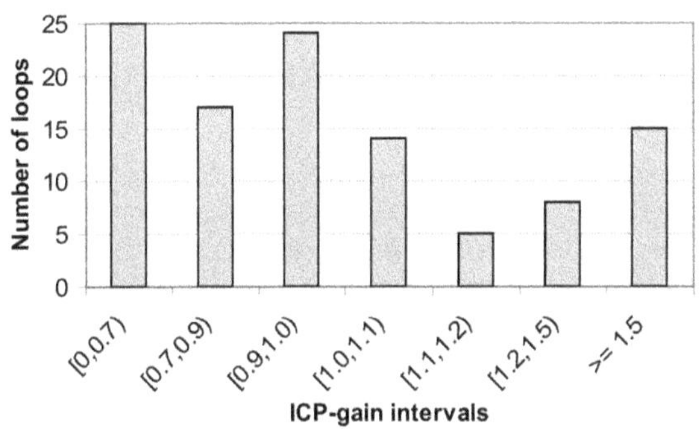

Figure 2: Histogram of 108 loops using $ICP\text{-}gain_{32}$ for the Opteron system.

combine ICP with the existing parallelism, and coalition threading (CT) means we make an intelligent decision about which type of parallelism to apply to each loop.

We evaluate these techniques on each of the 108 loops in our applications, using between 1 and 32 total threads (and cores). All comparisons throughout the paper apply for the same total number of threads (cores). So, the data point for 32 threads means either 32 main threads (traditional), or 16 main threads with one helper thread (par-ICP), or 1 main thread with 31 helper threads (seq-ICP). We consider other cases of par-ICP (more than one helper thread) in Section 5.2.1.

We see four different behaviors across the loops. Figure 1 compares the performance for four loops that represent these four classes of behaviors. The first class (a) are loops for which traditional threading performs better regardless of thread counts. For loops in class (b), par-ICP consistently outperforms traditional threading. The third class, (c), contains loops that scale poorly (or negatively) even for small thread counts with traditional threading. Behavior for the fourth class, (d), changes as the number of threads increases, despite the fact that these loops tend to have good scalability. In particular, par-ICP loses for small thread counts, but wins for large thread counts. All of these four loops are from one application, *SP*, demonstrating the importance of applying coalition threading on a per-loop basis.

Since all our benchmarks are parallel to start with, ICP alone (seq-ICP) is never the best choice for large core counts. In the more general case, seq-ICP would be an attractive case for many loops that lack parallelism. In our experiments, seq-ICP speeds up almost all of our loops (90 out of 108) over sequential execution, but never over parallel execution; thus we do not consider seq-ICP as an option for the compiler in this paper.

We introduce the term $ICP\text{-}gain_T$ for a loop to compare performance between traditional parallelization and par-ICP. It is the ratio of the maximum speedup using par-ICP and the maximum speedup using traditional threading while using no more than T threads in total. So, for 32 threads, if a loop gets maximum speedup of 16× using traditional threading and maximum speedup of 20× using par-ICP, the loop has an $ICP\text{-}gain_{32}$ of 1.25. In the case of coalition threading, we seek to apply par-ICP for only those loops that have $ICP\text{-}gain_T > 1$.

Figure 2 shows the histogram of the 108 loops to represent the impact of applying par-ICP on each loop in the Opteron system.

The x-axis shows different intervals of *ICP-gain*$_{32}$, and the y-axis shows the number of loops in that category. Applying par-ICP outperforms traditional threading in 42 loops in Opteron. There are 15 loops that gain at least 50% or more, and 7 loops see speedup as high as 2× or more on top of traditional parallelization.

There are a large number (38 out of 108) of loops where the difference between par-ICP and traditional is within $\pm 10\%$. The most common trend we see is for the par-ICP gains to increase with core counts, in fact we observe quite a few cases where the curves appear to be reaching a crossover point just at the limit of cores. Thus, as we continue to scale the number of cores, we expect the number of applications for which coalition threading is profitable to also increase.

Next, we try to understand the factors that cause some of the loops to scale better using par-ICP than traditional threading.

5.2 Understanding loop behavior

We analyze all 108 loops to identify the most common factors that cause the diverse behavior when we evaluate both traditional threading and par-ICP on each loop.

There are some loops where traditional threading always outperforms coalition threading, as shown in Figure 1(a). For these loops, adding more main threads provide better performance than using ICP, even if ICP has something to offer. The 59 loops in this class achieve 19% speedup on average when we apply ICP in the single-threaded case with one helper thread, but if we use that thread for parallel execution, we get, on average, an 83% speedup. These are highly parallel loops with little or no synchronization overhead, few coherence misses, and high instruction level parallelism (ILP) that hides the effect of memory latency, if any.

Conversely, Figure 1(b) represents the set of loops where par-ICP always outperforms traditional threading. This includes both loops that scale well and those that do not. The common factor is that ICP is highly effective in all of these cases. For the 16 loops in this category, executing in parallel gives 1.2× speedup on average for two threads ($N = 2, M = 0$), while ICP gives an average speedup of 1.9× using just one main thread and one helper thread ($N = 1, M = 1$). For some loops, we even see speedup as high as 3.5×. These loops have a significant number of L2 misses per instruction, and have little memory level parallelism.

In our analysis, we also find several loops that scale poorly for traditional threading (overlaps with the prior category in some cases). These loops stop scaling beyond some thread count or even start scaling negatively, as in Figure 1(c). We observe three main causes for such behavior. First, some loops have limited scalability because there are not enough iterations to distribute over all threads. This creates load imbalance and does not amortize the cost of parallelism with only one iteration per thread. Second, there are some loops where computation increases significantly (linearly in some cases) with the number of threads. For example, threads can have a private copy of the shared data and can update that copy independently and merge afterward instead of using locks to access that shared data. Finally, some loops execute barriers very frequently and so synchronization time dominates the execution time as the loop is scaled. In all these three cases, par-ICP always works better than traditional parallelism for higher thread counts.

Some loops (total 33) exhibit more complex behavior. Their behavior changes more slowly with the thread counts, as in Figure 1(d). For small thread counts, performance for traditional and par-ICP is similar or par-ICP performs worse. But for larger thread counts, par-ICP starts outperforming traditional threading and the performance gap grows. This is often just a sub case of the previous category, but with lower synchronization overheads that are just starting to be exposed with high thread counts. We see just a couple of counterexamples (2 loops from *LU* benchmark), where the opposite happens – par-ICP wins for smaller thread counts but loses for larger thread counts. These two loops show super linear parallel scalability when enough cores are used to fit the working set in the L2 caches, making prefetching less effective at those core counts.

5.2.1 *Multiple helper threads*

We also measure performance using more than one helper thread per main thread. Multiple helper threads can be effective when applied to the single-threaded case. In our experiments, the speedup (averaged over all 108 loops) improves to 1.49× from 1.38× when we add one more helper thread ($N = 1, M = 2$ instead of $N = 1, M = 1$). However, in most cases, this improvement cannot compensate the reduced parallelism because of the decrease in the number of main threads. Additionally, more helper threads saturate off-chip bandwidth in some cases and we do not see the same degree of speedup as we scale to higher thread counts.

We found three loops where multiple helper threads provided better performance than using a single helper thread for the same total number of threads (e.g., $N = 8, M = 2$ works better than $N = 16, M = 1$). These loops each had poor scalability as in Figure 1(c). Using more threads for ICP reduced the number of main threads and improved performance. Even in these cases, the gains were small. So, we restrict ourselves to one helper thread per main thread in the remainder of the paper. This also has the benefit of significantly reducing the decision space for the compiler.

6. HEURISTICS TO APPLY COALITION THREADING

Coalition threading is the process of making a decision about when to apply what type of parallelism to each loop. Because we filter our benchmarks for existing parallelism, we focus here on deciding between traditional parallelism and par-ICP. For the more general case, seq-ICP must also be considered.

Predicting when par-ICP is profitable for a loop, then, is essential. Our compiler tool chain profiles (single-threaded) and analyzes each loop to determine how to extract the most performance using the available CPUs. Depending on the loop's characteristics, it will either apply par-ICP or traditional threading. This section describes the heuristics that our compilation framework uses.

We use a standard machine learning technique, linear classification [8], to develop our heuristics. It exploits profile information that we capture from the single-thread execution of the application to classify loops. We describe this next.

6.1 Linear Classification

A linear classifer [8] is a simple and robust binary classifier widely used in machine learning. It uses a hyperplane of n-1 dimension to best separate a set of n-dimensional points to two classes. The linear classifier library like *liblinear* [8] automatically extracts a weight vector from the input training set to represent the hyperplane. For a particular test point, the classifier computes the dot product of the weight vector and the feature vector of the test point and makes a decision based on that. The number of points that the

Name	Description	Name	Description
PO	Parallelization overhead	BRANCH	No of branches per instruction
CDR	Chunk data reuse	IPC	Instructions per cycle
L2MI	L2 misses per instruction	DRAM	DRAM accesses per instruction
TLBL2IN	L2 misses for TLB walking per instruction	FETCH	Per instruction stalls for not fetching
DTLBIN	TLB misses per instruction	DISP	Per instruction stalls for not dispatching
SSE	No of arithmetic operations per instruction	LSQS	Per instruction stalls for load store queue full

Table 3: List of 12 loop characteristics that we measure for the classification.

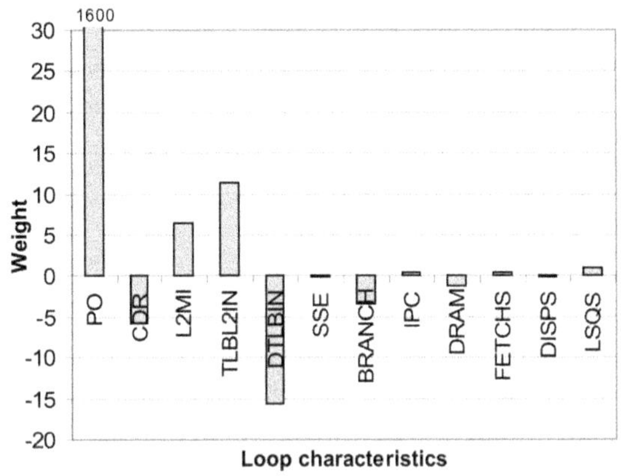

Figure 3: Weight vector generated by the linear classifier that represents correlation.

hyperplane can accurately classify to the correct class determines the accuracy of the classifier.

In our case, we consider each loop as an n-dimensional point where n is the number of loop characteristics or features that we measure. There are 12 such characteristics, shown in Table 3. These characteristics capture two main things – factors that impact the scalability of traditional parallelism and factors that impact the effectiveness of ICP. Parallelization overhead falls in the first category, while CDR and microarchitectural characteristics (IPC, L2MI, etc.) fall in the second category.

We use hardware performance counters to measure all microarchitectural features. For PO and CDR, we use simple profiling. PO computes the number of barrier or lock executions per instruction while executing with one thread. A high PO implies the loop is unlikely to scale well. We also assign a large PO value to the loops that have limited software parallelism and loops where the computation increases linearly with the number of threads. These special loops also scale poorly with additional threads.

CDR is the percent of data that the main thread chunk shares with the helper thread chunk, when the application runs with one main thread. Write sharing is more expensive than read sharing [12] because of the expensive cache to cache transfers. Thus, we give it more weight and calculate data reuse as: $read\_sharing + k \times write\_sharing$. The value of k depends on how expensive coherence misses are. In our setup, any value of 2 or above works well. CDR varies from 0 to 50% for our loops.

We evaluate our linear classifier in two steps – first we try to find out the features that have strong correlation, and then we measure the effectiveness of the best linear classifier.

6.1.1 Correlation of loop characteristics with the classification

We analyze the weight vector of the linear classifier to understand the correlation of the loop characteristics. The magnitude of the weight defines how strong the correlation is. On the other hand, the sign indicates whether the correlation is positive or negative. In our case, positive correlation indicates a bias toward applying par-ICP.

To analyze the correlation, we construct the linear classifier using all 108 loops and 12 characteristics and compute the weight vector. We do 10-fold cross validation to avoid any bias and take the average weight over all 10 classifiers. For 10-fold cross validation, the data is partitioned into 10 subsets. Each classifier uses a different subset for testing while the remaining 9 subsets are used for training. The cross validation accuracy is the percent of data that are correctly classified. The cross validation accuracy in this case is 79%. There are few parameters (e.g., cost for incorrect classification) which we can tune during the training phase of the classifier. For all of our experiments, we tune these parameters to get the best accuracy.

Figure 3 shows the weight of the characteristics in the classifier. The strong positively correlated characteristics are PO, TLBL2IN, and L2MI, while CDR, DTLBIN, BRANCH exhibit negative correlation. Thus, a loop that has large PO, L2MI, TLBL2IN but low CDR, DTLBIN is most likely to gain from par-ICP. This figure demonstrates several interesting things. First, IPC and different types of stalls (fetch, dispatch) have negligible correlation with the decision process. These are complex metrics and depend on several things like branch misprediction, cache misses, data dependency, resource conflict, etc., but ultimately they do not provide concrete information useful for the classification.

BRANCH has a negative correlation because a high rate of branches indicates irregular code where it is difficult to prefetch the correct data – e.g., they are more likely to contain control-dependent loads or load addresses. L2MI and TLBL2IN have strong positive correlation since ICP primarily converts L2 misses into L2 hits. DRAM and DTLBIN have negative correlation. This is a little surprising since we expect all types of misses to have positive correlation. This is impacted by some cases where the loops are very memory intensive and the data sets are very large, requiring multiple helper threads for ICP to be effective – threads which are better used for traditional parallelism in those cases.

As expected, PO limits the scalability of traditional parallelization, and has strong positive correlation. Similarly, CDR reduces the effectiveness of ICP and has negative correlation.

Since several of the parameters have little impact on the outcome of the classifier, we can simplify it (and the required profiling) by removing some of the metrics. We remove the five characteris-

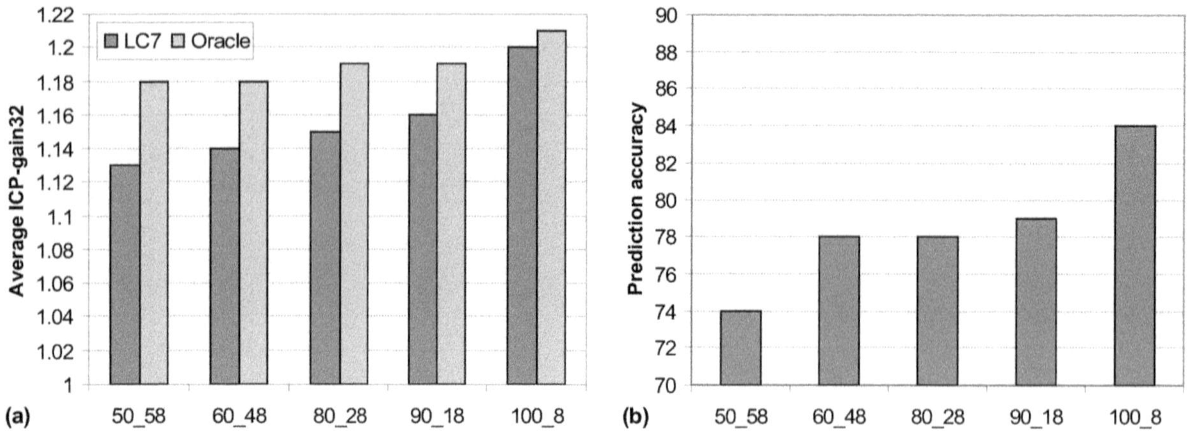

Figure 4: Average $ICP\text{-}gain_{32}$ (a) and prediction accuracy (b) for LC7 using different combinations of training and test set sizes (shown on the x-axis). The first number represents the training set size.

tics (SSE, IPC, FETCH, DISP, and LSQS) that have the smallest correlation and construct the linear classifier with the remaining seven characteristics. The 10-fold cross validation accuracy, in this case, improves to 84%; thus, ignoring the characteristics that are not heavily correlated removes the noise and builds a better linear classifier. On the other hand, skipping some of the important characteristics and picking others does decrease the accuracy, e.g., using PO, CDR, L2MI, SSE and BRANCH decreases the accuracy to 69%. Our best linear classifier uses 7 characteristics – PO, CDR, L2MI, TLBL2IN, DTLBIN, DRAM, and BRANCH. We refer to this classifier as LC7.

6.1.2 *Linear classifier performance*

This section measures the effectiveness of our best linear classifier, LC7, using standard evaluation techniques for machine learning. We randomly pick k loops to train the linear classifier and use the rest of (108-k) loops to test it. While training the classifier, we assume nothing about the test loops and use cross validation for the train loops to avoid bias towards the training set. To cancel out the effect of randomization, for a particular training size of k, we repeat the procedure 20 times to pick different sets of training and test loops, and then take the average of the outcomes.

There are two metrics that we measure for the test set – average $ICP\text{-}gain_{32}$ and the percent of loops correctly classified in the test set, i.e. prediction accuracy. We compare our results with the oracle classifier which has prediction accuracy of 100%. Figure 4 shows the average $ICP\text{-}gain_{32}$ and prediction accuracy for different values of k. Here, the first value indicates the size of the training set while the second one indicates the size of the test set.

We use different training sizes from 50 to 100. The prediction accuracy improves with the train size, because the classifier can capture more information. However, even if we use 50 loops for training and the other 58 loops for testing, we get very good accuracy of 74%. Considering the average $ICP\text{-}gain_{32}$, LC7 loses 5% performance compared to the oracle classifier. For a training set size of 100 loops, the accuracy improves to 84% and LC7 performs just 1.2% less well than the oracle.

We also do another test, where we use all 108 loops to construct the linear classifier and use that to predict the same 108 loops. In this case, the accuracy is 87% and LC7 provides around 1.4% less gain than the oracle classifier. This demonstrates two things – the loops are not linearly classifiable, so we can expect some error, and yet LC7 performs close to the oracle classifier.

For further information, we analyze the loops that LC7 correctly classifies. LC7 can more accurately classify the loops which are highly sensitive to the correct decision – the performance variation between applying par-ICP and traditional is large. If we only consider the loops where par-ICP either wins or loses by at least 5%, LC7 classifies 91% of loops correctly. The accuracy improves to 98% when we consider at least 25% performance variation. This is significant, because the linear classifier does not use any information regarding the possible performance gain or loss. This also explains why LC7 closely follows the oracle in terms of the average $ICP\text{-}gain_{32}$ despite selecting the less effective technique 13% of the time.

Other Decision Heuristics.

In an attempt to simplify the decision process for the compiler, we alternatively take the correlation data learned from the linear classifier, and use that to construct a simple decision matrix. Specifically, we are able to take just four of our highly correlated metrics (PO, CDR, L2MI, and DTLBIN), apply an experimentally derived threshold for each, and classify each loop according to whether it is high or low with respect to these four metrics. By doing so, we are able to replicate the accuracy of the linear classifier. The advantage of this construction is that it uses only four profile measurements and simple table lookup. However, since it does not provide gains above the linear classifier, we do not show the specific results here.

6.2 Application Level Impact

This section analyzes the impact of applying coalition threading (CT) to the applications. There can be several dominant loops in an application, so we have four different schemes to consider – apply seq-ICP to all loops, apply traditional parallelism to all loops, apply par-ICP to all loops and apply the combination of traditional parallelism and par-ICP as suggested by our heuristic. We call the last scheme *heuristic CT* which applies par-ICP to the set of loops chosen by the heuristic and applies traditional threading to the rest. For heuristic CT, our coalition threading framework uses the LC7 heuristic described earlier. We also implement *oracle CT* that ap-

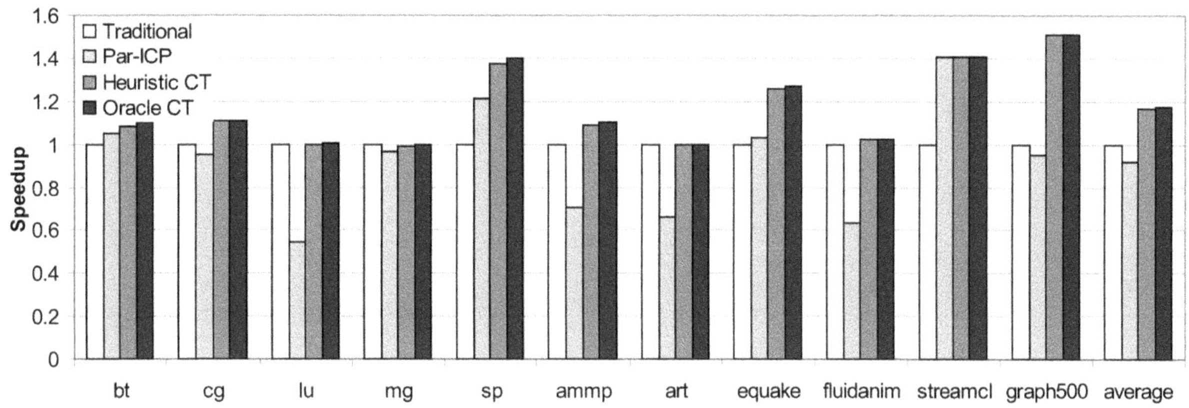

Figure 6: The graph compares speedup (normalized to best traditional performance) of oracle CT and heuristic CT with other techniques in Opteron. The improvement is as high as 51%.

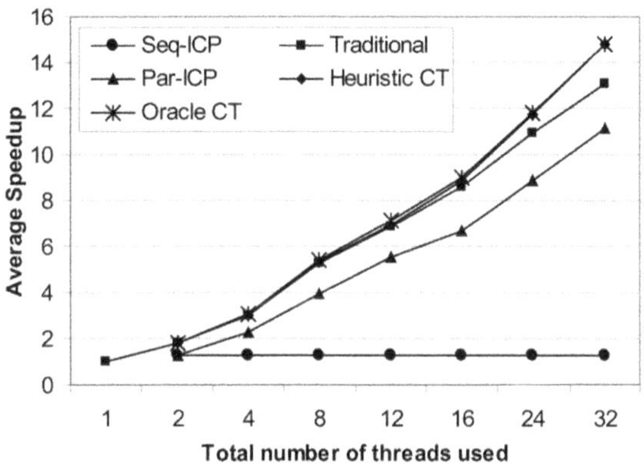

Figure 5: The scalability of the speedup averaged over all benchmarks using different techniques.

plies coalition threading using the oracle heuristic to evaluate the performance of the LC7 heuristic at the application level.

Figure 5 shows the effect of applying all the schemes on our benchmarks in the Opteron system. The y-axis here denotes the average speedup over all benchmarks for a particular number of threads. The seq-ICP scheme cannot compete with other schemes, because most of them scale with traditional threading, whereas seq-ICP scales only marginally beyond 2 cores. Par-ICP scales better than traditional threading and gradually catches up – 28% performance loss for 2 threads vs. 15% loss for 32 threads. The impact of par-ICP is more prominent in case of heuristic CT. For all thread counts, heuristic CT outperforms traditional threading. The improvement is 1% for 4 threads, but reaches 13% for 32 threads. As expected, the utility of coalition threading increases with core count. There is no reason to expect this trend does not continue. Figure 5 also shows the strength of the LC7 heuristic. It performs almost the same as the oracle heuristic.

Next, in Figure 6, we compare the performance of heuristic CT with par-ICP, traditional threading, and oracle CT across all benchmarks. The values on the y-axis are normalized to the best possible speedup by traditional threading using no more than 32 cores.

In the Opteron machine, we see gain as high as 21% for *SP* and 40% for *streamcluster* while using the par-ICP scheme. Oracle CT improves performance further from 21 to 40% for *SP* by filtering the loops that do not get any benefit from par-ICP. However, for *streamcluster*, both the key loops get benefit from par-ICP and oracle CT gives the same speedup as the par-ICP scheme. *Graph500* shows the importance of using a good heuristic. For this application, heuristic CT provides 51% speedup vs. the 5% loss by par-ICP. Overall, the oracle CT gives an average of 17.4% gain across all benchmarks, and an average gain of 21% considering only the nine benchmarks where we apply par-ICP to at least one loop. Compared to that, heuristic CT gives an average of 16.7% gain across all benchmarks and performs very close to the oracle CT. The small number of loops where our heuristic does not make the correct decision have negligible impact on the overall application run-time. So our developed heuristic is nearly as effective as the oracle heuristic.

7. CONCLUSION

This paper describes Coalition Threading, a hybrid threading technique that combines traditional parallelism with non-traditional parallelism, and demonstrates heuristics to find the best combination, which can be used to direct a parallel compiler. We analyze the effectiveness of coalition threading using inter-core prefetching as the non-traditional component and observe that for a number of parallel loops, adding ICP on top of traditional threading outperforms traditional threading alone. Our results show that in a 32-core Opteron system, there are 20 loops out of 108 where coalition threading provides more than 30% improvements on top of the best possible speedup by traditional threading. Coalition threading has a strong impact on application level scalability (up to 51% performance gain in some cases) when we apply the right technique to the right set of loops. Our best heuristic makes the correct decision 87% of the time and can accurately identify 98% of the loops where the correct decision is critical. Heuristic-based coalition threading gives an average of 17% improvements across our benchmarks and is only 0.7% less than what an oracle provides.

Acknowledgments

The authors would like to thank the anonymous reviewers for many useful suggestions. This work was supported by NSF grants CCF-1018356 and CCF-0643880 and by SRC Grant 2086.001.

8. REFERENCES

[1] V. Aslot, M. Domeika, R. Eigenmann, G. Gaertner, W. B. Jones, and B. Parady. Specomp: A new benchmark suite for measuring parallel computer performance. In *Workshop on OpenMP Applications and Tools*, 2001.

[2] D. H. Bailey, E. Barzcz, L. Dagum, and H. D. Simon. NAS parallel benchmark results. *IEEE Concurrency*, 1993.

[3] C. Bienia, S. Kumar, J. P. Singh, and K. Li. The parsec benchmark suite: characterization and architectural implications. In *Proceedings of International Conference on Parallel Architectures and Compilation Techniques*, 2008.

[4] B. Chapman, G. Jost, and R. v. d. Pas. *Using OpenMP: Portable Shared Memory Parallel Programming (Scientific and Engineering Computation)*. The MIT Press, 2007.

[5] R. Chappell, J. Stark, S. Kim, S. Reinhardt, and Y. Patt. Simultaneous subordinate microthreading (ssmt). In *Proceedings of the International Symposium on Computer Architecture*, 1999.

[6] J. Collins, D. Tullsen, H. Wang, and J. Shen. Dynamic speculative precompuation. In *Proceedings of the International Symposium on Microarchitecture*, 2001.

[7] J. Collins, H. Wang, D. Tullsen, C. Hughes, Y.-F. Lee, D. Lavery, and J. Shen. Speculative precomputation: Long-range prefetching of delinquent loads. In *Proceedings of the International Symposium on Computer Architecture*, 2001.

[8] R.-E. Fan, K.-W. Chang, C.-J. Hsieh, X.-R. Wang, and C.-J. Lin. Liblinear: A library for large linear classification. *J. Mach. Learn. Res.*, 9:1871–1874, June 2008.

[9] M. I. Gordon, W. Thies, and S. Amarasinghe. Exploiting coarse-grained task, data, and pipeline parallelism in stream programs. In *Proceedings of the International Conference on Architectural Support for Programming Languages and Operating Systems*, 2006.

[10] K. Z. Ibrahim, G. T. Byrd, and E. Rotenberg. Slipstream execution mode for cmp-based multiprocessors. In *Proceedings of the International Symposium on High Performance Computer Architecture*, 2003.

[11] M. Kamruzzaman, S. Swanson, and D. M. Tullsen. Software data spreading: leveraging distributed caches to improve single thread performance. In *Proceedings of the ACM SIGPLAN Conference on Programming Language Design and Implementation*, 2010.

[12] M. Kamruzzaman, S. Swanson, and D. M. Tullsen. Inter-core prefetching for multicore processors using migrating helper threads. In *Proceedings of the International Conference on Architectural Support for Programming Languages and Operating Systems*, 2011.

[13] D. Kim and D. Yeung. Design and evaluation of compiler algorithm for pre-execution. In *Proceedings of the International Conference on Architectural Support for Programming Languages and Operating Systems*, 2002.

[14] S. Liao, P. Wang, H. Wang, G. Hoflehner, D. Lavery, and J. Shen. Post-pass binary adaptation for software-based speculative precomputation. In *Proceedings of ACM SIGPLAN Conference on Programming Language Design and Implementation*, 2002.

[15] J. Lu, A. Das, W.-C. Hsu, K. Nguyen, and S. G. Abraham. Dynamic helper threaded prefetching on the sun ultrasparc cmp processor. In *Proceedings of the International Symposium on Microarchitecture*, 2005.

[16] C.-K. Luk. Tolerating memory latency through software-controlled pre-execution in simultaneous multithreading processors. In *Proceedings of the the International Symposium on Computer Architecture*, 2001.

[17] E. Lusk and A. Chan. Early experiments with the openmp/mpi hybrid programming model. In *Proceedings of the International Conference on OpenMP in a new era of parallelism*, 2008.

[18] P. Marcuello, A. González, and J. Tubella. Speculative multithreaded processors. In *12th International Conference on Supercomputing*, 1998.

[19] F. Mueller. A library implementation of posix threads under unix. In *In Proceedings of the USENIX Conference*, 1993.

[20] D. J. Quinlan, M. Schordan, B. Philip, and M. Kowarschik. The specification of source-to-source transformations for the compile-time optimization of parallel object-oriented scientific applications. In *14th Workshop on Languages and Compilers for Parallel Computing*, 2001.

[21] C. G. Quiñones, C. Madriles, J. Sánchez, P. Marcuello, A. González, and D. M. Tullsen. Mitosis compiler: an infrastructure for speculative threading based on pre-computation slices. In *Proceedings of the ACM SIGPLAN Conference on Programming Language Design and Implementation*, 2005.

[22] B. W. B. J. A. A. C. U. G. C. Richard C. Murphy, Kyle B. Wheeler. Introducing the graph 500. May 2010.

[23] G. S. Sohi, S. E. Breach, and T. N. Vijaykumar. Multiscalar processors. In *Proceedings of the International Symposium on Computer Architecture*, 1995.

[24] M. A. Suleman, M. K. Qureshi, and Y. N. Patt. Feedback-driven threading: power-efficient and high-performance execution of multi-threaded workloads on cmps. In *Proceedings of the International Conference on Architectural Support for Programming Languages and Operating Systems*, 2008.

[25] K. Sundaramoorthy, Z. Purser, and E. Rotenberg. Slipstream processors: improving both performance and fault tolerance. *SIGPLAN Not.*, 35(11), 2000.

[26] W. Zhang, B. Calder, and D. M. Tullsen. An event-driven multithreaded dynamic optimization framework. In *Proceedings of the International Conference on Parallel Architectures and Compilation Techniques*, 2005.

[27] W. Zhang, D. Tullsen, and B. Calder. Accelerating and adapting precomputation threads for efficient prefetching. In *Proceedings of the International Symposium on High Performance Computer Architecture*, 2007.

[28] C. Zilles and G. Sohi. Execution-based prediction using speculative slices. In *Proceedings of the the International Symposium on Computer Architecture*, 2001.

Shared Memory Multiplexing: A Novel Way to Improve GPGPU Throughput

Yi Yang
North Carolina State University
Raleigh, NC
yyang14@ncsu.edu

Ping Xiang
North Carolina State University
Raleigh, NC
pxiang@ncsu.edu

Mike Mantor
Advanced Micro Devices
Orlando, FL
Michael.Mantor@amd.com

Norm Rubin
Advanced Micro Devices
Boxborough, MA
Norman.Rubin@amd.com

Huiyang Zhou
North Carolina State University
Raleigh, NC
hzhou@ncsu.edu

ABSTRACT

On-chip shared memory (a.k.a. local data share) is a critical resource to many GPGPU applications. In current GPUs, the shared memory is allocated when a thread block (also called a workgroup) is dispatched to a streaming multiprocessor (SM) and is released when the thread block is completed. As a result, the limited capacity of shared memory becomes a bottleneck for a GPU to host a high number of thread blocks, limiting the otherwise available thread-level parallelism (TLP). In this paper, we propose software and/or hardware approaches to multiplex the shared memory among multiple thread blocks.

Our proposed approaches are based on our observation that the current shared memory management reserves shared memory too conservatively, for the entire lifetime of a thread block. If the shared memory is allocated only when it is actually used and freed immediately after, more thread blocks can be hosted in an SM without increasing the shared memory capacity. We propose three software approaches to enable shared memory multiplexing and implement them using a source-to-source compiler. The experimental results show that our proposed software approaches effectively improve the throughput of many GPGPU applications on both NVIDIA GTX285 and GTX480 GPUs (an average of 1.44X on GTX285, 1.70X on GTX480 with 16kB shared memory, and 1.26X on GTX480 with 48kB shared memory). We also propose hardware support for shared memory multiplexing, which incurs minor hardware changes to existing hardware and enables significant performance improvements (an average of 1.53X) to be achieved with very little change in GPGPU code.

Categories and Subject Descriptors

B.3.2 [**Memory Structures**]: Design Styles – *shared memory*

General Terms

Performance, Design, Experimentation.

Keywords

GPGPU, Shared memory, Dynamic management.

1. INTRODUCTION

Modern many-core graphics processor units (GPUs) rely on thread-level parallelism (TLP) to deliver high computational throughput. To mitigate the impact of long latency memory accesses, besides TLP, software managed on-chip local memory is included in state-of-art GPUs. Such local memory, called shared memory in NVIDIA GPUs and local data share in AMD GPUs, has limited capacity. As a shared resource among threads, shared memory is one of the key factors to determine how many threads can run concurrently on a GPU.

State-of-art GPUs manage shared memory in a relatively simple manner. When a group of threads (called a thread block or workgroup) is to be dispatched, the shared memory is allocated based on the aggregate shared memory usage of all the threads in the thread block (TB). When a TB finishes execution, the allocated shared memory is released. When there is not sufficient shared memory for a thread block, the TB dispatcher is halted.

There are two major limitations to the aforementioned shared memory management. First, the allocated shared memory is reserved throughout the lifetime of a TB, even if it is only utilized during a small portion of the execution time. Second, when the shared memory size (e.g., 16kB) is not a multiple of the shared memory usage (e.g., 9kB) of a TB, a fraction of shared memory (e.g., 7kB) is always wasted. These two limitations reduce the number of TBs that can concurrently run on a GPU, which may impact the performance significantly as there may not be sufficient threads to hide long latencies of operations such as memory accesses.

In this paper, we first characterize the usage of shared memory in GPGPU (general purpose computation on GPUs) applications and make an important observation that many GPGPU applications only utilize shared memory for a small amount of time compared to the lifetime of a TB. Then, we propose novel ways to multiplex shared memory so as to enable a higher number of TBs to be executed concurrently. These schemes include three software approaches, namely VTB, VTB_pipe, CO-VTB, and one hardware solution. Our software approaches work on existing GPUs and they essentially combine two original TBs into a new TB and add if-statements to control time multiplexing of the allocated shared memory between the two original TBs. Our hardware solution incurs minor changes to existing hardware and supports dynamic shared memory allocation and de-allocation so as to enable shared memory multiplexing with very little change in GPGPU code.

Our experimental results on NVIDIA GTX285 and GTX480 GPUs show remarkable performance gains from our proposed software approaches, up to 1.95X and 1.44X on average on GTX285 and up to 2.19X and 1.70X on average on GTX480. We also evaluate our hardware proposal using the GPGPUsim simulator [1], which shows up to 2.34X and an average of 1.53X performance enhancement.

Our work makes the following contributions. (1) We characterize shared memory usage among GPGPU applications and highlight that many GPGPU applications utilize shared memory only for a limited portion (an average of 25.6%) of the execution time of a TB; (2) we propose three software approaches to time multiplex shared memory among TBs; (3) we propose a simple hardware approach to support dynamic shared memory management; and (4) we show that our proposed software- and hardware-based shared memory multiplexing approaches are highly effective and significantly improve the performance.

The remainder of the paper is organized as follows. In Section 2, we present a brief background on GPGPU architecture and highlight the importance of shared memory. We characterize the shared memory usage of GPGPU applications in Section 3. In Section 4, we present our three software approaches to multiplex shared memory. Section 5 discusses our hardware solution. The experimental methodology is addressed in the Section 6 and the results are presented in Section 7. Related work is discussed in Section 8. Section 9 concludes our paper.

2. BACKGROUND

State-of-art GPUs use many-core architecture to deliver high computational throughput. One GPU consists of multiple streaming multiprocessors (SMs) in NVIDIA GPU architecture or computer units (CUs) in AMD GPU architecture. Each SM/CU in turn includes multiple streaming processors (SPs) or thread processors (TPs). Threads running on GPUs follow the single program multiple data (SPMD) model and are organized in a hierarchy. A GPU kernel is launched to a GPU with a grid of thread blocks (TBs) using the NVIDIA CUDA terminology [10], which are called workgroups in OpenCL [12]. Threads in a TB form multiple warps, with each running in the Single Instruction Multiple Data (SIMD) mode. One or more TBs run concurrently on one SM, depending on the resource requirement of a TB.

On-chip shared memory is a critical resource for GPGPU applications. The shared memory provides a mechanism for threads in the same TB to communicate with each other. It also serves as a software managed cache so as to reduce the impact of long latency memory accesses. Since each SM has limited amount of shared memory, for many GPGPU applications, the usage of shared memory of a TB determines how many TBs can run concurrently, i.e., the degree of thread level parallelism (TLP). Besides shared memory, the register usage of each thread is another critical factor to determine the number of threads that can run concurrently. In state-of-art GPUs, both shared memory and register files (RFs) are managed similarly. When a TB is to be dispatched to an SM, the TB dispatcher allocates the shared memory and registers based on the aggregate usage of all the threads in the TB. The allocated shared memory and registers are released when the TB finishes execution. When there is not sufficient resource available in either shared memory or RF in an SM, the resource is not allocated and no TB will be dispatched to the SM.

Between shared memory and RFs, current GPUs have higher capacity in RFs. For example, on NVIDIA GTX285 GPUs, each SM has 16kB shared memory and a 64kB RF. On NVIDIA GTX480 GPUs (i.e., the Fermi architecture), each SM has a 128kB RF and a 64kB hybrid storage that can be configured as a 16kB L1 cache+48kB shared memory or a 48kB L1cache+16kB shared memory. The latest NVIDIA GPU, GTX680 (i.e., the Kepler architecture), has the same size of shared memory per SM as GTX480 and a 256kB RF. With a high number of SPs and a larger RF in each SM, the Kepler architecture is designed to host more concurrent thread blocks/threads in each SM than the Fermi architecture, thereby increasing the pressure on shared memory. On AMD HD5870 GPUs, each CU contains 32kB shared memory (called local data share) and a 256kB RF. As a result, for many GPGPU applications, shared memory presents a more critical resource to limit the number of TBs/threads to run concurrently on an SM.

3. CHARACTERIZATION OF SHARED MEMORY USAGE

To understand how GPGPU applications utilize shared memory, we select and study ten benchmarks, which have shared memory variables in the source code, as shown in Table 1. Among the benchmarks, MC, SP, MM, CV, RD and TP are from NVIDIA SDK [11]. FFT and HG are from AMD SDK [2]. STO [13] is from the GPGPUSim infrastructure [1]. We implemented the GPU kernel for MV, which has similar performance to CUBLAS 4.0 [8]. For each benchmark, the shared memory usage of a TB as well as the number of threads in a TB is reported in Table 1. Also included is the number of TBs that can run concurrently in an SM with 16kB shared memory.

Table 1. Benchmarks used in experiments

Benchmarks	Shared memory size per TB (Bytes)	Threads per TB	Threads (TBs) per SM	Actual shared memory usage per SM (Bytes)
Matrix vector multiplication (MV)	4268	32	96 (3)	4268x3 = 12804
Fast Fourier Transform (FFT)	8736	64	64 (1)	8736x1 = 8736
MarchingCubes (MC)	9324	32	32 (1)	9324x1 = 9324
StoreGPU (STO)	16304	128	128 (1)	16304x1 = 16304
ScalarProd (SP)	4144	64	192 (3)	4144x3 = 12432
Histogram (HG)	8224	64	64 (1)	8224x1 = 8224
Convolution(CV)	8300	128	128 (1)	8300x1 = 8300
Matrix Multiplication (MM)	2084	256	1024 (4)	2084x4 = 8336
Transpose (TP)	4260	128	384 (3)	4260x3 = 12870
Reduction (RD)	540	128	1024 (8)	540x8 = 4320

From Table 1, we can classify the benchmarks into two categories. The first category, including MV, FFT, MC, STO, SP, HG and CV, has the characteristics that the number of threads, which can execute concurrently in a SM, is severely limited by the shared memory capacity. The second category, including MM, TP, and RD, has the characteristics that either the shared memory usage of each TB is small or each TB has a large number of threads. For the benchmarks in the second category, the shared memory is not a bottleneck for TLP. Therefore, the target of our proposed approaches is the workloads in the first category. Another interesting observation from Table 1 is that for all workloads in the first category, except STO, the shared memory can be severely underutilized, as shown in the last column of Table 1, although the limited shared memory size is the cause for limited thread-level parallelism (TLP). The reason is that when a TB is to be dispatched, all its required shared memory needs to be available. Therefore, if the remaining shared memory is not enough for a TB, it is always wasted.

Next, for all the benchmarks in Table 1, we use simulation to determine how long the shared memory is utilized in a TB (see Section 6 for the detailed experimental methodology). Since the compiler may schedule the shared memory accesses to interleave with other type instructions to improve instruction-level parallelism (ILP), if we simply consider the lifetime of shared memory usage as between the first instruction writing to the shared memory and the last instruction reading from the shared memory, we may find that the shared memory is used for almost the entire lifetime of kernel execution. To isolate the usage of shared memory from other parts of the kernel code, we insert '__syncthreads()' instructions before the first *write/define* to and after the last *read/use* from the shared memory. We denote a code region surrounded by our inserted '__syncthreads()' as a shared memory access region. A redefine of the shared memory variables will start a new shared memory access region. Here, any define or use of shared memory variables is based on all the threads in a TB. Then, we use the accumulated execution time of all shared memory access regions as the duration for shared memory usage. In Figure 1, we show the ratio of the duration of shared memory usage over the overall execution time of a TB. For each benchmark, this ratio is an average across all its TBs.

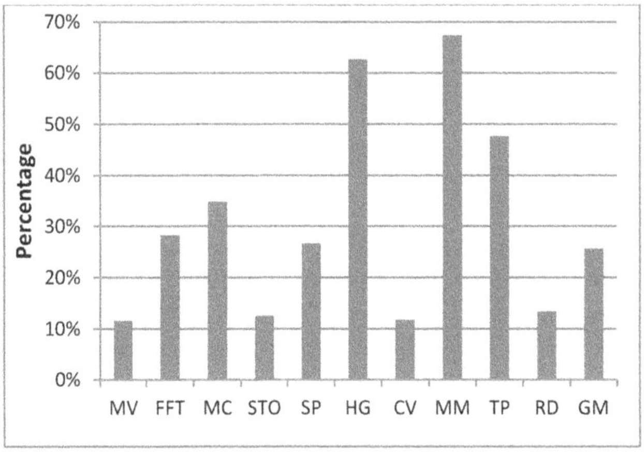

Figure 1. The portion of the execution time, during which the allocated shared memory is actually utilized, of a thread block for GPGPU applications.

As shown in Figure 1, using the geometric mean (GM) for all the benchmarks, the shared memory is only used in 25.6% of the execution time, which means that TBs do not need to use the allocated shared memory during the 74.4% of their execution time. Among these benchmarks, MM and TP have high TLP and they use the shared memory often during the lifetime of a TB. RD has high TLP but its performance bottleneck is global memory accesses; therefore the shared memory is idle most of the time. HG spends most of the execution time on accessing data in the shared memory, thereby showing the high ratio in Figure 1. For the remaining benchmarks, the TLP is limited by the shared memory capacity although their allocated shared memory is only used for a very limited amount of time compared to the lifetime of a TB.

4. SHARED MEMORY MULTIPLEXING: SOFTWARE APPROACHES

As discussed in Section 3, many GPGPU applications suffer from insufficient TLP due to the limited shared memory capacity. In this section, we propose three software approaches to time multiplex shared memory to boost TLP. The key idea of these three approaches is the same: we combine multiple original TBs into a larger one and introduce control flow to manage how the shared memory is accessed among the original TBs. The difference among the three approaches lies in how to overlap shared memory accesses with other parts of the code and whether the combined TB will use more shared memory than an original TB. To illustrate the proposed approaches, we use the FFT as a running example. Figure 2 shows the pseudo code of the kernel function, which implements a 1K-point FFT through a sequence of 4-point FFT (FFT4 functions) and data interchange through shared memory (loadFromSM and saveToSM functions). In loadFromSM, threads load data from shared memory. In saveToSM threads save data to the shared memory. '__syncthreads()' is used to ensure the order of the shared memory accesses. We also include the sequence number as a parameter of FFT4, loadFromSM and saveToSM functions to show the different parts of the code. With this implementation, each TB has 64 threads and uses 8736-Byte shared memory (8192 Bytes for data, additional bytes for padding to avoid bank conflicts and a few bytes reserved by CUDA). This shared memory usage is obtained from the NVCC compiler.

```
loadFromGlobal();
FFT4(0);
saveToSM(0);   //define by multiple threads in a TB
 __syncthreads();
loadFromSM(0); //use by multiple threads in a TB
FFT4(1);
 __syncthreads();
saveToSM(1);   //(re)define by multiple threads in a TB
 __syncthreads();
loadFromSM(1); //use by multiple threads in a TB
....
FFT4(4);
writeToGlobal();
```

Figure 2. The pseudo code of a 1k-point FFT implementation, which uses 8736-Byte shared memory per thread block and there are 64 threads per thread block.

4.1 Virtual Thread Block (VTB)

In this approach, we first isolate the part(s) of a kernel function that accesses shared memory variables. Second, we combine two original TBs into a new one. Here, we refer to an original TB as a virtual TB. In other words, after TB combination, one TB contains two virtual TBs. Third, we introduce the control flow "if(v_tb_id==0)" and "if(v_tb_id ==1)" to manage which virtual TB will access the shared memory at a time. The amount of the required shared memory of the combined TB remains the same as either of the virtual TBs.

For the FFT code example, the code after we apply VTB is shown in Figure 3. The 'if-statements' on lines 4, 6, 8, and 10 are introduced to ensure that only one virtual TB is accessing the allocated shared memory at a time. The 'syncthreads()' function on line 7 implicitly marks the last use of the shared memory of virtual TB 0 so that virtual TB 1 can use the shared memory immediately afterwards.

```
int v_tb_id = threadIdx.x/64; //virtual thread block id
loadFromGlobal();
FFT4(0);
if (v_tb_id==0) saveToSM(0); //def. from threads in v_tb_0
__syncthreads();
if (v_tb_id==0) loadFromSM(0);//use. from threads in v_tb_0
__syncthreads();
if (v_tb_id==1) saveToSM(0); //def. from threads in v_tb_1
__syncthreads();
if (v_tb_id==1) loadFromSM(0);//use. from threads in v_tb_1
FFT4(1);
....
FFT4(4);
writeToGlobal();
```

Figure 3. The pseudo code of a 1k-point FFT implementation using VTB. Each thread block uses 8736-Byte shared memory and there are 128 threads in each thread block.

Next, we illustrate the reason why our proposed VTB can improve the GPU throughput and also highlight its overhead. Assuming a GPU with 16kB shared memory in each SM, since each TB requires more than 8kB shared memory, two TB dispatched to the same SM have to execute back to back with the code in Figure 2. This execution process is shown in Figure 4a. For the purpose of clarity, in Figure 4 we only show the execution time corresponding to the global memory access, the first 4-point FFT and the data exchange via the shared memory. The remaining code in the kernel function simply repeats 4-point FFT and data exchange multiple times. With the code in Figure 3, the combined TB is equivalent to the two original TBs. Due to the increased TLP, the execution time of the function loadFromGlobal() and FFT4() of 128 threads is significantly less than the back-to-back execution of the same functions for 64 threads, as shown in Figure 4b. However, to control the accesses to shared memory between the two virtual TBs, additional synchronization functions are added to ensure correctness. Besides the latency to perform such '__syncthread()' functions, the barrier also limits the compiler's capability to schedule instructions across the barriers, which may result in reduced instruction-level parallelism (ILP) and additional register usage. The added control flow instruction "if(v_tb_id==0)" has minimal overhead as it does not generate any control divergence within a warp since all 64 threads in the same virtual TB will follow the same direction and each warp has 32 threads on NVIDIA GPUs. The global memory access functions 'loadFromGlobal' and 'writeToGlobal' benefit from VTB as the increased TLP translate to increased memory-level parallelism (MLP).

From Figure 4, we can also see that when a virtual TB accesses the shared memory, the other virtual TB is forced to be idle due to the control flow and the '__syncthread()' functions. Our proposed second and third software approaches address this limitation and we include the execution time information of these approaches in Figure 4c and 4d for comparison. We discuss these two approaches in detail in Sections 4.2 and 4.3.

Note that although Figure 3 and Figure 4 show the case of combining two original TBs into one, we can apply the same principle to combine more than two TBs. The optimal number of TBs to combine is dependent on how many concurrent threads can run on an SM. Typically, combining two TBs is sufficient to reap most performance benefits. Among all the benchmarks in our study, only MarchingCubes (MC) benefits from combining more than two TBs (we combined 4 TBs for MC using our proposed VTB approach).

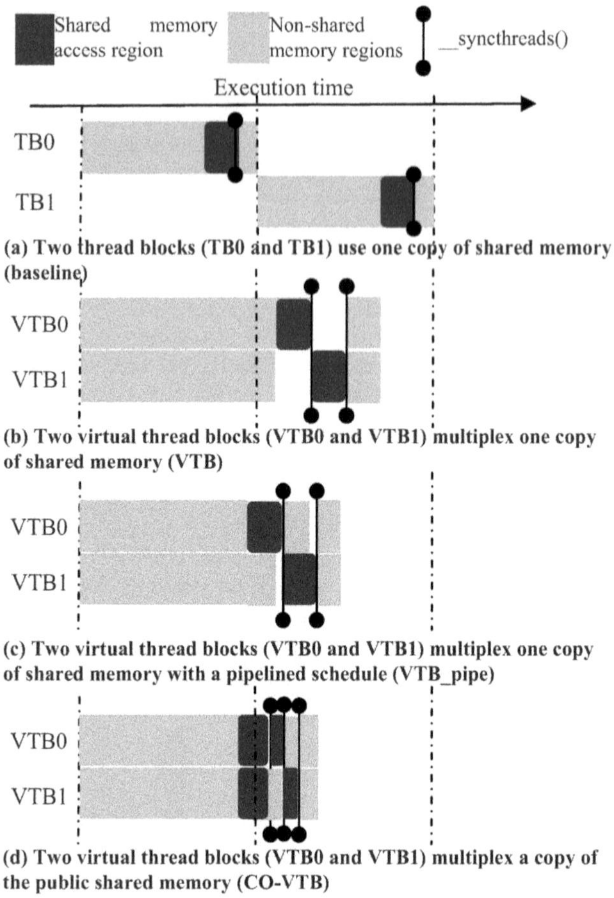

(a) Two thread blocks (TB0 and TB1) use one copy of shared memory (baseline)

(b) Two virtual thread blocks (VTB0 and VTB1) multiplex one copy of shared memory (VTB)

(c) Two virtual thread blocks (VTB0 and VTB1) multiplex one copy of shared memory with a pipelined schedule (VTB_pipe)

(d) Two virtual thread blocks (VTB0 and VTB1) multiplex a copy of the public shared memory (CO-VTB)

Figure 4. A comparison of execution time of the baseline to our proposed software approaches: (a) the baseline, (b) VTB, (c) VTB_pipe, and (d) CO-VTB.

4.2 Pipelined Virtual Thread Block (VTB_PIPE)

As discussed in Section 4.1, VTB combines two virtual TBs into a larger one and it ensures that only one virtual TB is accessing the shared memory by forcing the other virtual TB to be idle. To reduce such idle cycles, we propose to overlap computation with shared memory accesses. To do so, we make the first virtual TB to run faster than the second one using an 'if(v_tb_id==0)' statement. Then, when the first virtual block reaches the code section of shared memory access, the second virtual TB continues its computation instead of being forced idle. When the second virtual block reaches the code section of shared memory accesses, the first will continue to run ahead. This process is similar to letting the two virtual TBs to go through a pipeline. Therefore, we refer to this approach as pipelined VTB (VTB_pipe).

For the FFT example, the code after we apply our proposed VTB_pipe is shown in Figure 5. From Figure 5, we can see that initially the two virtual TBs will both execute the 'loadFromGlobal()' function. Then, the 'if(v_td_id==0)' statements on lines 3 and 4 as well as the '__syncthreads()' on line 5 enable virtual TB 0 to execute the 'FFT4()' and 'saveToSM' functions, making it running ahead of virtual TB1. The code on line 6 and line 7 shows the overlapping between the function 'loadFromSM()' of virtual TB0 and the 'FFT4()' function of virtual TB1. Since virtual TB1 is lagging behind, when it reads from the shared memory via 'loadFromSM()' on line 11, the virtual TB0 proceeds to compute its next 4-point FFT, the 'FFT4()' on line 12. The execution process is shown in Figure 4b. Due to the overlapping between shared memory accesses and computation, we can reduce the idle cycles experienced by virtual TBs.

```
1. int v_tb_id = threadIdx.x/64;
2. loadFromGlobal();
3. if (v_tb_id==0) FFT4(0);
4. if (v_tb_id==0) saveToSM(0);
5. __syncthreads();
6. if (v_tb_id==0) loadFromSM(0);
7. else FFT4(0);
8. __syncthreads();
9. if (v_tb_id==1) saveToSM(0);
10. __syncthreads();
11. if (v_tb_id==1) loadFromSM(0);
12. else FFT4(1);
13. __syncthreads();
14. if (v_tb_id==0) saveToSM(1);
15. __syncthreads();
16. if (v_tb_id==0) loadFromSM(1);
17. else FFT4(1);
18. ....
19. FFT4(4);
20. writeToGlobal();
```

Figure 5. The pseudo code of a 1k-point FFT implementation using VTB_pipe. Each thread block uses 8736-Byte shared memory and there are 128 threads in each thread block.

The complexity of VTB_pipe, however, is that we may need to partition the non-shared memory access code section to create small computational/global memory access tasks so that they can overlap with shared memory accesses. The ideal case is that the small computational tasks have similar execution latency to the shared memory accesses and can completely utilize the otherwise idle cycles. In the FFT example, the FFT4 is a convenient choice and does not require such partition. For other benchmarks such as Histogram (HG), loop peeling is used to create such a computational/global memory access task to overlap with the shared memory accesses. Similar to the VTB approach, we can choose to combine more than two original TBs. However, synchronization among more than two TBs becomes difficult to manage. Therefore, we choose not to combine more than two TBs for our VTB_pipe approach.

4.3 Collaborative Virtual Thread Block (CO_VTB)

In both VTB and VTB_pipe, a few original TBs are combined to time multiplex the allocated shared memory, thereby significantly improving TLP. For some applications, the TLP improvement is sufficient to hide instruction execution latencies. For others, there exist additional opportunities. As discussed in Section 3, if the shared memory size is not a multiple of the shared memory usage of a TB, part of shared memory is always wasted. Neither VTB nor VTB_pipe addresses this issue as they do not alter the shared memory usage of a TB. To effectively utilize such otherwise wasted shared memory, we propose to let two TBs to collaboratively utilize the shared memory and refer to this approach as collaborative virtual thread blocks (CO-VTB). In CO-VTB, we partition the shared memory usage of a TB into two parts, private and public, and apply the VTB (or VTB_pipe) approach only on the public part. For example, if the original shared memory usage of a TB is 9kB, an SM with 16kB shared memory can only host 1 TB. If we partition the shared memory usage of a TB into a 7kB private part and a 2kB public part, when we combine two TBs, each uses 7kB private shared memory each (a total of 14kB) and both time multiplex the 2kB public shared memory, thereby utilizing the 16kB shared memory effectively. Figure 4d illustrates the execution of our proposed CO-VTB approach.

Next, we use the benchmark, MatchingCube, to show the code changes for CO-VTB. For the benchmark FFT, CO-VTB involves too much code change, which incurs high performance overhead. The simplified pseudo code of the baseline MatchingCube kernel is shown in Figure 6a. From the code, we can see that each TB has 32 threads and uses 9216-Byte (=24*32*3*4) shared memory. The code after we apply CO-VTB is shown in Figure 6b. Now, one TB has 2 virtual TBs and there are 64 threads in a TB. The shared memory array is partitioned into two parts: the private arrays 'vertlist_v0' and 'vertlist_v1', which are combined into a single array 'vertlist', and the public array 'vertlist2', which is multiplexed by the two virtual TBs. Either private array has the size of 6144(=16*32*3*4) Bytes and the public array size is 3072(=8*32*3*4) Bytes. So, the overall shared memory usage of a TB becomes 15360 (= 2*6144+3072) Bytes. The register variable 'reg' is introduced to temporarily hold the data to be written to the public part of the shared memory. Additional code is inserted to check the array index (the variable 'edge') to determine whether the data resides in the private or public part of shared memory and then either the array 'vertlist' (private) or the array 'vertlist2' (public) is used accordingly.

As shown from the code example in Figure 6, there is overhead involved in the CO-VTB approach, including additional register variables and additional code. For kernel functions like FFT, the complex array access patterns introduce too much overhead when a shared memory array is partitioned to private and public parts. Therefore, CO-VTB is utilized selectively, only for arrays with relatively simple access patterns. Due to this complexity, we also choose not to combine more than two TBs.

5. SHARED MEMORY MULTIPLEXING: A HARDWARE SOLUTION

As discussed in Section 4, our proposed software approaches improve TLP by merging original TBs and explicitly managing the shared memory accesses among them. The advantage of the software approaches is that they work well with current GPUs. The disadvantage, however, is the overhead introduced to manage the shared memory. In this section, we propose a hardware solution to managing shared memory.

In GPUs, the TB dispatcher dispatches TBs onto SMs. For each SM, it maintains a shared memory management (SMM) table, as shown in Figure 7. The SMM table has multiple entries and each entry keeps three fields, the TB id, the size, and the starting address. When a TB is to be dispatched to an SM, the TB dispatcher goes through the SMM table of the SM to determine whether there is enough free shared memory. If so, the dispatcher allocates the required shared memory by filling an entry in the SMM table with the TB id and setting its size field to the required shared memory size of the TB. The starting address field is determined and then passed to the TB so that every shared memory access in the TB will use this starting address as the base address. When a TB finishes execution, the dispatcher releases the allocated shared memory by invalidate the corresponding SMM table entry. Since the shared memory is allocated through the lifetime of a TB, we refer to such shared memory management as 'static' allocation and de-allocation.

```
#define NTHREADS 32
__global__ void generateTriangles() {
  //each TB uses 4*3*24*32 = 9216 byte share memory.
  __shared__ float3 vertlist[24][NTHREADS];
  // store the result of function f1 into shared memory
  for (i=0; i<24; i++) vertlist [i][threadIdx.x]= f1(i);
  for(i=0; i<numVerts; i++) {
    uint edge = tex1Dfetch(triTex, cubeindex*16 + i);
    // use function f2 perform computation on shared memory
    pos[index] = f2(vertlist[edge][ threadIdx.x]);
  }
}
```

(a) The pseudo code of MarchingCubes, for which each thread block uses 9216-Byte shared memory and has 32 threads.

```
#define NTHREADS 32
__global__ void generateTriangles() {
// each virtual TB uses 6144-byte private shared memory.
//__shared__ float3 vertlist_v0[16][ NTHREADS];
//__shared__ float3 vertlist_v1[16][ NTHREADS];
//Both private parts are combined into a single array vertlist
  __shared__ float3 vertlist[2][16][NTHREADS];
// accessing the private part of shared memory
  for (i=0; i<16; i++) vertlist [v_tb_id][i][v_t_id]=f1(i);
  float3 reg[8];
  for (i=16; i<24; i++) reg[i-16] = f1(i);
  __syncthreads();
// two virtual TBs multiplex 3072-byte public shared memory.
  __shared__ float3 vertlist2[8][NTHREADS];
  if (v_tb_id==0) {
   for(i=0; i<8; i++) vertlist2[i][v_t_id]= reg[i];
   for(i=0; i<numVerts; i++) {
    uint edge = tex1Dfetch(triTex, cubeindex*16 + i);
// check whether the data is in private or public shared memory
    if( edge<16) pos[index] =
           f2(vertlist[v_tb_id][edge][v_t_id])
    else pos[index] = f2(vertlist2[edge-16][v_t_id]); } }
  __syncthreads();
  if (v_tb_id==1) { ... }
}
```

(b) The pseudo code of MarchingCubes using CO-VTB. Each thread block uses 2*6144+3072=15360 Byte shared memory and there are 64 threads in each thread block.

Figure 6. The simplified pseudo code of MarchingCubes, (a) the baseline kernel code; (b) the code after we apply CO-VTB.

Valid	TB id	Size	Starting Address
1	6	4kB	0
1	10	4kB	4096
	...	...	

Figure 7. A shared memory management (SMM) table.

To enable dynamic shared memory management, we propose to extend the TB dispatcher so that the shared memory management is exposed to and can be controlled by software. Since shared memory allocation and de-allocation affect all the threads in a TB, we propose to associate shared memory management with the existing '__syncthreads()' function and the new syntax of the function becomes '*__syncthreads(int opt, unsigned &base_addr, unsigned size)*'. It still serves as a barrier to synchronize all the threads in a TB. When the parameter 'opt' is 1, it invokes the TB dispatcher to allocate the shared memory for 'size' bytes. The TB dispatcher uses the same allocation process by going through the corresponding SMM table. If there is enough free shared memory, an entry in the SMM table is updated and its 'starting address' field is passed to the 'base_addr' variable to be used by subsequent shared memory accesses. If there is no sufficient shared memory to be allocated, the TB will be stalled until another TB frees its allocated shared memory. If the parameter 'opt' is '-1', the TB dispatcher performs shared memory de-allocation using the 'base_addr' parameter. It searches the SMM table entries to find the matching 'starting address' with the 'base_addr' and invalidates the table entry. If the parameter 'opt' is '0', the other two parameters ('base_addr' and 'size') are ignored and '__syncthreads' operates as a regular barrier. To simplify the design, we choose not to allow nested shared memory allocation so as to avoid any potential deadlock issue. We also require that for a kernel function, the size of dynamic allocation and de-allocation to be the same so as to avoid fragmentation.

The code change to utilize our proposed dynamic shared memory management is very little. It only needs a shared memory allocation at the beginning and de-allocation at the end of each memory access code region. For the FFT kernel, the code after such changes is shown in in Figure 8.

```
loadFromGlobal();
FFT4(0);
__syncthreads(1, &base_addr , 8376); //allocation
saveToSM(0);        //define by multiple threads in a TB
__syncthreads(0, 0, 0); //synchronization
loadFromSM(0);    //use by multiple threads in a TB
__syncthreads(-1, &base_addr , 8376); //de-allocation

FFT4(1);
....
writeToGlobal();
```

Figure 8. The pseudo code for 1k-point FFT kernel using the hardware supported dynamic shared memory management. Each TB allocates and de-allocates 8376-byte shared memory and contains 64 threads.

The dynamic shared memory allocation and de-allocation in the FFT kernel shown in Figure 8 enables an SM to exploit higher degrees of TLP. Figure 9 illustrates this effect with two TBs running on an SM. Although the shared memory (16kB) on the SM is not large enough for the aggregate requirement from the two TBs (2x8376=16752B), our proposed dynamic allocation enables them to run concurrently and ensures that the two allocation calls will be served one after the other.

From Figure 9, it can be seen that the key performance advantages of our dynamic shared memory management include: (1) higher degrees of TLP to hide instruction latencies, and (2) reduced overhead of '__syncthreads()' as the barrier is limited to a TB and doesn't affect other TBs. In comparison, in our software approaches, such a barrier will affect both virtual TBs. Furthermore, dynamic allocation and de-allocation naturally enables overlap between shared memory accesses of one TB and non-shared memory code in another as long as they do not reach allocation at the same time. This is the reason why we do not need the code changes of our VTB or VTB_pipe approaches.

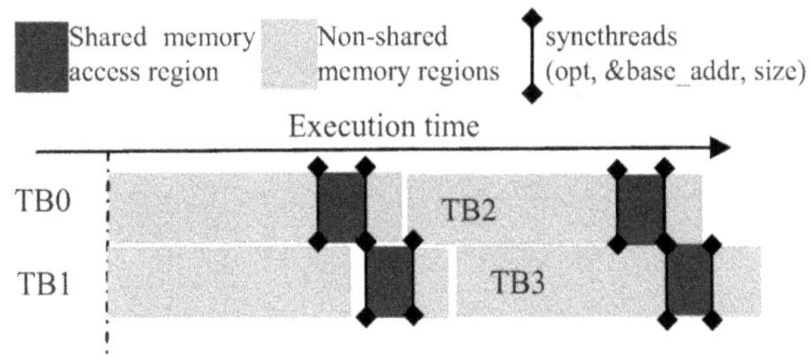

Figure 9. Two TBs running concurrently on an SM using dynamic shared memory management.

With the hardware supported shared memory management, we do not need to combine TBs. A TB can be dispatched to an SM as long as other resource requirements such as registers are satisfied. As a result, there might be too many TBs dispatched to an SM. We propose to use a counter to track how many TBs are running on an SM and stall TB dispatching when this counter reaches a threshold. If we denote the maximum number of TBs that can be dispatched to an SM using the static shared memory management as K, the threshold setting of $K+2$ or $K+3$ achieves good performance (See Section 7.2). In other words, allowing an SM to run 2 or 3 more TBs concurrently usually improves TLP sufficiently.

With our proposed hardware solution, the TB dispatcher can support both static and dynamic shared memory management. We propose to let either the run-time or compiler to determine which mechanism to be used. If the static management is selected for the purpose of quality of service, the dynamic management instructions are ignored. Static and dynamic shared memory management can also be used together to support collaborative TBs, similar to the idea exploited in CO-VTB. We refer to this hardware supported collaborative TB approach as CO-HW. Like CO-VTB, we need to change the kernel code to partition the shared memory usage into the private part and the public part. Unlike CO-VTB, we do not need to use VTB or CO-VTB on the public part. Instead, we insert dynamic allocation and de-allocation instruction to multiplex the public part. When a kernel is launched to a GPU, the compiler or the run-time provides the sizes of both the private part and the public part to the TB dispatcher. Static shared memory management is used for the private part and dynamic shared memory management is used to multiplex the public part. For example, a TB originally uses 6kB shared memory and an SM with 16kB shared memory can host two such TBs using static shared memory management. After partition, a TB uses 4kB private and 2kB public shared memory. With 16kB shared memory, three TBs can run concurrently using a total of 12kB (=4kBx3) private shared memory. The remaining 4kB is used as public shared memory among the three TBs. The same SMM table is used to manage shared memory as shown in Figure 10, where the first three entries are allocated when the three TBs are dispatched and the last two are allocated/de-allocated with the '__syncthreads(opt, &base_addr, size)' instructions.

Valid	TB id	Size	Starting Address
1	0	4kB	0
1	1	4kB	4096
1	2	4kB	8192
1	0	2kB	12288
1	1	2kB	14436

Figure 10. The SMM table manages shared memory usage for collaborative TBs. The first three entries are for the private shared memory of the 3 TBs. The last two entries are for the public shared memory.

Due to static management, the private part is allocated when a TB is dispatched and is de-allocated when it completes execution. The public part is managed based on the dynamic allocation and de-allocation instructions. The only constraint, which the TB dispatcher enforces, is that when a TB is dispatched, the total amount of the private parts of currently running TBs in an SM cannot exceed (the size of overall shared memory – the size of the public part of a TB). The purpose is to ensure that there is at least one set of public shared memory available to be used among the TBs.

Our proposed hardware solution simply exposes the existing shared memory management in the TB dispatcher to the software and enables it to be controlled by the extended '__syncthreads()' instructions. The code change is to insert '__syncthreads(1, &base_addr, size)' at the beginning of shared memory access regions and '__syncthreads(-1, &base_addr, size)' at the end. For CO-HW, this region is where the public shared memory part is accessed. Therefore, we argue that this solution has low overhead in both hardware and software changes. The effectiveness is evaluated in Section 7.2.

6. EXPERIMENTAL METHODOLOGY

To evaluate our proposed software approaches, we use both NVIDIA GTX 480 and NVIDIA GTX285 GPUs with CUDA SDK 4.0. Because the shared memory size is configurable on GTX 480 GPUs, we present two sets of results: one with 48kB shared memory and the other with 16kB shared memory. As discussed in Section 3, the focus of our proposed approaches is the category of applications, which have low TLP due to the limited capacity of shared memory in an SM. Therefore, among all the workloads in Table 1, our experiments do not include MM, TP, and RD as they have high TLP already and are not affected by our approaches. We implemented our proposed VTB and VTB_pipe using a source-to-source compiler, Cetus [14]. For VTB, the compiler searches defines and uses of shared memory variables among all the threads in a TB. The code between the first define and the last use is treated as a shared memory access region. Re-defines to shared memory variables are used to help to determine the last uses in a region. Then, the compiler generates the code for virtual TB ids and the control flow to determine which virtual TB accesses the shared memory. For VTB_pipe, we add annotations manually to denote the section of code to overlap with shared memory access regions and the compiler generates the final code. For CO-VTB, we generate the code manually due to the complexity of partitioning shared memory variables into private and public parts. Also, as discussed in Section 5.3, not all workloads are suitable to CO-VTB due to the associated overheads. Among the workloads, we applied CO-VTB to MC, STO, and HG.

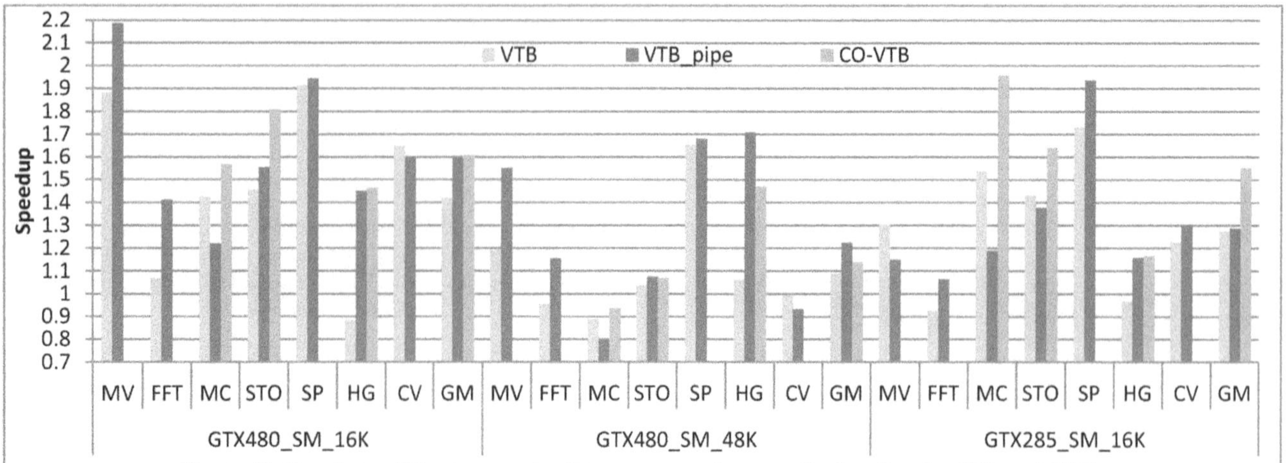

Figure 11. Speedups of the proposed software approaches over the baseline for different GPUs.

To model our proposed hardware support, we extend the GPGPUsim V3.0 simulator [1] to support our proposed dynamic shared memory management instructions (i.e., the extended '__syncthreads()' instruction). The simulator models an NVIDIA GTX285 GPU, which has 16kB shared memory and a 64kB register file on each SM. The off-chip memory frequency is set to 1100MHz. We manually inserted the dynamic allocation and de-allocation instructions in the workloads. For the CO-HW approach, we used very similar code to CO-VTB except the part using virtual TB ids as we do not need to combine two TBs. We also inserted the dynamic allocation and de-allocation instructions surrounding the code region that accesses the public shared memory.

7. EXPERIMENTAL RESULTS

7.1 Evaluation of Software-Based Shared Memory Multiplexing

In our first experiment, we evaluate the performance improvements from our proposed software approaches, VTB, VTB_pipe and CO-VTB. In Figure 11, we report the speedups of these three approaches over the baseline implementation. For each benchmark, we examine three GPU configurations, GTX 480 with 16kB shared memory (labeled "GTX480_SM_16K"), GTX 480 with 48kB shared memory (labeled "GTX480_SM_48K") and GTX 285 with 16kB shared memory (labeled "GTX285_SM_16K"). From the figure, we can make some interesting observations. First, among the three software approaches, CO-VTB achieves highest performance on average, using geometric mean (GM). However, as discussed in Section 6, not all workloads are suitable for this approach. VTB_pipe achieves higher performance than VTB on average as it can overlap shared memory accesses with other parts of code. The benchmark, MC, is an exception since the shared memory accesses dominate its execution and the overlapping effect from VTB_pipe fails to offset the overhead. Since different workloads may favor different shared memory multiplexing approaches, in order to achieve the best performance, we can generate three versions of optimized code using VTB, VTB_pipe and CO-VTB and select the best performing one. Second, among three GPU configurations, highest performance gains are achieved on GTX 480 with 16kB shared memory and the average speedups are 1.42X, 1.60X, 1.61X for VTB, VTB_pipe and CO-VTB, respectively. If we select the best version for each benchmark, the average performance gain reaches 1.70X. The reason is that compared to GTX285, GTX480 has a higher number of SPs. One instruction from a warp will keep the SP busy for 4 cycles on GTX285 compared 2 cycles on GTX480. Therefore, compared to GTX285, TLP is more critical for GTX480. Third, the increased shared memory capacity on GTX480 with 48kB shared memory enables an SM to host more TBs. The improved TLP in turn reduces the benefit of our proposed software schemes. For example, for the benchmark CV, each TB has 128 threads and uses 8300 Bytes of shared memory. As a result, 16kB shared memory can only host 1 TB while 48kB shared memory can host 5TBs (or 640 threads). Nevertheless, our proposed approaches remain effective and the achieved speedups are 1.09X, 1.22X, 1.14X on average for VTB, VTB_pipe, and CO-VTB, respectively. Selecting the best version for each benchmark provides a 1.26X speedup on average.

As two of our benchmarks, FFT and MV, are implemented in NVIDIA libraries, we compare our implementation of FFT to CUFFT4.0 and MV to CUBLAS4.0 on GTX480. For MV, we keep the width of the input matrix as 1024 and vary the height from 8K to 128K. The reason is that the height of the input matrix determines the number of threads for MV. The throughput comparison to CUBLAS4.0 is shown in Figure 12.

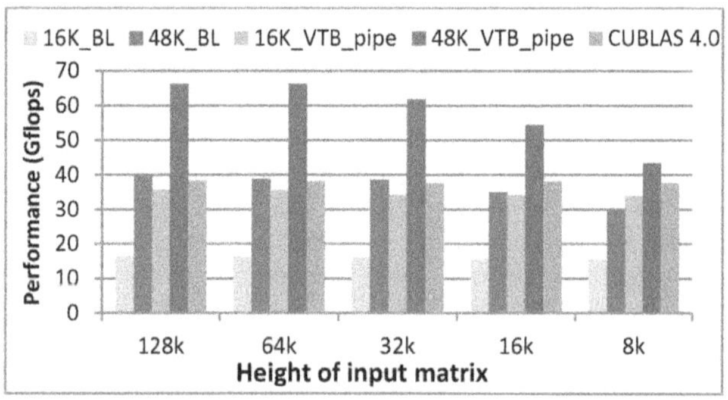

Figure 12. Performance comparison of MV among the baseline (xK_BL), VTB_pipe (xK_VTB_pipe) and CUBLAS 4.0 on GTX 480. 'xK' denotes the size of shared memory.

In Figure 12, the results with label '16K_BL' and '48K_BL' are our baseline implementation running on GTX480 with 16kB shared memory and 48kB shared memory, respectively. Our VTB_pipe results are labeled as '16K_VTB_pipe' and '48K_VTB_pipe' for the two shared memory configurations of GTX480. From the results, we can see that our baseline implementation running on GTX 480 with 48kB shared memory has similar performance to CUBLAS. With our VTB_pipe approach on GTX480 with 16kB shared memory, we can achieve similar performance to CUBLAS. On the GTX480 configuration with 48kB shared memory, our VTB_pipe approach outperforms CUBLAS by up to 74% and 52% on average.

For 1K-point FFT, we use batch execution [7] to evaluate the throughput and vary the batch size from 128 to 2048. The throughput results are reported in Figure 13.

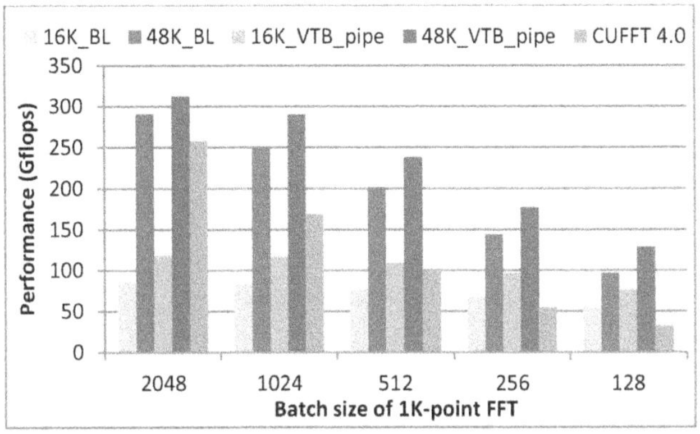

Figure 13. Performance comparison of FFT among the baseline (xK_BL), VTB_pipe (xK_VTB_pipe) and CUFFT 4.0 on GTX 480. 'xK' denotes the size of shared memory.

From the figure, we can see that our baseline implementation running on GTX480 with 16kB shared memory outperforms CUFFT [9] for small batch sizes and not as good as CUFFT for large batch sizes. With the 48kB shared configuration, our baseline implementation consistently outperforms CUFFT. The average throughput of '48K_BL' is 168.3 GFLOPS compared to the average of 72.4 GFLOPS throughput of CUFFT. Our VTB_pipe further improves the throughput by up to 33% and achieves the average throughput of 205.9 GFLOS (a 2.84X speedup over CUFFT).

7.2 Evaluation of Hardware-Supported Shared Memory Multiplexing

To evaluate the effectiveness of our proposed hardware solution, we first measure the performance of the baseline implementation (i.e., the static shared memory management) and the one with hardware support for dynamic shared memory management. Here, we use execution time (in the unit of cycles) rather than instruction per cycle (IPC) since we insert the dynamic allocation and de-allocation instructions into the code. The speedups of our hardware-supported dynamic shared memory management (labeled 'HW') over the baseline are shown in Figure 14. We also report the performance results of CO-HW, in which the shared memory usage is partitioned into statically managed private and dynamically managed public parts, in the figure (labeled 'CO_HW').

From Figure 14, we can see that our hardware supported dynamic allocation and de-allocation can significantly improve the performance, up to 2.34X and 1.53X on average, over the baseline static shared memory allocation. Similar to the software-based CO-VTB approach, we manually modified the code of MC, STO and HG for CO-HW. From Figure 14, it can be seen that CO-HW achieves up to 1.88X and an average of 1.42X speedups over the baseline. As discussed in Section 5, our hardware support dynamic shared memory management ('HW') eliminates some overheads of VTB or VTB_pipe. As a result, between HW and CO-HW, CO-HW remains more effective for MC but not for STO and HG. In contrast, for their software counterparts, CO-VTB typically performs much better than VTB or VTB-pipe.

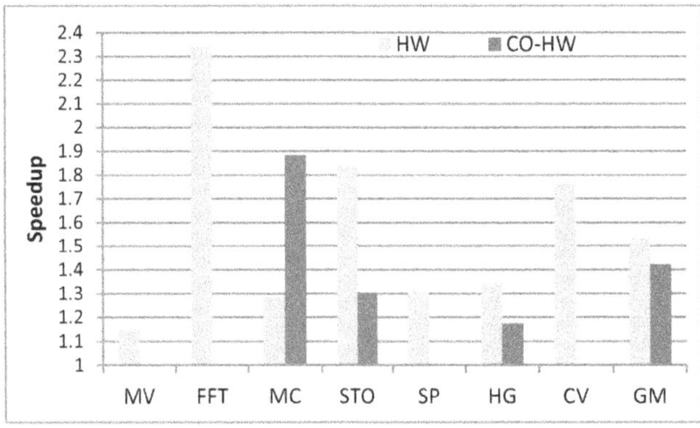

Figure 14. Speedups of hardware-supported dynamic shared memory management over baseline.

As discussed in Section 5, using dynamic shared memory management, many TBs can be dispatched to an SM if the shared memory is the only resource bottleneck. This may generate too much contention for multiplexing shared memory. A counter scheme is proposed in Section 5 to control the number of concurrent TBs that can be dispatched to an SM. If we use K to denote the maximum number of TBs that can be supported using the static shared memory management, we vary the upper bound of this counter from $K+1$ to $K+3$ and show the performance impact in Figure 15. In other words, we use dynamic shared memory management to allow an SM to host 1~3 more TBs. From the figure, we can see that on average, hosting 1 more TB ('K+1') does not provide sufficient TLP. Although hosting 2 or 3 more TBs in an SM shows similar performance, individual benchmarks show different trends. FFT and MC favor more TLP while HG and MV do not. Overall, our results suggest that either $K+2$ or $K+3$ is a fine choice as the maximum number of TBs to be allowed to run concurrently on an SM.

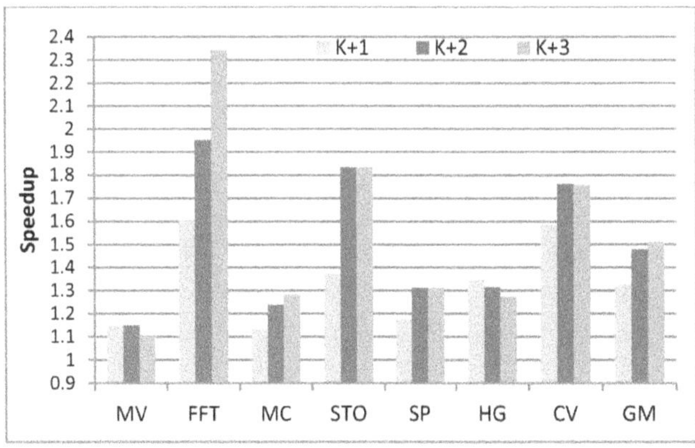

Figure 15. The impact of the maximum number of TBs to be allowed to run in an SM.

8. RELATED WORK

On-chip shared memory is a critical resource for GPGPU applications. Previous works mainly focus on utilizing shared memory to achieve coalesced memory accesses [3][4][5][15][16][17][18][19][20], to provide data exchange among threads [7], to use shared memory as software managed cache [18], etc. Although it is well known that heavy usage of shared memory may limit TLP [6][18], it is common that the benefits of using shared memory overweigh the shortcomings of reduced TLP. As a result, many GPGPU workloads as shown in Section 3 have exhibited high shared memory usage. This is also a reason why the latest NVIDIA Fermi architecture (e.g., GTX 480 GPUs) provides larger shared memory and an L1 cache. However, as shown in Section 7, the high number of SPs in an SM in GTX480 (and even higher number of SPs in GTX680) makes TLP more important to hide instruction execution latencies. In contrast, our work improves TLP without sacrificing the usage of shared memory.

9. CONCLUSION

In this paper, we propose novel software and hardware approaches to multiplex shared memory. Our approaches are based on our observation that for the GPGPU applications with heavy use of shared memory, the duration of time, when the shared memory is utilized, is actually low. Our experimental results confirm that the shared memory is utilized for only 25.6% of the execution time of a TB. Therefore, there exist significant opportunities to time multiplex shared memory. Among our software approaches, VTB is simplest and it combines two TBs into a new one and adds control flow to ensure only one original TB accesses the shared memory at a time. VTB_pipe reduces the performance overhead of VTB by overlapping non-shared memory access regions (e.g., computation or global memory accesses) with shared memory accesses. CO-VTB partitions the shared memory data into a private part and a public part and only applies VTB/VTB_pipe upon the public part. Our proposed hardware support essentially exposes the existing shared memory management to software and enables software to control when to perform allocation and de-allocation. Our experimental results show that our proposed software schemes improve the performance significantly on current GPUs. We evaluate our hardware solution using the GPGPUsim simulator and the results show that it improves the performance remarkably with very little change in GPGPU code.

10. ACKNOWLEDGEMENTS

We thank the anonymous reviewers for their insightful comments to improve our paper. This work is supported by a NSF project 1216569, a NSF CAREER award CCF-0968667 and a gift fund from AMD Inc.

11. REFERENCES

[1] A. Bakhoda, G. Yuan, W. W. L. Fung, H. Wong, and T. M. Aamodt. Analyzing CUDA workloads using a detailed GPU simulator. In IEEE International Symposium on Performance Analysis of Systems and Software, April 2009.

[2] AMD Accelerated Parallel Processing SDK V2.3, 2011

[3] B. Jang, D. Schaa, P. Mistry and D. Kaeli. Exploiting memory access patterns to improve memory performance in data-parallel architectures. In IEEE Transactions on Parallel and Distributed Systems, 2010.

[4] E. Z. Zhang, Y. Jiang, Z. Guo, K. Tian, and X. Shen. On-the-fly elimination of dynamic irregularities for GPU computing. In International Conference on Architectural Support for Programming Languages and Operating Systems, 2011.

[5] G. Ruetsch and P. Micikevicius, Optimize matrix transpose in CUDA. NVIDIA, 2009.

[6] J. Sim, A. Dasgupta, H. Kim, and R. Vuduc, A Performance Analysis Framework for Identifying Performance Benefits in GPGPU Applications. In Proc. ACM SIGPLAN Symposium on Principles and Practice of Parallel Programming, 2012.

[7] N. Govindaraju, B. Lloyd, Y. Dotsenko, B. Smith, and J. Manferdelli. High performance discrete Fourier transforms on graphics processors. In Proc. Supercomputing, 2008.

[8] NVIDIA CUDA Toolkit 4.0 CUBLAS Library, 2011

[9] NVIDIA CUDA Toolkit 4.0 CUFFT Library, 2011

[10] NVIDIA CUDA C Programming Guide 4.0, 2011.

[11] NVIDIA GPU Computing SDK 4.0, 2011.

[12] OpenCL, http://www.khronos.org/opencl/

[13] S. Al-Kiswany, A. Gharaibeh, E. Santos-Neto, G. Yuan, and M. Ripeanu. StoreGPU: exploiting graphics processing units to accelerate distributed storage systems. In International Symposium on High Performance Distributed Computing, 2008.

[14] S. I. Lee, T. Johnson, and R. Eigenmann. Cetus – an extensible compiler infrastructure for source-to-source transformation. In Workshops on Languages and Compilers for Parallel Computing, 2003

[15] S. Ryoo, C. I. Rodrigues, S. S. Stone, S. S. Baghsorkhi, S. Ueng, J. A. Stratton, and W. W. Hwu. Optimization space pruning for a multi-threaded GPU. In Proc. International Symposium on Code Generation and Optimization, 2008.

[16] S. Ryoo, C. I. Rodrigues, S. S. Baghsorkhi, S. S. Stone, D. B. Kirk, and W.W. Hwu. Optimization principles and application performance evaluation of a multithreaded GPU using CUDA. In Proc. ACM SIGPLAN Symposium on Principles and Practice of Parallel Programming, 2008.

[17] V. Volkov and J. W. Benchmarking GPUs to tune dense linear algebra. In Proc. Supercomputing, 2008.

[18] Y. Yang, P. Xiang, J. Kong and H. Zhou. A GPGPU Compiler for Memory Optimization and Parallelism Management. In ACM SIGPLAN conference on Programming Language Design and Implementation, 2010.

[19] Y. Yang, P. Xiang, M. Mantor and H. Zhou. Fixing Performance Bugs: An Empirical Study of Open-Source GPGPU Programs. In International Conference on Parallel Processing, 2012.

[20] Y. Zhang, J. Cohen, and J. D. Owens. Fast Tridiagonal Solvers on the GPU. In Proc. ACM SIGPLAN Symposium on Principles and Practice of Parallel Programming, 2010.

Introducing Hierarchy-awareness in Replacement and Bypass Algorithms for Last-level Caches

Mainak Chaudhuri
Indian Institute of Technology
Kanpur 208016, India
mainakc@iitk.ac.in

Jayesh Gaur
Intel Architecture Group
Bangalore 560103, India
jayesh.gaur@intel.com

Nithiyanandan Bashyam
Intel Architecture Group
Bangalore 560103, India
nithiyanandan.bashyam@intel.com

Sreenivas Subramoney
Intel Architecture Group
Bangalore 560103, India
sreenivas.subramoney@intel.com

Joseph Nuzman
Intel Architecture Group
Haifa 31015, Israel
joseph.nuzman@intel.com

ABSTRACT

The replacement policies for the last-level caches (LLCs) are usually designed based on the access information available locally at the LLC. These policies are inherently sub-optimal due to lack of information about the activities in the inner-levels of the hierarchy. This paper introduces cache hierarchy-aware replacement (CHAR) algorithms for inclusive LLCs (or L3 caches) and applies the same algorithms to implement efficient bypass techniques for exclusive LLCs in a three-level hierarchy. In a hierarchy with an inclusive LLC, these algorithms mine the L2 cache eviction stream and decide if a block evicted from the L2 cache should be made a victim candidate in the LLC based on the access pattern of the evicted block. Ours is the first proposal that explores the possibility of using a subset of L2 cache eviction hints to improve the replacement algorithms of an inclusive LLC. The CHAR algorithm classifies the blocks residing in the L2 cache based on their reuse patterns and dynamically estimates the reuse probability of each class of blocks to generate selective replacement hints to the LLC. Compared to the static re-reference interval prediction (SRRIP) policy, our proposal offers an average reduction of 10.9% in LLC misses and an average improvement of 3.8% in instructions retired per cycle (IPC) for twelve single-threaded applications. The corresponding reduction in LLC misses for one hundred 4-way multi-programmed workloads is 6.8% leading to an average improvement of 3.9% in throughput. Finally, our proposal achieves an 11.1% reduction in LLC misses and a 4.2% reduction in parallel execution cycles for six 8-way threaded shared memory applications compared to the SRRIP policy.

In a cache hierarchy with an exclusive LLC, our CHAR proposal offers an effective algorithm for selecting the subset of blocks (clean or dirty) evicted from the L2 cache that need not be written to the LLC and can be bypassed. Compared to the TC-AGE policy (analogue of SRRIP for exclusive LLC), our best exclusive LLC proposal improves average throughput by 3.2% while saving an average of 66.6% of data transactions from the L2 cache to the on-die interconnect for one hundred 4-way multi-programmed workloads. Compared to an inclusive LLC design with an identical hierarchy, this corresponds to an average throughput improvement of 8.2% with only 17% more data write transactions originating from the L2 cache.

PACT'12, September 19–23, 2012, Minneapolis, Minnesota, USA.

Categories and Subject Descriptors

B.3 [**Memory Structures**]: Design Styles

General Terms

Algorithms, design, measurement, performance

Keywords

Last-level caches, replacement policy, bypass algorithm

1. INTRODUCTION

The replacement policy for a particular level of a cache hierarchy is usually designed based on the access information (frequency, recency, etc.) available only at that level of the hierarchy. Such a level-centric design methodology for the last-level cache (LLC) fails to incorporate two important pieces of information. First, the reuses taking place in the inner-levels of a hierarchy are not propagated to the LLC. Past research showed that propagating even a small fraction of these reuses to the LLC can significantly increase the traffic in the on-die interconnect [7]. Second, the clean evictions from the inner-levels are usually not propagated to the LLC in an inclusive or a non-inclusive/non-exclusive hierarchy.

This paper, for the first time, studies the possibility of using an appropriately chosen subset of L2 cache evictions as hints for improving the replacement algorithms of an inclusive LLC (or L3 cache) in a three-level hierarchy. The central idea is that when the L2 cache residency of a block comes to an end, one can estimate its future liveness based on its reuse pattern observed during its residency in the L2 cache. Particularly, if we can deduce that the next reuse distance of such a block is significantly beyond the LLC reach, we can notify the LLC that this block should be marked a potential victim candidate in the LLC. An early eviction of such a block can help retain more blocks in the LLC with relatively shorter reuse distances. In a hierarchy with an exclusive LLC, this liveness information can be used to decide the subset of the L2 cache evictions that need not be allocated in the LLC.

To estimate the merit of making an inclusive LLC aware of the L2 cache evictions, we conduct an oracle-assisted experiment where the LLC runs the two-bit SRRIP policy [8] (this is our baseline in this paper). The two-bit SRRIP policy fills a block into the LLC with a re-reference prediction value (RRPV) of two and promotes it to RRPV of zero on a hit. A block with RRPV three (i.e., large re-reference distance) is chosen as the victim in a set. If none exists, the RRPVs of all

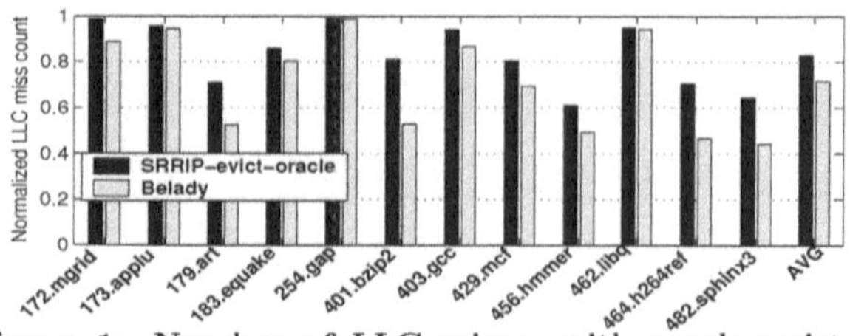

Figure 1: Number of LLC misses with oracle-assisted LLC replacement policies normalized to baseline SRRIP in an inclusive LLC.

the blocks in the set are increased in steps of one until a block with RRPV three is found. Ties are broken by victimizing the block with the least physical way id.[1] In our oracle-assisted experiment, on an L2 cache eviction of a data block[2], a next forward use distance oracle determines the relative order between the next forward use distances of the evicted block and the current SRRIP victim in the LLC set where the L2 cache victim belongs to. If the next forward use distance of the L2 cache victim is bigger, it is marked a potential victim by changing its RRPV to three in the LLC.

The left bar in each group of Figure 1 shows the number of LLC misses of this oracle-assisted policy normalized to the baseline SRRIP. The bar on the right in each group shows the number of LLC misses in Belady's optimal algorithm [1, 20] normalized to the baseline. These experiments are carried out on an offline cache hierarchy simulator that takes as input the entire L2 cache access trace of twelve single-threaded applications drawn from SPEC 2000 and SPEC 2006 suites. The L2 cache access trace of each application is collected for a representative set of one billion dynamic instructions chosen using the SimPoint toolset [22]. The cache hierarchy consists of 32 KB 8-way L1 instruction and data caches, a 256 KB 8-way L2 cache, and a 2 MB 16-way inclusive LLC. The L1 and L2 caches implement LRU replacement policy. Overall, Belady's optimal policy saves 28.5% of the LLC misses (refer to the AVG group), while the oracle-assisted SRRIP policy with L2 cache eviction hints can save about 17% of the baseline LLC misses. As a result, this policy can bridge close to two-third of the gap between Belady's optimal and the baseline SRRIP. Of course, this potential can be realized only if we can accurately learn which L2 cache evictions should be used to update the RRPV rank in the target LLC set and the solution to this problem forms the crux of our proposal.

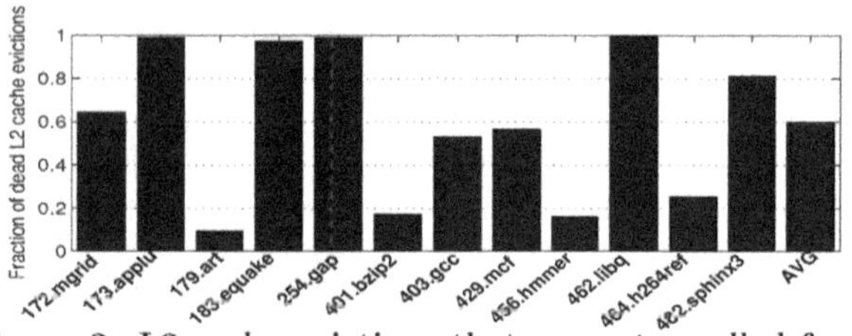

Figure 2: L2 cache evictions that are not recalled from the LLC in baseline SRRIP policy.

To further justify the data in Figure 1, we show in Figure 2 the percentage of blocks evicted from the L2 cache that are never recalled by the core from the time they are evicted from the L2 cache until they are evicted from the LLC. These data show that almost 60% of the blocks evicted from the L2 cache turn out to be dead in the LLC (refer to the AVG group). Such a block could be marked a potential LLC replacement candidate at the time it is evicted from the L2 cache provided we can separate it from the live blocks. Early replacement of such dead blocks can improve performance if the application has a good number of live blocks that can now stay longer in the LLC and enjoy additional reuses.

[1] SRRIP is known to outperform NRU and LRU [8].

[2] We do not apply our policy proposal to instruction blocks.

The fact that 60% of the L2 cache evictions are dead corresponds well with the already known fact that the blocks brought into the LLC have low use counts [21]. For the data in Figure 2, the average use count per LLC block is about 1.67 (reciprocal of dead percentage). In summary, the L2 cache eviction stream is rich in information regarding liveness of the cache blocks. Accurate separation of the live blocks from the dead ones in the L2 cache eviction stream can bridge a significant portion of the gap between the baseline and the optimal replacement policy for the LLC.

In Section 2, we present our cache hierarchy-aware replacement (CHAR) algorithms for inclusive LLCs. Figure 3 shows a high-level implementation of our CHAR algorithm for inclusive LLCs. The dead hint detector hardware is part of the L2 cache controller. It consumes the L2 cache eviction stream and identifies the eviction addresses that should be sent to the LLC as dead hints. As usual, it sends all dirty evictions to the LLC, some of which may be marked as dead hints. We note that the general framework of CHAR algorithms is not tied to any specific LLC replacement policy.

Section 2 also discusses how our CHAR proposal seamlessly applies to exclusive LLCs as well. In such designs, we use the dead hints to decide which blocks evicted from the L2 cache can be bypassed and need not be allocated in the exclusive LLC (blocks are allocated and written to an exclusive LLC when they are evicted from the L2 cache). This leads to bandwidth saving in the on-die interconnect and effective capacity allocation in the LLC. Further, we show that simple variants of our CHAR proposal can be used to dynamically decide if a block should be cached in exclusive mode or non-inclusive/non-exclusive mode in the LLC. The former mode optimizes the effective on-die cache capacity, while the latter trades cache capacity for on-die interconnect bandwidth by tolerating controlled amount of duplication of contents between the LLC and the L2 cache.

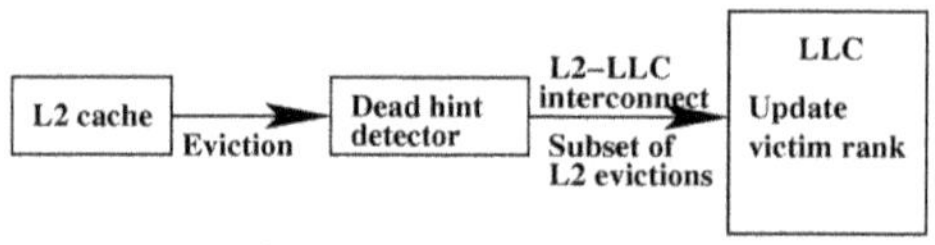

Figure 3: Implementation of CHAR algorithm.

Our execution-driven simulation methodology and results for single-threaded, multi-programmed, and shared memory parallel workloads are discussed in Sections 3 and 4. For inclusive LLCs, CHAR achieves 10.9%, 6.8%, and 11.1% reductions in LLC misses respectively for these workload classes compared to the baseline SRRIP policy. This leads to an average IPC improvement of 3.8% for the single-threaded applications, an average throughput improvement of 3.9% for the multi-programmed workloads, and an average reduction of 4.2% in parallel execution cycles for the shared memory applications. For exclusive LLCs, the best CHAR proposal achieves an average throughput improvement of 3.2% compared to the two-bit TC-AGE baseline (analogue of SRRIP for exclusive LLC) [5] while saving 66.6% data write transactions from the L2 cache to the on-die interconnect for the multi-programmed workloads.

1.1 Related Work

A large body of research work exists in the domain of replacement policies for inclusive LLCs. However, almost all of these consider the LLC in isolation and design the algorithms based on information available locally at the LLC. Only a few published studies explore hierarchy-aware (sometimes called global) replacement policies for inclusive LLCs. The first such study explored a number of global replacement policies where different types of access hints from the inner-level are sent to the LLC [26]. It showed that the advantage of such global schemes is limited to specific scenarios. A subsequent study further analyzes the limited utility of access hint-based global replacement schemes using a reuse distance argument [4].

A recent work shows that inner-level access hints can improve performance of an inclusive LLC significantly for a selected set of multi-programmed workloads if the on-die interconnect bandwidth is not a constraint [7]. This study also proposes two techniques, namely, early core invalidation (ECI) and query-based selection (QBS) to infer the temporal locality of inner-level accesses without sending access hints to the LLC. At the time of an LLC eviction, ECI invalidates the next LLC victim block from the L1 and L2 caches so that the LLC can observe any short-term temporal locality of this block before it is evicted from the LLC. QBS probes the L1 and L2 caches when an eviction decision is taken in the LLC to infer the usefulness of the current LLC victim and accordingly modifies the selection of LLC victims. In all the inclusive LLC configurations used in this paper, we keep the inclusion overhead low by maintaining an 8:1 capacity ratio between the LLC and the L2 cache [7], thereby eliminating most of the negative effects of inclusion victims. A recent work [27] explores an orthogonal dimension of the problem by proposing global cache management schemes to decide which level of the hierarchy in a two-level cache an incoming block should be placed in. Our proposal significantly differs from all these existing proposals. Our policy learns to identify a subset of blocks evicted from the L2 cache that can be made potential victim candidates in the LLC.

Our proposal shares some similarities with the dead block predictors. The existing dead block predictors predict the last access or the last burst of accesses to a block [6, 12, 13, 14, 16, 18]. These predictors usually require partial or full program counters (PC) to construct the necessary correlations with liveness of cache blocks. A recent work constructs a PC-less dead-on-fill predictor for use in cache bypassing by dynamically segmenting the LLC between referenced and not referenced blocks [11]. PC-less light-weight dead block predictors exploiting the fill order of LLC blocks have also been proposed [2]. Our basic CHAR proposal infers the death of an LLC block at the time it is evicted from the L2 cache and does not rely on program counter information. We briefly explore how to extend this basic CHAR design to take into account PC-based correlations.

Our proposal relies on estimation of reuse distance patterns in the L2 cache eviction stream. L2 cache eviction patterns have been used to arrive at bypass decisions and assign insertion ages to the non-bypassed blocks in the context of exclusive L3 caches [5]. LLC insertion and replacement policies based on static and dynamic re-reference interval prediction (SRRIP and DRRIP) have been explored [8]. A recent proposal improves the re-reference interval prediction of RRIP by exploiting LLC fill PC signatures (SHiP-PC), memory region signatures (SHiP-Mem), and instruction trace signatures (SHiP-ISeq) [24]. Another recent work shows how to extend RRIP to manage LLCs shared between CPU workloads and GPGPU workloads in a CPU-GPU heterogeneous environment [17]. Further, the PACMan family of policies is shown to outperform the RRIP policy in the presence of hardware prefetching by judicious design of RRPV insertion and update algorithms for prefetch fills and prefetch hits [25]. Prediction of reuse distances or next-use distances by correlating with program counters has also been studied [10, 19].

A recent proposal explores a set dueling-based solution to deliver performance close to an exclusive LLC while saving on-die interconnect bandwidth by dynamically switching the entire LLC between non-inclusive/non-exclusive and exclusive modes based on the outcome of the duel [23]. We show that our best CHAR proposal for exclusive LLC can dynamically decide the caching modes of different classes of blocks in the LLC at a fine grain.

2. CHAR ALGORITHMS

This section details our proposal on cache hierarchy-aware replacement (CHAR). The high-level flow diagram of CHAR is shown in Figure 3. Section 2.1 presents the design of the dead hint detector that identifies dead blocks in the L2 cache eviction stream in the context of an inclusive LLC. Section 2.2 explores the relationship of this design with PC-based dead block predictors. In Section 2.3, we discuss how the same dead hint detector design can be used in the context of an exclusive LLC.

2.1 Dead Hint Detector

The dead hint detector relies on the reuse behavior experienced by the blocks residing in the L2 cache to decide whether a block is likely to be recalled in future from the LLC after it is evicted from the L2 cache. To better learn a summary of this reuse behavior, we classify an L2 cache block (data block only) into one of five categories at the time of its eviction from the L2 cache. Such a classification is expected to separate the blocks with different liveness/death patterns.

2.1.1 Classification of L2 Cache Blocks

The classification of the L2 cache blocks is based on an approximate estimation of reuse distances inferred from their L2 cache usage patterns. This classification is invoked when a block is evicted from the L2 cache. The following four attributes ($A_0, \ldots, A_3$) are used to classify an L2 cache block.

- (A_0) The type of the request that filled the block in the L2 cache (prefetch or demand).
- (A_1) The request that filled the block in the L2 cache was a hit or a miss in the LLC.
- (A_2) Number of demand uses (including the fill if it was a demand fill) enjoyed by the block during its residency in the L2 cache.
- (A_3) The L2 state of the block when it is evicted from the L2 cache.

Table 1 summarizes the class definitions, while Figure 4 shows how a block can transition from one class membership to another during its residency in the L2 cache. For example, a block belongs to C_0 if a) it is filled into the L2 cache by a prefetch request that misses in the LLC, b) it fails to experience any demand hit during its residency in the L2 cache, and c) it is evicted from the L2 cache in a clean state (E or S in a MESI protocol). On the other hand, a block is categorized as a C_2 block if a) it is filled into the L2 cache by a prefetch or a demand request that misses in the LLC, b) it enjoys exactly one demand use during its residency in the L2 cache (if it was filled by a demand request, it does not experience any demand hit), and c) it is evicted from the L2 cache in modified state.

Table 1: L2 cache block classification

Class	A_0	A_1	A_2	A_3
C_0	Prefetch	Miss	0	E/S
C_1	X	Miss	1	E/S
C_2	X	Miss	1	M
C_3	X	Miss	≥ 2	X
C_4	X	Hit	X	X

The C_0 class is relevant only if a hardware prefetcher is turned on and this class separates the potential premature or incorrect prefetches from rest of the blocks.[3] The remaining four classes separate the L2 cache blocks into different reuse distance bins. Beyond the L1 cache hits, a C_1 block is expected to have most of its natural reuse distances bigger than the reach of the L2 cache, since it fails to experience any demand hits while residing in the L2 cache. The C_2 blocks are

[3] In our simulation model, the prefetched blocks are brought into the LLC and the L2 cache, but not into the L1 cache.

similar to the C_1 blocks, except that the former class is modified and the latter is clean. We find that in several applications, separation of C_1 blocks from the C_2 blocks improves the identification of dead blocks in the L2 cache eviction stream. The C_3 blocks are likely to have a reuse cluster falling within the reach of the L2 cache. Finally, the C_4 blocks are likely to have a reuse cluster within the LLC reach.

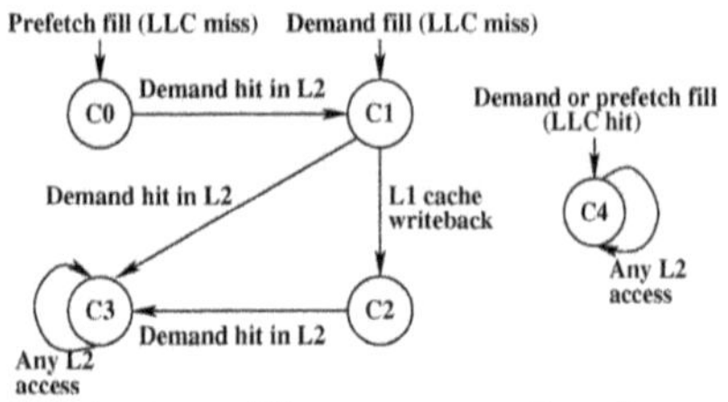

Figure 4: State transitions among the classes of the L2 cache blocks.

Our classification of the L2 cache blocks is inspired by the classification based on trip count and use count of cache blocks presented in an earlier study in the context of a cache hierarchy with an exclusive LLC [5]. According to the terminology used in that study, the set $C_0 \cup C_1 \cup C_2 \cup C_3$ contains the zero trip count blocks i.e., the blocks that are filled in the L2 cache for the first time during their residency in the hierarchy. The C_4 blocks have positive trip counts because they are recalled at least once from the LLC. As a result, C_4 is a subset of $C_0 \cup C_1 \cup C_2 \cup C_3$.

Table 2 shows how our five classes of cache blocks can be encoded in the L2 cache with just two extra state bits (S_1, S_0) per L2 cache block (as opposed to three bits per L2 cache block in [5]). Figure 4, through the class transitions, unambiguously defines the state transitions of these two bits on hits and writebacks to L2 cache blocks.[4]

Table 2: Class encoding in the L2 cache

State M	State S_1	State S_0	Class
X	0	0	C_0
0	0	1	C_1
1	0	1	C_2
X	1	0	C_3
X	1	1	C_4

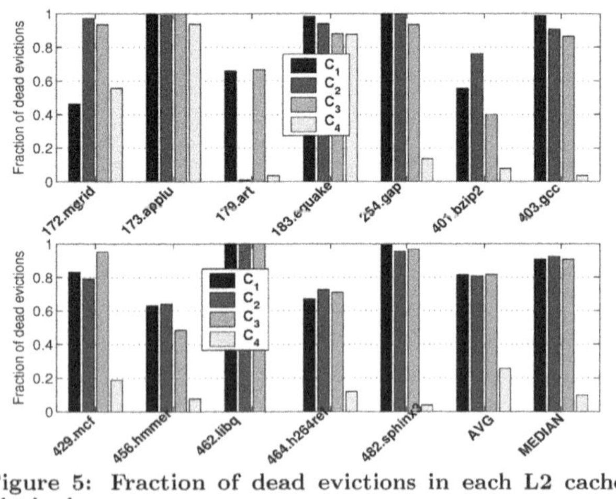

Figure 5: Fraction of dead evictions in each L2 cache block class.

Figure 5 quantifies the benefit of implementing the aforementioned classification of the L2 cache blocks. It shows the fraction of dead L2 cache evictions in each class for the non-prefetched baseline configuration on the single-threaded applications (32 KB 8-way LRU L1 caches, 256 KB 8-way LRU L2 cache, 2 MB 16-way SRRIP LLC). Naturally, the C_0 class is non-existent in non-prefetched executions. Overall, the C_1, C_2, and C_3 classes have very high fractions of dead blocks, while the C_4 blocks are mostly live (see the average and median groups of bars). By looking at the average or median data, one may be tempted to merge the C_1, C_2, and C_3 classes, given that they behave similarly. However, since C_4 is a subset of $C_1 \cup C_2 \cup C_3$, it is necessary to use a finer-grain partitioning of the set $C_1 \cup C_2 \cup C_3$ to identify the blocks that eventually get promoted to C_4. Also, there are applications where the C_1, C_2, and C_3 classes behave very differently. For example, in 172.mgrid, the likelihood of finding a dead block in C_1 evictions is below 0.5. The same is applicable to the C_3 evictions of 401.bzip2. On the other hand, the C_2 evictions coming out of the L2 cache in 179.art are primarily live. As a result, it is necessary to dynamically learn the reuse probability (same as live fraction) of each class of blocks evicted from the L2 cache and based on these probabilities we need to classify a block evicted from the L2 cache as dead or live. To save hardware resources necessary for this learning, our dead hint detector statically classifies all C_4 evictions as live because dead blocks are usually a minority in the C_4 class. The learning algorithm for the remaining four classes ($C_0, \ldots, C_3$) is presented next.

2.1.2 Learning Dead Evictions

The goal of the learning algorithm is to estimate the reuse probabilities of the L2 cache block classes. If the estimated probability of a class falls below an appropriate threshold, the blocks belonging to that class are identified as dead when they are evicted from the L2 cache and this hint is propagated to the LLC. To effectively learn these probabilities, each class C_k ($k \in \{0, 1, 2, 3\}$) maintains two saturating counters, namely, the eviction counter (E_k) and the live counter (L_k). An eviction counter E_4 is also maintained for class C_4. All these counters reside in the L2 cache controller. Further, sixteen LLC sample sets per 1024 LLC sets are dedicated for learning E_k and L_k. These LLC sample sets always execute the baseline SRRIP replacement policy. The L2 cache controller is made aware of the hash function for determining if an L2 cache fill or eviction address maps to an LLC sample set. E_k keeps track of the number of L2 cache evictions belonging to class C_k and mapping to the LLC sample sets. L_k keeps track of which of these E_k evictions are recalled from the LLC (these are the live evictions). The total number of L2 cache evictions mapping to the LLC sample sets is maintained in a saturating counter N_E residing in the L2 cache controller.

Tables 3 and 4 show the actions of the L2 cache controller on an eviction and a fill, respectively. These actions are in addition to the usual ones such as sending a writeback to the LLC on evicting a dirty block from the L2 cache, etc.. The L2 cache eviction actions depend on whether the evicted address maps to an LLC sample set and the class of the evicted block. The L2 cache fill actions depend on whether the filled address maps to an LLC sample set and two attributes of the fill e.g., fill type (demand/prefetch) and hit/miss in the LLC. When a block mapping to one of the LLC sample sets is evicted from the L2 cache, its class id (k) and address (A) are sent to the LLC. The LLC stores the class id with the block. This storage is needed only for the sample sets in the LLC. The LLC, on a hit to a block in one of the sample sets, sends two pieces of additional information along with the fill message: the last stored class id (k) of the block and one bit signifying a hit in the LLC. This value of k is used to update L_k, as shown in the first and third rows of Table 4.

From Tables 3 and 4, we conclude that the estimated reuse probability of class C_k is L_k/E_k, which is the collective hit

[4] In our model, a block is filled into the L2 cache in either S or E state and it can transition to M state only if the L1 data cache writes the block back to the L2 cache.

Table 3: L2 cache block eviction flow (address A)

Class	Maps to LLC sample set	Does not map to LLC sample set
$C_k, k \in \{0,1,2,3\}$	E_k++, N_E++, send A and k to LLC	Invoke dead block detection algorithm
$C_k, k = 4$	E_4++, N_E++, send A and k to LLC	—

Table 4: L2 cache block fill flow (last class id k, if hit in LLC sample set)

Fill attribute	Maps to LLC sample set	Does not map to LLC sample set
Demand hit in LLC	L_k++ if $k \neq 4$, fill in L2 cache as C_4	Fill in L2 cache as C_4
Demand miss in LLC	Fill in L2 cache as C_1	Fill in L2 cache as C_1
Prefetch hit in LLC	L_k++ if $k \notin \{0,4\}$, fill in L2 cache as C_4	Fill in L2 cache as C_4
Prefetch miss in LLC	Fill in L2 cache as C_0	Fill in L2 cache as C_0

rate of the blocks belonging to class C_k, as learned from the LLC sample sets executing the baseline SRRIP policy. Notice, however, that a prefetch fill in the L2 cache does not update the live counter of C_0, even if the filled block hits in an LLC sample set (third row of Table 4). This is because such a block was filled into the L2 cache last time by a prefetch request and got evicted as a C_0 block without experiencing a demand hit. If this block is again prefetched into the L2 cache, we speculate that this is likely to be a premature or incorrect prefetch and do not update the live counter of C_0.

Finally, we present our dead block detection algorithm. This algorithm dynamically estimates an appropriate threshold t such that if $L_k/E_k < t$ or equivalently $L_k < tE_k$, we identify a block belonging to class C_k as dead when it is evicted from the L2 cache. One reasonable choice for t at any point in time during execution would be the baseline hit rate of the LLC. Such a dynamic choice would guarantee that if any class of blocks has hit rate lower than the current baseline LLC hit rate, the blocks in that class would be marked dead as and when they are evicted from the L2 cache. This algorithm would evict the less useful blocks from the LLC early and create more space in the LLC for the blocks that are contributing more heavily toward LLC hit rate. A highly accurate online estimate of the baseline LLC hit rate is E_4/N_E because E_4 approximates the number of LLC hits to the sampled sets and N_E approximates the total number of LLC accesses to the sampled sets.

To simplify the hardware, we approximate the E_4/N_E ratio such that t turns out to be a reciprocal of power of two. Therefore, we can synthesize $L_k < tE_k$ using a shifter and a comparator. The approximation is done by dividing the possible values of E_4 into four ranges, namely, $[0, N_E/8]$, $(N_E/8, N_E/4]$, $(N_E/4, N_E/2]$, and $(N_E/2, N_E]$. On each L2 cache eviction, we first determine the range the current value of E_4 falls in. If it falls in the lowermost range i.e., $[0, N_E/8]$, we approximate it to half of the upper bound of the range. If it falls in any of the remaining ranges, we approximate it to the lower bound of the range, which is also half of the upper bound of the range. Finally, we determine t as $\tilde{E}_4/N_E$ where $\tilde{E}_4$ is the approximate value of E_4. This leads to the following definition of t.

$$t = \begin{cases} 1/16 & \text{if } E_4 \leq N_E/8 \\ 1/8 & \text{if } N_E/8 < E_4 \leq N_E/4 \\ 1/4 & \text{if } N_E/4 < E_4 \leq N_E/2 \\ 1/2 & \text{if } E_4 > N_E/2 \end{cases} \quad (1)$$

The computation of t may require further tuning. For certain workload classes, $t = 1/2$ may turn out to be very aggressive. In such situations, we recommend merging the last two ranges in Equation (1) i.e., $t = 1/4$ if $E_4 > N_E/4$. Similarly, the last three ranges can be merged, if necessary. Also, a carefully chosen static value of t can offer reasonably good performance. A static value of 1/8 achieves excellent performance for our selection of workloads. In this study, we present results assuming Equation (1) for computing t dynamically.

2.1.3 Few Implementation Details

The L2 cache, on evicting a data block, first queries the L1 data cache. If the query hits in the L1 data cache, the L1 data cache retains the block (our L2 cache is non-inclusive/non-exclusive of the L1 caches). Only those L2 cache data evictions that do not hit in the L1 data cache are passed on to the dead hint detector. The dead hint detector receives the address and the class of each such L2 cache eviction. It decides if the block is dead in the LLC by determining the current value of t and applying the dead hint detection algorithm (only for blocks not mapping to LLC sample sets). If the block is identified as dead, its address is sent to the LLC in a special dead hint message. The LLC, on receiving a dead hint message, sets the RRPV of the block to three. It also clears the bit position corresponding to the evicting core in the coherence bitvector of the block, since neither L1 cache nor L2 cache of the evicting core has the block. This saves a future back-invalidation message.[5] If the LLC receives an eviction message from the L2 cache for a block mapping to one of its sample sets, it stores the class id of the block found in the eviction message.

The combined hardware overhead of our CHAR proposal involves two extra state bits per L2 cache block, ten counters in the L2 cache controller ($L_0, \ldots, L_3$, E_0, ..., E_4, and N_E), negligible logic overhead to implement the additional actions in the L2 cache controller on eviction and fill (Tables 3 and 4), the logic of the dead hint detector in the L2 cache controller, three extra bits per LLC block for the sample sets to store class id, and handling of dead hints to non-sampled sets and eviction messages to sampled sets in the LLC. Note that our proposal does not involve any dynamic dueling between CHAR and baseline SRRIP policies, even though we use a small number of sampled sets in the LLC to dynamically learn the reuse behavior of the SRRIP policy. The L_k, E_k, and N_E counters are halved periodically whenever the total number of L2 cache evictions mapping to the LLC sampled sets reaches a value of 127. We also experimented with halving intervals of 255, 1023, and 2047, but did not see any significant swing in performance. With a halving interval of 127, we need eight bits for each of the ten counters and seven bits for the counter that keeps track of the halving interval.

The CHAR algorithms seamlessly apply to multi-core scenarios without any change, since each core would have its own CHAR hardware attached to its private L2 cache controller. The sample sets in the shared LLC would be shared by all the threads.

For shared memory programs, we do not apply CHAR to the shared blocks, since the current proposal does not have the global view necessary to detect the death of shared blocks. We rely on the inclusive LLC for detecting the read-shared and read/write-shared blocks. When a request from a core

[5] We simulate a bitvector-based directory coherence protocol. The L1 and L2 caches are private to each core and the LLC is shared. Each LLC tag is extended to maintain the coherence states and sharing bitvector in the inclusive LLC design.

hits in the LLC and the requested block is currently shared by another core (as indicated by the sharing bitvector directory), the LLC marks this block shared using an additional state bit per LLC block. Once marked, this bit remains set until the block is evicted from the LLC. Dead hints received for the blocks with this bit set are ignored by the LLC. Also, as soon as a block mapping to the LLC sample sets is identified as shared, it is upgraded to class C_4 in the LLC so that it does not update the L_k counters of any of the sharing cores. This policy will be referred to as CHAR-S.

2.1.4 Controlling Dead Hint Rate

Our dead hint generation algorithm tries to victimize the blocks belonging to the classes that have collective hit rates lower than the baseline LLC hit rate. However, there are situations where the overall baseline hit rate is reasonably high, but some of the classes are undergoing a phase transition and have low hit rates. The blocks belonging to these classes will be reused in near-future if we can retain them. CHAR cannot infer this by looking at the current hit rates of these classes and can hurt performance by sending premature dead hints to the LLC. The SPEC 2000 application 172.mgrid exhibits a few such phases. To address this problem, we incorporate a dead hint rate divider D with each core's L2 cache controller that sends out every D^{th} dead hint to the LLC. The value of D is always a power of two, and ranges between one and 256, inclusive. In all simulations, we initialize D to one. In the following, we discuss how D is adjusted dynamically.

We ear-mark sixteen LLC sample sets (different from the sixteen baseline samples) per 1024 LLC sets to monitor the relative number of hits experienced by CHAR compared to the baseline samples. This is done using a saturating counter residing in the L2 cache controller. The counter is initialized to the midpoint M of the range of the counter e.g., M is 2^{n-1} for an n-bit counter. The counter is incremented whenever the L2 cache receives a fill that hits in one of the CHAR sample sets of the LLC. The counter is decremented whenever the L2 cache receives a fill that hits in one of the baseline sample sets of the LLC.

After every eight halving intervals, we check the status of this counter. If the counter value is at least $M+T_{gb}$, we halve D to double the dead hint rate because CHAR is performing better than the baseline. Note, however, that the minimum value of D is one. If the counter value is less than or equal to $M-T'_{gb}$, we quadruple D provided the LLC hit rate is at least 3/8 i.e., E_4 is at least $N_E/4+N_E/8$; otherwise, D is left unchanged. The rationale is that we do not decrease the dead hint rate if the baseline LLC hit rate is anyway small. Note that this particular hit rate threshold (i.e., 3/8) may require tuning depending on the workload set under consideration. The guard-band thresholds, T_{gb} and T'_{gb}, are used to avoid potentially spurious adjustments in D and are set to 8 and 32 in this study. The dead hint rate division algorithm is conservative in the sense that it increases D much faster (though with a bigger guard-band) than it decreases D so that the performance penalty is low in the phases where CHAR becomes too aggressive. In multi-core configurations, the CHAR sample sets in the shared LLC are shared by all the threads and each private L2 cache controller maintains its own dead hint rate divider. To implement this algorithm, we use a 16-bit saturating counter for relative hit count monitoring (i.e., M is set to 2^{15}) and a 9-bit dead hint rate divider.

2.2 Code Space Correlation and CHAR-PC

Past research on dead block predictors has established a strong correlation between program counters (PCs) of the load/store instructions and the death patterns of the data blocks, as already discussed in Section 1.1. Figure 6 explores the relationship between the program counters of the instructions that bring the blocks of different classes into the L2 cache in the baseline configuration (32 KB 8-way LRU L1 caches, 256 KB 8-way LRU L2 cache, and 2 MB 16-way SRRIP LLC) for the single-threaded programs with the hardware prefetcher disabled. We focus only on the classes C_1, C_2, and C_3 that can source dead hints in a non-prefetched execution. Let PC_k be the set of program counters that cause the blocks, which eventually get classified as C_k blocks, to be filled into the L2 cache. Figure 6 shows $|PC_k \cap PC_{k'}|$ as a fraction of $|PC_k \cup PC_{k'}|$ for all ordered pairs (k, k') with $k, k' \in \{1, 2, 3\}$. It is very encouraging to find that the load/store instructions that bring C_1 blocks into the L2 cache overlap very little with those that bring C_2 and C_3 blocks (see the average and median groups). The implication is that our PC-less classification of L2 cache blocks can effectively capture differing code space signatures for the pairs (C_1, C_2) and (C_1, C_3). However, the classes C_2 and C_3 share a sizable proportion of program counters. Further examination of this behavior revealed that the blocks that are written to and do not belong to C_4 are consumed in either near-future (C_3) or far-future (C_2). The dirty C_4 blocks have reuses in intermediate-future such that the reuse distance is within the LLC reach. Therefore, we conclude that our classification can successfully partition the dirty cache blocks based on their next use distance, which the code signature fails to do.

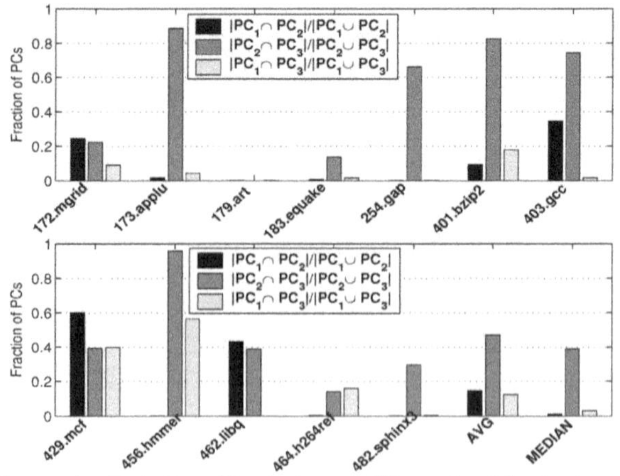

Figure 6: Relationship between L2 cache block classes and code space.

While our classification correlates well with code space signatures, further improvements may be possible if we can split a class of blocks based on L2 cache fill PCs. For example, suppose the set PC_1 has two program counters, say, PC_{11} and PC_{12}. The blocks filled into the L2 cache by the instruction at PC_{11} may behave differently from those filled by the instruction at PC_{12}. Clustering these both types of blocks into a single class would lower the overall prediction accuracy. To resolve this issue, we propose CHAR-PC, a PC-based extension to CHAR. CHAR-PC maintains, for each class C_k with $k \in \{1, 2, 3\}$, an eight-entry fully associative table T_k for storing the lower 14 bits of the PCs (after removing the lowest two bits) of the instructions that bring the C_k blocks into the L2 cache. Each entry of T_k has a valid bit, a 14-bit fill PC signature, and a three-bit saturating counter.

When a block is filled into the L2 cache, the 14-bit fill PC signature is stored with the L2 cache block. When a block mapping to an LLC sample set is evicted from the L2 cache, its class C_k is determined and T_k is looked up with its PC signature. If the signature is not found in T_k, an entry is allocated by invoking the not-recently-used (NRU) replacement policy and the saturating counter for that entry is initialized to zero. If the entry is found in T_k, the saturating counter for that entry is decremented by one. The fill PC signature and the class id of the evicted block are sent to the LLC. The LLC stores these along with the blocks mapping to the sample sets. When a block mapping to an LLC sample set is filled into the L2 cache as a result of an LLC hit, the last class id (k) and the last fill PC signature of the block are supplied by the LLC. At this point, T_k is looked up with the last fill PC signature and if the entry is found, its saturating counter is incremented by one.

Finally, the dead block prediction takes place when a block not mapping to an LLC sample set and belonging to C_k with $k \in \{1, 2, 3\}$ is evicted from the L2 cache. T_k is looked up with the fill PC signature of the block. If the entry is found and the saturating counter has a value zero, the block is predicted dead and a dead hint is propagated to the LLC. The signature length, the saturating counter size, and the prediction threshold of zero have been borrowed from the SHiP-PC proposal [24]. In Section 4, we show that CHAR-PC, which exploits the cross product of our classification and L2 cache fill PC signature, improves performance beyond SHiP-PC.

2.3 Application to Exclusive LLC

A block is allocated in an exclusive LLC when it is evicted from the L2 cache and it is de-allocated from the LLC on a subsequent hit or replacement. Since every L2 cache eviction (clean or dirty) must be sent to the LLC for allocation, an exclusive LLC design consumes much bigger on-die interconnect bandwidth compared to an inclusive LLC design. However, the dead hints of the CHAR algorithm can be used to identify the blocks that can be dropped by the L2 cache and need not be sent to the LLC for allocation. This is known as selective cache bypassing. In the following, we discuss the working of the CHAR algorithm in an exclusive LLC. Our baseline exclusive LLC allocates all L2 cache evictions and decides the insertion age of a block based on the two-bit TC-AGE policy [5]. This policy is the analogue of SRRIP for exclusive LLCs. It inserts all C_0, C_1, C_2, and C_3 blocks at age two and the C_4 blocks at age zero. Note that a block is in C_4 class if and only if it has experienced at least one LLC hit. The LLC replacement policy is same as the inclusive SR-RIP replacement policy (i.e., it victimizes a block with age three).[6]

In CHAR algorithm for exclusive LLC, every L2 cache eviction address is first sent to the LLC to update the coherence directory (the data is not sent at this point). The dead hint (one bit) for the block is sent to the LLC along with this message. If the block is not marked dead, the LLC requests the block from the L2 cache for allocation. If the block is marked dead, but there is an invalid way available in the target LLC set, a request for the block is sent by the LLC to the L2 cache. However, in this case, the block is filled at age three in the LLC. If the block is marked dead and there is no invalid way available in the target LLC set, the LLC sends a bypass command to the L2 cache. If the L2 cache receives a bypass command for a dirty block, it sends the block directly to the memory controller over the interconnect. On the other hand, if it receives a bypass command for a clean block, it drops the block and eliminates the data transaction. In summary, the CHAR algorithm allocates all live blocks in the LLC with an insertion age dictated by the TC-AGE policy. It also allocates a dead block at the highest possible age provided an invalid way is available in the target LLC set. All other dead blocks are either dropped (if clean) or sent to the memory controller (if dirty) by the L2 cache.

Since the CHAR algorithm classifies the C_4 blocks as live, these blocks are always allocated in the LLC. A block moves to the C_4 class as soon as it experiences a hit in the LLC and it remains in the C_4 class during its residency in the cache hierarchy. As a result, a C_4 block may get repeatedly allocated in and de-allocated from the LLC on its every trip between the L2 cache and the LLC. This leads to unnecessary wastage of on-die interconnect bandwidth.

[6] We use the term "age" instead of "RRPV" in this discussion to conform to the terminology used in the prior work on exclusive LLC management [5]. Age can be considered synonymous to RRPV in this discussion.

We address this inefficiency by observing that a block allocated in the LLC should not be de-allocated on a hit because it is a live block and will have to be allocated again when it is evicted from the L2 cache. In other words, live blocks should be cached in non-inclusive/non-exclusive mode to save on-die interconnect bandwidth. However, if a C_4 block is evicted from the LLC by the time it is evicted from the L2 cache, it must be re-allocated in the LLC at age zero so that the live blocks are retained in the cache hierarchy. Also, if such a block is evicted in the dirty state from the L2 cache, it must be sent to the LLC to update the LLC copy. In all other cases, the L2 cache can drop a C_4 block. Finally, the age of a C_4 block in the LLC is changed to zero when it is evicted from the L2 cache so that the block, being live, gets the highest level of protection in the LLC.

We explore three variations of this basic policy that eliminates the unnecessary data transactions involving the C_4 blocks. While these policies do not de-allocate a block from the LLC on a hit, they update the age of the block in the LLC differently at the time of the hit. The first policy, CHAR-C4, leaves the age of the block unchanged at the time of hit. The second policy, CHAR-C4-MAX, updates the age of the block to the maximum possible i.e., three. The third policy, CHAR-C4-MIN, updates the age of the block to the minimum possible i.e., zero. All three policies continue to fill cache blocks from memory directly into the L2 cache and a block is considered for allocation in the LLC only when it is evicted from the L2 cache and the dead hint detector identifies it as live. Among these three policies, CHAR-C4-MIN offers the best protection for C_4 blocks and is expected to have the highest bypass rate (percentage of blocks dropped by the L2 cache) because it reduces the chance of a C_4 block getting evicted from the LLC before it is evicted from the L2 cache. On the other hand, CHAR-C4-MAX is expected to have a bypass rate that is higher than CHAR but lower than CHAR-C4 and CHAR-C4-MIN. Since all these three policies reduce the effective on-die cache capacity, their relative performance depends on the sensitivity of the workloads toward cache capacity and on-die interconnect bandwidth.

3. EVALUATION METHODOLOGY

We carry out our execution-driven simulations on a MIPS ISA simulator. We model an out-of-order issue core running at 4 GHz with 4-wide front-end and 8-wide commit. The core model has an 18-stage pipeline with 128-entry re-order buffer, 160-entry integer and floating-point register files, and a hybrid branch predictor similar to the Alpha 21264 tournament predictor. The front-end of the core has a 256-set 4-way branch target buffer, a 32-entry return address stack, and a 32-entry branch stack allowing 32 in-flight branch instructions. The issue unit of the core has a 32-entry integer queue, a 32-entry floating-point queue, and a 64-entry load/store queue. The execution unit of each core is equipped with six integer ALUs, three FPUs, and two load/store units.

Each core has private L1 and L2 caches. The L1 instruction and data caches are 32 KB 8-way with LRU replacement policy. In the inclusive LLC model, the capacity ratio between the LLC and the L2 cache is maintained at 8:1 in all our configurations to keep the inclusion overhead low [7]. Our single-threaded applications are simulated on a 256 KB 8-way L2 cache with LRU replacement policy and a 2 MB 16-way LLC. The 4-way multi-programmed workloads are simulated on a 4-core model with each core having a 256 KB 8-way private L2 cache. The LLC is 8 MB 16-way and shared among all the cores. The 8-way threaded shared memory programs are simulated on an 8-core model with each core having a 128 KB 8-way private L2 cache. The LLC is 8 MB 16-way and shared among all the cores. In all the multi-core configurations, the LLC banks and the cores sit on a bidirectional ring that has a single-cycle hop time. Each hop has a core and an LLC bank. The L2 cache of a core connects to the router in each ring hop through a 32-entry outgoing message queue. The LLC in the single-threaded and multi-programmed models has banks of size 2 MB with access latency of eight cycles (tag+data). The model used to evaluate the shared memory programs has 1 MB LLC banks with seven-cycle access latency (tag+data). Each LLC bank can keep track of 16 outstanding misses. All the levels in the cache hierarchy have 64-byte block size.

Table 5: Storage overhead of CHAR

States	ST	Mprog	Shm
States in L2C	8192 bits	32768 bits	32768 bits
Counters in L2C	112 bits	448 bits	896 bits
LLC samples	1536 bits	6144 bits	6144 bits
TOTAL	1.20 KB	4.80 KB	4.86 KB

Table 5 summarizes the extra storage overhead of CHAR (as discussed in Sections 2.1.3 and 2.1.4) for the three cache configurations used to evaluate single-threaded (ST), multi-programmed (Mprog), and shared memory (Shm) workloads. It is clear that this overhead is a small percentage (less than 0.1%) of the total storage devoted to the cache hierarchy. The CHAR-S implementation would need one extra shared bit per LLC block in the Shm configuration. This would increase the overhead of the Shm configuration to 20.86 KB, which is still less than 0.3% of the LLC capacity.

We model an aggressive memory system with four single-channel memory controllers clocked at 2 GHz with a round robin mapping of consecutive cache blocks on the controllers. Each controller implements the FR-FCFS scheduling policy and connects to an 8-way banked DDR3-1600 DIMM. The 800 MHz DRAM part has 64-bit burst length and 9-9-9-27 (tCAS-tRCD-tRP-tRAS) access cycle parameters.

We model per-core multi-stream stride prefetchers that keep track of sixteen simultaneous streams and prefetch into the LLC and the L2 cache. The prefetcher attached to the L2 cache injects a prefetch request on an L2 cache miss as well as on a demand hit to a prefetched L2 cache block.

The exclusive LLC model uses the same configuration as the inclusive LLC model. Since there is no inclusion overhead in exclusive LLC models, the per-core private L2 cache capacity is increased to 512 KB (with a corresponding increase in access latency) to improve baseline performance.

Table 6: Baseline inclusive LLC MPKI

mgrid	applu	art	equake	gap	bzip2
2.92	4.62	6.51	13.93	3.60	1.18
gcc	mcf	hmmer	libq	h264ref	sphinx3
5.35	28.84	0.34	11.38	0.31	7.43

We select twelve single-threaded applications (shown in Figure 1) from SPEC 2000 and SPEC 2006 suites. The selected twelve applications represent a fair distribution of LLC miss savings achievable by Belady's optimal algorithm. The savings range from 1.1% in gap to 55.9% in sphinx3 (see Figure 1). The applications also represent a wide range of LLC misses per kilo instructions (MPKI) for the baseline SRRIP policy, as shown in Table 6. We simulate one billion dynamic instructions chosen using the SimPoint toolset [22] from each application executed on the ref input set.

The single-threaded applications are mixed to prepare one hundred 4-way heterogeneous multi-programmed workloads. In each workload, each thread is executed for 500 million representative dynamic instructions. If a thread finishes executing its set of instructions early, it continues to run beyond that point so that the LLC contention can be modeled correctly. However, performance is reported based on the first 500 million instructions retired by each thread.

We pick six shared memory kernels and applications for preliminary evaluation in this paper. These are FFT (256K complex double points), Radix-sort (4M points, radix 32), and Ocean (514×514 grid) from SPLASH-2, Art (MinneSPEC input [15]) and Equake (MinneSPEC input, ARCHduration 0.5) from SPEC OMP, and FFTW (4096×16×16 complex double points) [3]. All the applications are executed in entirety on eight cores (one thread per core).

4. SIMULATION RESULTS

We present the results for the single-threaded applications on the inclusive LLC model first with the hardware prefetcher disabled to understand how each application performs in isolation. Next we discuss the multi-core results for heterogeneous workload mixes as well as shared memory applications with and without the hardware prefetcher enabled. We conclude this section with a discussion of the results for the exclusive LLC model with the hardware prefetcher enabled.

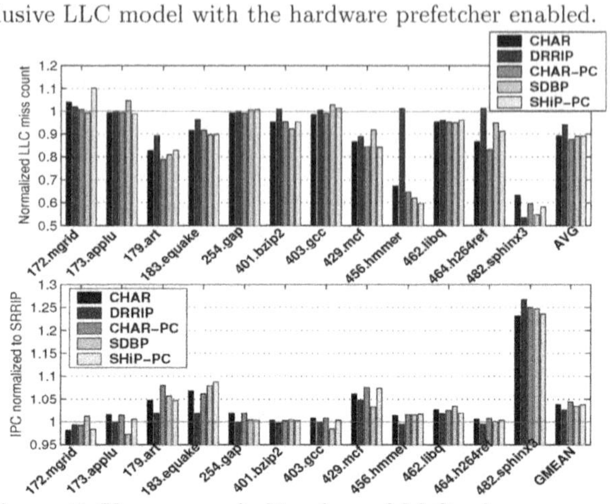

Figure 7: Upper panel: Number of LLC misses normalized to SRRIP. Lower panel: IPC normalized to SRRIP.

4.1 Inclusive LLC Model

In the following, we discuss the performance of CHAR on the inclusive LLC model.

4.1.1 Single-threaded Applications

Figure 7 compares the performance of CHAR, DRRIP [8], CHAR-PC, SDBP [12], and SHiP-PC [24]. The last three policies require the program counter of the load/store instructions. SDBP is the state-of-the-art dead block prediction technique that correlates death of a cache block with the last-touch PC of the block. We do not exercise the LLC bypass component of SDBP so that strict inclusion is maintained between the LLC and the L2 cache. SHiP-PC is the state-of-the-art PC-correlated LLC insertion policy that improves the re-reference interval prediction of SRRIP and DRRIP. The upper panel of Figure 7 compares the policies in terms of the number of LLC misses (lower is better) normalized to SRRIP, while the lower panel shows normalized IPC (higher is better). CHAR enjoys noticeable reductions in LLC misses in art, equake, bzip2, mcf, hmmer, libquantum, h264ref, and sphinx3. On average, CHAR reduces the number of LLC misses by 10.9%, while DRRIP exhibits a 5.8% reduction in LLC misses. The reduction in LLC misses achieved by CHAR-PC is 12.4%. Interestingly, CHAR achieves reductions in LLC misses similar to the SDBP and SHiP-PC policies without requiring any program counter information. This further confirms the finding of Section 2.2 that our L2 cache block classification captures the code space signatures quite well. Referring back to Figure 1, we find that CHAR and CHAR-PC still leave significant room for improvement.

As shown in the lower panel of Figure 7, the IPC gains correspond well with the LLC miss reductions. The IPC improvements achieved by CHAR and CHAR-PC are 3.8% and 4.4%, respectively. The corresponding improvements of DRRIP, SDBP, and SHiP-PC are 2.7%, 3.5%, and 3.8%, respectively. Given the small benefit of CHAR-PC in comparison with CHAR and the added complexity of CHAR-PC, we do not pursue CHAR-PC any further.

Table 7: LLC hit distribution

Policy	C_1	C_2	C_3	C_4	Ins.	Total
CHAR	0.11	0.08	0.04	0.76	0.01	1.00
DRRIP	0.07	0.05	0.01	0.75	0.01	0.89
SRRIP	0.09	0.05	0.01	0.52	0.01	0.68
SRRIP-Or	0.26	0.13	0.21	0.78	0.04	1.42
Belady	0.34	0.17	0.14	0.85	0.02	1.52

To further understand the sources of LLC hits in CHAR and DRRIP, Table 7 shows the average distribution of LLC hits normalized to CHAR among the L2 cache block classes and instructions for the non-prefetched execution of the single-threaded applications. To collect this data, every block evicted from the L2 cache is classified as C_1, C_2, C_3, C_4, or instruction and this is also recorded in the LLC. A subsequent LLC hit to such a block belonging to a category increments the hit count of the corresponding category. We show the average of this hit distribution for CHAR, DRRIP, SRRIP, oracle-assisted SRRIP (SRRIP-Or), and Belady's optimal policy normalized to CHAR. The last two rows correspond to the two policies discussed in Figure 1. Compared to SRRIP, both DRRIP and CHAR significantly improve the volume of hits enjoyed by the C_4 blocks (recall that the C_4 blocks are predominantly live). DRRIP achieves this while sacrificing some of the hits in the C_1 class. The RRPV duel of DRRIP inserts *all* blocks in the LLC with RRPV of either two or three during an execution phase. Therefore, it is expected that during the phases dominated by a mix of C_1, C_2, and C_3 blocks, DRRIP would probably insert all blocks with RRPV three, even though inserting some of these with RRPV two could have improved performance. CHAR can enjoy such selectivity because it learns to send dead hints based on the reuse probabilities of different classes of blocks. As a result, it improves the volume of hits across all the four classes. Overall, DRRIP and SRRIP experience 11% and 32% less LLC hits compared to CHAR. The last two rows of Table 7 point out that further characterization of the C_1, C_2, and C_3 classes is necessary to exploit the remaining performance potential.

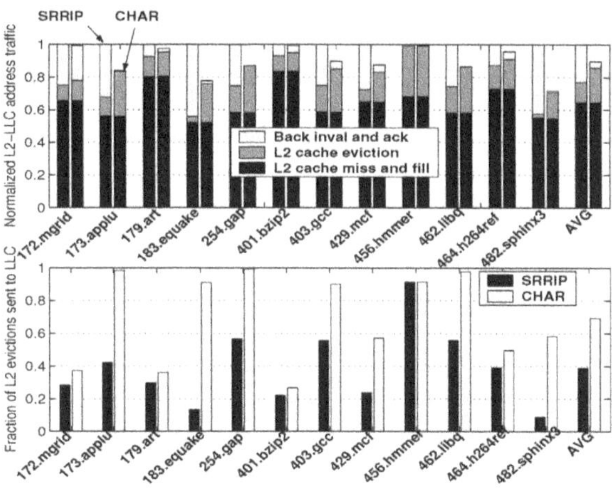

Figure 8: Upper panel: Address traffic in L2-LLC interconnect normalized to SRRIP. Lower panel: L2 cache eviction addresses sent to LLC.

Before closing the discussion on the single-threaded applications, we examine the L2-LLC address traffic in the presence of the dead hints generated by CHAR. We divide the traffic into three parts: a) L2 cache miss requests and the L2 cache fills, b) L2 cache evictions (in SRRIP, these are only the dirty block evictions, while in CHAR, these also include the eviction messages to the LLC sample sets and the dead hints to the non-sample sets), c) back-invalidations and their acknowledgments exchanged at the time of an LLC eviction.

The upper panel of Figure 8 shows the address traffic in the L2-LLC interconnect normalized to SRRIP. Both SRRIP and CHAR have the same volume of traffic due to L2 cache misses and L2 cache fills. Although CHAR increases the L2 cache eviction traffic (as expected), it dramatically reduces the traffic due to back-invalidations. The reduction in back-invalidations in CHAR is observed for two reasons. First, due to less number of LLC misses in CHAR, LLC evictions are less in number leading to a lower volume of back-invalidations. Second, a dead hint message clears the coherence bitvector position of the core sending the dead hint. When such a block is evicted from the LLC, no back-invalidation is generated. On average, CHAR enjoys 10% less address traffic on the L2-LLC interconnect compared to SRRIP. The lower panel of Figure 8 further quantifies the fraction of L2 cache eviction addresses sent to the LLC by SRRIP and CHAR. On average, SRRIP sends 38.9% of all L2 cache evictions to the LLC (these are dirty cache block evictions) and CHAR sends 69.5% of all L2 cache evictions to the LLC. It is important to note that a dead hint is a dataless message and inflates only the address traffic, unlike the dirty block evictions.

4.1.2 *Multi-core Workloads*

For heterogeneous workload mixes, we present three different metrics to summarize the performance and fairness of several policies. Normalized average IPC (or throughput) i.e., $\frac{\sum_i IPC_i^{NEW}}{\sum_i IPC_i^{SRRIP}}$ summarizes the improvement in average throughput of the mix when a policy "NEW" replaces the baseline SRRIP, where IPC_i is the IPC of thread i ($0 \le i \le 3$). We use $min_i \frac{IPC_i^{NEW}}{IPC_i^{SRRIP}}$ as a conservative fairness metric that captures the minimum throughput improvement enjoyed by any thread in a mix. A policy "NEW" is considered at least as fair as the baseline SRRIP policy if this metric is at least 1.0 meaning that no thread has suffered from a slowdown due to introduction of the new policy. Finally, we evaluate the normalized LLC miss count as $\frac{\sum_i M_i^{NEW}}{\sum_i M_i^{SRRIP}}$, where M_i is the number of LLC misses experienced by thread i during the execution of its first 500 million instructions. For shared memory applications, we execute each application completely and compare the policies in terms of the execution time of the parallel computation.

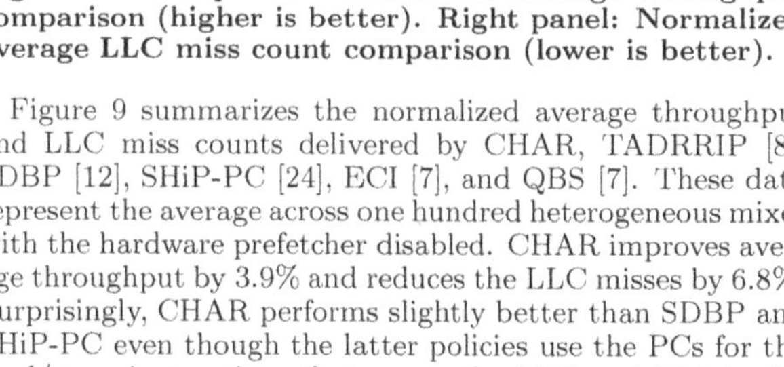

Figure 9: Left panel: Normalized average throughput comparison (higher is better). Right panel: Normalized average LLC miss count comparison (lower is better).

Figure 9 summarizes the normalized average throughput and LLC miss counts delivered by CHAR, TADRRIP [8], SDBP [12], SHiP-PC [24], ECI [7], and QBS [7]. These data represent the average across one hundred heterogeneous mixes with the hardware prefetcher disabled. CHAR improves average throughput by 3.9% and reduces the LLC misses by 6.8%. Surprisingly, CHAR performs slightly better than SDBP and SHiP-PC even though the latter policies use the PCs for the load/store instructions that access the LLC and fill into the LLC, respectively. The SDBP and SHiP-PC policies significantly reduce the LLC miss counts of several non-memory-intensive mixes and as a result, these two policies save more

LLC misses compared to CHAR, but they fail to convert these savings into throughput improvement. These results once again underscore the effectiveness of CHAR in capturing the code space signatures of LLC access patterns. CHAR does not have the complexity of carrying the PC information through the load-store pipeline, the L1 and L2 cache controllers, the on-die interconnect, and the LLC controller. Also, the SDBP and SHiP-PC policies need additional storage to maintain the PC signatures and the predictor tables.

Thread-aware DRRIP (TADRRIP) improves throughput by 3.1% and reduces the LLC miss count by 3.1%, on average. In Section 4.1.1, we have already explained how the fine-grain cache block classification of CHAR helps it enjoy more LLC hits compared to the DRRIP policy.

Finally, for completeness, we discuss the results of ECI and QBS (these policies were discussed in Section 1.1). For our workload mixes and simulated configurations, we do not expect ECI or QBS to deliver noticeable performance improvements. Only 2.5% of the back-invalidations sent at the time of LLC evictions in baseline SRRIP hit in the L1 or the L2 cache. As a result, at the time of an LLC eviction, the block has already been evicted from the core caches with a likelihood of 0.975. Hence, it is impossible for QBS to infer much about the temporal locality of the block by querying the core caches. Overall, QBS improves the average throughput by only 0.23% compared to the baseline SRRIP. For ECI, only 1.5% of early-invalidated blocks are recalled by the cores before they are evicted from the LLC leading to an average throughput improvement of 0.46% compared to the baseline SRRIP. The original study [7] reported that QBS performs better than ECI and we believe that we observe the opposite trend due to selection of different workload mixes.

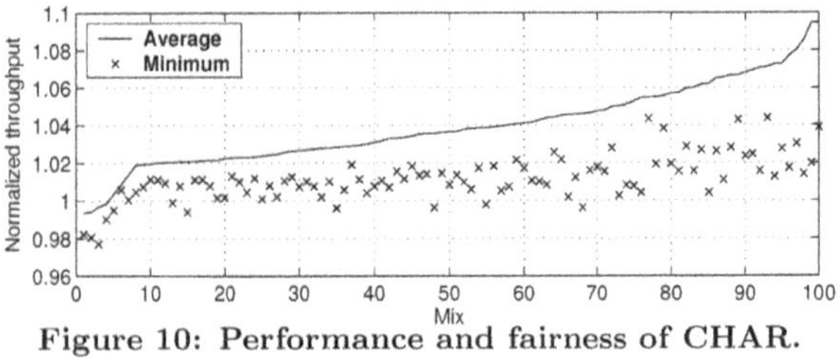

Figure 10: Performance and fairness of CHAR.

Figure 10 shows the details of the normalized average and minimum throughput delivered by CHAR for each of the mixes. The mixes are arranged in the increasing order of throughput improvement. The average throughput profile ranges from a loss of 1.0% to an improvement of 9.5%. The minimum throughput profile also looks very encouraging as only 11 of the 100 mixes have minimum improvement below 1.0. The minimum throughput improvement of any thread ranges from 0.98 to 1.04, averaging at 1.01. Overall, CHAR remains at least as fair as SRRIP while offering a throughput improvement of 3.9% and an LLC miss saving of 6.8%.

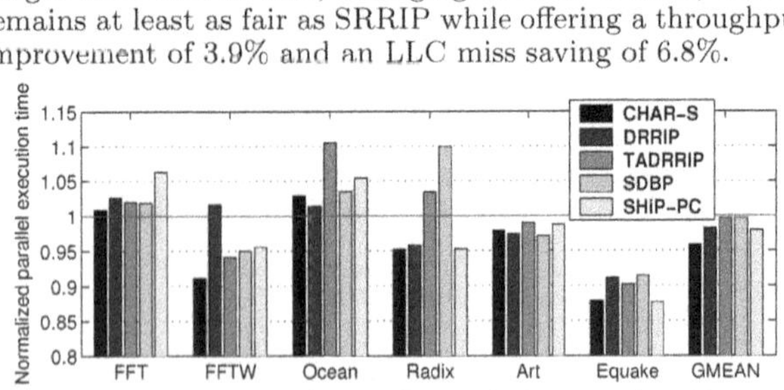

Figure 11: Comparison of parallel execution time.

Figure 11 presents the parallel execution time (lower is better) of CHAR-S, DRRIP, TADRRIP, SDBP, and SHiP-PC normalized to SRRIP for the shared memory applications. CHAR-S achieves noticeable savings in FFTW, Radix-sort, Art, and Equake. On average, it saves 4.2% execution time compared to the baseline. This performance gain comes from an 11.1% reduction in LLC misses. The reductions in execution time achieved by DRRIP, TADRRIP, SDBP, and SHiP-PC are 1.8%, 0.4%, 0.4%, and 2.1%, respectively.

4.1.3 *Interaction with Hardware Prefetching*

All the results presented up to this point pertain to configurations with the hardware prefetcher disabled. In this section, we evaluate the performance of our policy proposal in the presence of a multi-stream hardware prefetcher. This would also validate the efficiency of our algorithm in identifying and managing the blocks belonging to the C_0 class.

Table 8: Comparison between CHAR and PACMan-DYN-Global relative to SRRIP

Metric	CHAR	PACMan-DYN-Global
Throughput improvement	5.3%	2.8%
LLC demand misses saved	15.0%	11.5%
DRAM requests	8.8% less	4.8% more

Prefetching alone improves the average throughput of SRRIP by 20.6% for the hundred heterogeneous mixes. Table 8 further compares CHAR and PACMan-DYN-Global [25] for these mixes in terms of average throughput improvement, the number of LLC demand misses saved, and the total volume of DRAM requests relative to SRRIP with the hardware prefetcher enabled. PACMan is a family of RRPV insertion and RRPV update policies that was shown to outperform DRRIP and SDBP in the presence of hardware prefetching [25]. CHAR improves average throughput by 5.3% and significantly improves the effectiveness of the prefetcher by reducing the LLC demand miss count by 15.0% compared to the prefetched SRRIP. We find that compared to SRRIP, the CHAR algorithm evicts 11.3% less C_0 blocks from LLC. This is primarily due to dynamic learning of the usefulness of C_0 blocks in the LLC. The prefetched blocks that experience demand hits much later than they are prefetched into the hierarchy must be identified and retained in the LLC. These are a subset of the C_0 blocks. CHAR dynamically monitors the collective reuse probability of the C_0 blocks and learns to retain them if they are useful.

PACMan-DYN-Global delivers a throughput improvement of 2.8% compared to prefetched SRRIP. This policy dynamically selects one of the two algorithms, namely, PACMan-H and PACMan-HM. None of these policies upgrade the RRPV of a block on prefetch hits in the LLC. As a result, the blocks that can potentially enjoy multiple prefetch hits in the LLC followed by demand hits in the L2 cache get prematurely evicted from the LLC. Note that even though CHAR does not increment the live counter of C_0 class if a C_0 block experiences a prefetch hit in the LLC, it does increment the live counters of C_1, C_2, and C_3 classes if a block belonging to any of these three experiences a prefetch hit in the LLC. Further, CHAR always upgrades the RRPV of a block in the LLC on a prefetch hit following the SRRIP policy. A common pattern experienced by a live block in CHAR is the following. The block is prefetched into the L2 cache (filled as C_0 in the L2 cache). It enjoys demand hit(s) in the L2 cache and is evicted as a C_1, C_2, or C_3 block from the L2 cache. Later the block is again prefetched from the LLC and it enjoys further demand hits. While CHAR can retain such blocks in the LLC, PACMan-DYN-Global fails to do so because it does not upgrade the RRPVs on prefetch hits in the LLC.

Overall, we find that PACMan-DYN-Global is too aggressive in filtering prefetch-induced LLC pollution and in the process it often loses useful prefetched blocks early resulting in an eventual increase in the memory controller congestion because several prematurely evicted useful prefetches will have to be fetched/prefetched again. This fact is substantiated by the last row of Table 8. CHAR saves 8.8% DRAM requests compared to SRRIP, while PACMan-DYN-Global increases the memory traffic by 4.8%. The increased pressure on the memory controllers leads to loss in performance for several mixes when running with PACMan-DYN-Global.

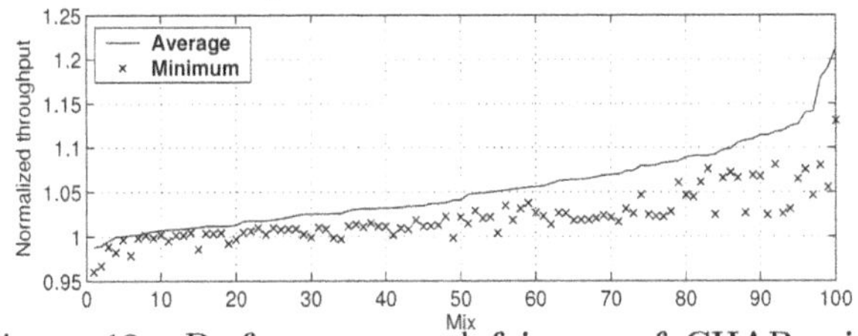

Figure 12: Performance and fairness of CHAR with prefetcher enabled.

Figure 12 shows the details of throughput improvement and fairness of CHAR for the heterogeneous mixes relative to SRRIP with the hardware prefetcher enabled. The mixes are arranged in the increasing order of throughput improvement. The throughput profile ranges from a loss of 1.2% to an improvement of 21.3%. The average throughput improvement achieved by CHAR is 5.3%. The minimum throughput improvement of any thread ranges from 0.96 to 1.13, averaging at 1.02. Only 16 mixes have minimum throughput improvement below 1.0. These data confirm that even in the presence of prefetching, CHAR continues to achieve significant performance improvement compared to SRRIP.

For the shared memory parallel programs, prefetching alone reduces the execution time of SRRIP by 15.6%. CHAR-S achieves a further 2.2% reduction in execution time relative to prefetched SRRIP. Thread-oblivious PACMan-DYN [25] and thread-aware PACMan-DYN-Global respectively achieve 1.1% and 0.4% reduction in parallel execution time.

4.2 Exclusive LLC Model

We summarize our results for the exclusive LLC model in Figure 13. All the simulations are done with the hardware prefetcher enabled. The leftmost panel shows the average throughput of one hundred 4-way multi-programmed mixes for a non-inclusive (NI) LLC model [7, 23] and TC-AGE, CHAR, CHAR-C4, CHAR-C4-MAX, and CHAR-C4-MIN policies implemented on the exclusive LLC model. The throughput results are normalized to an inclusive LLC model. The inclusive, non-inclusive, and exclusive LLC models have identically designed cache hierarchies (32 KB 8-way private L1 instruction and data caches, 512 KB 8-way private L2 cache, 8 MB 16-way shared LLC). The inclusive and the non-inclusive LLCs implement the two-bit SRRIP policy. The NI LLC model is identical to the inclusive LLC model, except that on an LLC eviction the NI model does not invalidate the copy of the block in the L2 and L1 caches. The performance gain of the NI model over the inclusive model arises from elimination of back-invalidations, while the performance gap between the NI model and the TC-AGE policy running on the exclusive LLC model stems from the added effective capacity of the exclusive LLC. Overall, CHAR-C4 delivers the best performance improving the average throughput by 8.2% over the inclusive model and 3.2% over the TC-AGE exclusive model. The CHAR, CHAR-C4-MAX, and CHAR-C4-MIN policies deliver performance close to CHAR-C4.

The middle panel of Figure 13 shows the bypass fractions for CHAR, CHAR-C4, CHAR-C4-MAX, and CHAR-C4-MIN. This fraction corresponds to the fraction of L2 cache evictions dropped by the L2 cache controller and not sent to the LLC or memory controllers in the exclusive LLC model. While CHAR bypasses 14.8% blocks on average, the other three policies that switch the C4 blocks to non-inclusive/non-exclusive mode enjoy more than 60% bypass rates. CHAR-C4 bypasses 66.6% of the L2 cache evictions.

The rightmost panel of Figure 13 quantifies the number of data write transactions from the L2 cache to the on-die

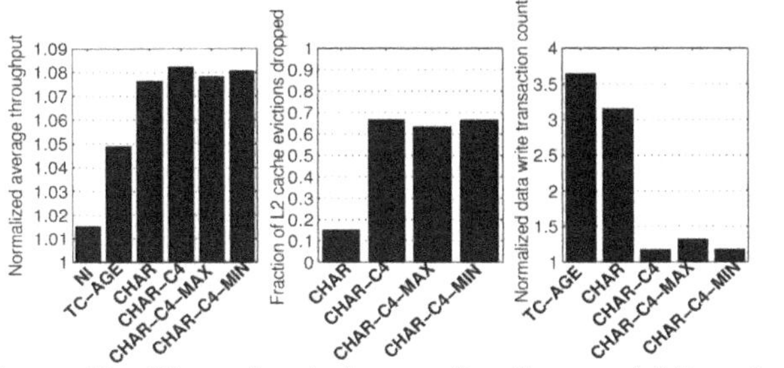

Figure 13: Throughput, bypass fraction, and L2 cache to interconnect data traffic in exclusive LLC model for multi-programmed workloads with prefetcher enabled.

interconnect in the exclusive LLC policies relative to the inclusive LLC model. For an exclusive LLC, these are the data transactions to LLC or memory controllers originating from L2 cache evictions that could not be bypassed. For an inclusive LLC, these are dirty writebacks from the L2 cache to the LLC. While TC-AGE generates 3.6 times data write transactions relative to the inclusive LLC model, the CHAR-C4 policy generates only 17% more writes to the LLC. As mentioned in Section 2.3, the TC-AGE policy does not exercise any bypass algorithm. Overall, CHAR-C4 is the best policy among the ones we have evaluated for an exclusive LLC. It improves the average throughput by 8.2% while generating only 17% more data writes to the LLC compared to an identically sized inclusive LLC hierarchy.

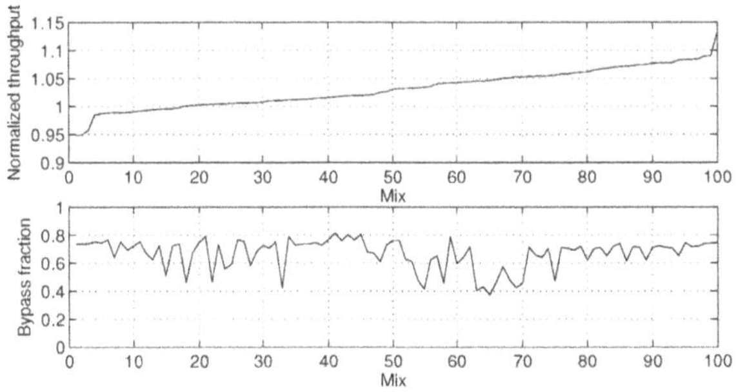

Figure 14: Throughput normalized to TC-AGE and bypass fraction of CHAR-C4 policy.

Figure 14 shows the details of throughput (upper panel) and bypass fraction (lower panel) of the CHAR-C4 policy for the heterogeneous mixes. The throughput is normalized to the TC-AGE policy. The mixes are arranged in the increasing order of normalized throughput. The throughput profile varies from a loss of 5.1% to a gain of 13.3%, while the bypass fraction is between 0.37 and 0.81. In other words, the CHAR-C4 policy can save 37% to 81% (average 66.6%) on-die data write traffic originating from the L2 cache evictions while delivering a throughput improvement of up to 13.3% (average 3.2%) relative to TC-AGE.

5. SUMMARY

This paper proposes hierarchy-aware replacement and allocation/bypass policies for LLCs in a three-level cache hierarchy. The proposal uses a carefully chosen subset of the L2 cache evictions as hints to improve the quality of replacement and allocation in inclusive and exclusive LLCs, respectively. When a data block is evicted from the L2 cache, it is passed on to a dead hint detector. The dead hint detector decides if the block should be marked a potential victim in an inclusive LLC, provided the block has already been evicted from the L1 data cache. A similar decision is used to identify L2 cache evictions that need not be allocated in an exclusive LLC and can be bypassed. Central to the dead hint detector logic is an approximate reuse distance-based classification of L2 cache blocks and estimation of reuse probability of each of these classes. If the reuse probability of a class falls below a threshold, any block belonging to that class is marked a potential victim/bypass candidate for inclusive/exclusive LLC when the block is evicted from the L2 cache.

We evaluate our policy proposal on single-threaded, multi-programmed, and shared memory workloads. In an inclusive LLC, our cache hierarchy-aware algorithm offers an average throughput improvement of 5.3% for one hundred 4-way multi-programmed mixes compared to a baseline SRRIP policy with a well-tuned multi-stream hardware prefetcher enabled. Our best proposal for exclusive LLC improves the average throughput of one hundred 4-way multi-programmed mixes by 8.2% compared to an identical inclusive LLC hierarchy while bypassing 66.6% of the L2 cache evictions. As a result of this high bypass rate, this policy introduces only 17% more data write transactions into the on-die interconnect compared to an identical inclusive LLC hierarchy.

6. ACKNOWLEDGMENTS

This research effort is funded by Intel Corporation. The authors thank Praveen Vishakantaiah from Intel India and Koby Gottlieb from Intel Israel for their financial support and continued encouragement.

7. REFERENCES

[1] L. A. Belady. A Study of Replacement Algorithms for a Virtual-storage Computer. In *IBM Systems Journal*, **5**(2): 78–101, 1966.

[2] M. Chaudhuri. Pseudo-LIFO: The Foundation of a New Family of Replacement Policies for Last-level Caches. In *Proceedings of the 42nd International Symposium on Microarchitecture*, pages 401–412, December 2009.

[3] M. Frigo and S. G. Johnson. The Design and Implementation of FFTW3. In *Proceedings of the IEEE*, **93**(2): 216–231, February 2005.

[4] R. V. Garde, S. Subramaniam, and G. H. Loh. Deconstructing the Inefficacy of Global Cache Replacement Policies. In *7th Annual Workshop on Duplicating, Deconstructing, and Debunking*, held in conjunction with the *35th International Symposium on Computer Architecture*, June 2008.

[5] J. Gaur, M. Chaudhuri, and S. Subramoney. Bypass and Insertion Algorithms for Exclusive Last-level Caches. In *Proceedings of the 38th International Symposium on Computer Architecture*, pages 81–92, June 2011.

[6] Z. Hu, S. Kaxiras, and M. Martonosi. Timekeeping in the Memory System: Predicting and Optimizing Memory Behavior. In *Proceedings of the 29th International Symposium on Computer Architecture*, pages 209–220, May 2002.

[7] A. Jaleel et al. Achieving Non-Inclusive Cache Performance with Inclusive Caches. In *Proceedings of the 43rd International Symposium on Microarchitecture*, pages 151–162, December 2010.

[8] A. Jaleel et al. High Performance Cache Replacement using Re-reference Interval Prediction (RRIP). In *Proceedings of the 37th International Symposium on Computer Architecture*, pages 60–71, June 2010.

[9] A. Jaleel et al. Adaptive Insertion Policies for Managing Shared Caches. In *Proceedings of the 17th International Conference on Parallel Architecture and Compilation Techniques*, pages 208–219, October 2008.

[10] G. Keramidas, P. Petoumenos, and S. Kaxiras. Cache Replacement Based on Reuse Distance Prediction. In *Proceedings of the 25th International Conference on Computer Design*, pages 245–250, October 2007.

[11] S. Khan, Z. Wang, and D. A. Jimènez. Decoupled Dynamic Cache Segmentation. In *Proceedings of the 18th International Symposium on High Performance Computer Architecture*, pages 235–246, February 2012.

[12] S. Khan, Y. Tian, and D. A. Jimènez. Dead Block Replacement and Bypass with a Sampling Predictor. In *Proceedings of the 43rd International Symposium on Microarchitecture*, pages 175–186, December 2010.

[13] S. Khan et al. Using Dead Blocks as a Virtual Victim Cache. In *Proceedings of the 19th International Conference on Parallel Architectures and Compilation Techniques*, pages 489–500, September 2010.

[14] M. Kharbutli and Y. Solihin. Counter-based Cache Replacement and Bypassing Algorithms. In *IEEE Transactions on Computers*, **57**(4): 433–447, April 2008.

[15] A. J. KleinOsowski and D. J. Lilja. MinneSPEC: A New SPEC Benchmark Workload for Simulation-Based Computer Architecture Research. In *Computer Architecture Letters*, **1**(1), January 2002.

[16] A-C. Lai, C. Fide, and B. Falsafi. Dead-block Prediction & Dead-block Correlating Prefetchers. In *Proceedings of the 28th International Symposium on Computer Architecture*, pages 144–154, June/July 2001.

[17] J. Lee and H. Kim. TAP: A TLP-aware Cache Management Policy for a CPU-GPU Heterogeneous Architecture. In *Proceedings of the 18th International Symposium on High Performance Computer Architecture*, pages 91–102, February 2012.

[18] H. Liu et al. Cache Bursts: A New Approach for Eliminating Dead Blocks and Increasing Cache Efficiency. In *Proceedings of the 41st International Symposium on Microarchitecture*, pages 222–233, November 2008.

[19] R. Manikantan, K. Rajan, and R. Govindarajan. NUcache: An Efficient Multicore Cache Organization Based on Next-Use Distance. In *Proceedings of the 17th IEEE International Symposium on High-performance Computer Architecture*, pages 243–253, February 2011.

[20] R. L. Mattson et al. Evaluation Techniques for Storage Hierarchies. In *IBM Systems Journal*, **9**(2): 78–117, 1970.

[21] M. K. Qureshi et al. Adaptive Insertion Policies for High Performance Caching. In *Proceedings of the 34th International Symposium on Computer Architecture*, pages 381–391, June 2007.

[22] T. Sherwood et al. Automatically Characterizing Large Scale Program Behavior. In *Proceedings of the 10th International Conference on Architectural Support for Programming Languages and Operating Systems*, pages 45–57, October 2002.

[23] J. Sim et al. FLEXclusion: Balancing Cache Capacity and On-chip Bandwidth with Flexible Exclusion. In *Proceedings of the 39th IEEE/ACM International Symposium on Computer Architecture*, pages 321–332, June 2012.

[24] C-J. Wu et al. SHiP: Signature-Based Hit Predictor for High Performance Caching. In *Proceedings of the 44th International Symposium on Microarchitecture*, pages 430–441, December 2011.

[25] C-J. Wu et al. PACMan: Prefetch-Aware Cache Management for High Performance Caching. In *Proceedings of the 44th International Symposium on Microarchitecture*, pages 442–453, December 2011.

[26] M. Zahran. Cache Replacement Policy Revisited. In *6th Annual Workshop on Duplicating, Deconstructing, and Debunking*, held in conjunction with the *34th International Symposium on Computer Architecture*, June 2007.

[27] M. Zahran and S. A. McKee. Global Management of Cache Hierarchies. In *Proceedings of the 7th Conference on Computing Frontiers*, pages 131–140, May 2010.

Efficient Techniques for Predicting Cache Sharing and Throughput

Andreas Sandberg
Uppsala University
Sweden
andreas.sandberg@it.uu.se

David Black-Schaffer
Uppsala University
Sweden
david.black-schaffer@it.uu.se

Erik Hagersten
Uppsala University
Sweden
erik.hagersten@it.uu.se

ABSTRACT

This work addresses the modeling of shared cache contention in multicore systems and its impact on throughput and bandwidth. We develop two simple and fast cache sharing models for accurately predicting shared cache allocations for random and LRU caches.

To accomplish this we use low-overhead input data that captures the behavior of applications running on real hardware as a function of their shared cache allocation. This data enables us to determine how much and how aggressively data is reused by an application depending on how much shared cache it receives. From this we can model how applications compete for cache space, their aggregate performance (throughput), and bandwidth.

We evaluate our models for two- and four-application workloads in simulation and on modern hardware. On a four-core machine, we demonstrate an average relative fetch ratio error of 6.7% for groups of four applications. We are able to predict workload bandwidth with an average relative error of less than 5.2% and throughput with an average error of less than 1.8%. The model can predict cache size with an average error of 1.3% compared to simulation.

Categories and Subject Descriptors

C.4 [**Performance of Systems**]: Modeling Techniques

General Terms

Measurement, Performance

Keywords

Cache Sharing, Modeling, Performance

1. INTRODUCTION

The shared cache in contemporary multicore processors has been repeatedly shown to be a critical resource for application performance [13, 15, 18, 8, 14]. This has motivated a significant amount of research into modeling the impact of cache sharing with the goal of understanding applications' interactions through the shared cache and for providing insight to schedulers and runtime systems [15, 20, 11, 10].

This work presents two models for predicting cache allocations, bandwidth requirements, and performance of application mixes in the presence of a shared last-level cache. The models are developed for random replacement and LRU caches, but are shown to be accurate for the pseudo-LRU caches of modern Intel processors.

These models take into account the complexities of modern hardware (such as out-of-order execution and hardware prefetchers) by leveraging input data that incorporates the applications' behavior on real hardware. This input data consist of the applications' fetch and hit rates, IPCs, and hit ratios as a function of their cache allocation, and can be acquired with low overhead on modern multicore machines [6]. This low-overhead data is in contrast to many existing methods for modeling cache sharing which rely on expensive data such as stack distance traces [2, 4, 3, 17].

To model cache sharing we use an application's fetch and hit rates as a function of cache size to determine how much of its data is reused for a given cache allocation, and how often that data is reused. With this information we can model how multiple applications compete for shared cache space. The model then uses a numerical solver to find a stable solution that determines the final cache allocations. Once we know the cache allocations we can use our input data to predict performance (throughput) and bandwidth requirements for mixes of co-scheduled applications.

This ability to model cache sharing and predict its impact on performance and bandwidth is important for scheduling and performance analysis on complex systems. Such modeling forms the basis for resource-aware placement in modern memory hierarchies, scheduling on heterogeneous architectures, and for making runtime decisions on future chips in the presence of power constraints (e.g., dark silicon). By combining low-overhead data that reflects the complexities of the real hardware and a simple sharing model we are able to quickly and accurately predict sharing and performance, which is essential for such goals.

This paper makes the following contributions:

- We present a statistical cache-sharing model for random caches that uses high-level, low-overhead input data.

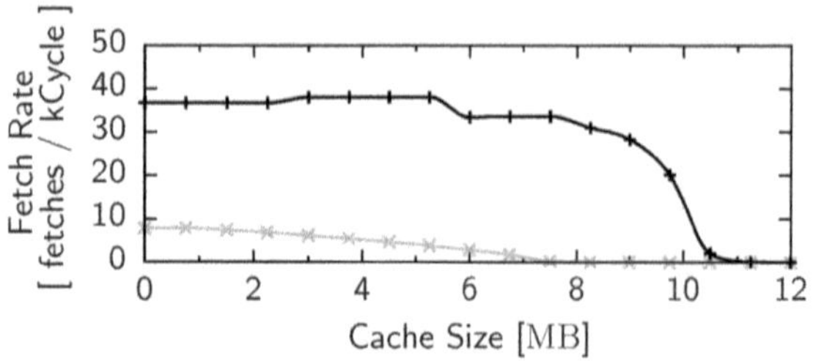

Figure 1: Example Cache Pirate data showing fetch rate as a function of cache size for two applications.

- We extend the model to LRU caches by deriving aggregate data reuse information from the input data, and using this to model competition for cache space based on the data reuse frequencies of each application.
- We demonstrate the accuracy of the model for predicting cache sharing and fetch ratios for mixes of two and four co-scheduled applications through simulation and on real hardware.
- We demonstrate the ability to accurately predict performance (IPC) and bandwidth requirement of application mixes on real hardware.

2. MODELING CACHE SHARING

Consider two applications sharing a cache. Their behavior with respect to the shared cache can intuitively be thought of as two flows of liquid filling an overflowing glass. The two in-flows correspond to fetches into the cache and the liquid pouring out of the glass corresponds to the replacement stream from the cache. If the in-flows are constant, the system will eventually reach a steady state. At steady state, the concentrations of the liquids in the glass are constant and proportional to their relative inflow rates. Furthermore, the outflow rates of the liquids are proportional to their concentrations. This very simple analogy describes the behavior of random caches.

Describing LRU caches requires data reuse to be considered since data reused *frequently enough* will stick in the cache and avoid replacement. In the liquid analogy above, data reused frequently enough can be thought of as ice cubes that never leave the glass. The threshold for how frequently data needs to be reused to exhibit "sticky" behavior varies between sharing situations.

2.1 Low-Overhead Input Data

The goal of our cache sharing models is to find the amount of cache allocated to each application in a mix of co-scheduled applications at steady state. This requires per-application information about fetch[1] rate and data reuse characteristics for all applications as well as how that information is affected by cache contention. In order for this information to accurately describe the target system, it needs to take into consideration effects from complex dynamic hardware, such as super-scalar out-of-order execution and hardware prefetching.

[1]The term *fetch* is used extensively in this paper to describe a movement of data from memory to cache caused by either a cache miss or prefetching activity.

Cache Pirating [6] is a method to capture our required input data on the target hardware. In Cache Pirating, the studied application is co-scheduled to share a cache with a small cache-intensive micro benchmark, the Pirate. The Pirate is designed to steal only cache, leaving other shared resources untouched. In a single run, the amount of cache the Pirate steals is varied, while the effects on the studied application are measured using hardware performance counters. The application's miss rate, fetch rate, hit rate, miss ratio, fetch ratio, hit ratio, memory bandwidth, CPI, etc., *as a function of cache size*, can be measured with an average overhead of 5.5%.

Cache Pirating typically measures sensitivity by stealing a whole way at a time, while our models assume continuous data. We therefore interpolate the measured data using monotone cubic splines [7]. We chose this interpolation method over linear interpolation because the resulting function estimates the behavior in applications with sharp steps in their fetch rate curves (e.g., applications with a small fixed data set) more accurately by making the edges sharper. Figure 1 shows an example of data produced using Cache Pirating: Fetch rate as a function of cache size for two applications, measured in 16 discreet steps and interpolated with monotone cubic splines.

The following section describes how the fetch rate and hit rate information measured using Cache Pirating is used to determine the amount of cache allocated to each application in a sharing situation. Knowing the amount of cache allocated to each application allows us to predict additional performance metrics. In Section 4 we show how throughput and bandwidth demand can be predicted using knowledge about cache allocations and the data from Cache Pirating.

2.2 Modeling Random Caches

In random caches, sharing only depends on two events: fetches into the cache and replacements. At steady state, the amount of data an application installs into the cache is equal to the amount of data evicted from that application's cache allocation; that is, the application's fetch rate (fetches per cycle) must equal its replacement rate (replacements per cycle). An application's replacement rate is proportional to the total fetch rate, F, into the cache and its replacement probability. Since replacements are random, the replacement probability is proportional to the amount of cache allocated to the application. For a shared cache of size C and an application, n; the application's fetch rate, f_n, and cache allocation, c_n, are related according to:

$$\begin{cases} f_n = F\dfrac{c_n}{C} \\ C = \sum_i c_i \end{cases} \tag{1}$$

We can solve the equation system above, given that we have each application's fetch rate as a function of cache size, using readily available equation system solvers.

2.3 Modeling LRU Caches

LRU caches, unlike random caches, use access history to replace the item that has been unused for the longest time. We refer to the duration of time a cache line has been unused as its *age*. Whenever there is a replacement decision, the oldest cache line is replaced.

In practice, we can not determine the age of individual

cache lines based on our input data. Instead, we look at *groups* of cache lines with the same maximum *age*[2] and let the groups from different applications compete for cache space.

Cache lines that are fetched into the cache but are evicted before they are reused are put in a separate group and handled differently. After the initial fetch into the cache, the age of these cache lines increases whenever *any* application fetches new data into the cache. This allows us to treat them as one group common to all applications, with one common age. We will refer to these cache lines as *volatile* since they are evicted from the cache before they are reused.

Cache lines which are reused before they are evicted from the cache are referred to as *sticky* cache lines since their reuse makes them resilient to eviction. Normally an application reuses more data in the cache when the amount of cache the application has access to grows. This means that some data is *potentially* sticky and only becomes sticky when the application has access to enough cache. The amount of sticky and volatile data in the cache therefore depends on how much cache an application has access to, which is a function of what other applications are co-executing.

To explain the LRU model, we will first describe how to model sharing within the volatile group and how the age of the group is determined. We will then describe how sticky groups are modeled, and finally how our solver uses this information to determine cache sharing.

2.3.1 Modeling Volatile Data

When applications do not reuse their data before it is evicted from the cache, LRU caches degenerate into FIFO queues with data moving from the MRU position to the LRU position before being evicted. Similar to random replacement, the amount of cache allocated to an application will be proportional to its fetch rate. This observation allows us to use the method devised for random replacement to model cache sharing for volatile data. Assuming that we know the amount of cache available to volatile data[3], C^v, we can solve Equation 1 for the volatile part of the cache. This allows us to estimate the amount of volatile data, c^v, each application has.

Since sticky data and volatile data from different applications compete for cache space, we need to be able to compare their maximum age. Because the cache degenerates into a FIFO queue for volatile data, the maximum age of volatile elements can be determined using Little's law [9].[4] Assuming that we know the total size of the volatile part of the cache, C^v, and the *total* fetch rate into the cache, the maximum age of all volatile cache lines, A^v, is:

$$A^v = \frac{C^v}{F} \tag{2}$$

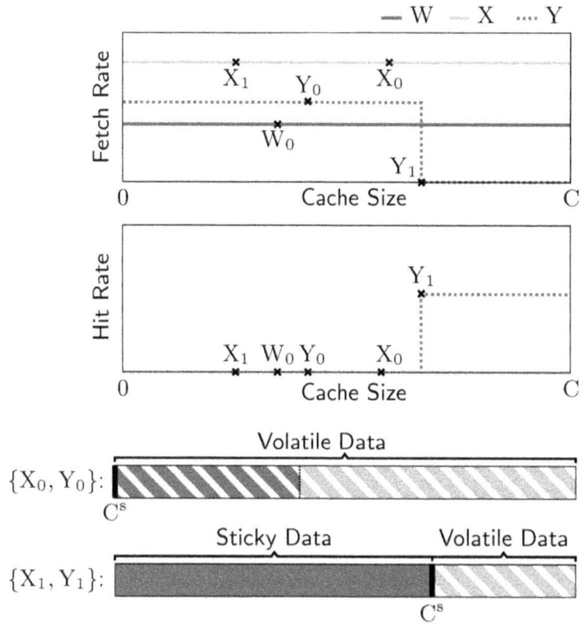

Figure 2: Fetch and hit rate curves for three sample applications. Application W and X always miss in the shared cache, while Y misses only when it has less than $c_n(Y_1)$ space in the cache. The cache allocations for the two stable cache sharing configurations of X and Y are shown below.

Example 1: Consider application X and application W in Figure 2. Both of the applications have fetch rates that are independent of cache size and X has twice the fetch rate of W. Since the hit rate is zero for both of them, neither reuses any data in the cache (i.e., all data is volatile). Using the random replacement model for the volatile data, we conclude that X gets twice the cache allocation of W (i.e., X uses two thirds of the cache) causing the applications to stabilize at the solution $\{X_0, W_0\}$. Since the entire cache is filled with volatile data, the maximum age of volatile elements is described by:

$$A^v = \frac{C^v}{F} = \frac{C}{f(X_0) + f(W_0)}$$

□

2.3.2 Modeling Sticky Data

In most cases, there is both sticky and volatile data in the cache at the same time. Unlike volatile data, sticky data stays in the cache because it is reused while it is in the cache. When sticky and volatile cache lines compete for cache space, the decision to let a sticky cache line remain sticky depends on its age. A sticky cache line becomes volatile if it is older than the oldest volatile cache line. In our model, we make this decision for entire groups of cache lines with the same maximum age. A group of sticky cache lines with the same maximum age, a^s, is allowed to stay in the cache as sticky cache lines if it is younger than the oldest volatile cache line:

$$a^s < A^v \tag{3}$$

Similar to volatile data, we can estimate the maximum

[2]At any given moment, the cache lines in a group will have different ages. It therefore only makes sense to talk about the maximum age of a group.

[3]We can estimate the amount of sticky data each application has, and therefore whatever is left of the cache is used for volatile data.

[4]Little's law sets up a relationship between the number of elements in a queue (size), the time spent in the queue (maximum age) and the arrival rate (fetch rate). The total arrival rate into the queue is the sum of all fetch rates, F, in the system.

age for a group of sticky data using Little's law if we know the size of the group and its reuse rate. This can best be illustrated with an example:

Example 2: Application Y in Figure 2 does not reuse any data (its hit rate is zero) when it has access to less cache than $c(Y_1)$. However, it reuses all its data when it has access to more cache (its fetch rate is zero). This means that it has one group of potentially sticky data. The size of the group is $c(Y_1)$ and the aggregate reuse rate of all elements in the group is its hit rate, $h(Y_1)$.

When Y starts it will bring its entire data set into the cache and start reusing it, causing the data to become sticky. If X is then started, it will first install data into the unused part of the cache. The size of Y's sticky data set will at this point be $c(Y_1)$ and the rest of the cache will be filled with data belonging to X. Since X does not reuse its data, all its data will be volatile. We obtain the ages of sticky, a^s, and volatile, A^v, elements when they start to compete for cache as follows:

$$a^s = \frac{c(Y_1)}{h(Y_1)}$$

$$A^v = \frac{C^v}{F} = \frac{C - c(Y_1)}{f(X_1)}$$

$\{X_1, Y_1\}$ is a stable cache sharing configuration if Y's sticky cache lines are younger than X's volatile cache lines. This means that Y is reusing its data set frequently enough to prevent X from pushing it out of the cache.

An interesting feature of this benchmark combination is that it can have two stable cache sharing configurations. If X starts first and is allowed to fill the cache with its volatile data, when Y starts, it will have to compete with X to bring its data into the cache. At this point, the entire cache consists of volatile data since Y has not installed enough of its data to be able to reuse it before it is evicted from the cache. Since X has a higher fetch rate than Y, it fetches data faster and will therefore get more cache than Y. In this case, Y will never fit its entire group of potentially sticky data, and its data it will instead remain volatile. Both $\{X_0, Y_0\}$ and $\{X_1, Y_1\}$ are therefore valid sharing configurations, depending on the starting order. □

In the examples so far, both of the benchmarks in a pair have either had sticky or volatile data, but not both. Real applications typically have both sticky and volatile data in the cache at the same time:

Example 3: Application Z in Figure 3 has two drops in its fetch rate curve, which means that it has two groups of potentially sticky data. This can happen in applications reusing two arrays of different size. For a cache size of $c(Z_0)$, the application is able to fit its first group of data in the cache (the fetch rate drops just before $c(Z_0)$) and that group becomes sticky. If the application has access to more cache than $c(Z_1)$, its fetch rate drops to zero and all of its data becomes sticky. In order to calculate the age, a^s, of a group of sticky data, we need to know how much that group contributes to the total hit rate and how big the group is. Assuming that we know the amount of sticky data in an application, c^s, as a function of cache size (we will show how

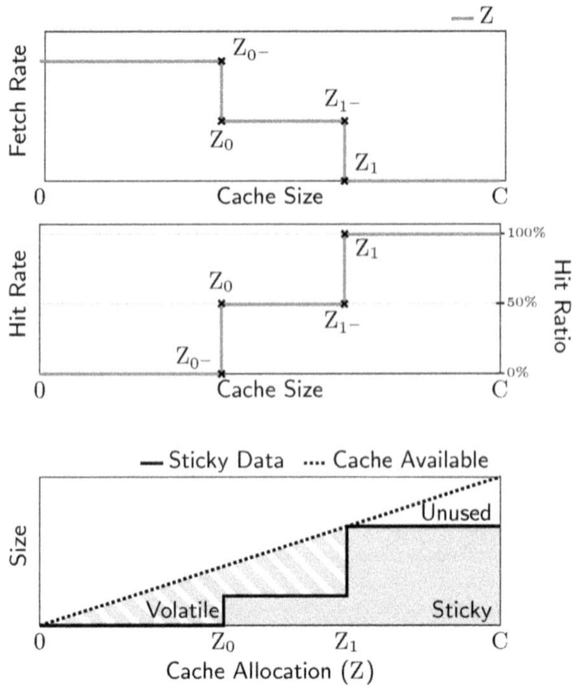

Figure 3: Z has two groups of sticky data of different sizes. When a group of sticky data starts to fit in the cache, the fetch rate starts to drop and the hit ratio increases. Whenever the hit ratio increases, the amount of volatile data at that point decreases (it becomes sticky) by the same relative amount.

to estimate this in Section 2.3.3), we can calculate $a^s(Z_0)$ as:

$$a^s(Z_0) = \frac{c^s(Z_0) - c^s(Z_{0-})}{h(Z_0) - h(Z_{0-})}$$

□

The age derived in the example above is simply a finite difference approximation of a differential equation. In general, the access rate for sticky elements is defined as:

$$a^s(c) = \frac{dc^s}{dh} \qquad (4)$$

Equation 4 is actually a simplification that assumes that an application's execution rate does not change with cache size. However, execution rate generally increases as an application gets access to more cache. This variation is accurately captured in our Cache Pirate input data. Not compensating for the change in execution rate leads an erroneous estimate of a block's contribution to the total hit rate. We address this by using the difference in *hit ratio* (hits per memory access) which is execution rate independent. We then scale the difference in *hit ratio* with the application's *accesses rate* (which is execution rate dependent) to get the block's contribution to the total hit rate.

2.3.3 Estimating Sticky Group Sizes

The amount of sticky data can be estimated from how an application's hit ratio changes with its cache allocation. The relative change in hit ratio is proportional to the relative change in the sticky data.

Example 4: As seen in Figure 3, Z's hit ratio increases in two steps. This means that it has two groups of potentially sticky data. When it has access to less cache than $c(Z_0)$, the hit ratio is zero and it has no sticky data. The amount of sticky data can be broken down into three different cases based on the cache allocation c:

$0 \le c < c(Z_0)$
Since the hit ratio is zero, there is no sticky data.

$c(Z_0) \le c < c(Z_1)$
When the amount of cache is increased to $c(Z_0)$, the hit ratio increases from 0% to 50% (i.e., 50% of the fetches become hits). We would therefore expect 50% of the volatile data to become sticky. Since the amount of volatile data just before Z_0 is $c(Z_0)$, the amount of sticky data in this range is $\frac{1}{2}c(Z_0)$.

$c(Z_1) \le c$
At $c(Z_1)$, all of the fetches become hits. The sticky data set size is therefore $c(Z_1)$.

Using Z's hit ratio function, $\hat{h}$, the reasoning above can be generalized into:

$$\frac{c^s(Z_x) - c^s(Z_{x^-})}{c(Z_x) - c^s(Z_{x^-})} = \frac{\hat{h}(Z_x) - \hat{h}(Z_{x^-})}{1 - \hat{h}(Z_{x^-})}$$

□

The difference approximation above can be generalized into the following differential equation:

$$\frac{dc^s}{dc}\frac{1}{c - c^s} = \frac{d\hat{h}}{dc}\frac{1}{1 - \hat{h}} \tag{5}$$

2.3.4 *Putting It All Together*

We have described how an LRU cache can be modeled by splitting it into groups of cache lines with the same maximum age. Volatile data is treated as a separate group of data where the maximum age is determined by the *total* fetch rate into the cache. Each application's sticky data is allowed to stay in the cache as sticky data as long as its maximum age is lower than the maximum age of any application's volatile data, otherwise it becomes volatile. This leads to the following requirement, which must hold for every application, n, at steady state:

$$a^s_n < A^v \tag{6}$$

If the requirement does not hold for an application, its sticky data that is too old to remain sticky becomes volatile.

Volatile data in the cache can be modeled using the model derived for random replacement (Equation 1), that is:

$$f_n = F\frac{c^v_n}{C^v} \tag{7}$$

The total amount of cache an application has access to is the sum of its sticky and volatile cache allocations:

$$c_n = c^s_n + c^v_n \tag{8}$$

Using the requirements defined above, we can find a sharing solution using a numerical solver. The solver starts with an initial guess, wherein the application that starts first has

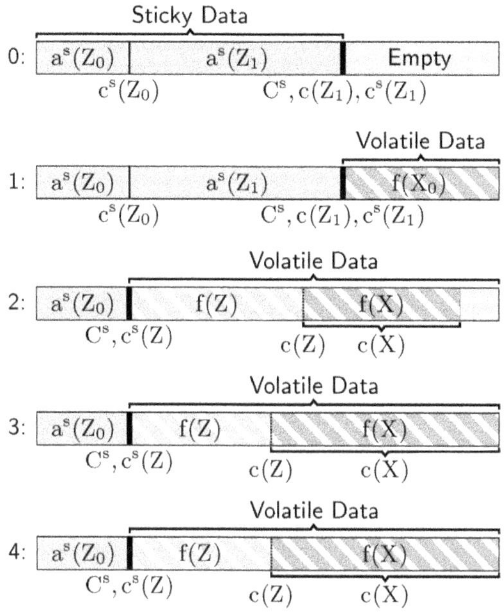

Figure 4: Solver steps for determining cache sharing when running example applications X and Z from Figure 2 and Figure 3 together. (See Example 5.)

access to the entire cache[5] and the other applications do not have access to any cache. The initial guess corresponds to the state of the cache just before a new application is started, which enables us to find the correct solution if the application mix has multiple solutions.

The solver then lets all applications compete for cache space by enforcing the age requirement between sticky and volatile cache lines. If the age requirement can not be satisfied for an application, the solver shrinks that application's cache allocation until the remaining sticky data satisfies the age requirement. If multiple applications fail to satisfy the age requirement, we shrink the application with the oldest cache lines. The cache freed by the shrinking operation is then distributed among *all* applications by solving the sharing equations for the volatile part of the cache.

The process of shrinking and growing the amount of cache allocated to the applications is repeated until the solution stabilizes (i.e., no application changes its cache allocation significantly).

Example 5: Assume that we run application Z from Figure 3 and X from Figure 2. Z starts first. The solver will then make the following decisions (illustrated in Figure 4):

0. Since Z starts first, it is given access to all cache and all its sticky data will fit in the cache. This is the initial guess.

1. X starts and the random sharing equations are solved for the volatile part of the cache. X fills the entire volatile part of the cache with its data since Z has a fetch rate of 0.

[5]The start order can be generalized to more than two applications by first determining the sharing for two applications and using that as the initial guess when start the next application and so on.

Cache line size	64 B
L1 latency	3 cycles
L1 associativity	16
L1 size	64 kB
L2 latency	30 cycles
L2 associativity	16
L2 size	8 MB
Memory latency	200 cycles

Table 1: M5 Simulator parameters

2. Based on the access rates and group sizes, we compute that Z's oldest sticky cache lines are now older than the oldest volatile cache line (i.e., the age requirement does not hold). Z can therefore not keep all its sticky data in the cache. The solver decides to shrink Z until the age condition can be satisfied. The condition is satisfied when the second sticky group becomes volatile.
3. Sharing in the volatile part of the cache is updated using the random model.
4. When the age conditions are satisfied, applying the random model to the volatile part of the cache does not change cache allocations and a stable solution is found.

□

3. EVALUATION (SIMULATOR)

3.1 Experimental Setup

To evaluate the quality of the model, we simulated a simple in-order quad-core processor without prefetching using M5 [1]. The simulated processor implemented a snooping MOESI protocol with all L1 caches connected to a shared L2 cache through a common bus. The simulator does not enforce inclusion between cache levels. The detailed parameters are listed in Table 1.

To obtain the input data for the model, we simulated each application running in isolation and changed the L2 size from 512 kB to 8 MB in steps of 512 kB and measured its cache behavior.

We evaluated our models against three different L2 replacement policies: random replacement, LRU, and the pseudo-LRU algorithm used in the Intel Nehalem microarchitecture [6]. We included the pseudo-LRU policy to determine if our LRU model generalizes to the hardware we use for evaluating the model in Section 4.1. In our experiments, this pseudo-LRU algorithm behaved very similar to normal LRU, so we will limit our discussion to random and LRU.

We selected benchmarks with time-stable behavior from SPEC CPU2006 and PARSEC, and tried to select applications with a wide variety of fetch rate behaviors. Applications with high fetch rates or fetch rates that change significantly when their cache allocation changes are particularly interesting because they are affected by cache contention the most. To avoid unstable start-up behavior, all benchmarks were fast forwarded 85 billion instruction before starting the simulation. The subsequent 2 billion memory accesses were used to drive the simulation.

To further stress our models, we included the two classes of microbenchmarks shown in Figure 5. The first class,

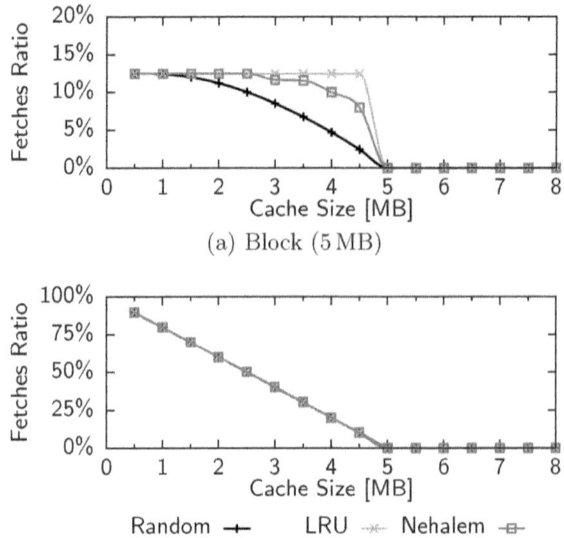

(b) Random (5 MB)

Figure 5: Shared cache fetch ratios for the block and random microbenchmarks.

App 0	App 1	App 2	App 3
block 5 MB	random 3 MB	streamcluster	bodytrack
bodytrack	soplex	astar	lbm
bodytrack	streamcluster	blackscholes	lbm
lbm	leslie3d	astar	bodytrack
libquantum	block 5 MB	random 5 MB	random 7 MB
libquantum	lbm	astar	bodytrack
random 5 MB	streamcluster	astar	leslie3d
random 7 MB	lbm	leslie3d	bodytrack
random 3 MB	block 5 MB	lbm	astar
streamcluster	leslie3d	soplex	bodytrack

Table 2: Mixes of four applications

block, repeatedly accesses its data in a sequential order. This behavior causes the fetch ratio for LRU caches to drop sharply when the cache size is larger than the data set size. The block benchmark is particularly challenging for the LRU model for two reasons: First, since it has a sharp edge on the fetch ratio curve, estimating group ages is hard as it involves taking a derivative of the curve at the point of the sharpest drop off. Second, as seen in Example 2, such benchmarks have a tendency to induce multiple stable sharing configurations in a given pair of benchmarks. The correct configuration generally depends on which application started first.

The *random* microbenchmark class accesses its entire data set randomly. This causes the fetch ratio to decrease linearly with cache size. An interesting observation is that all three replacement policies behave the same in this case. One of the main reasons to include this benchmark is that its steep fetch ratio curve means that a small error in estimating cache allocation will translate into a large error in fetch ratio. For example, a 1 MB error in predicted cache allocation would lead to a fetch ratio error of 20 percentage points, which is larger than the fetch ratio of most normal applications.

We ran all pairs of the following benchmarks from PARSEC: *blackscholes, bodytrack, streamcluster*; SPEC CPU2006: *astar, LBM, leslie3d, libquantum, soplex*; and the following microbenchmarks: *block (3 MB, 5 MB, 7 MB), random (3 MB, 5 MB, 7 MB)*. Since the simulation time needed to simulate all possible combinations of four applications would be prohibitive, we limited our study to the groups shown in Table 2.

3.2 Simulation Results

3.2.1 Random Replacement

We simulated a random replacement cache and measured the cache allocation and fetch ratio per co-scheduled application. Figure 6a shows the predicted cache size versus simulated cache size and predicted fetch ratio versus simulated fetch ratio for all pairs of applications. The better a prediction, the closer it is to the diagonal. As seen in the figure, there is an excellent agreement between the amount of cache used by the applications and that predicted by the random model. The average error in cache size prediction as a fraction of the total cache size was 0.8%.

Some applications, such as the microbenchmarks in Figure 5, change their fetch ratio significantly when there is only a slight change in cache size. The effect an error in cache size has on the memory system will therefore depend on the shape of an application's miss ratio curve. In order to more accurately assess how the model predicts cache performance, we also evaluated how well the model predicts fetch ratio. We define the relative fetch ratio error as the absolute difference in predicted and simulated fetch ratio over the simulated fetch ratio. It makes little sense to look at relative errors for benchmarks with small fetch ratios, since with a fetch ratio close to zero, even an insignificant error will cause the relative error to explode. Excluding benchmarks with a simulated fetch ratio less than 0.5%, we measure a relative fetch ratio error of 6.1%. The average absolute error for the excluded benchmarks was 0.04%, which corresponds to an insignificant difference in performance.

As seen in Figure 6c, groups of four applications can be predicted with similar accuracy. In this case, the average error in cache size was 0.9% and the average relative error in fetch ratio was 3.3%.

3.2.2 LRU Replacement

Figure 6b shows the predicted and simulated behavior for pairs of applications with LRU replacement. The scatter plot compares the simulator solutions with their predicted counterparts. The average error in predicted cache size was 0.9% and the average relative error for the fetch ratio prediction was 5.4%. Similar to the random replacement case, we excluded applications with a fetch ratio lower than 0.5% from the fetch ratio average. The average absolute error for the excluded benchmarks was 0.05%. The model accurately solves the more complex task of modeling cache sharing for LRU caches, even the microbenchmarks with sharp edges in their fetch ratio curves can be handled accurately.

As seen in Figure 6d, the average error for groups of four applications is similar to when modeling random replacement. The average error in cache size in this case is 1.3% and the average relative error in fetch ratio is 4.2%.

The solver typically finds a solution within 5 to 10 iterations. Our prototype Python-based solver normally finds a solution in less than 100 ms.

3.2.3 Multiple LRU Sharing Solutions

As seen in Section 2.3, some combinations of applications can result in multiple stable sharing configurations. It turns out that such benchmark combinations are uncommon, and

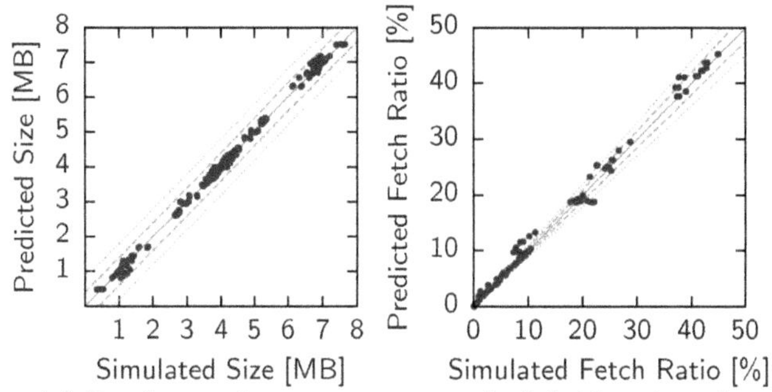

(a) Random replacement, two co-scheduled benchmarks

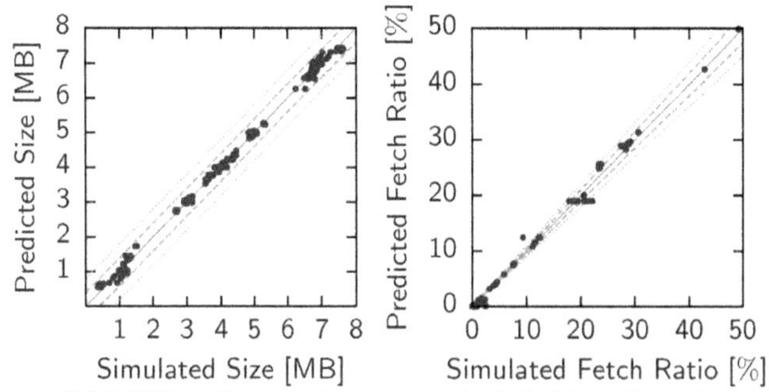

(b) LRU replacement, two co-scheduled benchmarks

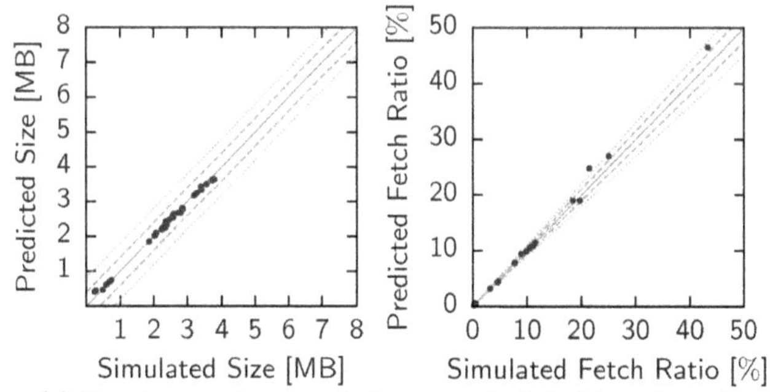

(c) Random replacement, four co-scheduled benchmarks

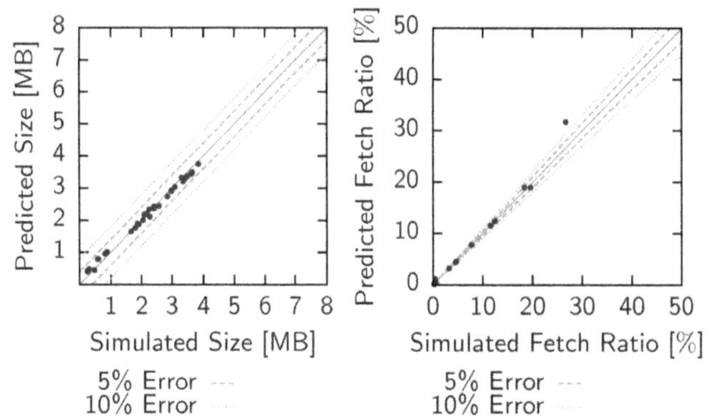

(d) LRU replacement, four co-scheduled benchmarks

Figure 6: Predicted vs. simulated sharing and fetch ratio

we only observed such behavior for microbenchmarks running in the simulator. In order for a pair of applications to have multiple stable sharing configurations, at least one of the applications must have a sharp knee in its fetch rate curve. In that case, the configuration the simulator finds will depend on

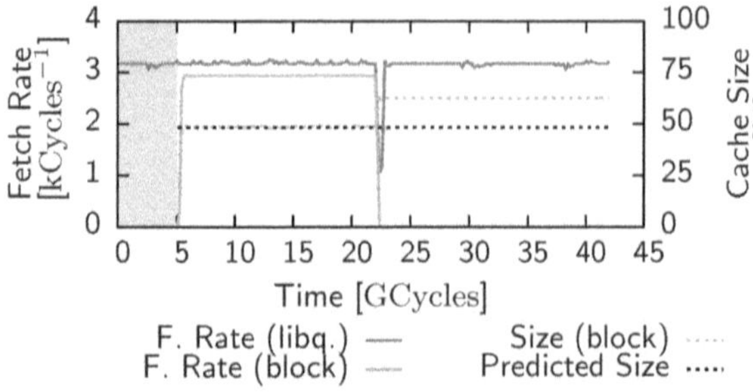

Figure 7: Fetch rate and cache sharing as a function of time for libquantum and the 5 MB block microbenchmark. The shaded part of the graph is the warm-up period where libquantum is executes in isolation.

the start order of the applications. To find such application pairs, we ran every application pair twice, starting one of the applications 5 billion cycles after the other.

Out of the 98 benchmark pairs, the simulator found multiple stable solutions in three cases, all involving the 5 MB block microbenchmark. The model accurately found both solutions in all of these cases by modeling the start order of the applications.

In two benchmark pairs, the simulator found a stable solution, but later switched to a different solution. This can occur for applications, which despite having fairly time stable behavior, have short hiccups where their fetch rate temporarily drops. Figure 7 shows the 5 MB block microbenchmark running together with libquantum. In this case, libquantum started first and was allowed to execute in isolation for 5 billion cycles before the block microbenchmark was started. When the block application starts, its fetch rate immediately rises and stays high since it is unable to make its data sticky. Later libquantum has a short drop in its fetch rate which allows the block microbenchmark to install its entire data set into the cache and stabilize at the second solution. The model, being unaware of libquantum's time-varying behavior, predicts that the simulator will stay in the first solution.

In addition to the five benchmark pairs where the simulator found multiple solutions, our model found an additional solution in four other benchmark pairs. As in the cases where the simulator found multiple solutions, all of these cases involved the 5 MB block microbenchmark. The main reason for the additional solutions found by the model is input data limitations. The model uses sparse data collected for a limited set of cache sizes for each benchmark. This makes it feasible to apply the model to real-world systems, but causes numerical problems for benchmarks with sharp edges in their fetch rate curves. For example, inaccuracies in the input data caused the model to predict two sharing configurations when running the 5 MB block microbenchmark together with the 7 MB random microbenchmark.

4. EVALUATION (HARDWARE)

4.1 Experimental Setup

Our evaluation system consisted of a 2.4 GHz Intel Xeon E5620 system (Westmere) with 4 cores and 6 GB DDR3 memory. Each core has a private 32 kB L1 data cache and a

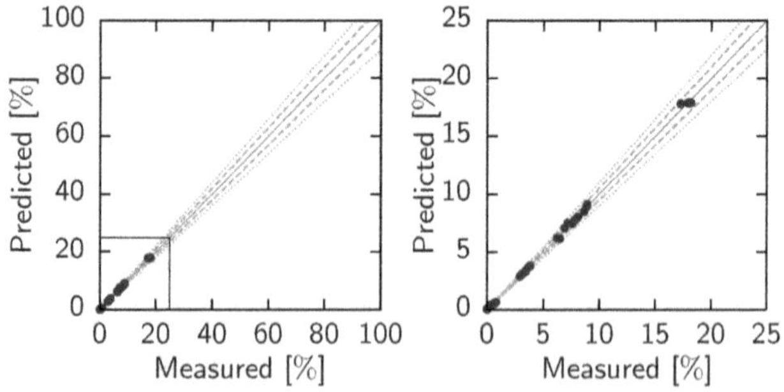

(a) Two co-scheduled benchmarks

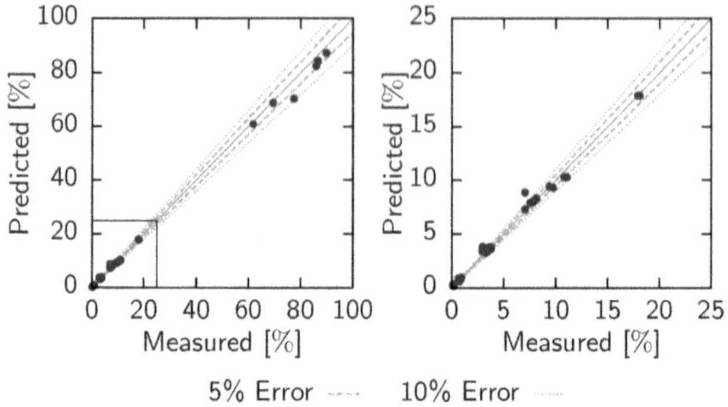

(b) Four co-scheduled benchmarks

Figure 8: Predicted vs. measured fetch ratio for applications running on an Intel Xeon E5620 based system.

private 256 kB L2 cache. All four cores share a 12 MB 16-way L3 cache with a pseudo-LRU replacement policy.

Our cache sharing model requires information about application fetch rate, access rate and hit ratio as a function of cache size. We used Cache Pirating [6] to measure this data for different cache sizes in steps 16 steps of 768 kB (the equivalent of one way) up to 12 MB.

We used the same benchmarks in the hardware study and the simulation study. However, we increased the size of the microbenchmarks' data set by 50% to better stress the 50% larger shared last-level cache.

While measuring the microbenchmarks, we discovered that the Cache Pirate slightly overestimates working set sizes. The average error in working set for the random microbenchmark was 256 kB due to the Pirate application and the monitoring framework using some of the shared cache. We compensated for this error by shrinking the total cache size in the model by this amount and offsetting the input data.

4.2 Results

Figure 8a compares the predicted and measured fetch ratio of pairs of co-scheduled applications. We do not show the amount of cache allocated to each application since there is no accurate way to measure this on the hardware. Unlike the simulator, we only found one solution for each benchmark pair. We believe that the reason for this is that the fetch rate curves of the applications running on our reference hardware do not have as sharp edges as in the simulator. The average relative error in predicted fetch ratio was 7.1%. Similar to the simulator evaluation, we excluded applications with a fetch ratio lower than 0.5% from the average. Figure 8b

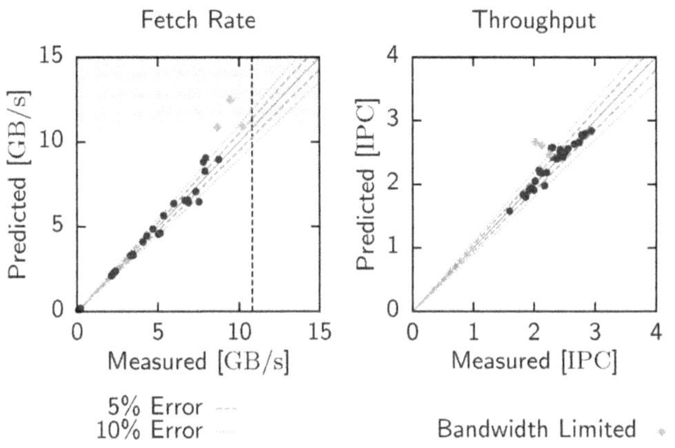

Figure 9: Estimated bandwidth vs. measured bandwidth and estimated IPC vs. measured IPC for pairs of benchmarks running on an Intel Xeon E5620 based system. The gray area indicates the bandwidth limit.

shows the results for groups of four co-scheduled applications. The average fetch ratio error was 6.7%.

4.3 Estimating Bandwidth and Throughput

Knowing how applications share cache allows us to predict other performance metrics, such as bandwidth requirements and throughput. The data measured using Cache Pirating contains information about each application's individual CPI and bandwidth requirement as a function of cache size. Since we can predict each application's cache allocation, we can trivially find its *bandwidth demand*. Assuming that a mix is not bandwidth limited, we can calculate the combined IPC of the mix (throughput) and its expected bandwidth usage.

Knowing the combined bandwidth demand of an application mix can guide a scheduler to avoid mixes with bandwidth demands too close to the system's bandwidth limitation. For mixes well below that limitation, our throughput estimates should be accurate enough to find the best mixes.

We estimated the real-world bandwidth limit of our reference system to approximately 12 GB/s using the STREAM benchmark [12]. We consider an application mix to be bandwidth limited if it uses more than 90% of the maximum bandwidth.

Figure 9 compares the combined bandwidth and throughput of our estimation with the corresponding numbers measured on real hardware. As seen in the figure, as long as the estimated bandwidth is low enough (below 11 GB/s), our bandwidth estimate is quite accurate. Excluding the mixes with a too high bandwidth demand, we can predict the bandwidth of a mix with an average relative error of less than 5.9% and throughput with an average error less than 2.5%.

5. RELATED WORK

Cache sharing models can be divided into two categories: trace driven and high-level data driven. The trace driven models generally use memory access traces or stack distance[6] traces. The benefit of using traces is that they contain detailed information about the execution. Unfortunately, acquiring a memory access trace is slow and storage intensive. Using high-level data, such as sampled memory accesses or statistics provided by performance counters, has become a common approach to reduce data collection overhead.

There are several models [2, 4, 3, 17] using stack distance traces. Chandra et al. [2] pioneered the field with a statistical model that estimates the probability that an access becomes a miss by prolonging its stack distance with the expected number of accesses performed by other applications. One drawback with their model is that it assumes that an application's execution rate is independent of the amount of cache it has access to. Chen and Aamodt [4, 3] extended Chandra's model by including variable execution rate. They also improved the accuracy of the model for low cache associativity by taking the access distribution across sets into account.

The method most similar to ours is CAMP [19] by Xu et al. They use high-level input data, similar to the input data used by our model to model sharing among pairs of applications. However, their model depends on a linear approximation of CPI as a function of fetch ratio. Such an approximation is often inaccurate for processors with out-of-order execution and prefetching. We do not need to model execution rate as this is implicit in our input data. Xu et al. also evaluate two simpler models, which assume that an application's cache share is either proportional to its access rate or its fetch rate. The latter is equivalent to the model we use for random caches, but is applied to LRU caches and approximates fetch rates using their linear execution rate model.

Eklöv et al. proposed a statistical cache sharing model [5] using memory access samples, which can be measured with low overhead. They use a performance model similar to the one used by Xu et al. to estimate the relative execution rate of co-scheduled applications and merge the sampled access streams from each of them. Unfortunately, since they use a linear approximation of execution rate, they suffer from the same drawbacks as the model by Xu et al.

Two recent works focus on estimating how resource contention affects performance. Mars et al. [10] use a stress benchmark to induce contention in an application and then measure its slowdown. The slowdown is used as a contention-sensitivity metric which can be used to guide schedulers. Unlike our method, they do not try to estimate the performance of specific combinations of applications. Instead they focus on a general classification of applications as either being sensitive or insensitive to contention. The approach by Van Craeynest and Eeckhout [16] is more similar to our method in that they estimate the throughput of mixes of applications. A major difference between our methods is that they depend on a single high-fidelity simulation to generate the application profiles used by their model, whereas we measure our input data with low overhead on the target system.

6. FUTURE WORK

We are currently working on extending our models to handle time-varying application behavior. A simple approach would be to slice applications into time windows and estimate sharing between windows. Such an approach would work, however, the amount of data needed would most likely be prohibitively large. Instead, we envision using phase infor-

[6]A stack distance is the number of *unique* between two accesses to the same cache line.

mation, which would enable us to analyze larger regions of stable behavior.

Another exciting direction is to extend the model to more accurately predict throughput for bandwidth limited mixes. This, however, most likely requires a detailed analytical performance model of the processor or performance data as a function of bandwidth.

7. ACKNOWLEDGMENTS

The simulations were performed on resources provided by the Swedish National Infrastructure for Computing (SNIC) at Uppsala Multidisciplinary Center for Advanced Computational Science (UPPMAX). This work was financed by the CoDeR-MP project and the UPMARC research center.

8. REFERENCES

[1] N. L. Binkert, R. G. Dreslinski, L. R. Hsu, K. T. Lim, A. G. Saidi, and S. K. Reinhardt. The M5 Simulator: Modeling Networked Systems. In *Proc. Annual International Symposium on Microarchitecture (MICRO)*, 2006.

[2] D. Chandra, F. Guo, S. Kim, and Y. Solihin. Predicting Inter-thread Cache Contention on a Chip Multi-Processor Architecture. In *Proc. International Symposium on High-Performance Computer Architecture (HPCA)*, 2005.

[3] X. Chen and T. Aamodt. Modeling Cache Contention and Throughput of Multiprogrammed Manycore Processors. *IEEE Transactions on Computers*, PP(99), 2011.

[4] X. E. Chen and T. M. Aamodt. A First-Order Fine-Grained Multithreaded Throughput Model. In *Proc. International Symposium on High-Performance Computer Architecture (HPCA)*, 2009.

[5] D. Eklöv, D. Black-Schaffer, and E. Hagersten. Fast Modeling of Cache Contention in Multicore Systems. In *Proc. International Conference on High Performance and Embedded Architecture and Compilation (HiPEAC)*, 2011.

[6] D. Eklöv, N. Nikoleris, D. Black-Schaffer, and E. Hagersten. Cache Pirating: Measuring the Curse of the Shared Cache. In *Proc. International Conference on Parallel Processing (ICPP)*, 2011.

[7] F. N. Fritsch and R. E. Carlson. Monotone Piecewise Cubic Interpolation. *SIAM Journal on Numerical Analysis*, 17(2):238, 1980.

[8] A. Jaleel, W. Hasenplaugh, M. Qureshi, J. Sebot, J. Simon Steely, and J. Emer. Adaptive Insertion Policies for Managing Shared Caches. In *Proc. International Conference on Parallel Architectures and Compilation Techniques (PACT)*, 2008.

[9] J. D. C. Little. A Proof for the Queuing Formula: $L = \lambda W$. *Operations Research*, 9(3):383–387, 1961.

[10] J. Mars, L. Tang, and M. L. Soffa. Directly Characterizing Cross Core Interference Through Contention Synthesis. In *Proc. International Conference on High Performance and Embedded Architecture and Compilation (HiPEAC)*, 2011.

[11] J. Mars, N. Vachharajani, R. Hundt, and M. L. Soffa. Contention Aware Execution. In *Proc. International Symposium on Code Generation and Optimization (CGO)*, 2010.

[12] J. D. McCalpin. STREAM: Sustainable Memory Bandwidth in High Performance Computers. Tech. rep., University of Virginia, 1991–2007. http://www.cs.virginia.edu/stream/.

[13] M. K. Qureshi and Y. N. Patt. Utility-Based Cache Partitioning: A Low-Overhead, High-Performance, Runtime Mechanism to Partition Shared Caches. In *Proc. Annual International Symposium on Microarchitecture (MICRO)*, 2006.

[14] A. Sandberg, D. Eklöv, and E. Hagersten. Reducing Cache Pollution Through Detection and Elimination of Non-Temporal Memory Accesses. In *Proc. High Performance Computing, Networking, Storage and Analysis (SC)*, 2010.

[15] D. Tam, R. Azimi, L. Soares, and M. Stumm. Managing Shared L2 Caches on Multicore Systems in Software. In *Proc. Workshop on the Interaction between Operating Systems and Computer Architecture (WIOSCA)*, 2007.

[16] K. Van Craeynest and L. Eeckhout. The Multi-Program Performance Model: Debunking Current Practice in Multi-Core Simulation. In *Proc. International Symposium on Workload Characterization (IISWC)*, 2011.

[17] X. Xiang, B. Bao, T. Bai, C. Ding, and T. Chilimbi. All-Window Profiling and Composable Models of Cache Sharing. In *Proc. Symposium on Principles and Practice of Parallel Programming (PPoPP)*, 2011.

[18] Y. Xie and G. H. Loh. Dynamic Classification of Program Memory Behaviors in CMPs. In *Proc. Workshop on Chip Multiprocessor Memory Systems and Interconnects (CMP-MSI)*, 2008.

[19] C. Xu, X. Chen, R. P. Dick, and Z. M. Mao. Cache Contention and Application Performance Prediction for Multi-Core Systems. In *Proc. International Symposium on Performance Analysis of Systems & Software (ISPASS)*, 2010.

[20] S. Zhuravlev, S. Blagodurov, and A. Fedorova. Addressing Shared Resource Contention in Multicore Processors via Scheduling. In *Proc. Internationla Conference on Architectural Support for Programming Languages and Operating Systems (ASPLOS)*, 2010.

Optimal Bypass Monitor for High Performance Last-level Caches

Lingda Li, Dong Tong, Zichao Xie, Junlin Lu, Xu Cheng
Microprocessor Research and Development Center, Peking University, Beijing, China
{lilingda, tongdong, xiezichao, lujunlin, chengxu}@mprc.pku.edu.cn

ABSTRACT

In the last-level cache, large amounts of blocks have reuse distances greater than the available cache capacity. Cache performance and efficiency can be improved if some subset of these distant reuse blocks can reside in the cache longer. The bypass technique is an effective and attractive solution that prevents the insertion of harmful blocks.

Our analysis shows that bypass can contribute significant performance improvement, and the optimal bypass can achieve similar performance compared to OPT+B, which is the theoretical optimal replacement policy. Thus, we propose a bypass technique called *Optimal Bypass oni tor OB* , which makes bypass decisions by learning and predicting the behavior of the optimal bypass. OBM keeps a short global track of the incoming-victim block pairs. By detecting the first reuse block in each pair, the behavior of the optimal bypass on the track can be asserted to guide the bypass choice.

Any existing replacement policy can be extended with OBM while requiring negligible design modification. Our experimental results show that using less than 1.5KB extra memory, OBM with the NRU replacement policy outperforms LRU by 9.7% and 8.9% for single-thread and multi-programmed workloads respectively. Compared with other state-of-the-art proposals such as DRRIP and SDBP, it achieves superior performance with less storage overhead.

Categories and Subject Descriptors

B.3.2 [**Memory Structures**]: Design Styles—*cac e mem ories*

General Terms

Design, Performance

Keywords

Optimal Bypass, Replacement, Last-level Cache

PACT'12, September 19–23, 2012, Minneapolis, Minnesota, USA.

1. INTRODUCTION

Energy efficiency is treated as a critical metric in modern processor design, and future processors tend to integrate larger last-level caches (LLCs) due to their high energy efficiency [3]. However, the cache management policy is critical to the processor performance and efficiency. The commonly-used Least Recently Used (LRU) policy and its approximations perform poorly for LLCs because most of the temporal locality is filtered by inner-level caches. This paper focuses on improving the LLC performance and efficiency with very low hardware cost[1].

As shown in Figure 1, the reuse distances of numerous LLC blocks (cache lines) are greater than the cache size, which leads to the poor performance of LRU policy. Such kinds of cache blocks are called *istant re se locks* in this paper. A good LLC management policy should retain cache blocks with high temporal locality in the LLC first, and then avoid thrashing caused by distant reuse blocks. In order to achieve such goals, various replacement policies [12, 27, 38] attempt to insert distant reuse blocks into the LRU position. Dead block prediction techniques [10, 19, 20, 21, 22] try to identify distant reuse blocks to evict them earlier. Several adaptive methods [12, 27, 28, 32] dynamically change between different replacement policies to accommodate to the changing access patterns. However, such proposals either cannot achieve significant performance improvement, or require significant hardware overhead and large modification to the cache structure. There is still large potential space for the exploration of the LLC management policies.

Bypass is an effective and attractive technique. Figure 2 shows that on average 81.2% of blocks are not reused before eviction in a 2MB LLC. Among them, 25.6% of blocks are never accessed again, and they should be bypassed rather than being inserted into the LLC. For the remaining 55.6% of blocks, Belady's OPT [2] with bypass (OPT+B), which is the theoretical optimal replacement policy, inserts the blocks with minimal reuse distances to fill up the cache at first, and then bypasses the others to avoid thrashing. Besides, our experiments show that the optimal bypass, which bypasses the incoming block if its reuse distance is larger than or equal to that of the victim block selected by the baseline replacement policy, can achieve similar performance improvement compared to OPT+B. Thus, bypass can make significant contribution to the LLC performance. Moreover, bypass can save energy consumption due to the reduction of replacement and writebacks.

[1]Unless stated otherwise, cache refers to the last-level cache in this paper.

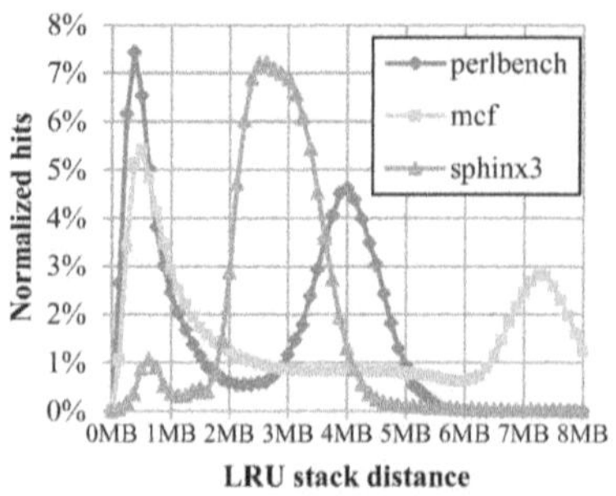

Figure 1: Normalized hit distribution in the stack of a 64-way 8MB LRU LLC. This figure shows lots of blocks have reuse distances larger than 2MB.

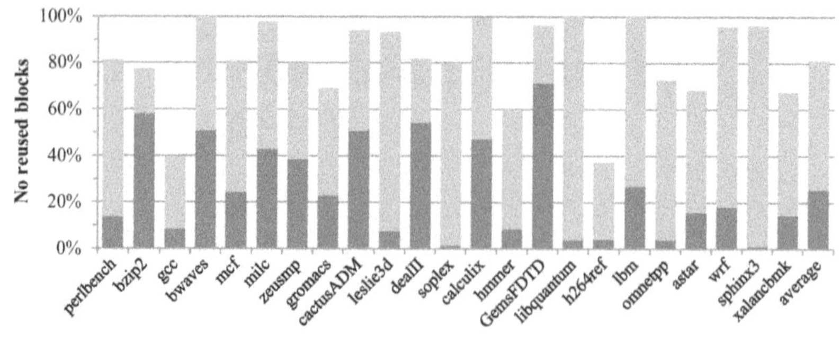

Figure 2: Percentage of distant reuse blocks in a 2MB LRU LLC. This figure shows that over a memory-intensive subset of SPEC CPU2006 benchmarks, 81.2% of blocks are not reused before eviction. Among them 25.6% of blocks are never accessed again, and they should be bypassed to improve cache performance and efficiency.

In this paper, we propose a bypass technique called *Optimal Bypass onitor* OB , which learns and predicts the behavior of the optimal bypass to make bypass decisions. OBM uses a small *Replacement istory a le* R   to keep track of the recent incoming-victim block pairs. On each cache access, the current incoming block and victim candidate will compare with the RHT content to assert the behavior of the optimal bypass on a recorded pair. A PC indexed *Bypass ecision Co nter a le* B C of saturating counters is used to learn which operation, bypass or replacement, is dominated under the optimal bypass recently and determine whether bypass should be used.

OBM can be applied to the current LLC design with any replacement policy, and it requires negligible modification to the existing cache design. Furthermore, OBM is both thread-aware and prefetch-aware.

We evaluate OBM with NRU, LRU, and SRRIP [12]. Our evaluation shows that they all improve cache performance significantly while requiring only less than 1.5KB extra storage. Among them, OBM with NRU performs well enough and requires minimal hardware cost. On average it outperforms LRU by 9.7% and 8.9% for single-thread and multi-programmed workloads respectively in the absence of prefetching, and it can also improve performance significantly in the presence of prefetching. Compared to other state-of-the-art proposals including DRRIP [12], SDBP [19], and DSB [6], OBM with NRU has superior performance while requiring less storage overhead.

The rest of this paper is organized as follows. Section 2 demonstrates the motivation of OBM. Section 3 describes the design and implementation of OBM. We show the experimental methodology and analyze the results in Section 4 and 5. Section 6 discusses some related work. Finally, the paper is concluded in Section 7.

2. MOTIVATION

Bypass is a promising technique for LLCs due to its high performance and efficiency, and thus we aim to design an LLC bypass technique in this paper. In order to understand how bypass should work, we first study OPT [2] with bypass (OPT+B), which is the theoretical optimal replacement policy for minimal misses. On a miss, among all victim candidates, OPT selects the block with the largest reuse distance for replacement. After enhanced with bypass, OPT+B does not replace any block if the reuse distance of the incoming block is larger than or equal to that of any victim candidate.

Figure 3 illustrates the behavior of OPT+B for four representative cache access patterns [12]. Let a_i donate a cache block. $(a_1, a_2, a_3, \ldots, a_n)$ denotes an access sequence from block a_1 to block a_n, and $(a_1, a_2, a_3, \ldots, a_n)^I$ denotes that an access sequence repeats I times.

For cache friendly access patterns, OPT+B behaves as normal replacement policies to insert all incoming blocks because of their good locality. For streaming access patterns, since there is no temporal locality for any block, OPT+B bypasses all incoming blocks. Although these bypasses cannot improve performance, the power used for replacement can be saved to improve efficiency.

While the performance of LRU and its approximations is close to that of OPT+B for cache friendly and streaming patterns, they perform poorly for the remaining two access patterns. For thrashing access patterns, OPT+B first places a subset of the working set into the cache. Then, the rest of blocks are bypassed to avoid thrashing. In mixed access patterns, blocks with different locality are mixed together. The accesses to blocks with poor locality are called *scans* because their insertion evicts good blocks in the cache. For the example in Figure 3, OPT+B retains d_1 and d_2 which have the best locality and a subset of e_i, while bypasses the rest. Our analysis of OPT+B shows that bypass plays an important role on improving the LLC performance and efficiency.

OPT+B uses both the optimal replacement and optimal bypass to improve cache performance. However, the optimal bypass itself can have similar performance compared to OPT+B. The optimal bypass compares the reuse distances of the incoming block and the victim block, which is selected by the baseline replacement policy. If the incoming block has a larger or equal reuse distance, it will be bypassed by the optimal bypass. Otherwise it replaces the victim. Figure 4 shows that for a 16-way 2MB LLC, the optimal bypass with LRU (LRU+OB) reduces average misses by 23.5% compared to LRU, and it bridges roughly four-fifths of the gap between LRU and OPT+B. Compared to other recent proposals like DRRIP [12] and SDBP [19], it outperforms them dramatically.

Cache friendly access pattern $(a_1, a_2, a_3, a_4)^I$

Access	a_1	a_2	a_3	a_4	a_1	...
Cache		a_1	a_1	a_1	a_1	a_1
			a_2	a_2	a_2	a_2
				a_3	a_3	a_3
					a_4	a_4
Behavior	R	R	R	R	H	H
Burst type	Replace					

Streaming access pattern $(b_1, b_2, b_3, b_4, ...)$

Access	b_1	b_2	b_3	b_4	...
Cache	a_1	a_1	a_1	a_1	a_1
	a_2	a_2	a_2	a_2	a_2
	a_3	a_3	a_3	a_3	a_3
	a_4	a_4	a_4	a_4	a_4
Behavior	B	B	B	B	B
Burst type	Bypass				

Thrashing access pattern $(c_1, c_2, c_3, c_4, c_5, c_6)^J$

Access	c_1	c_2	c_3	c_4	c_5	c_6	...	c_5	...
Cache	a_1	c_1	c_1	c_1	c_1	c_1	c_1	c_1	c_1
	a_2	a_2	c_2	c_2	c_2	c_2	c_2	c_2	c_2
	a_3	a_3	a_3	c_3	c_3	c_3	c_3	c_3	c_3
	a_4	a_4	a_4	a_4	c_4	c_4	c_4	c_4	c_4
Behavior	R	R	R	R	B	B	H	B	H or B
Burst type	Replace				Bypass				

Mixed access pattern $[(d_1, d_2)^2, e_1, e_2, e_3, e_4]^K$

Access	d_1	d_2	d_1	d_2	e_1	e_2	e_3	e_4	...	e_3	e_4	...
Cache	c_1	d_1	d_1	d_1	d_1	d_1	d_1	d_1	d_1	d_1	d_1	d_1
	c_2	c_2	d_2	d_2	d_2	d_2	d_2	d_2	d_2	d_2	d_2	d_2
	c_3	c_3	c_3	c_3	c_3	e_1	e_1	e_1	e_1	e_1	e_1	e_1
	c_4	c_4	c_4	c_4	c_4	c_4	e_2	e_2	e_2	e_2	e_2	e_2
Behavior	R	R	H	H	R	R	B	B	H	B	B	H or B
Burst type	Replace						Bypass					

Note: H: hit; R: replacement; B: bypass.

Figure 3: The behavior of OPT+B for representative cache access patterns using a 4-entry cache.

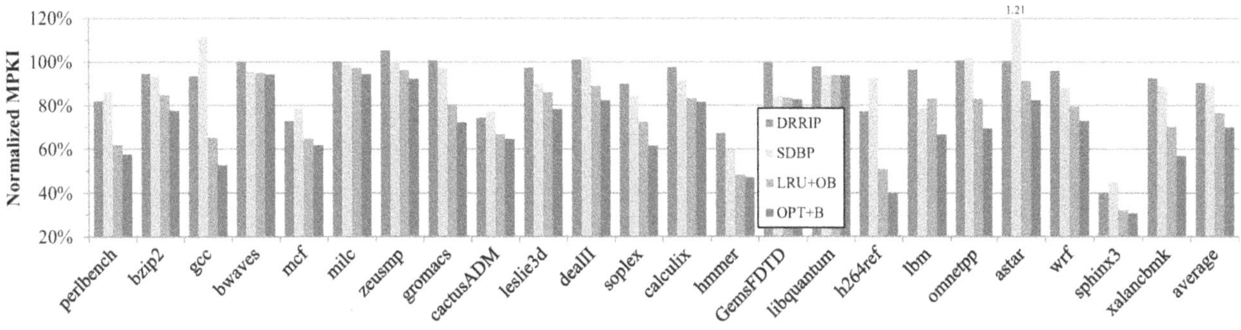

Figure 4: Normalized LLC MPKI for LRU+OB and OPT+B.

Although it is still impractical to implement the optimal bypass due to the need of future information, we can learn the past behavior of the optimal bypass to predict its future behavior. Therefore, to achieve high performance, the proposed bypass technique should behave similarly to the optimal bypass.

3. OPTIMAL BYPASS MONITOR

Our goal is to design a new bypass technique, which can make proper bypass decisions by dynamically learning and predicting the behavior of the optimal bypass. Thus, we propose *Optimal Bypass onitor OB* .

3.1 Overview

On a cache miss, the optimal bypass determines whether or not to use bypass based on the reuse distances of the incoming block (IB) and its corresponding victim block (VB), which is selected by the baseline replacement policy. Therefore, to learn the behavior of the optimal bypass, we propose *Replacement istory a le R* to keep track of IB-VB pairs on cache misses. Then according to the relative reuse order on a recorded pair, the behavior of the optimal bypass on that pair can be asserted:

- If IB is accessed earlier, the reuse distance of IB is smaller than that of VB. For that IB-VB pair, the optimal bypass should replace VB with IB;
- If VB is accessed earlier, the reuse distance of IB is larger than that of VB. For that IB-VB pair, the optimal bypass should bypass IB;
- If neither IB nor VB is accessed in the future, the reuse distances of IB and VB are both infinite, and the optimal bypass should also bypass IB.

These three conditions are called *Optimal Bypass ssertion s*, because we can assert the behavior of the optimal bypass by detecting the occurrence of one certain condition.

Table 1 shows three Optimal Bypass Assertions. Since Assertion 3 is impossible to detect, we consider that Assertion 3 is satisfied when IB and VB both have reuse distances larger than the cache size. This conversion is reasonable because if both blocks are not reused before eviction, IB should be bypassed to improve efficiency. Our experiments show that the probability of each assertion occurrence is 12.9%, 78.7%, and 8.4% respectively under LRU. Therefore, all assertions are essential to learn the behavior of the optimal bypass accurately.

Using Optimal Bypass Assertions, we can learn the behavior of the optimal bypass on the RHT content, and then saturating counters called *Bypass ecision Co nters B Cs* are employed to record the learning results. All BDCs are kept in the *Bypass ecision Co nter a le B C* , and they are initialized to -1. When the behavior of the optimal bypass on a recorded pair is detected, the signature of IB in that pair is used to index the BDCT to update its corresponding BDC. If Assertion 1 is satisfied, the BDC is decreased by 1; if Assertion 2 or 3 is satisfied, it is increased by 1.

On a miss, the incoming block consults the BDCT to find out whether it should be bypassed. If the BDC indexed by its signature is greater than or equal to 0, it indicates that the optimal bypass uses more bypasses for blocks with that signature recently, and thus OBM predicts that the incoming block should be bypassed. Otherwise, it indicates that replacement is the dominant behavior of the optimal bypass for blocks with that signature recently, and OBM predicts that the incoming block should be placed in the cache.

Table 1: Optimal Bypass Assertions to detect the behavior of the optimal bypass.

	Action on IB-VB pair	Reuse distance relationship	optimal bypass behavior
Assertion 1	Current incoming block hits IB.	IB's reuse distance < VB's reuse distance	Replacement
Assertion 2	Current incoming block hits VB.	IB's reuse distance > VB's reuse distance	Bypass
Assertion 3	Current victim block hits IB.	IB's reuse distance > cache size and VB's reuse distance > cache size	Bypass

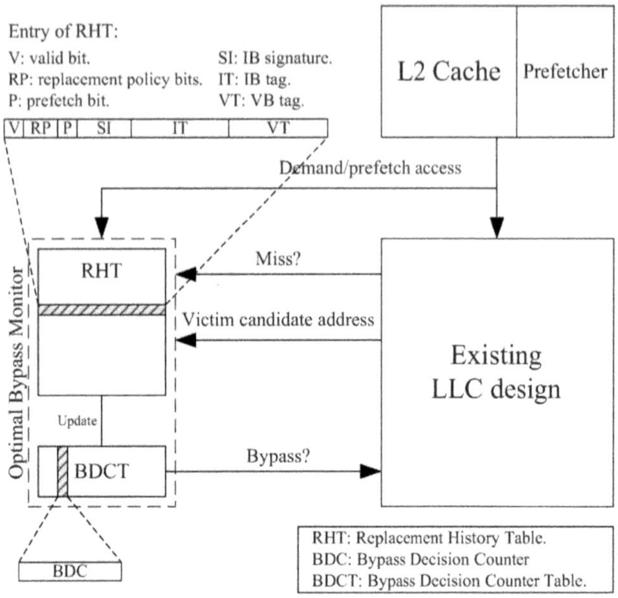

Figure 5: The structure of OBM.

```
On an access to block x:
if x is a demand access
    for each valid entry A in the corresponding set of RHT
        if x.tag == A.IT    // Assertion 1
            BDCT[A.SI]--;
            Invalidate A;
        else if x.tag == A.VT    // Assertion 2
            BDCT[A.SI]++;
            Invalidate A;
if x misses in the cache
    y = Select_Victim_Candidate();
    for each valid entry A in the corresponding set of RHT
        if y.tag == A.IT    // Assertion 3
            BDCT[A.SI]++;
            Invalidate A;
    if RHT.Record(x) == true
        B = RHT.Select_Victim(x);    // Select an entry to record x
        B.SI = x.signature;
        B.IT = x.tag;
        B.VT = y.tag;
    if BDCT[x.signature] >= 0
        Bypass x;
    else
        Replace y with x;
```

Figure 6: The algorithm of OBM.

Figure 5 and 6 illustrate the structure and algorithm of OBM respectively. OBM requires only a little necessary information from the baseline LLC, and it uses a signal to inform the LLC whether to bypass the current miss or not. Therefore, the existing LLC design does not need to be changed.

OBM can be used with any deterministic replacement policy. It can also potentially cooperate with non-deterministic replacement policies like the random policy. However, because the random policy chooses victim blocks randomly, which makes the behavior of the optimal bypass less predictable, OBM with the random policy does not work as well as OBM with other policies, although it still outperforms L-RU. Thus, we only evaluate the performance of OBM with some deterministic replacement policies, including the Not Recently Used policy (NRU), LRU, and SRRIP [12].

3.2 Implementation Details

The RHT can be organized as fully-associate, set-associate, or direct-associate. In practice we use a 16-way set-associate RHT. Each RHT entry contains 6 fields: a valid bit indicates whether the entry is valid, and an RHT entry is invalidated when the behavior of the optimal bypass on it is detected; the RP bits are used to implement the replacement policy of RHT, which is similar to LRU; the P bit introduces prefetch awareness; the SI bits keep the signature of IB; IT and VT store the tag of IB and VB respectively. We also use partial tags to reduce the RHT storage overhead, and IT and VT store the lower 21 bits of tags instead of the whole tags.

To reduce the storage overhead, it is not necessary to record all misses in the RHT. A miss should be recorded only if there are invalid entries in the corresponding set of RHT or a low probability is satisfied. Our experiments show that, for a 16-way 128-entry RHT and a 16-way 2MB LLC, OBM can perform well when 1/512 of misses are recorded.

Various kinds of block signatures can be used to index the BDCT, such as memory address, instruction program counter (PC), or many others [35]. Previous studies have shown that methods using PC can be more effective than other methods. Therefore, we use the instruction PC which causes the miss as the signature to update and consult the BDCT. For a 1024-entry BDCT, the lower 10 bits of PC are used to index the BDCT. Like all PC based methods [17, 19, 20, 21, 23, 35, 37], the shortened PC is delivered along with the request through the cache hierarchies.

3.3 Thread-awareness

OBM is naturally thread-aware because of its PC based design. Since OBM makes bypass decisions based on the behavior of the optimal bypass, it can implicitly partition the shared LLC to minimize the total misses. The program with poor locality will have more blocks bypassed, and thus its cache space is released to improve the performance of programs with good locality.

3.4 Prefetch-awareness

Prefetch is an important feature in modern high performance processors, and a simple extension is proposed to make OBM prefetch-aware. Demand and prefetch accesses usually have different behavior. For instance, in a thrash-

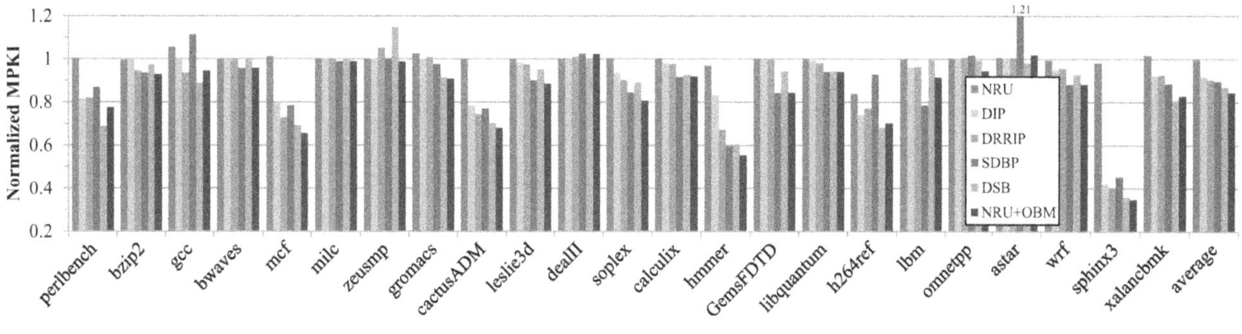

Figure 7: Reduction in MPKI normalized to LRU.

ing access pattern, demand accesses have large reuse distances and should be bypassed, while prefetch accesses are expected to be used soon and should be inserted. Therefore, it is reasonable to make bypass decisions for demand and prefetch accesses separately. In the prefetch-aware OBM, we assign an additional BDC for each core, which is dedicated for prefetch accesses. The prefetch bit (P in Figure 5) in the RHT entry indicates whether the entry records a prefetch access, and the signature field is used to store the core number of the incoming block instead of the shortened PC when recording a prefetch access.

4. EXPERIMENTAL METHODOLOGY

4.1 Simulator

The simulator we used is CMP$im, a Pin based trace-driven x86 simulator. We use a modified version which is provided for the 1st JWAC Cache Replacement Championship. It models an out-of-order, 4-wide, and 8-stage pipeline with a 128-entry instruction window. The microarchitecture parameters of memory hierarchies are shown in Table 2, which are similar to Intel Core i7 [11]. The L1 and L2 caches are private to each core. In single-core configuration, the LLC (L3 cache) is 16-way 2MB for single-thread workloads. In 4-core configuration, the LLC is 16-way 8MB for multi-programmed workloads. It also models a stream hardware prefetcher in each L2 cache, and the prefetched blocks are inserted into both the L2 and L3 caches.

Table 2: Parameters of memory hierarchies

Parameter	Configuration
L1 ICache	64B blocks, 32KB, 4-way, 1 cycle, LRU
L1 DCache	64B blocks, 32KB, 8-way, 1 cycle, LRU
L2 Cache	64B blocks, 256KB, 8-way, 10 cycles, LRU
Last-level Cache	64B blocks, 2MB per core, 16-way, 30 cycles
Memory Latency	200 cycles
RHT	128-entry, 16-way
BDCT	4-bit BDC, 1-entry per core+1024-entry

4.2 Benchmarks

We use SPEC CPU2006 benchmarks [9] with the first reference inputs to do evaluation. These benchmarks are compiled using GCC 4.5.2 with -O2 optimizations. We use PinPoints [26] to obtain a single representative one billion instructions for each benchmark. Among these benchmarks, gamess, namd, povray, sjeng, tonto, and specrand are not evaluated because their working sets are so small that their misses are mostly compulsory misses, and the performance improvement is less than 1% when the cache size increases from 2MB to 32MB under LRU. The rest of 23 benchmarks are used in our experiments[2].

For multi-programmed workloads, we choose four benchmarks out of our memory-intensive set of SPEC CPU2006 at random to combine into a mix workload. Totally, we create 15 mix workloads. Simulations run until all benchmarks have executed one billion instructions. If one benchmark finishes its one billion instructions early, it restarts from the beginning to continue modeling the contention of four cores. Our experimental methodology is similar to other recent work.

5. RESULTS AND ANALYSIS

5.1 OBM with NRU

At first we evaluate the performance of Optimal Bypass Monitor in the absence of hardware prefetching. Figure 7 shows misses per thousand instructions (MPKI) normalized to LRU for OBM with NRU (NRU+OBM) and other techniques. Besides the baseline NRU and NRU+OBM, we also investigate the recently proposed techniques including DIP [27], DRRIP[3] [12], sampling dead block prediction (SDBP) [19], and dueling segmented LRU with adaptive bypassing (DSB)[4] [6]. While the MPKI of NRU is similar to that of LRU, NRU+OBM reduces MPKI by 15.5% compared to LRU on average, and the best reduction is 65.1% for sphinx3. NRU+OBM also outperforms other proposals: DIP reduces 8.2% of MPKI on average, while the reduction is 9.7% for DRRIP, 10.4% for SDBP, and 13.0% for DSB.

Figure 8 shows the speedup over LRU. The speedup is computed by dividing the IPC of various proposals by the IPC of LRU. The geometric mean speedup of NRU+OBM is 9.7%, while it is 4.9% for DIP, 6.0% for DRRIP, 6.3% for SDBP, and 7.5% for DSB. Moreover, the performance degradation is less than 0.5% compared to the baseline NRU for all benchmarks. Our results show that NRU+OBM can deliver significantly superior performance compared to other recent work.

[2]Our infrastructure cannot address gobmk, and previous work has reported that gobmk is not memory-intensive.

[3]We use 2-bit SRRIP and DRRIP in this paper because it performs slightly better in our experiments.

[4]We use its second configuration which is reported to perform best in their paper.

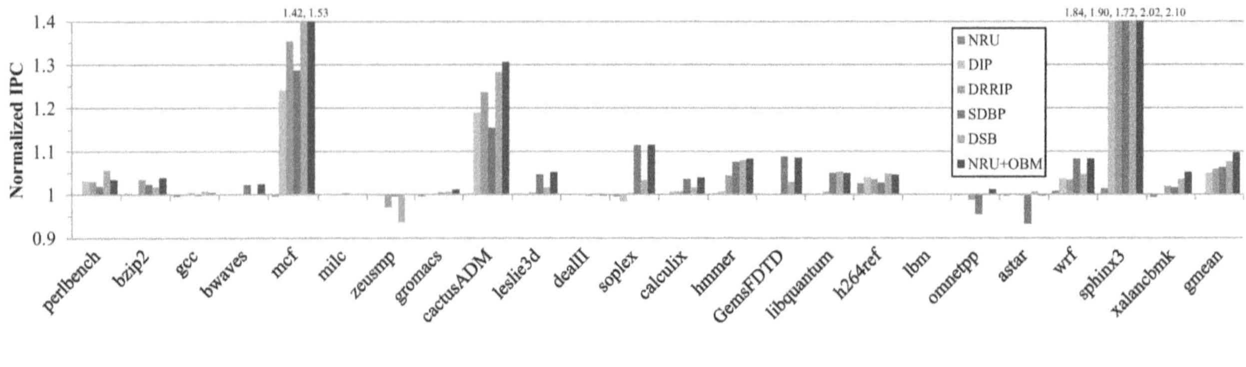

Figure 8: Speedup for various policies.

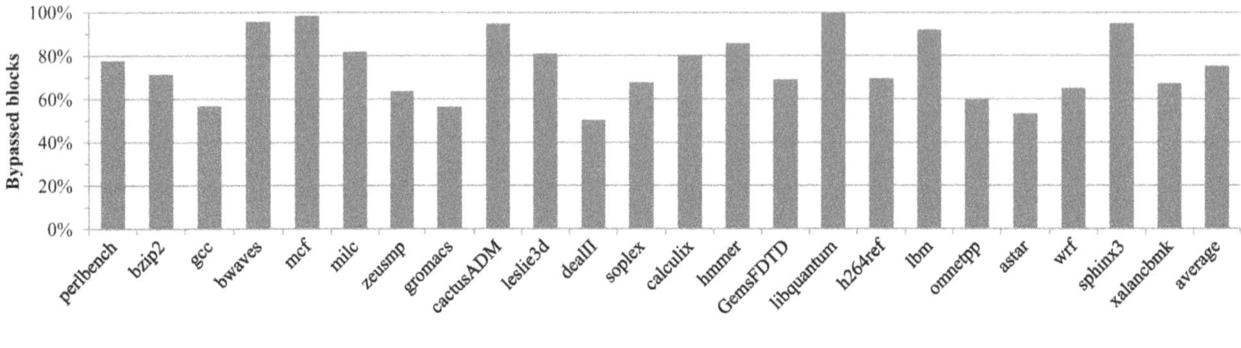

Figure 9: Percentage of bypassed blocks.

Figure 9 shows the fraction of bypassed cache blocks for NRU+OBM. It shows that on average 75.2% of incoming blocks are bypassed. For benchmarks which have a large fraction of blocks not reused in Figure 2 such as cactusADM, libquantum, and sphinx3, most incoming blocks are bypassed and OBM performs well for them. Even for benchmarks which LRU performs well enough like zeusmp, dealII, and astar, roughly half of the misses are bypassed. Although these bypasses do not help to improve the performance, they reduce the writeback number of dirty victim blocks. As a result, the contention on shared system buses is reduced, and the power used to write back dirty victim blocks is saved, too.

5.2 OBM with Other Replacement Policies

Besides NRU, we also investigate the performance of OBM with LRU and SRRIP. The results are similar to those of NRU+OBM. LRU+OBM outperforms LRU by 9.5%, and the reduction in MPKI is 14.6% on average. SRRIP+OBM outperforms LRU by 9.4% and reduces MPKI by 15.5%. Compared to SRRIP, SRRIP+OBM outperforms by 7.7%. These results show that OBM can cooperate with various replacement policies well. Among these replacement policies, NRU needs the least storage and is the simplest, while the performance of NRU+OBM is comparable to that of LRU+OBM and SRRIP+OBM. Therefore, we mainly focus on the study of NRU+OBM in the following experiments.

5.3 Sensitivity to the Size of RHT and BDCT

Figure 10 studies the sensitivity of NRU+OBM performance to different size of RHT and BDC using a 1024-entry BDCT. The number of RHT entries is changed from 16 to 1024 while the associativity is fixed at 16, and the probability of recording misses in the RHT is adjusted accordingly. The number of BDC bits is changed from 2 to 5. Figure 10 shows that a 128-entry RHT with 4-bit BDCs can perform sufficiently well. A small RHT with large BDCs performs poorly because the learning process is slower. On the other hand, a large RHT with small BDCs also degrades performance because BDCs are easily affected by accidental events and become more sensitive.

Figure 11 studies the performance sensitivity to the BDCT size when using a 128-entry RHT and 4-bit BDCs. The results show that a 1024-entry BDCT is enough and more entries are not necessary. We also notice that even a 16-entry RHT with a 128-entry BDCT and 3-bit BDCs can achieve a significant speedup of 8.2% compared to LRU, which requires only 0.17KB extra storage.

5.4 Sensitivity to the Cache Size

Figure 12 shows the speedup of NRU+OBM for different cache sizes. We vary the size of LLC from 512KB to 8MB and the associativity is fixed at 16. The speedup is normalized to the speedup of LRU for the specified cache size. We show the speedup for five representative benchmarks and the geometric mean speedup for all 23 benchmarks. The figure shows that the performance gain of OBM for small caches is limited because there is less wasted space to place distant reuse blocks such as soplex and libquantum. While for large caches, the performance gain decreases because there are fewer distant reuse blocks and the working set is more likely to fit into the cache such as perlbench and hmmer. However, NRU+OBM can still achieve a geometric mean speedup of

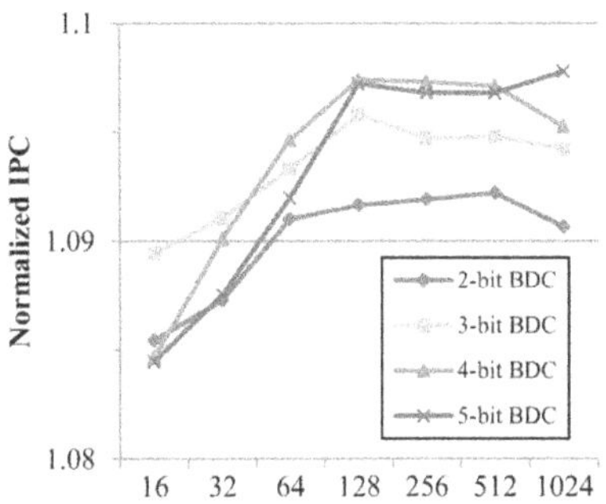

Figure 10: Sensitivity to the size of RHT and BDC.

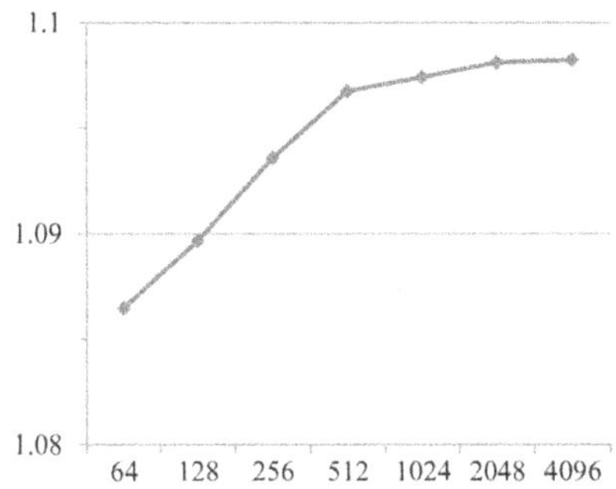

Figure 11: Sensitivity to the size of BDCT.

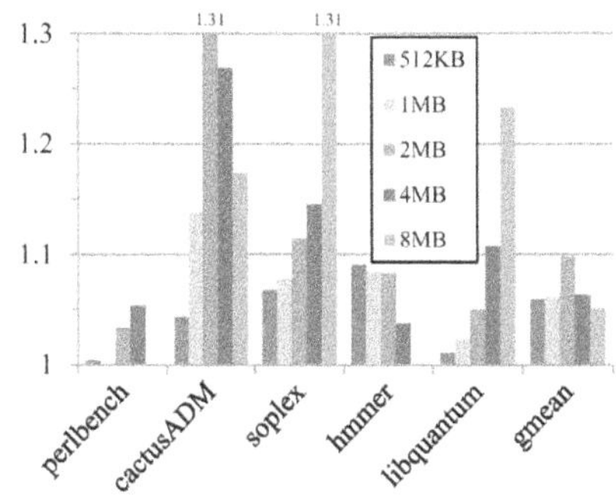

Figure 12: NRU+OBM for different cache sizes.

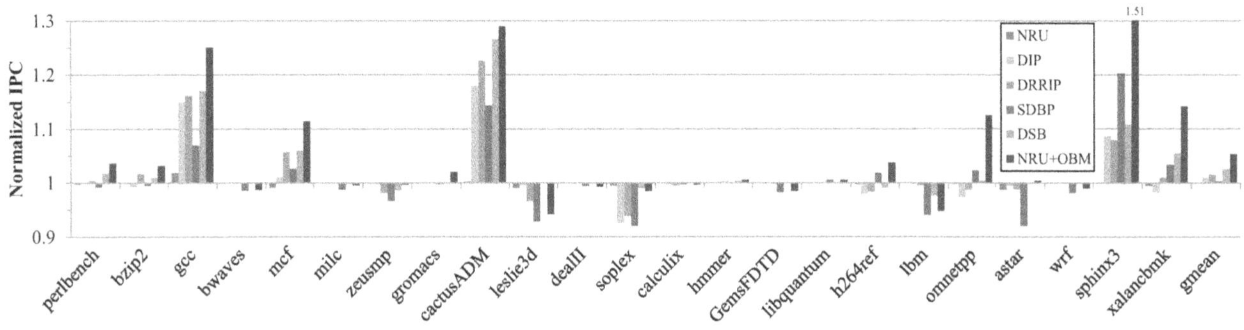

Figure 13: Speedup in the presence of prefetching.

5.1% for an 8MB LLC. Therefore, we conclude that OBM is scalable to different cache sizes.

5.5 LRU Insertion Instead of Bypass

It is straightforward to apply OBM in non-inclusive and exclusive LLCs, but to satisfy inclusion, bypass cannot be used. In order to apply OBM in inclusive LLCs, a reasonable choice is to insert the incoming block into the LRU position instead of bypassing it [27]. The reason is that when bypass is not allowed, if the reuse distance of the incoming block is larger than or equal to that of any victim candidate, OPT will insert it into the LRU position so that it can be evicted on the next miss. Therefore, we modify OBM to *Optimal RU insertion onitor O* . OLM uses the penultimate victim block instead of the real victim block to train the RHT. Our experiments show that with the same configuration, the speedup of NRU+OLM is 8.9%. Although it underperforms NRU+OBM slightly, it still outperforms other recent work.

5.6 Results in the presence of prefetching

Next, we evaluate the performance of OBM when the hardware prefetcher is enabled. Figure 13 shows that NRU+OBM reduces average MPKI by 16.2% and achieves a performance gain of 5.3% compared to LRU in the presence of prefetching. It doubles the performance gain of other recent proposals due to its ability to make bypass decisions for demand and prefetch accesses separately. Compared to LRU without prefetching, it can outperform by 66.1%. The experiments of SRRIP+OBM and LRU+OBM show similar results in the presence of prefetching.

5.7 Results for Multi-threaded Workloads

Figure 14(a) shows the weighted speedup normalized to LRU for various techniques on 15 multi-programmed workloads in the absence of prefetching. The weighted speedup is computed as the formula $\sum_{i=1}^{4} \frac{IPC_i}{SingleIPC_i}$, where *in le* C_i is got when program i runs alone on an 8MB LRU-managed LLC. NRU+OBM can achieve a normalized weighted speedup of 8.9% on geometric mean, while it is 6.8% for SDBP which performs best among various state-of-the-art techniques. NRU+OBM improves 14 out of 15 mix workloads more than 1%, and does not degrade performance for any workload. In the presence of prefetching, the performance gain of NRU+OBM is 6.2% compared to that of LRU with prefetching, which is twice the performance gain of other proposals in which SDBP performs best and outperforms LRU by 3.1%.

Figure 14(b) summarizes the results for OBM with other replacement policies. For LRU+OBM, the weighted speedup is 9.3% and 6.1% without and with prefetching respectively. For SRRIP+OBM it is 9.6% and 6.3%. SRRIP+OBM performs best for multi-programmed workloads because SRRIP can reduce the conflicts between the accesses of different cores by evicting no reuse blocks earlier. These results show that OBM is also an effective technique in multi-core environment.

5.8 Storage, Latency, and Power

Table 3 compares the storage overhead of various techniques for the 2MB LLC used in single-thread experiments. Each RHT entry consists of 1 valid bit, 4 bits for implementing the replacement of RHT, 1 prefetch bit, 10-bit signature, 21-bit IT and 21-bit VT, and each BDC needs 4 bits. It to-

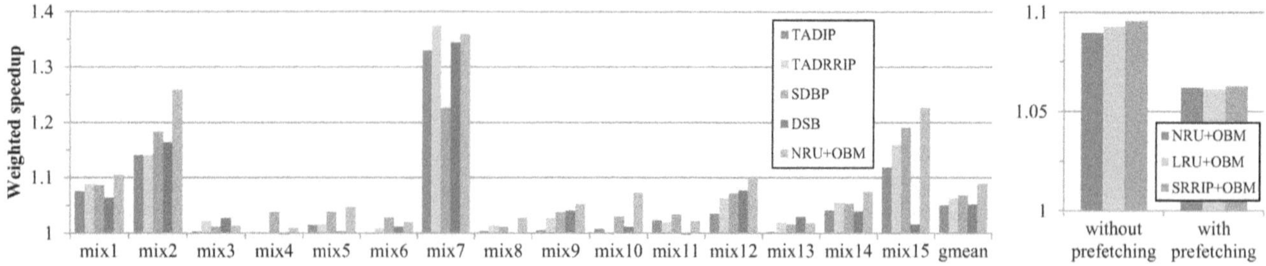

(a) NRU+OBM and other proposals without prefetching. (b) Others.

Figure 14: Normalized weighted speedup for multi-programmed workloads.

Table 3: Storage overhead of various techniques for a 16-way 2MB LLC.

	Speedup[1]	Speedup with prefetching[1]	Storage per block	Extra storage	Total
LRU	1	1.577	4 bits	0	16KB
NRU	1.001	1.575	1 bit	0	4KB
DIP	1.049	1.593	4 bits	10 bits	16KB
DRRIP	1.060	1.601	2 bits	10 bits	8KB
SDBP	1.063	1.582	5 bits	9.75KB	29.75KB
DSB	1.075	1.618	5 bits	11.35KB	31.35KB
NRU+OBM	1.097	1.661	1 bit	1.41KB	5.41KB

[1] The speedup is normalized to LRU without prefetching.

tally consumes $((1+4+1+10+21+21)\times 128+4\times(1024+1))$ bits $= 1.41$KB of extra storage to implement OBM for single-core configuration, which is less than 0.1% of the total storage of a 2MB LLC. For 4-core configuration, only 3 extra BDCs are needed. Compared to other recent proposals, NRU+OBM requires the lowest storage overhead.

We use CACTI 6.5 [25] to simulate the latency and power under 32nm process technology. We model the RHT as the tag array of a 32-way associative cache with 256 blocks. The access time of the 2MB LLC is 1.30ns, while the access time of RHT and BDCT is 0.14ns and 0.19ns respectively. It is fast enough to fit well in the access time of LLC. Consequently, OBM does not affect the access latency of LLC.

The dynamic access energy of LLC is 0.72nJ, and the leakage power is 678.4mW. While OBM has a dynamic access energy of 0.003nJ, and a leakage power of 3.5mW. Assuming the CPU frequency is 3GHz, according to our experiment, the LLC is accessed every 60.5ns on average. Consequently, OBM only consumes 0.51% of the power budget of LLC. What's more, since OBM can reduce LLC misses and thus the execution time of programs, actually it reduces the energy consumption of the memory system and processors.

6. RELATED WORK

Extensive research has been done to improve the LLC performance, and we will discuss some of the primary studies, which are most relevant to our work.

Replacement: Lots of LLC replacement policies try to retain some fraction of the working set in caches to avoid thrashing. DIP [27] attempts to insert most distant reuse blocks into the LRU position when the working set is larger than the cache size. Pseudo-LIFO [4] prioritizes to evict blocks on the top of fill stack to keep blocks in the bottom longer. A recent proposal guides replacement by explicitly predicting the reuse distance with a PC based predictor [17]. RRIP [12] can further identify frequently accessed blocks and retain them longer in the cache. Using signatures based on PC or instruction sequences, SHiP [35] proposes a re-reference interval predictor to improve performance. PACMan [36] extends RRIP to be prefetch-aware. Shepherd cache [29] uses two separate caches to record the relative access order of blocks, and then emulates the replacement and bypass decisions of OPT+B.

Dead Block Prediction: Dead block prediction tries to identify distant reuse blocks, also known as dead blocks in their papers. By evicting or bypassing dead blocks preferentially, the remaining blocks could reside longer in caches. Dead block prediction can be classified into three categories based on how to identify dead blocks: trace based [18, 19, 21], time based [10], and counter based [20]. Cache burst predictor [22] makes prediction for continuous access sequences rather than individual accesses to improve prediction accuracy. SDBP [19] samples a part of sets to reduce conflicts in the predictor for high accuracy.

Bypass: A few researchers have proposed bypass techniques for cache management. Based on how to predict distant reuse blocks, these studies can be classified into PC based [5, 8, 33] and address based [13, 15, 30, 31]. LRF [37] combines PC based and address based methods to improve performance. Annex caches [14] and PCC [34] filter no reuse blocks before they are brought into the main cache. Dead block prediction and bypass techniques mentioned above are all based on the assumption that all distant reuse blocks are useless. However, as we have shown, many blocks among them are actually useful and should be retained in caches.

DSB [6] records the incoming block and the victim block for each set on a miss. Then it adjusts the bypass probability based on which one is accessed first. As stated above, OBM does not use bypass based on a probability, and three Optimal Bypass Assertions are used to learn the behavior of the optimal bypass. Since we collect replacement pairs globally, not for each set, our storage overhead is much lower. Moreover, OBM makes prediction based on PC to improve performance. A bypass and insertion algorithm for exclusive LLCs was presented recently [7]. It classifies blocks based on their access number in the L2 cache and the hit number in the LLC. NUcache [23] dedicates a part of LLC to keep distant reuse blocks. Only blocks accessed by selected PCs are inserted into the dedicated part, and the others are bypassed.

Some researchers have proposed similar policies using some kinds of incoming-victim block relationship. They study the characteristic of accesses using metrics which are either similar to Assertion 1 and 2 [6], or similar to Assertion 1 and 3 [19, 35, 37]. However, since such proposals do not assert the behavior of the optimal bypass, and they only use a fraction of the three Optimal Bypass Assertions, they are not as accurate as OBM.

Others: Victim caches [16] use a small fully-associative buffer to improve direct-associative cache performance. However, as shown in Figure 1, the LLC blocks usually have rather large reuse distances, which makes victim caches ineffective for LLCs [18].

7. CONCLUSION

Since the reuse distances of numerous blocks are larger than the cache capacity, the commonly-used LRU and its approximations perform poorly for LLCs. Many previous proposals attempt to address this problem, which either have limited performance or require significant hardware overhead and large modification to the existing cache design. Based on the analysis of the optimal bypass, this paper proposes *Optimal Bypass onitor OB* . By keeping track of a short replacement history, OBM accurately learns the recent behavior of the optimal bypass to make bypass decisions. Our experiments show that OBM can cooperate well with various replacement policies including NRU, LRU, and SRRIP. Especially, OBM with NRU achieves a significant speedup for both single-thread and multi-programmed workloads, in both cases whether prefetching is enable or not. It also outperforms other state-of-the-art proposals including DIP, DRRIP, SDBP, and DSB. OBM only consumes less than 1.5KB extra storage and does not need to change the original design of LLC.

To the best of our knowledge, the idea that learns the behavior of the optimal bypass to guide the LLC management is firstly proposed. We believe that OBM can be widely used in other relative research areas, such as memory and storage management [1, 24].

8. ACKNOWLEDGMENTS

We would like to thank the anonymous reviewers for their helpful comments. This work is supported by the National Science and Technology Major Project of the Ministry of Science and Technology of China under grant 2009ZX01029-001-002-2.

9. REFERENCES

[1] S. Bansal and D. S. Modha. Car: Clock with adaptive replacement. In *F* , 2004.

[2] L. A. Belady. A study of replacement algorithms for a virtual-storage computer. *B ystems o rnal*, 5(2):78–101, 1966.

[3] S. Borkar and A. A. Chien. The future of microprocessors. *Comm n C* , 54:67–77, 2011.

[4] M. Chaudhuri. Pseudo-lifo: the foundation of a new family of replacement policies for last-level caches. In *CRO* , 2009.

[5] C.-H. Chi and H. Dietz. Improving cache performance by selective cache bypass. In *C* , 1989.

[6] H. Gao and C. Wilkerson. A dueling segmented lru replacement algorithm with adaptive bypassing. In *W C* , 2010.

[7] J. Gaur, M. Chaudhuri, and S. Subramoney. Bypass and insertion algorithms for exclusive last-level caches. In *C* , 2011.

[8] A. González, C. Aliagas, and M. Valero. A data cache with multiple caching strategies tuned to different types of locality. In *C* , 1995.

[9] J. L. Henning. Spec cpu2006 benchmark descriptions. *RC Comp t rc it ews*, 34:1–17, 2006.

[10] Z. Hu, S. Kaxiras, and M. Martonosi. Timekeeping in the memory system: predicting and optimizing memory behavior. In *C* , 2002.

[11] Intel. Intel core i7 processor. http://www.intel.com/products/processor/corei7/.

[12] A. Jaleel, K. B. Theobald, S. C. Steely, Jr., and J. Emer. High performance cache replacement using re-reference interval prediction (rrip). In *C 7*, 2010.

[13] J. Jalminger and P. Stenstrom. A novel approach to cache block reuse predictions. In *C* , 2003.

[14] L. John and A. Subramanian. Design and performance evaluation of a cache assist to implement selective caching. In *CC 7*, 1997.

[15] T. Johnson, D. Connors, M. Merten, and W.-M. Hwu. Run-time cache bypassing. *Comp ters, ransactions on*, 48(12):1338–1354, 1999.

[16] N. P. Jouppi. Improving direct-mapped cache performance by the addition of a small fully-associative cache and prefetch buffers. In *C 7*, 1990.

[17] G. Keramidas, P. Petoumenos, and S. Kaxiras. Cache replacement based on reuse-distance prediction. In *CC 5*, 2007.

[18] S. M. Khan, D. A. Jiménez, D. Burger, and B. Falsafi. Using dead blocks as a virtual victim cache. In *C* , 2010.

[19] S. M. Khan, Y. Tian, and D. A. Jimenez. Sampling dead block prediction for last-level caches. In *CRO* , 2010.

[20] M. Kharbutli and Y. Solihin. Counter-based cache replacement and bypassing algorithms. *Comp ters, ransactions on*, 57(4):433–447, 2008.

[21] A.-C. Lai, C. Fide, and B. Falsafi. Dead-block prediction & dead-block correlating prefetchers. In *C* , 2001.

[22] H. Liu, M. Ferdman, J. Huh, and D. Burger. Cache bursts: A new approach for eliminating dead blocks and increasing cache efficiency. In *CRO* , 2008.

[23] R. Manikantan, K. Rajan, and R. Govindarajan.

Nucache: An efficient multicore cache organization based on next-use distance. In *C 7*, 2011.

[24] N. Megiddo and D. S. Modha. Arc: A self-tuning, low overhead replacement cache. In *F* , 2003.

[25] N. Muralimanohar, R. Balasubramonian, and N. Jouppi. Cacti 6.0: A tool to understand large caches. *Researc Report*, 2007.

[26] H. Patil, R. Cohn, M. Charney, R. Kapoor, A. Sun, and A. Karunanidhi. Pinpointing representative portions of large intel itanium programs with dynamic instrumentation. In *CRO 7*, 2004.

[27] M. K. Qureshi, A. Jaleel, Y. N. Patt, S. C. Steely, and J. Emer. Adaptive insertion policies for high performance caching. In *C* , 2007.

[28] M. K. Qureshi, D. N. Lynch, O. Mutlu, and Y. N. Patt. A case for mlp-aware cache replacement. In *C* , 2006.

[29] K. Rajan and G. Ramaswamy. Emulating optimal replacement with a shepherd cache. In *CRO* , 2007.

[30] J. Rivers and E. Davidson. Reducing conflicts in direct-mapped caches with a temporality-based design. In *C* , 1996.

[31] J. A. Rivers, E. S. Tam, G. S. Tyson, E. S. Davidson, and M. Farrens. Utilizing reuse information in data cache management. In *C* , 1998.

[32] R. Subramanian, Y. Smaragdakis, and G. H. Loh. Adaptive caches: Effective shaping of cache behavior to workloads. In *CRO* , 2006.

[33] G. Tyson, M. Farrens, J. Matthews, and A. R. Pleszkun. A modified approach to data cache management. In *CRO* , 1995.

[34] S. Walsh and J. Board. Pollution control caching. In *CC 5*, 1995.

[35] C. Wu, A. Jaleel, W. Hasenplaugh, M. Martonosi, S. Steely Jr, and J. Emer. Ship: Signature-based hit predictor for high performance caching. In *CRO* , 2011.

[36] C. Wu, A. Jaleel, M. Martonosi, S. Steely Jr, and J. Emer. Pacman: Prefetch-aware cache management for high performance caching. In *CRO* , 2011.

[37] L. Xiang, T. Chen, Q. Shi, and W. Hu. Less reused filter: improving l2 cache performance via filtering less reused lines. In *C* , 2009.

[38] Y. Xie and G. H. Loh. Pipp: Promotion/insertion pseudo-partitioning of multi-core shared caches. In *C* , 2009.

Lossless and Lossy Memory I/O Link Compression for Improving Performance of GPGPU Workloads

Vijay Sathish†, Michael J. Schulte‡, Nam Sung Kim†

†The University of Wisconsin-Madison, WI, U.S.A. ‡Advanced Micro Devices, TX, U.S.A.

sathish@wisc.edu, michael.schulte@amd.com, nskim@engr.wisc.edu

Abstract

State-of-the-art graphic processing units (GPUs) provide very high memory bandwidth, but the performance of many general-purpose GPU (GPGPU) workloads is still bounded by memory bandwidth. Although compression techniques have been adopted by commercial GPUs, they are only used for compressing texture and color data, not data for GPGPU workloads. Furthermore, the microarchitectural details of GPU compression are proprietary and its performance benefits have not been previously published. In this paper, we first investigate required microarchitectural changes to support lossless compression techniques for data transferred between the GPU and its off-chip memory to provide higher effective bandwidth. Second, by exploiting some characteristics of floating-point numbers in many GPGPU workloads, we propose to apply lossless compression to floating-point numbers after truncating their least-significant bits (i.e., lossy compression). This can reduce the bandwidth usage even further with very little impact on overall computational accuracy. Finally, we demonstrate that a GPU with our lossless and lossy compression techniques can improve the performance of memory-bound GPGPU workloads by 26% and 41% on average.

Categories and Subject Descriptors

C.1.2 **[Multiple Data Stream Architectures (Multiprocessors)]**: Single-instruction-stream, multiple-data-stream processors (SIMD)

General Terms

Performance, Design

Keywords

Graphics processing units, lossless and lossy data compression.

1. Introduction

To reduce the performance impact of long latency off-chip memory accesses, GPUs rely on many threads in flight to hide memory latency. A GPU's hardware scheduler simply switches to a different thread group when the current group is waiting for data to return from its off-chip memory. Since these context switches are lightweight and involve practically no overhead for GPUs, the memory access latency can be effectively hidden for workloads with many threads. However, as the ratio of memory instructions to compute instructions increases, this technique becomes less effective. Workloads exhibiting such a behavior can be classified as memory-bound workloads.

PACT'12, September 19–23, 2012, Minneapolis, Minnesota, USA.

Clearly, one way to improve the performance of these workloads is to improve the memory bandwidth by integrating more memory channels (i.e., memory controllers (MCs) and their memory I/O links (i.e., I/O circuits and pins, and interconnects)) and/or increasing their frequencies. The technical challenges, however, include limits in off-chip memory speeds and the number of I/O pins, neither of which scale well with technology scaling for a given chip package. Moreover, individual memory channels constitute a notable fraction of the power consumption in computing platforms (e.g., 25W for four DDR3 memory channels for a 4GB total capacity [1]), which can limit bandwidth and frequency increases under a given platform power constraint.

Considering such challenges, we can improve the memory bandwidth by utilizing the available memory channels more efficiently. As an effective alternative, in this paper, we propose a GPU architecture supporting lossless and lossy compression techniques for data transferred through the memory I/O links. Although compression techniques have been adopted by commercial GPUs [2], they are customized for compressing texture and color data. Furthermore, the microarchitectural details for GPU data compression are proprietary and its performance benefits have not been previously published.

The key contributions of this paper are as follows. First, we demonstrate the potential of a hardware-based lossless compression technique to improve the performance of GPUs by showing the compressibility of the data stored in GPU's off-chip memory (Section 2). Second, we propose necessary microarchitectural enhancement to support lossless and lossy compression for data transferred through the GPU memory I/O links (Section 3). The compression technique and implementation for GPUs are different than those for CPUs [3,4,5,6] because they exploit (i) a programming model and platform architecture unique to GPUs, which allows the compression to be transparent to existing workloads and compilation tools, and (ii) the impact of compression latency on performance is not as critical for GPUs as it is for CPUs. Furthermore, our lossy compression technique exploits the observation that reducing the precision of floating-point (FP) numbers incurs very little accuracy loss for many GPGPU workloads [7,8]; we apply lossless compression after truncating some least-significant bits (LSBs) of FP data to reduce the bandwidth usage even further while producing acceptable results for many GPGPU workloads in recognition, mining, synthesis (RMS) and physics simulation domains. Finally, we demonstrate the performance improvements of the GPU supporting lossless and lossy compression techniques, respectively (Section 4).

2. The Case for GPU Memory I/O Link Compression

GPUs typically provide much higher off-chip memory bandwidth and shorter latency than CPUs by using more memory channels and faster memory (e.g., GDDR); each channel is controlled by a MC. For example, 4-8 MCs are integrated in NVIDIA GPUs. However, many GPU workloads can still benefit from more memory channels (i.e., higher bandwidth). Figure 1 shows the performance speedup of 16 GPU workloads when the number of MCs (i.e., memory

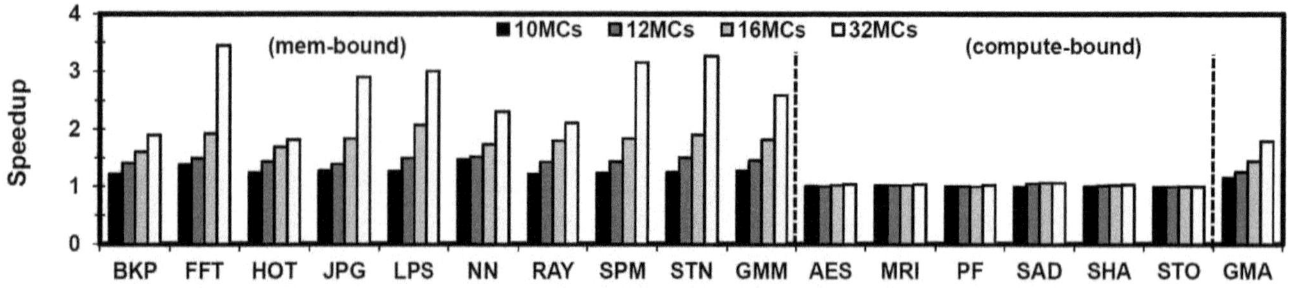

Figure 1: Speedup when varying the number of MCs, relative to a baseline GPU with 8 MCs.

channels) is increased from 8 to 10, 12, 16, and 32. While compute-bound workloads (i.e., AES, MRI, PF, SAD, SHA, and STO) show little or no performance improvement, memory-bound workloads (i.e., BKP, FFT, HOT, JPG, LPS, NN, RAY, SPM, and STN) significantly benefit from higher memory bandwidth provided by more meory channels; GMM and GMA denote the geometric mean speedup of memory-bound and all workloads, respectively. Doubling the number of memory channels increases the geometric mean of the performance of memory-bound workloads by 81%. See Section 4.1 for the benchmark descriptions, properties, and simulation methodology.

Figure 2 shows pseudo code for (a) an NVIDIA CUDA application, and (b) the corresponding data flow between a CPU (i.e., host) and a GPU (i.e., device). The CPU initializes the data for the GPU, stores them in the CPU DRAM (i.e., CPU main memory), and initiates a memory copy transaction by invoking the "CUDAMemCpy" function. Once the GPU acknowledges the transaction, the GPU's DMA controller begins to copy the data, which go through the GPU's on-chip interconnect and MCs to the GPU DRAM; see the dotted arrow lines in the "HostToDevice" direction.

After the DMA controller finishes the copy transaction, the CPU launches a GPU kernel and the GPU begins computations. During the kernel execution, streaming multiprocessors (SMs), each of which is comprised of 8-32 CUDA cores, read/write data from/to the GPU DRAM through the on-chip interconnect and MCs; see the solid arrow lines in the "MemRdWr" direction. After the GPU finishes the kernel execution, it invokes another "CUDAMemCpy," requesting the DMA controller to copy the computed results back to the CPU DRAM; see the dotted arrow lines in the "DeviceToHost" direction. During the memory copy transactions from the CPU DRAM to the GPU DRAM, the data can be compressed on the fly if the compressors, which are integrated with the GPU MCs, provide sufficiently high bandwidth.

When an SM requests a memory read (i.e., a 128-byte block per request), an MC begins to fetch 16-byte compressed data chunks from the GPU DRAM in burst mode (i.e., 4 bytes per transfer). Since the number of transferred 16-byte chunks for the compressed 128-byte block is fewer than for the uncompressed block, the effective bandwidth and latency between the GPU and its off-chip memory are improved; the compressors and decompressors should support higher throughput than the memory channels. Then, the compressed block can be decompressed in the MC using the decompressors, and the decompressed 128-byte block is sent back to the SM; the gray-shaded region in Figure 2-(b) represents the region where the data resides in compressed form.

Figure 3 plots the average compression ratio of data copied from the CPU DRAM to the GPU DRAM; a single block is considered as a single independent unit for compression, and the size of a single block is denoted by block size. We applied a compression algorithm presented by Chen *et al.* [9] to every block transferred to the GPU DRAM. On average, the volume of the data can be compressed to approximately a half of the uncompressed size for 128-byte blocks. In turn, this can improve the effective (or perceived) bandwidth by a factor of two.

Finally, integrating the CPU and GPU on the same chip can enable them to share the same memory and may not require data transfers between them. However, high-end GPUs will still continue to be discrete devices (i.e., they are not likely to be integrated with CPUs in the same chip) because of power and thermal constraints.

```
//main routine that executes on the CPU
int main(void){
    .
    .
    // initializes data
    .
    .
    // initiates the data transfer to the GPU
    cudaMemcpy(..., MemcpyHostToDevice);

    // invokes the kernel
    foo <<<n_blocks, block_size>>> (...);

    // initiates the data transfer to the CPU
    cudaMemcpy(...,MemcpyDeviceToHost);
    .
    .
```

(a)

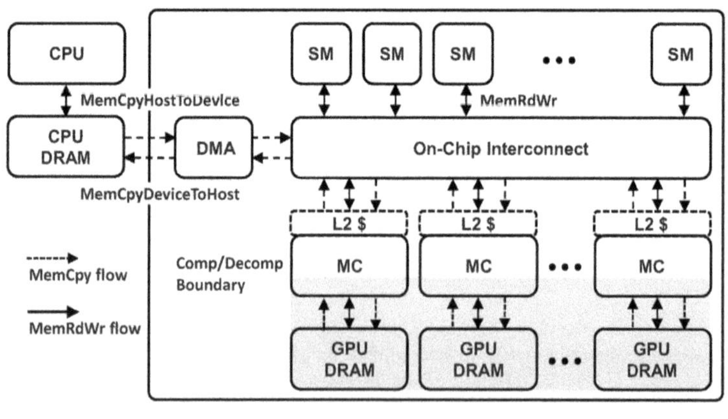

(b)

Figure 2: (a) Pseudo code using CUDA. (b) The data transfer flows between a host CPU and a GPU device; some GPUs have on-chip L2 caches.

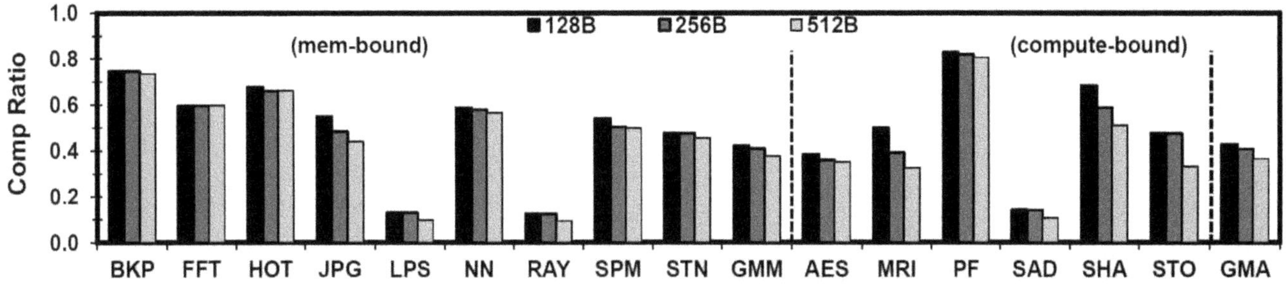

Figure 3: Average compression ratio, which is defined as the size of the compressed blocks over the size of the uncompressed blocks, when varying unit block size over which the compression algorithm is applied.

3. Microarchitectural Enhancement for Memory I/O Link Compression

There are two important observations for supporting hardware-based memory I/O link compression to mitigate the memory bandwidth and latency issues for GPUs. First, the data values for some GPU workloads are likely to be highly correlated, resulting in high compression ratios as shown in Section 2. This can potentially improve the perceived bandwidth and latency. Second, threads running on an SM are executed as a group (i.e., warp) in a single instruction multiple thread (SIMT) fashion. Consequently, each warp, which is comprised of 32 threads, generates 128-byte memory accesses. Thus, GPUs allow a larger block size for compression than CPUs, potentially leading to a higher compression ratio.

3.1 General Requirements

In this paper, we make the compressed data residing in the GPU's DRAM transparent to the GPU's SMs by compressing and decompressing data with dedicated hardware in the GPU's MCs. Moreover, the host CPU is also completely isolated from the compressions and decompressions. Thus, this architectural change places no need for modifications to the rest of the system. The objective of the proposed compression technique for GPUs is not to increase the effective capacity of the GPU DRAM, but to improve the effective bandwidth and/or latency. Thus, our design still allocates 128 bytes per block in the GPU's DRAM, even though compressing a 128-byte block results in fewer than 128 bytes, as illustrated in Figure 4(a); the space saved due to compression is left unused to eliminate the complications often associated with space compaction and writing to compressed data.

3.2 Impact on Memory Bandwidth and Latency

In Figure 4(a), for the purpose of illustration, we assume that (i) GDDR3 has a burst length of four with a 4-byte bus width (16 bytes per burst) [10], and (ii) the throughput of our decompressor is 16 bytes per cycle with a 1-cycle latency [9]. Although the frequency of the decompressor can be 1.2GHz in a 65nm technology [9] and the frequency of GDDR3 and the MCs is 800MHz, we assume that the decompressor is operating at 800MHz. For example, when a 128-byte block is compressed to two 16-byte chunks (i.e., compression ratio = 0.25), a compressed 16-byte chunk from each burst read yields 64 uncompressed bytes on average. In this case, the bandwidth usage and latency are reduced to 1/4 and 2/3 of fetching a 128-byte block. While a compressed data block from a context is being decompressed, a memory access by another context can be interleaved to maximize the usage of the memory I/O links (and thus the bandwidth). Since these two data blocks are independent, they can also be decompressed in parallel with an additional decompressor.

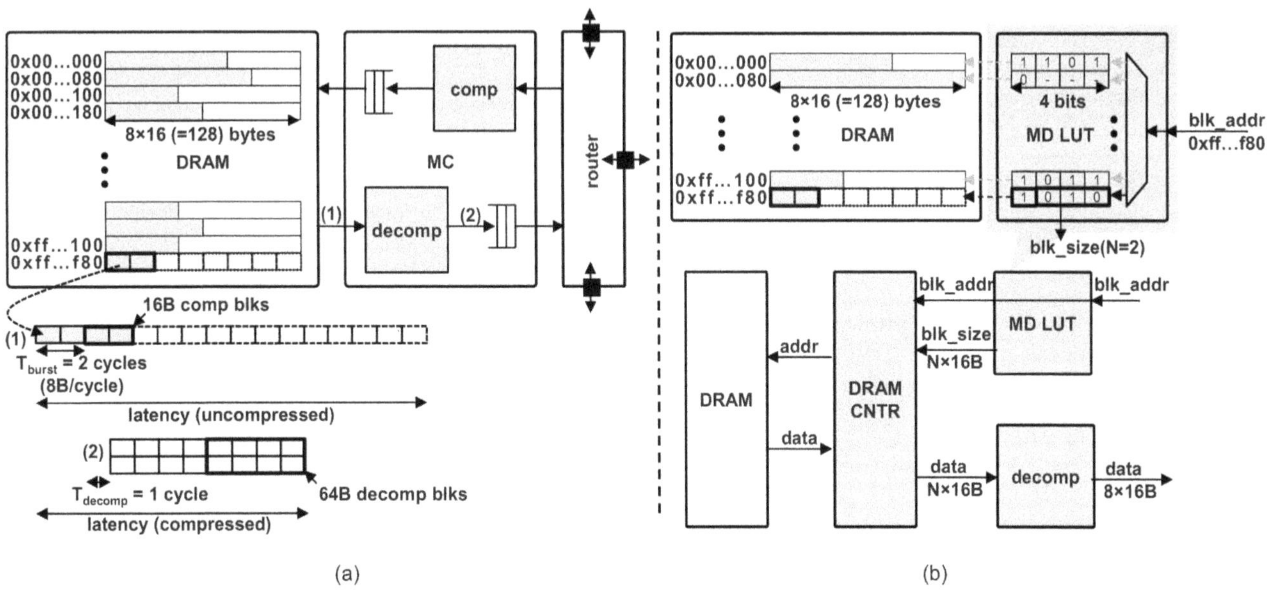

Figure 4: (a) Data flow for compression and the corresponding DRAM read and decompression transaction for 128 bytes compressed to two 16-byte blocks. In the figure, GDDR3 has a burst length of 4 with a 4-byte bus width (16 bytes per burst) [10]; and the throughput of our compressor and decompressor is 4 bytes/cycle and 16 bytes/cycle, respectively with a 1-cycle latency [9]. (b) Interaction between DRAM, DRAM controller, metadata LUT, and decompressor, where N is the number of compressed 16-byte chunks to fetch, instead of the full 8 16-byte chunks.

3.3 Metadata Cache

Need for compression metadata: There are two important reasons to maintain metadata information for every original 128-byte block stored in the GPU's DRAM. First, we need to store 1 bit per original 128-byte block to indicate whether or not the block is compressed; it is not always possible to compress every original 128-byte block to a block with fewer than 128 bytes. Second, we need to fetch only the compressed 16-byte chunks from the corresponding 128-byte block space. Although fetching the empty unused chunks in a full 128-byte block space is not harmful, it will nullify the bandwidth and latency benefit that we are seeking to maximize. Since the number of 16-byte compressed chunks per 128-byte block can vary from 1 to 8, we use three more bits per 128-byte block to indicate the number of 16-byte chunks in each block.

The need for metadata raises the question of how and where the metadata can be allocated, stored, and accessed. When the data blocks are being copied for the first time from the CPU's DRAM to the GPU's DRAM by the GPU's DMA controller, look-up-table (LUT) entries that contain metadata information for all the transferred 128-byte blocks, are populated on the fly during the compression process. The entries will be updated later if writes change the number of 16-byte compressed chunks. We also need to ensure that each MC only holds metadata information for the blocks belonging to that particular MC's address space; the consecutive LUT entries within a MC correspond to consecutive original 128-byte blocks belonging to the MC's address space.

Naïve implementation of metadata LUT: For the naïve implementation of the LUT, we assume the presence of a perfect cache to store all the metadata information. In Figure 4(b), for all read requests, the LUT returns the number of compressed 16-byte chunks (N) for a given block address (blk_addr). Then, the DRAM controller fetches N 16-byte chunks instead of 8 16-byte chunks. No matter what the value of N is, N 16-byte chunks are always decompressed into 8 16-byte chunks (i.e., the original 128-byte block). However, the GPU's DRAM can be up to 4GB for 32-bit addressing. Thus, we need 16MB (= 4GB / 128B × 4b) for LUT storage considering 4 bits of metadata information per original 128-byte block. Although the LUT size is just 0.4% of the total GPU memory space, it is very large for an on-chip memory, and thus not practical. On the other hand, if the LUT is located in the GPU's DRAM, the effective latency of memory accesses will increase considerably since each read or write requires two memory accesses, first for the metadata and then for the actual data.

Metadata cache: In this paper, we devise a microarchitectural technique to allocate the metadata information in the GPU DRAM, but cache the most-recently-used metadata information on the chip. This reduces the on-chip memory usage and the latency penalty of accessing metadata stored in the GPU's off-chip memory. Since we adopt a static one-to-one mapping of metadata information based on the data block's address, we reserve 16MB (this is sufficient for 32-bit addressing) of the GPU's DRAM from a known base address during the GPU initialization. When a particular data request address is provided to the MC, the metadata information corresponding to the block always maps to a location in the reserved 16MB space.

MSHR for metadata cache: Caching metadata utilizes a dedicated small two-way set-associative cache and a miss status handling register (MSHR) tables per MC. The metadata requests are placed by the MCs on behalf of the compressors or decompressors to the GPU's DRAM. Returning metadata responses from the GPU's DRAM are used to update the metadata caches and are not forwarded to any of the SMs. The hardware overhead of adding such a cache and a MSHR table per MC is negligible compared to storing all the metadata on chip; we provide a detailed analysis showing the cycle time, area and power consumption of a metadata cache and a MSHR table later in Section 4.1. Whenever a request for metadata misses, an MSHR entry, which is used to prevent duplication of metadata requests in flight, is allocated (if it has not already been allocated previously) and the request is sent to the GPU's DRAM.

Technically, the original 128-byte block request associated with the missed metadata must stall until the metadata returns and is parsed by the *request size modifier* that converts 8 16-byte accesses to N 16-byte access. This is to ascertain whether or not a block is compressed, and if so, how many 16-byte chunks need to be fetched from the GPU's DRAM. However, stalling memory requests for a metadata cache miss wastes precious memory bandwidth. Thus, the read request instead proceeds as a request for a full 128-byte block. This conservative sizing of data requests on a metadata cache miss ensures that memory bandwidth is never wasted due to stalling behind metadata requests. However, we note that the received 128-byte block has to stall at the decompressor until the metadata returns to verify whether or not the data block was compressed. Since metadata requests are always given priority over read/write requests, this stall period should be short. We also note that metadata responses returning from the GPU's DRAM require a separate virtual network to ensure that they never get blocked behind stalled data responses that are waiting for their corresponding metadata responses, as this would lead to a deadlock scenario.

3.4 Lossy Compression Technique

The impact of reducing the precision of FP data on computing accuracy has been widely studied for media, RMS, and physics simulation domain workloads [7,8]; truncating some LSBs of FP data before computing with them results in very little loss in overall accuracy while reducing a considerable amount of chip area and/or power consumption of FP units (FPUs). Furthermore, GPUs already support two different FP computation modes: IEEE compliant and non-compliant FP computations where the latter is much faster than the former at the cost of a small accuracy loss [11]. Since the LSBs in the data transferred from the GPU's off-chip memory are going to be truncated before computations in such a computing method, we observe that the GPU does not need to bring in the LSBs of the FP data. We hypothesize that this can also reduce the memory bandwidth usage significantly with a negligible loss in accuracy.

The main challenge, however, is that many GPGPU workloads use a mix of both integer (INT) and FP data and truncating INT data, unlike FP data, may have detrimental effects on accuracy (and sometimes may lead to erroneous execution states). Therefore, we propose to apply lossy compression only to FP data. Considering the CUDA programming style, which often transfers a set of data with the same data type from/to the GPU's off-chip memory using the CUDAMemCpy function as shown in Figure 5(a), we can selectively apply lossy compression only to FP data. For a programmer to specify the number of LSBs to be truncated for a set of FP data, we modify the *CUDAMemCpy* function interface; in Figure 5(a) we truncate the 8 LSBs of array "bd" copied to the GPU off-chip memory.

Figure 5(b) illustrates the hardware support for lossy compression. For example, if we truncate 8 out of 24 mantissa bits in every 32-bit single precision FP datum in a 128B block, effectively we shrink it to 96B, reducing the bandwidth usage by 25%; two extra bits in each MD LUT entry record the number of truncated LSBs, which is needed for decompression later. In addition to the truncation, we apply the lossless compression technique to the remaining 96B. This results in a 32B compressed block in this example. Note

```
int   *a = new int[N*N];
float *b = new float[N*N];

for(int i = 0; i < M*M; ++i)
    a[i] = i; b[i] = 1.0f;

int *ad; float   *bd;
const int intsize = N*N*sizeof(int);
const int fpsize = N*N*sizeof(float);

cudaMalloc((void**)&ad, intsize);
cudaMalloc((void**)&bd, fpsize);

//existing cudaMemcpy code
//cudaMemcpy(ad, a, intsize, HostToDevice);
//cudaMemcpy(bd, b,  fpsize, HostToDevice);

//new cudamMemcpy to support lossy compression
cudaMemcpy(ad, a, intsize, 0, HostToDevice);
cudaMemcpy(bd, b,  fpsize, 8, HostToDevice);
```

(a)

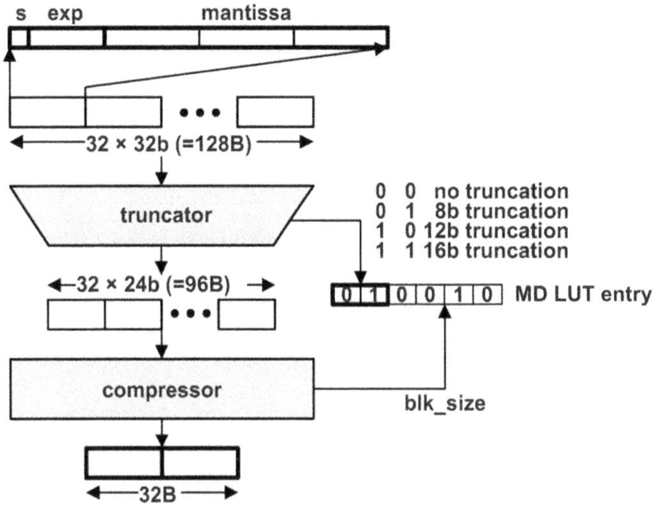

(b)

Figure 5: (a) cudaMemcpy example code and (b) hardware support for lossy compression.

that some applications require greater accuracy and use double-precision FP arithmetic. In this case, the proposed lossy compression can be an optional feature that programmers can turn on (e.g., to accelerate initial solution searches for large problem spaces).

3.5 MC Microarchitecture

Figure 6 illustrates the microarchitectural changes required for each MC to support a hardware-based memory-link compression technique. The GPU's DRAM (using NVIDIA's architectural convention) is partitioned into four different address spaces depending on the properties and caching patterns of the underlying data. The *global address space* stores the data arrays used for computation and can be both read from and written into. The read-only *texture address space* stores graphics textures and read only data structures. The read-only *constant address space* stores constants required during computation while a *local address space* is used to manage register spills (register data sent back from the SMs to the GPU's DRAM). Our proposed architecture only supports compression of the global and texture spaces, which represent the bulk of the memory traffic. Therefore, only requests prefixed with a "*g*" (global or texture space) in Figure 6 need to pass through the compressor and decompressor.

The requests prefixed "*l*" represent traffic to local and constant address spaces and safely bypass the compression scheme. The abbreviations "*rd*," "*wr*," "*req*," and "*resp*" refer to read, write, request, and response. For example, "*g_wr*" refers to a global write initiated by an SM. If a write is to a full 128-byte block, it passes through the compressor before getting written to the GPU's

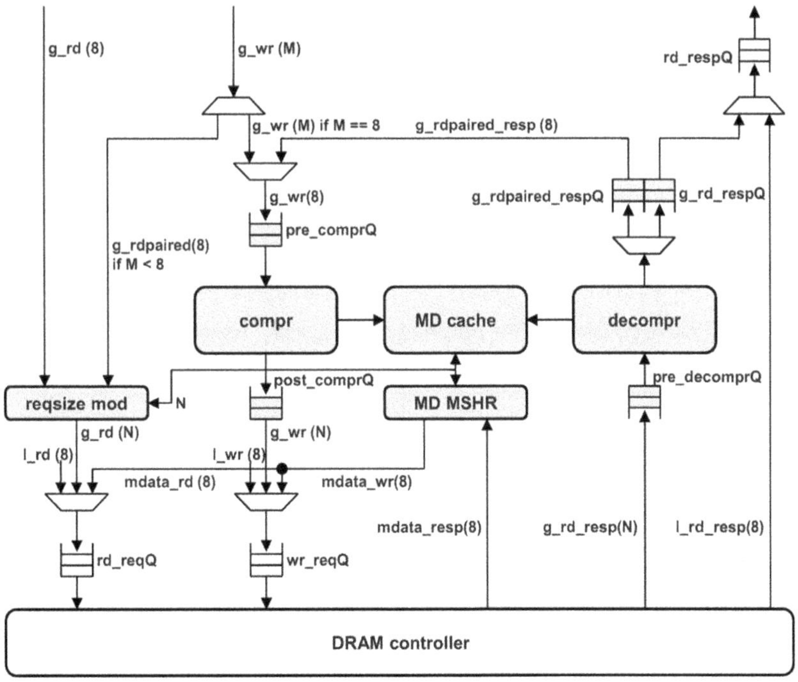

Figure 6: MC microarchitecture to support compression and decompression. The gray-color blocks are components added to an existing MC. The numbers in the parentheses represent the number of 16-byte chunks.

Table 1: Description of abbreviations used in Figure 6.

g_rd/wr (l_rd/wr)	global (local) read/write request by SM
g_rdpaired	global read request by either SM or MC as part of read-modify-write operation
md_rd/wr	MD line read/write request by MD MSHR in response to MD cache miss/dirty line eviction
g_rd_resp (l_rd_resp)	global data (local data) from DRAM in response to g_rd (l_rd) or g_rdpaired
g_rdpaired_resp	global data after decompression in response to g_rdpaired
md_resp	MD line from DRAM in response to md_rd
rd/wr_reqQ	A physical queue staging all read/write requests to the DRAM controller
pre/post_compQ	A logical queue staging g_wr(16) and g_wr(N) data before/after compression
pre _decompQ	A physical queue staging g_rd or g_rdpaired response data before decompression
g_rd/rdpaired_respQ	A physical queue staging g_rd/g_rdpaired response data after decompression
rd_respQ	A physical queue staging all read response data returning to SMs from MC

DRAM. However, a partial write, which is smaller than 128 bytes, needs to be converted to a read request (marked "*g_rdpaired*") followed by an update and write back with decompression and compression operations in between. Such an operation can be costly and is the main reason for potential performance degradations with a larger block size than the L1 cache line size (i.e., 128 bytes). The compressor also needs to update the corresponding metadata entry in the LUT after compression for the write. The request size modifier ("*reqsize mod*" in Figure 6) block is used to modify the read request size by reading the metadata cache to ascertain the number of compressed 16-byte chunks that need to be fetched from the GPU's off-chip memory, and thus plays an important role in the memory traffic reduction. Table 1 describes the abbreviations used in Figure 6.

4. Evaluation

4.1 Methodology

GPU architecture simulation: In this study, we analyze the performance of a GPU using GPGPU-Sim, which was validated against NVIDIA's Quadro FX 5800 and showed more than 90% performance correlation [12]. Our baseline GPU is configured to simulate NVIDIA's Quadro FX 5800 [13] with an enhanced number of streaming multiprocessors (SMs) and MCs to model recent high-end GPUs like the GTX580; see Table 2 for detailed simulation parameters. We modify GPGPU-sim to model a GPU architecture supporting our compression technique. Note that NVIDIA's GTX580 has 16 SMs operating while our baseline GPUs have 42 to 60 SMs, but GTX580 has 32 CUDA cores per SM while Quadro FX5800 has 8 CUDA cores per SM. That is, GTX580 has 512 CUDA cores, while our GPUs have 336 to 480 CUDA cores. We use 16 benchmarks from the GPGPU-Sim [12], Rodinia [14], Parboil2 [15] and ERCBench [16] benchmark suites. Their characteristics are summarized in Table 3.

Compressor/decompressor throughput, power, and area models: We assume that the architecture uses the compressor and decompressor hardware design proposed in [9], and our proposed microarchitectural enhancements described in Section 3. Table 4 summarizes the frequencies, throughputs per cycle, power consumption, and area of a compressor and a decompressor designed with a 65nm technology. The compressor is pipelined with a 3-cycle initial latency and it can compress 64 bits per cycle. The decompressor is not pipelined and it can decompress 128 bits per cycle. The combined power consumption of 8 decompressor and compressor pairs (one pair per MC) is 0.24% of the maximum power consumption of a Quadro FX 5800 that typically consumes 187W. Similarly, the area overhead is negligible (the Quadro FX 5800 die area is close to $500mm^2$).

Metadata cache and its MSHR timing, power, and area models: We use CACTI 6.5 with the 65nm technology itrs-hp option to evaluate the cycle time, power, and area overhead of metadata caches and their MSHR tables. The area per 32-entry metadata cache with 128-byte line size is less than $0.05mm^2$. The maximum cycle time is less than 800ps and the total power consumption is roughly 10mW at 800MHz.

4.2 Results

Performance improvement with compression /decompression using perfect LUT: Figure 7 shows the performance speedup trend as the throughput per cycle of decompressors is varied from 4 to 32 bytes per cycle; the maximum throughput per cycle of decompressors from [9] is 16 bytes per cycle at 1.2GHz while the MCs operates at 800MHz. Assuming a perfect metadata LUT and

Table 2: Simulation parameters (see [12] for details).

# of SMs	42~60	# of Memory Channels	8
SM Freq	1.30GHz	Memory Freqquency	800MHz (GDDR3)
On-chip Interconnect Freq	0.65GHz	Memory Bandwidth	102.4 GB/s
Warp Size	32	Bus Width per Channel	4 (Bytes/Cycle)
SIMD Width	8	Memory Controller	FR-FCFS
Max # of Threads per SM	1024	Branch Divergence	Immediate post dominator
Max # of CTAs per SM	8	Warp Scheduling	Round Robin
# of Registers per SM	16384	Const. Cache Size per SM	8 KB
L1$ Memory per SM	32KB	Texture Cache Size per SM	8 KB
Metadata cache	32 entries (128 bytes/entry)	Metadata MSHR	10 entries
pre _compQ	32 entries (8 bytes/entry)	pre/post_decompQ/ *_resQ	32 entries (16 bytes/entry)

Table 3: Benchmark summary.

Benchmark	Acronym	Property	Working Set Size	Working Set Data Composition
Back Propagation	BKP	memory-bound	55MB	single-precision FP
Fast Fourier Transform	FFT		165MB	single-precision FP
HotSpot	HOT		13MB	single-precision FP
JPEG encoder/decoder	JPG		7MB	single-precision FP
Leukocyte	LKT		20MB	single-precision FP / INT
3D Laplace solver	LPS		33MB	single-precision FP
Neural Network	NN		11MB	single-precision FP
Ray Tracing	RAY		76MB	single-precision FP / INT
Sparse Matrix Vector Multiplication	SPM		40MB	single-precision FP / INT
3D Stencil Operation	STN		328MB	single-precision FP
AES encryption/decryption	AES	compute-bound	4MB	INT
Magnetic Resonance Imaging Q	MRI		3MB	FP
Particle Filter	PF		116MB	double-precision FP
Sum of Absolute Difference	SAD		18MB	INT
SHA 1 encryption	SHA		7MB	INT
StoreGPU	STO		1MB	INT

Table 4: Hardware parameters for compressor/decompressor designed with a 65nm technology [9].

Compressor		Decompressor	
Maximum frequency	1.25GHz	Maximum frequency	1.2GHz
Throughput/cycle	64 bits	Throughput/cycle	128 bits (16 bytes)
Power consumption	32.63mW	Power consumption	24.14mW
Area	0.043mm^2	Area	0.043mm^2

16 bytes per cycle for the throughput of decompressors, the proposed technique improves the geometric mean of performance for memory-bound workloads by 26%. FFT and STN show good initial compression ratios (i.e., the compression ratio achieved during the initial data transfer from the CPU's DRAM to the GPU's DRAM) in Section 2, but their compression ratios become close to 1 as the workload progresses, which means little or no compression is achieved, as the execution of workloads progresses. This results in little or no improvement in performance for such workloads. The proposed compression technique does not improve the performance of compute-bound workloads notably, but it does not negatively impact their performance either; PF was categorized as a compute-bound workload in Section 2 where the bandwidth was increased to identify compute- and memory-bound workloads, but the compression technique improves its performance. This is because the compression technique also reduces DRAM access latency; we observe that PF performance increases when the frequency of MC is increased.

Impact of metadata cache size on performance: To analyze the impact of metadata cache size on the performance of GPUs, we vary the number of entries from 4 to 32. The miss rates are high if the number of metadata cache entries is either 4 or 8. However, the geometric mean of the miss rates become less than 2% if the number of metadata cache entries is 16. When the performance of a GPU using perfect on-chip metadata LUTs is compared to that of a GPU using metadata caches, we observe that the 16-entry metadata data caches result in a geometric mean performance degradation of roughly 1%. Note that most compute-bound workloads have relatively high miss rates. This is because their memory accesses are not frequent enough to exercise metadata caches, resulting in high miss rates caused by compulsory misses. Furthermore, 32-entry metadata caches have a negligible impact on performance relative to perfect on-chip metadata LUTs. This is because (i) data accesses by SMs show very high *spatial* locality, (ii) the metadata cache retrieves 128 bytes of metadata information per metadata cache miss, and (iii) a 32-entry metadata cache per MC exceeds the entire data caching capacity of our baseline GPU. Since we need only four-bit metadata for each 128B data block and the number of 128B data blocks covered by one metadata cache line is 128 × 8 bits / 4 bits = 256, each 128-byte metadata cache line contains the metadata for 256 × 128-byte data blocks (i.e., 32KB worth of data blocks). Thus, a 32-entry metadata cache in each MC can contain the metadata for 32 × 256 × 128-byte data blocks (i.e., 1MB worth of data blocks). Since each MC has one 32-entry metadata cache and our baseline GPU has total eight MCs, eight 32-entry metadata caches contain the metadata for 8MB worth of data blocks. Note that the total L1 capacity in our baseline GPU is at most 1.875MB for L1 caches (i.e., 32KB × 60 SMs) (and another baseline GPU supporting L2 caches has 2MB for L2 caches (i.e., 256KB × 8 MCs)). Thus, a 32-entry metadata cache per MC exceeds the entire data caching capacity of our baseline GPU.

Impact of the number of decompressors per MC on performance: An MC can access multiple DRAM banks. In such a case, multiple decompressors may reduce the latency of decompression. Otherwise, the 16-byte chunks from the second bank must wait until the decompression of all the 16-byte chunks from the first bank is completed. However, our experiments using decompressors with 16 bytes per cycle throughput show that the performance of a GPU with two decompressors per MC shows only marginal performance increase (~1%) compared to a GPU with one decompressor per MC across all the workloads we examine. This is because the throughput (i.e., bandwidth) of a single decompressor

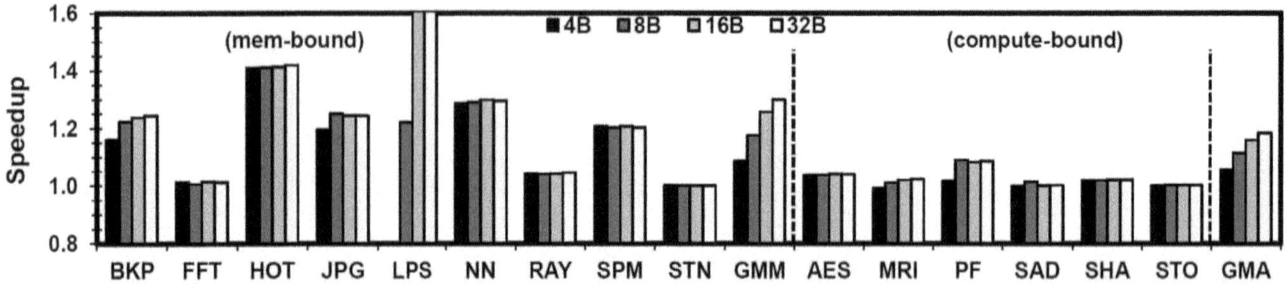

Figure 7. Performance speedup when varying throughput/cycle of decompressors. A perfect metadata LUT and 60 SMs are assumed.

is already twice as high as the memory bandwidth. In situations where the throughput of the decompressor is close to or less than the memory bandwidth, having multiple decompressors may be useful.

Impact of the peak bandwidth to peak compute ratio on performance: The peak bandwidth to peak compute ratio is a key measure to check whether or not the memory bandwidth is balanced with the compute capability. A GTX580 has 512 cores (16 SMs × 32 cores per SM) operating at 1.55GHz and it has a bandwidth over compute ratio (BCR) of 0.24, while our baseline GPUs have 336 to 480 cores (42 to 60 SMs × 8 cores per SM) operating at 1.3GHz and BCR ranging from 0.26~0.16.

Figure 8 shows performance speedup with the compression technique when varying the number of SMs in a GPU when we fix the memory bandwidth to the value shown Table 2; the speedup of 42-, 48-, 54-, and 60-SM GPUs with compression is relative to the performance of 42-, 48-, 54-, and 60-SM GPUs without compression, respectively. The overall relative improvement with 42 SMs is slightly lower than with 60 SMs, which demonstrates that the compression technique can still be effective for a GPU with higher BCR since most memory-bound workloads congest the MCs even with much fewer SMs. These memory-bound workloads can easily congest the MCs even with 48 SMs; Lee *et al.* [17] show that just 32 SMs could generate enough memory accesses to congest the MCs. The geometric mean of speedup for all the memory-bound workloads for 42, 48, 54, and 60 SMs is 22%, 24%, 27%, and 26 %, respectively. Note that the speedup trends of some workloads such as FFT, JPG, and RAY have slight ups and downs as the number of SMs increases. This is because the performance of the baseline 42-, 48-, 54-, and 60-SM GPUs, which do not support compression, does not increase linearly with more SMs. Finally, the BCR is lower for our baseline GPU with 60 SMs than the GTX580, but we expect that future GPUs will have lower BCRs.

Performance improvement with L2 caches + compression/decompression: Figure 9 plots the speedup when varying L2 cache size. We measure the performance speedup of a GPU supporting the proposed compression technique (32-entry MD caches and 16 bytes per cycle decompressor throughput) with 32KB, 64KB, 96KB, and 256KB L2 caches per MC (total 256KB, 512KB, 768KB, and 2MB L2 caches); the NVIDIA Fermi architecture supports a 768KB total L2 cache capacity [11]. Then, we plot the performance speedup of the GPU relative to our baseline GPU that neither has L2 caches nor supports the compression technique. The geometric mean performance speedup of the memory-bound workloads is about 88% when a GPU with a 768KB L2 cache supports the compression technique. For roughly half of workloads we examined (i.e., JPG, NN, BKP, HOT, LPS, and SPM), the performance of a GPU supporting the compression technique with 768KB L2 caches is higher than or comparable to that of a GPU with 2MB L2 caches only. To isolate the performance increase contributed by the compression technique, we stack the speedup numbers shown in Figure 9 on top of the speedup numbers obtained with a GPU that has the same size L2 caches but does not support the compression technique. JPEG, RAY, BKP, HOT, LPS, and SPM show notable improvements over using L2 caches only. The compression technique increases the geometric mean of performance of a GPU with a 768KB L2 cache by 37% for memory-bound workloads.

Note that the compression technique without L2 caches improves the performance by only 26% while the improvement with the compression technique and L2 caches is nearly 37%. This can be explained by the following observations we made based on simulation statistics. First, the L2 miss rates of some workloads are reduced with the compression technique, because highly compressed blocks arrive earlier than their uncompressed counterparts, and the subsequent memory accesses for the blocks do not experience misses. Second, L2 caches filter some or many accesses to the DRAM, reducing the contentions for accessing the memory channels. This allows the MCs and the compression technique to work

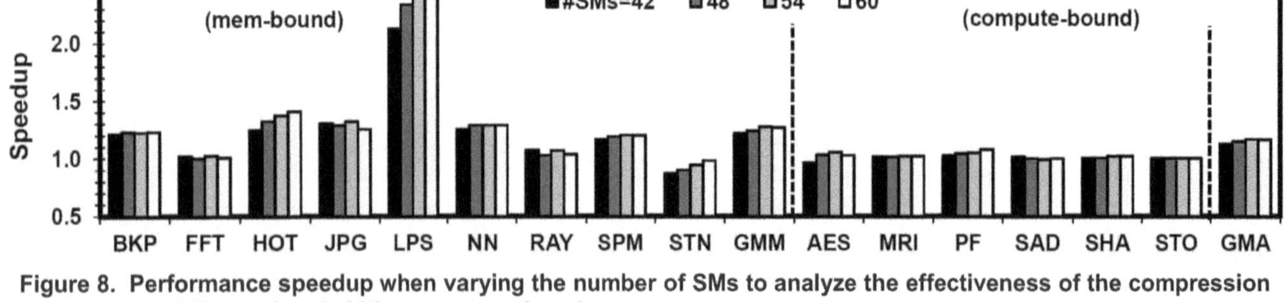

Figure 8. Performance speedup when varying the number of SMs to analyze the effectiveness of the compression technique for different bandwidth-compute ratio values.

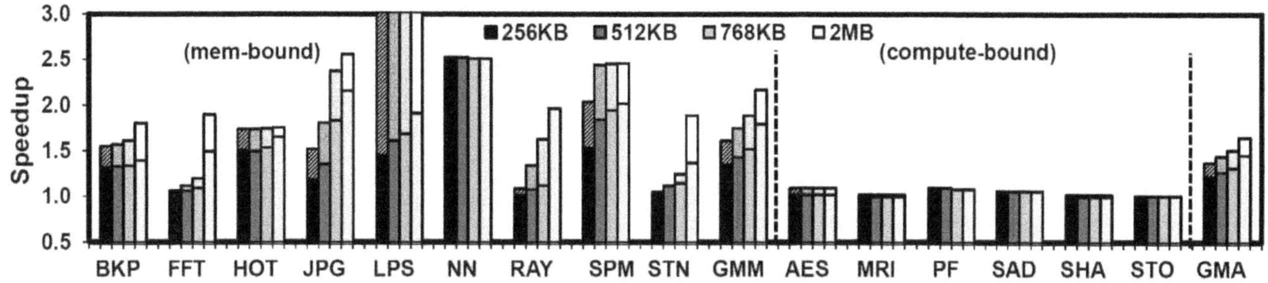

Figure 9. Performance speedup when varying L2 cache size combined with the compression/decompression technique. The results are normalized to a GPU without L2 caches or the compression/decompression technique.

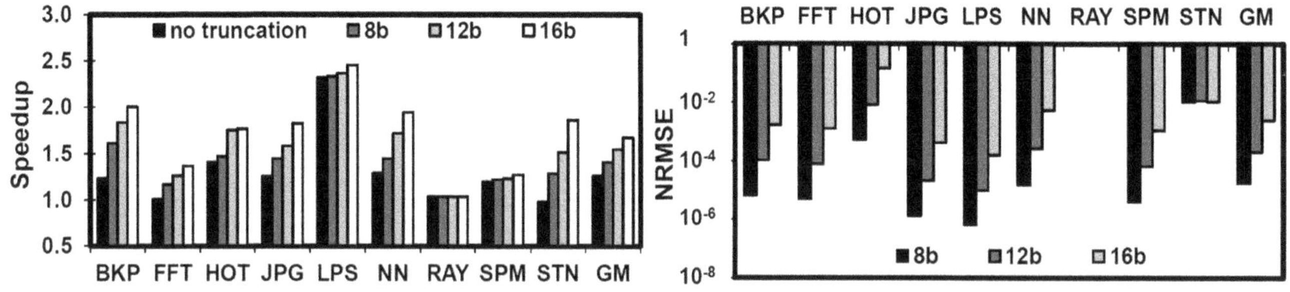

(a) (b)

Figure 10: (a) Speedup when varying the number of LSBs truncated and (b) normalized root mean square error (NRMSE) of all the final data transferred back to the CPU at the end of kernel executions.

more efficiently for servicing the same number of accesses. On the other hand, if the MCs are flooded with too many concurrent requests, their service efficiency goes down substantially and the compression technique shows less benefit. Finally, the compression technique improves the effective memory bandwidth and latency. This leads to less memory contention and allows L2 caches to handle misses more efficiently, leading to a synergistic effect of more efficient services for memory requests.

Impact of lossy compression on performance and overall computing accuracy: Figure 10(a) shows the performance speedup as the number of truncated LSBs increases for the memory-bound workloads. The GPU with more LSBs truncated provides higher performance improvement for most workloads except for RAY; the performance of RAY is limited by many simultaneous memory accesses rather than high memory bandwidth usage and the truncation does not improve the performance since the LSBs of the data are already zero. The compression after truncating 8~16 LSBs improves the geometric mean performance by 41%~61%, which is 15%~41% higher than the lossless compression alone. Meanwhile, as demonstrated in Figure 10(b), the impact on overall computing accuracy (i.e., the geometric mean of normalized root-mean-square error (NRMSE)) is 10^{-5} to10^{-3} for truncated single-precision data; we obtain the NRMSE values for all the final data transferred back to the CPU at the end of the kernel executions using double precision arithmetic. Note that RAY shows no error even after the lower 16-bits are truncated since the original input data applied to the FP units have zeros in their 16 LSBs. This is because RAY only utilizes the upper 8 bits of the mantissa for its input data. Thus, RAY is excluded when calculating the geometric mean of the NRMSE values.

5. Related Work

Hardware-based memory data compression techniques have been primarily employed either to increase the effective memory size by memory compaction, or to increase the effective cache size. Chen *et al.* used a variant of the Lempel-Ziv (LZ) compression algorithm to propose a scheme that dynamically partitions the cache into sections of different compressibility [3]. Alameldeen *et al.* showed that an adaptive dynamic scheme that chooses between holding compressed or uncompressed data in the L2 can improve the performance of memory-intensive workloads while constraining the performance degradation of other workloads to an acceptable level [4]. Zhang *et al.* show that supplementing a direct mapped cache with a small frequent value cache can greatly reduce the cache miss rate [18]. The frequent value cache is basically a smaller direct-mapped cache dedicated to holding frequent benchmark values. IBM's XMT technology employs a hardware parallelized derivative of the LZ sequential algorithm to achieve on the fly content compression [5]. The input data is divided into 1KB blocks before applying parallelized compression. However, their primary goal was not to improve the memory bandwidth but to increase the main memory capacity due to data compaction.

Some researchers have also employed hardware-based compression to reduce communication bandwidth between general purpose processors and off-chip DRAM. Benini *et al.* proposed a data compression scheme to reduce memory traffic in general purpose processor systems [19]. Data is stored in a compressed form in the main memory but uncompressed in the cache. They use a differential compression scheme to achieve on-the-fly compression (decompression) of data from (to) the cache to (from) the DRAM. Finally, Thuresson *et al.* quantified what type of value locality is exploited by each compression scheme and demonstrated that a new compression scheme exploiting value locality can free up a considerable percentage of the memory bandwidth [6]. Montrym and Moreton described the architecture of the GeForce 6800 [2]. Although they mentioned that compression techniques are used for texture depth and color data, but they neither disclose any microachitecture details for supporting the compression techniques nor provide a performance analysis.

6. Conclusion

Although GPUs support very high memory bandwidth and hide long memory access latency using many in-flight threads, the performance of many GPU workloads is still memory-bound. Furthermore, improving the bandwidth and latency is often limited by package, interconnect, and power constraints. Facing such challenges, in this paper, we propose a GPU architecture supporting hardware-based memory I/O link compression techniques for the data residing in the GPU's DRAM. First, we demonstrate that many GPU workloads are memory-bound but their data exhibit high compression ratios. Second, we show that GPUs assisted by high-throughput and low-latency compressors and decompressors integrated with metadata caches can improve the performance of many memory-bound workloads by 26% on average for GPUs with L1 caches but without L2 caches. We also show that the power and area of the proposed compression techniques are negligible compared to those of a GPU. Third, we evaluate compression support for GPUs with integrated L2 caches. Due to the synergistic effects between L2 caches and the compression technique, the performance of a GPU adopting 768KB L2 caches and the proposed compression technique is (i) an average of 37% higher than that of a GPU with the same size L2 caches but without the compression technique, and (ii) comparable to that of a GPU with 2MB L2 caches and no compression in many memory-bound workloads that we examined. Fourth, we investigate how a lossy compression technique can be applied to GPGPU workloads and evaluate its effectiveness. This technique leverages the observation that the reduced precision of FP data in GPGPU workloads does not notably impact the overall computing accuracy; truncating the 8 LSBs before the compression improves the performance by 41% while the RMSE for the final results is less than 10^{-3}. Finally, although compression techniques have been adopted by commercial GPUs, they are only used for compressing texture and color data, not data for GPGPU applications; the microarchitectural details for those GPU compression techniques are proprietary and their performance benefits have not been previously published.

Acknowledgement

We would like to thank Prof. David Wood (the University of Wisconsin-Madison), Mike O'Connor (AMD), and Jay Owen (AMD) for their valuable comments and supports. We also would like to thank Prof. Robert Dick and Xi Chen who assisted us to evaluate his compression hardware for this study. This work is supported in part by an SRC grant (Task ID: 2080.001), NSF grants (CCF-095360, CCF-1016262, CNS-1217102), Hiran Mayukh Award, IBM Faculty Award, and generous gift grants from AMD.

References

[1] Rambus, "Challenges and Solutions for Future Main Memory," 2009.

[2] J. Montrym and H. Moreton, "The GeForce 6800," *IEEE Micro*, vol. 25, no. 2, pp. 41-51, Mar-Apr 2005.

[3] D. Chen, E. Peserico, and L. Rudolph, "A Dynamically Partitionable Compressed Cache," in *Singapore-MIT Alliance Symp.*, 2003.

[4] A.R. Alameldeen and D.A. Wood, "Adaptive Cache Compression for High Performance Processors," in *IEEE/ACM Int. Symp. on Comp. Arch. (ISCA)*, 2004, pp. 212-223.

[5] B. Abali *et al.*, "Memory Expansion Technology (MXT): Software Support and Performance," *IBM J. Research and Development*, vol. 45, no. 2, pp. 287-301, Mar 2001.

[6] M. Thuresson, L. Spracklen, and P. Stenstrom, "Memory-Link Compression Schemes: A Value Locality Perspective," *IEEE T. on Computers*, vol. 57, no. 7, pp. 916-927, Jul 2007.

[7] T. Yeh, G. Reinman, S. Patel, and P. Faloutsos, "Fool me twice: Exploring and exploiting error tolerance in physics-based animation," *ACM Trans. Graph.*, vol. 29, no. 1, p. Article 5, Dec 2009.

[8] J. Tong, D. Nagle, and R. Rutenbar, "Reducing Power by Optimizing the Necessary Precision/Range of Floating-Point Arithmetic," *IEEE T. on Very Large Scale Integr. (VLSI) Syst.*, vol. 8, no. 3, pp. 273-285, Jun 2000.

[9] Xi Chen, Yang L., R.P. Dick, Li Shang, and H. Lekatsas, "C-Pack: A High-Performance Microprocessor Cache Compression Algorithm," *IEEE T. on Very Large Scale Integration (VLSI) Systems*, vol. 18, no. 8, pp. 196-1208, Aug 2010.

[10] GDDR3 Specific SGRAM Functions. [Online]. http://www.jedec.org/standards-documents/docs/sdram-3110507

[11] C.M. Wittenbrink, E. Kilgariff, and A Prabhu, "Fermi GF100 GPU Architecture," *IEEE Micro*, vol. 31, no. 2, pp. 50--59, Mar 2011.

[12] A. Bakhoda, G. Yuan, W W.L. Fung, H. Wong, and T.M. Aamodt," Analyzing CUDA Workloads using a Detailed GPU Simulator," in *IEEE Int. Symp. Perf. Analysis of Syst. and Software (ISPASS)*, 2009, pp. 163-174.

[13] Specification for Nvidia Quadro FX 5800. [Online]. http://www.nvidia.com/object/product_quadro_fx_5800_us.html

[14] S. Che *et al.*, "Rodinia: A Benchmark Suite for Heterogeneous Computing," in *IEEE Int. Symp. on Workload Characterization (IISWC)*, 2009, pp. 44-54.

[15] Parboil Benchmark Suite. [Online]. http://impact.crhc.illinois.edu/parboil.php.

[16] D.W. Chang et al., "ERCBench: An Open-Source Benchmark Suite for Embedded and Reconfigurable Computing," in *IEEE Int. Conf. on Field Programmable Logic and App. (FPL)*, 2010, pp. 408 -413.

[17] J. Lee, P. Ajgaonkar, and N.S. Kim, "Analyzing throughput of GPGPUs exploiting within-die core-to-core frequency variation," in *IEEE Int. Symp. on Performance Analysis of Syst. and Software (ISPASS)*, 2011, pp. 237-246.

[18] Y. Zhang, J. Yang, and R. Gupta, "Frequent Value Locality and Value-centric Data Cache Design," in *ACM Int. Conf. Arch. Support for Programming Lang. and Operating Syst. (ASPLOS)*, 2009, pp. 150-159.

[19] L. Benini, D. Bruni, B. Ricco, A. Macii, and E. Macii, "An Adaptive Data Compression Scheme for Memory Traffic Minimization in Processor-Based Systems," in *IEEE Int. Conf. on Circuits and Syst (ICCAS)*, May 2002, pp. 866-869.

Multi2Sim: A Simulation Framework for CPU-GPU Computing

Rafael Ubal† ubal@ece.neu.edu
Byunghyun Jang‡ * bjang@cs.olemiss.edu
Perhaad Mistry† pmistry@ece.neu.edu
Dana Schaa† dschaa@ece.neu.edu
David Kaeli† kaeli@ece.neu.edu

†Electrical and Computer Engineering Dept.
Northeastern University
360 Huntington Ave., Boston, MA 02115

‡Computer and Information Science Dept.
University of Mississippi
P. O. Box 1848, University, MS 38677

ABSTRACT

Accurate simulation is essential for the proper design and evaluation of any computing platform. Upon the current move toward the CPU-GPU heterogeneous computing era, researchers need a simulation framework that can model both kinds of computing devices and their interaction. In this paper, we present Multi2Sim, an open-source, modular, and fully configurable toolset that enables ISA-level simulation of an x86 CPU and an AMD Evergreen GPU. Focusing on a model of the AMD Radeon 5870 GPU, we address program emulation correctness, as well as architectural simulation accuracy, using AMD's OpenCL benchmark suite. Simulation capabilities are demonstrated with a preliminary architectural exploration study, and workload characterization examples. The project source code, benchmark packages, and a detailed user's guide are publicly available at *www.multi2sim.org*.

Categories and Subject Descriptors

C.1.2 [**Computer Systems Organization**]: Processor Architectures—*Multiple Data Stream Architectures*; B.1.2 [**Hardware**]: Control Structures and Microprogramming—*Control Structure Performance and Design Aids*

Keywords

GPU, AMD, Evergreen ISA, Multi2Sim

*This work was done while the author was with AMD.

PACT'12, September 19–23, 2012, Minneapolis, Minnesota, USA.

1. INTRODUCTION

GPUs have become an important component of High Performance Computing (HPC) platforms by accelerating the ever demanding data-parallel portions of a wide range of applications. The success of GPU computing has made microprocessor researchers in both academia and industry believe that CPU-GPU heterogeneous computing is not just an alternative, but the future of HPC. Now, GPUs are showing up as integrated accelerators for general purpose platforms [8, 5, 9]. This move attempts to leverage the combined capabilities of multi-core CPU and many-core GPU architectures.

As CPU-GPU heterogeneous computing research gains momentum, the need to provide a robust simulation environment becomes more critical. Simulation frameworks provide a number of benefits to researchers. They allow pre-silicon designs to be evaluated and performance results to be obtained for a range of design points. A number of CPU simulators supporting simulation at the ISA level have been developed [11, 14] and successfully used in a range of architectural studies. Although there are tools that are currently available for simulating GPUs at the intermediate language level (e.g., PTX) [12, 13], the research community still lacks a publicly available framework integrating both fast functional simulation and cycle-accurate detailed architectural simulation at the ISA level that considers a true heterogeneous CPU-GPU model.

In this paper we present Multi2Sim, a simulation framework for CPU-GPU computing. The proposed framework integrates a publicly available model of the data-parallel AMD Evergreen GPU family [3][1] with the simulation of superscalar, multi-threaded, and multicore x86 processors. This work also offers important insight into the architecture of an AMD Evergreen GPU, by describing our models of instruction pipelines and memory hierarchy, to a deeper extent than previous public work, to the best of our knowledge, has done before.

Multi2Sim is provided as a Linux-based command-line toolset, designed with an emphasis on presenting a user-friendly interface. It runs OpenCL applications without any source code modifications, and provides a number of instrumentation capabilities that

[1] AMD has used the Evergreen ISA specification for the implementation of its mainstream Radeon 5000 and 6000 series of GPUs.

enable research in application characterization, code optimization, compiler optimization, and hardware architecture design. To illustrate the utility and power of our toolset, we report on a wide range of experimental results based on benchmarks taken from AMD's Accelerated Parallel Processing (APP) SDK 2.5 [1].

The rest of this paper is organized as follows. Section 2 introduces the functional simulation model in Multi2Sim. Section 3 presents the Evergreen GPU architecture and its simulation. Section 4 reports our experimental evaluation. We summarize related work in Section 5, and conclude the paper in Section 6.

2. THE MULTI2SIM PROJECT

The Multi2Sim project started as a free, open-source, cycle-accurate simulation framework targeting superscalar, multi-threaded, and multicore x86 CPUs. The CPU simulation framework consists of two major interacting software components: the *functional simulator* and the *architectural simulator*. The functional simulator (i.e., *emulator*) mimics the execution of a guest program on a native x86 processor, by interpreting the program binary and dynamically reproducing its behavior at the ISA level. The architectural simulator (i.e., *detailed* or *timing simulator*) obtains a trace of x86 instructions from the functional simulator, and tracks execution of the processor hardware structures on a cycle-by-cycle basis.

The current version of the CPU functional simulator supports the execution of a number of different benchmark suites without any porting effort, including single-threaded benchmark suites (e.g., SPEC2006 and Mediabench), multi-threaded parallel benchmarks (SPLASH-2 and PARSEC 2.1), as well as custom self-compiled user code. The architectural simulator models many-core superscalar pipelines with out-of-order execution, a complete memory hierarchy with cache coherence, interconnection networks, and additional components.

Multi2Sim integrates a configurable model for the commercial AMD Evergreen GPU family (e.g., Radeon 5870). The latest releases fully support both functional and architectural simulation of a GPU, following the same interaction model between them as for CPU simulation. While the GPU emulator provides traces of Evergreen instructions, the detailed simulator tracks execution times and architectural state.

All simulated programs begin with the execution of CPU code. The interface to the GPU simulator is the Open Compute Language (OpenCL). When OpenCL programs are executed, the host (i.e., CPU) portions of the program are run using the CPU simulation modules. When OpenCL API calls are encountered, they are intercepted and used to setup or begin GPU simulation.

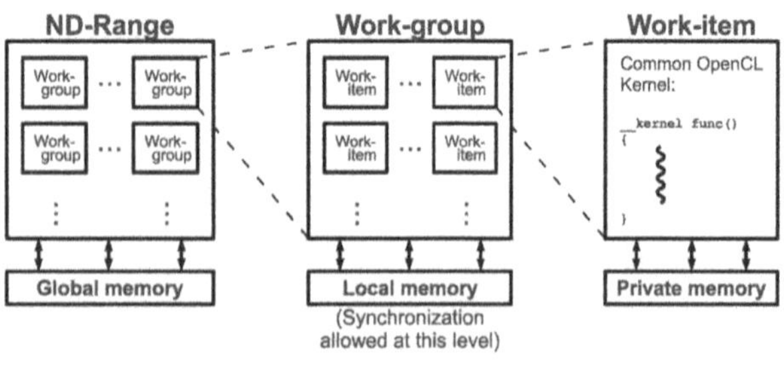

Figure 1: OpenCL programming and memory model.

2.1 The OpenCL Programming Model

OpenCL is an industry-standard programming framework designed specifically for developing programs targeting heterogeneous computing platforms, consisting of CPUs, GPUs, and other classes of processing devices [7]. OpenCL's programming model emphasizes parallel processing by using the *single-program multiple-data* (SPMD) paradigm, in which a single piece of code, called a *kernel*, maps to multiple subsets of input data, creating a massive amount of parallel execution.

Figure 1 provides a view of the basic execution elements hierarchy defined in OpenCL. An instance of the OpenCL kernel is called a *work-item*, which can access its own pool of *private memory*. Work-items are arranged into *work-groups* with two basic properties: i) those work-items contained in the same work-group can perform efficient synchronization operations, and ii) work-items within the same work-group can share data through a low-latency *local memory*. The totality of work-groups form the *ND-Range* (grid of work-item groups) and share a common *global memory*.

2.2 OpenCL Simulation

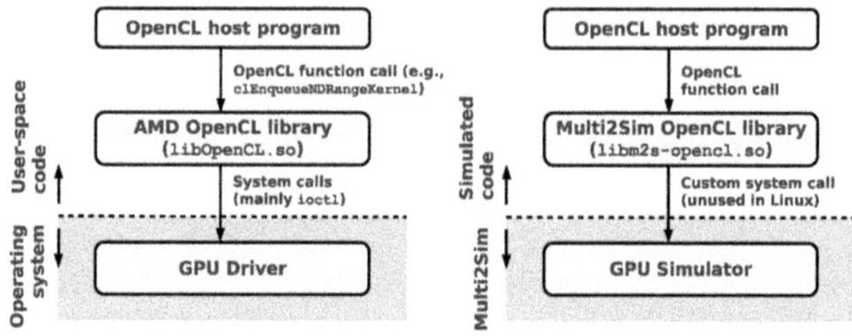

a) Execution on native device b) Execution on Multi2Sim

Figure 2: Comparison of software modules of an OpenCL program: native AMD GPU based heterogeneous system versus Multi2Sim simulation framework.

The call stack of an OpenCL program running on Multi2Sim differs from the native call stack starting at the OpenCL library call, as shown in Figure 2. When an OpenCL API function call is issued, our implementation of the OpenCL runtime (`libm2s-opencl.so`) handles the call. This call is intercepted by the CPU simulation module, which transfers control to the GPU module as soon as the guest application launches the device kernel execution. This infrastructure allows unmodified x86 binaries (precompiled OpenCL host programs) to run on Multi2Sim with total binary compatibility with the native environment.

3. ARCHITECTURAL SIMULATION OF AN AMD EVERGREEN GPU

This section presents the architecture of a generic AMD Evergreen GPU device, focusing on hardware components devoted to general purpose computing of OpenCL kernels. As one of the novelties of this paper, the following block diagrams and descriptions provide some insight into the instruction pipelines, memory components, and interconnects, which tend to be kept private by the major GPU vendors, and remain undocumented in currently available tools. All presented architectural details are accurately modeled on Multi2Sim, as described next.

3.1 The Evergreen GPU Architecture

A GPU consists of an *ultra-threaded dispatcher*, an array of independent *compute units*, and a *memory hierarchy*. The ultra-threaded dispatcher processes the ND-Range and maps waiting

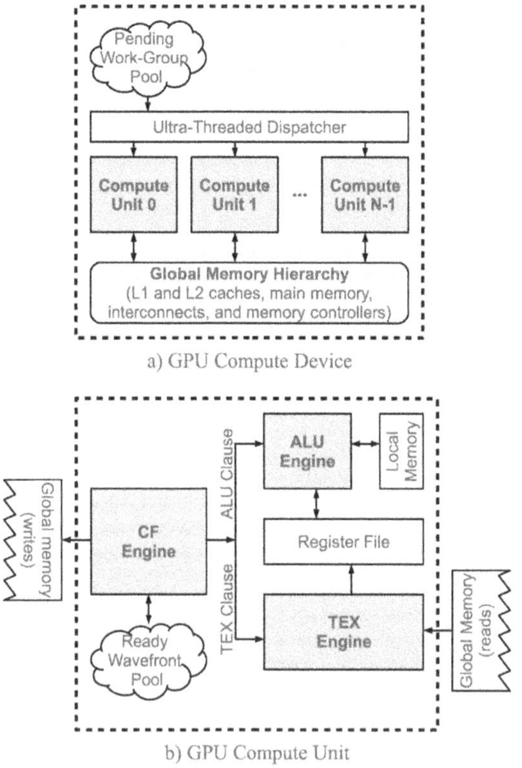

Figure 3: Block diagram of the GPU architecture.

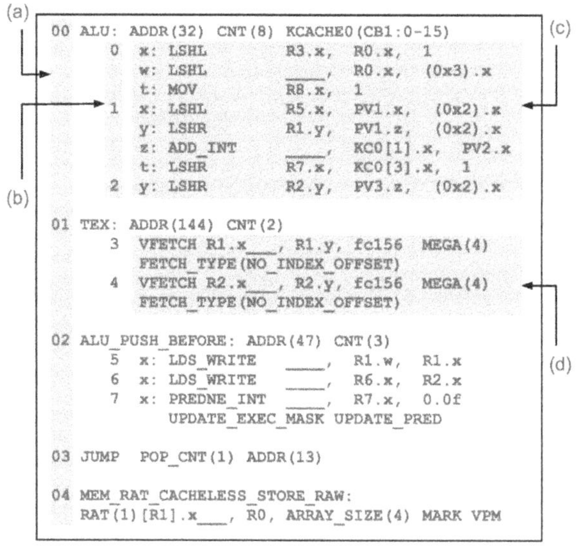

Figure 4: Example of AMD Evergreen assembly code: (a) main CF clause instruction counter, (b) internal clause instruction counter, (c) ALU clause, (d) TEX clause.

work-groups onto available compute units. Once a work-group is assigned to a compute unit, it remains in the compute unit until its execution completes. As a work-group executes, work-items fetch and store data through the global memory hierarchy, formed of two levels of cache, interconnects, and memory controllers. Figure 3a shows a block diagram of the Evergreen family compute device.

A compute unit consists of three *execution engines*, a *local memory*, and a *register file*. The three execution engines, called *control flow* (CF), *arithmetic-logic* (ALU), and *texture* (TEX) engines, are devoted to execute different portions of an OpenCL kernel binary, referred to as CF, ALU, and TEX clauses, respectively (see Section 3.2). A block diagram of the compute unit is illustrated in Figure 3b.

The ALU engine contains a set of *stream cores*, each devoted to the execution of one work-item's arithmetic operations. ALU instructions are organized as 5-way VLIW bundles, created at compile time. Each instruction in a VLIW bundle is executed on one of the 5 VLIW lanes forming the stream core.

An Evergreen GPU defines the concept of a *wavefront* as a group of work-items executing in a Single-Instruction Multiple-Data (SIMD) fashion. Each instruction is executed concurrently by every work-item comprising a wavefront, although each work-item uses its private data for the computations. This model simplifies instruction fetch hardware by implementing a common front-end for a whole wavefront.

3.2 The Evergreen Instruction Set Architecture (ISA)

When the GPU functional simulator receives the OpenCL kernel to execute, an emulation loop starts by fetching, decoding, and executing Evergreen instructions. The basic format of the AMD Evergreen ISA can be observed in the sample code from Figure 4.

Evergreen assembly uses a clause-based format. The kernel execution starts with a CF instruction. CF instructions affect the main program control flow (such is the case for CF instruction `03`), write data to global memory (`04`), or transfer control to a secondary clause, such as an ALU clause (`00`, `02`), or a TEX clause (`01`). ALU clauses contain instructions performing arithmetic-logic operations and local memory accesses, while TEX clauses are exclusively devoted to global memory read operations.

ALU instructions are packed into VLIW bundles. A VLIW bundle is run one at a time on a stream core, where each ALU instruction label reflects the VLIW lane assigned to that instruction. An ALU instruction operand can be any output from the previously executed VLIW bundle using the *Previous Vector* (`PV`) or the *Previous Scalar* (`PS`) special registers. Finally, *constant memory* is an additional globally accessible storage initialized by the CPU, which can also be used as ALU instruction operands (`KC`).

From our discussion above of Evergreen ISA characteristics, we can observe a couple of important differences from working with higher level intermediate languages, such as AMD's IL [4] or NVIDIA's PTX [6]. For example, in AMD's Evergreen ISA there is a limited number of general purpose registers, so there are restrictions on how to form VLIW bundles, and there are specific rules to group machine instructions forming clauses. In general, there are many properties of the ISA run directly by the machine that need not be considered working with an intermediate language. Thus, significant performance accuracy can be gained with ISA-level simulation.

3.2.1 *Kernel Execution Model*

When an OpenCL kernel is launched by a host program, the ND-Range configuration is provided to the GPU. Work-groups are then created and successively assigned to compute units when they have available execution resources. The number of work-groups that can be assigned to a single compute unit is determined by four hardware limitations: *i*) the maximum number of work-groups supported per compute unit, *ii*) the maximum number of wavefronts per compute unit, *iii*) the number of registers on a compute unit, and *iv*) the amount of local memory on a compute unit. Maximizing the number of assigned work-groups per compute unit is a performance-sensitive decision that can be evaluated on Multi2Sim.

Each work-group assigned to a compute unit is partitioned into wavefronts, which are then placed into a *ready wavefront pool*. The CF engine selects wavefronts from the wavefront pool for execution, based on a *wavefront scheduling* algorithm. A new wavefront starts running the main CF clause of the OpenCL kernel binary, and subsequently spawns secondary ALU and TEX clauses. The wavefront scheduling algorithm is another performance sensitive parameter, which can be evaluated with Multi2Sim.

When a wavefront is extracted from the pool, it is only inserted back in when the executed CF instruction completes. This ensures that there is only a single CF instruction in flight at any time for a given wavefront, avoiding the need for branch prediction or speculative execution in case flow control is affected. The performance penalty for this serialization is hidden by overlapping the execution of different wavefronts. Determining the extent to which overlapping execution is occurring and the cause of bottlenecks are additional benefits of simulating execution with Multi2Sim.

3.2.2 Work-Item Divergence

In a SIMD execution model, *work-item divergence* is side-effect generated when a conditional branch instruction is resolved differently for any work-items within a wavefront. To address work-item divergence present during SIMD execution, the Evergreen ISA provides each wavefront with an *active mask*. The active mask is a bit map, where each bit represents the active status of an individual work-item in the wavefront. If a work-item is labeled as inactive, the result of any arithmetic computation performed in its associated stream core is ignored, preventing the work-item from changing the kernel state.

This work-item divergence strategy attempts to converge all work-items together across all possible execution paths, allowing only those active work-items whose conditional execution matches the currently fetched instruction flow to continue execution. To support nested conditionals and procedure calls, an *active mask stack* is used to push and pop active masks, so that the active mask at the top of the stack always represents the active mask of the currently executing work-items. Using Multi2Sim, statistics related to work-item divergence are available to researchers (see Section 4.3).

3.3 The Instruction Pipelines

In a compute unit, the CF, ALU, and TEX engines are organized as instruction pipelines. Figure 5 presents a block diagram of each engine's instruction pipeline. Within each pipeline, decisions about scheduling policies, latencies, and buffer sizes must be made. These subtle factors have performance implications, and provide another opportunity for researchers to benefit from experimenting with design decisions within Multi2Sim.

The CF engine (Figure 5a) runs the CF clause of an OpenCL kernel. The *fetch* stage selects a new wavefront from the wavefront pool on every cycle, switching among them at the granularity of one single CF instruction. Instructions from different wavefronts are interpreted by the *decode* stage in a round-robin fashion. When a CF instruction triggers a secondary clause, the corresponding execution engine (ALU or TEX engine) is allocated, and the CF instruction remains in the *execute* stage until the secondary clause completes. Other CF instructions from other wavefronts can be executed in the interim, as long as they do not request a busy execution engine. CF instruction execution (including all instructions run in a secondary clause, if any) finishes in order in the *complete* stage stage. The wavefront is returned to the wavefront pool, making it again a candidate for instruction fetching. Global memory writes are run asynchronously in the CF engine itself, without requiring a secondary engine.

The ALU engine is devoted to the execution of ALU clauses from the allocated wavefront (Figure 5b). After the *fetch* and *decode* stages, decoded VLIW instructions are placed into a *VLIW bundle buffer*. The *read* stage consumes the VLIW bundle and reads the source operands from the register file and/or local memory for each work-item in the wavefront. The *execute* stage issues an instance of a VLIW bundle to each of the stream cores every cycle. The number of stream cores in a compute unit might be smaller than the number of work-items in a wavefront. Thus, a wavefront is split into *subwavefronts*, where each subwavefront contains as many work-items as there are stream cores in a compute unit. The result of the computation is written back to the destination operands (register file or local memory) at the *write* stage.

The TEX engine (Figure 5c) is devoted to the execution of global memory fetch instructions in TEX clauses. The TEX instruction bytes are stored into a TEX instruction buffer after being fetched and decoded. Memory addresses for each work-item in the wavefront are read from the register file and a read request to the global memory hierarchy is performed at the *read* stage. Completed global memory reads are handled in order by the *write* stage. The fetched data is stored into the corresponding locations of the register file for each work-item. The lifetime of a memory read is modeled in detail throughout the global memory hierarchy, as specified in the following sections.

3.4 Memory Subsystem

The GPU memory subsystem contains different components for data storage and transfer. With Multi2Sim, the memory subsystem is highly configurable, including customizable settings for the number of cache levels, memory capacities, block sizes, number of banks, and ports. A description of the memory components for the Evergreen model follows:

Register file (GPRs). Multi2Sim provides a model with no contention for register file accesses. In a given cycle, the register can be accessed by the TEX and ALU engines simultaneously by different wavefronts. Work-items within and among wavefronts always access different register sets.

Local Memory. A separate local memory module is present in each compute unit, and is modeled in Multi2Sim with a configurable latency, number of banks, ports, and allocation chunk size. In an OpenCL kernel, accesses to local memory are defined by the programmer by specifying a variable's scope, whose accesses are then compiled into distinct assembly instructions. Contention to local memory is modeled by serializing accesses to the same memory bank whenever no read or write port is available. Also, memory access coalescing is considered by grouping those accesses from different work-items to the same memory block.

Global memory. The GPU global memory is accessible by all compute units. It is presented to the programmer as a separate memory scope, and implemented as a memory hierarchy managed by hardware in order to reduce access latency. In Multi2Sim, the global memory hierarchy has a configurable number of cache levels and interconnects. A possible configuration is shown in Figure 6a, using private L1 caches per compute unit, and multiple L2 caches that are shared between subsets of compute units. L1 caches provide usually a similar access time as local memory, but they are managed transparently by hardware, similarly to how a memory hierarchy is managed on a CPU.

Interconnection networks. Each cache in the global memory hierarchy is connected to the lower-level cache (or global memory) using an interconnection network. Interconnects are organized as

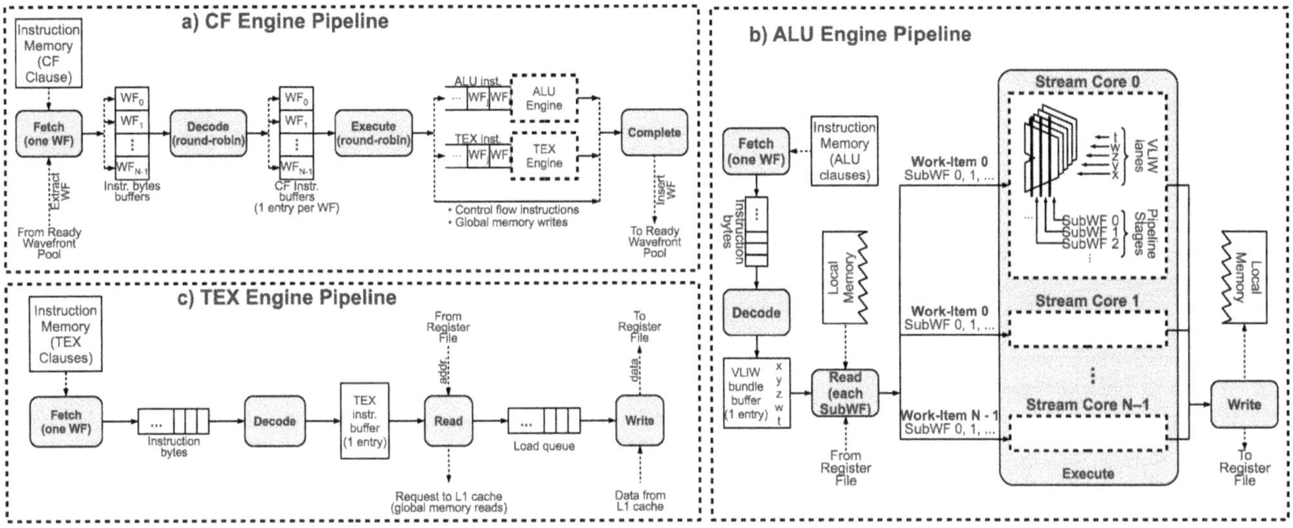

Figure 5: Block diagram of the execution engine pipelines.

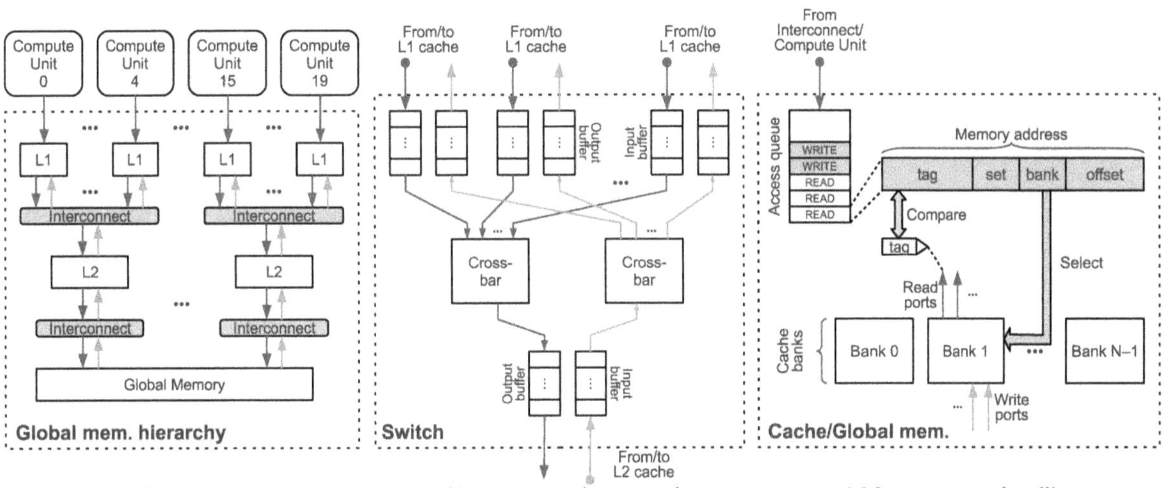

a) Cache hierarchy b) Interconnection network c) Memory access handling

Figure 6: Components of the GPU global memory hierarchy, as modeled in Multi2Sim.

point-to-point connections using a switch, whose architecture block diagram is presented in Figure 6b. A switch contains two disjoint inner subnetworks, each devoted to package transfers in opposite directions.

Cache access queues. Each cache memory has a buffer where access requests are enqueued, as shown in Figure 6c. On one hand, access buffers allow for asynchronous writes that prevent stalls in instruction pipelines. On the other hand, memory access coalescing is handled in access buffers at every level of the global memory hierarchy (both caches and global memory). Each sequence of subsequent entries in the access queue reading or writing to the same cache block are grouped into one single actual memory access. The coalescing degree depends on the memory block size, the access queue size, and the memory access pattern, and is a very performance sensitive metric measurable with Multi2Sim.

4. EXPERIMENTAL EVALUATION

This section presents a set of experiments aimed at validating and demonstrating the range of functional and architectural simulation features available with Multi2Sim. All simulations are based on a baseline GPU model resembling the commercial AMD Radeon 5870 GPU, whose hardware parameters are summarized in Table 1.

For the simulator performance studies, simulations were run on a machine with four quad-core Intel Xeon processors (2.27GHz, 8MB cache, 24GB DDR3). Experimental evaluations were performed using a subset of the AMD OpenCL SDK [1] applications, representing a wide range of application behaviors and memory access patterns [16]. The applications discussed in this paper are listed in Table 2, where we include a short description of the programs and the corresponding input dataset characteristics.

4.1 Validation

Our validation methodology for establishing the fidelity of the GPU simulator considered the correctness of both the functional and architectural simulation models, though we follow two different validation methodologies. For the functional simulator, the correctness of the instruction decoder is validated by comparing the

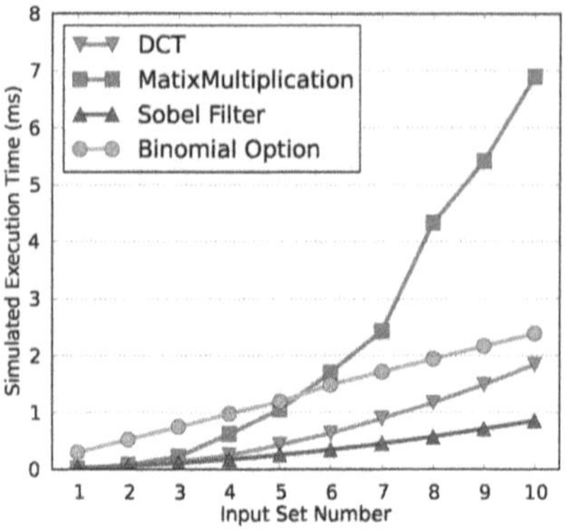

a) Simulated execution time reported by Multi2Sim.

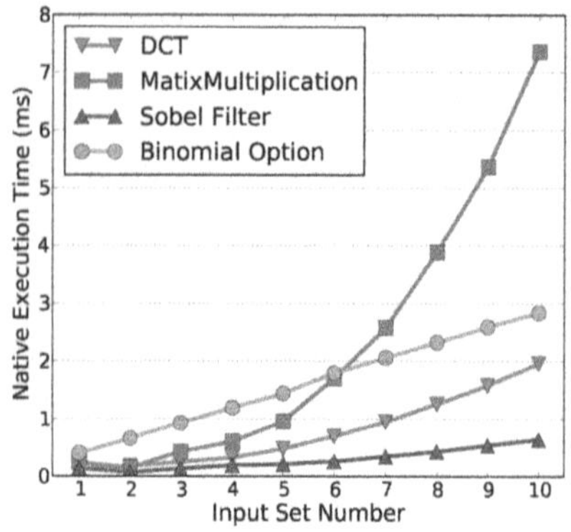

b) Native execution time on the AMD Radeon 5870.

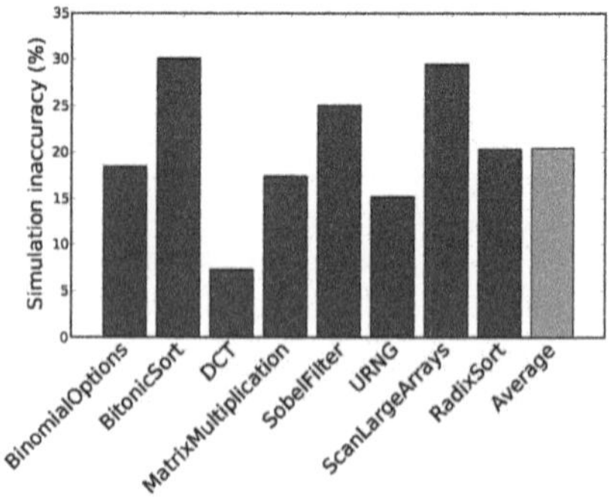

c) Average error percentage between the native execution time and simulated execution time for APP SDK benchmarks.

Figure 7: Validation for the architectural simulation, comparing simulated and native absolute execution times.

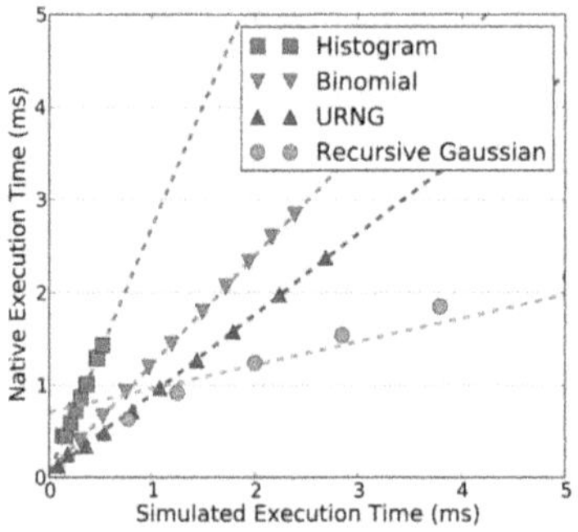

a) Correlation between simulated execution times and native execution times.

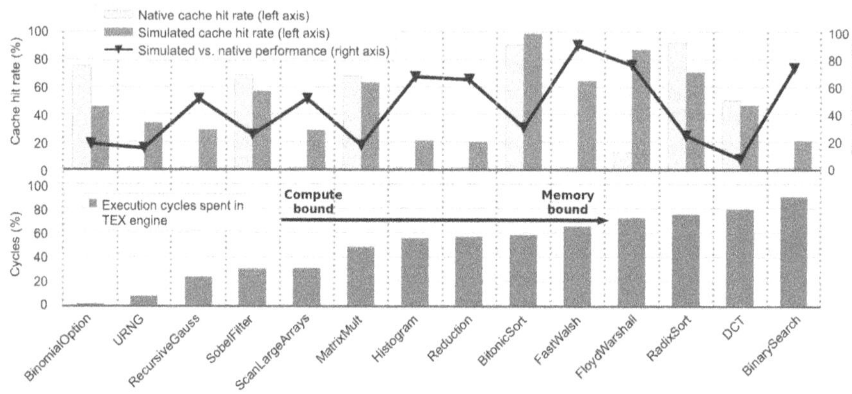

b) Comparison of cache hit rate in simulated and native executions, along with measured difference in overall execution time. Workloads are sorted from compute bound to memory bound.

Figure 8: Validation for architectural simulation, comparing trends between simulated and native execution times.

disassembled code to the Evergreen output that is generated by the AMD compiler. We also validate the correctness of each benchmark's execution by comparing the simulated application output with the output of the application run directly on the CPU. All simulations generate functionally correct results for all programs studied and input problem sets.

Regarding the fidelity of the architectural model, Multi2Sim's performance results have been compared against native execution performance (native here refers to the actual Radeon 5870 hardware), using ten different input sizes within the ranges shown in Table 2 (column *Input Range*). Since our architectural model is cycle-based, and the native execution is measured as kernel execution time, it is challenging to compare our metrics directly. To convert simulated cycles into time, we use the documented ALU clock frequency of 850MHz of the 5870 hardware. The native execution time is computed as the average time of 1000 kernel executions for each benchmark. Native kernel execution time was measured using the AMD APP profiler [2]. The execution time provided by the APP profiler does not include overheads such as kernel setup and host-device I/O [2].

Figure 7a and Figure 7b plot simulated execution time and native execution time performance trends, respectively (only four benchmarks are shown for clarity). Figure 7c shows the percentage difference in performance for a larger selection of benchmarks. The value shown for each benchmark in Figure 7c is the average of the absolute percent error for each input of the benchmark. For those cases where simulation accuracy decreases, Figure 8 shows detailed trends, leading to the following analysis.

In Figure 8a, we show the correlation between the native execution time and the simulated execution time for the studied benchmarks. For some of the benchmarks (e.g., *Histogram* or *RecursiveGauss*), execution times vary significantly. However, we still see a strong correlation between each of the native execution points and their associated simulator results for all benchmarks. In other words, a change in the problem size for a benchmark has the same relative performance impact for both native and simulated executions. The linear trend-line is represented using a curve-fitting algorithm that minimizes the squared distances between every data point and itself. For the benchmarks that are modeled accurately using the simulator, the data points lie on the 45° line. The reason for the occurrence of divergent slopes can be attributed to the lack of precise representation of the memory hierarchy in the 5870 GPU, including the following factors:

Table 1: **Baseline GPU simulation parameters.**

Compute Device Configuration		
Compute resources	# of compute units (CU)	20
	# of stream cores (SC) / CU	16
	# of processing elements / stream core	5
	Total # of processing elements	**20*16*5 = 1600**
Register file	# of vector registers	16,384
	# of 32 bit registers / vector	4
	Total amount of register memory	**16k*4*4=256KB**
Local memory	# of banks	32
	Block Size	16B
	# of Read / Write ports (1 per SC)	16R / 16W
	Total amount of local memory	**32kB**

Global Memory Configuration		
L1 Cache (one per CU) Accessed by 16 SCs	# of banks	32
	Associativity	8 way
	Latency (cycles)	1
	Block Size	64B
	# of Read / Write ports	16R / 16W
	Total L1 cache size	**8KB**
L2 Cache (each shared between 5 CUs)	# of L2 caches	4
	# of banks	32
	Associativity	8 way - set
	Latency (cycles)	10
	Block Size	256B
	# of Read / Write ports	2R / 2W
	Total L2 cache size	**4x128KB =512KB**
Main memory	# of banks	128
	Bus width	256B / cycle
	Latency (cycles)	100
	Global memory size	**1GB**

Table 2: List of OpenCL benchmarks used for experiments. Column *Input base* contains the baseline problem size used, and column *Input range* contains the range of problem sizes used during simulator validation.

Benchmark	Input feature	Inp. base	Input range
BinarySearch	Array Size	1M	2k - 2M
BinomialOption	Num. of options	640	64 – 640
BitonicSort	Vector size	4k	512 – 10k
DCT	Matrix size	1024x1024	128x128–1280x1280
DwtHaar1D	Array size	256k	1k – 512k
FastWalsh	Array size	640	1k – 512k
FloydWarshall	Num. of nodes	128	64 – 512
Histogram	Array size	1M	16k - 2M
MatrixMult	Matrix sizes	1024x1024	128x128–1280x1280
RadixSort	Array size	32k	8k - 128k
RecursiveGauss	Image size	512x512	256x256–1536x1536
Reduction	Array size	4M	400k – 4M
ScanLargeArrays	Array size	1M	512 – 2M
SobelFilter	Image size	1024x768	256x256–1536x1536
URNG	Image size	1024x768	256x256–1536x1536

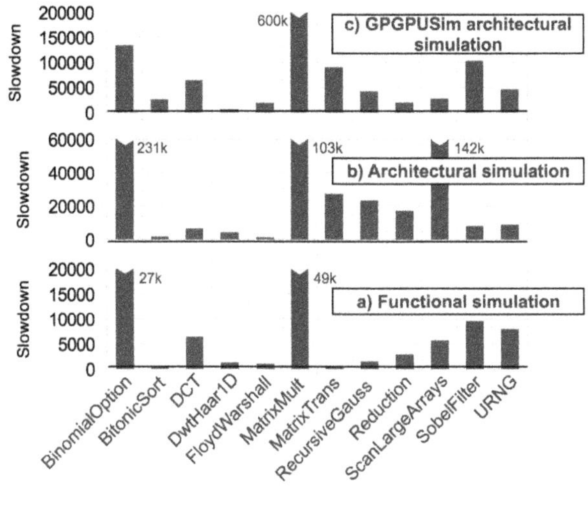

Figure 9: Simulation slowdowns over native execution for functional and architectural simulation.

Specialized Memory Path Design. The AMD Radeon 5870 consists of two paths from compute units to memory [2], each with different performance characteristics. The *fast path* performs only basic operations, such as loads and stores for 32-bit data types. The *complete path* supports additional advanced operations, including atomics and stores for sub-32-bit data types. This design has been deprecated in later GPU architectures for a more conventional layout [17], which is similar to the one currently implemented in Multi2Sim.

Cache Interconnects. The specification of the interconnection network between the L1 and L2 caches has not been published. We use an approximation where four L2 caches are shared between compute units (Table 1).

Cache Parameters. The latency and associativity of the different levels of the cache hierarchy are not known. Some sources of simulation inaccuracy can be attributed to cache parameters, as shown in Figure 8, where the percent error is minimum for the cases where the native cache hit ratios and simulated cache hit ratios vary the least.

4.2 Simulation Speed

For the benchmarks used in this paper, Multi2Sim's simulation overhead is plotted in Figure 9 as a function of the slowdown over native execution time. The average functional simulation slowdown is 8700× (113s), and the average architectural simulation time is 44000× (595s). It should be noted that simulation time is not necessarily related to native execution time (e.g., simulating one 100-cycle latency instruction is faster than simulating ten 1-cycle instructions), so these results only aim to provide some representative samples of simulation overhead.

Simulation performance has been also evaluated for an architectural simulation on GPGPUSim, an NVIDIA-based GPU simulator [10]. This simulator has been used as experimental support for recent studies on GPU computing, exploring alternative memory controller implementations [18] and dynamic grouping of threads (work-items) to minimize thread divergence penalty [15], for example. To enable this comparison, the APP SDK benchmarks were adapted to run on GPGPUSim. Figure 9c shows the performance slowdown over native execution, which averages about 90000× (1350s).

4.3 Benchmark Characterization

As a case study of GPU simulation, this section presents a brief characterization of OpenCL benchmarks carried out on Multi2Sim, based on instruction classification, VLIW bundle occupancy, and control flow divergence. These statistics are dynamic in nature, and are reported by Multi2Sim as part of its simulation reports.

Figure 10a shows Evergreen instruction mixes executed by each OpenCL kernel. The instruction categories are control flow instructions (jumps, stack operations, and synchronizations), global memory reads, global memory writes, local memory accesses, and arithmetic-logic operations. Arithmetic-logic operations form the bulk of executed instructions (these are GPU-friendly workloads).

Figure 10b represents the average occupancy of VLIW bundles executed in the stream cores of the GPU's ALU engine. If a VLIW instruction uses less than 5 slots, there will be idle VLIW lanes in the stream core, resulting in an underutilization of available execution resources. The Evergreen compiler tries to maximize the VLIW slot occupancy, but there is an upper limit imposed by the available instruction-level parallelism in the kernel code. Results show that we rarely utilize all 5 slots (except for *SobelFilter* thanks to its high fraction of ALU instructions), and the worst case of only one single filled slot is encountered frequently.

Finally, Figure 10c illustrates the control flow divergence effect among work-items. When work-items within a wavefront executing in a SIMD fashion diverge on branch conditions, the entire wavefront must go through all possible execution paths. Thus, frequent work-item divergence has a negative impact on performance. For each benchmark in Figure 10c, each color stride within a bar represents a different control flow path through the program. If a bar has one single stride, then only one path was taken by all work-items for that kernel. If there are n strides, then n different control flow paths were taken by different work-items. Notice that different colors are used here with the only purpose of delimiting bar strides, but no specific meaning is assigned to each color. The size of each stride represents the percentage of work-items that took that control flow path for the kernel. Results show benchmarks with the following divergence characteristics:

- No control flow divergence at all (*URNG*, *DCT*).
- Groups of divergence with a logarithmic decreasing size due to different number of loop iterations (*Reduction*, *DwtHaar1D*).
- Multiple divergence groups depending on input data (*BinomialOption*[2]).

4.4 Architectural Exploration

The architectural GPU model provided in Multi2Sim allows researchers to perform large design space evaluations. As a sample of the simulation flexibility, this section presents three case studies, where performance significantly varies for different input parameter values. In each case, we compare two benchmarks with respect to their architectural sensitivity. Performance is measured using the number of instructions per cycle (IPC), where the instruction count is incremented by one for a whole wavefront, regardless of the number of comprising work-items.

Figure 11a shows performance scaling with respect to the number of compute units. The total memory bandwidth provided by global memory is shared by all compute units, so increasing the number of compute units decreases the available bandwidth per executed work-group. The available memory bandwidth for the device in this experiment only increases between compute unit counts which are a multiple of 5 when a new L2 is added (Table 1). When the total bandwidth is exhausted, the trend (as seen between 10-15 and 15-20 compute units) flattens. This point is clearly observed when we increase the number of compute units in compute-intensive kernels with high ALU-to-Fetch instruction ratios (e.g., *URNG*) and less so in memory-intensive benchmarks (e.g., *Histogram*).

Figure 11b presents the performance achieved by varying the number of stream cores per compute unit. In the *BinomialOption* kernel we observe a step function, where each step corresponds to a multiple of the wavefront size (64). This behavior is due to the fact that the number of stream cores determines the number of subwavefronts (or time-multiplexed slots) that stream cores deal with for each VLIW bundle. When an increase in the number of stream cores causes a decrease in the number of subwavefronts (e.g., 15 to 16, 21 to 22, and 31 to 32), performance improves. When the number of stream cores matches the number of work-items per wavefront, the bottleneck due to a serialized stream core utilization disappears. This effect is not observed for *ScanLargeArrays* due to a lower wavefront occupancy.

Figure 11c plots the impact of increasing the L1 cache size. For benchmarks that lack temporal locality and exhibit large strided accesses in the data stream, performance is insensitive to increasing cache size, as seen in *Reduction*. In contrast, benchmarks with locality are more sensitive to changes in the L1 cache size, as observed for *FloydWarshall*.

5. RELATED WORK

While numerous mature CPU simulators at various levels are available, GPU simulators are still in their infancy. There continues to be a growing need for architectural GPU simulators that model a GPU at the ISA level. And in the near future, we will see a more pressing need for a true CPU-GPU heterogeneous simulation framework. This section briefly summarizes existing simulators targeting GPUs.

Barra [12] is an ISA-level functional simulator targeting the NVIDIA G80 GPUs. It runs CUDA executables without any modification. Since the NVIDIA's G80 ISA specification is not publicly available, the simulator relies on a reverse-engineered ISA provided by another academic project. Similar to our approach, Barra intercepts API calls to the CUDA library and reroutes them to the simulator. Unfortunately, it is limited to GPU functional simulation, lacking an architectural simulation model.

GPGPUSim [10] is a detailed simulator that models a GPU architecture similar to NVIDIA's architecture. It includes a shader core, interconnects, thread block (work-group) scheduling, and memory hierarchy. Multi2Sim models a different GPU ISA and architecture (Evergreen). GPGPUSim can provide us with important insight into design problems for GPUs. However, Multi2Sim also supports CPU simulation within the same tool enabling additional architectural research into heterogeneous architectures.

Ocelot [13] is a widely used functional simulator and dynamic compilation framework that works at a virtual ISA level. Taking NVIDIA's CUDA PTX code as input, it can either emulate or dynamically translate it to multiple platforms such as x86 CPUs, NVIDIA GPUs, and AMD GPUs. Ocelot has objectives different than GPU architectural simulation, so there is an extensive functionality not provided or targeted by Multi2Sim, which makes them complementary tools.

[2]The darker color for *BinomialOption* is caused by many small divergence regions represented in the same bar.

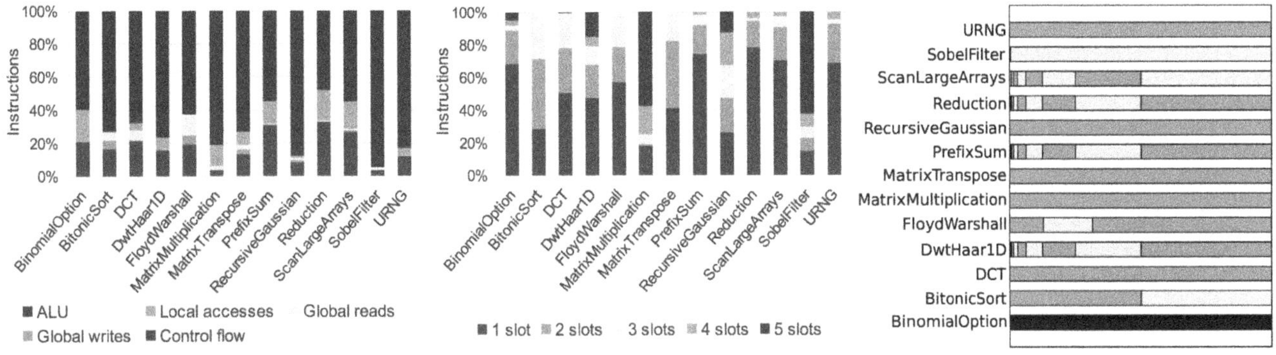

a) Classification of instruction types. b) VLIW bundles occupancy. c) Control flow divergence.

Figure 10: Examples of benchmarks characterization, based on program features relevant to GPU performance. IPC is calculated as total number of instructions the for entire kernel, divided by total cycles to execute the entire kernel.

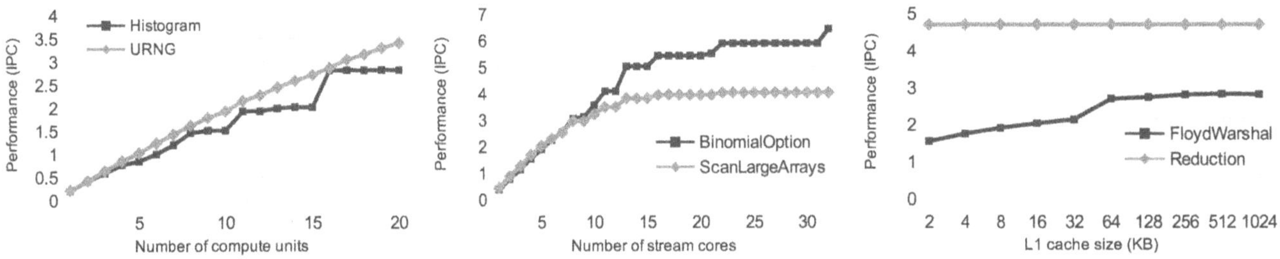

a) Scaling the number of compute units. b) Scaling the number of stream cores. c) Scaling L1 cache size.

Figure 11: Architectural exploration, showing results for those benchmarks with interesting performance trends.

When compared to previous work, Multi2Sim is unique in the following aspects. First, it models the native ISA of a commercially available GPU. Second, it provides an architectural simulation of a real GPU with tractable accuracy. Third, Multi2Sim is a CPU-GPU heterogeneous simulation framework, which can be used to evaluate upcoming architectures where the CPU and GPU are merged on silicon and share a common memory address space [8].

6. CONCLUSIONS

In this paper we have presented Multi2Sim, a full-fledged simulation framework that supports both fast functional and detailed architectural simulation for x86 CPUs and Evergreen GPUs at the ISA level. It is modular, fully configurable, and easy to use. The toolset is actively maintained and is available as a free, open-source project at *www.multi2sim.org*, together with packages of benchmarks, a complete user guide, and active mailing lists and forums.

Ongoing work for Multi2Sim includes expanding benchmark support by increasing Evergreen ISA coverage. Future releases will include a model for the AMD Fusion architecture, where the CPU and GPU share a common global memory hierarchy and address space. Supporting shared memory for heterogeneous architectures highlights the potential of Multi2Sim, as no other simulator can provide useful architectural statistics in this type of environment. Current development also includes support for OpenGL applications and exploration into OpenCL language extensions. Since Multi2Sim is currently being used by a number of leading research groups, we believe this is a great opportunity to accelerate research on heterogeneous, parallel architectures.

Acknowledgments

This work was supported in part by NSF Award EEC-0946463, and through the support and donations from AMD and NVIDIA. The authors would also like to thank Norman Rubin (AMD) for his advice and feedback on this work.

7. REFERENCES

[1] AMD Accelerated Parallel Processing (APP) Software Development Kit (SDK). http://developer.amd.com/sdks/amdappsdk/.

[2] AMD Accelerated Parallel Processing OpenCL Programming Guide (v1.3c).

[3] AMD Evergreen Family Instruction Set Arch. (v1.0d). http://developer.amd.com/sdks/amdappsdk/documentation/.

[4] AMD Intermediate Language (IL) Spec. (v2.0e). http://developer.amd.com/sdks/amdappsdk/documentation/.

[5] Intel Ivy Bridge. http://ark.intel.com/products/codename/29902/Ivy-Bridge.

[6] NVIDIA PTX: Parallel Thread Execution ISA. http://developer.nvidia.com/cuda-downloads/.

[7] OpenCL: The Open Standard for Parallel Programming of Heterogeneous Systems. www.khronos.org/opencl.

[8] The AMD Fusion Family of APUs. http://fusion.amd.com/.

[9] The NVIDIA Denver Project. http://blogs.nvidia.com/.

[10] A. Bakhoda, G. Yuan, W. Fung, H. Wong, and T. Aamodt. Analyzing CUDA Workloads Using a Detailed GPU Simulator. In *Proc. of the Int'l Symposium on Performance Analysis of Systems and Software (ISPASS)*, Apr. 2009.

[11] N. L. Binkert, E. G. Hallnor, and S. K. Reinhardt. Network-Oriented Full-System Simulation Using M5. *6th Workshop on Computer Architecture Evaluation using Commercial Workloads (CAECW)*, Feb. 2003.

[12] S. Collange, M. Daumas, D. Defour, and D. Parello. Barra: A Parallel Functional Simulator for GPGPU. In *Proc. of the 18th Int'l Symposium on Modeling, Analysis and Simulation of Computer and Telecommunication Systems (MASCOTS)*, Aug. 2010.

[13] G. Diamos, A. Kerr, S. Yalamanchili, and N. Clark. Ocelot: a Dynamic Optimization Framework for Bulk-Synchronous Applications in Heterogeneous Systems. In *Proc. of the 19th Int'l Conference on Parallel Architectures and Compilation Techniques*, Sept. 2010.

[14] P. S. M. et. al. Simics: A Full System Simulation Platform. *IEEE Computer*, 35(2), 2002.

[15] W. W. L. Fung, I. Sham, G. Yuan, and T. M. Aamodt. Dynamic Warp Formation and Scheduling for Efficient GPU Control Flow. In *Proc. of the 40th Int'l Symposium on Microarchitecture*, Dec. 2007.

[16] B. Jang, D. Schaa, P. Mistry, and D. Kaeli. Exploiting Memory Access Patterns to Improve Memory Performance in Data-Parallel Architectures. *IEEE Transactions on Parallel and Distributed Systems*, 22(1), Jan. 2011.

[17] M. Houston and M. Mantor. AMD Graphics Core Next. http://developer.amd.com/afds/assets/presentations/2620_final.pdf.

[18] G. L. Yuan, A. A. Bakhoda, and T. M. Aamodt. Complexity Effective Memory Access Scheduling for Many-Core Accelerator Architectures. In *42nd Int'l Symposium on Microarchitecture*, Dec. 2009.

A Yoke of Oxen and a Thousand Chickens for Heavy Lifting Graph Processing

Abdullah Gharaibeh, Lauro Beltrão Costa, Elizeu Santos-Neto, Matei Ripeanu
Department of Electrical and Computer Engineering, The University of British Columbia
{abdullah, lauroc, elizeus, matei}@ece.ubc.ca

ABSTRACT

Large, real-world graphs are famously difficult to process efficiently. Not only they have a large memory footprint but most graph processing algorithms entail memory access patterns with poor locality, data-dependent parallelism, and a low compute-to-memory access ratio. Additionally, most real-world graphs have a low diameter and a highly heterogeneous node degree distribution. Partitioning these graphs and simultaneously achieve access locality and load-balancing is difficult if not impossible.

This paper demonstrates the feasibility of graph processing on heterogeneous (i.e., including both CPUs and GPUs) platforms as a cost-effective approach towards addressing the graph processing challenges above. To this end, this work *(i)* presents and evaluates a performance model that estimates the achievable performance on heterogeneous platforms; *(ii)* introduces TOTEM – a processing engine based on the Bulk Synchronous Parallel (BSP) model that offers a convenient environment to simplify the implementation of graph algorithms on heterogeneous platforms; and, *(iii)* demonstrates TOTEM'S efficiency by implementing and evaluating two graph algorithms (PageRank and breadth-first search). TOTEM achieves speedups close to the model's prediction, and applies a number of optimizations that enable linear speedups with respect to the share of the graph offloaded for processing to accelerators.

Categories and Subject Descriptors

D.1.3 [**Programming Techniques**]: Concurrent Programming – *Parallel Programming*; D.3.4 [**Programming Languages**]: Processors – *Run-time Environments*; D.4.8 [**Operating Systems**]: Performance – *Measurements, Modeling and Prediction*; G.2.2 [**Discrete Mathematics**]: Graph Theory – *Graph Algorithms*.

General Terms

Algorithms, Performance, Design, Experimentation.

Keywords

Heterogeneous Systems, GPU, Graph Algorithms, Breadth-first Search, PageRank, TOTEM.

1. INTRODUCTION

Graphs are the core data structure for problems that span a wide set of domains, from mining social networks, to genomics, to business and information analytics. In these domains, key to our ability to transform raw data into insights and actionable knowledge is the ability to process large graphs efficiently and at a reasonable cost. Imagine, for example, an advertising system for an online social network with hundreds of millions of users.

PACT'12, September 19–23, 2012, Minneapolis, Minnesota, USA.

Many challenges make processing large graphs difficult. First, these workloads imply a large memory footprint (a "Mini" graph based on the Graph500 benchmark taxonomy [19] requires 137GB of memory). Second, most graph algorithms lead to a memory access pattern that has poor locality, data-dependent parallelism and a low compute–to-memory access ratio. Finally, most real-world graphs have a low-diameter and a highly heterogeneous node degree distribution (i.e., they are 'power-law') [2] thus partitioning them for access locality and load-balancing is difficult: processing graphs with low-diameter typically leads to a variable amount of parallelism available across execution rounds; while node degree heterogeneity causes imbalanced work across vertices.

Single-node[1] graph processing has a long history [1,12,14,17]. Yet, graph processing on single nodes is fundamentally limited not only by a node's memory size but also, and more importantly from a performance perspective, by memory access latency. Efficient single-node graph processing is, at the same time, a prerequisite to any efficient solution to process larger graphs on shared-nothing architectures (e.g., clusters).

This paper investigates the feasibility and the comparative advantages of supporting graph processing on heterogeneous, GPU-accelerated nodes. Moreover, in the spirit of building abstractions to hide complexity, it presents a generic graph-processing engine that leverages such platforms.

Two reasons make us believe that commodity heterogeneous nodes (e.g., GPU accelerated nodes) are an attractive building block to assemble a platform for high-performance, low-cost graph processing. First, GPUs bring massive hardware-supported multithreading able to hide memory access latency – a major performance bottleneck for this class of problems. Second, heterogeneous architectures that host processing units optimized for both fast sequential processing as well as for bulk processing match well the heterogeneous structure of graph workloads that need to be processed in practice. We expand on the opportunities and the challenges of using heterogeneous architectures in Section 2.

The following high-level questions guide our investigation:

Q1. *What are the general challenges to support graph processing on a single-node GPU-accelerated system?* In particular, *is it*

[1] We use *node* to refer to computing elements, and *vertex* to refer to the graph element.

feasible to efficiently use both the traditional CPU cores and GPU(s) for graph processing?

Q2. *Assuming that a low-level engine can efficiently process large graphs on GPU-accelerated nodes, what could an abstraction that aims to simplify the task of implementing graph algorithms look like?*

While we make preliminary progress on these relatively generic issues, this paper makes the following concrete contributions:

- We present a performance model that captures the key characteristics of a GPU-accelerated platform and the graph processing workload (Section 3). Given the characteristics of today's platforms (e.g., processing rates, memory space, and communication cost) the model demonstrates that *it is beneficial to offload part of the graph workload to a GPU*. Moreover, as we demonstrate, the model can serve as a tool to guide optimization efforts, system configuration, and provisioning.
- We present TOTEM, an open-source generic graph processing engine for GPU-accelerated platforms (Section 4)[2]. Our proposed design efficiently uses all CPU and GPU cores on a given node. Guided by the performance model, TOTEM applies a number of algorithm-agnostic optimizations that lead to performance improvements. One key optimization we introduce is reducing communication overhead by over an order of magnitude by aggregating messages at the source processor.
- We evaluate (Section 5) two key graph processing algorithms that are building blocks for a number of relevant applications: PageRank and breadth-first search (BFS). These two algorithms stand at the two extremes of a key performance factor for graph algorithms: the computation-to-communication ratio. We demonstrate linear speedups for both algorithms with respect to the proportion of the graph that is offloaded to a GPU.

The importance of this work comes from all these three contributions. Firstly, the performance model not only encourages the design of GPU-offloading techniques, but can guide hardware purchase and software design decisions for various classes of graph-related problems. Secondly, this work is the first to demonstrate the feasibility of using, in parallel, all CPU and GPU processors of a heterogeneous platform for a key class of irregular problems: graph processing. Finally, the processing engine we provide, TOTEM, offers an efficient and easy to use environment to develop graph applications that can benefit from acceleration.

Overall, our work is a basic building block towards an environment dedicated to processing graphs on large-scale machines (i.e., GPU-accelerated clusters, similar to the recent top entries in the Top500 supercomputer list). To this end, scaling out to multi-node systems is one of the main directions of future work (we elaborate on this in Section 6).

[2] The code can be found at: http://netsyslab.ece.ubc.ca

2. GRAPH PROCESSING ON HETEROGENEOUS ARCHITECTURES: OPPORTUNITY AND CHALLENGES

Large-scale graph processing faces two main difficulties. First, *large memory footprint:* efficient graph processing requires the whole graph to be present in memory, where for practical applications, graphs occupy from few gigabytes to terabytes of space. Second, *high memory access latency* combined with a *low computation to memory access ratio:* the major overhead of processing a graph is fetching the state of the vertices (e.g., a vertex iterates over its neighbors' state); because of poor locality and the scale of the workload, caches and prefetching are of little value, and most accesses are served by main memory.

The opportunity: GPU-acceleration has the potential to bring, at a low cost, the key advantage of massive, hardware-supported multithreading. In fact, a commodity GPU has much higher memory bandwidth and supports orders of magnitude more hardware threads and in-flight memory requests compared to traditional CPU processors. Additionally, properly mapping the graph-layout and the algorithmic tasks between the CPU(s) and the GPU(s) holds the promise to exercise each of these computing units where they perform best: CPUs for fast sequential processing (e.g., for the few high degree nodes of a power-law graph) and GPUs for the bulk parallel processing (e.g., for the many low-degree nodes).

Indeed, past work [5,8,10,12,16] demonstrates that GPU offloading offers tangible benefits compared to traditional multiprocessors for graph processing. However, *previous work assumes the entire graph fits in the GPU memory.* This is a major limitation as GPUs support up to one order of magnitude less memory space than the host (a trend that has been observed in the past ten years, and announcements of future GPU models indicate that this trend will continue at least in the medium term).

Hong et al. [8] work is, perhaps, the closest to this work in the spirit of enabling an application to harness the opportunities offered by a heterogeneous architecture, yet Hong et al. still assume that the GPU memory can hold the entire graph. In particular, they present a BFS implementation on a GPU-accelerated platform. They divide the processing into a first phase done on the CPU (as, at the beginning, only limited parallelism is available), and a second phase that starts once enough parallelism is exposed, at which point the whole graph is transferred to the GPU to accelerate processing.

The challenges: *This work investigates the feasibility of accelerating graph processing while partitioning the graph between the processing elements.* Moreover, in the spirit of building abstractions to hide complexity, it presents a graph-processing engine that leverages such platforms. To this end, we need to address a number of major challenges that we discuss in turn below:

First, the large amount of data to be processed, and the need to communicate between processors put pressure on two scarce resources: the GPUs' on-board memory and the host to GPU transfer bandwidth. Intelligent data placement solutions are needed to reduce memory pressure and limit generated transfer traffic. The ability to overlap communication with computation and to directly communicate between GPUs attached to the same host offer good prospects to mitigate some of these obstacles.

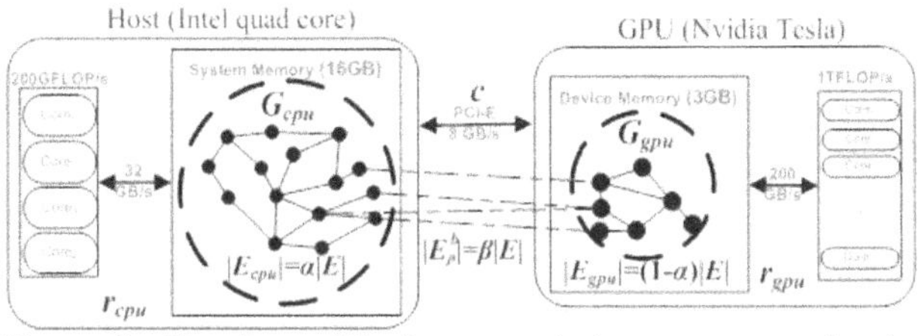

Figure 1: Graph partitioning on a heterogeneous node: An illustration of the model's parameters and their values for today's commodity components.

Second, to achieve good performance on GPUs, the application should match the SIMD computing model. As graph problems exhibit data-dependent parallelism, traditional implementations of graph algorithms lead to low memory access locality. Nevertheless, GPUs are able to hide memory access latency via massive hardware multithreading that, with careful design of the graph data structure, can reduce the impact of these factors.

Finally, mapping high-level abstractions (e.g., vertex-centric processing) and APIs to facilitate application development to the low level engine while limiting the efficiency loss, is an additional challenge.

Our methodology: To address these challenges, our methodology consists of the following interrelated steps:

- *Performance modeling.* We focus on assessing the feasibility of accelerating graph processing through partitioning and offloading a partition to the GPU. We take into account a number of key aspects such as the parallel processing model, the characteristics of the processing elements and the interconnect. It is worth noting that the model is agnostic to the precise graph algorithm and the model can be used to answer more complex resource provisioning and configuration questions.
- *Engine design and prototyping.* Informed by the performance model and the type of algorithms we aim to support, we design and prototype the building blocks of the graph processing engine (TOTEM). This includes defining the engine's programming model and interface.
- *Algorithm prototyping.* We prototype two graph algorithms on top of the engine. We evaluate the performance of the system to demonstrate the feasibility of graph partitioning and offloading to GPUs and validate and refine the performance model.

3. PERFORMANCE MODEL

The model aims to answer the following question: *Is it beneficial to partition and process the graph on both the host and the accelerator (when compared to processing only on the host)?*

In particular, we consider a heterogeneous node that consists of two processing elements $P = \{p_{cpu}, p_{acc}\}$, the CPU and an accelerator (e.g., a GPU) (Figure 1). The model can be easily generalized to a mix of multiple CPUs and accelerators. However, for the sake of simplicity, we use the setup with only two processing units for the rest of this section.

The model makes the following assumptions:

(i) Each processing element has its own local memory. The processing elements are connected by a bidirectional interconnect with communication rate c measured in edges per second (E/s) -- this is a reasonable unit as the time complexity of a large number of graph algorithms depends on the number of edges in the graph. However, the same model can be recast in terms of vertex-centric algorithms by normalizing by the number of vertices instead of edges.

(ii) The processing model is bulk synchronous parallel (BSP). Processing proceeds in rounds of concurrent computation and communication at the processing elements. Note that the performance model is agnostic to the architecture of each processing element.

(iii) p_{cpu} has enough memory to load and process the complete graph. The question is whether it is useful to partition the graph and process part of it on p_{acc}. p_{acc} has limited memory compared to p_{cpu}, and can not load and process the complete graph at once.

(iv) p_{acc} has higher graph processing rate than p_{cpu}. This is based on published results [8,12], which we validated independently.

(v) In addition to participating in graph processing, p_{cpu} schedules the workload (e.g., partitions the graph) and gathers the results. The model assumes these overheads are negligible compared to the algorithm processing time.

Let $G = (V, E)$ be a directed graph, where V is the set of vertices and E is the set of directed edges. $|V|$ and $|E|$ represent the number of vertices and edges, respectively.

The time it takes to process a partition of G, $G_p = (V_p, E_p) \subseteq G$ on a processing element p, is given by:

$$t(G_p) = \frac{|E_p^b|}{c} + \frac{|E_p|}{r_p} \tag{1}$$

where r_p is the processing rate of processor p (in E/s), and $E_p^b \subseteq E_p$ represents the subset of *boundary edges* – edges where either the source or the destination vertex is not located in p's local memory.

Equation 1 estimates the time required to process a partition as a combination of the time it takes to communicate possible updates through boundary edges (communication phase) plus the time it takes to process the edges in that given partition on processor p (computation phase). Intuitively, the higher the processing rate of a processing element, the lower is the processing time. Similarly, the less communication a processing element needs to access the edges in its partition, the lower is the processing time.

Now, we build on Equation 1 and define the makespan[3] of a graph workload G on a given platform P as follows:

$$m_P(G) = \max_{p \in P}\{t(G_p)\} \tag{2}$$

The intuition behind Equation 2 is that the performance of a parallel system is limited by its slowest component. Since, as discussed before, we assume that (*i*) the host processes its

[3] Makespan: the completion time of the last workload partition [13].

partition slower than the accelerator (i.e., $r_{cpu} < r_{acc}$) and that (*ii*) the host has more memory and is assigned a larger partition, the time spent on processing the CPU partition is always higher than that of the GPU partition (i.e., $t(G_{cpu}) > t(G_{gpu})$). Hence, the speedup of processing a graph on a heterogeneous platform (compared to processing it on the host only) can be calculated by Equation 3, as follows:

$$s_P(G) = \frac{m_{\{cpu\}}(G)}{m_P(G)} = \frac{m_{\{cpu\}}(G)}{m_{\{cpu\}}(G_{cpu})} = \frac{|E|/r_{cpu}}{|E^b_{cpu}|/c + |E_{cpu}|/r_{cpu}} \quad (3)$$

To understand the gains resulted from moving a portion of the graph to the accelerator, we rewrite Equation 3 by introducing two parameters that characterize the '*quality*' of the graph partition. Let α be the share of edges (out of the total number of graph edges $|E|$) assigned to the host, similarly let β be the percentage of *boundary* edges (i.e., the edges that cross the partition). Introducing these parameters, we have:

$$s_P(G) = \frac{|E|/r_{cpu}}{\beta|E|/c + \alpha|E|/r_{cpu}} = \frac{c}{\beta r_{cpu} + \alpha c} = \frac{1}{\frac{\beta \cdot r_{cpu}}{c} + \alpha} \quad (4)$$

As expected, Equation 4 predicts that a high communication rate, c, improves the speedup. In fact, if c is set to infinity, the speedup can be approximated as $1/\alpha$. This is intuitive, as in this case the communication overhead becomes negligible compared to the time spent on processing the CPU's share of edges, α.

Figure 1 presents an illustration of the model and reasonable values for models' parameters for today's commodity heterogeneous platforms. We discuss them in turn next:

Communication rate (c) is directly proportional to the bus bandwidth and inversely proportional to the amount of data transferred per edge. The GPU is typically connected to the host via a PCI-E bus. The commonly used PCI Express 2.0 has a measured transfer bandwidth of 4GB/sec. If we assume the data transferred for each graph edge is a 4-byte value, the transfer rate c becomes 1 Billion E/s – or BE/s.

CPU's processing rate (r_{cpu}) depends on the CPU's characteristics, the graph algorithm, and the graph topology. We discuss possible values below in Table 1.

Percentage of boundary edges (β) depends on the graph partitioning between the processing elements. In the worst case all edges cross the partition.

The share of the graph that stays on the CPU (α) is configurable, but is constrained by the memory space available on the processing elements (for example, larger memory on the GPU allows for offloading a larger partition, hence smaller α).

We now explore the effect of changing the CPU processing rate or the percentage of boundary edges on the predicted speedup. Figure 2 shows the speedup predicted by the model (Equation 4) for different values of α, while varying the CPU processing rate (left plot) and the percentage of boundary edges (right plot).

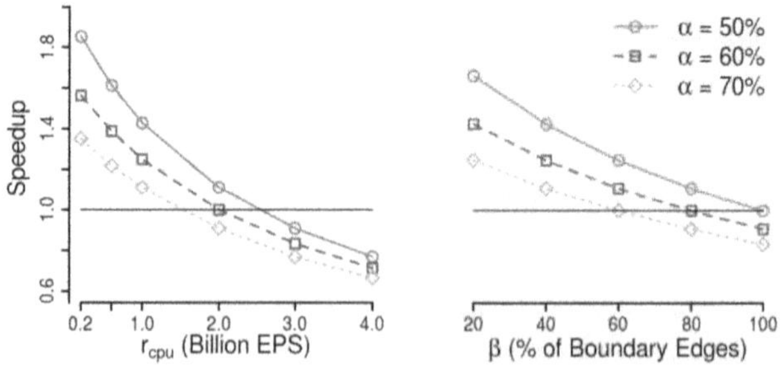

Figure 2: Predicted speedup (values below one indicate slowdown). Left: while varying the CPU's processing rate (β is set to 20%). Right: while varying the percentage of boundary edges (r_{cpu} is set to 0.5 BE/s). For both plots, the communication rate is 1 BE/s.

Note that we keep at least half of the graph on the CPU (i.e., $\alpha > 50\%$) as a conservative measure to ensure that the assumption $t(G_{cpu}) > t(G_{gpu})$ (which allows us to transform from Equation 2 to Equation 3) always holds. Note that this constraints the speedup to 2x or lower.

Figure 2 shows that as r_{cpu} (left plot) or β (right plot) increase, the speedup decreases. For CPU processing rate above 1 BE/s or a graph partition that leads to larger or equal to 60% of boundary edges, the speedup decreases (with slowdown in some cases). This is because the communication overhead becomes significant. Figure 2 (right) also presents a hypothetical worst case where all of the edges are boundary edges (e.g., a bipartite graph where the partition cuts each edge). Even in this case, and due to the high communication rate c, the slowdown is not that significant, in fact, for $\alpha = 50\%$, no slowdown is predicted.

Figure 3 evaluates the effect of the amount of transferred data per edge on the predicted speedup. The speedup significantly drops as we double the amount of transferred data. However, having a low percentage of boundary edges, β, helps addressing this problem. Section 4.2 presents optimizations that aim to lower β (for practical cases we obtain an effective β as low as 3%).

To put in perspective the gains predicted by the model, and make sure we use values anchored in reality, we look at the estimated CPU processing rates based on the performance of the BFS algorithm benchmarks. Table 1 shows the best published parallel BFS performance results on a single CPU-only node for a power-law graph with 1Billion edges. BFS is a simple graph traversal algorithm with minimal per vertex processing. The processing rate for other more compute intensive algorithms, like Single Source Shortest Path (SSSP) and PageRank, is expected to be lower.

Nonetheless, as shown in the last column, offloading only 30% of the graph to a GPU offers tangible speedups (up to 1.39x).

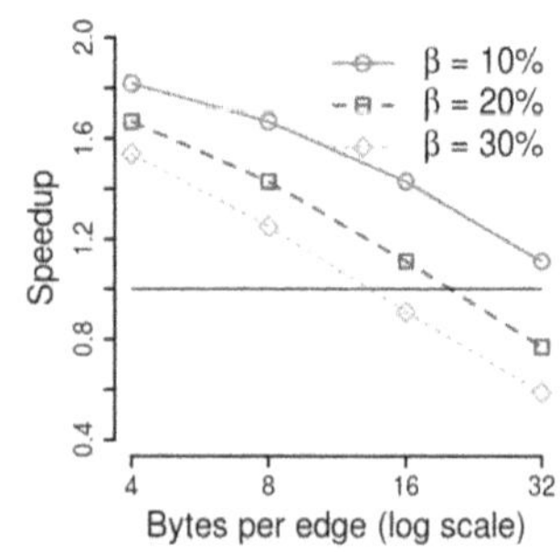

Figure 3: Predicted speedup while varying the transferred data per edge (α is set to 50% and the transferred bandwidth to 4GB/sec (PCI-E bandwidth)).

Table 1: Best published parallel BFS performance results (in ME/s) on a CPU-only node for an RMAT graph with $|V|$ = 32M and $|E|$=1B. The last column shows the performance and speedup predicted by the model if 30% of the workload is offloaded to a GPU (i.e., α = 70%). β is set to 3% (discussed in Section 4.2).

Ref.	Platform	Hardware Threads	r_{cpu} (ME/s)	Predicted rate with GPU (Speedup)
[1,8]	dual- Intel X5570	16	650	903 (1.39x)
	four- Intel X7500	32	1,050	1,435 (1.37x)

More importantly, Table 1 allows us to get a sense of whether adding a GPU to the system brings higher benefits compared to adding extra CPU sockets. It is clear that the predicted speedup that results from adding a GPU to the dual-socket platform (i.e., 903 ME/s) leads to a performance that is comparable to the four-socket platform (i.e., 1050 ME/s), but at a lower price and energy point.

Considering the region of the plots where the parameters are set to values that represent realistic scenarios (650 ME/s ≤ r_{cpu} ≤ 1050 ME/s) we observe in Figure 2 that the model predicts speedups above one. Hence, we conclude that *it can be beneficial to have an engine to partition and process the graph on both the host and the accelerator.*

The model proposed here enables estimating the performance gained by replacing certain processing elements by accelerators (and vice-versa). As we have shown, there are practical scenarios where it is beneficial to add accelerators to graph processing platforms. The next challenge is to provide a framework that allows application programmers to write graph algorithms that make the most out of such heterogeneous platforms. We describe TOTEM, our proposal to address such challenge, in the next section.

4. TOTEM

To enable application programmers to leverage heterogeneous architectures, we design TOTEM – a graph processing engine for heterogeneous and multi-GPU single-node systems. This section presents TOTEM's programming model (Section 4.1) and implementation (Section 4.2).

4.1 Programming Model

TOTEM adopts a Bulk Synchronous Parallel (BSP) [15] parallel computation model and divides processing into rounds (*supersteps* in BSP terminology). Each superstep consists of three phases executed in order: *computation*, *communication* and *synchronization*. In the computation phase, each processor (in our case the CPU and the GPU(s)) executes asynchronously computations based on values stored in their local memories. In the communication phase, the processors exchange messages that are necessary to update their statuses before the next computation phase starts. The synchronization phase guarantees the delivery of the messages. Specifically, a message sent at superstep i is guaranteed to be available in the local memory of the destination processor only at superstep i+1.

```
totem_config_t config = {
    graph,
    partitioning_algo,
    init_func,
    kernel_func,
    msg_reduce_func,
    finalize_func,
  };
totem_config(&config);
totem_execute();
```

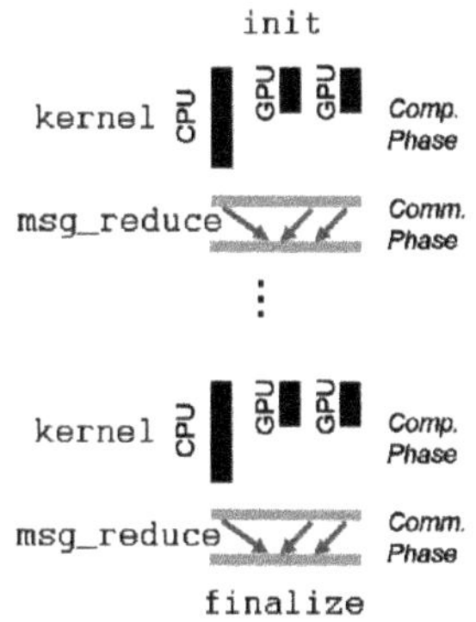

Figure 4: A simplified TOTEM configuration and how the callbacks map to the BSP execution model.

Adopting the BSP model allows to circumvent the fact that the GPUs are connected via the high-latency PCI-Express bus. In particular, batch communication matches well BSP, and this enables TOTEM to hide (some of) the bus latency.

Computation phase. TOTEM initially partitions the graph and assigns each partition to a processing unit. In each compute phase of a superstep, the processing units work in parallel, each executing the user-specified kernel on the set of vertices that belong to its assigned partition.

Communication phase. TOTEM enables the partitions to communicate via boundary edges. The engine stores messages sent to remote vertices in local buffers that are transferred in the communication phase to the corresponding remote partitions. As the performance model shows, reducing communication overhead is paramount to improve performance. The engine achieves such reduction by aggregating at the source processor messages targeted to the same remote destination vertex. The aggregation is performed based on a user-provided function. Note that the synchronization phase is performed implicitly as part of the communication phase.

Termination. The engine terminates execution when all partitions vote to finish in the same superstep. At this point the engine invokes a user-specified function to collect and merge the results from all partitions.

4.2 Implementation

TOTEM is open-source, and is implemented in C and CUDA. A client configures TOTEM to execute a graph algorithm by implementing a number of callback functions executed at different points in the BSP execution model.

Figure 4 shows a simplified configuration of TOTEM. The engine creates one partition for the host and a partition for each GPU. The `init_func` allows the client to allocate algorithm-specific state (such as the cost array in BFS or the rank array in PageRank), the `kernel_func` callback performs the core computation of the algorithm, the `msg_reduce_func` callback defines how a message received from a boundary edge updates a vertex's state (e.g., update the vertex's state with the sum of the two in the case of PageRank, or the minimum in SSSP). Finally, the `finalize_func` callback enables the client to release state allocated at initialization. TOTEM accepts other configuration parameters, most notably is the graph partitioning algorithm the engine should use.

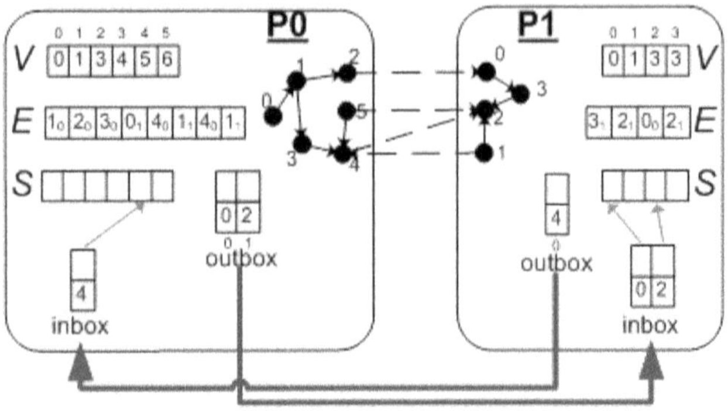

Figure 5: An illustration of the main data structures and the communication infrastructure in a two-way partitioning scenario.

All callbacks are invoked per partition. If the partition is GPU resident, the engine ensures that the execution context is correctly set such that CUDA calls invoked from the callback are executed on the corresponding GPU.

A number of important aspects related to TOTEM's design and implementation are worth discussing; however, space constraints allow us to only discuss two topics: the data structures used and the communication via boundary edges.

Graph representation. Graph partitions are represented as Compressed Sparse Rows (CSR) in memory [3], a space efficient graph representation that uses $O(|V| + |E|)$ space. Figure 5 shows an example of two-way partitioning setup. The arrays $\boldsymbol{V}$ and $\boldsymbol{E}$ represent the CSR data structure. In each partition, the vertex ids span a linear space from zero to $|V_p|$-1. A vertex id together with a partition id represents a global id of a vertex. A vertex accesses its edges by using its id as an index in $\boldsymbol{V}$ to fetch the start index of its neighbors in $\boldsymbol{E}$.

The array $\boldsymbol{E}$ stores the destination vertex of an edge, which includes the partition id (shown in the figure as subscripts) encoded in the high-order bits. In the case of boundary edges, the value stored in $\boldsymbol{E}$ is not the remote neighbor's id, rather it is an index to its entry in the outbox buffer (discussed later). To simplify state management, a vertex in a directed graph has access only to its outgoing edges, which is sufficient for most graph algorithms. Note that undirected edges can be represented in this graph data structure using two directed edges, one in each direction.

The array $\boldsymbol{S}$ represents the algorithm-specific local state of each vertex, it is of length $|V_p|$, and is indexed using vertex ids. Note that a similar array of length $|E_p|$ can be created if the state is required to be per edge rather than per vertex.

The processing of a vertex typically consists of iterating over its neighbors. A neighbor id is fetched from $\boldsymbol{E}$, and is used to access $\boldsymbol{S}$ for local neighbors, or the outbox buffer for the remote ones. Typically, accessing the state of a neighbor (either in $\boldsymbol{S}$ or in the outbox buffer) is done via atomic operations as multiple vertices may simultaneously try to update the state of a common neighbor.

To improve pre-fetching, the set of neighbors of each vertex in $\boldsymbol{E}$ are sorted and are placed such that the local edges are processed first (entails accessing $\boldsymbol{S}$), and then the boundary edges (entails accessing the outbox buffers).

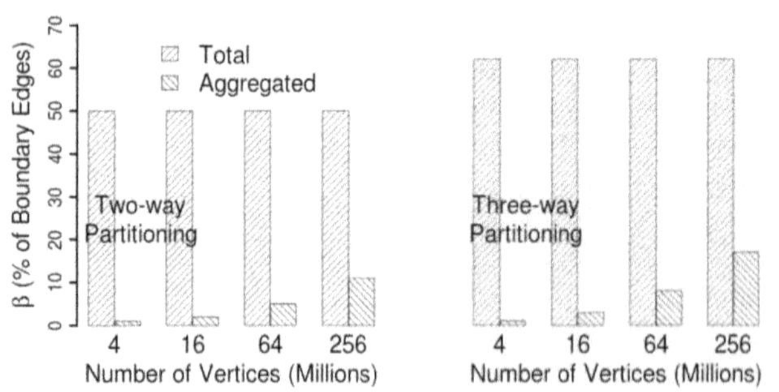

Figure 6: resulted β with and without aggregation while varying the number of vertices, and using a random partitioning algorithm. ($|E|$ = 512M).

Communication via boundary edges. A challenge for a graph processing engine for heterogeneous and multi-GPU setups is how to keep the cost of communication low. TOTEM addresses this problem by using local buffers and aggregation functions. As mentioned in section 4.1, messages sent via boundary edges in the computation phase of a superstep are temporarily stored and, if possible, aggregated in local buffers that are transferred in the communication phase.

TOTEM maintains two sets of buffers for each processing element (Figure 5). The outbox buffers have an entry for each remote neighbor, while the inbox buffers have an entry for each local vertex that is remote to another partition. An in/outbox buffer is composed of two arrays: one maintains the remote vertex id and the other stores the messages.

The outbox buffer in a partition is symmetric to an inbox buffer in another. Therefore, in the communication phase, only the message array is transferred. Once transferred, TOTEM uses the user-defined aggregation function to update the remote neighbors' state in the $\boldsymbol{S}$ array at the remote partition with the new values. Similar to $\boldsymbol{E}$, the entries in the inbox buffers are sorted by vertex ids to improve pre-fetching and cache efficiency when doing the update.

Optimizing access to boundary edges. To show the benefit of aggregating the communication along boundary edges, we test a naïve graph partitioning algorithm (i.e., random partitioning) and compare how much communication would happen with and without aggregation. Figure 6 shows β resulted from two- and three- way partitioning of a power-law graph (e.g., setup with one and two GPUs, respectively). The x-axis varies $|V|$ while keeping $|E|$ constant at 512M, hence varying the density of the graph (the density decreases as $|V|$ increases).

Increasing the number of partitions for the naïve partitioning increases β (from 50% for two partitions to 62% for three) as the probability of having a remote neighbor increases. More importantly, β is significantly reduced (between 3% to 16%) by aggregating boundary edges that have the same remote destination vertex. Note that decreasing the density of the graph reduces the opportunity for aggregation. However, even for a highly sparse graph, denoted by the most right data point in Figure 6, aggregation is still beneficial, reducing β by four times.

The worst case inputs are the Erdos-Renyi purely random graphs (The power-law RMAT graphs are advantageous as multiple edges from the same partition will point to the high degree vertexes and thus enable aggregation). Most graphs processed in practice, however, are power-law, thus this optimization is likely to be useful.

Finally, it is important to mention that aggregation works for algorithms where it is possible to reduce, at the source partition, into one value the values sent to the same remote vertex. For example, the "visited" status in BFS, minimum "distance" in SSSP and "rank" sum in PageRank.

Nonetheless, for algorithms where aggregation is not feasible, careful partitioning [9] has the potential to minimize the number of boundary edges, and reducing the communication overhead.

Summary of optimizations. In the following we summarize the main optimizations used by TOTEM. (they have been discovered through an iterative exploration process and provide sizeable gains. Lack of space prevents us to present a detailed evaluation of the performance impact of each of these optimizations).

(i) A compressed graph representation to reduce the memory footprint.

(ii) Aggregating boundary edges to reduce communication overhead. This technique has been used in cluster setups [11], and we show its application and effectiveness on heterogeneous platforms.

(iii) Sorting vertex ids in the inbox buffers to improve pre-fetching and cache efficiency when updating the vertices' local state.

(iv) Processing the local and remote edges separately to improve data access locality.

Limitations. Two main limitations related to the current implementation of TOTEM are worth mentioning. First, the implementation assumes fixed structure graphs, as the used CSR data structure makes it expensive to support updates to the graph structure during the algorithm execution (e.g., creation of new edges or vertices). This is a tradeoff. CSR enables a lower memory footprint and efficient iteration over the graph's elements (vertices and edges), which are essential for performance. Any other graph data structure that aims to enable mutable graphs will have to have some form of dynamic memory management (e.g., linked lists), which is expensive to support, particularly on GPUs.

The second limitation is related to the way communication is performed. During the communication phase of each superstep, the current implementation copies the whole outbox buffer of a partition to the inbox buffer of a remote partition assuming that there is a message to be sent via every edge between the two partitions. This is efficient for algorithms that communicate via each edge in every superstep, such as PageRank. However, this may be considered an overhead for other algorithms that communicate only via a selective set of edges in each superstep. For example, in the level-synchronized BFS algorithm, at a given superstep, only the vertices at the *frontier* communicate data via their outgoing edges. Additional compression techniques could be employed to lower the communication volumes.

Summary. The current implementation is space efficient, and simplifies the communication phase at the expense of adding communication overhead for some algorithms. An alternative implementation that enables selective communication via boundary edges, on the other hand, will avoid communicating inactive edges, but requires maintaining additional state (e.g., a bitmap to identify active remote edges or a thread-safe queue), and communicating a destination vertex id along with each message. We chose the former solution for its simplicity and acceptable performance, which is demonstrated in the next section.

5. EVALUATION

Goals. The evaluation aims to show the benefits of a heterogeneous platform compared to a platform based solely on CPUs. Particularly, it aims to address the following questions.

First, *how does TOTEM compare to the performance predicted by the model described in Section 3?* Such comparison allows us to validate the model and understand, for each use case, how much room is possibly left for optimizations.

Second, *how do the workload characteristics affect the performance predicted by the model and the one achieved by TOTEM?* We focus on one graph characteristic, graph density as it affects the communication overhead – a key overhead in distributed memory platforms.

Third, *how does TOTEM scale when increasing the number of GPUs?* New commodity systems are able to host multiple GPUs, which can be harnessed to offload larger part of the graph, and achieve better overall performance.

Workload. We use graphs generated using Recursive MATrix (R-MAT) scale-free graph generation algorithm [4], a graph generator adopted by the Graph500 benchmark. We use the benchmark's default configuration parameters (A=0.57, B=0.19, C=0.19 and D=0.05). In all experiments, we use a random partitioning algorithm. Finally, for each data point, we present the average over 20 runs.

Algorithms. We implemented two graph algorithms on top of TOTEM. We look at these algorithms as representatives of the two ends of the computation-to-communication ratio spectrum. First, PageRank, has a relatively high computation-to-communication ratio, and is less sensitive to communication overhead and memory access latency. The algorithm is based on the one described in [11]. It is worth noting that, to the best of our knowledge, this is the first work to implement and evaluate PageRank on GPUs.

Second, BFS, which has a low computation-to-communication ratio. BFS mainly does memory lookups with no major computation; hence it is more sensitive to memory access latency. The kernel implementation of BFS is based on the one described in [7].

Due to space constraints, we do not present the implementation of the algorithms. Also, all figures show two side-by-side plots for PageRank (left) and BFS (right).

Expected model prediction accuracy. We expect the model to predict better for PageRank than BFS. This is because PageRank is more computationally intensive; hence it will be less sensitive to the overheads introduced by TOTEM and not modeled (e.g., sub-optimal communication efficiency and extra memory lookups to handle boundary edges).

Testbed. We conduct the experiments on a machine with the following characteristics: dual-socket Intel Xeon (E5520) clocked at 2.27GHz per core, 16GB of host memory, two Tesla C2050 NVIDIA GPU (448 cores clocked at 1.1GHz, 3GB of memory). The cards are connected to the host via a PCI Express 2.0 x16

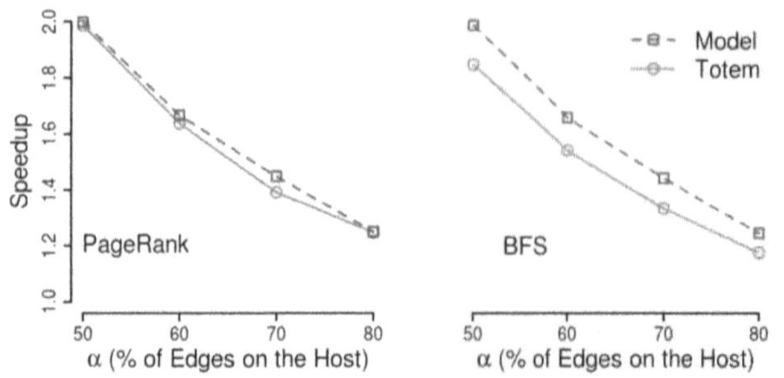

Figure 7: Predicted and achieved speedup while varying the percentage of edges on the host. (|V|=32M, |E|=1B).

bus. The machine runs Fedora14, CUDA release 4.1 and driver version 64-285.05.33. TOTEM and the algorithms were compiled using g++ 4.5.1 with "-O3" option. OpenMP was used to parallelize the CPU code. Finally, all CPU-side processing was performed on the two CPU sockets.

5.1 TOTEM and the Performance Model

We first compare the speedup achieved by TOTEM and predicted by the model by offloading part of a graph to one GPU only. Figure 7 shows the speedup while varying α (|V| = 32M and |E| = 1B). The observed r_{cpu} is 155ME/s for BFS (which is comparable to latest numbers reported on a similar CPU model [8]), and 81ME/s for PageRank. *The observed β is 50%, but after aggregation, which both algorithms apply, β is reduced to only 2%.*

The plot shows that the achieved speedup follows the pattern predicted by the model. Also, as expected, the prediction is better for PageRank than for BFS.

Nonetheless, offloading 50% of the edges, which is the maximum we were able to fit on the GPU's 3GB device memory, offers tangible gains: out of the maximum possible 2x speedup indicated by the model, PageRank achieves 98%, while BFS achieves 84% of this maximum speedup.

To understand on which phase (computation or communication) and processor (CPU or GPU) the bulk of time is spent, we look at the breakdown of total execution time. Figure 8 shows the percentage of time spent on each phase. Two points are worth discussing.

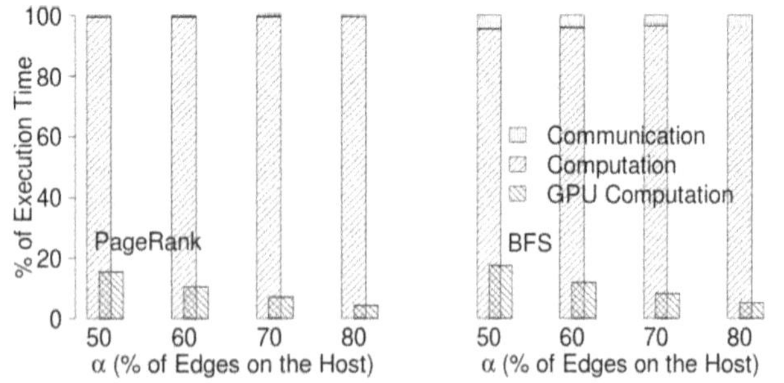

Figure 8: Breakdown of execution time. The computation phase is dominated by the processing of the CPU partition. The GPU partition, processed concurrently, is shown for comparison.

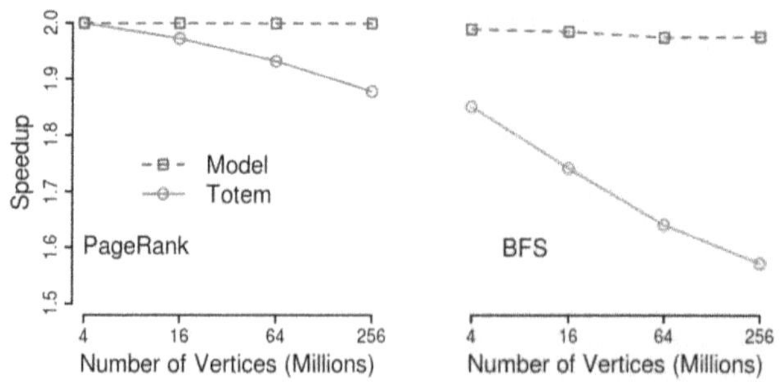

Figure 9: Predicted and achieved speedup while varying graph density. The number of vertices is indicated on the x-axis. (|E| = 512M). The higher the number of vertices, the lower is the graph's density. Note the compressed y-axis.

First, the GPU processes its partition at a faster rate such that processing the CPU partition will remain the main bottleneck even when using a high-end CPU. For example, in the case of BFS, the GPU is 5 to 20 times faster. Recent published work on high-end dual-socket CPU, and using a highly tuned BFS kernel, (shown in Table 1) promises an at most 4x speedup compared to our measured CPU performance for the same workload. This indicates that our assumption that the GPU finishes its processing faster will hold in practice.

Second, the CPU-GPU communication overhead is almost 20x lower than the computation. This is due to the aggressive aggregation of boundary edges which efficiently diminishes this overhead. Therefore, even when using a high-end CPU (and assuming 4x computation speedup), the computation will remain the main bottleneck.

5.2 The Effect of Workload Characteristics

To expose the effect of communication overhead, Figure 9 shows the predicted and achieved speedup while varying the density of the graph (by varying |V| and keeping |E| constant at 512M). Figure 6 (left) shows the observed β.

Figure 9 shows that the achieved speedup for both PageRank and BFS deviate from the model as the graph density is reduced. Figure 10 shows the predicted (based on Equation 1) and measured time spent on the communication and computation phases *for the data point where the deviation is the highest*, |V| = 256M.

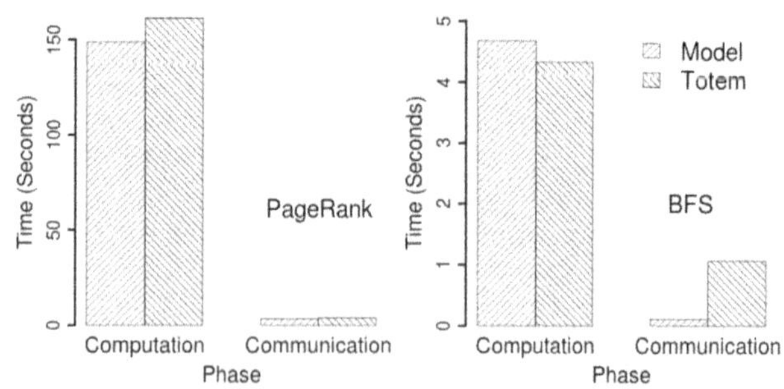

Figure 10: Predicted and measured time spent on the computation and communication phases for the datapoint where the deviation form the model is the highest (|V| = 256M, |E| = 512M).

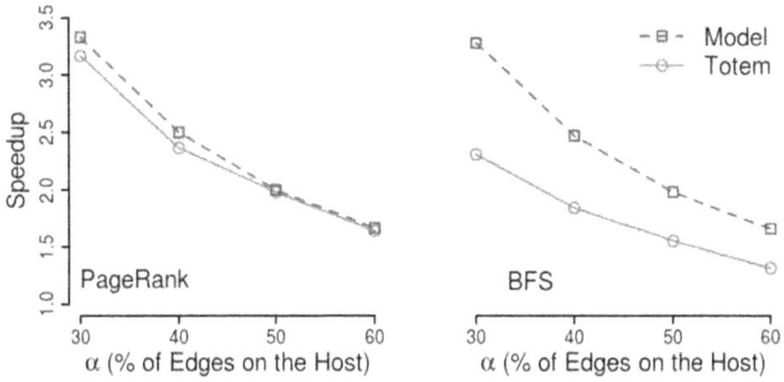

Figure 11: Predicted and achieved speedup after adding a second GPU. Note that having a second GPU allows using lower values of α as more edges can be offloaded. (|V|=32M, |E|=1.5B).

In the case of BFS, the deviation in speedup is due to communication. As mentioned before, reducing the density of the graph while applying aggregation increases β; hence the communication overhead increases. Two factors generate this deviation. First, for the model, we set c, the communication throughput, to the PCI-E bus bandwidth. However, other practical factors affect the communication throughput, such as pre- and post-transfer overheads. TOTEM has a post-transfer overhead of delivering the messages from the inbox buffer to the destination vertices' local state, which is not captured by the model. The second factor is related to a limitation in TOTEM's implementation (discussed at the end of Section 4.2) that results in extra transferred data, and almost an order of magnitude difference between predicted and measured communication.

In the case of PageRank, the computation phase dominates, and the small, less than 10%, speedup prediction error is generated by the achieved computation time which is sub-linear with respect to the offloaded proportion of the graph.

5.3 Adding a Second GPU

Adding a second GPU enables offloading a larger portion of the graph which, according to the model, provides additional speedup. Figure 11 shows the predicted and achieved speedup for a setup with two GPUs. In this experiment, we increased the number of edges of the graph to |E|=1.5B (|V|=32M). At α=30%, each GPU partition fills the GPU's device memory.

The figure shows that the model's prediction matches the achieved speedup for PageRank, while the memory-bound BFS deviates more from the model, yet it follows the trend indicated. As discussed in Section 4.2, increasing the number of partitions increases β, hence the communication overhead. Similar to the reason presented above, the deviation in the case of BFS is mainly the result of extra communication incurred by TOTEM's implementation. As α increases, less workload is offloaded, hence the number of boundary edges is reduced, rendering a lower communication overhead which results in better prediction accuracy.

Nevertheless, the results show that TOTEM is able to efficiently harness the added GPU, achieving linear speedup for PageRank and sublinear speedup for BFS.

6. SUMMARY AND DISCUSSION

GPU-acceleration is now a popular approach; however it has not been explored often for irregular applications. This paper investigates the feasibility of processing large graphs on single-node, GPU-accelerated heterogeneous platforms. In particular, the focus is on understanding whether (and in what scenarios) it is beneficial to harness GPUs to aid graph processing. In the following, we summarize the contributions of the paper and our plans to extend them.

Performance modeling. We presented a simple, yet effective performance model that helps estimating the benefits of offloading part of the graph workload. Given the current characteristics of heterogeneous platforms, the model shows that it is beneficial to partition the graph workload and process it on a heterogeneous platform, and highlights the importance of minimizing the communication overhead to improve the overall performance.

Notwithstanding the model's simplicity and its demonstrated usefulness, it can be improved (at the cost of making it more complex). For example, the model assumes that the processing rate r_{cpu} is constant, determined by a benchmark independent of the graph characteristics of the actual workload. A more accurate modeling of r_{cpu} would take into account the characteristics of the partition. To address this issue, we plan to analyze the effect of workload characteristics (e.g., degree distribution and graph structure) on obtained performance. We plan to perform controlled experiments on diverse hardware while varying graph characteristics, and feed the results to a machine learning approach to better predict r_{cpu} for partitions with specific characteristics.

Most importantly, considering the hardware characteristics as parameters in this machine learning methodology has the potential to predict what is more beneficial, adding more CPU sockets or accelerators, given a workload pattern and energy or dollar budget; hence providing valuable information needed for efficient system provisioning.

A graph processing engine for heterogeneous platforms. We presented the design and implementation of TOTEM, a graph processing engine for heterogeneous single-node platforms. We discussed a number of design decisions and optimizations TOTEM applies and their tradeoffs. TOTEM's importance, however, comes not only from enabling harnessing single-nodes, but also as a building block to harness GPU-accelerated clusters which have become common in the HPC space. For instance, three of the first five supercomputers in the latest (November, 2011) Top500 supercomputer list host GPUs [20] and heterogeneous architectures are increasingly popular [18].

Furthermore, TOTEM can be used as a back-end module of a domain specific language (DSL) for graph processing. For example, it can be used to extend the DSL developed by Hong et al. for graph analysis which currently targets only symmetric shared-memory platforms [6].

Our plan is to extend TOTEM to harness GPU-accelerated clusters. Shared-nothing architectures that aggregate heterogeneous nodes, that is, clusters of GPU-accelerated nodes, can offer a cost-efficient, yet high performance graph processing platform. The fact that new commodity nodes can support multi-hundred gigabytes of memory space, offers the opportunity to aggregate large memory space using smaller number of components; therefore, reducing the inter-node communication cost. At the same time, adding GPUs to each node offsets the loss in parallelism resulted from reducing the number of nodes.

Performance evaluation. We implemented and evaluated two graph algorithms on top of TOTEM. Our evaluation demonstrated the efficacy of the performance model, and the important gains offered by offloading part of the workload to one or more GPU.

We plan to extend our evaluation to more sophisticated graph partitioning algorithms than random partitioning. The ideal here is a low-cost partitioning technique that leads to partitions such that the generated workload for a partition matches well the strength of the processing element the partition is allocated to (e.g., assign the few high-degree nodes of a power-law graph to fast sequential processor, the CPU, and the many nodes with a limited number of neighbors to the GPU).

Finally, we consider two future evaluation directions. First, investigating the tradeoffs offered by emerging heterogeneous architectures with shared memory between the CPU and the GPU, which eliminate the high-latency PCI-E communication bus (e.g., AMD Fusion). At a first look, the potential seems limited: as presented in the evaluation section, aggregation significantly reduces the communication overhead, eliminating it as a bottleneck. Moreover, since graph problems are memory-bound, integrated platforms have all processing elements compete to access the memory system, as opposed to platforms based on discrete GPUs. Still, such architectures can benefit from partitioning algorithms that map the graph partitions to the heterogeneous characteristics of the hardware. The second direction is to compare the energy and performance aspects of heterogeneous and symmetric architectures. Recent CPU models (e.g., Intel's Sandy Bridge) offer higher hardware multithreading and better memory bandwidth, two key improvements for graph processing. We believe that the performance model and its planned extensions will allow this type of exploration.

7. ACKNOWLEDGMENTS

We thank Greg Redekop and Samer Al-Kiswany for their insightful comments on earlier versions of this paper and for helping with early implementations of the algorithms we have used.

8. REFERENCES

[1] Agarwal, V., Petrini, F., Pasetto, D., and Bader, D.A. Scalable Graph Exploration on Multicore Processors. *SuperComputing*, (2010).

[2] Barabasi, A.-L. Linked: How Everything Is Connected to Everything Else and What It Means. *Recherche 67*, (2003).

[3] Barrett, R., Berry, M., Chan, T.F., et al. *Templates for the Solution of Linear Systems: Building Blocks for Iterative Methods, 2nd Edition*. SIAM, 1994.

[4] Chakrabarti, D., Zhan, Y., and Faloutsos, C. R-MAT□: A Recursive Model for Graph Mining. *SDM*, (2004).

[5] Harish, P., Narayanan, P., Aluru, S., Parashar, M., Badrinath, R., and Prasanna, V. Accelerating Large Graph Algorithms on the GPU Using CUDA. *HiPC*, (2007).

[6] Hong, S., Chafi, H., Sedlar, E., and Olukotun, K. Green-Marl: A DSL for Easy and Efficient Graph Analysis. *ASPLOS*, (2012).

[7] Hong, S., Kim, S.K., Oguntebi, T., and Olukotun, K. Accelerating CUDA graph algorithms at maximum warp. *PPoPP*, (2011).

[8] Hong, S., Oguntebi, T., and Olukotun, K. Efficient Parallel Graph Exploration on Multi-Core CPU and GPU. *PACT*, (2011).

[9] Karypis, G. and Kumar, V. A Fast and High Quality Multilevel Scheme for Partitioning Irregular Graphs. *SIAM Journal on Scientific Computing 20*, 1 (1998).

[10] Katz, G.J. and Kider Jr, J.T. All-pairs shortest-paths for large graphs on the GPU. *SIGGRAPH/EUROGRAPHICS*, (2008).

[11] Malewicz, G., Austern, M.H., Bik, A.J.., et al. Pregel: a system for large-scale graph processing. *SIGMOD*, (2010).

[12] Merrill, D., Michael, G., and Grimshaw, A. Scalable GPU Graph Traversal. *PPoPP*, (2012).

[13] Pinedo, M.L. *Scheduling: Theory, Algorithms, and Systems*. Springer Verlag, 2012.

[14] Scarpazza, D.P., Villa, O., and Petrini, F. Efficient Breadth-First Search on the Cell/BE Processor. *IEEE TPDS 19*, 10 (2008).

[15] Valiant, L.G. A bridging model for parallel computation. *Communications of the ACM 33*, 8 (1990).

[16] Vineet, V. and Narayanan, P.J. CUDA cuts: Fast graph cuts on the GPU. *Conference on Computer Vision and Pattern Recognition Workshops*, IEEE (2008).

[17] Xia, Y. and Prasanna, V.K. Topologically Adaptive Parallel Breadth-First Search on Multicore Processors. *ICPDCS*, (2009).

[18] *TITAN: Paving the Way to Exascale*. 2011.

[19] Graph500. 2012. http://www.graph500.org.

[20] Top500. 2012. http://www.top500.org/.

The Evicted-Address Filter: A Unified Mechanism to Address Both Cache Pollution and Thrashing

Vivek Seshadri[†] vseshadr@cs.cmu.edu
Onur Mutlu[†] onur@cmu.edu
Michael A Kozuch[*] michael.a.kozuch@intel.com
Todd C Mowry[†] tcm@cs.cmu.edu

[†]Carnegie Mellon University [*]Intel Labs Pittsburgh

ABSTRACT

Off-chip main memory has long been a bottleneck for system performance. With increasing memory pressure due to multiple on-chip cores, effective cache utilization is important. In a system with limited cache space, we would ideally like to prevent 1) cache pollution, i.e., blocks with low reuse evicting blocks with high reuse from the cache, and 2) cache thrashing, i.e., blocks with high reuse evicting each other from the cache.

In this paper, we propose a new, simple mechanism to predict the reuse behavior of missed cache blocks in a manner that mitigates both pollution and thrashing. Our mechanism tracks the addresses of recently evicted blocks in a structure called the *Evicted-Address Filter* (EAF). Missed blocks whose addresses are present in the EAF are predicted to have high reuse and all other blocks are predicted to have low reuse. The key observation behind this prediction scheme is that if a block with high reuse is prematurely evicted from the cache, it will be accessed soon after eviction. We show that an EAF-implementation using a Bloom filter, which is cleared periodically, naturally mitigates the thrashing problem by ensuring that only a portion of a thrashing working set is retained in the cache, while incurring low storage cost and implementation complexity.

We compare our EAF-based mechanism to five state-of-the-art mechanisms that address cache pollution or thrashing, and show that it provides significant performance improvements for a wide variety of workloads and system configurations.

Categories and Subject Descriptors

B.3.2 [**Design Styles**]: Cache memories

General Terms

Design, Experimentation, Measurement, Performance.

Keyword

Caching, Memory, Pollution, Thrashing, Insertion policy

1. INTRODUCTION & MOTIVATION

Off-chip main memory has long been a bottleneck for system performance. Many modern applications demand increasingly more bandwidth and reduced latency from main memory. In addition, with the evolution of chip-multiprocessors, multiple applications run simultaneously on the same chip, increasing the pressure on the memory subsystem. In most modern processor designs, such concurrently running applications share the on-chip last-level cache [1, 2, 3, 22]. As a result, effective use of the available cache space is critical for high system performance.

Ideally, to ensure high performance, the cache should be filled only with blocks that have high temporal reuse – blocks that are likely to be accessed multiple times within a short time interval. However, as identified by prior work (e.g., [17, 19, 34, 35]), two problems degrade cache performance significantly. First, cache blocks with little or no reuse can evict blocks with high reuse from the cache. This problem is referred to as *cache pollution*. Second, when there are a large number of blocks with high reuse, they start evicting each other from the cache due to lack of space. This problem is referred to as *cache thrashing*. Both pollution and thrashing increase the miss rate of the cache and consequently reduce system performance. Prior work proposed to modify the cache insertion policy to mitigate the negative effects of pollution and thrashing [16, 17, 19, 34, 35, 53, 55].

To prevent cache pollution, prior approaches [19, 34, 53, 55] predict the reuse behavior of missed cache blocks and insert blocks predicted to have low reuse with a low priority – e.g., at the least-recently-used (LRU) position for the LRU replacement policy. This ensures that such low-reuse blocks get evicted from the cache quickly, thereby preventing them from polluting the cache. To predict the reuse behavior of missed cache blocks, these mechanisms *group* blocks based on the program counter that accessed them [34, 55] or the memory region to which the blocks belong [19, 55]. The mechanisms subsequently learn the reuse behavior of each group and use that to predict the reuse behavior of an individual cache block. As such, they do not distinguish between the reuse behavior of blocks within a group.

To prevent thrashing, recent prior work [35] proposed the use of a thrash-resistant bimodal insertion policy (BIP). BIP inserts a majority of missed blocks with low priority (at the LRU position) and a small fraction of blocks with high priority (at the most-recently-used (MRU) position). By doing so, a fraction of the working set can be retained in the cache, increasing the hit rate when the working set is larger than the cache size. When multiple threads share the cache, prior approaches [16, 17] learn the thrashing behavior of individual threads using a technique called set-dueling [35, 36], and use BIP for those threads that are determined to suffer from thrashing. As such, these approaches do not distinguish between the reuse behavior of cache blocks within a thread.

The Problem: In this work, we observe that previous proposals are not effective in preventing both pollution and thrashing at the same time. On one hand, proposals that address cache pollution do not distinguish between the reuse behavior of blocks that belong to

PACT'12, September 19–23, 2012, Minneapolis, Minnesota, USA.

the same group. As a result, these mechanisms can lead to many mispredictions when the reuse behavior of an individual block does not correlate with the reuse behavior of the group to which it belongs. Moreover, these approaches do not have any inherent mechanism to detect and prevent thrashing. If a large number of blocks are predicted to have high reuse, they will evict each other from the cache. On the other hand, since proposals that address thrashing use thread-level behavior to detect thrashing, they cannot distinguish between high-reuse blocks and low-reuse blocks within a thread. As a result, they either insert low-reuse blocks of a non-thrashing thread with high priority and hence, pollute the cache, or they repeatedly insert high-reuse blocks of a thrashing thread with the bimodal insertion policy, potentially leading to cache under-utilization. Since approaches to prevent pollution and approaches to prevent thrashing both modify the cache insertion policy using different mechanisms, it is difficult to combine them to address both problems concurrently. Our goal in this work is to design a mechanism that seamlessly reduces both pollution and thrashing to improve system performance.

Our Approach: To prevent cache pollution, one would like to predict the reuse behavior of a missed cache block and prevent low-reuse blocks from polluting the cache by choosing an appropriate cache insertion policy. As such, we take an approach similar to prior work, but unlike prior work which predicts the reuse behavior of a *group* of blocks, we predict the reuse behavior of *each* missed block based on *its own* past behavior. Unfortunately, keeping track of the behavior of all blocks in the system would incur large storage overhead and lookup latency. We eliminate this high cost by taking advantage of the following observation: *If a block with high reuse is prematurely evicted from the cache, it will likely be accessed soon after eviction. On the other hand, a block with low reuse will not be accessed for a long time after eviction.* This observation indicates that it is sufficient to keep track of a small set of recently evicted blocks to predict the reuse behavior of missed blocks – blocks evicted a long time ago are unlikely to have high reuse. To implement this prediction scheme, our mechanism keeps track of *addresses* of recently evicted blocks in a hardware structure called the *Evicted-Address Filter* (EAF). If a missed block's address is present in the EAF, the block is predicted to have high reuse. Otherwise, the block is predicted to have low reuse.

Cache thrashing happens when the working set is larger than the cache. In the context of EAF, there are two cases of thrashing. First, the working set can be larger than the aggregate size of the blocks tracked by the cache and the EAF together. We show that this case can be handled by using the thrash-resistant bimodal insertion policy [35] for low-reuse blocks, which ensures that a fraction of the working set is retained in the cache. Second, the working set can be larger than the cache but smaller than the aggregate size of the blocks tracked by the cache and the EAF together. In this case, thrashing can be mitigated by restricting the number of blocks predicted to have high reuse to a value smaller than the number of blocks in the cache. We find that implementing EAF using a Bloom filter enables this effect by forcing the EAF to be periodically cleared when it becomes full. Doing so results in the EAF predicting only a portion of the working set to have high reuse, thereby mitigating thrashing. We describe the required changes that enable the EAF to mitigate thrashing in detail in Section 2.3, and evaluate them quantitatively in Section 7.4.

Thus, our mechanism can reduce the negative impact of *both* cache pollution and thrashing using a single structure, the Evicted-Address Filter.

Summary of Operation: Our mechanism augments a conventional cache with an Evicted-Address Filter (EAF) that keeps track of addresses of recently evicted blocks. When a block is evicted from the cache, the block's address is inserted into the EAF. On a cache miss, the cache tests whether the missed block address is present in the EAF. If yes, the block is predicted to have high reuse and inserted with a high priority into the cache. Otherwise, the block is predicted to have low reuse and inserted with the bimodal insertion policy. When the EAF becomes full, it is completely cleared. We show that EAF naturally lends itself to a low-cost and low-complexity implementation using a Bloom filter (Section 3.2).

Using EAF to predict the reuse behavior of missed cache blocks has three benefits. First, the hardware implementation of EAF using a Bloom filter has low overhead and complexity. Second, the EAF is completely outside the cache. As a result, our mechanism does not require any modifications to the existing cache structure, and consequently, integrating EAF in existing processors incurs low design and verification cost. Third, EAF operates only on a cache miss and does not modify the cache hit operation. Therefore, it can be favorably combined with other techniques that improve performance by monitoring blocks while they are in the cache (e.g., better cache replacement policies).

We compare our EAF-augmented cache (or just EAF-cache) with five state-of-the-art cache management approaches that aim to prevent pollution *or* thrashing: 1) Thread-aware dynamic insertion policy [16] (TA-DIP), 2) Thread-aware dynamic re-reference interval prediction policy [17] (TA-DRRIP), 3) Signature-based Hit Prediction using Instruction pointers (SHIP) [55], 4) Run-time cache bypassing [19] (RTB), and 5) Miss classification table [9] (MCT). Our evaluations show that EAF-cache significantly outperforms all prior approaches for a wide variety of workloads and on a number of system configurations.

We make the following contributions:

- We show that keeping track of a small set of recently evicted blocks can enable a new and low-cost per-block reuse prediction mechanism.
- We provide a low-overhead, practical implementation of a new cache insertion policy based on Evicted-Address Filters (EAF), which mitigates the negative impact of both cache pollution and thrashing.
- We compare the EAF-cache with five state-of-the-art cache management mechanisms using a wide variety of workloads and show that EAF-cache provides better overall system performance than all of them (21% compared to the baseline LRU replacement policy and 8% compared to the best previous mechanism, SHIP [55], for a 4-core system). We also show that EAF-cache is orthogonal to improvements in cache replacement policy, by evaluating it in conjunction with two different replacement policies.

2. THE EVICTED-ADDRESS FILTER

As mentioned before, our **goal** in this work is to devise a mechanism to prevent both cache pollution and thrashing. Unlike prior approaches, instead of predicting the reuse behavior of a missed cache block indirectly using program counter, memory region or application behavior, our approach predicts the reuse behavior of a missed block based on *its own past behavior*. This can be achieved by remembering the history of reuse behavior of every block based on its past accesses. However, keeping track of the reuse behavior of *every* cache block in the system is impractical due to the associated high storage overhead.

In this work, we make an observation that leads to a simple per-block reuse prediction mechanism to address cache pollution. We first describe this observation and our basic mechanism. We show that a naïve implementation of our basic mechanism 1) has high storage and power overhead, and 2) does not address thrashing. We then describe an implementation of our mechanism using a Bloom filter [6], which addresses both of the above issues.

2.1 Addressing Cache Pollution

> **Observation:** *If a cache block with high reuse is prematurely evicted from the cache, then it will likely be accessed soon after eviction. On the other hand, a cache block with little or no reuse will likely not be accessed for a long time after eviction.*

The above observation indicates that to distinguish blocks with high reuse from those with low reuse, it is sufficient to keep track of a set of recently evicted blocks. Based on this, our mechanism augments a cache with a structure that tracks the *addresses* of recently evicted blocks in a FIFO manner. We call this structure the **Evicted-Address Filter** (EAF). On a cache miss, if the missed block address is present in the EAF, it is likely that the block was prematurely evicted from the cache. Therefore, the cache predicts the block to have high reuse. On the other hand, if the missed block address is not present in the EAF, then either the block is accessed for the first time or it was evicted from the cache a long time ago. In both cases, the cache predicts the block to have low reuse.

Depending on the replacement policy used by the cache, when a missed block's address is present in the EAF, the block (predicted to have high reuse) is inserted with a high priority, which keeps it in the cache for a long period – e.g., at the most-recently-used (MRU) position for the conventional LRU replacement policy. In this case, the corresponding address is also removed from the EAF, as it is no longer a recently evicted block address. This also allows the EAF to track more blocks, and thus make potentially better reuse predictions. When a missed block address is not present in the EAF, the block (predicted to have low reuse) is inserted with a low priority such that it is less likely to disturb other blocks in the cache – e.g., at the LRU position.

The size of the EAF – i.e., the number of recently evicted block addresses it can track – determines the boundary between blocks that are predicted to have high reuse and those that are predicted to have low reuse. Intuitively, blocks that will be reused in the cache should be predicted to have high reuse and all other blocks should be predicted to have low reuse. For this purpose, we set the size of the EAF to be the same as the number of blocks in the cache. Doing so ensures that if any block that can be reused gets prematurely evicted, it will be present in the EAF. This also ensures any block with a large reuse distance will likely not be present in the EAF. Section 7.4 analyzes the effect of varying the size of the EAF.

In summary, the EAF keeps track of as many recently evicted block addresses as the number of blocks in the cache. When a block gets evicted from the cache, the cache *inserts* its address into the EAF. On a cache miss, the cache *tests* if the missed block address is present in the EAF. If yes, it *removes* the address from the EAF and inserts the block into the cache set with a high priority. Otherwise, it inserts the block with a low priority. When the EAF becomes full, the cache *removes* the least-recently-evicted block address from the EAF (in a FIFO manner).

Although the EAF-based mechanism described above, which we refer to as the *plain-EAF*, can distinguish high-reuse blocks from low-reuse blocks, it suffers from two problems: 1) a naïve implementation of the plain-EAF (a set-associative tag store similar to the main tag store) has high storage and power overhead, and 2) the plain-EAF does not address thrashing.

> **Observation:** *Implementing EAF using a Bloom filter addresses the first problem, as a Bloom filter has low storage and power overhead. In addition, we observe that a Bloom-filter-based EAF implementation also mitigates thrashing.*

We defer a detailed description of the Bloom filter and how it enables a low-overhead implementation of EAF to Section 3. We first provide a deeper understanding of why the plain-EAF suffers from the thrashing problem (Section 2.2) and how a Bloom-filter-based EAF implementation mitigates thrashing (Section 2.3).

2.2 The Problem with Large Working Sets

Consider an application that accesses a working set larger than the cache size in a cyclic manner. In the context of EAF, there are two possible cases.

Case 1: The working set is larger than the aggregate size of blocks tracked by the cache and EAF together. In this case, *no* missed block's address will be present in the EAF. Therefore, all missed blocks will be predicted to have low reuse and inserted into the cache with a low priority. This leads to cache under-utilization as no block is inserted with a high priority, even though there is reuse in the working set.[1] In this case, we would like to always retain a fraction of the working set in the cache as doing so will lead to cache hits at least for that fraction.

Case 2: The working set is smaller than the aggregate number of blocks tracked by both the cache and EAF together. In this case, every missed block's address will be present in the EAF. As a result, every missed block will be predicted to have high reuse and inserted into the cache with a high priority. This will lead to blocks of the application evicting each other from the cache. However, similar to the previous case, we would like to always retain a fraction of the working set in the cache to prevent this problem.

The above discussion indicates that simply using the plain-EAF for predicting the reuse behavior of missed blocks would degrade cache performance when the working set is larger than the cache because using the plain-EAF causes cache under-utilization (Case 1) and does not address thrashing (Case 2).

To address the cache under-utilization problem (Case 1), we insert blocks predicted to have low reuse with the bimodal insertion policy (BIP) [35], as opposed to always inserting them with a low priority. BIP inserts a small fraction of blocks with a high priority and the remaining blocks with a low priority, retaining a fraction of the large working set in the cache. As a result, using BIP for low-reuse blocks allows EAF to adapt to working sets larger than the cache size and the EAF size combined. In the following section, we describe our solution to address cache thrashing (Case 2).

2.3 Addressing Cache Thrashing

The reason why the plain-EAF suffers from thrashing is that it does not have any mechanism to prevent a large number of high-reuse blocks from getting into the cache with a high priority. To mitigate thrashing, the plain-EAF should be augmented with a mechanism that can restrict the number of blocks predicted to have high reuse. Such a mechanism would ensure that not all blocks of a large working set are inserted into the cache with a high priority, and thereby prevent them from evicting each other from the cache. We show that implementing EAF using a Bloom filter achieves this goal.

EAF using a Bloom Filter: Note that the EAF can be viewed as a *set* of recently evicted block addresses. Therefore, to reduce its storage cost, we implement it using a Bloom filter, which is a *compact* representation of a set, in this case, a set of addresses. However, a

[1] We assume that the cache is already filled with some other data.

Bloom filter does not perfectly match the requirements of the plain-EAF. As summarized in Section 2.1, the plain-EAF requires three operations: *insertion*, *testing* and *removal* of an address. Although the Bloom filter supports the insertion and testing operations, it does not support removal of an individual address (Section 3.1). Therefore, to make the plain-EAF implementable using a Bloom filter, we slightly modify the plain-EAF design to eliminate the need to remove an individual address from the EAF. As described in Section 2.1, there are two cases when an address is removed from the EAF. First, when a missed block address is present in the EAF, the cache removes it from the EAF. In this case, we propose to simply *not remove* the address from the EAF. Second, when the EAF becomes full, the least-recently-evicted address is removed from the EAF, in a FIFO manner. In this case, we propose to *clear* the EAF completely, i.e. remove all addresses in the EAF, as the Bloom filter supports such a *clear* operation (Section 3.1). With these two changes, the EAF design becomes amenable for low-cost implementation using a Bloom filter.

Serendipitously, we also found that the changes we make to the plain-EAF design to enable its implementation with a Bloom filter has the benefit of mitigating thrashing. To see why this happens, let us examine the effect of the two changes we make to the plain-EAF. First, *not removing* a cache block address from the EAF ensures that the EAF becomes full even when a thrashing working set fits into the cache and the EAF together. Second, once the EAF becomes full, its gets *cleared*. These two changes together enable the periodic clearing of the EAF. Such periodic clearing results in only a fraction of the blocks of a thrashing working set to get predicted as high-reuse blocks, retaining only that fraction in the cache. This improves the cache hit-rate for such a working set, and thereby mitigates thrashing.

In summary, we propose three changes to the plain-EAF to handle working sets larger than the cache size: 1) insert low-reuse blocks with the *bimodal insertion policy*, 2) *not remove* a missed block address from the EAF, when it is present in the EAF, and 3) *clear* the EAF when it becomes full. We evaluate and analyze the effect of each of these three changes in Section 7.4. Hereafter, we use "EAF" to refer to an EAF with all the above proposed changes. In Section 7.7, we evaluate other possible changes to the plain-EAF design that also mitigate thrashing. We find that those designs perform similarly to the EAF design we proposed in this section.

2.4 Putting it All Together

Figure 1 summarizes our EAF-based cache management mechanism. There are three operations involving the EAF. First, when a block is evicted from the cache, the cache *inserts* the block's address into the EAF ❶. Second, on a cache miss, the cache *tests* whether the missed block address is present in the EAF ❷. If so, the cache inserts the missed block with a high priority, otherwise it inserts the block with the bimodal policy. Third, when the EAF becomes full – i.e., when the number of addresses in the EAF is the same as the number of blocks in the cache – the cache clears the EAF ❸.

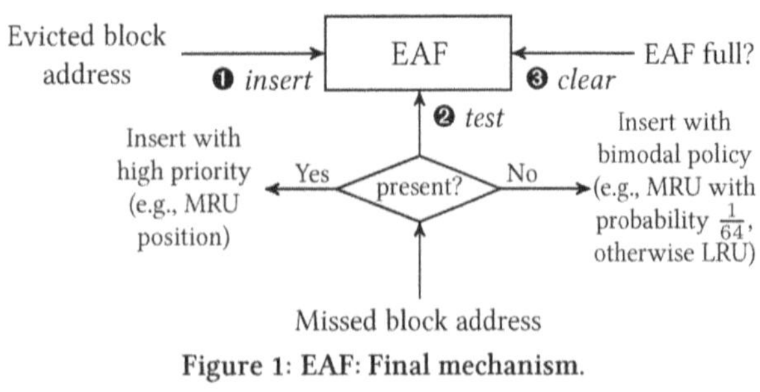

Figure 1: EAF: Final mechanism.

2.5 Handling LRU-friendly Applications

When a block with high reuse is accessed for the first time, it will not be present in the EAF. In this case, the EAF will falsely predict that the block has low reuse. Hence, the block will likely get inserted with a low priority (due to BIP) and get evicted from the cache quickly. As a result, for an LRU-friendly application – i.e., one whose most recently accessed blocks have high reuse – EAF-cache incurs one additional miss for a majority of blocks by not inserting them with high priority on their first access. In most multi-core workloads with LRU-friendly applications, we find that this does not impair performance as the cache is already filled with useful blocks. However, we observe that, for some workloads with *all* LRU-friendly applications, EAF-cache performs considerably worse than prior approaches because of the additional mispredictions.

To address this problem, we use set-dueling [35, 36] to determine if the system as a whole benefits from an always-high-priority insertion policy. The cache chooses two groups of 32 random sets. A missed block that belongs to a set of the first group is always inserted with the priority chosen based on the EAF prediction. A missed block that belongs to a set of the second group is always inserted with high priority. A saturating counter is used to keep track of which group incurs fewer misses. Blocks that do not belong to either of the groups are inserted with the policy that leads to fewer misses. We call this enhancement *Dueling-EAF (D-EAF)* and evaluate its performance in Section 7. Our results indicate that D-EAF mitigates the performance loss incurred by EAF-cache for workloads with all LRU-friendly applications and does not significantly affect performance of other workloads.

3. PRACTICAL IMPLEMENTATION

As described in Section 2.3, the EAF is designed to be implementable using a Bloom filter [6]. In this section, we describe the problems with a naïve implementation of the EAF that forced us to consider alternate implementations. We follow this with a detailed description of the hardware implementation of a Bloom filter, which has much lower hardware overhead and complexity compared to the naïve implementation. Finally, we describe the implementation of EAF using a Bloom filter.

A naïve implementation of the EAF is to organize it as a set-associative tag store similar to the main tag store. Each set of the EAF can keep track of addresses of the most recently evicted blocks of the corresponding cache set. However, such an implementation is not desirable for two reasons. First, it incurs a large storage overhead as it requires a separate tag store of the same size as the main tag store. Second, testing whether an address is present in the EAF requires an associative look-up. Although the test operation is not on the critical path, associative look-ups consume additional power.

3.1 Bloom Filter

A Bloom filter is a probabilistic data structure used as a compact representation of a set. It allows three simple operations: 1) *insert* an element into the set, 2) *test* if an element is present in the set, and 3) *remove all* the elements from the set. The *test* operation can have false positives – i.e., the Bloom filter can falsely declare that an element is present in the set even though that element might never have been inserted. However, the false positive rate can be controlled by appropriately choosing the Bloom filter parameters [6].

The hardware implementation of a Bloom filter consists of a bit-array with m bits and a set of k hash functions. Each hash function maps elements (e.g., addresses) to an integer between 0 and $m - 1$. Figure 2 shows one such implementation with $m = 16$ and $k = 2$. To insert an element into the set, the Bloom filter computes the

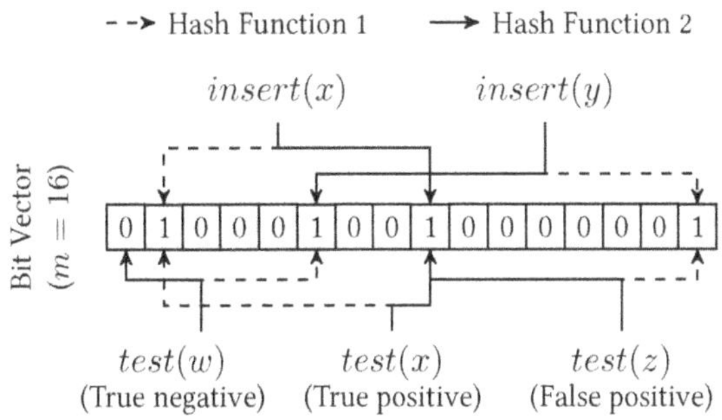

Figure 2: Hardware implementation of a Bloom filter using a bit vector of size 16 and two hash functions. The insert operations are performed before the test operations.

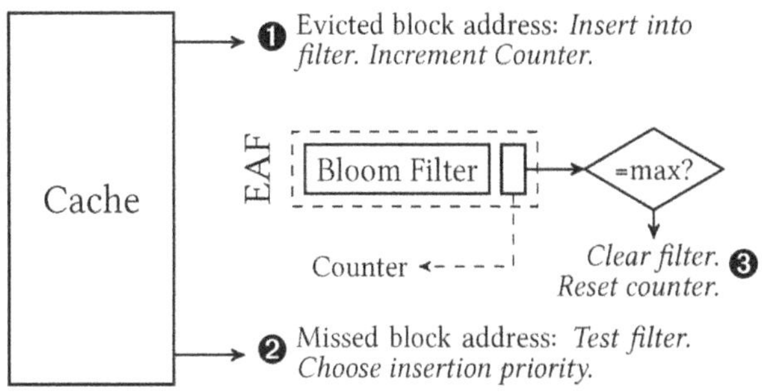

Figure 3: EAF implementation using a Bloom filter and a counter. The figure shows the three events that trigger operations on the EAF.

values of all the k hash functions on the element, and sets the corresponding bits in the bit-array – e.g., in the figure, inserting the element x sets the bits at locations 1 and 8. To test if an element is present in the set, the Bloom filter computes the values of all the k hash functions on the element, and checks if *all* the corresponding bits in the bit-array are set. If so, it declares that the element is present in the set – e.g., $test(x)$ in the figure. If any of the corresponding bits is not set, the filter declares that the element is not present in the set – e.g., $test(w)$ in the figure. Since the hash functions can map different elements to the same bit(s), the bits corresponding to one element could have been set as a result of inserting other elements into the set – e.g., in the figure, the bits corresponding to the element z are set as a result of inserting elements x and y. This is what leads to a *false positive* for the test operation. Finally, to remove all the elements from the set, the Bloom filter simply resets the entire bit-array. Since multiple elements can map to the same bit, resetting a bit in the Bloom filter can potentially remove multiple elements from it. This is the reason why an individual element cannot be removed from a Bloom filter.

Since a Bloom filter does not directly store elements, it generally requires much smaller storage than a naïve implementation of a set. In addition, all operations on a Bloom filter require only indexed lookups into the bit-array, which are more energy efficient than associative lookups.

3.2 EAF Using a Bloom Filter and a Counter

As described in Section 2.3, the EAF is designed so that the three operations associated with it, namely, *insert*, *test*, and *clear*, match the operations supported by the Bloom filter. In addition to the Bloom filter required to implement the EAF, our mechanism also requires a counter to keep track of the number of addresses currently inserted into the Bloom filter. This is required to determine when the EAF becomes full, so that the cache can clear it.

Figure 3 shows the operation of an EAF implemented using a Bloom filter and a counter. Initially, both the Bloom filter and the counter are reset. When a cache block gets evicted, the cache inserts the block's address into the Bloom filter and increments the counter. On a cache miss, the cache tests if the missed block address is present in the Bloom filter and chooses the insertion policy based on the result. When the counter reaches the number of blocks in the cache, the cache resets both the counter and the Bloom filter.

For our Bloom filter implementation, we use the H_3 class of hash functions [41]. These functions require only XOR operations on the input address and, hence, are simple to implement in hardware.

3.3 Hardware Implementation Cost

Implementing EAF on top of a conventional cache requires three additional hardware structures: 1) a *bit-array* for the Bloom filter, 2) a *counter* that can count up to the number of blocks in the cache, and 3) peripheral logic structure to determine the insertion priority of each missed cache block. The primary source of storage overhead is the bit-array required to implement the Bloom filter.

The number of bits required for the bit-array scales linearly with the maximum number of addresses expected to be stored in the Bloom filter, which in our case, is same as the number of blocks in the cache (C) (as described in Section 2.1). We set the number of bits in the bit-array to be αC, where α is the average number of bits required per address stored in the Bloom filter. We will discuss the trade-offs of this parameter shortly. For a system where cache block size is B and the size of each cache tag entry is T, the storage overhead of EAF compared to the cache size is given by:

$$\frac{\text{Bloom filter size}}{\text{Cache size}} = \frac{\alpha C}{(T+B)C} = \frac{\alpha}{T+B} \quad (1)$$

The false positive probability (p) of the Bloom filter is given by (as shown in [12]):

$$p = 2^{-\alpha \ln 2} \quad (2)$$

Since the false positive rate of the Bloom filter directly affects the accuracy of EAF predictions, the parameter α presents a crucial trade-off between the storage overhead of EAF and its performance improvement. From Equations (1) and (2), it can be seen that as α increases, the storage overhead also increases, but the false positive rate decreases. We find that, for most systems we evaluate, setting α to 8 provides the performance benefits of an EAF with no false positives (Section 7.4). For a 2-MB last-level cache with 64-byte block size, this amounts to a modest 1.47% storage overhead. Our evaluations show that, for a 4-core system, EAF-cache provides 21% performance improvement compared to the baseline.

4. ADVANTAGES & DISADVANTAGES

As we will show in Section 7, EAF-cache, which addresses both pollution and thrashing, provides the best performance compared to five prior approaches. In addition, EAF-cache has three advantages.

Ease of hardware implementation: As Figure 3 shows, EAF-cache can be implemented using a Bloom filter and a counter. Bloom filters have low hardware overhead and complexity. Several previous works [8, 29, 33, 40] have proposed the use of Bloom filters in hardware for various applications. Therefore, our EAF implementation using a Bloom filter incurs low design and implementation cost.

No modifications to cache design: Since both the Bloom filter and the counter are outside the cache, our mechanism does not require any modifications to the cache. This leads to low design and verification effort for integrating EAF into existing processor designs.

Mechanism	Addresses Pollution?	Addresses Thrashing?	Storage Overhead	Changes to Cache?	Modifies Cache Hit Behavior?
TA-DIP [16]	No	Yes	2 bytes per application	No changes to cache	No changes to cache hits
TA-DRRIP [17]	Partly	Yes	2 bytes per application	No changes to cache	No changes to cache hits
SHIP [55]	Yes	No	4-16KB prediction table*, 1.875KB instruction tags	Requires storing program counter in the tag store	Updates to the prediction table
RTB [19]	Yes	No	3KB for a 1024 entry MAT*	No changes to cache	Updates to the memory access table
MCT [9]	Yes	No	1 KB miss classification table	No changes to cache	No changes to cache hits
EAF-Cache	Yes	Yes	16KB for Bloom filter	No changes to cache	No changes to cache hits

Table 1: Storage overhead and implementation complexity of different mechanisms (for a 1MB 16-way set-associative cache with 64B block size). *In our evaluations, we use an infinite size table for both SHIP and RTB to eliminate interference caused by aliasing.

No modifications to cache hit operation: Finally, EAF operates only on a cache miss. The cache hit operation remains unchanged. Therefore, EAF can be combined with mechanisms that improve cache performance by monitoring only cache hits – e.g., the cache replacement policy. As an example, we show that EAF-cache provides better performance with an improved cache replacement policy (Section 7.3).

One shortcoming of EAF-cache is its storage overhead compared to certain other prior approaches [9, 16, 17] to address cache thrashing or pollution individually (see Table 1). However, as we show in Section 7, EAF-cache significantly outperforms these techniques, thereby justifying its additional storage overhead.

5. QUALITATIVE COMPARISON TO PRIOR WORK

We qualitatively compare our proposed mechanism, the EAF-cache, with five state-of-the-art high-performance mechanisms to address cache pollution or thrashing. The fundamental difference between the EAF-cache and prior approaches is that *unlike the EAF-cache, previous mechanisms do not concurrently address the negative impact of both pollution and thrashing.* As a result, they do not obtain the best performance for all workloads. Table 1 lists the previous mechanisms that we compare with the EAF-cache. The table indicates whether each mechanism addresses pollution and thrashing, along with its implementation complexity. We now describe each mechanism individually.

Thread-Aware Dynamic Insertion Policy (TA-DIP) [16] addresses the thrashing problem by determining thrashing at a thread granularity. It does so by using set-dueling [35, 36] to determine if a thread incurs fewer misses with the conventional LRU policy or the bimodal insertion policy (BIP). *All* blocks of a thread are inserted with the policy that has fewer misses. As a result, TA-DIP cannot distinguish between high-reuse blocks and low-reuse blocks within a thread. When following the LRU policy, this can lead to low-reuse blocks polluting the cache. When following BIP, this can lead to high-reuse blocks getting repeatedly inserted with the bimodal insertion policy, causing a low cache hit rate. As a result, TA-DIP does not provide the best performance when blocks within a thread have different reuse behavior.

Thread-Aware Dynamic Re-Reference Interval Prediction (TA-DRRIP) [17] improves upon TA-DIP by using a better replacement policy than LRU, RRIP. Unlike the LRU policy, which inserts all incoming blocks with the highest priority (MRU position), RRIP inserts all incoming blocks with a lower priority. This allows RRIP to reduce the performance degradation caused by low-reuse blocks, when compared with LRU. However, as identified by later work [55], TA-DRRIP does not completely address the pollution problem as it monitors the reuse behavior of a block *after* inserting the block into the cache. In addition, like TA-DIP, since TA-DRRIP operates at a thread (rather than a block) granularity, it suffers from the shortcomings of TA-DIP described before.

Signature-based HIt Prediction (SHIP) [55] addresses the pollution problem by using program counter information to distinguish blocks with low reuse from blocks with high reuse. The key idea is to group blocks based on the program counter that loaded them into the cache and learn the reuse behavior of each group using a table of counters. On a cache miss, SHIP indexes the table with the program counter that generated the miss and uses the counter value to predict the reuse behavior of the missed cache block. SHIP suffers from two shortcomings: 1) blocks loaded by the same program counter often may not have the same reuse behavior. In such cases, SHIP leads to many mispredictions, 2) when the number of blocks predicted to have high reuse exceeds the size of the cache, SHIP cannot address the resulting cache thrashing problem.[2]

Run-time Cache Bypassing (RTB) [19] addresses cache pollution by predicting reuse behavior of a missed block based on the memory region to which it belongs. RTB learns the reuse behavior of 1KB memory regions using a table of reuse counters. On a cache miss, RTB compares the reuse behavior of the missed block with the reuse behavior of the to-be-evicted block. If the missed block has higher reuse, it is inserted into the cache. Otherwise, it bypasses the cache. As RTB's operation is similar to that of SHIP, it suffers from similar shortcomings as SHIP.[3]

Miss Classification Table (MCT) [9] also addresses the cache pollution problem. MCT keeps track of one most recently evicted block address for each set in the cache. If a subsequent miss address matches this evicted block address, the miss is classified as a conflict miss. Otherwise, the miss is classified as a capacity miss. MCT inserts only conflict-missed blocks into the cache, anticipating that they will be reused. All other blocks are inserted into a separate buffer. MCT has two shortcomings. First, for a highly associative last-level cache, keeping track of only one most recently evicted block per set leads to many conflict misses getting falsely predicted as capacity misses, especially in multi-core systems with shared caches. Second, naïvely extending MCT to keep track of more evicted blocks can lead to the number of predicted-conflict-miss blocks to exceed the number of blocks in the cache. In such a scenario, MCT cannot address the resulting thrashing problem.

In contrast to previous approaches, our proposed mechanism, the **EAF-Cache**, is designed to address *both* cache pollution and thrashing with a single structure, the Evicted-Address Filter. Instead of indirectly predicting the reuse behavior of a cache block using the

[2]We also implemented single-usage block prediction [34] (SU), which also uses the program counter to identify reuse behavior of missed blocks. Both SU and SHIP provide similar performance.

[3]The SHIP paper [55] also evaluates mechanisms that use memory regions and other signatures to group blocks. The paper identifies that program counter-based grouping provides the best results. We reach a similar conclusion based on our experimental results.

Core		4 Ghz processor, in-order x86
L1-D Cache		32KB, 2-way associative, LRU replacement policy, single cycle latency, 64B block size
Private L2 Cache		256KB, 8-way associative, LRU replacement policy, latency = 8 cycles, 64B block size
L3 Cache	1-core	1 MB, 16-way associative, latency = 21 cycles, 64B block size
	2-core	Shared, 1 MB, 16-way associative, latency = 21 cycles, 64B block size
	4-core	Shared, 2 MB, 16-way associative, latency = 28 cycles, 64B block size
Main memory		DDR2 parameters, Row hits = 168 cycles, Row conflicts = 408 cycles, 4 Banks, 8 KB row buffers,

Table 2: Main configuration parameters used for our simulations

Name	L2-MPKI		Sens.		Name	L2-MPKI		Sens.		Name	L2-MPKI		Sens.		Name	L2-MPKI		Sens.	
ammp	5.76	M	36%	H	fma3d	1.14	L	5%	M	lucas	3.11	L	0%	L	vpr	6.13	M	46%	H
applu	1.92	L	2%	L	galgel	7.94	M	17%	M	mcf	49.58	H	26%	H	wupwise	1.33	L	1%	L
art	40.56	H	52%	H	gcc	4.08	L	3%	M	mgrid	3.14	L	5%	M	xalancbmk	10.89	H	16%	M
astar	25.49	H	6%	M	GemsFDTD	16.57	H	1%	L	milc	12.33	H	0%	L	zeusmp	5.77	L	1%	L
bwaves	15.03	H	0%	L	gobmk	1.92	L	2%	L	omnetpp	12.73	H	10%	M	**Server Benchmarks**				
bzip2	7.01	M	32%	H	h264ref	1.52	L	5%	M	parser	2.0	L	18%	H	apache20	5.8	L	9%	M
cactusADM	4.4	L	8%	M	hmmer	2.63	L	2%	L	soplex	25.31	H	18%	H	tpcc64	11.48	H	31%	H
dealII	1.51	L	9%	M	lbm	24.64	H	1%	L	sphinx3	14.86	H	9%	M	tpch2	17.02	H	31%	H
equake	9.22	M	6%	M	leslie3d	14.02	H	7%	M	swim	17.7	H	46%	H	tpch6	3.93	L	23%	H
facerec	4.61	L	18%	H	libquantum	14.31	H	1%	L	twolf	10.21	M	56%	H	tpch17	13.97	H	26%	H

Table 3: Benchmark classification based on intensity (L2-MPKI) and sensitivity (Sens.). (L - low, M - Medium, H - High). Intensity: L2-MPKI < 5 (Low); > 10 (High); Rest (Medium). Sensitivity: Perf. Degradation < 5% (Low); > 18% (High); Rest (Medium)

behavior of the application, program counter or memory region as a proxy, the EAF-cache predicts the reuse behavior of each missed cache block based on *the block's own past behavior*. As described in Section 2.3, the EAF-cache also mitigates thrashing by retaining only a fraction of blocks of a thrashing working set in the cache. As a result, EAF-cache adapts to workloads with varying working set characteristics, and as we will show in our quantitative results, it significantly outperforms prior approaches.

6. METHODOLOGY

We use an in-house event-driven x86 simulator for our evaluations. Instruction traces were collected by running the benchmarks on top of the Wind River Simics full system simulator [4], which are then fed to our simulator's core model. Our framework faithfully models all memory-related processor-stalls. All systems use a 3-level cache hierarchy similar to some modern architectures [2, 22]. The L1 and L2 caches are private to individual cores and the L3 cache is shared across all the cores. We do not enforce inclusion in any level of the hierarchy. All caches use a 64B block size. Writebacks do not update the replacement policy state.

Other major simulation parameters are provided in Table 2. The cache sizes we use for our primary evaluations (1MB for 2-core and 2MB for 4-core) were chosen to account for the small working set sizes of most of our benchmarks. Section 7.5 presents results with larger cache sizes (up to 16MB). For all mechanisms, except baseline LRU and DIP, the last-level cache uses the re-reference interval prediction replacement policy [17]. For our EAF proposals, we assume that the operations on the EAF can be overlapped with the long latency of memory access (note that all EAF operations happen only on a last-level cache miss).

For evaluations, we use benchmarks from the SPEC CPU2000 and CPU2006 suites, three TPC-H queries, one TPC-C server and an Apache web server. All results are collected by running a representative portion of each benchmark for 500 million instructions [49]. We classify benchmarks into nine categories based on their cache sensitivity (low, medium, or high) and memory intensity (low, medium, or high). For measuring cache sensitivity, we run the benchmarks with a 1MB last-level cache and a 256KB last-level cache and use the performance degradation as a metric. We define a benchmark's memory intensity as its misses per 1000 instructions (MPKI) on a 256KB L2 cache. We do not consider benchmarks with L2-MPKI less than one for our studies as they do not exert significant pressure on the last-level cache. Table 3 shows the memory intensity and cache sensitivity of different benchmarks used in our evaluations along with the criteria used for classifying them.

We evaluate multi-programmed workloads running on 2-core and 4-core CMPs. We generate nine categories of multi-programmed workloads with different levels of aggregate intensity (low, medium, or high) and aggregate sensitivity (low, medium, or high).[4] We evaluate the server benchmarks separately with ten 2-core and five 4-core workload combinations. In all, we present results for 208 2-core and 135 4-core workloads.[5]

We evaluate system performance using the weighted speedup metric [50], which is shown to correlate with the system throughput [11]. We also evaluate three other metrics, namely, instruction throughput, harmonic speedup [28], and maximum slowdown [25, 26], in Section 7.6 for completeness.

$$\text{Weighted Speedup} = \sum_i \frac{IPC_i^{shared}}{IPC_i^{alone}}$$

7. RESULTS

7.1 Single-core Results

Figure 4 compares the performance, instructions per cycle (IPC), for different benchmarks with different mechanisms.[6] The percentages on top of the bars show the reduction in the last-level cache misses per kilo instruction of D-EAF compared to LRU. We draw two conclusions from the figure.

First, D-EAF, with its ability to address both pollution and thrashing, provides performance comparable to the better of the previous

[4]We compute aggregate intensity/sensitivity of a workload as the sum of individual benchmark intensities/sensitivities (low = 0, medium = 1, high = 2).

[5]We provide details of individual workloads in our tech report [47].

[6]For clarity, results for DIP and RTB are excluded from Figures 4 and 5 (left) as their performance improvements are lower compared to the other mechanisms. We also don't present single-core results for benchmarks where all mechanisms perform within 1% of the baseline LRU. Our tech report provides the full results [47].

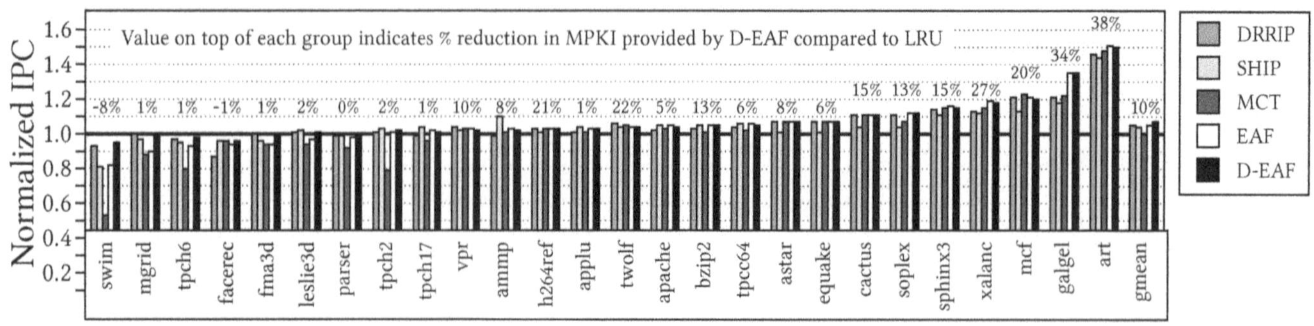

Figure 4: System performance: Single-core system

best mechanisms to address pollution (SHIP) or thrashing (DRRIP) for most benchmarks. On average, D-EAF provides the best performance across all benchmarks (7% IPC improvement over LRU). In fact, except for benchmarks *swim*, *facerec* and *parser*, D-EAF always reduces the miss rate compared to the LRU policy. As the figure shows, MCT considerably degrades performance for several benchmarks. This is because MCT keeps track of only one most recently evicted block address per set to identify conflict misses. This leads to many conflict-miss blocks to get falsely predicted as capacity misses (as described in Section 5). As a result, such blocks are inserted with low priority, leading to poor performance. This effect becomes worse in a multi-core system, where there is interference between concurrently running applications.

Second, as expected, for LRU-friendly benchmarks like *swim* and *mgrid*, EAF degrades performance considerably. This is because, when a block is accessed for the first time, EAF predicts it to have low reuse. However, the most recently accessed blocks in these benchmarks have high reuse. Therefore, EAF incurs one additional miss for most blocks. D-EAF identifies this problem and inserts all blocks of such applications with high priority, thereby mitigating the performance degradation of EAF. For example, in case of *swim*, D-EAF reduces the MPKI by 18% compared to EAF. We conclude that D-EAF, with the ability to dynamically adapt to different benchmark characteristics, provides the best average performance.

7.2 Multi-core Results

In multi-core systems, the shared last-level cache is subject to varying access patterns from the concurrently-running applications. In such a scenario, although pollution or thrashing caused by an application may not affect its own performance, they can adversely affect the performance of the concurrently-running applications. Therefore, the cache management mechanism should efficiently handle all the access patterns to provide high system performance. The EAF-cache with its ability to concurrently handle both cache pollution and thrashing provides better cache utilization than prior approaches that were designed to handle only one of the two problems. As a result, we find that the EAF-cache significantly outperforms prior approaches for multi-programmed workloads (on both 2-core and 4-core systems).

Performance by workload categories: Figure 7 shows the absolute weighted speedup for our 4-core system grouped based on different workload categories (as described in Section 6).[7] The percentage on top of the bars show the improvement in weighted speedup of D-EAF compared to the LRU policy. For SPEC workloads, as expected, overall system performance decreases as the intensity of the workloads increases from low to high.[8] Regardless, both EAF and D-EAF outperform other prior approaches for all workload categories (21% over LRU and 8% over the best previous mechanism, SHIP). The figure also shows that within each intensity category, the performance improvement of our mechanisms increases with increasing cache sensitivity of the workloads. This is because the negative impact of cache under-utilization increases as workloads become more sensitive to cache space. Although not explicitly shown in the figure, the performance improvement of D-EAF over the best previous mechanism (SHIP) also increases as the cache sensitivity of the workloads increases.

For server workloads, D-EAF improves weighted speedup by 17% compared to the LRU policy. These workloads are known to have *scans* [17] (accesses to a large number of blocks with no reuse) which pollute the cache, making pollution the major problem. This is the reason why SHIP and RTB, which were designed to address only cache pollution, are able to perform comparably to D-EAF for these workloads. In contrast, TA-DIP, which is designed to address only cache thrashing, offers no improvement over LRU.

We conclude that our EAF-based approach is better than other prior approaches for both SPEC and server workloads and its benefits improve as workloads become more sensitive to cache space.

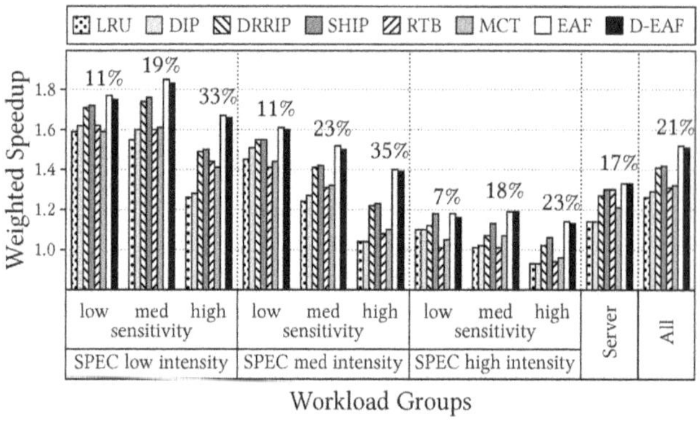

Figure 7: 4-core system performance for different workload categories. The value on top of each group indicates % improvement in weighted speedup provided by D-EAF compared to LRU.

Overall performance analysis: Figures 5 and 6 plot the performance improvements of the different approaches compared to the baseline LRU policy for all 2-core and 4-core workloads, respectively. The workloads are sorted based on the performance improvement of EAF. The goal of these figures is *not* to indicate how different mechanisms perform for all workloads. Rather, the figures show that both EAF and D-EAF (thick lines) significantly outperform all prior approaches for most workloads.

[7]We do not include the results for 2-core workloads due to space constraints. The observed trends for them are similar to those for 4-core workloads. We include these results in our tech report [47].

[8]Our server benchmarks have little scope for categorization. Therefore, we present average results for all server workloads.

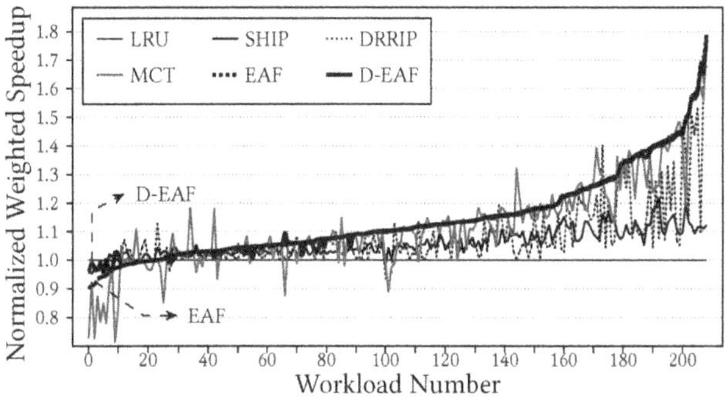

Figure 5: System performance: 2-core

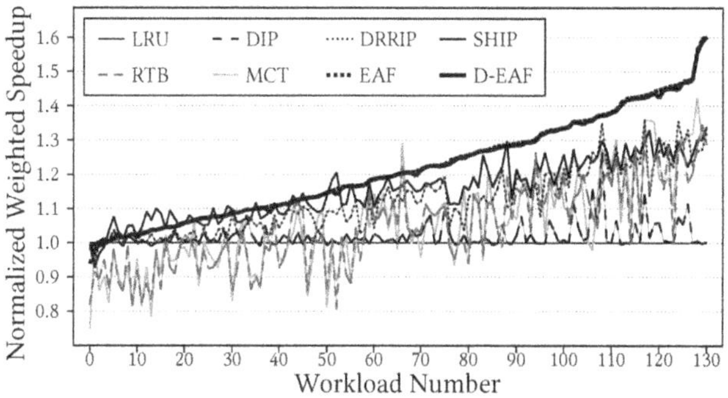

Figure 6: System performance: 4-core

Two other observations can be made from these figures. First, there is no consistent trend in the performance improvement of the prior approaches. Different approaches improve performance for different workloads. This indicates that addressing only cache pollution or only cache thrashing is not sufficient to provide high performance for all workloads. Unlike these prior approaches, EAF and D-EAF, with their ability to address both problems concurrently, provide the best performance for almost all workloads. Second, there is no visible performance gap between EAF and D-EAF for the majority of the workloads except for a small set of LRU-friendly 2-core workloads (indicated in the far left of Figure 5), where D-EAF performs better than EAF. This is because, for most workloads (even with LRU-friendly applications), the cache (with only EAF) is already filled with high-reuse blocks. As a result, the additional misses caused by EAF for LRU-friendly applications do not significantly affect performance. But, as evidenced by our results for single-core and the small fraction of LRU-friendly 2-core workloads, D-EAF is more robust in terms of performance than EAF.

7.3 Interaction with the Replacement Policy

As EAF-cache modifies only the cache insertion policy, it can be used with any cache replacement policy. Figure 8 shows the benefits of augmenting our EAF mechanism to 1) a cache following the LRU replacement policy, and 2) a cache following the RRIP [17] policy for all 4-core workloads. As the figure shows, EAF-cache consistently improves performance in both cases for almost all workloads (11% on average for LRU and 12% for RRIP). We conclude that the benefits of EAF-cache are orthogonal to the benefits of using an improved cache replacement policy.

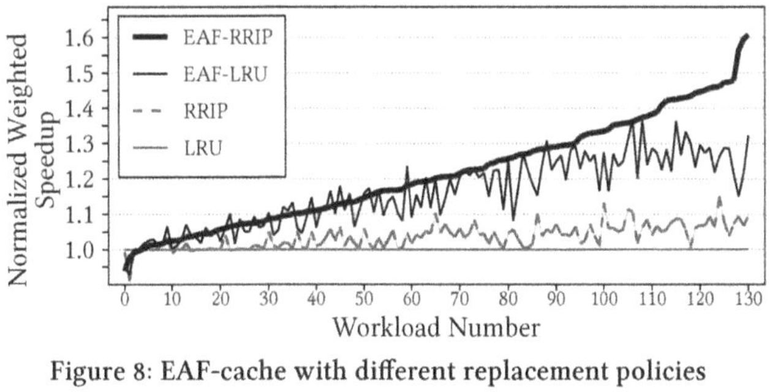

Figure 8: EAF-cache with different replacement policies

7.4 Effect of EAF Design Choices

EAF size – Number of evicted addresses: The size of the EAF – i.e., the number of evicted addresses it keeps track of – determines the boundary between blocks that are considered to be recently evicted and those that are not. On one hand, having a small EAF increases the likelihood of a high-reuse block getting incorrectly predicted to have low reuse. On the other hand, a large EAF increases the likelihood of a low-reuse block getting incorrectly predicted to have high reuse. As such, we expect performance to first increase as the size of the EAF increases and then decrease beyond some point. Figure 9 presents the results of our experiments studying this trade-off. As indicated in the figure, the performance improvement of EAF peaks when the size of the EAF is approximately the same as the number of blocks in the cache. This concurs with our intuition (as mentioned in Section 2.1) – sizing the EAF to be around the same size as the number of blocks in the cache ensures that a block that can potentially be reused in the cache will likely be predicted to have high reuse while a block with a larger reuse distance will likely be predicted to have low reuse.

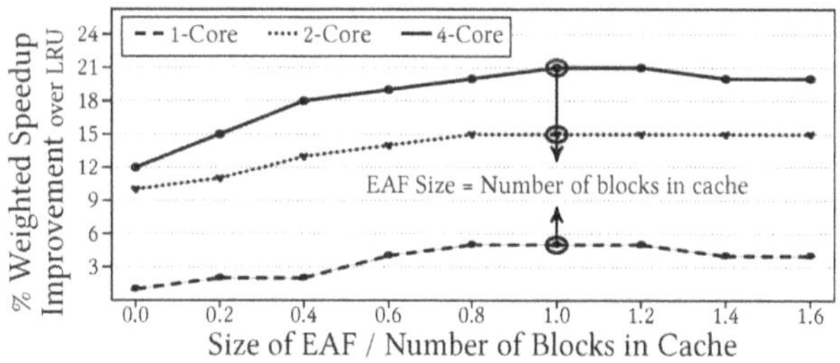

Figure 9: Sensitivity to EAF size

Storage overhead of the Bloom filter: As described in Section 3.3, for a fixed EAF size, the parameter α associated with the Bloom filter presents a trade-off between the false positive rate and the storage overhead of the Bloom filter. A large value of α leads to a low false positive rate but incurs high storage overhead. On the other hand, a small value of α incurs small storage overhead but leads to a high false positive rate. As a false positive can result in an actually low-reuse block to be predicted to have high reuse, the choice of α is critical for performance. Figure 10 shows the effect of varying α on performance, when the EAF size is the same as the number of blocks in the cache. The figure also shows the corresponding storage overhead of the Bloom filter with respect to the cache size. As α increases, performance improves because false positive rate decreases. However, almost all of the potential performance improvement of having a perfect EAF (EAF with no false positives) is achieved with $\alpha = 8$ (1.47% storage overhead).

Effect of EAF policies for cache thrashing: In Section 2.3, we proposed three changes to the plain-EAF, to address cache thrashing: 1) using the *bimodal insertion policy* (BIP) for low-reuse blocks (B), 2) *not removing* a block address when it is present in the EAF (N), and 3) *clearing* the EAF when it becomes full (C). Figure 11 shows the performance improvement of adding all combinations of these policies to the *plain-EAF* (described in Section 2.1). Two observations are in order.

First, the *not remove* (+N) and the *clear* (+C) policies individually improve performance, especially significant in the 4-core system.

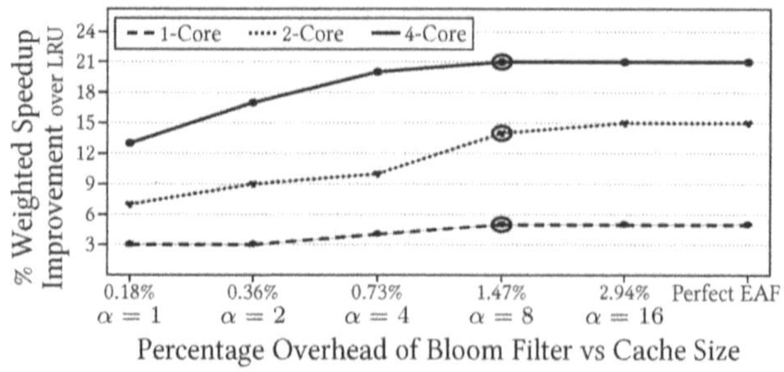

Figure 10: Sensitivity to Bloom filter storage overhead

However, applying both policies together (+NC) provides significant performance improvement for *all* systems. This is because, when the working set is larger than the cache size but smaller than the aggregate size of the blocks tracked by the cache and EAF together, the *not remove* (+N) policy is required to ensure that the EAF gets full, and the *clear* (+C) policy is required to clear the EAF when it becomes full. Second, the best performance improvement is achieved for all systems when *all* the three policies are applied to the EAF (+NCB), as doing so improves the hit-rate for both categories of large working sets (as discussed in Section 2.2).

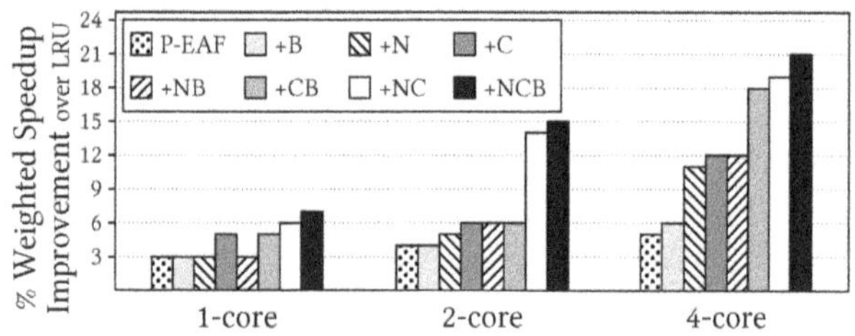

Figure 11: Effect of changes to plain-EAF (P-EAF)

7.5 Sensitivity to System Parameters

Varying Cache Size: Figure 12 plots the performance improvements of SHIP (best previous mechanism), EAF and D-EAF compared to LRU for different cache sizes for multi-core systems. The performance improvement of different mechanisms decreases with increasing cache size. This is expected because with increasing cache size, cache under-utilization becomes less of a problem. However, the EAF-cache provides significant performance improvements even for 8MB/16MB caches, and better performance than SHIP for all cache sizes.

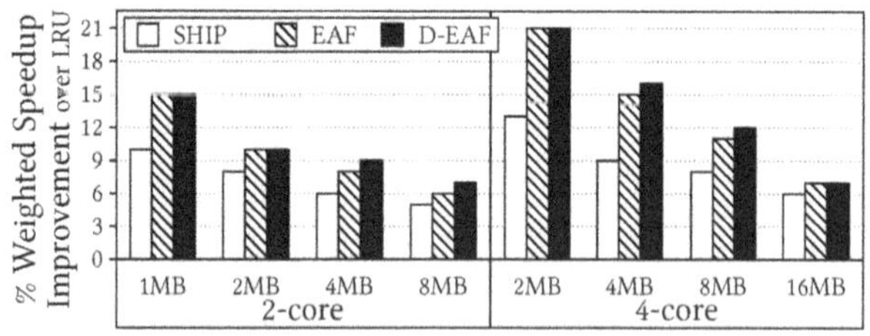

Figure 12: EAF-cache with different cache sizes

Varying Memory Latency: Figure 13 shows the effect of varying the memory latency. For ease of analysis, we use a fixed latency for all memory requests in these experiments. As expected, system throughput decreases as the memory latency increases. However, the performance improvement of EAF-cache increases with increasing memory latency, making it a more attractive mechanism for future systems, which are likely to have higher memory access latencies due to contention.

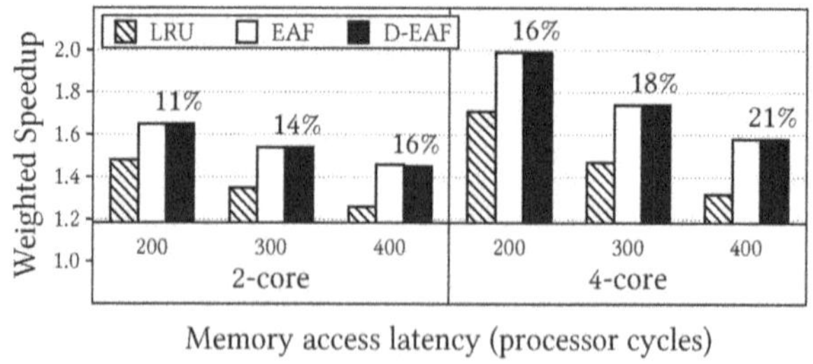

Figure 13: EAF-cache with different memory latencies. The value on top of each group indicates % weighted speedup improvement of D-EAF compared to LRU.

7.6 Multi-core Systems: Other Metrics

Table 4 shows the percentage improvement of the EAF-cache over the baseline LRU policy and the best previous mechanism, SHIP, on four metrics: weighted speedup [11, 50], instruction throughput, harmonic speedup [28] and maximum slowdown [25, 26]. For both 2-core and 4-core systems, EAF-cache significantly improves weighted speedup, instruction throughput and harmonic speedup, and also considerably reduces the average maximum slowdown. We conclude that EAF-cache improves both system performance and fairness compared to prior approaches.

Metric	2-core		4-core	
	+ LRU	+ SHIP	+ LRU	+ SHIP
Weighted Speedup	15%	6%	21%	8%
Instruction Throughput	14%	6%	22%	7%
Harmonic Speedup	15%	6%	29%	6%
Max. Slowdown Reduction	16%	7%	31%	8%

Table 4: Improvement of EAF on different metrics

7.7 Alternate EAF Designs

In this section, we describe two different approaches to mitigate cache pollution and thrashing by making slight modifications to the proposed EAF design: 1) Segmented-EAF, and 2) Decoupled-Clear-EAF. We describe these two designs below and compare their performance to our original EAF-cache design.

Segmented-EAF: The plain-EAF (described in Section 2.1) and the EAF (with the three changes described in Section 2.3) are two ends of a spectrum. While the former removes just one block address when the EAF becomes full, the latter clears the entire EAF when it becomes full. One can think of an approach which clears a fraction of the EAF (say $\frac{1}{2}$) when it becomes full. This can be accomplished by segmenting the EAF into multiple Bloom filters (organized in a FIFO manner) and clearing only the oldest one when the EAF becomes full. We call this variant of the EAF *Segmented-EAF*. A Segmented-EAF trades off the ability to mitigate thrashing (number of addresses removed from the EAF) with the ability to mitigate pollution (amount of information lost due to clearing).

Decoupled-Clear-EAF: In EAF-cache, the number of blocks that enter the cache with high priority is reduced by clearing the EAF when it becomes full. However, this approach requires the size of the EAF to be around the same as the number of blocks in the cache, so as to limit the number of blocks predicted to have high-reuse between two EAF-clear events. This restricts the EAF's visibility of recently evicted blocks. However, having a larger visibility can potentially allow EAF to better identify the reuse behavior of more cache blocks. The *Decoupled-Clear-EAF* addresses this visi-

Design	1-core	2-core	4-core
EAF	7%	15%	21%
Segmented-EAF	6%	13%	21%
Decoupled-Clear-EAF	6%	14%	21%

Table 5: Comparison of EAF with other design alternatives

bility problem by decoupling the size of the EAF from determining when the EAF is cleared. In this approach, the EAF keeps track of more addresses than the number of blocks in the cache (say 2×). An additional counter keeps track of the number of blocks inserted with high priority into the cache. The EAF is cleared on two events: 1) when it becomes full, and 2) when the number of high-priority blocks reaches the number of blocks in the cache.

Table 5 compares the performance improvement (over baseline LRU) of the above designs with our proposed EAF design. Our results indicate that there is not much performance gap (less than 2%) across all three designs. We conclude that all the three heuristics perform similarly for our workloads. We leave an in-depth analysis of these design points and other potential designs as future work.

8. RELATED WORK

The primary contribution of this paper is the EAF-cache, a low-complexity cache insertion policy that mitigates the negative impact of both cache pollution and thrashing, by determining the reuse behavior of a missed block based on the block's own past behavior. We have already provided qualitative and quantitative comparisons to the most closely related work on addressing pollution or thrashing [9, 16, 17, 19, 34, 55], showing that EAF-cache outperforms all these approaches. In this section, we present other related work.

A number of cache insertion policies have been proposed to prevent L1-cache pollution [43, 53]. Similar to some approaches we have discussed in our paper [19, 34, 55], these mechanisms use the instruction pointer or the memory region to predict the reuse behavior of missed blocks. As we showed, our EAF-based approach provides better performance than these prior approaches as it can address both pollution and thrashing simultaneously.

Prior work has proposed compiler-based techniques (e.g., [10, 42, 54]) to mitigate the negative impact of pollution and thrashing by either modifying the data layout or by providing hints to the hardware – e.g., non-temporal load/store in x86 [14]. However, the scope of such techniques is limited to cases where reuse and/or locality of accesses can be successfully modeled by the programmer/compiler, which often corresponds to array accesses within loop nests. Our EAF-cache proposal can potentially improve performance for a much broader set of memory accesses, and hence complements these compiler-based techniques.

Much prior research (e.g., [13, 17, 23, 27, 39, 46]) has focused on improving the cache replacement policy. Researchers have also proposed mechanisms to improve cache utilization (e.g., [38, 45, 44, 48, 57]) by addressing the set imbalance problem (i.e., certain cache sets suffer many conflict misses while others are under-utilized). The EAF-cache can be combined with any of these mechanisms to further improve performance.

A number of page replacement policies have been proposed to improve virtual memory performance (e.g., [5, 18, 20, 30, 32]). As these mechanisms were designed for software-based DRAM buffer management, they usually employ complex algorithms and assume large amounts of storage. As a result, applying them to hardware caches incurs higher storage overhead and implementation complexity than the EAF-cache.

Jouppi proposed victim caches [21] to improve the performance of direct mapped caches by reducing the latency of conflict misses. A victim cache stores recently evicted cache blocks (including data) in a fully associative buffer. As a result, it has to be a small structure. In contrast, our proposed EAF mechanism is a reuse predictor which keeps track of *only addresses* of a larger number of recently evicted blocks. As such, the two techniques can be employed together.

Cache partitioning is one technique that has been effectively used to improve shared-cache performance [37, 51, 52, 56] or provide QoS in multi-core systems with shared caches [7, 15, 24, 31]. The mechanisms to improve performance use partitioning to provide more cache space to applications that benefit from the additional space. For QoS, the proposed approaches ensure that applications are guaranteed some minimum amount of cache space. Since blocks with low reuse contribute neither to system performance nor to fairness, these mechanisms can be employed in conjunction with the EAF-cache, which can filter out low-reuse blocks to further improve performance or fairness. Evaluation of this is part of our future work.

9. CONCLUSION

Efficient cache utilization is critical for high system performance. Cache pollution and thrashing reduce cache utilization and consequently, degrade cache performance. We show that prior works do not concurrently address cache pollution and thrashing.

We presented the EAF-cache, a mechanism that mitigates the negative impact of *both* cache pollution and thrashing. EAF-cache handles pollution by keeping track of addresses of recently evicted blocks in a structure called the *Evicted-Address Filter* (EAF) to distinguish high-reuse blocks from low-reuse blocks. Implementing the EAF using a Bloom filter naturally mitigates the thrashing problem, while incurring low storage and power overhead. Extensive evaluations using a wide variety of workloads and system configurations show that the EAF-cache provides the best performance compared to five different prior approaches.

We conclude that EAF-cache is an attractive mechanism that can handle both cache pollution and thrashing, to provide high performance at low complexity. The concept of EAF provides a substrate that can enable other cache optimizations, which we are currently exploring.

ACKNOWLEDGEMENTS

Many thanks to Chris Wilkerson, Phillip Gibbons, and Aamer Jaleel for their feedback during various stages of this project. We thank the anonymous reviewers for their valuable feedback and suggestions. We acknowledge members of the SAFARI and LBA groups for their feedback and for the stimulating research environment they provide. We acknowledge the generous support of AMD, Intel, Oracle, and Samsung. This research was partially supported by grants from NSF, GSRC, Intel University Research Office, and Intel Science and Technology Center on Cloud Computing. We thank Lavanya Subramanian, David Andersen, Kayvon Fatahalian and Michael Papamichael for their feedback on this paper's writing.

REFERENCES

[1] AMD Phenom II key architectural features. `http://goo.gl/iQBfK`.

[2] Intel next generation microarchitecture. `http://goo.gl/3eskx`.

[3] Oracle SPARC T4. `http://goo.gl/KZSnc`.

[4] Wind River Simics. `www.windriver.com/producs/simics`.

[5] S. Bansal and D. S. Modha. CAR: Clock with adaptive replacement. In *FAST*, 2004.

[6] B. H. Bloom. Space/time trade-offs in hash coding with allowable errors. *ACM Communications*, 13, July 1970.

[7] J. Chang and G. S. Sohi. Cooperative cache partitioning for chip multiprocessors. In *ICS*, 2007.

[8] Y. Chen, A. Kumar, and J. Xu. A new design of Bloom filter for packet inspection speedup. In *GLOBECOM*, 2007.

[9] J. Collins and D. M. Tullsen. Hardware identification of cache conflict misses. In *MICRO*, 1999.

[10] C. Ding and K. Kennedy. Improving effective bandwidth through compiler enhancement of global cache reuse. *JPDC*, 2004.

[11] S. Eyerman and L. Eeckhout. System-level performance metrics for multiprogram workloads. *IEEE Micro*, 2008.

[12] A. Goel and P. Gupta. Small subset queries and Bloom filters using ternary associative memories, with applications. In *SIGMETRICS*, 2010.

[13] E. G. Hallnor and S. K. Reinhardt. A fully associative software managed cache design. In *ISCA*, 2000.

[14] Intel. Intel 64 and IA-32 architectures software developer's manuals, 2011.

[15] R. Iyer. CQoS: A framework for enabling QoS in shared caches of CMP platforms. In *ICS*, 2004.

[16] A. Jaleel, W. Hasenplaugh, M. Qureshi, J. Sebot, S. Steely, Jr., and J. Emer. Adaptive insertion policies for managing shared caches. In *PACT*, 2008.

[17] A. Jaleel, K. B. Theobald, S. C. Steely, Jr., and J. Emer. High performance cache replacement using re-reference interval prediction. In *ISCA*, 2010.

[18] S. Jiang and X. Zhang. LIRS: An efficient low inter-reference recency set replacement policy to improve buffer cache performance. In *SIGMETRICS*, 2002.

[19] T. Johnson, D. Connors, M. Merten, and W.-M. Hwu. Run-time cache bypassing. *IEEE TC*, 1999.

[20] T. Johnson and D. Shasha. 2Q: A low overhead high performance buffer management replacement algorithm. In *VLDB*, 1994.

[21] N. P. Jouppi. Improving direct-mapped cache performance by the addition of a small fully-associative cache and prefetch buffers. In *ISCA*, 1990.

[22] R. Kalla, B. Sinharoy, W. Starke, and M. Floyd. Power7: IBM's next-generation server processor. *IEEE Micro*, 2010.

[23] G. Keramidas, P. Petoumenos, and S. Kaxiras. Cache replacement based on reuse-distance prediction. In *ICCD*, 2007.

[24] S. Kim, D. Chandra, and Y. Solihin. Fair cache sharing and partitioning in a chip multiprocessor architecture. In *PACT*, 2004.

[25] Y. Kim, D. Han, O. Mutlu, and M. Harchol-Balter. ATLAS: A scalable and high-performance scheduling algorithm for multiple memory controllers. In *HPCA*, 2010.

[26] Y. Kim, M. Papamichael, O. Mutlu, and M. Harchol-Balter. Thread cluster memory scheduling: Exploiting differences in memory access behavior. In *MICRO*, 2010.

[27] H. Liu, M. Ferdman, J. Huh, and D. Burger. Cache bursts: A new approach for eliminating dead blocks and increasing cache efficiency. In *MICRO*, 2008.

[28] K. Luo, J. Gummaraju, and M. Franklin. Balancing thoughput and fairness in SMT processors. In *ISPASS*, 2001.

[29] M. J. Lyons and D. Brooks. The design of a Bloom filter hardware accelerator for ultra low power systems. In *ISLPED*, 2009.

[30] N. Megiddo and D. S. Modha. ARC: A self-tuning, low overhead replacement cache. In *FAST*, 2003.

[31] K. J. Nesbit, J. Laudon, and J. E. Smith. Virtual private caches. In *ISCA*, 2007.

[32] E. J. O'Neil, P. E. O'Neil, and G. Weikum. The LRU-K page replacement algorithm for database disk buffering. In *SIGMOD*, 1993.

[33] J.-K. Peir, S.-C. Lai, S.-L. Lu, J. Stark, and K. Lai. Bloom filtering cache misses for accurate data speculation and prefetching. In *ICS*, 2002.

[34] T. Piquet, O. Rochecouste, and A. Seznec. Exploiting single-usage for effective memory management. In *ACSAC*, 2007.

[35] M. K. Qureshi, A. Jaleel, Y. Patt, S. Steely, and J. Emer. Adaptive insertion policies for high performance caching. In *ISCA*, 2007.

[36] M. K. Qureshi, D. N. Lynch, O. Mutlu, and Y. N. Patt. A case for MLP-aware cache replacement. In *ISCA*, 2006.

[37] M. K. Qureshi and Y. N. Patt. Utility-based cache partitioning: A low-overhead, high-performance, runtime mechanism to partition shared caches. In *MICRO*, 2006.

[38] M. K. Qureshi, D. Thompson, and Y. N. Patt. The V-way cache: Demand based associativity via global replacement. In *ISCA*, 2005.

[39] K. Rajan and G. Ramaswamy. Emulating optimal replacement with a shepherd cache. In *MICRO*, 2007.

[40] R. Rajwar, M. Herlihy, and K. Lai. Virtualizing transactional memory. In *ISCA*, 2005.

[41] M. V. Ramakrishna, E. Fu, and E. Bahcekapili. Efficient hardware hashing functions for high performance computers. *IEEE TC*, 1997.

[42] G. Rivera and C.-W. Tseng. Compiler optimizations for eliminating cache conflict misses. Technical Report UMIACS-TR-97-59, University of Maryland, College Park, 1997.

[43] J. Rivers and E. S. Davidson. Reducing conflicts in direct-mapped caches with a temporality-based design. In *ICPP*, 1996.

[44] D. Rolan, B. B. Fraguela, and R. Doallo. Adaptive line placement with the set balancing cache. In *MICRO*, 2009.

[45] D. Rolan, B. B. Fraguela, and R. Doallo. Reducing capacity and conflict misses using set saturation levels. In *HiPC*, 2010.

[46] D. Sanchez and C. Kozyrakis. The ZCache: Decoupling ways and associativity. In *MICRO*, 2010.

[47] V. Seshadri, O. Mutlu, M. A. Kozuch, and T. C. Mowry. The Evicted-Address Filter: A unified mechanism to address both cache pollution and thrashing. Technical Report SAFARI 2012-002, CMU, 2012.

[48] A. Seznec. A case for two-way skewed-associative caches. In *ISCA*, 1993.

[49] T. Sherwood, E. Perelman, G. Hamerly, and B. Calder. Automatically characterizing large scale program behavior. In *ASPLOS*, 2002.

[50] A. Snavely and D. M. Tullsen. Symbiotic jobscheduling for a simultaneous multithreaded processor. In *ASPLOS*, 2000.

[51] H. S. Stone, J. Turek, and J. L. Wolf. Optimal partitioning of cache memory. *IEEE TC*, Sep. 1992.

[52] G. E. Suh, S. Devadas, and L. Rudolph. A new memory monitoring scheme for memory-aware scheduling and partitioning. In *HPCA*, 2002.

[53] G. S. Tyson, M. K. Farrens, J. Matthews, and A. R. Pleszkun. A modified approach to data cache management. In *MICRO*, 1995.

[54] Z. Wang, K. S. McKinley, A. L. Rosenberg, and C. C. Weems. Using the compiler to improve cache replacement decisions. In *PACT*, 2002.

[55] C.-J. Wu, A. Jaleel, W. Hasenplaugh, M. Martonosi, S. Steely Jr., and J. Emer. SHIP: Signature-based hit predictor for high performance caching. In *MICRO*, 2011.

[56] Y. Xie and G. H. Loh. PIPP: Promotion/insertion pseudo-partitioning of multi-core shared caches. In *ISCA*, 2009.

[57] D. Zhan, H. Jiang, and S. C. Seth. STEM: Spatiotemporal management of capacity for intra-core last level caches. In *MICRO*, 2010.

A Software Memory Partition Approach for Eliminating Bank-level Interference in Multicore Systems

Lei Liu[1,2], Zehan Cui[§1,2], Mingjie Xing[1], Yungang Bao[1], Mingyu Chen[1], Chengyong Wu[1]
[1]State Key Laboratory of Computer Architecture, Institute of Computing Technology, Chinese Academy of Sciences
[2]Graduate School of Chinese Academy of Sciences
Beijing, China
{liulei2010, cuizehan, baoyg, cmy, cwu}@ict.ac.cn

ABSTRACT

Main memory system is a shared resource in modern multicore machines, resulting in serious interference, which causes performance degradation in terms of throughput slowdown and unfairness. Numerous new memory scheduling algorithms have been proposed to address the interference problem. However, these algorithms usually employ complex scheduling logic and need hardware modification to memory controllers, as a result, industrial venders seem to have some hesitation in adopting them.

This paper presents a practical software approach to effectively eliminate the interference without hardware modification. The key idea is to modify the OS memory management subsystem to adopt a page-coloring based bank-level partition mechanism (BPM), which allocates specific DRAM banks to specific cores (threads). By using BPM, memory controllers can passively schedule memory requests in a core-cluster (or thread-cluster) way.

We implement BPM in Linux 2.6.32.15 kernel and evaluate BPM on 4-core and 8-core real machines by running randomly generated 20 multi-programmed workloads (each contains 4/8 benchmarks) and multi-threaded benchmark. Experimental results show that BPM can improve the overall system throughput by 4.7% on average (up to 8.6%), and reduce the maximum slowdown by 4.5% on average (up to 15.8%). Moreover, BPM also saves 5.2% of the energy consumption of memory system.

Categories and Subject Descriptors

B.3.1 [Semiconductor Memories]: Dynamic memory (DRAM), Static memory (SRAM); C.4 [Computer Systems Organization]: Performance of Systems-Design studies; D.4.1[Operating System]: Process Management-Scheduling; D.4.2[Operating System]: Storage Management-Main Memory;

General Terms

Management, Performance, Design

Keywords

Main Memory, Multicore, Interference, Data Allocation, Memory Scheduling, Bank, Partition

1. INTRODUCTION

On multicore platforms, DRAM memory system shared by all cores usually suffers from the memory contention and interference problem, which can cause serious performance degradation and unfairness of the overall system. Specifically, modern multicore machines consist of many components, such as processing cores, prefetchers and DMA engines, which can generate memory requests with different characteristics and priorities. For example, different cores can generate memory-intensive and non-intensive requests simultaneously; prefetchers' requests are of low priority and DMA engines' requests are sequential. If memory controllers are unable to distinguish these different requests, interference inevitably occurs.

A number of recently proposed scheduling algorithms [18, 19, 25, 26, 27, 30], leveraging the abovementioned different characteristics information, have been demonstrated to be able to effectively reduce the memory contention and interference. For instance, TCM [18], which classifies threads into memory-intensive group and non-intensive group and uses different policies for the two groups, is shown to exhibit both performance and QoS improvements for overall system.

Although some memory scheduling algorithms are claimed to be easily integrated into memory controllers [18, 19, 22, 25, 29, 30], they usually introduce complex hardware logic and require extra storage in memory controllers to store per core (or per thread) information, which can be an obstacle to the scalability of on-chip core number. Therefore, industrial venders seem to have some hesitation in adopting aggressive scheduling algorithms.

In this paper, we propose a software approach to effectively eliminate the memory contention and interference problem without any hardware modification to memory controllers. Our approach is inspired by two observations that 1) DRAM bank-level conflict is a major reason of the memory contention and interference problem and 2) the demanded bank amount for a thread is limited (typically less than 16 banks).

Intuitively, inter-thread bank-level conflicts can be eliminated by exclusively mapping a thread's data to specific banks. We adopt this basic idea and modify the physical pages allocation of OS memory management subsystem. Therefore the physical pages in specific banks can be exclusively mapped to a specific thread (or core). For example, if OS maps thread 1's data to 4 banks (e.g., bank 0~3) and maps thread 2's data to 12 banks (e.g., bank 4~15), memory controllers will deliver all memory requests of thread 2 to only bank 4~15 and will not affect thread 1 whose memory requests are delivered to only bank 0~3. By doing this mapping,

[§] Co-first author

the bank-level inter-thread memory contention and interference are eliminated. We call this approach Bank-level Partition Mechanism (BPM), which is an extension of page-coloring.

Although the OS page-coloring technique is not new, the distinct advantage of BPM is that it exposes both cache and memory bank-level information to OS. We implement BPM in Linux 2.6.32.15 kernel and run multi-programmed/threaded workloads on 4-core and 8-core real machines to evaluate BPM. Experimental results show that BPM can improve the overall system throughput by 4.7% (up to 8.6%), reduce the maximum slowdown by 4.5% (up to 15.8%) on average. Besides, we find that BPM can also save 5.2% of the energy consumption of memory system.

In summary, we make the following contributions:

(1) We observe that the demanded bank amount for a thread is limited, which means that a thread's performance would not be improved even if more banks are assigned to it. Empirical studies show that 8 ~ 16 banks are enough for one thread.

(2) We propose a new practical page-coloring based Bank-level Partition Mechanism (BPM) to effectively eliminate the memory contention and interference problem without any hardware modification to memory controllers.

(3) We implement BPM in Linux 2.6.32.15 kernel for evaluation. Experimental results show that BPM can improve the overall system throughput by 4.7% (up to 8.6%), reduce the maximum slowdown by 4.5% (up to 15.8%) and save 5.2% of the energy consumption of memory system.

(4) We find that the product of the sum of all threads' memory bandwidth and the standard deviation of each thread's row-buffer locality (i.e., Sum(BW)*Stdev(RBL)) is a good indicator for predicting BPM's performance improvement. This indicator probably can be used to evaluate system performance in a shared environment.

The rest of this paper is organized as follow. In Section 2, we introduce the background of DRAM system, and our motivation on this work. In Section 3, we present our BPM in detail. The methodology and metrics are discussed in Section 4. We evaluate BPM in Section 5. In Section 6, we discuss related work and conclude in Section 7.

2. Background and Motivation

2.1 DRAM System

We briefly describe DRAM memory systems and OS memory management mechanism. Our description is based on DDR3 SDRAM systems, and it is generally applicable to some other DRAM types that employ bank/page-mode.

DRAM Organization: Modern memory system consists of multiple independent banks, each of which contains at least one 2-dimensional storage array. Banks can work in a parallel way, hence, memory requests to different banks can be served concurrently [25, 27, 33].

However, since each bank has only one row buffer, only one row is accessible in a bank at any time. Typically, DDR3 chip's row buffer is 1KB~2KB size. Once a request to a bank arrives, if the required row is in the row-buffer, MC[1] can immediately issue a read/write command. Otherwise, a row buffer conflict occurs so that the MC needs to firstly issue a precharge command to write back the content in the row-buffer and then issue an active command to fetch the required row into row buffer before issuing a read/write command. Obviously, row buffer conflict results in longer memory request latency (may more than two times) than the row buffer hit case. Requests from different threads seldom go to same rows, so the row buffer conflict occurs more frequently on multicore platform than single thread computing environment.

Bank-Level Parallelism (BLP) and Bank Sharing: BLP means that multiple banks can serve memory requests concurrently and independently because they are physically independent. BLP can often help make full use of banks and improve memory bandwidth. Hence, memory system usually employs a bank-interleaved address mapping schema to take the advantages of BLP [17, 25, 27, 33, 38], which is meant to share all banks to all cores in a multicore system. Nevertheless, such bank-sharing schema brings interference among threads because one bank may receive memory requests from different cores, which probably have different memory access characteristics. Therefore, the bank conflicts between cores become more and more frequent as the core number increasing.

OS Memory Management: Nowadays, Linux kernel's memory management system uses a buddy system to manage physical memory pages. In the buddy system, the continuous 2^{order} pages (called a block) are organized in the free list with the corresponding order, which ranges from 0 to a specific upper limit. When a program accesses an unmapped virtual address, a page fault occurs and OS kernel takes over the following execution wherein the buddy system identifies the right order free list and allocates one block (2^{order} physical pages) for that program. Usually the first block of a free list is selected but the corresponding physical pages are undetermined [8].

2.2 Multicore-Posed Challenges and Current Solutions

Multicore architecture poses two major challenges on memory system: 1) Interference. Usually a single thread's memory requests have good locality and can exhibit good row buffer hit rate. But the locality is significantly reduced in a multicore machine wherein multiple threads can issue memory requests to the memory system. Row buffer hit rate also decreases sharply, leading to poor overall system performance. For example, Udipi et al. [37] illustrate that the row buffer hit rate decreases significantly from 1 core (over 60%) to 16 cores (35%). 2) Unfairness. Conventional memory controller's scheduling algorithms (e.g., FR-FCFS [15, 33]) favor processing those memory requests with good row buffer locality in order to improve row buffer hit rate. Therefore, memory intensive applications, which have better locality can obtain higher priority than memory non-intensive applications. For instance, Mutlu et al. [27] illustrate that the slowdowns for some memory non-intensive applications can increase by 7.74X for 4-core system and even 11.35X for 8-core system whereas the memory intensive application experiences the slowdowns of only 1.04X and 1.09X respectively.

One major reason of the two problems is that memory controllers are unable to identify one thread's distinct access pattern from other threads' pattern in a multiple-threaded mixed memory requests stream. To address these challenges, numerous new memory scheduling algorithms have been proposed to effectively reduce the memory contention and interference. For instance, the

[1] MC is short for Memory Controller.

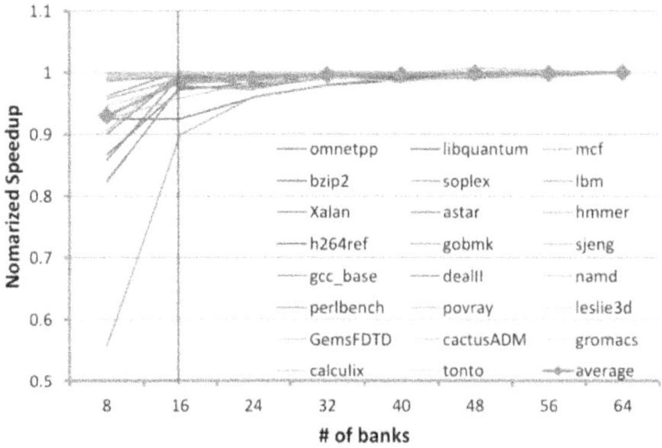

Figure 1. The correlation between application performance and bank amount. The blue line is the "watershed", which indicates all benchmarks can achieve 90% of its maximum performance with only 16 banks.

state-of-the-art scheduling algorithm, Thread Clustering Memory Scheduling (TCM), which classifies threads into memory-intensive group and non-intensive group and uses different policies for the two groups, exhibits both performance and QoS improvements for overall system [18]. Another important reason is DRAM bank-level conflict. As mentioned above, because all banks are shared by all cores, one bank can receive memory requests from different cores with different memory access characteristics. Unfortunately, even the state-of-the-art scheduling algorithms are unable to fully eliminate the interference problem unless banks are not shared among cores. Some partition approaches are proposed in order to eliminate interference at cache-level [23] and channel level [30], but the contention in terms of bank-level still remains. Recent research proposes a bank level partition among multi-programmed workloads [28, 32]. Yet, their work is not deployed in real hardware. Besides, they do not take into account the relationship between cache and bank partition.

Although those solutions are claimed to be easily integrated into memory controllers, they usually introduce complex hardware logic and require extra storage in memory controllers to store per core (or per thread) information [18, 19, 25-27, 30]. For example, TCM [18] requires additional 4 Kbits storage in a memory controller to support 24 cores, additional logic to rank threads and a central meta-controller to gather global information of multiple memory controllers. Besides, because the thread number in a system is usually much more than the core number, there probably exist frequent context-switches, which require a sophisticated hardware thread-behavior monitoring mechanism. Therefore, industrial venders seem to have some hesitation in adopting aggressive scheduling algorithms. Then, a question is raised: ***Can we use a software approach to achieve the similar effect as these hardware solutions do?***

2.3 Our Insights

Intuitively, the inter-thread bank-level conflicts can be fully eliminated by exclusively mapping a thread's data to specific banks. But doing so will reduce the available bank amount for one thread, thus it is important to know how available bank amount influences the thread's performance.

We perform experiments on an Intel i7-860 machine with 64 banks (125MB per bank) to analyze the correlation between bank amount and application's performance (details of experimental setup are in Section 4). For one application, we fix the available banks from 8 banks to 64 banks and see its performance changes. Figure 1 illustrates the results of 23 benchmarks from SPEC2006 [2]. Surprisingly, we find that **the necessary amount of banks one program requires is limited**, for example 16 banks in our experiments. Providing more banks (e.g., all 64 banks) than the necessary amount (e.g., 16 banks) to a program will not yield significant performance improvement.

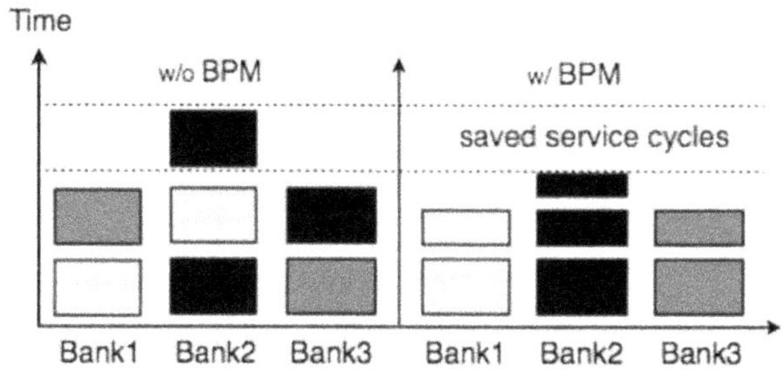

Figure 2. The Comparison between interleaved address mapping and BPM. Different colors mean that the requests are from different threads.

In fact, usually a single core is unable to generate enough concurrent memory requests due to the combination of many factors such as memory dependency, high cache hit rate and limited number of MSHRs. Nevertheless, most modern systems always interleave memory requests across banks in order to take the advantages of bank-level parallelism, thus one program can access all banks, largely exceeding its necessary bank amount. As a result, those programs, which are sharing all banks only suffer from memory interference rather than obtain any performance gain.

This insight inspires us that it is feasible to partition banks into several groups and designate specific bank groups to specific threads so as to eliminate inter-thread bank conflicts. Based on the key insight, we propose a software approach, OS page-coloring based bank-level partition mechanism (BPM), to effectively eliminate the memory contention and interference problem without any hardware modification to memory controllers.

3. Bank-Level Partition Mechanism (BPM)

3.1 Overview of BPM

The key idea of BPM is that OS memory management system uses a page-coloring mechanism to partition banks into several groups and maps each thread (process) to a specific bank group. Consequently, memory controllers can passively schedule memory requests in a thread-cluster (or core-cluster) way, i.e., scheduling one thread's memory requests to pre-specific banks.

3.1.1 Advantages

OS page-coloring technique is a well-known technique for cache partition [23]. But the distinct advantage of BPM allows OS to partition memory space based on the underlying memory bank-level information. Because memory controllers also schedule memory requests at bank-level, the OS partition effect can be indirectly propagated to memory controllers.

Figure 2 illustrates an example. The smaller blocks mean row buffer hits, which result in shorter latencies. Assume there are three threads (different colors) issuing memory requests to DRAM banks. For conventional page allocation without BPM (the left), these requests are delivered to all banks, resulting in many row buffer conflicts. With BPM (the right), one thread's memory

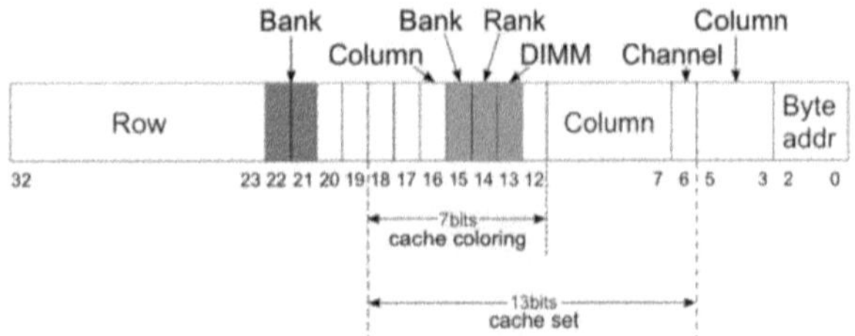

Figure 3. Address Mapping policy of our platform. The Bank bits are divided into two separate parts. One is overlapped with Cache set bits; another is independent.

requests are mapped to its specific bank so that row buffer conflicts are eliminated between threads (processes).

Specifically, BPM brings the following advantages:

(1) BPM is an entirely software approach, so that it is easier to be implemented in modern systems. Since software is more flexible than hardware, more partition policies can be explored to achieve better performance.

(2) It is easier for OS to monitor threads' behavior than hardware, which requires additional storage and logic. Contemporary processors provide powerful performance counters to monitor system behavior, and the state-of-the-art tools such as LiMit [12] are already able to precisely monitor per-thread behavior (e.g., cache miss rate, memory bandwidth etc.) with negligible overhead. BPM can easily leverage this kind of information for exploring various partition policies.

(3) Moreover, BPM can facilitate improving other OS functionalities. For example, OS's process management module can utilize BPM partition information to guide process scheduling. BPM can also be implemented in Virtual Machine Monitor (VMM) to partition memory space for virtual machines in order to improve VM isolation effect.

3.1.2 Principle

A physical address contains several common bits, which denote both OS page index and bank index, so these bits are referred to as ***bank color bits***. For instance, if a physical address has 4 bank color bits, then there are 2^4=16 bank colors. ***Partition*** means that BPM exclusively assigns banks with the same color to a thread such that those banks can be accessed only by the specific thread. Note that a thread can possess multiple bank colors. Here is a concrete example. Our experimental machine has 4GB/8GB DDR3 main memory with 32/64 banks. Usually, the OS page size is 4KB, so the low 12 bits are page offset and the OS physical page index bits are bit 12~32. Figure 3 illustrates the 5 bank color bits of our platform, i.e., bit 13~15 and bit 21~22. Therefore, there are 32 colors, and each color represents 1 bank for 4GB memory or 2 banks for 8GB memory.

Each OS page index (bit 12~32) also contains 5 bank color bits which designate one color, thus each physical page belongs to one bank color. When a thread applies for one page, BPM first checks which bank colors are possessed by the thread, then picks a bank color, and finally allocates a physical page with the color for the thread.

3.2 Cache Partition

Figure 3 illustrates that bit 13~15 are used for both bank coloring and cache coloring. Therefore, the last level cache with physical index is also partitioned into 2^3 = 8 groups. As a result, we could

Algorithm1: Discover Bank Bits
Input: The address bits; **Output:** BANK{}, which contains all bank bits.

```
BEGIN
/* STEP 1: Detect row address bits */
/*Based on the idea that row miss causes larger latency*/
1. FOR each bit x IN address bits
2. DO
3.     Generate 2 memory requests, one's x bit is 0, and
       another's x bit is 1;
4.     Access the two addresses (uncached) in turn and record the
       latency (repeat at least 10000000 times);
5. END FOR
6. The latency will be easily clustered into two groups;
7. Put the group with higher latency into Row{} // row miss
8. The left parts are put into Remain{} // row hit
9. Call Step 2

/*STEP 2: Detect column address bits*/
/*Based on the idea that bank parallelism outperforms row miss */
1. FOR each bit y IN Remain{}
2. DO
3.     Choose an x from Row{};
4.     Generate 2 requests, one's x and y bit are both 0, and
       another x and y bit are both 1;
5.     Access the two address (uncached) in turn and record
       the latency (repeat at least 10000000 times);
6. END FOR
7. The latency will be easily clustered into two groups;
8. Put the group with higher latency into Column{} //row miss
9. The left parts are put into Remain{} //mapped to different banks
10. IF there is no XOR policy THEN
11.    Put Remain{} into BANK{}
12.    Output BANK{}
13. ELSE
14.    Call STEP 3
15. ENDIF

/*STEP 3: Detect XOR Policy (Optional)*/
/*Many MCs employ XOR to improve performance*/
1. FOR each pair <u,v>, u,v IN Remain{}
2. DO
3.     Generate 2 memory requests, one's u and v bit are both 0, and
       another's u and v bit are both 1; the other bits are identical;
4.     Access the two address (uncached) in turn and record the latency
       (repeat at least 10000000 times);
5. END FOR
6. The latency will be easily clustered into one or two groups;
7. IF there is only one groups THEN
8.     XOR is not employed
9. ELSE
10.    Put the group of <u,v> pairs with higher latency into BANK{},
       Delete all u, v in that group from Remain{} //row miss
11. END IF
12. Put Remain{} into BANK{}
13. Output BANK{}
END
```

gain the benefits from both cache partition and bank partition. On the other hand, since there are two extra bits (21~22) for bank coloring, BLP can also be orthogonal to cache partition.

3.3 Discover bank bits by software method

In order to employ BPM, we need to obtain the memory address mapping information so as to extract the bank bits. We can look up address mapping in vendors' manuals. However, address mapping in a memory controller is not fixed and can be configured by BIOS at boot time. A memory controller always supports various address mapping policies. Some hardware tools can be used (such as HMTT [5]) to figure out address mapping policy, but it is impossible to deploy this approach for massive normal machines. In order to solve this problem, we propose a practical software method (**Algorithm1**) to discover the address mapping policy as well as bank bits on any machines.

The approach is based on two observations that: 1) the latency of row buffer misses is much longer than the latency of row buffer hits (refer to STEP 1); 2) concurrent accesses to two different banks (BLP) still result in lower latency than row buffer conflict within a bank (refer to STEP 2). We verify our algorithm by a hybrid memory trace tool (HMTT) [5], which is able to monitor memory signals over memory buses. The verification results show that our algorithm works well on various platforms. Thus, this algorithm can be embedded into OS boot phase to collect the address mapping information, which can be used for BPM setup.

3.4 Implementation

We implement BPM in Linux kernel 2.6.32.15. The kernel uses a buddy system to manage the free physical pages, which are organized as different orders (0~11) of free lists (refer to Section 2.1). We modify the original free list organization into a hierarchy way: for each order of free page list, we re-organize the free pages to form 32 colored free lists according to the 5 bank bits. Each process has its own colors (i.e., a group of banks). When a page fault occurs, the OS kernel will search a colored free list and allocate a page for the process. This is transparent to applications so that programmers do not need to modify programs.

For multi-programmed workloads, bank colors are assigned to each program. For multi-threaded workloads, we enhance OS kernel with new APIs for programmers to perceive the underlying bank colors so that programmers can map threads' data into different colors on their demand.

The overhead of the searching color operation is negligible. Experimental results show that the average kernel time accounts for only 0.3% for all workloads.

4. Methodology and Metrics

4.1 Hardware and software platform

We conduct our experiments on a machine, which has 4 cores, 2.8GHz Intel Core i7-860 processor with a shared 8MB 16-way associative last level cache and 8GB DDR3 main memory. The processor incorporates Hyper-Threading technology, so we can run 8 threads concurrently.

We use CentOS Linux 5.4 with kernel 2.6.32.15. The memory system is 8GB with 64 banks (each bank is 125MB). There are 5 bank bits, so the memory is divided into 32 colors, and each color represents 2 banks bundled together across dual-channel. In our experiments, colors are statically assigned to processes/threads at their starting time. Modern multi-thread servers often have enough memory for their running threads [11]. Therefore, we also disable OS swap. Moreover, for most experimental workloads, the memory capacity of 0.5~1GB (4~8 banks) is enough.

We use Perfmon2 [1] and its corresponding libpfm library to access the performance counters to gather architectural information, such as memory bandwidth and last level cache miss rate. For memory system, because DIMMs are directly plugged into motherboard and it is difficult to measure memory power consumption, we adopt an in-house hardware tool [10], which consists of a wrapper card for each DIMM. The wrapper card is plugged into motherboard's DIMM slot and memory power consumption can be measured precisely via the sensors embedded into the wrapper card. It should be noted that the wrapper card does not affect the memory access at all.

4.2 Benchmarks

We use the SPEC CPU2006 benchmarks for evaluation. We compile each benchmark using gcc 4.1.2 with -O3 optimizations. From these benchmarks, we randomly generate multi-programmed workloads each of which contains 4/8 applications (due to space limitation, we omit a table depicting all workloads' characteristics). We employ a multi-threaded benchmark streamcluster from PARSEC 2.1 [7]. We use the notion of "Miss Per Kilo-Instruction (MPKI) > 1" to define memory-intensive applications. We use ref input size for the SPEC benchmarks and the native for PARSEC.

In our experiments, for each benchmark in 4-programmed workloads, each program has 8 colors (i.e., 16 banks/2GB); for 8-programmed workloads, each program has 4 colors (i.e., 8 banks/1GB).

4.3 Metrics

We use ***Weighted Speedup*** [18] (WS) to measure system throughput and use ***Maximum Slowdown*** (MS) [18] for fairness. We also report ***Improvement*** compared with the normal environment without BPM.

$$\text{Weighted Speedup(WS)} = \sum \frac{RUNTIME_{ALONE}}{RUNTIME_{SHARED}}$$

$$\text{Maximum Slowdown(MS)} = Max\left\{\frac{RUNTIME_{SHARED}}{RUNTIME_{ALONE}}\right\}$$

$$\text{Improvement\_ws} = \frac{WS_{BPM} - WS_{No-BPM}}{WS_{No-BPM}}$$

$$\text{Improvement\_fairness} = \frac{MS_{No-BPM} - MS_{BPM}}{MS_{No-BPM}}$$

5. Results

5.1 Overall system performance

In this experiment, we use static uniform partition policy. Figure 4 combines the improvement of both the fairness and system throughput across all 20 workloads. According to Figure 4, BPM can improve weighted speedup by 4.7% on average, and reduce the maximum slowdown (unfairness) by 4.5% on average.

The improvement of Weighted Speedup is steady for all workloads and no workload's performance degrades. We firstly study these 4-programmed workloads (workload 11~20 in Figure 4). BPM can achieve a maximum weighted speedup by up to 5.9% for workload_11, which consists of 462.libquantum (MPKI = 50, RBL[2] = 99.22%), 403.gcc (MPKI = 0.4), 447.dealII (MPKI = 0.5), 444.namd (MPKI = 0.3). For the four benchmarks in workload_11, 462.libquantum is obviously a memory intensive application, specifically a stream-like program (RBL = 99.22%), while the other three are memory non-intensive. In normal configuration without BPM, where memory accesses are interleaved across banks, 462.libquantum causes substantial row buffer conflicts due to its stream characteristics, affecting the other three applications'

[2] RBL (Row Buffer Locality) is equivalent to row buffer hit rate.

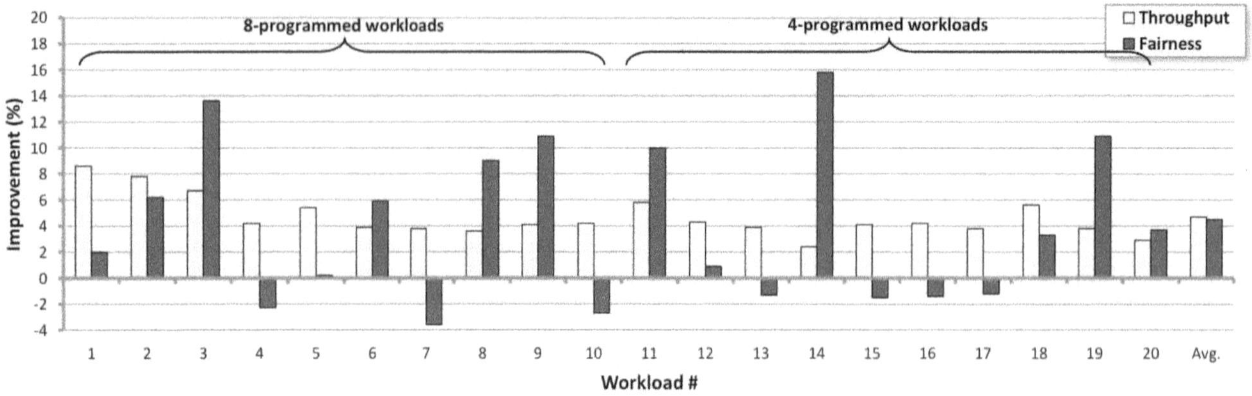

Figure 4: The Overall system performance of BPM across 20 workloads. The x-axis denotes the workload number, and the y-axis shows both the improvement of fairness and system throughput. Baseline is the conventional Linux kernel without BPM.

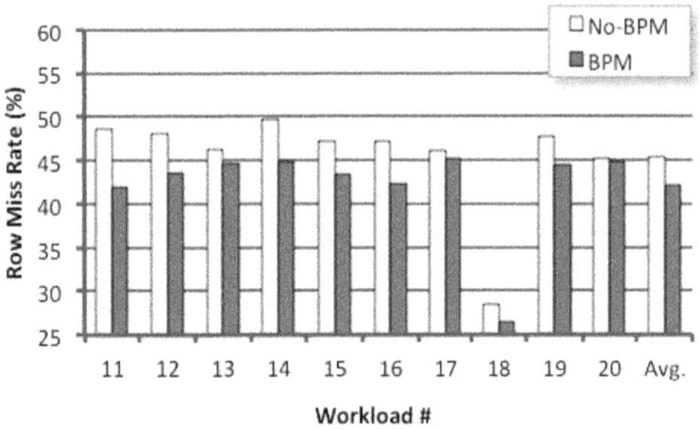

Figure 5. Row buffer miss rate across 10 workloads

row buffer hit rate. Figure 5 shows the row buffer miss rate is almost 50% for workload_11. However, when using BPM, each application has 8 dedicated bank-colors (16 banks) and their memory requests can only be delivered to those banks. According to Figure 1, the performance for the four benchmarks decrease very slightly from 64 banks to 16 banks (92% for 462.libquantum and 99% for others). Since the memory interference is fully eliminated (the overall row buffer miss rate reduces by about 10% in Figure 5), the overall system performance is improved. In 8-programmed workloads, we find the workload_1 can achieve the maximum improvement by 8.6%. Wokload_1 also includes 462.libquantum, and it is a heavy memory-intensive workload (all programs' MPKI > 2). The more intensive the threads are, the more interference on banks there would be. Thus, BPM would exhibit better improvements by totally eliminating the bank-level interference in such an environment.

For the Fairness metric, workload_11 exhibits 10% improvement and workload_14 improves by even 15.8%. We find that workload_14 comprises of 462.libquantum, 456.hmmer (MPKI = 5.7), 403.gcc, 444.namd. The only difference between workload_11 and workload_14 is replacing 447.dealII (MPKI = 0.5) with 456.hmmer. Obviously, when workload_14 runs on normal environment, there will be more memory interference because 456.hmmer issues more memory requests than 447.dealII. As mentioned before, current memory controllers favor processing those memory requests that have good row buffer locality, thus memory intensive applications, which are more likely to have good locality, can obtain higher priority than

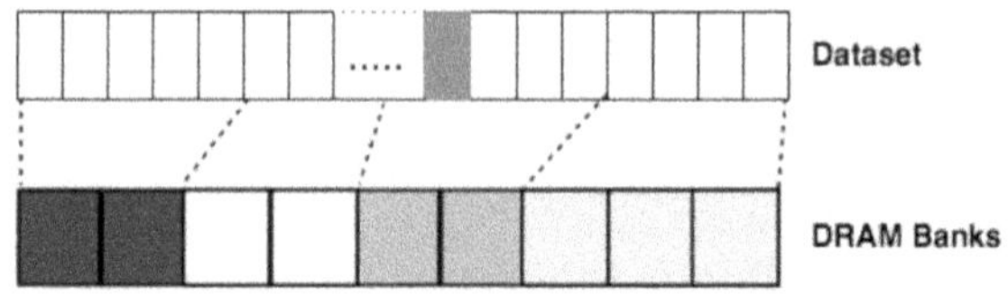

Figure 6: Thread Level Coloring. The above array is mapped to different bank colors. The colored rectangle in dataset represents shared data.

memory non-intensive applications. The more memory intensive applications are there, the less opportunities do non-intensive applications get their memory requests been served. Therefore, the unfairness problems always occur in modern multicore systems. Obviously, BPM can effectively eliminate this unfairness.

It should be noted that there are several workloads exhibiting worse fairness, i.e., workload_13, workload_15, workload_16 and workload_17. We find that those workloads have a common benchmark 429.mcf (MPKI = 99.8), which is an extreme memory intensive application. But the interesting thing is that when reducing bank amount from 64 to 16, unlike 462.libquantum whose performance decreases by 8%, the performance of 429.mcf almost does not decrease (only 2%). Therefore, BPM can improve 429.mcf's performance even more than other non-intensive applications, leading to a slight unfairness. For 8-programmed workloads, the average improvement of system throughput is 5.3% (up to 8.6%), which are slightly better than 4-programmed workloads (4.1%). This implies that BPM is able to exhibit better performance improvements in a worse interference scenario.

5.2 Multi-threaded workload

In practical, many servers are used to run multi-threaded workloads. We use streamcluster of PARSEC [7] to evaluate BPM. Its coloring scheme is nearly the same as that of multi-programmed workloads. We use Native dataset (200000 *5 points) as input in our experiment. For a stream of these input points, they are divided into N chunks according to core number, the first N-1 chunks contains the same amount of points, while the N*th* chunk collects the rest points. Because streamcluster itself is a typical data parallelism computing multi-threaded program, we could partition the dataset in a straightforward way (Figure 6). We get performance gains by 1.7% and 2.3% on 4/8-thread separately. The improvement is less than that of multi-programmed workloads because there is too much shared data among threads

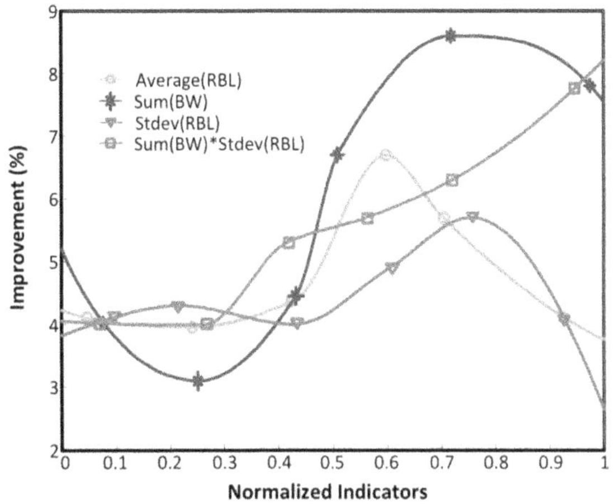

Figure 7. The correlation of BPM improvements and four indicators.

(the colored rectangle in dataset in Figure 6). In our straightforward partition, the shared data belongs to blue banks. When other threads access the shared data, inter-thread bank conflicts occur. There are two ways to improve multi-threaded applications: 1) designing a better partition policy and 2) leveraging a dynamic color adjustment mechanism. We will do further study on these issues in the future work.

5.3 What affects the BPM?

In this subsection, we study the correlation between workloads' characteristics and performance improvements. We investigate four indicators derived from memory bandwidth (BW) and row buffer locality (RBL) of individual benchmarks, which are collected by perfmon [1] when the benchmarks are running alone. Given a workload, we calculate the following four indicators: 1) The indicator Average(RBL) is the weighted average of the 4/8 programs' RBL, where BW is the weight. This indicates the overall row buffer locality of the workload. 2) The indicator Sum(BW) is the sum of the 4/8 programs' BW. This indicates the intensity of the workload. 3) The indicator Stdev(RBL) is the weighted standard deviation of the 4/8 programs' RBL. This indicates the difference of locality among programs. 4) Sum(BW)*Stdev(RBL) is the combination of the two indicator stated before.

Figure 7 illustrates four curves, which represent the correlation between the improvements of BPM and the four indicators respectively. To fit them into one figure, we normalized the value of all the four indicators into range (0, 1). Besides, there are 6 points on each curve; each point represents one workload or the average of multi workloads, which have close indicator values. According to the figure, none of the indicators can match the improvements of BPM perfectly except ***Sum(BW)*Stdev(RBL)*** – as the indicator increases, the improvements of BPM also increase steadily. Actually, we can use ***Sum(BW)*Stdev(RBL)*** to indicate the interference degree of a multi-programmed workload. The more interference is there, the more improvement can be achieved by BPM.

5.4 Page-Policy and Power

There are two page policies in memory system, open-page policy and close-page policy. Usually, open-page policy has better performance than close-page policy. But recent studies show that the row-buffer locality in multicore systems is sharply decreased to a lower level [35, 37]. Therefore, some server machines have to compromise to adopt close-page policy. Our experiments show that BPM can revive open-page policy in multicore systems. In our experiments, we change the page policies of the experimental machine and measure the system throughput improvement. Figure 8 shows that open-page with BPM outperforms close-page by 6.3% in terms of weighted speedup. This implies that if we partition banks appropriately, open-page policy can still be employed in heavily threads computing environment.

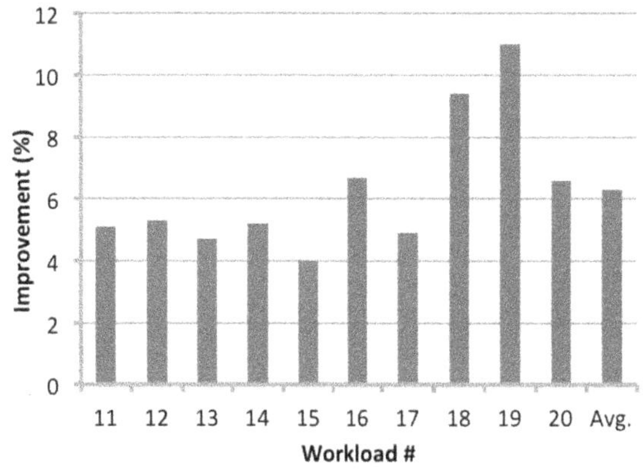

Figure 8. Improvement of weighted speedup of Open-Page policy with BPM over Close-Page policy.

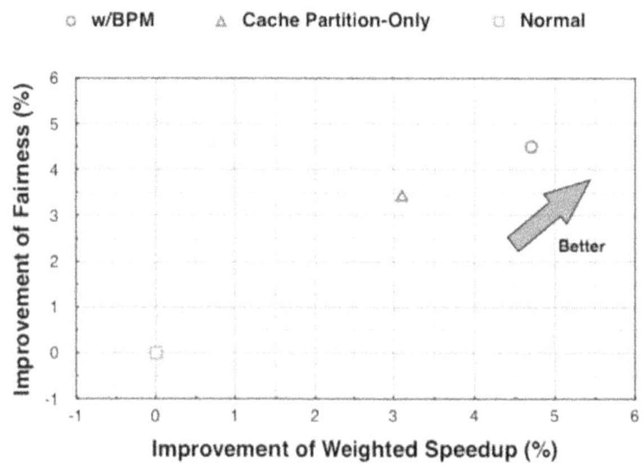

Figure 9. BPM vs. Cache-Partition-Only across 20 workloads on average (Toward right top is better)

The active operation is the most power-consuming operation in the DRAM system [3, 37], because it has to move an entire row from array to a row buffer. BPM can lower the power consumption of DRAM because of the reduced row buffer conflict miss rate (as illustrated in Figure 5). As mentioned in 4.1, we measure the power consumption by real hardware, so we can get the real value of power savings on memory system. Our experimental results show that BPM with open-page policy can save up to 5.2% of memory power consumption, better than the configurations without BPM.

5.5 Comparison between Bank and Cache

As mentioned in Section 3.2, there are 3 common bits for both bank partition and cache partition and 2 extra bits for bank-partition only. This mechanism allows us to evaluate the effect of

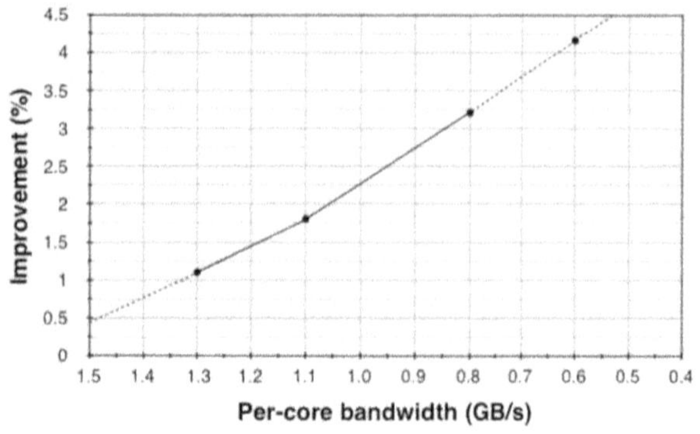

Figure 10. The correlation of BPM improvements and per-core Bandwidth

different partition schemes on real machines. Figure 9 illustrates the comparison between cache-partition-only and BPM, which embraces cache partition. When only adopting cache partition with 8 colors (3 bits), both system throughput and fairness are improved slightly (3.1% and 3.4%). Furthermore, when the two extra bits are used to form 32 bank colors (still 8 cache colors), the performance is further improved (4.7% and 4.5%), which proves that BPM is orthogonal to cache partition.

5.6 The Correlation between BPM improvements and Per-core bandwidth

Off-chip memory bandwidth is limited by the pin count of micro-processor chip and thereby is considered as the major bottleneck of the scalability of on-chip core number [6, 34]. Since the core number is still increasing, memory bandwidth per core is decreasing, which causes more and more serious interference. In order to evaluate the influence of different per-core bandwidth on our BPM approach, we emulate different bandwidth scenarios by varying memory frequency from 1333 to 800 MHz so that the per-core bandwidth decreases form 1.3GB/s to 0.8GB/s.

Figure 10 illustrates that the correlation of performance improvements and per-core bandwidth is negative: BPM performs better when per-core bandwidth is less. In fact, our previous experiments also provide evidences from another perspective. For example, when we enable Hyper-Threading on the experimental machine, the per-thread memory bandwidth halves, but the overall system throughput still improve from 4.1% (4-programmed) to 5.3% (8-programmed). Therefore, BPM is a promising approach for future many-core architecture that arguably has even less per-core bandwidth.

6. Related work

There are a number of related studies.

Thread Scheduling. Scheduling algorithms DI and DIO proposed in [39] aimed to distribute threads to get an even distribution of miss rate among multiple caches, which avoid severe contention on cache, memory controller, memory bus and prefetching hardware. Similar mechanisms are also proposed in [11, 21]. This method can alleviate contention, but cannot eliminate the bank interference among threads.

Cache Partition. Either hardware based cache partition [13, 14, 31, 36] or software page coloring based cache partition [4, 8, 23, 24] are employed to partition shared cache to concurrent running threads, which can eliminate the interference between multi-threads and hence reduce conflict at cache level. However, other resources such as MC, memory bus, and DRAM are also shared and confronted with contention and interference.

Channel Partition. Data of different threads are mapped into different channels according to their memory access behavior in [30], which can eliminate the interference between threads at channel level. However, channel partition cannot be applied to system with cache line interleaving policy between channels [30], which limit its applicable scope. Furthermore, there are usually more threads than channels in a system, so some threads have to be assigned to the same channel, which still interference with each other. Besides, channel partition actually partitions the bandwidth of memory system into several portions. Since the total number of portions is limited by channel amount, which is usually small, it is challenging to seek a balance among channels so as to ensure no bandwidth wasted.

Thread-based Memory Scheduling. Memory controllers are designed to distinguish the memory access behavior at thread-level in [16, 18, 19, 25, 27], so that scheduling modules can adjust their scheduling policy at the running time. TCM [18], which dynamically groups threads into two clusters (memory intensive and non-intensive), and assign different scheduling policy to different group, is the best scheduling policy, which aim to address fairness and throughput at the same time. Yet, this method needs modification to memory controller, and the overhead at running time cannot be neglected.

Row buffer optimization. In [35], frequently accessed data of different rows are dynamically migrated into row buffer, which can improve the row buffer usage and performance; power consumption is also lowered by reducing the operations of precharge and active. In [20], the content in row-buffer will be precharged after 4 times access, which target at the reduction of row-buffer conflicts.

Comparison with BPM. To the best of our knowledge, this is the first work that implements and evaluates bank level partition in reality. Our work is quite different from the previous work [28, 32]. First, we do not need to modify hardware, and our mechanism can be deployed on any Linux platforms. Second, our page-coloring mechanism takes both cache and bank bits information into account, which can eliminate both cache-level and bank-level conflicts, and ensure the fairness between threads.

7. Conclusion

We present Bank-level Partition Mechanism (BPM), a new approach to eliminate the interference between threads and improve the overall system performance. BPM achieves this goal by assign different group of banks to different threads to eliminate inter-thread bank-level interference. This leads to the reduction of row buffer misses as well as the energy consumption of memory system. To the best of our knowledge, BPM is the first bank level partition that is implemented on real machines and can be used in real multicore computing environment.

Our experimental evaluations show that BPM can improve system throughput and reduce unfairness due to the elimination of interference between threads. Our analysis also shows that BPM can be an effective mechanism on future manycore platforms on which per-core bandwidth is decreasing.

8. Acknowledgments

We would like to thank the anonymous reviews for their valuable feedback. Lei Liu, Mingjie Xing and Chengyong Wu are supported by the National Natural Science Foundation of China under grants No. 60873057, 60921002 and 61033009; the National High Technology Research and Development Program of China (863 Program) under grants No. 2012AA010902; the National Basic Research Program of China (973 Program) under grant No. 2011CB302504; and the National Science and Technology Major Project of China under grants No. 2009ZX01036-001-002 and 2011ZX01028-001-002. Zehan Cui, Yungang Bao and Mingyu Chen are supported by the National Natural Science Foundation of China under grants No. 60903046, 60921002, 60925009, 61003062. the National Basic Research Program of China (973 Program) under grants No.2011CB302502.

9. References

[1] Hewlett-Packed Development Company. Perfmon project. http: //www.hpl.hp.com/research/linux/ perfmon.

[2] Standard Performance Evaluation Corporation. http://www.spec.org/cpu2006/CINT2006/.

[3] N. Aggarwal et al. Power Efficient DRAM Speculation. In HPCA-14, 2008.

[4] R. Azimi, D. K. Tam, L. Soares, and M. Stumm. Enhancing Operating System Support for Multicore Processors by Using Hardware Performance Monitoring. In ACM SIGOPS Operating Systems Review 43(2): 56-65, 2009.

[5] Y. Bao et al. HMTT: A Platform Independent Full-System Memory Trace Monitoring System. In SIGMETRICS-08, 2008

[6] S. Beamer et al. Re-Architecting DRAM Memory Systems with Monolithically Integrated Silicon Photonics. In ISCA-37, 2010.

[7] C. Bienia, S. Kumar, J. P. Singh, and K. Li. The PARSEC benchmark suite: Characterization and architectural implications. Technical Report TR-811-08, Princeton Univ., Jan. 2008.

[8] S. Cho, and L. Jin. Managing Distributed, Shared L2 Caches through OS-Level page Allocation. In MICRO-39, 2006.

[9] J. Carter, IBM Power Aware Systems. Personal Correspondence, 2011.

[10] Z.Cui, Y.Zhu, Y.Bao and M.Chen. A Fine-grained Component-level power measurement method. In PMP,2011.

[11] G. Dhiman, G. Marchetti, and T. Rosing. vGreen: a System for Energy Efficient Computing in Virtualized Environments. In Proceedings of International Symposium on Low Power Electronics and Design. In ISLPED-2009.

[12] J. Demme et al, Rapid Identification of Architectural Bottlenecks via Precise Event Counting. In ISCA, 2011

[13] G. E. Suh, S. Devadas, and L. Rudolph. A New Memory Monitoring Scheme for Memory-Aware Scheduling and Partitioning. In HPCA-8, 2002.

[14] G. E. Suh, L. Rudolph, and S. Devadas. Dynamic partitioning of shared cache memory. In Journal of Supercomputing, 28(1), 2004.

[15] I. Hur and C. Lin. Memory scheduling for modern microprocessors. ACM Transactions on Computer Systems, 25(4), December 2007.

[16] R. Iyer et al, QoS policy and architecture for cache/memory in CMP platforms. In SIGMETRICS-07, 2007.

[17] C. J. Lee et al. Improving memory bank-level parallelism in the presence of prefetching. In MICRO-42, 2009.

[18] Y. Kim, M. Papamicheal and O. Mutlu. Thread Cluster Memory Scheduling: Exploiting Differences in Memory Access Behavior. In MICRO-43, 2010.

[19] Y. Kim et al. ATLAS: A scalable and high-performance scheduling algorithm for multiple memory controllers. In HPCA-16, 2010.

[20] D. Kaseridis, J. Stuecheli, and L. K. John. Minimalist Open-page: A DRAM Page-mode Scheduling Policy for the many-core Era. In MICRO-44, 2011.

[21] R. Knauerhase, P. Brett, B. Hohlt, T. Li, and S. Hahn. Using OS Observations to Improve Performance in Multicore Systems. In Micro-41, 2008.

[22] G. L. Yuan et al. Complexity effective memory access scheduling for many-core accelerator architectures. In MICRO-42, 2009.

[23] J. Lin, Q. Lu, X. Ding, Z. Zhang, X. Zhang, and P. Sadayappan. Gaining Insights into Multicore Cache Partitioning: Bridging the Gap between Simulation and Real Systems. In HPCA-14, 2008.

[24] J. Liedtke, H. Haertig, and M. Hohmuth. OS-Controlled Cache Predictability for Real-Time Systems. In RTAS-3, 1997.

[25] O. Mutlu and T. Moscibroda. Parallelism-aware batch scheduling: Enhancing both performance and fairness of shared DRAM systems. In ISCA-35, 2008.

[26] T. Moscibroda and O. Mutlu. Memory performance attacks: Denial of memory service in multi-core systems. In USENIX Security, 2007.

[27] O. Mutlu and T. Moscibroda. Stall-time fair memory access scheduling for chip multiprocessors. In MICRO-40, 2007.

[28] W. Mi, X. Feng, J. Xue, and Y. Jia. Software-hardware cooperative DRAM bank partitioning for chip multiprocessors. In Proc. the 2010 IFIP Int'l Conf. Network and Parallel Computing (NPC), Sep. 2010.

[29] C. Natarajan, B. Christenson, and F. Briggs. A Study of Performance Impact of Memory Controller Features in Multi-Processor Environment. In Proceedings of WMPI, 2004.

[30] S. Prashanth et al. Reducing Memory Interference in Multicore Systems via Application-Aware Memory Channel Partitioning. In Micro-44, 2011.

[31] M. K. Qureshi, and Y. N. Patt. Utility-based cache partitioning: A low-overhead, high-performance, runtime mechanism to partition shared caches. In MICRO-39, 2006.

[32] M. K. Jeong, D. H. Yoon et al. Balancing DRAM Locality and Parallelism in Shared Memory CMP Systems. In HPCA-18, 2012.

[33] S. Rixner, W. J. Dally, U. J. Kapasi, P. R. Mattson, and J. D. Owens. Memory access scheduling. In ISCA-27, 2000.

[34] B. Rogers et al. Scaling the Bandwidth Wall: Challenges in and Avenues for CMP Scaling. In ISCA-42, 2009.

[35] K. Sudan, N. Chatterjee, D. Nellans, M. Awasthi, R. Balasubramonian, and A. Davis. Micro-Pages: Increasing DRAM Efficiency with Locality-Aware. In ASPLOS-2010.

[36] H. S. Stone, J. Turek, and J. L. Wolf. Optimal Partitioning of Cache Memory. In IEEE Transactions on Computers, 41(9), 1992.

[37] A. Udipi et al. Rethinking DRAM design and organization for energy-constrained multi-cores. ISCA, June 2010.

[38] Z. Zhang, Z. Zhu, and X. Zhang. A permutation-based page interleaving scheme to reduce row-buffer conflicts and exploit data locality. In MICRO-33, 2000.

[39] S. Zhuravlev, S. Blagodurov, and A. Fedorova. Addressing shared resource contention in multicore processors via scheduling. In ASPLOS-XV, 2010.

Base-Delta-Immediate Compression: Practical Data Compression for On-Chip Caches

Gennady Pekhimenko† gpekhime@cs.cmu.edu
Vivek Seshadri† vseshadr@cs.cmu.edu
Onur Mutlu† onur@cmu.edu
Michael A. Kozuch* michael.a.kozuch@intel.com
Phillip B. Gibbons* phillip.b.gibbons@intel.com
Todd C. Mowry† tcm@cs.cmu.edu
†Carnegie Mellon University *Intel Labs Pittsburgh

ABSTRACT

Cache compression is a promising technique to increase on-chip cache capacity and to decrease on-chip and off-chip bandwidth usage. Unfortunately, directly applying well-known compression algorithms (usually implemented in software) leads to high hardware complexity and unacceptable decompression/compression latencies, which in turn can negatively affect performance. Hence, there is a need for a simple yet efficient compression technique that can effectively compress common in-cache data patterns, and has minimal effect on cache access latency.

In this paper, we introduce a new compression algorithm called **Base-Delta-Immediate (BΔI)** compression, a practical technique for compressing data in on-chip caches. The key idea is that, for many cache lines, the values within the cache line have a low dynamic range – i.e., the differences between values stored within the cache line are small. As a result, a cache line can be represented using a base value and an array of differences whose combined size is much smaller than the original cache line (we call this the **base+delta** encoding). Moreover, many cache lines intersperse such base+delta values with small values – our BΔI technique efficiently incorporates such **immediate** values into its encoding.

Compared to prior cache compression approaches, our studies show that BΔI strikes a sweet-spot in the tradeoff between compression ratio, decompression/compression latencies, and hardware complexity. Our results show that BΔI compression improves performance for both single-core (8.1% improvement) and multi-core workloads (9.5% / 11.2% improvement for two/four cores). For many applications, BΔI provides the performance benefit of doubling the cache size of the baseline system, effectively increasing average cache capacity by 1.53X.

Categories and Subject Descriptors: B.3.2 [**Design Styles**]: Cache Memories; E.4 [**Coding and Information Theory**]: Data compaction and compression

General Terms:
Performance, Experimentation, Measurement, Design.

Keywords: Cache compression, Caching, Memory.

1. INTRODUCTION

To mitigate the latency and bandwidth limitations of accessing main memory, modern microprocessors contain multi-level on-chip cache hierarchies. While caches have a number of design parameters and there is a large body of work on using cache hierarchies more effectively (e.g., [11, 17, 20, 21]), one key property of a cache that has a major impact on performance, die area, and power consumption is its *capacity*. The decision of how large to make a given cache involves tradeoffs: while larger caches often result in fewer cache misses, this potential benefit comes at the cost of a longer access latency and increased area and power consumption.

As we look toward the future with an increasing number of on-chip cores, the issue of providing sufficient capacity in shared L2 and L3 caches becomes increasingly challenging. Simply scaling cache capacities linearly with the number of cores may be a waste of both chip area and power. On the other hand, reducing the L2 and L3 cache sizes may result in excessive off-chip cache misses, which are especially costly in terms of latency and precious off-chip bandwidth.

One way to potentially achieve the performance benefits of larger cache capacity without suffering all disadvantages is to exploit *data compression* [2, 10, 12, 13, 33, 34]. Data compression has been successfully adopted in a number of different contexts in modern computer systems [14, 35] as a way to conserve storage capacity and/or data bandwidth (e.g., downloading compressed files over the Internet [24] or compressing main memory [1]). However, it has not been adopted by modern commodity microprocessors as a way to increase effective cache capacity. Why not?

The ideal cache compression technique would be *fast*, *simple*, and *effective* in saving storage space. Clearly, the resulting compression ratio should be large enough to provide a significant upside, and the hardware complexity of implementing the scheme should be low enough that its area and power overheads do not offset its benefits. Perhaps the biggest stumbling block to the adoption of cache compression in commercial microprocessors, however, is *decompression latency*. Unlike cache *compression*, which takes place in the background upon a cache fill (after the critical word is supplied), cache *decompression* is on the critical path of a *cache hit*, where minimizing latency is extremely important for performance. In fact, because L1 cache hit times are of utmost importance, we only consider compression of the L2 caches and beyond in this study (even though our algorithm could be applied to any cache).

Because the three goals of having *fast*, *simple*, and *effective* cache compression are at odds with each other (e.g., a very simple scheme may yield too small a compression ratio, or a scheme with a very high compression ratio may be too slow, etc.), the challenge is to find the right balance between these goals. Although several cache compression techniques have been proposed in the past [2, 6, 8, 12, 33], they suffer from either a small compression ratio [8, 33], high hardware complexity [12], or large decompression latency [2, 6, 12, 33]. To achieve significant compression ratios while minimizing hardware complexity and decompression latency, we propose a new cache compression technique called **Base-Delta-Immediate (BΔI)** compression.

1.1 Our Approach: BΔI Compression

The key observation behind **Base-Delta-Immediate (BΔI)** compression is that, for many cache lines, the data values stored within the line have a *low dynamic range*: i.e., the relative difference between values is small. In such cases, the cache line can be represented in a compact form using a common *base* value plus an array of relative differences ("*deltas*"), whose combined size is much smaller than the original cache line. (Hence the *"base"* and *"delta"* portions of our scheme's name).

We refer to the case with a single arbitrary base as *Base+Delta* (B+Δ) compression, and this is at the heart of all of our designs. To increase the likelihood of being able to compress a cache line, however, it is also possible to have *multiple bases*. In fact, our results show that for the workloads we studied, the best option is to have *two bases*, where one base is always *zero*. (The deltas relative to zero can be thought of as small *immediate* values, which explains the last word in the name of our BΔI compression scheme.) Using these two base values (zero and something else), our scheme can efficiently compress cache lines containing a mixture of two separate dynamic ranges: one centered around an arbitrary value chosen from the actual contents of the cache line (e.g., pointer values), and one close to zero (e.g., small integer values). Such mixtures from two dynamic ranges are commonly found (e.g., in pointer-linked data structures), as we will discuss later.

As demonstrated later in this paper, BΔI compression offers the following advantages: (i) a *high compression ratio* since it can exploit a number of frequently-observed patterns in cache data (as shown using examples from real applications and validated in our experiments); (ii) *low decompression latency* since decompressing a cache line requires only a simple masked vector addition; and (iii) *relatively modest hardware overhead and implementation complexity*, since both the compression and decompression algorithms involve only simple vector addition, subtraction, and comparison operations.

This paper makes the following contributions:

- We propose a new cache compression algorithm, Base-Delta-Immediate Compression (BΔI), which exploits the low dynamic range of values present in many cache lines to compress them to smaller sizes. Both the compression and decompression algorithms of BΔI have low latency and require only vector addition, subtraction and comparison operations.

- Based on the proposed BΔI compression algorithm, we introduce a new compressed cache design. This design achieves a high degree of compression at a lower decompression latency compared to two state-of-the-art cache compression techniques: Frequent Value Compression (FVC) [33] and Frequent Pattern Compression (FPC) [2], which require complex and long-latency decompression pipelines [3].

- We evaluate the performance benefits of BΔI compared to a baseline system that does not employ compression, as well as against three state-of-the-art cache compression techniques [2, 33, 8]. We show that BΔI provides a better or comparable degree of compression for the majority of the applications we studied. It improves performance for both single-core (8.1%) and multi-core workloads (9.5% / 11.2% for two- / four-cores). For many applications, compression with BΔI provides the performance benefit of doubling the uncompressed cache size of the baseline system.

2. BACKGROUND AND MOTIVATION

Data compression is a powerful technique for storing large amounts of data in a smaller space. Applying data compression to an on-chip cache can potentially allow the cache to store more cache lines in compressed form than it could have if the cache lines were not compressed. As a result, a compressed cache has the potential to provide the benefits of a larger cache at the area and the power of a smaller cache.

Prior work [2, 33, 9] has observed that there is a significant amount of redundancy in the data accessed by real-world applications. There are multiple patterns that lead to such redundancy. We summarize the most common of such patterns below.

Zeros: Zero is by far the most frequently seen value in application data [4, 9, 33]. There are various reasons for this. For example, zero is most commonly used to initialize data, to represent NULL pointers or false boolean values, and to represent sparse matrices (in dense form). In fact, a majority of the compression schemes proposed for compressing memory data either base their design fully around zeros [9, 8, 15, 31], or treat zero as a special case [2, 32, 34].

Repeated Values: A large contiguous region of memory may contain a single value repeated multiple times [23]. This pattern is widely present in applications that use a common initial value for a large array, or in multimedia applications where a large number of adjacent pixels have the same color. Such a repeated value pattern can be easily compressed to significantly reduce storage requirements. Simplicity, frequent occurrence in memory, and high compression ratio make repeated values an attractive target for a special consideration in data compression [2].

Narrow Values: A narrow value is a small value stored using a large data type: e.g., a one-byte value stored as a four-byte integer. Narrow values appear commonly in application data due to over-provisioning or data alignment. Programmers typically provision the data types in various data structures for the worst case even though a majority of the values may fit in a smaller data type. For example, storing a table of counters requires the data type to be provisioned to accommodate the maximum possible value for the counters. However, it can be the case that the maximum possible counter value needs four bytes, while one byte might be enough to store the majority of the counter values. Optimizing such data structures in software for the common case necessitates significant overhead in code, thereby increasing program complexity and programmer effort to ensure correctness. Therefore, most programmers over-provision data type sizes. As a result, narrow values present themselves in many applications, and are exploited by different compression techniques [2, 32, 16].

Other Patterns: There are a few other common data patterns that do not fall into any of the above three classes: a table of pointers that point to different locations in the same memory region, an image with low color gradient, etc. Such data can also be compressed using simple techniques and has been exploited by some prior proposals for main memory compression [32] and image compression [28].

In this work, we make two observations. First, we find that the above described patterns are widely present in many applications

	Characteristics			Compressible data patterns			
	Decomp. Lat.	Complex.	C. Ratio	Zeros	Rep. Val.	Narrow	LDR
ZCA [8]	**Low**	**Low**	Low	✔	×	×	×
FVC [33]	High	High	Modest	✔	Partly	×	×
FPC [2]	High	High	**High**	✔	✔	✔	×
BΔI	**Low**	Modest	**High**	✔	✔	✔	✔

Table 1: Qualitative comparison of BΔI with prior work. LDR: Low dynamic range. Bold font indicates desirable characteristics.

(SPEC CPU benchmark suites, and some server applications, e.g., Apache, TPC-H). Figure 1 plots the percentage of cache lines that can be compressed using different patterns.[1] As the figure shows, on average, 43% of all cache lines belonging to these applications can be compressed. This shows that there is significant opportunity to exploit data compression to improve on-chip cache performance.

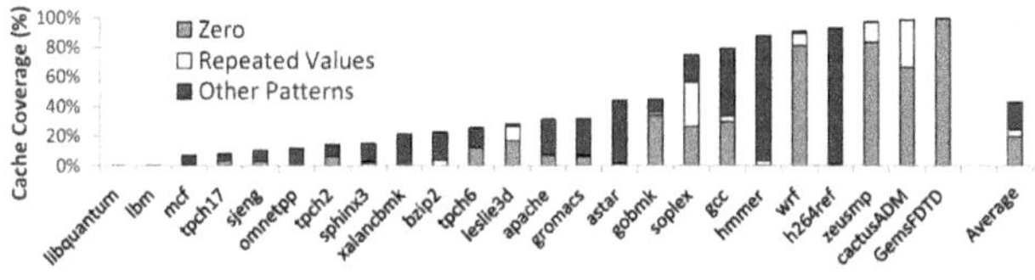

Figure 1: Percentage of cache lines with different data patterns in a 2MB L2 cache. "Other Patterns" includes "Narrow Values".

Second, and more importantly, we observe that all the above commonly occurring patterns fall under the general notion of *low dynamic range* – a set of values where the differences between the values is much smaller than the values themselves. Unlike prior work, which has attempted to exploit each of these special patterns individually for cache compression [2, 33] or main memory compression [9, 32], our **goal** is to exploit the general case of values with *low dynamic range* to build a simple yet effective compression technique.

Summary comparison: Our resulting mechanism, base-delta-immediate (BΔI) compression, strikes a sweet-spot in the tradeoff between decompression latency (Decomp. Lat.), hardware complexity of the implementation (Complex.), and compression ratio (C. Ratio), as shown in Table 1. The table qualitatively compares BΔI with three state-of-the-art mechanisms: ZCA [8], which does zero-value compression, Frequent Value Compression (FVC) [33], and Frequent Pattern Compression (FPC) [2]. (These mechanisms are described in detail in Section 6.) It also summarizes which data patterns (zeros, repeated values, narrow values, and other low dynamic range patterns) are compressible with each mechanism. For modest complexity, BΔI is the only design to achieve both low decompression latency and high compression ratio.

We now explain the design and rationale for our scheme in two parts. In Section 3, we start by discussing the core of our scheme, which is *Base+Delta (B+Δ)* compression. Building upon B+Δ, we then discuss our full-blown BΔI compression scheme (with multiple bases) in Section 4.

3. BASE + DELTA ENCODING: BASIC IDEA

We propose a new cache compression mechanism, *Base+Delta* (B+Δ) compression, which unlike prior work [2, 8, 33], looks for compression opportunities at a cache line granularity – i.e., B+Δ either compresses the entire cache line or stores the entire cache line in uncompressed format. The key observation behind B+Δ is that many cache lines contain data with low dynamic range. As a result, the differences between the words within such a cache line can be represented using fewer bytes than required to represent the words themselves. We exploit this observation to represent a cache line with low dynamic range using a common *base* and an array of *deltas* (differences between values within the cache line and the common base). Since the *deltas* require fewer bytes than the values themselves, the combined size of the *base* and the array of *deltas* can be much smaller than the size of the original uncompressed cache line.

The fact that some values can be represented in base+delta form has been observed by others, and used for different purposes: e.g. texture compression in GPUs [28] and also to save bandwidth on CPU buses by transferring only deltas from a common base [10]. To our knowledge, no previous work examined the use of base+delta representation to improve on-chip cache utilization in a general-purpose processor.

To evaluate the applicability of the B+Δ compression technique for a large number of applications, we conducted a study that compares the effective compression ratio (i.e., effective cache size increase, see Section 7 for a full definition) of B+Δ against a simple technique that compresses two common data patterns (zeros and repeated values[2]). Figure 2 shows the results of this study for a 2MB L2 cache with 64-byte cache lines for applications in the SPEC CPU2006 benchmark suite, database and web-server workloads (see Section 7 for methodology details). We assume a design where a compression scheme can store up to twice as many tags for compressed cache lines than the number of cache lines stored in the uncompressed baseline cache (Section 5 describes a practical mechanism that achieves this by using twice the number of tags).[3] As the figure shows, for a number of applications, B+Δ provides significantly higher compression ratio (1.4X on average) than using the simple compression technique. However, there are some benchmarks for which B+Δ provides very little or no benefit (e.g., *libquantum*, *lbm*, and *mcf*). We will address this problem with a new compression technique called BΔI in Section 4. We first provide examples from real applications to show why B+Δ works.

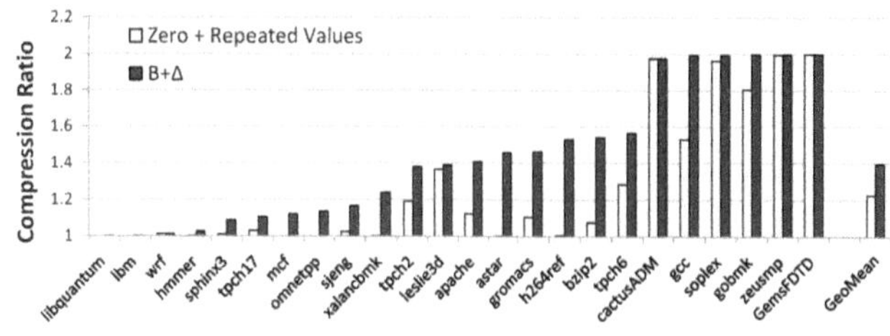

Figure 2: Effective compression ratio with different value patterns

3.1 Why Does B+Δ Work?

B+Δ works because of: (1) regularity in the way data is allocated in the memory (similar data values and types grouped together), and (2) low dynamic range of cache/memory data. The first reason is typically true due to the common usage of arrays

[1]The methodology used in this and other experiments is described in Section 7. We use a 2MB L2 cache unless otherwise stated.

[2]Zero compression compresses an all-zero cache line into a bit that just indicates that the cache line is all-zero. Repeated value compression checks if a cache line has the same 1/2/4/8 byte value repeated. If so, it compresses the cache line to the corresponding value.

[3]This assumption of twice as many tags as the baseline is true for all compressed cache designs, except in Section 8.3.

to represent large pieces of data in applications. The second reason is usually caused either by the nature of computation, e.g., sparse matrices or streaming applications; or by inefficiency (over-provisioning) of data types used by many applications, e.g., 4-byte integer type used to represent values that usually need only 1 byte. We have carefully examined different common data patterns in applications that lead to B+Δ representation and summarize our observations in two examples.

Figures 3 and 4 show the compression of two 32-byte[4] cache lines from the applications *h264ref* and *perlbench* using B+Δ. The first example from *h264ref* shows a cache line with a set of narrow values stored as 4-byte integers. As Figure 3 indicates, in this case, the cache line can be represented using a single 4-byte base value, 0, and an array of eight 1-byte differences. As a result, the entire cache line data can be represented using 12 bytes instead of 32 bytes, saving 20 bytes of the originally used space. Figure 4 shows a similar phenomenon where nearby pointers are stored in the same cache line for the *perlbench* application.

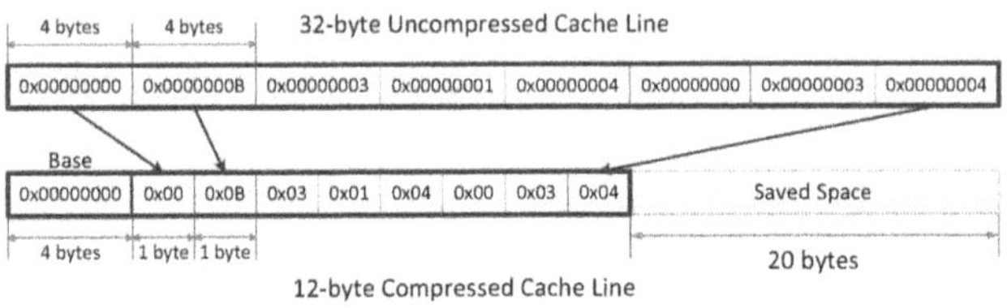

Figure 3: Cache line from *h264ref* compressed with B+Δ

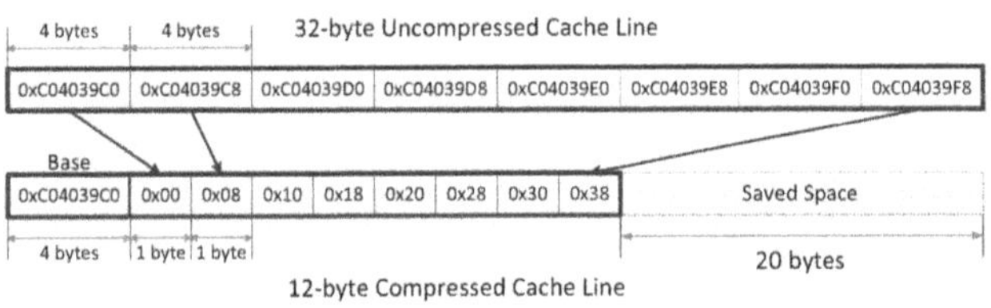

Figure 4: Cache line from *perlbench* compressed with B+Δ

We now describe more precisely the compression and decompression algorithms that lay at the heart of the B+Δ compression mechanism.

3.2 Compression Algorithm

The B+Δ compression algorithm views a cache line as a set of fixed-size values i.e., 8 8-byte, 16 4-byte, or 32 2-byte values for a 64-byte cache line. It then determines if the set of values can be represented in a more compact form as a base value with a set of differences from the base value. For analysis, let us assume that the cache line size is C bytes, the size of each value in the set is k bytes and the set of values to be compressed is $S = (v_1, v_2, ..., v_n)$, where $n = \frac{C}{k}$. The goal of the compression algorithm is to determine the value of the base, B^* and the size of values in the set, k, that provide maximum compressibility. Once B^* and k are determined, the output of the compression algorithm is $\{k, B^*, \Delta = (\Delta_1, \Delta_2, ..., \Delta_n)\}$, where $\Delta_i = B^* - v_i \; \forall i \in \{1, .., n\}$.

Observation 1: The cache line is compressible *only if* $\forall i, \max(\text{size}(\Delta_i)) < k$, where $\text{size}(\Delta_i)$ is the smallest number of bytes that is needed to store Δ_i.

In other words, for the cache line to be compressible, the number of bytes required to represent the differences must be strictly less than the number of bytes required to represent the values themselves.

[4]We use 32-byte cache lines in our examples to save space. 64-byte cache lines were used in all evaluations (see Section 7).

Observation 2: To determine the value of B^*, either the value of $\min(S)$ or $\max(S)$ needs to be found.

The reasoning, where $\max(S)$/$\min(S)$ are the maximum and minimum values in the cache line, is based on the observation that the values in the cache line are bounded by $\min(S)$ and $\max(S)$. And, hence, the optimum value for B^* should be between $\min(S)$ and $\max(S)$. In fact, the optimum can be reached only for $\min(S)$, $\max(S)$, or exactly in between them. Any other value of B^* can only increase the number of bytes required to represent the differences.

Given a cache line, the optimal version of the B+Δ compression algorithm needs to determine two parameters: (1) k, the size of each value in S, and (2) B^*, the optimum base value that gives the best possible compression for the chosen value of k.

Determining k. Note that the value of k determines how the cache line is viewed by the compression algorithm – i.e., it defines the set of values that are used for compression. Choosing a single value of k for all cache lines will significantly reduce the opportunity of compression. To understand why this is the case, consider two cache lines, one representing a table of 4-byte pointers pointing to some memory region (similar to Figure 4) and the other representing an array of narrow values stored as 2-byte integers. For the first cache line, the likely best value of k is 4, as dividing the cache line into a set of of values with a different k might lead to an increase in dynamic range and reduce the possibility of compression. Similarly, the likely best value of k for the second cache line is 2.

Therefore, to increase the opportunity for compression by catering to multiple patterns, our compression algorithm attempts to compress a cache line using three different potential values of k simultaneously: 2, 4, and 8. The cache line is then compressed using the value that provides the maximum compression rate or not compressed at all.[5]

Determining B^*. For each possible value of $k \in \{2, 4, 8\}$, the cache line is split into values of size k and the best value for the base, B^* can be determined using Observation 2. However, computing B^* in this manner requires computing the maximum or the minimum of the set of values, which adds logic complexity and significantly increases the latency of compression.

To avoid compression latency increase and reduce hardware complexity, we decide to use the *first* value from the set of values as an approximation for the B^*. For a compressible cache line with a low dynamic range, we find that choosing the first value as the base instead of computing the optimum base value reduces the average compression ratio only by 0.4%.

3.3 Decompression Algorithm

To decompress a compressed cache line, the B+Δ decompression algorithm needs to take the base value B^* and an array of differences $\Delta = \Delta_1, \Delta_2, ..., \Delta_n$, and generate the corresponding set of values $S = (v_1, v_2, ..., v_n)$. The value v_i is simply given by $v_i = B^* + \Delta_i$. As a result, the values in the cache line can be computed in parallel using a SIMD-style vector adder. Consequently, the entire cache line can be decompressed in the amount of time it takes to do an integer vector addition, using a set of simple adders.

4. BΔI COMPRESSION

4.1 Why Could Multiple Bases Help?

Although B+Δ proves to be generally applicable for many applications, it is clear that not every cache line can be represented

[5]We restrict our search to these three values as almost all basic data types supported by various programming languages have one of these three sizes.

in this form, and, as a result, some benchmarks do not have a high compression ratio, e.g., *mcf*. One common reason why this happens is that some of these applications can mix data of different types in the same cache line, e.g., structures of pointers and 1-byte integers. This suggests that if we apply B+Δ with multiple bases, we can improve compressibility for some of these applications.

Figure 5 shows a 32-byte cache line from *mcf* that is not compressible with a single base using B+Δ, because there is no single base value that effectively compresses this cache line. At the same time, it is clear that if we use two bases, this cache line can be easily compressed using a similar compression technique as in the B+Δ algorithm with one base. As a result, the entire cache line data can be represented using 19 bytes: 8 bytes for two bases (`0x00000000` and `0x09A40178`), 5 bytes for five 1-byte deltas from the first base, and 6 bytes for three 2-byte deltas from the second base. This effectively saves 13 bytes of the 32-byte line.

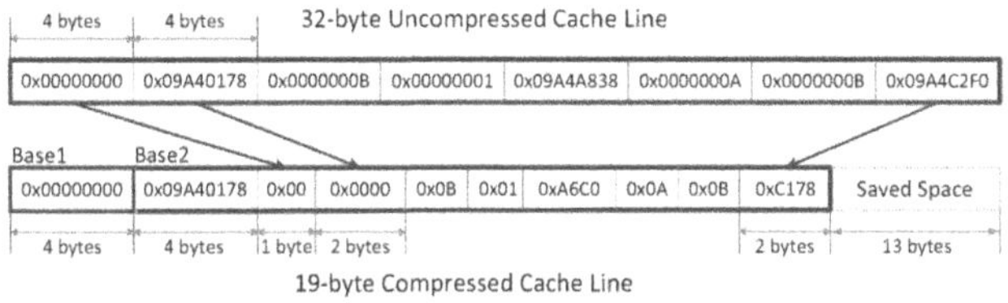

Figure 5: Cache line from *mcf* compressed by B+Δ (two bases)

As we can see, multiple bases can help compress more cache lines, but, unfortunately, more bases can increase overhead (due to storage of the bases), and hence decrease effective compression ratio that can be achieved with one base. So, it is natural to ask *how many bases are optimal for B+Δ compression*?

In order to answer this question, we conduct an experiment where we evaluate the effective compression ratio with different numbers of bases (selected suboptimally using a greedy algorithm). Figure 6 shows the results of this experiment. The "0" base bar corresponds to a mechanism that compresses only simple patterns (zero and repeated values). These patterns are simple to compress and common enough, so we can handle them easily and efficiently without using B+Δ, e.g., a cache line of only zeros compressed to just one byte for any number of bases. We assume this optimization for all bars in Figure 6.[6]

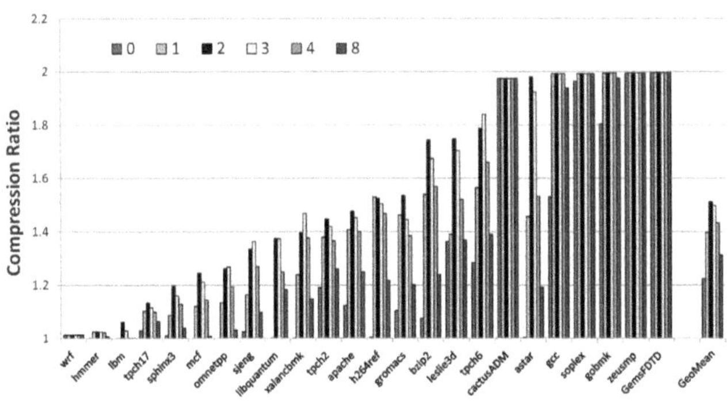

Figure 6: Effective compression ratio with different number of bases. "0" corresponds to zero and repeated value compression.

Results in Figure 6 show that the empirically optimal number of bases in terms of effective compression ratio is 2, with some benchmarks having optimums also at one or three bases. The key conclusion is that B+Δ with two bases significantly outperforms B+Δ with one base (compression ratio of 1.51 vs. 1.40 on average), suggesting that it is worth considering for implementation. Note that having more than two bases does not provide additional improvement in compression ratio for these workloads, because the overhead of storing more bases is higher than the benefit of compressing more cache lines.

Unfortunately, B+Δ with two bases has a serious drawback: the necessity of finding a second base. The search for a second arbitrary base value (even a sub-optimal one) can add significant complexity to the compression hardware. This opens the question of how to find two base values efficiently. We next propose a mechanism that can get the benefit of compression with two bases with minimal complexity.

4.2 BΔI: Refining B+Δ with Two Bases and Minimal Complexity

Results from Section 4.1 suggest that the optimal (on average) number of bases to use is two, but having an additional base has the significant shortcoming described above. We observe that setting the second base to zero gains most of the benefit of having an arbitrary second base value. Why is this the case?

Most of the time when data of different types are mixed in the same cache line, the cause is an aggregate data type: e.g., a structure (`struct` in C). In many cases, this leads to the mixing of wide values with low dynamic range (e.g., pointers) with narrow values (e.g., small integers). A first arbitrary base helps to compress wide values with low dynamic range using base+delta encoding, while a second zero base is efficient enough to compress narrow values separately from wide values. Based on this observation, we refine the idea of B+Δ by adding an additional implicit base that is always set to zero. We call this refinement **Base-Delta-Immediate** or **BΔI** compression.

There is a tradeoff involved in using BΔI instead of B+Δ with two arbitrary bases. BΔI uses an implicit zero base as the second base, and, hence, it has less storage overhead, which means potentially higher average compression ratio for cache lines that are compressible with both techniques. B+Δ with two general bases uses more storage to store an arbitrary second base value, but can compress more cache lines because the base can be any value. As such, the compression ratio can potentially be better with either mechanism, depending on the compressibility pattern of cache lines. In order to evaluate this tradeoff, we compare in Figure 7 the effective compression ratio of BΔI, B+Δ with two arbitrary bases, and three prior approaches: ZCA [8] (zero-based compression), FVC [33], and FPC [2].[7]

Although there are cases where B+Δ with two bases is better — e.g., *leslie3d* and *bzip2* — on average, BΔI performs slightly better than B+Δ in terms of compression ratio (1.53 vs. 1.51). We can also see that both mechanisms are better than the previously proposed FVC mechanism [33], and competitive in terms of compression ratio with a more complex FPC compression mechanism. Taking into an account that B+Δ with two bases is also a more complex mechanism than BΔI, we conclude that our cache compression design should be based on the refined idea of BΔI.

Now we will describe the design and operation of a cache that implements our BΔI compression algorithm.

[6] If we do not assume this optimization, compression with multiple bases will have very low compression ratio for such common simple patterns.

[7] All mechanisms are covered in detail in Section 6. We provide a comparison of their compression ratios here to give a demonstration of BDI's relative effectiveness and to justify it as a viable compression mechanism.

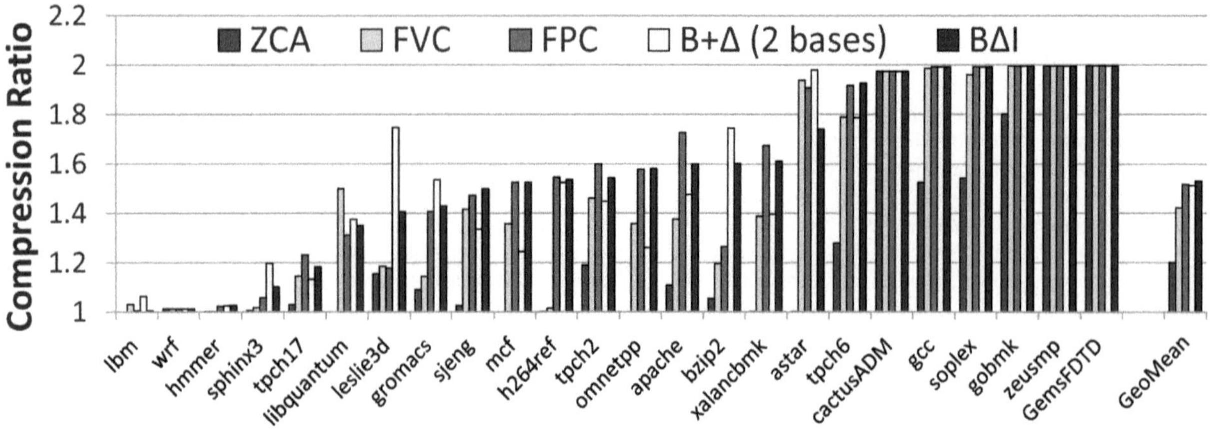

Figure 7: Compression ratio comparison of different algorithms: ZCA [8], FVC [33], FPC [2], B+Δ (two arbitrary bases), and BΔI. Results are obtained on a cache with twice the tags to accommodate more cache lines in the same data space as an uncompressed cache.

5. BΔI: DESIGN AND OPERATION

5.1 Design

Compression and Decompression. We now describe the detailed design of the corresponding compression and decompression logic.[8] The compression logic consists of eight distinct compressor units: six units for different base sizes (8, 4 and 2 bytes) and Δ sizes (4, 2 and 1 bytes), and two units for zero and repeated value compression (Figure 8). Every compressor unit takes a cache line as an input, and outputs whether or not this cache line can be compressed with this unit. If it can be, the unit outputs the compressed cache line. The compressor selection logic is used to determine a set of compressor units that can compress this cache line. If multiple compression options are available for the cache line (e.g., 8-byte base 1-byte Δ and zero compression), the selection logic chooses the one with the smallest compressed cache line size. Note that all potential compressed sizes are known statically and described in Table 2. All compressor units can operate in parallel.

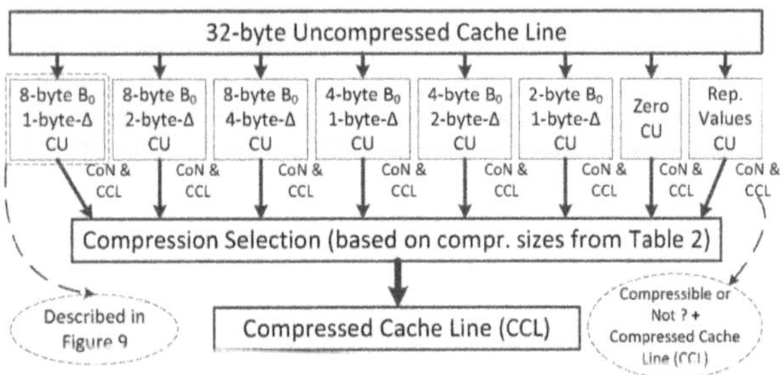

Figure 8: Compressor design. CU: Compressor unit.

Figure 9 describes the organization of the 8-byte-base 1-byte-Δ compressor unit for a 32-byte cache line. The compressor "views" this cache line as a set of four 8-byte elements (V_0, V_1, V_2, V_3), and in the first step, computes the difference between the base element and all other elements. Recall that the base (B_0) is set to the first value (V_0), as we describe in Section 3. The resulting difference values ($\Delta_0, \Delta_1, \Delta_2, \Delta_3$) are then checked to see whether their first 7 bytes are all zeros or ones (1-byte sign extension check). If so, the resulting cache line can be stored as the base value B_0 and the set of differences $\Delta_0, \Delta_1, \Delta_2, \Delta_3$, where each Δ_i requires only 1 byte. The compressed cache line size in this case is 12 bytes instead of the original 32 bytes. If the 1-byte sign extension check returns false (i.e., at least one Δ_i cannot be represented using 1 byte), then the compressor unit cannot compress this cache line. The organization of all other compressor units is similar. This compression design can be potentially optimized, especially if hardware complexity is more critical than latency, e.g., all 8-byte-base value compression units can be united into one to avoid partial logic duplication.

[8]For simplicity, we start with presenting the compression and decompression logic for B+Δ. Compression for BΔI requires one more step, where elements are checked to be compressed with zero base; decompression logic only requires additional selector logic to decide which base should be used in the addition. We describe the differences between BΔI and B+Δ designs later in this section.

Name	Base	Δ	Size	Enc.	Name	Base	Δ	Size	Enc.
Zeros	1	0	1/1	0000	Rep.Values	8	0	8/8	0001
Base8-Δ1	8	1	12/16	0010	Base8-Δ2	8	2	16/24	0011
Base8-Δ4	8	4	24/40	0100	Base4-Δ1	4	1	12/20	0101
Base4-Δ2	4	2	20/36	0110	Base2-Δ1	2	1	18/34	0111
NoCompr.	N/A	N/A	32/64	1111					

Table 2: BΔI encoding. All sizes are in bytes. Compressed sizes (in bytes) are given for 32-/64-byte cache lines.

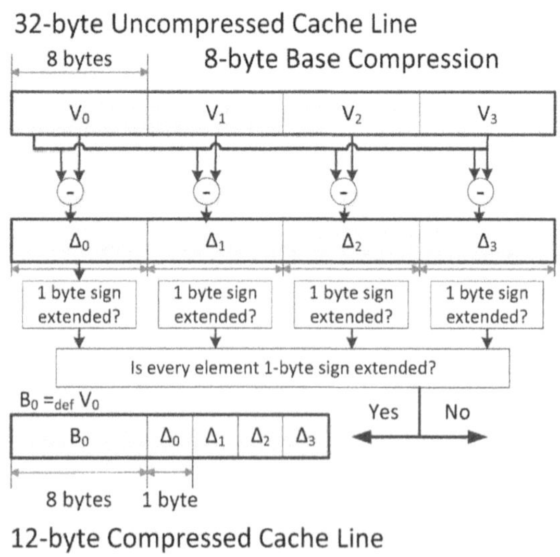

Figure 9: Compressor unit for 8-byte base, 1-byte Δ

Figure 10 shows the latency-critical decompression logic. Its organization is simple: for a compressed cache line that consists of a base value B_0 and a set of differences $\Delta_0, \Delta_1, \Delta_2, \Delta_3$, only additions of the base to the differences are performed to obtain the uncompressed cache line. Such decompression will take as long as the latency of an adder, and allows the BΔI cache to perform decompression very quickly.

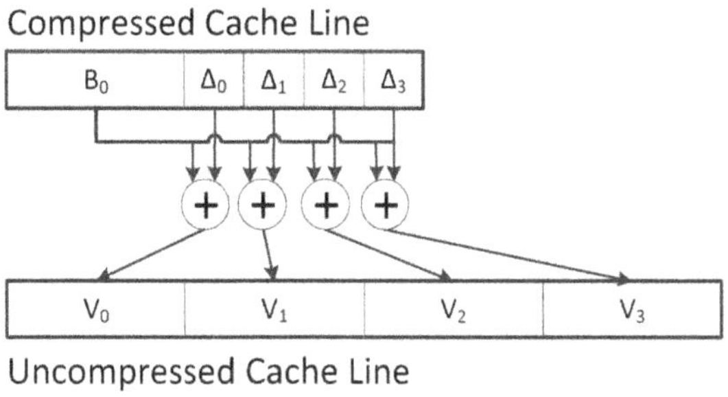

Figure 10: Decompressor design

BΔI Cache Organization. In order to obtain the benefits of compression, the conventional cache design requires certain changes. Cache compression potentially allows more cache lines to be stored in the same data storage than a conventional uncompressed cache. But, in order to access these additional compressed cache lines, we need a way to address them. One way to achieve this is to have more tags [2], e.g., twice as many,[9] than the number we have in a conventional cache of the same size and associativity. We can then use these additional tags as pointers to more data elements in the corresponding data storage.

Figure 11 shows the required changes in the cache design. The conventional 2-way cache with 32-byte cache lines (shown on the top) has a tag store with two tags per set, and a data store with two 32-byte cache lines per set. Every tag directly maps to the corresponding piece of the data storage. In the BΔI design (at the bottom), we have twice as many tags (four in this example), and every tag also has 4 additional bits to represent whether or not the line is compressed, and if it is, what compression type is used (see "Encoding" in Table 2). The data storage remains the same in size as before ($2\times32 = 64$ bytes), but it is separated into smaller fixed-size segments (e.g., 8 bytes in size in Figure 11). Every tag stores the starting segment (e.g., Tag_2 stores segment S_2) and the encoding for the cache block. By knowing the encoding we can easily know the number of segments used by the cache block.

Storage Cost Analysis. This cache organization potentially allows storing twice as many cache lines in the same data storage, because the number of tags in a set is doubled. As a result, it requires modest increase in the tag store size (similar to some other designs [3, 11, 22]. We analyze the storage overhead in terms of raw additional bits in Table 3 for a baseline 16-way 2MB cache. We have also used CACTI 5.3 [29] to estimate the additional latency and area cost of our proposed cache organization, using parameters for the 32nm technology node. Cache access latency increases by 1-2 cycles (depending on cache size) for a 4GHz processor. On-chip cache area increases by 2.3%, but this increase is small compared to the 137% increase in area, which occurs if we double both the tag store and the data store size (by doubling the associativity).[10]

[9] We describe an implementation with the number of tags doubled and evaluate sensitivity to the number of tags in Section 8.

[10] As we show in Section 8, BΔI with our proposed cache organization achieves performance that is within 1-2% of a cache that has double the tag and data store size.

	Baseline	BΔI
Size of tag-store entry	21 bits	32 bits (+4–encoding, +7–segment pointer)
Size of data-store entry	512 bits	512 bits
Number of tag-store entries	32768	65536
Number of data-store entries	32768	32768
Tag-store size	84kB	256kB
Total (data-store+tag-store) size	2132kB	2294kB

Table 3: Storage cost analysis for 2MB 16-way L2 cache, assuming 64-byte cache lines, 8-byte segments, and 36 bits for address space.

Cache Eviction Policy. In a compressed cache, there are two cases under which multiple cache lines may need to be evicted because evicting a single cache line (i.e., the LRU one in a cache that uses the LRU replacement policy) may not create enough space for the incoming or modified cache line. First, when a new cache line (compressed or uncompressed) is inserted into the cache. Second, when a cache line already in the cache is modified such that its new size is larger than its old size. In both cases, we propose to use a slightly modified version of the LRU replacement policy wherein the cache evicts multiple LRU cache lines to create enough space for the incoming or modified cache line.[11] such a policy can increase the latency of eviction, it has negligible effect on performance as evictions are off the critical path of execution. Note that more effective replacement policies that take into account compressed cache line sizes are possible – e.g., a policy that does not evict a zero cache line unless there is a need for space in the tag store. We leave the study of such policies for future work.

BΔI Design Specifics. So far, we described the common part in the designs of both B+Δ and BΔI. However, there are some specific differences between these two designs.

First, BΔI compression happens (off the critical path) in two steps (vs. only one step for B+Δ). For a fixed Δ size, *Step 1* attempts to compress all elements using an implicit base of zero. *Step 2* tries to compress those elements that were not compressed in Step 1. The first uncompressible element of Step 1 is chosen as the base for Step 2. The compression step stores a bit mask, 1-bit per element indicating whether or not the corresponding base is zero. Note that we keep the size of Δ (1, 2, or 4 bytes) the same for both bases.

Second, BΔI decompression is implemented as a masked addition of the base (chosen in Step 2) to the array of differences. The elements to which the base is added depends on the bit-mask stored in the compression step.

5.2 Operation

We propose using our BΔI design at cache levels higher than L1 (e.g., L2 and L3). While it is possible to compress data in the L1 cache [33], doing so will increase the critical path of latency-sensitive L1 cache hits. This can result in significant performance degradation for applications that do not benefit from compression.

We now describe how a BΔI cache fits into a system with a 2-level cache hierarchy (L1, L2 and main memory) with the L2 cache compressed using BΔI – note that the only changes are to the L2 cache. We assume all caches use the writeback policy. There are four scenarios related to the compressed L2 cache operation: 1) an L2 cache hit, 2) an L2 cache miss, 3) a writeback from L1 to L2, and 4) a writeback from L2 to memory.

First, on an L2 hit, the corresponding cache line is sent to the L1 cache. If the line is compressed, it is first decompressed before it is sent to the L1 cache. Second, on an L2 miss, the corresponding

[11] On average, 5.2% of all insertions or writebacks into the cache resulted in the eviction of multiple cache lines in our workloads.

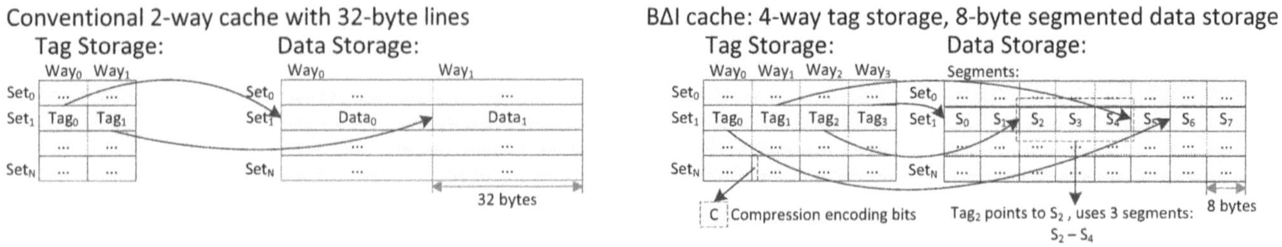

Figure 11: BΔI vs. conventional cache organization. Number of tags is doubled, compression encoding bits are added to every tag, data storage is the same in size, but partitioned into segments.

cache line is brought from memory and is sent to the L1 cache. In this case, the line is also compressed and inserted into the L2 cache. Third, when a line is written back from L1 to L2, it is first compressed. If an old copy of the line is already present in the L2 cache, the old (stale) copy is invalidated. The new compressed cache line is then inserted into the L2 cache. Fourth, when a line is written back from L2 cache to memory, it is decompressed before it is sent to the memory controller. In both second and third scenarios, potentially multiple cache lines might be evicted from the L2 cache based on the cache eviction policy described in Section 5.1.

6. RELATED WORK

Multiple previous works investigated the possibility of using compression for on-chip caches [34, 2, 8, 15, 11, 6] and/or memory [32, 1, 9]. All proposed designs have different tradeoffs between compression ratio, decompression/compression latency and hardware complexity. The spectrum of proposed algorithms ranges from general-purpose compression schemes e.g., the Lempel-Ziv algorithm [35], to specific pattern-based schemes, e.g., zero values [8, 15] and frequent values [33].

The fundamental difference between BΔI and previous cache compression mechanisms is that whereas prior techniques compress data at word granularity – i.e., each word within a cache line is compressed separately, BΔI compresses data at cache-line granularity – i.e., all the words within a cache line are compressed using the same encoding or all the words within a cache line are stored uncompressed. As a result, BΔI provides two major advantages. First, the decompression of all words in the same cache line can be performed in parallel (using a masked vector addition), since the starting point of each word is known in the compressed cache line. In contrast, compressing each word within a cache line separately, as in prior works, typically serializes decompression as different words can be compressed to different sizes, making the starting point of each word in the compressed cache line dependent on the previous word. Second, BΔI exploits correlation across words within a cache line, which can lead to a better compression ratio – e.g., when cache line consists of an array of pointers. Prior works do not exploit this correlation as they compress words individually. As already summarized in Table 1, different prior works suffer from one or more of the following shortcomings, which BΔI alleviates: 1) high decompression latency, 2) low effective compression ratio, and 3) high hardware complexity. We now describe the prior designs in more detail.

6.1 Zero-based Designs

Dusser et al. [8] propose Zero-Content Augmented (ZCA) cache design where a conventional cache is augmented with a specialized cache to represent zero cache lines. Decompression and compression latencies as well as hardware complexity for the ZCA cache design are low. However, only applications that operate on a large number of zero cache lines can benefit from this design. In our experiments, only 6 out of 24 applications have enough zero data to benefit from ZCA (Figure 7), leading to relatively small performance improvements (as we show in Section 8).

Islam and Stenström [15] observe that 18% of the dynamic loads actually access zero data, and propose a cache design called Zero-Value Canceling where these loads can be serviced faster. Again, this can improve performance only for applications with substantial amounts of zero data. Our proposal is more general than these designs that are based only on zero values.

6.2 Frequent Value Compression

Zhang et al. [34] observe that a majority of values read or written by memory operations come from a small set of frequently occurring values. Based on this observation, they propose a compression technique [33] that encodes frequent values present in cache lines with fewer bits. They apply this technique to a direct-mapped L1 cache wherein each entry in the cache can store either one uncompressed line or two compressed lines.

Frequent value compression (FVC) has three major drawbacks. First, since FVC can only compress frequent values, it cannot exploit other commonly found patterns, e.g., narrow values or stride patterns in application data. As a result, it does not provide a high degree of compression for most applications as shown in Section 8. Second, FVC compresses only the frequent values, while other values stay uncompressed. Decompression of such a cache line requires sequential processing of every element (because the beginning of the next element can be determined only after the previous element is processed), significantly increasing the latency of decompression, which is undesirable. Third, the proposed mechanism requires profiling to identify the frequent values within an application. Our quantitative results in Section 8 shows that BΔI outperforms FVC due to these reasons.

6.3 Pattern-Based Compression Techniques

Alameldeen and Wood [2] propose frequent pattern compression (FPC) that exploits the observation that a majority of words fall under one of a few compressible patterns, e.g., if the upper 16 bits of a 32-bit word are all zeros or are all ones, all bytes in a 4-byte word are the same. FPC defines a set of these patterns [3] and then uses them to encode applicable words with fewer bits of data. For compressing a cache line, FPC first divides the cache line into 32-bit words and checks if each word falls under one of seven frequently occurring patterns. Each compressed cache line contains the pattern encoding for all the words within the cache line followed by the additional data required to decompress each word.

The same authors propose a compressed cache design [2] based on FPC which allows the cache to store two times more compressed lines than uncompressed lines, effectively doubling the cache size when all lines are compressed. For this purpose, they maintain twice as many tag entries as there are data entries. Similar to frequent value compression, frequent pattern compression also requires serial decompression of the cache line, because every word can be compressed or decompressed. To mitigate the decompression latency of FPC, the authors design a five-cycle decompression pipeline [3]. They also propose an adaptive scheme which avoids compressing data if the decompression latency nullifies the benefits of compression.

Chen et al. [6] propose a pattern-based compression mechanism (called C-Pack) with several new features: (1) multiple cache lines can be compressed into one, (2) multiple words can be compressed in parallel; but parallel decompression is not possible. Although the C-Pack design is more practical than FPC, it still has a high decompression latency (8 cycles due to serial decompression), and its average compression ratio is lower than that of FPC.

7. EVALUATION METHODOLOGY

We use an in-house, event-driven 32-bit x86 simulator whose front-end is based on Simics [18]. All configurations have either a two- or three-level cache hierarchy, with private L1D caches. Major simulation parameters are provided in Table 4. All caches uniformly use a 64B cache block size and LRU policy for replacement. All cache latencies were determined using CACTI [29] (assuming a 4GHz frequency), and provided in Table 5. We also checked that these latencies match the existing last level cache implementations from Intel and AMD, when properly scaled to the corresponding frequency.[12] For evaluations, we use benchmarks from the SPEC CPU2006 suite [26], three TPC-H queries [30], and an Apache web server (shown in Table 6, whose detailed description is in Section 8). All results are collected by running a representative portion of the benchmarks for 1 billion instructions.

Processor	1–4 cores, 4GHz, x86 in-order
L1-D cache	32kB, 64B cache-line, 2-way, 1 cycle
L2 caches	0.5–16 MB, 64B cache-line, 16-way
L3 caches	2–16 MB, 64B cache-line, 16-way
Memory	300 cycle latency

Table 4: Major parameters of the simulated system

Size	Latency	Size	Latency	Size	Latency
512kB	15	1MB	21	2MB	27
4MB	34	8MB	41	16MB	48

Table 5: Cache hit latencies used in simulations (in cycles). BΔI caches have +1 cycle for 0.5–4MB (+2 cycle for others) on a hit/miss due to larger tag stores, and +1 cycle for decompression.

Metrics. We measure performance of our benchmarks using IPC (instruction per cycle), effective compression ratio (effective cache size increase, e.g., 1.5 for 2MB cache means effective size of 3MB), and MPKI (misses per kilo instruction). For multi-programmed workloads we use the weighted speedup [25] as the performance metric: ($\sum_i \frac{IPC_i^{shared}}{IPC_i^{alone}}$). For bandwidth consumption we use BPKI (bytes transferred over bus per thousand instructions [27]).

Effective compression ratio for all mechanisms is computed without meta-data overhead. We add all meta-data to the tag storage, e.g., for BΔI, we add four bits to encode the compression scheme, and a bit mask to differentiate between two bases. We include these in the tag overhead, which was evaluated in Section 5. Our comparisons are fair, because we do not include this overhead in compression ratios of previous works we compare to. In fact, the meta-data overhead is higher for FPC (3 bits for each word).

We conducted a study to see applications' performance sensitivity to the increased L2 cache size (from 512kB to 16 MB). Our results show that there are benchmarks that are almost insensitive (IPC improvement less than 5% with 32x increase in cache size) to the size of the L2 cache: dealII, povray, calculix, gamess, namd, milc, and perlbench. This typically means that their working sets mostly fit into the L1D cache, leaving almost no potential for any L2/L3/memory optimization. Therefore, we do not present data for these applications, although we verified that our mechanism does not affect their performance.

Parameters of Evaluated Schemes. For FPC, we used a decompression latency of 5 cycles, and a segment size of 1 byte (as for BΔI) to get the highest compression ratio as described in [3]. For FVC, we used static profiling for 100k instructions to find the 7 most frequent values as described in [33], and a decompression latency of 5 cycles. For ZCA and BΔI, we used a decompression latency of 1 cycle.

We also evaluated BΔI with higher decompression latencies (2-5 cycles). BΔI continues to provide better performance, because for most applications it provides a better overall compression ratio than prior mechanisms. When decompression latency of BΔI increases from 1 to 5 cycles, performance degrades by 0.74%.

Internal Fragmentation. In our simulations, we assumed that before every insertion, we can shift segments properly to avoid fragmentation (implementable, but might be inefficient). We believe this is reasonable, because insertion happens off the critical path of the execution. Previous work [2] adopted this assumption, and we treated all schemes equally in our evaluation.

8. RESULTS & ANALYSIS

8.1 Single-core Results

Figure 12a shows the performance improvement of our proposed BΔI design over the baseline cache design for various cache sizes, normalized to the performance of a 512KB baseline design. The results are averaged across all benchmarks. Figure 12b plots the corresponding results for MPKI also normalized to a 512KB baseline design. Several observations are in-order. First, the BΔI cache significantly outperforms the baseline cache for all cache sizes. By storing cache lines in compressed form, the BΔI cache is able to effectively store more cache lines and thereby significantly reduce the cache miss rate (as shown in Figure 12b). Second, in most cases, BΔI achieves the performance improvement of doubling the cache size. In fact, the 2MB BΔI cache performs better than the 4MB baseline cache. This is because, BΔI increases the effective cache size *without* significantly increasing the access latency of the data storage. Third, the performance improvement of BΔI cache decreases with increasing cache size. This is expected because, as cache size increases, the working set of more benchmarks start fitting into the cache. Therefore, storing the cache lines in compressed format has increasingly less benefit. Based on our results, we conclude that BΔI is an effective compression mechanism to significantly improve single-core performance, and can provide the benefits of doubling the cache size without incurring the area and latency penalties associated with a cache of twice the size.

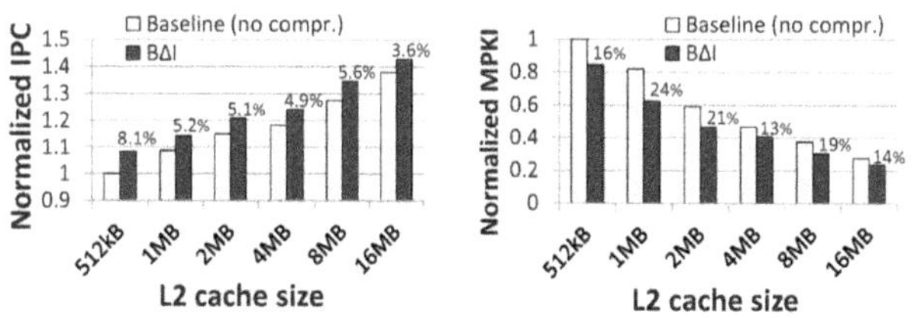

(a) IPC (b) MPKI

Figure 12: Performance of BΔI with different cache sizes. Percentages show improvement over the baseline cache (same size).

[12]Intel Xeon X5570 (Nehalem) 2.993GHz, 8MB L3 - 35 cycles [19]; AMD Opteron 2.8GHz, 1MB L2 - 13 cycles [5].

Cat.	Name	Comp. Ratio	Sens.	Name	Comp. Ratio	Sens.	Name	Comp. Ratio	Sens.	Name	Comp. Ratio	Sens.
LCLS	gromacs	1.43 / L	L	hmmer	1.03 / L	L	lbm	1.00 / L	L	libquantum	1.25 / L	L
	leslie3d	1.41 / L	L	sphinx	1.10 / L	L	tpch17	1.18 / L	L	wrf	1.01 / L	L
HCLS	apache	1.60 / H	L	zeusmp	1.99 / H	L	gcc	1.99 / H	L	GemsFDTD	1.99 / H	L
	gobmk	1.99 / H	L	sjeng	1.50 / H	L	tpch2	1.54 / H	L	cactusADM	1.97 / H	L
	tpch6	1.93 / H	L									
HCHS	astar	1.74 / H	H	bzip2	1.60 / H	H	mcf	1.52 / H	H	xalancbmk	1.61 / H	H
	omnetpp	1.58 / H	H	soplex	1.99 / H	H	h264ref	1.52 / H	H			

Table 6: Benchmark characteristics and categories: Comp. Ratio (effective compression ratio for 2MB BΔI L2) and Sens. (cache size sensitivity). Sensitivity is the ratio of improvement in performance by going from 512kB to 2MB L2 (L - low ($\leq$ 1.10) , H - high (> 1.10)). For compression ratio: L - low ($\leq$ 1.50), H - high (> 1.50). Cat. means category based on compression ratio and sensitivity.

8.2 Multi-core Results

When the working set of an application fits into the cache, the application will not benefit significantly from compression even though its data might have high redundancy. However, when such an application is running concurrently with another cache-sensitive application in a multi-core system, storing its cache lines in compressed format will create additional cache space for storing the data of the cache-sensitive application, potentially leading to significant overall performance improvement.

To study this effect, we classify our benchmarks into four categories based on their compressibility using BΔI (low (LC) or high (HC)) and cache sensitivity (low (LS) or high (HS)). Table 6 shows the sensitivity and compressibility of different benchmarks along with the criteria used for classification. None of the benchmarks used in our evaluation fall into the low-compressibility high-sensitivity (LCHS) category. We generate six different categories of 2-core workloads (20 in each category) by randomly choosing benchmarks with different characteristics (LCLS, HCLS and HCHS).

Figure 13 shows the performance improvement provided by four different compression schemes, namely, ZCA, FVC, FPC, and BΔI, over a 2MB baseline cache design for different workload categories. We draw three major conclusions.

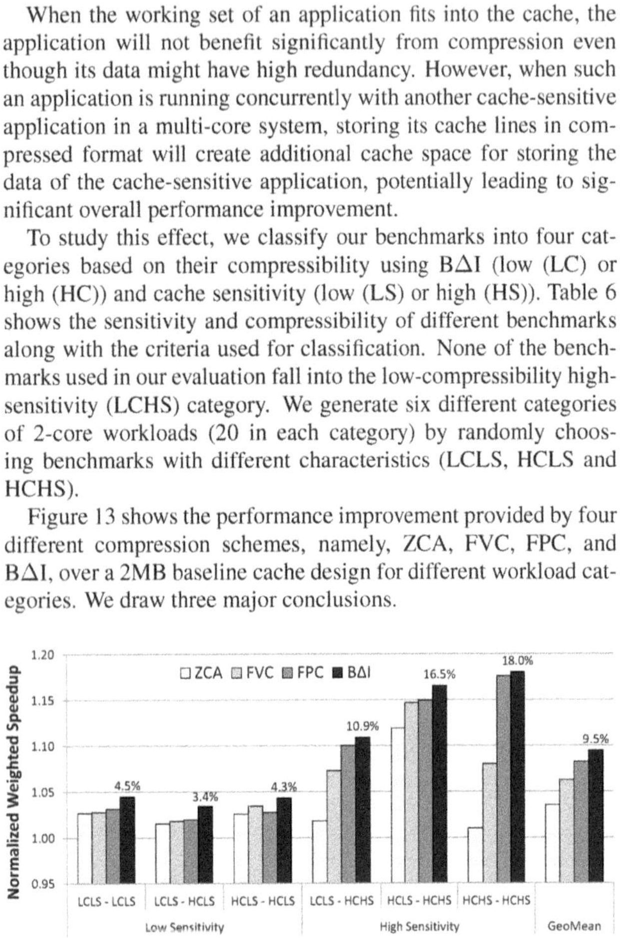

Figure 13: Normalized weighted speedup for 2MB L2 cache, 2-cores. Percentages show improvement over the baseline uncompressed cache.

First, BΔI outperforms all prior approaches for all workload categories. Overall, BΔI improves system performance by 9.5% compared to the baseline cache design.

Second, as we mentioned in the beginning of this section, even though an application with highly compressible data may not itself benefit from compression (HCLS), it can enable opportunities for performance improvement for the co-running application. This effect is clearly visible in the figure. When at least one benchmark is sensitive to cache space, the performance improvement of BΔI increases with increasing compressibility of the co-running benchmark (as observed by examining the bars labeled as High Sensitivity). BΔI provides the highest improvement (18%) when *both* benchmarks in a workload are highly compressible and highly sensitive to cache space (HCHS-HCHS). As the figure shows, the performance improvement is not as significant when neither benchmark is sensitive to cache space irrespective of their compressibility (as observed by examining the bars labeled Low Sensitivity).

Third, although FPC provides a degree of compression similar to BΔI for most benchmarks (as we showed in Section 4.2, Figure 7) its performance improvement is lower than BΔI for all workload categories. This is because FPC has a more complex decompression algorithm with higher decompression latency compared to BΔI. On the other hand, for high sensitivity workloads, neither ZCA nor FVC is as competitive as FPC or BΔI in the HCLS-HCHS category. This is because both ZCA and FVC have a significantly lower degree of compression compared to BΔI. However, a number of benchmarks in the HCLS category (*cactusADM*, *gcc*, *gobmk*, *zeusmp*, and *GemsFDTD*) have high occurrences of zero in their data. Therefore, ZCA and FVC are able to compress most of the cache lines of these benchmarks, thereby creating additional space for the co-running HCHS application.

We conducted a similar experiment with 100 4-core workloads with different compressibility and sensitivity characteristics. We observed trends similar to the 2-core results presented above. On average, BΔI improves performance by 11.2% for the 4-core workloads and it outperforms all previous techniques. We conclude that BΔI, with its high compressibility and low decompression latency, outperforms other state-of-the-art compression techniques for both 2-core and 4-core workloads, likely making it a more competitive candidate for adoption in modern multi-core processors.

We summarize BΔI performance improvement against the baseline 2MB L2 cache (without compression) and other mechanisms in Table 7.

Cores	No Compression	ZCA	FVC	FPC
1	5.1%	4.1%	2.1%	1.0%
2	9.5%	5.7%	3.1%	1.2%
4	11.2%	5.6%	3.2%	1.3%

Table 7: Average performance improvement of BΔI over other mechanisms: No Compression, ZCA, FVC, and FPC.

8.3 Effect on Cache Capacity

Our proposed BΔI cache design aims to provide the benefits of increasing the cache size while not incurring the increased latency of a larger data storage. To decouple the benefits of compression using BΔI from the benefits of reduced latency compared to a larger cache, we perform the following study. We compare the performance of the baseline cache design and the BΔI cache design by progressively doubling the cache size by doubling the cache associativity. We fix the latency of accessing all caches.

Figure 14 shows the results of this experiment. With the same access latency for all caches, we expect the performance of the BΔI

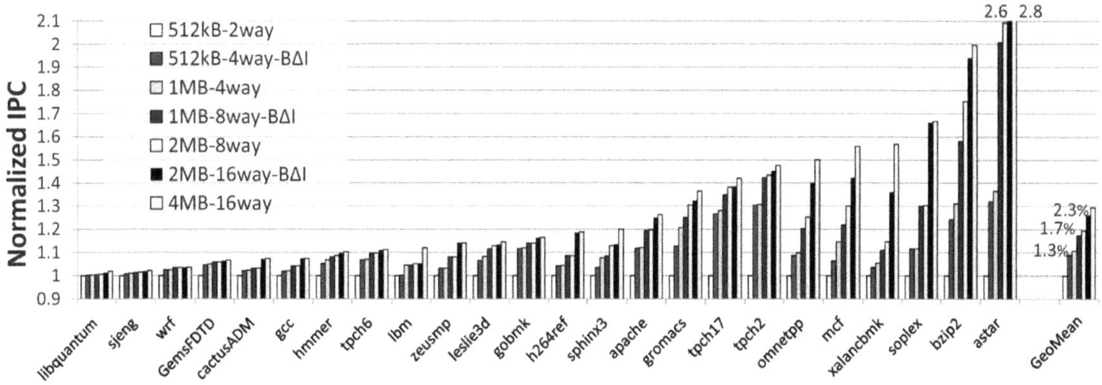

Figure 14: IPC comparison of BΔI against lower and upper limits in performance (from 512kB 2-way - 4MB 16-way L2 cache). Percentages on the GeoMean bars show how close BΔI gets to the performance of the cache with twice the size (upper limit).

cache (with twice the number of tags as the baseline) to be strictly between the baseline cache of the same size (lower limit) and the baseline cache of double the size (upper limit, also reflected in our results). However, with its high degree of compression, the BΔI cache's performance comes close to the performance of the twice as-large baseline cache design for most benchmarks (e.g., *h264ref* and *zeusmp*). On average, the performance improvement due to the BΔI cache is within 1.3% – 2.3% of the improvement provided by a twice as-large baseline cache. We conclude that our BΔI implementation (with twice the number of tags as the baseline) achieves performance improvement close to its upper bound potential performance of a cache twice the size of the baseline.

For an application with highly compressible data, the compression ratio of the BΔI cache is limited by the number of additional tags used in its design. Figure 15 shows the effect of varying the number of tags (from 2× to 64× the number of tags in the baseline cache) on compression ratio for a 2MB cache. As the figure shows, for most benchmarks, except *soplex*, *cactusADM*, *zeusmp*, and *GemsFDTD*, having more than twice as many tags as the baseline cache does not improve the compression ratio. The improved compression ratio for the four benchmarks is primarily due to the large number of zeros and repeated values present in their data. At the same time, having more tags does not benefit a majority of the benchmarks and also incurs higher storage cost and access latency. Therefore, we conclude that these improvements likely do not justify the use of more than 2X the tags in the BΔI cache design compared to the baseline cache.

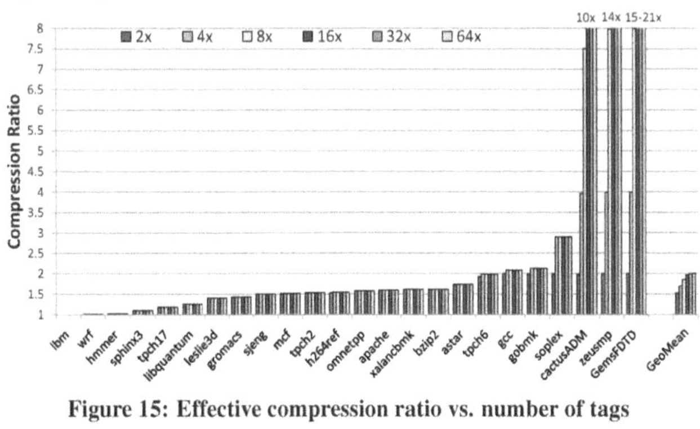

Figure 15: Effective compression ratio vs. number of tags

8.4 Effect on Bandwidth

In a system with a 3-level cache hierarchy, where both the L2 and the L3 caches store cache lines in compressed format, there is an opportunity to compress the traffic between the two caches. This has two benefits: (1) it can lead to reduced latency of communication between the two caches, and hence, improved system performance, and (2) it can lower the dynamic power consumption of the processor as it communicates less data between the two caches [7]. Figure 16 shows the reduction in L2-L3 bandwidth (in terms of bytes per kilo instruction) due to BΔI compression. We observe that the potential bandwidth reduction with BΔI is as high as 53X (for *GemsFDTD*), and 2.31X on average. We conclude that BΔI can not only increase the effective cache size, but it can also significantly decrease the on-chip traffic.

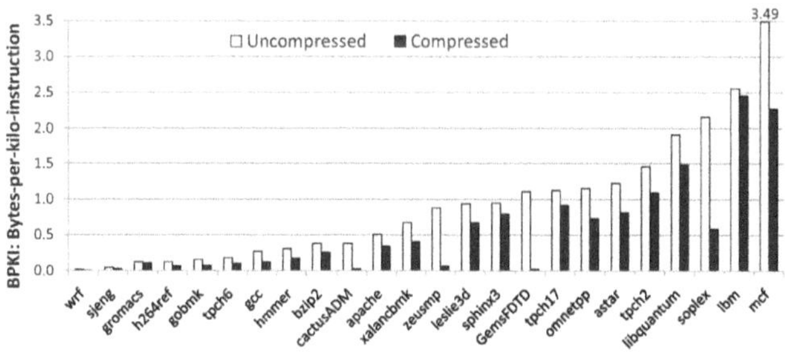

Figure 16: Effect of compression on bus bandwidth (in terms of BPKI) between L2 (256kB) and L3 (8MB)

8.5 Detailed Comparison with Prior Work

To compare the performance of BΔI against state-of-the-art cache compression techniques, we conducted a set of studies and evaluated IPC, MPKI, and effective compression ratio (Figure 7) for single core workloads, and weighted speedup (Figure 13) for two- and four-core workloads.

Figure 17 shows the improvement in IPC using different compression mechanisms over a 2MB baseline cache in a single-core system. As the figure shows, BΔI outperforms all prior approaches for most of the benchmarks. For benchmarks that do not benefit from compression (e.g, *leslie3d*, *GemsFDTD*, and *hmmer*), all compression schemes degrade performance compared to the baseline. However, BΔI has the lowest performance degradation with its low 1-cycle decompression latency, and never degrades performance by more than 1%. On the other hand, FVC and FPC degrade performance by as much as 3.1% due to their relatively high 5-cycle decompression latency. We also observe that BΔI and FPC considerably reduce MPKI compared to ZCA and FVC, especially for benchmarks with more complex data patterns like *h264ref*, *bzip2*, *xalancbmk*, *hmmer*, and *mcf* (not shown due to space limitations).

Based on our results, we conclude that BΔI, with its low decompression latency and high degree of compression, provides the best performance compared to all examined compression mechanisms.

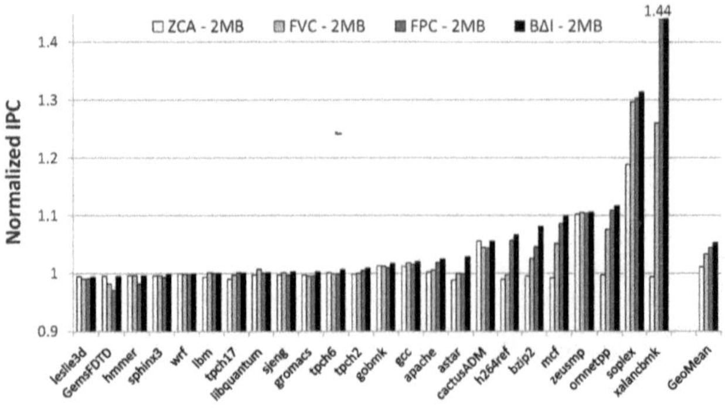

Figure 17: Performance of BΔI vs. prior work for a 2MB L2 cache

9. CONCLUSIONS

This paper presents BΔI, a new and simple, yet efficient hardware cache compression technique that provides high effective cache capacity increase and system performance improvement compared to three state-of-the-art cache compression techniques. BΔI achieves these benefits by exploiting the low dynamic range of in-cache data and representing cache lines in the form of two base values (with one implicit base equal to zero) and an array of differences from these base values. We provide insights into why BΔI compression is effective via examples of existing in-cache data patterns from real programs. BΔI's key advantage over previously proposed cache compression mechanisms is its ability to have low decompression latency (due to parallel decompression) while still having a high average compression ratio.

We describe the design and operation of a cache that can utilize BΔI compression with relatively modest hardware overhead. Our extensive evaluations across a variety of workloads and system configurations show that BΔI compression in an L2 cache can improve system performance for both single-core (8.1%) and multi-core workloads (9.5% / 11.2% for two/four cores), outperforming three state-of-the-art cache compression mechanisms. In many workloads, the performance benefit of using BΔI compression is close to the performance benefit of doubling the L2/L3 cache size. We conclude that BΔI is an efficient and low-latency data compression substrate for on-chip caches in both single- and multi-core systems.

Acknowledgments

Many thanks to Brian Hirano, Matt Pharr, and Ron Babich for their feedback during various stages of this project. We thank the anonymous reviewers for their feedback. We acknowledge members of the SAFARI and LBA groups for their feedback and for the stimulating research environment they provide. We acknowledge the generous support of AMD, Intel, Oracle, and Samsung. This research was partially supported by NSF (CCF-0953246, CCF-1212962), GSRC, Intel University Research Office, Intel Science and Technology Center for Cloud Computing and NSERC PGS-D. We thank Greg Ganger, Kayvon Fatahalian and Michael Papamichael for their feedback on this paper's writing.

REFERENCES

[1] B. Abali, H. Franke, D. E. Poff, R. A. Saccone, C. O. Schulz, L. M. Herger, and T. B. Smith. Memory expansion technology (MXT): software support and performance. *IBM JRD*, 2001.

[2] A. R. Alameldeen and D. A. Wood. Adaptive cache compression for high-performance processors. In *ISCA-31*, 2004.

[3] A. R. Alameldeen and D. A. Wood. Frequent pattern compression: A significance-based compression scheme for L2 caches. *Tech. Rep., University of Wisconsin-Madison*, 2004.

[4] S. Balakrishnan and G. S. Sohi. Exploiting value locality in physical register files. In *MICRO-36*, 2003.

[5] J. Chen and W. A. Watson-III. Multi-threading performance on commodity multi-core processors. In *Proceedings of HPCAsia*, 2007.

[6] X. Chen, L. Yang, R. Dick, L. Shang, and H. Lekatsas. C-pack: A high-performance microprocessor cache compression algorithm. In *IEEE TVLSI*, Aug. 2010.

[7] R. Das, A. Mishra, C. Nicopoulos, D. Park, V. Narayanan, R. Iyer, M. Yousif, and C. Das. Performance and power optimization through data compression in network-on-chip architectures. In *HPCA*, 2008.

[8] J. Dusser, T. Piquet, and A. Seznec. Zero-content augmented caches. In *ICS*, 2009.

[9] M. Ekman and P. Stenström. A robust main-memory compression scheme. In *ISCA-32*, 2005.

[10] M. Farrens and A. Park. Dynamic base register caching: a technique for reducing address bus width. In *ISCA-18*, 1991.

[11] E. G. Hallnor and S. K. Reinhardt. A fully associative software-managed cache design. In *ISCA-27*, 2000.

[12] E. G. Hallnor and S. K. Reinhardt. A unified compressed memory hierarchy. In *HPCA-11*, 2005.

[13] D. W. Hammerstrom and E. S. Davidson. Information content of CPU memory referencing behavior. In *ISCA-4*, 1977.

[14] D. Huffman. A method for the construction of minimum-redundancy codes. 1952.

[15] M. M. Islam and P. Stenström. Zero-value caches: Cancelling loads that return zero. In *PACT*, 2009.

[16] M. M. Islam and P. Stenström. Characterization and exploitation of narrow-width loads: the narrow-width cache approach. In *CASES*, 2010.

[17] A. Jaleel, K. B. Theobald, S. C. Steely, Jr., and J. Emer. High performance cache replacement using re-reference interval prediction (rrip). In *ISCA-37*, 2010.

[18] P. S. Magnusson, M. Christensson, J. Eskilson, D. Forsgren, G. Hållberg, J. Högberg, F. Larsson, A. Moestedt, and B. Werner. Simics: A full system simulation platform. 2002.

[19] D. Molka, D. Hackenberg, R. Schone, and M. Muller. Memory performance and cache coherency effects on an Intel Nehalem multiprocessor system. In *PACT*, 2009.

[20] M. K. Qureshi, A. Jaleel, Y. N. Patt, S. C. Steely, and J. Emer. Adaptive insertion policies for high performance caching. In *ISCA-34*, 2007.

[21] M. K. Qureshi, M. A. Suleman, and Y. N. Patt. Line distillation: Increasing cache capacity by filtering unused words in cache lines. In *HPCA-13*, 2007.

[22] M. K. Qureshi, D. Thompson, and Y. N. Patt. The V-Way cache: Demand based associativity via global replacement. ISCA-32, 2005.

[23] Y. Sazeides and J. E. Smith. The predictability of data values. In *MICRO-30*, 1997.

[24] A. B. Sharma, L. Golubchik, R. Govindan, and M. J. Neely. Dynamic data compression in multi-hop wireless networks. In *SIGMETRICS*, 2009.

[25] A. Snavely and D. M. Tullsen. Symbiotic jobscheduling for a simultaneous multithreaded processor. *ASPLOS-9*, 2000.

[26] SPEC CPU2006 Benchmarks. http://www.spec.org/.

[27] S. Srinath, O. Mutlu, H. Kim, and Y. N. Patt. Feedback directed prefetching: Improving the performance and bandwidth-efficiency of hardware prefetchers. In *HPCA-13*, 2007.

[28] W. Sun, Y. Lu, F. Wu, and S. Li. DHTC: an effective DXTC-based HDR texture compression scheme. In *Graphics Hardware*, 2008.

[29] S. Thoziyoor, N. Muralimanohar, J. H. Ahn, and N. P. Jouppi. CACTI 5.1. Technical Report HPL-2008-20, HP Laboratories, 2008.

[30] Transaction Processing Performance Council. http://www.tpc.org/.

[31] L. Villa, M. Zhang, and K. Asanovic. Dynamic zero compression for cache energy reduction. In *MICRO-33*, 2000.

[32] P. R. Wilson, S. F. Kaplan, and Y. Smaragdakis. The case for compressed caching in virtual memory systems. In *USENIX ATC*, 1999.

[33] J. Yang, Y. Zhang, and R. Gupta. Frequent value compression in data caches. In *MICRO-33*, 2000.

[34] Y. Zhang, J. Yang, and R. Gupta. Frequent value locality and value-centric data cache design. *ASPLOS-9*, 2000.

[35] J. Ziv and A. Lempel. A universal algorithm for sequential data compression. *IEEE Transactions on Information Theory*, 1977.

Hardware Acceleration in the IBM PowerEN Processor: Architecture and Performance

Anil Krishna, Timothy Heil[†], Nicholas Lindberg[‡], Farnaz Toussi, Steven VanderWiel [*]

Systems and Technology Group, IBM
{krishnaa,farnaz,svw}@us.ibm.com

[†]Microsoft IEB
timheil@microsoft.com

[‡]Milwaukee Institute
nlindberg@mkei.org

ABSTRACT

Computation at the edge of a datacenter has unique characteristics; it deals with streaming data from multiple sources, often requiring repeated application of several standard algorithmic kernels. The demand for high data rates and power efficiency points toward hardware acceleration of key functions. These accelerators must be tightly integrated with general purpose computation to keep invocation overhead and latency low. The accelerators must be easy for software to use, and the system must be flexible enough to support evolving networking standards.

In this paper, we describe and evaluate the architecture of IBM's PowerEN processor, with a focus on its on-chip hardware accelerators.

PowerEN unites the throughput of application-specific accelerators with the programmability of general purpose cores on a single coherent memory architecture. Hardware acceleration improves throughput by orders of magnitude in some cases compared to equivalent computation on the general purpose cores. By offloading work to the accelerators, general purpose cores are freed to simultaneously work on computation less suited to acceleration.

Categories and Subject Descriptors

C.3 [**Computer Systems Organization**]: SPECIAL-PURPOSE AND APPLICATION-BASED SYSTEMS

Keywords

PowerEN, Accelerator, Architecture, Performance, XML, Pattern Matching, Crypto, Compression

1. INTRODUCTION

Transistor size and integration continue to scale according to Moore's Law. However, the slowdown in the scalability of transistor power and diminishing returns of microarchitectural complexity have given rise to multi-core processor chips over the past decade. Further improvements in energy-proportional computing have been proposed and achieved using heterogeneity in multi-core chips [11, 16]. Domain specific software can exploit heterogeneity further by embracing domain specific hardware accelerators [25]. Hardware acceleration has been identified as a key approach to continue to scaling performance in the future [2, 9].

As networking continues to mature, more and more function is being embedded in the network itself. *Edge-of-network* applications represent a growing class of workloads with unique characteristics that blur the boundaries between server and network applications. Such applications include cyber security, network intrusion detection, database acceleration, online transaction processing request checking and normalization, service oriented architecture acceleration, and TCP/FTP/HTTP offload. These functions are typically highly parallel in nature, work with streaming data and stress cryptography, compression and pattern scanning algorithms, as well as network function. Hardware acceleration presents an opportunity to greatly enhance both the performance and energy efficiency of edge-of-network functions compared to handling them via traditional, general-purpose computing.

There has been substantial work in industry over the last decade to address this computation domain by companies such as Cavium [5], NetLogic [3], Tilera [28] and others. Such SOCs attack network applications by integrating tens of simple, efficient cores with a bevy of domain-specific accelerators. This highlights the fact that edge-of-network processing is becoming an key differentiator in data center performance. In this paper we describe the architecture of IBM's PowerEN processor [4, 10, 12, 15, 23], focusing on how the architecture enables hardware acceleration.

The rest of this paper is organized as follows. Section 2 provides a high-level overview of PowerEN, highlighting its unique architectural features and its general purpose cores. Sections 3, 4, 5, 6 and 7 describe the architecture and performance of the Host Ethernet Adapter, the Pattern-Matching accelerator, the Cryptography accelerator, the Compression and Decompression accelerator, and the XML accelerator respectively. Section 9 summarizes the findings and concludes.

2. ARCHITECTURE OF POWEREN

The PowerEN processor was designed to meet the demands of next-generation networks. It integrates 16 general purpose, multi-threaded processor cores with an array of accelerators.

The PowerEN architecture is accelerator friendly. It provides architectural and microarchitectural features that let software easily and efficiently use the hardware accelerators. In this section, we describe the high level microarchitecture of the PowerEN chip, and the control and data flow in a typical usage scenario. We then describe architectural ex-

[*]All authors were with IBM when working on this paper

PACT'12, September 19–23, 2012, Minneapolis, Minnesota, USA.

Table 1: Overview of PowerEN Capabilities

Unit	Capability	Performance
A2 Processor Core	4 threads, scalar FP, dual-issue, 16KB I- and D-caches	2.3GHz
L2 Cache	2MB shared by four cores, 8-way set associative	
Memory	4x channels, 64b+ECC each	Up to 1600MHz DDR-3
Cryptography	Encryption, Decryption, Authentication, Asymmetric Math, Asynchronous Data Mover, Random Number Generator	up to 50Gbit/s (symmetric) and 10M ops/sec (asymmetric math)
Compression and Decompression	LZ77 and Huffman coding/decoding	9Gbit/s (average across Canterbury Corpus suite)
Host Ethernet Adapter	Packet preclassification, automatic packet queue management	4x 10Gbit/s ports
Pattern Matching Engine	Up to 1024 pattern contexts. 1000's of regular expressions per context. 8 simultaneous scans	73Gbit/s peak. 15Gbit/s to 40Gbit/s typical.
XML	XML Parsing, XPATH evaluation, Schema validation and more	>10 Gbit/s (average across 14 workloads studied)

tensions in PowerEN that allow software to use the accelerators efficiently.

2.1 PowerEN Chip Overview

The PowerEN chip consists of a collection of 16 general purpose cores, two memory controllers each with two channels and a collection of accelerators (Host Ethernet Adapter, Multi-Pattern Matching, Compression/Decompression, Cryptographic Data Mover and XML Processing). All components are interconnected via a coherent interconnect. Table 1 summarizes PowerEN components, and their capabilities[1].

The *A2* general purpose cores are 64-bit PowerPC Book-E architecture compliant and are designed for throughput computing. An A2 core supports in-order execution and dual issue from up to 4 active hardware threads in a fine-grained simultaneous multi-threaded fashion. Each A2 has a 16KB L1-I and L1-D cache, and a group of 4 A2s share a 2MB L2 cache.

2.2 Example Use Case

Figure 1 shows a typical PowerEN use scenario. A packet stream coming in over the 4 10Gbit/s Ethernet ports is received by the Host Ethernet Adapter (HEA) (Arrow 1). The HEA is able to strip the packet of the appropriate headers from the lower-layers of the network stack before depositing the payload into software data structures either in memory or, preferably, directly into the L2 cache space on-chip. The latter, called *cache injection*, is shown in the figure (Arrow 2). The arrival of the packet awakens a software thread running on the general purpose core (Arrow 3). To decrypt the packet, the software thread sets up the necessary control data structures needed to communicate with the Cryptographic Data Mover (CDM), and sends the request to the CDM (Arrow 4). The control data structures and the command to wake up the CDM accelerator are standardized across all accelerators, and are part of the PowerEN ISA. The control data structure primarily identifies three things - the input data buffer (address, size), the output data buffer (address, size) and the operation to perform (for example, which decryption algorithm, and, if applicable, the decryption key to use). All addresses are specified as virtual addresses. Each accelerator has a Memory Management Unit (MMU) to translate the virtual addresses to physical addresses. This makes it straightforward for user-level software to set up these control structures. The CDM unit pulls the control data and input data from, in this case, an L2 cache (Arrow 5). All accelerator accesses participate in the interconnect's cache coherence protocol, ensuring correct operation regardless of the physical location of requested cache lines. The CDM writes the output data, as it is generated, to the appropriate location pointed to by the control block (Arrow 6). The CDM also writes to specific fields in the control block to indicate completion (Arrow 7). Software observes completion by simply reading the appropriate virtual address. In typical scenarios, decrypted data may be further processed by additional accelerators (decompression, pattern matching, XML parsing, etc.) using a similar handshake. Finally, the output data may be sent back out through the HEA.

[1]PowerEN fits into different power envelopes ranging from 25W to 75W via frequency/voltage scaling, all reported numbers assume nominal frequency/voltage settings

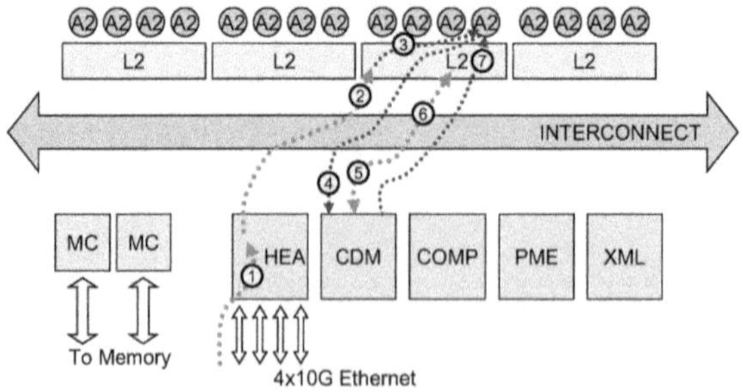

Figure 1: PowerEN Chip Overview

2.3 Accelerator-Friendly Architecture

The above example illustrates many of PowerEN's architectural enhancements, which simplify accelerator invocation and reduce startup overheads.

The PowerEN ISA defines a new instruction, called *Initiate Coprocessor Store Word* or *icswx* (pronounced ik-switch). The icswx instruction copies a 64B aligned co-processor request block (CRB) to the target accelerator. The CRB contains all the parameters for the command, such as, target accelerator, command to execute, and input and output data addresses.

Process identification information is securely added to the CRB prior to transmission, allowing the accelerator to run in the same virtual address space as the invoking thread. Each accelerator has an associated MMU, including a TLB and hardware translation table walker, so accelerators can perform their own address translation with minimal software involvement. This information includes the virtual partition identifier and the process identifier for the invoking address space. By providing both IDs, the accelerator is able to concurrently run requests from different processes on different virtualized operating systems.

Each accelerator is directly attached to the coherent interconnect (called *PBus*) and participates in the hardware coherence protocol. Accelerators are, therefore, able to read or write all the data they need without special software support such as pinning virtual pages or DMAing data in to and out of the accelerator.

Each accelerator has a hardware queue to hold a handful of CRBs. Should this queue overflow, further CRBs will be rejected by the accelerator. The rejection is reported back to software through a condition code set by the icswx instruction, placed in the same condition registers set by normal compare instructions in the PowerPC architecture.

To minimize this occurrence, the PowerEN accelerators can extend the hardware queue into main memory. The *spill/fill feature* spills excess CRBs to a queue in memory, from which they are filled as CRBs are completed. Other than initial configuration of the spill/fill queues, software is uninvolved in this process. While this can increase parallelism, it does increase memory and bus bandwidth, so some applications may not find it beneficial. The test results reported in the following sections do not use the spill/fill feature.

Since all accelerator activity involves data movement, managing data movement within the system is a major focus of the PowerEN bus architecture. Besides traditional optimizations, such as prefetching and cache line locking, PowerEN provides a number of accelerator-friendly optimizations.

Data produced by an accelerator or ingressed onto the chip from the HEA is not sent out to DRAM. Rather, accelerators can be configured to place generated data in a specific L2 cache, or spread it uniformly across all L2 caches. This dramatically reduces memory bandwidth requirements compared to traditional models. In a traditional system, every hop to and from every accelerator would require writing and reading the data to and from memory. In PowerEN, all data stays on the chip.

Furthermore, accelerators can update data in L2 caches in place. This is useful, for instance, when accelerators report completion. Accelerators typically report completion by writing a status bit in memory. The bit is checked by software using normal loads. Rather than forcing the line to memory, the status bit is updated in place in the L2 cache where it resides – typically the L2 cache of the core that submitted the request, and which will check for completion. Hence, rather than being in memory distant from the consumer, the status ends up exactly where it is needed.

To make polling on completion status even more efficient, PowerEN provides the wait-on-reservation instruction. Wait-on-reservation will stall a thread for many cycles, until a store is detected. This prevents polling loops from interfering with the other threads running on the same core. The wait-on-reservation instruction is also useful for inter-thread communication structures, such as locks.

2.4 Accelerator Software Architecture

Historically, software communicated with devices via a kernel-level device driver. The driver performed two basic functions - security checks and device abstraction. In PowerEN, security checks have moved into the hardware. Accelerators access memory using the same virtual addresses as the invoking process, and the same page-level protections apply. Device abstraction allows applications to be written to a higher-level standard API, while giving hardware vendors the freedom to innovate. In PowerEN, device abstraction occurs through the user-level libraries typically used to invoke the accelerator.

PowerEN's Software Development Kit (SDK) provides standard libraries supporting encryption/decryption (OpenSSL, OpenVPN) and compression/decompression (zlib). Multi-pattern search is a developing area, and standard APIs for this function are not mature. PowerEN provides a custom interface for this function. The interface to program the Host Ethernet Adapter is also based on a custom-developed user-level library code.

Finally, the libcopl library provides an efficient low-level interface to the accelerators. This allows application developers to port PowerEN function to their own internal APIs efficiently. A uniform architecture simplifies the software interfaces to heterogenous accelerators, allowing the application layer to take full advantage of their capabilities.

3. HOST ETHERNET ADAPTER

The HEA unit provides network connectivity through four Ethernet ports, each configurable as either 1Gbit/s port or a 10Gbit/s port. The HEA provides a number of important packet acceleration functions, including:

- Programmable packet pre-classification
- Check-sum validation (IP header, TCP, UDP)
- Automatic packet scattering/gathering over 128 send or receive queues
- Hardware-assisted packet queue management

The HEA communicates with software through *queue pairs*, each of which contains a receive queue and a send queue. Each logical receive-queue can contain up to three internal queues to efficiently handle different packet sizes.

When the HEA receives a packet from the network, it selects a queue pair based on a hash of the 5-tuple.[2] This spreads work across many threads, such that they can work largely independently; yet it still ensures that inter-packet dependencies are enforced. Within the selected logical receive-queue, the HEA places the packet on the correct internal receive-queue based on the packet size.

To transmit a packet, software places the packet on a send-queue, and notifies the HEA. For large packets, the packet buffer used for reception can also be used for transmission, accelerating applications such as security, which tend to retransmit packets with few modifications.

3.1 Performance

Figure 2 illustrates HEA throughput with minimum software overhead. An Ixia Ethernet test system [14] was used to drive or receive packets in to or out of PowerEN in order to measure peak packet throughputs. All packets are IPv4 packets (IPv6 is also supported), and minimal packet classification is done. For transmit tests throughput is measured using Ixia's tracing capability to measure the elapsed time and total number of bytes received on Ixia. For receive tests the HEA timestamp associated with each frame was used to compute the elapsed time and the number of bytes received.

For small packet sizes, HEA sustains 12Gbit/s to 28Gbit/s in each direction. However, for packets of 320B and larger, HEA supports nearly 100% utilization on all four Ethernet ports simultaneously. Since typical Internet packet mixes have an average packet size of around 384B, the HEA will support the full port bandwidth for realistic traffic patterns.

[2] i.e. protocol, source address and port, destination address and port.

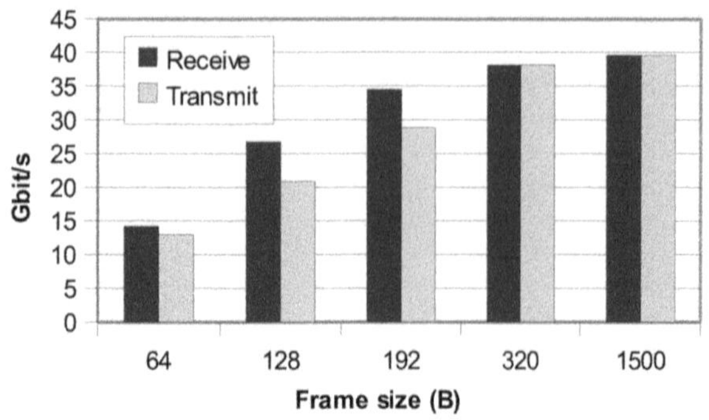

Figure 2: HEA transmit and receive bandwidth

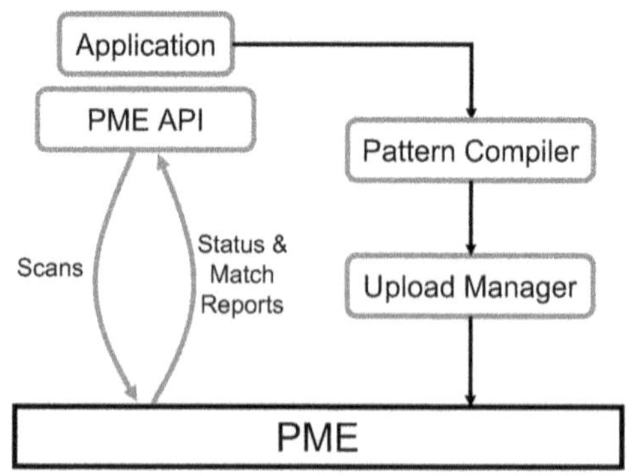

Figure 3: PME Software Stack

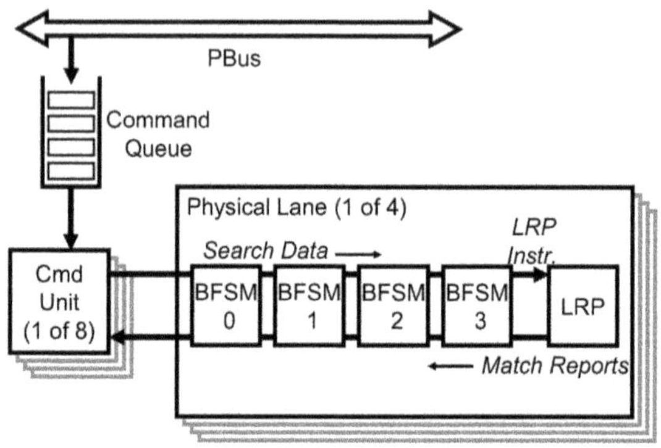

Figure 4: PME Architecture

4. PATTERN MATCHING ENGINE

The pattern matching engine (PME) scans input data for large numbers of regular expressions. Typical applications group tens to thousands of expressions into *pattern contexts*, and may contain hundreds of such pattern contexts. Given an input byte stream, the PME reports all match locations for all patterns in a particular context. Theoretical peak throughput is 73.6 Gbit/s. Realistic workloads typically obtain 15 Gbit/s to 45 Gbit/s.

Supported regular expression constructs include:

- Bounded/unbounded repeat operators (`{...}`, `*`, `+`)
- Wild-cards, character classes, case-insensitivity (`[]`, `.`)
- Alternatives (|)
- Start-anchored, end-anchored, unanchored patterns (`^`, `$`)

The only hardware feature specific to ASCII encoding is case-insensitivity. The PME is therefore suitable for scanning any byte-oriented data stream.

4.1 Software Interface

Figure 3 shows the PME software stack. Pattern contexts are compiled into an internal form understood by the hardware.

Compiled contexts are uploaded to the PME via the PME *Upload Manager* (UM). Application software then submits searches. During the performance critical search function applications interact directly with the PME engine through icswx, embedded in the PME search library. Match reports and completion status are produced by the PME into normal user memory, and processed by the application using normal loads and stores.

Network traffic can be scanned one packet at a time, without first reassembling traffic streams. To accomplish this the PME saves scan state at the end of one data buffer, and then restores that state before the next packet is scanned. The results produced are identical to scanning both packets at once. State is stored in normal user memory, so the number of active network flows is bounded only by system memory size.

This capability creates dependencies between successive scans. These hazards are checked and enforced by the PME. Software can submit multiple dependent scans in parallel, and the PME will ensure they are performed in the correct order.

4.2 Accelerator Design

The PME follows a RISC design philosophy. Simple hardware performs a minimal number of critical functions as fast as possible. An intelligent compiler makes efficient use of hardware primitives.

Like many modern multi-pattern-search engines [6, 17, 24, 26, 27], the PME contains both NFA and DFA features (Figure 4). The core engine, the *B-FSM* [30] is a DFA state walking engine. Four of these are combined together into a *physical lane*. The compiler will optimally distribute patterns across the B-FSMs to prevent the state-explosion that DFA-based algorithms are prone to.

State explosion is further avoided via the *local-result processor* (LRP). While the B-FSMs can identify many patterns directly, some regular expression constructs, such as the common `.*` construct, cannot be encoded efficiently on the B-FSM. Patterns are broken into sub-expressions at such constructs, and the B-FSMs search for these sub-expressions. When a sub-expression is found, the B-FSM forwards an instruction to the LRP, which determines when all the sub-expressions have been identified in the correct order. The LRP then reports the pattern match.

When a context becomes too large to fit efficiently on four B-FSMs and/or one LRP, the compiler will break the context into multiple sub-contexts. Similar to the dispersal across the B-FSMs, the compiler intelligently distributes patterns to minimize pressure on the B-FSMs and LRPs.

This dramatically reduces the size of the resulting compiled context, but does come at a cost. To the hardware, these sub-contexts look like independent contexts that happen to scan the same data. The PME search library must submit a separate scan for each sub-context in the logical context.

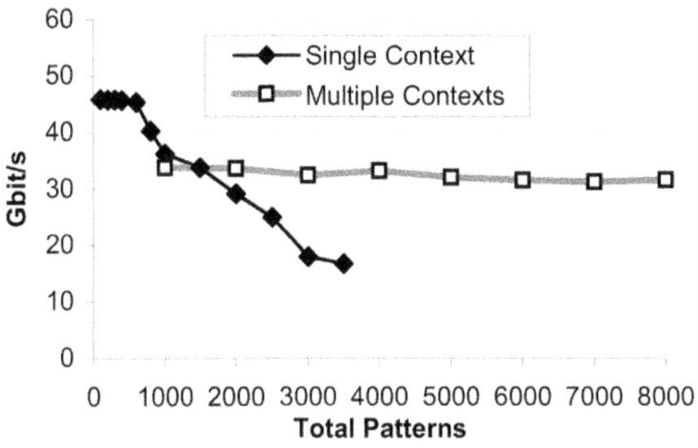

Figure 5: PME Performance: Simple string patterns

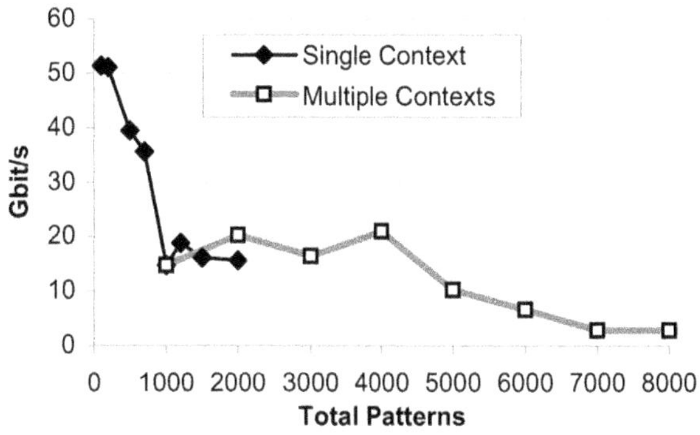

Figure 6: PME Performance: Complex patterns

To improve the performance of large contexts, a single PME icwsx command can invoke two scans.

Four independent physical lanes are instantiated on the PME. Furthermore, each physical lane is time-multiplexed between two virtual lanes, each of which can run an independent search. Thus the PME can work on eight scans simultaneously from the same or different software threads or processes. Each of the eight virtual lanes can scan one byte every other cycle at 2.3GHz.

The PME contains 512KB of SRAM cache for compiled pattern rules, organized as 32KB of cache per B-FSM. A B-FSM can read the rules required to process a single character in a single cycle, as long as the rules are in its local cache. When a rule miss occurs, the rule is fetched from main memory. While the rule is being fetched, the scan is disengaged from the virtual lane, which may be assigned to a different scan, reducing the effective miss penalty.

If a context is frequently used, it may benefit from more bandwidth than that provided by a single physical lane. In this case, the upload manager can replicate the context across multiple physical lanes. This requires replicating the rules in the B-FSM caches, thereby reducing the effective cache capacity. The UM seeks to maximize throughput, balancing the cost of increased rule miss rate, vs. improved load balancing across the physical lanes. The search application is uninvolved in this optimization. Replication is done asynchronously and transparently by the UM, based on hardware-assisted profiling of context and rule usage.

4.3 Performance

Figures 5 and 6 illustrate the performance of the PME for a wide range of synthetic workloads. Multi-pattern search workloads containing large numbers of complex patterns are not publicly available at this time. By using synthetic workloads, we can vary key parameters, and make the set publicly available [13].

Performance is measured using multi-threaded user-level Linux applications that leverage the libcopl library. The tests stream scans from 32 threads, an excessive number designed to ensure the PME is saturated. We measure the steady-state bandwidth on the processor threads using the processor's timebase register over about 20K scans. These measurements are verified using performance counters on the PME engine. The average of three measurements is reported.

The figures show the performance in Gbit/s on the y-axis and total number of patterns on the x-axis. The number of patterns are increased either by adding more patterns to a

Table 2: Example patterns from the complex pattern sets

<table>
<tr><th>Example Pattern</th><th>Description</th></tr>
<tr><td>6zfe4t0ikumP</td><td>Simple string pattern</td></tr>
<tr><td>cbPvd(WT)?</td><td>Extended string pattern with optional element</td></tr>
<tr><td>^jVC6(Wj|zq|A7)vX[^\n\r]* 3FFh3GA0z</td><td>Two string elements with separator, front-anchored</td></tr>
<tr><td>E[a-z]kRqDMf.*xbgyHH.* 9Ia3UbnPdhW4tq[A-Z]</td><td>Three string elements with separators</td></tr>
</table>

single context (Single Context), or by increasing the number of fixed-sized contexts (Multiple Contexts). In the later case, each context contains 1000 patterns.

The simple string patterns (Figure 5) consist of patterns made up of a uniform distributions of upper and lower case letters and digits. Each pattern is 10 characters long. All are case sensitive. None are anchored.

The complex pattern sets (Figure 6) consist of a mix of simple strings, extended string-like elements and *separator* elements. The extended string-like elements contain broad character classes (*[a-z]* , *[A-Z]* , *[0-9]*), alternatives (*(abc|xyz|123)*) and optional components (*abc(123)?*). They represent 35% of all string elements. In addition, 20% of patterns contain multiple such string-like elements separated by wildcards and repeat constructs (*.* , *.** , *[^"]*"*, *[^\n\r]**, ...). Of the patterns, 50% are case insensitive, and 20% are front-anchored (*^*). Table 2 shows several example patterns from the complex pattern sets.

The input data is also an important factor affecting pattern matching performance. Most of the input characters are chosen from a random uniform distribution over letters and digits. However, random data does not stress the B-FSMs realistically because they will not tend to traverse a wide variety of DFA states. By interspersing byte sequences that match the initial pieces of the patterns, the B-FSMs are driven to explore a much wider variety of states, stressing the rule cache hierarchy. The distance between such sequences is an exponential distribution with a mean of 100 characters. The length of matching sequences is exponential with a mean of 2. The target pattern for the pattern-based sequence is random uniform over all patterns in the pattern context. All scans are 1000B long.

Where multiple contexts are used, searches are distributed in a uniform random distribution over the contexts. This is a worst case situation. Applications with multiple contexts commonly use a few contexts frequently, and many rarely.

For a single context of simple patterns (Figure 5), performance is a constant 45 Gbit/s up to 600 patterns. In this range, there are no rule misses. Beyond this performance starts to fall due to increasing miss rate. At 1000 patterns (36 Gbit/s) a single logical lane is full. After this two logical lanes are used[3], reducing the miss rate, but at the cost of more physical scans. The trend continues resulting in a gentle decline in performance as patterns are added, culminating with 3500 patterns on four logical lanes at 17 Gbit/s.

With multiple contexts, performance remains constant at about 33 Gbit/s out to 8000 patterns, even though the number of rules increases as contexts are added. This is due to physical lane replication described previously. With a single context, the UM replicates that context on all four physical lanes for maximum throughput. Essentially four contexts are being cached. With two contexts, replication is reduced to two copies, again yielding four cached contexts and leaving the effective cache pressure unchanged, even though the number of live rules have doubled . Four contexts are similar. Each physical lane can comfortably hold 2 large, heavily used contexts. Hence, 8 contexts result in similar performance.

The complex pattern sets show similar trends, but put more pressure on the LRP and B-FSM rule cache hierarchy (Figure 6). Approximately 500 patterns, rather than 1000, fit in a logical lane. Performance is flat (51 Gbit/s) up to 200 patterns. Every 500 patterns, another logical lane is added, trading off increasing miss rate for additional scans. Performance degrades reasonably to 16 Gbit/s with 2000 patterns on four logical lanes. Note that the 1000 pattern point is relatively low, due apparently to random variation in the synthetic pattern set.

The multi-context results are relatively flat up to 4000 patterns (4 contexts). Replication again plays a key role in this region. Each context with 1000 patterns is compiled into two sub-contexts. Similar to the multi-context simple string results, the upload manager puts four copies of each sub-context on each of the four physical lanes, physically caching eight total sub-contexts. With two contexts, the upload manager switches to replicating each context twice. In fact, with two logical contexts, four total sub-contexts, the UM has some flexibility to decide which sub-contexts are paired on the physical lanes, leading to a lower miss rate and better performance (20 Gbit/s, up from 15 Gbit/s).

There is a dip again with three contexts, because six sub-contexts don't pack cleanly on four physical lanes. Two contexts are unreplicated, and one is replicated twice. As with two contexts, performance increases again with four contexts. Each context is unreplicated, and the eight sub-contexts are packed on the four physical lanes.

Performance is therefore relatively flat, varying between 15 Gbit/s and 20 Gbit/s from one to four contexts. After this point, the miss rate increases, and performance slopes off as shown.

In summary, the PME is capable of scanning data at 15 to 50 Gbit/s on multiple contexts containing as many as 8000 patterns. A RISC design philosophy couple with tight integration produced a flexible high-performance pattern matching accelerator capable of handling a rich regular expression language at wire-speed.

5. CRYPTOGRAPHIC DATA MOVER ACCELERATOR

Encryption, decryption, and authentication of streaming data at the edge of a datacenter can substantially free up general purpose compute resources inside the datacenter. The Cryptographic Data Mover (CDM) is capable of handling a wide range of cryptographic algorithms, often at wire speeds, including combinations of two operations (encryption and authentication) in a single command.

In addition to accelerating cryptography the CDM also supports block data moves (generic DMA) at over 60 Gbit/s, and random number generation at 12K 64-bit numbers per second.

5.1 Accelerator Design

The CDM is composed of eight *channels*. Each channel contains one or more *algorithm engines*, and a DMA engine to stream data in and out of the algorithm engines. Only one algorithm engine is active within a channel at a time. Each algorithm engine is capable of handling one or a small subset of the supported algorithms. Algorithm engines are replicated across the channels to meet throughput targets for each algorithm.

The CRB indicates which algorithm is required. For a given algorithm, there are a fixed subset of applicable channels – those containing the appropriate algorithm engine. The CDM will select the next available, applicable channel to handle the CRB request.

The channel works on the incoming data in a pipelined fashion. The DMA unit in the channel starts fetching the packet data. The algorithm engine will begin work as soon as a sufficient minimum amount of data has arrived. The output data is DMAed back to the destination address, as pointed to by the CRB, as it is generated.

5.2 Performance

The performance tests are written as user-level code under Linux, leveraging the libcopl library provided with the PowerEN Software Development Kit. Each test submits requests of a particular size for one particular cryptographic algorithm. The requests are submitted from a programmable number of software threads, spaced uniformly across the 64 available hardware threads. We vary both the packet size and the number of software threads to investigate how these parameters affect throughput. We only show the encryption rates; the rate of encryption and decryption are equal for these cryptographic algorithms.

The steady state icswx acceptance rate directly correlates with the steady state icswx completion rate, and this is used to measure throughput. We validate this measurement using both hardware performance counters on the CDM, and the processor timebase register.

We first enumerate the absolute throughput achieved for each algorithm tested. We then discuss the relative advantage of acceleration compared to running code on the general purpose cores.

5.2.1 Accelerator Throughputs

Figure 7 and Figure 8 show the absolute throughputs measured for the individual symmetric encryption and authentication (message digest or hashing) algorithms, including combined operations (last six workloads in Figure 8). The results do not show all possible sub-functions within each algorithm. For example, AES supports a handful of different flavors. We just consider one (ECB) with a 128-bit key size. This was a conscious decision to help focus on insights, while gaining a reasonably good feel for the performance ranges. Each stacked bar indicates the throughput that can be reached by increasing the number of threads participat-

[3]The proto-type compiler logical lane selection heuristics are still being tuned. The number of logical lanes was selected using command-line switches.

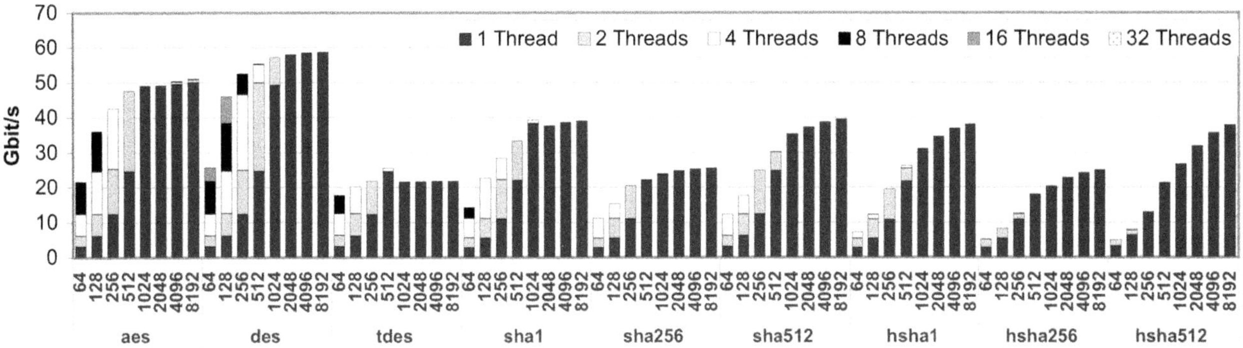

Figure 7: Best-case throughputs for individual, symmetric, crypto algorithms. x-axis is payload size in Bytes.

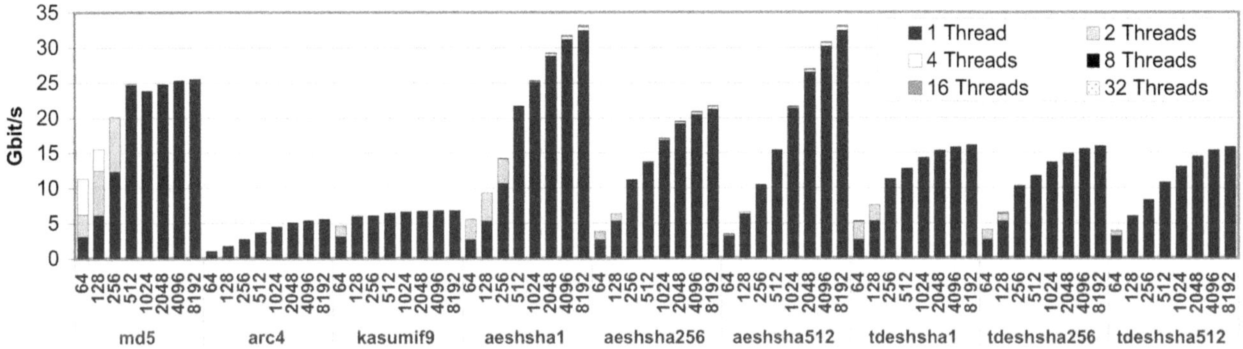

Figure 8: Best-case throughputs for symmetric, crypto algorithms including combined encryption/authentication algorithms. x-axis is payload size in Bytes.

ing in sending work to the accelerator. For each algorithm the figure also shows the throughput improvements as the size of the payload per CRB increases. As can be seen, often, only 1 to 4 threads (out of the 64 on a chip) are needed to keep the accelerator well fed with work - only AES and DES need 8 or 16 threads, and that too only for payloads which are 128B or smaller. As the payload size increases the number of threads needed decreases; fewer threads are able to keep the accelerator busy if each request demands more work. This allows the other threads to be used for other useful work.

The CDM supports a wide range of asymmetric mathematical functions, used to accelerate asymmetric cryptographic algorithms including Rivest-Shamir-Aldeman(RSA) and Elliptic Curve Cryptography (ECC) [7, 8, 29]. The asymmetric operations are basically modular arithmetic operations - addition, subtraction, multiplication, inversion, reduction, exponentiation and exponentiation based on the Chinese Remainder Theorem (CRT) - done on operands belonging to different Galois Fields (GF). In Figure 9 operations labeled M* operate on operands in GF(2^m). In Figure 10 operations labeled M2* operate on ECC operands over GF(2^m); operations labeled P* operate on operands in GF(P), and operations labeled P2* operate on ECC operands over GF(P).

Unlike the symmetric algorithms, these operations are not done over variable-sized input data. Instead the operations are mathematical functions performed over input operands of well defined sizes. Performance for these operations is therefore measured in operations per second, rather than in bits per second.

5.2.2 *Acceleration Advantage*

We used an internal software tool called *sslbench* to measure performance with and without acceleration. Sslbench uses the OpenSSL library to submit work. This makes it easy to compare accelerator and software performance, by either linking against the PowerEN-specific version of OpenSSL (with accelerator support), or, the generic software-based version of OpenSSL. This allows us to measure the latency of encrypting a large, 32KB payload with and without acceleration for a number of algorithms.

Figure 11 and Figure 12 summarize our findings. Figure 11 shows the performance of the tests that offload work to the accelerator, as more and more software threads are employed. The results are normalized to the best performance we could get using the software-only approach; in most cases the software-only approach required employing all 64 threads available on chip for best performance. The main take away from this figure is that for most algorithms acceleration can improve performance by nearly an order of magnitude, while engaging much fewer A2 threads than the purely software option would require. Indirectly, this also indicates a potentially significant power advantage by freeing up the general purpose cores. That said, we found one algorithm, rc4 (and its variant, rc4_40) for which by using sufficiently large number of threads the software-only approach does better than acceleration.

A different way to compare the performance with and without acceleration is to employ a fixed number of software threads in both cases. Figure 12 shows such a comparison with 8 A2 threads engaged. In one case the 8 threads run

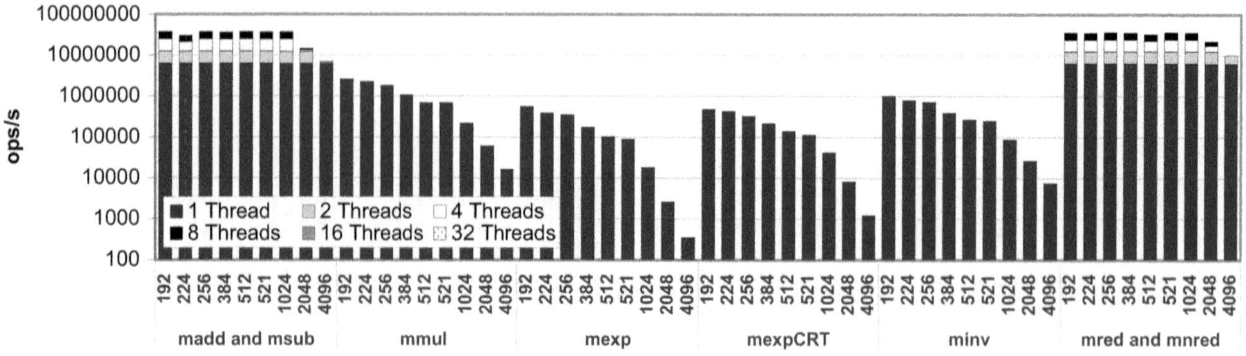

Figure 9: Best-case throughputs for asymmetric m* crypto algorithms. x-axis is operand size.

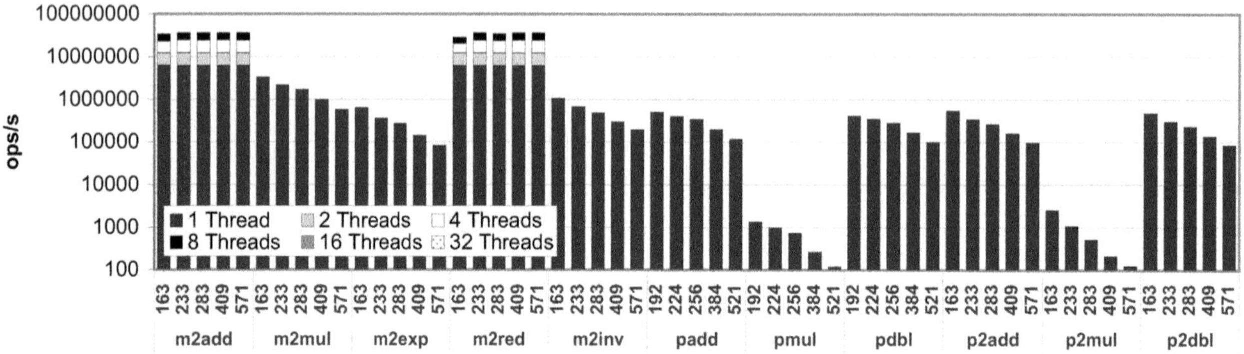

Figure 10: Best-case throughputs for asymmetric m2*, p* and p2* crypto algorithms. x-axis is operand size.

the cryptographic algorithm on the A2 cores; in the other, the same 8 threads are used only to set up CRBs and offload work to the accelerator. The performance advantage of acceleration shown in this figure are likely conservative. Fewer than 8 threads may be able to fully engage the accelerators, where as software performance will degrade proportionally with fewer threads.

6. COMPRESSION ACCELERATOR

Data compression and decompression are extremely important for highly streamlined datacenter applications, often utilized in both high traffic networking and disk management to yield higher efficiency by shrinking data footprints. The nature of these algorithms lend themselves to hardware acceleration, and several standalone compression/decompression hardware engines have emerged to offload these operations [1, 19].

The PowerEN compression/decompression accelerator supports up to 8 Gbit/s of simultaneous compression and decompression bandwidth, using the RFC 1951 [22] compliant DEFLATE/INFLATE algorithms, based on LZ77 and Huffman coding. As they share the same base algorithm functionality, the engine is also capable of handling zlib (RFC1950 [20]) and gzip (RFC1952 [21]) stream operations as well.

The accelerator can work on multiple compress/decompress commands at once from the same or multiple threads from the same or multiple processes. Furthermore, a single data stream can be submitted in separate pieces. Compressed packet streams do not need to be reassembled prior to decompression, nor be completed prior to compression and transmission.

For compression, the engine emphasizes speed, latency, and die area over maximum compression ratios – only static Huffman encoding is supported. For decompression, both static and dynamic Huffman decoding are supported using a 32KB history table, as required by the standards. The engine contains a 4KB history cache to cache recently used history during decompression. In the time during which missing history is fetched from memory the engine does not stop. Instead, a "hole" is created in the output stream, which is filled once the missing history returns from memory.

6.1 Performance

Performance is gauged using the Canterbury Corpus benchmark set [18]. The benchmark set contains 11 files chosen specifically to stress various aspects of compression and decompression, and to deliver representative results. The testcases are single threaded. All reported results are averaged over 20 runs. An enhanced version of the zlib library capable of utilizing the accelerator was used. All measurements of time rely on the processor's timebase register. Table 3 lists each file's size before and after compression with gzip -9, as well as the compression ratio. The compression ratio ranges from 2.43 (xargs.1) all the way up to 9.83 (ptt5), with a harmonic mean of 2.26[4]. Results are sorted by this compression ratio throughout this section.

[4]The harmonic mean corresponds to an average input made up of equal parts of each component, and is used throughout this section.

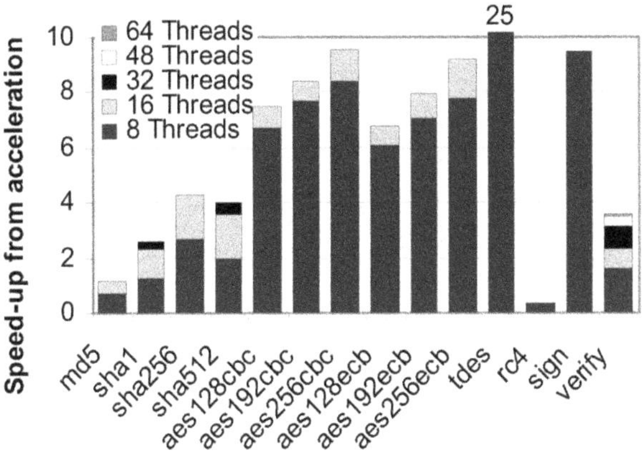

Figure 11: Performance advantage of acceleration

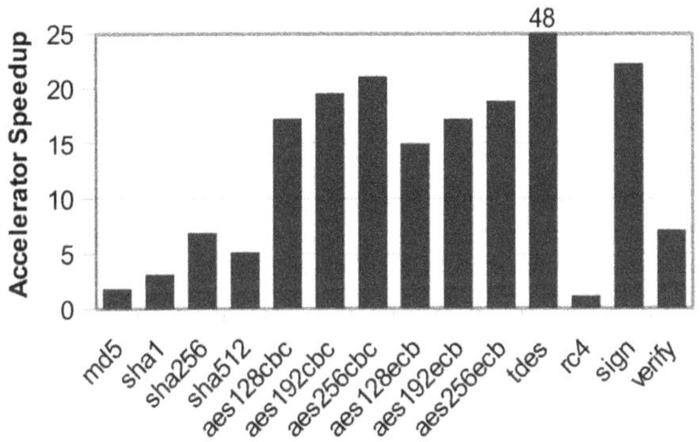

Figure 12: Performance advantage of acceleration when engaging 8 threads

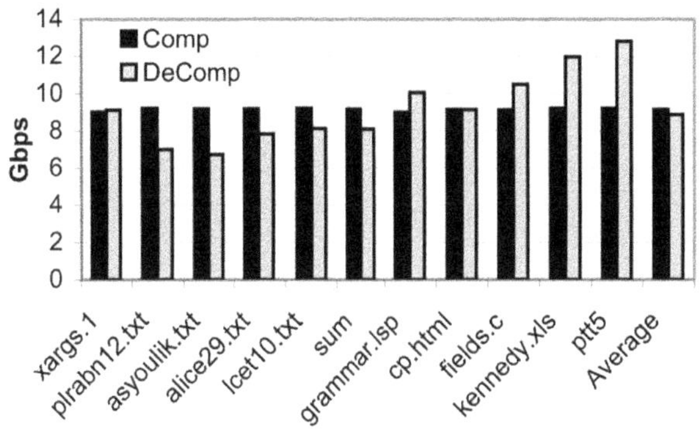

Figure 13: Absolute Throughputs

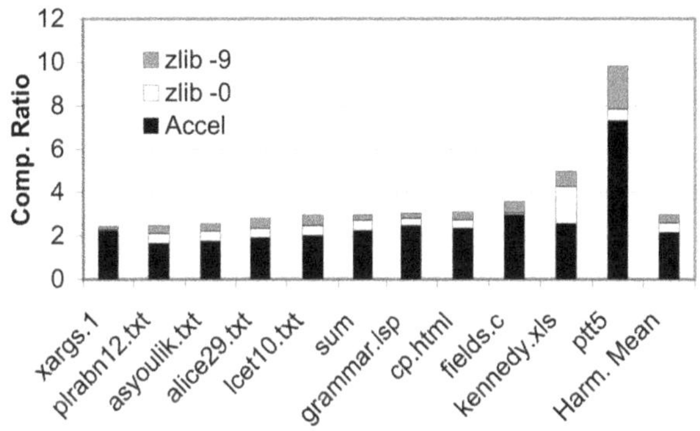

Figure 14: Compression Ratios HW vs. SW

6.1.1 *Throughput*

Figure 13 illustrates the raw bandwidth (measured in terms of the uncompressed data stream) of the accelerator for each file in the Canterbury Corpus benchmark set. The average reported compression bandwidth is 9.1 Gbit/s, and given the straightforward static Huffman coding, is fairly constant.

Decompression has an average bandwidth of 8.9 Gbit/s, but varies by almost a factor of two from 6.7 Gbit/s (asyoulik.txt) all the way up to 12.8 Gbit/s (ptt5). The general upward trend across the graph demonstrates that high compression ratios lead to better decompression rates, as fewer history buffer reads are required.

While a full end to end application that simultaneously engages multiple accelerator engines was beyond the scope of this work, a subset of such a test was attempted involving the HEA, CDM and the compression unit. This corresponded to a case where a packet stream received over the HEA is first encrypted and then compressed before being retransmitted out. The overall throughput was, as expected, limited by the lowest performing individual accelerator in that case, which happened to be the compression unit. This provides a glimpse at how PowerEN's efficient data movement avoids creating additional performance bottlenecks when multiple accelerators are chained together in a pipelined fashion.

Table 3: Workload file sizes and compression ratios

File	Orig. Size	Comp. Size	Comp. Ratio
xargs.1	4227	1736	2.43
plrabn12.txt	481861	194332	2.48
asyoulik.txt	125179	48778	2.57
alice29.txt	152089	54170	2.81
lcet10.txt	426754	144439	2.95
sum	38240	12838	2.98
grammar.lsp	3721	1222	3.05
cp.html	24603	7940	3.10
fields.c	11150	3115	3.58
kennedy.xls	1029744	207029	4.97
ptt5	513216	52221	9.83
HMean			**3.17**

6.1.2 *Comparison to Software*

Accelerator and software performance can be directly compared using the zlib library on the PowerEN processor core. Figure 14 shows the difference in compression ratios between the software and hardware implementations. As expected, software with dynamic Huffman encoding and variable levels of compression, achieves higher compression ratios than the accelerator. On average, the accelerator produces compressed files 22% larger than zlib -0, and 42% larger than zlib -9. However, the resulting increase in throughput is enormous.

Table 4 shows the speedup of the accelerator over zlib. Decompression averages 22 times faster. The ptt5 input, with its high compression ratio, does relatively well with software (only 14x slower). Other than this, there is little trend to the data.

Compression is even more impressive. Compared to zlib -0, the accelerator is more than 100 times faster. With level-9 compression, zlib is more variable in performance, resulting in a wide range of speedups from 169x (grammar.lsp) to 7842x (kennedy.xls), with a harmonic mean of 464x. The mean drops only slightly to 424x if the high outlier (kennedy.xls) is removed.

Table 4: Throughput Ratios HW vs. SW

File	Decomp	Comp zlib -0	Comp zlib -9
xargs.1	30.9	116.3	345.6
plrabn12.txt	24.2	131.9	919.0
asyoulik.txt	23.6	106.9	560.4
alice29.txt	22.5	121.4	722.1
lcet10.txt	22.1	129.9	650.3
sum	22.3	89.3	2416.0
grammar.lsp	30.7	115.1	169.4
cp.html	21.3	90.7	249.3
fields.c	21.7	99.0	244.5
kennedy.xls	19.8	137.7	7842.7
ptt5	14.2	105.4	2183.7
HMean	**22.1**	**110.9**	**464.3**

In summary, compared to a general purpose processor core, the accelerator provides a 20x performance improvement on decompression. On compression, the accelerator yields hundreds to thousands of times more bandwidth. Offloading compression/decompression leaves processor cores available for more suitable tasks, and enables wire-speed processing rates.

7. XML ACCELERATOR

7.1 Architecture

The XML accelerator parses XML documents, and can, optionally, post-process the results in different ways. Post-processing can include schema validation, Xpath matching and filtering, and other streamable XML processing options. The accelerator receives documents to parse in chunks (of up to 64KB) and generates output incrementally, as a collection of 4KB buffers, as the document is parsed. There are two main output formats - TLA (Type-Length-Attribute) format, which can be incrementally consumed by the software application, and the Tree format, which is intended to be used by the software once the entire document is processed. The size of the output is highly variable depending on the the output format requested, the post processing being performed, and the characteristics of the document itself. A 64KB chunk of input can generate anywhere from 1 to 32 4KB output buffers.

The accelerator can parse multiple documents simultaneously - and both the input document chunks and output data buffers can be interleaved. The accelerators can handle a large number of simultaneously live *sessions*, each of which is associated with one document and is identified by a unique *session ID*. Software communicates with the hardware accelerator by setting up a Coprocessor Request Buffer (CRB) structure in memory and using the icswx command. The first CRB associated with the processing of a new document requests that the accelerator open a new *session*. From that point on, all input data transfers from the software to the accelerator and output data or responses from the accelerator to software are tagged with the unique *session ID*. The *session ID* can be reused once the processing of the document currently associated with it completes.

The accelerator also contains a post processing engine (PPE) that may be optionally engaged to perform in-line post processing on the parsed document chunks. The PPE can suppress or selectively include parts of the result document in the final output, switch output formats mid-stream, or insert tags that annotate specific items in the result. The PPE is a programmable microcontroller with its own internal Instruction Set Architecture(ISA) and can execute sophisticated post processing operations on the parsed output. If the PPE is to be used for a document, the CRB that opens a new session must indicate this and also point

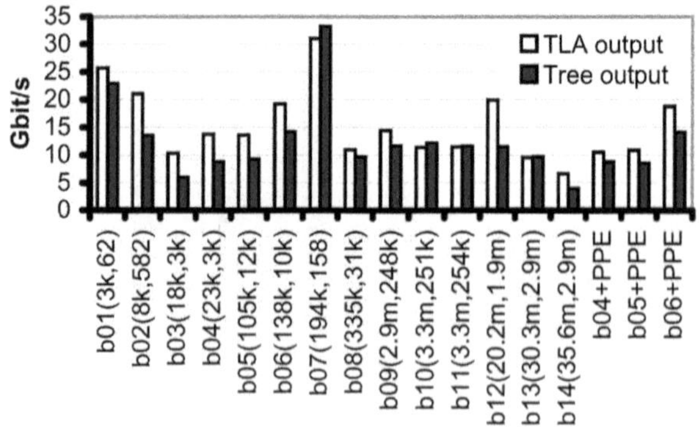

Figure 15: Throughputs for XML workloads when generating TLA and TREE output (size in bytes and number of TLAs in workload shown along x-axis)

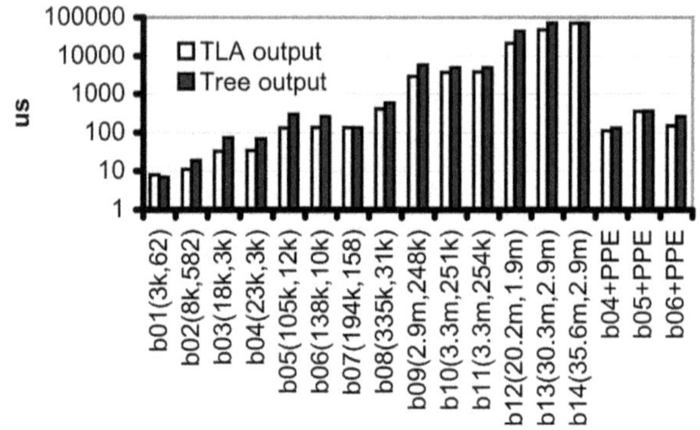

Figure 16: Latency to process XML documents (size in bytes and number of TLAs in workload shown along x-axis)

to the pre-compiled PPE program in memory to be used in the post-processing step.

The accelerator can be used by up to four processes at a time, be they across different Virtual Machines or within a single Operating System. The accelerator can handle 4 separate virtual-to-physical address mappings.

Internally, the accelerator implements 4 accelerator engine pipelines that can parse, post-process and generate output buffers in parallel. There is some function that is shared by these pipelines - address translation, data ingress and egress, request queuing etc. Load balancing is achieved by statically and predictably associating any given session ID to only one of the parallel pipelines.

7.2 Performance

We measured performance of the XML accelerator using 14 realistic workloads. Each workload repeatedly processes a unique, real-life, XML document. The testcases that exercise the accelerators were written as multi-threaded (1 to 4 threads) C programs running under Linux. The library used to communicate with the XML accelerator was a kernel-level library, although a corresponding, lightweight, user-level library is currently under development. Time is measured using the processor timebase register. These results illustrate the range of performance numbers that may be expected, although the actual performance depends on the characteristics of the document itself.

Figure 15 shows the throughputs of processing the workloads studied. The x-axis shows the size of each XML file and the number of TLAs in it. The first 14 pairs of bars correspond to parsing the input XML file in the XML Unit's Parse engine. The last 3 pairs of bars correspond to the case where the the input XML file is sent through the Parse engine followed by the Packet Processing Engine. For most workloads, the XML accelerator is able to sustain a throughput of over 10 Gbit/s.

In addition to throughput, the latency of document processing is an important performance metric for the XML unit. Figure 16 shows the latencies of processing a document under each of the workloads studied. The processing latency is dependent on the size of the file, the output format (tree format takes longer) and the post processing steps if any (last 3 workloads).

8. ACKNOWLEDGMENTS

This work benefited from the contributions of the whole PowerEN team at IBM; in particular, we thank Brian Bass, William McNeil, Heather Achilles, Ken Inoue, Kay Muller, Sairam Kamaraju, Shaul Yifrach, James Xenidis, Chris Arges, David Maze, Kelly Carpenter, Randall Kunkel, Thomas McSweeney, Shane Lardinois, Srinivasan Ramani, James Appleman, Stephen Eaton, James Tate, David Moscrip and many others for their technical advice, tools support and lab support. We would also like to thank Ahmad Samih and Yan Solihin for their high level feedback and suggestions.

9. CONCLUSION

Edge-of-network applications represent a growing class of workloads with unique characteristics compatible with hardware acceleration of key functions - compression, encryption, authentication, intrusion detection and XML processing. Hardware acceleration has also been described as a key approach to continued energy-proportional performance scaling.

In this paper we describe the hardware acceleration features in IBM's PowerEN processor, a processor that targets this application space. We highlight the architectural features of PowerEN that simplify software so its hardware acceleration capabilities can be used efficiently. We also measure and report quantitative performance data for each of the hardware accelerators in PowerEN, across a range of test cases. The accelerators typically provide 10Gbit/s to 40Gbit/s of accelerated function, often orders of magnitude faster than software. This leaves many software threads free to address computation that is not conducive to acceleration.

PowerEN exemplifies the new direction in application-specific SOCs. Heterogenous computation dispersed across processors and hardware accelerators, tightly integrated with well-architected low-latency user-level interfaces, will enable SOCs to sustain wire-speed processing for generations to come.

10. REFERENCES

[1] AHA. AHA367-PCIe GZIP Compression/Decompression. http://www.aha.com/show_prod.php?pid=38, 2010.
[2] S. Borkar and A. A. Chien. The future of microprocessors. *Commun. ACM*, 54, 2011.
[3] Broadcom Inc. XLP800 Series. http://www.broadcom.com/products/Processors/Data-Center/XLP800-Series, 2012.
[4] J. Brown, S. Woodward, B. Bass, and C. Johnson. IBM Power Edge of Network processor: A wire-speed system on a chip. *Micro, IEEE*, 31(2), 2011.
[5] Cavium Inc. Octeon. http://www.cavium.com/OCTEON_MIPS64.html, 2010.
[6] Cavium Networks. Nitrox DPI CN17XX L7 Content Processor Family. Product Brief, 2009.
[7] Certicom Research, Standards for Efficient Cryptography. SEC 1: Elliptic Curve Cryptography, version 1.0. http://www.secg.org/collateral/sec1_final.pdf , 2000.
[8] Certicom Research, Standards for Efficient Cryptography. SEC 2: Recommended Elliptic Curve Domain Parameters, version 1.0. http://www.secg.org/collateral/sec2_final.pdf , 2000.
[9] H. Esmaeilzadeh, E. Blem, R. St. Amant, K. Sankaralingam, and D. Burger. Dark silicon and the end of multicore scaling. *SIGARCH Comput. Archit. News*, 39, 2011.
[10] H. Franke, J. Xenidis, C. Basso, B. M. Bass, S. S. Woodward, J. D. Brown, and C. L. Johnson. Introduction to the wire-speed processor and architecture. *IBM Journal of Research and Development*, 54(1), 2010.
[11] H. P. Hofstee. Power efficient processor architecture and the cell processor. In *the 11th Intl. Symp. on High-Performance Computer Architecture*, Washington, DC, USA, 2005. IEEE Computer Society.
[12] Hubertus Franke. The IBM Power Edge of Network Processor. http://www.cercs.gatech.edu/iucrc10/material/franke.pdf, 2010.
[13] IBM. PowerEN PME Public Pattern Sets Wiki. (URL removed to preserve the anonymity of the authors. URL to be provided in the final version.), 2012.
[14] IXIA Inc. XM12 High Performance Chassis. http://www.ixiacom.com/products/display?skey=ch_optixia_xm12, 2012.
[15] C. Johnson, D. Allen, B. Jeff, V. Steve, H. Russ, A. Heather, C. Chen-Yong, M. George, F. Hubertus, X. Jimi, and B. Claude. A Wire-Speed Power Processor: 2.3 GHz 45nm SOI with 16 Cores and 64 Threads. In *Intl. Solid State Circuits Conf. (ISSCC), 2010*, 2010.
[16] R. Kumar, D. M. Tullsen, and N. P. Jouppi. Core architecture optimization for heterogeneous chip multiprocessors. In *15th international conference on Parallel architectures and compilation techniques*, PACT '06, New York, NY, USA, 2006. ACM.
[17] S. Kumar, B. Chandrasekaran, J. Turner, and G. Varghese. Curing regular expressions matching algorithms from insomnia, amnesia, and acalulia. In *3rd ACM/IEEE Symp. on Architecture for networking and communications systems*, Princeton, New Jersey, USA, 2009.
[18] Matt Powell. Canterbury Corpus. http://corpus.canterbury.ac.nz/ , 2000.
[19] NetLogic Microsystems. XLS608 Processor. http://www.netlogicmicro.com/Products/ProductBriefs/MultiCore/XLS608.htm , 2010.
[20] Network Working Group. RFC 1950 Standard. http://www.ietf.org/rfc/rfc1950.txt , 1996.
[21] Network Working Group. RFC 1950 Standard. http://www.ietf.org/rfc/rfc1952.txt , 1996.
[22] Network Working Group. RFC 1951 Standard. http://www.ietf.org/rfc/rfc1951.txt , 1996.
[23] D. Pasetto, K. Lynch, R. Tucker, B. Maguire, F. Petrini, and H. Franke. Ultra low latency market data feed on IBM PowerEN. *Comput. Sci.*, 26, 2011.
[24] D. Pasetto, F. Petrini, and V. Agarwal. Tools for very fast regular expression matching. *IEEE Computer*, 2010.
[25] Rui Hou and Lixin Zhang and Huang, M.C. and Kun Wang and Franke, H. and Yi Ge and Xiaotao Chang. Efficient Data Streaming with On-chip Accelerators: Opportunities and Challenges. In *the 17th Intl. Symp. on High-Performance Computer Architecture*, 2011.
[26] R. Smith, C. Estan, S. Jha, and S. Kong. Deflating the big bang: Fast and scalable deep packet inspection with extended finite automata. In *ACM SIGCOMM 2008 Conf. on Data Communication*, Seattle, Washington, USA, 2008.
[27] Y. Tang, T. Xue, J. Jiang, and B. Liu. Deflation DFA: Remembering history is adequate. In *2010 IEEE Intl. Conf. on Communications*, Cape Town, South Africa, 2010.
[28] Tilera Inc. TILE-Gx Processor Family. http://www.tilera.com/products/processors/TILE-Gx_Family, 2012.
[29] US Department of Commerce/National Institute of Standards and Technology. FIPS PUB 186-3, Digital Signature Standard (DSS). http://csrc.nist.gov/publications/fips/fips186-3/fips_186-3.pdf , 2009.
[30] J. van Lunteren. High-performance pattern-matching for intrusion detection. In *The 25th IEEE Conf. on Computer Communications*, Barcelona, Spain, 2006.

Workload and Power Budget Partitioning for Single-Chip Heterogeneous Processors

Hao Wang[†], Vijay Sathish[†], Ripudaman Singh[†], Michael J. Schulte[‡], and Nam Sung Kim[†]
[†]The University of Wisconsin-Madison, WI, U.S.A. [‡]Advanced Micro Devices, TX, U.S.A.
{hwang223, sathish, rsingh27, nskim3}@wisc.edu michael.schulte@amd.com

Abstract

With technology scaling, manufacturers are integrating both CPU and GPU cores in a single chip to improve the throughput of emerging applications. To maximize the throughput of a single-chip heterogeneous processor (SCHP), the chip power budget shared between the CPU and GPU must be effectively utilized. At the same time, the CPU and GPU in an SCHP must each satisfy its own power constraint. Furthermore, the power budget allocated to the CPU and GPU impacts performance. In this paper, using a detailed cycle-level SCHP simulator, we first demonstrate that the joint optimization of workload and power budget partitioning between the CPU and GPU can provide 13% higher throughput than the optimization of workload partitioning alone under a fixed power budget allocation to the CPU and GPU. Second, we propose an effective runtime algorithm that can determine near-optimal or optimal combinations of workload and power budget partitioning. The algorithm exploits the runtime power efficiencies of the workload executed on the CPU and the GPU. Using the detailed cycle-level SCHP simulator, we show that within five to eight kernel invocations the algorithm can achieve 96% of the maximum throughput obtained by an exhaustive search algorithm. Finally, we demonstrate comparable throughput improvements when we apply the algorithm to a commercial computing system with an SCHP.

Categories and Subject Descriptors

C.1.2 **[Multiple Data Stream Architectures (Multiprocessors)]**: Single-instruction-stream, multiple-data-stream processors (SIMD)

General Terms

Performance, Design

Keywords

Single-chip heterogeneous processor, voltage/frequency/core scaling, power constraint.

1. Introduction

Technology scaling has reduced the area, delay, and power consumption of CMOS devices, allowing manufacturers to integrate more devices per chip. With more devices available for integration, manufacturers have introduced multi- and many-core processors that exploit thread- and application-level parallelism to satisfy the ever-increasing performance demands of emerging applications. With this approach, however, the number of cores per chip is often limited by power and thermal constraints that do not scale with device scaling [1]. This in turn will eventually limit the maximum performance that can be delivered by future many-core processors. Thus, improving power efficiency of cores has become one of the most critical priorities for designing high-performance many-core processors.

In recent years, GPUs have become more programmable [2]. They also provide much higher power efficiency than CPUs for parallel compute-intensive applications. To fully exploit the potential of GPUs for a wide variety of general-purpose applications, programming frameworks such as NVIDIA's Compute Unified Device Architecture (CUDA) [3] and the Open Computing Language (OpenCL) [4] have been proposed. In a heterogeneous computing system comprised of discrete CPU and GPU devices, the parallel portions of compute-intensive workloads typically execute on the GPU, and the serial portions typically execute on the CPU. CPUs often provide much higher performance than GPUs when executing code with limited parallelism and complex control flows.

Many computing systems have both a CPU and a GPU. However, a heterogeneous computing system, which is comprised of discrete CPU and GPU components, requires data transfer between the CPU and GPU through slow chip-to-chip interconnects (i.e., PCIe). This significantly diminishes the potential performance and power efficiency benefits of heterogeneous computing systems. To avoid the performance bottleneck due to data transfers through the chip-to-chip interconnects, new architectures such as AMD's Llano processor [5] and Intel's Sandy Bridge processor [6] integrate both the CPU and GPU in a single chip.

Recent studies demonstrate that workload partitioning between the CPU and GPU can improve the overall throughput or power efficiency of a heterogeneous computing system (comprised of discrete CPU and GPU components) [7,8,9,10]. Such workload partitioning can also improve the overall throughput of SCHPs. However, the CPU and GPU must share a chip power budget due to their integration on a single chip, and the CPU or GPU must also satisfy its own power constraint due to thermal and reliability constraints. The relative performance of a CPU or GPU is often proportional to its power consumption (i.e., assigned power), yet the CPU and GPU exhibit different performance and power efficiencies depending on the characteristics of the executed workload. Therefore, joint optimization of both workload and power budget partitioning between the CPU and GPU can help to increase the overall throughput of SCHPs.

Note that in current SCHPs neither the CPU nor the GPU can consume the entire chip power budget. In other words, the power budget of the CPU or GPU alone is always lower than the power budget of the entire SCHP. Hence, assigning the entire workload to either the CPU or GPU is not an effective way to maximize the overall throughput of SCHPs.

To maximize the overall throughput of SCHPs, this paper makes the following specific contributions:

PACT'12, September 19–23, 2012, Minneapolis, Minnesota, USA.

- We demonstrate that joint optimization of both workload and power budget partitioning between the CPU and GPU can lead to considerably higher throughput than optimization of workload partitioning alone with fixed power budget allocations to the CPU and GPU.
- We propose an effective runtime algorithm that can determine near-optimal or optimal workload and power budget partitioning within a small number of kernel invocations. The runtime algorithm, which can be implemented as a part of the OpenCL runtime layer, exploits the runtime power efficiency ratio between the CPU and GPU when executing a given workload.
- We demonstrate the effectiveness of the proposed runtime algorithm using both (i) a detailed cycle-level SCHP simulator that integrates gem5 and GPGPU-Sim and (ii) a commercial computing system with an AMD Trinity processor, also known as an accelerated processing unit (APU).

The remainder of this paper is organized as follows. Section 2 presents background information. Section 3 describes our experimental methodology. Section 4 demonstrates the potential throughput improvements achieved by joint optimization of workload and power budget partitioning. Section 5 describes our proposed runtime algorithm and evaluates its effectiveness. Section 6 describes related work. Section 7 concludes this paper.

2. Background

OpenCL extends C to provide a language to access and manage heterogeneous computational resources [4]. OpenCL is designed to efficiently support parallel execution on single or multiple programmable processors (e.g., GPUs, CPUs, DSPs, FPGAs) using a data- and task-parallel computing model. OpenCL allows any processors in the computing system to act as peers by abstracting the specifics of the underlying hardware. The software stack of OpenCL is composed of: (i) a platform layer that queries and selects compute devices (e.g., CPUs and GPUs) in the platform, initializes the compute device(s), and creates compute contexts and work-queues; (ii) a runtime layer that manages computational resources and executes compute kernels; and (iii) a compiler that supports a subset of ISO C99 with appropriate language extensions and compiles/builds executable compute kernels online or offline.

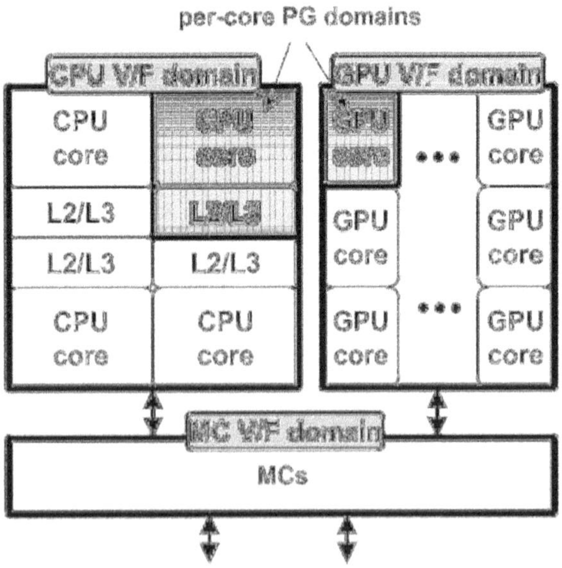

Figure 1: Block diagram of a SCHP comprised of CPU and GPU cores. The memory controllers (MCs) are shared by both the CPU and GPU cores.

Figure 1 shows a block diagram of an SCHP, similar to processors from AMD and Intel. For example, AMD's Llano APU integrates four x86 Stars CPU cores and eighty VLIW-5 Radeon GPU cores in a single chip in 32nm technology [5]. Each CPU core supports out-of-order execution and has a 1MB L2 cache. Each GPU core is comprised of four stream cores, a special-function stream core, a branch unit, and a register file. The CPU and GPU cores share two DDR3 1866 memory controllers (MCs) and the chip-level power budget of 100W [5].

For efficient power management, SCHPs typically support separate voltage/frequency (V/F) domains for the CPU and GPU cores. They also provide power-gating (PG) devices for each CPU and GPU core (or each group of GPU cores). These two features allow an SCHP to dynamically allocate its total power budget between the CPU and GPU under the chip power constraints [6,11].

Traditionally, dynamic voltage/frequency scaling (DVFS) has been widely used to optimize performance under a power constraint [12]. However, as multi-/many-core processors running multiple threads and/or applications emerge, dynamically varying the number of on/off (or active/inactive) cores based on the degree of parallelism and/or problem size in the application can also provide opportunities to optimize performance under a power constraint. This is known as dynamic core scaling (DCS) [13,14]. It has been demonstrated that the DCS can be effectively combined with DVFS (i.e., providing dynamic voltage/frequency/core scaling (DVFCS)) to optimize performance in multi-thread and multi-program applications. This paper extends [13,14] by applying DVFCS in a single-chip heterogeneous computing environment, in which both the workload and chip power budget are partitioned across the CPU and GPU to maximize the overall throughput.

3. Experimental Methodology

3.1 SCHP Simulator

In this study, the CPU and GPU are integrated into a single chip and share common MCs to service memory access requests from both the CPU and GPU. Because this leads to memory access contentions, it is critical to build a detailed cycle-level simulator to accurately model the effects of the shared main memory bandwidth between the CPU and GPU, as well as the memory access contentions. Our integrated simulator infrastructure has been developed based on widely-used simulators: gem5 [15] and GPGPU-Sim [16] for modeling the CPU and GPU, respectively. In developing this infrastructure and considering the current heterogeneous computing model, we recognize that we are mainly interested in the interactions between the CPU and GPU at the MCs. This is because the CPU and GPU are running parallel independent threads and hence do not interact directly with each other except for the interactions through the off-chip main memory.

To model the interactions at the MCs, we use a shared memory programming model in the Linux OS. In our study, the CPU and GPU execute data-parallel threads from the same compute kernel, but on statically partitioned datasets. As in the current AMD Llano APU architecture [5], the CPU and GPU caches do not maintain an explicit coherence protocol. Defining a GPU memory hole in the memory map of the CPU, and having all the data that the GPU may access lie in the (physically mapped) memory hole, eliminates the need for coherence mechanisms; while the CPU cores have separate L1 and L2 caches that are coherent with main memory, the GPU cores have private L1 caches that only support a weak consistency model.

We use gem5 to model the cores and memory subsystem in which a MEOSI directory protocol is supported by Ruby [15]. We use GPGPU-Sim to model the stream multiprocessors (SMs) and on-chip interconnect within the GPU, and we completely remove GPGPU-Sim's memory subsystem and DRAM model. This leaves only a set of request and response queues per MC; GPGPU-Sim communicates with the memory subsystem of gem5 to service its main memory accesses indirectly by using an instantiation of shared memory structures.

There are two requirements for the integrated gem5 and GPGPU-Sim processes to correctly model SCHP behavior. The first is for the two processes to operate in lockstep. The second is to provide a mechanism for GPGPU-Sim to place requests to gem5's memory subsystem on a cache miss, and receive correctly-timed responses from gem5's memory subsystem. In order to ensure that both simulators are running in lock-step, gem5 provides periodic SM-blocking ticks and memory ticks to GPGPU-Sim. The communications of these ticks between the two simulators are realized using shared memory structures in the Linux OS. gem5 issues one blocking tick for all SMs in GPGPU-Sim, but one memory tick per MC in GPGPU-Sim. gem5 triggers SMs or MCs in GPGPU-Sim by setting a flag. It then blocks itself until GPGPU-Sim completes the execution of a GPU cycle and resets the flag to unblock gem5.

There is one set of memory request and response queues per MC. On each memory tick received for a particular MC, GPGPU-Sim pushes a pending request, in FIFO order, from its internal queue into the request queue of the MC. Similarly, it pops pending read responses, if there are any, in FIFO order from the response queue and pushes them into its internal response queue to be returned to an appropriate SM. The memory ticks for the individual MCs do not need to arrive in any pre-determined order, because gem5 is an event-driven simulator, but each MC is guaranteed to receive one tick for each logical memory tick. Once a pending memory tick is reset by GPGPU-Sim, gem5 executes its portion of the memory tick. This involves the corresponding MC popping any GPU memory requests present in the shared memory and pushing them into the request queues inside gem5. Similarly, gem5 also pops any responses intended for the GPU from its own response queues and pushes them into the shared response queue. Once the GPU's requests are in gem5, gem5 uses an arbitration policy to determine whether to schedule a CPU request or a GPU request on each memory cycle. The responses may also be returned out of order based on the scheduling policy implemented in gem5. Secondary communication mechanisms involve provisions for gem5 to detect if GPGPU-Sim completed early and therefore suspend the mechanism to issue SM and memory ticks to GPGPU-Sim.

3.2 Baseline Processor Configurations

In this study, we configure our simulator to model an SCHP with 4 CPU cores. We set the number of GPU SMs based on a recent discrete GPU; NVIDIA's GT260M, which has a similar peak throughput as the GPUs integrated in Intel's and AMD's SCHPs. The GT260M has 12 SMs with 396GFLOPs of throughput and consumes 38W at the nominal operating V/F [17]. Table 1 summarizes the key configuration parameters.

We assume that the total chip power budget allowed for both the CPU and GPU is 100W. To model CPU and GPU power consumption, we first apply the configuration parameters from Table 1 to the CPU and GPU power models from [18] and [19], respectively. This allows us to calculate the *ratio* between dynamic and leakage power of CPU cores and GPU SMs at nominal V_{DD} (0.9V). Following the modeling methodology presented in [13], we obtain the frequency and leakage scaling factors by estimating the delay of a 24-stage FO4 inverter chain and a dummy leakage circuit that includes a large number of NOT (50%), NAND (30%), and NOR (20%) gates using SPICE and a 32nm technology model [20] at different V_{DD} levels.

With (i) the ratio between dynamic and leakage power at the nominal V_{DD}, (ii) frequency and leakage scaling factors as functions of voltage, and (iii) the known power consumption of the CPU and GPU at the nominal V_{DD}, we can calculate the power consumption of the CPU and GPU as a function of V/F and the number of active CPU cores and GPU SMs; Table 2 tabulates the frequency and power consumption of a CPU core and a GPU SM for different voltages.

Considering such an SCHP under power constraints, we establish four initial evaluation configurations for our study: (i) GPU-oriented, (ii) CPU-oriented, (iii) GPU-only, and (iv) CPU-only. Configurations (i) and (ii) allocate more power budget to the GPU and CPU, respectively, while configurations (iii) and (iv) use only either the GPU or the CPU in the SCHP. In configuration (i), 3 CPU cores at 0.9V/2.9GHz and 12 SMs at 0.9V/600MHz are active and consume 60W and 40W, respectively. In configuration (ii), 4 CPU cores at 0.9V/2.9GHz and 6 SMs at 0.9V/600MHz are active and consume 80W and 20W, respectively. In configuration (iii) only 12 SMs are active and consume 40W 0.9V/600MHz. In configuration (iv), 4 CPU cores are active and consume 80W at 0.9V/2.9GHz. The maximum power consumption allowed is 80W for the CPU and 63W for the GPU. This occurs by running the CPU/GPU at 0.99V, the maximum voltage allowed under thermal and reliability constraints.

In this paper, we assume that the power consumption of other on-chip components (e.g., I/O, MCs, and other peripheral components), which are connected to different power domains, is constant regardless of V/F and the number of active CPU cores and

Table 1: Key configuration parameters for our single-chip heterogeneous processor.

# of CPU cores	4	# of GPU SMs	12
CPU freq/volt	1.67-3.44GHz/0.72-0.99V	GPU freq/volt	350-710MHz/0.72-0.99V
CPU core fetch/issue/retire	4/4/4	GPU # of registers per SM	16384
CPU IL1 and DL1	64KB/2-way/64B 2 cycles	GPU # of threads per SM	1024
CPU L2 per core	1MB/16-way/64B 20 cycles	GPU # of CTAs per SM	8
CPU store buffer	16 per core	GPU L1$ per SM	32KB
CPU core BTB	8K/4-Way per core	GPU SIMD Width	8
CPU branch mis-pred. penalty	14 cycles	GPU Warp Size	32
CPU MSHR	20 per core	GPU branch divergence	Immediate post dominator
Memory freq	1866MHz (DDR3)	# of MC/scheduling policy	2/FR-FCFS

Table 2: Voltage versus frequency and power consumption of a CPU core and GPU SM.

Voltage (V)	Freq (GHz)		Power (Watts)	
	CPU	GPU	CPU	GPU
0.72	1.67	0.35	7.1	1.2
0.75	1.89	0.39	8.7	1.4
0.78	2.09	0.43	10.4	1.7
0.81	2.31	0.48	12.4	2.1
0.84	2.51	0.52	14.6	2.4
0.87	2.70	0.56	17.1	2.8
0.90	2.90	0.60	20.0	3.3
0.93	3.07	0.64	23.2	3.9
0.96	3.26	0.68	27.0	4.5
0.99	3.44	0.71	31.4	5.2

GPU SMs; we only consider the power consumption of the CPU and GPU after excluding this fixed power component for the total chip power budget and consumption.

3.3 Evaluated Workloads

We use ten benchmarks (Back Propagation, Breadth-First Search, CFD Solver, Heart Wall Tracking, HotSpot, Leukocyte Tracking, LU Decomposition, Needleman-Wunsch, K-means, and SRAD) from Rodinia, a benchmark suite for heterogeneous computing covering a wide range of parallel communication patterns and synchronization techniques [21]. The abbreviation for each benchmark and its input data sizes are described in Table 3.

Each benchmark is either an application executing one or several parallel kernels many times, or a kernel that is called iteratively in real applications. For example, CFD Solver, which is the first case, executes two kernels 2000 times by default; and HotSpot, which corresponds to the second case, updates the temperature profile for one small time step, and should be called iteratively to estimate the processor temperature based on a simulated power trace for a certain period of time. Because the parallel code portions of the program dominate the total execution time, we focus on improving the throughput of the parallel code portions, which are implemented as CUDA or OpenCL kernels.

4. Joint Optimization of Workload and Power Budget Partitioning

4.1 The Need to Use Both the CPU and GPU

In an SCHP a proper partitioning of the workload between the CPU and GPU can improve overall throughput. There are two reasons for this. First, the performance of the CPU (or GPU) varies based on its power consumption when DVFS is employed. Second, the CPU (or GPU) alone cannot consume the total chip power budget due to its thermal and/or maximum voltage constraints.

Consequently, the CPU and GPU should operate in parallel to consume the entire chip power budget and thus maximize overall application throughput. To adjust the power allocation between the CPU and GPU within the chip power budget, we explore two options: (i) dynamic core scaling (DCS) enabled by per-core and per-SM PG devices and (ii) dynamic voltage/frequency scaling (DVFS) enabled by two separate V/F domains; one for the CPU and one for the GPU.

Under such conditions, instead of assigning all the work (i.e., threads) to the GPU, whose maximum throughput is limited by its power constraint (i.e., 63W in our baseline), we can assign some work to the CPU such that the remaining chip power budget (i.e., 37W out of 100W in our baseline) can be fully used to maximize the overall throughput. For the DCS option, all 12 GPU SMs are active and consume 40W while only 3 CPU cores operating at the nominal V/F consume 60W. Alternatively, 4 CPU cores can consume 60W at lower V/F, leaving 40W for the GPU.

Table 3: The full name of each benchmark, its corresponding abbreviation, and its input data size.

Benchmark	Abbrev.	Input Data Size
Back Propagation	BPR	131,072 input nodes
Breadth-First Search	BFS	1,000,000 nodes
CFD Solver	CFD	200k elements
Heart Wall Tracking	HWT	609×590 pixels / frame
HotSpot	HOT	1024×1024 data points
Leukocyte Tracking	LKT	480×640 pixels / frame
LU Decomposition	LUD	512×512 data points
Needleman-Wunsch	NW	2048×2048 data points
K-means	KMN	20,4800 points, 34 features
SRAD	SRAD	2048×2048 data points

4.2 Power Allocation through DCS

Figure 2 plots the maximum throughput of different SCHP configurations for all the benchmarks we examine. For CPU- and GPU-oriented configurations, we simulated 16 workload partitioning points (i.e., from 6.25% to 100% of the workload assigned to the GPU) for each benchmark, and pick the percentage value that maximizes throughput. The optimal percentage values for all the benchmarks are tabulated in Table 4.

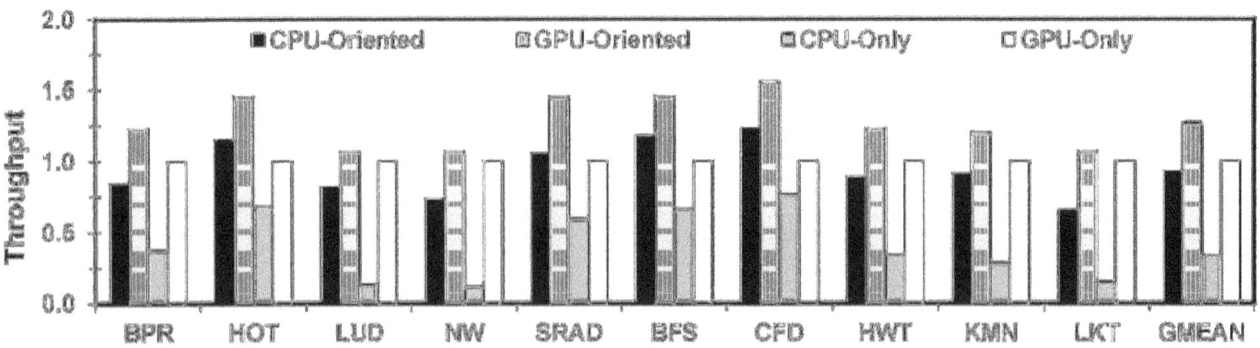

Figure 2: Throughput of different SCHP configurations with fixed power budgets. Throughput is normalized to GPU-only.

Table 4: Percentage of workload assigned to GPU to optimize the throughput of each configuration.

Bench mark	CPU-oriented	GPU-oriented	Bench mark	CPU-oriented	GPU-oriented
BPR	56.3%	81.3%	LKT	81.3%	93.8%
BFS	43.8%	68.8%	LUD	87.5%	93.8%
CFD	37.5%	62.5%	NW	87.5%	93.8%
HWT	62.5%	81.3%	KMN	68.8%	81.3%
HOT	43.8%	68.8%	SRAD	43.8%	68.8%

The throughputs in Figure 2 are normalized to that of the GPU-only configuration in which all the CPU cores are disabled and all GPU SMs are active. On average (using the geometric mean), the GPU-oriented configuration, which uses the full power budget of the SCHP, exhibits 27% higher throughput than the GPU-only configuration. In comparison, the CPU-oriented configuration, which also uses the full power budget of the heterogeneous processor, has 7% lower throughput than the GPU-only configuration. The CPU- and GPU-oriented configurations show 177% and 278% higher throughput than the CPU-only configuration, respectively. This supports our earlier argument: to maximize the throughput of an SCHP, the workload should be partitioned between the CPU and GPU and executed using both the CPU and GPU.

4.3 Power Budget Partitioning Using DVFCS

Figure 3(a) and (b) plot the relative execution time versus the percentage of work assigned to the GPU for HotSpot and Heartwall, respectively. These benchmarks are chosen because the optimal percentages of work assigned to the GPU of the remaining benchmarks is between those of these two benchmarks. In addition to the CPU- and GPU-oriented configurations, we apply DVFS and DCS simultaneously (i.e., DVFCS). This allows us to explore more fine-grain power allocations between the CPU and GPU depending on the workload characteristics.

For DVFCS at each workload partitioning point, we initially perform an exhaustive search for all possible combinations of (i) V/F of the CPU and GPU and (ii) the number of active CPU cores and GPU SMs, while satisfying the chip, CPU, and GPU power constraints. In HotSpot, the highest throughput is achieved with 68.75% of the work assigned to twelve active GPU SMs operating at 0.96V/680MHz and consuming 54.1W. The rest of the work (31.25%) is assigned to four active CPU cores operating at 0.78V/2.09GHz and consuming 41.5W. In Heartwall, the highest throughput is achieved with 87.5% of the work assigned to twelve active GPU SMs operating at 0.99V/710MHz and consuming 62.8W. The rest of the work (12.5%) is assigned to four active CPU cores operating at 0.75V/1.89GHz and consuming 34.2W.

In both HotSpot and Heartwall, the minimum execution time (i.e., maximum throughput) is achieved when both the CPU and GPU finish the assigned work approximately at the same time because the total execution time of an SCHP is the maximum of the CPU and GPU execution times. In other words, one finishing the given work much earlier than the other leads to worse performance since all the available resources and power budget are not fully and efficiently utilized. The optimal DVFCS configurations provide 13% and 54% higher throughput than the GPU- and CPU-oriented configurations, respectively, while using lower V/F for the CPU and allocating more power to the GPU to make it run faster than either the CPU- or GPU-oriented configurations. Depending on how efficiently the CPU and GPU

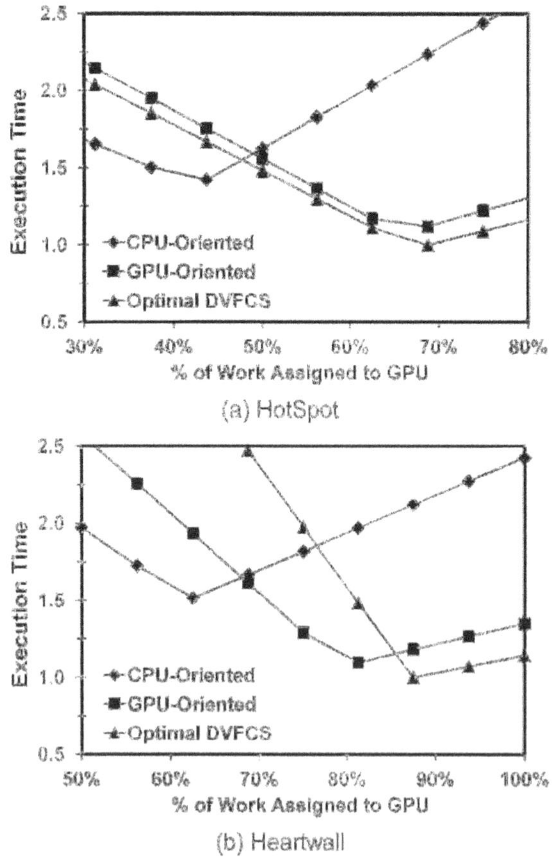

Figure 3: Execution time versus percentage of work assigned to the GPU.

can each process a given workload, the optimal configuration assigns more work (and thus more power) to either the CPU or GPU. This clearly demonstrates that proper workload and power budget partitioning based on workload characteristics is a key to maximize the overall throughput of SCHPs.

Figure 4 shows the throughput improvement with optimal DVFCS for all the benchmarks we examine. The throughput is normalized to the GPU-oriented configuration. Compared to the results of the optimal workload partitioning under the fixed power budget for the CPU and GPU (i.e., the CPU- and GPU-oriented configurations), the joint optimization of workload and power budget partitioning delivers up to 19% (and on average 13%) higher throughput than the GPU-oriented configuration, and up to 94% (and on average and 54%) higher throughput than the CPU-oriented configuration. Table 5 summarizes the optimal percentage of work assigned to the GPU and the optimal processor configurations (i.e., the number of active CPU cores and GPU SMs, and the operating V/F and power consumption of the CPU and GPU) for all the benchmarks. In columns (2) to (5) of Table 5, the numbers in parenthesis are the value for the GPU.

4.4 Insight into Joint Optimization of Workload and Power Budget Partitioning Using DVFCS

To gain insight into developing an effective runtime DVFCS algorithm that can determine the optimal configurations (i.e., the optimal percentage of work to assign to the GPU, number of active CPU cores and GPU SMs, and their V/F values), we plot the power efficiency ratio of the CPU to the GPU for the different configurations used to generate Figure 4. We define power efficiency at the optimal workload partitioning point, where both

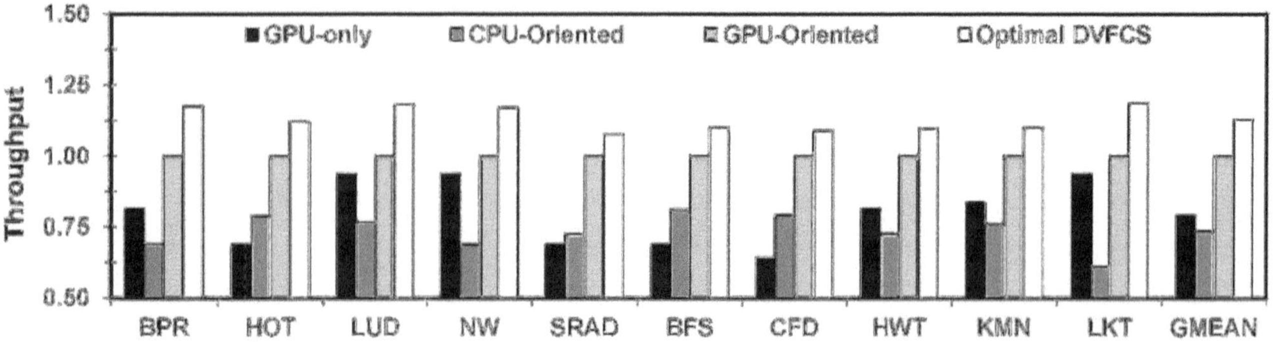

Figure 4: Throughput improvement with fixed power budgets and optimal DVFCS. Throughput is normalized to GPU-Oriented.

the CPU and GPU exhibit the same execution time for a given workload, as follows:

$$\frac{P_{EFF\_CPU}}{P_{EFF\_GPU}} = \frac{W_{CPU} / P_{CPU}(V_{CPU}, F_{CPU}, N_{CPU})}{W_{GPU} / P_{GPU}(V_{GPU}, F_{GPU}, N_{GPU})} \quad (1)$$

where P_{EFF_CPU} and P_{EFF_GPU} are the power efficiency of the CPU and GPU; W_{CPU} and W_{GPU} are the percentage of work assigned to the CPU and GPU; and P_{CPU} and P_{GPU} are the power consumption of the CPU and GPU as a function of the number of active CPU cores and GPU SMs (N_{CPU} and N_{GPU}) and their V/F values (V_{CPU}/F_{CPU} and V_{GPU}/F_{GPU}).

As we can observe from the results shown in Figure 5, the power efficiency ratios are very low for the CPU- and GPU-oriented configurations; on average 0.14 for both configurations. Such a low ratio indicates that the CPU is using its power less efficiently than the GPU, and therefore more power should be shifted to GPU so that the SCHP can use the limited power budget more efficiently to improve overall throughput. As the CPU operates at lower V/F to allocate more power to the GPU, it becomes more power-efficient. Note that power efficiency increases as the operating voltage decreases. This is because power is reduced super-linearly while frequency (and the performance of compute-bound applications) is degraded close to linearly.

On the other hand, as the GPU shifts to a higher V/F operating point by exploiting the power transferred from the CPU, the power efficiency of the GPU decreases. After the DVFCS optimization, we observe that the power efficiency ratios significantly improve. We note that throughput can be maximized by allocating more power from a less power-efficient device to a more power-efficient device. This increases the power efficiency ratio; the average power efficiency ratio with the optimal DVFCS is increased from 0.14 to 0.34. Theoretically, the optimal DVFCS technique should perfectly balance the power efficiency between the CPU and GPU, but (i) the limited V/F levels due to the minimum operating V/F constraint for the CPU and the maximum operating V/F constraint for the GPU, (ii) discrete V/F levels, and (iii) discrete workload partitioning points prevent the optimal DVFCS from reaching the perfectly balanced point (i.e., a power efficiency ratio of 1.0) in Figure 5.

To validate this argument, we plot the power efficiency ratio of HotSpot in Figure 6, as we allow more V/F levels by providing both lower minimum and higher maximum operating V/F levels for the CPU and GPU. The number of baseline V/F levels is 10. To support 12 (or 14) V/F levels, we decrease the minimum operating voltage from 0.72V to 0.69V (or 0.66V) and increase the maximum operating voltage from 0.99V to 1.02V (or 1.05V), which adds two

Table 5: Optimal (1) percentage of work assigned to the GPU, (2) number of CPU cores (GPU SMs), (3) voltage in Volts, (4) frequency in GHz, and (5) power consumption of the CPU (GPU) in Watts.

	(1)	(2)	(3)	(4)	(5)
BPR	81.3	4(12)	0.78(0.96)	2.09(0.68)	41(54)
BFS	68.8	4(12)	0.78(0.96)	2.09(0.68)	41(54)
CFD	68.8	4(12)	0.75(0.99)	1.89(0.71)	34(63)
HWT	87.5	3(12)	0.75(0.99)	1.89(0.71)	26(63)
HOT	68.8	4(12)	0.78(0.96)	2.09(0.68)	41(54)
LKT	93.8	3(12)	0.78(0.99)	2.09(0.71)	31(63)
LUD	93.8	2(12)	0.87(0.99)	2.70(0.71)	34(63)
NW	93.8	3(12)	0.78(0.99)	2.09(0.71)	31(63)
KMN	87.5	3(12)	0.78(0.99)	2.09(0.71)	31(63)
SRAD	75.0	3(12)	0.81(0.99)	2.31(0.71)	37(63)

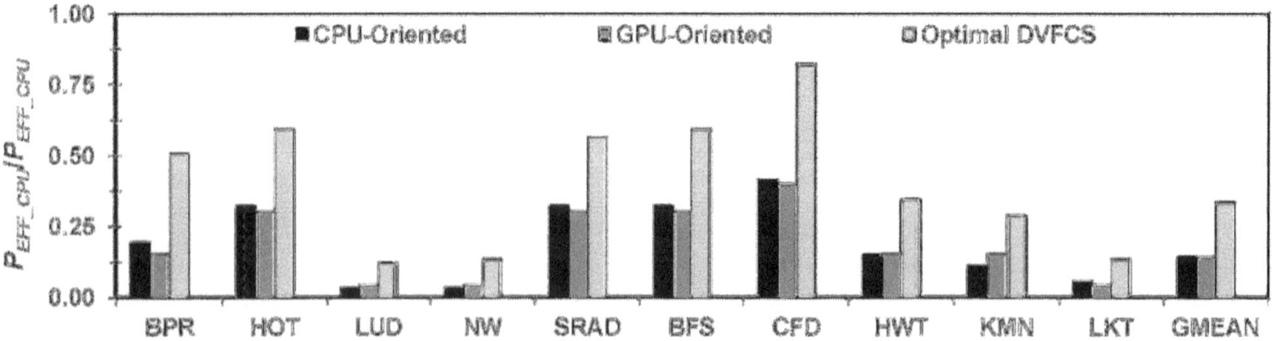

Figure 5: Power efficiency ratio of the CPU to the GPU for different processor configurations.

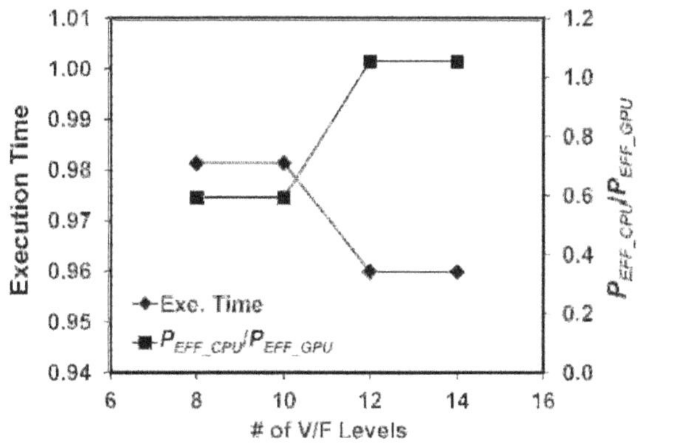

Figure 6: Execution time and power efficiency ratio of Hotspot when varying the number of V/F levels.

(or four) more V/F levels for DVFS. We can observe that the power efficiency of the CPU comes closer to that of the GPU as the number of supported V/F levels is increased from 10 to 12. However, increasing the number of V/F levels to 14 does not reduce the execution time further because we have already reached the optimal operating point where the power efficiencies of the CPU and GPU has been already balanced with the 12 V/F levels.

The key point is that the CPU and GPU have different performance and power efficiency characteristics that scale differently based on workload characteristics when varying V/F levels, the number of CPU cores, and the number of GPU SMs. This provides the opportunity to improve the overall throughput of power-constrained SCHPs through DVFCS. Furthermore, comparing the power efficiency of the CPU and GPU provides a promising basis for an effective runtime DVFCS algorithm for workload and power budget partitioning that does not need to collect instruction-level statistics.

5. Runtime DVFCS Algorithm

According to the analysis performed in the previous section, the basic idea of the runtime DVFCS algorithm is to adaptively adjust the power efficiency between the CPU and GPU through DVFCS such that the overall throughput is maximized for a given workload. To develop a runtime DVFCS algorithm, we need to answer the following two questions:

- What percentage of work should we assign to the CPU and GPU, respectively?
- Which knob, DVFC or DCS, should we use first to adjust power efficiency?

In this section, we, answer these two questions, describe the proposed runtime DVFCS algorithm, and evaluate the effectiveness of the proposed runtime DVFCS algorithm using both the detailed cycle-level simulator and a commercial computing system with an AMD Trinity APU.

5.1 Optimization Solution Space Analysis

First, as shown in Figure 3, the execution time of both the CPU and the GPU scales linearly with the percentage of work assigned for most benchmarks. This is because the input data size is large enough; even 6.25% (1/16) of the workload can fully occupy the computing resources and thus its execution time is approximately equal to 6.25% of the total execution time.

Due to this linear relationship, the optimal workload partitioning point for given V/F levels for the CPU and the GPU, the number of the CPU cores, and the number of GPU SMs can be determined after each invocation of a kernel in the main execution loop of the benchmark. Suppose the current invocation assigns X_i % of the workload to the GPU and $(100 - X_i)$% to the CPU, and the CPU and GPU execution times are T_{GPU} and T_{CPU}, respectively. Then, the optimal workload partitioning point for the next invocation (X_{i+1} % of work on the GPU) can be calculated by simply solving Eq. 2:

$$T_{GPU}\cdot\frac{X_{i+1}}{X_i} = T_{CPU}\cdot\frac{100-X_{i+1}}{100-X_i} \qquad (2)$$

To obtain X_{i+1} as a function of X_i ,T_{CPU}, and T_{GPU}, Eq. 2 can be rearranged as follows:

$$X_{i+1} = \frac{T_{CPU}\cdot X_i}{(T_{CPU}-T_{GPU})\cdot X_i + T_{GPU}} \qquad (3)$$

Second, both the CPU and GPU are generally more power efficient when operating at lower V/F. We plot HotSpot's execution time versus power efficiency ratio for different numbers of CPU cores and GPU SMs in Figure 7. Each point represents one valid configuration (i.e., V/F of the CPU and GPU, the number of CPU cores, and the number of GPU SMs) that satisfies the chip, CPU, and GPU power constraints and delivers higher throughput than the CPU-oriented configuration. Figure 7 demonstrates that using more CPU cores at lower V/F levels gives higher throughput than the CPU-oriented configuration

A similar trend is also observed in all other benchmarks. Therefore, we use the following strategy for our proposed runtime DVFCS algorithm. When we need to allocate less power to the CPU (or GPU), we lower its V/F level first. If the V/F level is

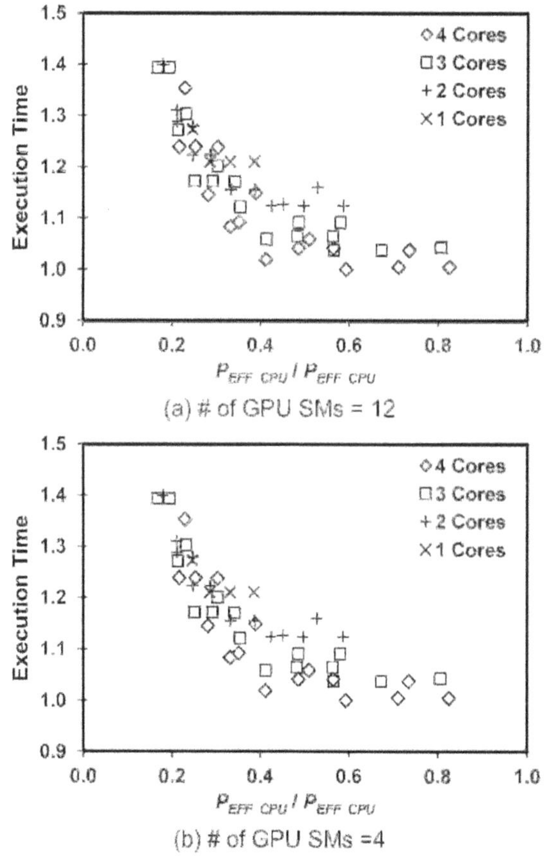

Figure 7: HotSpot's execution time versus power efficiency ratio for different numbers of CPU cores and GPU SMs.

Algorithm 1: Runtime DVFCS algorithm.

```
Initialize: W_GPU = 0.5, W_CPU = 0.5;
Conf = [N_CPU=N_CPU_TOT, V/F_CPU=nom, N_GPU=N_GPU_TOT, V/F_GPU=nom];     // init. config (V/F, # of CPU cores, and # of GPU SMs)
Is_Final_VF = Is_Final_N_GPU = Is_Final_N_CPU = FALSE;                   // init. flags to indicate whether or not the searches of V/F,
                                                                          // # of CPU cores, and # of GPU SMs values are completed.
[T_GPU, T_CPU] = get_exe_time(W_GPU, W_GPU, Conf);                       // get exe. time of CPU and GPU after the first kernel launch
while(!Is_Final_N_GPU || !Is_Final_N_CPU || !Is_Final_VF) {              // repeat until the search is completed
     while(!Is_Final_VF) {                                               // search V/F level first
          if(Worse || V/F_MIN == V/F_MAX)                                // worse throughput or no more V/F value to adjust:
               Is_Final_VF = TRUE; break;                                // stop V/F binary search and set Is_Final_VF flag
          W_GPU_op = get_ W_GPU_op(T_GPU, T_CPU, W_GPU, W_CPU);          // find the optimal partitioning point using Eq.(3)
          W_CPU_op = 1 - W_GPU_op;
          P_EFFGPU = W_GPU_OP / P_GPU(N_GPU, V/F_GPU);                   // calculate power efficiency of CPU and GPU at given
          P_EFFCPU = W_CPU_OP / P_CPU(N_CPU, V/F_CPU);                   // workload partitioning point
          if(P_EFFGPU < P_EFFCPU)                                        // higher CPU power efficiency:
               V/F_MAX = V/F_CPU;                                        // allocate more power to CPU (binary search w/ higher V/F)
          else                                                           // lower CPU power efficiency:
               V/F_MIN = V/F_CPU;                                        // allocate less power to CPU (binary search w/ lower V/F)
          V/F_CPU = (V/F_MIN + V/F_MAX) / 2;
          V/F_GPU = get_GPU_VF(P_TOT, P_CPU(V/F_CPU, N_GPU), N_GPU);     // calculate V/F of GPU satisfying total power budget
          [T_GPU, T_CPU] = get_exe_time(W_GPU_OP, W_GPU_OP, Conf);       // get exe. time of CPU and GPU for new workload partitioning
     }                                                                   // and config
     if(Is_Final_VF && !Is_Final_N_CPU){                                 // search # of CPU cores after completing V/F search
          N_CPU--; V/F_CPU++;                                            // decrease # of CPU cores/ increase V/F for the same power
          [T_GPU, T_CPU] = get_exe_time(W_GPU_OP, W_GPU_OP, Conf);       // get exe. time of CPU and GPU for new config
          if(Worse)                                                      // worse throughput or no more N_CPU to adjust:
               Is_Final_N_CPU = 1; continue;                             // stop N_CPU search
          else                                                           // better throughput
               Is_Final_VF = 0;                                          // repeat the tuning for V/F
     }
     if(Is_Final_VF && Is_Final_N_CPU && !Is_Final_N_GPU){               // repeat searching # of GPU cores similar to searching # of
          N_GPU--; V/F_GPU++;                                            // CPU cores after completing a search for CPU
          [T_GPU, T_CPU] = get_exe_time(W_GPU_OP, W_GPU_OP, Conf);
          if(Worse)
               Is_Final_N_GPU = 1; continue;
          else
               Is_Final_VF = 0;
     }
}
Opt_conf = Config;
```

already at the lowest possible level but the power efficiency ratio still indicates less power should be assigned to the CPU (or GPU), we begin to turn off CPU cores (or GPU SMs). Similarly, when we need to allocate more power to the CPU (or GPU), we activate the disabled CPU cores (or GPU SMs) first. Only after there are no more available CPU cores (or GPU SMs), we begin to increase its V/F if we still need to allocate more power to either the CPU (or GPU). To set the V/F level and the number of CPU cores (or GPU SMs), we apply a binary search method for the given range of V/F levels and the number of available CPU cores (or GPU SMs). To avoid a local optimum, we run an additional iteration with fewer cores after the V/F level is found to see whether or not we can obtain a higher throughput with fewer CPU cores (or GPU SMs). Because the solution points are not very close to the optimal point, it is unlikely that the runtime DVFCS algorithm converges to a local minimum. Summarizing the above discussion, Algorithm 1 shows our runtime DVFCS algorithm.

Algorithm 1, which can be implemented as a part of a runtime system (e.g., the OpenCL runtime layer), can be invoked every time a kernel is launched. Once the throughput improvement converges, the algorithm no longer changes the V/F levels, the number of the CPU cores, or the number of GPU SMs. However, if the algorithm observes a notable throughput change, it will begin to adjust the V/F levels, the number of the CPU cores, and the GPU SMs.

5.2 Evaluation of Runtime DVFCS Algorithm

Figure 8 plots the throughput from our cycle-level SCHP simulator for all the benchmarks based on four different configurations: (i) the GPU-oriented configuration, (ii) the configuration selected by

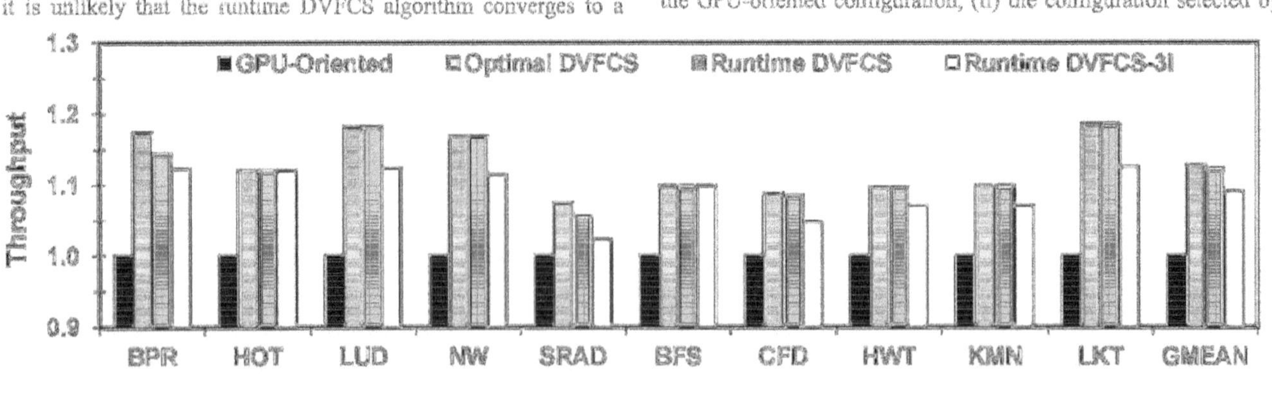

Figure 8: Normalized throughput comparisons using the detailed cycle-level simulator.

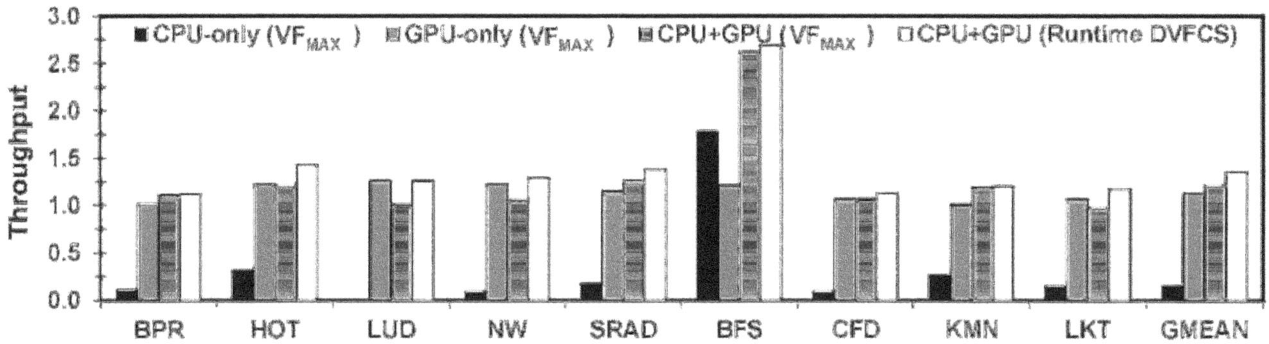

Figure 9: Normalized throughput comparisons using a commercial computing system with an AMD Trinity APU.

an exhaustive search method (denoted by "Optimal DVFCS"), (iii) the configuration selected by running the proposed runtime DVFCS algorithm until it converges (denoted by "Runtime DVFCS"), and (iv) the configuration selected by running DVFCS for only three iterations (denoted by "Runtime DVFCS-3I"). The optimized configurations selected by DVFCS leads to 12% higher throughput on average than the GPU-oriented configuration, while the optimal configurations after the exhaustive search is on average 13% higher; only the results for BPR and SRAD using the proposed runtime DVFCS algorithm are slightly worse than using the exhaustive search.

Our experiment shows that our runtime DVFCS algorithm takes 5 to 8 iterations (6.8 iterations on average) to achieve the optimal DVFCS configuration for eight of the twelve workloads. Moreover, Figure 8 shows that significant throughput improvements are achieved after just 3 iterations, with an average throughput improvement of 9.1%. This indicates that the overhead of the runtime algorithm is negligible considering that many GPGPU applications execute the same kernels many times for *the same size input set*; for example, HotSpot and Heartwall repeat the execution of the same kernel(s) for a specified time window and a specified number of frames, respectively.

We also demonstrate the effectiveness of the proposed runtime DVFCS algorithm using a commercial computing system with an AMD Trinity APU. The Trinity APU has (i) 4 CPU cores with four 16KB 4-way associative L1 data caches, two 64KB 2-way associative L1 instruction caches, and a shared 4MB 16-way L2 cache and (ii) 6 GPU compute units (CUs), each of which has 64 stream-cores. We use AMD internal software that enables us to vary V/F of the CPU and GPU, the number of active CPU cores, and the number of GPU CUs. We set the nominal frequency for the CPU and GPU to 3.4GHz and 633MHz, respectively.

Figure 9 plots the throughput of all the benchmarks based on four different configurations: (i) CPU-only operating at the maximum V/F level (denoted by "CPU-only (VF_{MAX})"), (ii) GPU-only operating at the maximum V/F level (denoted by "GPU-only (VF_{MAX})"), (iii) CPU+GPU at the nominal V/F levels using all available CPU cores and GPU CUs (denoted by "CPU+GPU (VF_{NOM})"), and (iv) CPU+GPU at the V/F levels using the number of CPU cores and GPU CUs determined by the proposed runtime DVFCS algorithm (denoted by "CPU+GPU (Runtime DVFCS)"); Heartwall is excluded from Figure 9 because of a bug in its OpenCL version. The throughput of each configuration is normalized to that of the GPU-only configuration running at the nominal V/F level. The throughput of CPU- and GPU-oriented configurations, which are explored with the detailed cycle-level simulator in the earlier analyses, are not compared in Figure 9. This is because these two configurations can be regarded as sub-optimal solutions of the entire solution space explored by the runtime DVFCS algorithm. On average, the proposed runtime DVFCS algorithm can provide 35% higher throughput than the GPU-only configuration operating at the maximum V/F level and 12% higher throughput than the CPU+GPU configuration operating at the nominal V/F level. One of the main reasons the Trinity APU yields lower throughput improvements for some benchmarks than the simulated SCHP is that the Trinity APU supports fewer V/F levels than the simulated SCHP. These results confirms our key findings of this study using the detailed cycle-level simulator: (i) joint optimization of workload and power budget partitioning through DVFCS can provide higher throughput than the assignment of all the workload to the GPU or partitioning only the workload and using a static power budget allocation, and (ii) our runtime DVFCS algorithm is effective for a variety of GPGPU applications.

6. Related Work

C. Luk *et al.* proposed a technique that adaptively partitions a given workload between the CPU and GPU in a heterogeneous computing system to improve the overall throughput of a heterogeneous computing system [7]. The execution times of a given kernel on the CPU and GPU are estimated based on a performance model trained by a profiling method and the workload is partitioned between the CPU and GPU to minimize the total execution time. Wang and Ren evaluated a workload partitioning algorithm to improve the overall power efficiency of a heterogeneous computing system based on an Intel CPU and an AMD GPU [10]. Unlike our study, in these two studies the target heterogeneous computing system is comprised of a CPU and a GPU that are two separate chips. Therefore, sharing the power budget between the CPU and GPU was not considered.

J. Li *et al.* proposed a runtime DVFC scaling algorithm that minimizes the power consumption of a general-purpose *homogeneous* chip multiprocessor under a performance constraint [14]. The power/performance characteristics of applications were analyzed to effectively prune the optimization search space and it was demonstrated that their runtime DVFC scaling algorithm produces near-optimal solutions. J. Lee *et al.* proposed a runtime algorithm that scales (i) the number of active SMs and (ii) the V/F of both SMs and on-chip interconnects/caches to maximize the throughput of a *homogeneous* GPU under a power constraint [13].

The prior studies focus on either adaptively partitioning work between two heterogeneous processors on separate chips to optimize performance or DVFCS of homogeneous processors to reduce power consumption or improve throughput. In comparison, we target an SCHP and maximize the throughput under a power constraint by exploiting different performance/power trade-offs between the CPU and GPU. Furthermore, our novel runtime DVFCS algorithm improves the effectiveness of the workload partitioning technique by jointly applying a DVFCS technique to both the CPU and GPU. This allows the SCHP to utilize the given power budget more effectively and flexible, leading to higher throughput under the power constraints.

7. Conclusion

In this paper, we consider an SCHP, in which the CPU and GPU have independent V/F domains and CPU cores and GPU SMs have independent PG devices, respectively. Since the CPU and GPU are on the same chip, they share the chip power budget while each must satisfy its own power constraint. In such an SCHP, we first demonstrate that its overall throughput can be significantly improved by jointly optimizing workload and power partitioning between the CPU and GPU; we perform an exhaustive search of (i) the percentage of work assigned to the CPU and GPU, (ii) the V/F of the CPU and GPU, and (iii) the number of active CPU cores and GPU SMs while satisfying the chip, CPU, and GPU power constraints. This achieves 13% throughput improvement over the SCHP configuration operating both the CPU and GPU at the nominal V/F levels. Second, we propose an effective runtime DVFCS algorithm that compares the power efficiency of the CPU with that of the GPU for a given workload and power budget partitioning; our algorithm can find a optimal or near-optimal configuration within 5-8 iterations while most of the kernels in the workloads we evaluated are often executed more than a thousand times. Finally, we confirm the key findings of this study using a detailed cycle-level SCHP simulator and measurements from a commercial computing system with an AMD Trinity APU.

Acknowledgement

We would like to thank our AMD colleagues, Lloyd Bircher, Mike O'Connor, Jay Owen, and Madhu Sravana Sibi Govindan for their valuable comments and technical support for the measurement using a system with a Trinity APU. This work is supported in part by an SRC grant (Task ID: 2080.001), NSF grants (CCF-095360, CCF-1016262, CNS-1217102), IBM Faculty Award, and generous gift grants from AMD.

References

[1] H. Esmaeilzadeh, E. Blem, R. St. Amant, K. Sankaralingam, and D. Burger, "Dark silicon and the end of multicore scaling," in *IEEE Int. Symp. on Comp. Arch. (ISCA)*, 2011, pp. 365--376.

[2] J. Nickolls and W.J. Dally, "The GPU Computing Era," *IEEE Micro*, vol. 30, no. 2, pp. 56 -69, Mar-Apr 2010.

[3] NVIDIA. What is CUDA? [Online]. http://www.nvidia.com/object/cuda_home_new.html

[4] OpenCL - The open standard for parallel programming of heterogeneous systems. [Online]. http://www.khronos.org/opencl/

[5] A. Branover, D. Foley, and M. Steinman, "AMD Fusion APU:Llano," *IEEE Micro*, vol. 32, no. 2, pp. 28-37, Mar-Apr 2012.

[6] M. Yuffe, E. Knoll, M. Mehalel, J. Shor, and T. Kurts, "A fully integrated multi-CPU, GPU and memory controller 32nm processor," in *IEEE Int. Solid-State Circuits Conf. (ISSCC)*, 2011, pp. 264-266.

[7] Chi-Keung Luk, Sunpyo Hong, and Hyesoon Kim, "Qilin: Exploiting parallelism on heterogeneous multiprocessors with adaptive mapping," in *IEEE/ACM International Symposium on Microarchitecture (MICRO)*, 2009, pp. 45-55.

[8] M. Linderman, J. Collins, H. Wang, and Meng T., "Merge: a programming model for heterogeneous multi-core systems", ACM Int. Conf. on Architectural Support for Programming Languages and Operating Systems (ASPLOS), 2008, pp. 287-296.

[9] P. Wang *et al.*, "EXOCHI: Architecture and Programming Environment for a Heterogeneous Multi-core Multithreaded System," in *ACM SIGPLAN Conf. on Programming Language Design and Implementation (PLDI)*, pp. 156-166.

[10] G. Wang and X. Ren, "Power-Efficient Work Distribution Method for CPU-GPU Heterogeneous System," in *IEEE Parallel and Dist. Proc. with Applications (ISPA)*, 2010, pp. 122-129.

[11] D Foley et al., "AMD'S Llano Fusion APU," in *IEEE/ACM Symp. on High Performance Chips (HOTCHIPS)*, 2011.

[12] C. Isci, A. Buyuktosunoglu, C.-Y. Cher, P. Bose, and M. Martonosi, "An Analysis of Efficient Multi-Core Global Power Management Policies: Maximizing Performance for a Given Power Budget," in *IEEE Int. Symp. on Microarch. (MICRO)*, 2006, pp. 347 -358.

[13] J. Lee, V. Sathish, M. Schulte, K. Compton, and N.S. Kim, "Improving Throughput of Power-Constrained GPUs Using Dynamic Voltage/Frequency and Core Scaling," in *IEEE/ACM Int. Conf. on Parallel Architectures and Compilation Techniques (PACT)*, 2011, pp. 111-120.

[14] J. Li and J.F. Martinez, "Dynamic power-performance adaptation of parallel computation on chip multiprocessors," in *IEEE/ACM Int. Symp. on High-Performance Computer Architecture (HPCA)*, 2006, pp. 77- 87.

[15] N. Binkert *et al.*, "The gem5 simulator," *ACM SIGARCH Comp. Arch. News*, vol. 39, no. 2, pp. 1-7, Aug 2011.

[16] A. Bakhoda, G. Yuan, W. W. L. Fung, H. Wong, and T. M. Aamodt, "Analyzing CUDA Workloads using a Detailed GPU Simulator," in *IEEE International Symposium on Performance Analysis of Systems and Software (ISPASS)*, 2009.

[17] NVIDIA. GeForce GTS 260M Specification. [Online]. http://www.geforce.com/hardware/notebook-gpus/geforce-gts-260m/specifications

[18] C. Shuai *et al.*, "Rodinia: A Benchmark Suite for Heterogeneous Computing," *IEEE Int. Symp. on Workload Characterization (IISWC)*, Oct. 2009.

[19] Sheng Li *et al.*, "McPAT: an integrated power, area, and timing modeling framework for multicore and manycore architectures," in *IEEE Int. Symp. on Microarch. (MICRO)*, 2009, pp. 469-480.

[20] S. Hong and H. Kim, "An integrated GPU power and performance model. ," in *IEEE/ACM Int. Symp. on Computer Architecture (ISCA)*, 2010, pp. 280-289.

[21] W. Zhao and Y. Cao, "New generation of Predictive Technology Model for sub-45nm early design exploration," *IEEE T. on Electron Devices*, vol. 53, no. 11, pp. 2816-2823, Nov 2006.

[22] NVIDIA, "NVIDIA's Next Generation CUDA Compute Architecture: Fermi,".

Database Analytics Acceleration using FPGAs

Bharat Sukhwani[§], Hong Min[§], Mathew Thoennes[§], Parijat Dube[§],
Balakrishna Iyer[†], Bernard Brezzo[§], Donna Dillenberger[§], Sameh Asaad[§]

[§]IBM T. J. Watson Research Center
Yorktown Heights, NY, 10598

[†]IBM Santa Teresa Lab
555 Bailey Ave, San Jose, CA 95141

{bharats, hongmin, tardis, pdube, balaiyer, brezzo, engd, asaad}@us.ibm.com

ABSTRACT

Business growth and technology advancements have resulted in growing amounts of enterprise data. To gain valuable business insight and competitive advantage, businesses demand the capability of performing real-time analytics on such data. This, however, involves expensive query operations that are very time consuming on traditional CPUs. Additionally, in traditional database management systems (DBMS), the CPU resources are dedicated to mission-critical transactional workloads. Offloading expensive analytics query operations to a co-processor can allow efficient execution of analytics workloads in parallel with transactional workloads.

In this paper, we present a Field Programmable Gate Array (FPGA) based acceleration engine for database operations in analytics queries. The proposed solution provides a mechanism for a DBMS to seamlessly harness the FPGA compute power without requiring any changes in the application or the existing data layout. Using a software-programmed query control block, the accelerator can be tailored to execute different queries without reconfiguration. Our prototype is implemented in a PCIe-attached FPGA system and is integrated into a commercial DBMS platform. The results demonstrate up to 94% CPU savings on real customer data compared to the baseline software cost with up to an order of magnitude speedup in the offloaded computations and up to 6.2x improvement in end-to-end performance.

Categories and Subject Descriptors

C.3 [Special-purpose and application-based systems];
H.2.4 [Database Management]: Systems

Keywords

Relational database, analytics, FPGA, acceleration

1. INTRODUCTION

We find ourselves, today, in the midst of the widespread adoption of analytics in the business world. Whether it is to stock store shelves just-in-time, set airline ticket prices to maximize yield, or purchase hedge contracts on fuel prices to make a transportation company's forthcoming quarter's budget more predictable, rapid analysis of transactional data in corporate database management systems has become a business necessity. Snapshot warehousing, such as in [1], is the existing practice where a snapshot of data is taken from an online transaction processing (OLTP) system to a warehouse system for decision support analysis.

Snapshot warehousing has been acceptable in the past when updates to the database were infrequent. Performing analysis on a month old, week old or day old snapshot of business data was good enough for making executive decisions pertaining to business. Interpersonal networking, the empowering of individuals by personal communication devices and the wide use of social media networking has changed the dynamics of the marketplace. Increasingly, businesses are finding themselves required to respond to changes in market conditions in real time. For example, an airline may have the luxury of no more than a few minutes to respond to fare modifications by its competitor. Real time analytics is the capability to process analytical queries and other operations directly on transactional data.

Injecting expensive analytics query operations into the data operating environment also poses challenges. One challenge is that system resources such as CPU and I/O have to be shared between transactional and analytical workloads. Normally, transactional workloads have stringent Service Level Agreements (SLAs); further, because these are directly tied to revenue generation, they are often the primary focus of the business. Analytical workloads need to run against the same data without impacting the SLA of the transaction workloads. Meeting this challenge requires consideration of both CPU and I/O resource issues.

In this paper we focus on the CPU issue. We propose a hardware acceleration approach that offloads and accelerates some of the most CPU-intensive query operations on an FPGA. Our architecture enables the FPGA to retrieve DBMS in-memory data, which is mostly up-to-date, perform expensive query operations, and send the results back to the database engine. The accelerator has been made customizable by architecting a query control block, and making the FPGA logic behave as an interpreter of the query control block. In this sense, one principle of object oriented programming, late binding, has been implemented on the FPGA, making it versatile for DBMS queries. The presented work includes the following key contributions:

- an architecture that integrates an FPGA into a host system and processes data extracted from the memory of a DBMS,
- the design and prototype of FPGA functions including data decompression and predicate evaluation, both of which consume considerable CPU cycles on conventional processor architectures,
- a software integration approach that enables FPGA-based acceleration for an existing DBMS,
- experimental and performance observations from our integrated prototype.

The rest of the paper is organized as follows. Section 2 outlines the previous work. Section 3 introduces related background information on database systems. In section 4, we present the overview of our proposed architecture and system integration. Section 5 describes the FPGA design of the data decompression and predicate evaluation functions. Section 6 describes software integration of the FPGA-based accelerator into an existing DBMS system. Section 7 presents our experiments and results. Section 8 concludes the paper with discussions and future work.

2. PREVIOUS WORK

Over the years, there have been many efforts to speed up query processing in database management systems. As the increase in the speed of processors diminishes each year, further focus has been placed on parallelization techniques.

One approach is to increase the number of processors [2] and threads [3] exploited by the DBMS. The problem here lies in how to partition the data, metadata, updates and data deltas to reduce memory conflicts and contention between cores [4]. Moreover, suboptimal utilization of the cores in large multi-core systems results in power inefficiencies [5].

Single Instruction Multiple Data (SIMD) operation provides data level parallelism by processing multiple data entities in a single instruction [6][7]. Effective SIMD exploitation, however, requires the DBMS data to be laid out in specific formats and packed tightly into 64 or 128 bit registers. This requires extra processing or compilation for each database table [6]. Further work has been done to exploit Graphics Processing Units (GPUs) to aid database sort operations [8]. GPUs offer a relatively fixed architecture, however, leading to limitations similar to those of SIMD architectures.

Prior work [9][10][11] use FPGAs for parallel query processing. One of the differentiators of our work is the enablement of FPGAs to execute different queries without reconfiguration. This is different than the compilation-based approach [12] which first compiles queries into a hardware description and then synthesizes into FPGA circuit.

Data warehouse appliances such as the Netezza Performance Server [13] or the IBM DB2 Analytics Accelerator (IDAA) [14] also use FPGAs to accelerate query operations. In the former, the FPGA is in the I/O path, hence requiring a write-through I/O protocol which would increase the IOPS to unacceptable levels in an OLTP system. In IDAA, data from an OLTP system is periodically copied, which is appropriate for applications without stringent real time analytics needs.

3. DBMS DATA PAGE PROCESSING

3.1 Relational Database Tables and Pages

In relational DBMS, records are stored in objects called tables. Records are often referred to as rows, and record attributes are called columns (or fields). Table 3-1 is a simplified illustration of a three-row table with six attribute columns (PhoneNumber, FirstName, LastName, Age, State, SalesTotal($)) per row.

Table 3-1 Example "Customers" table

Phone Number	First Name	Last Name	Age	State	SalesTotal($)
212-111-1111	Ann	Smith	25	NY	250.54
212-111-0000	Steve	Jones	31	NY	500.00
203-222-2222	Emily	Brown	29	CT	900.01

Typically, the physical unit of storage and I/O processing of a non in-memory database table is a page. All pages in a table are the same size such as 4KB, 8KB, 16KB, 32KB etc. A database has designated memory space, called buffer cache or buffer pool (BP), for temporarily storing the data pages. All relational data operations get the data pages from the BP and the I/O operations between the BP and the disk are managed transparently. When a page is updated, including insertions and deletions, its BP image is committed first, before eventually being written to the disk. Enabling processing of the latest data in the BP is the main reason that our accelerator is connected to the memory instead in the I/O path, as is done in [13].

3.2 Page Format

In transactional database systems, data is typically stored in a row-based layout where all the columns of a row are stored in contiguous storage. A page is a collection of slots that each contains a row [15]. At the end of a page, there is an array whose entries contain the offsets of the rows within the same page. The pair <pageID, slot number> is often referred to as record ID (RID), which uniquely identifies a row within a table. Figure 3-1 illustrates such page format.

When processing a row in a table, the corresponding page is read from the buffer pool (if necessary, disk I/O is involved) and the row offset is used to extract the row from the page. If a row is deleted, its corresponding slot number holds an invalid value.

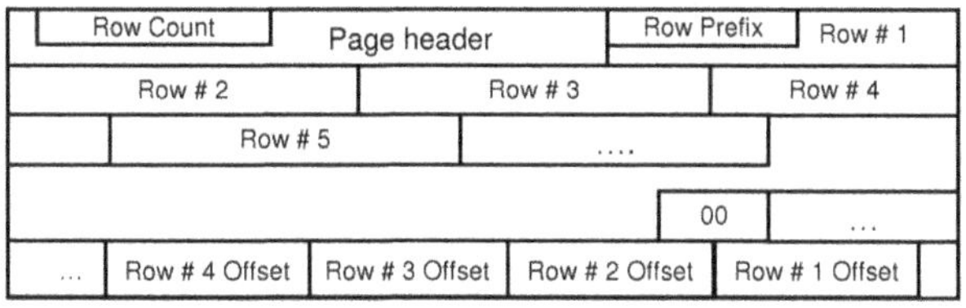

Figure 3-1 Example page format

3.3 SQL Predicate Evaluation

Structured Query Language (SQL) has become the de facto standard language for schema definition, data manipulation and data query for relational DBMS. Large high throughput enterprise class OLTP applications based on SQL power a huge number of commercial applications today.

SQL predicate evaluation refers to the process of retrieving those DBMS table rows that qualify under some criteria. The query typically may require logical inequality or equality comparisons of fields from records against constants, or test set containment for a field in a record. For example, the SQL statement *"SELECT salesTotal FROM Customer WHERE state ='NY' AND age <30"* asks for sales dollar amount from all customers in state 'NY' that are younger than 30 years old from the example Table 3-1.

Efficient access to one or few records is usually achieved in DBMS by means of an I/O efficient B+ tree index data structure based on the data retrieval key. B+ tree indexes have also been explored to retrieve large number of records.

In a DBMS that supports OLTP and analytics simultaneously, the indexes that support OLTP serve the purpose to speed up OLTP. Any indexes that are intended merely to speed up analytics, however, have a detrimental impact on OLTP because insert, update, delete operations on records could entail index updates, resultant CPU and I/O consumption and hence impact on OLTP throughput. A mechanism is needed to accelerate the evaluation of SQL predicates on relational data without building B+ tree indexes specifically to accelerate their execution.

3.4 Data Compression and Decompression

Since the early 90's, data compression has been embedded into DBMS [16]. Since OLTP applications typically only access a single or a small number of related rows, good OLTP systems select the database row as the unit of compression. DBMS data structures allow database logic to find the row; the DBMS merely decompressed the row before processing it. In the absence of indexes, the DBMS has to scan the table, decompress each row, and then apply SQL predicates against the decompressed row. The decompression technique built into the DBMS we worked with is typical of common DBMS in that decompression proceeds by taking some part of the input string and matching it against strings in a dictionary and retrieving its decompressed representation. Concatenating various decompressed fragments reproduces the decompressed row.

From a processor CPU consumption perspective, predicate evaluation against each row becomes an intensive operation as the number of predicates increase, especially against a very large number of rows. Furthermore, decompression, being a per-byte operation, significantly increases required CPU cycles. Reducing the cost of both predicate evaluation and decompression on the processor executing OLTP is critical to maintain OLTP performance.

4. DATABASE ACCELERATOR ON FPGA - SYSTEM OVERVIEW

Figure 4-1 shows the high-level system architecture for the FPGA-accelerated DBMS. The prototyped system is implemented on a PCIe-attached FPGA card and is integrated with a commercial database system. The FPGA operates on DBMS' in-memory data and writes the results back into the host CPU's main memory. Data is transferred between the FPGA and the host using direct memory access (DMA) operations. Once the DBMS sends a job request to the FPGA, all the DMA operations are initiated by the FPGA without any intervention from the host CPU.

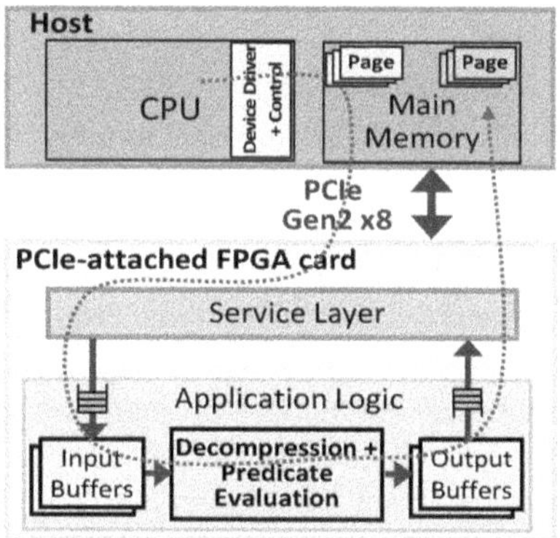

Figure 4-1 System overview of the FPGA accelerator

The FPGA solution has been structured in a modular fashion. There are two distinct pieces of logic that implement the required functionality. The service layer provides all of the logic that interfaces to the PCIe, DMA engines and job management logic. The application logic implements just the functions required to process database queries on the FPGA. A set of well defined interfaces exists between the two that include data buses for input and output data, queues for DMA requests, and control signals.

On the host CPU, a job queue is maintained and the device driver and service layer logic cooperate to dispatch the jobs to the FPGA. Once a job has been dispatched, the service layer passes the job structures to the application logic and signals it to begin. From then on, the service layer only processes the DMA requests and updates the status of the jobs to the host. This structure allows the application logic to be developed independent of the service layer.

To maximize the overall performance, the service layer must perform data transfers at full PCIe bandwidth and the application layer must process the data at the rate sustained by the service layer. For our current bus interface, the peak bandwidth is 3.2 GB/sec (16B at 200 MHz); maintaining such rate is a challenge and must be addressed at all levels.

The first challenge is to maximize the available bus bandwidth; this is addressed in a number of ways. First, a set of job structures, which are passed to the application logic, are created for each job; these specify the DMA addresses of all the data for the job. Second, a set of queues between the service layer and the application logic is implemented that allow the application logic to queue up DMA requests, thereby maximizing the use of the DMA engines. Finally, multiple input and output buffers enable double buffering, thereby completely hiding the host-FPGA transfer latencies. With these techniques, we achieve a data transfer rate of up to 2.7 GB/sec over the PCIe bus.

Next, the FPGA must consume the 16B of data delivered every cycle. The predicate evaluation/decompression engine is designed to consume 1B every clock cycle. Replicating this engine sixteen times will enable the FPGA to consume all data being delivered. For uncompressed data, this results in a balance system. For compressed data, however, creating a balanced system becomes more difficult. For data compressed down to 40% of its original size, for example, the 16 bytes transferred on the PCIe per cycle expands to 40 bytes, consequently requiring a 2.5-fold increase in the number of engines to sustain the uncompressed bandwidth. Simply increasing the number of parallel engines may require more logic resources than the capacity of a given FPGA. Our FPGA design is thus architected such that the number of engines can be traded against the complexity of the query handled by each engine. Thus for very high levels of compression, high throughput can still be maintained, albeit for relatively simpler queries.

5. QUERY PROCESSING ON FPGA

The query processing engine on the FPGA is designed with two goals in mind: to support the most common cases in the target database system and to achieve maximum performance from the available hardware resources. Consequently, the size of the largest predicate supported, the database page buffer size and the decompression dictionary buffer size were chosen based on real-life customer workloads. While these sizes are fixed in the current design, supporting other sizes is trivial.

Figure 5-1 shows the overall architecture for database row processing on FPGA. The design is architected to exploit parallelism at various levels. The core computational unit is a predicate evaluation unit (PE), which evaluates a single predicate by comparing two up to 64-bit long quantities: a stored predicate value supplied by the query and a row field streamed in from main memory. All the predicates within a row are evaluated concurrently by the multiple instances of PEs inside a row scanner (Figure 5-4). The number of PEs inside a row scanner is configurable at synthesis time.

Multiple database rows are processed concurrently using parallel instances of row decompression and predicate evaluation logic within a *scan tile* (see Figure 5-1). Obtaining a balanced system with multiple parallel execution units requires careful rate matching and data staging. A scan tile forms a balanced unit for scanning the rows. It encapsulates the entire design flow for scanning database rows on the FPGA; the design can be scaled simply by replicating the tiles.

A scan tile contains 8 row scanners, each preceded by a decompressor, plus buffers to store the input and output database pages, logic to extract the rows from the input pages and logic to write the qualified rows in the output buffers in a database-specific page format. Each input and output page buffer is 4KB in size, to match the target database page size. Each instance of the expansion dictionary is 32 KB and is shared by two decompression units; both have concurrent access to the dictionary using two independent read ports.

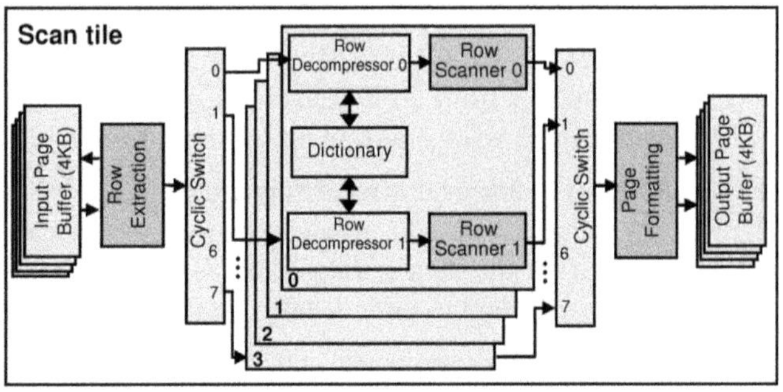

Figure 5-1 Architecture for row processing on FPGA

A scan tile scans one database page at a time. More than one page can be scanned in parallel by having multiple independent scan tiles on the FPGA. Processing at full PCIe bus bandwidth requires a minimum of two tiles, provided the pages are uncompressed or have a small compression ratio. Utilizing full bus bandwidth for highly compressed pages would require larger number of parallel scan tiles. For a given FPGA area, the number of tiles can be traded against the number of PEs within each row scanner. Depending on the query complexity and the compression ratio, different hardware configurations can be used. In one configuration, we instantiate 2 tiles for a total of 16 row scanners, each with 64 PEs, thus decompressing 16 rows concurrently and evaluating 1024 predicates in parallel. A query with fewer predicates, on the other hand, can allow more tiles and thus higher page-level parallelism. This flexibility to exploit parallelism at different granularities is an essential part of the design as it allows different database queries to obtain the highest performance from the available FPGA resources. Since generating an FPGA image is a time-consuming process, we pre-generate FPGA bit files for a variety of different hardware configurations and load the one that is best-matched to the given workload, where a workload is a collection of different queries.

5.1 Row Decompression on FPGA

In our design, the compressed rows are decompressed on-the-fly on the FPGA before being fed to the predicate evaluation logic. Performing decompression on the FPGA brings numerous benefits. First, database pages can be sent directly from the host to the FPGA without the need to pre-filter and decompress on the host. Secondly, offloading decompression to the FPGA increases the amount of computation per datum transferred to the FPGA. Thirdly, efficient parallel hardware implementation of the decompression algorithm results in improved performance. Finally, transferring compressed rows increases the "effective" PCIe transfer bandwidth. This is especially important since the overall accelerator performance is often limited by the available host-to-FPGA data transfer bandwidth. Depending on the compression ratio, transferring compressed rows increases the effective bandwidth by a factor of 2 to 5.

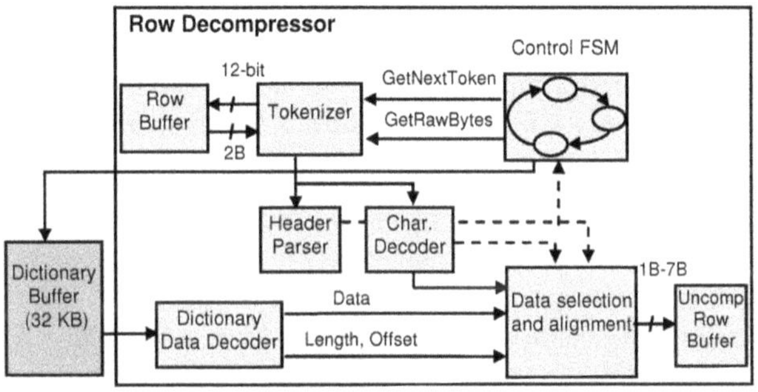

Figure 5-2 Row decompression logic on FPGA

As mentioned in section 3, our target row decompression algorithm performs dictionary-based expansion. A compressed row consists of one or more 12-bit compressed symbols (tokens); a symbol may either represent a character of the uncompressed row or a pointer to a dictionary entry, which in turn may contain up to 7 characters of the uncompressed row. The decompression operation essentially involves decoding all the compressed symbols in a row and building the uncompressed row by *stitching* together character data from each of them.

Row decompression logic on FPGA is shown in Figure 5-2. During an initial setup phase, the expansion dictionary is downloaded from the host into the dictionary buffers on the FPGA. This is a one-time process; it need not be repeated for each job, unless the table and hence the dictionary changes. During the scan phase, as the database pages are streamed to the FPGA, rows are extracted and stored in the row buffer. This extra buffering is required for rate matching between the decompressor and the row extraction logic and to provide each decompressor instance dedicated access to its respective rows in parallel to the rest. At the output of the decompression logic is an uncompressed row buffer which stores the decompressed rows. It provides a variable-bytes write interface, from 1 to 7 bytes, to support variable output rates from the decompressor.

A given database page may contain compressed rows mixed with rows in raw form; the decompression logic thus works in two modes – decompression mode and pass-through mode. As a new row is fetched from the row buffer, the header parser determines if the row is compressed or raw. If raw, the row is simply passed along to the uncompressed row buffer, two bytes per cycle. Even though a raw row can be copied over faster, only two bytes are transferred per cycle to keep a common read interface from the row buffer for both raw data as well as compressed tokens. This reduces extra multiplexing at the output of the row buffer. Note that reading just 2 bytes a cycle does not cause any starvation of the downstream predicate evaluation logic since it consumes data at a rate of 1 byte per cycle.

For compressed rows, the tokenizer module fetches the compressed token from the row buffer, one token at a time, as requested by the controller FSM. For a character-type token, the 8-bit character data is decoded from the token and written into the uncompressed row buffer. For a dictionary token, the controller reads the 8-byte entry from the dictionary.

A dictionary entry can be *unpreceded* or *preceded* and is decoded appropriately by the dictionary data decoder. An *unpreceded* entry contains up to 7 bytes of data and a length field. It is a terminal entry, indicating that the current token has been fully decompressed. A *preceded* entry contains up to 5 bytes of data and its length. Additionally, it contains a pointer to the next *chaining* dictionary entry that must be decoded to continue decompressing the current token, and an offset that indicates the relative position of the data bytes from the current entry within the complete uncompressed data for the token. Decompression of a compressed token is continued until an unpreceded entry is found, at which point the next token is fetched from the row buffer.

Optimal implementation of the decompressor design on the FPGA requires the operations described above to be staged in pipelined fashion. This, however, presents a potential problem – since the algorithm is not purely feed-forward, a new token cannot be fetched until the previous one is completely decompressed. Similarly, a new dictionary entry cannot be read until the current one has been read and decoded. These lead to empty cycles or *bubbles* between consecutive token reads and dictionary reads. This is not a problem as long as the average output rate of the decompressor is higher than 1 byte per cycle, which is the rate at which the predicate evaluation logic consumes data. For data with a very high compression ratio, this rate is easily achieved. For data with a lower compression ratio, however, where each compressed token expands to a few bytes, the average rate may drop below one byte per cycle, leading to stalling of the predicate evaluation pipeline.

We address this issue by adding token prefetch logic in the tokenizer, wherein the 8 next tokens are prefetched and stored in a FIFO. With this approach, the next token is ready for processing as soon as the current one is finished. When the entire row is fully decompressed, any outstanding tokens in the FIFO are flushed and a new set of tokens is prefetched from the next compressed row. Figure 5-3 shows the effect of adding the prefetch logic on the overall pipeline utilization, for a specific real-life workload. Adding the prefetcher results in a more than 50% reduction in row decompression time; for the 165 byte long rows, the average row decompression time is reduced from 190 cycles to 80 cycles, bringing the average decompressor output rate well above the required 1 byte/cycle. Actual savings and the average output rate, of course, are dependent on the compression ratio and the number of tokens to be analyzed to decompress a row of certain length. The worst case of compression arises where a token does not access the dictionary and simply generates a single byte. With prefetching, such tokens can be processed in a single cycle, thus maintaining a throughput of 1 byte/cycle.

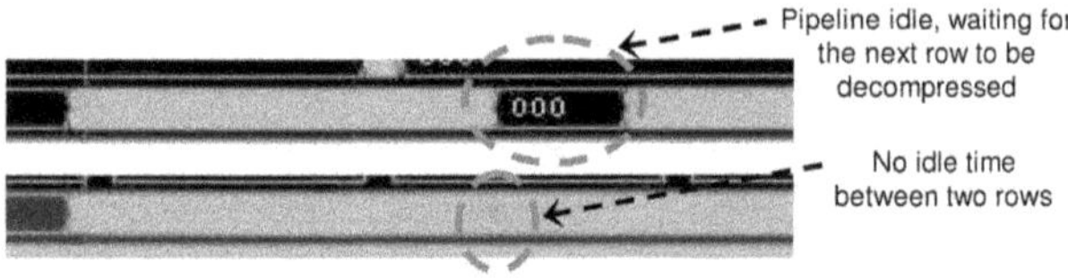

Figure 5-3 Effect of prefetching on pipeline utilization

Note that similar optimization is not possible on the dictionary read side since the reads from the dictionary are not from sequential locations and depend on the value of the pointer. This, however, is a concern only for the dictionary tokens that generate three or fewer bytes of data. Such tokens would appear in data with a very low compression ratio and can potentially lead to sub-optimal utilization of the predicate evaluation pipelines.

5.2 Predicate Evaluation on FPGA

Once the rows are decompressed, they are sent to downstream predicate evaluation logic for filtering based on the query predicates. A row scanner is used to evaluate the database rows against the query (Figure 5-4). It consists of a chain of independent predicate evaluation units and a reduction network (RN). Each PE evaluates a single predicate on a particular column of the database row. The reduction network then reduces the outputs of the PEs, as per the query, to a 1-bit qualify signal.

To evaluate a query on the FPGA, each PE must perform a specific operation on specific bytes of the database row, and the reduction network must combine the outputs of the PEs in a certain manner. The operation to perform and the fields to evaluate are specific to a given query and change with the query. Generating a new FPGA hardware image for each query and reprogramming the FPGA is not viable since synthesis and place-and-route typically take hours to finish. Reprogramming the FPGA with a pre-generated FPGA image is plausible, though for queries that operate on relatively small amounts of data, the reconfiguration time may dominate the overall processing time. Moreover, even a slight change in the query would require regeneration of the FPGA image and reconfiguration of the FPGA.

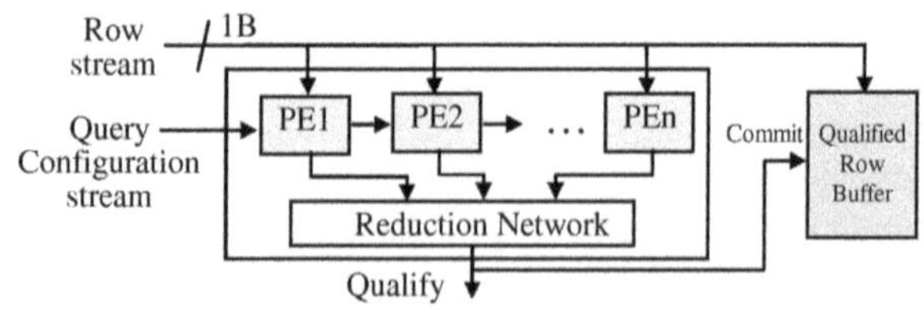

Figure 5-4 Row scanner for evaluating database rows

To address this issue, we designed the row scanner such that a given hardware image can be tailored to a variety of different queries. To that end, each PE is designed to perform 1 of 6 inequality operations; the actual operation to be performed is chosen during the query load time. Moreover, some of the PEs can also be disabled and excluded from participating in the query. Similarly, the reduction network is constructed as a binary tree of reduction units. Each reduction unit is a 2 to 1 reducer capable of performing one of 6 1-bit operations between the two inputs: AND, OR, NOT a, NOT b, PASS a, or PASS b.

During the query load phase, the configuration options are propagated down the PE chain and the reduction tree. PEs are configured using 5 options: (i) enable, to indicate whether the current PE is being used, (ii) predicate value, the constant against which the row field is compared, (iii) the inequality operation to be performed, (iv) offset of the first byte of the desired field within the row and (v) length of the field. A reduction unit has only one configuration option: the operation to perform between two predicates.

During the scan phase, database rows are streamed over the PEs, one byte per cycle. Streaming at a granularity of 1 byte is essential since fields in a row can be of varying length and may start at any byte position within the row. To reduce the latency of evaluating a row, the streaming bytes are broadcast to all the PEs as opposed to being rippled down the chain. Further, they are also *speculatively* written into the qualified row buffer; this write is later committed or invalidated based on whether the row qualifies. Since broadcasting requires large fan out, we use a register tree to feed all the PEs concurrently while keeping the fan out low.

As the row is streamed in, each PE captures the required bytes (using the start offset and length fields), evaluates its respective predicate and outputs a 1-bit match/mismatch signal. These funnel down the reduction network to generate the row qualify signal. For PEs disabled during the query load phase, the corresponding reduction unit either disables itself (if both the PEs feeding into it are disabled) or replaces the output from the disabled unit with the default pertaining to the function programmed into the reduction unit (e.g. 1 for an AND operation).

For an N-byte long row, it takes N + log2(n_{PE}) cycles to qualify the row, where n_{PE} is the number of PEs in the row scanner. At that point, the row, if qualified, is committed into the qualified row buffer. The qualified rows from different row scanners are copied over to the output page buffer by the page formatting logic (see Figure 5-1), at a rate of 16 bytes per cycle. Formatted pages are sent to the host for further processing. Note that the FPGA returns the rows in uncompressed form, for direct consumption by the DBMS. This does not affect the processing rate on the FPGA since the filtering of the database rows typically results in lower bandwidth requirements on the return path.

6. SOFTWARE ENABLEMENT FOR FPGA ACCELRATION

Enabling FPGA acceleration for a DBMS is an end-to-end effort. One aspect of this effort is to restructure the data flow. Secondly, the capability of transforming a DBMS query into a format that the FPGA accelerator can interpret for dynamic self-re-customization is also critical for accelerating various workloads without the need for reconfiguring the FPGA.

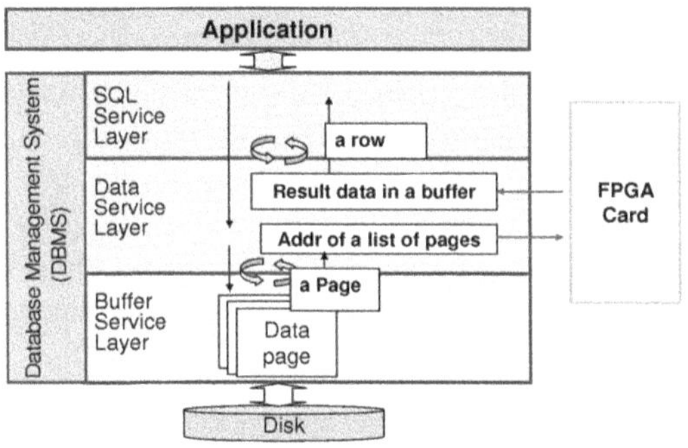

Figure 6-1 Block operation to enable FPGA acceleration

6.1 Block Level Data Operation

An important design aspect for integration performance is to reduce the *chattiness* during the interactions between the host and the accelerator. For this purpose, we introduce a block level data operation within the DBMS query processing engine. More specifically, a long running predicate evaluation query is divided into multiple jobs for an FPGA to process sequentially. Each job consists of a number of data pages as input for the FPGA to read, and an output buffer into which the FPGA writes the results. Both data transferring actions are initiated by the FPGA.

Figure 6-1 illustrates the changes made for enabling the block level data processing, as opposed to a traditional one page or one row at a time processing flow. For FPGA acceleration, a list of BP pages (addresses) is obtained by the Data Service Layer in DBMS and read by the FPGA. For output data from the FPGA, the DBMS pre-allocates a large enough buffer that is filled by the FPGA engine with its results. The data format in this output buffer conforms to the structure that is understood by DBMS processing engine for further downstream processing so additional data copy and formatting software can be avoided.

6.2 DBMS-FPGA Communication Protocol

Communication between the DBMS and the FPGA is achieved through a series of control blocks that are passed from the host to the FPGA. These carry the necessary information for describing the operations and data transfers.

6.2.1 DMA Addressing

Since the FPGA does not have direct addressability to host memory, all in-memory data blocks and control information blocks need to be transferred to the FPGA via DMA over PCIe. When constructing the communication protocol between software and the FPGA, the DMA addresses for the memory are used instead of the host addresses, as shown throughout this section.

6.2.2 Host Control Block

A query may be broken up into multiple jobs. A job is submitted to the FPGA via a host control block (HCB), which encapsulates the job information but is independent of the application logic. The HCB is interpreted by the service layer in the FPGA; it carries information such as whether the current HCB is the last job in the queue, the DMA address of the query control block (see 6.2.3), as well as updatable fields indicating an active job's status. A queue of HCBs is maintained which allows more jobs to be queued while a job is active on the FPGA. FPGA will continue to the next job in the queue, if one is available, when the current one is completed.

6.2.3 Query Control Block

A query control block (QCB) is a data structure that is used to tailor the FPGA application logic to a specific query. To address different invocation scenarios, we devise two formats of the QCBs. Both formats contain an address list of the input data pages to be processed and the address of the output buffer. The first format, shown as QCB1 in Figure 6-2, is used when the FPGA needs to interpret new query instructions and customize its internal logic. It thus also contains predicate function information and an address list of the 8 4K dictionary pages to be loaded. When the second format, shown as QCB2 in Figure 6-2, is used, the FPGA performs the same task as in the previous job on a different set of data. This saves the time needed to re-customize the FPGA logic and reload the dictionary.

To process more data pages per job than the limit imposed by a single QCB, a query control data continuation block (QCDCB), shown in Figure 6-2, enables more input pages to be chained to a job. The last entry in QCB's data list points to the next QCDCB when this is needed.

6.2.4 Query Mapping to FPGA Engines

To express predicate instruction to the FPGA, QCB1 contains a list of predicate function control blocks and a list of reduction control blocks. A predicate function control block, shown in Figure 6-3, is a 16 byte data structure that has information on the column, the comparison operator and the constant to compare against the column value that personalizes each PE.

Reduction control blocks, logically structured as a tree for the RN, contain the Boolean operations information among the simple predicates in a complex predicate expression.

Figure 6-4 shows an example mapping of a predicate expression to the PEs and the reduction network.

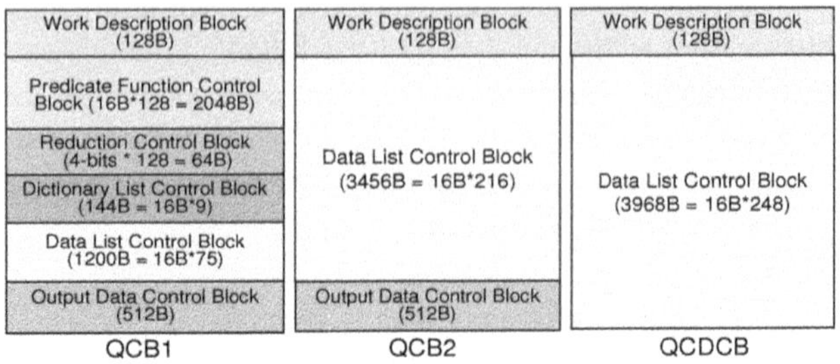

Figure 6-2 Different formats of the query control block

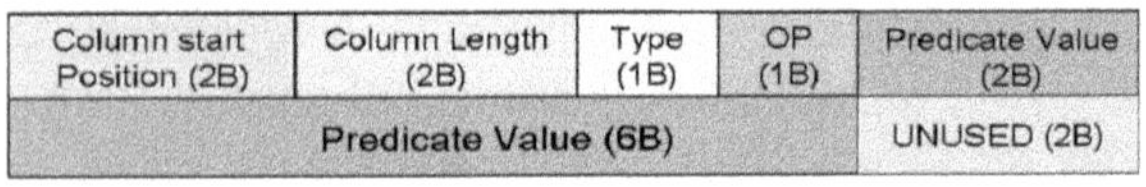

Figure 6-3 16B predicate function control block

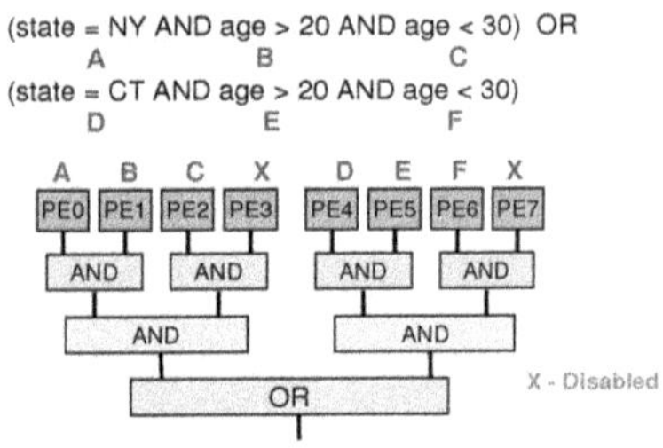

Figure 6-4 Mapping predicate expression to PE and RN

6.3 Transforming Query to QCBs

SQL provides rich syntaxes to express data relations. Predicate expression are not limited to just comparisons and Boolean operations. For example, expression *"WHERE state IN ('NY', 'CT') AND age between 20 AND 30"* tests set containment for field "state" and it can not be directly mapped to PEs and RUs as is. However, existing SQL parsing and transformation capabilities in the DBMS are capable of converting the predicate into the comparison and Boolean only expressions shown in Figure 6-4 and representing it in an internal format [17]. A realistic approach for query transformation integration is to inject the FPGA QCB build function into the query processing flow such that it can take advantage of the transformed expression for its input. It is then straightforward for the QCB build function to map the transformed expression to predicate function control blocks and correct topology in the reduction network.

7. EXPERIMENTS AND RESULTS

Our prototype is built upon a commercial DBMS running on a 3.8GHz multi-core super scalar system. Our target FPGA system is a PLDA XpressGX4LP card [18] with an Altera Stratix IV GX530 FPGA. The card communicates with the host system over a PCIe gen2 x8 interface.

Table 7-1 FPGA resource requirements

Tiles	PEs	Logic	ALUTs	Registers	Memory Bits
1	16	9%	24637 (6%)	27338 (6%)	2179840 (10%)
	32	16%	39893 (9%)	48949(12%)	
	64	30%	70,240 (17%)	91114 (21%)	
2	16	19%	47,877 (11%)	54,318 (13%)	4359680 (21%)
	32	33%	76,681 (18%)	97,441 (23%)	
	64	59%	136149 (32%)	181750 (43%)	
4	16	38%	95,795 (23%)	108269 (25%)	8,719,360 (41%)
	32	66%	152,687(36%)	194416 (46%)	

Table 7-1 lists the FPGA resource requirements for the different configurations of the database acceleration engine. This does not include the service layer, which occupies a fixed area of around 25% of the target FPGA. For a given number of tiles, the logic requirements increase proportionately with the number of PEs within a row scanner, while the memory requirements remain unchanged. Increasing the number of tiles, on the other hand, increases the number of row scanners, leading to higher logic as well as memory requirements. While the former is due to the increased number of PEs, the latter results from having more dictionary and data staging buffers. With 64 PEs per row scanner, the current FPGA can support up to 2 tiles; 4 tiles can be instantiated with fewer PEs per scanner.

We now present the results of evaluating our FPGA-based accelerator for database systems, using three metrics: CPU savings, speedup on offloaded computations, and overall end-to-end speedup. Additionally, we discuss the cost and relative merit of invoking the FPGA kernel. In our experimental workload, the data is derived from real customer database tables, and the query operations include decompression and predicate evaluation, which are two of the most CPU intensive functions. Both the baseline and hardware-accelerated versions of the code are single-threaded and run on a single processor core. All the measurements were taken with the data in buffer pools and do not include disk I/O time. Measurements were taken with both uncompressed and compressed rows; the uncompressed row lengths for the two workloads evaluated (customer 1 and customer 2 in Figure 7-2) are 165 bytes and 229 bytes, with the average compression space savings of 80% and 50% respectively.

CPU savings represent the CPU runtime reduction obtained by offloading the computations from the CPU to the FPGA. This is an important metric since it effectively represents freeing-up of the CPU resources for online transaction processing in real-time analytics systems. Figure 7-1 shows the savings obtained while processing 468K database pages of uncompressed data and 101K pages of compressed data from customer 1 workload, for a range of data qualification ratios. Note that the reduced CPU time shown for the FPGA-assisted database system does not include the time spent on the FPGA to perform the actual computations.

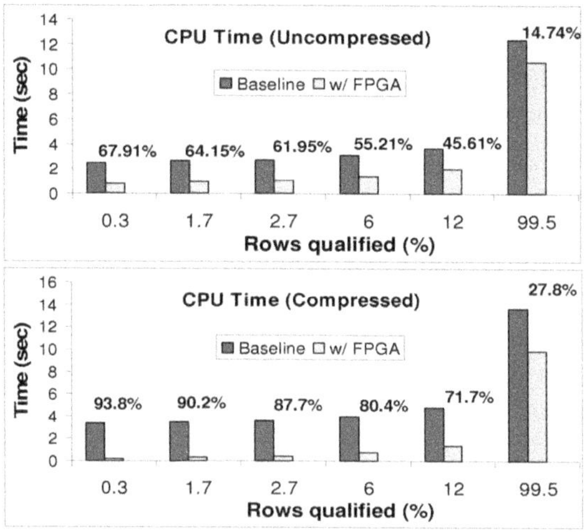

Figure 7-1 CPU savings obtained from FPGA offload

As shown, for compressed data, an 27.8% to 93.8% reduction in CPU time is obtained, while the reduction is between 14.7% and 67.9% for uncompressed data. This difference is expected; for uncompressed data, no decompression operation is involved, so the offload, and hence the savings is smaller. Moreover, for both compressed and uncompressed data, the savings are higher when a smaller fraction of rows qualify. This is due to the post-processing of the qualified data by the CPU, such as moving data to application buffer. When a larger fraction of rows qualify, there is more processing on the CPU and hence lower overall CPU savings. Overall, both compressed and uncompressed cases achieve significant saving of CPU resources, which in turn can be diverted to OLTP work.

Next we compare the raw power of the FPGA to that of the host processor in performing the same work, expressed in Figure 7-2 in terms of 'rows processed per second', for compressed and uncompressed data from two customer workloads. Also shown is the *effective* uncompressed data processing throughput achieved by the FPGA for each case. The FPGA design was instantiated with 4 scan tiles, for a total of 32 row scanners, and runs at 200 MHz. Note that the processing rate shown here measures just the offloaded computations and is thus independent of data characteristics such as qualification ratio. These measurements do, however, include the time for host-FPGA data transfers.

As shown, the FPGA achieves speedups of 10.7x and 6.7x on compressed data, whereas the speedups on uncompressed data are relatively modest. The reason is as follows: for uncompressed data, the overall performance is limited by the data transfer bandwidth; therefore, in this case, the FPGA engines are starved and not fully utilized. With uncompressed transfer bandwidth of 2.6GB/sec, the design achieves pipeline utilization of just 37%. In other words, the row scanners on the FPGA are idle for 63% of the time, waiting for data. Transferring compressed data, on the other hand, results in data expansion on the FPGA, thus leading to higher effective uncompressed bandwidth, thereby overcoming the effects of the PCIe limitation. For customer 2 workload, where the data is compressed down to 50%, the effective bandwidth is 4.8GB/sec and the FPGA engines achieve 75.7% of their peak performance. Here, all the available raw bandwidth has been utilized and the overall performance is still limited by PCIe. For customer 1 data, however, which is compressed down to 20%, the effective bandwidth is 6.8GB/sec with the actual transfer bandwidth of just 1.5GB/sec. In this case, the design achieves 98.5% pipeline utilization and the performance is limited by the available FPGA resources.

As can be seen, compression plays an important role; due to the high compression ratio, even a portion of the available bus bandwidth is sufficient to saturate the predicate evaluation engines on the FPGA. Higher PCIe utilization and further performance improvement can be achieved by instantiating more scan tiles on the FPGA. Data with a smaller compression ratio, alternatively, can utilize higher PCIe bus bandwidth to achieve high data processing rate. Note that the actual and effective bandwidths for uncompressed data are one and the same.

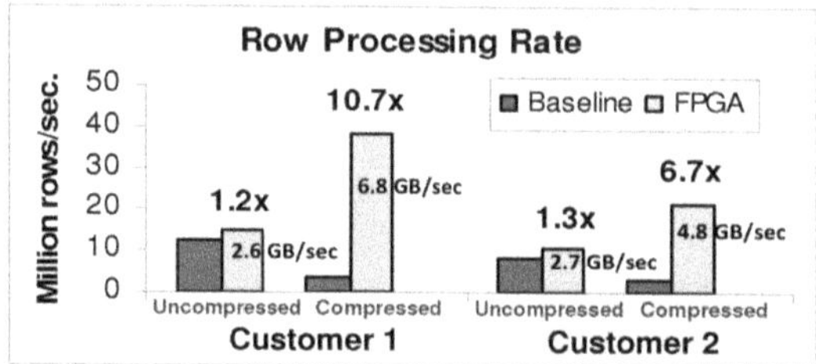

Figure 7-2 FPGA speedup over the baseline software

To evaluate the ultimate benefit of the proposed approach to an end customer, we measure the improvements on the end-to-end query response time. Figure 7-3 plots response times for compressed and uncompressed data. The dataset used is the same as that reported in Figure 7-1. The measured time includes data transfer time, the time for pre and post processing of the data on the host CPU and the time spent on the FPGA accelerator.

Again, the end-to-end response time is dependent on the filtering ratio, due to the post-processing of the qualified data. For compressed data, the graph shows similar trend as that for CPU savings – larger end-to-end speedups for lower qualification ratio, with speedups in the range of 1.2x to 6.2x for various filtering ratios. Uncompressed data, on the other hand, does not show any improvement in response time. This is mainly due to two reasons: first, the amount of processing that is offloaded is not enough to amortize the costs associated with invoking the FPGA routine and second, the computation-only speedup obtained from the FPGA is modest, as discussed earlier, due to the bus bandwidth limitations. While the latter can be addressed by tuning the current PCIe DMA interface or using a higher bandwidth bus, addressing the former requires offloading more computations to the FPGA. These include some of the post processing operations performed by the CPU. Nonetheless, the fact that there is no regression in response time in the uncompressed case still makes offloading an effective improvement due to CPU savings. More importantly, the compressed data performance is particularly significant in that most enterprise customers do compress their large tables for storage savings.

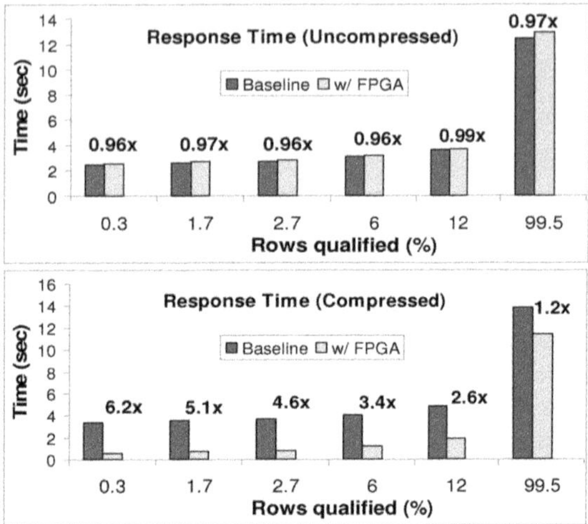

Figure 7-3 Query response time improvement

As is clear from the above discussions, offloading the decompression operation to the FPGA is crucial to obtaining overall performance improvement. Our FPGA design performs streaming, on-the-fly decompression of the compressed rows, thereby offsetting PCIe bus bandwidth limitations without incurring any performance penalties for large, throughput-centric analytics workloads.

Finally, we discuss the overhead of calling the FPGA routine. Since sending a query to the FPGA incurs some start-up cost, we performed experiments to find the minimum query data size needed to offset that cost and obtain an overall performance benefit. In terms of absolute time, the CPU cost for FPGA invocation is around 50 to 100 milliseconds on this processor. Based on our experiments, this cost gets offset for tables with 4000 to 10,000 uncompressed pages or 400 to 1,000 compressed pages. For smaller queries, invoking the FPGA routine does not pay off and the original software path should be used instead. A future work in deploying this acceleration technology to DBMS is to enhance the query optimizer such that it can select the appropriate execution path between software and the acceleration based on database statistics and the optimizer's analysis of the query.

8. CONCLUSIONS AND FUTURE WORK

We have presented an FPGA-accelerated database system for evaluating expensive analytics queries. The results show up to 94% savings of CPU resources and up to an order of magnitude speedup in the offloaded computations on the tested workload. We presented a general approach for an existing DBMS to seamlessly leverage the FPGA accelerator and validated with a prototype that integrates the accelerator into a commercial DBMS and achieves significant end-to-end performance improvements.

As part of our future work, we are investigating offload of other database computations to the FPGA to further improve the overall performance. Moreover, in our current work, we focused on the issue of CPU resources while running analytics queries in parallel with mission-critical transactional work. While CPU is the most critical resource in such environments, in some cases, I/O resources can also affect the overall performance. Addressing this also forms a part of our future work.

9. REFERENCES

[1] http://www.teradata.com/

[2] Krueger, J., et. al. "Fast Updates on Read Optimized Databases Using MultiCore CPUs" Proceedings of the VLDB Endowment, Vol. 5, No. 1, August 2012.

[3] Low, B., Ooi, B., and Wong, C., "Exploration on Scalability of Database Bulk Insertion with Multi-threading" Int. J. New Computer Architectures and Their Applications, 2011.

[4] Horikawa, T., "An Unexpected Scalability Bottleneck in a DBMS: A Hidden Pitfall in Implementing Mutual Exclusion", Parallel and Distributed Computing and Systems, 2011.

[5] Scofield, T. C., et. al., "XtremeData dbX: An FPGA-Based Data Warehouse Appliance" Computing in Science and Engineering, IEEE 2010.

[6] Johnson, R., Raman, V., Sidle, R., Swart, G. "Rowwise Parallel Predicate Evaluation" Proc. Int. Conf on VLDB'08.

[7] Zhou, J. and Ross, K. A., Implementing Database Operations Using SIMD Instructions", ACM SIGMOD, 2002, 145-156.

[8] Satish N., et. al., "Fast sort on CPUs and GPUs: a case for bandwidth oblivious SIMD sort". ACM SIGMOD, 2010.

[9] Leung, K., Ercegovac, M., and Muntz, R. "Exploiting Reconfigurable FPGA for Parallel Query Processing in Computation Intensive Data Mining Applications" In UC MICRO Technical Report Feb. 1999.

[10] Mueller, R. and Teubner, J. "FPGA: What's in it for a Database?." In ACM SIGMOD, 2009, 999-1004.

[11] Mueller, R., Teubner, J. and Alonso, G., "Data processing on FPGAs", Proceedings of the VLDB Endowment, v.2 n.1, August 2009.

[12] Mueller, R., Teubner, J. and Alonso, G., "Glacier: a query-to-hardware compiler", In ACM SIGMOD'2010, 1159-1162.

[13] http://www.netezza.com/

[14] http://www-01.ibm.com/software/data/db2/zos/analytics-accelerator

[15] Ramakrishnan, R., and Gehrke, J. Database Management Systems. McGraw-Hill, 3rd edition.

[16] Iyer, B. and Wilhite, D. 1994. Data Compression Support in Databases. In Proceedings of Int. Conf on VLDB.

[17] Lorie, R.A., and Nilsson, J.F.. 1979. "An access specification language for a relational data base system", IBM J. Res. Dev.

[18] http://www.plda.com/prodetail.php?pid=184

LumiNOC: A Power-Efficient, High-Performance, Photonic Network-on-Chip for Future Parallel Architectures

Cheng Li, Mark Browning, Paul V. Gratz and Samuel Palermo
{seulc, mabrowning, pgratz, spalermo}@tamu.edu
Department of Electrical and Computer Engineering, Texas A&M University, College Station, Texas 77843-3128

ABSTRACT

Achieving scaling performance as core counts increase to the hundreds in future chip-multi-processors (CMPs) requires high performing, yet energy-efficient interconnects. Silicon nanophotonics is a promising replacement for electronic on-chip interconnect due to its high bandwidth and low latency, however, prior techniques have required high static power for the laser and ring thermal tuning. We propose a novel nano-photonic NoC architecture, LumiNOC, optimized for high performance and power-efficiency. In a 64-node NoC under synthetic traffic, LumiNOC enjoys 50% lower latency at low loads and 40% higher throughput per Watt on synthetic traffic, versus other reported photonic NoCs. LumiNOC reduces latencies 40% versus an electrical 2D mesh NoCs on the PARSEC shared memory, multithreaded benchmark suite.

Categories and Subject Descriptors

C.1.2 [**Multiple Data Stream Architectures**]: Interconnection arch.

Keywords

CMP; NoC; Synthetic/Realistic Workload; Power Efficiency

1. INTRODUCTION

Monolithic silicon photonics have been proposed as a scalable alternative to meet future many-core systems bandwidth demands, however, current photonic NoC (PNoC) architectures suffer from high static power demands, high latency and low efficiency, making them less attractive than their electrical counterparts. For example, conventional photonic crossbars [1, 2], achieve nearly uniform latency and high bandwidth, however, channels are dedicated to each node and cannot be flexibly shared by the others. Due to the unbalanced traffic distribution in realistic workloads, channel bandwidth cannot be fully utilized. This leads to inefficient energy usage, since the static power is constant regardless of traffic load. Over-provisioned channels also implies higher ring resonator counts, which must be maintained at the appropriate trimming temperature, consuming on-chip power. In addition, many photonic NoCs globally route waveguides in a bundle, connecting all the tiles in the CMP. The long waveguide leads to significant laser power losses over the long distance. Moreover, the power and overhead introduced by the separated arbitration channels or networks in previous photonic NoCs can lead to further power efficiency losses. In future latency and power constrained CMPs, these characteristics will hobble the utility of photonic interconnect. In this paper we propose LumiNOC, a novel PNoC architecture which addresses the power wasted due to channel overprovisioning, while reducing latency and maintaining high bandwidth. LumiNOC makes three contributions: *First*, instead of conventional, globally distributed, photonic channels, requiring high laser power, we propose a novel channel sharing arrangement composed of sub-sets of cores in photonic subnets. *Second*, we propose a novel, purely photonic, distributed arbitration mechanism, dynamic channel scheduling, which achieves extremely low-latency without degrading throughput. *Third*, our photonic network architecture leverages the same wavelengths for channel arbitration and parallel data transmission, allowing efficient utilization of the photonic resources, lowering static power consumption.

PACT'12, September 19–23, 2012, Minneapolis, Minnesota, USA.
ACM 978-1-4503-1182-3/12/09.

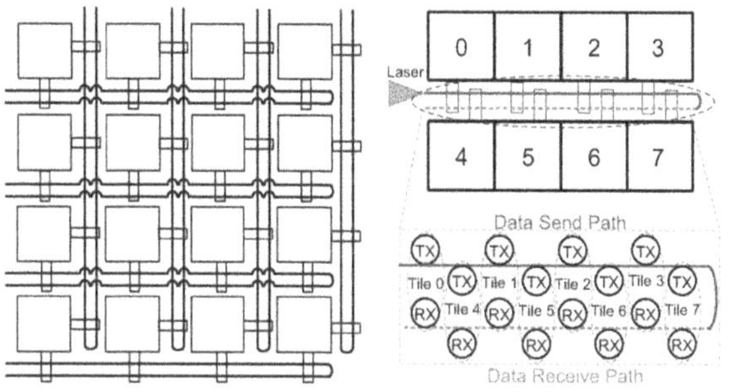

(a) (b)

Figure 1: (a) LumiNOC interconnection of CMP with 16 tiles, (b) One-row subnet of eight nodes. Circles (TX and RX) represent groups of rings; one dotted oval represents a tile.

2. LUMINOC ARCHITECTURE

The LumiNOC design breaks the network into several smaller networks (subnets) with shorter waveguides. Fig. 1a shows an example of this subnet inter-connected 16-node CMP system. All tiles are interconnected by two different subnets, one horizontal and one vertical. If a sender and receiver do not reside in the same subnet, transmission requires a hop through an intermediate node's electrical router. In this case, transmission experiences longer delay due to the extra O/E-E/O conversions and router latency.

Fig. 1b details the shared channel for a LumiNOC one-row subnet design. Each tile contains W modulating "Tx rings" and W receiving "Rx Rings", where W is the number of wavelengths multiplexed in the waveguide. Since the optical signal uni-directionally propagates in the waveguide from its source at off-chip laser, each node's Tx rings are connected in series on the "Data Send Path", shown in a solid line from the laser, prior to connecting each node's Rx rings on the "Data Receive Path", shown in a dashed line. In this "double-back" waveguide layout, modulation by any node can be received by any other node; furthermore, the node which modulates the signal may also receive its own modulated signal, a feature that is leveraged in our collision detection scheme in the arbitration phase. The same wavelengths are leveraged for arbitration and parallel data transmission. At any given time a multi-wavelength channel with N nodes may be in one of three states: **Idle** - All wavelengths are un-modulated and the network is quiescent. **Arbitration** - One more sender nodes are modulating N copies of the arbitration flags; one copy to each node in the subnet (including itself) with the aim to gain control of the channel. **Data Transmission** - Once a sender has established ownership of the channel, it modulates all channel wavelengths in parallel for data transmission.

To send a packet, a node first waits for the channel to enter the **Idle** state. Then, it places the link in the **Arbitration** state and modulates a copy of the arbitration flags to the appropriate arbitration wavelengths for each of the N nodes. A "1-hot" source address serves as collision detection mechanism: since the subnet is operated synchronously, any time multiple nodes send overlapping arbi-

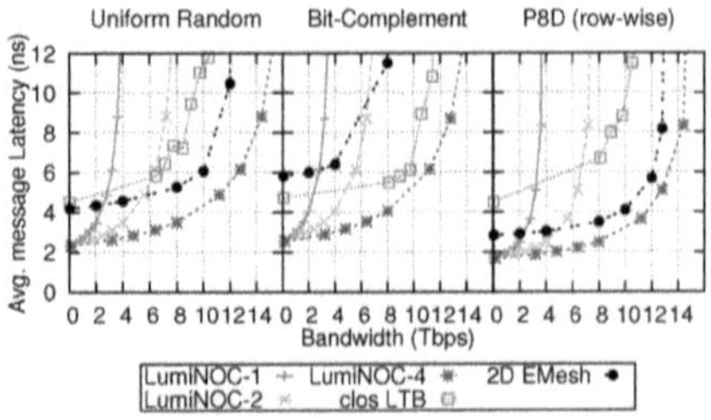

Figure 2: LumiNOC vs. Clos LTBw and electrical network under synthetic workloads.

Literature		ELP (W)	TTP (W)	ERP (W)	EO/OE (W)	ITP (Tbps)	RTP (Tpbs)	TP (W)	**RTP/W (Tbps/W)**
EMesh [3]		NA	NA	NA	NA	10	3.0	26.7	**0.1**
Corona [2]		26.0	21.00	0.52	4.92	160	73.6	52.4	**1.4**
FlexiShare [1]		5.80	11.00	0.13	0.60	20	9.0	17.5	**0.5**
Clos [4]		3.30	0.14	0.10	0.54	18	10.0	4.1	**2.4**
LumiNOC	1-Layer	0.35	0.33	0.13	0.30	10	4.0	1.1	**3.6**
	2-Layers	0.73	0.65	0.26	0.61	20	8.0	2.3	**3.4**
	4-Layers	1.54	1.31	0.52	1.22	40	16.0	4.6	**3.4**

Table 1: Power efficiency comparison of different photonic NoC architectures.

tration flags, the "1-hot" precondition is violated and all nodes are aware of the collision. We leverage self-reception of the arbitration flag: right after sending, the node monitors the incoming arbitration flags. If uncorrupted, then the sender succeeded arbitrating the channel and the channel proceeds to the **Data Transmission** phase. If the arbitration flags are corrupted (>1 is hot), then a conflict occurred. In this event, conflicting nodes back-off a specified number of cycles dependent upon their node id and the current clock cycle, and attempt arbitration again.

3. IMPLEMENTATION AND EVALUATION

We develop a baseline physical implementation of the general LumiNOC architecture for the evaluation of LumiNOC against competing PNOC architectures. We assume a 400 mm^2 chip implemented in a 22nm CMOS process and containing 64 square tiles that operate at 5GHz. Each tile contains a processor core, private caches, a fraction of the shared last-level cache, and a router connecting it to one horizontal and one vertical photonic subnet. The effective waveguide length is 4.0 cm, yielding a propagation delay of 2.7 cycles at 10GHz network frequency. The wavelengths per waveguide is limited to 32 to reduce the ring through loss. To evaluate this implementation's performance, we use a cycle-accurate, microarchitectural-level network simulator. The network was simulated under both synthetic and realistic workloads. LumiNOC designs with 1, 2, and 4 Network Layers are simulated to show results for different bandwidth design points.

Synthetic Workload Results: in Fig. 2, the LumiNOC design is compared against the electrical and Clos networks under *uniform random*, *bit complement*, and *P8D*. The figure shows the low-load latencies of the LumiNOC design are much lower than the competing designs. This is due primarily to the lower diameter of the LumiNOC topology, destinations within one subnet are one "hop" away while those in a second subnet are two. The 1-layer network saturates at 4Tbps realistic throughput as determined by analyzing the offered vs accepted rate.

The different synthetic traffic patterns bring out interesting relationships. On the *P8D* pattern, which is engineered to exploit the physical locality inherent in the LumiNOC and Clos designs, all have universally lower latency than on other patterns. However, while both the electrical and LumiNOC network have around 25% lower low-load latency than uniform random, Clos only benefits by a few percent from this optimal traffic pattern. At the other extreme, the electrical network experiences a 50% increase in no-load latency under the bit-complement pattern compared to uniform random while both Clos and the LumiNOC network are only marginally affected. This is due to the LumiNOC having a worst-case hop count of 2 and not all routes go through the central nodes as in the electrical network. Instead, the intermediate nodes are well distributed through the network under this traffic pattern. However, as the best-case hop count is also 2 with this pattern, the LumiNOC network experiences more contention and the saturation bandwidth is decreased as a result.

Realistic Workload Results: Fig. 3 shows the performance of the LumiNOC network in 1-, 2- and 4-layers, normalized against the performance of the baseline electrical NoC. Even with one layer, the average message latency is about 10% lower than the electrical

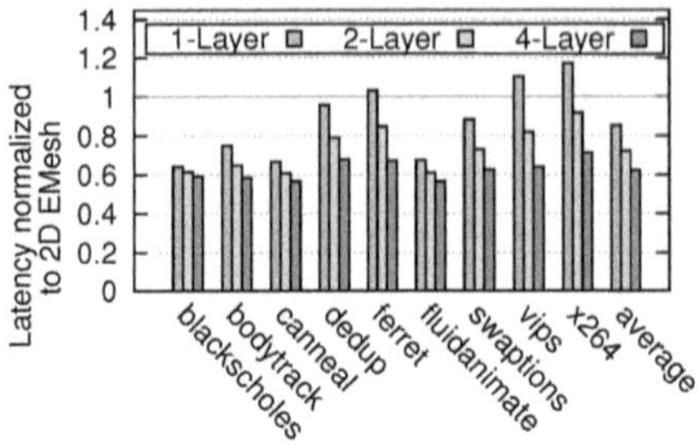

Figure 3: Message Latency in PARSEC benchmarks for LumiNOC compared to electrical network.

network. With additional network layers, LumiNOC has approximately 40% lower average latency. These results are explained by examining the bandwidth-latency curves in Fig. 2. The average offered rates for the PARSEC benchmarks are of the order of 0.5Tbps, so these applications benefit from LumiNOC's low latency while being well under even the 1-layer, LumiNOC throughput.

Power Efficiency: in order for a fair comparison versus other reported PNoC architectures, we refer to the photonic loss of various photonic devices reported by Joshi et al. [4] and Pan et al. [1]. Total power (TP) consists of the electrical laser power, thermal tuning power required to maintain microring resonant at the work wavelength, electrical router power, and electrical to optical/optical to electrical conversion power. Power efficiency is compared in Table 1. **ITP** is the ideal throughput of the design, while **RTP** is the maximum throughput of the design under a uniform random workload as shown in Fig. 2. A 2GHz electrical 2D-mesh [3] was scaled to 8×8 nodes operating at 5GHz, in a 22nm CMOS process, to compare against the photonic networks.

The table shows that LumiNOC has the highest power efficiency of all designs compared in RTP/Watt, increasing efficiency by ~40% versus the nearest competitor, Clos [4]. By reducing wavelength multiplexing density, utilizing shorter waveguides, and leveraging the data channels for arbitration, LumiNOC consumes the least electrical laser power (ELP) among all the compared architectures. A 4-layer LumiNOC consumes ~1/4th the ELP of a competitive Clos architecture, of nearly the same throughput.

4. CONCLUSIONS

In this work, LumiNOC addresses power inefficiencies issues of prior photonic NoCs by adopting a shared-channel, photonic on-chip network with a novel, in-band arbitration mechanism to efficiently utilize power, achieving a high performance and scalable interconnect with extremely low latency.

References

[1] Y. Pan et al., "FlexiShare: Channel Sharing for an Energy-Efficient Nanophotonic Crossbar," *HPCA*, pp. 1-12, 2010.
[2] D. Vantrease et al., "Corona: System Implications of Emerging Nanophotonic Technology," *ISCA*, pp. 153-164, 2008.
[3] J. Howard et al., "A 48-Core IA-32 Processor in 45 nm CMOS Using On-Die Message-Passing and DVFS for Performance and Power Scaling," *JSSC*, vol. 46, no. 1, pp. 173-183, Oct., 2011.
[4] A. Joshi et al., "Silicon-Photonic Clos Networks for Global On-Chip Communication," *NOCS*, pp. 124-133, 2009.

Acceleration of Bulk Memory Operations in a Heterogeneous Multicore Architecture

JongHyuk Lee
University of Houston
Houston, TX 77004, USA
jonghyuk.lee@daum.net

Ziyi Liu
University of Houston
Houston, TX 77004, USA
brian.zy.liu@gmail.com

Xiaonan Tian
University of Houston
Houston, TX 77004, USA
daniel.xntian@gmail.com

Dong Hyuk Woo
Intel Labs
Santa Clara, CA 95054, USA
dong.hyuk.woo@intel.com

Weidong Shi
University of Houston
Houston, TX 77004, USA
larryshi@ymail.com

Dainis Boumber
University of Houston
Houston, TX 77004, USA
dainis.boumber@gmail.com

ABSTRACT

In this paper, we present a novel approach of using the integrated GPU to accelerate conventional operations that are normally performed by the CPUs, the bulk memory operations, such as memcpy or memset. Offloading the bulk memory operations to the GPU has many advantages, i) the throughput driven GPU outperforms the CPU on the bulk memory operations; ii) for on-die GPU with unified cache between the GPU and the CPU, the GPU private caches can be leveraged by the CPU for storing moved data and reducing the CPU cache bottleneck; iii) with additional lightweight hardware, asynchronous offload can be supported as well; and iv) different from the prior arts using dedicated hardware copy engines (e.g., DMA), our approach leverages the exiting GPU hardware resources as much as possible. The performance results based on our solution showed that offloaded bulk memory operations outperform CPU up to 4.3 times in micro benchmarks while still using less resources. Using eight real world applications and a cycle based full system simulation environment, the results showed 30% speedup for five, more than 20% speedup for two of the eight applications.

Categories and Subject Descriptors

C.0 [**Computer Systems Organization**]: General—System architectures; C.1.3 [**Processor Architectures**]: Other Architecture Styles—Heterogeneous (hybrid) systems

General Terms

Design, Performance

Keywords

Bulk memory operation, GPU, Heterogeneous multicore architecture, SIMD

1. INTRODUCTION

General purpose computing on GPUs (GPGPUs) has become a widely adopted architectural solution to build high performance computing systems, e.g. three out of the top 5 machines in TOP500 were built using GPGPUs as accelerators, as of January 2012. Despite such rapid evolution, we are facing yet another revolutionary change: an integrated GPU, i.e. CPUs and GPUs are integrated into the same package or even into the same die. In this paper, we are interested in how to utilize the integrated GPU to accelerate conventional operations (i.e., bulk memory operations such as memcpy or memset) that are normally performed by the CPUs, thus to improve application and overall system performance and resource utilizations without changing or rebuilding the application codes. In particular, we are interested in improving the performance of workloads that run on the server machines of commercial data centers. Besides computation requirements, these applications typically process a large volume of data, and devote large percentage of their processing time to I/O and manipulating the data.

PACT'12, September 19–23, 2012, Minneapolis, Minnesota, USA.
ACM 978-1-4503-1182-3/12/09.

2. ARCHITECTURE AND DESIGN

Our baseline architecture is a heterogeneous platform that has multiple CPU cores and GPU cores on a chip as shown in Figure 1. These heterogeneous processing units have different characteristics. First, a CPU core is a traditional, superscalar out-of-order core that is optimized for reducing the latency of each instruction through many architectural techniques such as branch prediction, data forwarding, and speculative instruction scheduling. Such a CPU core has a private instruction L1 cache and a private data L1 cache.

On the other hand, a GPU like SIMD core is a highly-multithreaded, wide SIMD core that is optimized for improving the overall throughput rather than latency. As a result, it does not support fancy speculation techniques. Rather, it is designed to consume less power and less area such as a multi-banked register file (rather than a multi-ported register file of an out-of-order core) to improve the overall throughput under a given power and area budget. In particular, a GPU core groups a large number of threads (for example, 256 threads) into one scheduling unit, termed a "warp", and executes the same instruction over those threads simultaneously. Furthermore, because a GPU core supports heavy multithreading among those warps and because it supports many more relaxed consistency model, it can support much more in-flight memory instructions than a CPU core, which goes through a private instruction and data L1 cache as shown in Figure 1. Note that different threads of a warp can issue non-coalesced memory requests. Our GPU L1 data cache models performs memory coalescing.

In our baseline, CPU cores and GPU cores share several

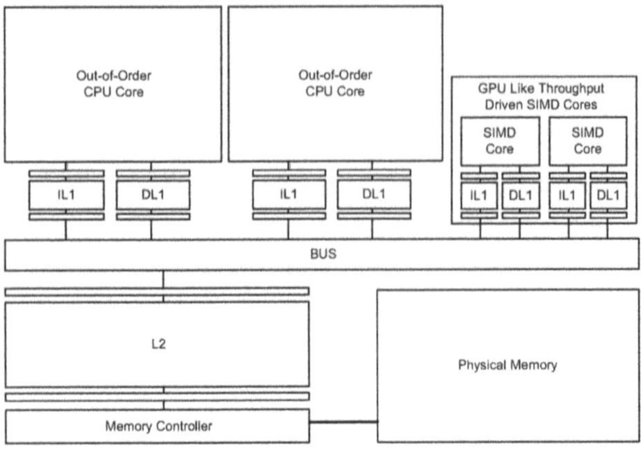

Figure 1: CPU Integrated with Throughput Driven GPU Like SIMD Cores

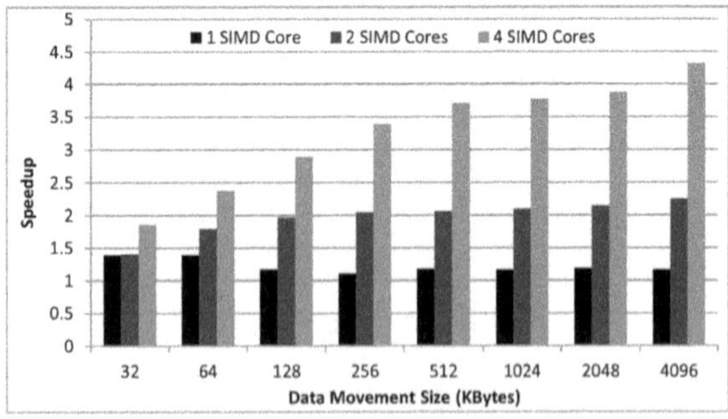

Figure 2: Speedup with Number of Cores for Different Data Movement Sizes

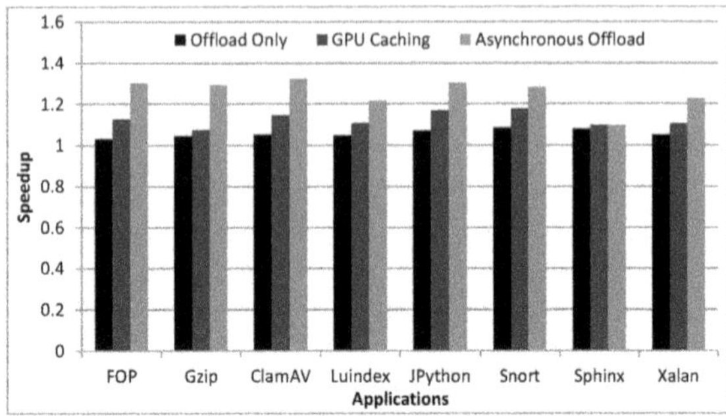

Figure 3: Speedup of Offloading Bulk Memory Operations to the Integrated GPU like Cores

on-die resources. First, private L1 caches of both CPU and GPU cores are connected through an on-die bus sharing its bus bandwidth. Second, the on-die shared bus is connected to a large, shared L2 cache as shown in Figure 1. Lastly, CPU and GPU memory requests that miss in the L2 cache as well as dirty cache lines that need to be written-back from the L2 cache go through a shared memory controller. In addition to such shared resources, both CPU and GPU share the off-chip bus bandwidth and main memory space.

After bulk memory operation functions are called, the GPU aware memory copy function can decide whether the operations should be offloaded to the GPU cores. Often this decision can be based on the size of data movement. When deciding that the data movement operations should be offloaded, the GPU aware library will parallelize the data movement by creating multiple independent GPU threads and dispatch them to the integrated GPU cores. Compared with the CPU threads, GPU threads are much more lightweight and can be created with very little overhead. Furthermore, this process can be accelerated using a hardware engine that takes size, source and destination addresses of the data movement, and automatically creates the parallel GPU threads.

3. EXPERIMENTS AND ANALYSIS

To evaluate our solution, we used a functional full system emulator, Simics [2], combined with a cycle based architecture simulator that can model a heterogenous multi-core. FeS2 [1] is a timing-first, multiprocessor, x86 simulator, implemented as a module for Simics. MV5 [3] is a cycle based architecture simulator for heterogenous multi-core such as a processor integrating OOO CPU cores with large number of GPU like array-style SIMD cores. We combined MV5 with FeS2 where the GPU is simulated using MV5's infrastructure and the x86 workload is simulated by FeS2. In full system simulation, we apply the described bulk memory operation offloading to the GNU libc and the kernel (Linux kernel version 2.6.32.31).

As shown in Figure 2, for memory movement micro benchmarks, the speedup over CPU can be as much as 4.3 times depending on the workload sizes and the GPU configurations.

As shown in Figure 3, evaluation based on eight popular CPU benchmark applications with real-world input dataset shows that we can significantly improve the overall performance of those applications. When offload is combined with GPU caching and asynchronous support, the speedup is more than 30% for five, and more than 20% for two of the eight real world applications.

4. CONCLUSIONS

In this paper, we proposed and presented a novel architectural support to improve the bulk memory operation performance for the CPU applications in a CPU-GPU heterogenous multicore processor. With very lightweight system and architectural support, our solution can take advantage of the most likely idle on-die GPU to improve the performance of bulk memory operations.

5. ADDITIONAL AUTHORS

Additional authors: Yonghong Yan (University of Houston, email: `yanyh@cs.uh.edu`) and Kyeong-An Kwon (University of Houston, email: `kyeongan@cs.uh.edu`).

6. REFERENCES

[1] Fes2: A full-system execution-driven simulator for x86. `http://fes2.cs.uiuc.edu/index.html`, 2007.

[2] Magnusson, P., Christensson, M., Eskilson, J., Forsgren, D., Hallberg, G., Hogberg, J., Larsson, F., Moestedt, A., and Werner, B. Simics: A full system simulation platform. *Comp ter 5*, 2 (Feb 2002), 50–58.

[3] Meng, J., and Skadron, K. Avoiding cache thrashing due to private data placement in last-level cache for manycore scaling. In *rocee in s o t e international con erence on Comp ter esi n* (Piscataway, NJ, USA, 2009), ICCD'09, IEEE Press, pp. 282–288.

Integrating Nanophotonics in GPU Microarchitecture

Nilanjan Goswami[1] Zhongqi Li[1] Ajit Verma[1] Ramkumar Shankar[2] Tao Li[3]

[1]{nil, zhongqi, aejeet}@ufl.edu, [3]taoli@ece.ufl.edu
University of Florida
Gainesville, USA

[2]ramkumar@qualcomm.com
Qualcomm Inc.
San Diego, USA

ABSTRACT

As high-performance computing device, the GPU has exposed bandwidth and latency bottlenecks in on-chip interconnect and off-chip memory access. To eliminate such bottlenecks, we employ silicon nanophotonics and 3D stacking technologies in GPU microarchitecture. This provides higher communication bandwidth and lower latency signaling mechanisms at reduced power. Furthermore, to insulate the performance of the GPU compute cores from the interconnect bottlenecks we propose a novel interconnect aware thread scheduling scheme to alleviate the traffic congestion. We evaluate a 3D stacked GPU with 2048 SIMD cores having photonic interconnect. The photonic multiple-write-single-read crossbar network with 32B channel bandwidth on average, achieves 96% power reduction. We anticipate that for emerging workloads and microarchitectures the implications of the proposed ideas are far reaching in terms of power and performance.

Categories and Subject Descriptors

C.1.2 [**Computer Systems Organization**]: Multiprocessors – Interconnection Architectures

General Terms

Design, performance.

1. INTRODUCTION

Recent advancements in CMOS process based silicon nanophotonics have substantially mitigated the power, latency and bandwidth problem. 3D stacking technology provides low latency and high bandwidth cross-layer communication in a compact form. With significant bandwidth demand in GPU, it is anticipated that power consumption will reach a point at which electrical interconnect and memory subsystem design will become infeasible. On the contrary, optically connected GPU shader cores and memory interface in 3D-stacked multi-layer chip seems to be an attractive alternative. In this paper, we explore a novel 3D-stacked GPU microarchitecture based on silicon nanophotonics technology. The GPU chip has a shader core layer, a cache layer, and a built-in optically connected on-chip network layer. The optical network layer possesses dense wavelength division multiplexed (DWDM) high-speed interconnect for core to memory communication. In addition, on-chip memory controllers communicate with the off-chip memory using DWDM links. Furthermore, instruction scheduling (here issue of memory requests) has direct impact on on-chip interconnect traffic. Hence, we propose a novel instruction scheduling policy that helps in alleviating interconnect traffic congestion.

*PACT'*12, September 19–23, 2012, Minneapolis, Minnesota, USA.
ACM 978-1-4503-1182-3/12/09.

2. MOTIVATION

Emerging GPGPU and graphics workloads are expected to have more computation load for shader cores and will exert more traffic to on-chip interconnect and memory controller. Figure 1 shows a Hotspot 5.0 based temperature profile (Matrix Transpose benchmark) of a GPU with 16 shader cores and 6 memory controllers connected using 2D-mesh interconnect. It asserts that on-chip network and memory controller components dissipate maximum power (in turn heat). Moreover, according to ITRS projection 80% of chip power will be consumed by interconnect. We propose novel power-efficient photonic GPUs that leverage optical medium for on/off-chip data transfer.

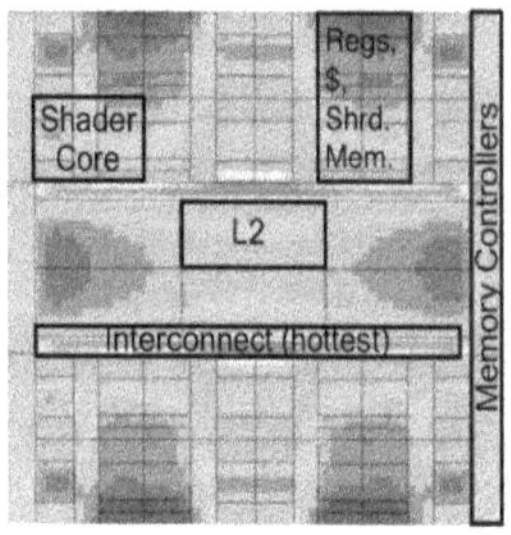

Figure 1: GPU chip temperature profile.

Our investigation of interconnect load for various GPGPU workloads using GPGPU-Sim simulator [1] reveals bursty traffic behavior. This suggests that the GPU shader cores are executing several memory instructions at a stretch for large number of threads. For example, shader core (S_i) cache miss generates interconnect traffic when it executes a thread-batch (Nvidia: *warp* and AMD: *wavefront*) (W_k) and encounters a memory instruction (I_p). If memory access pattern is random, then serving a cache miss will not result in a cache hit for the rest of the threads in the warp. Moreover, in case of memory miss, a new warp is scheduled to execute on the SIMD pipeline due to SIMD lock-step execution policy. For a large number of threads, it is expected that the next warp will also execute instruction I_p. Due to random memory access pattern, repeated execution of memory instruction warps will create on-chip network congestion. To avoid such scenarios, the warps should be scheduled in interleaved fashion, so that an instruction causing on-chip network congestion is avoided when non-memory instructions are available in the thread scheduler. We have explored a hardware solution to the shader core thread scheduler.

3. NANOPHOTONIC GPU DESIGN

3.1 Shader Core Microarchitecture

Silicon nanophotonics technology enabled GPU uses multiple DWDM based waveguides to optically connect multiple shader cores and off-chip memory arrays. To meet area constraints and improve heat dissipation capabilities, we separate shader core layer and L2 cache/memory interface layer and use face-to-face bonding to connect the two layers. We incorporate a separate silicon nanophotonic optical layer that transfers the optical signals to enable shader core and memory controller communication. We use through silicon vias (TSV) to connect the L2 cache layer and optical layer. TSVs also provide clocking, power and ground signals. The optical layer includes laser source, coupler, resonators and optical interface to the off-chip memory. We use silicon nanophotonic waveguides to communicate between on-chip memory controllers and off-chip memory arrays with optimized the DRAM chip organization. Figure 2 shows the simplified layout of the GPU optical interconnection network layer design. Efficient interfacing of optically connected off-chip memory motivates layout of the silicon waveguide. We use many-writer-single-reader (MWSR) photonic crossbar to connect the clusters using 128 waveguides (16 channels × 4 waveguides/channel × 2 directions) in both directions (shader core to memory controller and memory controller to shader core). Each waveguide is capable of propagating 64 wavelengths (64 bits per clock, i.e. 32B per clock period in each direction) of light using DWDM. With 5 GHz clock, all the 16 channels can achieve raw interconnect bandwidth of 40.96 Tb/s. The dedicated floor for optical interconnect in 3D GPU allows us to place these waveguides in the serpentine structure, where the waveguide pitch is as low as 5.5µm. The optical interconnect incorporates MWSR based crossbar that requires arbitration mechanism, which are used in token ring LAN system arbitration to resolve the read requests sent by multiple shader nodes. An alternative to MWSR is single-writer-multiple-read (SWMR) crossbar, which is relatively power hungry. The static power of the crossbar is estimated as 0.33W. The dynamic energy consumption is estimated as 200 fJ/bit for data transmission and the dynamic power for arbitration is negligible.

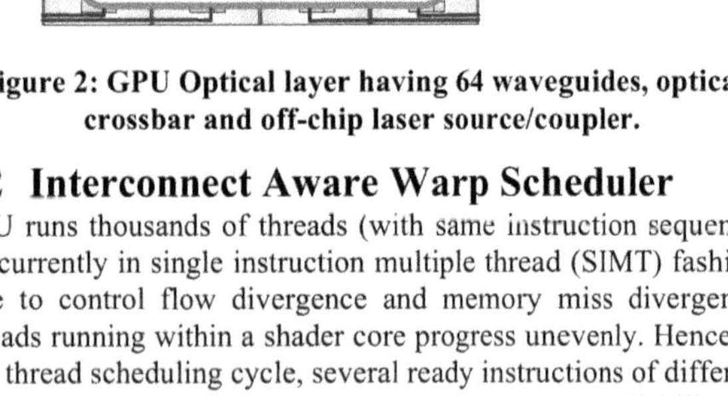

Figure 2: GPU Optical layer having 64 waveguides, optical crossbar and off-chip laser source/coupler.

3.2 Interconnect Aware Warp Scheduler

GPU runs thousands of threads (with same instruction sequence) concurrently in single instruction multiple thread (SIMT) fashion. Due to control flow divergence and memory miss divergence, threads running within a shader core progress unevenly. Hence, at any thread scheduling cycle, several ready instructions of different types (ALU/memory access) are present. The availability of different types of instructions at the scheduling cycle varies due to the instruction mix of the GPGPU program. Based on the last level cache miss information, we design a novel thread scheduler that can interleave the memory access requests in between arithmetic operations. In addition to reducing on-chip optical network congestion, the proposed scheme also hides the memory access latency of various on-chip memories whenever possible. We carryout the operation in two stages: warp classification and deterministic scheduling. When the warp with a certain PC completes the decode stage of the shader core pipeline, the instruction classification for all the other warps with the same PC is obtained. Using the information, our scheme deterministically saves the memory access latencies of several cache (off-chip memory, texture, and constant) misses by knowing the instruction classification at the scheduling stage.

4. RESULTS AND CONCLUSION

Figure 3 shows the speedup and power consumption characteristics of the different designs. On average, SWMR crossbar shows almost 87% power saving and 1% performance degradation as compared to electrical 16B mesh baseline. As expected, average MWSR power saving is comparatively higher (98%) with only 2% performance degradation. Memory intensive workloads benefits most due to the optical interconnect. BFS shows maximum power saving of 89% due to its heavy memory access in MWSR. We recommend MWSR based crossbar with 32B channel bandwidth as the best solution that comes with 96% power saving and 1% average increase in performance. On average, SWMR 16B crossbar has 0.04% lower performance than 16B electrical mesh, but as we increase the bandwidth to 32B and 64B the performance increase is 3% and 5% respectively. Maximum performance increase is observed in BFS (17%) with 64B channel bandwidth. However, MWSR based crossbar shows almost 4% improvement in performance, which is attributed to the large amount delay experienced by the packets to grab the destination token.

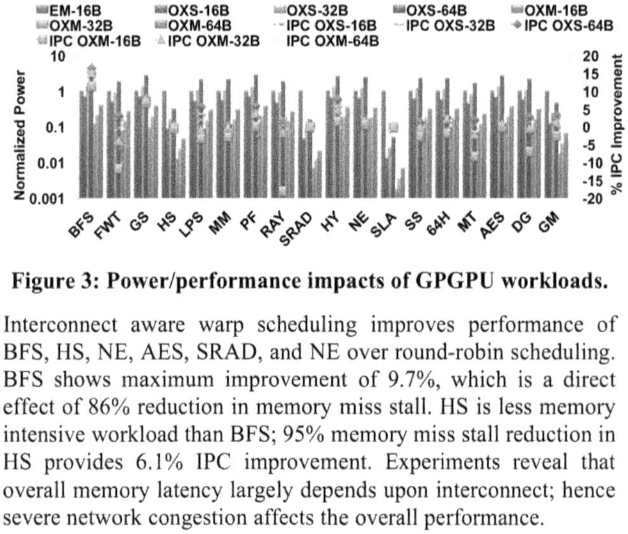

Figure 3: Power/performance impacts of GPGPU workloads.

Interconnect aware warp scheduling improves performance of BFS, HS, NE, AES, SRAD, and NE over round-robin scheduling. BFS shows maximum improvement of 9.7%, which is a direct effect of 86% reduction in memory miss stall. HS is less memory intensive workload than BFS; 95% memory miss stall reduction in HS provides 6.1% IPC improvement. Experiments reveal that overall memory latency largely depends upon interconnect; hence severe network congestion affects the overall performance.

5. ACKNOWLEDGEMENT

This work is supported in part by NSF grants 1117261, 0937869, 0916384, 0845721(CAREER), 0834288, 0811611, 0720476, and by Microsoft Research Trustworthy Computing, Safe and Scalable Multi-core Computing Awards. Authors acknowledge UF HPC center for providing computational resources.

6. REFERENCES

[1] Bakhoda, A.; Yuan, G.L.; Fung, W.W.L.; Wong, H.; Aamodt, T.M.; "Analyzing CUDA workloads using a detailed GPU simulator," *IEEE International Symposium on Performance Analysis of Systems and Software*, pp.163-174, 26-28 April 2009.

Branch and Data Herding: Reducing Control and Memory Divergence for Error-tolerant GPU Applications

John Sartori and Rakesh Kumar
University of Illinois at Urbana-Champaign

ABSTRACT

Control and memory divergence between threads in the same execution bundle, or warp, can significantly throttle the performance of GPU applications. We exploit the observation that many GPU applications exhibit error tolerance to propose branch and data herding. Branch herding eliminates control divergence by forcing all threads in a warp to take the same control path. Data herding eliminates memory divergence by forcing each thread in a warp to load from the same memory block. To safely and efficiently support branch and data herding, we propose a static analysis and compiler framework to prevent exceptions when control and data errors are introduced, a profiling framework that aims to maximize performance while maintaining acceptable output quality, and hardware optimizations to improve the performance benefits of exploiting error tolerance through branch and data herding. Our software implementation of branch herding on NVIDIA GeForce GTX 480 improves performance by up to 34% (13%, on average) for a suite of NVIDIA CUDA SDK and Parboil [7] benchmarks. Our hardware implementation of branch herding improves performance by up to 55% (30%, on average). Data herding improves performance by up to 32% (25%, on average). Observed output quality degradation is minimal for several applications that exhibit error tolerance, especially for visual computing applications. For a more detailed exposition of this work, see [6].

Categories and Subject Descriptors
D.m [Software]: Miscellaneous
General Terms: Design, Performance, Reliability
Keywords: GPGPU, Error Tolerance, High Performance, Control Divergence, Memory Divergence

1. BRANCH AND DATA HERDING

The nature of SIMD execution requires that groups of parallel threads that execute together (warps) must execute the same instruction in lockstep. While the SIMD nature of execution allows the processor design to be relatively simple, application performance may suffer significantly whenever threads in the same warp behave differently due to control or memory divergence [5, 4]. Control divergence results in serialized execution of divergent control paths, leaving execution resources idle and throttling parallelism. Similarly, memory divergence causes a warp to stall until the longest memory request for a vector load completes before executing any dependent instructions. Recent work has shown that control and memory divergence between threads within a warp cause significant performance bottlenecks for many GPU applications [3, 2].

We draw on the observation that many GPU applications produce acceptable outputs even if a small number of threads in a SIMD execution unit are forced to go down the wrong control path or are forced to load from an incorrect (albeit spatially local) address. This is not surprising, considering that many GPU applications are data-intensive. Similarly, the fraction of branches that diverge tends to be small (even though the corresponding performance degradation is large). We exploit these observations to propose two novel optimizations – *branch herding* and *data herding*. Branch herding eliminates control divergence by herding all threads in a warp onto the same control path taken by the majority of threads. This prevents serialization of branch paths that causes execution resources to remain idle for threads on the inactive control path. Data herding eliminates memory divergence by forcing each thread in a warp to load from the most popular memory block accessed by a warp load, allowing all the loads to be coalesced into a single memory request. This reduces the number of memory stalls. This also reduces bandwidth pressure, as fewer blocks need to be loaded from memory. With the aid of static and profiling-based analyses, branch and data herding are applied discriminately to safely increase performance while maintaining acceptable output quality.

2. SAFETY, PERFORMANCE, AND OUTPUT QUALITY ASSURANCE

It is well-known that several data-parallel applications exhibit error tolerance [1, 8, 9]. To efficiently exploit this error tolerance through branch or data herding, the challenges lie in (1) guaranteeing that loading the wrong data or taking the wrong branch path will not cause an exception, and (2) maximizing performance improvement while maintaining acceptable output quality. In this section, we describe a *static analysis and compiler framework* that guarantees (1) by identifying branches and data that are safe for herding, and a *profiling framework* that targets (2) by identifying the subset of safe branches and data for which herding increases performance while maintaining acceptable output quality.

The first step in identifying safe branches and data for herding is to identify *vulnerable operations* that, if affected by an error, *might* cause exceptions. After identifying vulnerable operations, we trace through the control and data dependence graphs of a program to identify the branches and data that the vulnerable operations depend on. Then, to guarantee freedom from exceptions, we do not allow the compiler to insert herding directives for the branches and data identified as unsafe during static analysis. Preventing herding of "unsafe" branches and data ensures that errors induced by herding will only impact output quality.

After identifying which branches and data can be safely herded, we next identify which can be profitably herded. Our profiling framework starts with no branches/loads herded, progressively marks a larger fraction of candidate branches/loads for herding, and at each step profiles the program for a set of test inputs to characterize the space of output quality degradation and performance vs. number of herded branches/loads.

PACT'12, September 19–23, 2012, Minneapolis, Minnesota, USA.
ACM 978-1-4503-1182-3/12/09.

```
// Static Safety Analysis
Generate Abstract Syntax Tree AST(A) for Application A
Search AST(A) to identify Vulnerable Operations VO
foreach(Vulnerable Operation v ∈ VO)
    Trace Control and Data Dependencies of v to classify Safe/Unsafe Branches/Data
// Quality and Performance-targeted Profiling
Profile A and identify Divergent, Safe Branches/Loads as Herding Candidates C
Herded Branches/Loads H = ∅
Baseline Output Quality Degradation,Performance = Q(∅), P(∅)
foreach(Candidate c ∈ C)
    foreach(Test Input t)
        Profile Output Quality Degradation Q(H + c, t), Performance P(H + c, t)
    if(∃ t such that P(H + c, t) > P(H, t))
        Approximate Quality Degradation Bound B(H + c) = max[Q(H + c, t)|t
        H += c
// Runtime Quality Monitoring
User specifies desired maximum Output Quality Degradation Q_max
Use Profiling Data to find maximum Herding Thresh-
old T_h such that B(T_h) ≤ Q_max
Count Herding Instances I_h and disable herding when I_h == T_h
```

Figure 1: Pseudocode describing safety, performance, and output quality assurance framework.

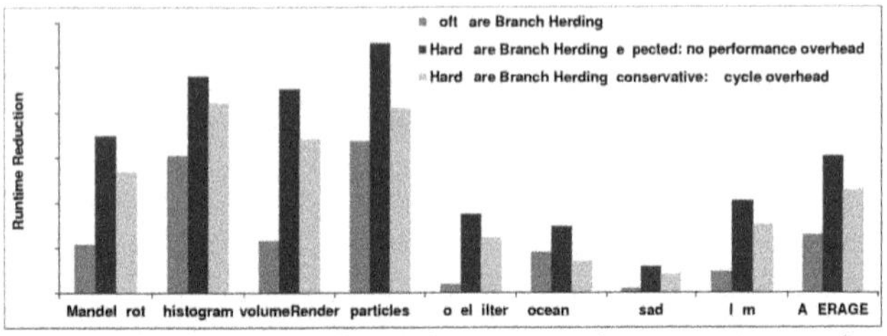

Figure 2: Potential performance improvement for software and hardware branch herding.

From this sampling we can determine an approximate upper bound on output quality degradation corresponding to a given amount of herding by selecting the worst case degradation observed for a given amount of herded branches/loads. During runtime, performance counters [5] track the number of herded branches/loads and disable branch/data herding before the specified approximate threshold has been exceeded. To enable profiling and quality monitoring, the programmer should mark the variable in the code that represents output quality and specify the desired approximate bound on output quality degradation. Figure 1 presents pseudocode describing the control flow of our safety, performance, and output quality assurance framework for branch and data herding.

3. RESULTS

Branch herding increases the performance of GPU applications that normally exhibit control divergence by preventing the serialization of branch paths and eliminating overheads associated with divergent branch handling. Figure 2 shows potential performance gains for branch herding for applications that normally exhibit control divergence. Our branch herding implementation targets only safe branches that exhibit divergence *and* show benefits from branch herding. Therefore, performance improvements are significantly higher than any naïve branch herding implementation that targets all static branches.

Since branch herding exploits error tolerance to eliminate divergence, it may result in output quality degradation. Table 1 compares output quality degradation for the benchmarks with and without branch herding, using the quality metrics incorporated by the original benchmark writers.

Table 1: Output quality degradation (%) for branch herding compared to original

% Mismatch	Mandelbrot	histogram	volRender	particles
Original	0.03	0.00	6.72	18.24
Branch Herding	1.87	5.82	7.61	18.24
% Mismatch	SobelFilter	oceanFFT	sad	lbm
Original	0.00	0.03	0.00	6.7E-7
Branch Herding	6.00	0.03	0.42	5.6E-5

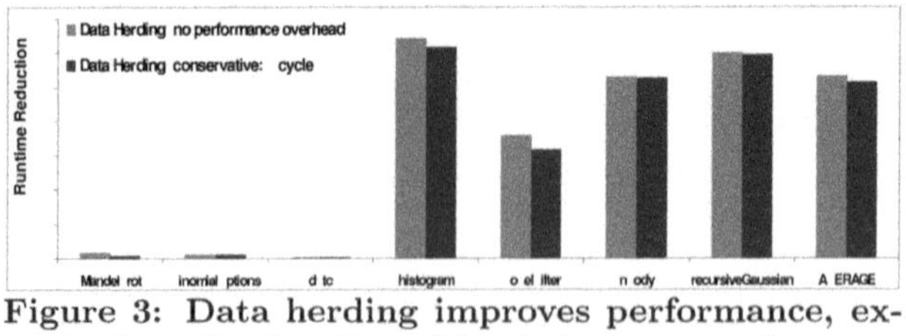

Figure 3: Data herding improves performance, except when the fraction of loads is very small.

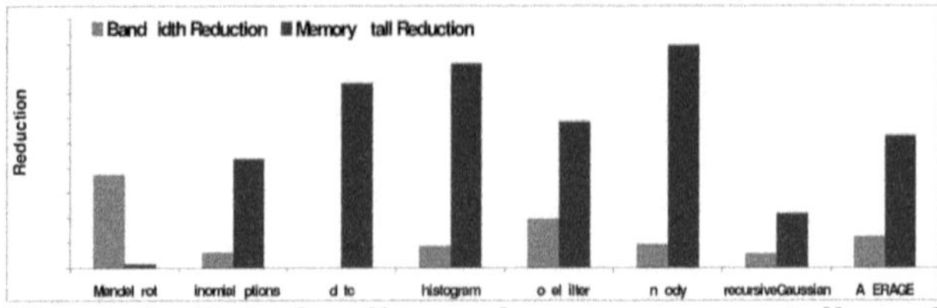

Figure 4: Data herding reduces memory stalls and bandwidth usage due to divergent memory requests.

Figure 3 shows potential for performance improvements for various benchmarks with data herding. For the three benchmarks that do not see benefits for data herding, less than 0.2% of dynamic instructions are loads. Output quality degradation associated with data herding is compared against original output quality degradation in Table 2.

Data herding achieves performance benefits for two reasons. First, all non-coalesced loads to the herded data will be coalesced into a single memory request. This reduces memory bandwidth usage and contention for resources. Reduced bandwidth and contention can also reduce the latency of memory requests. Second, since only one memory request is made for a load, memory divergence is eliminated, and warps do not spend cycles waiting for additional requests to finish after the first request returns. Figure 4 quantifies the impact of data herding in terms of bandwidth reduction and reduction of cycles that ready warps spend stalled and waiting for outstanding memory requests.

4. REFERENCES

[1] S. Byna, J. Meng, A. Raghunathan, S. Chakradhar, and S. Cadambi. Best-effort semantic document search on GPUs. In *GPGPU*, pages 86–93, 2010.

[2] W. Fung, I. Sham, G. Yuan, and T. Aamodt. Dynamic warp formation and scheduling for efficient GPU control flow. In *MICRO*, pages 407–420, 2007.

[3] J. Meng, D. Tarjan, and K. Skadron. Dynamic warp subdivision for integrated branch and memory divergence tolerance. In *ISCA*, pages 235–246, 2010.

[4] NVIDIA. *NVIDIA Compute PTX: Parallel Thread Execution*, 2009.

[5] NVIDIA. *NVIDIA CUDA Programming Guide, Vers. 3.0*, 2010.

[6] J. Sartori and R. Kumar. Branch and data herding: Reducing control and memory divergence for error-tolerant gpu applications. *Multimedia, IEEE Transactions on*, 2012.

[7] The IMPACT Research Group. Parboil benchmark suite. http://impact.crhc.illinois.edu/parboil.php.

[8] G. Varatkar and N. Shanbhag. Energy-efficient motion estimation using error-tolerance. In *ISLPED*, pages 113–118, 2006.

[9] T. Yeh, P. Faloutsos, M. Ercegovac, S. Patel, and G. Reinman. The art of deception: Adaptive precision reduction for area efficient physics acceleration. In *MICRO*, pages 394–406, 2007.

Table 2: Output quality degradation (%) for data herding compared to original

% Mismatch	Mandelbrot	histogram	nbody	binomialO
Original	0.02	0.00	0.00	3.8E-5
Data Herding	0.99	0.6	0.95	3.8E-5
% Mismatch	SobelFilter	dxtc	recursiveGauss	–
Original	0.00	0.019	0.00	–
Data Herding	1.81	0.019	0.00	–

Layout-oblivious Optimization for Matrix Computations

Huimin Cui
SKL Computer Architecture, Institute of Computing Technology, CAS
Beijing, China
cuihm @ict.ac.cn

Qing Yi
Depart. of Computer Science
University of Texas at San Antonio
San Antonio, TX, USA
qingyi@cs.utsa.edu

Jingling Xue
School of Computer Science and Engineering,
University of New South Wales
Sydney, NSW, Australia
jingling@cse.unsw.edu.au

Xiaobing Feng
SKL Computer Architecture, Institute of Computing Technology, CAS
Beijing, China
fxb@ict.ac.cn

ABSTRACT

Most scientific computations serve to apply mathematical operations to a set of preconceived data structures, e.g., matrices, vectors, and grids. In this paper, we use a number of widely used matrix computations from the LINPACK library to demonstrate that complex internal organizations of data structures can severely degrade the effectiveness of compilers optimizations. We then present a data layout oblivious optimization methodology, where by isolating an abstract representation of computations from complex implementation details of their data, we enable these computations to be much more accurately analyzed and optimized through varying state-of-the-art compiler technologies.

Categories and Subject Descriptors:
D.3.4 [Processors]: Compilers, Optimization

Keywords : Compiler, Optimization, Packed matrix, High-performance computing

1. INTRODUCTION

A majority of scientific computation kernels typically serve to apply a sequence of domain-specific operations to a preconceived set of compound data structures, e.g., matrices, vectors, grids, and graphs. To effectively optimize these computations, a compiler must be able to correctly decipher the dependence relations among statements operating on different data. While compilers have used *dependence analysis* as the foundation of optimization for more than thirty years, the accuracy of dependence analysis could be severely degraded by complex data structures. Take the well-understood dense matrix multiplication for instance. When a non-rectangular matrix is stored in a *packed* layout such as those in Figure 1(b), the array subscripts used to reference different elements of the matrix could become extremely complex, which could easily overwhelm the internal dependence analysis of a compiler and thus thwart all optimizations to the matrix computation code.

We present a layout-oblivious optimization methodology to overcome these difficulties. In particular, using a normalization algorithm, our method seeks to isolate the high level semantics of operations from the organization details of compound data structures and thereby to derive an abstract specification of operations to be applied to the data. The simplified computation can then be accurately analyzed and optimized through varying state-of-the-art compiler technologies. Finally, the optimized operations are combined with the previously isolated implementation details of their data to generate the final optimized code of the original computation.

2. THE OVERALL APPROACH

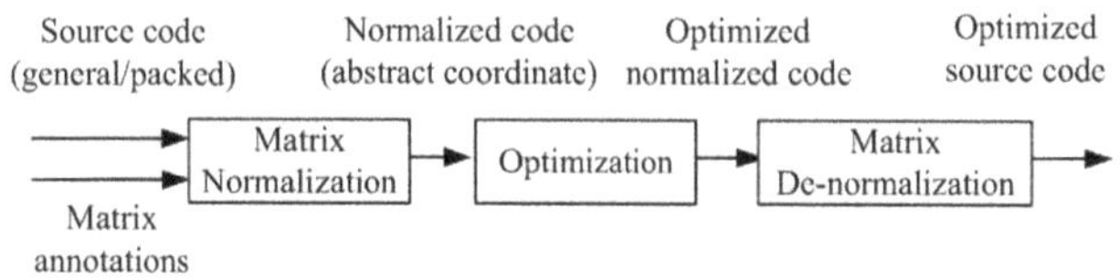

Figure 2: Overview of our approach.

Figure 2 shows an overview of our approach, which takes two inputs, the computational kernel to be optimized and a set of annotations that define the internal organization of matrices used in the kernel. It produces optimized code through the following steps:

1. **Matrix normalization.** This step seeks to isolate the high level semantics of matrix operations from implementation details of matrices within the input computation, by automatically converting all the relevant array references to a higher level representation which uses (row,column) coordinates to access each abstract matrix.

[1]This work is partially supported in part by the Chinese National Basic Research Grant 2011CB302504, the Innovation Research Group of NSFC 60921002, the National Science and Technology Major Projects of China 2011ZX01028-001-002, State 863 project 2012AA010902, the US National Science Foundation under Grants 0833203 and 0747357, and the US Department of Energy under Grant DE-SC001770.

PACT'12, September 19–23, 2012, Minneapolis, Minnesota, USA.
ACM 978-1-4503-1182-3/12/09.

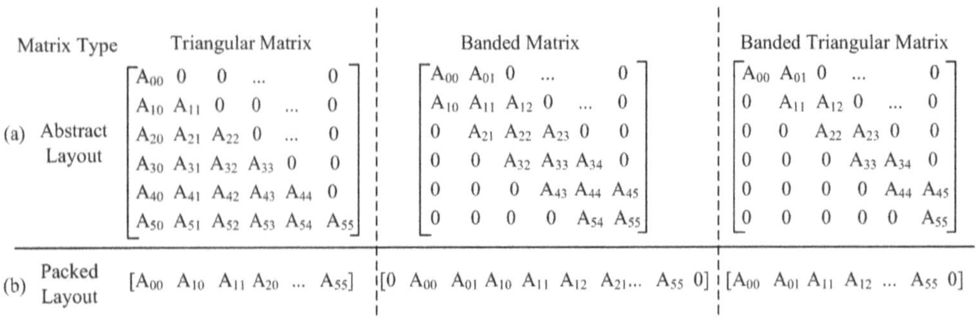

Figure 1: Layout example for triangular, banded and banded triangular matrices.

```
(1) Function definition:
    %fun_name(p1,...pn) = e1 if (c)
                        | e2 otherwise;
(2) Type definition:
    @type_name(p1,...,pn) =
            @matrix : (row:[l..u],col:[l..u])=> e;
(3) Variable annotation:
    $x : @type_name(e1,...en);

* p1,...,pn: parameter names;
* e, e1, e2, ..., en: integer expressions;
* c : a boolean expression;
* [l..u] : an integer type with values ≥ l and ≤ u;
* fun_name: the name of a local function;
* type_name: type name of special matrices;
* x: name of a matrix variable in the input code;
```

Figure 3: Matrix Annotation Language

2. **Optimization.** This step applies state-of-the-art compiler optimizations, e.g., parallelization, tiling [3], array copying, unroll-and-jam, and scalar replacement, to the normalized code, which operates on abstract matrices. Note that some layout-sensitive optimizations, e.g., SSE vectorization, require array addresses to be aligned and thus need to be turned off in this step.

3. **Matrix de-normalization.** This step takes the optimized code from Step(2) and modifies all the references of abstract matrix coordinates to instead access the corresponding locations in their original condensed matrix storage forms.

3. MATRIX ANNOTATIONS

Figure 3 shows our matrix annotation language designed to allow programmers to easily define the intended semantics of data structures in matrix computations, including three different statements: function definitions, type definitions, and variable annotations.

Function Definitions. Shown at line (1) of Figure 3, function definitions are used by our annotation language to express complex non-linear functions which may be required to annotate access functions of different matrix storage forms.

Type Definitions. Shown at line (2) of Figure 3, type definitions are used by our annotation language to define a special matrix form and specify how to locate each matrix element at an arbitrary (row, col) coordinate in the condensed storage layout. Here, @*matrix* is a keyword and $(row[l1..u1], col[l2..u2])$ specifies the *coordinate* parameters of an abstract matrix.

Variable Annotation. Shown at line (3) of Figure 3, variable annotations in our language serve to declare additional type information for matrix variables inside a given input code, especially those that use special storage forms. These matrix annotations can be embedded inside the input code by enclosing them in C language comments if desired, so that they can be ignored by other compilers.

4. EXPERIMENTAL RESULTS

We have implemented our layout-oblivious approach using the POET language [4], and used the Pluto [1] and the EPOD [2] source-to-source C compilers to optimize triangular matrix multiply variants - mm.tri.abs and mm.tri.packed, which represent a triangular matrix in the abstract and packed layout, respectively.

We used the `icc` compiler version 11.0 to compile the sources to machine code with the `-openmp` and `-fast` options. We evaluated the benchmarks using randomly initialized 2048*2048 matrices, and carried out all of our experiments on an 8-core Intel platform with two 2.33GHz quad-core Xeon 5410 processors. Each processor has 32KB L1 data cache per core, 32KB L1 instruction cache per core, and 6MB L2 unified data/instruction cache shared by all cores.

	icc	EPOD	EPOD+LO	Pluto	Pluto+LO
abstract	0.04	102.7	102.7	12.3	12.3
packed	0.04	0.04	94.1	0.04	11.9

Table 1: Performance results for triangular matrix multiply using our approach with EPOD and Pluto, in GFLOPS.

Table 1 shows the performance results when using our approach together with EPOD and Pluto. With our layout-oblivious optimization approach, the computational kernels which originally cannot be analyzed by compilers can benefit from normalizing its data accesses and become optimizable.

5. REFERENCES

[1] U. Bondhugula, A. Hartono, J. Ramanujan, and P. Sadayappan. A practical automatic polyhedral parallelizer and locality optimizer. In *PLDI*, 2008.

[2] H. Cui, J. Xue, L. Wang, Y. Yang, X. Feng, and D. Fan. Extendable pattern-oriented optimization directives. In *CGO*, 2011.

[3] J. Xue. *Loop Tiling for Parallelism.* Kluwer Academic Publishers, Boston, 2000.

[4] Q. Yi. Poet A scripting language for applying parameterized source-to-source program transformations. *SPE*, 2011.

Boost.SIMD: Generic Programming for Portable SIMDization

Pierre Estérie
LRI, Université Paris-Sud XI
Orsay, France
pierre.esterie@lri.fr

Mathias Gaunard
Metascale
Orsay, France
mathias.gaunard@metascale.org

Joel Falcou
LRI, Université Paris-Sud XI
Orsay, France
joel.falcou@lri.fr

Jean-Thierry Lapresté
IP (Institut Pascal), Université Blaise Pascal
Clermont-Ferrand, France
lapreste@univ-bpclermont.fr

Brigitte Rozoy
LRI, Université Paris-Sud XI
Orsay, France
rozoy@lri.fr

ABSTRACT

SIMD extensions have been a feature of choice for processor manufacturers for a couple of decades. Designed to exploit data parallelism in applications at the instruction level and provide significant accelerations, these extensions still require a high level of expertise or the use of potentially fragile compiler support or vendor-specific libraries. In this poster, we present BOOST.SIMD, a C++ template library that simplifies the exploitation of SIMD hardware within a standard C++ programming model.

Categories and Subject Descriptors

C.1.2 [**Processor Architectures**]: Multiple Data Stream Architectures (Multiprocessors)—*Single-instruction-stream, multiple-data-stream processors (SIMD)*; D.2.2 [**Software Engineering**]: Design Tools and Techniques—*Software libraries*

Keywords

SIMD, C++, Generic Programming, Template Metaprogramming

1. MOTIVATIONS

Since the late 90's, processor manufacturers have provided specialized processing units called multimedia extensions or Single Instruction Multiple Data (SIMD) extensions. The introduction of this feature has allowed processors to exploit the latent data parallelism available in applications by executing a given instruction simultaneously on multiple data stored in a single special register. Today's processor architectures offer rich SIMD instruction sets working with larger and larger SIMD registers. For example, the AVX extension introduced in 2011 enhances the x86 instruction set for the Intel Sandy Bridge and AMD Bulldozer micro-architectures by providing a distinct set of 16 256-bit registers. Similary, the forthcoming Intel MIC Architecture will embed 512-bit SIMD registers and embedded systems also integrate such features like NEON ARM extensions. However, programming applications that take advantage of the SIMD extension remains a complex task. Programmers that use low-level intrinsics have to deal with a verbose programming style which is burying the initial algorithms in architecture specific implementation details. Furthermore, these efforts have to be repeated for every different extension that one may want to support, making design and maintenance of such applications very time consuming. Different approaches have been suggested to limit these shortcomings. On the compiler side, **autovectorizers** implement code analysis and transform phases to generate vectorized code [2, 4]. Compilers are able to detect code fragments that can be vectorized but they struggle when the classical code is not presenting a clear vectorizable pattern (complex data dependencies, non-contiguous memory accesses, aliasing or control flows). Other compiler-based systems use code directives to guide the vectorization process by enforcing loop vectorization. The ICC and GCC extension **`#pragma simd`** is such a system. To use this mechanism, developers explicitly introduce directives in their code, thus having a fine grain control on where to apply SIMDization. However, the generated code quality will greatly depend on the used compiler. Another approach is to use **libraries** like Intel MKL. Those libraries offer a set of domain-specific routines that are optimized for a given architecture. This solution suffers from a lack of flexibility as the proposed routines are optimized for specific use-cases that may not fulfill arbitrary code constraints.

PACT'12, September 19–23, 2012, Minneapolis, MN, USA.
ACM 978-1-4503-1182-3/12/09.

2. THE BOOST.SIMD LIBRARY

The main issue of SIMD programming is the lack of proper abstractions over the usage of SIMD registers. This abstraction should not only provide a portable way to use hardware-specific registers but also enable the use of common programming idioms when designing SIMD-aware algorithms.

2.1 SIMD register abstraction

The first level of abstraction introduced by BOOST.SIMD is the `pack` class. For a given type `T` and a given static integral value `N` (`N` being a power of 2), a `pack` encapsulates the best type able to store a sequence of `N` elements of type `T`.

For arbitrary `T` and `N`, this type is simply `std::array<T,N>` but when `T` and `N` matches the type and width of a SIMD register, the architecture-specific type used to represent this register is used instead. By default, `pack` will automatically select a value that will trigger the selection of the native SIMD register type. The `pack` class handles these low-level SIMD register type as regular objects with value semantics, which includes the ability to be constructed or copied from a single scalar value, list of scalar values, iterator or range. In each case, the proper register loading strategy (splat, set, load or gather) will be issued. This abstraction is coupled with a large set of functions covering the classical set of operators along with a sensible amount (200+) of mathematical functions and utility functions like constant generators and arithmetic/IEEE 754/reductions functions. A fundamental aspect of SIMD programming relies on the effective use of fused operations like multiply-add on VMX extensions or sum of absolute differences on SSE extensions. `pack` relies on *Expression Templates* [1] to capture the Abstract Syntax Tree (AST) of large `pack`-based expressions and performs compile-time optimization on this AST. These optimizations include the detection of fused operation and replacement or reordering of reductions versus elementwise operations. Moreover, the AST-based evaluation process is able to merge multiple function calls into a single inlined one, contrary to solutions like MKL where each function can only be applied on the whole data range at a time. This increases data locality and ensures high performance for any combination of functions.

2.2 C++ Standard integration

Realistic applications usually require functions applied over a large set of data. To support such a use case, the library provides a set of classes to integrate SIMD computation inside C++ code relying on the C++ Standard Template Library (STL) components, thus reusing its generic aspect to the fullest. Based on Generic Programming [3], the STL is based on the separation between data, stored in various `Containers`, and the way one can traverse these data, thanks to `Iterators` and algorithms. Boost.SIMD reuses existing STL Concepts to adapt STL-based code to SIMD computations by providing SIMD-aware allocators, iterators for regular SIMD computations and hardware-optimized algorithms. The hardware implementation of SIMD processing units introduces constraints related to memory handling. Performance is guaranteed by accessing the memory through dedicated `load` and `store` intrinsics that perform register-length aligned memory accesses. This constraint requires a special memory allocation strategy via OS and compiler-specific function calls. Boost.SIMD provides a STL compliant allocator dealing with this kind of alignment. The `simd::allocator` class wraps these OS and compiler functions in a simple STL-compliant allocator. Usually, modern C++ programming style based on Generic Programming leads to an intensive use of various STL components like Iterators. Boost.SIMD provides iterator adaptors that turn regular random access iterators into iterators suitable for SIMD processing. These adaptors act as free functions taking regular iterators as parameters and return iterators that output `pack` whenever dereferenced. These iterators are then usable directly with common STL algorithms such as `transform` or `fold`. The code keeps a conventional structure which facilitates the usage of template functors for both scalar and SIMD cases, maximizing code reuse.

3. THE RGB2YUV ALGORITHM

The RGB and YUV models are both color spaces with three components that encode images or videos. Unlike RGB, the YUV color space takes into account the human perception of the colors. The RGB2YUV algorithm fits the data parallelism requirement for SIMD computation. The comparison shown in Table 1 shows the performance of Boost.SIMD against scalar C++ code and SIMD reference code. The implementation is realized in single precision floating-point and the results are presented in cycles per point (cpp).

Table 1: Results for RGB2YUV algorithm in *cpp*

Size	Version	SSE4.2	AVX	Altivec
256^2	Scalar C++	29.23	21.46	42.51
	Ref. SIMD	6.48	2.80	29.05
	Boost.SIMD	6.51	2.45	29.01
	Speedup	4.49	8.76	1.47
	Overhead	0.04%	-14.3%	0.1%

The speedups obtained with SEE4.2 and AVX are superior to the expected ×4 and ×8 on such extensions and no overhead is added by Boost.SIMD. A slowdown appears with Altivec due to the lack of a level 3 cache which causes the SIMD unit to wait constantly for data from the main memory. For a size of 64^2 on the PowerPC, Boost.SIMD performs at 4.65 cpp against 36.32 cpp for the scalar version giving a speedup of 7.81 which confirms the memory limitation of such an architecture. The latent data parallelism in the algorithm is fully exploited and the benchmarks corroborate the ability of the library to generate effecient SIMD code.

4. CONCLUSION

SIMD instruction sets are a technology present in an ever growing number of architectures. Despite the performance boost that such extensions usually provide, SIMD has been usually underused. Losing the ×4 to ×16 speed-ups they may provide in HPC applications is starting to be glaring. We presented Boost.SIMD, which aims at simplifying the design of SIMD-aware applications while providing a portable high-level API, integrated with the C++ Standard Template Library and solves the problem of portable SIMD code generation.

5. REFERENCES

[1] K. Czarnecki, U. W. Eisenecker, R. Glück, D. Vandevoorde, and T. L. Veldhuizen. Generative programming and active libraries. In *Generic Programming*, pages 25–39, 1998.

[2] J. Shin. Introducing control flow into vectorized code. *Parallel Architectures and Compilation Techniques, International Conference on*, 0:280–291, 2007.

[3] A. Stepanov and M. Lee. The standard template library. Technical Report 95-11(R.1), HP Laboratories, 1995.

[4] H. Wang, H. Andrade, B. Gedik, and K.-L. Wu. A code generation approach for auto-vectorization in the spade compiler. In *LCPC'09*, pages 383–390, 2009.

Speculative Parallelization Needs Rigor

—Probabilistic Analysis for Optimal Speculation of Finite-State Machine Applications

Zhijia Zhao, Bo Wu and Xipeng Shen
Computer Science Department
College of William and Mary, VA, USA
{zzhao,bwu,xshen}@cs.wm.edu

ABSTRACT

Software speculative parallelization has shown effectiveness in parallelizing certain applications. Prior techniques have mainly relied on simple exploitation of heuristics for speculation. In this work, we introduce probabilistic analysis into the design of speculation schemes. In particular, by tackling applications that are based on Finite State Machine (FSM) which have the most prevalent dependences among all programs, we show that the obstacles for effective speculation can be much better handled with rigor. We develop a probabilistic model to formulate the relations between speculative executions and the properties of the target computation and inputs. Based on the formulation, we propose two model-based speculation schemes that automatically customize themselves with the best configurations for a given FSM and its inputs. The new technique produces substantial speedup over the state of the art.

Categories and Subject Descriptors

D.3.4 [**Software**]: Programming Languages

Keywords

Speculative Parallelization, FSM, DFA

1. INTRODUCTION

Parallelization is key to computing efficiency and scalability. Many programs, however, are hard to parallelize for their data dependences. A typical solution is to circumvent the dependences through speculation. Prior speculative parallelizations have mainly relied on simple use of heuristics. In this work, we explore rigorous analysis for tapping into the full potential.

Particularly, we concentrate on applications that are based on Finite-State Machine (FSM)—when it comes to the prevalence of dependences, FSM is truly unbeatable. An example is the FSM in Figure 1 for matching regular expression $([01]^*00[01]^*11[01]^*)^{10}$. Dependences exist between every two steps of an FSM computation. They effectively chain through the computation, making parallelization difficult.

Enabling FSM parallelization has some immediate value, given that FSM forms the core of many important applications, including lexing in web browsers, intrusion detection in networking security, Huffman decoding in multimedia processing and string pattern matching in document processing. Further, it will shed insights on circumvention of dependences in general, benefiting parallelization of other types of programs.

The key difficulty for parallelizing FSM applications is to determine the starting state for each thread. Researchers have attempted to circumvent the difficulty by speculation—letting a thread T_i guess the correct starting state to process segment S_i. A random guess is subject to large errors. Researchers have found it helpful to do a **lookback** [1,2] —that is, thread T_i runs the FSM on a number of ending symbols (called a *suffix*) of the preceding segment S_{i-1}, and uses the ending state as the speculated starting state for processing its own segment S_i. The lookback helps speculation by offering some context. For instance, for the FSM in Figure 1, if the suffix of S_{i-1} is "11", a lookback will always finish at an even-numbered state. Hence, the lookback successfully prevents the speculation from taking those impossible states.

However, performance benefits from lookback is inconsistent as the "heuristic" bars in Figure 2 shows. The main reason is the lack of rigor in the designs of speculation, reflected in multiple dimensions. The *first* is in the length of the suffix to examine by a lookback. A longer suffix exposes more context, but at the same time incurs more overhead. The *second* dimension is in the selection of the state for starting a lookback. The *third* dimension is in the usage of lookback results. All prior studies used the initial state as the lookback starting state, the ending state of a lookback as the speculated state for processing the next segment, and empirically chose the lookback length. Are these always the best choices? Without rigorous ways to treat these factors and dimensions in the design, existing parallelizations are vulnerable to FSM complexities, resulting in the inconsistent speedups.

2. MODEL-BASED FSM SPECULATION

We present the first principled understanding of FSM parallelization so that the parallelization can best match with the properties of an FSM and its inputs. We start with enhancing the understanding of lookback, the key operation for speculation accuracy.

2.1 Essence of Lookback

Lookback is essentially a process that tries to use the context (i.e., a suffix) to improve the knowledge about the

PACT'12, September 19–23, 2012, Minneapolis, Minnesota, USA.
ACM 978-1-4503-1182-3/12/09.

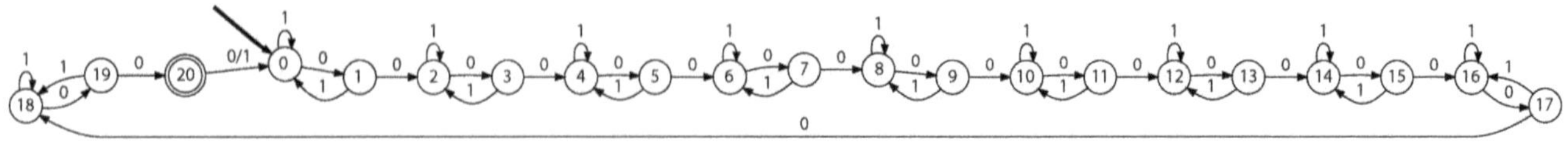

Figure 1: An FSM for matching regular expression $([01]^*00[01]^*11[01]^*)^{10}$, where 10 is the repetition times.

chance for a state to be the correct state at a speculation point. For convenience, we introduce the term *feasibility* as the probability for state s to be the correct state at a speculation point.

Without consideration of contexts, statistically, the feasibility of a state s at every speculation point is the same, approximately equaling the frequency for the FSM to visit that state in normal executions. We call these probabilities *context-free feasibilities*. Accordingly, feasibilities after a input string is processed are called *conditional feasibilities*.

Estimating conditional feasibility through brute-force profiling is infeasible due to the large condition space. We observe that state transitions essentially lead to an incremental propagation of conditional feasibilities, with contexts enriched gradually. Accordingly, we design a probabilistic model to derive each state's feasibility during lookback. It is described in our technical report [3].

2.2 Model-Based Speculative Parallelization

Based on conditional feasibility, we develop a *Makespan Formula*, which computes the statistical expectation of the performance of a lookback-based speculative parallel execution of an FSM. It provides the foundation for choosing appropriate parameters in designing speculation schemes.

With the Makespan Formula, we develop two novel, model-based speculation schemes: *All-State Lookback* and *Single-State Lookback*. In all-state lookback, the lookback uses the complete state set as the starting state set—that is, during the lookback, each thread other than the first processes a suffix for $|S|$ times (S stands for state set), each time starting with a different state. The single-state lookback starts lookback from a single carefully chosen state.

Facilitated by the Makespan Formula, our design automatically finds the parameter values so that the two models can best meet the probabilistic properties of the FSM and inputs,. These parameters include lookback length, the state to start a lookback, and the best way to use the lookback results for speculative parallelization. We prove the optimality through a series of rigorous inference [3].

3. EVALUATION

The implementations of the two speculation schemes both consist of a profiler and a controller. The controller runs online. By feeding information collected by the profilers to the analytic models described in the previous section, it configures the speculation schemes on the fly to suite the properties of the FSM and inputs. The profiler can run either online or offline. To make the model-based speculative schemes easy to use, we develop a library named *OptSpec* which integrates the all-state and single-state speculative schemes and the online and offline profiling procedures together.

We evaluate the proposed techniques on seven FSM applications, with different complexities, including XML processing (*lexing* and *xval*), mathematics (*div*), Huffman decoding (*huff*), and string pattern matching (*str1*, *pval*, and *str2*). Figure 2 shows that our techniques (single-state online/offline, all-state online/offline) boost the performance by more than a factor of 4 over the state of the art (heuristic 1 and 2 are two versions of a recent technique that uses simple lookback for speculation [2]).

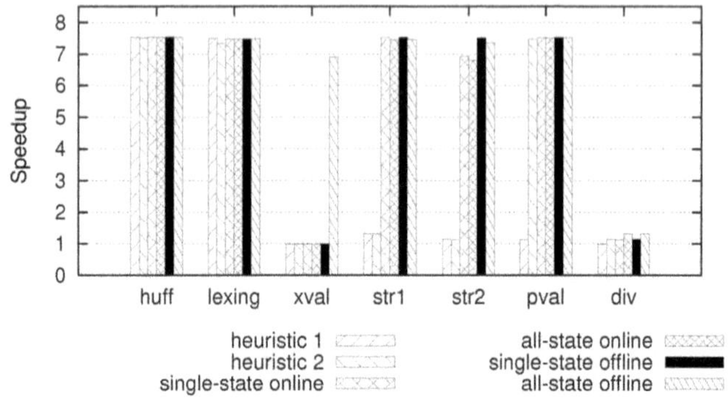

Figure 2: Speedup over the default sequential (8 threads, Intel Xeon E5620).

4. CONCLUSION

This paper introduces formal analysis into the design of speculative parallelization. It reveals the essential connections between the design of speculation schemes and the characteristics of FSM and their inputs. It provides two model-based speculation schemes, with suitable configurations automatically determined. Experiments show that the new techniques outperform the state of the art substantially. The findings may apply to applications beyond FSM, prompting more studies in shifting speculative parallelization to a rigorous paradigm.

Acknowledgement

We thank Ras Bodik for his valuable suggestions. This material is based upon work supported by the NSF grant (0811791), NSF CAREER, DOE Early Career, and IBM CAS Fellowship. Any opinions, findings, and conclusions or recommendations expressed in this material are those of the authors and do not necessarily reflect the views of NSF, DOE, or IBM.

5. REFERENCES

[1] C. Jones, R. Liu, L. Meyerovich, K. Asanovic, and R. Bodik. Parallelizing the web browser. In *HotPar*, 2009.

[2] P. Prabhu, G. Ramalingam, and K. Vaswani. Safe programmable speculative parallelism. In *PLDI*, 2010.

[3] Z. Zhao, B. Wu and X. Shen. Probabilistic Models towards Optimal Speculation of Finite State Machine Applications. *WM-CS-2011-03*, 2011.

Supporting Stateful Tasks in a Dataflow Graph

Vladimir Gajinov*†,1 Srdjan Stipić*†,1 Osman S. Unsal†,1
Tim Harris†,2 Eduard Ayguadé*†,1 Adrián Cristal§‡,1

* Universitat Politecnica de Catalunya, †Barcelona Supercomputing Center, † Microsoft Research Cambridge,
§ Artificial Intelligence Research Institute, ‡ Spanish National Research Council
1 {name}.{surname}@bsc.es, 2 tharris@microsoft.com

ABSTRACT
This paper introduces Atomic Dataflow Model (ADF) - a programming model for shared-memory systems that combines aspects of dataflow programming with the use of explicitly mutable state. The model provides language constructs that allow a programmer to delineate a program into a set of tasks and to explicitly define input data for each task. This information is conveyed to the ADF runtime system which constructs the task dependency graph and builds the necessary infrastructure for dataflow execution. However, the key aspect of the proposed model is that it does not require the programmer to specify all of the task's dependencies explicitly, but only those that imply logical ordering between tasks. The ADF model manages the remainder of inter-task dependencies automatically, by executing the body of the task within an implicit memory transaction. This provides an easy-to-program optimistic concurrency substrate and enables a task to safely share data with other concurrent tasks. In this paper, we describe the ADF model and show how it can increase the programmability of shared memory systems.

Categories and Subject Descriptors
D.1.3 [**Concurrent Programming**]: Parallel Programming.

Keywords
Dataflow, Transactional Memory, Parallelization.

1. INTRODUCTION
Current multicore processors are for the most part built on top of the shared memory architecture. However, shared memory programming can be quite difficult. The programmer has to reason about not one, but many threads of execution that concurrently access potentially shared data. Often, the costs of data access synchronization prevent a shared-memory program performance from scaling to high core counts. Moreover, solutions to this problem require significant programmer effort which defeats the objective to exert parallel programming to the general programming community.

Lately, there has been a resurgence of interest into the dataflow model (Perez, Badia, & Labarta, 2008; Diavastos, Trancoso, Lujan, & Watson, 2011) due to its ability to efficiently exploit parallelism. The main characteristic of the dataflow model is that the execution of an operation is constrained only by the availability of its input data. Following a single assignment rule the dataflow model is able to extract all the parallelism inherent in the program.

We argue that dataflow and shared memory programming can be integrated into a more versatile programming model which can provide a user with more expressive concurrency abstractions that are sufficiently easy to reason about. Accordingly, this paper introduces Atomic Dataflow Model (ADF) - a programming model for shared-memory systems that combines aspects of dataflow programming with the use of explicitly mutable state. The key idea is that computation is triggered by the flow of data

PACT'12, September 19–23, 2012, Minneapolis, Minnesota, USA.
ACM 978-1-4503-1182-3/12/09.

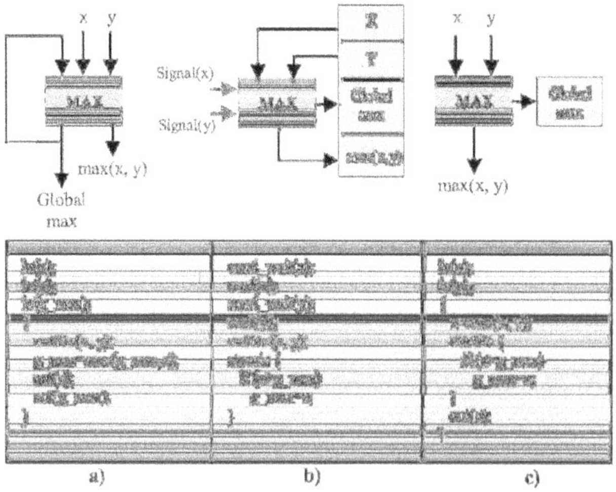

Figure 1: Max function with the global maximum: a) dataflow, b) shared memory and c) ADF implementation.

between ADF components (tasks) but that, within a component, execution occurs by making atomic updates to the common mutable state. Following the algorithm, the programmer delineates a program into a set of tasks and defines explicit dependencies between them. The ADF model manages implicit inter-task dependencies automatically, by executing each task transactionally, which guarantees atomic shared memory updates from within the task. This leads to a flexible form of parallelism in which computation can be carried out in a pure dataflow fashion, in a common task-based style of shared memory programming, or in a combination of these two methods. Therefore, compared to each of the aforementioned techniques alone, the ADF model can represent a wider range of problems naturally.

To illustrate the advantages of the ADF model let us consider a simple example from Figure 1. Given two input streams of integers, x and y, the goal is to discover which of the current values of these two streams is larger, but we would also like to find the global maximum of all values received on both streams. Dataflow model handles the input streams naturally, but in order to maintain the global maximum the state of the previous execution has to be provided as an input for the next execution - Figure 1a. This means that the state has to be copied after each invocation of the MAX node. On the contrary, shared memory model treats the global maximum as the mutable state which can be updated in-place - Figure 1b. Still, we need to synchronize access to this data in order to allow safe updates by concurrent threads. The issue with the shared memory implementation is how to deal with input data streams. A typical solution is to rely on some form of conditional waiting, i.e. conditional variables, transactional memory retry mechanism or message channels through which we implement coordination between different threads of execution. Ultimately, the ADF model, being the combination of the previous two models, can handle both of the above problems naturally. Figure 1c illustrates the idea: we handle the streams and find the current maximum in a dataflow fashion, while the global maximum is treated as a mutable state.

2. THE ADF MODEL DESCRIPTION

Atomic dataflow model is based on execution of tasks which are scheduled according to the dataflow principles, when their input dependencies are satisfied. As such, the ADF task operates as a macro dataflow actor which processes one set of data, produces output data and then waits for the new matching set of input data.

Every ADF program starts with the initialization of the ADF runtime system. This also creates a pool of worker threads whose function is to execute enabled dataflow tasks. Then, the main thread creates all ADF tasks defined by a programmer and generates initial data values which are necessary to start the new dataflow execution, after which it starts the dataflow execution using the following ADF pragma directive:

```
#pragma adf_start
```

The main thread waits for the end of the dataflow execution, which is entirely self-scheduled, using the second ADF directive:

```
#pragma adf_taskwait
```

The basic building blocks in the ADF model are ADF tasks. The ADF task is characterized partly with explicitly defined input data dependency and partly with a mutable state that it can access. The ADF runtime system uses data dependency information to construct task graph that governs the execution of program tasks. In addition, the ADF task can safely access and update the mutable common state since the task body is enclosed in an implicit memory transaction which guarantees the atomicity of the task execution.

A task is defined using the *adf_task* pragma directive with the following syntax:

```
#pragma adf_task  [ trigger_set (<set>) ]
                  [ until (exit_condition) ]
                  [ relaxed ]
                  {  < task_body >   }
```

Basically, a programmer uses *adf_task* directive to transform a sequential program into the parallel form. For example, the following code fragment shows the implementation of the function from Figure 1 which uses this directive.

```
#pragma adf_task  trigger_set(x,y) until(done)
{
     z = max(x,y);
     if (z > g_max)
          g_max = z;
}
```

The *trigger_set* clause is used to define data dependencies for the task. Each data from the trigger set is associated with an implicit buffer which stores different values of the data item and enables asynchronous execution of producer and consumer tasks.

The ADF runtime system schedules tasks based on the availability of the trigger set data. A consumer task blocks if its input dependencies are not satisfied and waits for the producer task to commit new data values. When the input is ready, a consumer ADF task atomically processes the data, commits the changes and returns to the beginning of the task to wait for new data. During commit, the consumer task may produce the data needed by some other ADF task, which then processes the data further. Since each

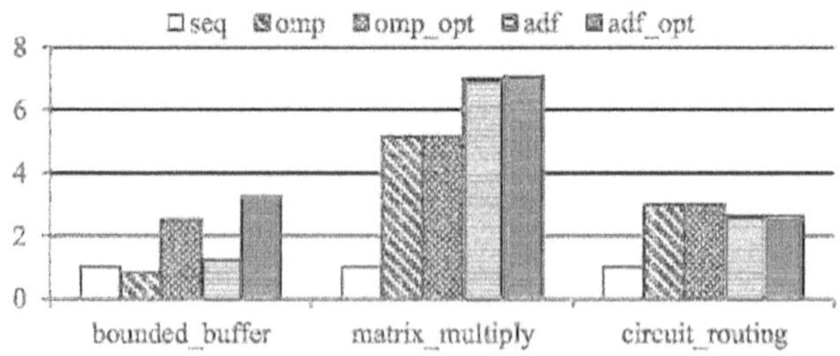

Figure 2: Speedup of parallel implementations.

ADF task is triggered only when a new data value is produced, a program is thus executed in a dataflow fashion. An important aspect of the ADF model is that it separates the transactional execution from the dataflow coordination. In case of abort as a result of conflicting changes to the shared mutable state, the task restarts a transaction using the same set of input values.

Usually, dataflow execution stops once it achieves the goal of the calculation; e.g. when the product of two matrices has been found. However, there are cases when the execution should proceed until some external signal is received. For example, a game server runs indefinitely processing clients' requests and terminates only when it is explicitly shutdown. In such case, the exit condition for a task can be defined using the *until* clause.

Finally, using the *relaxed* option it is possible to switch off the implicit TM synchronization of the task body. The implicit transaction guarantees the atomicity of the task execution in regard to the shared memory operations, but in some cases a programmer can provide more optimal synchronization by inserting transactions manually within the body of the task.

3. CONCLUSION

In Figure 2, we compare the performance of benchmark applications parallelized using the ADF model against the performance of the corresponding sequential and task-based OpenMP implementations. We implement two versions of parallel applications: one with implicit task transactions and the other with optimally placed transactions. The results show that added expressiveness of the ADF model also results in improved performance. Our ongoing experiments suggest that the model is suitable for parallelization of the Producer-Consumer type of applications as well as for applications that exhibit irregular parallelism. In the future, we plan to evaluate the ADF model using a wide range of applications and experiment with different implementations of the ADF runtime system.

4. ACKNOWLEDGMENTS

We thankfully acknowledge the support of Microsoft Research though the BSC-Microsoft Research Centre, the European Commission through the HiPEAC-3 Network of Excellence, the Spanish Ministry of Education (TIN2007-60625, and CSD2007-00050) and the Generalitat de Catalunya (2009-SGR-980).

5. REFERENCES

Diavastos, A., Trancoso, P., Lujan, M., & Watson, I. (2011). Integrating Transactions into the Data-Driven Multi-threading Model using the TFlux Platform. Galveston Island, TX: *The first workshop on Data-Flow Execution Models for Extreme Scale Computing (DFM)*.

Perez, J. M., Badia, R. M., & Labarta, J. (2008). A dependency-aware task-based programming environment for multi-core architectures. *Proceedings of the 2008 IEEE International Conference on Cluster Computing*, (pp. 142-151).

MaSiF: Machine Learning Guided Auto-tuning of Parallel Skeletons

Alexander Collins
a.collins@ed.ac.uk

Christian Fensch
c.fensch@ed.ac.uk

Hugh Leather
hleather@inf.ed.ac.uk

University of Edinburgh, School of Informatics

ABSTRACT

We present MaSiF, a novel tool to auto-tune parallelization parameters of skeleton parallel programs. It reduces the cost of searching the optimization space using a combination of machine learning and linear dimensionality reduction. To auto-tune a new program, a set of program features is determined statically and used to compute k nearest neighbors from a set of training programs. Previously collected performance data for the nearest neighbors is used to reduce the size of the search space using Principal Components Analysis. This results in a set of eigenvectors that are used to search the reduced space.

MaSiF achieves 88% of the performance of the oracle, which searches a random set of 10,000 parameter values. MaSiF searches just 45 points, or 0.45% of the optimization space, to achieve this performance. MaSiF provides an average speedup of 1.18x over parallelization parameters chosen by a human expert.

Categories and Subject Descriptors

D.1.3 [**Programming Techniques**]: Concurrent Programming—*Parallel programming*

General Terms

Measurement, Performance, Experimentation

Keywords

Auto-tuning, FastFlow, Machine Learning, Multi-core, Parallel Skeletons

1. INTRODUCTION

Parallel skeletons provide a predefined set of parallel templates that can be combined, nested and parameterized with sequential code to produce complex parallel programs. The implementation of each skeleton includes parameters that have a significant effect on performance; so carefully tuning them is vital. The optimization space formed by these parameters is complex, non-linear, exhibits multiple local optima and is program dependent. This makes manual tuning impractical. Effective automatic tuning is therefore essential for the performance of parallel skeleton programs.

PACT'12, September 19–23, 2012, Minneapolis, Minnesota, USA.
ACM 978-1-4503-1182-3/12/09.

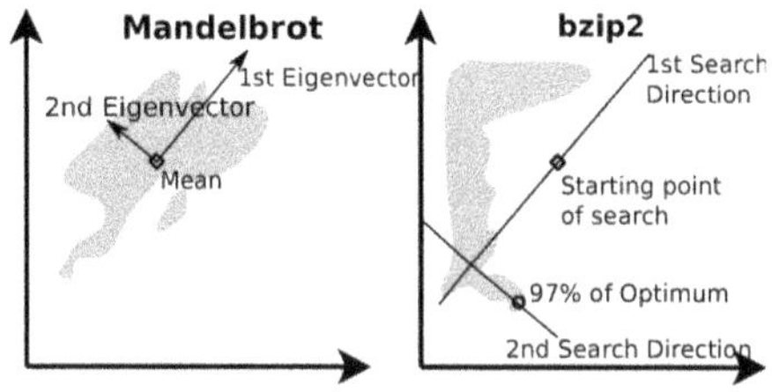

Figure 1: Optimizing a new program using eigenvector search (right) using training data from a similar program (left).

We present MaSiF, a tool that auto-tunes the FastFlow parallel skeleton framework [1]. We have identified five implementation parameters within FastFlow that have an effect on performance. MaSiF auto-tunes them using machine learning guided search applied to performance data for a subset of the parameter space collected a priori. Given a new program, a set of static features are extracted that categorize its behavior. A nearest neighbor classifier then chooses k programs from the training set that are the closest match for the new program.

The best performing points in the optimization space for these k programs are collected together. Dimensionality reduction is applied to these points, to produce a reduced sized search space. The search is then performed within this smaller space, along the directions of greatest variation in the best points provided by the dimensionality reduction.

Our results show that MaSiF achieves 88% of the performance of the oracle, which searches a random set of 10,000 parameter values. MaSiF searches just 45 parameter values on average. MaSiF also achieves an average speedup of 1.18× over parallelization parameters chosen by a human expert. These results demonstrate that our technique is effective at automatically optimizing parallel skeleton programs without the need for human expertise.

2. MOTIVATION

Figure 1 illustrates how we optimize a new program (bzip2), given training data from a similar program (mandelbrot). The left plot in Figure 1 shows the optimization space of the mandelbrot program with 2 parallelization parameters. Shaded areas mark parallelization parameter values that obtain 95% or more of the best performance. Applying Principal Components Analysis (PCA) [2] to these best parameter values provides a mean and two eigenvectors. These are shown in the plot.

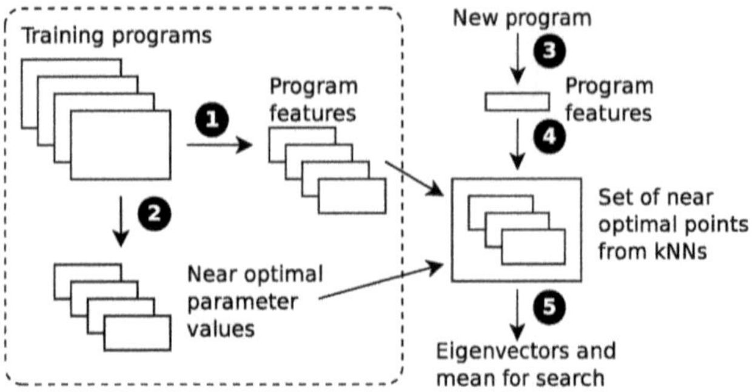

Figure 2: Schematic of how machine learning guides the search. The dotted box indicates the offline training phase. ❶ Extract program features from training programs. ❷ Find a set of near optimal parameter values for each training program, by measuring a random subset of the space. ❸ Extract program features from the new program. ❹ Compute the k-nearest neighbors, using the program features, to create a set of near optimal parameter values for all nearest neighbors. ❺ Apply PCA to the set of near optimal parameter values. The resulting mean and eigenvectors are used to perform the search.

The right plot in Figure 1 shows the optimisation space of a different program: bzip2, with the same 2 parallelization parameters as the mandelbrot program. Again, the grey shaded area indicates parameter values with 95% or more of the best available performance. Even though the optimization space looks completely different, we can apply a search to optimise bzip2 using the mean and eigenvectors from mandelbrot. Starting at that mean, we exhaustively search along the first eigenvector in both directions to find the best point. From there, we now search along the direction of the second eigenvector. The search finds a point that obtains 97% of the best available performance.

This motivating example shows that the eigenvectors provided by the PCA for one program can be used to guide the search in the optimisation space of a different program, if the programs are a good match. In Section 3, we show how similar programs can be found.

3. AUTO-TUNING USING MaSiF

MaSiF starts by collecting all 'near optimal' parameter values from similar training programs, using machine learning detailed in Figure 2. We define 'near optimal' parameter values as those at 95% or more of the best performance of the oracle (a random search over 10,000 parameter values).

Applying PCA to this set of parameter values provides a new set of orthogonal basis vectors, or eigenvectors, for the parameter space.

PCA also returns a measure of the variance of the data in the direction of each eigenvector, called the eigenvalues. These are used to scale the eigenvectors so that they cover the region of the space where the majority of the 'near optimal' parameter values lie. The search space is reduced by only searching within the plane defined by the two eigenvectors that capture the most variation. The search space is further reduced by searching along each eigenvector in turn, as discussed in Section 2.

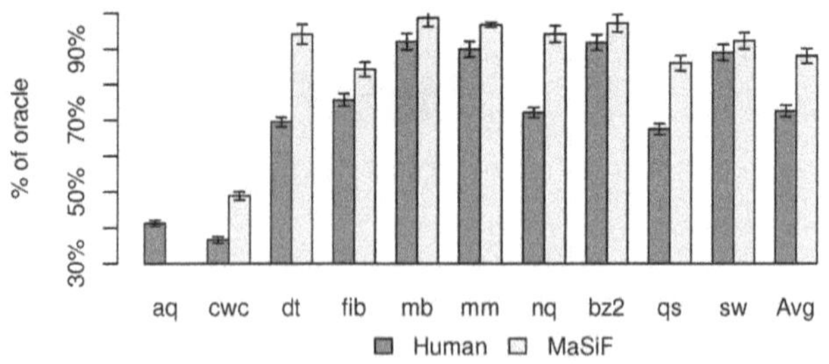

Figure 3: The percentage of the oracle performance achieved by a human expert and MaSiF. MaSiF searches along two eigenvectors, exploring 45 parameter values on average. The error bars show 99% confidence intervals for the mean.

4. RESULTS

We evaluate MaSiF using a 32-core shared memory machine and 10 existing skeleton parallel programs implemented using FastFlow.

Figure 3 shows the percentage of the oracle performance achieved by MaSiF and parallelization parameters chosen by the FastFlow authors. This plot demonstrates that MaSiF achieves performance closer to the oracle than the expert in all but one case. For 7 of the 10 programs, MaSiF achieves at least 90% of the oracle performance, and in some cases is close to 100%. On average over all programs, MaSiF achieves 88% of the oracle performance.

It is important to note that MaSiF only measures the performance at 45 points on average, in order to obtain this performance. This is far fewer than the size of the space, which consists of 127,008 points.

5. CONCLUSIONS AND FUTURE WORK

We have demonstrated that MaSiF achieves 88% of the performance of the oracle; which searches a random subset of the entire space. The results also show that MaSiF provides a 1.18× speedup over human expert chosen parameters, on average over all programs.

These results show that MaSiF does not significantly impact the maximum possible performance achievable—in fact it does better than a human expert—whilst markedly reducing the number of parameters that need to be searched. The PCA space reduction reduces the size of the search space by 275× on average, and searching along just two eigenvectors reduces the space by 1,925×.

Our technique is fully automatic and not constrained to only work with FastFlow. It can be easily adapted to tune different parameters. In the future, we will investigate searching the reduced parameter space at runtime. We will also investigate more sophisticated techniques to improve over the exhaustive search along each eigenvector.

6. REFERENCES

[1] M. Aldinucci, M. Torquati, and M. Meneghin. FastFlow: Efficient parallel streaming applications on multi-core. Technical Report TR-09-12, Università di Pisa, Dipartimento di Informatica, Italy, 2009.

[2] C. M. Bishop. *Pattern Recognition and Machine Learning*. Information Science and Statistics. Springer, 2006.

TMNOC: A Case of HTM and NoC Co-design for Increased Energy Efficiency and Concurrency

Lihang Zhao, Woojin Choi, Jeff Draper
Information Sciences Institute
University of Southern California
Marina del Rey, CA 90242
{lihangzh, woojinch, draper}@isi.edu

ABSTRACT

Hardware Transactional Memory (HTM) designs must implement conflict detection to guarantee the correctness of transaction execution. A conflict occurs when more than one transaction access the same data and at least one of them attempts to modify the data. The corresponding conflict detection mechanism usually works at a cacheline level that fits naturally into the cache coherence protocol. Thus, the inter-transaction communication for conflict detection is usually mapped onto the coherence communication controlled by the directory-based coherence protocols. In this paper, we identify inefficiency introduced by such mappings. The net effect of such inefficiency is excessive on-chip network traffic that consumes substantial dynamic power as packets are switched over the routers and links. We present TMNOC, a HTM and Network-on-Chip (NoC) co-design to improve network energy efficiency. The on-chip network, instead of a passive communication substrate, proactively filters out transactional requests that waste energy yet having no contribution to the progress of transactions. Experiment results show that TMNOC reduces energy consumption of the on-chip network by 14.5% on average (up to 38%) across a wide range of transaction applications.

Categories and Subject Descriptors

C.1.2 [**Processor Architecture**]: Parallel processors

Keywords

Hardware Transactional Memory, On-chip Network, Chip Multiprocessor, Energy Efficiency

1. INTRODUCTION

Concurrent accesses from different processing units to shared memory must be orchestrated correctly as well as efficiently. Hardware Transactional Memory (HTM) is an optimistic concurrency control mechanism proposed to increase productivity in parallel programming. A transaction is defined as a sequence of memory operations that either executes completely or has no effect [1]. When more than one transaction try to access the same data and at least one of them tries to modify the data, a conflict occurs. As one of the two major design choices to detect conflicts, the eager scheme ensures conflicts being detected progressively as transactions execute. When a conflict is detected, it is resolved immediately to maintain the "single-write-multiple-reader" invariant. Eager conflict detection designs typically piggyback onto the cache coherence protocol to reduce implementation overhead. Figure 1 illustrates how a conflict is detected eagerly using the directory-based MESI protocol. The requesting transaction (R) issues a GETX (request for exclusive access) to the home directory ①, which replies to the requester with the number of sharers ②. Then, the directory forwards the request to all the current sharers that hold a replica of the requested data ③. Meanwhile, the block state in the directory is changed to busy (*i.e.* upcoming requests to the same data are not serviced). Upon receiving the request, the sharer transactions check their read and write sets to detect conflicts. If the sharer transaction detects a conflict and has a higher priority in the conflict resolution policy, it sends a Nack (negative acknowledgement) to the requestor ④. Upon receiving the response messages from all the sharers, the requestor sends an UNBLOCK message to the directory ⑤. Since the request is nacked, the requesting transaction is stalled and keeps retrying until all the sharer transactions have released isolation on the data.

While this conflict detection scheme is straightforward and widely-adopted in eager HTM designs, it simply maps the inter-transaction communication onto coherence communication without being optimized towards the properties of transaction execution. As conflicting transactions are stalled, they keep retrying the nacked requests until higher priority transactions holding the data in their read or write set have finished execution. Those nacked retries generate excessive network traffic by initiating communication between the requesters and the directory, the directory and all

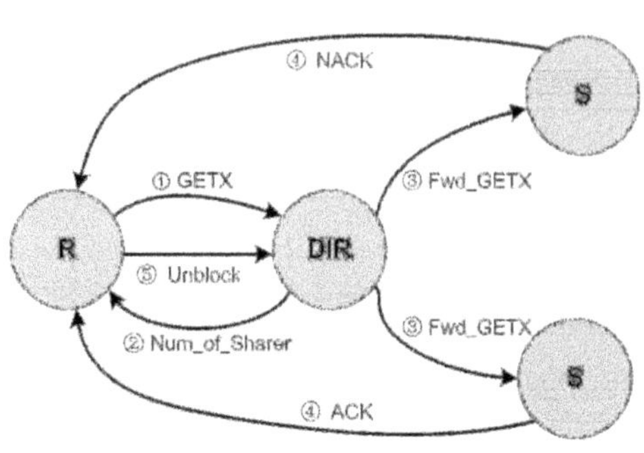

Figure 1: Illustration of eager conflict detection using directory-based coherence protocol.

PACT'12, September 19–23, 2012, Minneapolis, Minnesota, USA.
ACM 978-1-4503-1182-3/12/09.

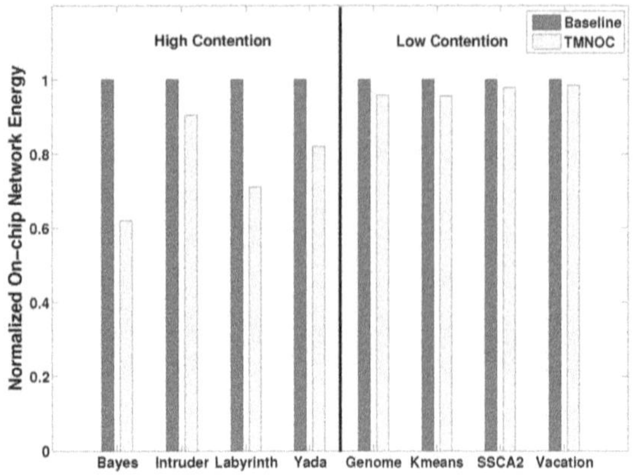

Figure 2: On-chip network energy consumption. Normalized to baseline.

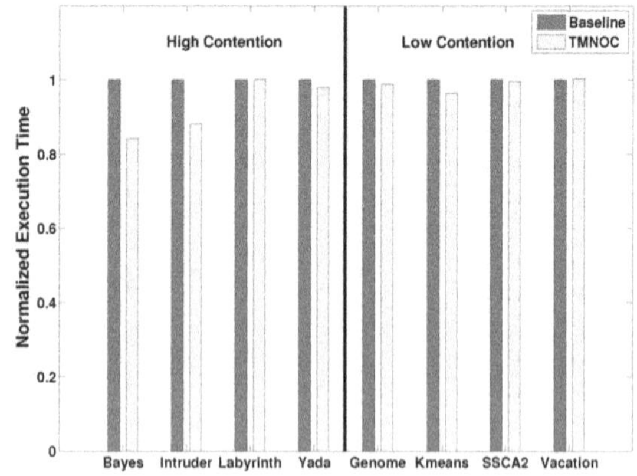

Figure 3: Overall performance. Normalized to baseline.

the sharers, and the sharers and the requesters. Since the nacked retries do not contribute to the progress of transaction, the network traffic is unnecessary. Moreover, it could lead to energy inefficiency as well as performance loss.

2. TMNOC

We propose TMNOC to reduce conflict detection traffic using a TM-aware on-chip network. This mechanism can be integrated into HTM designs piggybacking conflict detection on directory-based coherence protocols [5, 2]. The on-chip network is augmented to monitor transaction conflicts using dedicated storage in routers. When a router sees NACK messages between transactions, it keeps copies of those messages in its local NACK buffer. When a router sees data request messages from transactions, it consults its NACK buffer to speculate on the probability of the requests being nacked by the receiving transaction. If the probability is sufficiently high, the router drops the message and sends a NACK to the requesting transaction. Proactively dropping the transaction requests eliminates subsequent communication thus reducing network traffic, which is translated into energy savings and reduced network latency. Upon a miss prediction, the requesting transaction can attain data access permission later through retrying the request.

Correctness of transaction execution is guaranteed since the net effect of TMNOC is preventing potential conflicting transactions from committing new states into the memory, while forward progress is completely determined by the HTM design. Meanwhile, router latency is not penalized as TMNOC-specific operations can be performed in parallel with route computation, VC arbitration and SW arbitration.

3. EVALUATION

In our experiment, a 16-tile chip multiprocessor is used as the baseline architecture. LogTM-SE [5] is used as the baseline HTM design. The on-chip router microarchitecture is based on the canonical wormhole router with virtual-channel flow control [4]. The TMNOC design (to be described in detail in a future paper) is evaluated using cycle accurate full-system simulation.

Figure 2 presents the energy consumption of the on-chip network. TMNOC reduces on-chip network energy consumption in all eight STAMP benchmarks [3]. More network energy can be saved in high contention benchmarks as NACK and request retry are more frequent. Figure 3 presents the overall execution time. On average, performance is improved by 4.3% due to reduced coherence traffic delivered by the on-chip network.

4. CONCLUSION

Conflict detection is a critical design dimension in HTM systems. Eager conflict detection typically piggybacks onto the coherence protocol to reduce implementation overhead. However, the mismatch between the coherence protocol and transactional behavior could lead to energy inefficiency in the on-chip network. In this work, it is identified that the nacked retries of transaction requests could incur unnecessary network traffic that wastes energy and link resources. The proposed TMNOC design filters out unnecessary network traffic by enabling enroute on-chip routers to proactively nack transaction requests that have a high probability to be nacked by transactions currently holding the data. Experimental results indicate the effectiveness of the TMNOC in reducing network energy consumption.

5. REFERENCES

[1] A.-R. Adl-Tabatabai, C. Kozyrakis, and B. Saha. Unlocking concurrency. *ACM Queue*, 4:24–33, December 2006.

[2] M. Lupon, G. Magklis, and A. Gonzalez. A dynamically adaptable hardware transactional memory. In *Proceedings of the 43rd International Symposium on Microarchitecture*, 2010.

[3] C. C. Minh, J. Chung, C. Kozyrakis, and K. Olukotun. Stamp: Stanford transactional applications for multi-processing. In *IEEE Intl Symp on Workload Characterization*, 2008.

[4] L.-S. Peh and W. Dally. A delay model for router microarchitectures. *Micro, IEEE*, 21(1), jan/feb 2001.

[5] L. Yen, J. Bobba, M. R. Marty, K. E. Moore, H. Volos, M. D. Hill, M. M. Swift, and D. A. Wood. Logtm-se: Decoupling hardware transactional memory from caches. In *Proceedings of International Symposium on High Performance Computer Architecture*, 2007.

Application-aware Prefetch Prioritization in On-chip Networks

Nachiappan Chidambaram Nachiappan[†] Asit K. Mishra[§] Mahmut Kandemir[†]
Anand Sivasubramaniam[†] Onur Mutlu[‡] Chita R. Das[†]
[†]The Pennsylvania State University [§]Intel Corp. [‡] Carnegie Mellon University
{nachi, kandemir, anand, das}@cse.psu.edu {asit.k.mishra@intel.com} {onur@cmu.edu}

ABSTRACT

Data prefetching is an effective technique for hiding memory latency. When issued prefetches are inaccurate, performance can degrade. Prior research provided solutions to deal with inaccurate prefetches at the cache and memory levels, but not in the interconnect of a large-scale multiprocessor system. This work introduces *application-aware* prefetch prioritization techniques to mitigate the negative effects of prefetching in a network-on-chip (NoC) based multicore system. The idea is to rank prefetches from different applications based on their potential utility for the application and propensity to cause interference to other applications. Our evaluation shows that this approach provides significant performance improvements over a baseline that does not distinguish between prefetches from different applications.

Categories and Subject Descriptors: C.1.2[Computer Systems Organization] Multiprocessors; Interconnection architectures;
General Terms: Design, Performance
Keywords: Interconnect, Multicore, Prefetching

1. INTRODUCTION

Memory access latency is a major limiter of computer system performance. A widely-used technique to tolerate this latency is prefetching, a method that predicts the memory accesses that will be made by a processor and fetches the data before it is requested by the processor. This technique has been shown to be very effective when prefetch accuracy, coverage and timeliness are reasonably high [10]. Unfortunately, not all prefetch requests are accurate (or, useful, i.e., will be needed by the processor). An inaccurate prefetch request wastes system resources (such as memory and interconnect bandwidth, cache space) and degrades performance by delaying demand or useful prefetch requests. As recent work has shown, uncontrolled aggressive prefetching can be ineffective in bandwidth-limited and cache-space-limited multi-core systems [8, 3, 4] because it causes significant interference between cores in shared caches and main memory.

A critical shared resource in scalable multi-core systems is the on-chip interconnect/network (NoC), which is the communication substrate that connects the cores and caches, carrying private-cache-miss traffic and coherence traffic (requests and responses). Inaccurate prefetch requests waste NoC resources (bandwidth, buffers, etc) and delay other requests while traversing the NoC. In fact, we find that aggressive prefetching can cause significant congestion in the NoC and the resulting uncontrolled interference between applications significantly degrades overall system performance in some workloads.

While previous works [8, 7, 10, 3, 4] developed techniques to alleviate the negative effects of aggressive prefetching in caches and memory controllers via intelligent prioritization or prefetcher throttling mechanisms, little work considered such effects in the NoC. Our goal in this work is to examine the effects of aggressive prefetching in NoC-based multi-core systems and develop techniques to mitigate the negative effects of prefetching in the NoC. To this end, we propose an application-aware prefetch prioritization mechanism for NoC routers that differentiates between the prefetches from different applications and prioritizes prefetches from those applications where prefetching 1) is more likely to improve the performance of the application, 2) is likely to not cause significant interference to other applications.

2. MOTIVATION

Aggressive prefetching in an NoC-based system can cause network congestion because the prefetcher can inject a significant number of inaccurate prefetches into the network. These inaccurate prefetches can delay not only demand requests but also useful prefetch requests. To investigate the effect of aggressive prefetching in an NoC-based multicore system, we implemented a version of the aggressive, state-of-the-art stream prefetcher described in [10] on a 64-core 2D mesh based NoC.[1]

Figure 1(a), (b), (c) show respectively the prefetch accuracy, network latency increase due to prefetching, and IPC delta with the prefetcher over no prefetching across a set of multiprogrammed workloads. Each workload consists of 64 concurrently-executed copies of a SPEC 2006 benchmark. Results are averaged across all SPEC workloads, but the figure shows a subset. Overall, with an average prefetch accuracy of 43%, we see an average network latency increase of 170% due to a 45% increase in network traffic (not shown). Although the prefetcher improves average performance, we find it degrades performance by more than 10% on 8 of the 26 evaluated workloads.

We find two major problems contribute to the performance degradation: 1) prefetch requests are sometimes prioritized over demands in NoC routers (our baseline does not distinguish between them), 2) useless or less beneficial prefetch requests for one application are sometimes prioritized over useful or more beneficial prefetch requests for another in NoC routers.

Previous works [8, 7, 4] tackled the first problem: they developed policies to adaptively prioritize between prefetch and demand requests in memory controllers and caches such that likely-inaccurate prefetch requests do not get prioritized over demand requests. In our evaluations, we find that prioritizing demands over prefetches in the network (as done in [9]) provides better performance than treating prefetches and demands equally (shown as Demand-first in Figure 2). Adapting previous dynamic prioritization policies [8, 7, 4] to the NoC context can provide even better performance, but we leave this to future work as our goal is to focus on the second problem above.

To our knowledge, previous works did not tackle the second problem: different applications' prefetch requests have different impact on application performance and system performance.

[1]Our baseline uses the standard XY-routing algorithm, has 4 memory controllers located at the corners, and does not differentiate between prefetch and demand requests in the routers.

PACT'12, September 19–23, 2012, Minneapolis, Minnesota, USA.
ACM 978-1-4503-1182-3/12/09.

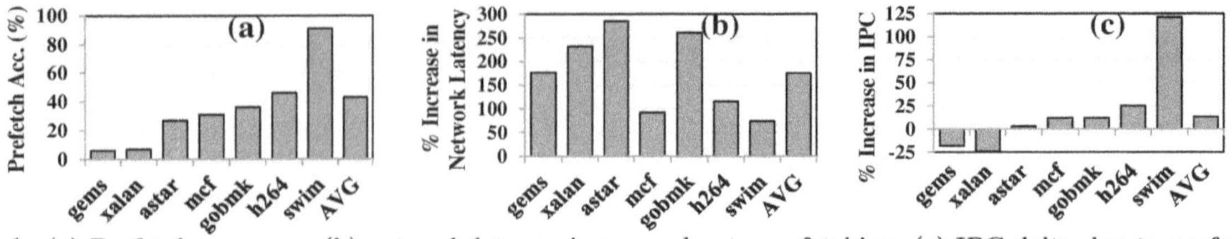

Figure 1: (a) Prefetch accuracy, (b) network latency increase due to prefetching, (c) IPC delta due to prefetching.

The major question we aim to answer is: *how should prefetch requests of different applications be prioritized in the network routers?*

3. MECHANISM

Ideally, one would like to prioritize prefetches of those applications that benefit the most from prefetching and do not cause harm to other applications due to prefetching. Again, ideally, one would like to deprioritize the prefetches of those applications that benefit the least from prefetching but cause significant performance degradation to other applications due to their prefetches. We observe that the benefit an application gains from prefetching and the harm it causes due to prefetching can be approximated by observing two metrics for the application: prefetch accuracy and prefetch count.

Our policy is based on two insights. First, an application that has high prefetch accuracy is more likely to benefit from prefetching because its prefetches are more likely to be useful. Second, an application that injects fewer prefetches into the network is less likely to harm other applications because its prefetches are less likely to interfere with other applications' requests.

Using these two insights, we develop a mechanism that categorizes applications into four categories, either statically or dynamically, based on whether the application's 1) prefetch accuracy is high or low, and 2) prefetch count is high or low. Prefetches from those applications with high prefetch accuracy but low prefetch count are given the highest priority because such applications are the most likely to benefit from prefetching and the least likely to harm others due to prefetching. Conversely, prefetches from those applications with low prefetch accuracy and high prefetch count are given the least priority. In-between these two extremes, applications with high accuracy and high prefetch count are given priority over those with low accuracy and low prefetch count. If two applications happen to be in the same category, their prefetches are prioritized using the default prioritization policy of the router (e.g., age-based or round-robin).

Static vs. Dynamic: An application's prefetch accuracy and prefetch count category can be estimated statically or dynamically. In the static version of our policy, a profile run determines in which of the four categories an application falls. In the dynamic version, hardware collects these metrics periodically and at the end of a period (i.e., time quantum) assigns each application to one of the four categories. For the next quantum, the network routers use the assigned category of an application to appropriately prioritize prefetches from that application.

Results: Figure 2 shows the performance improvement of our static and dynamic application-aware prefetch prioritization mechanisms (AppAware-S and AppAware-D, respectively) over the baseline system that uses round-robin prioritization in routers, as described in [1]. In our mechanisms, demands are always prioritized over prefetches. For comparison, we also show the performance improvement with two different policies: 1) one that only prioritizes demands over prefetches but employs round-robin prioritization across different prefetches (Demand-first), and 2) an unimplementable policy in which prefetch requests never contend with each other or with demands, which provides an upper bound on what is achievable with our techniques. The results are averaged across 12 heterogeneous multiprogrammed workloads, where each workload consists of a combination of different SPEC benchmarks running together. We show five representative workloads in the figure.

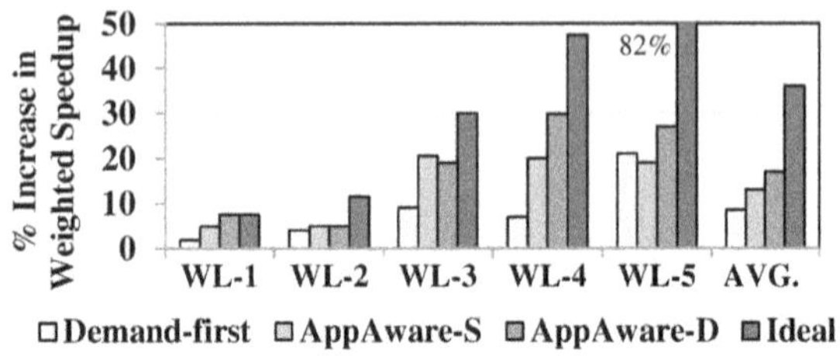

Figure 2: Performance of app-aware prefetch prioritization.

Figure 2 leads to three major conclusions: 1) Application-aware prioritization among prefetches, static or dynamic, provides significant performance improvement over policies that do not distinguish between prefetches, 2) Our dynamic policy performs better than the static one as it can adapt to changes in application and prefetcher phase behavior (improving performance by 9% over Demand-first), 3) Although our mechanism bridges more than one third of the gap between Demand-first and Ideal, there is still significant performance to be gained by eliminating the negative effects of prefetching in the NoC.

4. CONCLUSIONS

We showed differentially prioritizing between prefetches from different applications in an NoC based system significantly improves system performance. Our future work includes analyzing our techniques and combining them with other application-aware prioritization techniques in NoC routers (e.g., [1, 5, 2, 6]).

References

[1] R. Das et al. Application-Aware Prioritization Mechanisms for On-Chip Networks. In *MICRO-42*, 2009.

[2] R. Das et al. Aergia: Exploiting packet latency slack in on-chip networks. In *ISCA-37*, 2010.

[3] E. Ebrahimi et al. Coordinated control of multiple prefetchers in multi-core systems. In *MICRO-42*, 2009.

[4] E. Ebrahimi et al. Prefetch-aware shared-resource management for multi-core systems. In *ISCA-38*, 2011.

[5] B. Grot et al. Preemptive Virtual Clock: A Flexible, Efficient, and Cost-effective QOS Scheme for Networks-on-a-Chip. In *MICRO-42*, 2009.

[6] B. Grot et al. A QoS-Enabled On-Die Interconnect Fabric for Kilo-Node Chips. *IEEE Micro*, May/June 2012.

[7] C. J. Lee et al. Improving memory bank-level parallelism in the presence of prefetching. In *MICRO-42*, 2009.

[8] C. J. Lee et al. Prefetch-aware memory controllers. *IEEE Transactions on Computers*, 2011.

[9] J. Lee et al. Exploiting mutual awareness between prefetchers and on-chip networks in multi-cores. In *Poster Session, PACT*, 2011.

[10] S. Srinath et al. Feedback directed prefetching: Improving the performance and bandwidth-efficiency of hardware prefetchers. In *HPCA-13*, 2007.

ReCaP: A Region-Based Cure for the Common Cold Cache

Jason Zebchuk
University of Toronto
zechuk@eecg.toronto.edu

Harold W. Cain
IBM T.J. Watson Research Center
tcain@us.ibm.com

Vijayalakshmi Srinivasan
IBM T.J. Watson Research Center
viji@us.ibm.com

Andreas Moshovos
University of Toronto
moshovos@eecg.toronto.edu

Categories and Subject Descriptors

C.1.0 [**Processor Architectures**]: General

Keywords

Cache Restoration, Memory Bandwidth, Memory Energy, Virtualization

1. INTRODUCTION

Server consolidation, virtual desktop infrastructure (VDI) environments, and cloud computing trends dominate the landscape of new server purchases. Virtualization has many benefits: it increases utilization, improves security, lowers costs, and reduces management overheads. In some cases, the number of virtual machines consolidated onto a single processor has grown faster than the number of hardware threads. For example, IBM has reported a case study of consolidating 3,900 servers onto only 30 systems [7] and VMWare case studies have reported consolidation ratios from 4:1 to 15:1 [9]. The number of partitions on each machine is expected to continue to increase [1].

Multiprogrammed virtualization allows multiple virtual machines to time-share a single core. However, this fine-grain sharing comes at a cost. Each time slice a virtual machine gets scheduled, it effectively begins with a "cold" cache, since any cache blocks it accessed in the previous slice have likely been evicted by other virtual machines. The shorter the interval assigned to each virtual machine and the larger the on-chip caches the higher the performance impact of the "cold" cache effect. In some scenarios, the execution interval for each partition has to be kept relatively short to meet QoS constraints and provide real-time interactive response times. For instance, the PowerVM partition manager will allocate some portion of a 10 ms dispatch window to each active partition, such that a system with five partitions, for example, might execute each one for only 2 ms at a time.

Daly and Cain recently explored the effects of multiprogrammed virtualization and found that it can reduce performance by as much as 40% compared to running applications in isolation [4]. Our results of Figure 1 show slowdowns of up to 35% for some applications from SPEC CPU 2000. Accordingly, there is significant potential to regain performance by attacking the "cold" cache effect.

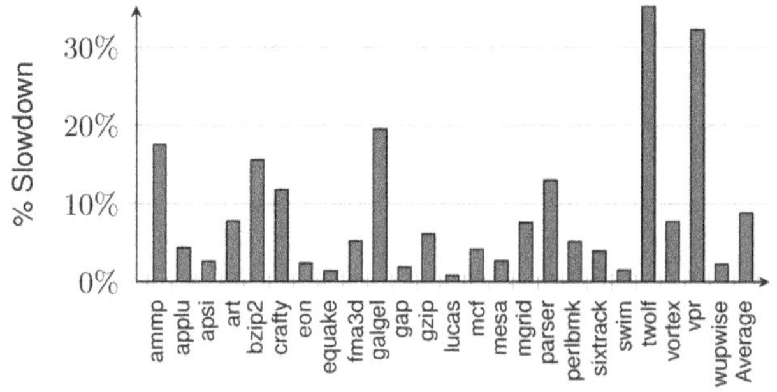

Figure 1: Slowdown due to multi-programmed virtualization.

We propose a *Region-Based Cache Restoration Prefetcher* (RECAP), a bandwidth-efficient prefetcher that reduces the "cold" cache effect caused by multiprogrammed virtualization. RECAP groups blocks into regions and limits prefetching to those regions that are more likely to be see further hits. RECAP exploits the following two observations: (1) blocks that experienced hits are more likely to be reused again, and (2) coarser regions of memory that contain at least one block with reuse are likely to contain other blocks that will be touched again. RECAP provides a robust prefetcher that improves performance by up to 35% for some applications while never incurring more than a 38% bandwidth overhead or more than a 1.5% slowdown. Compared to other prefetchers designed for multiprogrammed virtualization, RECAP provides comparable performance benefits while using an average of 19% to 21% less bandwidth, and an average of 8% less power in the off-chip memory and last-level cache.

2. RECAP

RECAP conserves bandwidth through two key mechanisms. First, it prefecthes only those blocks which it predicts to be useful after a partition switch. Second, it uses a space-efficient representation of block addresses when writing and reading the list of blocks to prefetch for a partition. By conserving bandwidth, RECAP minimizes the power consumption and contention for off-chip memory.

To identify blocks that are likely to be useful to prefetch, we observe that blocks in the cache that have experienced cache hits are likely to see additional reuse in the future,

PACT'12, September 19–23, 2012, Minneapolis, Minnesota, USA.
ACM 978-1-4503-1182-3/12/09.

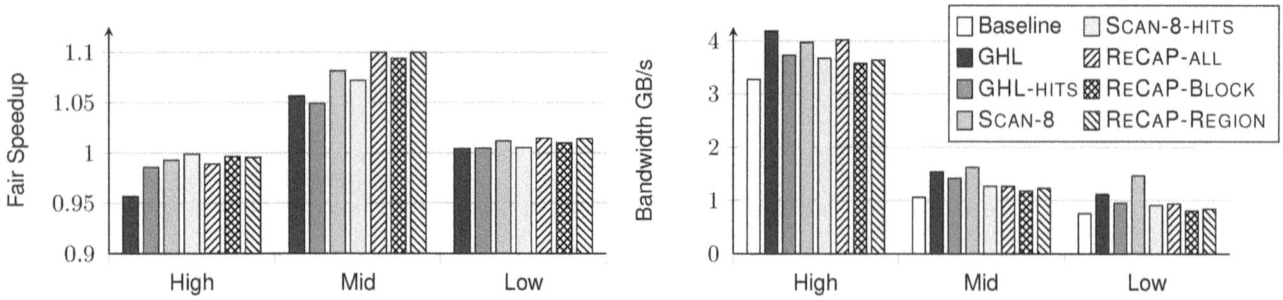

(a) Fair Speedup

(b) Average Bandwidth

Figure 2: Speedup and Bandwidth averaged for the three workload mixes.

while blocks that have never seen any cache hits are less likely to experience future reuse.

RECAP exploits common behaviour within coarse-grain regions of memory to use memory space and bandwidth efficiently. RECAP groups data blocks into contiguous 4 KB regions (most systems use 4K pages) of memory and uses bit-vectors to identify individual blocks within a given region. Assuming 64-byte cache blocks, 4 KB regions and 46-bit physical addresses, up to 64 cache blocks can be identified using a 34-bit *region tag* and a 64-bit vector for an overhead of 1.5 bits per block. For the workloads studied the regions present in the cache at the time of a partition switch contained an average of 17 blocks each. This results in an overhead of 5.6 bits per block, seven times less than the 40 bits required for simply listing the block addresses. Thus, RECAP's approach significantly reduces the bandwidth to read or write a list of blocks to prefetch, and it also allows a relatively small hardware structure to track a large number of cache blocks to consider for potential prefetching.

3. PERFORMANCE AND BANDWIDTH

We constructed three workloads, each consisting of eight partitions running different SPEC CPU 2000 applications within equal portions of a 10ms dispatch window. The workloads are labelled as high/mid/low based on the L2 cache MPKI for each application running in isolation. Simulations modeled a single-core, 4-way out-of-order single-thread processor with a stride prefetcher, 64KB 4-way L1 caches, and a 2MB 16-way inclusive unified L2 cache running Solaris 8. The simulator is based on the full-system simulator *Flexus* [6], which uses WindRiver Simics [5], and a DRAMSim2 [8] timing model.

We model GHL [3], CRP [4] and RECAP L2 prefetchers with a 32-entry main memory write-back buffer. There can be up to four outstaning prefetches to avoid excessive contention with demand accesses. We scaled the GHL structures in proportion to the L2 cache size, resulting in a 2K entry on-chip LRU structure and a 30K in-memory FIFO. We model CRP with a scanning prefetcher since less than 1.5% of cache blocks survive consecutive intervals for our workloads, On each partition switch, the cache was scanned and blocks were recorded in MRU order. We present results for SCAN-8 that scans the eight most recently used ways since it achieves the best overall speedup. All three RECAP variants we consider track up to 1K regions on-chip: RECAP-BLOCK, RECAP-REGION and RECAP-ALL prefetch blocks that have block reuse, have region reuse, or all blocks respectively. We propose two hybrid predictors that adapt RECAP's reuse based prediction mechanism to work with the GHL and CRP prefetchers. GHL-HITS is only updated for cache hits so it only prefetches blocks with block reuse. SCAN-8-HITS only prefetches reused blocks.

Figure 2 shows the fair speedup [2] and bandwidth for the three workload mixes. The baseline system for these results is running the same virtualized workload with only a stride prefetcher. Overall, RECAP-REGION achieves a mean speedup of 3.5% across the three workloads, which is 0.7% more than SCAN-8, and 3% more than GHL. Of the three prefetchers, GHL performs the worst.

As Figure 2(b) shows, RECAP-REGION's performance advantage is combined with a significant reduction in bandwidth. On average RECAP-REGION uses 17% less bandwidth than GHL and 19% (or 0.4 GB/s) less bandwidth than SCAN-8. This results in an overhead of only 12%, or 0.2 GB/s, compared to the baseline design with only a stride prefetcher. Both GHL and SCAN-8 can impose large bandwidth overheads that result in some performance losses.

4. REFERENCES

[1] B. Botelho. Virtual machines per server, a viable metric for hardware selection? Web Article.

[2] J. Chang and G. S. Sohi. Cooperative cache partitioning for chip multiprocessors. In *ICS*, 2007.

[3] H. Cui and S. Sair. Extending data prefetching to cope with context switch misses. In *Proc. of the IEEE Int'l Conf. on Computer Design*, 2009.

[4] D. Daly and H. Cain. Cache restoration for highly partitioned virtualized systems. In *HPCA*, 2012.

[5] J. Engblom et al. Full-system simulation from embedded to high-performance systems. In R. Leupers and O. Temam, editors, *Processor and System-on-Chip Simulation*, pages 25–45. Springer US, 2010.

[6] N. Hardavellas et al. Simflex: A fast, accurate, flexible full-system simulation framework for performance evaluation of server architecture. *SIGMETRICS*, 2004.

[7] IBM Corporation. *Shrinking 3900 Distributed Servers to 30 Linux Mainframes*, Aug. 2007. Press Release.

[8] P. Rosenfeld et al. Dramsim2: A cycle accurate memory system simulator. *IEEE CAL*, 2011.

[9] VMWare Inc. *Enabling End-to-End Virtualization Solutions for Mid-market and Enterprise Customers: Featured Case Studies.*

Power-efficient Computing for Compute-intensive GPGPU Applications

Syed Zohaib Gilani
University of Wisconsin-Madison
Madison, WI, USA
gilani@wisc.edu

Nam Sung Kim
University of Wisconsin-Madison
Madison, WI, USA
nskim3@wisc.edu

Michael Schulte
AMD Research
Austin, TX, USA
michael.schulte@amd.com

ABSTRACT
The peak performance of graphics processing units (GPUs) has traditionally been increased by increasing the number of compute resources and/or their frequency. However, these approaches significantly increase the power consumption of GPUs. Consequently, modern high-performance GPUs are power constrained and must employ more power efficient approaches for performance improvements in future processors. In this paper we propose three power-efficient techniques for improving the performance of GPUs. First, we observe that many GPGPU applications are integer instruction intensive. For such applications, we propose to utilize the fused multiply-add (FMA) units to fuse dependent integer instructions into a composite instruction, improving power efficiency and performance by reducing the number of fetched/executed instructions. Secondly, GPUs often perform computations that are duplicated across multiple threads. We dynamically detect such instructions and execute them in a separate scalar pipeline. Finally, the register file bandwidth in GPUs is a critical resource that is optimized for 32-bit instruction operands. However, many operands require considerably fewer bits for accurate representation and computations. We propose a sliced GPU architecture that improves performance of the GPU by dual-issuing instructions to two 16-bit execution slices. Overall, our techniques result in more than a 25% (geometric mean) power efficiency improvement.

Categories and Subject Descriptors:
D.3.3 [**Multiple Data Stream Architectures (Multiprocessors)**]: Single-instruction-stream, multiple-data-stream processors (SIMD)

Keywords:
GPU, power efficiency, low-power.

1. INTRODUCTION
Graphics processing units (GPUs) are massively parallel processors that offer a large pool of execution units, high-bandwidth memories and thousands of hardware threads. Although originally designed for graphics applications, the high compute power and memory bandwidth of GPUs is also being used to accelerate general purpose (GPGPU) applications that can efficiently utilize GPU resources.

PACT'12, September 19–23, 2012, Minneapolis, Minnesota, USA.
ACM 978-1-4503-1182-3/12/09.

The peak compute performance of a GPU is a function of its compute resources and its operating frequency. Consequently, the peak compute performance of GPUs has traditionally been improved by increasing the number of compute resources and/or their frequency. However, modern GPUs are typically power-constrained (e.g., a GeForce® 8800 consumes 280W [1]) and cannot afford to increase compute resources or frequency within their power and thermal budgets [2]. Moreover, as power supply voltage scaling diminishes the energy cost per instructions must be decreased to achieve performance improvements in future processors [3].

The compute resources of GPUs are organized into groups, such as streaming multiprocessors (SMs) in NVIDIA GPUs. Each SM is composed of a single-instruction multiple-thread (SIMT) pipeline that consists of execution units, main register file (MRF), fetch, decode and scheduling (FDS) logic, and memories. For compute-intensive applications, more than 85% of the total GPU dynamic power may be consumed by the SMs [4]. The FDS logic, MRF and execution units can contribute to more than 45% of an SM's dynamic power [4]. Reducing the power consumption of these architectural components is thus imperative for a power efficient GPU architecture.

2. PROPOSED APPROACHES

2.1 Composite instructions
GPUs are optimized for FP intensive 3D graphics. Consequently, the execution pipelines in GPUs are typically composed of FP fused multiply-add (FMA) units [5,6,7]. However, the massive parallelism and high memory bandwidths of GPUs are also utilized to accelerate integer-intensive applications. To support integer instructions in the same pipeline, the FMA unit is enhanced with logic to perform integer arithmetic, bitwise and logical operations. We exploit the resources of FMA units to combine pairs of dependent integer instructions into composite instructions that can be efficiently mapped to the FMA pipeline. These composite instructions are formed by the compiler and thus they reduce the total number instructions in a kernel. Composite instructions directly impact the FDS, execute and MRF power consumption of the SM and also provide a significant performance improvement.

2.2 Exploiting computational redundancy
Many GPGPU applications exhibit considerable computational redundancy. This redundancy arises when an instruction has the same result across all the threads in a single-instruction multiple-thread (SIMT) group. For many GPGPU applications, redundant computations constitute from 10% to 50% of the overall dynamic instructions. The sources of this computational redundancy are the duplicated control instructions in different threads, operations with constants, memory address

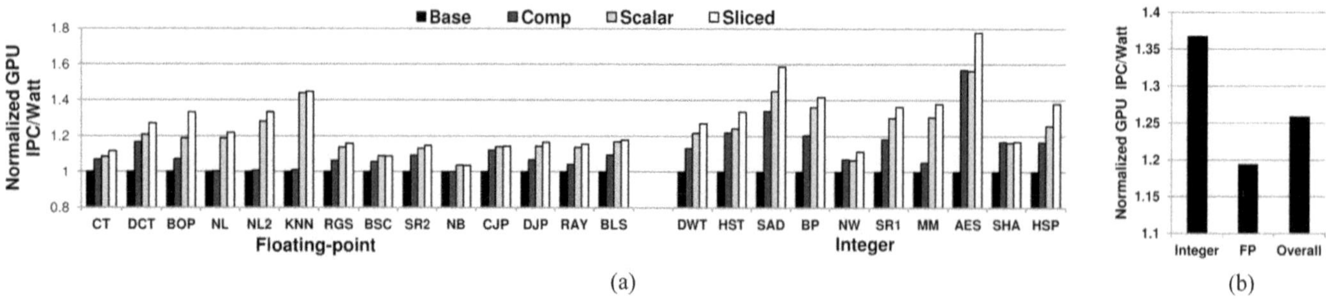

Figure 1: GPU IPC per Watt: (a) All benchmarks (b) Geometric means of benchmarks

calculations and the inherent redundancy in the pixel data in image and video processing applications.

We exploit the computational redundancy within a warp, by dynamically detecting instructions that produce the same results across all the threads in the warp. A scalar bit is added for each SIMT register in the MRF. The scalar bit is set if all physical registers within the SIMT registers contain the same value. A SIMT instruction has compute redundancy if all of its operands have the scalar bit set. These instructions are then issued to a separate scalar pipeline and their source and destination registers are kept in a separate scalar RF. The scalar pipeline provides significant performance improvements and also reduces the energy consumption due to the elimination of redundant computations and a reduction in MRF accesses. The baseline GPU assumed in this study (NVIDIA® Quadro FX5800) can issue up to two instructions per thread every cycle [8]. We utilize the same dual-issue capability for our approach, except we use it to issue computationally redundant instructions to a scalar unit for power and performance improvements.

2.3 Sliced GPU architecture

GPUs are optimized to perform operations on 32-bit data values. However, many operands do not completely utilize the 32-bit resources of the SM pipeline and MRF. This data trend can be utilized to reduce the MRF access energy and improve instruction throughput by slicing the MRF banks and the execution data-path into two 16-bit wide slices. This allows the GPU to issue two instructions with 16-bit operands instead of a single instruction with 32-bit operands, effectively improving the instruction throughput and the energy consumption of the MRF and execution units. While some GPUs provide support for 16-bit data types, these data types are used only for storage (i.e. to reduce memory bandwidth pressure). Moreover, the use of these data types requires the programmer to explicitly specify the proper data-type. Our approach dynamically detects short bit-width operands and schedules them on half bit-width slices.

3. EVALUATION

The impact of our proposed approaches on power efficiency is shown in Figure 1. Power efficiency is determined as the instructions per cycle (IPC) per Watt for the entire GPU. Due to the limited power overhead of our approaches, the performance improvements achieved improve the power efficiency of the GPU significantly. For integer benchmarks, our approaches exhibit more than 35% (geometric mean) improvement in power efficiency while for FP benchmarks the power efficiency increases by 19% (geometric mean). Across both integer and FP benchmarks, our approaches achieve more than a 25% (geometric mean) power efficiency improvement.

4. CONCLUSIONS

We proposed three techniques that significantly improve the power efficiency of GPU architectures. We exploited the resources of the execution pipeline to form composite instructions that reduced the power consumption of critical resources (FDS, MRF, EU) and also improved performance significantly. Exploiting computational redundancy with a scalar unit provided additional performance and power improvements. Finally, a sliced GPU architecture was employed to take advantage of short bit-width operands. Together, our techniques improved performance by 15% (geometric mean) and power efficiency by 25%.

REFERENCES

[1] GeForce 8800 & NVIDIA CUDA: A new architecture for computing on the GPU. [Online]. www.gpgpu.org

[2] J. Lee et al., "Improving throughput of power-constrained GPUs using dynamic voltage/frequency and core scaling," in *International Conference on Parallel Architectures and Compilation Techniques*, 2011, pp. 111-120.

[3] ITRS. (2011) International technology roadmap for semiconductors.

[4] S. Hong and H. Kim, "An integrated GPU power and performance model," in *International Symposium on Computer Architecture*, 2010, pp. 280--289.

[5] Advanced Micro Devices. Heterogeneous Computing: OpenCL™ and the ATI Radeon™ HD 5870 ("Evergreen") architecture. [Online]. http://developer.amd.com/gpu_assets/Heterogeneous_Computing_OpenCL_and_the_ATI_Radeon_HD_5870_Architecture_201003.pdf

[6] L. Seiler et al., "Larrabee: a many-core x86 architecture for visual computing," *ACM Transactions on Graphics*, vol. 27, no. 3, pp. 18:1--18:15, 2008.

[7] E. Lindholm et al., "NVIDIA Tesla: A Unified Graphics and Computing Architecture," *IEEE Micro*, vol. 28, pp. 39-55, 2008.

[8] H. Wong et al., "Demystifying GPU microarchitecture through microbenchmarking," in *IEEE International Symposium on Performance Analysis of Systems & Software (ISPASS)*, 2010, pp. 235-246.

Off-Chip Access Localization for NoC-Based Multicores*

Wei Ding
The Pennsylvania State University, University Park
wzd109@cse.psu.edu

Mahmut Kandemir
The Pennsylvania State University, University Park
kandemir@cse.psu.edu

Yuanrui Zhang
Intel
yuanrui.zhang@intel.com

Emre Kultursay
The Pennsylvania State University, University Park
euk139@cse.psu.edu

ABSTRACT

In a network-on-chip based multicore, an off-chip data access needs to travel through the on-chip network, spending considerable amount of time within the chip (in addition to the memory access itself). Further, it also causes additional delays for on-chip accesses by creating contention on network resources. In this paper, we propose a compiler-guided off-chip data access localization strategy to ensure that, an off-chip access traverses a small number of links (hops) to reach the memory controller which governs the memory bank that holds the requested data. The results collected clearly emphasize the importance of localizing off-chip accesses.

Categories and Subject Descriptors

C.4 [**Computer Systems Organization**]: Performance of Systems; B.3.2 [**Hardware**]: Memory StructuresDesign Styles

General Terms

Algorithms, Design, Experimentation, Management, Performance

Keywords

network-on-chip, data locality, memory controller, compiler

1. INTRODUCTION

As the number of cores on a single chip is increasing, designers are moving away from bus-based interconnects to *on-chip networks*. As shown in Figure 1, a state-of-the-art NoC (network-on-chip [2]) is constructed from multiple point-to-point data links connected by switches such that messages can be relayed from any source node to any destination node over several links by making routing decisions at the switches. Such a design brings several advantages from the scalability, complexity, power and reliability perspectives compared to conventional buses [2]. As a result, optimizing NoC based multicore systems has received considerable attention lately. The proposed strategies include careful design of cache access/lookup strategies [3] and on-chip accesses localization [6, 8]. While these optimizations are certainly important and can provide significant performance and power benefits, they do

*This research is supported in part by NSF grants #1213052, #1147388, #1017882, #0963839, #0720645, #0811687, #0702519, and a grant from Microsoft Corporation.

PACT'12, September 19–23, 2012, Minneapolis, Minnesota, USA.
ACM 978-1-4503-1182-3/12/09.

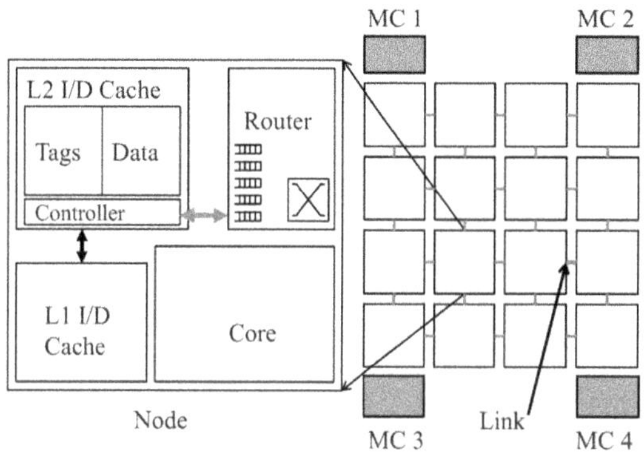

Figure 1: Basic structure of a two-dimensional 4×4 NoC based multicore with 4 memory controllers (MCs). Each node hosts a processor core, private L1 data/instruction caches, an L2 cache (bank) which can be private or shared, and a router through which it gets connected to the neighboring nodes. Physical address space is distributed across memory controllers (MC1, MC2, MC3, and MC4) by the hardware.

not have much impact on *off-chip* accesses, which can also be very important due to the following reasons:

- Since off-chip accesses must travel through the on-chip network to reach their target memory controllers, they can spend significant amount of time in the network, depending on the network congestion and the distance between the node that makes the off-chip request and the target memory controller.
- Since off-chip accesses and on-chip accesses share the same on-chip network, they contend for the same links and routers/buffers. Consequently, off-chip accesses also cause additional delays for on-chip cache accesses, further affecting the application performance.

Because of these reasons, optimizing off-chip data accesses can be very important in practice. In an NoC based multicore with per-core private L2 caches, as shown in Figure 2(a), when an L1 miss is detected, a request is sent to the local L2 cache. In case of an L2 miss, this request is forwarded to a centralized L2 tag directory, which is cached in the memory controller (MC) that the requested data is mapped to (path 1). The directory decides whether to get the data from another on-chip L2 cache (in which case we have an on-chip data access), or issue an off-chip memory request. In the latter case, the memory controller schedules this request (path 2), and the response from the corresponding memory bank is sent to the private L2 cache (path 3). Clearly, the cost of an off-chip

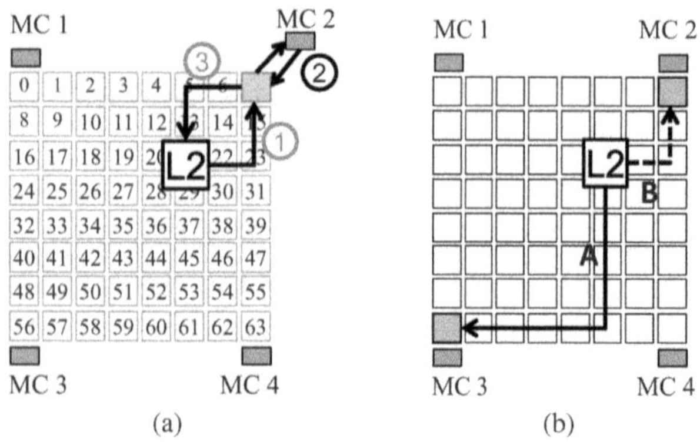

Figure 2: (a) Flow of a memory access on an NoC based multicore with private L2 caches. The number attached to a node represents its core ID. (b) The concept of off-chip access locality.

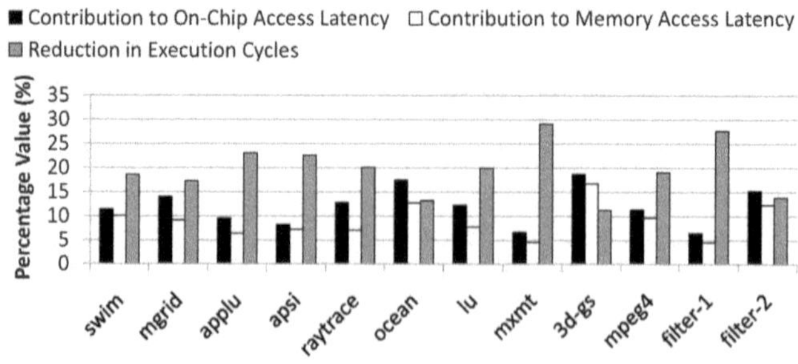

Figure 3: The impact of localized accesses on application performance (page interleaving).

access in an NoC-based system is mainly a function of two parameters: (1) the time spent in the network, and (2) the time spent in memory controller and in accessing the memory bank.[1] In fact, our initial experiments show that, in an 8×8 multicore, cumulative network latency can be comparable to the memory access latency, which means *the network latency can play a significant role in off-chip accesses.* This latency can be reduced by improving the *locality of off-chip accesses.* What we mean by "improving locality" in this context is "reducing the distance" between the requester of an off-chip data element and the memory controller that manages the block/page that holds the data. Figure 2(b) illustrates this concept in an 8×8 NoC based multicore. For the off-chip data access that follows path *A*, the distance between the requester of the data and the node that is connected to the memory controller that holds the data is 10 links, whereas the distance for the off-chip access through path *B* is only 4 links. Clearly, everything else being equal, the L2 shown in this figure would prefer to satisfy most of its off-chip data requirements from the nearest memory controller which is the one on the top-right corner. Motivated by this, we propose a compiler-guided and OS-supported data transformation and placement strategy that *improves the locality of off-chip accesses* in NoC based multicores with private last level (L2) caches.

2. DATA-TO-MC MAPPING

Note that, how physical address are mapped to controllers (e.g., cache-block interleaving versus page interleaving) is dictated by the hardware. However, a compiler-guided data transformation can either directly or indirectly (with the help of OS) control the mapping between the data and memory controller(s). In particular, a carefully designed data transformation can help to minimize the distance between the requesting cores/L2s and the memory controllers that hold requested data elements. Our proposed optimization framework consists of two components, namely, *data transformation* and *OS-level page allocation.* In the first component, we apply data transformation to rearrange the data elements on the virtual address space. In cases where a cache-block interleaving (i.e., cache-block level of distribution of physical addresses across memory controllers) is adopted, a desired mapping between data and memory controllers(s) can be achieved based on this transformed layout (such that the off-chip accesses can be localized). The second component is needed only when page interleaving is adopted. In this component, we modify the OS-level page allocation algorithm based on the layout obtained in the first component. The modified scheme assigns a physical address space for each page such that the data elements (within each page) can be mapped to the desired memory controller.

[1] The impact of this component can be reduced through smart memory controller scheduling algorithms as proposed in [4, 5], which is orthogonal to our work.

3. EXPERIMENTS

We used a set of multithreaded programs in SPECOMP [1] and SPLASH2 suites [7], with affine loops, as well as five kernel computations that are frequently used in embedded computing domain. The impact of these localized accesses on application performance is quantified in Figure 3. The first bar in this graph plots the contributions of the off-chip accesses to the on-chip access latency. We see that the average value for this parameter is about 12.1%. The second bar for each benchmark gives contributions of network latency to overall data access latency. We observe about 9.5% reduction in the value of this parameter. Finally, the last bar plots the percentage reduction (improvement) in execution latencies. Our approach saves about 18.2% performance, when averaged across all 12 application programs.

4. REFERENCES

[1] V. Aslot et al. SPEComp: A new benchmark suite for measuring parallel computer performance. *OpenMP Shared Memory Parallel Programming*, 2001.

[2] L. Benini and G. D. Micheli. *Networks on Chips: Technology and Tools.* Elsevier Inc., 2006.

[3] C. Kim et al. An adaptive, non-uniform cache structure for wire-delay dominated on-chip caches. *Proc. of ASPLOS*, 2002.

[4] Y. Kim et al. ATLAS: A scalable and high-performance scheduling algorithm for multiple memory controllers. *Proc. of HPCA*, 2010.

[5] Y. Kim et al. Thread cluster memory scheduling: Exploiting differences in memory access behavior. *Proc. of MICRO*, 2010.

[6] Q. Lu et al. Data layout transformation for enhancing data locality on NUCA chip multiprocessors. *Proc. of PACT*, 2009.

[7] S. C. Woo et al. The SPLASH-2 programs: Characterization and methodological considerations. *Proc. of ISCA*, 1995.

[8] Y. Zhang et al. A data layout optimization framework for NUCA-based multicores. *Proc. of MICRO*, 2011.

Many-Thread Aware Instruction-Level Parallelism: Architecting Shader Cores for GPU Computing

Ping Xiang, Yi Yang, Mike Mantor[#], Norm Rubin[#], Huiyang Zhou

Dept. of Electrical and Computer Engineering
North Carolina State University
Raleigh, NC,USA
{pxiang, yyang14, hzhou}@ncsu.edu

[#]Graphics Products Group
AMD Inc.
Orlando, FL, USA
{michael.mantor, norman.rubin}@amd.com

Categories and Subject Descriptors
C.1.4 [**Processor Architectures**]: Parallel Architectures

General Terms
Performance, Design, Experimentation

Keywords
GPGPU, Heterogeneous, ILP, Energy

1. INTRODUCTION

The design philosophy of many-core architectures such as graphics processing units (GPUs) is to exploit thread-level parallelism (TLP) to achieve high throughput. Compared to central processing unit (CPU) designs, GPU-like many-core architectures spend the on-die area mainly for computational/instruction execution logic rather than caches or complex instruction processing, such as register renaming and out-of-order execution, to extract instruction-level parallelism (ILP). Each core in a GPU, referred to as a shader core (SC), is a relatively simple in-order multi-threaded processor, which relies on TLP to overcome pipeline hazards. In this paper, we propose to architect SCs for GPU-like many-core processors to achieve both high performance and high energy- and area-efficiency.

We first revisit the ILP techniques for in-order processors, including data bypassing/forwarding, scoreboards, and branch prediction, to gain insight on how they interact with throughput-oriented many-core architectures. Similar to CPUs, data bypass in a GPU accelerates execution of producer and consumer instruction pairs from the same thread (warp); a scoreboard checks data independency to support the 'stall-on-use' policy, i.e., the pipeline is not stalled by a long latency instruction such as a cache miss, instead it is stalled by the consumer instruction of the loaded value; and branch prediction aims to reduce the impact of control hazards. Since GPU-like many-core architectures execute instructions in the single-instruction multiple-thread (SIMT) mode, there are new challenges and opportunities to implement these ILP techniques. We propose the many-thread aware ILP designs and analyze their impacts on performance, area, and power/energy consumption. Modern GPUs may have implemented some ILP techniques like bypass or scoreboard. But the implementation details have not been disclosed and our study provides insights to such designs. More importantly, our proposed scoreboard design supports *precise interrupts*. The reason is that with GPUs being widely used for general purpose computation, they need to support virtual memory. In addition, in the server environment, GPUs will need to provide the context switch capability in order to run multiple tasks, which also requires precise interrupts.

PACT'12, September 19–23, 2012, Minneapolis, Minnesota, USA.
ACM 978-1-4503-1182-3/12/09.

2. MANY-THREAD AWARE INSTRUCTION-LEVEL PARALLELISM FOR SHADER CORES

In this section, we present our many-thread aware ILP designs. The microarchitecture of a streaming multiprocessor (SM) in a GPU is presented in Figure 1. In an SM, there is a warp scheduler selecting and issuing instructions from 'ready' warps, meaning that the next instruction from this warp has all its dependencies resolved. Each entry in the warp scheduler contains the information of a warp. Using the program counter (PC) field, it reads the instruction from the instruction buffer. During decode, the TB id, the warp id and the thread id are used to generate the mapping from logical register numbers to physical register numbers for SCs to read from and write to the physical register file. An issued instruction will be executed by multiple SCs for all the threads in a warp. Depending on the type of the instruction, it either goes through the ALU pipeline or the memory pipeline. The ready field of a warp scheduler entry is cleared when an instruction is issued from this warp. When an instruction reaches the write back stage, it uses its warp id to set the 'ready' bit of the corresponding warp scheduler entry.

2.1 Handling Data Hazards

In pipeline designs, data bypassing is an effective way to reduce the penalty of read-after-write data hazards. In an SM of a GPU, once an instruction is issued from a warp, the same instruction will be executed by the SCs for all the threads in that warp. Given the warp size of 32 and the number of SCs as 8 in an SM, the SCs will be fully utilized if one instruction can be issued every four cycles. As a result, it presents a different tradeoff for data bypassing compared to single-threaded pipelines. Considering a pair of immediate producer ($f1 = f2 + f3$) and consumer ($f4 = f1 + f5$) instructions, these two instructions can be issued back-to-back without data bypassing if latency of the producer instruction is fewer than 4 cycles. If the producer execution latency is 4 cycles, however, the dependent instruction can only be issued when there is a data bypass path. If the producer execution latency is 8 cycles, the pipeline requires at least two warps to fully utilize the pipeline with a data bypass path. In our experiments, we assume that the ALU instructions have 8-cycle latency as it is consistent with the AMD GPUs which require two wavefronts (warps) to make the pipeline busy when there is such a producer-consumer pair in the code [1]. Note that the bypass path is within a SC ALU pipeline and there is no need to bypass data across different SCs.

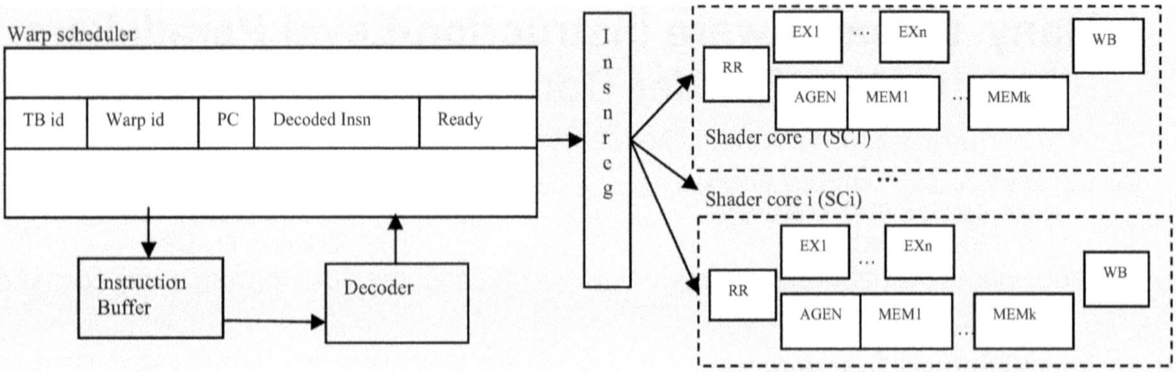

Figure 1. The microarchitecture of a streaming multiprocessor (SM) in a GPU. RR stands for register read, EX for execution, AGEN for address generation, WB for write back, multiple EX or MEM stages account for multi-cycle latency.

When a long latency instruction, such as a cache-missing load, is issued from one warp, the stall-on-use policy, i.e., issuing subsequent independent instructions from the same warp until the consumer of the loaded value, provides opportunities to hide the latency beyond leveraging the independent warps in the same SM. To support such a stall-on-use policy, the following issues need to be addressed carefully. First, as discussed in Section 1, we argue that precise interrupts are required for next generation GPUs and we need to support in-order instruction commit or write back. Second, we need an efficient way to check data dependencies to enable independent instructions to be executed. Third, as a warp contains multiple (32) threads, control divergence (i.e., not all the threads in a warp have the same control flow) complicates the handling of data dependence. We propose a cost-effective design that addresses all these challenges.

Our proposed scoreboard is a fully-associative structure with a small number of entries, maintaining the information of issued-but-not-yet-committed instructions. To support precise interrupts, outstanding instructions' execution results (or loaded values) are kept in the scoreboard rather than updating the register file out-of-order. If each warp has its own scoreboard, we can manage the scoreboard as a circular buffer, similar to the reorder buffer in CPU designs, to achieve in-order commit (i.e., update the register file in order). However, this approach adds too much overhead as an SM can support high number of concurrent warps (e.g. 32). Therefore, we propose to share the scoreboard among all the warps in an SM. Due to such sharing, we introduce the pointers in the warp scheduler and the scoreboard to maintain the order of outstanding instructions in each warp.

2.2 Handling Control Hazards

After a warp issues a branch instruction, if there are no other ready warps, it may impose a control hazard. In GPUs, control hazards have different characteristics compared to single-threaded CPUs. First, the branch target can be computed promptly in GPUs. Due to the SIMD execution mode of a warp (8 SCs executing an instruction for 32 threads), fetching one instruction in every four cycles is sufficient to keep the pipeline busy. During the 4 cycles of IF stage, the branch target can be computed. Even with 16 SCs in an SM, there are 2 cycles to generate the target. Therefore, there is no need for a branch target buffer (BTB) as commonly used in CPU designs. It also means that unconditional branches should impose no control hazards. Second, for conditional branches, branch divergence among the threads in a warp makes it friendly to branch prediction. For non-divergent branches, we study both hardware-based dynamic predictors such as gshare predictors [2] and software-based static predictors.

Our experimental results show that the ILP enhancing techniques are particularly effective for applications with high resource requirement in registers or shared memory, which limits the number of threads that can run concurrently, thereby limiting the capability for TLP to hide pipeline hazards. On the other hand, for applications that TLP alone can achieve high hardware utilization, the ILP techniques are not highly effective.

To efficiently handle such workload-dependent behavior, we also propose heterogeneous GPU-like many-core architectures, which contain two types of cores, one with the ILP techniques and the other without. This heterogeneous architecture is particularly useful for concurrent kernel execution, which is supported by latest GPUs such as NVIDIA Fermi architecture [3] for general purpose computation. When concurrent kernels have different characteristics, the heterogeneous design improves both the throughput and energy efficiency compared to homogenous GPU designs (all SCs with/without ILP enhancing techniques).

3. CONCLUSIONS

We propose many-thread aware ILP designs, including data bypassing, scoreboards, and branch prediction. We show that for applications, whose resource requirements prevent GPUs from running a sufficient number of concurrent threads, the ILP techniques can significantly improve the performance. We then propose heterogeneous GPU architectures to include both ILP cores (i.e., cores with the ILP techniques) and TLP cores (i.e., cores without them). Our results show that the proposed heterogeneous GPUs have higher performance and energy-efficiency than homogenous GPUs based on either ILP cores or TLP cores.

4. REFERENCES

[1] AMD R700-Family Instruction Set Architecture Reference Guide, February 2011.

[2] S. McFarling, Combining branch predictors, Digital Western Research Lab (WRL) Technical Report, 1993.

[3] NVIDIA CUDA Programming Guide 4.1, 2011

PS-Dir: A Scalable Two-Level Directory Cache

Joan J. Valls*, Alberto Ros†, Julio Sahuquillo*, María E. Gómez*, and José Duato*

*Department of Computer Engineering
Universitat Politècnica de València (Spain)
joavalmo@fiv.upv.es, {jsahuqui,megomez}@disca.upv.es

† Dept. de Ingeniería y Tecnología de Computadores
Universidad de Murcia (Spain)
aros@ditec.um.es

ABSTRACT

As the number of cores increases in both incoming and future chip multiprocessors, coherence protocols must address novel hardware structures in order to scale in terms of performance, power, and area. It is well known that most blocks accessed by parallel applications are private (i.e., accessed by a single core). These blocks present different directory requirements and behavior than shared blocks. Based on this fact, this paper proposes a two-level directory cache that tracks shared blocks in a small and fast first-level cache and private blocks in a larger and slower second-level cache, namely Shared and Private caches, respectively. Speed and area reasons suggest the use of eDRAM technology much dense but slower than SRAM technology for the Private cache, which in turn brings energy savings. Experimental results for a 16-core system show improvements in performance by 11.1%, in area by 25.4%, and in energy consumption by 20.5% compared to a conventional directory cache.

Categories and Subject Descriptors

B.3.2 [**Memory Structures**]: Design Styles—*Cache memories*; C.1.2 [**Processor Architectures**]: Multiple Data Stream Architectures (Multiprocessors)

Keywords: Multicore, cache coherence, directory protocol, two-level directory, private/shared blocks.

1. INTRODUCTION AND MOTIVATION

Chip-multiprocessors (CMPs) have dominated a wide spectrum of the microprocessor market, ranging from embedded to supercomputers, since a few years ago. The on-chip core counts in CMPs have rapidly grown and it is expected to reach several hundreds of cores in the following years [1]. Most CMPs allow the shared memory programming model and implement a cache coherence protocol to maintain data coherence among the processor caches. The use of directory-based protocols is the commonly preferred approach, since this approach represents the most scalable alternative by keeping track of every cached memory block in the system to avoid broadcasting messages.

Traditionally, directory caches have kept track of both shared and private blocks all together. However, both types of blocks have different requirements in terms of area and latency. First, directory entries of shared blocks are accessed by several cores while entries of private blocks are accessed

PACT'12, September 19–23, 2012, Minneapolis, Minnesota, USA.
ACM 978-1-4503-1182-3/12/09.

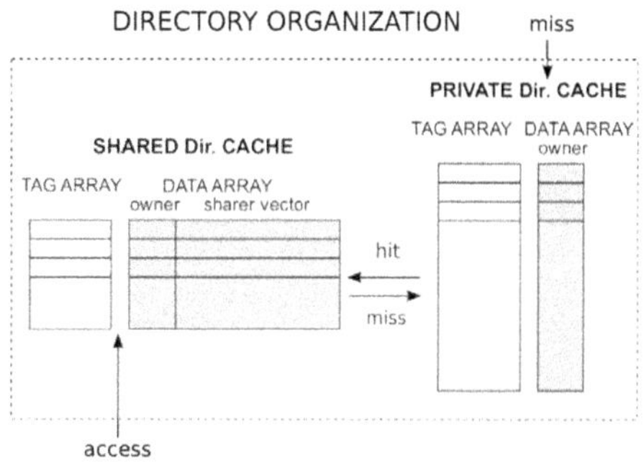

Figure 1: Private-Shared directory organization.

only in they are evicted from the processor cache and requested again. Second, to keep track of private blocks, the area-demanding sharing vector is not required. Finally, as recently stated [2], most of the accessed blocks in parallel workloads are private.

In this paper we propose a novel directory cache organization which discerns between private and shared blocks. PS-Dir (Private/Shared Directory) is organized in two independent caches, namely the Private cache and the Shared cache, aimed at tracking coherence of private and shared blocks, respectively. The Shared cache is designed with the same fields as a typical directory cache but with much lower number of entries, attending to the low fraction of expected shared blocks; but fast due to the high lookup rate expected. In contrast, the Private cache has a higher number of entries but it does not includes a sharing vector, thus allowing scalability. Additionally, while the Shared cache should be implemented in typical SRAM technology for speed reasons, the Private cache can use eDRAM technology [5], which although slower, it incurs less energy consumption and area than SRAM. eDRAM technology has been already used to implement large caches in some recent commercial processors like the IBM Power7 [3].

Experimental results for a 16-core CMP show that PS-Dir improves performance by 11.1% compared to a conventional directory due to the separate treatment of private and shared blocks, while reducing its area by 18.85%. In addition, when eDRAM technology is considered for the Private cache this area reduction becomes 25.39%. In terms of energy, PS-Dir allows energy savings by 20.5%.

2. THE PRIVATE/SHARED DIRECTORY

Figure 1 depicts the proposed organization consisting of the Private cache and the Shared cache, as well as the main fields required for each cache structure. As observed, both the height (number of entries) and the width (bits per entry) of both directory caches differ. The different height is because most of the blocks are private, so the Private cache has been designed with more entries. The width differs because the sharer vector, whose size does not scale with the core count, is only implemented in the small Shared cache.

The proposal considers the Private cache as the default cache, that is, on a directory miss the block is assumed to be private and fetched into the Private cache. On subsequent accesses to a private block, the processor will find it in its L1 cache (in case of no eviction), so no additional directory access will be done. On the other hand, when a private block is removed from the processor cache, the protocol can invalidate the associated directory entry. Thus, a subsequent access to that block would result in a directory miss. This means that the Private cache access time does not affect the performance of private blocks since these blocks are provided directly to cores by the NUCA slice or main memory.

If a block in the Private cache is accessed by a core other than the owner, the block becomes shared and therefore, it is moved to the Shared cache and the sharing vector is updated accordingly. From then on and until eviction, coherence of this block is tracked in the Shared cache. Evictions from the Shared cache are removed from the directory.

The proposal reduces area by design with respect to conventional caches since entries in the Private cache are narrower. In addition power is also reduced by accessing smaller cache structures sequentially. Nevertheless, the use of two independent organizations with different design goals (speed for the Shared and capacity for the Private) suggests that the use of specific technologies could provide our proposal further energy and area savings. This work explores the use of eDRAM technology in the Private cache which leads to important area and leakage savings.

3. EXPERIMENTAL EVALUATION

The proposal has been evaluated with full-system simulation using Virtutech Simics, the GEMS toolkit [4], and a wide range of scientific applications from both the SPLASH-2 and the PARSEC benchmark suite. We simulate a 16-tile CMP with 2-cycle, 64KB, 4-way L1 instruction and data caches, and a shared (NUCA) LLC cache with 512KB and 8-way per tile. Each LLC bank is accessed in 6 cycles (2 for accessing only the tags).

Different configurations for PS-Dir have been evaluated and compared to a conventional directory (*single cache* configuration) with the same number of entries as an L1 processor cache, i.e., 1× coverage ratio. The coverage ratio indicates the number of directory entries per processor cache entry. Different coverage ratios have been evaluated ranging from 1× to 0.125×. We used the CACTI 6.5 toolto estimate access time, area requirements, and power consumption of the different cache structures for a 32nm technology node.

Performance. Every time a directory entry is evicted, invalidation messages are sent to processor caches for coherence purposes. These invalidations will cause *coverage* misses upon a subsequent memory request to those blocks, impacting on the final performance. Reductions in the number of coverage misses translate into improvements in execution time. As observed in Figure 2, a PS-Dir with a 1× coverage ratio reduces execution time on average by 11.1%. Alternatively, if reducing silicon area is a design goal, one can opt for reducing the area overhead of the directory with-

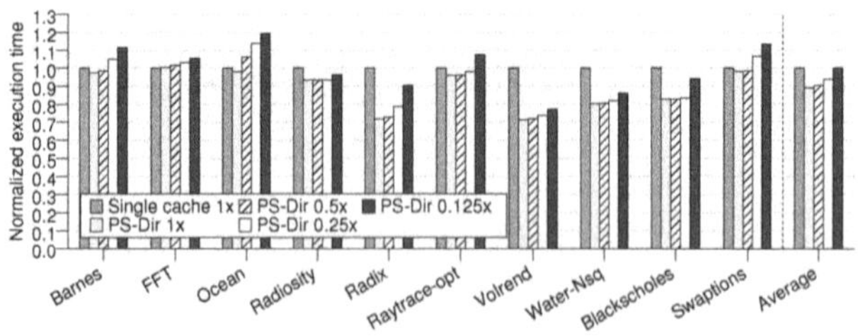

Figure 2: Normalized performance with respect to a conventional single-cache directory.

out losing performance. The 0.125× PS-Dir achieves the same performance as a single cache.

Area. PS-Dir reduces area even for the 1× configuration. This is because the Private cache does not include a sharing vector. In fact, the 1× PS-Dir with the SRAM Private cache saves 18.8% of area compared to the single cache. In addition, when eDRAM technology is considered these reductions increase up to 25.4%. Moreover, when the directory coverage ratio is reduced (0.5× and 0.25×), area savings significantly increase up to 80.2% for the 0.25× configuration, while still improving the system performance.

Energy. The PS directory also attacks by design the energy consumption, specially leakage, due to its area reduction. The 1× and 0.5× PS-Dir configurations consume more dynamic energy per access than the conventional cache, but this is highly offset by the much lower leakage consumed. Leakage is reduced from 19% for the SRAM 1× PS-Dir up to 86% for the eDRAM 0.25× PS-Dir. Regarding total directory energy, the 1× PS-Dir can save around 20.5% of the energy consumption of the single cache directory. Smaller coverage ratios lead to less energy consumed at the cost of performance degradation.

4. CONCLUSIONS

This work proposes the PS directory, which uses two different directory cache structures tailored to the behavior of the blocks they track: the Shared directory cache, aimed at keeping track of shared blocks is small and fast, and a larger Private directory cache, aimed at tracking private blocks, which does not store the sharing vector. Compared to a single directory cache with the same number of entries and considering a 16-core system, the PS directory improves performance by 11.1%, area by 25.4%, and energy by 27%.

5. ACKNOWLEDGMENTS

This work has been supported by the Spanish MICINN, as well as European Commission FEDER funds, under Grants CSD2006-00046 and TIN2009-14475-C04.

6. REFERENCES

[1] S. Bell, et al. TILE64™ processor: A 64-core SoC with mesh interconnect. In *ISSCC*, pages 88–598, Jan. 2008.

[2] B. Cuesta, A. Ros, M. E. Gómez, A. Robles, and J. Duato. Increasing the effectiveness of directory caches by deactivating coherence for private memory blocks. In *38th ISCA*, pages 93–103, June 2011.

[3] R. Kalla, B. Sinharoy, W. J. Starke, and M. Floyd. Power7: IBM's Next-Generation Server Processor. *IEEE Micro*, 30:7–15, 2010.

[4] M. M. Martin, et al. Multifacet's general execution-driven multiprocessor simulator (GEMS) toolset. *Computer Architecture News*, 33(4):92–99, Sept. 2005.

[5] R. E. Matick and S. E. Schuster. Logic-based eDRAM: Origins and rationale for use. *IBM Journal of Research and Development*, 49(1):145–165, 2005.

Inference and Declaration of Independence: Impact on Deterministic Task Parallelism*

Foivos S. Zakkak, Dimitrios Chasapis, Polyvios Pratikakis, Angelos Bilas
Institute of Computer Science, Foundation for Research and Technology—Hellas
Heraklion, Crete, Greece

Dimitrios S. Nikolopoulos
School of EEECS, Queen's University of Belfast, Belfast, Northern Ireland, UK

ABSTRACT

We present a set of static techniques that reduce runtime overheads in task-parallel programs with implicit synchronization. We use a static dependence analysis to detect non-conflicting tasks and remove unnecessary runtime checks. We further reduce overheads by statically optimizing task creation and management of runtime metadata. We implemented these optimizations in SCOOP, a source-to-source compiler for such a programming model and runtime system. We evaluate SCOOP on 10 representative benchmarks and show that our approach can improve performance by 12% on average.

Categories and Subject Descriptors

D.3.4 [**Programming Languages**]: Optimization

Keywords

task parallelism; static analysis

1. INTRODUCTION

Thread-based programming is a low-level abstraction for describing parallel computations, close to the underlying hardware model of processor cores and communication via shared memory variables. Multithreaded programs require the programmer to reason about all thread interactions and manually synchronize conflicting threads, which is difficult and error prone. Task-based parallelism offers a higher level abstraction to the programmer, making it easier to express parallel computation. Early task-parallel programming models, such as Cilk and OpenMP raise the level of abstraction for expressing parallelism, but still require explicit synchronization. Recent task-based programming models use implicit synchronization, using a task's memory footprint, either inferred by the system or declared by the programmer, to avoid concurrent accesses, or even achieve fully deterministic execution [1, 4].

Statically prohibiting concurrent access to shared memory among parallel tasks is too restrictive, as in many cases only a few instances of conflicting tasks will actually conflict. For this reason, even existing statically verifiable non-dependent task models relax the requirement for strictly non-overlapping task memory footprints. Instead, they use dynamic techniques to detect and correct conflicts at runtime [2].

However, dynamic dependence analysis incurs a high overhead compared to hand-crafted synchronization. It requires a complex runtime system to manage and track memory allocation, check for conflicts, and schedule parallel tasks. Often, the runtime cost of checking for conflicts in pessimistic, or rolling back a task in optimistic runtimes becomes itself a bottleneck, limiting the achievable speedup.

This work aims to alleviate the overhead of dynamic dependence analysis without sacrificing the benefit of implicit synchronization. We use a static dependence analysis to detect and remove runtime dependence checks when unnecessary. We make the following contributions:

- We develop a static analysis that detects independent task arguments and reduces runtime overhead in task-parallel programs with implicit synchronization.
- We implement our analysis in SCOOP, a compiler that extends C with parallel tasks and task-footprint annotations, similar to OpenMP and SMPSs [3]. SCOOP targets the BDDT runtime dependence analysis, improving its performance by inferring and removing unnecessary runtime checks.
- We evaluate the efficiency and precision of the analysis on a representative set of task-parallel benchmarks. SCOOP found 28 out of 31 independent task-arguments in all benchmarks, improving performance by 12% on average and by up to 40%.

2. DESIGN AND IMPLEMENTATION

We have implemented our analysis in SCOOP, a compiler for task-parallel programs with implicit synchronization. We use the BDDT runtime system to schedule tasks and perform the runtime dependence checks that cannot be statically eliminated.

SCOOP is structured as three modules. The first extends the C front-end with support for OpenMP-like `#pragma` directives to define tasks and SMPSs-like syntax to define task footprints. The syntax for declaring task footprints supports strided memory access patterns, so that we can describe multidimensional array tiles as task arguments. When not explicitly given, we assume that the size of a task argument is the size of its type.

*The research leading to these results has received funding from the European Community's Seventh Framework Programme [FP7/2007-2013] under the ENCORE Project (www.encore-project.eu), grant agreement n° 248647.

PACT'12, September 19–23, 2012, Minneapolis, Minnesota, USA.
ACM 978-1-4503-1182-3/12/09.

Benchmark	LOC	Tasks	Total Args	Scalar Args	Analysis Time (s)	Graph Nodes	Safe Args	BDDT (ms)	SCOOP (ms)	Speedup
Black-Scholes	3564	1	8	1	3.17	1790	7	1618	963	1.68
Ferret	30145	1	2	0	699.05	85128	2	3344	3344	1.00
Cholesky	1734	4	16	8	1.06	7571	0	983	981	1.00
GMRES	2661	18	72	20	2.21	7957	9	16640	13947	1.19
HPL	2442	11	63	35	1.47	9330	0	1628	1574	1.03
Jacobi	1084	1	6	0	0.74	3980	0	11499	11588	0.99
SMPSs-FFT	2278	8	36	25	1.17	9270	0	1077	1042	1.03
SPLASH-FFT	2935	4	12	4	1.72	9750	7	2028	1849	1.10
Multisort	1215	2	8	4	1.02	4016	0	3683	3446	1.07
Intruder	6452	1	5	1	19.89	16855	3	12572	10332	1.22

Table 1: Benchmark description, analysis performance, and impact on execution

The second SCOOP module uses a type-system to generate points-to and control flow constraints, and then solves them to infer argument independence. To increase the analysis precision, we use a context-sensitive, field sensitive points-to analysis, and a context-sensitive control flow analysis. Moreover, in several benchmarks tasks within loops access disjoint parts of the same array. However, the points-to analysis treats all array elements as one abstract location, producing false aliasing and causing such safe arguments to be missed. To rectify this, in part, we have implemented a simple loop-dependence analysis that discovers when different loop iterations access non-overlapping array elements. This (orthogonal) problem has been extensively studied in the past, resulting in many techniques that can be applied to improve the precision of this optimization.

The final SCOOP phase transforms the input program to use BDDT for creating tasks, disabling BDDT's runtime dependence checks for inferred or declared independent arguments. During code generation, we optimize the output code by producing custom code to interact with the dependence analysis and scheduler, instead of using generic BDDT API calls. This way, SCOOP is able to optimize away loops, `va_args`, some conditionals, and treat scalar arguments specially (by value), further reducing the runtime overhead of creating a task, compared to a generic API for task creation.

BDDT uses a region-based allocator to support dynamic memory allocation in tasks, and allow for tasks that operate on complex data structures. Hence, SCOOP handles task footprints that include dynamic regions specially. Specifically, the task footprint language allows several task arguments to belong to a dynamic region; the task footprint then includes the region instead of the individual arguments, and SCOOP registers only the region descriptor with the dependence analysis.

3. EVALUATION

We evaluate SCOOP on 10 benchmarks and measure the precision and performance of the analysis, as well as the impact of the resulting optimization on execution time and scalability. The left part of Table 1 shows the characterization of each benchmark. The first columns show the size of the source code processed by SCOOP, the number of static task definitions, the number of the total arguments used by the tasks, and the number of the scalar arguments, which are not processed by the static analysis, respectively.

The middle part of Table 1 shows the performance and precision of the static analysis. Namely, the next three columns show the total running time of the static dependence analysis, the number of nodes in the constraint graph, and the number of independent task arguments inferred by the analysis. Note that Ferret, the largest benchmark, creates the largest constraint graph, causing an analysis time of over 11 minutes, as context sensitive analysis is cubic in the size of the constraint graph. To assess the precision of the analysis, we manually examined all benchmarks for independent arguments. We discovered three additional task arguments we believe are independent in GMRES. SCOOP fails to detect these because GMRES uses complex array indexing expressions that cannot be handled by the simple "doall" analysis implemented in SCOOP.

The right part of Table 1 shows the effect of SCOOP on the total running time of all benchmarks on 32 cores. Specifically, the last three columns show the total running time in milliseconds when using BDDT to perform runtime dependence analysis on all task arguments of all tasks, the total running time for the benchmark compiled with SCOOP, where the runtime dependence analysis is disabled for any arguments found safe by the static analysis, and the speedup factor gained by applying SCOOP for each benchmark.

Overall, the average performance improvement from applying SCOOP on all benchmarks is 12%, although this value is not representative, as actual impact greatly varies among benchmarks; the dependence analysis is able to infer safe task arguments only in Black-Scholes, Ferret, GMRES, SPLASH-FFT and Intruder. In these benchmarks, inferring independent arguments has a large impact on the overhead and scalability of the dependence analysis, producing substantial speedup over the original BDDT versions for four benchmarks. The reduction of dependence analysis overhead is not noticeable in Ferret because the tasks are very coarse grain. On the other hand, the analysis did not discover any safe task arguments in the other five benchmarks, which do not gain any significant benefit from SCOOP, other than that resulting from custom code generation.

4. REFERENCES

[1] M. J. Best et al. Synchronization via scheduling: Techniques for efficiently managing shared state. In PLDI'11.

[2] R. L. Bocchino et al. Safe nondeterminism in a deterministic-by-default parallel language. In *POPL*, 2011.

[3] J. Perez et al. A dependency-aware task-based programming environment for multi-core architectures. In *ICCC*, 2008.

[4] G. Tzenakis et al. BDDT: block-level dynamic dependence analysis for deterministic task-based parallelism. In *PPoPP*. Poster paper.

Application-to-Core Mapping Policies to Reduce Memory Interference in Multi-Core Systems

Reetuparna Das* Rachata Ausavarungnirun† Onur Mutlu† Akhilesh Kumar‡ Mani Azimi‡
*University of Michigan †Carnegie Mellon University ‡Intel Labs
reetudas@umich.edu rachata, onur@cmu.edu akhilesh.kumar, mani.azimi@intel.com

Abstract

How applications running on a many-core system are mapped to cores largely determines the interference between these applications in critical shared resources. This paper proposes application-to-core mapping policies to improve system performance by reducing inter-application interference in the on-chip network and memory controllers. The major new ideas of our policies are to: 1) map network-latency-sensitive applications to separate parts of the network from network-bandwidth-intensive applications such that the former can make fast progress without heavy interference from the latter, 2) map those applications that benefit more from being closer to the memory controllers close to these resources. Our evaluations show that both ideas significantly improve system throughput, fairness and interconnect power efficiency.

Categories and Subject Descriptors: C.1.2[Computer Systems Organization] Multiprocessors; Interconnection architectures; C.1.4[Parallel Architectures] Distributed architectures
General Terms: Design, Algorithms, Performance
Keywords: Multicore, scheduling, interconnect, memory

1. INTRODUCTION

One important use of multi-core systems is to concurrently run many diverse applications. Managing critical shared resources, such as the on-chip network (NoC), among co-scheduled applications is a fundamental challenge. In a large many-core processor, which core is selected to execute an application could have a significant impact on system performance because it affects contention and interference among applications. Performance of an application critically depends on how its network packets *interfere* with other applications' packets in the interconnect and memory, and how far away it is executing from shared resources such as memory controllers.

While prior research (e.g., [9, 14, 13]) tackled the problem of how to map tasks/threads *within* an application onto cores, the interference behavior *between* applications in the NoC is less well understood. Current operating systems are unaware of the on-chip interconnect topology and application interference characteristics at any instant of time, and employ naive methods while mapping applications to cores. For instance, Linux 2.6.x [1] assigns a static numbering to cores and chooses the numerically-smallest core when allocating an idle core to an application. This leads to an application-to-core mapping that is oblivious to application characteristics and inter-application interference, causing two major problems.

First, overall performance degrades when applications that interfere significantly with each other get mapped to closeby cores. Second, an application may benefit significantly from being mapped to a core that is close to a shared resource (e.g., a memory controller), yet it can be mapped far away from that resource (while another application that does not benefit from being close to the resource is mapped closeby the resource), reducing system performance. To solve these two problems, in this work, we develop intelligent application-to-core mapping policies that are aware of application characteristics and on-chip interconnect topology.

PACT'12, September 19–23, 2012, Minneapolis, Minnesota, USA.
ACM 978-1-4503-1182-3/12/09.

2. OVERVIEW OF MAPPING POLICIES

Our policies are built upon two major observations. First, we observe some applications are more *sensitive* to interference than others: when interfered with, network-sensitive applications slow down more significantly than others [3]. Thus, system performance can be improved by separating (i.e., mapping far away) network-sensitive applications from aggressive applications that have high demand for network bandwidth.

Second, an application that is *both memory-intensive and network-sensitive* gains more performance from being close to a memory controller than one that does not have either of the properties (as the former needs fast, high-bandwidth memory access). Thus, system performance can be improved by mapping such applications to cores close to memory controllers.

We sketch our proposed mapping schemes with illustrations. Detailed descriptions of our policies can be found in a technical report [5]. Figure 1(a) shows the logical layout of a many-core processor interconnected with an 8x8 mesh NoC. Corner tiles consist of the memory controllers (triangles). Every other tile consists of a core, L1 cache and L2 cache bank. We divide the 8x8 mesh into four 4x4 clusters (marked by dotted lines).

1. Clustering In our policies, cores are clustered into subnetworks to reduce interference between applications mapped to different clusters. Applications mapped to a cluster predominantly access the memory controller within that cluster (and share the L2 cache slices within that cluster). To enable this, the system software's page mapping policies should be changed [5]. Clustering not only reduces interference between applications mapped to different clusters, but also 1) reduces overall congestion in the network, 2) reduces average distance packets traverse to get to the memory controllers or shared caches. Our results show most of the NoC packets of an application can be restricted to the application's cluster, with our page mapping algorithm, called Cluster-CLOCK [5].

2. Mapping Policy between Clusters An important question is which applications should be mapped to which clusters, as the answer affects which applications contend with each other. To illustrate the importance of this, Figure 1(b), (c), (d) show three possible application-to-core mappings. Each core tile in the figure is shaded according to the network intensity of the application: a darker tile corresponds to an application with a higher *L1 misses per thousand instructions (MPKI)*, i.e., a more network-intensive one. Figure 1(b) shows a possible random mapping of applications to clusters (called RND). This mapping is exemplary of policies usually employed in existing general-purpose systems. Unfortunately, it does not take into account 1) how applications mapped to the same cluster would interfere with each other, 2) balance of network and memory load across clusters, and as a result leads to high contention and relatively low system performance.

Figure 1(c) illustrates an example of a *balanced* mapping (called BL), which equally divides the network load among clusters. The idea is to distribute applications to clusters such that the sum of MPKIs in each cluster is similar across clusters. BL can achieve better performance than RND as it more effectively utilizes NoC and memory bandwidth. However, we find BL is not the best-performing mapping because it can map network-sensitive applications to the same cluster as network-intensive ones, leading to significant interference against, and thus slowdowns for, network-sensitive applications.

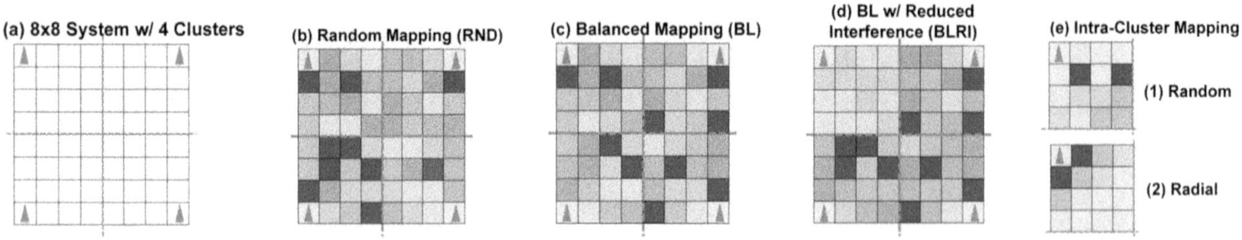

Figure 1: Visual examples of clustering and different inter-cluster and intra-cluster mapping policies

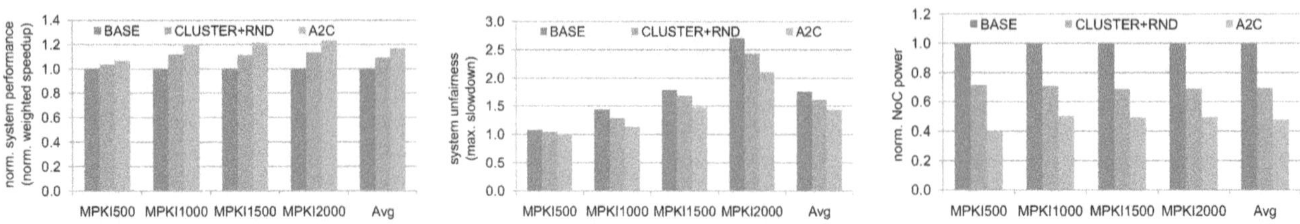

Figure 2: (a) System performance (b) system unfairness and (c) interconnect power of A2C for 128 workloads

Our proposal, *Balanced mapping with Reduced Interference (BLRI)* is shown in Figure 1(d). BLRI attempts to protect interference-sensitive applications from others by assigning them their own cluster (the top left cluster) while trying to preserve load balance in the rest of the network (i.e., among more network-intensive applications). BLRI can improve performance significantly because it can keep the slowdowns of the most latency-sensitive applications under control.

3. Mapping Policy within a Cluster After mapping applications to different clusters, a question remains: *which core within a cluster* should an application be mapped to? Figure 1(e) shows two possible intra-cluster mappings for a single cluster. *Random* mapping is not the best as it is agnostic to application characteristics. In contrast, our proposed mapping (*Radial*), places applications radially in concentric circles around the memory controller in decreasing order of a metric that considers both network-intensity and network sensitivity of an application. Darker (inner and closer) tiles represent network-intensive and interference-sensitive applications; lighter (outer and farther) tiles represent lower intensity applications with low sensitivity. We found the former type of applications benefit from being close to the memory controller, and this policy therefore improves performance.

Putting It All Together Our final policy, A2C, operates periodically by invoking the above three steps in order. It uses BLRI mapping across clusters and Radial mapping within a cluster. Our technical report [5] provides the policy details, examines tradeoffs, and describes implementation issues.

3. EVALUATION

We evaluate A2C using an instruction-trace-driven, cycle-level x86 CMP simulator [3, 4, 5] that models cores (with limited instruction window), interconnect, and memory. Our baseline configuration has 60 cores and 4 memory controllers connected with a 2D, 8x8 mesh NoC. We also use a detailed functional model for virtual memory management to study page access and page fault behavior of our workloads. The baseline page allocation and replacement policy is CLOCK [10]. We use our Cluster-CLOCK policy [5] to enforce clustering, which slightly reduces the page fault rate (an effect *not* included in performance results presented below).

We evaluate three systems: 1) the baseline with random mapping of applications to cores without clustering (BASE), 2) our enhanced system using clustering and Cluster-CLOCK, and random mapping of applications to cores (CLUSTER+RND), 3) our final system with A2C. We evaluate 128 multiprogrammed workloads of 35 diverse applications. Workloads are categorized into four groups based on their network intensity measured in terms of last-level cache MPKI.

Figures 2(a) and 2(b) respectively show system performance (higher is better) and system unfairness [11] (lower is better). Solely using clustering (CLUSTER+RND) improves weighted speedup by 9.3% over the baseline (BASE). A2C improves weighted speedup by 16.7% over the baseline, while reducing unfairness by 22%. Figure 2(c) shows the normalized average interconnect power consumption (lower is better). Clustering reduces power consumption by 31.2% over baseline; A2C by 52.3%. The clustering of traffic to memory controllers, reduced inter-application interference with A2C, and mapping network-intensive applications close to memory controllers altogether largely reduce the average hop count, and hence the energy spent in moving data over the interconnect.

4. CONCLUSION

We showed that mapping applications to cores in a manner that is aware of applications' characteristics significantly improves system performance, fairness, and energy-efficiency. Our policies are synergistic with interference reduction methods in NoC (e.g., [3, 7, 4, 16, 8]) and memory (e.g., [12, 2, 6, 15]), and we intend to examine this interaction in future work.

References

[1] Linux source code (version 2.6.39). http://www.kernel.org.

[2] M. Awasthi et al. Handling the problems and opportunities posed by multiple on-chip memory controllers. In *PACT-19*, 2010.

[3] R. Das et al. Application-Aware Prioritization Mechanisms for On-Chip Networks. In *MICRO-42*, 2009.

[4] R. Das et al. Aergia: Exploiting packet latency slack in on-chip networks. In *ISCA-37*, 2010.

[5] R. Das et al. Application-to-core mapping policies to reduce interference in on-chip networks. In *Carnegie Mellon SAFARI Technical Report No. 2011-001*, 2011.

[6] E. Ebrahimi et al. Fairness via source throttling: A configurable and high-performance fairness substrate for multi-core memory systems. In *ASPLOS-XV*, 2010.

[7] B. Grot et al. Preemptive Virtual Clock: A Flexible, Efficient, and Cost-effective QOS Scheme for Networks-on-a-Chip. In *MICRO-42*, 2009.

[8] B. Grot et al. A QoS-Enabled On-Die Interconnect Fabric for Kilo-Node Chips. *IEEE Micro*, May/June 2012.

[9] J. Hu et al. Energy-aware mapping for tile-based NoC architectures under performance constraints. In *ASPDAC*, 2003.

[10] S. Jiang et al. CLOCK-Pro: an effective improvement of the CLOCK replacement. In *USENIX*, 2005.

[11] Y. Kim et al. ATLAS: A scalable and high-performance scheduling algorithm for multiple memory controllers. In *HPCA-16*, 2010.

[12] Y. Kim et al. Thread cluster memory scheduling: Exploiting differences in memory access behavior. In *MICRO-43*, 2010.

[13] T. Lei and S. Kumar. A two-step genetic algorithm for mapping task graphs to a network on chip architecture. In *Euromicro*, 2003.

[14] S. Murali and G. D. Micheli. Bandwidth-constrained mapping of cores onto NoC architectures. In *DATE*, 2004.

[15] S. Muralidhara et al. Reducing memory interference in multi-core systems via application-aware memory channel partitioning. In *MICRO-44*, 2011.

[16] G. Nychis et al. Next generation on-chip networks: What kind of congestion control do we need? In *HotNets-9*, 2010.

Bandwidth Bandit: Quantitative Characterization of Memory Contention

David Eklov, Nikos Nikoleris, David Black-Schaffer and Erik Hagersten
Uppsala University, Department of Information Technology
{david.eklov, nikos.nikoleris, david.black-schaffer, erik.hagersten}@it.uu.se

ABSTRACT

Applications that are co-scheduled on a multi-core compete for shared resources, such as cache capacity and memory bandwidth. The performance degradation resulting from this contention can be substantial, which makes it important to effectively manage these shared resources. This, however, requires quantitative insight into how applications are impacted by such contention.

In this paper we present a quantitative method to measure applications' sensitivities to different degrees of contention for off-chip memory bandwidth on real hardware. We then use the data captured with our profiling method to estimate the throughput of a set of co-running instances of a single threaded application.

Categories and Subject Descriptors: C.4 [Performance of Systems]: Modeling techniques

General Terms: Measurement, Performance

Keywords: Memory contention, Performance Prediction

1. APPLICATION SENSITIVITY TO MEMORY CONTENTION

Previous work [1, 3] has highlighted the correlation between an application's off-chip bandwidth demand and its sensitivity to memory contention. To investigate this we profiled seven benchmarks on a quad core Intel Xeon E5520 machine. We picked five benchmarks from SPEC CPU2006 and two from PARSEC which have high bandwidth demands. First, we ran them in isolation and measured their baseline IPC and off-chip bandwidth. Second, we co-ran them with a stress application that consumes bandwidth but no other shared resources (e.g., cache capacity) and measured their slowdowns. The stress application's access rate was configured such that the total bandwidth reaches 90% of the system's saturation bandwidth. Figure 1 shows the benchmarks' slowdowns and their baseline bandwidths.

The graph in Figure 1(a) shows hardly any correlation between the slowdowns and the baseline bandwidths. For example, Canneal and Streamcluster have the lowest (but different) baseline bandwidths, but large (and very similar) slowdowns, while Lbm and Soplex have virtually the same baseline bandwidth, but very different slowdowns. The graph in Figure 1(b) shows the correlation between the slowdowns and the corresponding baseline IPCs. This graph

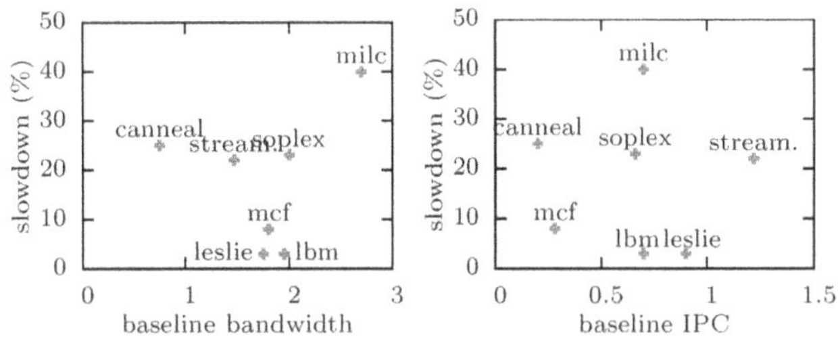

Figure 1: Correlation of slowdown under memory contention with baseline bandwidth (left) and IPC (right). Both baseline bandwidth and performance are poor indicators of sensitivity to memory contention.

shows even less correlation. Neither the baseline bandwidth nor the baseline IPC are good indicators of an application's sensitivity to memory contention.

From a performance point of view the memory hierarchy can be described by two metrics: its latency and bandwidth. These two metrics are intimately related. Using Little's law, the average bandwidth achieved by an application can be expressed as follows:

$$bandwidth = transfer\_size \times \frac{MLP}{latency}, \qquad (1)$$

where MLP is the average Memory Level Parallelism, that is, the average number of concurrent memory requests it has in-flight, and *latency* is the average time to complete the application's memory accesses. The above equation clearly illustrates that the bandwidth consumed by an application is determined by both its memory access *latency* and its memory *parallelism*. While the bandwidth of an application largely determines how much contention it generates, its sensitivity to off-chip memory contention is instead determined by its *latency-* and *bandwidth-sensitivity*.

The fact that an application's performance can be limited by either latency, bandwidth or both is widely understood. However, it is not always obvious when and by how much these factors impact application performance. To this end we introduce the Bandwidth Bandit, a general, quantitative, profiling method which enables us to measure how an application's performance is impacted by contention for shared off-chip memory resources, and determine the application's degree of latency- and bandwidth-sensitivity.

2. THE BANDWIDTH BANDIT

The Bandwidth Bandit works by co-running the application whose performance we want to measure (the *Target*)

PACT'12, September 19–23, 2012, Minneapolis, Minnesota, USA.
ACM 978-1-4503-1182-3/12/09.

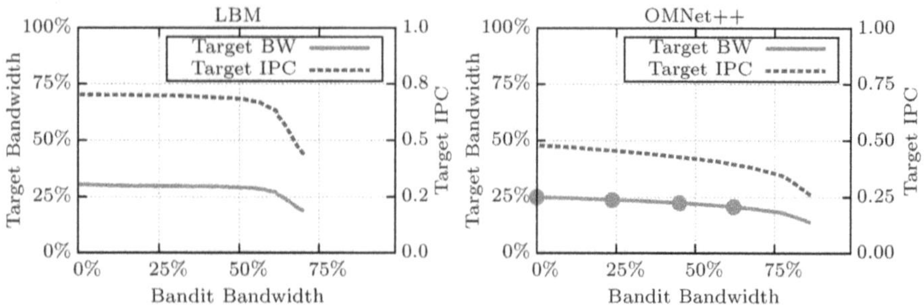

Figure 2: Bandwidth Bandit data: Performance and bandwidth as a function of memory contention.The slope of the IPC data indicates the application's sensitivity to memory contention. Bandwidths are presented as a percentage of the saturation bandwidth.

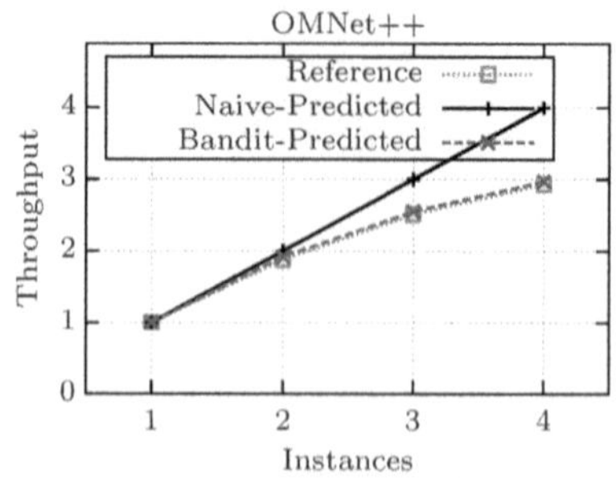

Figure 3: Normalized throughput.

with a *Bandit* application that generates contention for the shared off-chip memory resources. Importantly, the Bandit does not consume any other shared resources, such as cache capacity. This allows us to study the impact of contention for off-chip memory resources in isolation. To accomplish this, the Bandit accesses memory at a specified rate and in a controlled pattern that ensures that it generates the desired amount and type of contention. By measuring the Target's performance while varying the amount of contention generated by the Bandit, we obtain the Target's performance as function of contention for memory resources. A detailed discussion of how to implement the Bandit application can be found in [2].

2.1 Results

Figure 2 shows the data obtained using the Bandwidth Bandit on a quad core Intel Xeon E5520 (Nehalem) machine for two SPEC2006 benchmarks: Lbm and OMNet++. Lbm's bandwidth and IPC are virtually flat up to the point where the total bandwidth (Target + Bandit) levels off, which indicates that the off-chip bandwidth has saturated. Beyond the point where the bandwidth saturates, Lbm's bandwidth and IPC decrease proportionally to the amount of bandwidth the bandit steals. This indicates that Lbm is initially latency-insensitive but becomes bandwidth-sensitive when the off-chip bandwidth saturates. On the other hand, OMNet++'s bandwidth and IPC start to decrease almost immediately, long before the bandwidth saturates. This indicates that it is latency-sensitive.

3. ESTIMATING THROUGHPUT

In this section we show how the data obtained with the Bandwidth Bandit can be used to estimate the throughput of a set of co-running instances of a single threaded application.

When co-running multiple instances of the same application, all instances get an equal amount of bandwidth. Therefore, finding how much bandwidth one of the co-running instances gets, amounts to finding the (x, y)-point on its bandwidth graph where $y = x$, $y = 2x$ and $y = 3x$ for two, three and four co-running instances, respectively. These equations can be easily solved using standard fixed-point methods. The solutions of are marked with circles in Figure 2(b).

To find the IPC of one of the co-running instances, we first compute the total bandwidth of its co-runners, T (the sum of their individual bandwidths). Then, we use the first instance's IPC curve to find its IPC when its co-runners have a total bandwidth of T. Since we are co-running multiple instances of the same application, all co-runners have the same IPC, and the overall throughput is therefore the sum of the co-running applications' individual IPCs.

Figure 3 shows the throughput predicted using the Bandwidth Bandit ("Bandit-Predicted") and the hardware reference throughput ("Reference"). It also shows a "naive" throughput prediction ("Naive-Predicted"). Because the baseline bandwidth demand of OMNet++ is slightly less than 25% of the saturation bandwidth, which is less than the system peak bandwidth, we would not expect four instances to saturate the bandwidth. Therefore, without any additional information, our best (although naive) prediction would be that the throughput scales linearly.

This result shows the significance of using the data captured by the Bandwidth Bandit when predicting throughput.

4. CONCLUSIONS

The Bandit Bandwidth is a quantitative method to measure applications' sensitivity to contention for off-chip memory bandwidth. With the Bandwidth Bandit we were able to draw the following conclusions: 1) Latency sensitive applications are likely to experience large slowdowns (up to 25%) before the off-chip memory bandwidth is saturated; 2) On the other hand, the performance of applications that are not latency sensitive is not significantly affected until the off-chip memory bandwidth becomes saturated; 3) Neither the baseline bandwidth nor performance is a good indicator of how sensitive an application is to off-chip memory contention. This highlights the need for methods which can quantify applications' sensitivity to contention for off-chip memory resources.

5. REFERENCES

[1] T. Dey, W. Wang, J. W. Davidson, and M. L. Soffa. Characterizing multi-threaded applications based on shared-resource contention. In *Proc. of ISPASS*, 2011.

[2] D. Eklov, N. Nikoleris, D. Black-Schaffer, and E. Hagersten. Design and evaluation of the bandwidth bandit. Technical Report 2012-003, Department of Information Technology, Uppsala University, 2012.

[3] L. Tang, J. Mars, N. Vachharajani, R. Hundt, and M. L. Soffa. The impact of memory subsystem resource sharing on datacenter applications. In *Proc. of ISCA*, 2011.

Speculative Dynamic Vectorization for HW/SW Co-designed Processors

Rakesh Kumar[1], Alejandro Martínez[2], Antonio González[1, 2]
[1] Dept. of Computer Architecture, Universitat Politècnica de Catalunya, 08034 Barcelona, Spain
[2] Intel Barcelona Research Center, Intel Labs, 08034, Barcelona, Spain
rkumar@ac.upc.edu, alejandro.martinez@intel.com, antonio.gonzalez@intel.com

ABSTRACT

Hardware/Software (HW/SW) co-designed processors have emerged as a promising solution to the power and complexity problems of modern microprocessors. These processors utilize dynamic optimizations to improve the performance. However, vectorization, one of the most potent optimizations, has not yet received the deserved attention. This paper presents a speculative dynamic vectorization algorithm to explore its potential.

Categories and Subject Descriptors

C.1.2[Computer System Organization]: Multiprocessor-SIMD

Keywords

HW/SW Co-designed processor, Vectorization, Speculation

1. INTRODUCTION

SIMD accelerators are ubiquitous in modern microprocessors. However, compiler´s inability to reorder ambiguous memory references severely limits vectorization opportunities, hence leading to inefficient utilization of these accelerators.

This paper presents a speculative dynamic vectorization algorithm that speculatively reorders ambiguous memory references to uncover vectorization opportunities. The hardware checks for any memory dependence violation due to speculative vectorization and takes corrective action in case of violation. The algorithm does not require any compiler or operating system support. Moreover, it can vectorize legacy code which was not compiled for any SIMD accelerator.

2. ALGORITHM

The software layer of our co-designed processor is called Emulation Software Layer (ESL). ESL operates in three translation modes for generating host code from guest x86 code: Interpretation Mode (IM), Basic Block Translation Mode (BBM) and Superblock Translation Mode (SBM).

2.1 Pre-Vectorization Steps

2.1.1 Superblock Creation

ESL starts by interpreting guest x86 instruction stream in IM. When a basic block is executed more than a predetermined number of times, ESL switches to BBM. In this mode, the whole basic block is translated and stored in the code cache and the rest of the executions of this basic block are done from the code cache. Moreover, branch profiling information for direction and target of the branches is also collected. Once the execution of a basic block exceeds another predetermined threshold, ESL creates a bigger optimization region, called superblock, using the branch profiling information collected during BBM. A superblock generally includes multiple basic blocks following the biased direction of branches or unrolled loops.

2.1.2 Pre-optimizations

First of all, the superblock is converted into Static Single Assignment (SSA) form to remove anti and output dependences. Then, the optimizations Constant Propagation, Copy Propagation, Constant Folding, Common Sub-expression Elimination and Dead Code Elimination are applied. The next step is to generate the Data Dependence Graph (DDG). During DDG creation, we perform memory disambiguation analysis and consecutiveness analysis. If memory disambiguation analysis cannot prove that a pair of memory operations will never/always alias, it is marked as "may alias". In case of reordering, the original memory instructions are converted to speculative memory operations. Similarly, consecutiveness analysis finds adjacent memory accesses and marks them for vectorization.

2.2 Vectorization

The vectorizer packs together a number of independent scalar instructions, which perform the same operation, and replaces them with one vector instruction. Before describing the algorithm, we define a set of conditions that a pair of instructions must satisfy to be included in the same pack. The instructions:

- must be performing the same operation.
- must be independent.
- must not have been included in another pack.
- If the instructions are load/store, they must be accessing consecutive memory locations.

Vectorization starts by marking First Load and First Store instructions. First Load/Store instructions are those for which there are no other loads/stores from/to adjacently previous memory locations. For example, if there is a 64-bit load instruction I_L that loads from a memory location [M] and there is no 64-bit load instruction that loads from address [M – 8], we call I_L First Load.

Vectorization begins by packing consecutive stores. Once a pack of stores is created, their predecessors are packed before packing other stores, if they satisfy the packing conditions. Moreover if the last store in the pack has a next adjacent store, it is marked as First Store so that a new pack can start from it.

Once all the stores are packed and their predecessor/ successors chains have been followed, we check for remaining load instructions that satisfy the packing conditions and pack them in the same way as stores.

Vectorization starting from adjacent loads/stores has an obvious limitation: if a superblock does not have any consecutive loads/stores, nothing can be vectorized. To tackle this problem,

PACT'12, September 19–23, 2012, Minneapolis, Minnesota, USA.
ACM 978-1-4503-1182-3/12/09.

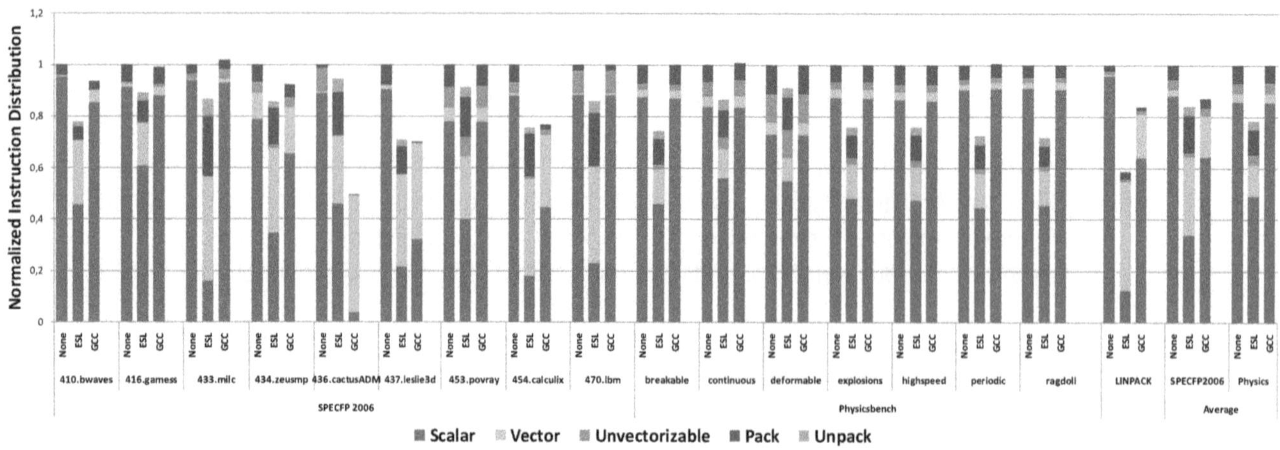

Figure 1 Dynamic Instruction Distribution: Without Vectorization, ESL Vectorization and GCC Vectorization

after packing all loads/stores and their predecessors/successors, we check if still there are some arithmetic instructions which can be packed together. If yes, we vectorize them and follow their predecessor/successor trees. This allows us to partially vectorize loops with interleaved memory accesses.

While traversing the predecessor/successor tree, if we find out that the predecessors of a pack cannot be vectorized, a Pack instruction is generated. This Pack instruction collects the results of all the predecessors into a single vector register and feeds the current pack. Similarly, if all the successors of a pack cannot be vectorized, an Unpack instruction is generated. This Unpack instruction distributes the result of the pack to the scalar successor instructions.

3 SPECULATION AND RECOVERY

Since, memory operations play an important role in vectorization, by freely reordering them, consecutive memory references can be packed together. This not only helps in utilizing memory bandwidth but also in vectorization of their dependent arithmetic operations.

ESL labels each load/store instruction with a sequence number in original program order. During vectorization or instruction scheduling, if a pair of load-store or store-store instructions that may alias is reordered, the original load/store instructions are converted to speculative load/store instructions.

To support the speculative execution, we have two sets of architectural registers in the hardware: the working set and the shadow registers. Before starting the execution of speculative code, a copy of the working set is saved into the shadow registers. Moreover, during the execution of speculative code, store instructions write into a store buffer instead of directly writing to the memory.

During the execution, if the hardware detects:

- that a speculative memory instruction with higher sequence number is executed before another speculative memory instruction with lower sequence number and
- they access overlapping memory locations,

an exception in raised. In this case, the contents of the store buffer are flushed; register values from the shadow registers are copied to the working set; and the execution is restarted in Interpretation Mode. On the other hand, in case of successful execution of speculative code, values in the store buffer are forwarded to the memory and the contents of the shadow registers are discarded.

If the rate of speculation failures exceeds a predetermined limit in a particular superblock, it is recreated without reordering ambiguous memory references.

4 PERFORMANCE EVALUATION

To evaluate the proposed algorithm, we use DARCO [2], which is an infrastructure for evaluating co-designed virtual machines. DARCO executes guest x86 binary on a PowerPC-like RISC host architecture. The proposed algorithm was implemented in Emulation Software Layer (ESL) of DARCO. In our experiments, we assume that the host architecture supports a vector size of 128-bits. Moreover, we vectorize only the floating point operations.

We use a set of applications from SPECFP2006 and Physicsbench benchmarks suites and LINPACK for the evaluation. All the benchmarks are compiled with gcc-4.5.3 with -O3 -fomit-frame-pointer -ffast-math -mfpmath=sse -msse3 flags.

4.1 FP Dynamic Instruction Elimination

Figure 1 compares the dynamic instruction reduction by our algorithm and that of GCC [1]. Dynamic instruction stream includes: Scalar and vector floating point instructions, unvectorizable instructions and Pack/Unpack instructions.

As the figure shows, we are able to reduce, on average, 16%, 22% and 41% of dynamic instructions and compared to GCC, we are able to eliminate, on average, 3%, 22% and 25% more dynamic instructions for SPECFP2006, Physicsbench and LINPACK respectively. The behavior of Physicsbench is really interesting for both vectorization techniques. GCC practically does not find any SIMD parallelism in Physicsbench because of the extensive use of pointers in this benchmark suite. Moreover, these benchmarks consist of complex control flow in the frequently executed loops and GCC fails to vectorize them. However, our algorithm shows a dynamic instruction reduction of 22%. This shows that we are able to find significant vectorization opportunities even in the cases where GCC fails to vectorize anything.

Our experimental results also show that memory speculation doubles the dynamic instruction stream coverage of vectorization.

5 REFRENCES

[1] Auto-vectorization in GCC. URL http://gcc.gnu.org/projects/tree-ssa/vectorization.html

[2] D. Pavlou et al. DARCO: Infrastructure for Research on HW/SW co-designed Virtual Machines. In *AMAS-BT'11, held in conjunction with ISCA-38*, June 2011.

Fine-Grained Parallel Traversals of Irregular Data Structures

Bin Ren,[*] Gagan Agrawal
Dept. of Computer Science and Engineering
The Ohio State University
{ren,agrawal}@cse.ohio-state.edu

James R. Larus, Todd Mytkowicz,
Tomi Poutanen[†], Wolfram Schulte
Microsoft Research
{larus,toddm,tomipout,schulte}@microsoft.com

ABSTRACT

Fine-grain *data parallelism* is increasingly common in mainstream processors in the form of long vectors and on-chip GPUs. This paper develops compiler and runtime support to exploit such data parallelism for non-numeric, non-graphic, irregular parallel tasks that perform simple computations while *traversing* many independent, irregular data structures, like trees and graphs. We vectorize the traversal of trees and graphs by treating a set of irregular data structures as a parallel control-flow graph and compiling the traversal into a domain-specific bytecodes. We produce a SIMD interpreter for these bytecodes, so each lane of a SIMD unit traverses one irregular data structure. Despite the overhead of interpretation, we demonstrate significant increases in single-core performance over optimized baselines.

Categories and Subject Descriptors

D.1.3 [**Programming Techniques**]: [Concurrent Programming — Parallel Programming]

Keywords

Irregular Data Structure, Fine Grained Parallelism, SIMD

1. INTRODUCTION

Fine-grain, data parallelism is increasingly prevalent in mainstream processors (e.g. x86 and ARM), as the width of vector instructions increases and GPUs are integrated on chip. Fine-grained data-parallel hardware is widely used in programs that have *regular* data access patterns (e.g. graphics, image and video processing, signal processing, etc.).

In general, programs that rely on irregular, pointer-based data structures, such as trees and graphs, benefit little from SIMD execution because of the mismatch between the strict, lockstep behavior of SIMD parallelism and the dynamic, data-driven behavior of programs that manipulate irregular data structures.

This paper starts to bridge this gap by demonstrating an approach to speeding up important, latency-sensitive algorithms using SIMD execution. In general, our approach is able to speed up applications that independently traverse *many* instances of pointer-based data structures. These applications arise in domains as diverse as machine learning (e.g. random forests), compilation (e.g. parsing), intrusion detection (e.g. regular expressions).

[*]Work completed while intern at Microsoft Research

[†]Affiliation: Microsoft

PACT'12, September 19–23, 2012, Minneapolis, Minnesota, USA.
ACM 978-1-4503-1182-3/12/09.

Effective parallelization of independent traversals of irregular data structures on a SIMD unit requires addressing two key challenges. First, to reduce the memory bottlenecks that choke performance of modern processors, we demonstrate how to organize many irregular data structures in memory so as to increase spatial locality. Second, to enable SIMD execution, we demonstrate how to turn fine-grained task parallelism—in the form of traversing many irregular data structures—into fine-grained data parallelism by emulating a MIMD machine in SIMD hardware.

In this paper, we develop compiler and runtime support to address these challenges and demonstrate that our approach is effective by speeding up two random forest implementations by over 10X across many inputs.

2. IRREGULAR DATA STRUCTURES

Many programs perform simple data-driven traversals of irregular trees and graphs. When these programs visit a node of the tree or graph, they optionally perform an *operation* on a node and then might evaluate an *expression* to select the next node to visit. We will denote the operation(s) performed at a leaf node (e.g. one that does not have children) n as $\mathcal{W}(n)$ and the computations at the non-leaf, or internal node, as $\mathcal{T}(n)$.

To make this concrete, consider a binary tree traversing: each node of a binary tree is either an internal node or a leaf node. At an internal node (n), a traversal executes $\mathcal{T}(n) := input < n.threshold$ and branches to the left or right child depending on whether $input$ is less than node n's $threshold$. Likewise, at a leaf node (n), the traversal terminates by storing a node n's $value$ field into a global variable (e.g. $\mathcal{W}(n) := counter \leftarrow n.value$).

2.1 Parallel Traversal of Fine-Grained Tasks

It is difficult to exploit fine-grained data parallelism when traversing a single irregular data structure because there is little parallelism *within* a single traversal. However, when traversing *many* irregular data structures we can execute $\mathcal{T}(n)$ and $\mathcal{W}(n)$ in parallel. For example, when traversing two binary trees, we *could* execute $\mathcal{T}(n)$ for the two trees in a single SIMD unit; $\mathcal{T}(n)$ is a simple comparison of two concrete values and each lane of a SIMD unit could do that comparison in parallel.

To accomplish this, we execute all of the sequential traversals in parallel; we first execute $\mathcal{T}(n)$ for all root nodes n giving us a set of successor nodes ns. Next we evaluate $\mathcal{T}(n)$ for all n in ns, and so on, until we reach leaf nodes. At a leaf node n, we evaluate $\mathcal{W}(n)$. Since different traversals might have different lengths, at certain levels a mixture of $\mathcal{T}$ and $\mathcal{W}$ can occur.

In effect, we turn fine-grained task parallelism (e.g. each traversal of a single irregular data structure is one task) into fine-grained *data* parallelism by executing $\mathcal{T}(n)$ and $\mathcal{W}(n)$ in lockstep in the SIMD unit.

2.2 SIMD Interpretation of $\mathcal{T}(n)$ and $\mathcal{W}(n)$

To traverse many independent fine-grained data structures in parallel, we build a traversal-specific *virtual machine*, where the intermediate language or *bytecodes* of the virtual machine, are operations from $\mathcal{T}(n)$ and $\mathcal{W}(n)$. For example, when traversing two binary trees, the two operations map to SIMD implementations of *compare* for internal nodes and *store* for leaf nodes. For each binary tree, we build a syntax-directed compiler to traverse the trees and re-write every internal node into a bytecode that implements $\mathcal{T}(n) = compare$ (parameterized by the node's threshold) and any leaf node into a bytecode that implements $\mathcal{W}(n) = store$ (parameterized by the value contained in the leaf node), resulting in an executable program.

To execute this program, the virtual machine simultaneously visits the first node for *all* fine-grained tasks and executes their respective first instruction, resulting in the second node for all tasks, and so on, until all tasks have reached and evaluated a leaf. In other words, the virtual machine executes every $\mathcal{T}(n)$ in parallel across all root nodes. Because of the SIMD hardware, the virtual machine must execute each bytecode type (e.g. $\mathcal{T}(n)$ and $\mathcal{W}(n)$) as it cannot assume all SIMD lanes contain the same type of instructions. The virtual machine then masks away the results of bytecodes whose types are not represented by the current operation.

In effect, the virtual machine is using interpretation to emulate a MIMD machine with SIMD, a topic that has been studied in the past [5, 2, 1, 4].

3. EXPERIMENTAL EVALUATION

In this section we demonstrate the efficacy of our SIMD interpreter by demonstrating that it significantly speeds up two random forest applications. Random forests are a popular machine learning technique which traverse many independent decision trees in order to classify an input. We apply our approach to two implementations of random forests: one used in a latency critical capacity (online-service) at Microsoft and ALGLIB, a widely used open source implementation.

Methods: We conduct experiments on an Intel Xeon E5420 CPU (2.5GHz frequency and SSE-4). We use the Intel ICC (Intel Parallel Composer 2011) compiler and for each experiment, we run the program 30 times and calculate the mean.

Data: We evaluate the impact of our approach by comparing our SIMD implementation against the baselines listed above. To compare against ALGLIB, we use four datasets from UCI Machine Learning Repository[3]—Poker, Shuttle, Abalone, and Satellite. To compare against the Microsoft product we use production data for that product.

For both applications, we use the respective applications to train random forests and then compile those forests into bytecodes to execute on our SIMD interpreter.

SIMD Interpreter: Our SIMD interpreter traverses 4 trees in parallel, one for each lane of the SIMD unit. To improve spatial locality during the traversals, we design three new data layouts to take advantage of any *bias* in a traversal. By bias we mean a node is more likely to traverse to one child over the other. The random forests created from Shuttle and Satellite have a slight left bias, while the Microsoft dataset has a severe left bias.

Our layouts are: LL (Level by Level layout across many trees), SLL (Sorted Level by Level layout by separating the left part and the right part of each level across many trees), and DLL (Depth first Level by Level layout by organizing the left most of all trees together while keeping the right part in a depth first manner).

Evaluation: Our SIMD interpreter provides a significant single-core performance benefit (**Figure 1** (a)). A bar on this graph gives the speedup (y-axis) of our approach over ALGLIB and Microsoft's random forest implementation, respectively for each of our five

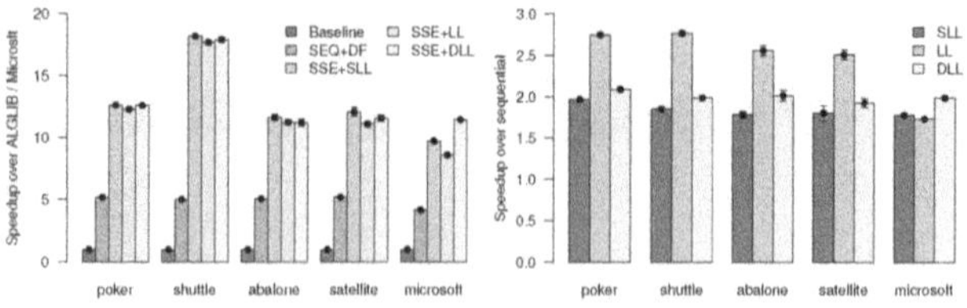

(a) (b)

Figure 1: (a) Speedup with Our Approach (over Baseline Implementations and (b) SSE Speedups with Different Data Layouts)

datasets (x-axis). Each data set has five bars, one bar for each of memory layout of the irregular data structure. The baseline (darkest bar per dataset) provides the performance of the baselines (ALGLIB and Microsoft, respectively). The SEQ+DF bar refers to a sequential version of our interpreter evaluated on a depth first layout (DF) of the random forest nodes. We use a DF layout because that is the layout used by both of the baselines and allows us to evaluate the overhead of our sequential interpreter. The other three bars per dataset refer to the SIMD interpreter running on the other data layouts.

Figure 1 (a) demonstrates that our transformed dense layouts and SIMD interpreter provide significant speedups over the baseline implementations of this irregular application: we see more than a 10X speedup over the baseline implementations on all 5 datasets. We include the SEQ+DF implementation because we are interested in showing how much speedup we get from SIMD after linearization; on the UCI datasets SIMD increases performance by a factor of 3, while on the internal dataset SIMD increases performance by a factor of more than 2.

Impact of SIMD: To understand the impact of our SIMD interpreter we compare the runtime of our sequential interpreter against our SIMD version. To ensure this comparison is fair, we hold the layout constant. A bar on Figure 1 (b) shows the speedup of our SIMD interpreter over our sequential one (y-axis) for each dataset (x-axis). The speedup from SIMD (with 4 SIMD lanes) range between 2 and 2.8, demonstrating significant speedups from our SIMD implementation.

4. CONCLUSIONS

This paper shows how to extract SIMD parallelism from applications that traverse irregular data structures such as trees and graphs. As SIMD execution units become more common and capable in the near future, it becomes increasingly pressing to find general techniques to exploit the power of this hardware in new and broader contexts. This paper describes one such approach, which is to traverse and compute on multiple, independent, irregular data structures in parallel using a targeted virtual machine running on a SIMD vector processor.

5. REFERENCES

[1] Guy E. Blelloch, Siddhartha Chatterjee, Jonathan C. Hardwick, Jay Sipelstein, and Marco Zagha. Implementation of a portable nested data-parallel language. *Journal of Parallel and Distributed Computing*, 21(1):4–14, April 1994.

[2] H. G. Dietz and W. E. Cohen. A massively parallel mimd implemented by simd hardware? Technical report, Purdue University, 1992.

[3] A. Frank and A. Asuncion. UCI machine learning repository, 2010.

[4] Jonathan C. Hardwick. An efficient implementation of nested data parallelism for irregular divide-and-conquer algorithms. In *Proceedings of the First International Workshop on High-Level Programming Models and Supportive Environments*, pages 105–114, April 1996.

[5] Reinhard von Hanxleden and Ken Kennedy. Relaxing simd control flow constraints using loop transformations. In *PLDI*, pages 188–199, 1992.

High-Performance Analysis of Filtered Semantic Graphs *

Aydın Buluç†, Armando Fox+, John R. Gilbert*, Shoaib Kamil+†, Adam Lugowski*†,
Leonid Oliker, Samuel Williams
Lawrence Berkeley National Laboratory, +University of California at Berkeley,
and *University of California at Santa Barbara
abuluc@lbl.gov, fox@cs.berkeley.edu, gilbert@cs.ucsb.edu, skamil@cs.berkeley.edu,
alugowski@cs.ucsb.edu, loliker@lbl.gov, swwilliams@lbl.gov

ABSTRACT

High performance is a crucial consideration when executing a complex analytic query on a massive semantic graph. In a semantic graph, vertices and edges carry "attributes" of various types. Analytic queries on semantic graphs typically depend on the values of these attributes; thus, the computation must either view the graph through a *filter* that passes only those individual vertices and edges of interest, or else must first materialize a subgraph or subgraphs consisting of only the vertices and edges of interest. The filtered approach is superior due to its generality, ease of use, and memory efficiency, but may carry a performance cost.

In the Knowledge Discovery Toolbox (KDT), a Python library for parallel graph computations, the user writes filters in a high-level language, but those filters result in relatively low performance due to the bottleneck of having to call into the Python interpreter for each edge. In this work, we use the Selective Embedded JIT Specialization (SEJITS) approach to automatically translate filters defined by programmers into a lower-level efficiency language, bypassing the upcall into Python. We evaluate our approach by comparing it with the high-performance C++ /MPI Combinatorial BLAS engine, and show that the productivity gained by using a high-level filtering language comes without sacrificing performance.

Categories and Subject Descriptors

D.1.3 [**Software**]: Programming Techniques—*Concurrent Programming, Parallel programming*

Keywords

Domain Specific Languages, Graph Analysis, SEJITS, KDT, High-performance computing

1. INTRODUCTION

In a semantic graph, edges and/or vertices are labeled with *attributes* that may represent a timestamp, a type of relationship, or a mode of communication. An analyst (i.e. a user of graph analytics) may want to run a complex workflow over a large graph, but wish to only use those graph edges whose attributes pass a filter defined by the analyst. For example, in a graph where vertices represent Twitter users and edges represent "following" or "retweeting" relationships, the analyst may want to search through vertices reachable from a particular user via the subgraph consisting only of "retweet" edges with timestamps earlier than a given date.

Filters raise performance issues for large-scale graph analysis. In many applications, running a filter across an entire graph data corpus to materialize the filtered graph as a new object for analysis can be prohibitively expensive and creates storage problems. Moreover, the time spent during materialization is typically not amortized by many graph queries because the user modifies the query (or just the filter) during interactive data analysis. The alternative is to filter edges and vertices "on the fly" during execution of the complex graph algorithm. A graph algorithms expert can implement an efficient on-the-fly filter as a set of primitive Combinatorial BLAS [2] operations coded in C++ , but filters written at the higher-productivity KDT [5] level, as graph operations in Python, incur a significant performance penalty.

Our solution to this challenge is to apply Selective Just-In-Time Specialization techniques from the SEJITS approach [3]. We define an embedded domain-specific language (DSL) that uses a subset of Python to define semantic graph filters, and use the SEJITS methodology to implement the translation necessary for filters written in that subset to run as efficiently as the low-level C++ code. As a result, we are able to demonstrate that SEJITS technology significantly accelerates Python graph analytics codes written in KDT and running on clusters and multicore CPUs.

2. KDT FILTERS IN PYTHON

In KDT, any graph algorithm can be performed with an edge filter. A filter is a unary predicate on an edge that returns true if the edge is to be considered, or false if it is to be ignored. The KDT user writes a filter predicate as a Python function or lambda expression of one input that returns a boolean value.

KDT filters are applied directly to the lowest-level KDT structures; all operations on these structures then respect the filter. This means that all algorithms automatically respect filters with no modifications required. Additional filters can be added and removed at any time, with filter predicates evaluated in the order they are added. KDT supports two approaches for filtering semantic graphs: ***materializing filters*** and ***on-the-fly filters***.

*This work was supported in part by NSF grant CNS-0709385, by DOE grant DE-AC02-05CH11231, and by grants from Intel Corporation and Microsoft Corporation.
†Corresponding authors.

PACT'12, September 19–23, 2012, Minneapolis, Minnesota, USA.
ACM 978-1-4503-1182-3/12/09.

When a ***materializing filter*** is placed on a graph (or matrix or vector), the entire graph is traversed and a copy is made that includes only the edges that pass the filter. This touches every element only once and potentially doubles the memory requirements. By contrast, every primitive operation (e.g. semiring scalar multiply) applies an ***on-the-fly filter*** to its inputs when it is called. No copy is made, rather every primitive operation accesses the graph through the filter and behaves as if the filtered-out edges were not present. Only the filter predicates are stored. Each filtered element may be touched multiple times, but, depending on algorithm, some may not be touched at all.

3. SEJITS AND FILTERS

In order to mitigate the slowdown caused by defining filter predicates in Python, which results in a serialized upcall into Python for each operation, we opt to instead use the Selective Embedded Just-In-Time Specialization (SEJITS) approach [3]. By defining an embedded DSL for KDT filters, and translating it to C++ , we avoid performance penalties while still allowing users the flexibility to specify filters in Python. We use the Asp[1] framework to implement our DSL.

In the usual KDT case, filters are written as simple Python functions. Since KDT uses Combinatorial BLAS at the low level to perform graph operations, each operation at the Combinatorial BLAS level must check to see whether the vertex or edge should be taken into account, requiring a per-vertex or per-edge upcall into Python.

We define an embedded domain specific language for filters, and allow users to write their filters in this DSL, expressed as a subset of Python with normal Python syntax. At instantiation, the filter source code is introspected to get the Abstract Syntax Tree (AST), and then is translated into low-level C++ . Subsequent applications of the filter use this low-level implementation, sidestepping the serialization and cost of upcalling into Python. Formal definition of our domain-specific language and several examples of filters written in Python can be found in our technical report [1].

4. EXPERIMENTS

We use synthetically-generated R-MAT [4] graphs with a very skewed degree distribution. An R-MAT graph of scale N has 2^N vertices and approximately $edgefactor \cdot 2^N$ edges. Our *edgefactor* is 16, and R-MAT seed paratemeters a, b, c, and d are $0.59, 0.19, 0.19, 0.05$, respectively. After generating this non-semantic (boolean) graph, edge payloads are artificially introduced using a random number generator in a way that ensures target filter permeability. The edge type is a struct that is composed of a boolean isfollower flag, a timestamp, the number of retweets. Our technical report [1] contains experiments on graphs from real social network interactions on a distributed memory supercomputer.

The parallel scaling of our approach and the relative performance of three methods is shown in Figure 1. The experiment is run on Mirasol, a single node platform composed of four Intel Xeon E7-8870 processors. The sustained stream bandwidth is about 30 GB/s per socket. Mirasol has 256 GB 1067 MHz DDR3 RAM. We use OpenMPI 1.4.3 with GCC C++ compiler version 4.4.5, and Python 2.6.6.

CombBLAS achieves remarkable linear scaling with increasing process counts (34-36X on 36 cores), while SEJITS+KDT closely tracks its performance and scaling. Single core KDT runs did not finish in a reasonable time to report. We do not report performance of materialized filters as they were the slowest by a large margin.

[1] https://github.com/shoaibkamil/asp/wiki/

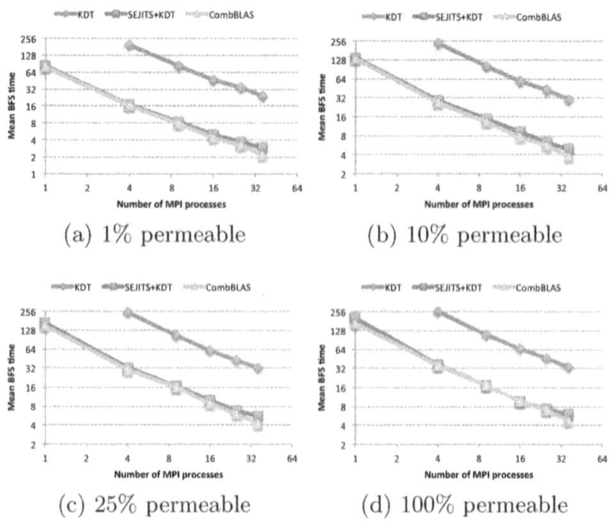

(a) 1% permeable (b) 10% permeable (c) 25% permeable (d) 100% permeable

Figure 1: Parallel 'strong scaling' results of filtered BFS on Mirasol, with varying filter permeability on a synthetic data set (R-MAT scale 23). Both axes are in log-scale, time is in seconds.

5. CONCLUSION

The KDT graph analytics system achieves customizability through user-defined filters, high performance through the use of a scalable parallel library, and conceptual simplicity through appropriate graph abstractions expressed in a high-level language. We showed that the performance hit of expressing filters in a high-level language can be mitigated by Just-in-Time Specialization. In particular, our embedded DSL for filters enables Python code to achieve comparable performance to a pure C++ implementation.

6. REFERENCES

[1] A. Buluç, A. Fox, J. Gilbert, S. Kamil, A. Lugowski, L. Oliker, and S. Williams. High-performance analysis of filtered semantic graphs. Technical Report UCB/EECS-2012-61, May 2012.

[2] A. Buluç and J.R. Gilbert. The Combinatorial BLAS: Design, implementation, and applications. *International Journal of High Performance Computing Applications (IJHPCA)*, 25(4):496–509, 2011.

[3] B. Catanzaro, S.A. Kamil, Y. Lee, K. Asanović, J. Demmel, K. Keutzer, J. Shalf, K.A. Yelick, and A. Fox. SEJITS: Getting Productivity and Performance With Selective Embedded JIT Specialization. In *PMEA*, 2009.

[4] J. Leskovec, D. Chakrabarti, J. Kleinberg, and C. Faloutsos. Realistic, Mathematically Tractable Graph Generation and Evolution, Using Kronecker Multiplication. In *PKDD*, pages 133–145, 2005.

[5] A. Lugowski, D. Alber, A. Buluç, J. Gilbert, S. Reinhardt, Y. Teng, and A. Waranis. A Flexible Open-Source Toolbox for Scalable Complex Graph Analysis. In *SDM'12*, pages 930–941, April 2012.

Energy-Efficient Cache Partitioning For Future CMPs

Karthik T. Sundararajan
School of Informatics
University of Edinburgh
t.s.karthik@ed.ac.uk

Timothy M. Jones
Computer Laboratory
University of Cambridge
timothy.jones@cl.cam.ac.uk

Nigel P. Topham
School of Informatics
University of Edinburgh
npt@staffmail.ed.ac.uk

ABSTRACT

The demand for high performance computing systems requires processor vendors to increase the number of cores per chip multiprocessor (CMP). However, as their number grows, the core-to-way ratio in the last level cache (LLC) increases, presenting problems to existing cache partitioning techniques which require more ways than cores. Further, effective energy management of the LLC becomes increasingly important due to its size.

In this paper we propose an LLC energy-saving scheme for high-performance, many-core processors. It partitions the data within the cache into shared and private regions. Applications only access the ways containing the type of data that they require, realising dynamic energy savings. Any ways that are not within the shared or private regions can be turned off to save static energy.

Categories and Subject Descriptors

B.3.2 [**Memory Structures**]: Cache memories, Shared memory

General Terms

Design, Management, Performance

Keywords

Cache partitioning, LLC management, Energy-efficient cache

1. INTRODUCTION

The last level cache (LLC) within a chip multiprocessor (CMP) is the largest cache within the processor, and is often shared among all cores on the chip. It accounts for a significant fraction of the total processor power budget, therefore decreasing its energy consumption realizes significant system benefits. However, it is a critical structure for performance, standing between the rest of the processor and long-latency main memory. Therefore, any energy-saving scheme for the LLC should cause minimal or no performance degradation.

Recently cache partitioning for performance has received significant interest within the community [6, 8]. However, this work takes a different approach. Instead of partitioning based on the requirements of each core, we partition based on the *type of data* that is being accessed — shared or private. This paper proposes an Energy-efficient Cache Partitioning architecture (ECP), which is shown in Figure 1. We identify and separate private and shared data, justifying the former to the left-hand side of the cache and the latter to the right. When an access requires private data, only the ways on the left of the cache need to be activated, and vice-versa for shared requests. This way alignment of data allows us to realise significant dynamic energy savings. Further, we monitor the cache usage of each core in the system and dynamically restrict the size of the private region for each one. This means that ways in the center of the cache become unused and can be turned off for static energy savings. To our knowledge, we are the first to propose separate partitioned cache regions for private and shared data.

PACT'12, September 19–23, 2012, Minneapolis, Minnesota, USA.
ACM 978-1-4503-1182-3/12/09.

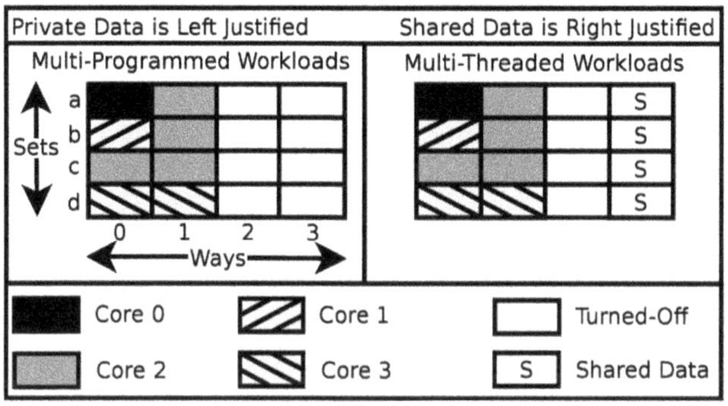

Figure 1: Example data layouts for differing workloads in ECP.

2. THE ECP ARCHITECTURE

There are two parts to ECP. The first is the monitoring of cache usage for each individual core. This allows us to determine the optimal number of cache ways to assign to each core to maintain high performance but enable significant energy reduction. The second part actually implements the way assignments and to gain energy benefits. We assume a serially-accessed last level cache, as is the norm. Therefore dynamic energy savings come from the tag side only.

Figure 2 gives an overview of ECP. All accesses from the higher-level caches pass through the directory on their way to the LLC. Over an interval containing a fixed number of instructions, these accesses are monitored by the cache usage logic and are then used to make partitioning decisions. These are written into the access permission registers

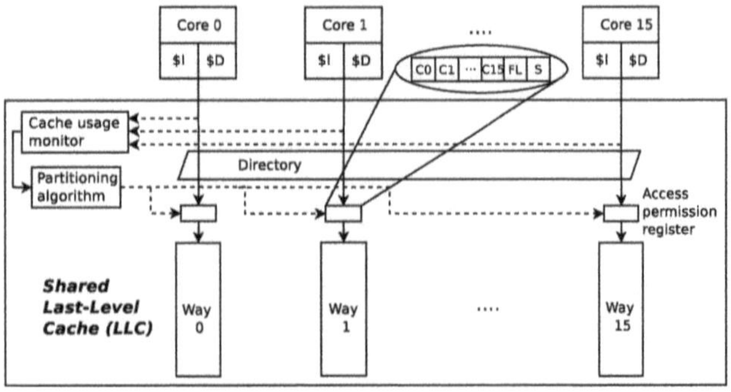

Figure 2: An overview of the region aware cache partitioning (RECAP) architecture.

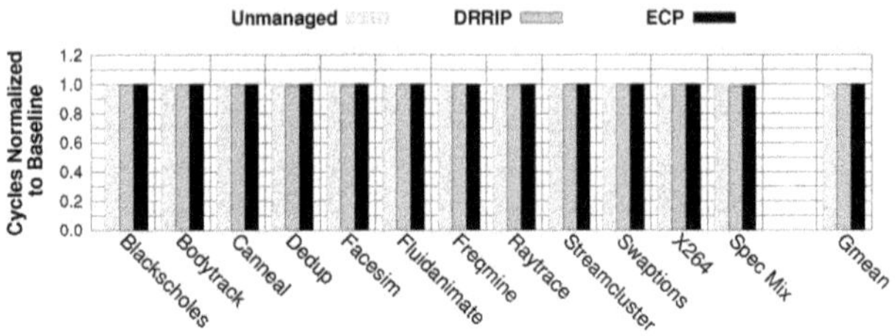

Figure 3: Performance with an 8MB, 16-way cache.

(APRs) that sit before the cache ways, to control which cores have access to each way. Data that is private to a particular thread is kept left-justified in the cache (i.e., in the low-numbered ways) whereas shared data is kept right-justified (i.e., in the high-numbered ways).

3. EXPERIMENTAL METHODOLOGY

We implemented our partitioned cache architecture in gem5 [2]. We simulated an x86-based in-order processor running an SMP-enabled Linux kernel version 2.6.28. We modelled a 16-core system to fully evaluate the effects of sharing and partitioning the last level cache. All level 1 caches are private and all processors share a common level 2 cache. To obtain energy information we used Cacti [7] at 45nm. Finally, as in prior work [4], we assumed a 5 million cycle phase interval for monitoring and partitioning decisions. We ran Parsec benchmarks [1] for our multi-threaded applications and a random mix of benchmarks from SPEC CPU2006 [5] for our multi-programmed workload.

4. EVALUATION ON A 16-CORE SYSTEM

Figures 3-5 show the performance and energy consumption for each application and mix. It is clear that there is very little performance change for any workload when using DRRIP [3] or ECP, although DRRIP achieves a performance improvement of 1.8% in *spec mix*. When all cores contend for the cache, DRRIP preserves parts of the working set that lead to better performance. However, for DRRIP to work effectively it needs more cache ways than there are cores, which is not the case in this setup.

On the other hand, ECP achieves significant dynamic and static energy savings that cannot be realised by DRRIP, since it only targets performance. This leads to a mean dynamic energy reduction of 84% across our workloads.

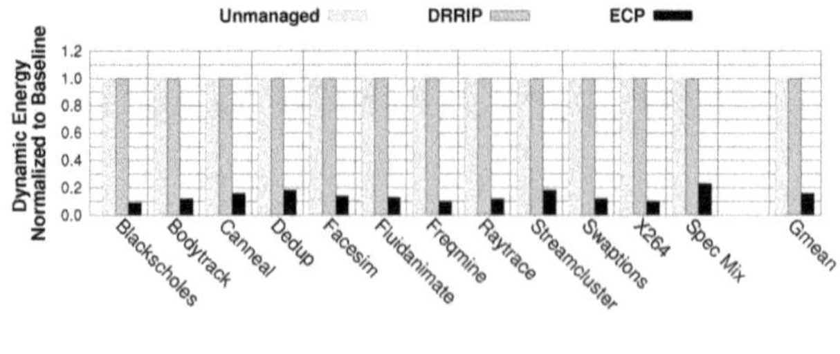

Figure 4: Dynamic energy with an 8MB, 16-way cache.

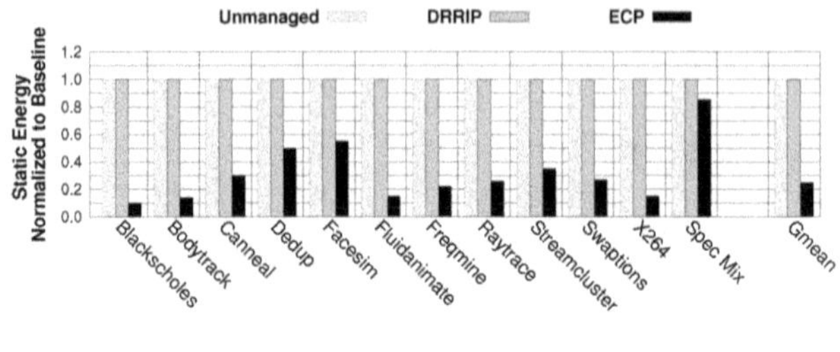

Figure 5: Static energy with an 8MB, 16-way cache.

Static energy reductions are also large, shown in Figure 5. On average a 75% reduction in static energy is achieved across all workloads.

5. CONCLUSION

We have proposed an energy-efficient cache partitioning scheme for both multi-programmed and multi-threaded applications running within a shared last-level CMP cache. Our approach maintains high performance while saving significant dynamic and static energy. This is achieved by partitioning the cached data into private and shared regions, and only allowing cores to access the ways containing the data type that they seek. Unused ways can be turned off for static energy savings.

We have evaluated our scheme on a 16-core system with a 16-way LLC, showing that it achieves 84% dynamic and 90% static energy savings with no performance loss.

6. REFERENCES

[1] C. Bienia. *Benchmarking Modern Multiprocessors*. PhD thesis, Princeton University, January 2011.

[2] N. Binkert et al. The gem5 simulator. *SIGARCH Comput. Archit. News*, May 2011.

[3] A. Jaleel et al. High performance cache replacement using re-reference interval prediction (RRIP). In *ISCA*, 2010.

[4] M. K. Qureshi and Y. N. Patt. Utility-based cache partitioning: A low-overhead, high-performance, runtime mechanism to partition shared caches. In *MICRO*, 2006.

[5] SPEC Corporation. SPEC CPU2006. http://www.spec.org/cpu2006/.

[6] G. E. Suh et al. Dynamic partitioning of shared cache memory. *The Journal of Supercomputing*, 28, 2004.

[7] S. Thoziyoor et al. Cacti 5.1. Technical Report HPL-2008-20. *HP Laboratories Palo Alto*, 2008.

[8] Y. Xie and G. H. Loh. PIPP: Promotion/insertion pseudo-partitioning of multi-core shared caches. In *ISCA*, 2009.

A Low-Overhead Dynamic Optimization Framework for Multicores*

Christopher W. Fletcher†, Rachael Harding†, Omer Khan‡, and Srinivas Devadas†
†Massachusetts Institute of Technology; Cambridge, MA, USA
‡University of Connecticut; Storrs, CT, USA
{cwfletch, rhardin, devadas}@mit.edu, khan@uconn.edu

ABSTRACT

This paper argues for a "less is more" design philosophy when integrating dynamic optimization into a multicore system. The primary insight is that dynamic optimization is inherently *loosely-coupled* and can therefore be supported on multicores with very *low-overhead* by using a Partner core. We exploit this property by designing a dynamic optimizer composed of a two-core partnership that requires a minimal amount of dedicated hardware and is resilient to (a) reducing the Partner core's clock frequency, (b) changing the Partner core's placement on the multicore die and (c) varying the latency of dynamic optimization operations.

Categories and Subject Descriptors

C.5 [**Computer Systems Organization**]: Computer System Implementation—*General*

Keywords

Dynamic optimization, Multicores, Helper threads

1. INTRODUCTION

This paper presents a low-overhead dynamic optimization framework for multicores. A dynamic optimizer (a) monitors an application (App) for *hot* program paths at runtime, (b) re-compiles hot paths into optimized/contiguous traces [1] and (c) provides the application a mechanism to execute from within traces.

Dynamic optimization is a naturally *loosely-coupled* yet memory-intensive process. The canonical dynamic optimization flow consists of two entities: the App which runs in one context and a Helper thread which monitors the App and provides recompilation support once hot paths are detected. Like prefetching, dynamic optimization can take place in the background; the App does not depend on the Helper thread to make forward progress. This non-blocking property makes multicores well suited to support dynamic optimization because the App and Helper thread can be run on separate App and Partner cores, putting less pressure on the App core's private memory hierarchy and pipeline. To put this in perspective, dynamic optimizers traditionally need a large amount of memory (over 50 KBytes) to track, store and expand traces [1, 3, 5], which is comparable in size to today's L1 caches. The open question is whether a Helper thread running on a separate Partner core can *rate match* the App core; that is, can it run in the background and still deliver traces that the App will be able to use.

Duesterwald et al. made an important observation that when profiling application hot paths, simple heuristics achieve on par the same quality of results as complex heuristics, yet incur significantly less storage [2]. Our work extends this result by exploiting how the dynamic optimization process is *latency and noise tolerant* due to hot paths being repetitive by nature.

To exploit latency and noise tolerance, we show how to implement dynamic optimization on a multicore with very small area, power and performance overheads (Section 2). In particular we show how with little dedicated hardware, large inter-core network latencies and a reduced power envelope, the Partner core can still detect, expand and return a majority of program hot paths before the main application changes phase (Section 3).

2. SYSTEM ARCHITECTURE

Our system changes program execution at *run-time only* and works with unmodified application binaries. Once an application is loaded onto the App core, the operating system spawns a fixed Helper thread on some other core (the Partner core). The high-level system is shown in Figure 1 and is broken into the following main components:

(1) Network. A mechanism for the App core to send data to the Partner core, and vice versa. In our system, the network behaves like a first-in-first-out queue which can be replaced by a conventional Network on Chip (NoC).

(2) Hot path FSM (App core). A hardware finite state machine (FSM) that detects candidate hot paths and writes messages describing those hot paths to the network. The FSM starts a new message when (a) it is not in the middle of building another message and (b) the App fetches a backwards branch (as done in [2]), sees a function call, or a trace currently executing on the App core exits. Each hot path message consists of the PC address for the start of the hot path, a bit vector representing up to 16 taken/not-taken consecutive branch directions on the path (BR), and a path length field (each message is $\sim$ 64 bits in size). If the network between cores is full when a message is ready to be sent, the message is dropped (instead of being stored in a dedicated table).

(3) Helper thread (Partner core). A software routine that reads and records hot path messages from the network. When a message has been seen *enough* times (8 in this paper), the Helper thread uses the message's PC and BR to reconstruct the sequence of dynamic instructions that make up the hot path, optimizes those instructions as a trace, caches the trace in the Partner core data cache, and sends the trace back to the App core through the network. Each trace is $\leq$ 128 instructions in length (longer traces are cut short) and the Helper thread stalls while it waits for traces to be sent through the network to the App core.

*This material is based upon work supported by the National Science Foundation Graduate Research Fellowship under Grant No. 1122374.

PACT'12, September 19–23, 2012, Minneapolis, Minnesota, USA.
ACM 978-1-4503-1182-3/12/09.

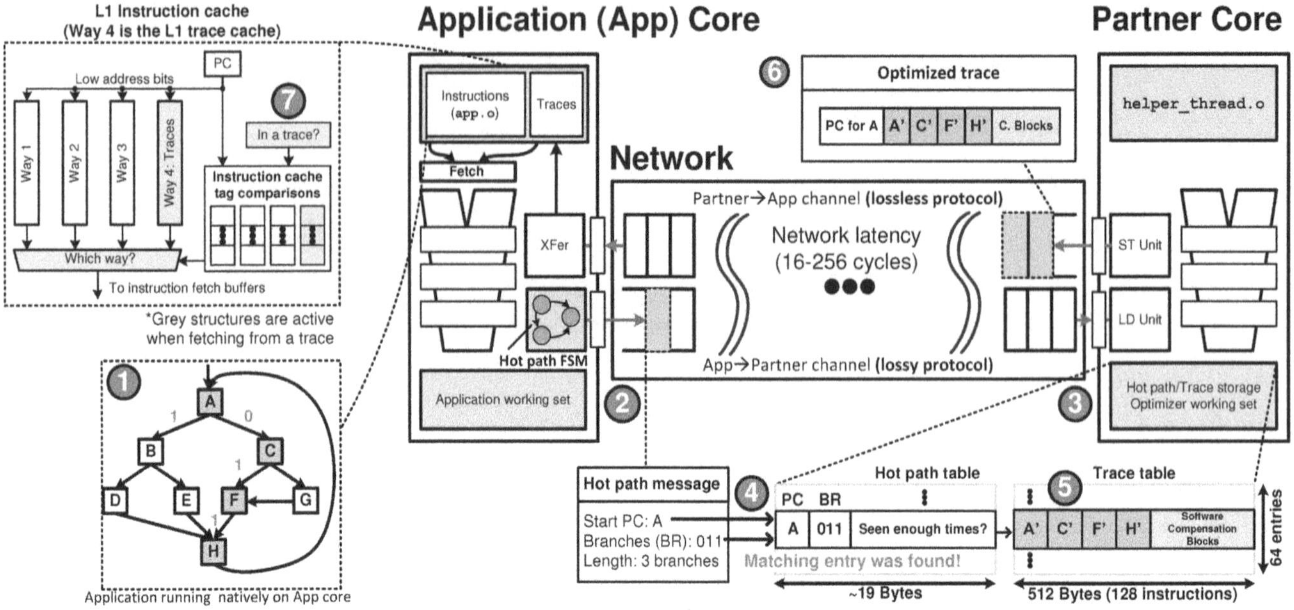

Figure 1: An end-to-end example showing our system optimize the small loop shown in (1). ((1)-(2)) The hot path FSM detects that $\{A, C, F, H\}$ is hot (H is a backwards branch) and sends a hot path message to the Partner core. The Helper thread reads the hot path message ((3)), sees that the message has been seen enough times to warrant optimization ((4)), and ((5)) creates an optimized trace for the message. Finally, the trace and its start PC are sent back to the App core ((6)) and fetched in place of regular instructions ((7)).

(4) L1 trace cache (App core). A hardware buffer from which traces, sent by the Partner core, can be fetched and executed in place of regular instructions. We implement the L1 trace cache as a way in the L1 instruction (I)Cache, managed as a direct-mapped structure with a small number of entries (16 for this paper). The direct-mapped lookup is cheap in terms of dedicated hardware cost ($\sim$ 14 Bytes) and combinational latency (several additional gate delays). When the Helper thread is disabled, the trace way can be used to store normal instructions.

3. RESULTS

We evaluate our system over the SPEC06-int benchmark suite using the SESC simulator [4], and simulate for 3 billion instructions with a 1-20 billion instruction warmup depending on the benchmark. Both the App and Partner core have mid-range core models (2-issue out-of-order with a 64-entry reorder buffer) with a private/shared cache hierarchy (32 KB, 4-way, single-cycle L1 I/D caches and a 1 MB, 8-way, 10 cycle unified L2 cache).

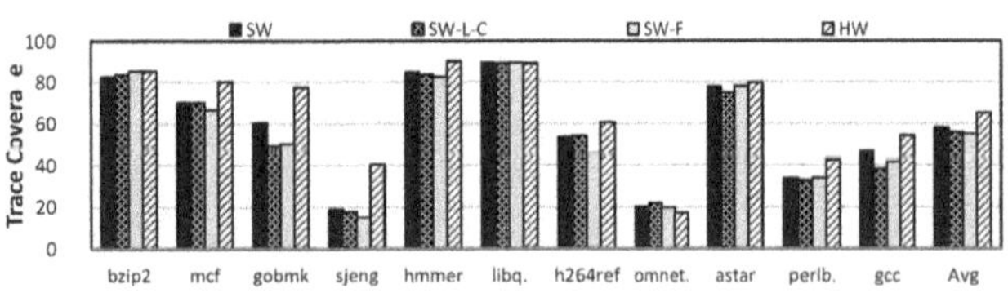

Figure 2: Trace coverage for the representative system design points discussed in Section 3.

Figure 2 shows the *trace coverage* (the percent of dynamic instructions executed from within traces) for each benchmark. Higher trace coverage is better: a dynamic optimizer's effectiveness scales with how many instructions the App executes from within traces. SW implements a software-based Helper thread on a Partner core that is adjacent to the App core on the chip (inter-core latency = 16 cycles). SW-L-C is the same as SW, but the Partner core is scheduled to the "other side" of the chip (the latency and capacity in the network is 256 cycles and 256 buffer slots, respectively). SW-F is the same as SW, but the Partner core clock frequency is 10× less than the App core and network. HW is an *idealized* Helper thread that performs the same dynamic optimization routine as SW but in a single cycle and with no network latency/bandwidth overheads. Furthermore, HW assumes a fully associative L1 trace cache (which avoids conflict misses but requires a dedicated fully-associative lookup on the App core).

Overall, SW, SW-L-C and SW-F maintain competitive trace coverage with HW (and have a 7.2%, 9.2% and 9.9% difference, respectively). As another point of comparison, SW attains on average 5.8% more coverage on bzip2, mcf and gcc relative to [3], which also evaluates these benchmarks and assumes large hardware structures to support the trace collection process. Most benchmarks (all except bzip2, omnet and h264ref) show slight dips in coverage for SW-L-C/SW-F relative to SW, which is caused by the increase in round-trip trace collection latency. The three outlier benchmarks suffer from L1 trace cache thrashing: when round-trip latency increases, the Helper thread is able to process fewer hot paths per program phase, which leads to fewer L1 trace cache evictions. Especially for omnet, which has repetitive phases and many hot paths per phase, slowing down the Helper thread reduces the number of traces that are still hot yet evicted by (possibly cold) traces.

4. REFERENCES

[1] Vasanth Bala, Evelyn Duesterwald, and Sanjeev Banerjia. Dynamo: a transparent dynamic optimization system. In *Proceedings of the ACM SIGPLAN 2000 conference on Programming language design and implementation*, PLDI '00, 2000.

[2] Evelyn Duesterwald and Vasanth Bala. Software profiling for hot path prediction: less is more. *SIGPLAN Not.*, 2000.

[3] Sanjay J. Patel, Tony Tung, Satarupa Bose, and Matthew M. Crum. Increasing the size of atomic instruction blocks using control flow assertions. In *Proceedings of the 33rd annual ACM/IEEE international symposium on Microarchitecture*, MICRO 33, 2000.

[4] Jose Renau. Sesc: Superescalar simulator. Technical report, 2002.

[5] Weifeng Zhang, Brad Calder, and Dean M. Tullsen. An event-driven multithreaded dynamic optimization framework. In *Proceedings of the 14th International Conference on Parallel Architectures and Compilation Techniques*, PACT '05, 2005.

Making It Practical and Effective: Fast and Precise May-Happen-in-Parallel Analysis

Congming Chen
State Key Laboratory of Computer Architecture, CAS
Graduate University of CAS
Beijing, China
chencongming@ict.ac.cn

Wei Huo
State Key Laboratory of Computer Architecture, CAS
Beijing, China
huowei@ict.ac.cn

Xiaobing Feng
State Key Laboratory of Computer Architecture, CAS
Beijing, China
fxb@ict.ac.cn

ABSTRACT
May-Happen-in-Parallel (MHP) analysis is a very important and fundamental mechanism to facilitate concurrent program analysis. But the limitation of its efficiency keep it away from being practical and effective in analyzing large scale real world concurrent programs. We proposed a novel MHP algorithm by performing a reachability analysis on a so-called parallel reachability graph of a program. The MHP algorithm mainly comprises two phases: pre-computation of initial MHP information and top-down propagation of this information along the parallel reachability graph. Our algorithm is fast as it has a low complexity $O(|N|+|E|)$, in which N is the number of nodes in the parallel reachability graph and E is the number of edges in this graph. Our preliminary experiment on 13 concurrent programs indicates that our approach is extremely faster than two state-of-art approaches, respectively achieving a relative geometry average speed up of 395.53× and 136.37×, while yielding the same precision with these two approaches.

Categories and Subject Descriptors
D.3.4 [**Programming Languages**]: Processors - *Compilers*; F.3.2 [**Logics and Meanings of Programs**]: Semantics of Programming Languages - *Program Analysis*

General Terms
Algorithms, Performance, Languages

Keywords
may happen in parallel, concurrent, program analysis

1. INTRODUCTION
May-Happen-in-Parallel (MHP) analysis is a very important and fundamental mechanism which can facilitate many other techniques such as concurrent control flow and data flow analysis, concurrent program optimization, and even synchronization anomalies detection. Generally speaking, the problem of precise MHP analysis for all pairs of statements in a concurrent program is undecidable. Taylor[1] has proved that this problem is NP-complete given that all control paths in all threads are executable. Thus, most MHP algorithms are computing an approximate result.

Until now, many approaches have been proposed to compute MHP information for different concurrent programming models. However, the state-of-art approaches are still facing the efficiency obstacle when applying them to analyze large scale or even medium scale concurrent programs, for instance, most programs tested in previous works are less than 10KLOC[2], which is far smaller than the scale of real world programs. In the other side, popular programming models such as Java or POSIX Threads are difficult to analyze efficiently due to their low level concurrent syntax and complex concurrent structures[2].

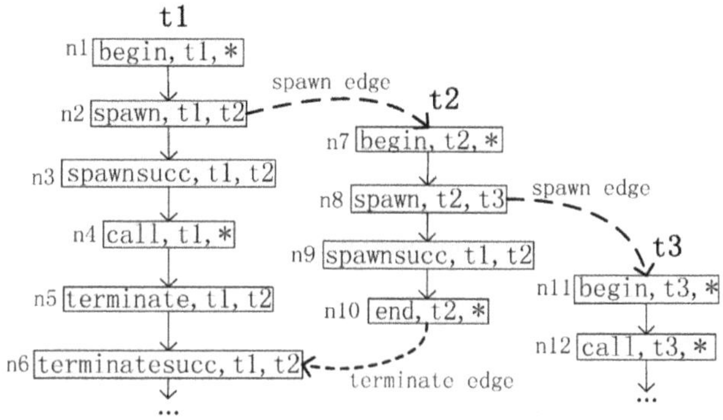

Figure 1: Simple PRG involved 3 threads

Before stating the motivation of our approach, we will introduce the primary program representation in our approach. Our main program representation is called Parallel Reachability Graph(PRG), which is a directed graph built by connecting different intra-threaded control flow graphs with kinds of edges. Each node n in PRG is represented as a triple $<O, Tl, Tt>$, where O is the operation performed by n, for example, we use operation *spawn* to create a new thread, we use operation *terminate* to terminate an existed thread. Tl is the local thread which n belongs to. Tt is the target thread on which n operates, and Tt will be set to "*" if n has no target thread. A simple PRG involved 3 threads is shown in figure 1 as our motivating example. Suppose we need to compute the MHP analysis results for node *n3*, then intuitively, we will find out that in threads *t2* and *t3*, all nodes which are reachable from *n7* but not dominated by *n3* may be executed in parallel with *n3*. Moreover, the MHP results of *n4* and *n5* are the same with *n3*, and thus, they can be simply computed by just propagating the MHP information from *n3*. In another word, the MHP results of *n4* and *n5* are determined by *n3*. Same rules can be applied to *n9* and *n10* in figure 1. The inspiration we get from this example is that different kinds of nodes have different influences on MHP analysis results. MHP information of certain nodes with concurrent syntax can be pre-computed by performing an elaborately designed inter-threaded reachability analysis, while the MHP information of nodes without concurrent syntax can be determined by this pre-computation. Therefore, there's no need to iteratively process each statement according to the predefined data flow equations as in Naumovich's approach[2] or exhaustively judge that whether each pair of statements in different threads may happen in parallel or not according to the predefined rules as in Barik's approach[4].

PACT'12, September 19-23, 2012, Minneapolis, Minnesota, USA.
ACM 978-1-4503-1182-3/12/09.

2. DESIGN and IMPLEMENTATION

For the sake of computing and preserving MHP results, each node n in PRG have a set $DEL(n)$ to preserve part of nodes which definitely cannot happen in parallel with n, and a set $M(n)$ to preserve all nodes may happen in parallel with n. A point worth emphasizing here is that $DEL(n)$ and $M(n)$ are not complementary.

Based on the above definitions and taking the motivation in section 1 as the fundamental principle of our approach, we present a MHP algorithm including two phases in this paper:

1. **Pre-computation**. In this phase, we compute the initial M_{init} set and DEL_{init} set for certain nodes by performing an elaborately designed reachability analysis and dominating analysis on PRG.

To compute DEL_{init} set for certain nodes, for each thread t, if t is terminated by another thread, then get *terminatesucc*(t), and set DEL_{init}(*terminatesucc*(t)) to include all nodes in thread t. At the same time, we also compute a node set comprises all nodes which are dominated by *terminatesucc*(t) in PRG, represented as *TerminateDom*(t). Notice that this process is recursive, which means if there is a thread ti which satisfies that *end*(ti) $\in$ *TerminateDom*(t), then *TerminateDom*(ti)$\subseteq$*TerminateDom*(t). For each thread t has a creation site, get *spawn*(t) and *begin*(t), we compute a node set comprises all nodes which are post reachable from *spawn*(t) in thread t, we define this node set as DEL_{init}(*begin*(t)).

To compute M_{init} set for certain nodes, for each node labeled as <*spawn*, *ti*, *tj*>, we compute all nodes dominated by *begin*(tj) in PRG, and preserve them in node set *LR*(*begin*(tj)) as the local reachable node set of *begin*(tj), *TerminateDom* sets will be used in this process. We also compute a node set to comprise all nodes which are reachable from *begin*(tj) in PRG, and preserve them in node set *R*(*begin*(tj)) as the reachable set of *begin*(tj). In a similar way, we get *LR*(*spawnsucc*(ti)) and *R*(*spawnsucc*(ti)) respectively. Finally, we compute M_{init}(*begin*(tj)) and M_{init}(*spawnsucc*(ti)) as the following equations indicate:

$$M_{init}(spawnsucc(tj)) := R(begin(tj)) \setminus LR(spawnsucc(tj))$$

$$M_{init}(begin(tj)) := R(spawnsucc(tj)) \setminus LR(begin(tj))$$

2. **Top-down propagation**. In this phase, we propagate the initial M sets and DEL sets along PRG in a top-down way, and each node will be visited only once. During the propagation, we distinguish that whether a given PRG node contains the *terminate* operation or not. If current node n is such a node, then we compute its M set and DEL set according to the following equations:

$$M(n) := (\bigcup_{p \in local-pred(n)} M(p)) \cup M_{init}(n)$$

$$DEL(n) := (\bigcup_{p \in pred(n)} DEL(p)) \cup DEL_{init}(n)$$

$$M(n) := M(n) \setminus DEL(n)$$

The propagation of M sets is confined to the local predecessors of n, since we do not merge M sets from different threads. Meanwhile, we eliminate $DEL(n)$ from $M(n)$ as the concurrent syntax of a *terminate* operation indicates. If n does not have *terminate* operation, then we use the following equations:

$$M(n) := (\bigcup_{p \in pred(n)} M(p)) \cup M_{init}(n)$$

$$DEL(n) := (\bigcap_{p \in pred(n)} DEL(p)) \cup DEL_{init}(n)$$

Finally, due to the concise reachability analysis and intuitive top-down propagation in above two phases, our approach achieves a low complexity $O(|N|+|E|)$, in which, N is the number of PRG nodes, and E is the number of edges in PRG.

In our preliminary experiment, we compared our approach with two state-of-art approaches[2][4]. Since the primary program representation used in [2] is Program Execution Graph, and the program representation used in [4] is Thread Creation Tree, we represented these two approaches as PEG and TCT respectively in our experiment. We implemented both of these approaches in an open source compiler framework[5], and adopted the optimization techniques proposed in [3] to reduce the size of program representation. We selected 13 programs in SPLASH2[6] as our benchmark, and ran our experiment on a Linux server with a 1.8GHz CPU and 2GB memory. Experimental data of relative speed up (in logarithm) between different approaches is shown in figure 2.

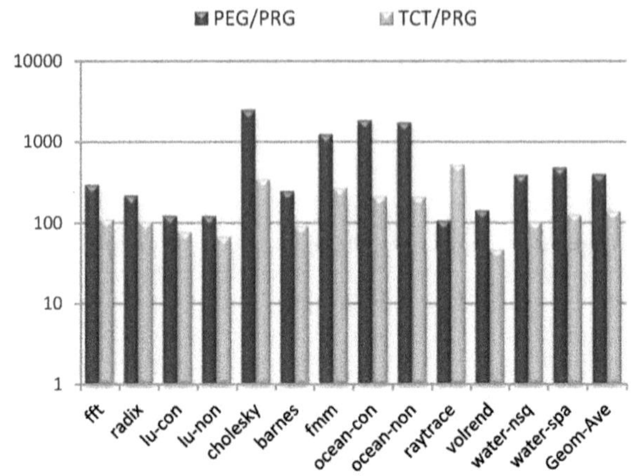

Figure 2: Relative speed up between PEG, TCT, PRG

For all programs in our experiment, our approach is extremely faster than both PEG approach and TCT approach, our approach gets a geometry average speed up of 395.53× compared with PEG approach and gets a geometry average speed up of 136.37× compared with TCT approach, while yielding the same precision with these two approaches. As a result, our approach can make MHP analysis more practical and effective.

3. ACKNOWLEDGMENTS

This work is supported by several Chinese Research Grants. The grant numbers are including: 2011CB302504, 60921002, 2011ZX01028-001-002, 2012AA010902.

4. REFERENCES

[1] Taylor, R.N.1983. Complexity of analyzing the synchronization structure of concurrent programs. Acta Inf. 57-84.

[2] Naumovich, G. Avrunin, G.S. Clarke, L.A. 1999. An efficient algorithm for computing mhp information for concurrent Java programs. *In Proceedings of the 7th ACM SIGSOFT international symposium on Foundations of software engineering*, Toulouse, France. DOI=http://doi.acm.org/10.1145/318773.319252.

[3] Li, L. Verbrugge, C. 2004. A practical mhp information analysis for concurrent Java programs. Technical Report. McGill University.

[4] Barik, R. 2005. Efficient computation of May-Happen-in-Parallel information for concurrent java programs. *In Proceedings of the 18th International Workshop Languages and Compilers for Parallel Computing*. Hawthorne, New York, DOI=http://doi.acm.org/10.1007/978-3-540-69330-7_11.

[5] The Open64 compiler framework: http://www.open64.net.

[6] Woo, S. Ohara, M. Torrie, E.1995. The SPLASH-2 Programs: Charact-erization and Methodological Considerations. *In Proceedings of the 22th International Symposium on Computer Architecture*. Santa Margherita Ligure, Italy. DOI= http://doi.acm.org/10.1145/223982.223990.

Mileage-based Contention Management in Transactional Memory

Woojin Choi, Lihang Zhao, and Jeff Draper
Information Sciences Institute / University of Southern California
Marina del Rey, CA 90242
{woojinch, lihangzh, draper}@isi.edu

Categories and Subject Descriptors

C.1.2 [**Multiple Data Stream Architectures (Multiprocessors)**]: Parallel processors

General Terms

Design, Experimentation, Performance

Keywords

Transactional memory, contention management, mileage

ABSTRACT

In Transactional Memory (TM), a conflict occurs when a memory block is accessed concurrently by two or more transactions and at least one of them is a write access. The management of conflicts significantly impacts TM performance. There are two alternative approaches for managing conflicts: Reactive Contention Management (RCM) [1] and Proactive Contention Management (PCM) [2]. Previous contention management schemes treat all transactions with no weights, and make a decision based on the information provided by the running transaction instance.

In this work, we suggest that all critical sections (transactions) are not equally performance-critical. Among the transactions from a program, some transactions are more important than others with respect to the performance of the implemented algorithm; e.g., the producer transaction in the producer-consumer relationship. It is worthy to distinguish the performance-critical transactions from others for speeding up the overall execution. For this purpose, we propose a mileage technique and show its effectiveness in the contexts of RCM and PCM.

To express the criticality of transactions, we define new instructions, `MILEAGE` and `MRSTCNT`. `MILEAGE` has one operand, mileage id (mid). A mid indicates how far a thread progresses and monotonically increases during the program execution. Each processor has a mileage unit. A mileage unit maintains the current mid and a mileage counter (mcnt), which tracks the number of times that `MILEAGE` has been executed with the current mid as its operand. When `MILEAGE` with a new mid is shown, that mid is stored in the mid register and the mcnt register is cleared. Every time the same mid appears again, the mcnt register is incremented. `MRSTCNT` is used to clear the mcnt register. When two threads contend with each other, the thread with the smaller mileage value (mid concatenated with mcnt) receives higher priority. `MILEAGE` and `MRSTCNT` were inserted manually based on source code analysis and performance profiling.

If a conflict is detected, one of conflicting transactions can continue its execution and the others stall or abort to maintain correctness. Traditional RCMs decide which transaction continues its execution based on information from the current instance. For example, age RCM selects the transaction that has started earlier and size RCM selects the transaction which has accessed more memory blocks [1]. The decision from mileage RCM is based on the relative importance of each transaction from the program flow (mid) as well as dynamic flow (mcnt). On a conflict, mileage RCM chooses the transaction with the smaller mileage value. From our experiments, mileage RCM provides prominent performance improvements with benchmarks that have performance critical transactions (*bayes* and *intruder*). Also, mileage RCM shows no severe speed-down across all the other benchmarks we evaluated. Mileage RCM achieves average speedups of 12.52% over age RCM (23.45% over size RCM).

Conflicts can be prevented by throttling the number of concurrently-running transactions. We propose Speculative Lock Insertion (SLI). After a transaction experiences aborts more than three times, it sets a global lock upon restart. If the transaction which holds the global lock commits, it resets the global lock. Every time a thread encounters a transaction, it first checks the global lock. If the global lock is set, the thread waits until it is released before starting a transaction. Otherwise, the transaction executes. In mileage-based SLI, the aborted transaction not only sets the global lock but also registers its mileage value. When a thread finds the lock is set, it compares its mileage value to that in the global location. If it has the smaller value, it starts execution, ignoring the lock. Because locking in SLI is for performance only, this does not impact correctness issues. The correctness is still maintained by the underlying TM system. From our experiments, mileage-based SLI achieves average speedups of 9.55% over Adaptive Transaction Scheduling [2].

PACT'12, September 19–23, 2012, Minneapolis, Minnesota, USA.
ACM 978-1-4503-1182-3/12/09.

1. REFERENCES

[1] A. Shriraman and S. Dwarkadas. Refereeing Conflicts in Hardware Transactional Memory. In *Proceedings of ICS*, 2009.

[2] R. M. Yoo and H.-H. S. Lee. Adaptive Transaction Scheduling for Transactional Memory Systems. In *Proceedings of SPAA*, 2008.

System-Level Power-Performance Efficiency Modeling for Emergent GPU Architectures

Shuaiwen Song
Virginia Tech
CS Department, KWII,
Blacksburg, VA, 24060
S562673@vt.edu

Kirk W. Cameron
Virginia Tech
CS Department, KWII,
Blacksburg, VA, 24060
Cameron@cs.vt.edu

Categories and Subject Descriptors

C.1.4 [**Processor Architectures**]: Parallel Architectures; C.4 [**Performance of Systems**]: Modeling Techniques

Keywords

Runtime statistical model, Power, Performance, System-wide energy consumption, Analytical Model, GPGPU, CUDA

1. INTRODUCTION

System and application design choices have profound impact on energy efficiency. Consider the rise of GPUs in emergent supercomputer design. Massive parallelism and high throughput offer the potential for improving performance. However, for systems with multiple GPUs power usage can easily triple. Therefore, we need to quantitatively understand power, performance, and their interactive effects to determine when the increased power use of a GPU is warranted.

In order to help application and system designers find power-performance bottlenecks and their causes, we need accurate models that balance abstraction and detail on emergent GPU architectures. The best available GPU power models are statistical- or simulation-based. Related statistical models use multiple linear regression (MLR) and hardware counter data to predict GPU power consumption in isolation. These models provide a good balance of abstraction and application/system detail but potentially ignore non-linear relationships between power and performance. This could lead to inaccuracy for individual kernel power prediction. Related simulation models use emulated performance data combined with detailed architectural information to predict integrated GPU power-performance efficiency. These models provide enough detail to explore architectural design but ignore application/system level information and require architectural schematics and expertise. Furthermore, both statistical- and simulation-based models require significant adaptation to support modern complex GPU architectures with true cache hierarchies. Therefore, we propose separate system-level power and performance models of modern GPU based systems that can be integrated to better understand the relationships between power and performance at scale. Our runtime hardware counter driven approach combines an analytical performance model for GPU based systems with a machine-learning-based artificial neural network (ANN) power model to form a power-performance efficiency model. Specifically, with the proposed models, users can:

- Predict optimal configurations to maximize efficiency for single GPU and GPU-based clusters.
- Explore and identify application and system bottlenecks for performance, power, and energy consumption, and explain the root causes.

2. DESIGN AND IMPLEMENTATION

The design of our Back Propagation Artificial Neural Network (BP-ANN) for GPU power modeling is illustrated in Figure 1.

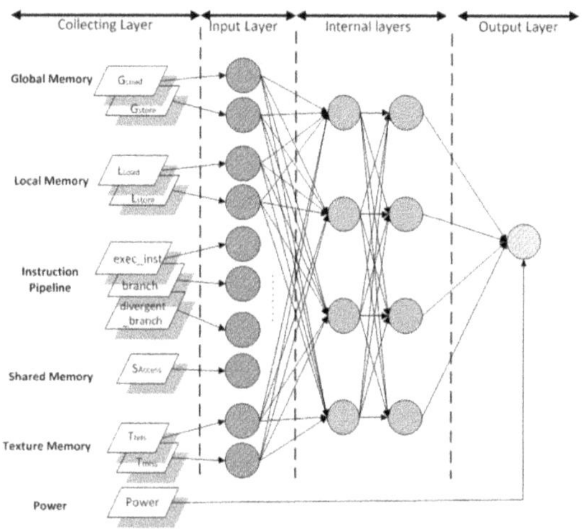

Figure 1: Design diagram for BP-ANN based GPU power model.

3. RESULTS

The experimental results show that our models are accurate for predicting power (within 2.1%) and performance (within 6.7%) for representative CUDA kernels running on Fermi based GPUs. Furthermore, results indicate that capturing non-linear effects between power and performance leads to improved accuracy over the best available GPU power models—MLR based approaches. Our models can also be simply used by programmers to identify power-performance bottlenecks. We apply our combined model to suggest the optimal number of GPU based cluster nodes for SHOC benchmarks from ORNL to achieve the best energy-performance efficiency on the Keeneland supercomputer.

PACT'12, September 19–23, 2012, Minneapolis, Minnesota, USA.
ACM 978-1-4503-1182-3/12/09.

Transactional Event Profiling in a Best-Effort Hardware Transactional Memory System

Matthew Gaudet, José Nelson Amaral
Dept. of Computer Science, University of Alberta
Edmonton, Alberta, Canada
mgaudet@ualberta.ca, jamaral@ualberta.ca

Categories and Subject Descriptors: B.8.2 [**Performance of Systems**]: Measurement Techniques
Keywords: Profiling, Transactional Memory

Introduction: Blue Gene/Q's (BG/Q) unique transactional memory system provides hardware isolation, atomicity and consistency for memory locations while leaving the details of the transactional programming system to software layers above the hardware [3]. This design allows for complex systems implemented as part of the software runtime. Here a profiling extension to the software runtime is presented.

Motivation: In TM systems, conflict resolution refers to the choice of which transaction will abort when two transactions conflict. In BG/Q it is the younger transaction that always aborts, and is decided by the hardware. Once a rollback is initiated after abortion, the BG/Q runtime system becomes involved and makes a decision to either retry the aborted transaction speculatively, or to execute an operation called *serialization*. A serialized transaction is forced to completion on retry, possibly at the expense of otherwise non-conflicting transactions, which will abort themselves if they conflict or attempt to commit.

A serialized transaction runs without speculation, which guarantees forward progress in the case of repeated failures, such as those caused by insufficient storage for speculative state. Serializing too little can cause persistent failures to repeat, wasting resources and slowing program execution. Serializing too often can abort transactions that otherwise should have committed, also wasting resources and slowing program execution. Static serialization decisions are inappropriate because the correct choice of when to serialize can vary depending on input data and on other transactions. Thus, we are investigating runtime adaptation heuristics.

Many TM implementations, including BG/Q, provide summary counters of the number of committed and aborted transactions. However, for the design of an adaptation heuristic, these summaries are imprecise.

Event Logging: I designed a software logging system that provides a high-resolution time-series view of transactional behaviour in programs run on BG/Q. This system provides both macro and micro views of transactional behaviour that have influenced our understanding of adaptation and subsumed simpler summary statistics.

Time-series analysis of transactional programs has been rare. Previous work has been done on Software Transactional Memory Systems, or has required specialized hardware to be added to the processors [4, 1, 2].

In my logging system, event logs are gathered by the TM runtime on events such as begin, rollback, serialization and commit. These events are stored in per-thread buffers, and are dumped to a log-file at the end of program execution. An event log consists of a list of 4-tuple events: (TS, T, TX, O), where: TS is the timestamp read from a high-resolution counter, T is an event type, TX is a unique identifier for each static transaction and O is the originating logical thread ID.

Event logs are imprecise because events may be lost due to a rollback before the logging is complete. Moreover, probe effects may change the behaviour under study. This imprecision is acceptable for analyses that use aggregates, and must be kept in mind when doing micro-level analysis.

Analysis: The raw event logs can undergo a variety of analyses. For instance: **1)** an instantaneous estimate of events-per-second aggregated by TX can identify phased executions. Similarly, aggregation on T reveals changes in transaction begin, commit, and rollback rates. **2)** Histograms of dynamic transaction lengths reveal the variability in the runtime of transactions and helps determine both transactions that dominate running time, and the multi-modal behaviour of some transactions. **3)** Analysis of the behaviour of individual dynamic transactions allows insight into the process by which an individual transaction is committed, and the timeline of events which lead to that point.

Results: When comparing long and short execution modes in BG/Q it becomes apparent that the *rate* of transactional events is very important. Long running mode often has higher sustained rates, leading to faster execution. Comparing summaries can lead to incorrect interpretations of scaling differences.

Visualizing how adaptation changes different phases of program behaviour, by comparing event logs of runs with adaptation enabled against those with adaptation disabled, is an important part of the design of an adaptation policy, because it can reveal pathologies otherwise invisible in summary data.

Conclusion: I have designed and implemented a new tool for development and tuning of transactional systems. The logs and visualizations provide a detailed view into the behaviour of TM applications.

References

[1] M. Ansari, K. Jarvis, C. Kotselidis, M. Luján, C. Kirkham, and I. Watson. Profiling Transactional Memory Applications. In *Parallel, Distributed, and Network-based Processing (PDP)*, pages 11–20, Feb 2009.

[2] H. Chafi, C. C. Minh, A. McDonald, B. D. Carlstrom, J. Chung, L. Hammond, C. Kozyrakis, and K. Olukotun. TAPE: a Transactional Application Profiling Environment. In *International Conference on Supercomputing (ICS)*, ICS '05, pages 199–208, New York, NY, USA, 2005. ACM.

[3] A. Wang, M. Gaudet, P. Wu, M. Ohmacht, J. N. Amaral, C. Barton, R. Silvera, and M. M. Michael. Evaluation of Blue Gene/Q Hardware Support for Transactional Memories. In *Parallel Architectures and Compilation Techniques (PACT)*, Sept 2012.

[4] F. Zyulkyarov, S. Stipic, O. S. Unsal, A. Cristal, T. Harris, I. Hur, and M. Valero. Profiling and Optimizing Transactional Memory Applications. *International Journal of Parallel Programming*, 40:25–56, February 2012.

PACT'12, September 19–23, 2012, Minneapolis, Minnesota, USA.
ACM 978-1-4503-1182-3/12/09.

Transparent Runtime Deadlock Elimination

Hari K. Pyla
Virginia Tech
Blacksburg, Virginia, United States
harip@vt.edu

Srinidhi Varadarajan*
Virginia Tech
Blacksburg, Virginia, United States
srinidhi@vt.edu

ABSTRACT

Thread based concurrent programming is hard due to the potential of concurrency bugs (e.g., data races, atomicity violations, deadlocks, and order violations). While data races and atomicity violations can be ameliorated with appropriate synchronization (a non-trivial problem in itself !), deadlocks require fairly complex avoidance techniques which may fail when the order of lock acquisition is not known apriori [2]. *The goal of this research is to present an efficient and practical system that transparently detects and eliminates deadlocks in real-world multi-threaded applications.*

Categories and Subject Descriptors

D.1.3 [**Programming Techniques**]: Concurrent Programming—*Parallel programming*; D.3.4 [**Programming Languages**]: Processors—*Run-time environments*

General Terms

Algorithms, Design, Languages, Performance and Reliability

Keywords

Deadlock Detection and Recovery, Concurrent Programming, Program Analysis, and Runtime Systems

1. INTRODUCTION

In practice, identifying a concurrency bug does not necessarily mean that it can be easily fixed. To properly fix the concurrency bug, the programmer must identify the root cause of the problem rather than simply observing how the bug manifests itself in the program's execution. Additionally, such bugs are often hard to reproduce. Properly fixing a concurrency bug may require a major software redesign. Recent studies have shown that the patches developed to fix a bug are themselves error-prone (70% of the time in their first release) and they introduce new bugs [1]. On average, a concurrency bug fix takes about 3 fixes (patches) before it is actually fixed [3, 1]. Unless we find mechanisms to enable a large number of programmers, representing a wide array of applications, to use these parallel shared memory platforms effectively, the potential of many-core will go unrealized.

In this research we present **Serenity**, a system that transparently and deterministically eliminates deadlocks at runtime in applications written in type-unsafe languages such as C, C++. Serenity operates by (a) associating memory updates with one or more locks guarding the updates and (b) containing (privatizing) the updates until all locks protecting the updates have been released. All memory updates within a critical section protected by one or more locks are performed atomically at the release of all surrounding locks. In such a system, deadlock detection can be performed at the acquisition of each lock and recovery merely involves selecting a victim lock and discarding all privatized memory updates performed subsequent to the acquisition of the victim.

Serenity transforms the program source to LLVM's IR and provides (a) efficient programming analysis techniques that infer the scope of a lock and (b) selective compile time instrumentation of the identified scope. Serenity's runtime system provides an efficient runtime shadowing technique to implement containment, thereby transparently and automatically eliminating deadlocks.

A comprehensive performance analysis using several applications shows that the scalability of Serenity is comparable to native thread execution with modest performance overhead.

The key contribution of this work is a practical system that can eliminate deadlocks in real-world applications. By providing usable and efficient deadlock detection and recovery for threaded code, Serenity provides a critical tool to programmers designing, implementing and debugging complex applications for emerging many-core platforms.

*Faculty Advisor

PACT'12, September 19–23, 2012, Minneapolis, Minnesota, USA.

2. REFERENCES

[1] G. Jin, L. Song, W. Zhang, S. Lu, and B. Liblit, Automated Atomicity-Violation Fixing, In PLDI '11, pages 389–400.

[2] H. K. Pyla and S. Varadarajan, Avoiding Deadlock Avoidance, In PACT '10, pages 75–86.

[3] H. Volos, A. J. Tack, M. M. Swift, and S. Lu, Applying transactional memory to concurrency bugs, In ASPLOS '12, pages 211–222.

Design of a Storage Processing Unit

Peng Li
University of Minnesota
Minneapolis, MN, 55455
lipeng@umn.edu

Kevin Gomez
Seagate Technology
Shakopee, MN, 55379
kevin.gomez@seagate.com

David J. Lilja
University of Minnesota
Minneapolis, MN, 55455
lilja@umn.edu

ABSTRACT

Researchers showed that performing computation directly on storage devices improves system performance in terms of energy consumption and processing time. For example, Riedel et al. [2] proposed an active disk which performs computation using the processor in a hard disk drive (HDD). Their experimental results showed that the active disk-based system had a factor of 2x performance improvement [2]. However, because the performance gap between the HDDs and CPUs becomes larger and larger, the active disk-based improvement is quite limited. As the role of flash memory increases in storage architectures, solid-state drives (SSDs) have gradually displaced the HDDs with higher access performance and lower power consumption. Researchers also proposed an active flash, which performs computation using a controller in the SSD [1]. However, the SSD controller needs to implement a flash translation layer to make the SSD as an emulated HDD for most operating systems. It also needs to communicate with a host interface to transfer required data. The additional computation power can be utilized is quite limited. To maximize the computation power on the SSD, we propose a processor design called storage processing unit (SPU).

Categories and Subject Descriptors

B.3.2 [**Memory Structures**]: Design Styles—*mass storage, primary memory*; C.1.2 [**Processor Architectures**]: Multiprocessors—*parallel processors, SIMD*

General Terms

Design

Keywords

Parallel architectures, memory systems, solid-state drive

1. THE PROPOSED SPU

Fig. 1 shows an SSD block diagram based on the proposed SPU. Besides the SSD controller, the SPU has additional N processors, where N is the number of flash channels in the SSD. Each of the N processors is connected to a single flash channel. The basic functions of these processors include error correction, channel encoding/decoding, and vector multiplication/addition. The design of the SPU leverages the multiple independent flash channels of the SSD, so that parallel computation can be performed in the SPU. To evaluate the proposed SPU, we implement a principal component analysis-based facial recognition algorithm on two different systems: a conventional SSD-based system (baseline system), and the SPU-based system. In the baseline system, the entire algorithm is implemented in a CPU. In the SPU-based system, 90% of the computation load is implemented in the SPU (10% in the CPU). Preliminary experimental results show that the SPU-based system has at least 4x speed-up and can save more than 50% energy compared to the baseline system.

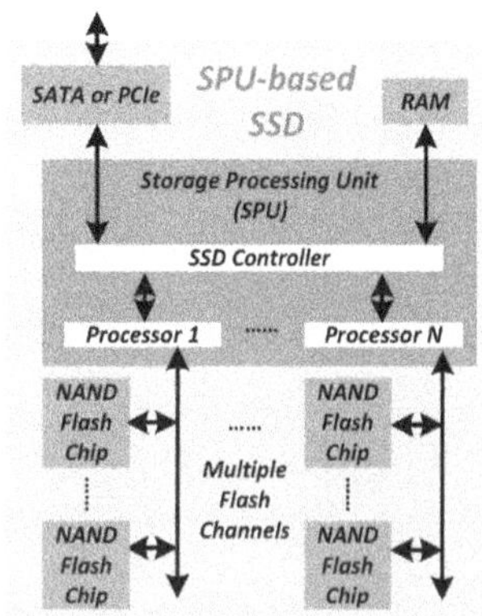

Figure 1: The SPU-based SSD.

The proposed SPU is a custom designed processor based on the latest multiple channel SSD architecture. The main contribution of our work is that we move computation to the storage device by exploiting the parallelism within the SSD. Compared to previous work, we design a specific processor instead of using existing ones to maximize the computation efficiency of the system. Compared to conventional systems, the SPU-based system reduces both processing time and energy consumption. The reduced energy allows for more scalability in a "cloud" like environment. Then the high power cost of a CPU is amortized over a large population of inexpensive processors in the SPU. This allows for significantly more compute resources in a given footprint of a system power budget. In summary, the proposed SPU will significantly benefit data-intensive and I/O-intensive applications in datacenters in terms of both processing time and energy consumption.

2. REFERENCES

[1] S. Boboila, Y. Kim, S. Vazhkudai, P. Desnoyers, and G. Shipman. Active flash: Out-of-core data analytics on flash storage. In *IEEE Symposium on Massive Storage Systems and Technologies (MSST 2011)*, 2011.

[2] E. Riedel, C. Faloutsos, and D. F. Nagle. Active disk architecture for databases. *Carnegie Mellon University Technical Report CMU-CS-00-145*, May 2000.

PACT'12, September 19–23, 2012, Minneapolis, Minnesota, USA.
ACM 978-1-4503-1182-3/12/09.

SkipCache: Miss-rate Aware Cache Management

Raghavendra K Tripti S Warrier Madhu Mutyam
PACE Laboratory, Department of Computer Science and Engineering
Indian Institute of Technology Madras, Chennai-36, India
{raghu, tripti, madhu}@cse.iitm.ac.in

ABSTRACT

It is common for computers to have multi-level caches. This piece of work revolves around one question: Are all levels needed by all applications during all phases of their execution?, especially in the multi programmed scenario where giving the entire cache to one application and depriving the other might actually increase the performance.

Categories and Subject Descriptors

B.3 [**Memory Structures**]: Cache memories

Keywords

Cache, Miss rate

Introduction and Motivation Prior works have looked at partitioning the cache giving lesser space to applications that are thrashing [4], tried to retain blocks that have higher chances of getting a hit again or bypassing blocks using predictors based on previous accesses to other levels of cache or the PC value [1, 3]. There are applications exhibiting high miss rates throughout their lifetime or at certain phases, even after applying techniques to reduce it. Those techniques, though very effective in bringing down the miss rates, might not work well for all workloads depending on the application footprint. Keeping this as the motivation, we classify phases of applications to be thrashing or non thrashing and accordingly bypass the entire cache, thereby gaining on three aspects: i) it would nullify the time taken to search for a block in the cache, ii) in a multi programmed workload the entire cache is made accessible to other applications which use it more effectively, iii) if all the applications/phases tend to be thrashing, it would result in completely switching off the cache thus gaining on power. To the best of our knowledge this work is first of its kind which explores bypassing the entire cache taking into account application behavior and with that technique as the cornerstone, studies the sharing of cache in multi programmed workloads.

Technique and Results To continuously track the miss rate of an application, we employ shadow tags per core. If the miss rate of an application crosses beyond a threshold, 0.8 a value which is determined empirically, any of its request that comes to the LLC is directly sent to the memory and cache blocks are directly fetched into the higher level. The cache blocks belonging to this application are invalidated in the LLC and there would be dirty blocks, to tackle which, we can either write them back to the main memory all at once and then proceed with bypassing or use a write-through cache. We employ the latter approach, since we find that using a write-through cache at the LLC does not significantly affect the performance and can be offset with the improvement gained by using the aforementioned technique. The shadow tags continue to monitor the application behavior and if the miss rate falls below the threshold, we again start using the cache. The application run is divided into phases of 50 million cycles and at the end of every phase, a decision is taken whether to use the cache or bypass it. This technique can be used on top of the existing cache optimization techniques already proposed in the literature.

We evaluate our technique on 2- and 4-core systems running multi-programmed workloads from a mix of SPEC CPU 2000 and 2006 benchmarks using the gem5 simulator. As our technique is miss rate aware, workloads with all possible mix of low (< 0.8) and high (> 0.8) miss rates are considered. We use 2MB (4MB) shared LLC for 2-core (4-core). Each core has a 32KB I-Cache and D-Cache, followed by an unified 256KB L2 cache. We fast-forward 9 billion, warm up for 1 billion and take statistics for the next 1 billion instructions. We report the performance improvement in terms of weighted speedup on top of RRIP [2], which we believe is state of the art technique to reduce miss rate of an application. We run 20 mixes of benchmarks for both 2- and 4-core simulations and get an average performance improvement of 11.14%, with a max speed-up of 25.41% for 2-core system and an average performance improvement of 11.17%, with a max speed-up of 20.61% for 4-core system.

Future work As part of future work i) we aim to reduce the overhead of shadow tags either by employing shadow tags only for few representative sets per core or by using the same shadow tags for more number of cores, each using the shadow tags at alternating phases ii) dynamically change the threshold by using feedback mechanism from the memory, taking into account DRAM and network congestion iii) look at the challenges of using this technique in a multi-threaded scenario where cache coherency comes into play.

References [1] G. Memik et al. Just Say No: Benefits of Early Cache Miss Determination. In HPCA, 2003.
[2] A. Jaleel et al. High performance cache replacement using re-reference interval prediction (RRIP). In ISCA, 2010.
[3] M. Hayenga et al. MadCache: A PC-aware cache insertion policy. In JWAC, 2010.
[4] Y. Xie et al. Scalable shared-cache management by containing thrashing workloads. In HiPEAC, 2010

PACT'12, September 19–23, 2012, Minneapolis, Minnesota, USA.
ACM 978-1-4503-1182-3/12/09.

Using Combined Profiling to Decide When Thread Level Speculation is Profitable

Arnamoy Bhattacharyya
University of Alberta
Edmonton, Alberta, Canada
arnamoy@ualberta.ca

ABSTRACT

Thread Level Speculation (TLS) speculatively executes parts of a program in parallel. Statically determined *may dependences* between *store-load* pairs prevent the compiler from speculatively executing parts of programs (e.g loop iterations or functions). If a compiler can determine that the probability of a *may dependence* occurring at runtime is low, then it can use TLS to execute the loop in parallel. This research will develop a *may dependence* profiling framework that is able to capture the effect of different inputs on the dependence behaviour of the program during runtime, using a technique called Combined Profiling (CP) [1]. The dependence profiling will be made efficient using the output from static analysis. TLS code generation strategies will be implemented in a version of the LLVM compiler that will generate code for the hardware support for TLS in the IBM BlueGene/Q (BG/Q) machine.

Categories and Subject Descriptors

D.1.3 [**Concurrent Programming**]: Parallel Programming

General Terms

Performance

Keywords

Thread Level Speculation, Loop Chunk

1. RESEARCH PROBLEM

(1) Given the BG/Q hardware support for TLS, could a dynamic analysis based on information gleaned from multiple runs of a program make better decisions about when to speculate than a strictly static analysis? **(2)** How can static dependence analysis be used to make dependence profiling more efficient and more effective in its ability to inform the compiler speculation decisions?

2. MOTIVATION AND BACKGROUND

For each *store-load* pair in a loop, if all are independent, the loop is parallel, if any pair is dependent, the loop is sequential. Speculation is concerned with *may dependences* which may or may not materialize at runtime. To decide when to speculate a loop with *may dependences*, a compiler has to weigh the benefit of a successful parallel execution against the overhead of thread creation and miss speculation. This decision can be based only on a static analysis, or it can also use information obtained through runtime profiling. Multiple runs of the program with different inputs should provide more precise information to estimate the probability of dependence materialization. Berube has proposed a technique called *Combined Profiling* (CP) to combine the information from multiple profiles for different inputs. This research will adapt CP to profile *may dependences.*

In the BG/Q the speculative state is stored in the L2 cache and the multiple speculative threads compete for this space in the same way that multiple threads compete for cache storage space in a non-speculative architecture. Therefore a more sophisticated analysis that takes into consideration the cache organization and the offsets of the memory references may be required to yield a better estimation of the profitability of speculating.

3. TECHNIQUES AND RESULTS

After the identification of speculation candidates, the proposed profiling framework resembles loop tiling. It first determines the memory footprint of a loop iteration. If the footprint size is greater than the speculative buffer size, the loop is not speculated. Otherwise the framework determines the number of iterations, a *chunk* of the loop, that can fit into one thread. For each chunk the framework profiles memory accesses by the *may-dependent store-load* pairs and records the probability of the dependence occurring at runtime. By querying a histogram built with the probabilities for multiple inputs, the compiler makes speculation decisions.

A preliminary examination of the SPEC CPU 2006 benchmark suite using the existing loop-dependence analysis pass in LLVM reveals that out of approximately 3 million store-load pairs that appear in loops, 46.7% are independent and 53.24% are regarded as may-dependent. This indicates that there is significant scope for the application of TLS to this set of benchmarks.

4. REFERENCES

[1] P. Berube and J. N. Amaral. Combined Profiling: A methodology to capture varied program behavior across multiple inputs. In *International Symposium on Performance Analysis of Systems and Software (ISPASS)*, pages 210 –220, New Brunswick, NJ, USA, April 2012.

PACT'12, September 19–23, 2012, Minneapolis, Minnesota, USA.
ACM 978-1-4503-1182-3/12/09.

Hardware Prefetchers for Emerging Parallel Applications

Biswabandan Panda
Computer Architecture and Systems Lab
CSE Department, IIT Madras, India
biswa@cse.iitm.ac.in

Shankar Balachandran
Computer Architecture and Systems Lab
CSE Department, IIT Madras, India
shankar@cse.iitm.ac.in

ABSTRACT

Hardware prefetching has been studied in the past for multiprogrammed workloads as well as GPUs. Efficient hardware prefetchers like stream-based or GHB-based ones work well for multiprogrammed workloads because different programs get mapped to different cores and are run independently. Parallel applications, however, pose a different set of challenges. Multiple threads of a parallel application share data with each other which brings in coherency issues. Also, local prefetchers do not understand the irregular spread of misses across threads. In this paper, we propose a hardware prefetching framework for L1 D-Cache that targets parallel applications. We show how to make efficient prefetch requests to the L2 cache by studying and classifying the patterns of L1 misses across all the threads. Our preliminary results show an improvement of 7% in execution time on an average on the PARSEC benchmark suite.

Categories and Subject Descriptors

B.3 [**Memory Structures**]: Cache memories

Keywords

Prefetching

1. DESIGN AND IMPLEMENTATION

We categorize miss patterns into three categories. A demand miss on a cache line from a particular thread is a (i) *Global Stride* (GS) miss if the line is at a stride S from another line that saw a demand miss from another thread; (ii) *Local Stride* (LS) miss if the line is at a stride S from another line that was missed from the same thread; (iii) *Producer_Consumer Shared* (PCS) miss if the miss to the same line happened in the other threads. The observation window is restricted to the last 32K cycles for this classification.

To alleviate the GS and PCS misses, we add two prefetchers called the GS prefetcher and the PCS prefetcher beside the L2 cache. LS misses are handled by the local prefetcher. **Prefetching Framework:** *GS* prefetcher uses a table indexed by tag-bits. Fig. 1 shows the structure of the GS table. Misses *miss1* and *miss2* originating from two different threads *tid1* and *tid2* are entered into the GS table. A miss from a thread other than *tid2* is called *miss3*. If the strides between subsequent pairs in these misses are the same (say S), a particular entry is trained.

Upper Tag	miss1	tid1	miss2	tid2	stride	Trained

Figure 1: GS Table

Subsequent misses to a trained entry results in a prefetch request to *miss_address* + S. The response from the L2 cache is sent to a hardware structure called the *filler* (which is private to each core). In the immediate future, if a demand miss occurs to the prefetched address, the data is transferred to L1 D-cache and deallocated from the respective *fillers*. *PCS* prefetcher maintains saturating counters, named PCS_{ij}, for every pair of threads. The PCS_{ij} counters are incremented when the PCS prefetcher observes trained entries in GS table with stride zero and they are decremented when the entries are evicted. For a demand miss from thread i, the *PCS* prefetcher issues prefetch responses as a *selective-broadcast* message to the fillers of those threads for which the PCS_{i*} counters have exceeded a threshold value.

Fig. 2 shows the overall design of our prefetching framework for a 2 core system which consists of *GS*, *PCS* and *LS* prefetchers.

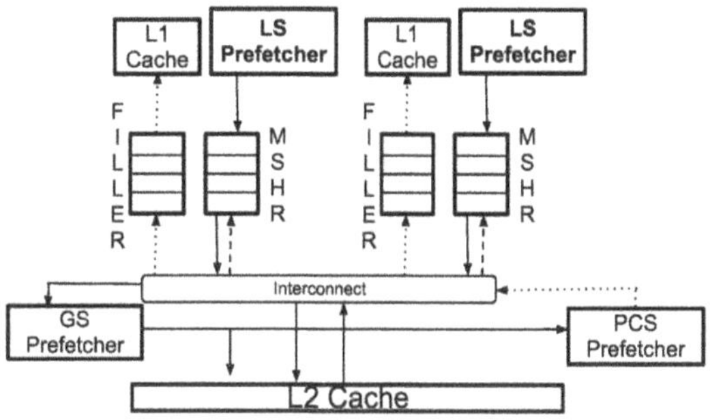

Figure 2: Prefetcher Framework

Preliminary Results: We use gem5 FS simulator to implement *GS* and *PCS* with L1 D-cache of size 32KB. We use stream-based prefetcher as the *LS* prefetcher. *GS* prefetcher uses a table of 256 entries. PCS prefetcher uses 3 bit PCS_{ij} counters per thread. We use PARSEC benchmarks with *sim-medium* as input set to evaluate our framework. Our framework outperforms the feedback-prefetcher [1] in terms of execution time by 4.2% and 7.1% on an average for 2-core and 4-core systems. The accuracy of *GS* and *PCS* is above 70% on an average. We believe that a collaborative framework between *GS*, *PCS* and *LS* prefetchers will further improve the performance.

[1] S. Srinath, O. Mutlu, H. Kim, and Y. N. Patt."Feedback directed prefetching: Improving the performance and bandwidth-efficiency of hardware prefetchers", in HPCA-13, 2007, pp. 63-74.

PACT'12, September 19–23, 2012, Minneapolis, Minnesota, USA.
ACM 978-1-4503-1182-3/12/09.

Strategies based on Green Policies to the Grid Resource Allocation

Fábio Coutinho
Federal University of Rio de Janeiro/UFRJ/PESC
PO. Box 68511, 21941-972, Rio de Janeiro/RJ, Brazil
+55 21 2562-8672
fabio@cos.ufrj.br

Luís Alfredo V. de Carvalho
Federal University of Rio de Janeiro/UFRJ/PESC
PO. Box 68511, 21941-972, Rio de Janeiro/RJ, Brazil
+55 21 2562-8658
luisalfredo@ufrj.br

ABSTRACT

This paper discusses strategies to the grid resource allocation in order to reduce energy consumption in a global perspective. We have implemented three green strategies: HGreen, GGreen and BOTEN. The former two strategies aim at reducing energy and were evaluated by simulation, whilst the latter intends simultaneously decreasing both energy and time.

Categories and Subject Descriptors

H.3.4 [**Information Storage and Retrieval**]: Systems and Software – *Distributed systems, Performance evaluation.*

Keywords

Grid Resource Allocation, Green Computing, Multiobjective.

1. INTRODUCTION

IT infrastructure affects the environment in different manners: designing, manufacturing, using and disposal. Regarding computers usage, the energy consumption has been considered an important factor of environmental impact. LHC is a good example of relevant physics experiment whose computer grid needs about 2.5MW just for sustain its major site located at CERN.

Over the last years, High Throughput Computing environments have lead task scheduling studies towards reducing the energy consumption. In section 3, we present scheduling strategies compromised with green policies in order to reduce the power consumption in global grid environments.

2. GRID ARCHITECTURE

Grid model herein has the LHC grid as a reference, i.e. a grid comprising several geographically distributed sites containing heterogeneous resources to the task execution from a meta-scheduler. Following grid characteristics should be highlighted:

(i) availability – grid machines are turned on all the time;

(ii) variable load – according to the moment, we have higher or lower load, consequently higher or lower energy consumption.

Due to the (i), we cannot switch off unused CPUs. The enforcement of DVS technique can disagree with the local site autonomy. In other words, resource global management cannot decrease the performance of a site machine in risk of being in opposition to the interest of this site.

PACT'12, September 19–23, 2012, Minneapolis, Minnesota, USA.
ACM 978-1-4503-1182-3/12/09.

3. GREEN STRATEGIES

3.1 HGreen

HGreen (**H**eavier Tasks on Maximum **Green** Resource) strategy [1] can be summarized as: *the heaviest tasks are allocated to the most energy-efficient resources*. For each grid resource is defined a metric denoted by eee (execution energy efficiency) that can be expressed by a benchmark.

3.2 GGreen

Unlikely HGreen, GGreen (**G**reedy **Green**) strategy does not use a single energy metric for each grid resource. Instead, GGreen makes measurements with respect to the power levels according to the resource load. Finally, GGreen prioritizes the allocation to the grid resource operating with the lowest power.

3.3 BOTEN

BOTEN (BiObjective Time and ENergy) is a multiobjective scheduling algorithm that reduces both energy consumption and execution time (makespan). BOTEN returns the minimal complete set of Pareto-optimal allocations in polynomial time.

4. COMPUTATIONAL EXPERIMENTS

HGreen and GGreen are evaluated by means of GridSim in order to simulate a grid with 6 resources. The simulation computed 50 batches containing 48 tasks (randomly generated) for three distinct scenarios executed in series of 12, 24, 36 and 48 tasks. Both strategies were compared with each other and against to a randomly task distribution view (1000 executions, see Figure 1).

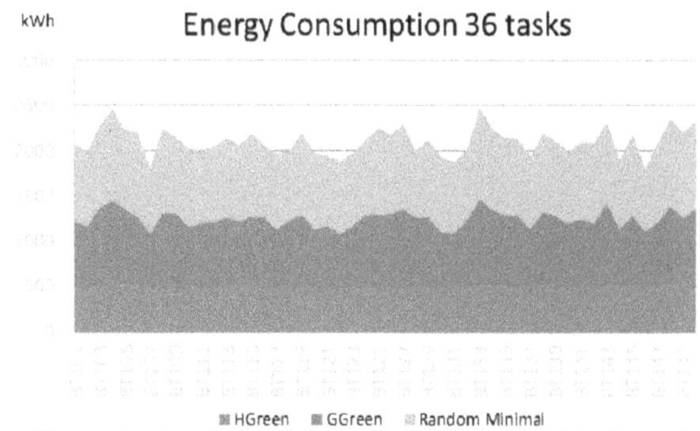

Figure 1. Results of a single scenario with 36 tasks series.

5. REFERENCE

[1] Fábio Coutinho, L. A. V. de Carvalho and R. Santana, "A Workflow Scheduling Algorithm for Optimizing Energy-Efficient Grid Resources Usage", in Proceedings of the IEEE DASC, Sydney, 2011, p. 642-649.

Linearly Compressed Pages: A Main Memory Compression Framework with Low Complexity and Low Latency

Gennady Pekhimenko, Todd C. Mowry, and Onur Mutlu
gpekhime@cs.cmu.edu, tcm@cs.cmu.edu, onur@cmu.edu

Categories and Subject Descriptors: B.3.2 [**Design Styles**]: Primary Memory, Cache Memories
Keywords: Main memory compression, cache compression

1. INTRODUCTION AND MOTIVATION

Main memory is a critical resource in modern systems. Its capacity must be sufficiently provisioned to prevent the target application's working set from overflowing into the backing store (e.g., hard disk, flash storage) that is slower by orders of magnitude compared to DRAM. Adding more DRAM to meet the increasing main memory demand is ideally not desirable, because this will significantly increase both the system's cost and the power consumption.

One potential way of addressing DRAM capacity problem is by using data compression. Data compression was previously used to increase the effective cache size [2, 3, 5, 6, 7], and DRAM capacity [1, 4], and to decrease bandwidth consumption [6]. One of the primary concerns with data compression is that *decompression* lies on the critical path of accessing any compressed data. To counter this problem, prior work [2, 6, 7] has proposed specialized compression algorithms that exploit some regular patterns present in in-memory data, and has shown that such specialized algorithms have high compression ratios while incurring relatively lower decompression latencies (1-5 cycles).

One of the primary reasons, why applying these works directly to main memory is difficult, is a virtual to physical page mapping. When a virtual page is mapped to a compressed physical page, the virtual page offset of a cache line can be different from the corresponding physical page offset since each physical cache line is expected to be smaller than the virtual cache line. In fact, where a compressed cache line resides in a main memory page is dependent on the sizes of the compressed cache lines that come before it in the page. As a result, accessing a cache line within a compressed page in main memory requires an additional layer of indirection to compute the location of the cache line in main memory. This indirection not only increases complexity and cost, but also can increase the latency of main memory access, and thereby degrade system performance.

Our goal in this work is to build a main memory compression framework that neither incurs the latency penalty nor requires power-inefficient hardware. To this end, we propose a new approach to compress pages, which we call *Linearly Compressed Pages* (LCP). The key idea of LCP is that if all the cache lines within a page are compressed to the *same size*, then the location of a cache line within a compressed page is simply the product of the index of the cache line and the compressed cache line size. Based on this idea, each compressed page has a target compressed cache line size. Cache lines that cannot be compressed to this target size are called *exceptions*. All exceptions, along with the metadata required to locate them, are stored separately on the same compressed page. We adapt two previously proposed compression algorithms (Frequent Pattern Compression [2] and Base-Delta-Immediate Compression [6]) to fit the requirements of LCP, and show that the resulting designs can significantly improve effective main memory capacity on a wide variety of workloads.

2. BACKGROUND

In summary, prior works on hardware-based main memory compression mitigate the performance degradation due to the main memory address computation problem by either adding large hardware structures (e.g., 32MB L2 cache) that consume significant area and power [1] or by using techniques that require energy-inefficient hardware and lead to wasted energy [4]. In contrast, in this work, we propose a new main memory compression framework that simplifies the nature of the main memory address computation, thereby significantly reducing the associated latency (compared to prior approaches) without requiring energy-inefficient hardware structures.

3. OUR APPROACH: KEY IDEA

The key idea of LCP is to *use a fixed size for compressed cache lines within a page* (which eliminates complex and long-latency main memory address calculation problem that arises due to variable-size cache lines), and still enable a page to be compressed even if not all cache lines within the page can be compressed to that fixed size (which enables high compression ratios). Since all the cache lines within a page are compressed to the same size, then the location of a compressed cache line within the page is simply the product of the index of the cache line within the page and the size of the compressed cache line – essentially a linear scaling using the index of the cache line.

It is clear, that some cache lines within a page may not be compressible to a specific fixed size (using some simple compression mechanism as BDI). Also, a cache line which is originally compressed to the target size may later become uncompressible due to a write. LCP stores such uncompressible cache lines of a page separately from the compressed cache lines (but still within the page), along with the metadata required to locate them.

There are two major benefits of having such a compressed page organization. First, it is possible to avoid the accesses to the special pages with metadata (as in MXT), and, hence, potentially avoid additional DRAM row misses. Second, when the data and the metadata are both located on the same page (e.g., 4kB in size), it is then possible to pipeline the requests to both of the them, since they are located on the same active DRAM row. Both these benefits decrease the negative effect of a higher access latency.

We also propose three simple optimizations to our LCP framework: (1) metadata cache, (2) memory bandwidth reduction, and (3) exploiting zero pages and zero cache lines.

References

[1] B. Abali and et al. Memory expansion technology (MXT): software support and performance. *IBM J. Res. Dev.*, 45:287–301, 2001.

[2] A. R. Alameldeen and D. A. Wood. Adaptive cache compression for high-performance processors. In *ISCA-31*, 2004.

[3] J. Dusser, T. Piquet, and A. Seznec. Zero-content augmented caches. In *ICS*, 2009.

[4] M. Ekman and P. Stenstrom. A robust main-memory compression scheme. In *ISCA-32*, 2005.

[5] E. G. Hallnor and S. K. Reinhardt. A unified compressed memory hierarchy. In *HPCA-11*, 2005.

[6] G. Pekhimenko and et al. Base-delta-immediate compression: A practical data compression mechanism for on-chip caches. In *PACT*, 2012.

[7] J. Yang, Y. Zhang, and R. Gupta. Frequent value compression in data caches. In *MICRO-33*, 2000.

PACT'12, September 19–23, 2012, Minneapolis, Minnesota, USA.
ACM 978-1-4503-1182-3/12/09.

Energy-Efficient Workload Mapping in Heterogeneous Systems with Multiple Types of Resources

Cong Liu
University of North Carolina at Chapel Hill
Dept. of Computer Science
cong@cs.unc.edu

Categories and Subject Descriptors

C.1.4 [**Processor Architectures**]: Parallel Architectures

General Terms

Algorithms, Measurement, Performance, Experimentation

1. ABSTRACT

Given the need to achieve higher performance without driving up power consumption, energy usage and heat dissipation, most chip manufacturers have shifted to multicore architectures. An important subcategory of such architectures are those that are heterogeneous in design. By providing heterogeneous processing elements with different performance and energy characteristics in the same system, heterogeneous architectures are expected to provide more flexibility for better energy efficiency. Indeed, prior work has shown that heterogeneous systems are able to reduce power and energy consumption compared to homogeneous systems. However, without power-aware application and data mapping methods that explicitly consider heterogeneity, such advantages cannot be fully exploited. Such methods are of interest for other reasons as well. For example, excessive power consumption may cause system unreliability (due to power constraints and local hot spots).

In work on homogeneous systems, much work has been directed at techniques that reduce power and energy consumption by applying dynamic voltage/frequency scaling (DVFS) techniques to lower CPUs' voltages/frequencies. With the growing prevalence of such heterogeneous architectures, there is a need to evolve such techniques so they can be applied in systems with different computing resources. One important category of applications that could benefit from such techniques is those that are time-sensitive; examples include data analytics, stock trading, avionics, real-time scoring of bank transactions, live video processing, etc. Such applications range from desktop-level systems to systems that require significant computational capacity. As an example of the latter, systems processing time-sensitive business transactions have been implemented by Azul Systems on top of the highly-parallel Vega3 platform, which consists of CPUs and GPUs with up to 864 cores. In this paper, such time-sensitive applications are our focus.

Our first contribution is to propose three power/energy-efficient mapping techniques that consider the characteristics of both resources and applications to make mapping decisions. These techniques can be applied both initially and when applications dynamically arrive at run-time. Additionally, by leveraging the fact that at run-time some applications typically exhibit actual execution times that are lower than their worst-case execution time, we propose and apply techniques to dynamically and aggressively reduce voltages/frequencies on multiple types of resources such as CPUs, GPUs, and FPGAs. Our overall strategy is based on several components: (*i*) *Static mapping:* an offline scheme for mapping the initial set of applications and computing the appropriate voltage/frequency to minimize power and energy consumption while meeting all deadlines, (*ii*) *Dynamic mapping:* an online scheme for dynamically mapping applications arriving at run-time and re-evaluating the voltage/frequency settings, and (*iii*) *Aggressive mapping:* a speculative voltage/frequency scaling scheme that aggressively reduces voltage/frequency by exploiting average-case execution time information. The intuitive idea behind our proposed techniques is to increase the likelyhood of assigning applications to their favorite type of resource, where an applicaion's *favorite type of resource* is the one that provides the fastest execution rate for this applications among all types of resources.

Our second contribution is to evaluate the proposed mapping algorithms by implementing them on a real CPU/GPU heterogeneous system and running several analytics workloads, such as Non-Negative Matrix Factorization (NMF), implemented using OpenCL. Experimental results using real power measurements demonstrate that our proposed algorithms can achieve much better power and energy efficiency than a performance-driven mapping algorithm earliest-response-time-first (ERF) that always maps applications to resources with the fastest response time. Fig. 1 shows that the proposed mapping algorithms greatly outperforms ERF with respect to energy efficiency.

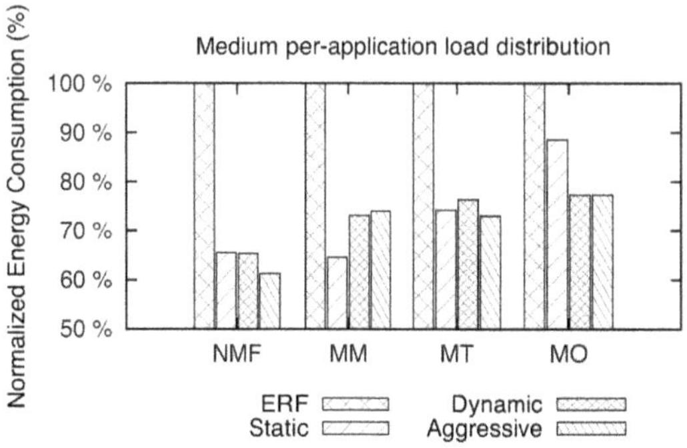

Figure 1: Energy consumption results under medium load distribution of the compared algorithms.

Phase-Based Scheduling and Thread Migration for Heterogeneous Multicore Processors

Lina Sawalha, Ronald D. Barnes
School of Electrical and Computer Engineering, The University of Oklahoma
{lina_sawalha, ron}@ou.edu

Heterogeneous multicore processors (HMPs) can provide better performance and reduced energy consumption than homogeneous ones [3]. Differences between cores provide different processing capabilities for different applications; a dynamic scheduler can exploit these differences to maximize performance and minimize energy consumption [5, 6] by adapting to fine changes in programs behavior. This work proposes new fine-grained online HMP schedulers using program phase identification. *However, exploiting fine-grained scheduling results in frequent thread migrations that can harm performance. OS context switching is time consuming (30–60μs [4]). To reduce context switching overhead, a context switching circuit that both accelerates thread switches among cores in HMPs and reduces switching cost within each core (multitasking) is introduced.*

Categories and Subject Descriptors

C.1.4 [**Processor Architectures**]: Parallel Architectures

Keywords

fine-grain scheduling, context switching, heterogeneous multicore

Dynamic scheduling approaches for HMPs fall into two categories: sampling [3] and prediction [1, 7]. Sampling approaches permute applications to cores to find the best-performing assignment. Sampling hurts performance and power due to time spent migrating threads through non-optimal assignments. Alternatively, prediction-based approaches estimate the performance for each application on different types of cores and choose the schedule with the best estimated performance. Prediction eliminates the cost of sampling but may result in sub-optimal scheduling decisions. We propose two new phase-identification-based online schedulers for HMPs that combine both approaches by *identifying* phases of execution (instruction sequences with similar behavior), sampling new phases, *recognizing* repeating phases and *reusing* recorded phase information to *predict* the best performing schedule. While previous approaches utilized only phase-change *detection* to begin evaluating new schedules, the proposed approaches recognize the current phase of each executing thread and reuse phase information recorded in a Signature History Table (SHT) when phases repeat. A Working Set Signature [2] is calculated over windows of executed instructions. A new phase is detected whenever two consecutive signatures differ by a threshold (0.5).

Sampled evaluation of each application on each type of processor is initiated upon each previously unencountered phase. New phases' signatures are stored in the SHT as a set along with the best schedule (*Phase_Sampling*) or individually along with the sampled IPC of each new phase on each core type (*Phase_IPC*). When phases recur, the schedule is retrieved from the SHT for *Phase_Sampling* and the best performing assignment is predicted based on the recorded IPCs for *Phase_IPC*. Figure 1 shows, ignoring switching and sampling cost, the weighted speedup (WS) of the two scheduling approaches compared with a heuristic sampling approach [3], the average WS of all static assignments and the optimal assignment. These simulated results were generated for a quad-core x86 processor, consisting of one in-order and three out-of-order cores. *Phase_Sampling* outperforms the other approaches but results in increased sampling since it requires a match of all phases across running applications to reuse a previously determined schedule. *Phase-IPC* yields a WS slightly below the heuristic but requires only half the sampling intervals. Similar approaches were also used for scheduling HMPs for reduced energy consumption [5].

Neglecting the cost of thread switching, finer-grained scheduling tends to result in higher performance. However, switching overhead makes it difficult to exploit this. A context switching circuit that greatly reduces the direct cost of switching (cost of copying processor state) is thus proposed. It is capable of switching all executing applications among all processor cores simultaneously and contains a *Shared Context Unit* (SCU) shared among a set of cores. The SCU is composed of a number of process control blocks, called context sets (CSs), that can be greater than the number of cores to support faster multitasking between different threads on each core. Each CS contains the basic execution environment (for x86-64, 584 bytes), debug registers, control registers, design specific registers, etc. (~1000 bytes). Using CACTI, a CS's area was estimated to 1971 nm^2 for a 32 nm process with each 8-byte access consuming 1.4 pJ. When the schedule changes, each core points to its new thread's CS via a crossbar switch. As the number of threads grows beyond the number of context sets, the OS is responsible for switching the context of the additional threads. The circuit takes up to m x n + $2m$ cycles, where n is the number of executing threads and m is the number of context sets, to switch cores to point to different CSs. By facilitating faster thread migration, the context switching circuit enables the proposed fine-grained scheduling algorithms to significantly improve the performance of HMPs (or to drastically reduce the sampling required to get similar performance) compared to previous heuristic sampling mechanisms.

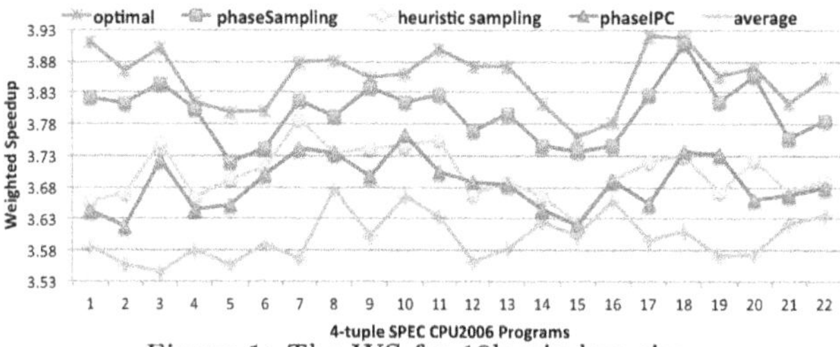

Figure 1: The WS for 10k window size.

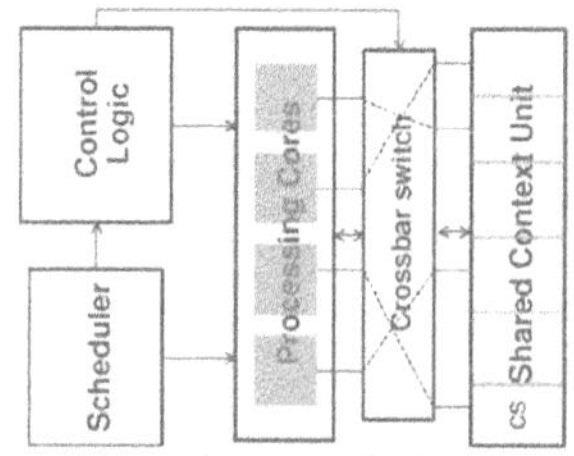

Figure 2: Fast Context Switching Circuit.

This material is based upon work supported by the National Science Foundation under Grant No. 1018771.

References

[1] K. V. Craeynest, et al. Scheduling heterogeneous multi-cores through performance impact estimation (PIE). In *ISCA'12*.

[2] A. S. Dhodapkar and J. E. Smith. Managing multi-configuration hardware via dynamic working set analysis. In *ISCA'02*.

[3] R. Kumar, et al. Single-ISA heterogeneous multi-core architectures for multithreaded workload performance. In *ISCA'04*.

[4] R. Ronen. The practical challenges of heterogneous architectures. Invited Talk at SHAW3'12.

[5] L. Sawalha and R. D. Barnes. Energy-efficient phase-aware scheduling for heterogneous multicore processors. In *IEEE GreenTech'12*.

[6] L. Sawalha, et al. Thread scheduling for heterogeneous multicore processors using phase identification. *SIGMETRICS PER*, 39(3):125–127, Dec. 2011.

[7] T. Sondag and H. Rajan. Phase-based tuning for better utilization of performance-asymmetric multicore processors. In *CGO'11*.

PACT'12, September 19–23, 2012, Minneapolis, Minnesota, USA.
ACM 978-1-4503-1182-3/12/09.

Author Index

www.ingramcontent.com/pod-product-compliance
Ingram Content Group UK Ltd.
Pitfield, Milton Keynes, MK11 3LW, UK
UKHW051414290926
15471UKWH00009B/1607

9 781450 318846